Bottom Line's

ULTIMATE HEALING

World's Greatest Treasury of Health Secrets

Bottom Line Books

www.BottomLineSecrets.com

Contents

6 • YOUR PRESCRIPTIONS

7 • LONGEVITY SECRETS

8 • BRAIN BOOSTERS

9 • HEART & STROKE HELP

10 • DIABETES & OTHER DISEASES

14 • HEALTHY RELATIONSHIPS

15 • YOUR SKIN & SENSES

16 • FOOD SMARTS

Preface

We are proud to bring you *Bottom Line's Ultimate Healing*. We trust that you'll find the latest discoveries, best treatments and safest solutions to your health concerns.

When you choose a Bottom Line Book, you are turning to a stellar group of experts in a wide range of specialties—medical doctors, naturopathic doctors, alternative practitioners, nutrition experts, research scientists, consumer-health advocates, exercise physiologists, mental health professionals and health-conscious chefs.

Whether it's cancer prevention, new heart therapies, breakthrough arthritis treatments or cutting-edge nutritional advice, our editors talk to the people who are creating the true innovations in health care.

How do we find all these top-notch medical professionals? Over the past two decades, we have built a network of literally thousands of leading physicians in both alternative and conventional medicine. They are affiliated with the premier medical institutions and the best universities throughout the world. We read the important medical journals and follow the latest research that is reported at medical conferences. And we regularly talk to our advisors in major teaching hospitals, private practices and government health agencies.

Bottom Line's Ultimate Healing is a result of our ongoing research and contact with these experts, and is a distillation of their latest findings and advice. We trust that you will enjoy the presentation and glean new, helpful information about the health topics that concern you and your family.

As a reader of a Bottom Line Book, please be assured that you are receiving reliable and well-researched information from a trusted source.

But, please use prudence in health matters. Always speak to your physician before taking vitamins, supplements or over-the-counter medication...changing your diet...or beginning an exercise program. If you experience side effects from any regimen, contact your doctor immediately.

The Editors, Bottom Line Books, Stamford, CT.

1

Health Care Essentials

Get Better Care from Your Doctor

Even people who are ordinarily savvy consumers lose their normal assertiveness at the examining room door—just when it's needed most.

The average internist sees 22 to 28 patients a day. In hectic medical environments, doctors barely have time to discuss their patients' major symptoms and complaints, much less minor health problems.

Traps to avoid...

***Trap 1:* Wasting time during the exam.** Most patients can provide a doctor with all the pertinent information in about 90 seconds—if they're mentally organized and make sure the doctor actually hears what they're saying.

Research shows that doctors interrupt patients, on average, after 23 seconds—and only 2% of patients get a chance to finish their opening statements.

Many people know to write down their symptoms and/or complaints ahead of time. But they make long, complicated lists that aren't much help during a short exam.

Helpful: Limit your written list to three main points—and keep the sentences short.

Example: "I've been having pain in my lower back," "I haven't been sleeping well" and "I'm having trouble with urination."

Hand a copy of the list to your doctor when he/she comes into the examining room. Reading a list while you're talking makes it easier for the doctor to process the information...and it ensures that you don't forget key points.

***Trap 2:* Not getting a second opinion.** Even though most people agree that second opinions are a good idea, only 20% of patients

Mehmet C. Oz, MD, founder and director of the Complementary Medicine Program and director of the Cardiovascular Institute at New York-Presbyterian Medical Center and professor and vice chairman of surgery at Columbia University, both in New York City, is coauthor of *You: The Smart Patient: An Insider's Handbook for Getting the Best Treatment.* Free Press.

actually seek them out—often because they are afraid of offending their doctors.

Getting a second opinion doesn't mean that you don't trust your doctor, or that his recommendations aren't valid. It just means that you're wisely exploring other treatment choices. One study found that 33% of second opinions resulted in a significant change in treatment. Health insurers usually pay for second opinions, especially for important procedures. It's a good idea to submit your request in writing to your insurer.

When to seek a second opinion…

•**If your doctor recommends any kind of surgery.**

•**If you have a condition that's uncommon or that's outside your doctor's main area of expertise.**

•**If a treatment doesn't seem to be working.** A patient with high blood pressure, for example, should show improvement within a few weeks. If that doesn't occur, a drug combination suggested by a different doctor might work better.

Useful: Use the Internet to look for scientific papers that have been written about your health problem. When you find a relevant study, write down the first author and last author listed at the end. The first author will be the doctor who did most of the research. The last author is usually the supervising physician. Both are good choices for a second opinion. Doctors who write papers for medical journals are usually among the country's top experts. Even if these doctors are not based in your area, they can probably provide a second opinion by phone if your doctor sends reports, test results, X-rays, etc.

Trap 3: **Not educating yourself on your condition.** Patients who do their research have basic knowledge that allows them to use their appointment time much more productively. Rather than wasting time discussing, say, the anatomy of the heart, you can inquire about the specifics of various treatments—for example, whether one class of drugs is better than another, different types of surgery, etc.

Important: When conducting research, Internet sites with URLs that end with ".edu" (educational institutions) or ".gov" (US government agencies) are among the most reliable. My favorite is *www.pubmed.gov,* sponsored by the National Library of Medicine and the National Institutes of Health.

Other research strategies…

•**Check when the information was updated.** Medical information that's more than two years old is ancient. Anything newer than that generally is timely.

•**Rely on Web sites that don't include advertising.** They are usually more reliable than those that do.

•**Don't trust information that suggests only one treatment plan.** That's often a tip-off that the information is biased and unreliable.

If you don't have time to do your own research, consider using a fee-based medical research service, such as The Health Resource, Inc. (800-949-0090, *www.thehealthresource.com*).

Trap 4: **Not understanding how to take your medication.** Only about half of all prescriptions are filled or taken correctly. In addition, medication errors—especially not identifying dangerous drug interactions—are among the most common preventable mistakes.

Smart idea: Go to the same pharmacy every time—and get to know the pharmacists. Someone who knows your health history is more likely to catch potential problems. The pharmacist might look at a new prescription and say something like, "You've never taken anything like this before. Let me call the doctor and check."

Other advice…

•**Choose a pharmacy that uses cross-checking software and medication-monitoring technology,** which checks for any potential drug interactions. (Just ask the staff if they use this technology.)

•**Ask your doctor to write detailed notes for you on the drug(s) you're taking.** Make sure you know the dose, when you're supposed to take it and how to take it (on an empty stomach, for example) and whether there are possible interactions with other drugs.

•**Inquire about age-related side effects.** A large study at Duke University found that more than 20% of older patients were given prescriptions for drugs that could cause serious side effects in people age 65 or older.

What Nurses Know—And Doctors Don't Tell You

Patricia Carroll, RN, Manchester Memorial Hospital, Eastern Connecticut Health Network, Manchester, CT, is the author of *What Nurses Know and Doctors Don't Have Time to Tell You: Practical Wisdom for Everyday Home Health Care.* Perigee.

Medical doctors are trained to treat illness, injury and disease with medication, surgery and/or hospitalization—but they rarely have time to give detailed self-care advice.

Nurses are usually the best people to offer this type of advice and help patients avoid dangerous medical mistakes.

Common mistakes…

•**Relying on an ear thermometer.** Ear thermometers use an infrared beam to gauge the temperature of the eardrum. They are accurate when trained nurses use them on unconscious patients, who aren't moving. Getting an accurate reading on a conscious patient, who is almost certain to move slightly, is less likely. When a patient moves, the infrared beam may shift off the eardrum, making the reading unreliable.

Rectal thermometers are still the gold standard for getting an accurate temperature reading. Digital oral thermometers also are reliable. But, according to a new study conducted at the University of Virginia Health System, you should not eat or drink anything for 15 to 25 minutes before taking the reading.

Forehead thermometers gauge the temperature in the temporal artery, which supplies blood to the temple and scalp, and are considered less reliable because proper placement and use can be tricky. Follow label instructions carefully.

•**Using silverware to measure liquid medicines.** Daily doses of certain medications —for example, the heart drug *digoxin* (Lanoxin) and anticonvulsant drugs, such as *phenytoin* (Dilantin)—must be measured precisely because there is a narrow range between optimal and toxic doses. Liquid drug doses are prescribed in milliliters but often are translated into teaspoons and tablespoons for convenience. However, the size of silverware teaspoons and tablespoons varies widely.

Ask your health-care provider to skip this translation. Measure out your prescribed dose in milliliters in a needleless syringe or a dosing spoon (a plastic device with a spoon on one end and measurements along the handle).

Check with your health-care provider for a needleless syringe. Or buy a dosing spoon, available at a drugstore for about $2. If you're not sure how to use these devices, ask a pharmacist or nurse for a demonstration.

•**Storing medicine in the bathroom medicine cabinet.** The humidity that commonly develops in a bathroom with a shower or bathtub increases the chances that your prescription or over-the-counter (OTC) drugs will break down quickly, losing their efficacy and possibly causing unwanted side effects, such as stomach upset or skin rash.

A box, placed in a linen closet near the bathroom, is the best place for your drugs because it keeps the medication cool and dry. (If you have children in your home, place the box on the top shelf, where it is out of reach.)

•**Taking pain relievers that contain caffeine instead of getting it from coffee.** The OTC pain reliever Excedrin contains *acetaminophen*, aspirin and caffeine. Anacin, another OTC pain reliever, contains buffered aspirin and caffeine. These drugs cost up to three times more than plain aspirin or acetaminophen.

Caffeine is added because aspirin and acetaminophen are absorbed up to 40% faster when taken with caffeine. However, a cup of caffeinated coffee contains about 135 mg of caffeine—compared with 64 mg to 130 mg per dose of pain reliever—and works just as well. Black tea, which contains 40 mg to 70 mg of caffeine per cup, also can be used.

If you use aspirin or acetaminophen, take it with a cup of coffee or tea in the morning to boost the drug's absorption. To avoid unwanted side effects, such as restlessness, do *not* drink coffee or tea at night.

Many people with arthritis suffer the most severe pain when they wake in the morning. Taking a pain reliever without caffeine allows you to take it at bedtime so it lasts until morning, without keeping you up at night.

What Your Doctor Should Ask You—But Won't

Leo Galland, MD, director, Foundation for Integrated Medicine, New York City. He is author of *The Fat Resistance Diet.* Broadway. *www.fatresistancediet.com.* Dr. Galland is a recipient of the Linus Pauling Award.

In the US, the typical doctor's office visit lasts seven to 10 minutes. During that time, the doctor reviews your medical history, asks questions about your symptoms, performs an exam and orders tests, if necessary.

This approach can be effective for emergencies or acute illnesses, such as earaches, bronchitis or chest pain. It doesn't work as well for chronic diseases, such as diabetes, arthritis, asthma or fatigue.

Reason: Doctors don't ask questions that reveal the key facts about a person's life that can significantly affect the development and progression of disease.

Example: One of my patients had severe rheumatoid arthritis. She failed to improve even with the latest, most powerful drugs. None of her doctors thought to ask about her diet, which was triggering the release of inflammatory chemicals that exacerbated her symptoms.

I ask my patients to complete a 20-page questionnaire before their initial visit with me. In many cases, their answers give important clues to an accurate diagnosis. Even if your doctor doesn't ask the questions listed below, you should bring up these issues with him/her during your appointment.

Questions your doctor should ask—but may not…

1. Have you ever felt better after avoiding particular foods? Up to 40% of *healthy* Americans report having an intolerance to one or more foods.

Why it matters: Millions of Americans react to wheat, dairy or other specific foods or food groups. Food intolerance is a frequent cause of diarrhea and other digestive problems. It also can cause fatigue and headache. Patients often suffer for years without being accurately diagnosed. The quality of a person's diet can have a significant impact on the risk for chronic or recurrent disease…energy levels, mood and body weight…recovery from infection…and the control of chronic disorders such as diabetes and high blood pressure.

What you can do: If you have unexplained symptoms, such as headache or diarrhea, keep a food diary to record everything you eat and drink over a three-day period, including spices and condiments such as pepper and mustard. The most common culprits are milk products, wheat, corn, yeast, sugar, artificial colors and flavors and spices. Eliminate a suspected problem food from your diet for five to seven days. Do your symptoms improve when you avoid the food? Do they get worse when you reintroduce it? If you find a problem food, ask your doctor whether you may have a food intolerance.

2. What are the major sources of stress in your life? Our bodies' nerves, hormones and immune cells work together to help us cope with emotional stress. In people who suffer chronic stress, this network becomes overwhelmed and stops working efficiently.

Why it matters: The body is designed to respond to stress and often benefits by becoming stronger. However, when people experience high levels of stress on a daily basis, the cost of responding to stress exceeds the benefit. This results in an increased risk for cardiovascular disease, infection, depression and other illnesses.

What you can do: It's impossible to eliminate stress altogether, but we all can learn to manage it more efficiently. For example, daily exercise—30 minutes of walking at a moderate to brisk pace—diminishes the effects of stress-related hormones.

3. Do you feel close to your family and/or friends? Doctors are often reluctant (or too busy) to ask about patients' personal lives. However, personal relationships are among the most important factors in preventing and treating disease.

Why it matters: Patients who are diagnosed with serious illnesses, including cancer and heart disease, live longer when they have a strong social network. Research also shows that people who are active in their communities or close to family and friends are less likely to get sick in the first place. A social support network also eases depression and protects you from the effects of daily stress.

What you can do: Take stock of your relationships with other people and nourish them by spending time with people you care about. If you are isolated, get involved in activities that help others.

4. How much personal control do you believe you have over your health? There are two primary ways that you can approach your health—you can rely on your doctor to tell you what to do…or you can actively participate in your health care.

Why it matters: Research shows that people are healthier and have better medical outcomes when they take responsibility for their own care…make important lifestyle changes… and generally put themselves in charge of their own health.

What you can do: The first step is to motivate yourself and make a commitment to yourself and those you love that you will be proactive in advocating for your own health. The second step is to learn what you can about the health conditions that affect you.

5. Do you have physical problems or certain personality traits that remind you of someone in your family? Your family medical history can help identify diseases that you may be predisposed to develop. Family history is an especially important risk factor for depression, heart disease, diabetes, high blood pressure and allergic and autoimmune disorders. Most cancers are not due to genetic risk factors, but to environmental exposures or diet.

Why it matters: A family history of a disease doesn't mean that you will develop that illness—but knowing your history, or just noticing similarities, makes it easier to predict and prevent future problems. For example, if you suffer from unexplained fatigue, weight gain or mood disturbances, and there is a history of thyroid problems in a close family member, such as a parent or sibling, your symptoms may be thyroid-related.

What you can do: Maintain a family tree that includes the health status and cause of death of grandparents, parents, aunts, uncles and siblings—and show it to your doctor.

Answers to Questions You Always Wanted to Ask

Billy Goldberg, MD, emergency medicine physician at Bellevue Hospital and New York University Medical Center, both in New York City, is coauthor of *Why Do Men Fall Asleep After Sex? More Questions You'd Only Ask a Doctor After Your Third Whiskey Sour.* Three Rivers.

We all have little things that we would like to ask our doctors—but we don't want to waste their time or we're too embarrassed to ask. *Here, an emergency room physician answers those questions…*

•Do carrots improve vision?

There is only a grain of truth to this—carrots are a good source of vitamin A, a lack of which can lead to blindness. However, most people get enough vitamin A in their diets with or without carrots.

The story that carrots really improve vision was started by Britain's Royal Air Force during World War II. The Brits didn't want Germany to figure out that they had developed improved radar systems, so they spread the word that the unprecedented nighttime accuracy of British fighter pilots was the result of eyesight sharpened by carrot consumption. Though the war has been over for 60 years, the carrot cover story remains widely believed.

Consuming excessive amounts of vitamin A in supplement form won't give you superior vision, but it could cause toxicity, with symptoms such as hair loss, fatigue and headaches.

•Why do men have nipples?

During the early weeks of embryonic development, both men and women are designed on the female template. Not until about six weeks after conception do male embryos begin to show male characteristics. By that point, males have nipples.

Men also have a small amount of breast tissue, which means it is possible for them to develop breast cancer. Men account for approximately one in every 100 cases of breast cancer. The first sign of male breast cancer usually is a breast lump, the same as it is for a woman.

•Why does urine smell funny after we eat asparagus?

Asparagus contains mercaptan, a sulfur compound that also is found in onions, garlic, rotten eggs and the secretions of skunks. In the case of asparagus, the odor isn't produced until the compound has been broken down by digestive enzymes. Interestingly, not everyone has the gene for the enzyme that breaks down mercaptan, so some people can consume asparagus without having their urine smell afterward. A study in *British Journal of Clinical Pharmacology* found that less than half of British people tested produced the odor, while all French people tested did.

•Does cracking knuckles lead to arthritis?

There's no connection. Knuckle cracking is relatively harmless—the loud noise is just bubbles popping in the synovial fluid surrounding the joint. Long-term knuckle cracking might stretch the ligaments surrounding the joint, causing a slight decrease in grip strength, but this isn't likely to become a significant problem.

•Why do we cry when we slice onions?

Cutting into an onion causes enzymes and amino acids in the onion to react together in a way that forms sulfenic acids. These sulfenic acids release a chemical called *syn-propanethial-S-oxide* into the air, which comes in contact with the nerve fibers of our corneas and stimulates our tear glands.

Attempts have been made to develop tear-free onions, but it turns out that when you remove the enzymes that lead to crying, you also remove the onion's flavor. Research continues, however, and a flavorful, tear-free onion might be available someday.

For the moment, the best ways to reduce onion tears are to chop under a steady stream of water or wear goggles.

•Why do we tend to feel hungry again only an hour or so after eating Chinese food?

Chinese food emphasizes white rice and noodles. These low-protein, high-carbohydrate foods cause blood sugar to peak, then fall quickly, leaving us hungry again. To avoid this, select Chinese dishes that contain lots of protein, such as chicken, beef, tofu and fish.

•What causes canker sores?

Canker sores, known to doctors as *recurrent apthous ulcers*, are the most common oral disease—yet we still don't know exactly what causes them.

Canker sores, which occur inside the mouth, are different from cold sores, which appear on the lips. Cold sores are caused by the herpes virus and are contagious. Canker sores are not contagious. Unfortunately, there is no treatment for canker sores.

•Do microwave ovens cause cancer?

There is no evidence that modern microwave ovens are capable of causing cancer. This relatively common fear springs from the fact that microwaves use radiation to cook. But while ionizing radiation, such as X-rays, can cause molecular damage, microwaves use nonionizing radiation, which does not, according to all evidence.

If nonionizing radiation did indeed cause cancer, we would have much bigger problems than our microwave ovens—all visible light is nonionizing radiation.

•Why does hair turn gray as we get older?

We lose hair color because the pigment cells in our hair follicles die off as we get older. The age at which this occurs is determined largely by heredity, though smoking or vitamin deficiency can speed up the process.

•Why do cucumber slices soothe puffy eyes?

Cucumbers are 90% water, and that water is likely to be nicely chilled when the vegetable has been stored in the refrigerator. The cold water constricts the blood vessels around the eyes and the puffiness decreases.

If cucumbers don't do the job, try black tea bags soaked in cold water. Not only will the cold water work, the tannic acid in the tea can help reduce swelling as well.

•Why do some people have "innie" belly buttons while others have "outies"?

There's a widespread misconception that the type of belly button you have is determined by the type of knot the doctor tied after you were delivered. I believed this myself—until I delivered my first baby and realized that no knot was involved. Clips are used to clamp off the umbilical cord, then it's cut. The type of belly button you're left with is just a matter of chance, determined by how you heal when the remainder of the umbilical cord dries up and falls off.

Some belly buttons do turn from innies to outies later in life, but that's usually due to hernias in the belly button region.

•Is it true that eating poppy seeds can make you fail a drug test?

Some drug tests do indeed label poppy seed fans as heroin addicts. The same plant that produces poppy seeds also is the source of opium, from which heroin is produced. As little as one teaspoon of poppy seeds might be enough to cause a positive test.

If you know that you're going to have to take a drug test, avoid poppy seeds for about five days. If you have failed a drug test and think that poppy seeds are responsible, there are more precise drug tests that can differentiate between heroin and poppy seeds, so it might be possible to retest your urine sample and prove your innocence.

■ ■ ■ ■

Screening Tests

Many medical tests become unnecessary as we get older. A test should be ordered only if the potential benefit outweighs the potential harm. For many older people who are in only fair or poor health, certain tests are likely to cause more harm, discomfort and anxiety than the diseases they might detect.

Example: Prostate-specific antigen (PSA) screening, which may detect prostate cancer, is not recommended for men with a life expectancy of less than 10 years. Older men in poor health will probably experience only the adverse effects of the screening, such as psychological distress, additional procedures due to false-positive results and/or the complications of treating clinically insignificant prostate cancer.

Self-defense: Ask your doctor about the benefits before getting tested for any condition.

Louise C. Walter, MD, assistant professor of geriatrics, University of California, San Francisco, and staff physician at San Francisco VA Medical Center.

Conditions Doctors Often Misdiagnose

Vicki Rackner, MD, a surgeon and clinical instructor at the University of Washington School of Medicine in Seattle, is the author of *The Biggest Skeleton in Your Doctor's Closet*. Medical Bridges.

Each year, up to 40% of Americans who are seen in an emergency room or intensive care unit are misdiagnosed. In some cases, a patient's condition is correctly diagnosed, and appropriate treatment is administered later. In other cases, the time that is lost through a misdiagnosis can be life-threatening.

Example: A patient who has painful abdominal cramping may be diagnosed with "gastroenteritis" (inflammation of the gastrointestinal tract) when the real culprit is a potentially fatal bowel obstruction.

Important: Listen to your intuition, but don't try to self-diagnose your problem. Get a complete evaluation from your doctor and a second opinion, if desired.

Often-misdiagnosed conditions…

Wrong diagnosis: **Gastroenteritis.** Gastroenteritis can be caused by ingesting food or water contaminated with a virus (Norwalk virus, adenovirus)…a bacterium (Salmonella, Escherichia coli)…a parasite (Giardia)…rare microorganisms (amoebas or parasitic worms)… or a food allergy. Gastroenteritis can result in cramping, vomiting and/or diarrhea.

But these symptoms also can characterize bowel obstruction (commonly caused by scar tissue from previous abdominal or pelvic surgery) …appendicitis…gallbladder disease…or antibiotic-associated colitis.

Self-defense: Do not accept a diagnosis of "gastroenteritis" if your symptoms include…

•Crampy abdominal pain that comes and goes. This could indicate a bowel obstruction.

•Pain that begins around the navel and migrates to the lower right abdomen. This could be appendicitis.

•Sudden pain in the upper-right abdomen after eating a high-fat meal. This symptom could be due to a gallbladder attack.

•**Severe diarrhea, abdominal pain and/ or fever.** These symptoms could be caused by pseudomembranous colitis, an inflammatory condition of the colon that occurs in some people who have used antibiotics. It's usually caused by overgrowth of the bacterium *Clostridium difficile*.

To diagnose your condition correctly, your doctor should take a thorough medical history and perform a physical exam. Tests may include blood work, X-rays and an ultrasound or computed tomography (CT) scan.

Wrong diagnosis: **Migraine.** More than 45 million people seek medical care each year for headaches. Many have a true migraine, a severe headache often accompanied by nausea, vomiting and/or extreme sensitivity to light and sound. Others have a tension or cluster headache.

In rare cases, a headache can signal a potentially serious condition, such as a stroke…a ruptured brain aneurysm (a weakened blood vessel that has burst)…a contusion (bruising of the brain)…a concussion (a head injury that can cause headache, confusion and amnesia)…a subdural hematoma (bleeding from veins between the outer and middle layers of tissue covering the brain, usually following a head injury)…a brain tumor…meningitis (a bacterial or viral infection of the membrane that surrounds the spinal cord and brain)…or a sinus infection.

Self-defense: Do not accept a diagnosis of "migraine" if your symptoms include…

•**Headache with confusion, weakness on one side of the body, double vision and/or trouble speaking.** This could indicate a stroke.

•**"The worst headache of my life" or a headache that "hits like a lightning bolt."** These are signs of a possible stroke or ruptured brain aneurysm.

•**Headache that gets worse after coughing, exertion, straining or sudden movement.** This can indicate a ruptured brain aneurysm.

•**Headache after a head injury, especially if the headache gets worse over the next day or two.** It could be a brain injury, such as a contusion, concussion or subdural hematoma.

•**New headache pain or changes in headache pattern** (location, intensity or frequency),

especially in people age 55 or older. This could signal a brain tumor.

•**Headache with a fever, stiff neck and/ or rash.** These are red flags for meningitis.

•**Headache after a recent sore throat, cold or flu.** This could indicate a sinus infection.

Ask your doctor whether you should be seen by a neurologist. Tests may include blood work, a CT or magnetic resonance imaging (MRI) scan, sinus X-rays or a spinal tap, in which a sample of the fluid that surrounds the brain and spinal cord is withdrawn with a needle and sent to a lab for analysis.

Wrong diagnosis: **Muscle strain.** Muscle strain often is diagnosed when a person overexerts himself/herself and then experiences pain and/or swelling.

Among the more serious conditions characterized by these symptoms are an infection…or an aortic dissection (a potentially fatal condition in which the inner layer of the wall of the aorta, the main artery of the body, tears).

Self-defense: Do not accept a diagnosis of "muscle strain" if your symptoms include…

•**Fever and/or a joint that is red and hot.** These are red flags for infectious arthritis (infection of the tissues of a joint).

•**A "ripping" or "tearing" sensation in the upper back.** This commonly occurs in patients who have suffered an aortic dissection.

An evaluation may include X-rays, a CT or MRI scan, blood tests and/or arthrocentesis (removal of joint fluid that is analyzed for bacteria, other microorganisms or gouty crystals).

Wrong diagnosis: **Pleurisy.** Pleurisy is an inflammation of the pleura, the lining of the lung and inner chest wall. This condition is often diagnosed when a sharp chest pain occurs during inhalation.

But chest pain also accompanies heart attack and pulmonary embolism (a blood clot that travels from a leg to the lungs). In addition, pleurisy usually has an underlying cause—such as influenza, pneumonia or fractured ribs—which doctors sometimes fail to identify.

Self-defense: Do not accept a diagnosis of "pleurisy" if your symptoms also include…

•**Shortness of breath, numbness in your arm and/or sweating.** These are all symptoms of a heart attack. In women, heart attack symptoms may include jaw pain, indigestion, back pain and/or fatigue.

•**Rapid heart rate, shortness of breath and/or sharp chest pain that worsens with deep breathing.** These could be red flags for a potentially fatal pulmonary embolism.

Your doctor may order a chest X-ray, electrocardiogram (EKG) or lung scan to look for blood clots.

Wrong diagnosis: **Rash.** Rashes are often harmless immune responses to a substance that a person touches or eats. They usually go away on their own or when treated with over-the-counter cortisone cream.

But rashes also can be due to a bacterial or viral infection.

Self-defense: Do not accept a diagnosis of "rash" if your symptoms also include…

•**Fever, chills, severe headache, aches and pains.** This can indicate an infection, such as Rocky Mountain spotted fever or scarlet fever.

•**Fatigue, muscle and joint stiffness, and a bull's-eye–shaped rash.** These are some signs of Lyme disease.

•**Chills, fever, nausea and/or fluid-filled blisters in a band on one side of the body.** These are signs of shingles.

Your doctor will perform a physical exam and order a blood test and/or other tests, if necessary.

Read This Before You Have "Minor" Surgery

Hector Vila, Jr., MD, assistant professor of oncology and anesthesiology, H. Lee Moffitt Cancer Center, Tampa, FL. *Archives of Surgery.*

Having plastic surgery, endoscopies and other minor surgeries in a doctor's office is risky, a study says.

"Our research compared adverse outcomes and deaths in physicians' offices with those in ambulatory surgical centers," explains study author Dr. Hector Vila, Jr., assistant professor of oncology and anesthesiology at the H. Lee Moffitt Cancer Center in Tampa, Florida. "We found a much higher death rate and a much higher injury rate when surgery was done in the physician's office," he adds.

THE STUDY

Vila and his colleagues studied all the deaths and injuries during surgery in doctors' offices reported to the Florida Board of Medicine from 2000 through 2002. They looked at similar data from ambulatory surgical centers during 2000, reported to the Florida Agency for Health Care Administration.

The study included all types of outpatient surgeries. Vila says most surgeries were plastic surgeries and endoscopies, a procedure using a fiber optic scope to look at the intestinal tract.

Vila's team found that the injury rate in doctors' offices was 66 per 100,000 operations, compared with five per 100,000 surgeries in ambulatory surgical centers. For death, the corresponding numbers were nine per 100,000 in doctors' offices and less than one per 100,000 in ambulatory surgical centers.

The researchers note that if all procedures had been done in surgical centers, approximately 43 injuries and six deaths would have been prevented each year. Vila believes that this problem is not confined to Florida.

CHECK THEIR CREDENTIALS

There are many reasons for the dramatic difference in death and injury rates, Vila says, including a lack of equipment and personnel, a lack of set procedures and the inability to deal with emergencies. "Sometimes it's the [lack of] credentials of the people performing the procedure or administering the anesthesia," Vila adds.

"To work in a hospital, a physician has to apply for privileges, but a private physician can do whatever he or she wants in his or her office," Vila says.

In addition, office surgeries are much cheaper than those done in ambulatory surgery centers.

Patients concerned with safety need to ask several questions before deciding to have surgery in their doctor's office, Vila advises.

"You should ask your doctor if he has the same standards as those used in the hospital or ambulatory surgical center. Are the physicians board-certified in the specialty that normally performs this procedure? Do they have the same equipment? Do they have emergency resuscitative equipment? Who is going to be giving the anesthesia? And, where will you be taken if there is an emergency?

"If you are unsure, then you should consider having your surgery in an ambulatory surgical center," Vila says.

The American College of Surgeons offers more information about surgical procedures and risk at *www.facs.org*. Click on "Public and Press."

Avoid Unnecessary Surgery

Charles B. Inlander, a consumer advocate and health-care consultant based in Fogelsville, PA. He was founding president of People's Medical Society, a consumer health advocacy group active in the 1980s and 1990s. He is the author of more than 20 books, including *Take This Book to the Hospital with You*. St. Martin's.

Few things are worse than having an unnecessary surgical procedure. Yet every year, millions of Americans have operations they do not need. In fact, the Congressional Committee on Energy and Commerce reports that 20% of all surgeries performed in the US are unnecessary. *Surgeries you may not need…*

• **Prostate removal.** The most common treatment for prostate cancer is removal of the prostate gland, but clinical studies show that the operation is of little benefit to men who have a life expectancy of 10 years or less because the cancer grows very slowly. This means that most men over age 75 have nothing to gain and may suffer from side effects of the surgery, such as incontinence and infection. Regardless of a man's age, he should seek several medical opinions (including that of a urologist who does not perform surgery).

• **Cataract removal.** More than a decade ago, the Agency for Healthcare Policy and Research warned that many of the operations performed to remove a cataract were not necessary. The National Institutes for Health suggests that cataract removal is best performed if your vision has been reduced to at least 20/150—even with glasses. Yet each year, hundreds of thousands of Americans have the surgery even though their eyesight is

far better than that. In many cases, surgery will not improve sight and can cause infection. For a more impartial view, get a second opinion from an optometrist (a health-care provider licensed to provide a broad range of eye-care services), rather than a surgical ophthalmologist (a medical doctor who specializes in eye disease).

• **Gallbladder removal.** Since the late 1980s, the number of gallbladder surgeries has increased by 40%. The reason is the advent of minimally invasive laparoscopic surgery. This procedure can be done in an outpatient setting and is quicker (conventional surgery typically requires three days in the hospital), more convenient and more profitable for doctors. But it is often not necessary. Before agreeing to gallbladder removal consult an experienced internist about nonsurgical options, such as a special diet or the gallstone-dissolving medication *ursodiol* (Actigall).

• **Wisdom tooth extraction.** This is the granddaddy of all unnecessary surgeries, as about half of all wisdom tooth extractions are unnecessary. For decades, major dental organizations and journals have criticized the removal of wisdom teeth that are symptom free. To protect yourself, any time a dentist recommends having your wisdom teeth removed, get a second opinion from another dentist. If wisdom teeth are impacted, infected or are causing other teeth to shift, surgery may be necessary. But many times they will not cause any problems, and you can save yourself a lot of time, money and pain.

"Full-Body" CT Scans

Mark A. Stengler, ND, naturopathic physician in private practice, La Jolla, CA…adjunct associate clinical professor at the National College of Natural Medicine, Portland, OR…author of 16 books, including *The Natural Physician's Healing Therapies* (Bottom Line Books) and coauthor of *Prescription for Natural Cures* (Wiley)…and author of the *Bottom Line/Natural Healing* newsletter.

It wasn't so long ago that a Cat scan—a computerized X-ray technique, also called a CT (for "computed tomography") scan—seemed very exotic. In fact, if you're age 35 or older, there were no CT scanners in clinical use when you were born. Today, of course, CT scans are commonplace.

Now there's an even more advanced, and highly touted, version—electron beam computed tomography (EBCT), often (erroneously) referred to as a full-body scan. EBCT scans examine the abdominal cavity and chest (including coronary arteries and lungs). These scans are available in cities nationwide and are being promoted as a way to detect coronary artery disease and other abnormalities, including tumors and aneurysms in the chest, abdomen and pelvic area. In many states, a prescription is not required to get a scan. Even if you're healthy, you can just contact an imaging center and ask—and pay—for the test. The idea is to find trouble before any symptoms appear.

EBCT scans use very rapidly processed X-rays that capture images in a fraction of a second. This allows for clear, freeze-frame pictures of the heart and arteries while the heart is beating. Images are captured from many angles, allowing a three-dimensional view of the heart as well as other organs and systems.

The test is painless. While the patient lies on a table, an overhead scan machine takes images in an open environment—not in an enclosed space as with some other CT and magnetic resonance imaging (MRI) scans. Testing usually takes 10 to 15 minutes. Typically, a center's radiologist or cardiologist determines if there are any visible abnormalities and reviews the results with the patient within minutes. Upon your request, a copy of the report and images can be sent to your primary care doctor.

One purpose of an EBCT scan is to determine the amount of calcium buildup in the lining of the arteries, including the coronary arteries. Several studies, including one conducted at the respected Cooper Institute in Dallas and published in the *American Journal of Epidemiology*, have shown a correlation between the degree of calcification and the severity of hardening of the arteries, known as atherosclerosis. A low level of calcium buildup in the arteries means that your risk for coronary artery disease is low. A high level means that you are at higher risk for cardiovascular problems in the future.

There are a few downsides to EBCT scans. One is the radiation exposure from the X-rays—which can be two to 10 times more than that of a standard X-ray. Radiation is a known risk factor

for cancer (although the risk appears small with occasional scans). The EBCT scan also may result in "false positives"—meaning that doctors may spot a suspected lesion that requires follow-up tests, possibly even an invasive biopsy, and it may turn out to be nothing serious. Lastly, many insurance companies don't cover EBCT preventive screening. A scan costs $850 to $1,500.

Despite the financial cost, I do recommend that people age 40 and older get a preventive EBCT screening. If the results are normal, then follow up with another in five to 10 years. The test is even more important for those with a strong family history of heart disease or cancer. While EBCT scanning is not foolproof, it can help detect life-threatening diseases that are best treated with early intervention.

■ ■ ■ ■

Future Hospitals

New hospitals under construction will likely have only private rooms.

Reason: Patients in private rooms have up to 45% lower risk for hospital-acquired ("nosocomial") infections than patients who share hospital rooms.

Richard A. Van Enk, PhD, director, infection control and epidemiology, Bronson Methodist Hospital, Kalamazoo, MI, and leader of a study of infection rates in private rooms, published in *The Architecture of Hospitals*. NAI.

Hospitals' Hidden Killers: Blood Clots

Steven Deitelzweig, MD, chairman, department of hospital medicine and vice president of medical affairs, Ochsner Clinic Foundation, New Orleans.

Samuel Goldhaber, MD, director, Venous Thromboembolism Research Group, Brigham and Women's Hospital and professor of medicine, Harvard University Medical School, both in Boston.

Doctors at the Ochsner Clinic Foundation in New Orleans have started a campaign against two conditions that are responsible for 10% of all hospital deaths each year.

One of these conditions is *deep vein thrombosis* (DVT), which occurs when a blood clot forms in the leg and blocks the flow of blood. This can lead to potentially life-threatening pulmonary embolisms, which are caused when a clot breaks free, travels upward through the body and lodges in a lung. If the clot is large enough, it can cause sudden death.

Approximately 600,000 Americans develop pulmonary embolisms every year, and 200,000 people die from them. The American College of Chest Physicians says it may be the most preventable cause of hospital death.

WHO'S AT RISK?

People hospitalized for long periods of time are particularly at risk because blood can collect in their legs and increase the probability of a clot forming.

Air travelers can also be prone to the condition because of the long hours spent cramped in a seat, experts say.

Those with cancer, chronic heart or respiratory failure, and an inherited or acquired predisposition to clotting and varicose veins also have an increased risk. So do people who are obese, as well as women who are pregnant or are using birth control pills or hormone-replacement therapy.

Symptoms of DVT can include leg pain, swelling, tenderness, discoloration or redness. Often, though, there are no symptoms.

Dr. Samuel Goldhaber, director, Venous Thromboembolism Research Group at Brigham and Women's Hospital in Boston, says the conditions are difficult to diagnose.

WHAT CAN BE DONE

Dr. Steven Deitelzweig, Ochsner's chairman of the department of hospital medicine, and his colleagues have developed a clinical assessment tool to help identify people who are at risk for developing DVT. The various risk factors—obesity, heart failure, infections, lung problems, prolonged immobility—are put on a grid. Everyone admitted to the hospital is assessed and put in a category of low, medium or high risk.

People who have two risk factors get treated with nonpharmacological devices, such as compression stockings.

If a person has at least three risk factors, or two risk factors and a history of stroke or cancer, they get at least one blood-thinning drug.

How to Choose the Right Hospital

Charles B. Inlander, a consumer advocate and healthcare consultant based in Fogelsville, PA. He was founding president of People's Medical Society, a consumer health advocacy group active in the 1980s and 1990s. He is the author of more than 20 books, including *Take This Book to the Hospital with You*. St. Martin's.

If you assume that hospitals are roughly equivalent in the quality of care they offer, you could be making a deadly mistake. Most people are not aware of the differences among the various types of hospitals. *What you should know...*

There are two major categories of hospitals—specialty hospitals and general hospitals.

•**Specialty hospitals** focus on either one type of medical condition, such as cancer or eye problems, or deal exclusively with a specific category of patients, such as women or children.

Advantage: Greater access to applicable new technology and treatment techniques.

Disadvantage: Since not all communities have specialty hospitals, you may have to travel a great distance to use one.

Best used for: Complicated problems, such as major heart surgery, or rare conditions, such as certain cancers.

•**General hospitals** deal with a wide variety of medical conditions.

Advantage: General hospitals are better equipped to handle unexpected medical situations that may occur in the course of treatment.

Disadvantage: They may not be expert in rare or unique problems.

A general hospital can be a community hospital or a medical center…

•**Community hospitals** typically have fewer than 250 beds but are fully equipped to handle most medical conditions.

Advantage: Because they have fewer patients and shorter lengths of stay, on average, community hospitals have lower infection rates than larger hospitals.

Disadvantage: They may not have as many highly trained specialists.

Best used for: Routine treatment and surgery, such as appendectomy.

•**Medical centers** are large institutions that are typically, though not always, affiliated with universities.

Advantage: Medical centers offer state-of-the-art intensive care and coronary care.

Disadvantage: Because medical centers typically have sicker patients who get less personalized attention, higher infection rates are often reported at these facilities.

Best used for: Complicated conditions requiring medical experts in a number of specialties—for example, cardiology and endocrinology—and/or rare conditions that require comprehensive diagnostic services.

Community hospitals and medical centers can be classified as teaching or nonteaching facilities…

•**Teaching hospitals** provide teaching programs for medical students, interns (students still in training) and residents (doctors learning specialties).

Advantage: Access to cutting-edge technology and renowned expertise (that's why students come there).

Disadvantage: Students are learning on you! Therefore, you are often treated as a condition, not a person. There are no studies indicating that teaching hospitals are better than nonteaching hospitals, so choose the type of facility that best meets your needs.

•**Nonteaching hospitals** are strictly care facilities.

Advantage: Less intrusive care.

Disadvantage: Usually fewer specialties are offered.

Best used for: People who are being treated for non-life-threatening conditions.

What You Should Do if You Receive Poor Medical Care

Charles B. Inlander, a consumer advocate and health-care consultant based in Fogelsville, PA. He was founding president of People's Medical Society, a consumer health advocacy group active in the 1980s and 1990s. He is the author of more than 20 books, including *Take This Book to the Hospital with You.* St. Martin's.

In my almost 40 years of helping consumers with health-care problems, the number-one reason that people have contacted me is to find out where to file a complaint about a doctor, hospital, nurse or pharmacist. In most cases, the individual is not interested in filing a medical malpractice lawsuit. Rather, he/she simply wants to report shoddy business practices, including billing problems, or poor health care.

Filing a complaint is relatively easy. But knowing where to file can be tricky. All complaints are investigated. Results vary from state to state, and from board to board, but you will be notified of the outcome, which could include suspension or revocation of the health-care provider's license. *Here's how and where to file a complaint when you have a gripe against a health-care practitioner or a facility…*

•**State licensing board.** If you have a complaint against a doctor, contact the state medical licensing board in the state where the problem occurred. All doctors must be licensed by the state in which they practice. You can find the address, phone number and Web site of the medical licensing board in your state at *www.aimmembers.org/boarddirectory.*

Filing a complaint against a nurse or a pharmacist also is done at the state level. The National Council of State Boards of Nursing lists all the boards and their contact information at *www.ncsbn.org.* Click "Boards of Nursing" on their home page. The National Association of Boards of Pharmacy also lists each state board at *www.nabp.net*. Click "Boards of Pharmacy" on the home page. Hospitals and nursing homes are usually licensed by a division of a state's health department. If you do not have access to a computer, call your state's governor's office for the phone number of the board you are trying to reach.

•**Attorney general's office.** If you have a complaint about a doctor's bill or you suspect fraudulent billing, you also should file a complaint with your state's attorney general's office. You can find contact information from the National Association of Attorneys General at *www. naag.org*. Click "The Attorneys General" on the homepage. The attorney general investigates and litigates all business and criminal charges that might need to be brought against a licensed doctor or facility. The attorney general's office may refer some criminal complaints to your local district attorney's office.

•**Medicare.** If you are a Medicare or Medicaid beneficiary and have a complaint against a doctor or hospital for matters relating to your insurance, call Medicare at 800-633-4227 to file your complaint. They will pass it along to the appropriate government agency.

All complaints should be made in writing. To ensure a proper investigation, include the full name of the offending party…tell where, when and what time the incident occurred…and include statements of witnesses, if available. Also include copies of bills and other pertinent paperwork, if requested.

■ ■ ■ ■

Longer ER Waits

Emergency room waiting times are getting longer. Because of rising patient volume, the average amount of time a patient waited to see a physician in the ER increased from 38 minutes in 1997 to 47 minutes in 2004 (the most recent statistics available). According to the National Center for Health Statistics, more than 1.1 billion visits were made to emergency departments, doctors' offices and hospital outpatient centers in 2004.

National Center for Health Statistics, Hyattsville, MD.

How to Stay Safe In the Hospital

David J. Sherer, MD, a board-certified anesthesiologist in clinical practice at Kaiser Permanente, Chevy Chase, MD, is author of *Dr. David Sherer's Hospital Survival Guide: 100+ Ways to Make Your Hospital Stay Safe and Comfortable.* Claren.

As many as 195,000 patients die each year in US hospitals because of medical errors, according to a study by HealthGrades, a leading health-care rating company. Here's how to stay safe next time you're in the hospital. If you're too incapacitated by your illness or injury to do these things for yourself, a family member can do many of them for you.

1. Keep a list of prescribed medications with dosages. You can get this list from the attending physician (the doctor in charge of your case), an intern, resident or nurse. Receiving the wrong medication is one of the most common—and dangerous—hospital errors. When a hospital staff member hands you a pill or starts to hook an intravenous (IV) bag to your arm, ask what you're being given. *If the drug isn't on the list of medications you have been prescribed…*

•Ask "What does this treat?" If the answer isn't a condition that you think you have, double-check that the drug provider knows your name and birthday, to confirm you're the patient he/she thinks you are.

•Make sure it's not a drug with a similar name. If you've been prescribed Zantac and someone's trying to give you Xanax or you take Celebrex but the nurse shows up with Cerebyx, someone may have misheard the instructions and provided the wrong medication.

•If you're allergic to any medications, make a sign to this effect and post it over your hospital bed. *Example:* "Allergic to Penicillin."

Also, if it is a drug you've been prescribed but you previously received a different dosage, make sure the change was intentional.

2. Label yourself. If you're in the hospital for an operation on a limb, a lung or anything else that you have more than one of on or in your body, use a marker or ballpoint pen to write "this arm," "this leg" or just "yes" on the side that should go under the knife, so there is no confusion in the operating room. (At some hospitals, your surgeon will sign his initials to the body part in advance of your operation.) Don't use an "X" to mark the spot, because an "X" is ambiguous—it could be misinterpreted as "not here."

3. Schedule your hospital stay wisely. New interns, residents and medical school students begin assignments at teaching hospitals in early July. If possible, postpone elective procedures until a different time, when young medical professionals have more experience.

If you can't avoid a July stay in a teaching hospital, be wary about what you let interns and medical students do. If one wants to draw blood, insert a catheter or perform another common hospital task, ask how many times he/she has done it before. If the answer doesn't fill you with confidence, insist that a nurse or resident take over.

Also, at any time of the year, try to schedule your surgery for early in the day. By the end of a long day, even the most skilled surgeons aren't at the top of their game. Also, because patients aren't allowed to eat or drink before surgery, a late operation means extra hours of hunger, thirst and worry.

4. Get to know the staff. A wide range of doctors, nurses, physician's assistants, interns, residents, orderlies and others might be involved in your care. Whenever a new face arrives, politely ask his name and what his role is, unless his name tag makes this obvious, then engage in some friendly conversation.

If you make a personal connection with everyone involved in your care, it reduces the odds that you'll be mistaken for a different patient with potentially dangerous results. It also increases the odds that you'll get prompt care. Because most hospital patients are preoccupied with their health problems, the few who remain composed, personable and interested in the hospital staff often are treated more favorably.

5. Know who should do what. Find out when you can expect your attending physician to visit your bedside, and save any questions you have until then. Answers you receive from anyone else might not be definitive.

Don't let a UAP (also known as unlicensed assistive personnel or nurse assistant) insert an IV or catheter, change a sterile dressing, give you a shot or feed you through a tube. Such tasks should be handled by trained medical staff, such as a registered nurse. Check the person's name tag. If there's no designation, such as RN, ask what his training is.

6. Select the right surgeon. Unless it is an emergency, you shouldn't necessarily settle for the first surgeon you're sent to. *When you meet with a surgeon for a consultation, ask...*

•Are you board-certified in this specialty? Or check this on the Web site of the American Board of Medical Specialties (*www.abms.org*). You will have to register, but it is free.

•How many times have you performed this exact procedure? You want someone who has done it hundreds or even thousands of times. If the procedure is rare, you at least want a surgeon who performs it dozens of times per year.

7. Find the right hospital. If your surgeon has privileges at more than one hospital in your area, the annual "America's Best Hospital Guide" of *US News and World Report* (*www.usnews.com* and click on "Rankings" on the right, then on "Best Hospitals") can help you decide which facility is best for a given procedure. Be aware that your health insurance might limit you to a particular hospital or restrict your choice of surgeons.

8. Plan for the unexpected *before* you wind up in a hospital. Ask your doctor now which emergency room in your region he considers the best, assuming that there's more than one. (Of course, in situations where every second counts, the closest ER is almost always the best choice.)

9. Speak up. Make no effort to conceal your pain in a crowded emergency room—the ER staff might equate a quiet patient with a low-priority medical problem and treat others ahead of you. If you must wait, let the staff know if the pain gets worse...you have trouble breathing...feel increasingly lightheaded...or lose feeling in, or control over, part of your body.

10. Encourage bedside visitors. Visitors don't just keep you company in the hospital. They can keep an eye on the quality of your care when you're unable to do so yourself. And because hospital employees know that family members keep an eye on what's going on, more visitors tend to mean more attention from the staff.

11. Warn your anesthesiologist of any loose teeth. A loose tooth could be knocked out during intubation (when a breathing tube is placed in your windpipe), causing a potentially serious infection if the tooth reaches your lungs. Also, ask your doctor about removing any dentures or artificial teeth before you're taken to the operating room.

■ ■ ■ ■

Insurance for High Risk

Thirty-four states guarantee health insurance to residents through high-risk pools. Rules vary.

Caution: Three states popular with retirees —Arizona, Florida and Nevada—don't have open high-risk pools. If you want to move to one of these states or a state without a high-risk pool, be sure you have private insurance or wait until you qualify for Medicare.

Details at *www.communicatingforamerica. org*.

Communicating for America, Fergus Falls, MN.

Survive a Trip to the Emergency Room

Joel Cohen, MD, medical director of MD Room-Service/DoctorCare, a house call practice in Scottsdale, AZ. He has practiced emergency care and internal medicine for 15 years and is author of *ER: Enter at Your Own Risk—How to Avoid Dangers Inside Emergency Rooms.* New Horizon.

To experience true chaos, just visit an emergency room. Through those metal doors is a busy, often disorganized place that can be hazardous to your health.

ERs are overcrowded and understaffed. You may be treated by an overworked medical student, an exhausted intern or a doctor trained in a field unrelated to your problem.

Obtaining high-quality emergency care fast can be vital after an accident or when a chronic illness, such as heart disease or asthma, suddenly becomes life threatening. But in a surprising number of situations, you'll have enough leeway to *choose* your ER.

Key: Know how to go to the right place at the right time for the right reasons—and be treated by the right caregiver. *Here's how...*

PREPARATION IS IMPORTANT

Get ready for the ER visit that you hope you'll never need. *Do your homework...*

•**Visit all ERs within 30 minutes of your home.** If your condition demands exceptional treatment, arriving in a half hour may be better than being transferred from another hospital later.

Look around. Would you feel well cared for?

Snowbird alert: If you have multiple homes or travel to the same places frequently, also do this exercise in these locations.

•**Identify facilities geared to your health problems.**

Example: If you have a heart condition, locate the ER with the best cardiac service. Your ultimate plan will be to ask an ambulance driver to take you there if your condition, such as symptoms of a mild heart attack, permits.

It surprises many people to learn that you often can get an ambulance crew to take you to the hospital of your choice. If the ambulance must go elsewhere or your condition demands faster treatment, the paramedic will say so.

Find the best ERs: Ask your primary care doctor, pulmonologist, cardiologist or other specialist where to find local high-level trauma or teaching hospitals. Ask the public relations departments at nearby hospitals for brochures promoting the hospitals' areas of expertise. Read hospital Web sites. Consult Castle Connolly Medical Ltd., a guide to top doctors and hospitals (212-367-8400, ext. 16, *www.castleconnolly.com*).

Cost: $24.95 for a one-year membership.

•**Wear a tag, necklace or bracelet identifying your medical status.**

Examples: Diabetes, medication allergies, need for dialysis. Wearing this information on a medical alert tag will help ensure that you receive appropriate care. Also, medical personnel will be able to retrieve your health information by calling the tag sponsor.

Information: MedicAlert (888-633-4298, *www.medicalert.org*)...Bodyguard Medical I.D. Tags (800-383-7790, *www.medicalidtags.com*).

KEEP THESE ER AIDS IN YOUR WALLET

Regularly update information that could be lifesaving in the ER. *Don't leave home without a...*

• **List of your drug allergies** (or the statement "no known drug allergies").

• **List of all current medications,** prescription and nonprescription (herbs, vitamins, antacids), including dose and reason.

• **Health insurance and/or Medicare card.**

• **Miniature copy of your baseline electrocardiogram** (ECG), laminated. Take your ECG readout to a copy place, reduce it to wallet size and cover it with self-stick clear plastic sheets, sold at stationery and office supply stores.

Why: Comparing a new ECG with an old one can increase accuracy in diagnosing heart problems.

• **Research your health insurance plan's emergency coverage.** Must you report an ER visit within 24 hours? What if you're out of town or taken to an out-of-plan hospital? Having this information on hand will save precious time when admitted to an ER.

• **Maintain a relationship with a trusted physician.** In an emergency, your doctor may help you decide whether an ER visit is warranted...meet you there or consult by phone...recommend a specialist if you need one...find you a local doctor if you're out of town.

KNOW WHEN TO GO

For flu, a twisted ankle, longtime bad back or repeat kidney stone pain, call your doctor for an appointment. Consider going to a good walk-in urgent-care center (their quality varies tremendously) if your doctor isn't available and your insurance covers it. If you can, avoid ERs on Mondays and on Friday and Saturday nights, the busiest times.

Do head for the ER if you're experiencing unbearable or worst-ever pain...profuse bleeding...unfamiliar or severe chest pain, shortness of breath or abdominal pain...sudden arm or leg numbness or weakness...any other signs of a stroke or heart attack (see below).

STEALTH SYMPTOMS

If you are having a stroke or heart attack, the sooner you reach an ER that has the appropriate technology and expertise, the better. When given within about three hours for stroke, six hours for a heart attack, clot-busting drugs may save your life or reduce disability. Optimal stroke treatment can make the difference between paralysis and a little weakness.

Little-known symptom: In older women, shortness of breath is a more common primary heart attack symptom than chest pain.

Other subtle heart symptoms: Weakness ...fatigue...unfamiliar indigestion...jaw or upper back pain.

Information: American Heart Association (800-242-8721, *www.americanheart.org*)...National Heart, Lung, and Blood Institute (301-592-8573, *www.nhlbi.nih.gov/actintime*).

Subtle stroke symptoms: Severe headache... facial tingling...drooping mouth...unexplained dizziness.

Information: American Stroke Association (888-478-7653, *www.strokeassociation.org*).

THE BEST CARE ONCE THERE

At the ER, contribute to the quality of your care. *Be sure to...*

• **Enter riding.** Patients arriving by ambulance get much faster attention than walk-ins. Don't let a friend drive you unless waiting for an ambulance would take too long.

• **Focus on one or two chief complaints.** The more vague you are, the less seriously your problem will be taken.

Example: Mention the new sharp pain in your side, not your arthritic hip.

• **Help the staff to help you.** Don't accept every test or treatment suggested without a discussion. Ask the doctor treating you in the ER to help you decide whether the potential gains of any proposed intervention justify possible risks.

• **Identify yourself and your circumstances often.** Ask what you're being given and why. To a nurse adding medication to your IV line, say, "Do you know about my drug allergies?" Don't assume that everyone has read your chart.

• **Be wary.** Reject medications and prescriptions proposed without logical, compelling reasons. Refuse any risky or unnecessary test or treatment.

Reasons: Older people are especially vulnerable to complications from invasive procedures... standard adult drug dosages can be too strong for older people.

If you are sensitive to drugs or you have kidney or liver problems, tell every ER staff member who treats you.

•**Don't leave too soon.** An ER staff eager to "clear the board" may want to send you home although you feel the same as or worse than when you arrived. Explain that you still feel bad. Ask the person discharging you, "Are you an attending physician here? Will you discuss my case with my family doctor?" You can also ask to speak to the attending physician yourself, but he/she may not be available.

TAKE AN ADVOCATE

It's hard to advocate for yourself in the midst of a health emergency. A relative, friend or neighbor can make sure your needs are met… scrutinize your care…discuss options…make phone calls…take detailed notes. Staff are more vigilant when someone is watching.

Your advocate can request the business card of every doctor who sees you…the name of every nurse who treats you…the name of every test that you're given. You may need these details later in the day or for your records.

Self-defense: With an "ER buddy," visit ERs together and compare notes. Show each other where your relevant medical papers are kept, such as health-care proxies naming the person who can make health decisions for you. Agree to accompany each other to the ER if needed.

Avoid Deadly Errors in the Hospital

Michael F. Roizen, MD, chief wellness officer at the Cleveland Clinic, OH, is coauthor of *YOU: The Smart Patient* (Free Press). Dr. Roizen has cowritten *YOU: The Owner's Manual* (HarperCollins), and served on the boards of five nonprofit foundations. He is former chair of a Food and Drug Administration advisory committee and has published over 160 peer-reviewed papers.

The hospital is one of the most dangerous places you'll ever go. Patients are exposed to bacteria and viruses…subjected to tests and procedures with high risks…and given drugs that should be closely monitored—but sometimes aren't.

Between 44,000 and 98,000 Americans die annually from hospital errors. Although patients can't control everything that happens in the hospital, they can lower their risks more than they realize.

Example: Use only a hospital that's accredited by The Joint Commission. Accreditation means the hospital is evaluated every three years to ensure that it meets the best standards in cleanliness, infection control, drug administration guidelines, etc. More than 15,000 health-care facilities are accredited—but many aren't. To check, go to *www.qualitycheck.org*, or call 630-792-5800. *Other ways to stay safe…*

PICK THE BEST HOSPITAL

Teaching hospitals affiliated with major medical universities tend to have the latest technology and best-trained staff. If you require major surgery (such as a transplant operation) or have a life-threatening condition (such as an aortic aneurysm or pancreatic cancer), a teaching hospital is your best option. Smaller hospitals are fine for patients with "routine" health problems, such as pneumonia or a broken leg.

Warning: In the summer months, teaching hospitals are largely staffed by new residents and interns. Their lack of experience can adversely affect patient care. If you can, avoid teaching hospitals during the first two weeks of July, when the new school year begins. *Other points to consider…*

•**Is it a "magnet" hospital?** Medical centers with outstanding nursing programs earn this designation from the American Nurses Credentialing Center (800-284-2378, *www.nursecredentialing.org*). Patients in these hospitals benefit from improved care…less staff turnover…and high-quality physicians, who are more likely to work at a hospital with magnet status.

•**Are there full-time *intensivists* and *hospitalists*?** Intensivists are doctors who specialize in treating critically ill patients. Hospitalists are doctors who treat only hospital patients. Both types of specialists provide superior hospital care and don't maintain private practices "on the side."

•**How often does the hospital perform the procedure you're undergoing?** The best outcomes usually occur at hospitals where a given procedure is performed most often, on average.

Examples: A top-flight hospital will perform at least 500 open-heart procedures annually…100 carotid-artery grafts or surgeries …and 25 mastectomies.

CHOOSE THE BEST SURGEON

Only use a surgeon who is board certified in the specialty related to your operation—neurosurgery, cardiac surgery, etc. Look for the letters "FACS" (Fellow, American College of Surgeons) after his/ her name. This means that the surgeon has been evaluated for competence and ethical standards.

Helpful: Call the hospital anesthesiology department, and ask one of the anesthesiologists which surgeon he would pick. (Anesthesiologists often are free between 3 pm and 5 pm.) They know all the surgeons and have no reason not to give a straight answer.

Once you have some recommendations, choose a surgeon who does only a few types of procedures. Research has shown that surgeons who specialize—in nerve-sparing prostate surgery, for example—have better results and fewer complications than the national average.

Caution: Don't shave your surgical site before surgery. You'll wind up with thousands of invisible nicks that increase the risk for infection. Let the operating room staff do it. They use special creams that prevent nicks.

Important: Ask the anesthesiologist to provide a blanket (if it won't get in the way) to keep you warm during surgery. Patients who maintain normothermia (normal body temperature) have a lower risk for infection and other complications.

PREVENT HOSPITAL INFECTIONS

Each year, an estimated two million hospital patients develop an infection. With the emergence of antibiotic-resistant bacteria, even a minor initial infection can be fatal.

We all know the importance of hand washing, so insist that visitors (including nurses and doctors) wash their hands before touching you. A quick rinse doesn't help. Studies show that you must wash vigorously with soap and warm water for at least 15 seconds to remove all bacteria. As an alternative, hand-sanitizing gel, which is now located outside many hospital rooms, may be used by visitors.

Other self-defense strategies…

•**Keep a bottle of hand-sanitizing gel at your bedside.** Use this hand cleanser yourself before eating.

•**Beware of the TV remote control.** One study found that remote controls in hospitals have three times more bacteria than doorknobs or nurse call buttons. To protect yourself, cover the TV remote with a new hospital glove. You'll still be able to change the channels.

•**Ask about the stethoscope.** Doctors and nurses are supposed to clean their stethoscopes with alcohol between patients—but some get too busy and forget. Uncleaned stethoscopes have been linked to hospital infections.

DRUG PROTECTION

Drug mistakes—giving the wrong drug, a dangerous drug combination or the wrong dose—often occur in hospitals. Ask your primary care doctor to supervise all of your health care, including drug prescriptions. If that isn't possible, ask one of the hospitalists to do it. Patients with one supervising doctor face fewer risks.

Each time you're given medication: Show your ID bracelet. To ensure that you're getting the right drug (medical test or procedure), ask the nurse to check your ID wrist bracelet.

Also, ask the nurse to tell you what each drug is and why you're taking it. Don't take a drug unless you're sure it's the one that you're supposed to be taking. If you're receiving a medical test or procedure, confirm that it's the correct one.

Finally, ask a family member or friend to help monitor your daily care. This is especially important if you are not able to do so.

Are You Being Overcharged for Medical Care?

Sid Kirchheimer, an investigative reporter and author of the "Scam Alert" column in *AARP Bulletin*, is author of *Scam Proof Your Life: 377 Smart Ways to Protect You and Your Family from Ripoffs, Bogus Deals & Other Consumer Headaches.* Sterling.

Three-quarters of hospital bills have overcharges, and the average overcharge is about $1,000. Doctors, too, are handing inflated bills to patients.

Good news: It's simple to fight back.

If your health insurance completely covers hospital and doctor visits, these steps might not be necessary, though making the extra effort to eliminate overcharges can help bring down medical costs for everyone. Also, be aware that your insurance coverage might not be as comprehensive as you think—call your insurance carrier or review the exclusions section of your policy.

DOCTORS' BILLS

To avoid paying more than you should…

•**Negotiate.** If you have no health insurance, ask your doctor for a discount. Only 13% of patients ever make this request, but when they do, the majority secure a lower price, according to a survey of 2,118 adults conducted by Harris Interactive.

Ask the doctor in person. Requests made by phone or to an office assistant rarely work.

Keep in mind that insurance companies typically pay doctors one-half to two-thirds of the billed amount. If you will be paying out-of-pocket, you can offer to pay somewhere in that range when negotiating a price.

•**Get blood tests done at a lab.** When your doctor does a blood test, he/she charges you for the office visit…plus an added fee for drawing your blood…plus the amount a lab charges to run the test.

Ask the doctor to waive his fees, or go directly to a lab to have the test done and pay only for the test (ask the doctor to supply any necessary paperwork).

Look in your local yellow pages under "Laboratories—Clinical, Medical, Diagnostic" or "Laboratories—Testing" for labs in your area.

•**Don't pay for the follow-up visit.** When you see a doctor about a health problem, you often have to see him again a few weeks later to confirm that the treatment was successful. Chances are, your doctor will look you over for a few seconds during this follow-up, pronounce you well—then bill you another $50 to $100 for the second appointment.

During your initial appointment, tell the doctor that you're paying out-of-pocket and ask if he'll waive or reduce the charge for the follow-up visit, assuming that it takes only a moment.

Many doctors will agree to this, particularly for regular patients.

•**Confirm that tests are necessary.** Doctors often order unnecessary medical tests out of fear that not conducting these tests might open the door for negligence lawsuits later. Unless your health insurance is picking up the entire bill, question whether recommended tests—including MRIs, CAT scans and X-rays—really are necessary. Ask what these tests will determine.

HOSPITAL OVERCHARGES

Here's how to spot overbilling on hospital bills…

•**Ask for a daily itemized bill.** When you check into the hospital, tell the staff member who takes down your insurance information that you want an itemized bill brought to your bed every day. Hospitals are required to provide this upon request.

When you receive these daily bills, review each listing (or ask a family member to do so for you). Were you billed for two doctor visits yesterday even though you saw a doctor only once? Were you billed for tests that you don't recall getting? Are there vague entries, such as "miscellaneous costs" or "lab fees?" Are there listings you can't understand? Tell the nurse you would like to speak with the hospital's patient advocate, then ask the advocate to explain any charge that isn't clear. You might be appalled by what you're told.

Examples: Some hospitals have been known to call a box of tissues a $12 "mucus recovery system" and a bag of ice cubes a $30 "thermal therapy kit."

Save the daily bills so you can reconcile them later with the final bill.

If the patient advocate won't help remove the mistakes and reduce egregious overcharges from your bill, hire an independent medical billing advocate. He/she will examine your bill and fight to remove any overcharges, usually in exchange for a percentage—typically 35%—of the amount he saves you.

To find a medical billing advocate: Contact Medical Billing Advocates of America (540-387-5870, *www.billadvocates.com*)… American Medical Bill Review (480-968-0374, *www.ambr.com*)…or Edward R. Waxman &

Associates (877-679-7224, *www.hospitalbillau diting.com*).

•**Bypass the hospital pharmacy.** Hospitals dramatically overcharge for drugs. A patient might be billed $5 to $10 for a pill that retails for 10 cents elsewhere.

If you are taking medications on an ongoing basis and are not fully covered by insurance, bring your drugs with you to the hospital.

When you consult with your doctor prior to entering the hospital, find out which drugs you're likely to be given during your stay. Ask the doctor to write you prescriptions so that you can buy these drugs at your local pharmacy in advance and avoid the hospital markup. Even if your doctor won't do this, you can bring any nonprescription pills you're told you'll need, such as vitamins.

If you must get drugs through the hospital pharmacy and your insurance isn't footing the bill, ask your doctor to specify generics whenever possible. When you get your itemized daily bill, double-check that you weren't charged for brand-name drugs instead.

•**Watch for double billing.** Hospitals often bill patients twice for certain things. If your bill lists sheets and pillows, ask the hospital's patient advocate if these items are included in your daily room rate. If you're billed for the scrubs, masks and gloves worn by surgical staff, find out if these were included in your bill for operating room time.

Also double-check the times on your operating room bill. Hospitals charge from $20 to $90 for every minute you're in the operating room, so if the time you spent in surgery is padded even a little, it will add a lot to your bill. Your anesthesia records will say how long your operation really lasted.

•**Don't pay for your last day.** Hospital patients are charged the full day's room rate for the day they check in—even if they arrive at 11:59 pm. In exchange, patients are not supposed to be charged for their last day, but hospitals often try to bill for the final day anyway. Sometimes these last-day room bills are simply removed when you complain, but there are hospitals that insist the last-day charge is legitimate for patients who aren't discharged by a certain hour, often noon.

During your hospitalization, ask the hospital's patient advocate whether you'll be billed for your room on the final day of your stay. If the answer is, "Yes, if you're not out by a certain hour," ask your doctor on the next-to-last day of your stay to give you your final checkup and discharge the following morning, rather than waiting until the afternoon. If the doctor says this doesn't fit his schedule, tell the patient advocate that you shouldn't have to pay because the delay is the doctor's fault.

Quality Medical Care at Great Savings

Rudy Rupak, founder of PlanetHospital, a foreign medical-treatment company based in Calabasas, CA, that arranges affordable surgeries overseas and offers free evaluations to those seeking surgery abroad.

More and more Americans are traveling to Europe, the Far East and Mexico for medical treatment.

Key reason: Low prices on top-quality care.

In the past, this kind of medical tourism has been associated with elective plastic surgery and experimental treatments not available in the US. But last year, more than 55,000 Americans went abroad for necessary but nonemergency operations, such as angioplasty, knee replacement and cataract surgery.* Less expensive labor and administrative costs make foreign treatment 50% to 75% cheaper. That can be a bargain even with the additional costs of airfare and accommodations. *Costs of medical procedures vary widely, within the US and internationally, but here are a few examples...*

•**Cataract surgery** in the US costs about $3,000 an eye...in Eastern Europe, it costs $1,200 an eye.

•**Repairing a herniated disk** in the US can range from $30,000 to $90,000...in Bangkok, Thailand, it starts at $3,500.

•**A total knee replacement** in the US is about $48,000...in India, $5,500.

•**Angioplasty** in the US, around $80,000...in Singapore, $15,000.

•**Root canal** in the US can range from $500 to $900...in Mexico, less than $300.

*US insurance companies currently do not pay for overseas surgery if it is not an emergency.

FINDING THE BEST

Flying thousands of miles from home for an operation is not for everyone, but it's worth exploring if you don't have adequate health insurance. Of course, you would want to use only top-quality foreign hospitals and physicians. *Here's how to find them…*

•**Start by word of mouth.** Ask friends and associates who have had medical procedures overseas for recommendations. Also ask doctors who specialize in the type of surgery you need.

•**Check with Partners Harvard Medical International** (PHMI). This is a self-supporting, not-for-profit subsidiary of Harvard Medical School. Its role is to extend internationally the school's tradition of improving the quality of health care. PHMI is affiliated with dozens of overseas medical institutions and hospitals. (617-535-6400, *www.hmi.hms.harvard.edu*)

•**Contact the Joint Commission International** (JCI), the global arm of the institution that accredits US hospitals. JCI hospitals have to meet rigorous standards of patient care, medication safety and infection control. (630-268-2900, *www. jointcommissioninternational.org*)

•**Choose a hospital with an international patient coordinator** on staff. He/she will help you coordinate doctor's appointments, diagnostics and treatment at the hospital, as well as arrange postoperative recuperation. He also can help with practical matters, such as airport pickup, currency exchange, hospital meal choices and interpreters if necessary.

•**Ask the foreign doctor/hospital for references** from Americans who have had the same type of treatment.

TOP FOREIGN HOSPITALS

These are foreign hospitals I would trust for myself and my family…

•**India.**

•*Apollo Hospitals.* Has hospitals in Delhi, Chennai and Hyderabad that cater to foreigners and specialize in heart-related procedures. *www. apollohospitals.com.*

•*Wockhardt Hospitals Group.* Has hospitals in Mumbai (formerly Bombay) and Bangalore that specialize in heart, eye, bone, brain and spinal surgery. Associated with PHMI. *www.wockhardt hospitals.net.*

•*The Max Hospital.* In New Delhi, offers state-of-the-art surgery for brain and pituitary tumors, aneurysms and vascular malformations. *www.maxhealthcare.in/corporate/index.html.*

•**Thailand.**

•*Bumrungrad Hospital.* Bangkok's leading health-care institution. Specialties include endocrinology, nephrology and neurology. *www.bum rungrad.com.*

•*Samitivej Hospitals.* Has branches in Bangkok and Chonburi. Specialties include cardiac and cancer surgery. *www.samitivej.co.th/index_en.aspx.*

•**Singapore.**

•*Parkway Group Healthcare.* Three hospitals specializing in cardiac surgery and neurosurgery —East Shore, Gleneagles and Mount Elizabeth. *www.ipac.sg/en/.*

•**Belgium.**

•*The De Smet Clinic.* In Ghent, specializes in hip-related surgery. *www.parkwayhealth.com.*

•**Mexico.**

•*Hospitales Angeles.* Has six hospitals in cities such as Tijuana and Juarez. Specializes in neurosurgery and dental surgery. *www.mediks. com* (site is in Spanish only).

GETTING QUALITY CARE

•**Ask for a full diagnosis** from your own doctor first. Develop a treatment plan you both feel comfortable with. Your doctor should be willing to forward all diagnostic information and communicate with the foreign surgeon to discuss your condition. Once you arrive, the foreign doctor also will evaluate you prior to surgery.

•**Bring a family member or friend.** You need someone for emotional support and to serve as your advocate. That person should bring with him/her your health-care power of attorney, which will be honored by international hospitals. This document allows him to make health decisions for you if you are unable to communicate your own wishes.

While a second person doubles the cost of the airfare, most foreign hospitals will allow a companion to stay as a guest in your room for no extra charge.

•**Know the costs.** Most international hospitals and/or health-care providers expect 50%

of their fee to book the surgery and the rest of the cost of treatment at the time of admission. If complications prevent you from returning home immediately, hospitals will accommodate you longer, but ask for the rates so that you can plan accordingly. Also, you should be able to change any airfare you book multiple times with minimal penalty.

Important: Check with your insurance company to make sure it will pay for the treatment of any complications once you arrive home.

•**Confirm that the hospital gives you the same rights** that you have in the US. Reputable hospitals and surgeons will guarantee these rights in writing before you travel overseas. *You should have the right to...*

•Receive complete and current information concerning your diagnosis, treatment and prognosis in terms that you can understand, including serious side effects or risks, problems related to recovery and the likelihood of success.

•Have access to all information contained in your medical records.

•Accept or refuse any treatment and be informed of the consequences of any such refusal.

•Request consultation with the hospital ethics/oversight committee regarding complaints and ethical issues involved in your care.

•Be transferred to another facility at your request or when it is medically appropriate.

•Examine your bill and receive an explanation of the charges.

•**Understand that your legal rights are limited** if medical malpractice is committed overseas. You cannot sue in American courts, and most foreign countries strictly limit malpractice damage awards.

Helpful: If your overseas doctor has a medical board certification in the US, you can complain to the board and seek sanctions.

■ ■ ■ ■

Interim Health Coverage

Between jobs and need health coverage? Your cheapest option might be a short-term policy. It is almost always less expensive than federally regulated COBRA, which extends your former employer's coverage.

To compare prices: Shop at sites such as *www.Insurance.com* and *www.eHealthInsurance.com.*

Important: If you have a preexisting condition, get COBRA and then see if you can get a short-term policy. After you get one, cancel COBRA.

Bob Hurley, senior vice president of carrier relations at eHealthInsurance, a leading site for finding, comparing and buying health insurance, Mountain View, CA. *www.ehealthinsurance.com.*

How to Speed Your Recovery in the Hospital

Marjory Abrams, publisher, newsletters, Boardroom Inc., 281 Tresser Blvd., Stamford, CT 06901.

A friend who just finished a two-week hospital stay after orthopedic surgery learned firsthand how much a patient can do to help—or occasionally hinder—recovery.

Take the simple act of breathing, for example. Pam Hagan, RN, notes that when patients are sedentary, lung secretions may build up, resulting in pneumonia. Pam, a nurse for more than 25 years and the chief programs officer for the American Nurses Association (*www.nursingworld.org*), encourages patients to cough frequently and vigorously—even if they don't feel the need.

Some hospital patients are given an inspirometer to help with breathing. Request it if you're not given one. The deeper you breathe, the higher the ball in the inspirometer rises. Use it often—your lungs will thank you for it.

Pam also urges patients confined to bed to flex their feet, do ankle rotations and perform other simple exercises. Ask a nurse or a physical therapist for suggestions.

Other things you can do...

•**Ring for assistance getting out of bed.** More than a million falls occur each year in US hospitals, at least 30% resulting in moderate to severe injuries. The biggest risks are falling when attempting to get to the bathroom or in the bathroom. Ask for help before the need is urgent. Painkillers, diuretics, laxatives, sedatives and other drugs can increase the risk of falling.

Also helpful: Keep the bed in a low position.

Drink to stay hydrated—to help prevent blood clots and increase the flow of secretions.

•**Eat nutritiously.** Poor nutrition can suppress the immune system, increasing the likelihood of medical complications. Pam encourages patients to request foods they like, as long as they comply with doctor-ordered limitations on salt and other restrictions. Ask to speak with the hospital dietitian if you have concerns. *Among the situations you may encounter…*

•**If you don't like what you get**—the meal, the flavor of your protein shake—request something else.

•**If you are hungry between meals** or want more of something, ask. My friend ate voluminous amounts of plain yogurt—which wasn't even on the menu.

Pam notes that sleep is a great healer, but hospital patients often don't get enough. *To get better shut-eye…*

•**Wear earplugs and/or an eye mask.**

•**Ask your night nurse to help you** into a comfortable sleeping position and turn off lights.

•**Make the nursing staff aware of your normal sleep schedule.** They may be able to adjust the timing of your medications or other nighttime interruptions.

•**If you feel you need a sleeping pill, ask your physician for one.** Talk with the nursing staff about pain medication, too. Day or night, preventing pain is easier than relieving it.

Have you noticed how frequently the word "ask" appears on this page? Optimal recovery requires a partnership between hospital professionals and patients. Communication is key.

■ ■ ■ ■

Hospital Care at Home

Treatments that were previously done only in a hospital, such as intravenous therapy or certain antibiotic therapies, now can be done at home by nurses. This may be useful for some patients who require careful short-term monitoring—for example, elderly people with chronic conditions, such as congestive heart failure and chronic obstructive pulmonary disease.

Advantages of home care: Greater comfort and less chance of infection. This type of care costs less than in-hospital care, but Medicare will pay for only a limited time, based on a doctor's orders.

Charles B. Inlander, a consumer advocate and health-care consultant based in Fogelsville, PA. He was founding president of People's Medical Society, a consumer health advocacy group active in the 1980s and 1990s. He is the author of more than 20 books, including *Take This Book to the Hospital with You*. St. Martin's.

■ ■ ■ ■

Insurance Shortfall

Limited-coverage health insurance plans don't cover major expenses if you become seriously ill. These plans—sometimes called *limited-benefit plans*—are offered by many small businesses that previously provided no coverage or whose employees could not afford more expensive coverage. They can cost as little as $40/month—hundreds of dollars less than the cost of a typical company health plan. The plans cover many routine services, such as doctor visits and medicines, but provide little or no coverage for emergencies and hospital care—and often cap annual payouts at $10,000 or less per person.

Charles B. Inlander, a consumer advocate and health-care consultant based in Fogelsville, PA. He was founding president of People's Medical Society, a consumer health advocacy group active in the 1980s and 1990s. He is the author of more than 20 books, including *Take This Book to the Hospital with You*. St. Martin's.

■ ■ ■ ■

Health Insurance for Your Co-ed

The right health insurance for students who are leaving college and who can no longer be covered under their parents' policies depends on the circumstances. Short-term coverage, which costs about $75/month and does not cover preexisting conditions, may be adequate for someone who is healthy and likely to find a job with benefits shortly after graduating from college. A comprehensive major medical plan with a low deductible can cost $400/month and may provide few benefits at a high cost for someone who is healthy. A major medical plan with a $1,000 deductible may be a better choice for the long term, for about $200/month. But first check with the college—some schools make inexpensive plans available for full-time students and alumni.

Robert Bland, chairman and founder, Insure.com, online insurance brokerage, Darien, IL.

More Fun Health Facts And Answers to Embarrassing Questions

Billy Goldberg, MD, emergency medicine physician at Bellevue Hospital and New York University Medical Center, both in New York City, is coauthor of *Why Do Men Fall Asleep After Sex? More Questions You'd Only Ask a Doctor After Your Third Whiskey Sour.* Three Rivers.

The human body is so complex that we can't come close to understanding everything that goes on inside of us. Emergency room physician Billy Goldberg, MD, answered some of the medical questions many people wonder about but often are embarrassed to ask. *Here, he answers more of those types of questions...*

•Why are men more likely to snore than women?

Women's airways are wider and less prone to collapse than men's airways—which allows for freer breathing. Also, men are more likely than women to gain fat around the neck, where it can squeeze the airway closed, causing snoring. And men are more likely to smoke or drink to excess, either of which can contribute to snoring.

Women are considerably more prone to snoring when they're pregnant. Blood flow to the nasal area can increase during pregnancy, causing the lining of the nose and throat to swell.

To reduce snoring: Adhesive nasal strips, marketed to athletes as a way to increase oxygen intake, have been shown to reduce snoring

for some people by opening nasal passages and making breathing easier. The Breathe Right brand is available at most drugstores. Also, consider losing weight and cutting down on smoking or drinking if these issues apply to you.

•Why do we lose our sense of taste when our noses are stuffed up?

Our sense of taste is quite limited. Human taste buds essentially are able to identify only sweet, salty, sour and bitter. All other information about a food's flavor reaches our brains through our sense of smell. A stuffed-up nose can't pick up odor molecules from food, so food tastes bland.

•Why do men fall asleep after sex?

Endorphins, gamma-aminobutyric acid and the hormones *oxytocin* and *prolactin* are released into a man's body after he has an orgasm. All of these hormones and chemicals have been found to contribute to sleepiness. Interestingly, these same chemicals are also released into women's bodies after orgasm. The difference might be that women are less likely to have orgasms when they have sex.

•Why do wintergreen LifeSavers spark when we bite them?

Put a wintergreen LifeSaver in your mouth, face a mirror, turn out the lights and bite into it with your lips open. You'll create tiny electrical fields and a small amount of ultraviolet light. The light is produced by molecules crashing together as your teeth fracture the sugar crystals in the mint. The scientific name for the process is *triboluminescence.* All hard candies will create some light, but the wintergreen flavoring, methyl salicylate, is fluorescent and adds the more visible, bright blue light.

•Does the black stuff that athletes wear under their eyes really help them?

An article in *Archives of Ophthalmology* confirms that eye-black grease does help. The color black applied to the cheeks slightly below the eyes absorbs sunlight that otherwise might reflect off the cheeks and interfere with the athlete's vision.

•Why do doctors tell men to "turn your head and cough" when they check for a hernia?

A hernia is a protrusion of an organ or other bodily structure through the body wall that normally contains it. The most common type of hernia is the inguinal hernia, which occurs in the groin area. Coughing increases abdominal pressure, so if there is an inguinal hernia, a section of the intestine will be forced through to where the doctor can feel it. This type of hernia is more common in men than in women.

Why turn the head? Because doctors don't like to be coughed on!

•Do bees die after they sting us?

Honeybees do. A honeybee's stinger is barbed and attached to its abdomen. When we're stung, the stinger lodges in our flesh and rips free from the bee's body, taking much of the bee's belly with it—a fatal wound. However, this does not apply to bumblebees. Their stingers do not typically remain in our skin when we're stung, so they can survive to sting again.

•Does hair grow back thicker after it is shaved off?

No. Shaving affects only the portion of the hair that's outside the skin, which is nothing but dead protein cells. It does not affect the hair follicles located deep within the skin, so there's no way that shaving could alter our hair growth rates or density.

•Why does breathing into a paper bag help us when we're hyperventilating?

It forces us to rebreathe the carbon dioxide that we just exhaled. This increases the carbon dioxide levels in our blood, which in turn slows our breathing rate.

The breathe-into-a-bag technique is a reasonable home remedy when rapid deep breathing is caused by anxiety or panic. However, hyperventilation occasionally is a symptom of a more serious problem, such as a heart attack, collapsed lung, blood clot in the lung or an aspirin overdose—and paper-bag breathing will not help.

Important: Seek medical help immediately if you have any reason to believe that you are experiencing anything more than simple anxiety or if the hyperventilation persists after five minutes of bag breathing.

•Why do we get goose bumps?

Goose bumps are caused by very tiny muscles at the base of each hair on our bodies, which contract and pull the hair erect. This is a mammalian response to cold—erect hair creates a layer of insulation—although this doesn't work well for people anymore, since we've lost most of our body hair. Goose bumps also can be a sympathetic nerve reflex that's related to the flight-or-fight response. A frightened animal's erect hairs might make it appear larger and thus more intimidating to an enemy.

•Why does inhaling helium make our voices sound funny?

Helium is less dense than air, so our vocal cords vibrate faster when they're in a helium-rich environment. Faster vibration produces a higher pitch.

•Why do some people sneeze when they look at the sun?

Between 10% and 25% of the population tends to sneeze, often repeatedly, when they look in the general direction of the sun. This is known as the photic *sneeze reflex*. (Don't test yourself by looking directly at the sun—that could damage your eyes.)

The unexpected response to excessive stimulation of the optic nerve is believed to be caused by an accidental crossing of nerve signals in the fifth cranial nerve nucleus. This trait seems to be genetic, so if you are a sun sneezer, others in your family are likely to be as well. It is considered a serious risk factor for combat pilots, but it doesn't affect the rest of us very much.

•If our natural body temperature is 98.6°F, why do 90° days feel hot to us?

Our bodies must work to maintain the proper temperature through a process called *thermoregulation*. When the temperature outside is cool, it's easy for us to release any excess heat, but as outside temperatures get closer to our body temperature, our bodies must work harder to keep us at 98.6°F. The extra effort we expend to maintain our normal temperature is what makes us feel uncomfortable.

What You Must Know Before Having Surgery

Charles B. Inlander, a consumer advocate and health-care consultant based in Fogelsville, PA. He was founding president of People's Medical Society, a consumer health advocacy group active in the 1980s and 1990s. He is the author of more than 20 books, including *Take This Book to the Hospital with You*. St. Martin's.

Each year, more than 80 million Americans undergo some type of surgery. Over the last 35 years, I have advised thousands of surgical patients on the information they should give their doctors and the questions that must be asked to ensure the best possible odds for a successful operation and recovery. *Here are the areas that are most often overlooked or cause confusion among patients…*

•**Medications and/or supplements before surgery.** If you take a blood thinner, such as *warfarin* (Coumadin), you will likely need to stop taking it three or more days before any major surgery, such as a coronary bypass or a hysterectomy, to prevent excessive bleeding. You will probably need to modify your medication schedule even for less invasive surgery, such as knee surgery or removal of a growth.

Caution: Do not assume that your surgeon knows the drugs and/or supplements you are taking. In fact, he/she probably doesn't. Give him a list of all your prescription and nonprescription drugs, such as aspirin or antacids, as well as all vitamins and other supplements that you take.

Self-defense: When your surgery is scheduled, ask your surgeon to write down the specific drugs and/or supplements you should *stop* taking before surgery and exactly how many days prior to the operation you should discontinue them. Also, be sure to mention any chronic conditions you have, such as diabetes, heart disease or allergies, which may affect the outcome of your surgery.

•**New drugs before surgery.** It's not uncommon that the surgeon will ask you to take an antibiotic (to prevent infection) or an anticoagulant drug (to prevent blood clots) several days before surgery.

Self-defense: Don't wait for the surgeon to tell you this. As soon as your operation is planned, ask about presurgery medications. Get this in writing as well.

•**Fasting.** Many types of surgeries require that you fast or go on a liquid-only diet the day prior to the procedure. Among other reasons, fasting is necessary to prevent the patient from vomiting and possibly choking. You also may need to take a laxative to empty your bowels before the operation.

Self-defense: When surgery is scheduled, ask your surgeon for a written schedule of when you should stop eating solid foods…when you should take a laxative (if necessary)…and when you must stop ingesting anything, including liquids.

•**Medical tests.** Presurgical tests may be required a few days before the operation to rule out any reasons to delay, alter or cancel the surgery. However, often, those same tests were performed only a week or two earlier to diagnose your condition.

Self-defense: Ask the surgeon or his staff to check whether you need to repeat a recently performed test. You have enough to do prior to surgery without going for unnecessary tests.

•**Conflicting instructions.** Your surgeon may tell you that it's okay to take a certain drug prior to surgery while one of your other doctors says to stop it.

Self-defense: When your surgeon gives you instructions that differ from what one of your other doctors has told you, ask that the doctors speak with each other and give you their joint recommendation.

2

Everyday Ailments

Natural Ways to Guard Against Colds, Flu— And Worse

Even people who pay close attention to their health often could be doing more to boost their immunity. Your body's immune system consists of specialized cells and chemicals that kill and/or inactivate viruses and other invaders. When viruses invade your body, they not only can trigger colds and the flu, but also Epstein-Barr infections (which have been implicated in hepatitis and certain cancers) and severe acute respiratory syndrome (SARS).

Latest development: Immunity researchers are confirming the profound importance of eating a healthful diet—and finding other helpful ways for you to protect yourself from viruses.

BEST DEFENSE

Some people forget that good nutrition is as important for strong viral immunity as it is for the health of your heart and arteries. And despite all the talk about eating healthfully, most people fall short in at least one key food group.

Best immunity-boosting diet…

•**Complex carbohydrates** should account for about 50% to 60% of your daily calories.

Good choices: Whole grains, such as brown and basmati rice, and legumes.

•**Vegetables and fruits** (preferably organic) —have one or two servings at each meal.

Good choices: Papaya, pineapple or peaches with breakfast…garden salad with fresh tomatoes with lunch…and steamed carrots and broccoli with dinner.

•**Fats** should account for 20% to 25% of your daily calories. Choose unsaturated oils that are rich in omega-3 fatty acids.

J.E. Williams, doctor of oriental medicine (OMD) and past academic dean of East West College of Natural Medicine in Sarasota, FL, is the author of *Viral Immunity: A 10-Step Plan to Enhance Your Immunity Against Viral Disease Using Natural Medicines.* Hampton Books. He is a member of the American Academy of Anti-Aging Medicine and a Fellow of the American Association of Integrative Medicine.

Good sources: Cold-water fish, such as salmon, mackerel and sardines…avocados…nuts (particularly walnuts and almonds) and seeds (particularly flax).

•**Protein** should make up about 20% of your diet.

Good choices: Protein from animal sources, such as fish, poultry, lean meat, low-fat milk and eggs. The vegetable protein found in grains and legumes (beans) also is nourishing. However, if you eat mostly plant-based proteins, take 12 g daily of whey protein (milk protein without fats or lactose) as a supplement.

If it's difficult to maintain this daily diet, I recommend taking supplements to compensate for any missing nutrients. In addition to a daily multivitamin, take 200 mg to 500 mg of vitamin C…400 international units (IU) of vitamin E…200 micrograms (mcg) of selenium…and 15 mg of zinc.

IMMUNITY-BOOSTING LIFESTYLE

Other ways to maximize your body's virus-fighting power…

•**Avoid fried foods.** Even an occasional serving of french fries or fried chicken can compromise your body's immunity. That's because fats are oxidized during the frying process, creating compounds that damage all cells, including those that fight viruses.

My advice: For optimal benefit from a generally healthful diet, avoid all fried foods. Grill (with low heat), boil, steam or bake your food instead.

•**Limit alcohol consumption.** Alcohol can depress immune function. Studies have linked excessive alcohol to susceptibility to lung infections, including bacterial pneumonia and tuberculosis.

My advice: Drink alcohol in moderation (up to one drink daily for women…two for men)—or not at all.

•**Drink pure water.** Most people don't consume enough water—or the right type. Water is one of the simplest ways to effectively flush toxins from the body and introduce the minerals as well as trace minerals that have been shown to support immune function.

Even though some experts don't believe that it's necessary to drink as many as eight eight-ounce glasses of water daily, I stand by this advice. If you exercise—even if you don't sweat—you need even more water because greater amounts of it are lost from the lungs due to exhalation. During winter, excessively heated rooms also deplete water from your body.

My advice: Don't include soda, juice or other sugary beverages in your daily water quota. Drink pure spring water, such as Evian or Volvic, or filtered tap water. It helps flush viruses from your body without the immune-depressing effects of sugar and other additives.

•**Get enough sleep.** A study published in *Nature Reviews Immunology* showed that insufficient sleep inhibits the production of chemicals, such as cytokines, which help boost the body's immunity. Not surprisingly, sleep deprivation is associated with increased rates of infection.

My advice: Most people need at least eight hours of sleep a night to restore normal body functions. If you feel rundown or are battling the early stages of a cold or other viral infection, try to get even more sleep.

Important: Just being in bed for eight hours does not count if you're having trouble falling asleep or are waking up during the night. If this occurs, ask your doctor for advice on improving the quality of your sleep.

•**Exercise—but not too much.** Regular exercise has been shown to neutralize inflammatory chemicals and improve the function of the body's natural killer cells—both key players in viral immunity.

But overly strenuous workouts, such as running a marathon, can have the opposite effect, triggering the production of *cortisol, adrenaline* and other stress hormones that suppress immune function and increase your odds of contracting an infection.

My advice: Up to one hour a day of moderate exercise (such as brisk walking, bicycling or swimming) is right for most people. Let your body be your guide—if you feel exhausted and generally worse after you exercise, cut back.

•**Take a sauna.** Dangerous chemicals from the environment, including the pesticides that we consume in nonorganic foods, cause an imbalance in the immune cells that fight viral infections. A sauna helps your body to release these chemicals via perspiration.

My advice: Take a dry sauna once or twice weekly. Don't exceed 20 minutes, and drink at least an extra quart of pure water to compensate for what you lose through perspiration.

Caution: Saunas may not be safe for people over age 65 or anyone who is weak or has a fever.

IMMUNITY-BOOSTING PLANTS

The leaves, stems and roots of some plants are concentrated sources of powerful antiviral compounds. Unless you have a chronic viral infection, such as chronic hepatitis, it's usually best not to take these on a regular basis.

However, if you're under considerable stress, feel rundown or are exposed to viral illnesses, consider taking one or more of the following supplements throughout cold and flu season…*

•**Astragalus.** Prized in Chinese medicine for its ability to restore the body's energy, this herb strengthens antiviral defenses by stimulating the production of interferon, a substance that inhibits viral growth.

Typical dose: As a tea, drink one cup twice daily.

To prepare: Simmer 30 g of dried astragalus root in one cup of water for 20 minutes. Or take two to three 500-mg capsules twice daily.

•**Ginseng.** This herb is known as an energy tonic, but it also stimulates the immune system.

Typical dose: Take a 250-mg capsule twice daily (choose a standardized extract containing 30% of the active ingredient ginsenosides per 250 mg).

Caution: Don't take ginseng if you have high blood pressure, a fever or an active infection. This herb also should be avoided by people who take a monoamine oxidase inhibitor (MAOI) antidepressant, such as *phenelzine* (Nardil) or *tranylcypromine* (Parnate).

•**Acemannan.** This aloe vera extract has been shown to increase the activity of virus-killing T-cells and stimulate the release of interleukin-1, an important immune system messenger chemical. Acemannan is available at most health-food stores in a product called Manapol, manufactured by Carrington Labs.

Typical dose: One 80-mg capsule one to three times daily.

*If you use prescription medication, are pregnant, nursing or have a chronic disease, such as diabetes or heart, liver or kidney disease, do not take any of these supplements without consulting your doctor.

Doctor's Warning on Steroidal Inhalers

Richard Firshein, DO, director of the Firshein Center for Comprehensive Medicine in New York City and author of *Reversing Asthma* (Warner) and *Your Asthma-Free Child* (Avery). Dr. Firshein has also written *The Nutraceutical Revolution* (Riverhead), was honored by the American Medical Association for work with asthmatic children, and is the founder and creator of *DrCity.com*.

Currently, steroidal inhalers are a standard treatment for asthma in children. Yet a study in *The New England Journal of Medicine* reported that these drugs have no long-term impact on the progression of asthma or on lung function in preschoolers. While symptoms were controlled during treatment, benefits disappeared when treatment was halted. Additionally, steroids have many dangerous side effects, with children in the study experiencing slowed growth when using steroidal inhalers. Bad for children. Bad for adults. What else to do?

Richard Firshein, DO, director of the Firshein Center for Comprehensive Medicine in New York City, explains his expert's take on steroids and safer, natural alternatives. He acknowledges that inhaled steroids are not a panacea, but they do play a helpful role when symptoms are particularly troublesome. For example, if a child is experiencing a high level of inflammation and/or wheezing and missing many school days, Dr. Firshein is apt to prescribe a corticosteroid inhaler for short-term use. However, he does not recommend these drugs on a long-term basis, and emphasized that his first line of defense is to prevent symptoms naturally. Patients with long-term asthma should consider Singulair or a bronchodilator on an "as needed" basis, he says.

BUILD A STRONG FOUNDATION

Asthma has many triggers. Among its possible triggers are airborne pollutants, secondhand smoke, allergens (dust mites, animal dander, mold, chemicals, foods, etc.) and cold air.

Also: Aspirin and NSAIDs can trigger an attack, as can a viral infection. To prevent asthma symptoms from occurring in the first place, rather than simply responding to them, Dr. Firshein stresses that you must make healthful changes—changes that reduce the exposure to the things that trigger asthma, and changes that strengthen the body's immune system to resist those triggers. That advice applies not only to children with asthma, but to asthma sufferers of all ages. Allergy shots have also been shown to reduce the sensitivity to allergy triggers such as dust, dust mites, pollen and pet dander.

To build a strong foundation, Dr. Firshein recommends…

•**Closely monitor your environment.** Go through your house carefully and remove possible triggers. For example, eliminate dust collectors such as wall-to-wall carpeting and heavy drapes…install an air filter to clean household air…frequently wash non-allergenic bedding and non-allergenic pillow and mattress covers …use a dehumidifier in damp basements and bathrooms and bedrooms…and avoid using air fresheners. Additionally, do not neglect school or work environments, where we spend so many hours of our lives. It's equally important to eliminate triggers here. Parents should speak directly to principals and teachers about a child's allergy triggers and have the necessary emergency procedures in place, should an attack occur.

•**Keep an eye on diet.** Dr. Firshein is particularly concerned with asthmatic children eating junk food, which he compares to an adult with heart disease eating fat-laden cheeseburgers and fries. He points out that junk foods promote inflammation, which promotes asthma. Instead, follow an anti-inflammatory diet rich in nutrient-dense whole foods such as fresh fruits and veggies (berries are especially rich in inflammation-fighting antioxidants), fish, nuts and seeds. Whenever possible, go with organic products.

•**Take immune-boosting supplements.** In particular, Dr. Firshein recommends vitamin C (1,000 mg), magnesium (500 mg), fish oil and a good multivitamin. When using inhaled steroids, which may compromise the bones, he also recommends a calcium-magnesium supplement (1,200 mg of calcium) for added protection.

Note: Dosages should be reduced in children by 50% to 75% of an adult dosage. In general, he finds that children respond much more rapidly to multivitamins than adults, allowing them to catch fewer colds and miss fewer school/work days, and gain heartier immunity overall with relatively simple supplementation.

•**Learn to breathe easy.** The Firshein Technique for Asthma Breathing is a series of exercises that teach children to stabilize their asthma. He finds that children above age five do particularly well with breathing exercises. Asthma sufferers often feel nervous and out of control when they approach a situation that they know brings on symptoms, such as exercise or cold air. These breathing exercises give individuals a sense of control over a situation, and also strengthen muscles in the diaphragm, which is crucial to controlling asthma.

Dr. Firshein recommends these simple exercises when encountering potential triggers…

•Breathe in through the nose for a count of five, and breathe out through the mouth for a count of seven.

•Next, breathe in deeply, and then blow out the air in a burst like you're blowing out a candle. This strengthens the lungs and diaphragm, explains Dr. Firshein.

•Now use your stomach. Lie down, and as you breathe in through the nose out through the mouth, consciously make your stomach expand.

•Try a rocking motion while standing, breathing in and rocking to one side then breathing out while rocking to the other side. Then switch. Air gets trapped in the lungs of people with asthma, so they cannot take in enough new oxygen, observes Dr. Firshein. Rocking back and forth helps the body use the ribcage more to expel the stale air so there's more room in the lungs.

•**Get plenty of exercise.** Exercise is doubly important for the asthmatic child, says Dr. Firshein. Breathing exercises work by reducing stress, improving oxygen intake and by strengthening the muscles that are used in respiration. If exercise is a trigger of asthma symptoms, the physician should closely monitor the exercise program. In some cases, breathing exercises may ease and prevent attacks. Using a peak flow meter is the most effective way to monitor breathing at home.

HOW TO INHALE
STEROIDS CORRECTLY

If you or your child must take steroids for a period of time, Dr. Firshein recommends a safer way to go about using them. Spacing devices provide an effective way of maximizing medication and minimizing deposits in the mouth. He cautions that steroids in dry powder form are difficult to inhale, with often as much as 90% of the powdered medication ending up in the mouth. When you swallow this, you are apt to experience greater side effects than with inhalation alone. To reduce side effects, following inhalation, rinse your mouth thoroughly.

A BETTER WAY

With side effects from steroids being so severe and their effectiveness being so limited, they should only be used when they are truly necessary. Using simple strategies that build a strong foundation for your health can lower risk of asthma attacks and cut back on the medication required to control them.

Good News for Asthmatics! Lower Doses of Steroids Work Just as Well

Neil C. Thomson, MD, professor of respiratory medicine, University of Glasgow, Scotland.
John J. Costa, MD, assistant clinical professor of medicine, Harvard Medical School, Boston.
British Medical Journal.

If you're among the 15% of all asthmatics who take high dosages of inhaled steroids, you may not need as much medicine as you think to keep your disease in check.

A Scottish study shows that patients with chronic, severe asthma can sharply reduce their dosages of inhaled steroids (to cut the risk of side effects) and still keep their condition under control.

The study was the first carefully controlled trial to show that this "step-down" approach works in chronic, severe cases of asthma.

Inhaled steroids are the recommended treatment for chronic asthma, but they are accompanied by a number of side effects, including weakened bones and eye problems, such as cataracts and glaucoma. For these reasons, doctors prefer to keep the dosage at a minimum.

The study included 259 adult asthma patients with symptoms severe enough to require an average of 1,400 micrograms per day of *beclomethasone*, or equivalent amounts of other steroids.

For the study, 130 patients began taking half of their previous dosage, while 129 continued their old dosage. As is common in such controlled studies, none of the patients were told how much they were taking.

After one year, results were as good for the reduced-dosage patients as they were for the higher-dosage patients, according to Dr. Neil C. Thomson, professor of respiratory medicine at the University of Glasgow, and leader of the study.

DOCTORS SHOULD FOLLOW UP ON TREATMENT

"The study is a welcome reminder that doctors treating asthma patients should look toward reducing steroid dosage," says Dr. John J. Costa, assistant clinical professor of medicine at Harvard Medical School in Boston, and a spokesman for the American Academy of Allergy, Asthma & Immunology (AAAAI).

Often, asthma patients go to their doctors when the disease flares up, and higher doses are prescribed to bring things back to normal, he says.

"The importance of this is to remind practitioners that often they see asthmatics and decide that a certain amount of medicine is needed to address what is going on at that moment. It may not be the amount of medicine needed when the patient is not in the middle of a flare-up," Costa says. "The doctor should follow up to see if it is possible to reduce the dosage."

■ ■ ■ ■

Inhaler Ban

Some asthma inhalers are banned by the US Food and Drug Administration as of January 2009. Inhalers that use atmosphere-damaging chlorofluorocarbons (CFCs) to dispense the medication *albuterol* will no longer be produced, marketed or sold in the US.

Karen Mahoney, spokesperson, US Food and Drug Administration, Rockville, MD.

Herbal Asthma Relief

Mark A. Stengler, ND, naturopathic physician in private practice, La Jolla, CA…adjunct associate clinical professor at the National College of Natural Medicine, Portland, OR…author of 16 books, including *The Natural Physician's Healing Therapies* (Bottom Line Books) and coauthor of *Prescription for Natural Cures* (Wiley)…and author of the *Bottom Line/Natural Healing* newsletter.

A study by researchers from New York and China found a combination of three Chinese herbal extracts to be an effective alternative to conventional asthma medicines. This combination of herbs—dubbed the Anti-Asthma Herbal Medicine Intervention, or ASHMI—included ling zhi (*Ganoderma lucidum*), ku shen (*Radix sophorae flavascentis*) and gan cao (*Radix glycyrrhizae uralensis*). In the US, these herbs are known as reishi, sophara root and licorice, respectively.

The four-week study focused on 91 people with moderate-to-severe asthma. Forty-six people were assigned to receive 12 ASHMI capsules per day (made of 20 g of ling zhi, 9 g of ku shen and 3 g of gan cao). Patients in this active treatment group also received placebo tablets similar in appearance to *prednisone*, an oral, manmade corticosteroid commonly used for suppressing inflammation caused by asthma. Patients in the control group received 20 mg of prednisone daily plus placebo herb capsules. Researchers measured lung function, inflammatory markers and side effects.

The effectiveness of prednisone on lung function was "slightly but significantly greater" than that provided by the herbs. However, the ASHMI had a beneficial effect on immune cell activity, while the immune cells of the people on prednisone were suppressed. Patients receiving ASHMI capsules also were less likely to have gastric discomfort than those receiving prednisone. The prednisone patients showed significant weight gain after four weeks of treatment as well.

My view: The study demonstrates that Chinese herbal therapy is effective (even if not quite as effective as prednisone) and less likely to cause side effects. Herbal therapy combined with good nutrition and supplements, such as magnesium, fish oil, vitamin C and the amino acid N-acetylcysteine, should be the first choice for people with asthma.

Caution: If you take prednisone, do not stop taking it without checking with your doctor.

Drug-Free Asthma Busters

Richard Firshein, DO, director of the Firshein Center for Comprehensive Medicine in New York City and author of *Reversing Asthma* (Warner) and *Your Asthma-Free Child* (Avery). Dr. Firshein has also written *The Nutraceutical Revolution* (Riverhead), was honored by the American Medical Association for work with asthmatic children, and is the founder and creator of *DrCity.com*.

Living with asthma does not have to be a life sentence with the drug companies. There are natural health-building ways to breathe free, drug free.

For the 20 to 40 million Americans who suffer from asthma, life can be very scary. In addition to dealing with debilitating and frightening attacks, many sufferers experience unpleasant side effects from the medications used to control the illness. "I've seen patients shaking, anxious, jittery, unable to concentrate and even complaining of chest pain—and they don't know it's their asthma medication," says New York City-based family physician Richard Firshein, DO, who specializes in complementary medicine. What's worse, some of the remedies fail to address the underlying causes, so sufferers continue to experience attacks.

The good news is that drug-free treatments abound, and they really work. "Alternative traditional therapies not only reduce or eliminate the need for medications, they also improve people's quality of life quite dramatically," says Dr. Firshein, author of *Reversing Asthma* (Warner).

Managing asthma, an allergic inflammation of the lungs, is increasingly important. The number of cases in this country is rising at an alarming rate—it has more than doubled just in the last 20 years.

Dr. Firshein calls on an arsenal of natural remedies and includes the manipulation of diet and environment and the addition of supplements, breathing exercises and acupuncture to help his patients live drug-free.

EXAMINE YOUR DIET

Asthma is a disease of inflammation, so it's especially important for sufferers to avoid foods that are triggers. Excessive sugar and salt are prime culprits, as are heavily processed foods that contain all kinds of chemicals.

In addition, individual asthmatics may find that they have other individual food allergies that trigger asthma attacks. To determine the problematic fare, Dr. Firshein recommends doing a "rotation diet" in which you avoid one of the major allergens—milk, corn, soy, wheat, eggs or nuts—for a four- to five-day period and see if symptoms abate. After you omit one item, reintroduce the food and see if you feel worse. When you have completed one food, try the next. "It's not foolproof," says Dr. Firshein, "but if you do it long enough, you might realize that you're only allergic to one or two things. Then you can feel so much better simply by avoiding those items," he says.

Dr. Firshein also recommends identifying your personal allergens with one of two tests—skin testing or a blood test called the radioallergosorbent test (RAST). In this test, substances known to trigger allergies are added to the blood sample and then the level of allergy antibodies is measured. The levels will be high if there is an allergic reaction. One of these tests, along with the rotation diet, should determine 80% of triggers, Dr. Firshein says.

NUTRITIONAL SHORTFALLS

Dr. Firshein, who also is author of *The Nutraceutical Revolution* (Riverhead), recommends talking to a doctor who specializes in nutrition about taking a well-balanced antioxidant, one that contains moderate amounts of vitamins A, C and E, the B vitamins, selenium and others. Several studies have drawn connections between low levels of antioxidants and higher levels of asthma. For example, many asthmatics have been shown to be deficient in magnesium, which acts as a natural bronchodilator. In other research, vitamin C has been found to reduce exercise-induced asthma.

TRY BREATHING

Most people don't know how to breathe properly. They breathe shallowly, allowing their chest to rise and fall with each breath. Abdominal breathing—using the diaphragm to draw air in and out—is, according to Dr. Firshein, "one of the most effective ways to strengthen weakened lungs and control attacks. Using your diaphragm helps you relax and gain control over your breathing, improving oxygenation," he says. "It can make a substantial difference."

With asthma, he explains, the problem is not that air can't get into the lungs—it is that it can't get out. The following breathing exercise helps constricted lungs pump air out more efficiently. "It's like a Heimlich maneuver for asthma sufferers, a natural bronchodilator," he says. *Do it for 10 minutes once or twice a day...*

1. Start by getting into a relaxed state of mind, by using meditation or imagining yourself lounging on a beach.

2. Breathe in deeply and visualize your stomach, not your chest, expanding. You even can place one hand on your stomach and one on your chest to ensure that your body is following along.

3. Start counting out your breaths—inhale on three counts, exhale on six counts. Blow air out through pursed lips.

This breathing technique is taught as "pranayama" by instructors in hatha yoga. It is the art of yogic breathing.

GO UNDER THE NEEDLE

The 1996 National Institutes of Health (NIH) Consensus Statement on Acupuncture found strong evidence that acupuncture can treat asthma effectively. Kim Jobst, MD, of Oxford University reports in an article for the *Journal of Alternative and Complementary Medicine* that, at the request of the NIH, he collected all the research on acupuncture and chronic lung diseases. Of the 16 studies he reviewed, he found that acupuncture was effective—reducing attacks and doses of drugs—in 62% of cases. Other research, including data from *The Journal of Traditional Chinese Medicine*, puts the success rate at closer to 75% or 80%.

Dr. Firshein finds acupuncture to be an important part of any nonconventional treatment for asthma because it's helpful in maintaining proper lung function. It works by stimulating certain responsive parts of the body's nervous system, which then transmit signals along the nerves and also produce biochemicals that influence other cells of the body. The nervous system also is linked to the hormonal system by way of the adrenal gland, so it can send healing signals to the body's every cell and system.

CONTROL YOUR ENVIRONMENT

Most asthmatics already know this, but it's good to mention that your home can have many triggers. Go through your house room by room to eliminate potential allergens, such as smoke, dust mites, mold, pet dander and water or chimney leaks. Also, install a carbon monoxide detector.

"It's very exciting to have all these different modalities for treating asthma," Dr. Firshein says. "It gives people a lot of options, a lot of choices, and they don't feel as threatened by the condition. They feel that they can do something to help themselves." Most important, these techniques look to cure the underlying ailments rather than simply suppress symptoms. Consider adding a physician formally schooled in these nonconventional modalities who can cooperate with your allergist or pulmonologist. It is a much more effective strategy for long-term health.

■ ■ ■ ■

Allergy Nation

Most Americans test positive for one or more allergens. The most common allergen is dust mites—27% of those tested responded positively. Reacting to an allergen doesn't necessarily mean that you will develop allergies, but there is a strong correlation between the two.

Samuel Arbes, DDS, PhD, adjunct assistant professor, dental ecology, University of North Carolina School of Dentistry, Chapel Hill, and leader of a survey of 10,500 individuals, reported in *Journal of Allergy and Clinical Immunology*.

■ ■ ■ ■

New Flu Test

A recently developed test diagnoses flu the same day. That is especially important for older people and those with compromised immune systems or chronic diseases, and it could help prevent complications.

Antiviral medicines generally shorten the course of the flu by one day if taken within 48 hours of initial symptoms. The best defense against flu is vaccination.

Katherine A. Poehling, MD, former assistant professor of pediatrics at Monroe Carell Jr. Children's Hospital, Vanderbilt University, Nashville, and leader of a study of influenza in more than 4,500 preschoolers, published in *The New England Journal of Medicine*.

Cure for Stomach Flu

Jamison Starbuck, ND, is a naturopathic physician in family practice in Missoula, Montana. She is past president of the American Association of Naturopathic Physicians and is a contributing editor to *The Alternative Advisor: The Complete Guide to Natural Therapies and Alternative Treatments*. Time-Life.

"Doctor, this is my third bout this winter! What can I do to get over it for good?" Ken was in obvious distress, holding his belly and rocking back and forth. Ken had "stomach flu"—a catchall phrase for *gastroenteritis,* an acute inflammation of the lining of the stomach and intestines characterized by nausea, vomiting, abdominal discomfort and diarrhea. It is usually caused by a viral or bacterial infection. He was suffering yet another episode of these acute symptoms after following the advice of his medical doctor. Now he was ready to try a natural approach.

When medical doctors treat gastroenteritis, they recommend bed rest, bland food and lots of fluids. They typically prescribe antibiotics when patients have high fevers. After a few days of symptoms, most people recover—or so they think. If gastroenteritis is treated conventionally, you may fail to *fully* recover.

Here's why: The organisms that cause the infection also inflame intestinal membranes, and vomiting and diarrhea may have eliminated both the "bad" and "good" bacteria found in the intestines. This is a setup to make you more susceptible to repeat infections.

My naturopathic approach…

•**Limit your diet.** To rest the gastrointestinal tract and speed healing, drink chicken or vegetable broth and eat baked apples and/or pears (the pectin in these fruits soothes the stomach and helps stop the diarrhea) until your symptoms abate. Avoid dehydration by consuming at least 72 ounces of water per day while you have the flu. Also, drink chamomile, peppermint, ginger, black or green tea. These teas have antinausea and antivomiting properties. Make a strong tea using two tea bags per 12 ounces of water. Drink three to six cups daily, preferably on an empty stomach.

•**Use a mustard poultice.** This will relieve nausea and vomiting.

What to do: Combine one tablespoon of mustard powder with one cup of flour. Stir in enough water to make a smooth paste. Saturate a piece of cotton cloth about the size of a face-cloth with hot water from the faucet, wring it out and spread the paste over the cloth. Place it (paste-side up) over your abdomen. Cover with a dry cotton cloth, and then a hot water bottle or heating pad. Leave the poultice in place for 30 minutes. Apply twice a day.

•**Take an herbal tincture.** Clinical trials confirm that the herbs Oregon grape root and geranium have antimicrobial properties, while slippery elm and licorice reduce inflammation and promote tissue growth in the intestine. Make a mixture of equal parts of these tinctures, which are sold individually at most health-food stores. Take 60 drops of the combined tinctures in two ounces of water, on an empty stomach, four times per day for up to five days.

•**Try probiotics.** *Lactobacillus acidophilus* and *Bifidobacterium bifidum* replenish "friendly" bacteria in the bowels. Probiotics are available at health-food stores in powder, liquid or capsules. Take 10 billion colony-forming units (CFUs) each of L. acidophilus and B. bifidum in four divided doses daily for the duration of the illness and for three weeks after your symptoms have resolved.

Epidemics Are on the Rise: How to Protect Yourself

Georges Benjamin, MD, professorial lecturer at George Washington University School of Public Health and executive director of the American Public Health Association (*www.apha.org*), both in Washington, DC. He is former secretary of the Maryland Department of Health and Mental Hygiene and a leading expert in emergency preparedness.

More than one-quarter of all deaths worldwide are caused by infectious diseases. In the US, more than 170,000 people die from these diseases each year—and the number is likely to get much higher. *In just the last few years...*

•**Reemerging diseases** that were nearly eradicated in the US, such as measles, malaria and tuberculosis, now are occurring in increasing numbers.

•**Influenza A H1N1,** known as the swine flu, was first detected in Mexico in April 2009. The virus has sparked a growing outbreak of illness among people both in the US and worldwide. As of June 2009, there is no vaccine to protect against this novel H1N1 virus (Centers for Disease Control and Prevention, June 3, 2009).

•**Bird (avian) flu** has killed more than half of those infected—though none of these cases has occurred in the US to date and most cases have resulted from people having direct contact with infected birds or contaminated surfaces. Should the virus mutate to permit human-to-human transmission, the death rate could rise into the millions.

•**Methicillin-resistant Staphylococcus aureus** (MRSA) now is the sixth-leading cause of death in the US. It is a strain of bacteria that causes an infection—often called "staph"—that can be deadly even when patients are treated with state-of-the-art antibiotics.

Here, Georges Benjamin, MD, executive director of the American Public Health Association, answers questions about the risks for infectious diseases...

•**Are epidemics on the rise?** Yes. Every two or three years, there's a new epidemic somewhere in the world. The term "epidemic" means that a particular health-related issue—an infectious disease, obesity, even car accidents—is occurring more often than expected. The frequency of epidemics seems to be increasing.

One of the reasons for the increase is that global warming has extended the population and range of mosquitoes, leading to increases in malaria, dengue fever and other mosquito-borne diseases.

In addition, human and animal populations worldwide are living in closer proximity than in the past. More than half of all infectious diseases can infect species other than their original hosts. Many of the most dangerous pathogens, including the virus that causes AIDS, originated in animals and only later developed the ability to infect humans.

A century ago, a disease in a remote area might sicken or kill a few dozen people and then "burn out." Now more than two billion people fly on airplanes every year. A deadly pathogen, such as Ebola virus, easily could spread into more populated areas and infect thousands—or worse.

•How dangerous is the next epidemic likely to be? It depends on the organism. In the best-case scenario, something such as a cold virus could mutate and gain the ability to infect more people than it had in the past. But because this virus isn't lethal, it would be more of a nuisance than anything else.

The most serious epidemics involve organisms that are both *highly transmissible* and *lethal*. The Spanish flu of 1918–1919 had both of these traits. It was readily passed from person to person, and it was uncommonly virulent. Worldwide, it killed between 20 million and 40 million people within about two years and has been called the most devastating epidemic in recorded history.

A disease that can be transmitted via indirect contact—for example, from inhaling airborne organisms from sneezes—is more likely to emerge as an epidemic than a disease that can be transmitted only under specific circumstances, such as hepatitis C from infected blood.

•If you had to guess, what epidemic is likely to be next? There's no way to know. Any infectious organism could be involved. Many bacterial infections (such as tuberculosis) have reached epidemic proportions, but we often can control these illnesses with antibiotics.

Viral infections are more worrisome. We have only a few antiviral drugs. Viruses replicate far more rapidly than bacteria, which means that they can develop drug resistance more quickly than bacteria. The same mechanism also allows them to mutate rapidly into more lethal forms.

•Is it likely that an epidemic will be caused by bioterrorism? It's a serious risk. People used to need specialized training and sophisticated equipment to produce or disseminate lethal agents. This is no longer the case. Knowledge in general is more widely available than it used to be, thanks to the Internet, and technology is more available and affordable.

It doesn't take much sophistication to launch a crude attack. In 1984, a religious cult in Oregon spiked area salad bars with a *Salmonella* culture. No one died, but more than 750 people were sickened. It was the largest bioterrorist attack in the US.

•What emergency supplies should we have on hand? We recommend stockpiling at least a three-day supply of nonperishable foods, such as canned meats, fish, beans, fruits and vegetables. Check the expiration dates every six months. Also, have on hand one gallon of water per person per day. Be aware that your water supply also needs to be rotated because microbes may build up in it. Also, try to keep prescriptions filled and pain relievers/fever reducers on hand.

•Should we stockpile antibiotics? You don't want to stockpile an antibiotic, because you don't know which one you are going to need.

•What will the authorities do? State health departments and the Centers for Disease Control and Prevention have surveillance systems that look for unusual symptoms or disease clusters that could indicate an emerging epidemic. In the early years of the AIDS crisis, it was noted that there was an increase in requests for a drug used to treat a rare fungal infection. This, along with an increase in unusual diseases later known to be associated with AIDS, indicated that a new organism was spreading fast.

Once a new (or reemerging) infectious disease has been identified, the goal is to both treat it and limit its spread. In addition to educating the public, public health officials might resort to isolation (keeping sick patients away from the general population to avoid infecting others) or quarantine (isolating people who have been exposed to an organism but who may or may not actually have the disease). There also will be a push to develop vaccines and other medications to treat the disease, protect healthy people and limit the spread of the disease.

•It almost sounds as if the government will have everything under control. What are your thoughts on that? There is a need for people to be as self-reliant as they can. Local officials will help as soon as they can, but the government cannot do everything. The greater the number of people who are self-reliant, the more help that will be available for those who are unable to help themselves.

■ ■ ■ ■

Flu Trouble

Sadness reduces the flu vaccine's effectiveness, according to British researchers.

Recent study: More than 30% of people over age 65 who received the flu vaccine and who were grieving over the loss of a loved one or were in an unhappy relationship had a significantly weakened response to two of the three flu strains included in the vaccine.

Anna Phillips, PhD, research fellow, school of sport and exercise sciences, University of Birmingham, Edgbaston, England, and lead researcher of a study of 184 flu-vaccine recipients over age 65, published in *Brain, Behavior and Immunity*.

■ ■ ■ ■

Legionnaires' Look-Out

Legionnaires' disease is on the rise, warns Janet E. Stout, PhD. This respiratory infection is caused by a bacteria most often found in the water-distribution and air-conditioning systems of large buildings and cruise ships. More than 20,000 cases occur nationwide each year. About one-quarter of those afflicted die. Symptoms—high fever, cough, headache and diarrhea—are similar to those of other illnesses, so the disease may go untreated until it is too late for antibiotics to work.

Self-defense: If you experience symptoms and recently have been in a hospital or hotel or on a cruise ship, ask to be tested for the disease.

Janet E. Stout, PhD, director of the Special Pathogens Laboratory and research assistant professor in the School of Medicine at University of Pittsburgh.

■ ■ ■ ■

Antibiotics vs. Viruses

Bronchitis can't be cured with antibiotics, according to recent research.

Bronchitis sufferers who were otherwise healthy did not get better any faster by taking antibiotics.

Possible reason: Most bronchitis infections are caused by viruses, which antibiotics don't fight.

Best treatment: Drink lots of fluids, and take pain and fever relievers, such as *acetaminophen*.

Paul Little, MD, professor of primary care research, University of Southampton, Highfield, England, and author of a study of 640 bronchitis patients, published in *The Journal of the American Medical Association*.

■ ■ ■ ■

Tick Fever Help

Rocky Mountain spotted fever can be spread by the common brown dog tick. Until recently, it was thought that only two less common ticks could transmit the disease, which is found across the country and has a fatality rate as high as 20% when untreated. Rocky Mountain spotted fever is especially severe in children. Symptoms, including fever, nausea, vomiting, muscle pain, lack of appetite, severe headache and a rash, appearing one to two weeks after infection.

Good news: Antibiotics are effective when given early.

Linda J. Demma, PhD, senior epidemiologist, Foodborne Diseases Active Surveillance Network, Centers for Disease Control and Prevention, Atlanta, and leader of a study of tick transmission of Rocky Mountain spotted fever, published in *The New England Journal of Medicine*.

■ ■ ■ ■

Allergy Alert

Allergies can cause surprising symptoms. Any part of the body can become swollen or inflamed. A person can feel lethargic or cranky...have mood changes, joint pain, an irritable bowel or intestinal cramps. Look for triggers—a specific place or time when symptoms occur, such as at work, after consuming certain foods or beverages or after exposure to inhalants, such as pollen. If you can't figure out the triggers on your own, see an allergist.

Thomas Brunoski, MD, specialist in food and environmental allergies and nutritional medicine, Westport, CT.

Winter Ailments: Folk Remedies for Colds, Coughs and Flu

Joan Wilen and Lydia Wilen are folk-remedy experts based in New York City. The sisters are coauthors of many books, including *Bottom Line's Healing Remedies: Over 1,000 Astounding Ways to Heal Arthritis, Asthma, High Blood Pressure, Varicose Veins, Warts and More!* Bottom Line Books. *www.BottomLineSecrets.com.*

Not every winter illness requires a trip to the doctor's office. The following time-tested folk remedies offer effective, inexpensive treatments for minor health complaints.

Important: Consult your doctor if your condition persists or grows worse.

COLDS

The average adult contracts between two and four colds each year, mostly between September and May. *Medical science has no cure for these highly contagious viral infections, but the following folk remedies can help ward off colds, ease symptoms and possibly shorten a cold's duration…*

•**Garlic.** Garlic contains *allicin*, which has been shown to reduce the severity of a cold. Eat four cloves of freshly crushed raw garlic three times a day until you have recovered.

•**Cinnamon, sage and bay.** Cinnamon contains compounds believed to reduce congestion. Sage can help sooth sore throats. Some Native American cultures have used bay leaves to clear breathing passages. Steep one-half teaspoon each of cinnamon and sage with a bay leaf in six ounces of hot water. Strain and add one tablespoon of lemon juice. Lemon helps reduce mucus buildup. If you like your tea sweet, add honey.

•**Chicken soup.** The Mayo Clinic has said in its health newsletter that chicken soup can be an excellent treatment for head colds and other viral respiratory infections for which antibiotics are not helpful.

FLU

Influenza is a potentially serious viral infection. People often mistake colds for the flu. Colds take hold gradually and are not usually accompanied by severe aches or a fever. The onset of the flu is sudden, and symptoms include fever, severe muscle aches and fatigue.

•**Garlic and cognac.** A shot of cognac is a popular flu remedy in Germany, where it's thought to ease symptoms and help the body cleanse itself. Garlic helps clear mucus, among other potential benefits. Peel and dice a half-pound of garlic. Add one quart of 90-proof cognac, and seal the mixture in an airtight bottle. Store in a cool, dark place for two weeks. Strain out the garlic, and reseal the liquid in the bottle. Prepare a new batch each year.

To treat the flu: Add 20 drops to eight ounces of water. Drink three glasses a day, one before each meal.

For prevention: Use 10 to 15 drops, instead of 20, per glass in flu season.

Important: This treatment is not advisable for people who have drinking problems or for children.

•**Sauerkraut.** Sauerkraut's concentration of lactic acid bacteria may weaken infections. Have two tablespoons of sauerkraut juice or about one-half cup of sauerkraut each day during flu season to reduce the chances of infection.

SORE THROATS

Experiment with these remedies until you find what works best for you…

•**Apple cider vinegar.** Vinegar is a powerful anti-inflammatory, and its acidity might help kill the bacteria that cause some sore throats. Add two teaspoons of apple cider vinegar to six ounces of warm water. Gargle with a mouthful, spit it out, then drink a mouthful. Continue this until the mixture is gone. Rinse your mouth with water to prevent the vinegar from eroding your teeth. Repeat the vinegar gargle every hour for as long as your sore throat persists.

•**Sage.** Sage is an anti-inflammatory. Add one teaspoon of dried sage to one six-ounce cup of boiling water. Steep for three to five minutes, strain, then gargle and swallow.

•**Lemon and honey.** Honey coats the throat, while lemon can temporarily reduce the mucus buildup that often accompanies a sore throat.

Squeeze one lemon, add a teaspoon of honey and drink. Repeat every two hours.

• **Tongue stretching.** Stick out your tongue for 30 seconds, relax it for a few seconds, then repeat four times. This is believed to increase blood flow to the throat, speeding the healing process.

COUGHS

Try these folk remedies to figure out which works best for you...

• **Lemon, honey and olive oil.** Honey and olive oil coat and soothe, while lemon reduces mucus. Heat one cup of honey, a half cup of olive oil and the juice of one lemon over a medium flame for five minutes. Turn off the heat, and stir for two minutes to blend the ingredients. Consume one teaspoon of the mixture every two hours.

• **Vinegar and cayenne pepper.** Cayenne pepper contains *capsaicin*, a proven painkiller, while vinegar serves as an anti-inflammatory. Add a half cup of apple cider vinegar and one teaspoon of cayenne pepper to one-half cup of water. Add honey if desired. Take one tablespoon when your cough acts up and another tablespoon before bed.

• **Horseradish and honey.** Horseradish can help loosen mucus, while honey coats the throat. Grate one teaspoon of fresh, peeled horseradish into two teaspoons of honey. Consume one teaspoon every two to three hours.

• **Ginger.** Ginger is an anti-inflammatory that contains gingerols, which provide pain-reducing and sedative benefits. Chew a piece of fresh, peeled gingerroot when you feel the cough acting up, usually in the evening before bed. Chew until the ginger loses its kick.

• **Licorice root tea.** Licorice relieves the pain of irritated mucous membranes. Drink licorice root tea as long as your cough persists.

Note: Don't try licorice root if you have high blood pressure or kidney problems.

Say Good-Bye to Hay Fever: Natural Remedies That Work

Mark A. Stengler, ND, naturopathic physician in private practice, La Jolla, CA...adjunct associate clinical professor at the National College of Natural Medicine, Portland, OR...author of 16 books, including *The Natural Physician's Healing Therapies* (Bottom Line Books) and coauthor of *Prescription for Natural Cures* (Wiley)...and author of the *Bottom Line/Natural Healing* newsletter.

Oh, the sneezing! About 35 million Americans suffer from upper respiratory tract symptoms due to airborne allergies. One of the most common is hay fever, which results from a reaction to pollen.

Pollen enters the nasal cavity and triggers a cascade of reactions that lead to the release of *histamine* and other inflammatory chemicals. This can cause sneezing, coughing and postnasal drip, a runny or congested nose and itchy, watery, red eyes with dark circles underneath. Hay fever can keep you awake at night, making you feel fatigued and generally terrible all day long.

The most widespread pollen allergen is ragweed. One plant can generate a million grains of pollen a day. Other offenders include sagebrush, redroot pigweed, lamb's quarter, Russian thistle (tumbleweed) and English plantain.

Even if none of the plants that cause hay fever are found in your area, you are still susceptible to exposure because the small, light, dry pollen grains are easily transported by wind. Scientists have found ragweed pollen two miles high in the air and up to 400 miles away from its original source.

PREVENTION STRATEGIES

Pollen season occurs during the spring, summer and fall, when pollen is released by trees, grasses and weeds. Pollen counts tend to be highest in the morning, especially on warm, dry, breezy days, and lowest during cool, rainy periods. The pollen concentration is available for most urban areas—check your newspaper. Another resource for pollen counts is the American Academy of Allergy, Asthma and Immunology's National Allergy Bureau at *www.aaaai.org*. You can monitor pollen levels and plan accordingly. For example, allergy sufferers should try to stay indoors with the windows closed when pollen levels are high.

You can wear a dust and pollen mask designed to stop pollen from entering the nasal passageways (available at most pharmacies). You can use a high-efficiency particulate air (HEPA) purifier in your house, especially in your bedroom since pollen counts increase during the night.

DRUG THERAPIES

Several pharmaceutical medications can be used to treat hay fever, all of which can have side effects.

We all know about antihistamines, which are used to control excess mucus and reduce itching and sneezing. Examples include the prescription drugs *fexo-fenadine* (Allegra), *desloratadine* (Clarinex) and *cetirizine* (Zyrtec) and the over-the-counter (OTC) medications *loratadine* (Claritin) and *diphenhydramine* (Benadryl). *Cromolyn sodium* (Nasalcrom) is an OTC nasal spray antihistamine.

Potential side effects of oral medications include drowsiness and impaired coordination. The nasal spray can cause cough, nasal congestion or irritation, nausea, sneezing, throat irritation and wheezing.

Decongestants are used for nasal congestion. A common OTC oral form is *pseudoephedrine* (Sudafed). *Phenylephrine* (NeoSynephrine, Sinex) is a widely used nasal spray. Decongestants may raise blood pressure, cause insomnia and irritability, and inhibit urinary flow. They should be avoided by people with high blood pressure and/or glaucoma (they can increase the eye's intraocular pressure). Decongestants should be taken for only a few days—long-term use causes increased blood vessel constriction, which worsens blood pressure.

Corticosteroid treatments contain small doses of steroids to reduce nasal inflammation and swelling. They prevent and treat most allergy symptoms. Common examples of prescription nasal corticosteroids include *fluticasone* (Flonase), *mometasone* (Nasonex) and *triamcinolone* (Nasacort). These nasal corticosteroid sprays can cause fungal infection of the sinuses and mouth.

Sometimes oral steroids are used for severe allergies. These are very powerful prescription medicines that should be used for only a short time (up to a few weeks). Short-term side effects may include weight gain, water retention, high blood pressure, mood swings and depression. Long-term side effects include increased risk for diabetes, cataracts, osteoporosis and muscle weakness.

I know firsthand the miseries of hay fever. *Fortunately, the natural approaches I describe below have worked extremely well for me* and *for my patients...*

NASAL RINSE

An effective technique for people prone to hay fever and/or sinusitis is nasal irrigation. This involves rinsing the nasal passages with a warm saline solution to reduce the concentration of pollen, dust and other allergens. It also helps to clear excess mucus from the nasal passageways. This is typically done with a neti pot, a small ceramic container with a narrow spout that allows you to pour water into your nostrils and sinus cavities. Neti pots are available at health-food stores for about $20.

To use a neti pot, mix one-quarter teaspoon of salt in a cup of warm water. Pour the solution into the neti pot. Tilt your head to the side, and insert the spout into the upper nostril. The solution will flow into the upper nostril and out the lower nostril. After a few seconds, remove the pot. With your head still tilted, blow through both nostrils. Do not cover one side of your nose—this will force the mucus and bacteria up into your sinuses. Repeat the rinse on the other side. It's messy, but it works. Use once daily for low-grade allergies and twice daily for acute allergies.

An easier alternative is Sinus Rinse. You open a packet of premeasured saline and baking soda, pour it into the bottle that comes with the kit and add warm water. Push the tip of the bottle into one nostril, and squeeze the bottle so the solution comes out the other nostril. Repeat with the other nostril. Do this once or twice daily. A kit containing 50 premixed packets is available from Allergy Solutions for $12.95 (800-491-4300, *www.allergysolution.com*).

Important: To avoid introducing bacteria into your nasal passageways, clean the tip of the neti pot (or Sinus Rinse bottle) with alcohol between uses.

HOMEOPATHIC HELP

Homeopathy treats hay fever by desensitizing the immune system to the offending pollen(s)—or the symptoms they trigger. This is based on the principle that "like cures like"—that is, substances that cause allergy symptoms can be used in a highly diluted form to alleviate those same symptoms.

For example, ragweed, oak and grasses can be taken as individual remedies or as part of a combination remedy. If you know that you are allergic to ragweed pollen, you can take homeopathic ragweed to minimize your response. An allergist can do skin testing to determine which allergens affect you.

Homeopathic remedies are somewhat similar to conventional allergy shots, in which minute doses of the substances you're allergic to are injected under the skin. The advantage of the homeopathic approach is that it is convenient (it requires dissolving some pellets or a liquid solution under your tongue) and relatively inexpensive ($10 to $20 a month).

Researchers at the Southwest College of Naturopathic Medicine and Health Sciences in Tempe, Arizona, conducted a four-week, double-blind clinical trial comparing homeopathic preparations with a placebo during the regional allergy season from February to May. Participants included 40 men and women, ages 26 to 63, diagnosed with moderate to severe seasonal allergy symptoms. Those taking the homeopathic preparations had a 38% reduction in symptoms, such as watery eyes and sneezing, compared with a 26% decline for those using the placebo.

There are two homeopathic remedies that I recommend for the treatment of hay fever. Which one you take depends on your symptoms. They are available at most health-food stores. The dosage is two pellets of a 30C potency twice daily.

•**Allium cepa** (from onion) is for those with watery and burning eyes…runny nose…sneezing.

•**Euphrasia** (from the eyebright plant) is for hay fever that mainly affects only the eyes, causing burning, tearing and redness.

If you don't know which homeopathic remedy to use, try Sabadil Allergy by Boiron, available at health-food stores for about $9. This formula contains six remedies commonly used for hay fever. The typical dose is two tablets dissolved in the mouth every 15 minutes for one hour, then two pellets three times daily.

CHOOSING SUPPLEMENTS

The right supplements also help control hay fever. *My recommendations…*

•**Quercetin,** a type of plant pigment known as a flavonoid, is nature's antihistamine, with anti-inflammatory and antioxidant properties. It is found in onions, apples and green tea. It works best at a starting dosage of 1,000 mg three times daily for five days, followed by a maintenance dosage of 500 mg two or three times daily. Quercetin is very safe, and side effects are uncommon. Quercetin also works well when combined with vitamin C, which may help reduce allergy symptoms in some individuals. A typical dose for hay fever is 3,000 mg to 5,000 mg of vitamin C daily. Reduce the dosage if you develop loose stools. If you have a history of kidney stones, consult your doctor before taking vitamin C supplements.

•**Stinging nettle leaf** is a popular herbal treatment for the relief of hay fever. I have seen it help some patients when used at the first sign of hay fever symptoms. A randomized, double-blind study conducted at the National College of Naturopathic Medicine in Portland, Oregon, involved 69 people with hay fever who took 300 mg of a stinging nettle leaf supplement or a placebo daily. Researchers found that after one week, 58% of those who took stinging nettle leaf had a reduction in symptoms, such as sneezing and itchy eyes, compared with 37% of those who received a placebo.

Interestingly, nettle leaves are a natural source of vitamin C and quercetin. Stinging nettle leaf supplements should be avoided by those with kidney disease because they have a diuretic (water-excreting) effect. The type of stinging nettle leaf used in the study mentioned above is available from Eclectic Institute and can be found at health-food stores.

•**N-acetylcysteine** (NAC) is a great supplement to use if you are suffering from postnasal drip or coughing as the result of mucous formation. I find that 500 mg twice daily is helpful for patients. Side effects, such as nausea, constipation and diarrhea, are rare.

GETTING STARTED

When using homeopathic remedies and supplements, it's best to start two weeks before allergy season and then continue until the end of the season if the treatment is helping. Try quercetin first. If you do not get relief within one week, try stinging nettle leaf, NAC and/or a homeopathic treatment.

A book that I especially like is *Sinus Survival: A Self-Help Guide*, by Rob Ivker, DO (Tarcher).

Uncommon Knowledge About the Common Cold

William Schaffner, MD, chairman of the department of preventive medicine at Vanderbilt University School of Medicine, Nashville, is a fellow of the Infectious Diseases Society of America, and a liaison member of the Advisory Committee on Immunization Practices of the Centers for Disease Control and Prevention. He is vice president of the National Foundation for Infectious Diseases Board of Directors.

The average American gets more than 100 colds in his/her lifetime, and scientists have amassed lots of information about the common cold. But misinformation still is widely circulated as fact. *Take the following quiz to see how much you really know about the common cold…*

•*True or False?* **Colds are mainly spread by coughs and sneezes.**

False: The viruses that cause colds usually are spread by hand-to-hand, hand-to-nose or hand-to-object contact. The *rhinovirus*, the most common cold virus, flourishes in mucous membranes. Someone infected with the virus rubs his nose or eyes, picking up the virus on his fingers. He then touches you or deposits the virus on another surface (doorknob, telephone, etc.). The virus can survive for 24 to 48 hours, so it can be readily picked up by the next person who comes along.

•*True or False?* **People with colds are highly contagious before they experience symptoms.**

True: You're most contagious in the 24 hours before symptoms start. You may feel healthy, but the virus is incubating—and spreading. Colds often are transmitted during this period because people who are infected aren't yet staying home—and other people aren't avoiding them the way they would someone who is coughing or sneezing.

•*True or False?* **Antimicrobial soap kills cold viruses.**

False: Antimicrobial soap kills bacteria, not the viruses that cause colds. The best protection against colds is to wash your hands often with warm, soapy water. It takes about a minute of washing to remove viruses from your hands.

Waterless alcohol-based hand sanitizers can be helpful when soap and water aren't available. Hand sanitizers such as Purell and Nexcare kill cold viruses, as do disposable alcohol towelettes.

•*True or False?* **Being cold increases the risk of getting a cold.**

False: Generations of moms have said, "Bundle up or you'll catch a cold"—but the best current evidence indicates that Mom was wrong.

In one well-regarded study, scientists divided volunteers into a "warm" group and a group that was damp and chilled. They exposed people in both groups to cold viruses. There was no difference in the incidence of subsequent colds between the two groups.

Opposing view: In a study reported in *Journal of Family Practice*, scientists did find an increase in colds in volunteers who soaked their feet in icy water for 20 minutes. This wasn't a controlled experiment, however. The scientists didn't know, for example, if the volunteers who got sick had more contact with people who already had colds than those who didn't get sick.

Cold weather brings an increase in colds, but being cold doesn't seem to be a factor.

•*True or False?* **Vitamin C has been proven to reduce the duration and/or severity of colds.**

False: Ever since the publication of Linus Pauling's book *Vitamin C and the Common Cold*, millions of Americans have attempted to prevent and/or treat colds by taking enormous amounts of vitamin C—as much as 1,000 milligrams (mg) every few hours. Since then, many studies have looked at the connection between colds and vitamin C. Most have been inconclusive—and many showed no benefit at all. In large doses, vitamin C inhibits the effects of *histamine*, a body chemical that causes sniffles and other cold symptoms. Yet there's no evidence that reducing histamine in this way has any effect on cold symptoms—and studies have not shown that it prevents colds.

Caution: Vitamin C is cleared through the kidneys. Taking large amounts can cause the vitamin to crystallize and result in kidney stones. Drink more water than usual if you decide to take extra vitamin C—and don't exceed 250 mg to 500 mg daily.

•*True or False?* Yellow or green mucus indicates a serious infection.

False: People who develop yellow or greenish mucus often rush to their doctors to ask for antibiotics because they believe that discolored mucus indicates a serious bacterial infection.

Colds can cause either clear, watery mucus or mucus that's thick and discolored. The coloration means that there's inflammation and more white blood cells. These immune cells are present in both viral and bacterial infections. Discolored mucus isn't a useful way to distinguish one from the other—and it doesn't mean that your cold is more serious or that it will last longer.

•*True or False?* We get fewer colds as we get older.

True: There are approximately 200 different viruses that cause colds. Each time your immune system is exposed to one of these viruses, it develops antibodies that make you immune to that particular strain. By the time you reach your 60s or 70s and have a lifetime of colds behind you, you have developed immunity to many—but not all—of the circulating cold viruses.

•*True or False?* Stress increases the likelihood of getting a cold.

False: There are theoretical reasons to think that emotional stress could increase the risk of getting a cold, but it has never been shown conclusively.

Studies have shown that chronic stress decreases the immune system's ability to suppress infections. But stress is ubiquitous—nearly everyone reports having stress in the days or weeks before a survey—so it's difficult to link it with illness.

•*True or False?* Hot tea eases cold symptoms.

True: Black and green tea both contain theophylline, a mild bronchodilator. Drinking tea when you have a cold may open the airways and make breathing easier. The heat and steam from the liquid also thin mucus and ease congestion.

Chicken soup also is a traditional remedy for colds—but don't expect too much. Though it provides extra fluids and the steam eases congestion, chicken soup cannot cure a cold, despite what many people think.

■■■■

Cold Threat

Common cold bacteria may cause blindness, says a noted ophthalmologist.

Recent study: The bacteria that causes respiratory infections, *Chlamydia pneumoniae*, was found in six of nine samples from patients who had age-related macular degeneration, the leading cause of blindness in people over age 55 in the US. C. pneumoniae also has been linked to coronary artery disease, heart attack and cerebrovascular disease (related to the blood supply to the brain).

Theory: The bacteria cause inflammation, a factor in the development of macular degeneration.

Self-defense: Eat a heart-healthy diet, and avoid smoking.

Joan W. Miller, MD, professor and chair, department of ophthalmology, Harvard Medical School, Boston, and senior author of a study, published in *Graef's Archive for Clinical and Experimental Ophthalmology.*

Killer Pneumonia Is on the Rise

Donald M. Yealy, MD, professor and vice-chair of emergency medicine at the University of Pittsburgh Medical Center/Presbyterian University Hospital, has written more than 150 articles, reviews and book chapters focusing on pneumonia.

If the recent flu seasons are typical, an estimated 30 million Americans will come down with the illness. That's bad enough—but many of these people will go on to develop *secondary pneumonia*, a much more serious condition.

Pneumonia, whether it follows another infection or occurs on its own (primary pneumonia), is the sixth leading cause of death in the US. More than 60,000 Americans die from it annually, and many more require hospitalization.

New danger: A rare—but particularly lethal—form of pneumonia is resistant to standard antibiotics. It is caused by the bacterium *methicillin-resistant Staphylococcus aureus* (MRSA), which has appeared in recent years in hospitals and increasingly in the wider community. The death rate from MRSA pneumonia is roughly double that of other pneumonias.

What you need to know…

WHO GETS PNEUMONIA?

Pneumonia is an illness of the lungs and respiratory system in which the *alveoli* (tiny sacs in the lungs) become inflamed and flooded with fluid. Pneumonia can be caused by bacteria, viruses or fungi. The viral form is the most common.

People get pneumonia in the same ways that they get the flu—by touching their eyes, nose or mouth after shaking hands, for example, with someone who has the virus on his/her hands—or through airborne droplets from coughs or sneezes.

Bacterial pneumonia is usually the most serious form. It is most commonly acquired by inhaling or aspirating bacteria. Hospital patients have a high risk of contracting bacterial pneumonia—their immune systems tend to be weakened, and germs are prevalent in this setting. Other vulnerable people include those with diabetes, heart or lung disease…adults age 65 and older…young children…and anyone who abuses alcohol or smokes.

Surprising new risk factor: People who take acid-suppressing heartburn drugs, such as *cimetidine* (Tagamet), *ranitidine* (Zantac), *omeprazole* (Prilosec) and *esomeprazole* (Nexium), have been found to be 27% more likely to develop pneumonia—especially hospital-acquired pneumonia—than people not taking such medication.

Researchers theorize that these drugs may increase a person's vulnerability to infection by reducing stomach acid, a major defense mechanism against pathogens ingested through the mouth. People should not use over-the-counter acid-reducing drugs for more than a few weeks unless they are prescribed by their doctors.

HOW IT'S DIAGNOSED

It can sometimes be difficult for patients to distinguish the symptoms of pneumonia from those caused by a cold or the flu. Therefore, anyone with a high fever (102° F or higher)…chills…a persistent cough…shortness of breath…and/or pain when inhaling should see a doctor right away.

What the doctor will look for…

•**Abnormal chest sounds** heard through a stethoscope. The doctor will listen for crackling sounds (rales) or rumblings (rhonchi), caused by air passing through mucus and/or other fluids in the lungs.

•**X-ray showing a cloudy area,** caused by fluid in the lungs.

Caution: An X-ray often will look normal in patients with early-stage pneumonia. A second X-ray is typically taken if symptoms do not improve in two to three days or worsen, especially if the first X-ray looked normal.

A sputum test is also recommended to identify the cause of the pneumonia—and help the doctor choose the best treatment. After an X-ray, it's the best test for diagnosing pneumonia, but only 20% to 25% of patients are able to bring up sputum (by coughing) for analysis.

TREATMENT

An antiviral drug, such as *oseltamivir* (Tamiflu), is sometimes prescribed for viral pneumonia. In viral pneumonia patients who are otherwise healthy, doctors may recommend the same therapy as for the flu—rest, plenty of liquids (up to one gallon daily) and medication to reduce fever and/or pain.

Because bacterial and viral pneumonia can appear quite similar, doctors typically err on the side of caution and assume that it's bacterial in origin when uncertain and prescribe antibiotics.

Studies show that older patients as well as those with underlying health problems do better when they're given antibiotics promptly—preferably within four to eight hours of the initial diagnosis. Most bacterial pneumonias are treated (orally or intravenously) with a *penicillin* antibiotic, such as *amoxicillin/clavulanic acid* (Augmentin)…a cephalosporin antibiotic, such as *cefaclor* (Ceclor) or *ceftriaxone* (Rocephin)…and/or *azithromycin* (Zithromax).

At-home treatment: Patients with pneumonia are sometimes advised to use an incentive spirometer (a tubelike device that patients breathe into, as hard as they can, at least two to three times a day). It increases pressure in the bronchial tubes and helps maintain open breathing passages.

Preventive: An incentive spirometer also can be used by patients who don't have pneumonia but who have underlying lung disease, such as chronic bronchitis, emphysema or some other obstructive lung disease. It helps keep the airways open and less vulnerable to pneumonia.

AN EMERGING THREAT

MRSA is primarily a skin infection that can enter the body through cuts or scrapes. MRSA was originally found only in health-care settings. In the 1990s, it began showing up in the general community. This form of infection has the prefix CA, denoting community-acquired.

CA-MRSA pneumonia isn't as dangerous as the hospital-acquired form. It's usually treated with the antibiotics *sulfamethoxazole* and *trimethoprim* (Bactrim). Hospital patients with MRSA-related pneumonia require a much stronger antibiotic—*vancomycin* (Vancocin), given intravenously.

Self-protection: CA-MRSA is spread by airborne droplets. It also can be present on drinking glasses, toothbrushes, etc. In community settings, such as health clubs, people should never share their personal items.

In the hospital: Patients should wash their hands after touching any object. MRSA can survive on doorknobs, faucet handles, bedrails, remote controls, telephones, food trays, etc. Patients also should wash after using the bathroom and before eating. For convenience, a 62% alcohol hand sanitizer gel can be used. Patients should insist that all medical personnel wash their hands before and after performing any procedure—and even before and after touching any object in the room.

PREVENTION

Not smoking and frequent hand-washing help prevent pneumonia.

Also important…

• **Annual flu vaccine.** People who don't get the flu are far less likely to get pneumonia. The Centers for Disease Control and Prevention (CDC) recommends the flu vaccine for adults age 50 and older…children ages six months to five years old…women who are pregnant during flu season (typically October to as late as May)…and health-care workers or others who have close contact with people in a high-risk group. However, flu vaccine, if available can help most people reduce risk.

Important: The FluMist nasal vaccine, which has been approved for healthy people ages five to 49, may be more effective than conventional flu shots. There appears to be a greater immune response in the nose, where the vaccine is administered. This can make it harder for an inhaled flu virus to cause infection.

Caution: FluMist is not recommended for people with asthma or lung disease.

• **Pneumococcal vaccine.** It's recommended for adults age 65 and older as well as for those with pneumonia risk factors, such as cardiovascular or lung disease, cancer or a previous illness with pneumonia. People with certain illnesses, such as kidney or severe lung disease, may need a second dose after five or more years.

What's Killing Older People?

Robert J.F. Laheij, PhD, epidemiologist, University Medical Center, Nijmegen, the Netherlands.

George Pankey, MD, director, infectious disease research, Ochsner Clinic Foundation, New Orleans.

The Journal of the American Medical Association.

Taking heartburn drugs for prolonged periods increases the risk of developing pneumonia, according to a Dutch study. According to study author, Robert J.F. Laheij, an epidemiologist at the University Medical Center in Nijmegen, these drugs work by reducing the production of stomach acid—less stomach acid lets more bacteria survive.

"There can be some kind of aspiration of bacteria into the airway," he explains. And while his study looked specifically at pneumonia, several previous studies have indicated an increase in other respiratory infections, such as influenza and bronchitis, from long-term use of heartburn drugs.

THE STUDY

In his population study of more than 364,000 people in the Netherlands national health insurance program, Laheij found that compared with similar people who were not taking heartburn drugs, the risk of pneumonia was nearly double among those taking heartburn drugs called *proton pump inhibitors* for prolonged periods.

And the risk was almost 66% higher for people regularly taking *histamine antagonists*, another type of drug used to fight heartburn.

Proton pump inhibitors—which include Nexium, Prevacid, Prevpac, Prilosec, Protonix and Aciphex—suppress approximately 90% of stomach acid production.

Histamine inhibitors act in a different way, blocking the histamine that stimulates cells to produce acid. They include *cimetidine* (Tagamet), *famotidine* (Pepcid), *nizatidine* (Axid) and *ranitidine* (Zantac).

INDISCRIMINATELY USED

Because some prescription heartburn medications are available in lower-priced generic forms, and others are sold over-the-counter, they are widely available and taken by millions. These drugs account for more than $20 billion in annual sales.

The easy availability of these heartburn medications is a big part of the problem, says Laheij. Two or three weeks of treatment is enough for most people to soothe heartburn, he says. But many people continue to take the medicine for much longer.

"My advice would be to use them as long as necessary and then stop them," he says.

"I don't think these drugs should be used indiscriminately, and I think they are," says Dr. George Pankey, director of infectious disease research at the Ochsner Clinic Foundation in New Orleans.

"Your doctor needs to know what you are taking," he adds.

"In this country, perhaps more than [in Europe], physicians do not know everything that a patient is taking, especially over-the-counter medications. If you are taking a lot of medications, tell your doctor," Pankey says.

To get additional information about proton pump inhibitors, check with Drug Digest on-line at *www.drugdigest.org*. Click on "Compare Drugs."

Exercise Improves Immunity

David Nieman, Dr.PH, director, Human Performance Lab, Appalachian State University, Boone, NC. Dr. Nieman was president of the International Society of Exercise Immunology for two terms, and is the author of nine books, including *Nutritional Assessment*. McGraw-Hill. He has also contributed over 200 peer-reviewed articles in books and journals.

If you want to avoid a nasty cold this winter, go for a nice, brisk walk. Studies have shown that people who walk briskly for 45 minutes most days of the week have just half the number of sick days caused by colds or sore throats as non-exercisers. David Nieman, Dr.PH, director of the Appalachian State University Human Performance Lab in Boone, North Carolina, has researched the impact of exercise on human cells for more than 20 years.

EXERCISE AND IMMUNE BOOSTING

Dr. Nieman says that moderate aerobic exercise creates favorable immune changes, including improvements in the killer T-cell function and improved immune system surveillance, which is the body's ability to detect and defend against pathogens. This improvement is triggered every time you exercise and lasts for one to three hours after the activity. The key, says Dr. Nieman, is frequency. Even though the change is just hours a day, over time it becomes protective. If you prefer, say, three 15-minute segments instead of 45 minutes, Dr. Nieman says it is probably equally effective as a cold fighter, but he can't confirm that until he completes research, now under way.

TOO MUCH OF A GOOD THING

Dr. Nieman does have one important caveat about exercise, however—beware of the more-must-be-better trap. Overexercising, which is 90-plus minutes per day or running 60 or more miles a week, increases vulnerability to illness. Marathon runners, for example, are six times more likely to get ill in the one to two weeks following a race because excessive exercise suppresses the immune system. Dr. Nieman says that it pops back up to normal quickly, but to get around the suppressed immunity period, superathletes need to be particularly careful to follow the rules of good health—avoid exposure to germs, eat healthfully and get enough sleep. In fact, studies have proven that lack of sleep as well as rapid weight loss and stress cause immune suppression.

Should you continue exercising if you are getting or have a cold or the flu? Not if you have fever, aches and pains that are symptomatic of flu or other systemic illnesses. Heavy exercising will make symptoms worse and last longer, says Dr. Nieman. In the case of a simple cold, though, exercise is neutral—it will neither hurt nor help you.

As to the old saw that cold weather can increase vulnerability to colds and flu, Dr. Nieman says it's unlikely, assuming that your body is not cold, so dress warmly.

His advice: Get out and move whatever the season—there is every reason to believe you are doing yourself a favor.

■ ■ ■ ■

Exercise Fights Colds

Researchers studied 160 overweight, sedentary women ages 18 to 85. Half walked for 45 minutes five days a week for 12 to 15 weeks, while the other half remained sedentary.

Result: The walkers who got colds had 40% to 50% fewer days of illness than nonwalkers who got colds.

Theory: Thirty to 60 minutes a day of moderate exercise, such as walking at a 15-minute-per-mile pace, spurs production of germ-killing cells called *neutrophils.*

Caution: Ninety minutes or more of high-intensity daily exercise, such as long-distance running, has the opposite effect, increasing stress hormones and immune dysfunction.

David C. Nieman, Dr.PH, director, Human Performance Lab, Appalachian State University, Boone, NC.

■ ■ ■ ■

Inoculations for Adults

Have a chickenpox vaccination if you have not had the disease, or aren't sure if you've had it. Get hepatitis B shots if you have been sexually active with more than one partner in the past six months. Have a flu shot annually after age 49 and a pneumoccocal shot once after age 64. Be vaccinated against measles, mumps and rubella if you were born in 1957 or later and have not had measles or mumps, or are not sure whether you had the diseases or a vaccination. Get a tetanus and diphtheria shot once every 10 years.

Raymond A. Strikas, MD, Seasonal and Pandemic Influenza Coorinator at the National Vaccine Program Office in the Department of Health and Human Services.

■ ■ ■ ■

Unstuffy Nose

Relieve a stuffy nose by alternately thrusting your tongue against the roof of your mouth, then pressing one finger between your eyebrows. This causes the vomer and ethmoid bones to move up and down, which helps loosen congestion. After 20 seconds or so, your sinuses will start to drain.

Lisa DeStefano, DO, department of osteopathic manipulative medicine, college of osteopathic medicine, Michigan State University, East Lansing.

■ ■ ■ ■

The Strep Attack

The most effective strep-throat treatment is a group of antibiotics called *cephalosporins,* sold as Cefpodoxime and Cefdinir. They work better in four to five days than *penicillin* or *amoxicillin* in 10 days. Children given penicillin were back at the doctor within three weeks 25% of the time…those treated with amoxicillin went back 18% of the time. Only 7% of children treated with cephalosporins saw the doctor a second time.

Michael Pichichero, MD, professor of microbiology and immunology, University of Rochester Medical Center, Rochester, NY, and leader of a review of treatment of more than 11,000 children with strep throat, reported in Interscience Conference on Antimicrobial Agents and Chemotherapy proceedings.

Immunity Boosters: Proven Ways to Stay Healthy

Michael F. Roizen, MD, chief wellness officer at the Cleveland Clinic, OH, and coauthor of *YOU: The Smart Patient* (Free Press). Dr. Roizen has cowritten *YOU: The Owner's Manual* (HarperCollins), and served on the boards of five nonprofit foundations. He is former chair of a Food and Drug Administration advisory committee and has published over 165 peer-reviewed papers.

It's amazing that we're not sick all the time. We are attacked more than 100 million times a day by viruses, bacteria and other disease-causing organisms. Our hands alone harbor up to two million germs. The only reason we're not continually sick is that the immune system is remarkably effective at recognizing and fighting threats.

Many harmful organisms are blocked by barriers, such as skin and mucous membranes, that prevent harmful organisms from getting into the body.

Those that get past the initial barriers are spotted by antibodies and attacked by a barrage of immune cells. The antibodies "remember" individual pathogens and attack and neutralize them during subsequent exposures.

FLAWS IN THE SYSTEM

The immune system isn't perfect, however. Immune cells aren't always effective—due to nutritional deficiencies, emotional stress and aging.

If the immune system has never been exposed to a particular virus or bacterium, it may not be able to mount an effective defense. Also, viruses and bacteria can develop their own defenses, which make them harder to detect and eliminate. In addition, the immune system can mistake healthy tissues for foreign invaders and launch an attack. This is what happens in autoimmune diseases, such as lupus.

Almost half of all deaths are due to infection or other immune-related problems. Even some cancers are caused by infectious organisms that break down the immune system.

Here's how to build up your immune system...

IMMUNITY BOOSTERS

Limiting exposure to harmful organisms is one of the best preventive measures. Wash your hands after you shake hands or touch surfaces that others have touched. Avoid people who are sneezing or coughing. These measures alone can significantly cut infection from colds or flu.

Also helpful...

• **Stay social.** People with active social lives and those who participate in religious or community groups are less likely to experience depression than those without social ties. Depression reduces immune response, mainly by inhibiting the activity of "attack" immune cells called T cells and B cells.

Get professional help if you're experiencing depression. The majority of depressed patients who receive medication or therapy improve within three months—and nearly all of them improve within six months.

• **Exercise daily—but don't overdo it.** People who get regular exercise and take care of themselves in other ways—eating nutritious meals, not smoking, etc.—can improve immune response. Symptoms of depression also can be reduced by exercise. Thirty minutes a day is optimal for most people.

Caution: Exercising more than two hours daily actually causes immunity to decline.

• **Manage stress.** Stress itself doesn't weaken immunity, but poor responses to stress—such as smoking, not eating healthfully and not exercising—are linked to infection. Not getting enough sleep is both a cause and a result of stress and can impair the activity of infection-fighting T cells and B cells.

Stress reducers: Set aside 20 minutes to listen to music or meditate...breathe deeply for a few minutes...go for a walk or engage in other exercise.

• **Get enough omega-3s.** The omega-3 fatty acids in nuts and fish have been shown to reduce depression and improve immunity. Have one-quarter cup of walnuts daily...three servings of fish weekly...or take two grams of a fish oil supplement daily.

• **Boost vitamin C.** Studies indicate that vitamin C may prevent infection by boosting levels of T cells and B cells. The optimal dosage is 500 milligrams (mg) twice daily. You can get this much vitamin C with several daily servings of vitamin C–rich foods, such as tomatoes, bell peppers and citrus fruits—or you can take a supplement.

• **Favor flavonoids.** These vitamin-like substances in fruits, vegetables and whole grains

49

minimize age-related declines in immune function. You need about 31 mg of flavonoids daily.

Best sources: Cranberry juice (13 mg per eight-ounce glass)…tomato juice (7.2 mg per eight-ounce glass)…apples (4.2 mg per medium apple)…strawberries (4.2 mg per cup)…broccoli (4.2 mg per cup)…onions (3 mg per small onion)…red wine (3 mg per five-ounce glass).

•**Avoid sugar.** Sugary foods, such as candy, cakes, cookies, etc., can drive blood glucose levels above 250 milli-moles per liter of blood (a normal level is between 65 and 140). Elevated blood sugar impairs the ability of immune cells to destroy bacteria.

How to Stop Staph

Jay R. Kostman, MD, chief, infectious diseases division, Penn Presbyterian Medical Center, Philadelphia.

Staph infections used to be a hospital-based problem, treatable with available antibiotics. Now they occur with increasing frequency outside of the hospital. The new, antibiotic-resistant strain of staph is known as MRSA, methicillin-resistant Staphylococcus Aureus. It is resistant to antibiotics such as *penicillin* and *amoxicillin* and it turns ordinary scrapes and cuts into potentially fatal problems.

According to Jay Kostman, MD, chief, infectious diseases division at the Penn Presbyterian Medical Center in Philadelphia, many common wound infections that would have responded to routine antibiotics are now MRSA infections, and they resist traditional treatment. Staph bacteria are everywhere, including on the body, but they're harmless unless there is a break in the skin. In places where people gather and literally rub shoulders, and sometimes towels (think gyms, Jacuzzis, and locker rooms), a cut, scrape or even a rug burn can be an invitation for the bacteria to hop in and cause trouble.

Athletic teams, children at camp and toddlers in day-care centers in close quarters are all vulnerable to the possibility of MRSA infection. It can also result from everyday falls on a sidewalk—or anywhere that provides an opportunity for the bacteria to penetrate the outer layers of the skin to the underlying tissue, perhaps eventually entering the blood stream.

HOW TO PROTECT YOURSELF

The first and best precaution is to cleanse all wounds thoroughly, even small ones. Cover with a bandage to keep the area clean, until healed. Dr. Kostman advises to wash minor cuts with soap and water or an antibacterial soap. A topical antibiotic such as Neosporin may be applied after cleaning, but OTC ointments should be used sparingly, as bacteria are becoming resistant to these everyday antidotes. For deeper injuries, seek medical attention immediately.

As a rule, careful cleaning protects against infection. But watch the wound as it heals to be sure no infection sets in, says Dr. Kostman. *Watch for these changes, which might signal infection…*

•**Pain or tenderness** at the site of the wound.

•**Fever,** even a slight one.

•**Redness around the wound** (especially red streaks running up from the wound site).

•**Drainage of pus.**

If any symptoms develop, see your doctor right away to be tested for MRSA or other bacteria. Several types of antibiotics are effective for MRSA. These include *trimethoprim-sulfamethoxazole* (Bactrim), *clindamycin* (Cleocin), and sometimes *linezolid* (Zyvox) or *vancomycin* (Vancocin). These medications must be taken for up to two weeks.

MRSA infections can both develop and escalate, including into a bloodstream infection, startlingly fast, sometimes in hours. This kind of rapidly moving infection is a medical emergency—do not wait for the next morning to call the doctor…get to the ER right away. Danger signals include a fever that reaches 102 degrees and is accompanied by shaking, chills, severe muscle aches and pains and altered thinking. Other infections may remain localized, says Dr. Kostman, typically showing up as an abscess with extreme tenderness and redness, similar in appearance to a boil.

Even after minor cuts and scrapes, remain vigilant for some time, because MRSA infection can develop even a few weeks later. As a rule, says Dr. Kostman, the danger of infection decreases sharply once a wound has closed, but even then it takes some time to be completely clear of risk.

3

Health Alerts

Symptoms You Should Never Ignore

We all experience troublesome symptoms from time to time, such as fatigue or digestive upset. These usually indicate mild conditions, but they can be a sign of dangerous problems. Complicating matters is that some symptoms are more likely to be serious for men, others for women. Symptoms and what they can mean…

DANGEROUS SYMPTOMS FOR MEN

Symptom: Shoulder pain.

Could be: Coronary artery disease.

Many men are sedentary during the week, then overdo it on weekends—and blame sudden shoulder pain on muscle strain. But shoulder pain that comes on suddenly often is a sign of coronary artery disease. In some cases, this is the only symptom. More often, men also will report that they are experiencing occasional shortness of breath and possibly subtle chest pain.

Important: Call 911 or get to an emergency room immediately if shoulder pain comes on suddenly for no obvious reason—or if it's accompanied by other symptoms. You could be having a heart attack.

Also: Ask your doctor, before an emergency arises, if you should take aspirin if you are having symptoms of a heart attack. Aspirin (chewed and swallowed) can reduce the severity of a heart attack.

Symptom: Persistent foot and hip pain.

Could be: Prostate cancer.

Nearly everyone experiences joint pain on occasion. It's usually due to overuse injuries or relatively mild "wear and tear" arthritis—joint pain that gets more common with age.

J. Edward Hill, MD, past president of the American Medical Association, board member of the Mississippi Department of Health and an adviser for the American Medical Association, *Family Medical Guide* (Wiley), is a family physician and a faculty member at the Family Medicine Residency Center, North Mississippi Medical Center, Tupelo.

51

However, a man who experiences joint pain that doesn't improve after a few days with the usual treatments, such as rest and over-the-counter analgesics, should get a complete checkup. This is especially important if the pain starts in the foot or ankle, then extends to the hip. It could indicate that prostate cancer has started to spread. Any delay could be life-threatening.

Also important: Men should see a doctor immediately if they notice any change in their urine or urinary habits—difficulty urinating, blood in the urine, etc. Men often assume that this is due to normal, age-related changes in the prostate gland—but changes in urinary habits also can indicate early-stage prostate cancer.

DANGEROUS SYMPTOMS FOR WOMEN

Symptoms: Slight numbness in an arm or leg, transient loss of balance, intermittent blurred vision.

Could be: Multiple sclerosis (MS).

Numbness, balance difficulties and vision changes are classic signs of MS, a disease that affects women about twice as often as men. Women often ignore the symptoms because they tend to come and go quickly—and they may occur so rarely that they don't seem serious. Many patients with MS report having symptoms up to seven years before being diagnosed.

MS symptoms usually get worse over time. Women who get early treatment—with drugs such as beta interferons, for example—usually have a marked reduction in symptoms and retain their ability to live normal lives.

Symptom: Minor abdominal/pelvic pain that comes and goes.

Could be: Ovarian cancer.

Most women of child-bearing age experience occasional discomfort in the abdomen or pelvic region. It's usually due to digestive distress or menstruation, but it also can be an early sign of ovarian cancer. The discomfort usually lasts a few days, then goes away for weeks or months. Because the pain tends to be minor and intermittent, most women ignore it—even when it occurs over the course of months or years.

Other possible symptoms of ovarian cancer: Abdominal swelling or bloating…indigestion and/or nausea…and/or urinary urgency.

The discomfort of menstrual or digestive conditions tends to occur in a predictable fashion—for example, at a certain time of the month or after eating certain foods. With ovarian cancer, the discomfort gets more persistent and severe as the cancer grows.

Important: Women experiencing this kind of pain should see a doctor right away. Ovarian cancer can be successfully treated when it is detected in the early stages. Because it causes only minor symptoms—or no symptoms at all, in some cases—only about 29% of patients are diagnosed before the cancer has spread. At that point, treatments are much less likely to be effective.

Symptoms: Unusual fatigue, shortness of breath.

Could be: Heart disease.

A woman's symptoms of heart disease or a heart attack are typically different than a man's. Women are unlikely to experience crushing chest pain or pain radiating down one or both arms. Instead, they are more likely to experience fatigue, difficulty breathing, pressure or pain in the upper abdomen or symptoms resembling indigestion.

A woman with heart disease may get short of breath or feel exhausted all the time. If you suspect you are having a heart attack, call for emergency medical help immediately.

Also: Ask your doctor, before an emergency arises, if you should take aspirin if you are having symptoms of a heart attack. Aspirin (chewed and swallowed) can reduce the severity of a heart attack.

■ ■ ■ ■

The Lowdown on Bedbugs

Bedbugs—small nocturnal insects that feed on human and animal blood—are a growing problem in hotels in the US and abroad, as well as in apartment houses, dormitories, sleep-away camps and other places. Unlike mosquitoes, bedbugs don't transmit disease—but their bites can cause irritation and discomfort. They do not attach themselves to people. They move from place to place via luggage, clothing and other items. *To protect yourself…*

When staying away from home: Pull back the bed sheets, and check the mattress seams and tufts. Look for live bugs that are about one-quarter to one-half-inch long and vary in color from reddish brown to nearly transparent. Also check for light brown, translucent molted skins…and pin-sized black spots (excrement). If possible, pull back the fabric headboard and inspect it, too. If signs are present, ask for another room.

Also: Keep your luggage in the bathroom until you have checked the bed.

When you return home: Leave luggage outside until you have inspected each item.

At home: If you find bedbugs on an article of clothing, comforters or other linens, wash them in 150° water. You may also want to call an exterminator. Do not bring used furniture or mattresses into your home.

Dini M. Miller, PhD, associate professor of entomology, Virginia Tech, Blacksburg, VA. Virginia Tech is one of only two US universities that raise bedbugs for research.

Organ Transplants Can Also Transfer Disease

Rona MacKie, MD, senior research fellow, University of Glasgow, Scotland.

Daniel G. Coit, MD, co-leader of the melanoma disease management team, Memorial Sloan-Kettering Cancer Center, New York City.

Robert A. Fisher, MD, professor of surgery, and director, Liver Transplantation and Transplantation Research, Virginia Commonwealth University Medical Center, Richmond.

The New England Journal of Medicine.

S ixteen years after a Scottish woman was diagnosed with melanoma, the deadly cancer was transferred to two more people via the woman's donated kidneys.

That incident and similar ones have resulted in stricter controls in some hospitals for organ transplants.

"It's very worrisome," says Dr. Rona MacKie, senior research fellow at the University of Glasgow in Scotland. "The amazing thing about this patient is the gap between having the melanoma diagnosed and giving her kidneys."

The time gap was twice as long as any other case, which testifies to the resilience of tumor cells in the bloodstream, MacKie says.

Although other cancers have been transferred with a transplanted organ, melanoma seems to be particularly dangerous.

"There is a significant risk in patients with melanoma, even after 10 or 15 years. It's not the same with other cancers," says Dr. Robert Fisher, director of liver transplantation and transplantation research at Virginia Commonwealth University Medical Center.

People who have had invasive melanoma should not donate organs. In fact, they are already prohibited from donating blood, according to the American Red Cross.

And although the transplant surgeons should have checked the Scottish woman's background, they could not reach her primary care physician.

THE TRANSPLANTS

In May 1998, a woman in Glasgow finally received the kidney that would enable her to go off dialysis. She seemed well until a year and a half later, when a routine mammography turned up a spot on the woman's left breast.

A biopsy uncovered something unusual: Secondary melanoma but no primary site. Secondary cancers are those that have spread from another part of the body. MacKie said there was no evidence of a primary melanoma, which is usually attached to a tumor.

Four months later, a second transplant patient arrived at the same hospital with a lump in his kidney that turned out—again—to be secondary melanoma with no indication of a primary site. His transplant and the woman's transplant were done only 24 hours apart.

The donor in both cases turned out to be the same person, a 62-year-old woman who had been treated for melanoma in 1982. After treatment, her doctors considered her cured of the cancer. She died 16 years later, ostensibly of a hemorrhage.

Both kidney recipients had the organs removed and were treated for melanoma, but only one survived.

HOW DID IT HAPPEN?

Although how this happened will never be known because an autopsy was not performed on the donor, two scenarios emerge as possibilities, says Dr. Daniel G. Coit, co-leader of the melanoma disease management team at Memorial Sloan-Kettering Cancer Center in New York City.

One scenario is that the donor actually died of undetected metastatic melanoma. The second is that individual melanoma cells were lurking in her body, waiting for the opportunity to flourish.

MacKie prefers the second scenario, and believes the cancer cells were lying dormant in the kidneys. Because transplant patients take immunosuppressant drugs to minimize the chances that the donated organ will be rejected, the weakened immune system may have encouraged the cancer growth.

Nicotine Vaccine Helps Smokers Quit

Kim D. Janda, PhD, professor of chemistry, The Scripps Research Institute, La Jolla, CA. Dr. Janda is the recipient of an NIH First Award.
Journal of the American Chemical Society.

A nicotine vaccine shows promise in ending nicotine addiction and helping smokers kick the habit, researchers say.

The vaccine allows the immune system to provide potent antibodies to remove nicotine from the body before it reaches the brain, says lead researcher Kim D. Janda, a professor of chemistry at The Scripps Research Institute in La Jolla, California.

The vaccine could act as a crutch for people trying to stop smoking by preventing nicotine from reaching the brain, Janda says.

Janda's team had already developed a successful cocaine vaccine, but when they first developed a nicotine vaccine, the researchers found it wasn't very effective.

Janda says the researchers didn't understand why the early nicotine vaccine was ineffective, since the nicotine and cocaine molecules are similar. When they went back and looked more closely, they found that the cocaine molecule was restricted in its movement but the nicotine molecule wasn't.

FURTHER STUDY NEEDED

The next step in the development of this new vaccine is to do more studies; it has only been tested in mice and rats. Once the researchers have more evidence that the vaccine is safe, it will be ready for clinical human trials.

The vaccine is designed to help smokers during the critical first 90 days of smoking cessation, when many relapse.

Epilepsy Drug Helps Alcoholics

Bankole A. Johnson, MD, PhD, former professor of psychiatry and pharmacology, deputy chairman of research and director of the South Texas Addiction Research and Technology Center, University of Texas Health Science Center, San Antonio. Dr. Johnson is currently professor and chairman of psychiatry at the University of Virginia, Charlottesville.
The Lancet.

I n what could be a breakthrough in the treatment of alcoholism, researchers say an antiseizure drug dramatically reduced drinking among alcoholics.

Alcoholics who took *topiramate* were six times as likely as those who took a placebo to abstain from drinking for at least four consecutive weeks during a 12-week study, say researchers at the University of Texas Health Science Center in San Antonio. Topiramate is a drug that the US Food and Drug Administration (FDA) approved for the treatment of epileptic and other seizures.

The study also found that those who took the placebo were four times as likely as those who took topiramate to drink heavily for 28 consecutive days.

MAY BE MOST EFFECTIVE

The dramatic results suggest that the drug may be more effective than any others currently being used to treat alcoholics, says lead researcher Dr. Bankole A. Johnson.

"The critical factor here is not only were all [of the subjects] heavily dependent on alcohol, but they were all still drinking heavily," says Johnson, director of the Health Science Center's South Texas Addiction Research and Technology Center.

Researchers defined drinking heavily as more than five drinks per day for men and more than four for women.

Johnson says existing drugs for alcoholism —*antabuse*, which makes patients sick if they drink, and *naltrexone*, which blocks the pleasure sensations from alcohol—are designed mainly to prevent a relapse among alcoholics who stop drinking.

Topiramate helps alcoholics quit by blocking the "high" from alcohol while reducing withdrawal symptoms and cravings, Johnson says.

Your Dental Visit Can Save Your Life

Alan Winter, DDS, a periodontist in private practice and associate professor of implant dentistry at the New York University College of Dentistry, both in New York City, has published more than a dozen medical journal articles on gum disease.

If you think that regular dental exams are just for your teeth and gums and aren't very important, you could be putting yourself in danger. Dentists are able to identify signs of a variety of serious diseases that affect other parts of the body.

Recent finding: About 78% of periodontists (dentists who specialize in the diagnosis and treatment of gum disease) have referred patients age 60 or older to be evaluated for diabetes, and 21% have made referrals for osteoporosis, according to a poll conducted by the American Academy of Periodontology. All dentists are trained to identify these diseases and others.

How can an oral exam yield such crucial health information? While you're sitting in the dentist's chair to be treated for tooth or gum problems, your dentist is also checking for signs of cancer and other diseases. By monitoring changes in your gum tissue, your dentist can look for oral manifestations of diseases or other serious health problems.

Adults should get dental exams at least twice a year, or three to four times if they have gum (periodontal) disease. During a thorough exam, a dentist inspects all the soft tissues, including the gums, tongue, palate and throat, and feels (palpates) the patient's neck and under the chin. Signs of possible health problems include ulcerations, thickened tissue, pigmentation changes and abnormal color or consistency of gums and other soft tissues.

No one should consider a dental exam an adequate screening of overall physical health. However, your dentist can serve as a valuable adjunct to your other doctors in helping to spot signs of serious medical conditions.

CANCER

Dentists can spot possible malignancies that form in the gums, palate, cheek or other soft tissues. They also can identify tumors in the jawbone, which either originated there or metastasized (spread) from the breasts, bones, lungs or elsewhere in the body.

Warning signs: A newly formed lesion (open sore) or bump anywhere in the mouth that doesn't go away after seven to 10 days… swelling of the gums…teeth that suddenly become loose…and/or nonspecific oral pain that doesn't seem to be related to a tooth problem. Less commonly, a cancerous lesion in the jawbone may be seen on an X-ray, but many people who have cancer that has spread to the jaw are already being treated by an oncologist or surgeon. On rare occasions, a dentist may be the first to identify such a metastasis.

Self-defense: If you have a bump or lesion that doesn't heal in seven to 10 days without treatment, see your dentist. He/she will decide whether you should see a specialist, such as a periodontist, oral surgeon or ear, nose and throat specialist.

Important: Although some bumps and lesions are cancerous, most are benign and due to canker sores, routine gum problems, root canal problems—or they are the result of trauma, such as hitting your gum with the head of your toothbrush. To reach a proper diagnosis, your dentist will do a thorough examination, get a detailed medical history and may even take a biopsy.

DIABETES

Periodontal disease develops over a period of years. If a dentist sees gum breakdown that is more rapid than expected or there has been extreme bone loss that can't be explained, diabetes should be suspected.

Warning signs: Poor healing after oral surgery, inflammation in the gums and other periodontal problems. These may be signs of diabetes or diabetes that is not well controlled. Such problems can occur because diabetes suppresses the immune system, which impairs the infection-fighting function of white blood cells.

Self-defense: If your dentist suspects diabetes, you should see your primary care doctor or an endocrinologist for a glucose tolerance test.

OSTEOPOROSIS

Most people associate osteoporosis with bone loss in the spine or hips, but it also can occur in the jawbone.

Warning sign: On an X-ray, the jawbone will look less dense than it should.

Self-defense: Follow up with your primary care doctor. A bone-density test may be needed.

Caution: Bisphosphonate drugs, such as *alendronate* (Fosamax), have been linked to osteonecrosis of the jaw—death of areas of jawbone. Most reports of this side effect are associated with bisphosphonates taken intravenously by cancer patients whose malignancy has spread to their bones, but a handful of cases have involved people who took the oral form of the medication.

A LINK TO HEART DISEASE

Contrary to what many people believe, dentists cannot diagnose heart disease based on the appearance of a person's gums. Much has been written about a possible link between gum disease and heart disease. However, the research that showed a connection was retrospective—that is, it reviewed the characteristics of a particular group.

One such study was conducted by Robert Genco, PhD, of the State University of New York at Buffalo, and colleagues at the University of North Carolina at Chapel Hill. The researchers noted that cumulative evidence supports—but does not prove—an association between periodontal infection and cardiovascular disease. In a recent Finnish study, people with gum disease were found to be 1.6 times more likely to suffer a stroke.

Additional research is needed to determine whether gum disease is, in fact, a risk factor for cardiovascular disease. In the meantime, it makes sense to keep your gums healthy to help minimize the possible risk for heart disease. Studies have shown that people with heart disease are more likely to smoke, not exercise regularly and/or have poor diets.

Dentists often send people with diagnosed heart disease for a cardiovascular evaluation.

Reason: These patients need to get medical clearance for dental surgery. During these evaluations, the cardiologist checks the patient's blood pressure, use of blood thinners and overall risk for heart attack and stroke. A cardiovascular evaluation also helps determine which anesthetic to use—an additive used in some anesthesia can stimulate the heart.

No More Eyestrain

Mark A. Stengler, ND, naturopathic physician in private practice, La Jolla, CA...adjunct associate clinical professor at the National College of Natural Medicine, Portland, OR...author of 16 books, including *The Natural Physician's Healing Therapies* (Bottom Line Books) and coauthor of *Prescription for Natural Cures* (Wiley)...and author of the *Bottom Line/Natural Healing* newsletter.

Anyone who spends extended time at a computer (an hour or more without a break) is vulnerable to blurred vision, red eyes, difficulty seeing long distances and headaches.

One of the first steps is to eliminate glare by tilting the screen away from light or getting an antiglare screen. These screens ($20 to over $100) are sold at office-supply and computer-accessory stores. Face your monitor away from windows and other bright light sources, and place it so the middle of the screen is slightly below eye level (about 20 degrees).

Take a five-minute break every 45 to 60 minutes to relax your eyes and body. Get up and walk around, and look away from bright light. Then sit in a relaxed position—for example, with your back straight and your hands on your knees, and take deep breaths. Perform a "cupping" technique to relax the eye muscles—place your cupped hands over your closed eyes, fingers resting on your forehead. Leave your hands there for one to two minutes while you relax.

The herbal extract bilberry (available at health-food stores and pharmacies) improves circulation to the eyes and reduces the redness and irritation that many people experience from computer use. Take 320 mg daily of a 25% *anthocyanoside* extract. For best results, take bilberry indefinitely.

Cell Phone Dangers

Rebecca Shannonhouse, editor of *Bottom Line Health.*

There are more than 260 million cell-phone users in the US—and researchers are now beginning to identify some of the associated risks.

While studies have shown that there appears to be no increase in the risk for brain cancer among cell-phone users, these devices may not be safe in all circumstances.

Driving while talking on a cell phone is dangerous—even if you're using a "hands-free" model. A new study indicates that motorists who talk on any type of cell phone show the same kind and degree of impairment—such as slowed reaction times—as drunken drivers.

People engaged in cell-phone conversations experience "inattention blindness"—even though they're looking at the road and traffic, their ability to process information drops by as much as 50%, explains Frank Drews, PhD, assistant professor of psychology at the University of Utah in Salt Lake City and coauthor of the study.

Some people argue that other distractions, such as putting on makeup or talking to a passenger, are equally risky, but Drews doesn't buy it. "I've never seen a driver putting on makeup in the car—but at least every fourth or fifth driver is on a cell phone."

Meanwhile, in London, a 15-year-old girl suffered severe injuries after being struck by lightning while talking on her cell phone. People struck by lightning are often not critically injured, but holding a cell phone to the ear during a storm can provide a conduit that allows electricity—more than 100 million volts, in some cases—to flow into the body.

These recent developments show that it pays to think before you pick up a cell phone.

■ ■ ■ ■

Recycle Cell Phones

Cell phones contain toxic substances that can contaminate water and soil. Lead, mercury and other potentially dangerous elements are used in the manufacture of cell phones.

Best: Don't throw away an old cell phone. Instead, talk to your service provider or a third-party cell-phone recycler, such as Collective Good (*www.collectivegood.com*), about recycling it.

Samuel A. Simon, founder, Telecommunications Research and Action Center, Washington, DC. *www.trac.org.*

Common Causes of Shoulder Injuries

Kevin D. Plancher, MD, a leading orthopedic surgeon and sports medicine specialist based in New York City, is associate clinical professor of orthopedics at Albert Einstein College of Medicine and attending physician at Beth Israel Hospital, both in New York City.

The shoulder is one of the most mobile joints in the body, capable of moving up to 180 degrees in a variety of planes, such as front to back and across the body. This versatility of movement aids performance in many activities and sports but leaves the shoulder uniquely vulnerable to painful and often debilitating injuries. In fact, shoulder problems account for 35% to 40% of all orthopedic injuries.

Shoulder troubles among athletes are common —but everyone is vulnerable. Even daily activities, such as household chores and yard work, can put tremendous strain on the shoulder joint.

Example: When carrying heavy boxes, people typically hold them well in front of the body, sometimes shoulder height or higher. These positions strain the shoulder and can result in soreness—or, in some cases, even permanent damage.

The most common shoulder injuries include *rotator cuff tears* (damage to the muscles/tendons that connect the upper arm bone, or humerus, to the shoulder blade)...*dislocations* (in which the humerus separates from the socket)...and *impingement syndrome* (the tendons of the rotator cuff get trapped between the roof of the shoulder, or acromion, and the head of the humerus).

Some injuries, such as a partial rotator cuff tear, near dislocation and impingement syndrome, improve when treated with ice for 20 minutes every three to four waking hours (do not put ice directly on the skin—use a towel) and/or over-the-counter anti-inflammatories, such as *ibuprofen* (Advil) or *naproxen* (Aleve). Follow label directions.

If these strategies don't relieve your acute shoulder pain within 72 hours, see an orthopedist or other sports medicine-trained physician. You may need a prescription painkiller, such as *hydrocodone* and *acetaminophen* (Vicodin) or *acetaminophen* and *codeine* (Tylenol with codeine)...physical therapy...and/or surgery to correct the problem.

Even though shoulder injuries can occur during virtually any activity that requires overhead or extensive shoulder movements, overexertion during exercise is still the most common trigger. The changes associated with aging, such as loss of muscle mass and diminished tendon flexibility, increase the risk for such joint damage.

Most common traps—and how to avoid them...

Trap 1: **Intermittent exercise.** Injuries often occur after people take a hiatus from a sport or start a new exercise or activity—for example, in the spring, when people who have been sedentary all winter spend long hours on the tennis court or working in the yard.

Muscles have "memory"—when skeletal muscle activity is repeated, the muscles remember that activity and can continue to perform at that level. That's why people who exercise regularly are not as prone to injury as "weekend warriors" (sedentary people who exceed their muscle memory on weekends).

Muscles and tendons require a longer warm-up time if you don't exercise daily. A good warm-up includes five minutes of a gentle version of the exercise you're planning to perform.

Example: Walking before jogging...simulating a tennis serve...swinging a golf club without hitting a ball.

My recommendation: Before exercising, also be sure to stretch your shoulders. To do this, take a long towel and place it over your shoulder. Grip the top end with your right hand, and the bottom end with your left hand. Pull it up and down 10 to 15 times, bringing your right elbow up toward the ceiling. Switch sides and repeat. This internal rotation stretch works the main muscles in the shoulders and helps prevent many injuries, including rotator cuff tears.

Important: Stretching before and after exercise is particularly important for people age 40 and older, regardless of their overall activity level. Stretching and warming up before exercise gets muscles ready for the activity. Stretching after exercise increases blood flow to help muscles heal and recover.

Trap 2: **Lifting weights overhead.** This is among the most popular exercises for strengthening the shoulders. It's also one of the most dangerous. Lifting heavy weights straight overhead while standing—often called a military press—exerts tremendous stress on the shoulders. This exercise is a common cause of impingement.

My recommendation: Use the incline press (which allows you to lift weights overhead while lying on an incline). It works the same muscles, but without placing so much stress on the shoulders. Even patients with a history of impingement usually can do incline lifts without discomfort or risk.

Trap 3: **Hands out of sight.** Studies show that when the hands and/or fingers are out of your peripheral line of vision when doing strength training, the benefits of the exercise are minimized and the risk for injury to shoulder muscles is greatly increased.

Example: You'll often see people lowering the bar on a pull-down machine behind the head. It's during that phase (when the hands disappear from sight) that the risk for subluxation (movement of the shoulder out of the joint) increases.

My recommendation: When exercising, always keep your hands in your direct or peripheral line of vision when looking straight ahead. When doing pull-downs, lower the bar in front of your head.

***Trap 4:* Too-wide grip.** Most upper-body exercise equipment includes some sort of bar with handles. The handles are typically positioned for a man of average height, shoulder-spread and reach length. For women and smaller men, the handle grips are usually too far apart. This puts excessive stress on the rotator cuff, which can cause damage and/or possible dislocation of the shoulder joint.

My recommendation: Grip the bars on exercise equipment no more than shoulder-width apart, regardless of where the handles are. The narrower grip reduces shoulder stress.

***Trap 5:* Overtraining.** Performing exercises that work the same muscles every day leads to injuries, because muscle fibers don't have a chance to recover.

My recommendation: Give the shoulders time to recover by doing a different kind of workout—aerobics, weight-lifting, sports, etc.—every other day. On weekends, pick an activity you haven't done during the week. If you were sedentary, vary the workout (for example, work the upper body for a half hour and then the lower body for a half hour). Giving specific muscles a day of rest promotes muscle healing and faster recovery—and reduces risk for soreness or injuries.

RED FLAGS

If you experience any of the following signs of shoulder injury—or any kind of acute shoulder pain and/or restricted movement for more than a few days—see an orthopedic physician…

•**Pain** when you are putting on a coat or when you're reaching around to the backseat of a car could be signs of impingement or rotator cuff irritation.

•**Inability to lift your arm** from your side and raise an object above shoulder height without arching your back. This can indicate a serious rotator cuff tear.

•**Inability to sleep on one shoulder** due to pain. It is often a sign of early-stage rotator cuff damage.

•**Pain when reaching for objects overhead.** This can indicate impingement or other shoulder problems.

Caution: If you experience severe shoulder pain, go to the hospital right away. You could have a dislocated shoulder.

Illustration by Shawn Banner.

Stay Safe in Your Own Backyard

Richard O'Brien, MD, spokesman for the American College of Emergency Physicians, is clinical instructor at Temple University School of Medicine in Philadelphia and an emergency physician at Moses Taylor Hospital, Scranton, PA.

The combination of warm weather and outdoor activities sends millions of Americans to emergency rooms each summer. Most of their injuries could have been prevented. *Here, an emergency room physician reveals the biggest dangers and how to avoid them…*

LAWN MOWERS

The lawn mower is probably the most dangerous tool around the house. A nine-year study published in *Annals of Emergency Medicine* reports an annual average of 74,000 emergency room visits due to lawn mower injuries. Most injuries are caused by debris flying into the bodies or eyes of lawn mower operators and bystanders. About one-third of lawn mower-related hospitalizations are due to injuries from the blades, including the loss of toes and/or fingers.

Self-defense: Remove twigs, sticks and rocks before mowing. Keep bystanders, especially children, away from the mower. Wear shoes—not sandals—long pants and safety goggles while mowing. Don't depend on glasses or sunglasses to protect eyes—they won't prevent debris from entering at the sides.

Also, wear hearing protection (ear plugs, ear mufflers, etc.). Don't use an iPod or similar portable music device—you really have to crank up the volume to hear the music, which can result in permanent hearing damage.

ELECTRIC HEDGE TRIMMERS

I see at least one patient a month who has been hurt by a hedge trimmer. It can cut off a finger instantly or cause a nasty injury—crushing tissue and bone—that is very difficult to repair.

Self-defense: Wear heavy leather or canvas gloves, sturdy shoes and long pants when using a trimmer. Don't overreach—you may lose your balance. Turn off the trimmer and unplug it before trying to clear it of stuck debris.

GARAGE DOORS

Some manual and electric garage doors have large, heavy springs on each side. A spring that suddenly loosens can hit your head with the force of a swinging baseball bat. A spring also can take off a finger.

Self-defense: Never attempt to repair or replace a garage door yourself. Hire an experienced professional to do it.

TICK BITES

Lyme disease gets most of the headlines, but ticks carry many other diseases, including ehrlichiosis and Rocky Mountain spotted fever, both bacterial infections that can cause fatigue, fever, severe muscle pain and headaches—and also can be life-threatening.

Self-defense: Removing a tick from your skin within 12 to 24 hours almost guarantees that you won't get sick. Grip the tick close to the skin with tweezers and pull it out. If part of the tick remains in the skin, try your best to remove it. If you're not able to remove it all, see a doctor. Wash the area well, and apply an antibiotic ointment to prevent infection.

If you're spending time in grassy or wooded areas, you can prevent most tick bites by using an insect repellent that contains DEET. Apply the repellent to exposed skin and clothing. A non-DEET repellent, Picaridin, is useful for people whose skin is sensitive to DEET. Also wear closed shoes rather than sandals…tuck long pants into socks…and wear a long-sleeved shirt, tucked in.

POISON IVY, OAK AND SUMAC

All of these plants contain *urushiol*, an oily substance that can cause an itchy rash in people who are sensitive to it. (To view the plants so you can identify them, go to *www.poisonivy.aesir.com*.)

As little as one-billionth of a gram of urushiol can cause the rash—so even brushing against one of these plants is a problem. The oil also can get on tools, gloves and clothing and stays active indefinitely, so it must be washed off.

Self-defense: If your skin comes into contact with one of the "poisons," wash the area immediately with soap and water. If you're outside and don't have access to soap or water, splash the area with any liquid—soda, beer, etc. If a rash develops, apply hydrocortisone ointment, available at drugstores. If the rash worsens, see a doctor.

CYCLING

Each year, bicycle accidents result in more than half a million visits to emergency rooms. More than 800 bicyclists die annually, many from head injuries.

Self-defense: Always wear a helmet, even if you (or your children) are riding close to home. Studies indicate that helmets are up to 85% effective in preventing head injuries. Helmets with visors are helpful for preventing facial lacerations. Be sure the helmet fits properly and is buckled snugly.

Warning: Most cycling deaths occur between 6 pm and 9 pm, when visibility is diminished. Wear reflective clothing to make yourself more visible.

SWIMMING

Drowning is a leading cause of accidental death in the US.

Reasons: People overestimate their swimming ability…panic in deep water or fast currents…or consume large amounts of alcohol before entering the water.

Self-defense: Enter unfamiliar water feet first to prevent head and neck injuries. Don't depend on flotation devices—they can fail and sink. Never drink alcohol before or while swimming.

Danger for women: The bacteria that cause urinary tract infections thrive in moist environments. Women who sit around in wet swimsuits give these organisms an opportunity to proliferate and migrate into the urethra—and possibly up into the kidneys, resulting in a potentially life-threatening infection. Change into dry clothing after you're done swimming. Also, drink lots of water—it increases urination, which helps flush bacteria from the urethra.

Protect Your Home from Dangerous Toxins

Mitchell Gaynor, MD, assistant clinical professor of medicine at Weill Medical College of Cornell University, and founder and president of Gaynor Integrative Oncology, both in New York City, is the author of *Nurture Nature/Nurture Health: Your Health and the Environment.* Nurture Nature.

As long as you breathe, eat and drink, you can't entirely escape environmental toxins. Research on the risks associated with these toxins is ongoing, but many scientists believe that existing evidence suggests that toxic buildup in our bodies contributes to the development of Parkinson's disease and may increase risk for some types of cancer and other serious conditions. A Centers for Disease Control and Prevention study that tested 10,000 men and women for the presence of 116 chemicals, including phthalates and dioxin, found that most Americans carried some combination of these toxins in small amounts in their blood.

TOXICITY IN THE HOME

Household sources of toxins that are under investigation…

•**Home furnishings.** *Polybrominated diphenylethers* (PBDEs), common ingredients in flame retardants that are used to treat upholstered chairs and sofas, foam mattresses and cushions, may be carcinogenic. PBDEs also may disrupt thyroid function and brain development.

What to do: When buying foam mattresses, upholstered furniture, etc., ask whether PBDEs were used during manufacturing.

•**Pressed wood and fiberboard,** which often are used in furniture and shelving, are common sources of *formaldehyde*, a gaseous compound that is used as a disinfectant. Formaldehyde has been found to be a probable carcinogen.

What to do: Look for solid-wood products or those carrying the seal of the American National Standards Institute (ANSI), which certifies that the item is low in formaldehyde emissions.

To find furniture and other products that are low in potentially dangerous chemical emissions, consult the Greenguard Environmental Institute, a nonprofit, independent organization that certifies low-emitting products, 800-427-9681, *www.greenguard.org.*

•**Cleaning products.** Most people use a wide variety of cleaning products, many of which contain toxic chemicals. Chlorine bleach is potentially carcinogenic and can damage the respiratory system. Among its by-products are *chlorinated hydrocarbons, chloroform* and *trihalomethanes,* all of which act like weak estrogens and cause breast cells to divide more rapidly. These by-products have been shown to cause breast tumors in animals.

What to do: Use commercial cleansers that are free of chlorine and most chemicals. Seventh Generation and Sun & Earth are two brands that are widely available at health-food stores.

Or use natural cleaning alternatives—baking soda to scrub sinks, tubs and toilets…white distilled vinegar in a pump-spray bottle to clean mirrors and windows. If you must use chlorine-containing cleaners, make sure the room is well-ventilated.

•**Pesticides.** Research has shown that pesticides increase risk for Parkinson's disease—and may be a cause of some cancers.

What to do: Use baits and traps instead of sprays. Try organic alternatives to toxic bug killers, including oil sprays, such as Sharpshooter, an all-natural insect killer containing plant oils…Burnout II, a natural herbicide that contains vinegar, clove and lemon…and corn gluten meal, a natural weed killer. All of these products are available at most garden centers that carry organic products.

For more information on pesticides and other toxic household products, visit the Web site of Earth Share (a nationwide network of environmental organizations) at *www.earthshare.org.*

•**Cosmetics.** *Para-phenylenediamine,* a chemical found in some dark hair dyes, increases risk for bladder cancer in humans, according to a study in the journal *Carcinogenesis. Other toxic ingredients used in cosmetics…*

•*Phthalates,* typically used as a solvent and plastic softener, have been linked to cancer and to birth defects of the male reproductive system. They are found in many shampoos and other hair products, cosmetics, deodorants and nail polish. To learn more about phthalates and get a list of products that contain them, go to *www.safecos metics.org,* a Web site of several consumer environmental groups.

•*Talc,* in talcum powder, has been linked to a 60% increase in the risk for ovarian cancer in women who use it in the genital area.

•*Propylene glycol,* an ingredient found in some moisturizing products and skin creams, is absorbed through the skin, and high levels may damage the kidneys and liver.

What to do: Read labels carefully. By law, cosmetic ingredients must be listed on the label, starting with those in largest amounts. Choose all-natural alternatives, such as products made with olive oil, safflower oil or oatmeal, whenever possible. To find hair products, lotions, deodorants and other products from companies that have replaced or are replacing toxic ingredients, go to *www.safecosmetics.org* (look for safe companies).

SELF-DEFENSE

Antioxidants such as vitamins C and E are known to promote health by scavenging free radicals (harmful by-products of metabolism), which damage our cells and contribute to cancer and other diseases.

But antioxidants have another role that is possibly even more important in protecting against environmental toxins. Antioxidants stimulate an area of the DNA called the *antioxidant responsive element* (ARE), which activates a gene that produces detoxifying enzymes. This is the body's way of breaking down carcinogens and other toxins.

In addition to commonly known antioxidant sources, such as brightly colored produce (carrots, beets, kale and tomatoes), be sure your diet contains…

•**Cruciferous vegetables,** such as cauliflower and brussels sprouts, which contain *sulforaphane*, a potent enzyme inducer.

•**Green tea,** an antioxidant source that is 20 times more potent than vitamin E, according to the American Chemical Society. Drink two to five cups daily.

•**Rosemary,** a source of *carnosol*, which has antioxidant and anticarcinogenic properties. Use rosemary in cooking, or drink one cup of rosemary tea daily.

•**Curry,** which contains curcumin and turmeric, two potent cancer-fighting herbs. Cook with curry three times a week.

■ ■ ■ ■

Alarm, Alarm

Fire danger remains even with smoke alarms. Standard US smoke alarms do not have the most effective signal to awaken older adults. Because many people age 65 and older have problems hearing high-pitched sounds, they are more likely to awaken to a mixed-frequency signal (500 to 2500 Hz), such as those found in some smoke alarms for the hearing impaired, rather than the more common high-pitched alarms.

Smart: Use an interconnected system that includes an alarm in each bedroom to increase the chance of being awakened in case of fire.

Dorothy Bruck, PhD, head of school of psychology, professor, Victoria University, Melbourne, Australia.

■ ■ ■ ■

Avoid Germs in Public Bathrooms

Use the first stall—it tends to be the least popular. Flush the toilet with your foot, then leave the stall quickly to avoid airborne bacteria. To be sure you are washing your hands long enough, sing the song *Happy Birthday to You* to yourself twice. Wash with comfortably lukewarm water—hotter water does not kill more germs. Use a paper towel to turn off the faucet and pull the door handle so that you don't pick up more germs after cleaning your hands.

Philip M. Tierno, Jr., PhD, director of clinical microbiology and diagnostic immunology, New York University Medical Center, New York City, and author of *The Secret Life of Germs.* Atria.

■ ■ ■ ■

Hospital Bed Warning

Hospital beds can trap patients between the rails and the mattress. Since 1985, more than 400 frail patients have become wedged in beds and died.

Self-defense: Check with the manufacturer to make sure that the bed meets current standards and that the parts fit together snugly. Read the Food and Drug Administration's safety recommendations at *www.fda.gov/cdrh/beds,* or order the brochure "A Guide to Bed Safety" at 888-463-6332.

Larry G. Kessler, ScD, director, USFDA Office of Science and Engineering Laboratories, Rockville, MD.

Are Silver Cars Safer?

Sue Furness, research fellow, University of Auckland School of Population Health, New Zealand.

Russ Rader, spokesman, Insurance Institute for Highway Safety, Arlington, VA.

British Medical Journal.

Choosing a color when you are purchasing a car may be more than just a reflection of your tastes and style. It also may affect how likely you are to be injured in an accident.

Researchers in New Zealand report that car color can have an impact on your chances of being injured in a road accident—and silver is the safest.

THE STUDY

After analyzing the statistics from a two-year study of more than 571 auto accidents in Auckland, epidemiologists at the University of Auckland found that the risk of having a serious injury was 50% lower in silver cars than in white, yellow, gray, red or blue vehicles.

The study also found that there was "a significant increased risk of a serious injury" in brown vehicles and a slightly increased risk in black and green cars.

"Our conclusions are valid for the location where the study was done," says Sue Furness, a research fellow working at the School of Population Health at the University of Auckland. But, she adds, "how valid they are for other settings is questionable because studies haven't been done elsewhere.

"Silver cars are becoming more popular with new-car buyers," she says. "Increasing the proportion of silver cars could be an effective passive strategy to reduce the burden of injury from car crashes."

SHOULD WE TAKE THIS SERIOUSLY?

The study was reported in the traditional Christmas issue of the *British Medical Journal* that is devoted to research that is decidedly off the beaten track. For example, another study is an analysis of how elderly and disabled pedestrians are depicted on road signs in 119 countries.

Russ Rader, a spokesman for the Insurance Institute for Highway Safety, is skeptical of the study—to say the least.

"The claim that car color could have this effect in reducing automobile accidents is preposterous, but there will be those people who read stories about this and actually think that it reflects reality," Rader says.

Vehicle color sometimes has been taken seriously in regard to highway safety. Some communities have the fire engines painted yellow rather than the more traditional red in the belief that they are more easily seen and identified, Rader acknowledges.

However, he adds, "There is no evidence that color has the kind of effect that the authors are finding. They have left out things like the driver's sex, vehicle engine size, vehicle age and ambient light conditions," all of which can affect auto safety, Rader says.

You can get real model-by-model—but colorless—auto safety statistics from the National Highway Traffic Safety Administration at *www. nhtsa.dot.gov/cars/problems*.

■■■■

Calming Scents

Certain scents reduce road rage. Drivers exposed to the smell of cinnamon and peppermint reported feeling less frustrated. Add two drops of peppermint and cinnamon oil to two cotton balls…wrap the cotton balls in a piece of cheesecloth…and put it under the car seat. The scent will last about a week.

Bryan Raudenbush, PhD, LPharm, associate professor of psychology, director of undergraduate research, psychology department, Wheeling Jesuit University, Wheeling, WV.

■■■■

Road Risks

Distracted driving causes 25% of the more than six million accidents reported to police in the US every year. Distractions include using a cell phone, eating, reading, chatting, shaving and changing CDs.

Most recent study: 91% of drivers surveyed admitted to engaging in some sort of risky behavior while driving.

National Highway Transportation Safety Administration statistics and driver survey by Mason-Dixon poll.

■ ■ ■ ■

Kids' Seats

Most child car seats are too loose, and children are strapped too loosely into them. A car seat must be installed so that there is no more than one inch of side-to-side or front-to-back movement. The child should be strapped in so that only one finger fits between the strap and his/her collarbone.

A child should be kept in a rear-facing seat until he weighs 30 to 35 pounds and as long as there is at least one inch of room between his head and the top of the car seat (though some groups recommend that a child should stay in a rear-facing seat until he is at least one year old and at least 20 pounds).

Children should start in booster seats when they weigh about 40 pounds and remain in them until they can wear a seat belt properly. This means that the lap portion rests firmly on the hip bone—low and snug on top of the thighs—when the child sits without slouching, with knees bending naturally over the edge of the seat. Children should not be out of booster seats until they are four feet nine inches tall, regardless of weight or age.

Alisa Baer, known as "The Car Seat Lady," based in New York City. www.thecarseatlady.com.

■ ■ ■ ■

Safety Seat Woes

Front seats of cars are not safe for children up to age 14—not age 12, as previously thought. Younger children are up to six times more likely to be injured than older kids when air bags deploy.

Reason: Bones and lean muscle protect the body, and age—not height or weight—determines their development.

Craig D. Newgard, MD, MPH, Center for Policy and Research in Emergency Medicine, Oregon Health and Sciences University, Portland, and author of a study of the effects of motor vehicle crashes on 3,790 children, published in Pediatrics.

■ ■ ■ ■

Drive Smart

If your hands fall asleep while you are driving, the problem could be that you are tightening the muscles that run down the front sides of your neck and attach to the collarbone. Sitting up tall and stretching your neck from side to side will help loosen these muscles and ease the nerve bundle that goes down the arm.

Lisa DeStefano, DO, chair, department of osteopathic manipulative medicine, college of osteopathic medicine, Michigan State University, East Lansing.

What to Do When an Elderly "Someone" Won't Stop Driving

Helen Kerschner, PhD, president and CEO of the Beverly Foundation, a California-based nonprofit organization that advocates for senior transportation, www. beverlyfoundation.org, is the former president of the American Association for International Aging and director of the University of New Mexico Center on Aging.

The comment, "I'm going to drive myself to the nursing home or the cemetery, whichever comes first" from an elderly driver shows what you might be up against when you try to persuade a parent, friend or other elderly person to stop driving.

But the effort can pay off. The US Department of Transportation reports that drivers over age 70 have higher rates of fatal accidents than do those in any other age group except teenagers.

While there are many individual exceptions, the chance of having an accident begins to increase around the age of 55, and the risk rises dramatically for people with diseases or who take medications that affect their motor skills, vision and/or judgment.

Still, many Americans think of driving as a fundamental right, and for older people, the car is often the last symbol of independence.

In trying to persuade a person to put away the car keys, you'll be attempting to influence a person who is probably accustomed to giving advice, not taking it. *Tactics that work...*

LAY THE GROUNDWORK

If possible, start your campaign before the danger of driving becomes immediate. Even if your loved one seems to be driving well, it's wise to suggest that he/she take a test to confirm the level of skill and/or take a refresher course for senior drivers. (AAA and many motor vehicle departments have information on the tests and courses.)

Advantage: These measures take some of the burden off you by letting drivers see their own shortcomings in a way that's difficult to deny.

Push your loved one to take a test or refresher course if you notice...

•**Friends no longer want to ride with him.**

•**Unexplained damage to the car,** such as scratches, dents or broken outside mirrors.

•**Incidents of confusion on well-known roads.**

•**An increase in accidents,** no matter who was at fault.

Reason: Accidents are often the result of a reduced ability to drive defensively.

AAA sells a compact disc, *Roadwise Review,* that lets people use a home computer to test themselves in such areas as physical flexibility, memory, visual acuity and information processing speed.

For information on how to order the disc, phone a local AAA office, listed in the phone book. Prices vary from state to state but are usually in the $10 to $15 range.

The AARP's $10 Driver Safety Program is aimed at people age 50 and older and is usually taught in two four-hour sessions on different days.

Information: 888-227-7669, *www.aarp.org/families/driver_safety.*

OVERCOMING OBJECTIONS

It's very common that a senior driver will balk at the idea of taking a test or refresher course. *Countermeasures...*

•**Offer to join** the person and take the test or course together. (With AAA's *Roadwise Review,* it is mandatory to take the test with someone else present in order to verify results.) The offer doesn't always work, but it's often successful.

•**Point out** that most insurance companies give a discount to people who take the AARP course. The markdown is usually about 10%.

RELY ON INFLUENCERS

Despite a poor test and pleas from family members, some seniors still won't give up driving. When that's the case, it's wise to ask for help from the people in authority whom they do listen to. Doctors are at the top of the list.

Contact your family member's physicians and discuss the situation with them. Many doctors are willing to tell older patients how their diminished eyesight, loss of motor skills or effects of a disability can increase the risk of a serious accident.

Not every physician, however, is knowledgeable in this area.

Smart move: Give doctors a copy of *Physician's Guide to Assessing and Counseling Older Drivers.* The book, developed by the American Medical Association and the National Highway Traffic Safety Administration, gives doctors a checklist of conditions that impair driving ability.

Some of the conditions might not be obvious to doctors who haven't dealt with the issue before.

Examples: Insomnia, which can cause drowsiness during the day, and foot problems, which can prevent the proper use of the brake and accelerator pedals.

The book, which is free, can be downloaded from the Internet or ordered for delivery by mail.

Information: 800-621-8335, *www.ama-assn.org/ama/pub/category/10791.html.*

If doctors don't succeed in persuading your loved one not to drive, turn to friends, relatives or members of the clergy for whom he/she has a deep respect.

DRIVING ALTERNATIVES

Almost all elderly people—even those urged by doctors and confronted by evidence of diminished skill—use a powerful argument against turning over the car keys. They say that there's no other way to get to places they have to go. This is a reasonable concern that should be respected.

If arguments about safety won't overcome this concern, be prepared by knowing about alternative types of transportation that can make a car unnecessary.

My organization, the Beverly Foundation, has more information on senior transportation programs. Go to *www.beverlyfoundation.org/senior_transportation_resource_store/index.html.*

Many elderly nondrivers require a combination of options...

•**Volunteer drivers.** Hundreds of volunteer driver programs have started up around the country, and more are being created each month. Typically sponsored by a charitable organization, these programs generally supply drivers to seniors free of charge. Many religious institutions also provide volunteer drivers.

The Beverly Foundation plans to post a directory of volunteer driver groups on its Web site. Until then, the best way to locate one is through local departments of senior services, churches and interfaith volunteer groups. If there isn't an appropriate option in your community, consider the possibility of promoting one.

•**Paratransit.** That's a term coined by federal officials for transportation systems for the disabled operated by many cities and counties throughout the country.

Depending on the jurisdiction, many minor disabilities associated with advanced age may qualify a person for paratransit.

Examples: Poor vision in one eye or lack of full mobility in a foot. To find out if a loved one would qualify, contact your local department of transportation.

•**Regular taxis.** Taxicabs are an obvious option, especially in suburbs and other areas outside the city. Taxis can be a relaxing way to travel, almost like having a chauffeur. (That's particularly true once you develop a relationship with a taxi company.)

The strongest argument is that taxis are a bargain. AAA estimates that the average cost of owning and operating a car is about $7,000 a year, or nearly $135 a week—enough to pay for many taxi rides.

•**Assisted-living apartments.** If your loved one is contemplating a move, ask him to consider an assisted-living apartment complex. Many of them operate their own transportation system for regular trips to grocery stores, malls and medical centers.

Few people have immediate success in persuading a senior to stop driving. But don't be discouraged. Before giving up, remember that if other friends and family members had been more persistent, some of the people cited in statistics on fatal accidents involving seniors might still be alive.

■ ■ ■ ■

Travel Advisory

Vehicle-related accidents are a major cause of accidental deaths of US citizens abroad. Especially in developing countries, taxi and bus drivers may take far more risks than in the US—overloading vehicles, ignoring stoplights, driving recklessly on mountain roads and failing to use headlights.

Self-defense: Avoid traveling at night, especially in rural areas. Sit in the backseat, and buckle up. Don't ride in taxis that don't have seat belts in the backseat.

Road safety information: Road reports for individual countries are available from Association for Safe International Road Travel (*www. asirt.org*).

Stuart R. Rose, MD, president, Travel Medicine, Inc., Northampton, MA, and author of International Travel Health Guide (Mosby). *www.travmed.com.*

■ ■ ■ ■

Travel Healthy

To stay healthy while traveling, take the right supplements, says Mark A. Stengler, ND. In addition to a multivitamin, take a *probiotic* (follow label instructions) on an empty stomach, starting three days before leaving and during the trip, to prevent diarrhea and related problems. *Garlic*—preferably aged garlic—reduces risk of respiratory and digestive infections. Take two capsules a day for two days before you leave, during the trip and for two days after. *Melatonin*—one to three milligrams—prevents jet lag and makes sleep easier. Take it the evening you arrive, at 9 pm in the time zone you are in, and for two or three more nights. Consult your physician before starting any supplements.

Mark A. Stengler, ND, naturopathic physician in private practice, La Jolla, CA...adjunct associate clinical professor at the National College of Natural Medicine, Portland, OR...author of 16 books, including *The Natural Physician's Healing Therapies* (Bottom Line Books) and coauthor of *Prescription for Natural Cures* (Wiley)...and author of the *Bottom Line/Natural Healing* newsletter.

Danger in the Water: Drink Safely When You Travel

Connie Lohsl, RN, BSN, is a nurse manager and travel-health specialist with Passport Health, Inc., a nationwide chain of travel-health franchises that provide low-cost immunizations and other travel-related services, based in Baltimore. *www.passporthealthusa.com.*

Unprepared travelers who hope to enjoy exotic locales often spend their days in a hotel bathroom instead. About 40% of all travelers experience some form of stomach upset from mild to debilitating diarrhea. For those with underlying kidney or heart problems, the dehydration from diarrhea can be life-threatening.

Check the Centers for Disease Control and Prevention Web site (*www.cdc.gov*) to find out which countries have safe drinking water. *They're rated by risk—high, intermediate and low…*

High risk: Africa, Mexico and Central America, South America, most of Asia and the Middle East, especially the rural areas. Hepatitis A is a concern in Russia.

Intermediate risk: South Africa, Eastern and Southern Europe.

Low risk: US, Canada, Japan, Northern Europe and Australia.

To stay safe…

• **Drink bottled water, but inspect it first.** In some countries, a container of bottled water costs $4 or more. Unscrupulous vendors may refill empties with tap water. Always check that the factory seal is intact. Buy carbonated water, if available—it's harder to fake.

• **Wipe bottles and cans dry before drinking.** Bottled and canned beverages may be kept cold in tubs filled with ice water. Moisture on the outside may contain organisms that can get into your mouth when you drink. Of course, don't add ice cubes to beverages unless you are sure they are made from uncontaminated water.

• **Use bottled water for brushing teeth.** Stand your toothbrush upright between uses so it isn't contaminated with water from the sink.

• **Drink bottled water on cruise ships and airplanes.** Nonbottled water could be contaminated. Coffee and tea made with boiling water should be safe.

• **Sterilize your water.** *Two ways…*

• Boiling. Put the water in a clean pot, bring it to a rolling boil, then remove it from the heat and let it cool. Transfer to a sterilized container. Boiling is the most reliable way to kill most disease-causing organisms.

• Use a water-filtration bottle. This can protect against bacteria, protozoa and lead. Some also filter viruses, including hepatitis A. Check the product label. Available at my Web site, *www.passporthealthusa.com*, or at any local passport office or camping supply store.

Cost: $20 to $100 or more.

• **Beware of swimming.** Swimming in the ocean is usually safe—few bacteria and parasites can survive in salt water. But lakes and other bodies of freshwater can have high levels of contamination—and some organisms pass directly through the skin.

Showering and toweling off soon after swimming will assist in removing parasites before they have a chance to burrow through the skin. Wearing swimming shoes can protect you from parasites and puncture wounds.

Well-maintained, chemically treated swimming pools generally are safe.

■ ■ ■ ■

Toxic Seafood Warning

Predatory tropical fish and subtropical reef fish, including amberjack, grouper, barracuda, hogfish, triggerfish, snapper, mullet and moray eels, can carry *ciguatoxin*, a seafood toxin that causes a food poisoning called ciguatera. The ciguatoxin does not affect the fish's taste, odor or color and is not eliminated by cooking. Those eating seafood in tropical areas such as Hawaii and the northern Caribbean are most at risk.

Victims experience cramping, diarrhea and nausea starting several hours after consumption. Headache, muscle pain, dizziness and tingling or numbing of the lips may follow. In extreme cases, sufferers can experience cold-hot reversal—hot things feel cold and vice versa. Symptoms last one to four weeks but may recur for up to six months. See a doctor immediately if you think you might be infected. Treatment with intravenous mannitol has been shown to relieve symptoms effectively.

Ewen Todd, PhD, former director of National Food Safety and Toxicology Center, Michigan State University, East Lansing. He was head of the Contaminated Foods Section of the Health Protection Branch of the Canadian government.

■ ■ ■ ■

Before You Go

Every traveler, regardless of destination, should get vaccinated against tetanus and hepatitis A. Hepatitis A virus is found in food and water, even in the US. Get revaccinated for tetanus every five years.

Also: Typhoid vaccination if going to Central or South America, Africa, India, Malaysia, Indonesia, Vietnam or the Mideast. Yellow-fever immunization if visiting tropical South America or subequatorial Africa. Polio booster if you haven't been vaccinated since childhood and are going to Africa, India, Pakistan, Malaysia, Indonesia or some parts of southern China. Influenza shot if visiting tropical areas in the southern hemisphere, where flu occurs year-round. Tuberculosis testing (PPD) should be done three to six months after travel to Central or South America, Africa, the Mideast, Eastern Europe and Russia.

Carol DeRosa, RN, senior vice president, clinical operations of Passport Health, Inc., provider of immunizations and travel consultations, Baltimore. 888-499-7277. *www.passporthealthusa.com.*

■ ■ ■ ■

In Any Language

Get your medical history in five languages. The Medistick carries your medical history —plus the medical histories of up to four more people—in a USB memory stick. Enter your information with the included software (for PCs only), and the histories are recorded in German, English, French, Italian and Spanish. Update information whenever necessary. Prices start at $60.00.

For more information see Medistick GmbH, *www.medistick.ch.*

Beware: Hotels, Hospitals And Health Clubs Can Make You Sick

Jeffrey C. May, owner of May Indoor Air Investigations LLC, an air-quality assessment company based in Tyngsborough, MA, has conducted indoor environmental investigations in thousands of buildings. He is a nationally recognized authority and speaker on indoor air quality and author of *My Office Is Killing Me! The Sick Building Survival Guide.* Johns Hopkins University Press.

Mold in homes has been linked to asthma, headaches, fatigue, skin irritations and increased cancer risk.

Important: Mold and other health-threatening irritants can be everywhere, including hotels, hospitals, health clubs and libraries.

You should suspect that you're in a sick building if you experience respiratory symptoms (coughing, sneezing, etc.) that come on soon after you enter that space.

Places to watch out for and steps to take…

HOTEL ROOMS

Carpeting and heating/cooling systems pose the biggest risks because they may be contaminated with mold and/or cleaning residues. *Helpful…*

•**Ask for a room on the second floor or higher.** The carpeted ground floor of a two-story motel is typically the dampest and most likely to be moldy. Avoid rooms located directly off an atrium that has a waterfall or a fountain and rooms near an indoor pool.

•**Turn off the air conditioner/heater fan.** The fan coils may have mold.

Helpful: Before booking a room, ask if the windows can be opened. Keeping windows open can reduce exposure to indoor contaminants.

•**Ask for synthetic bedding.** The feathers in bedding shed millions of tiny particles that can trigger asthma attacks and other respiratory problems.

•**Cover the carpet with adhesive plastic,** such as Pro Tect (800-545-0826, *www.pro-tect. com,* $44 for a 2' x 200' roll). It traps mold spores and particulate allergens and irritants. For a short stay, just cover the most used areas—the walking path around the beds and to the bathroom and entry.

• **Avoid hotels and motels undergoing renovation,** which may result in irritating dust or chemical emissions from new furniture and carpeting.

LIBRARIES

Books can harbor significant amounts of allergen-containing dust, particularly if they aren't used often. *If you experience symptoms after being at a library or taking home library books...*

• **Open and close the books vigorously once you get outside.** The air currents help remove allergens.

• **Vacuum the tops and sides** of the books when you get home. Use a high-efficiency particulate arrestance (HEPA) vacuum.

• **Examine the bindings of older,** hardcover books for white, yellow or other discolorations, all of which can indicate mold. Airing books outdoors in bright sunlight for two or three hours may help. If not, get different copies.

PUBLIC BATHROOMS

The chemical air fresheners in public bathrooms are a common cause of respiratory symptoms. More than 10% of Americans have some degree of chemical sensitivity. Air fresheners—as well as scented candles—are a particular problem because they're designed to disperse chemicals into the air.

In offices and hotels, ask the cleaning staff to avoid using fragranced products and cleaners with chemical odors. If you're in a hotel, you could also ask the housekeeping staff to skip your room.

Breathe through a folded paper towel or T-shirt when entering an area with a strong fragrance. Or use an N95 mask (available at hardware and medical-supply stores for about $1.25 each).

Be aware that the urinals in men's bathrooms often contain a block of *paradichlorobenzene* (the toxic substance that mothballs are made of), which can be extremely irritating to people with chemical sensitivities. If there is a window that vents to the outside, open it. A clean, well-ventilated restroom doesn't need chemicals to smell fresh.

ANTIQUES STORES

The backs and bottoms of old furniture often have mold. Even if an item has been kept in a dry place, it can harbor mold spores that are decades old. Consider wearing an N95 face mask when browsing in antiques stores.

After buying old furniture: If you notice a musty smell or are having symptoms, you may want to take the furniture outside and wipe unfinished surfaces with denatured alcohol. Apply a layer of clear finish to seal in mold spores and reduce mold growth. Mold growth on finished surfaces can be cleaned with any furniture cleaner (do this outdoors as well).

Caution: Don't do anything to an antique without consulting a dealer.

HEALTH CLUBS

Many fitness centers are warehouse-like structures that are built at or below ground level—an optimal environment for dampness and mold growth. If possible, join a health club that is above ground level—preferably one that can be ventilated with fresh air from open windows.

If there's a pool or hot tub, the smell of chlorine should not be so overpowering that it feels like your eyes or nose are burning. Chlorine and other pool disinfectants are a common cause of lung irritation. This problem can be worse in health clubs because people are exercising and breathing deeply.

HOSPITALS AND MEDICAL OFFICES

These often are modern, tightly sealed buildings, which, if the ventilation is inadequate, can result in high levels of indoor carbon dioxide. Medical and dental facilities also can trap large amounts of irritating chemical fumes—from anesthetics, disinfectants, etc.

If you notice strong smells: Wear a charcoal mask. (You can remove it during oral or nasal exams/treatments.) Unlike N95 masks, which trap only particles, charcoal masks also trap gases and chemical vapors. Single-use masks cost about $10. Reusable charcoal respirators with replaceable cartridges cost about $30 each. Both types are available at building-supply stores and some hardware stores.

A Pilot Answers Your Air Safety Questions

Meryl Getline, a pilot in Elizabeth, CO, with over 32 years of flying experience, including 15 as a captain with a major airline, is author of *The World at My Feet: The True (and Sometimes Hilarious) Adventures of a Lady Airline Captain* and the E-book *Ground School for Passengers* (both available at *FromtheCockpit.com*).

We trust our lives to airplanes and the pilots who fly them, but there is a lot that the average passenger doesn't know about modern aircraft. *We asked a veteran airline captain to answer some of the most common passenger questions...*

●**Where is the best place to sit on an airplane if you're prone to airsickness?**

The best spot is over the wing or a few rows in front of the wing. When a plane climbs or descends, it pivots on its center of gravity, which tends to be just in front of the wings. The closer you are to this point, the less you'll feel the movement, just as sitting in the middle of a seesaw subjects you to less movement than sitting at the end.

●**How do you prevent jet lag?**

I really don't suffer much from jet lag. I always observe local time, though many pilots keep their watches set to their hometown time and try to sleep accordingly. If you're traveling on business, this may be impractical.

The best advice is to stay well-hydrated and rest on the plane if you're traveling overnight and arriving in the morning. If you are traveling during the day, plan to read or watch a movie en route so that you're ready to sleep that night after you arrive.

●**Could the "autopilot" fly or land a plane without the pilots?**

Not really. Autopilot can't do much more than fly a programmed route or maintain the last heading or altitude entered by the pilots. Pilots are needed to manage the autopilot during the flight.

The autopilot sometimes plays a role in landings—it can keep the plane lined up with the centerline of the runway and even land the plane under certain conditions—but the pilot must control the air speed (even if autothrottles are used, they must be programmed and the speed monitored), flaps and landing gear. The autopilot plays no role at all in takeoffs, although some airplanes may employ autothrottles during takeoff.

●**How do I know that I can trust my pilot?**

Airline pilots are among the most thoroughly trained and tested professionals in the US. They also must go through rigorous retraining each year to remain certified. Any pilot at any airline in this country can be trusted to be a proficient flier.

The pilot certification process may not be as rigorous in some less-developed countries, however. Before you board a flight on a small airline in another country, consider checking the airline's safety record on the Web site *www.airsafe. com*. You can view accident reports and other statistics and reach your own conclusions.

●**Are air pockets dangerous?**

Not only are they not dangerous, they don't exist. The term "air pocket" was coined by a journalist during World War I, but he really just was referring to turbulence—irregular air currents that can shake aircraft around a bit.

When a plane "hits an air pocket" and seems to drop 1,000 feet, it really has just run into a little turbulence and probably dropped or climbed no more than 10 to 20 feet. Light turbulence is so common and inconsequential that experienced pilots scarcely notice it.

There is such a thing as "severe turbulence," which can be strong enough to injure passengers who aren't wearing their seat belts, but this is so rare that I have never encountered it in over 32 years of flying. Modern radar is advanced enough that pilots usually can steer clear of areas that have a high probability of moderate or severe turbulence.

Even when a plane does encounter severe turbulence, it won't crash because of it. When was the last time you read or heard of an airplane accident blamed on turbulence? If you're worried that a little turbulence will bring down your flight, watch one of those Discovery channel documentaries on "hurricane hunter" planes that fly right into the middle of huge storms and come out unscathed on the other side. A modern passenger jet is just as sturdy.

•In the movies, when a plane hits severe turbulence, the baggage compartments open up and luggage tumbles out. Would that happen in a real plane?

On occasion, if it gets really rough, an overhead compartment could open, especially if it isn't securely latched. I have never witnessed more than one compartment at a time come open due to turbulence, and I have only seen this once or twice.

•How dangerous is it when a plane gets struck by lightning?

My plane has been struck at least three times in my career. There's sometimes a bang, like a cannon going off, but it's not all that dangerous. The lightning charge simply travels around the plane's metal exterior, then off the "static wicks" (pencil-like protrusions) on the trailing edges and tips of the wings and tail.

It is true that lightning can cause problems for a plane's electrical systems. Once, on a flight from Oakland to Denver, a lightning strike knocked out my plane's power, but only for a few seconds. Even if the plane's main electrical system had been permanently disabled, we still had standby power. Some modern planes even are equipped with Ram Air Turbines (RATs), which use the airstream to power onboard electrical backup generators and hydraulic systems.

Between the emergency power systems and the extensive training that pilots receive, there's no reason to think that a plane would crash just because its main electrical system went out.

•What advice do you have for people who are afraid to fly?

I suggest that you consider the statistics regarding flying. It really is true that the drive to the airport is many, many times more dangerous than the flight. Personally, I feel far safer in a plane than I do in a car.

•Are some airports safer than others?

All US airports are safe, but some are more modern than others and thus probably a little safer.

Modern airports often have longer runways, easier-to-navigate approaches and more sophisticated electronics that allow pilots to land even with limited or no visibility.

Older airports, such as Chicago's Midway International Airport, Jackson Hole Airport, San Diego International Airport, New York City's LaGuardia Airport and Ronald Reagan Washington National Airport, are not this advanced, but I certainly wouldn't call them unsafe.

Ultramodern airports include Denver International Airport and Los Angeles International Airport.

•Has air travel security improved since 9/11?

Yes, mostly because the passengers themselves now are part of the security force. In the past, if a passenger started acting oddly, those seated near him/her would mind their own business. These days, if a passenger starts doing anything halfway suspicious, other passengers quickly alert a flight attendant.

■ ■ ■ ■

Beware of Ice!

Ice has more bacteria than the toilet water at some major fast-food restaurants.

Recent finding: Samples from served ice, self-serve ice machines and toilets at five fast-food restaurants were tested for bacteria and compared. Overall, toilet water fared better, although bacteria levels for all were in the acceptable range.

Jasmine Roberts, seventh-grade student, Tampa, whose project comparing bacteria in ice machines and public toilets won first place at the New Tampa School Science Fair.

■ ■ ■ ■

Wash Your Hands

Twenty-five percent of men and 10% of women leave restrooms without washing their hands. Hand washing is one of the easiest steps to staying healthy.

Best: Wash with soap under warm running water for at least 20 seconds after using the restroom, before eating, after counting money, after changing a diaper and after petting an animal.

Judy Daly, PhD, microbiologist, Primary Children's Medical Center, University of Utah, Salt Lake City, and former secretary, American Society of Microbiology.

■■■■

Less Than Fresh Air

Some air cleaners could make your air unhealthy.

Recent study: Some ionizing air filters expose users to high levels of ozone. Experts agree that exposure to ozone in excess of 80 parts per billion for eight hours or longer can cause coughing, wheezing and chest pain, and deaden the sense of smell. In a recent test, five ionizing room air cleaners performed poorly, and some emitted potentially harmful levels of ozone—Brookstone Pure-Ion V2, Sharper Image Professional Series Ionic Breeze Quadra S1737 SNX, Ionic Pro CL-369, Ioniz Air P4620 and Surround Air XJ-2000.

Best air cleaners: Friedrich C-90A and Whirlpool 45030—both effectively clean air and emit little ozone.

Mark Connelly, senior director, Consumer Reports, 101 Truman Ave., Yonkers, NY 10703, appliances & home improvement, and leader of a test of five ionizing air cleaners, one electrostatic precipitator and one HEPA air cleaner.

■■■■

Food Dangers for Your Dog

Table scraps can harm dogs. Grapes and raisins can cause vomiting, diarrhea and life-threatening kidney failure. Chocolate can be toxic to dogs—the darker the chocolate, the greater the risk. Sugarless gum and candy containing xylitol can cause a rapid drop in a dog's blood sugar, which can result in depression, loss of coordination and seizures. Onions can cause gastrointestinal irritation and anemia and can damage dogs' red blood cells—a single small whole onion can be fatal. Macadamia nuts can cause vomiting, depression, tremors and temporary paralysis of a dog's hind legs—though this usually clears up on its own without lasting effects.

Steven Hansen, DVM, Diplomate of the American Board of Veterinary Toxicology, senior vice president, ASPCA Animal Poison Control Center, Urbana, IL.

Before You Take Another Bite...Food Poisoning Self-Defense

Ewen Todd, PhD, former director, National Food Safety and Toxicology Center, Michigan State University, East Lansing, previously headed the Contaminated Foods Section of the Health Protection Branch of the Canadian government.

There are an estimated 76 million cases of foodborne illness in the US each year. Many victims think they have contracted a "stomach flu" and never realize that food was to blame.

Most foodborne illnesses cause a day or two of nausea, diarrhea, abdominal cramping and, sometimes, vomiting. But in the US, 325,000 cases a year are severe enough to lead to hospitalization and about 5,200 are fatal, according to the Centers for Disease Control and Prevention. Foodborne illnesses are particularly dangerous for children under age five, adults over age 70, pregnant women and people with weakened immune systems. *Here, the foods most likely to cause problems...*

POULTRY

More than 60% of the raw poultry sold in the US is thought to contain disease-causing bacteria, including...

•**Campylobacter,** which can cause up to a week of diarrhea, abdominal pain and fever starting two to five days after the tainted food is consumed.

•**Salmonella,** which can cause four to seven days of diarrhea, fever and abdominal pain starting 12 to 72 hours after eating the contaminated food. Other sources of salmonella include undercooked eggs.

Note: Commercially prepared mayonnaise is made from pasteurized eggs, which are heat-treated to kill bacteria.

In 5% to 15% of cases, salmonella bacteria can lead to reactive arthritis, an inflammatory condition that develops in response to infection in another part of the body. This condition can last weeks, months, even years.

When poultry is cooked all the way through, the bacteria are killed.

Safest: Cook poultry until juices run clear and there is no sign of pink. Even then poultry can become contaminated if not handled properly—for example, if cooked poultry is placed on a cutting board that hasn't been washed after uncooked poultry rested on it.

It used to be common practice to wash raw poultry prior to cooking, but this has been identified as risky because splashes and drips can spread bacteria throughout the kitchen.

STEWS & SOUPS

Stews, soups, sauces and gravies containing red meat or poultry—or their juices—can be a perfect breeding ground for the *Clostridium perfringens* bacteria. When these dishes are cooked, allowed to cool slowly and then rewarmed, the bacteria thrive. It can cause an unpleasant day of nausea and diarrhea starting within 24 hours of consumption. To reduce the risk, refrigerate stews, soups, sauces and gravies in small containers, which cool faster, soon after cooking.

GROUND BEEF

The *E. coli* bacteria sickens about 60,000 to 70,000 Americans every year. Most victims experience about a week of cramping and bloody diarrhea starting four to eight days after the tainted food is consumed. One of every 1,000 victims dies.

E. coli bacteria live naturally in the intestines of many animals, including cattle. During the slaughter and processing of cattle, the meat can accidentally come in contact with fecal matter.

Ground beef is riskiest. The E. coli bacteria can be present on the surface of any piece of raw beef, but steaks and roasts typically are sufficiently cooked to kill this surface bacteria—even when cooked rare. With ground beef, the surface of the meat gets ground up and can wind up in the middle of your burger. If the burger isn't cooked all the way through (to an internal temperature of 160°), bacteria can survive.

Important: If a steak has been punctured with a fork or knife prior to cooking, bacteria could find its way inside and survive. In that case, eat the meat only if it's cooked well-done.

Produce alert: E. coli also can be present in soil and has been found on lettuce, alfalfa sprouts and in unpasteurized apple juice and cider. Wash lettuce—even prewashed lettuce—carefully, and avoid sprouts (which are hard to clean) and unpasteurized juices.

DELI MEATS

Cold cuts, pâté and smoked fish are leading sources of the *Listeria* bacteria. Unpasteurized milk and milk products also can be contaminated. Listeria is found in soil and water. Animals also can carry the bacteria in their intestines. As a result, Listeria can spread to meat and dairy products. Ready-to-eat foods can become contaminated in the processing plant or en route from the plant.

There are about 2,500 cases of Listeria poisoning each year in the US, and about 20% of victims die, so it's important to be careful. Symptoms include fever, muscle aches and sometimes nausea or diarrhea.

Reduce your odds of infection by setting your refrigerator to just above freezing for storing deli meat, pâté and smoked fish. Consume or freeze these foods within four or five days of purchase.

LEFTOVERS

Discard leftovers that have been at room temperature for more than two hours or out in hot weather for more than an hour.

Use refrigerated leftovers within four days.

When reheating leftovers, bring them to an internal temperature of 165°. Reheat stews, soups, sauces and gravies to a boil.

If you think you have food poisoning: Drink lots of water and get plenty of rest. Don't use antidiarrheal medications—they may slow the elimination of bacteria from your system. Foodborne illness often improves within 48 hours. Call your doctor if you feel ill for longer than two or three days or if blood appears in your stool.

■ ■ ■ ■

Water Can Explode in a Microwave

When water is quickly heated far above its boiling point, the bubbles that normally form in boiling water don't form.

When such superheated, non-bubbling water is removed from a microwave and jiggled or touched with a spoon, the bubbles may then form suddenly and spray the water up and out of the cup or container—potentially causing serious burns. *Safety...*

• **Don't overheat water**—microwave it on high for no more than one minute, then test it.

• **Put food contents (tea bag, soup mix, etc.) in the water before heating it.** This will prevent super-heating.

• **Let a cup of heated water sit for a minute after taking it out of the microwave**—and don't put your face over it.

Reassurance: Conventional ranges and stoves pose a much greater risk of fire and burns than microwave ovens do.

Scott Wolfson, spokesman, US Consumer Product Safety Commission, Bethesda, MD, *www.cpsc.gov.*

■■■■

Health Club Hazard

Avoid germs at the gym. Germs, including potentially deadly antibiotic-resistant bugs, often are present at fitness clubs.

Self-defense: Minimize skin-to-equipment contact by keeping cuts clean and bandaged. Carry one towel for yourself and another to wipe down mats and other equipment before and after you use it. Use an alcohol-based hand sanitizer on your hands before and after your workout. Wash your workout clothes after every use.

Charles Gerba, PhD, professor of microbiology, epidemiology and biostatistics, departments of soil, water and environmental science, University of Arizona, Tucson.

■■■■

Sand Risk

Beach sand has five to 10 times more bacteria than adjacent water. Bacteria from bird droppings and human waste, such as *E. coli*, may survive longer in sand than in water because bacteria adhere to particles.

Self-defense: Wash hands after leaving the beach. Warn children not to put their hands in their mouths when digging in sand.

Walter McLeod, president, Clean Beaches Council, Washington, DC.

■■■■

Clean Veggies Safely

Remove pesticides and wax from fruits and vegetables. In a bowl or a basin, mix four tablespoons of table salt, four teaspoons of lemon juice and one quart of cool water. Soak fruits and vegetables for five to 10 minutes.

Exceptions: Soak leafy greens for two to three minutes…berries, one to two minutes. After soaking, rinse produce in plain cold water and dry.

Alternative: Veggie Wash. Made of 100% natural ingredients, it is available at supermarkets, health-food stores and on-line at *www.veggie-wash.com* (800-451-7096).

Joan Wilen and Lydia Wilen, authorities on folk remedies, New York City, and authors of *Bottom Line's Healing Remedies* and *Bottom Line's Household Magic, www.bottomlinesecrets.com.*

■■■■

Pollution Warning

Exposure to polluted air may cause premature death.

Recent finding: Elevated ozone levels were associated with spikes in the number of deaths in 95 areas around the country. People ages 65 to 74 had a slightly higher risk of death from pollution than younger people.

Self-defense: Check pollution forecasts at *www.epa.gov/airnow.* On days with high ozone concentrations, avoid congested streets, where car emissions cause ozone buildup, and don't exercise outside.

Michelle L. Bell, PhD, associate professor of environmental health, Yale School of Forestry & Environmental Studies, New Haven, CT, and lead author of a study comparing daily ozone levels and death rates, reported in *Journal of the American Medical Association.*

■■■■

Vaccinations Recommended

A childhood vaccine for bacterial pneumonia, among other invasive pneumococcal diseases, such as meningitis, is now recommended for all US children. The vaccine—Prevnar—is now available in 60 countries and has been shown to reduce the incidence of pneumococcal illnesses in adults as well.

Keith P. Klugman, MD, PhD, William H. Foege Chair, Rollins School of Public Health, Emory University, Atlanta, and leader of a study of more than 37,000 children in Soweto, South Africa, published in *Nature Medicine.*

■■■■

Autism Alert

Early signs of autism may be detected in high-risk children as young as 12 months who exhibit key behaviors associated with the disorder, such as lack of eye contact with parents, problems following an object visually and reduced social smiling. Until recently, parents had to wait until a child was two or three years old before he/she could be assessed for autism. A new research tool can identify these early signs of autism in babies who have a sibling with the disorder. More research is needed to evaluate whether screening is reliable this early in the general population. Earlier detection may lead to earlier intervention and improved outcomes for these children.

Jessica Brian, PhD, CPsych, clinician investigator, Bloorview Research Institute, Bloorview Kids Rehab, Toronto, Canada, and coauthor of a study of 150 infants, including 19 infants with early signs of autism, published in *International Journal of Developmental Neuroscience*.

■■■■

Bug Off Naturally

New herbal insect repellent—*oil of lemon eucalyptus*—now is on the Centers for Disease Control and Prevention's recommended list. But it must be reapplied more often than DEET or Picaridin (frequency depends on the concentration).

Warning: Just one mosquito bite can transmit West Nile virus or other infections. Apply repellent to exposed skin whenever you are outdoors, especially between dusk and dawn.

Emily Zielinski-Gutierrez, DrPH, behavioral scientist, Division of Vector-Borne Diseases, Centers for Disease Control and Prevention, Fort Collins, CO.

■■■■

A New Blood Test for TB

The *T-Spot TB test* is as accurate as the skin test and requires only one doctor visit, but it is not offered by all providers.

Who needs regular TB tests: Hospital workers and others who might come in close contact with TB...residents of long-term-care facilities...and those receiving immune-suppressing treatment, such as chemotherapy.

Testing also may be required by schools, colleges and other places where disease can spread quickly.

Peter Barnes, MD, director, Center for Pulmonary and Infectious Disease Control, University of Texas Health Center at Tyler. His study was published in *American Journal of Respiratory and Critical Care Medicine*.

■■■■

Better Emphysema Screening

Computed tomography (CT) scans are used to screen for emphysema, a progressive lung disease that enlarges the lung's air sacs, impairing oxygen delivery. In a study of eight nonsmokers and 11 smokers who did not have emphysema symptoms, such as shortness of breath and chronic cough, the patients inhaled "hyperpolarized" helium, a gas used with a new MRI technique that makes the lung sacs easier to view. The new technique detected signs of emphysema in smokers who were otherwise healthy, while the CT scans did not.

For more information, contact the International Society for Magnetic Resonance in Medicine, *www.ismrm.org/hng/* and see Information for Patients

Sean B. Fain, PhD, assistant professor of medical physics and radiology, University of Wisconsin, Madison.

How to Beat Yeast Infections (for Women and Men)

Jamison Starbuck, ND, is a naturopathic physician in family practice in Missoula, Montana. She is past president of the American Association of Naturopathic Physicians and is a contributing editor to *The Alternative Advisor: The Complete Guide to Natural Therapies and Alternative Treatments*. Time-Life.

We've got a man here who seems to have yeast. I don't know how to deal with it. You do, don't you? Over the years, I've received several calls like this from doctors or nurses in nearby clinics. Even though most medical doctors don't know how to treat yeast, naturopathic medicine has answers.

Candidiasis is the medical term for an overgrowth of the fungal organism *Candida albicans*, commonly known as yeast. The overgrowth occurs most often in the digestive tract, though yeast can flourish on the skin or in ear canals, sinus cavities and the vagina. Antibiotics, birth-control pills, anti-ulcer drugs and corticosteroids are common causes of candidiasis. Candidiasis can cause or worsen an array of conditions, including irritable bowel syndrome, vaginitis, prostatitis, eczema, psoriasis, hives, sinusitis, depression and chronic fatigue.

A stool culture is available to diagnose candidiasis, but it is often inaccurate. Therefore, I look for the cardinal signs of yeast—strong cravings for sweets (yeast feeds on sugar, so it may trigger this craving), gas, bloating, red and scaly skin rashes, rectal itching and generalized fatigue. I also review a patient's history of medication use for common candidiasis culprits. *If you have two or more candidiasis symptoms, follow these steps for one month...*

•**Improve your diet.** Avoid refined carbohydrates, including desserts, bread, pasta, chips and pretzels. Eliminate all juice, dried fruit and foods containing sugar, corn syrup, honey and maple syrup. Give up alcohol and artificial sweeteners. Curb your intake of starchy vegetables, such as white potatoes and corn. Reducing sugar and starches (which are converted in the body into sugar) starves the yeast. Eat only organic poultry, meat and dairy—other types may contain antibiotics, which worsen a yeast overgrowth. Freely consume all vegetables (excluding white potatoes and corn), protein (beans, soy and fish) and whole grains. Have two one-cup servings of fresh fruit daily.

•**Hydrate well.** Drink one-half ounce of water per pound of body weight daily, and limit caffeine to two cups of coffee or tea daily.

•**Use probiotics.** Take 4.5 billion colony-forming units (CFUs) of *L. acidophilus* and *B. bifidus* daily. These "good" bacteria, available at health-food stores, help with digestion and immune health. Antibiotics and other medications, such as antacids and corticosteroids, reduce these beneficial bacteria, allowing yeast to proliferate.

Finally, take a botanical antifungal preparation for a limited time in order to kill yeast and restore normal intestinal flora. Effective natural antifungals include *caprylic acid*, *Pau d'arco*, *Berberis vulgaris*, lavender and thyme. Single and combination formulas are available at health-food stores. Follow the label recommendations for daily dosing. Take the antifungal for one week, then stop it for 10 days. If your symptoms persist, repeat the antifungal for another seven days. Antifungals should be taken on an empty stomach.

If this program doesn't leave you feeling better within one month, see your doctor for an exam and evaluation.

■ ■ ■ ■

Air Freshener Warning

Room fresheners may cause headaches, depression and other maladies. A recent study finds that the "volatile organic compounds" found in aerosols such as air fresheners are associated with increased incidence of headache and depression among women, and higher levels of diarrhea, earache and other symptoms among young children. The study authors warn this may indicate heightened risk for other groups who are home a large percentage of their time, such as the elderly.

Safer: Use baking soda, lemons and other natural odor remedies. Don't use aerosols in confined spaces.

Alexandra Farrow, PhD, course director, School of Health Sciences & Social Care, Brunel University, Isleworth, England.

■ ■ ■ ■

Safe Water Rules

Don't try to drink an arbitrary daily amount of liquid, such as eight glasses of water. Urine color is a good indicator of hydration—it should be light yellow. Other beverages, such as juice, milk and soda, are treated as water by the body—even if they contain caffeine.

•**It is fine to drink tap water**—the US has some of the safest tap water in the world, and many bottled waters are simply filtered tap water.

•**If your home was built before 1986,** have your water tested for lead contamination.

•**If your water comes from a well,** have it tested for arsenic.

•**Use a filter** if you find that your water contains contaminants or has a taste you dislike.

Bottled-water caution: Reusing plastic bottles that have not been sterilized can expose you to high bacteria levels. Wash bottles in hot, soapy water or run them through a dishwasher. Store unopened bottled water in a cool, dark place to prevent damage to the containers from heat and light.

Steven Patch, PhD, authority on drinking water safety and director, Environmental Quality Institute, University of North Carolina, Asheville.

■ ■ ■ ■

Fall Prevention

A new study reveals that more than 300 women over age 70 with cataracts received cataract surgery within approximately four weeks or 12 months of diagnosis.

Result: Over 12 months, the rate of falling was reduced by 34% in the group who received surgery earlier, and their rate of fracture was 66% lower than in those who hadn't received surgery yet.

Self-defense: If possible, schedule cataract surgery as soon as possible.

Rowan Harwood, MD, consultant geriatrician, Nottingham University Hospital, Nottingham, England.

Protect Against Killer Food Allergies

Steve L. Taylor, PhD, professor of food science and director of the Food Allergy Research and Resource Program at the University of Nebraska, Lincoln, is a leading expert on food allergies and serves on the editorial boards of the *Journal of Food Protection* and the *Journal of Natural Toxins.*

Many people with food allergies have mild symptoms, such as a rash, runny nose or itchy eyes, when they eat small amounts of a problem food. But they may still be at risk for a potentially deadly reaction.

In the US, food allergies cause up to 30,000 emergency room visits and 200 deaths annually due to *anaphylaxis*, an acute reaction that can cause respiratory distress and/or a heart arrhythmia (irregular heartbeat).

Recent development: The Food Allergen Labeling and Consumer Protection Act, which went into effect in January 2006, requires food manufacturers to list eight major allergens on food labels to help people with food allergies identify and avoid problem foods.

IS IT REALLY AN ALLERGY?

Not all reactions to food are due to allergies. Tens of millions of Americans suffer from food *intolerance.* A food intolerance, such as a sensitivity to the lactose in milk, can begin in childhood. The most common symptom of lactose intolerance is gastrointestinal discomfort, including diarrhea, cramping and flatulence.

Food allergies affect about 11 million to 12 million Americans. With a food allergy, the immune system mistakenly identifies as harmful the various proteins—or even a single kind of protein—within one or more foods. This triggers a cascade of events that causes immune cells to respond to the "threat" by releasing large amounts of histamine and other chemicals that produce the allergic symptoms.

The most common food allergen is shellfish. Up to 2% of Americans are allergic to shrimp and/or other shellfish, such as lobster, crab and crayfish. This type of allergy often is ignored—primarily because most people tend to eat shellfish far less often than other allergenic foods, such as eggs, peanuts and fish.

TESTING FOR ALLERGIES

A food allergy usually can be diagnosed with a thorough medical history taken by an allergist.

The doctor will want to know…

•**When do symptoms occur?** Food allergies typically cause symptoms within a few minutes to several hours after exposure. Symptoms include stomach cramping, hives, lip swelling, runny nose, congestion and asthma. With a food intolerance, symptoms may not occur until the next day.

•**How much did you eat?** With food allergies, any exposure can trigger symptoms. For some patients, 1 mg—an amount that's almost impossible to see—will provoke an allergic response. A reaction can even be triggered by kissing—or sharing utensils with—someone who has eaten a substance to which you are allergic. A skin reaction can occur from touching the substance.

With a food intolerance, symptoms usually are linked to the amount consumed. Someone who's sensitive to milk, for example, can often drink a small amount without a reaction.

Two tests can identify most food allergies. *They are...*

•**Skin prick.** Extracts of suspected foods are pricked into the skin with a needle. The appearance of a rash within a few hours—or even a few minutes—indicates a food allergy.

Caution: The skin-prick test isn't advisable for patients with severe allergies. The tiny amounts of food used in the test could trigger a life-threatening reaction.

•**Radioallergosorbent test (RAST).** This blood test detects antibodies to specific food proteins. The test occasionally produces false positives—indicating an allergy where none is present. It's often combined with the skin-prick test for more accurate results.

TREATMENT

People with a history of serious food reactions must carry an EpiPen. Available by prescription, it's a self-injector that delivers a dose of *epinephrine*. Epinephrine stimulates the heart and respiration and helps counteract deadly anaphylaxis.

Important: Use the EpiPen immediately if you experience difficulty breathing or throat constriction. Even if you take the shot promptly, get to an emergency room as soon as possible for follow-up treatments.

Also helpful: Take an antihistamine, such as Benadryl, according to label instructions. It can lessen the severity of symptoms while you get to an emergency room.

New development: Omalizumab (Xolair), a medication currently used for asthma, appears to significantly blunt reactions in food-allergy patients who receive a monthly injection of the drug. In an early study, patients who reacted to trace amounts of peanuts were able to eat eight to 10 nuts without experiencing problems. Further studies must be completed to determine whether the FDA deems it an effective—and safe—therapy for food allergies.

AVOIDING PROBLEM FOODS

Because there isn't a cure for food allergies—and even trace amounts of a protein can trigger reactions—strict avoidance is the best defense...

•**Always read food labels**—even if you've safely eaten that product in the past. Manufacturers frequently change or add ingredients.

•**Ask about "hidden" ingredients in medications.** Some prescription and over-the-counter (OTC) drugs, as well as vitamins and supplements, contain milk proteins or other common food allergens. This information should be on the label, but check with your doctor or pharmacist before taking any medication or supplement.

•**Talk to the chef or restaurant manager when eating out.** The waiter or waitress doesn't always have accurate information about food ingredients and preparation. Ask to speak to the chef or manager instead and tell him/her what you're allergic to. Explain that *any* contact with the offending food can be *life-threatening*.

If you're allergic to shellfish, for example, tell the chef or manager you can't eat a hamburger that was cooked on the same grill used to cook shrimp.

Other hidden sources of food allergens: Cooking oils that are used to cook different foods...knives and cutting boards that aren't washed clean between uses.

•**Wear a medical alert bracelet/necklace.** Anaphylaxis can potentially cause a loss of consciousness within minutes. A medical alert bracelet/necklace lets medical personnel know that you require urgent treatment for your allergy.

■ ■ ■ ■

Lasting Effects

Marijuana is linked to mental illness. Children who use marijuana for the first time before age 12 are twice as likely to develop serious mental illness, such as depression and schizophrenia, later in life than those who don't use marijuana until after age 18.

The *National Survey on Drug Use and Health*, published by the Office of Applied Studies, Substance Abuse and Mental Health Services Administration, Rockville, MD.

■ ■ ■ ■
Tube Alert

Television breeds bullies. Children whose parents read to them and engage them in activities other than watching TV are less likely to become bullies. Emotional support from parents helps kids develop empathy, self-control and social skills, so they are less likely to intimidate others.

Frederick Zimmerman, PhD, investigator, Child Health Institute, University of Washington, Seattle, and leader of a study of 1,266 four-year-olds, published in *Archives of Pediatrics and Adolescent Medicine.*

■ ■ ■ ■
Patch Warning

Wearing a pain patch may cause fatal breathing problems. The FDA is investigating 120 deaths that may have been caused by an overdose or improper use of *fentanyl*, which is administered via a transdermal patch and is used by people who suffer from severe chronic pain.

Self-defense: If you wear the fentanyl patch, often sold as the Duragesic patch, contact your doctor.

Crystal Rice, spokesperson, Center for Drug Evaluation and Research, US Food and Drug Administration, Rockville, MD.

How to Prevent Golf Injuries

Frank Rabadam, DPT (doctor of physical therapy), who is certified by Back to Golf, a PGA- and LPGA-approved fitness and golf biomechanics program, is a certified Yoga for Golfers instructor and owner of Back Under Par LLC, a golf performance enhancement program.

The sedate pace of golf would seem to leave little room for injuries—but that's not so. According to one study, as many as one-third of the more than 25 million golfers in the US sustain significant injuries of the back, spine, shoulders, elbows or wrists while playing the sport. *Important...*

•**Warm up properly.** A study in the *British Journal of Sports Medicine* found that nearly 46% of golfers don't warm up. Those who do warm up usually perform little more than a few "air swings" before hitting the ball. Inadequate warm-up is a leading cause of injury.

Allow two to five minutes of aerobic warm-up activity—jogging in place, fast walking, etc.

Follow the aerobic workout with five to 10 minutes of gentle stretching—torso twists, chest stretches, etc. Include neck turns. Neck stiffness interferes with smooth body rotation during swings. Also, do stretches that target the hamstrings, such as lying leg lifts. Poor hamstring flexibility is a common cause of back pain.

Stretch one or two muscle groups at each hole while waiting for your turn. For more information on the best stretches and exercises for golfers, go to *www.yogaforgolfers.com*, which is run by fitness consultant Katherine Roberts. She is author of the book *Yoga for Golfers* (McGraw-Hill).

•**Be careful when lifting.** Golfers often get hurt before the first tee because they jerk their clubs out of the car trunk. Use your legs as well as your back when lifting the bag. On the course, pick up balls by kneeling rather than bending.

•**Practice good balance and posture.** Most neck and shoulder stiffness occurs when players hunch over the ball excessively, with their neck and shoulders too far forward. Work with a golf pro to optimize your posture and stance when addressing the ball. You want to maintain a neutral spine position, without excessive bending or extension.

•Limit your swing. Amateur golfers tend to "overswing"—using greater force than necessary. Instead, shorten your swing. End the backswing at about the 1:00 position, instead of 3:00.

•Strength train. Lifting weights to increase strength and endurance can significantly reduce the risk of golf injuries. Focus on strengthening the shoulders, upper back, and "core" muscles in the abdomen and lower back.

•Consider graphite clubs. They have more "give" and generate less vibration and shock than clubs with steel shafts. This is important when you accidentally hit the ground during hard drives, a cause of wrist and elbow injuries.

■ ■ ■ ■

Sunscreen Dose

Apply twice as much sunscreen as you think you need. FDA testing calls for about twice as much as most people apply.

To be able to count on the protection listed on the label, apply sunscreen, wait 20 minutes, then apply it again. It takes two to three tablespoons per application to cover exposed adult skin adequately. Look for sunscreens labeled "broad spectrum" or ones that protect against both UVA and UVB rays.

Vincent A. DeLeo, MD, chairman of clinical dermatology, St. Luke's-Roosevelt Hospital Center and Beth Israel Medical Center, New York City.

■ ■ ■ ■

Blood Sugar Risk

High blood sugar is a little-known risk patients should be aware of. Patients who have had a heart attack or stroke and who have even slightly elevated blood sugar—as little as one point beyond the normal range—are more likely to die in intensive care.

Self-defense: Make sure doctors monitor a loved one's blood glucose level before and after surgery. Get diabetes under control before any surgery.

Mercedes Falciglia, MD, assistant professor of medicine, University of Cincinnati College of Medicine, and lead author of a study of 216,000 patients, presented at a recent meeting of the American Diabetes Association.

■ ■ ■ ■

Croup Cuddle

Hold and calm a child with croup instead of exposing him/her to steam from a shower or kettle. Treatment with high or low humidity or mist therapy has no observable value. Soothing helps restore normal breathing in children whose croup is moderate to severe. Most croup attacks end within 30 minutes. Exposing the child to cool night air also can be helpful. If a child does not get better within 30 minutes or becomes pale or blue, get emergency help immediately.

Dennis Scolnik, MD, staff physician, department of pediatric emergency medicine, Hospital for Sick Children, Toronto, and leader of a study of 140 children with moderate to severe croup, published in Journal of the American Medical Association.

■ ■ ■ ■

ADHD Aid

New ADHD patch is available. The *Daytrana* patch, which is worn for nine hours per day by children with attention deficit-hyperactivity disorder, contains *methylphenidate*—the same stimulant found in Ritalin.

The patch is recommended for children ages six to 12 who have ADHD and may provide an alternative for those children who have trouble swallowing pills. It can be removed immediately if it causes side effects, such as nausea or irritability. Ask your child's pediatrician for more information.

Thomas Laughren, MD, director, division of psychiatry products, US Food and Drug Administration, Washington, DC.

■ ■ ■ ■

Raking Leaves? Protect Your Back

Stretch before you start raking—flex your back, shoulders and rib cage. Lift the rake and leaves with your legs, not your back (bend your knees and don't lean forward). Stretch when you are finished to cool down. Take a warm bath or get a massage to relax muscles.

Important: If you are not physically fit or have a history of injury or back pain, don't rake leaves or engage in any other heavy yard work. If you experience muscle spasms, radiating pain, numbness or tingling down the legs or arms after doing yard work, see a doctor. These symptoms may indicate a serious condition.

Steven Weiss, DO, osteopathic surgeon and medical director, The Medicine Lodge Clinic, New York City.

Surprising Leading Cause of Stress Disorder

J. Gayle Beck, professor of psychology, The State University of New York at Buffalo.

After the Crash: Psychological Assessment and Treatment of Survivors of Motor Vehicle Accidents, by Edward B. Blanchard, PhD, and Edward J. Hickling, PsyD. American Psychological Association.

Car accidents are a leading cause of post-traumatic stress disorder (PTSD), according to a book titled *After the Crash: Psychological Assessment and Treatment of Survivors of Motor Vehicle Accidents*.

PTSD is a common psychological ailment, affecting as many as five million Americans each year, according to the National Institute of Mental Health.

Symptoms of PTSD include reliving the traumatic incident through flashbacks or nightmares, sleep problems, depression, anxiety, irritability and anger.

The authors, psychologists Edward B. Blanchard, PhD, from the State University of New York (SUNY) at Albany, and Edward J. Hickling, PsyD, in private practice in Albany, New York, provide information from a new study of motor vehicle accident survivors and PTSD.

THE STUDY

The researchers followed up 161 car crash survivors for five years after they had their accidents. The study subjects were at least slightly injured and sought medical attention after their accidents.

In this group, 110 subjects were diagnosed with PTSD, and 60% of them also experienced major depression.

Practically all—95%—of the crash survivors had become anxious when driving and many avoided certain situations, such as driving at night or highway driving.

J. Gayle Beck, a professor of psychology at SUNY Buffalo who specializes in treating PTSD after an automobile crash, says that those are common behaviors for people who have lived through a serious accident.

"These people tend to refuse to drive or are unbelievably nervous drivers," Beck says.

And, she notes, a serious accident doesn't necessarily have to be one in which someone was seriously injured.

Any accident that scares someone or makes him/her believe that they might die has the potential to cause PTSD, she says, recalling a patient whose car rolled over. He was not seriously injured, but during the accident, he believed that he was going to die, and those memories haunted him.

According to Beck, PTSD isn't easy to diagnose. Many PTSD symptoms are not obvious. The most common symptom, for example, is having recurrent and intrusive thoughts about the accident. This may make the person appear to be unable to concentrate. Beck says people suffering from PTSD often are hyperactive and have trouble sleeping.

Clearer signs that someone may need help after they've been in an accident is refusing to drive or exhibiting very nervous or altered driving behavior.

Although these signs can be common right after an accident, if any symptoms persist for more than six months, it's time to get treatment, Beck says. The experts agree that cognitive behavioral therapy is helpful for many people, as is supportive psychotherapy. Beck says researchers are experimenting with new ways to treat PTSD. In her lab, she is using virtual-reality driving simulations as a way to get people with PTSD driving again.

To learn more about this disorder, visit the National Center for PTSD at *www.ncptsd.org*.

The "Clothing Cure" for Glaucoma

Robert Ritch, MD, professor of clinical ophthalmology, and chief, Glaucoma Service, The New York Eye and Ear Infirmary, New York City.

British Journal of Ophthalmology.

Ties that bind the neck may raise the risk of the eye disease glaucoma. A controversial study found that snug neckwear can increase intraocular pressure (IOP) in the eyes, possibly leading to glaucoma.

"If men wear tight neckties when their IOP is measured, it can raise their IOP," says Dr. Robert Ritch, lead author of the study and a professor of clinical ophthalmology at The New York Eye and Ear Infirmary.

DOUBLE TROUBLE

That double Windsor knot may be double trouble. If a person has moderate or severe glaucoma damage, the increase in IOP caused by a tight tie may worsen the damage. What's more, patients without glaucoma whose tight tie falsely increases IOP might end up being treated for glaucoma when they don't need to be. Although there are no reported cases of glaucoma being caused by a tight necktie, Ritch says it's theoretically possible.

Ritch became aware of the phenomenon during his regular practice. "I just noticed that some patients had tight neckties, and I just loosened their neckties and their IOP would go down several points," he says.

To quantify his observation, Ritch and his colleagues looked at 20 healthy men and 20 men with open-angle glaucoma, the most common form of the disease.

The researchers measured IOP first while the men weren't wearing neckties, then three minutes after they put on a tight necktie, and again three minutes after the tie was loosened.

Ritch's team found that in 70% of the healthy men, a tight necktie increased mean IOP, as it did in 60% of those with glaucoma.

Increases in IOP while wearing a tight necktie ranged from more than 2 to more than 4 mmHg (millimeters of mercury), compared with IOP readings when no ties were worn and after ties were loosened.

Ritch speculates that when a necktie exerts too much pressure on the jugular vein located in the neck, pressure is increased in the entire venous system, including in the eyes.

To learn more about glaucoma, visit the Glaucoma Research Foundation at *www.glau coma.org.*

■ ■ ■ ■

iPod Warning

If played too loudly, iPods can cause hearing loss and tinnitus (ringing in the ears). To protect your hearing, these and other personal stereo devices using earphones should not be audible to anyone standing near you. No matter what sort of earpiece you use, set the volume at about the level of a conversation with someone near you—the music should never get so loud that it causes discomfort and you have to turn down the volume.

Richard Tyler, PhD, audiologist and professor of otolaryngology and speech pathology and audiology, University of Iowa, Iowa City.

■ ■ ■ ■

Unusual Drug Reaction

Some drugs can trigger a rare skin disease called *Stevens-Johnson Syndrome* (SJS). Symptoms include red blotches, welts and pimple-like bumps either in one area of the body or all over. Eyelids may swell and eyes may turn red. The patient can have persistent fever or flu-like symptoms. SJS usually appears within one week of starting a new medication. The most common medications that cause SJS include drugs containing *sulfa*, nonsteroidal anti-inflammatory medications, anticonvulsants and drugs to treat gout. SJS is treated with antibiotics and steroids. In rare instances, it can result in blindness or death. There are roughly 600 to 2,000 cases of SJS annually.

C. Stephen Foster, MD, founder and director, Ocular Immunology and Uveitis Foundation, and clinical professor of ophthalmology, Harvard Medical School, Boston.

■ ■ ■ ■

Morning-After Pill Warning

The RU-486 pill can cause a rare but deadly infection in women who use it incorrectly. More than four deaths from sepsis—an infection of the bloodstream—have been reported since 2000, when the so-called "abortion pill" went on the US market. These infections occurred in women who inserted the second course of two pills vaginally, as some clinics recommend, rather than swallowing them, as the instructions state. The Food and Drug Administration says that the pill is safe when used properly and it will stay on the market.

Center for Drug Evaluation and Research, US Food and Drug Administration, Washington, DC.

■ ■ ■ ■

Deadly Heatstroke

People who become overheated—when spending hours in the sun—can lose their ability to sweat. This can cause heatstroke, in which body temperature soars to more than 104° F. Heatstroke is lethal. It can cause brain damage and/or cardiac arrest if body temperature isn't lowered immediately.

Self-defense: Drink a lot of fluids—at least one-half ounce per pound of body weight daily. Water and sports drinks are better than carbonated beverages. The carbonation makes it more difficult for the body to absorb fluids. Also, wear a hat and light-colored clothing.

Heatstroke warning signs: Dry mouth, dizziness, nausea, fatigue.

What to do: Find a cool, shaded area immediately. Get in front of an air conditioner or a fan, or get in your car and turn the air conditioner on high. If you don't feel better within a few minutes, have someone take you to a first-aid station or an emergency room.

■ ■ ■ ■

Oyster Alert

Raw oysters—particularly those from the Gulf Coast—are the main source of the *Vibrio* bacteria, which can cause three or four days of cramping, diarrhea, vomiting and fever starting one to four days after consumption. The bacteria can be fatal to people suffering from liver disease. You cannot tell whether an oyster is contaminated by its look, smell or taste.

Self-defense: Don't eat raw oysters.

Ewen Todd, PhD, former director of the National Food Safety and Toxicology Center at Michigan State University, East Lansing. He previously headed the Contaminated Foods Section of the Health Protection Branch of the Canadian government.

■ ■ ■ ■

Heart Attack Linked to Flu

An analysis of autopsy reports for nearly 35,000 people who died from heart disease over an eight-year period showed that the risk of dying from a heart attack increased by one-third during weeks of flu epidemics, compared with non-epidemic weeks.

Theory: Influenza causes inflammation, which can loosen plaques (fatty deposits) in coronary arteries and cause heart attacks.

If you have heart disease: Ask your doctor about getting an annual flu shot when the vaccine becomes available (usually in October or November).

Mohammad Madjid, MD, senior research scientist, Texas Heart Institute, Houston.

■ ■ ■ ■

Simple Flu Help

Ordinary soap and water eliminate the bird flu virus. So do hand sanitizers that contain alcohol.

Self-defense against respiratory viruses: Wash your hands before eating…after using the bathroom…and when you return home after being out.

William Schaffner, MD, chairman of the department of preventive medicine at Vanderbilt University School of Medicine, Nashville, is a fellow of the Infectious Diseases Society of America, and a liaison member of the Advisory Committee on Immunization Practices of the Centers for Disease Control and Prevention. He is vice president of the National Foundation for Infectious Diseases Board of Directors.

■ ■ ■ ■

Pass the Tissues, Please

The best way to blow your nose is to use paper facial tissues, not handkerchiefs, in which bacteria can grow.

Also: Use a tissue once, then throw it away. Blow gently—too much pressure can push infectious fluid into ears and sinuses. Press a finger outside one nostril, then blow through the open one. Repeat on the other side. Always wash your hands after blowing. Wait 10 minutes after waking in the morning before blowing your nose—congestion decreases after you get up from a prone position.

Murray Grossan, MD, otolaryngologist, Towers Ear, Nose and Throat Clinic, Cedars-Sinai Medical Center, Los Angeles.

How Depression Can Make You Sick...and Vice Versa

Charles Raison, PhD, assistant professor in the mind-body program, department of psychiatry and behavioral sciences at Emory University in Atlanta...and Esther Sternberg, MD, director of the integrative neural immune program at the National Institutes of Health in Rockville, Maryland. Dr. Sternberg is author of *The Balance Within: The Science of Connecting Health and Emotions* (Holt). *www.esthersternberg.com.*

It is an unfortunate double jeopardy—being sick can make you depressed...and being depressed can make you sick. New research shows that many chronic illnesses, including heart disease, diabetes and osteoporosis, have this two-way connection to depression.

Consequences can be grave. In a recent study, heart attack patients who were depressed had a two- to fourfold increased risk of dying within five years, compared with heart attack patients who were not depressed. In a global study from the World Health Organization involving 245,000 people, those with a chronic illness fared far worse if they also were depressed.

One in eight women experiences depression at some point, compared with only one in 16 men—a gender discrepancy due primarily to hormonal differences. That means it is especially important for women who are depressed to get regular checkups to screen for chronic illness...and for women who have a chronic disease to be alert for signs of depression.

EXPLAINING THE CONNECTION

Scientists are trying to discover how disease and depression interact. *What the evidence suggests...*

•**How disease can lead to depression:** Common sense tells us that a woman with a chronic illness might feel sad—but physiologically

speaking, the explanation may involve an overactive immune system.

Theory: Inflammation is part of the body's normal healing process...but if the immune system fails to turn off the inflammatory mechanism at the appropriate time, inflammation becomes long-lasting and widespread. This can alter metabolism and damage blood vessels, bones and other body tissues, bringing on a variety of chronic illnesses and disrupting the balance of *neurotransmitters* (brain chemicals) that affect mood, triggering depression.

Recent studies show that the following conditions may be linked to depression—cancer... heart disease...diabetes...fibromyalgia (a syndrome of widespread pain)...psoriasis (patches of scaly, red skin)...rheumatoid arthritis (an auto-immune disease)...and stroke.

•**How depression can lead to disease:** It is logical that a depressed woman may not take care of herself well enough to guard against illness, but this is only a partial explanation. Physiologically, depression is linked to high levels of stress hormones—which in turn may raise blood pressure and cholesterol levels...promote accumulation of harmful abdominal fat...impair digestion...and hamper immune function. Along with depression comes increased production of proteins called *cytokines,* which cause widespread inflammation. This can trigger changes in the brain that reduce its resistance to dementia.

Recent studies suggest that people who suffer from depression may be at increased risk for Alzheimer's disease...asthma...breast cancer...cardiovascular disease...diabetes...gastric ulcer...high blood pressure...osteoarthritis... osteoporosis...and thyroid disease.

DEFENSE AGAINST DEPRESSION

Getting relief from depression can help prevent chronic illness or make an existing illness easier to deal with. Yet even though up to 90% of depressed people can be treated effectively, only one in three seeks treatment. *To overcome depression...*

•**Develop realistic expectations.** You may pessimistically assume that your physical prognosis is worse than it really is...or you may be overly optimistic, then feel crushed if your progress is slow. Either attitude can negatively affect your motivation to participate actively in your own physical recovery.

What helps: Be proactive. Write down all of your questions about your condition, treatment and prognosis, and review them with your doctor.

•**Eat foods rich in omega-3 fatty acids.** Omega-3s reduce inflammation and aid neurotransmitter function. Research suggests that omega-3s may be better absorbed from food than from supplements.

What helps: Have at least four servings weekly of omega-3–rich foods.

•**Stay active.** Exercise releases *endorphins,* brain chemicals that lift mood and block pain.

What helps: Don't tell yourself, *I feel too lousy to work out.*

•**Strengthen social ties.** You may hesitate to tell loved ones how down your illness makes you feel for fear of burdening them—yet emotional support is vital to healing.

What helps: Remember that your illness affects your family and friends, too.

•**Know when to get professional help.** Many people incorrectly assume that depression is an unavoidable part of physical illness, so they don't seek treatment.

What helps: Learn the symptoms of depression—sleeping too much or too little, unintended weight gain or loss, low energy, persistent sadness, frequent crying, irritability, feelings of hopelessness, poor concentration, low libido or lack of interest in daily activities. If you have *any* thoughts of suicide or if you experience two or more of the symptoms above for more than two weeks, tell your doctor.

•**Consider psychotherapy.** A form called *cognitive behavioral therapy* helps depressed patients replace negative beliefs and behaviors with positive ones.

•**Try natural nonprescription supplements.** Sold at health-food stores, these may relieve mild-to-moderate depression. If you use pharmaceutical antidepressants or other medications, get your doctor's approval before taking natural supplements to avoid possible adverse interactions.

•**Consider pharmaceutical antidepressants.** These medications work by slowing the removal of neurotransmitters from the brain.

What helps: Antidepressants often are very effective, though it may take trial-and-error to find one that works for you and does not cause side effects.

■ ■ ■ ■

Sole Search

Wear the right shoe for walking workouts. Buy a shoe specifically designed for walking—it should be flexible at the ball of the foot, but not the arch. The heel should be cushioned. Buy in person, not on-line—from a knowledgeable salesperson at a store oriented toward runners and walkers. Buy a large-enough shoe—the listed size does not matter, but the fit does. Make sure there is at least a thumbnail's width from the end of your longest toe to the end of the shoe. The best time to have shoes fitted is at the end of the day because your foot swells during the day. Buy a new pair once the padding inside starts to lose its cushioning and stability—usually after about 500 miles.

Melinda R. Reiner, DPM, Syracuse, NY.

■ ■ ■ ■

Exercise Your Feet

Go barefoot or wear sandals whenever you can. Joints in feet stay properly lubricated when the small bones can move freely, which is not possible in closed shoes. Foot exercises also can keep feet healthy and prevent problems such as hammertoes.

Exercise examples: While sitting down, spread your toes as wide as possible and hold them open for five seconds at a time. This helps prevent muscle weakness that can cause toes to overlap. Lay a dish towel on the floor. Standing on one edge of the towel, scrunch it up inch by inch with your toes. Put some marbles in a wide bowl. Using one foot at a time, pick up the marbles and place them on the side or in another bowl.

Paul Chek, holistic health practitioner and certified neuromuscular therapist, Vista, CA.

4

Pain Relief

How to Control Chronic Pain

One in 10 Americans suffers from moderate to severe chronic pain, most often due to osteoarthritis, back ailments or injury. Unfortunately, pain is often *undertreated*.

Pain control is not a luxury—it is a medical necessity. Chronic pain can cause muscle weakness due to inactivity, insomnia and fatigue. Chronic pain can even "rewire" the nervous system, increasing your sensitivity to pain signals and causing pain in areas that were previously pain-free.

PAIN INVENTORY

Your doctor's ability to prescribe the right treatment depends on knowing exactly where, when and how your body hurts. *Before your next appointment, create a personal pain inventory by answering the following questions...*

•**Where is the pain?** Is it shallow and near the surface of your skin, or deep below the surface? Is it worse in any particular location, or equally bad all over?

•**When do you feel pain?** Is it worse in the morning or at night? Does it hurt all the time, or only when you move? Which movements cause pain? Is your pain affected by stress, changes in weather, exercise or sleep?

•**How bad is the pain?** Rate your pain on a scale of 0 to 10 (0 represents no pain, and 10 is the worst pain you've ever had). These ratings might change during the day—for example, you may wake up with level 3 pain, but progress to level 7 by evening. Or you may have no pain most of the time, but level 8 pain with specific movements, such as sitting down, standing up or walking.

•**What does the pain feel like?** Is it sharp, stabbing, dull, burning or throbbing?

•**How has the pain interfered with your life?** Does the pain interfere with your sleep?

Jennifer P. Schneider, MD, PhD, a Tucson, Arizona–based physician, board certified in internal medicine, addiction medicine and pain management, is the author of *Living with Chronic Pain: The Complete Health Guide to the Causes and Treatment of Chronic Pain*. Hatherleigh.

What activities or aspects of your life are limited by pain? Physicians use this information to determine how aggressively to treat the pain, so be honest and thorough in describing how your life has changed.

•**What relieves the pain?** What have you tried, and what worked? Include all prescription and over-the-counter (OTC) medications, ice packs, rest, applied pressure, herbal remedies, etc.

WORKING WITH YOUR DOCTOR

Most primary care physicians can diagnose and treat common causes of pain, such as back pain, headaches and osteoarthritis. Depending on your problem, your doctor may refer you to a neurologist, orthopedic surgeon, rheumatologist or other specialist. These doctors may determine that you need surgery or other procedures to treat the underlying cause of your pain.

People in pain tend to minimize movement because it hurts. But the less you move, the weaker your muscles become, which worsens the pain when you do try to move. To end this vicious cycle, engage in as much physical activity, such as walking, as you can.

Your doctor may need to experiment with different drugs to see which works best for you. Often, a "cocktail" of medications, instead of just one type, offers the best pain relief. For each medication prescribed, ask the doctor how soon it will begin working and what side effects you can expect. For example, some pain relievers cause constipation.

Make a follow-up appointment before leaving the office. You may need frequent visits while your medications are being adjusted. Once your pain is controlled, you will probably need to see your doctor less often. Prepare a new pain inventory before each visit.

MEDICATIONS TO CONSIDER

Potent pain-fighting therapies, many of which are underused…

•**Anti-inflammatory drugs.** Because these medications both relieve pain and decrease inflammation, they are typically used to treat arthritis and other painful conditions that cause inflammation. The pain reliever *acetaminophen* (Tylenol) does not treat inflammation. First-generation nonsteroidal anti-inflammatory drugs (NSAIDs) include *ibuprofen* (Motrin, Advil) and *naproxen* (Naprosyn, Aleve). These medications have side effects that can limit their use, including gastrointestinal bleeding and elevated blood pressure. A second-generation NSAID, such as the prescription COX-2 inhibitor *celecoxib* (Celebrex), is much less likely to cause bleeding, but may increase risk for heart attack and stroke. Your doctor should weigh the risks against the benefits when recommending anti-inflammatory medication.

•**Opioids.** These medications are typically used to treat moderate to severe pain. Opioids include codeine, morphine, *hydrocodone* (Vicodin), *fentanyl* patches (Duragesic), *oxycodone* (OxyContin), and *oxycodone* combined with *acetaminophen* (Percocet). These drugs have been so stigmatized by illicit drug use that many doctors are afraid to use them to ease pain in patients who are truly suffering.

When used as directed, opioids are no more dangerous than any other drugs and can be taken indefinitely, if needed. Although most patients taking opioid analgesics for more than about three weeks become physically dependent on them, few become addicted. Physical dependency means the body has become used to the drug, and when it is stopped, withdrawal symptoms, such as muscle pain, vomiting and diarrhea, can occur. This can be avoided if your doctor tapers the drugs slowly. Addiction occurs when there is a loss of control over the drug use, continued use of the drug despite negative consequences and a mental focus on getting and using more than the prescribed amount.

•**Topical analgesics.** Some types of pain, especially pain on the surface of the skin—such as from shingles or joint pain due to osteoarthritis—respond well to drugs that are absorbed through the skin. Examples include the *lidocaine* (Lidoderm) patch and *capsaicin* (Zostrix) cream.

•**Antidepressants.** *Venlafaxine* (Effexor) and *duloxetine* (Cymbalta) have been shown to relieve nerve pain, such as that from shingles, and diabetic neuropathy (nerve pain in the extremities).

•**Anticonvulsants.** Typically used to control seizures, *topiramate* (Topamax) eases migraines, and *gabapentin* (Neurontin) is helpful for those suffering from diabetic neuropathy or shingles pain.

■ ■ ■ ■

Cough Away Pain

In a new finding, coughing reduces the pain of a needle being inserted into the skin for local anesthetic, an intravenous (IV) line or when blood is drawn.

Reason: Coughing at the moment the needle is injected distracts a part of the brain that also perceives pain.

Important: Before trying this approach, ask the practitioner to observe whether you move your arm when you cough.

Taras I. Usichenko, MD, PhD, professor of anesthesiology, Ernst Moritz Arndt University, Greifswald, Germany.

What Relief! Natural Ways to Curb Your Pain

Mark A. Stengler, ND, naturopathic physician in private practice, La Jolla, CA...adjunct associate clinical professor at the National College of Natural Medicine, Portland, OR...author of 16 books, including *The Natural Physician's Healing Therapies* (Bottom Line Books) and coauthor of *Prescription for Natural Cures* (Wiley)...and author of the *Bottom Line/Natural Healing* newsletter.

Not long ago, a 60-year-old woman came to my office suffering from severe arthritis pain in both hands. I gave her a bean-sized dab of a homeopathic gel that she applied directly to the skin on her hands. After a few applications in the span of 30 minutes, her pain was reduced by 90%. She did not need to apply the gel again for two weeks.

I witnessed a similar result with a retired National Football League player. He had severe chronic hip pain from past injuries. With one application of the gel, his pain was relieved by 70% for two full days.

The relief that these people experienced has given them each a new lease on life. *But here's the best news*—unlike pharmaceutical pain relievers, which often cause gastrointestinal upset or damage to internal organs, natural therapies can reduce pain without adverse effects.

WHAT ARE YOU TAKING FOR PAIN?

Most Americans take too many pharmaceutical pain relievers. An estimated 175 million American adults take over-the-counter (OTC) pain relievers regularly. About one-fifth of Americans in their 60s take at least one painkiller for chronic pain on a regular basis.

There has been a lot of news about the life-threatening risks of anti-inflammatory medications such as *rofecoxib* (Vioxx) and *celecoxib* (Celebrex), two pain relievers that had been heavily prescribed by conventional doctors to treat the chronic pain of arthritis and similar conditions. Vioxx was pulled off the market by its manufacturer, Merck, following research that linked it to increased risk of heart attack and stroke. Celebrex is undergoing post-marketing clinical trials to determine whether it poses similar risks and now carries warnings about adverse effects, such as abdominal pain, diarrhea and edema (water retention).

Of course, pain-relieving drugs can be a blessing in the event of injury, severe acute migraines or diseases, such as terminal cancer. A number of years ago, when I had a wisdom tooth extracted, I received a local anesthetic. Afterward, I went to an acupuncturist for pain relief so I wouldn't need any painkillers. For about one hour after the acupuncture, I was fine—but then the pain-relieving endorphins wore off. I tried a few natural remedies, but when the pain became excruciating, I resorted to the OTC pain reliever *acetaminophen* (Tylenol). That did the trick.

But many people use painkillers on a regular basis for several months or even years, which increases the risk of dangerous side effects. For instance, people who rely on acetaminophen increase their risk of developing stomach ulcers, liver disease and kidney disease. If you regularly take Celebrex or an OTC nonsteroidal anti-inflammatory drug (NSAID), such as aspirin or *naproxen* (Aleve), you run the risk of kidney and stomach damage. Regular use of NSAIDs also increases risk of heart attack, according to the FDA.

BETTER RESULTS, FEWER RISKS

Before you take any remedy, it's important for your doctor to identify what is causing your pain. Remember, pain is your body's distress signal that something is being irritated or damaged. Sometimes we protect ourselves by reacting instinctively. If you touch something hot, for example, you eliminate the pain by quickly pulling back your hand.

But what if your back hurts? You may need a pain reliever—but back pain also can be a signal that you're harming your body by bending or sitting the wrong way. You may need to address the underlying cause to prevent further injury. Pain receptors are found in the skin, around bones and joints—even in the walls of arteries. If a muscle is torn, for example, a pain signal is released from fibers in the shredded tissue.

In light of the dangers from prescription and OTC drugs, what safe alternatives are available to you? There are many natural supplements that I recommend.

NATURE'S PAIN RELIEVERS

If you take prescription or OTC pain medication, work with a naturopathic physician, holistic medical doctor or chiropractor who will incorporate natural pain fighters into your treatment regimen. With his/her help, you may be able to reduce your dosage of pain medication (natural pain relievers can be used safely with prescription or OTC painkillers)—or even eliminate the drugs altogether.

Natural pain-fighting supplements are even more effective when combined with physical therapies, such as acupuncture, chiropractic, magnet therapy or osteopathic manipulation (a technique in which an osteopathic physician uses his hands to move a patient's muscles and joints with stretching, gentle pressure and resistance). Physiotherapy (treatment that uses physical agents, such as exercise and massage, to develop, maintain and restore movement and functional ability) also is helpful.

Here are—in no special order—the best natural pain relievers, which can be taken alone or in combination…

•**White willow bark extract** is great for headaches, arthritis, muscle aches and fever. In Europe, doctors prescribe this herbal remedy for back pain, and recent research supports this use. One study conducted in Haifa, Israel, involved 191 patients with chronic low-back pain who took one of two doses of willow bark extract or a placebo daily for four weeks. Researchers found that 39% of patients taking the higher dose of willow bark extract had complete pain relief, compared with only 6% of those who

were taking a placebo. The participants who benefited the most took willow bark extract that contained 240 mg of the compound *salicin*, the active constituent in this herbal remedy. (Aspirin is made from *acetylsalicylic acid*, which has many of the chemical properties of salicin.) However, aspirin can cause gastrointestinal ulceration and other side effects, including kidney damage. Willow bark extract is believed to work by inhibiting naturally occurring enzymes that cause inflammation and pain.

I recommend taking willow bark extract that contains 240 mg of salicin daily. In rare cases, willow bark extract can cause mild stomach upset. Don't take willow bark if you have a history of ulcers, gastritis or kidney disease. It also should not be taken by anyone who is allergic to aspirin. As with aspirin, willow bark extract should never be given to children under age 12 who have a fever—in rare instances, it can cause a fatal disease called Reye's syndrome. Willow bark extract has blood-thinning properties, so avoid it if you take a blood thinner, such as *warfarin* (Coumadin). For low-back pain, you may need to take willow bark extract for a week or more before you get results.

•**Methylsulfonylmethane (MSM)** is a popular nutritional supplement that relieves muscle and joint pain. According to Stanley Jacob, MD, a professor at Oregon Health & Science University who has conducted much of the original research on MSM, this supplement reduces inflammation by improving blood flow. Your cells have receptors that send out pain signals when they're deprived of blood. That's why increased blood flow diminishes pain.

MSM, a natural compound found in green vegetables, fruits and grains, reduces muscle spasms and softens painful scar tissue from previous injuries. A double-blind study of 50 people with osteoarthritis of the knee found that MSM helps relieve arthritis pain.

Start with a daily dose of 3,000 mg to 5,000 mg of MSM. If your pain and/or inflammation doesn't improve within five days, increase the dose up to 8,000 mg daily, taken in several doses throughout the day. If you develop digestive upset or loose stools, reduce the dosage. If you prefer, you can apply MSM cream (per the label instructions) to your skin at the painful area.

This product is available at health-food stores and works well for localized pain. MSM has a mild blood-thinning effect, so check with your doctor if you take a blood thinner.

•**S-adenosylmethionine (SAMe)** is a natural compound found in the body. The supplement is an effective treatment for people who have osteoarthritis accompanied by cartilage degeneration. SAMe's ability to reduce pain, stiffness and swelling is similar to that of NSAIDs such as ibuprofen and naproxen, and the anti-inflammatory medication Celebrex. There's also evidence that SAMe stimulates cartilage repair, which helps prevent bones from rubbing against one another. A 16-week study conducted at the University of California, Irvine, compared two groups of people who were being treated for knee pain caused by osteoarthritis. Some took 1,200 mg of SAMe daily, while others took 200 mg of Celebrex. It took longer for people to get relief from SAMe, but by the second month, SAMe proved to be just as effective as Celebrex.

Most patients with osteoarthritis and fibromyalgia (a disorder characterized by widespread pain in muscles, tendons and ligaments) who take SAMe notice improvement within four to eight weeks. Many studies use 1,200 mg of SAMe daily in divided doses. In my experience, taking 400 mg twice daily works well. It's a good idea to take a multivitamin or 50-mg B-complex supplement daily while you're taking SAMe. The vitamin B-12 and folic acid contained in either supplement help your body metabolize SAMe, which means that the remedy goes to work faster.

•**Kaprex** is effective for mild pain caused by injury or osteoarthritis. It is a blend of hops, rosemary extract and *oleanic acid*, which is derived from olive leaf extract. Rather than blocking the body's pain-causing enzymes, these natural substances inhibit pain-causing chemicals called *prostaglandins*.

In a study sponsored by the Institute for Functional Medicine, the research arm of the supplement manufacturer Metagenics, taking Kaprex for six weeks reduced minor pain by as much as 72%. I recommend taking one 440-mg tablet three times daily. Kaprex is manufactured by Metagenics (800-692-9400, *www.metagenics.com*),

the institute's product branch. The product is sold only in doctors' offices. To find a practitioner in your area who sells Kaprex, call the toll-free number. Kaprex has no known side effects and does not interact with other medications.

•**Proteolytic enzymes,** including *bromelain, trypsin, chymotrypsin, pancreatin, papain* and a range of protein-digesting enzymes derived from the fermentation of fungus, reduce pain and inflammation by improving blood flow. You can find these natural pain fighters at health-food stores in products labeled "proteolytic enzymes." Take as directed on the label. Bromelain, a favorite of athletes, is available on its own. Extracted from pineapple stems, bromelain reduces swelling by breaking down blood clots that can form as a result of trauma and impede circulation. It works well for bruises, sprains and surgical recovery. If you use bromelain, take 500 mg three times daily between meals.

Repair is a high-potency formula of proteolytic enzymes that I often recommend. It is manufactured by Enzymedica (to find a retailer, call 888-918-1118 or go to *www.enzymedica.com*). Take two capsules two to three times daily between meals. Don't take Repair or any proteolytic enzyme formula if you have an active ulcer or gastritis. Any enzyme product can have a mild blood-thinning effect, so check with your doctor if you take a blood thinner.

•**Pain Med** is the homeopathic gel that gave such quick relief to the patients I described at the beginning of this article. It is remarkably effective for relieving the pain of arthritis, muscle soreness and spasms, sprains, strains, stiffness, headaches (especially due to tension) as well as injuries, including bruises.

Pain Med is a combination of nine highly diluted plant and flower materials, including arnica, bryonia, hypericum and ledum. Like other homeopathic remedies, it promotes the body's ability to heal itself. A bean-sized dab works well for anyone who has pain. It should be spread on the skin around the affected area. Following an injury, use it every 15 minutes, for a total of up to four applications. As the pain starts to diminish, apply less often. Do not reapply the gel once the pain is gone. Pain Med does not sting, burn or irritate the skin. It is clear, has no odor, does not stain and dries quickly. Because it has so many uses and works so rapidly, Pain Med is a good first-aid remedy to have on hand. To order, contact the manufacturer, GM International, Inc., at 800-228-9850.

■■■■

Exercise Reduces Pain

Many people know running is an excellent exercise for general health, but they worry that it causes strain on ankles, knees, hips and legs that may lead to arthritis or other medical problems.

Reality: Research shows the reverse is true. Running strengthens joints and bones, and reduces risk of arthritis and skeletal problems.

New study: In 1984, 492 exercisers over age 50 joined a long-term study in which those who exercised (including running) at least two hours a week were matched with non-exercisers. Today, the exercisers report experiencing 25% less musculoskeletal pain than the non-exercisers.

Bonnie Bruce, DrPH, MPH, RD, senior research scientist, division of immunology & rheumatology, Stanford University, Palo Alto, CA.

No More NSAIDS: Safe And Natural Approaches To Headache Relief

Mark V. Wiley, OMD, PhD, practices Oriental medicine at Optimal Acu-Therapy in Philadelphia. Dr. Wiley is author of 10 books including *Outwitting Headaches.* The Lyons Press.

Mark A. Stengler, ND, naturopathic physician in private practice, La Jolla, California...adjunct associate clinical professor at the National College of Natural Medicine, Portland, Oregon...author of 16 books, including *The Natural Physician's Healing Therapies* (Bottom Line Books) and coauthor of *Prescription for Natural Cures* (Wiley)...and author of the *Bottom Line/Natural Healing* newsletter.

Front, back, inside, outside—not all headaches are the same. Of the 45 million Americans who suffer from chronic, recurring headaches, each have symptoms and headache triggers that differ. The most common headaches are tension-type, a catchall term for diffuse, mild to moderate pain over the head. Next come splitting migraines, afflicting 13% of Americans with symptoms such as nausea, pain around the eye, aura and throbbing in the temple area. Makers of *ibuprofen* (Advil, Motrin), *naproxen* (Aleve), among others, love headaches, because these nonsteroidal anti-inflammatory drugs (NSAIDs) are generally the first-line of defense in the multi-billion dollar headache market. However, as we all now know, NSAIDs come with significant risk when used regularly. What are better, safer options?

Mark V. Wiley, OMD, PhD, author of *Outwitting Headaches*, explains about headaches and how to cope with them. He says that it is not so much the particular label you put on a headache that is important, so much as taking a multi-pronged approach to returning your body to its natural, balanced state in which headaches are less likely to occur. After suffering from painful migraines himself for 27 years, he developed the following integrated mind/body approach to preventing headaches of all kinds.

IDENTIFY AND AVOID HEADACHE TRIGGERS

It is not normal—and is even harmful—to have headache after headache. You need to take action to break this destructive pattern, Dr. Wiley stresses. In his view, the key to ending headache pain is proactive avoidance of its causes rather than reactive treatment of symptoms. Major headache triggers include chemicals in food and beverages and even toxins in the body and air, dehydration, lack of exercise, as well as the stress you harbor and the sleep you miss. In order to reestablish what he calls cellular balance, he maintains that one must remove the toxins and stressors that tax the body, or learn to deal with them in new ways. For most people, this means a major lifestyle change.

What you can do: Start by looking at your diet. Eat more fresh and fewer processed foods. Also, try eliminating suspected food triggers one by one from your diet for two to three weeks, and monitor what happens with your headaches. Common culprits include cheeses such as Brie, feta and Gorgonzola, pickles, chocolate, dairy products (goat as well as cow), alcohol (beware the notorious "red wine headache"), processed meats (bologna, pepperoni, salami, hot dogs, etc.), onions, nuts, raisins and products that contain MSG, aspartame and tyramine.

DRINK PLENTY OF WATER

When we become dehydrated, the digestive system, lungs, liver and kidneys can no longer do their jobs as effectively, and this can lead to a headache.

What you can do: Drink plenty of water every day to help your body clear hazardous chemical residues and toxic buildup. Water cleanses the colon, flushes the liver and kidneys and empties the bowels. He recommends two quarts of bottled or filtered water daily, and cautions that caffeinated coffees and teas, carbonated sodas and sugar-filled fruit drinks and diet drinks don't count toward that total.

HOW TO BREAK STRESS PATTERNS

Stress, in its many forms, is a leading cause of headaches, Dr. Wiley observes. So, to control headaches, you must break the pattern of stress. Fortunately, there are many ways to go about doing this.

To reduce tension and tightness in the shoulders, neck and back, which can lead to a headache, see a massage therapist or do daily gentle stretches. A chiropractor can work with misalignments that can occur as a result of constantly tensed muscles…and acupuncture does wonders for keeping energy levels balanced. Dr. Wiley also recommends meditation and deep breathing to quiet the mind and relax the body's nervous systems. Others benefit from tai chi, yoga, qigong or other gentle exercises that stretch the body and soothe the soul. Find whatever stress releases work for you—it could be walking, biking, ice skating or whatever. Taking a multiple B vitamin, at least twice daily, also helps fight the stress reflex. For many people a magnesium supplement may be useful as well.

Dr. Wiley recommends an exercise for progressive relaxation.

What to do: Lie down comfortably with your arms at your sides, and inhale as you tense your toes. Hold for a moment, and then exhale as you consciously relax them. Gradually and slowly continue up the rest of the body, mindfully tensing and relaxing the feet, calves, thighs, etc., as you inhale and exhale.

TAKE A DEEP BREATH

In addition to stress relief, deep breathing ensures a continuous flow of fresh oxygen into the body. Many people breathe shallowly, which means they don't take in enough oxygen.

GET SUFFICIENT SLEEP

Everyone knows we get cranky and headachy when we don't get enough sleep. Your body uses serotonin to regulate sleep, and changes in serotonin levels can cause headaches. To prevent headaches, it's essential to establish deep and constant sleep patterns.

What you can do: Avoid caffeine six hours before bed, as well as overly stimulating activities such as intense exercise. Stop working at the computer at least an hour or more before bed. Instead, establish a regular, soothing routine, such as a warm bath and a good book before retiring. (As long as it is not a thriller type wherein the mind would be overstimulated before retiring, which can cause insomnia.)

Side sleeping is the best sleeping position if done correctly. To begin, side posture should mimic the fetal position. That is, both knees bent, and hands held close to the body. This is a normal and inherent sleeping posture. A pillow should be placed under the head and pulled to the shoulder for optimal neck support. The hands should be parallel and below the eyes. To avoid hip pain while sleeping on your side, place a pillow between your knees to create proper distance between them, thus keeping the hips in proper balance. The legs must be parallel, so the hips remain square and there is no strain on the lower back. If you were not previously a side sleeper, you can retrain your body by falling asleep in that position each night and then readjusting each time you wake up.

ENGAGE IN REGULAR EXERCISE

Exercise reduces stress, releases endorphins, improves blood flow, works through muscle tension and keeps the body firm and supple. Engaging in simple, regular activity such as brisk walks and simple stretches will go a long way toward preventing headaches, as well as improving overall health.

What you can do: Exercise at the same time every day, buddy up with a friend or group for accountability and support, and consider a trainer (if only for a few sessions) to help you establish a safe, personalized program. Even very easy, do-it-yourself stretches are beneficial for headache prevention. For example, try the chin-to-chest. To stretch and release tension in the shoulders and upper back, use your hands to gently push the back of the head forward to the chest. Repeat several times daily.

WHEN HEADACHES STRIKE AND YOU NEED RELIEF

With lifestyle changes, you can hopefully reduce the frequency and severity of your headaches. But, of course, on occasion a headache will arise and you may want immediate relief. Then what?

Mark Stengler, a naturopathic physician in La Jolla, California, suggests a number of options for immediate headache relief…

•**Mother Nature's aspirin.** Take 240 mg of salicin, the active component in white willow bark. This natural pain-relieving component, salicin, is the ingredient from which aspirin is derived. Do not take with NSAIDs.

•**Homeopathic medicines.** Options include Gelsemium sempervirens (Yellow Jessamine) for a dull, heavy pain at the back of the neck…Nux Vomica for headaches from stress…and Pulsatilla pratensis (Pasque Flower) for headaches around the menstrual cycle. For an acute headache, an average dosage consists of a 30C potency, four times daily.

•**A cup of tea.** Take a timeout with a soothing and relaxing cup of peppermint, chamomile or passionflower tea.

•**Herbal rub.** Gently massage peppermint or menthol cream into the temple area.

•**A compress.** Lie down in a darkened room and apply a compress to the painful area. Depending on the headache, some people prefer cold compresses, others warm.

•**Hydrotherapy.** Wrap a few ice cubes in a thin towel and apply to the back of the neck and upper back. At the same time, immerse your feet in a bucket of warm water for 10 minutes.

WHEN A HEADACHE MAY SPELL TROUBLE

While Dr. Wiley's strategy is effective for most headaches, there are times when headache pain requires immediate medical attention. *According to the National Institute of Neurological Disorders and Stroke (NINDS), you should seek prompt medical care if you experience any of the following…*

•**An abrupt, severe headache,** or a sudden headache associated with a stiff neck.

•**A headache associated with fever or convulsions,** or accompanied by confusion or loss of consciousness.

•**A headache following a blow to the head,** or associated with pain in the eye or ear.

•**Persistent headache** in a person who was previously headache-free.

•**Recurring headaches in children.**

YOU'RE IN CHARGE

At the end of the day, no physician and no drug alone can prevent headaches from occurring, Dr. Wiley asserts. You're in charge of your health and quality of life, and have the tools at hand to be headache-free. Using his program, Dr. Wiley believes that you will begin to see positive results within three weeks.

The Instant Migraine Eraser

Marvin D. Mansky, DDS, New York City.
Stephen D. Silberstein, MD, professor of neurology, Jefferson Medical College, and director, Jefferson Headache Center, Thomas Jefferson University, Philadelphia.

Can a mouth device prevent your head from throbbing? Maybe. The US Food and Drug Administration (FDA) has approved the *nociceptive trigeminal inhibition-tension suppression system* (NTI-tss) for the prevention of migraine and tension-type headache pain.

Dr. Marvin Mansky, a Manhattan dentist, admits he "didn't think [the NTI device] was a great idea" at first. But now, after he's used it to treat 350 patients—and wears one himself occasionally—he's a believer.

"It reduces the frequency and intensity of migraines dramatically," Mansky says. "For some, it stops the migraines completely."

THE DEVICE

Made of clear plastic, the inch-wide NTI device fits over two front teeth—usually, but not always, the top teeth.

It stops the teeth in the back from coming together and thus, prevents clenching—which the developer of the device, also a dentist, claims is the cause of many headaches.

According to the proponents of the NTI device, prolonged, intense clenching stresses the temporal muscles that work to open and close the jaw, often triggering migraine and tension headaches.

The first person Mansky fitted with one was a woman who had severe head pain. Immediately, he says, her pain, on a scale of one to 10, went from a 10 to a two, and within two weeks, all pain was gone.

For that relief, many people seem willing to pay roughly $600 for the tiny tooth protector. Mansky and other dentists around the country can mold and custom-fit the device in about an hour. Most people wear it only while sleeping, although some wear a slightly less obtrusive device during the day as well.

ANOTHER OPINION

However, Dr. Stephen D. Silberstein, a neurology professor at Thomas Jefferson University in Philadelphia and past president of the American Headache Society, disputes the connection between clenching and headaches.

"There's scientific evidence to show that only rarely does clenching ever produce headaches," Silberstein says.

Although he is unfamiliar with this particular device, Silberstein says it's "logical" that if it stops people from grinding their teeth, it would relieve any pain that stems from teeth grinding.

Responding to criticism of the device, its inventor—California dentist Dr. James P. Boyd—cites a study from Ireland that showed the jaw-clenching muscles in people who experience migraines were nearly 70% larger, as well as stronger, than the same muscles in people who did not have migraines. Boyd believes that points to a clear link between clenching and migraine headaches.

■ ■ ■ ■

How to Find Help for Your Migraines

Some migraines can be relieved with a dental device. Migraine pain usually stems from the trigeminal nerve, which also is involved in jaw clenching. When worn through the night, the *nociceptive trigeminal inhibition tension suppression system* (NTI-tss) dental mouthpiece reduces the intensity of clenching and frequency of migraines by 77%.

Cost: $600 and up. It may be covered by insurance, depending on your plan.

Find a dentist trained in NTI at *www.headache prevention.com* (click on "NTI Provider List").

Michael Steinberg, DDS, dentist in private practice, New York City.

■ ■ ■ ■

Migraine Relief

Migraines may be relieved when a minor heart defect is repaired. Research has found that when a hole in the heart called a patent foramen ovale was repaired in stroke patients, those who suffered migraines no longer had the headaches. If results of further studies are positive, this treatment may be available for migraine sufferers within several years.

Jonathan Tobis, MD, director of interventional cardiology research, David Geffen School of Medicine, University of California at Los Angeles.

Breakthrough Treatments For Rheumatoid Arthritis

Harry D. Fischer, MD, chief of the division of rheumatology at Beth Israel Medical Center and associate professor of clinical medicine at Albert Einstein College of Medicine, both in New York City, is coauthor of *What to Do When the Doctor Says It's Rheumatoid Arthritis*. Fair Winds Press.

Rheumatoid, or inflammatory, arthritis which affects an estimated two million Americans, typically occurs in the hands and feet, resulting in swelling, pain and joint deformities. It is an autoimmune disease (a malfunction in the immune system that causes the body to attack cells), which affects the synovium (the thin membrane that surrounds the joints). But rheumatoid arthritis isn't just about achy joints. It also can affect other parts of the body.

In severe cases, rheumatoid arthritis can cause dangerous heart inflammation (pericarditis)...

lung inflammation (pleurisy)...and sight-damaging eye inflammation (scleritis).

People with rheumatoid arthritis should be treated early not only to prevent permanent joint deformities but also to guard against the inflammation-related complications associated with the disorder. Most joint destruction caused by rheumatoid arthritis occurs in the first six to 12 months following diagnosis.

At one time, doctors mainly focused on relieving symptoms with pain medication.

Now: Drug therapies are aimed at curbing the progression of this debilitating disorder.

ARE YOU AT RISK?

Rheumatoid arthritis can occur at any age. About 75% of sufferers are women, which suggests that hormones may play a role in the disease. Some researchers believe that a viral or bacterial infection may trigger the disorder in some patients. Smoking and stress are thought to contribute to rheumatoid arthritis—but not cause it.

Rheumatoid arthritis is characterized by joint stiffness and swelling, often in symmetrical patterns on both sides of the body. Fatigue and a low-grade fever also may occur.

NEW TREATMENTS

Rheumatoid arthritis almost always requires drug therapy. Drugs can significantly reduce pain in more than half of patients and offer some relief to the others.

People who have rheumatoid arthritis should seek treatment from a rheumatologist (a medical doctor who specializes in the treatment of disease involving the joints, muscles and associated structures).*

Rheumatologists typically prescribe nonsteroidal anti-inflammatory drugs (NSAIDs), such as *ibuprofen* (Advil) and *naproxen* (Aleve), or the corticosteroid *prednisone*, to control the pain and inflammation associated with the condition.

A majority of rheumatoid arthritis sufferers also are prescribed a medication known as a disease-modifying anti-rheumatic drug (DMARD),

*To find a rheumatologist in your area, contact the American College of Rheumatology (404-633-3777, *www. rheumatology.org*).

which is designed to reduce pain and inflammation and slow progression of the disease.

•**Nonbiological DMARDs** are synthetic medications that have been available for many years. These drugs reduce joint damage. *Nonbiological DMARDs include...*

•*Methotrexate* (Rheumatrex). It suppresses the immune system and minimizes joint destruction. Most patients who take methotrexate experience reduced pain and joint swelling within weeks. It's among the best drugs for slowing the progression of rheumatoid arthritis.

Potential side effects include nausea, diarrhea and, in rare cases, liver scarring and/or inflammation. For this reason, periodic liver function tests are required.

•*Hydroxychloroquine* (Plaquenil). This antimalarial drug suppresses immune attacks on the joints. It's often combined with methotrexate for better results. This drug can cause nausea and decreased appetite and, in rare cases, retinopathy (a disorder of the retina, resulting in vision impairment). If you take this drug, you should have regular eye exams.

•*Sulfasalazine* (Azulfidine). This medication, often used for mild symptoms or in combination with other drugs for severe symptoms, can cause stomach upset, headache and, in some cases, a decrease in disease-fighting white blood cells.

Important: In addition to liver function tests, people who take nonbiological DMARDs require regular blood tests to monitor changes in blood counts.

•**Biological DMARDs** resemble substances that are naturally present in the body. Most patients who take these newer, more specifically targeted drugs experience improvements in a short time—and some even report a complete remission.

Three biologic agents are currently available that inhibit or block a cell protein known as *TNF-alpha*, which produces the inflammatory response.

•*Etanercept* (Enbrel). It is usually injected once or twice weekly.

•*Adalimumab* (Humira). It is given by injection once every two weeks, although it is sometimes given weekly.

•*Infliximab* (Remicade). This drug is taken in combination with methotrexate. It is given by intravenous (IV) infusion in a doctor's office, usually once every eight weeks. At times, it can be given as frequently as every four weeks.

These drugs may increase the risk for infection. They also can reactivate tuberculosis (TB) in patients who were previously exposed—even if they never had symptoms. A TB skin test is required prior to starting therapy.

Drawback: These drugs are extremely expensive, costing about $15,000 to $30,000 annually, depending on the dose.

NEW DRUG CHOICES

Several new drugs don't have the long-term data of the DMARDs, but they are an option for patients who don't respond to DMARDs.

•**Abatacept (Orencia).** Approved by the FDA in December 2005, abatacept inhibits the activity of *T-cells*, immune cells that play a central role in joint inflammation. It may increase risk for infection.

•**Rituximab (Rituxan).** Used for 10 years to treat lymphoma, this drug was recently approved to treat rheumatoid arthritis. It reduces *circulatory B-cells*, a type of white blood cell that has been shown to play a role in the development of rheumatoid arthritis. Rituximab is given by IV infusion every few months. It may increase infection risk.

Rheumatoid Arthritis May Cause Congestive Heart Failure

Paulo Nicola, MD, former research fellow, Mayo Clinic, Rochester, MN. General practioner, epidemiologist, Instituto de Medicina Preventiva School of Medicine, Lisbon University, portugal

William Wilke, MD, rheumatologist, Cleveland Clinic.

John Klippel, MD, rheumatologist, and president and chief executive officer, Arthritis Foundation.

Arthritis & Rheumatism.

A study conducted at the Mayo Clinic confirms that there's a strong link between rheumatoid arthritis (RA) and congestive heart failure, a condition in which the heart progressively loses its ability to pump blood.

Previous studies have shown the same link. However, this latest study "followed patients from the beginning of the disease, describing how the increase in heart-failure risk was present in the early stages and throughout," says Dr. Paulo Nicola, a research fellow at the Mayo Clinic in Rochester, Minnesota.

THE STUDY

Nicola and other Mayo researchers looked at 165 Minnesota residents who had rheumatoid arthritis and found that they were twice as likely to develop heart failure over a 15-year period than 116 residents of similar age and gender who did not have this autoimmune disease.

While the study was not designed to address the reason for an increase in heart failure, "several studies in the general population suggest that inflammation may be a direct cause of heart failure," Nicola notes.

Rheumatoid arthritis is a disease in which the body mistakenly attacks its own healthy tissues, causing painful inflammation and loss of joint function.

The inflammation that attacks the joints in rheumatoid arthritis is believed to foster the process in which fatty plaques in the walls of arteries burst, leading to clots that can block the blood vessels.

IMPLICATIONS

The results of the study showed the need for the aggressive treatment of risk factors for heart disease and stroke, such as high blood pressure and diabetes, in people who have rheumatoid arthritis, Nicola says.

"The clinician should be aware of the higher risk of heart failure and look for the early symptoms of heart failure even in people without cardiovascular risk factors," Nicola advises. "Treatment should be focused not only on the rheumatoid condition, but also on control of those risk factors."

The severity of arthritis in individual patients must also be considered, explains Dr. William Wilke, a rheumatologist at the Cleveland Clinic.

"A more active rheumatoid disease is a sign of greater risk of heart disease," he says.

"If we treat people aggressively with medications, such as methotrexate and tumor necrosis factor, we can significantly reduce the risk of heart disease," Wilke adds.

Nicola's research further stresses the importance of controlling RA quickly.

It also highlights rheumatoid arthritis "as a potentially life-threatening condition," says Dr. John H. Klippel, president and chief executive officer of the Arthritis Foundation.

"We've certainly become aware of cardiovascular disease as a risk factor for premature death in rheumatoid arthritis," Klippel says.

"People with rheumatoid arthritis have a life expectancy of roughly a decade less than those without the disease. At least one study has suggested that if one can get inflammation under control, there is increased survival," he says.

Faster Treatment for Rheumatoid Arthritis

Scott J. Zashin, MD, clinical assistant professor, division of rheumatology, University of Texas Southwestern Medical Center, Dallas, is author of *Arthritis Without Pain: The Miracle of TNF Blockers.* Sarah Allison.

Doctors used to recommend that patients "go slowly" in treating rheumatoid arthritis—start with nonsteroidal anti-inflammatory drugs (NSAIDs), such as *ibuprofen* (Advil, Motrin), followed by stronger drugs, as needed, over the years. This approach doesn't always work. In the past, up to 20% of patients with rheumatoid arthritis were disabled two years after diagnosis, and 50% were disabled 10 years after diagnosis.

Newer approach: Treatment with drugs called Tumor Necrosis Factor (TNF) blockers. People with rheumatoid arthritis have excessive amounts of the cell protein TNF-alpha. It mobilizes white blood cells, which travel to affected joints and cause inflammation, pain, stiffness and, eventually, joint damage. TNF blockers bind to *TNF-alpha*, rendering it inactive and relieving symptoms—sometimes in less than two weeks—and slowing down joint deterioration and deformity.

WHO SHOULD TAKE TNF BLOCKERS?

A newly diagnosed patient usually begins treatment with an NSAID, possibly combined with short-term steroid therapy. If that isn't effective within a few weeks, he/she might be given an antirheumatic drug, such as *hydroxychloroquine* (Plaquenil), *methotrexate* (Rheumatrex) or *sulfasalazine* (Azulfidine). If adequate results still aren't achieved in 12 to 24 weeks, the next step may be a TNF blocker. The FDA has approved three TNF blockers for rheumatoid arthritis. They appear to be equally effective. Your doctor can help you decide which is best for you.

• **Enbrel** (*etanercept*) is taken by self-injection, usually twice a week. It is not yet determined if a new once-a-week formula is as effective.

• **Humira** (*adalimumab*) also is taken by self-injection, usually once every two weeks.

• **Remicade** (*infliximab*) is given by intravenous infusion, usually in a doctor's office, once every six to eight weeks.

THE DOWNSIDE

TNF blockers are extremely expensive, costing at least $15,000 a year. You take them as long as the condition is active—often for life. The cost may be covered by insurance—check with your insurance company.

The drugs may cause itching, pain or swelling at the injection site. *More serious risks…*

• **Infection.** TNF blockers increase the risk of infection because they suppress the immune system. People who develop respiratory or other infections often are advised to discontinue the drugs until the infection is successfully treated. People who have insulin-dependent diabetes (type 1) have a high risk of infection and are not good candidates for TNF-blocker therapy.

Important: A tuberculosis (TB) skin test is required prior to starting a TNF blocker. TB can be activated in patients who have had any prior exposure, even if they never had symptoms of TB.

• **Cancer.** Some types of cancer, such as lymphoma, which affects the lymph system, have been associated with TNF blockers. But recent studies suggest that chronic inflammation, rather than the treatment, is responsible for the higher cancer risk.

The Greatest NEW Arthritis Cure

Gunther Spahn, MD, professor of internal and integrative medicine, Essen-Mitte Clinic, Essen, Germany.

Marc C. Hochberg, MD, MPH, professor of medicine, University of Maryland School of Medicine, Baltimore.

Marie Bonazinga, president, Leeches USA Ltd., Westbury, NY.

Annals of Internal Medicine.

L eech treatment relieves the excruciating knee pain of arthritis more effectively than conventional drug therapy, according to a study by German scientists.

It might seem like a story from many centuries ago, but the news appears to be the result of a carefully controlled, very modern medical trial.

THE STUDY

The study included 51 patients with severe arthritis-related knee pain. The 24 patients who had leeches applied to their joints reported an average reduction in pain from 53.5 to 19.3 on a standard scale used to measure pain. The reduction for those treated with *diclofenac*, a non-steroidal anti-inflammatory drug (NSAID), was much less, from 51.5 to 42.4, according to the report from physicians at the Essen-Mitte Clinic in Essen, Germany.

The pain relief received from leech therapy wore out after one week, but "differences for function, stiffness and total symptoms remained significant for leech therapy until the end of the study," which lasted 30 days, the report says.

There are many possible reasons for the beneficial results, says Dr. Gunther Spahn, a professor of internal and integrative medicine, who was a member of the study team.

"Leeches are a pharmaceutical company, injecting…many substances into the soft tissue," Spahn explains. "These substances may have an anti-swelling, anti-inflammatory and analgesic effect."

TOO EARLY TO PRESCRIBE

Dr. Marc C. Hochberg, professor of medicine at the University of Maryland School of Medicine, says, "I would hope it (leech therapy) would not be done until there are more data demonstrating safety and efficacy, especially in comparison with standard therapy."

A major problem with the study, he says, is that both groups of patients knew which treatment they were getting, which "raises concern about measurement bias," especially since the pain scores were based on patients' judgment.

A "more exciting" aspect of the study is that it might lead to better painkilling drugs based on an analysis of the molecules in leech saliva, Hochberg says.

Leeches had been used for centuries to get "the bad blood out," but the practice fell into disfavor by the 19th century. Today, leeches are used medically in this country, but on a very limited basis, according to Marie Bonazinga, president of Leeches USA Ltd., which sells them commercially.

You can learn about the medicinal leeches from the University of Michigan at *http://animal diversity.ummz.umich.edu.*

An Arthritis Therapy That Works—And No Drugs

Vijay B. Vad, MD, a sports medicine physician and researcher specializing in minimally invasive arthritis therapies at the Hospital for Special Surgery in New York City, is an assistant professor of rehabilitation medicine at Weill Medical College of Cornell University, also in New York City, and the author of *Arthritis Rx.* Gotham.

O nly about half of the people who suffer from osteoarthritis pain get significant relief from aspirin, *ibuprofen* (Advil) or other nonsteroidal anti-inflammatory drugs (NSAIDs)—and each year, an estimated 16,000 Americans die from gastrointestinal bleeding or other side effects from these medications.

New approach: Up to 80% of people who have osteoarthritis can experience significant improvement in pain and mobility—and reduce their need for medication and surgery—when they combine dietary changes, supplement use and the right kind of exercise. This program provides significant relief within six weeks.

DIET R$_x$

Inflammation in the body has been implicated in heart disease, diabetes and kidney disease—and it also contributes to osteoarthritis.

The incidence of arthritis has steadily risen since the early 1900s, when processed foods, such as packaged crackers, cereals, bread and snack foods, began to dominate the American diet—and more people started becoming obese. Most of these foods actually promote inflammation, which can cause joint and cartilage damage and aggravate arthritis pain.

Studies suggest that adding more foods with anti-inflammatory effects to the average American diet—and reducing foods that promote inflammation—can curb inflammation by 20% to 40%.

Best anti-inflammatory foods…

•**Apricots and berries** contain large amounts of antioxidants, chemical compounds that reduce inflammation.

•**Almonds** contain fiber, vitamin E and mono-unsaturated fats, all of which curb inflammation.

Other important steps…

•**Increase omega-3s.** These inflammation-fighting essential fatty acids are mainly found in cold-water fish, such as salmon, tuna, mackerel and sardines. At least three three-ounce servings of fish per week provide adequate levels of omega-3s.

People who don't like fish, or don't eat it often, can take fish-oil supplements or flaxseed oil.

My advice: Take 2 g to 3 g daily of a fish-oil supplement that contains *eicosapentaenoic acid* (EPA) and *docosahexaenoic acid* (DHA)…or one to three tablespoons daily of flaxseed oil.

Caution: Because fish oil taken at this dosage can have a blood-thinning effect, check with your doctor if you take a blood-thinning medication, such as *warfarin* (Coumadin).

•**Reduce omega-6s.** Most Americans get far too many of these inflammation-promoting fatty acids in their diets. A century ago, the ratio of omega-6 to omega-3 fatty acids was about 2:1 for the typical American. Today, it's about 20:1. This imbalance boosts levels of a chemical by-product, arachidonic acid, that triggers inflammation.

My advice: Because omega-6s are found primarily in red meats, commercially processed foods (described earlier) and fast foods, anyone with arthritis should avoid these foods as much as possible.

•**Give up nightshades.** Although the reason is unknown, tomatoes, white potatoes, eggplant and other foods in the nightshade family have been found to increase arthritis pain. It has been estimated that up to 20% of arthritis patients get worse when they eat these foods.

My advice: If you eat these foods and have arthritis pain, give them up completely for six months to see if there's an improvement.

SUPPLEMENT Rx

Americans spend billions of dollars annually on supplements to ease arthritis pain, but many of them are ineffective. *Best choices…*

•**Ginger.** The biochemical structure of this herb (commonly used as a spice) is similar to that of NSAIDs, making it a powerful anti-inflammatory agent. A study of 250 patients at the University of Miami School of Medicine found that ginger, taken twice daily, was as effective as prescription and over-the-counter drugs at controlling arthritis pain.

My advice: Add several teaspoons of fresh ginger to vegetables, salads, etc., daily or take a daily supplement containing 510 mg of ginger.

Caution: Ginger thins the blood, so consult your doctor if you take blood-thinning medication.

•**Glucosamine and chondroitin.** Taken in a combination supplement, such as Cosamine DS, these natural anti-inflammatories inhibit enzymes that break down cartilage and enhance the production of *glycosaminoglycans*, molecules that stimulate cartilage growth.

My advice: Take 1,500 mg of glucosamine and 1,200 mg of chondroitin daily. Or consider using a product called Zingerflex, which contains glucosamine and chondroitin as well as ginger.

Caution: If you have diabetes, consult your doctor before using glucosamine. It can raise blood sugar. Do not take glucosamine if you are allergic to shellfish.

EXERCISE Rx

Osteoarthritis pain weakens muscles, which diminishes joint support. The result is more inflammation and pain, and faster progression of the underlying disease.

Common exercises, including running and traditional forms of yoga, actually can *increase* pain by putting too much pressure on the joints. Patients benefit most from medical exercise, which includes modified versions of common strengthening and stretching exercises, supervised by a physical therapist.*

It's best to perform medical exercises under the guidance of a physical therapist for one to two months before beginning an exercise program at home. *Best choices…*

•**Medical yoga** improves joint strength and flexibility by strengthening muscles and moving joints through their full range of motion. Unlike conventional yoga, it does not require poses that put undue stress on the joints.

•**Pilates** combines yoga-like stretching and breathing control to strengthen the "core" muscles in the lower back and abdomen, as well as muscles in the hips. Like medical yoga, it puts very little pressure on the joints. A move called One-Leg Circle is typical of the Pilates exercises that are recommended for arthritis patients.

To perform One-Leg Circle…

•Lie on your back with your arms at your sides and your palms down. Tighten the abdominal muscles, press the lower back toward the floor and raise your right leg toward the ceiling. Point your toe.

•Rotate your right leg clockwise. Breathe in during half the rotation, then exhale during the other half. Then rotate the leg in the other direction. Repeat the sequence four times. Repeat with your left leg.

•**Healthy breathing.** Most of us take shallow breaths from the upper lungs—a breathing pattern that increases levels of stress hormones and heightens pain.

Better: Deep breathing, which promotes the release of pain-relieving chemicals called endorphins. Patients who breathe deeply for five minutes daily have less pain for several hours afterward. Practice deep breathing in addition to a regular exercise program.

Here's how…

•Sit in a chair with both feet flat on the floor. Close your mouth, place one hand on your stomach and breathe deeply through your nose until you can feel your stomach expanding. Hold your breath for 10 seconds.

*To locate a physical therapist in your area, contact the American Physical Therapy Association at 800-999-2782 or *www.apta.org.*

•Exhale through your nose, contracting your stomach until you've expelled as much air as possible. Hold the "emptiness" for a moment before inhaling again.

•Repeat the cycle for at least five consecutive minutes daily.

Arthritis Treatments That Work Very Well

John D. Clough, MD, retired rheumatologist in the department of rheumatic and immunologic disease at the Cleveland Clinic, is author of *Arthritis: A Cleveland Clinic Guide.* The Cleveland Clinic Press.

More than 21 million Americans suffer from osteoarthritis, a degenerative joint disease. That's the bad news. The good news—we know more about the disease now than ever before, including how to slow its progression.

CAUSES

There are many different forms of arthritis. Osteoarthritis is the most common form. When you have osteoarthritis, the cartilage that cushions the ends of the bones in your joints deteriorates. Over time, the cartilage may wear down completely, leaving bone rubbing on bone.

Osteoarthritis commonly affects the fingers, neck, lower back, hips and knees. *The exact cause of the disease isn't known, but the following are key risk factors…*

•**Advancing age.** People 45 years and older are at greater risk for the disease. In older people, the joint cartilage contains less fluid and may become brittle, which leads to deterioration.

•**Family history.** Heredity plays a role, especially in osteoarthritis of the hands. This particular type of osteoarthritis, which ultimately gives the fingers a gnarled appearance, is more common in women whose mothers also suffered from the condition.

•**Previous injury.** Not every joint injury causes a problem, but if you have had torn cartilage or a disruption of the ligaments in a major joint, then you are more likely to develop a problem in that area.

•**Obesity.** Being overweight puts unnecessary stress on weight-bearing joints—particularly hips and knees.

EARLY WARNINGS

Osteoarthritis often progresses slowly, but there can be early signs…

•**Joint pain during or after use,** after a period of inactivity or during a change in the weather.

•**Swelling and stiffness in a joint,** particularly after using it.

•**Joint instability,** especially noticeable in the knees, which can even take on a knock-kneed or bowlegged appearance as the cartilage deteriorates.

•**Bony lumps.** With osteoarthritis of the hands, these lumps (called Heberden's nodes and Bouchard's nodes) can appear on the middle or end joints of the fingers or at the base of your thumb.

PROTECT YOURSELF

There is no known cure for osteoarthritis, but lifestyle measures can help. *To prevent or slow progression of the disease…*

•**Lose weight.** While it's obvious that running and jumping can be hard on the joints, if you're overweight, even everyday tasks such as walking and climbing stairs can be problematic. Shed pounds, and you can ease the pressure on your weight-bearing joints.

•**Exercise.** Choose low-impact activities, such as walking, cycling and swimming, so that you don't put too much pressure on your joints.

If you've had a knee injury, it also pays to do quadricep-strengthening and hamstring-stretching exercises so that those muscles can better stabilize and operate the knee.

New finding: A study published in *Arthritis & Rheumatism* shows that people with knee osteoarthritis who exercised regularly for as long as 18 months had less disability and were able to walk much greater distances than people who dropped out of the program.

Check with your doctor before beginning a regular exercise program. He/she may recommend working with a physical therapist who can design an exercise program to meet your specific needs.

MEDICATIONS

Osteoarthritis sufferers have a range of treatment options…

•**Oral medications.** The most commonly used drugs for osteoarthritis are pain relievers, such as *acetaminophen* (Tylenol) and *nonsteroidal anti-inflammatory drugs* (NSAIDs), which fall into two categories…

•Nonselective NSAIDs. Drugs such as aspirin, *ibuprofen* (Advil), *diclofenac* (Voltaren) and *naproxen* (Aleve) are commonly used to treat the symptoms caused by inflammation (pain, swelling, redness, etc.), and they work very well for some people. However, long-term use of NSAIDs can cause problems ranging from stomach upset to gastrointestinal bleeding.

•Selective Cox-2 inhibitors. These drugs were originally touted as being less likely to cause gastrointestinal problems than traditional NSAIDs, but most have been pulled from the shelves because of potentially devastating side effects. *Rofecoxib* (Vioxx), for example, was pulled after a study showed that the drug predisposed people to heart attacks. Currently, there's only one Cox-2 inhibitor, *celecoxib* (Celebrex), still in use. Celebrex does not seem to cause the same heart risks as Vioxx.

New finding: In a paper published in the *Journal of the American Medical Association*, three researchers at Harvard University examined 114 clinical trials of Vioxx, Celebrex and other drugs. The researchers found that Celebrex was associated with lower blood pressure readings (unlike Vioxx, which was associated with higher blood pressure readings).

•**Injections.** In cases where a particular joint is acutely inflamed, a physician might opt to inject a corticosteroid preparation into the joint. This can provide rapid relief for up to several months, but long-term use of corticosteroids can be harmful to tissue and bones.

SUPPLEMENTS

Glucosamine and *chondroitin sulfate* play a role in the structure of cartilage and other connective tissue—and you can get them over-the-counter in supplement form. A massive study, known as the "Glucosamine/Chondroitin Arthritis Intervention Trial (GAIT)," coordinated by the University of Utah School of Medicine, found that in patients with moderate to severe pain, glucosamine and chondroitin provided statistically significant pain relief. However, the combination did not work any better than a placebo for the overall group of patients.

Also, a study suggests that glucosamine could potentially slow the progression of osteoarthritis of the knees, although not all studies of this supplement confirm this finding. More research is needed, but the supplements seem safe to use if you choose to try them.

Exception: People who are allergic to shellfish should steer clear of glucosamine, which is made from shellfish.

JOINT REPLACEMENT

In joint-replacement therapy (*arthroplasty*), the damaged joint is removed and replaced with a plastic or metal prosthesis. Joint replacement can be very effective, particularly for the major weight-bearing joints, such as the hips and knees, allowing you an active, pain-free life. Shoulder replacement also is effective, and the technology for smaller, more complex joints, such as the wrist and ankle, is improving.

■ ■ ■ ■

Pain in the Knee?

Acupuncture reduces pain from osteoarthritis of the knee.

Recent finding: Patients who received acupuncture 12 times in eight weeks experienced less pain and more functionality eight weeks after the treatment than those who received "sham" acupuncture or none at all. One year after treatment, both groups fared the same.

Claudia Witt, MD, vice director, project coordinator, complementary medicine, Institute of Social Medicine, Epidemiology, and Health Economics, Berlin, Germany, and leader of a study of 294 people with knee osteoarthritis.

What Does Acupuncture Really Do—And Feel Like?

Marjory Abrams, publisher, newsletters, Boardroom Inc., 281 Tresser Blvd., Stamford, CT 06901.

I started getting weekly acupuncture treatments to relieve chronic pain in my neck and lower back and to ease the acute pain that crops up in different places from one day to the next. I had tried physical therapy and chiropractic but was disappointed with the results.

The acupuncture has been very helpful. Though the pain is not gone, it is much less intense and acute pain subsides much more quickly.

Friends' ears always perk up when I mention acupuncture. Questions abound, especially about how it feels to have needles in my skin. Because I have had such success with the treatments, I wanted to share my experiences so that anyone considering acupuncture will know more about it.*

I go for treatment first thing in the morning. Usually, I lie on my back. The needles are inserted into the tops of my hands around my thumb and forefinger, my shins, the tops of my feet and at various spots on my head. Sometimes the needles hurt a bit when they go in, but that pain passes immediately. Then, as long as I don't move, I don't feel them at all. (I've never actually seen the needles inserted—I keep my eyes closed.)

Occasionally I feel a sort of oozy warmth when the needles are inserted—especially at the top of my head. Though wide awake when I arrive for treatment, I fall into a deep sleep while the needles are in.

Acupuncture needles are much thinner than the ones used for vaccinations. Though the needle size depends on where the needles are placed, my acupuncturist—Joan-Ellen Macredis, ND, LAc, a licensed acupuncturist and naturopathic physician in Stamford, Connecticut—says that most often they are only one or one-and-a-half inches long and no wider than a cat's whisker. The FDA requires that they be sterile, nontoxic and used only once and then safely discarded.

Each needle goes into a tubelike holder. The acupuncturist then taps the top of the holder to insert the needle about one-quarter inch into

*The premise of acupuncture: Energy, or *qi* (pronounced "chee"), runs through the body in channels, or meridians. When this energy is disturbed (either too much flow, too little or stuck), symptoms appear on an emotional and/or physical level. By inserting needles in acupuncture points, which lie along the meridians, the energy is balanced and the body begins to heal.

the skin. The holder is removed and the needle is left in place for about 20 minutes. In people with weaker energy, such as older people, Dr. Macredis uses fewer and finer needles and leaves them in for a shorter period of time.

Coworkers are surprised to see that I often leave the acupuncturist with several needles still in the top of my head and keep them in until I get home. My jaw dropped the first time Dr. Macredis suggested it, but it doesn't bother me now, because it really does relieve my pain. The results are literally instantaneous as soon as these needles are in. To remove them, I simply pull them out and discard them in a special container.

Dr. Macredis notes that acupuncture can be beneficial for many conditions, including asthma, carpal tunnel syndrome, headaches, osteoarthritis, tennis elbow and poststroke recovery. Not all insurers cover acupuncture, but many do (mine does). Be sure to ask. But don't be afraid to try acupuncture if insurance doesn't cover it. Some practitioners offer fees on a sliding scale.

To find a practitioner: Ask for referrals from physicians or friends (I found Dr. Macredis through colleagues at work).

The American Academy of Medical Acupuncture (*www.medicalacupuncture.org*) maintains a database of MDs who are certified to practice acupuncture—or you can use the database at the Web site of the American Academy of Acupuncture and Oriental Medicine (*www.aaaom.edu*) to find a licensed acupuncturist in your area.

■ ■ ■ ■

Rosehips for Arthritis

The anti-inflammatory properties of rosehips, found in wild dog rose (*Rose canina*), may help alleviate the pain and stiffness of arthritic joints. Rosehips are available at some health-food stores.

Best: Take 5 grams of rosehips daily.

Kaj Winther, MD, DMSc, head of department of clinical biochemistry, University Hospital Gentofte, Hellerup, Denmark, and leader of a study of 94 osteoarthritis patients, published in *Scandinavian Journal of Rheumatology.*

Do Arthritis Supplements Really Help?

Mark A. Stengler, ND, naturopathic physician in private practice, La Jolla, CA...adjunct associate clinical professor at the National College of Natural Medicine, Portland, OR...author of 16 books, including *The Natural Physician's Healing Therapies* (Bottom Line Books) and coauthor of *Prescription for Natural Cures* (Wiley)...and author of the *Bottom Line/Natural Healing* newsletter.

Many patients have asked me about the well-publicized Glucosamine/Chondroitin Arthritis Intervention Trial. This six-month, multicenter clinical trial tested glucosamine and chondroitin as a treatment for knee osteoarthritis.

In the study, 1,583 participants (average age 59) with knee osteoarthritis pain were randomly assigned to one of five treatment groups for 24 weeks...

Glucosamine alone (1,500 mg per day)...chondroitin alone (1,200 mg)...glucosamine and chondroitin (1,500 mg and 1,200 mg, respectively) ...200 mg of the prescription anti-inflammatory drug *celecoxib* (Celebrex)...or a placebo.

THE RESULTS

Researchers concluded that "glucosamine and chondroitin sulfate alone or in combination did not reduce pain effectively in the overall group of patients with osteoarthritis of the knee." As a result, many media outlets reported that glucosamine and chondroitin were ineffective for the treatment of osteoarthritis. While the combination wasn't effective for mild sufferers in the study, it was more effective than Celebrex for participants with moderate to severe osteoarthritis pain of the knees. Yet most of the mainstream media did not report this finding. Interestingly, for the group of patients with moderate to severe pain, Celebrex was only mildly more effective than the placebo.

My view: If you are being helped by these supplements, keep taking them. It's worthwhile to try them before taking Celebrex or a similar drug, since glucosamine and chondroitin have a much lower risk of side effects, such as digestive upset. Even if you have only mild pain, these supplements can help prevent cartilage breakdown so that the problem does not worsen.

For high-quality formulas, use brands sold at health-food stores.

Caution: Glucosamine and chondroitin may increase insulin resistance, so people with diabetes should monitor blood sugar levels carefully. The combination supplement should not be used by people with shellfish allergies.

■ ■ ■ ■

Cancer Pain Relief

Cancer patients who ordinarily used oral morphine for "breakthrough" pain (sudden moderate to severe pain that is not controlled by regular drug therapy) experienced 33% greater relief within 15 minutes of dissolving a lozenge containing the painkiller *fentanyl* (Actiq) in their mouths.

Theory: The fentanyl lozenge dissolves quickly, allowing it to pass into the central nervous system faster than oral pain medication, such as morphine.

Giovambattista Zeppetella, MD, medical director, St. Clare Hospice, Hastingwood, England. His study of 393 cancer patients was published in *The Cochrane Library*, John Wiley & Sons, 111 River St., Hoboken, NJ.

Fibromyalgia: Researchers Prove Pain Is Real

Thorsten Giesecke, MD, anesthesiologist and former research fellow, Cologne, Germany, at the University of Michigan, Ann Arbor.

Bruce Naliboff, PhD, clinical professor, David Geffen School of Medicine, University of California, Los Angeles (UCLA).

Arthritis & Rheumatism.

Fibromyalgia, a chronic pain illness, affects up to six million Americans, primarily women of childbearing age, according to the American College of Rheumatology.

Some experts believe that fibromyalgia patients who are also prone to emotional problems, such as depression and anxiety, are more likely to experience greater physical pain in areas called "tender points."

Common tender points are the front of the knees, the elbows, the hip joints, the neck and the spine. Some physicians also think that patients with emotional issues have more sleep disturbances, morning stiffness, irritable bowel syndrome and anxiety than patients with a more positive outlook.

But a recent study may change their ideas.

THE STUDY

Dr. Thorsten Giesecke, a former research fellow at the University of Michigan, and his colleagues evaluated 85 female and 12 male fibromyalgia patients. The patients answered a series of questions about their coping strategies and personality traits—particularly about their emotional well-being. They also were tested for sensitivity to pressure and pain.

The patients fell into three subgroups that refuted conventional wisdom.

The first subgroup consisted of 50 patients who had moderate levels of anxiety and depression. They also felt that they had moderate control over their pain, and they experienced low to moderate levels of pain.

The second group included 31 patients with high levels of anxiety and depression. They felt that they had the least control over their pain, and they had high levels of tenderness.

The third group, with 16 patients, reported the lowest levels of anxiety and depression and the highest control over their pain. Yet the testing showed that they experienced the highest levels of physical pain.

Some patients have extreme pain but no psychological problems, Giesecke explains, while others have moderate pain and fairly positive moods.

TAILORING TREATMENT

The findings may help tailor treatments to specific individuals. For example, antidepressants might not work well on group three, whose members were not depressed. They might benefit from exercise therapy instead, Giesecke says.

"It's easy to say it's all in their head," says Bruce Naliboff, a clinical professor at the UCLA David Geffen School of Medicine. The study will help prove that's not so, he adds.

To learn about the symptoms of fibromyalgia and how to manage this condition, visit *http://familydoctor.org*.

Yoga for Everyone

Susan Winter Ward, a Pagosa Springs, Colorado-based yoga instructor and the author of *Yoga for the Young at Heart: Accessible Yoga for Every Body.* New World Library.

Many people assume that they could never practice yoga because it requires so much flexibility. The truth is, inflexibility is actually one of the best reasons to do yoga.

Traditional yoga can be more challenging for people who suffer joint stiffness due to osteoarthritis or inactivity—the stretching as well as getting up and down from the floor, where some yoga poses are performed, can be difficult. But there is an alternative.

I've created a series of yoga exercises designed to be performed while seated in a chair.* These poses are accessible for people with physical handicaps, such as multiple sclerosis or muscular dystrophy. Chair yoga also can be done at your desk, or while traveling on a plane or a train.

The following series of exercises require little space and no equipment other than a firm, steady chair. When combined with cardiovascular exercise, such as brisk walking, and strength training, such as weight-lifting, chair yoga helps create a well-balanced exercise program. All inhalations and exhalations for these exercises should be done through the nose for a count of five.

For maximum benefits, practice the following exercises daily...

•**Breathing for relaxation.** Deep breathing brings extra oxygen into the lungs and bloodstream, both relaxing and energizing the body, and calming the mind.

What to do: Sit up straight. Place your right hand over your heart and your left hand over your stomach. Close your eyes and breathe in deeply. Exhale, then breathe in again, while focusing on lifting your chest and expanding your ribs. Inhale, then exhale while maintaining a straight spine. Repeat five to 10 times.

•**Butterfly curls.** These stretch the back of the neck, the spine, rib cage and arms.

What to do: Sitting toward the front of your chair, straighten your back and clasp your hands

*Check with your doctor before beginning this or any exercise program.

behind your head. Breathe in deeply and lengthen your spine while pulling your elbows back

and letting your rib cage expand. Keeping your back flat, exhale and curl your head forward, pulling your elbows gently toward each other. Take a few deep breaths, lifting your chest toward your chin as you inhale and dropping your chin toward your chest as you exhale. Repeat five times.

•**Windmill.** This relaxes the shoulders, neck and arms.

What to do: Sitting up straight, inhale as you raise your right arm overhead. Bend your

right elbow so that it points upward and your fingers touch your upper spine or neck. Exhale, then inhale again.

Next, stretch your left arm out to your left side and bend your elbow, bringing the back of your left hand to

your spine. Exhale, pressing your hands gently toward each other while keeping your back and shoulder blades flat. Inhale, lifting your chest and gently pressing your hands toward each other as you exhale. If you like, you can hold a belt or strap between your hands. Repeat three to five times.

•**Expand your heart.** This pose relaxes the back, shoulders and chest, and aids breathing by creating space in the rib cage for the lungs to expand.

What to do: Sitting toward the front of your chair, clasp your hands behind you at the waist.

With your elbows bent, press your shoulder blades together, lifting your chest. Inhale, drawing your elbows toward each other. Lengthen your spine as you inhale and lift your ribs away from your hips. Exhale as you press your knuckles down toward the chair

seat. Repeat three to five times, taking long, deep breaths.

•**Seated push-ups.** This exercise strengthens the arms, back and shoulders.

What to do: Sit near the front of your chair and put your hands on the front corners of the seat. Inhaling deeply, with your elbows in toward your sides, straighten your elbows and lift yourself off the seat of the chair. Keep your legs and shoulders relaxed and avoid pushing with your feet. Exhale as you slowly lower yourself. Repeat at least five times.

•**Spinal twist.** This stretches the rib cage and spine and eases back strain. It also aids digestion by massaging the stomach and intestines.

What to do: Sitting up straight, cross your right leg over your left and place your left hand on the inside of your left knee. Inhale deeply as you twist to the right, pulling your right elbow and shoulder around toward the back of the chair. Keeping your back straight, take three to five deep breaths as you hold the pose. Lengthen your spine by lifting through the top of your head with each inhalation, and twist a bit farther to the right with each exhalation. Return to center, then repeat on the opposite side.

•**Cervical stretch.** This pose stretches and relaxes the arms, wrists, hands, shoulders, back and chest. It counteracts the effects of typing and eases headaches due to shoulder tension.

What to do: Sitting near the front of your chair, inhale deeply and raise your arms overhead. Interlace your fingers, palms facing the ceiling. Exhale, pressing through the heels of your hands. Inhale again, tucking your chin in toward your throat. While holding this position, exhale and let your chin drop toward your chest. Breathe deeply three to five times, feeling the stretch down to your shoulder blades with each exhalation.

•**Hamstring stretch.** This stretches the backs of the thighs, releases low back tension, strengthens the back and abdomen, and improves digestion.

What to do: Sitting toward the front of your chair, place both feet flat on the floor. While keeping your back flat and chest lifted, clasp your left knee just below the kneecap with both hands and pull your thigh toward your rib cage. Hold for three to five breaths. Switch legs and repeat.

Illustrations by Shawn Banner.

■ ■ ■ ■

Quick Relief for Jaw Pain

Waking up with a sore jaw or a headache may indicate that you grind your teeth in your sleep. This condition, called *bruxism*, is primarily caused by stress. Symptoms include tooth sensitivity to hot and cold food and drinks as well as pain while chewing. Sinus congestion can cause severe pressure on dental roots, leading sufferers to grind their teeth or clench the jaw. Misaligned dental work can also trigger bruxism, leading to unconscious grinding. This grinding causes noticeable noise in only 30% of patients.

Your dentist can diagnose the problem by feeling muscle tension in the jaw and face… observing if teeth are worn or cracked…and viewing X-rays. Treatments include reshaping and polishing of tooth enamel to improve tooth alignment and/or the use of a mouth guard during periods of excessive grinding.

To ease jaw pain: Place your palm or fist under your chin and push up while barely opening your jaw against resistance. Hold for one to two seconds. Repeat 30 times, twice a day. This will stretch and strengthen jaw muscles, which helps alleviate pain.

Rob E. Sable, DDS, a restorative dentist in private practice in Alpharetta, Georgia.

Long-Lasting Relief for Neck Pain

Gerard P. Varlotta, DO, associate professor of rehabilitation medicine and director of sports rehabilitation at the Rusk Institute of Rehabilitation Medicine at New York University Medical Center in New York City.

There are very few upper-body movements that don't require use of the neck. That's why neck injury is one of the most common problems treated by orthopedists and physiatrists (doctors who specialize in rehabilitation medicine).

Most neck injuries are due to "onetime overload"—for example, putting too much strain on the neck by not keeping it in a neutral position while lifting a heavy object. Neck pain also can be caused by strain due to repetitive motions, such as twisting and turning the neck while exercising…muscle tension from stress…arthritic changes…or whiplash. Also, neck pain can be "referred" pain stemming from shoulder or elbow injuries or gallbladder disease.

Good news: Since neck pain usually includes muscle inflammation, it responds well to self-care. Even chronic pain usually can be relieved—and prevented—with simple exercises. Surgery is recommended in rare cases, such as those in which neck pain is accompanied by radiating arm pain and compression of a nerve.

REASONS FOR NECK PAIN

Severe neck pain usually comes on suddenly, but often there's an underlying irritation and/or weakness in the muscles. In most cases, the sufferer reports that the neck feels a little weak or sore, then suddenly worsens—after turning the head abruptly, for example.

When to get help: Neck pain that doesn't begin improving within 48 hours or is accompanied by neurological symptoms—tingling in the arms, hand weakness, loss of muscle strength, etc.—indicates a more serious problem. *Examples…*

•**Disk damage.** A herniated disk (the gelatinous material inside a disk pushes through the outer coating and presses against nearby nerves) can be excruciatingly painful and, in severe cases, cause permanent spinal cord damage.

Red flag: A loss of bowel and/or bladder control or any of the above neurological symptoms. See a doctor immediately.

•**Arthritic changes.** The joints in the neck can deteriorate or stiffen due to osteoarthritis or rheumatoid arthritis.

•**Whiplash.** Injury results when the head is jerked violently forward and backward, as can occur during a car accident.

The above problems are diagnosed during a physical exam, often in conjunction with an X-ray and/or magnetic resonance imaging (MRI) scan. Treatment involves controlling inflammation and restoring strength and range of motion.

RAPID PAIN RELIEF

In the absence of neurological symptoms, arthritis or traumatic injury, patients can assume that neck pain is probably due to muscle strain. *To reduce muscle inflammation and pain…*

•**Apply ice immediately.** It's the quickest way to reduce inflammation as well as pain—but only if you apply it within the first 24 to 48 hours. Hold a cold pack or ice cubes wrapped in a towel or washcloth to the painful area for 20 minutes once an hour throughout the day.

Important: Do not apply heat during the first two days after an injury. It relieves stiffness but can increase inflammation and pain.

•**Take the proper anti-inflammatory drug.** Over-the-counter *ibuprofen* (Advil) and *naproxen* (Aleve) are equally effective at relieving muscle pain and inflammation.

Main difference: Ibuprofen is a relatively short-acting drug—generally lasting four to six hours. Naproxen lasts eight to 12 hours. *Acetaminophen* (Tylenol) may help, but it mainly eases pain, not inflammation.

Caution: Ibuprofen and naproxen can cause stomach upset…acetaminophen can cause liver damage when combined with alcohol. Don't take any of these drugs for more than a week without consulting your doctor.

•**Stretch muscles often.** Stretching lengthens muscle fibers and reduces the tension caused by neck-related ergonomic problems, such as how you sit at a computer or hold a telephone. *Helpful…*

While standing or sitting, slowly lower your ear toward your shoulder. Stop when pain significantly increases. Hold the stretch for a few seconds, then relax. Switch to the other side. Repeat eight to 12 times, five times a day.

Bring your chin toward your shoulder, following the directions above.

Although chiropractic treatment can help alleviate pain that emanates from the neck joints, its effects are not long-lasting. Acupuncture also may be helpful but needs to be repeated until the pain dissipates.

LONG-TERM NECK CARE

Most people with chronic neck pain need to perform strengthening exercises (consult your doctor first) and change their posture.

Important: Don't sleep on your stomach—and don't raise your head too high with pillows. Both put excessive pressure on the neck.

Better: Sleep on your side with your head level—propped just high enough to keep your nose in line with your navel. The pillow (when compressed) should be just thick enough to support the side of your head without elevating it.

If you spend a great deal of time on the telephone, use a headset. Cradling a phone between the neck and shoulder is one of the most common causes of neck pain. Choose a headset that is comfortable for you. Good ones, such as those made by Plantronics, are available for $20 to $100 and up at electronics stores.

If you spend time at a desk, adjust your workstation. The center of a standard computer monitor should be directly at eye level (a bit lower if it's a large monitor)...your knees should be slightly lower than your hips...and use your chair's armrests when possible to avoid hunching forward.

Strengthen your neck and shoulders—they share some of the same muscles. Keeping these muscles strong makes them more flexible and less prone to injury. Perform eight to 12 repetitions of each of the following exercises three times, two to three days a week. Once you can do 12 repetitions easily, gradually increase the weight lifted.

•**Shrugs.** While standing straight with your arms down at your sides, hold a two-pound dumbbell (or a household object, such as a can of soup) in each hand. With palms facing your thighs, shrug your shoulders as high as possible, keeping your head straight. Hold for five seconds, then return to the starting position.

•**Flies.** Lie on your back on an exercise bench, with a two-pound dumbbell in each hand. Hold your hands out to the sides so that the weights are about even with your chest. Keeping your back straight, raise your arms over your chest in a semicircular motion until the weights touch in the middle over your chest. Lower them back to chest level in the same semicircular motion.

•**Side deltoid raise.** While standing straight with your arms down at your sides, hold a two-pound dumbbell or other weight in each hand, with your palms facing your thighs. Keeping your elbows slightly bent, raise your arms up and out to your sides until they're shoulder level (your palms will be facing the floor in this position). Hold for five seconds, then slowly lower the weights.

Illustrations by Shawn Banner.

Simple Relief for Neck Stiffness

Many patients ask me to recommend a natural treatment for neck stiffness. Supplements that work well include homeopathic *Rhus toxicodendron*—take two pellets of a 30C potency twice daily for two weeks. If there is improvement, continue taking it for another month.

Another option is the supplement *methylsulfonylmethane* (MSM). It is a natural compound that contains the mineral sulfur, which acts as an anti-inflammatory. MSM works better than over-the-counter anti-inflammatories, such as aspirin and ibuprofen, because it has an antispasm effect and improves circulation. Start with 3,000 mg of MSM and gradually increase to 5,000 mg, if necessary. You can take MSM indefinitely—the only negative side effect is possible digestive upset.

Another weapon is fish oil (1,000 mg daily of combined EPA-DHA). In a study published in *Surgical Neurology*, fish oil was given to patients with chronic neck and low-back pain. After an average of 75 days, 60% of subjects reported significant improvement, including reduction in pain and stiffness, and 59% were able to stop taking other pain medicine. Don't take fish oil if you use a blood-thinning medication, such as *warfarin* (Coumadin).

Soft tissue work by a massage therapist also can help relieve neck stiffness, as can acupuncture.

Mark A. Stengler, ND, naturopathic physician in private practice, La Jolla, CA...adjunct associate clinical professor at the National College of Natural Medicine, Portland, OR...author of 16 books, including *The Natural Physician's Healing Therapies* (Bottom Line Books) and coauthor of *Prescription for Natural Cures* (Wiley)...and author of the *Bottom Line/Natural Healing* newsletter.

■ ■ ■ ■

Better on Its Own

Sciatica pain often gets better on its own. There is no evidence that spinal decompression does any good. Anti-inflammatory drugs, cortisone shots and exercises that strengthen abdominal and back muscles may speed healing.

Also useful: Place a pillow behind your lower back while driving. Place a pillow under your knees when sleeping on your back—or between your knees when you sleep on your side.

David Borenstein, MD, is medical director, Spine and Sports Rehabilitation Center, Rehabilitation Institute of Chicago, and associate professor of clinical physical medicine and rehabilitation, Northwestern University Medical School, Chicago.

Relieve the Pain of a Pinched Nerve

David Borenstein, MD, clinical professor of medicine at George Washington University Medical Center, Washington, DC, is the author of *Back In Control: Your Complete Prescription for Preventing, Treating, and Eliminating Back Pain from Your Life.* M. Evans and Company.

Nerve pain is one of the worst kinds of pain. People with a pinched nerve (sometimes called a "stinger") may experience sharp, burning pain for anywhere from a few seconds to a few days or longer. The pain usually comes on suddenly and may disappear just as fast—only to return. There also might be temporary numbness or slight weakness.

A nerve gets "pinched" when surrounding tissue presses against it and causes inflammation of the nerve. Causes include repetitive motions, traumatic injuries and joint diseases, such as rheumatoid arthritis. The most common pinched nerves occur in the wrist, elbow, shoulder and foot. Nerve roots in the spinal canal also are vulnerable.

Red flag: Nerve pain that is accompanied by significant weakness or that doesn't improve within a few days needs to be checked by a physician. Excessive pressure on—or inflammation of—a nerve can result in loss of function and permanent damage.

SELF-HELP

To reduce the pain...

•**Stop repetitive movements.** A pinched nerve that's caused by performing the same movements over and over again usually will improve once the offending activity—leaning with your elbows on a counter, typing, working a cash register, etc.—is stopped for a few days. Avoiding these activities is also the best way to prevent a pinched nerve.

However, patients with job-related pain can't always afford to take time off. In that case, they should attempt to change their body position when doing the activity.

Example: Raising the back of a computer keyboard (most are adjustable) will enlarge the carpal tunnel in the wrist and reduce pressure on the nerve.

•**Ice the area.** Applying cold in the first 24 to 48 hours after nerve pain starts can reduce tissue swelling and nerve pressure. Use a cold pack or ice cubes wrapped in a towel. Hold against the affected area for about 15 minutes. Repeat every hour or two for a day or two.

•**Take an anti-inflammatory.** Over-the-counter analgesics that have anti-inflammatory properties, such as aspirin, *ibuprofen* and naproxen, reduce the body's production of chemicals that cause inflammation and swelling. Don't use *acetaminophen.* It will reduce pain but has little effect on inflammation.

•**Wear looser clothes.** It's fairly common for women to experience a pinched nerve in the outer thigh (*meralgia paresthetica*) from too-tight jeans or skirts...or foot pain (*tarsal tunnel syndrome*) from tight shoes.

MEDICAL CARE

Nerve pain that's severe or keeps coming back—or that's accompanied by other symptoms, such as a loss of bowel or bladder control—requires immediate medical care. Customized splints or braces can be used to minimize pressure on a nerve from repetitive movements. *Also helpful...*

•**An injection of a corticosteroid** into the painful area—or a short course of oral steroid therapy. These drugs reduce inflammation very quickly and provide short-term relief. The pain may disappear after a single treatment, but most patients need repeated courses. Sometimes, if pain is not relieved, acupuncture may be used in addition to medication and physical therapy.

•**Surgery is recommended** when the pain is severe or keeps coming back. The procedures vary depending on the part of the body affected.

■■■■

Better Back Pain Relief

For 12 weeks, adults with persistent lower-back pain either took gentle yoga classes, performed conventional aerobic and strengthening exercises or followed advice from a back pain self-help book as part of a recent study.

Result: After 12 weeks, the participants who performed the gentle yoga poses showed the most improvement in back-related dysfunction, such as difficulty walking up stairs.

Caution: Vigorous styles of yoga could worsen chronic back pain.

To find a yoga instructor experienced in helping people with back pain, consult the International Association of Yoga Therapists, 928-541-0004, *www.iayt.org.*

Karen J. Sherman, PhD, MPH, affiliate assistant professor, epidemiology, and senior investigator, Group Health Cooperative, Center for Health Studies, University of Washington School of Public Health and Community Medicine, Seattle.

A Simple 5-Step Plan to Get Rid of Back Pain… For Good

Miriam E. Nelson, PhD, associate professor at the Friedman School of Nutrition Science and Policy and director of the John Hancock Center for Physical Activity and Nutrition at Tufts University, Boston, is a fellow of the American College of Sports Medicine and author, with Lawrence Lindner, of *Strong Women, Strong Backs.* Putnam.

As many as 90% of all adults suffer back pain at some point in their lives. Back pain—lower-back pain, in particular—ranks fifth among the most frequent reasons for hospitalizations.

Worse for women: Their musculoskeletal systems—ligaments, vertebrae, spinal disks, etc.—are more delicate than men's and more vulnerable to injury. Women also tend to be less active, on average, than men, and a sedentary lifestyle is a common cause of back pain.

Most back problems are caused by prolonged sitting or by lifting heavy objects the wrong way, but other factors contribute to back pain, including excess body weight, stress and depression. Even smoking is a factor for reasons that aren't exactly clear.

Simple lifestyle measures—maintaining a healthy weight, not smoking and controlling stress and depression—can prevent many cases of back pain. Most important, though, are exercises that strengthen muscles in the back, chest, abdomen, hips and sides. These are the core muscles—the scaffolding that supports the spine and enables the back to flex and twist without injury. Strengthening these muscles can relieve pain and also prevent it.

A FIVE-STEP PLAN

The following workout, which takes no more than 20 minutes, targets all of the core muscles. It can be done three to five times weekly (unlike most strength-training workouts, which should be done no more than three times a week, because muscles need time to recover between sessions). These exercises can be done more often because the intensity is lower—and they're less likely than traditional workouts to cause back pain or other injuries.

For each of the following exercises…

•**Complete 10 repetitions,** rest for one minute, then complete another 10 reps. If you can complete only five or six reps, the intensity is too high and you should do only what you can comfortably manage.

•**Work up to an advanced progression.** This is a way to increase the exercise intensity by making the movements more difficult.

•**Always warm up**—by taking a brisk walk around the block or stepping quickly in place—for five minutes before doing the exercises.

STEP 1: ABDOMINALS

Most people's abdominal muscles are weaker than they should be. Strengthening the abdominals is among the best ways to prevent back pain.

Starting position: Lie on your back on the floor with your knees bent and the soles of your  feet flat on the floor. Lightly rest your hands on the lower part of the stomach.

The movement: Contract the abdominal muscles until you feel the small of the back pushing toward the floor. Imagine that you're pulling your belly button downward. Hold the "tense" position for three seconds, then relax.

Progression: Do almost the same exercise as above, with this difference. While the abdominal muscles are tight, raise the still-bent right leg a few inches off the floor and hold it up for three seconds, then place that leg down and raise the left leg for three seconds. The entire move will take 10 to 12 seconds.

STEP 2: CHEST MUSCLES

Along with abdominal exercises, chest workouts protect the back by strengthening the "front" of the core muscle groups.

Starting position: Stand facing a wall or a counter, about an arm's length away, with your feet hip-width apart and knees slightly bent. Put your palms on the wall (or lightly hold the edge of the counter).

The movement: Holding your body straight, bend at the elbows until you are leaning forward toward the wall or counter about 30 degrees. Pause in this position for a moment, then push with your arms until you're back in the starting position.

Progression: Work the same muscles with more intensity with a modified push-up. Lie facedown on the floor, with your palms directly next to your shoulders, elbows bent.

Keeping your knees on the floor, slowly push up only your chest. Keep your trunk in a straight line from your head to your knees. Push up until your shoulders are over your hands, but don't lock the elbows. Pause for a moment, then lower back down until your nose is about four inches from the floor. Keep your trunk in a straight line throughout the movements.

STEP 3: MIDBACK

Many exercises target the upper/lower back, but relatively few target the middle back—a common area for problems.

Starting position: Lie facedown on an exercise mat or carpet, with your arms straight out to the sides, perpendicular to the body.

The movement: Contract your shoulder blades to lift the arms up and slightly back. Hold the arms in the lifted position, and make four figure eights with the hands. Then lower your arms to the starting position.

Progression: Make the figure eights with the thumbs down or up…or while holding a balled-up sock in each hand…or with the little finger up or down. Varying the movement works different parts of the muscles.

STEP 4: UPPER BACK

This exercise increases shoulder strength as well as back strength.

Starting position: Tie a knot in the middle of an elastic exercise band (available at sporting-goods stores for $2 to $3). Place the knot over the top of a door, and then close the door to anchor the band in place. The two ends should be hanging down on the same side of the door. Sit in a chair facing the door, with your toes against the door. Hold one end of the band in each hand.

The movement: Slowly pull your hands down and in toward your chest. Keep your elbows pointed down and close to your body. Pause for a moment, then slowly let your arms extend back to the starting position.

Progression: When the exercise starts feeling easy, change to a higher-resistance band.

STEP 5: LOWER BACK

This is the area that gives most people problems.

Starting position: Lie facedown on an exercise mat or carpet. Reach your right hand in front of you, palm down. The left arm should be down alongside your body, with the palm up.

The movement: Slowly raise your right arm, chest and left leg about five inches off the floor. Keep your face down, so your spine is in a straight line. Keep your right leg and left hand on the ground. Pause for a moment, then return to the starting position.

Reverse the movement, raising your left arm, chest and right leg, and keeping the left leg and right hand on the floor.

Progression: Kneel on all fours. Raise your right arm straight in front of you while simultaneously raising the left leg straight behind.

Keep the abdominal muscles contracted. Pause, return to the starting position. Then reverse the movement.

OPTIONAL EXERCISE:
THIGHS, HIPS AND MORE

This optional exercise is a complex move that targets the upper legs as well as the trunk. It is good for improving stability and balance. The exercise requires the use of a stability ball, available at sporting-goods stores for about $20.

Starting position: Stand with your back to a wall, with the stability ball positioned between your back and the wall. Lean back against the ball, with your feet a bit more than hip-width apart. Hold your arms straight in front of you or crossed over your chest.

The movement: While keeping light pressure on the ball with your lower back, bend at the knees and slowly squat down—the ball will roll with the movement. Squat down as far as you comfortably can. The ball will then be positioned at about the midback.

Keeping pressure on the ball, contract the buttocks and slowly "roll" yourself up and back to the starting position.

Illustrations by Shawn Banner.

■ ■ ■ ■

Herbal Help for Back Pain

Back pain can be relieved with the herb devil's claw.

Recent study: A daily dose of 60 milligrams (mg) of *harpagosides*, found in devil's claw, is as effective in treating lower-back pain as a standard dose of the prescription drug Vioxx, which was linked to heart problems and removed from the market.

Caution: Do not take devil's claw if you are taking blood thinners or have any clotting disorders.

Joel J. Gagnier, ND, postgraduate fellow, Institute of Medical Sciences, University of Toronto, and leader of a metastudy of 12 previous studies of harpagosides, published in *BMC Complementary and Alternative Medicine.*

■ ■ ■ ■

Knee Repair

Removing all or part of a damaged meniscus (a pad of cartilage in the knee joint), a common procedure to ease arthritis pain, may result in further wear and tear on the joint and loss of cartilage in the knee.

Better: Except in some cases such as a locked knee, nonsurgical strategies to alleviate knee pain may be more effective. These include weight loss…braces…shoes that prevent foot pronation, or flattening…and anti-inflammatory drugs such as *ibuprofen* (Advil).

David J. Hunter, MD, PhD, assistant professor of medicine, Boston University School of Medicine.

■ ■ ■ ■

Relief for Leg Cramps

Many of my patients over age 50 tell me that they have recurrent lower leg cramps, usually in the evening. Their calf muscles seem to tighten up into a knot. Stretching does not alleviate the pain, though massaging the calves often helps.

The culprit is usually mineral deficiencies. This can happen even if you're taking a multivitamin. The three most common deficiencies, in order, are magnesium, calcium and potassium. All three are involved in nerve and muscle contraction. Blood tests can detect these deficiencies, but the tests often are not accurate.

The first thing to do is to consume foods rich in these minerals. Magnesium is found in whole grains, legumes and green, leafy vegetables. Good sources of calcium include broccoli, collard greens, kelp, yogurt and milk (unless you're dairy sensitive). Potassium-rich foods include apples, bananas, oranges, tomatoes and potatoes.

However, many of my patients get the best results by taking a combination supplement. Take a calcium (500 mg)/magnesium (250 mg) complex after dinner. For most people, this will resolve the problem within a day. If that doesn't help, a potassium deficiency may be the problem. Drink eight ounces of vegetable juice a day, such as low-sodium V8 juice.

Mark A. Stengler, ND, naturopathic physician in private practice, La Jolla, CA…adjunct associate clinical professor at the National College of Natural Medicine, Portland, OR…author of 16 books, including *The Natural Physician's Healing Therapies* (Bottom Line Books) and coauthor of *Prescription for Natural Cures* (Wiley)…and author of the *Bottom Line/Natural Healing* newsletter.

■■■■

Achilles Warning

Pain in the Achilles tendon could indicate cholesterol problems. People with hereditary high cholesterol are seven times more likely to report Achilles tendon pain lasting three days or more than people without the condition.

Self-defense: If Achilles tendon pain persists, have your cholesterol tested.

Paul N. Durrington, PhD, professor, University of Manchester division of cardiovascular and endocrine science, Manchester, England.

Do Your Muscles Cramp? You May Have Dystonia

Susan B. Bressman, MD, professor of neurology at Albert Einstein College of Medicine and chairperson of the department of neurology at Beth Israel Medical Center, both in New York City.

The neurological movement disorder known as dystonia causes muscles to contract uncontrollably, making parts of the body twist or twitch repeatedly, sometimes freezing in odd or painful postures. Dystonia, which affects more than 300,000 Americans, is the third most common movement disorder (Parkinson's disease is the first…and tremor is the second).

Most people who have dystonia go from doctor to doctor for years seeking a proper diagnosis. For many people, the condition is an annoyance they learn to live with. But sometimes dystonia can keep sufferers from participating in their hobbies…threaten careers…or even cause serious disability.

Good news: Although much about the condition remains a mystery, there are treatments that can vastly improve the lives of many sufferers.

TYPES OF DYSTONIA

When a single area of the body is affected, it's called focal dystonia. Writer's cramp (muscle contractions when you try to write) and occupational dystonia (muscle cramping that affects pianists and other musicians who use the same muscles repeatedly in their work) are two types that are known to most people.

Other forms of focal dystonia include…

• **Torticollis,** the most common type of dystonia, involves contraction of the muscles of the neck. The head is turned to the side, tilted toward either shoulder or pulled forward or backward. Muscles may cramp painfully.

• **Blepharospasm,** the next most common type, affects muscles around the eye. It can cause forceful blinking—or the eyes close altogether for sustained periods.

• **Generalized dystonia** is far less common —and it is potentially the most disabling form of the disorder. Usually beginning in childhood or adolescence, muscles all over the body are subject to uncontrollable movement.

WHAT GOES WRONG

Dystonia can strike at any age. Some cases appear to have a genetic cause—those that begin in childhood or adolescence, in particular, often can be traced to a mutation in a single gene, DYT1. If you inherited this mutated gene, you have a 30% chance of developing dystonia.

Some dystonias are caused by medication, including antipsychotic drugs such as *haloperidol* (Haldol) or *fluphenazine* (Prolixin)…*metaclopramide* (Reglan), which is prescribed for digestive problems…and *prochlorperazine* (Compazine), given for nausea. Neurological disorders, such as Parkinson's disease and stroke, may cause dystonia through their effect on the *basal ganglia*, clusters of nerve cells in the brain that are responsible for initiating and integrating movements.

TREATMENT BREAKTHROUGH

Dystonia is a chronic disorder that cannot be cured, but treatment has been revolutionized by the use of *botulinum toxin*. Two types of botulinum toxin are FDA approved for treating dystonia, *botulinum A* (Botox) and *botulinum B* (Myobloc). Botox also is commonly used by dermatologists to eliminate wrinkles, typically on the forehead and around the eyes, by causing temporary weakness to the muscles in those areas. When botulinum toxin is injected into specific muscles affected by dystonia, the abnormal movement can be largely diminished without causing paralysis. In some cases, improvements seem almost miraculous.

Example: At age 36, Leon Fleisher, a brilliant concert pianist, developed dystonia in his right hand. After 30 years of trying treatments that failed, botulinum toxin allowed him to again play with both hands.

Botulinum toxin typically remains effective for three to six months after an injection. Side effects can occur if the drug gets into the wrong muscle—an eyelid may droop, for example, or you could have difficulty swallowing.

DRUG TREATMENT

If dystonia doesn't respond to botulinum toxin or it is so widespread that botulinum toxin can't be used, other medications can be effective…

•**Anticholinergics,** drugs such as *benztropine* (Cogentin) and *trihexyphenidyl* (Artane), which are typically used to treat Parkinson's disease, block the neurotransmitter *acetylcholine*. The drugs bring effective relief from dystonia symptoms in 30% to 40% of patients, but side effects, including dry mouth, constipation and mental confusion, may limit their use.

•**Baclofen (Lioresal),** an antispasmodic often used for multiple sclerosis, also may be useful alone or in combination with other drugs.

THE SURGICAL OPTION

Dystonia that remains disabling despite other treatments may respond to a technique known as deep-brain stimulation (DBS). With DBS, electrodes are implanted in the *globus pallidus*, a part of the brain that regulates movement. A small device installed under the skin near the collarbone delivers electric pulses to stimulate these areas of the brain. Like any brain surgery, DBS carries some risk for complications, such as infection.

Another surgical procedure, selective denervation, is used for severe torticollis. Some nerves in the neck are cut, weakening muscles just enough to stop dystonia while preserving the capacity for normal movement.

COMPLEMENTARY THERAPIES

Nondrug, nonsurgical approaches also may be effective for dystonia. Physical therapy can stretch and ease the discomfort of muscles tightened by dystonia and increase range of motion.

No one knows why, but dystonia also may respond to "sensory tricks." Stimulating the affected—or a nearby—body part can reduce abnormal movements.

Examples: For blepharospasm, touching the skin alongside the eye, or looking down rather than up, can be effective…for torticollis, some patients have learned that wearing a scarf helps keep the head in an upright position.

For more information, contact the Dystonia Medical Research Foundation, 312-755-0198, *www.dystonia-foundation.org.*

Help for Swollen Ankles and Feet

Jamison Starbuck, ND, is a naturopathic physician in family practice in Missoula, Montana. She is past president of the American Association of Naturopathic Physicians and is a contributing editor to *The Alternative Advisor: The Complete Guide to Natural Therapies and Alternative Treatments.* Time-Life.

A patient recently visited my office, complaining of puffy calves, ankles and feet. We quickly discovered the cause—she had spent more than seven hours sitting on a flight returning from Europe. Other common causes of edema (water accumulation) in the calves, ankles and/or feet include dehydration, prolonged standing or excessive exposure to extreme temperatures (hot or cold). In these cases, the swelling lasts just a few hours or a day or two.

But edema also can be a symptom of more serious conditions, such as congestive heart failure, circulatory problems or kidney disease. Congestive heart failure leads to sodium retention, which causes an accumulation of fluid in the body. In kidney disease, salt and water retention may lead to swelling in the lower legs, the face and eventually the entire body.

If you have swollen legs and/or feet for more than two days, see your doctor. If you've recently had surgery or the swelling is only on one side or accompanied by skin discoloration, pain or heat, call your doctor's office and ask to be seen immediately. You may have a blood clot or an infection—both can be life-threatening. *Other causes of edema...*

•**Chronic disease.** Most people who have heart, circulatory or kidney problems benefit from taking a diuretic, a type of medication that helps your body eliminate water via the urine. Most conventional doctors prescribe a synthetic diuretic, such as *hydrochlorothiazide* (Microzide) or *furosemide* (Lasix). Because these drugs can raise cholesterol and triglyceride levels, I recommend dandelion instead. The root and leaf of dandelion are commonly used to treat liver disease, but the leaf alone is one of nature's best diuretics. Dandelion also reduces lipid (fat) levels and improves HDL "good" cholesterol.

What to do: Drink three eight-ounce cups of dandelion leaf tea per day until the swelling subsides. To prepare the tea, use two teaspoons of dried leaf or two tea bags per cup of boiling water. Steep covered for six minutes, and strain before drinking. If you prefer tincture, use ¼ teaspoon in two ounces of water, two times per day, at least 15 minutes before or after meals. Dandelion is safe and can be used on a regular basis. If you take blood-pressure medications or want to substitute dandelion for another diuretic, alert your doctor so he/she can monitor any interactions and help you determine the proper dose for you.

•**Dehydration.** If your feet and legs swell when you get overheated, travel by plane, drink alcohol or several cups of coffee or eat salty food, water is your best medicine. The puffiness can indicate that your body is dehydrated and that it's trying to retain water.

What to do: Drink at least ½ ounce of water per pound of body weight per day. Elevate your lower legs for 10 minutes each hour, and walk for 10 minutes once every two waking hours. The swelling should subside within a day.

■■■■

Home Pain Pumps

Portable pain pumps help surgical patients recover at home. The systems, commonly used after orthopedic surgery, deliver a preset amount of painkiller to the treatment area.

Advantage: Patients can avoid the dizziness, lethargy, nausea and other side effects of oral pain medications. Ask your doctor if a portable pain pump is right for you.

Frank C. Detterbeck, MD, professor and chief of thoracic surgery, surgical director of Yale thoracic oncology program, and associate director of clinical affairs, Yale Cancer Center, Yale University School of Medicine, New Haven, CT.

■■■■

Drug Side Benefit

Blood-pressure drugs fight headaches, but they should not be used solely to control headaches. An analysis of nearly 100 research studies shows that hypertension drugs cut incidence of headaches by an average of 33%. Beta-blockers—the class that includes *carvedilol* (Coreg) and *metoprolol* (Lopressor)—have the greatest effect. Other blood-pressure medications shown to reduce headaches include ACE inhibitors, such as *quinapril* (Accupril)...angiotensin II receptor antagonists, such as *losartan* (Cozaar)...and thiazides, such as *hydrochlorothiazide*.

Malcolm Law, FRCP, professor of epidemiology, Wolfson Institute of Preventive Medicine, University of London, England. His analysis of 94 studies involving 24,244 participants was published in *Circulation*.

■■■■

No More Needles?

Needles may become obsolete. The British company PowderMed has created a device that delivers vaccines without needles. The PMED is a flashlight-sized device that uses pressurized helium to shoot powdered vaccine just below the skin surface rather than into the muscle, as with needles. This results in less pain and better absorption. PowderMed is working on powdered vaccines for influenza, viral diseases and cancer.

Popular Science, 2 Park Ave., New York City 10016.

Foods Fight Headaches: What's Good to Eat and What's Bad

Elaine Magee, MPH, RD, registered dietitian, Pleasant Hill, CA, is the author of 25 books on nutrition, including *Tell Me What to Eat If I Have Headaches and Migraines.* New Page.

More than 45 million Americans annually seek medical treatment for frequent or severe headaches. Doctors have identified dozens of headache triggers, including stress, air pollution and weather changes, but one of the main triggers—especially for migraines—is diet.

At least 30% of migraine patients have one or more food triggers. In some cases, a single food may be responsible. Most patients have combination triggers—for example, red wine plus a high level of stress plus an extra cup of coffee in the morning.

Everyone who experiences migraines and other types of headaches should keep a food and lifestyle diary. Write down the foods and beverages you consume. Also note patterns that precede headaches—exercise activities, changes in sleep, stress level, menstrual cycle, etc. After a few weeks, review your diary and identify likely connections.

WHAT TO AVOID

•**Caffeine** is one of the main headache triggers. Some people get headaches when they consume any caffeine. Others get headaches when they consume less than they usually do and then need caffeine to relieve the headache.

If you drink coffee or other caffeinated beverages regularly, blood vessels in the brain become sensitized to the caffeine's effects. Eliminating or cutting back on caffeine causes rebound headaches in about half of patients.

People with chronic headaches often are advised to eliminate caffeine completely. Instead of quitting abruptly, gradually taper off. If you're used to drinking three cups of coffee a day, drink only two cups daily for a week. For several days after that, substitute decaf for one of your daily servings. Then dilute your regular coffee with decaf until you quit entirely.

•**High-fat foods.** Significantly reducing dietary fat decreases the frequency and intensity of headaches. Try to limit total fat intake to 20% of total calories. In particular, avoid saturated fats (mainly found in meats, fast food and full-fat dairy products) and trans fats (often called "partially hydrogenated oils" on labels and found in margarines, snack foods and packaged baked goods).

•**Tyramine** is a natural by-product of the amino acid tyrosine. Foods that are aged or fermented tend to be high in tyramine, which can cause vascular spasms that result in migraines.

Main offenders: Red wine, aged cheeses including blue and cheddar, deli meats and overripe bananas.

Stick with fresh meats and cheeses such as cottage cheese, ricotta and fresh mozzarella. White wine and beer have less tyramine than red wine—but any alcohol can trigger headaches.

•**Food additives,** including *monosodium glutamate* (MSG), nitrates and nitrites, dilate blood vessels and trigger migraines in people who are sensitive to these additives. Nitrates and nitrites are found mainly in processed meats, such as hot dogs, bacon and salami. MSG is added to literally thousands of processed foods. Check food labels, and avoid products that contain any of these additives.

FOODS THAT HELP

•**Omega-3 fatty acids.** The healthful fats in fish, flaxseeds and olive oil can reduce migraines by stimulating the production of body chemicals that inhibit inflammation in blood vessels in the brain.

Recommended: Two to three servings of fish weekly. Also, have one tablespoon daily of ground flaxseed (you can add it to cereal or smoothies or sprinkle on salads or yogurt). Cook with olive oil or canola oil, which contain more omega-3s than other vegetable oils.

•**Magnesium.** There is some evidence that adequate magnesium intake can help women prevent headaches (including migraines) associated with menstruation. The recommended daily intake for most women is 320 milligrams (mg). High-magnesium foods include whole grains, nuts, seeds, soy foods, legumes and dark green vegetables.

Examples: Almonds, two tablespoons (86 mg of magnesium)…artichoke, one medium (180 mg)…brown rice, two-thirds cup (57 mg)…peanut butter, two tablespoons (51 mg)…pumpkin seeds, two tablespoons (152 mg)…cooked spinach, one-half cup (78 mg)…tofu, one-half cup (118 mg).

•**Water** helps prevent dehydration—a common cause of headaches. Try to drink eight eight-ounce glasses every day.

The Best Pain-Relief Creams and Ointments

Beth E. Shubin Stein, MD, is an assistant attending sports medicine and shoulder surgeon with the Women's Sports Medicine Center at the Hospital for Special Surgery in New York City. Dr. Shubin Stein is a team physician for the U.S. Federation Cup tennis team.

If you suffer from chronic arthritis pain or have aching muscle strains or spasms after exercising, chances are you regularly take aspirin or another nonsteroidal anti-inflammatory drug (NSAID), such as *ibuprofen* (Advil) or *naproxen* (Aleve).

There is another option. Over-the-counter (OTC) topical pain relievers can be very effective without causing the stomach upset or gastrointestinal bleeding that may accompany oral pain medication.

Latest development: A topical form of the oral prescription NSAID *diclofenac* (Voltaren) is expected to undergo FDA review within a year or so. It is already available in Europe and Canada.

Meanwhile, a variety of OTC topical pain relievers are available now. The products below relieve arthritis, backache and muscle strain. Most are used three to four times daily. Follow label instructions.

Helpful: If one type of topical pain reliever doesn't work for you, try one from another class until you find a product that provides relief.

Caution: Keep these products away from your eyes, nose and other mucous membranes.

SALICYLATES

These aspirin-based products dull pain and curb the inflammation that often accompanies and worsens pain.

How they work: Topical salicylates inhibit the production of *prostaglandins,* substances in the body that cause pain and swelling when they are released in response to strains, sprains and other injuries. *Salicylates include…*

•**BenGay Ultra Strength Pain Relieving Cream.**

•**Aspercreme Analgesic Creme Rub with Aloe.**

•**Sportscreme Deep Penetrating Pain Relieving Rub.**

•**Flexall Maximum Strength Pain Relieving Gel.**

Warning: Do not use salicylates if you are sensitive or allergic to aspirin or take blood-thinning medication that might interact with them. Consult a doctor before applying a salicylate to a large area several times a day.

COUNTERIRRITANTS

These pain relievers give the sensation of warmth or coolness to mask pain.

How they work: Creating a secondary stimulus to diminish the feeling of pain reduces physical discomfort. It's what you do instinctively when you stub your toe, then grab it to apply pressure. Both competing sensations travel to your brain at the same time—but because only a limited number of messages can be processed at one time, the initial feeling of pain is diminished. *Counterirritants include…*

•**Icy Hot Pain Relieving Balm, Extra Strength.**

•**Tiger Balm Extra Strength Pain Relieving Ointment.**

•**Therapeutic Mineral Ice.**

In most cases, coolness is beneficial for acute injuries, such as sprains, while warmth eases stiffness.

Caution: People sensitive to heat or cold should avoid counterirritants.

CAPSAICINS

These products, which are a type of counterirritant, contain capsaicin, an extract of hot peppers that causes a burning sensation.

How they work: Unlike most other counterirritants, capsaicin inhibits the production of substance P, a chemical that sends pain messages to the brain via the nervous system. *Capsaicins include...*

- **Zostrix Arthritis Pain Relief Cream.**
- **Capzasin HP Arthritis Pain Relief Creme.**

LIDOCAINE

Lidoderm is a prescription-only patch that contains *lidocaine*, a topical anesthetic similar to the novocaine that dentists often use to numb the gums.

How it works: Lidocaine blocks signals at the skin's nerve endings. The Lidoderm patch (lidocaine 5%) is worn for 12 hours a day over a period of days. It slowly releases medication, so it has longer-lasting effects than other pain relievers and helps with pain that emanates from nerves near the surface of your skin, such as that caused by shingles or diabetic neuropathy.

Caution: Side effects include dizziness, headache and nausea. Allergic reactions are rare but may occur.

■ ■ ■ ■

No Heart Risk

Using *naproxen* (Aleve) as a painkiller has no risk of triggering a heart attack. It doesn't raise heart attack or stroke risk, unlike some other nonsteroidal anti-inflammatory drugs, such as Vioxx or Celebrex, and is inexpensive because generic versions are available.

Drawback: Naproxen can irritate the stomach, increase blood pressure slightly and/or adversely affect kidney function.

Steven Nissen, MD, chairman, department of cardiovascular medicine, and director of the Joseph J. Jacobs Center for Thrombosis and Vascular Biology, the Cleveland Clinic, and past president, American College of Cardiology, Washington, DC.

■ ■ ■ ■

Gallstone Risk

Eating bad fats increases the risk for gallstones.

New finding: A 14-year study of nearly 46,000 men found that those who consumed the most trans fats (4.5 g per day) had a nearly 25% higher risk for gallstone disease than those who ate the least amount of trans fats (1.4 g per day).

Theory: Trans fats increase LDL "bad" cholesterol and lower HDL "good" cholesterol, which may lead to gallstone formation.

Self-defense: Avoid trans fats by checking the nutrition label on processed foods, such as crackers, chips and baked goods.

Michael Leitzmann, MD, DPH investigator, National Cancer Institute, Bethesda, MD.

■ ■ ■ ■

Relief for Knee Osteoarthritis

In a new study, researchers performed magnetic resonance imaging (MRI) scans of the knee joints of 265 people with osteoarthritis of the knee to determine cartilage loss over a 30-month period and also measured the strength of the patients' quadricep (upper thigh) muscles.

Result: Patients who had stronger quadriceps had less cartilage loss behind the kneecap.

Theory: Strong quadriceps may help prevent excessive wear and tear on knee cartilage.

If you have knee osteoarthritis: Ask your doctor about quadricep exercises.

Shreyasee Amin, MD, MPH, associate professor of medicine, Mayo Clinic College of Medicine, Rochester, MN.

5

Over-the-Counter Remedies

Hidden OTC Dangers: Deciphering Labels

Over-the-counter (OTC) drugs can be purchased just as easily as a bottle of shampoo or a box of cereal—but that doesn't mean that they are harmless.

Few people realize that in some cases, OTC drugs contain the same amount of an active ingredient as that found in prescription medications. Using OTC drugs incorrectly—for example, taking them for too long or in excessive doses—can cause serious side effects.

Example 1: People with arthritis often treat their symptoms with OTC painkillers, such as *ibuprofen* (Advil) or *naproxen* (Aleve), for months or years—even though the label advises against taking these drugs for more than 10 consecutive days without consulting your doctor. The long-term use of such drugs greatly increases the risk for stomach bleeding as well as heart and/or kidney problems.

Example 2: If you have hypertension or heart disease, taking a cold remedy that contains *pseudoephedrine*, such as Sudafed, can cause a life-threatening problem such as atrial fibrillation (a heart-rhythm irregularity) or heart attack.

All OTC medications include a standardized "Drug Facts" label (on the outside of the packaging and also in an insert) that details the approved uses of the drug...active ingredients...how to use it...and possible risks. Even though OTC drug labels were simplified in 2002, the information is often confusing and printed in such small type that it's almost impossible to read.

Note: The FDA recently has required drug manufacturers to redesign prescription drug labels so that they are easier to read.

Important: Bring your reading glasses or a small magnifying glass with you and read the OTC drug label before leaving the store. If

Jack M. Rosenberg, PharmD, PhD, is director of the International Drug Information Center at the Arnold and Marie Schwartz College of Pharmacy Health Sciences at Long Island University in Brooklyn, NY.

you're purchasing from a drugstore, ask a pharmacist to explain any instructions that you don't understand.

What to look for...

ACTIVE INGREDIENT

This term refers to the medication that relieves symptoms. There might be dozens of drugs in a pharmacy that have the same active ingredient.

Example: Advil Cold & Sinus Liqui-Gels and Motrin Cold & Sinus caplets both contain 200 mg of ibuprofen and 30 mg of pseudoephedrine. Knowing the active ingredient makes it easy to comparison shop for the best price.

What you may not know: Manufacturers occasionally change the active ingredients in OTC products.

Example: The antidiarrheal drug Kaopectate once contained a type of clay called *attapulgite*. It was safe for patients who were taking blood-thinning medication. Kaopectate now contains *bismuth subsalicylate*, an aspirin-like ingredient that increases the risk for bleeding in patients taking blood thinners.

INACTIVE INGREDIENTS

This term refers to the chemicals that are used as preservatives, binders and colorants/flavors—but have no medical effects.

What you may not know: Some people are allergic to certain inactive (as well as active) ingredients.

Example 1: Hundreds of products, such as the OTC antihistamine *loratadine* (Alavert) and the OTC pain reliever Arthritis Strength BC Powder, contain the inactive ingredient lactose, a milk sugar that can trigger reactions in patients who are lactose intolerant.

Example 2: Gluten, a protein found in wheat, barley and rye, should be avoided by people with celiac disease, but starch, maltodextrin and other substances that could contain gluten are common inactive ingredients in both OTC and prescription medications, such as the OTC anti-gas drug Gas-X Regular Strength Chewable Tablets and the fiber supplement Senokot Wheat Bran.

USES

Known as "indications" on some labels, this term refers to the list of symptoms that a drug is designed to treat.

The FDA allows drug manufacturers to list only uses for which the medication has been proven to be safe and effective.

Example: The label on an antihistamine such as *diphenhydramine* (Benadryl) says the drug treats sneezing, runny nose and other allergy symptoms.

What you may not know: It can be risky to take drugs "off-label"—that is, taking a medication for uses other than the indications and/or directions found on the label.

Example: Taking high doses of the OTC B-vitamin niacin to lower cholesterol is an off-label use. Prescription niacin is approved for lowering cholesterol, but taking it without being monitored by your doctor can lead to liver damage.

WARNINGS

Many patients ignore the warnings on OTC medications because they assume the drugs must be safe or they wouldn't be sold without a prescription. Not true.

OTC drugs can cause side effects that are just as serious as those caused by prescription drugs. Aspirin and related drugs, for example, cause more than 100,000 hospitalizations annually in the US.

What you may not know: In addition to explaining the main risks of a medication, "warnings" may include information on who should not take the medication, when to consult your doctor if symptoms persist, when to take medications with foods (or when to avoid certain foods and beverages), whether it's safe to drive, etc.

Even if you've taken a particular OTC drug for years, check the warning label each time you purchase the medication. A drug that was safe when you first started taking it might cause problems if you've begun taking other medications or if the ingredients or your health needs have changed. Always check the expiration date.

FORMS AND FORMULATIONS

The label on an OTC drug lists the medication's form—tablet, capsule, caplet, etc. The form can affect how quickly the product works… what side effects occur…and how easy it is to take.

Examples…

•**Buffered analgesics** (pain relievers) are made slightly alkaline to protect the stomach. Patients who experience stomach irritation, pain or heartburn from aspirin or similar drugs might do better with a buffered product.

•**Caplets** are ordinary tablets in the shape of a capsule. They're easier to swallow than traditional tablets—an important point for patients who have trouble swallowing. Gelcaps, geltabs and capsules are coated with gelatin, making them also easier to swallow.

•**Timed-release capsules or tablets.** These drugs are designed with various types and layers of coatings around the active ingredients, which allows the medication to be released slowly, resulting in extended drug action.

An enteric-coated drug is treated so that it passes through the stomach unaltered and dissolves in the intestines. Enteric-coated medications take longer to work, so if you have a headache (and do not have a sensitive stomach), it may be better to take regular aspirin than enteric-coated aspirin.

•**Extra-strength drugs** contain a higher dose of the active ingredient. These medications, such as Extra Strength Tylenol, are helpful if the regular dose isn't adequate to control symptoms—and more convenient than taking two or more doses of a lower-dose product.

•**PM** (or night formulas), including some antihistamines or pain relievers, such as Excedrin PM, can cause drowsiness, so they're meant to be taken at night.

•**Suspension formulas** are liquid medications in which the active ingredient isn't dissolved. They require shaking before use (and typically indicate this on the label).

Example: The laxative Phillips Milk of Magnesia is an oral suspension medication.

Everyday Painkillers May Block Memory Loss!

Lon Schneider, MD, professor of psychiatry, neurology and gerontology, Keck School of Medicine, University of Southern California, Los Angeles.

Theo Palmer, PhD, associate professor of neurosurgery, Stanford University, Palo Alto, CA.

John C. Morris, MD, professor of neurology, and director, Alzheimer's Disease Research Center, Washington University School of Medicine, St. Louis, MO.

Science.

Two studies indicate that nonsteroidal anti-inflammatory drugs (NSAIDs), including aspirin and other aspirin-like drugs such as ibuprofen, can restore brain cell (neuron) production and decrease harmful levels of amyloid beta proteins by reducing inflammation.

Amyloid beta proteins form clumps in the brains of people who have Alzheimer's, and those clumps are suspected to cause or at least contribute to the disease. Amyloid beta-42 seems to be the most harmful form of these proteins.

The results of these two studies suggest that memory and learning problems in conditions such as Alzheimer's and other types of dementia, stroke and traumatic brain injury might be helped by a simple drug, a researcher says.

THE FIRST STUDY

In one study, Dr. Steven Paul and researchers from drugmaker Eli Lilly and Co. report that anti-inflammatory drugs can reduce the production of amyloid beta proteins, including amyloid beta-42.

These results support the notion that NSAIDs have a protective effect against future neurodegeneration, says Dr. Lon Schneider, a professor of psychiatry, neurology and gerontology at the University of Southern California.

Schneider believes trials are needed to see which NSAIDs might prevent dementia and treat head injury and stroke.

THE SECOND STUDY

In another study, a team led by Theo Palmer, an associate professor of neurosurgery at Stanford University, experimented with rats to see if reducing brain inflammation might have an effect on neuron production.

"The dogma for many decades has been that the brain doesn't replace neurons, but that is not true. There are regions of the brain that continue to make neurons throughout life. These new neurons are made by stem cells called precursors," Palmer says.

These new neurons may be important for memory and learning, he adds.

The team found that in rats with brain inflammation, the production of new neurons stopped. However, when they treated the rats with the anti-inflammatory drug indomethacin, the production of neurons was completely restored.

These results suggest that people who have Alzheimer's, stroke and brain injury might benefit from a simple drug such as indomethacin, Palmer says.

Dr. John Morris, director of the Alzheimer's Disease Research Center at Washington University School of Medicine, comments, "These reports suggest that commonly used anti-inflammatory drugs may lessen the toxic effects of brain inflammation believed to be important in Alzheimer's disease.

"However, neither study involved human subjects. Whether the positive effects shown in these experimental models translate to actual patients is far from clear," Morris says.

Get an explanation of how NSAIDs reduce inflammation at the American Academy of Orthopaedic Surgeons Web site, *www.aaos.org*.

■■■■

Aspirin vs. Stroke

Because aspirin can cause bleeding, it is typically avoided by people who have had a hemorrhagic stroke, which occurs when a blood vessel bursts in the brain.

New finding: In a study of 207 hemorrhagic stroke survivors, those who took an antiplatelet drug, such as aspirin, were not at increased risk for another hemorrhage.

Implication: Aspirin therapy may be appropriate for hemorrhagic stroke survivors who are at high risk for heart attack or ischemic stroke,

in which a blood clot blocks blood flow to the brain.

Anand Viswanathan, MD, PhD, assistant neurologist, neurology clinical trials unit, Massachusetts General Hospital, Boston.

The Dangerous Truth About Acetaminophen

Elham Rahme, PhD, assistant professor of medicine and scientific researcher, Research Institute of the McGill University Health Centre, Montreal, Quebec, Canada.
John Klippel, MD, rheumatologist, and president and chief executive officer, Arthritis Foundation.
Arthritis and Rheumatism.

Acetaminophen is often a first line of treatment for arthritis because it is believed to have fewer side effects than other painkillers.

But Canadian researchers have shown that in high doses, acetaminophen is just as likely to cause gastrointestinal (GI) problems, such as upset stomach and ulcers, as *nonsteroidal anti-inflammatory drugs* (NSAIDs), such as ibuprofen or naproxen.

"Physicians need to know that if they are increasing the dose of acetaminophen rather than switching to another medication because they think they will see fewer GI events, they should look at other options," says one of the study's authors, Elham Rahme, an assistant professor of medicine at the Research Institute of the McGill University Health Centre in Montreal.

Acetaminophen—the active ingredient in Tylenol, among other cold and headache products—is frequently recommended to manage the pain associated with arthritis.

HIGHER DOSE, GREATER RISK

After studying almost 50,000 arthritis patients, half of whom were taking acetaminophen, "we saw that there really is a difference," Rahme says.

"At the low dose of acetaminophen, GI events are much lower than in the NSAID group, but when you go to 2,600 milligrams [mg] a day and higher, there were similar rates of GI events," reports Rahme.

Rahme says the rate of stomach and intestinal troubles approximately doubled between the lowest dose (less than 650 mg per day) of acetaminophen and the highest dose (more than 3,250 mg daily).

The researchers started to see side effects at the equivalent of eight regular-strength or five extra-strength tablets a day.

Rahme says there are some limitations to the study. For example, there may have been a slight bias toward having GI problems because the patients included in the study were older and often on more than one medication. Many had already been on either acetaminophen or NSAID therapy. Rahme says the researchers tried to control for these variables and still saw more GI problems in patients on high doses of acetaminophen.

Dr. John Klippel, medical director of the Arthritis Foundation, wasn't surprised by the results of this study, but says that acetaminophen will probably remain the first line of treatment for many patients because it's cost-effective and still considered quite safe in low doses.

He cautions that consumers should check the label of any over-the-counter medication they are taking to be sure they're not getting extra doses of acetaminophen because it's contained in a lot of cold and headache preparations.

■ ■ ■ ■

Painkiller Risk

Combining painkillers can be dangerous. Patients regularly taking an over-the-counter nonsteroidal anti-inflammatory drug (NSAID), such as ibuprofen (Advil), and aspirin in the same day had two to three times the risk for ulcers and gastrointestinal (GI) bleeding as those who took either alone.

Theory: Acidity in the GI tract reaches more harmful levels when the painkillers are combined.

If you must take multiple painkillers: Ask your physician about adding a proton pump inhibitor (PPI), such as *lansoprazole* (Prevacid), to reduce stomach acid.

Joseph Biskupiak, PhD, research associate professor, department of pharmacotherapy, University of Utah, Salt Lake City.

The New Aspirin Breakthrough

Stefano Fiorucci, MD, professor of gastroenterology, University of Perugia, Italy.
Brett Bernstein, MD, director of endoscopy, division of digestive disease, Beth Israel Medical Center, and assistant professor of medicine, Albert Einstein College of Medicine, both in New York City.
Proceedings of the National Academy of Sciences.

A new formulation of aspirin, called NCX-4016, may be effective without damaging the stomach.

Millions of people are taking aspirin daily, largely because it has been shown to reduce the risk of heart attack and stroke.

However, aspirin also can damage the lining of the gastrointestinal tract.

In addition, some people take anti-inflammatory drugs called Cox-2 inhibitors for arthritis. Cox-2 inhibitors can exacerbate the stomach damage caused by regular aspirin.

People who are simultaneously exposed to Cox-2 inhibitors plus aspirin have a significantly higher risk of stomach damage, says Dr. Stefano Fiorucci, professor of gastroenterology at the University of Perugia in Italy.

THE STUDY

To see if NCX-4016 could prevent stomach damage from Cox-2 inhibitors, Fiorucci and his colleagues recruited 32 healthy volunteers.

Half received NCX-4016, plus the Cox-2 inhibitor *celecoxib*, which is sold under the brand name Celebrex. The other half got regular aspirin (100 milligrams) along with celecoxib.

At the end of the trial, participants in the regular aspirin group had approximately twice as much stomach damage as people in the NCX-4016 group.

The results suggest that NCX-4016 may be a safer alternative to regular aspirin for patients who also are taking Cox-2 inhibitors.

WHY IT WORKS

NCX-4016 differs from the old formulation of aspirin in that it releases nitric oxide, which increases blood flow in the body. One reason traditional aspirin can cause stomach damage is that it may decrease blood flow to the stomach lining, explains Dr. Brett Bernstein, director of ambulatory services in the division of digestive disease at Beth Israel Medical Center in New York City.

As a result, "substances that normally protect the stomach lining can't get to it," he says. "Nitric oxide opens up the blood flow, and therefore could protect the lining."

The Secret Cause Of Asthma?

R. Graham Barr, MD, DrPH, assistant professor of medicine and epidemiology, Columbia University, New York City.

Susan Redline, MD, professor of pediatrics, Case Western Reserve University, Cleveland.

American Journal of Respiratory and Critical Care Medicine.

Frequent use of the popular painkiller acetaminophen may increase a person's risk for developing asthma, a study says. But experts caution that it's far too early to tell consumers to avoid it.

Women who were taking acetaminophen at least 15 days a month for six years had a 63% higher risk of developing asthma compared with women who didn't use the analgesic, according to researchers.

Individual reactions to pain relievers vary. "We are not trying to say that all asthmatics should stop using acetaminophen," says study author Dr. R. Graham Barr, assistant professor of medicine and epidemiology at Columbia University.

Soaring rates of asthma across the United States have alarmed public health officials and puzzled asthma experts.

Scientists estimate that in the past 30 years, asthma cases approximately doubled in younger children, says Susan Redline, an asthma expert at Case Western Reserve University in Cleveland.

However, the exact cause of this steep climb remains unclear.

Rising rates of obesity—which can impair lung function—have been cited by experts as a possible culprit, as have indoor pollutants, such as dust mites and mold.

But the upswing in new asthma cases also coincided with the increasing popularity of over-the-counter acetaminophen, the researchers say. According to the American Medical Association, approximately 200 over-the-counter drugs contain acetaminophen.

THE STUDY

In their study, Barr and his colleagues examined data from the Nurses Health Study, which included nearly 122,000 adult women. As part of the study, each participant kept a record of her analgesic use, as well as the development of any new medical conditions, including asthma.

Among women who used acetaminophen for more than half of the days in a given month, "there was a significant increase—63%—in the risk of a new diagnosis of asthma," Barr says.

POSSIBLE EXPLANATION

Scientists know that acetaminophen lowers blood levels of a natural compound called *glutathione*. "Glutathione has an antioxidant effect in the body, particularly in the lungs," Barr explains. When glutathione levels plummet, "that may reduce the antioxidant defenses in the body and increase the possibility of developing asthma."

However, the study only demonstrates an association between acetaminophen and increased asthma—not a cause-and-effect relationship. And Barr notes that other analgesics such as aspirin, ibuprofen and nonsteroidal anti-inflammatory drugs (NSAIDs), such as *celexicob* (Celebrex), have also been shown to affect asthmatics in various ways.

"If individuals happen to notice that their asthma gets worse after they take aspirin or nonsteroidals or acetaminophen, it's worth reassessing that usage," Barr says. "But we're not making any blanket statements."

For information on controlling asthma symptoms, visit the Asthma and Allergy Foundation of America at *www.aafa.org*.

■ ■ ■ ■

OTC Risks

Acetaminophen may be a contributing cause of hypertension.

Recent finding: Women who take a daily dose of more than 500 milligrams of the aspirin-free painkiller—the equivalent of one extra-strength Tylenol—have double the risk of developing high blood pressure within three years. *Ibuprofen* (Advil and Motrin) and *naproxen* (Aleve) have been linked to hypertension, but until recently, acetaminophen was considered safe.

Best: Monitor blood pressure if you are taking these drugs.

Christie Ballantyne, MD, director of the Center for Cardiac Disease Prevention, Methodist DeBakey Heart Center, Houston.

The Secret Recipe for Hair Growth

Jane Buckle, RN, PhD, president, RJ Buckle Associates LLC, Hunter, NY.

When you hear the word "aromatherapy," you probably think of a scented bath or a fragrant candle.

But medical practitioners in the United States and around the world are using distilled oils of aromatic plants medicinally. Essential oils activate the *parasympathetic nervous system*, causing relaxation, which speeds healing.

AROMATHERAPY IN ACTION

Plant oils can be used in a warm bath…in a "carrier oil"—such as almond or sesame oil—for massage…or in a lotion.

The oil aromas can also be sniffed from a bottle…a cotton ball…or a *diffuser*—a machine that emits the aroma into the air.

Clinical and scientific studies support the use of aromatherapy as an adjunct to medical care for treating…

•**Anxiety.** Essential oils that were inhaled for three minutes relieved anxiety in men and women, according to research published in the *International Journal of Neuroscience.* Use rosemary, Roman chamomile or patchouli.

Typical treatment: Sniff one to three drops when anxious.

Caution: Avoid using rosemary if you have high blood pressure.

•**Bronchitis.** Use spike lavender.

Typical treatment: One drop of spike lavender in a bowl of three cups of boiling water. Drape a towel over your head, close your eyes and inhale the steam. Do this for five minutes, four times a day.

•**Hair loss.** In people with patchy hair loss due to *alopecia areata*, essential oils helped restore hair growth, notes an *Archives of Dermatology* study that used a carrier oil containing a mixture of thyme (two drops), rosemary (three drops), lavender (three drops) and cedarwood (two drops).

Typical treatment: Massage the mixture into the scalp for two minutes daily.

•**Headache.** Use peppermint. If pain isn't gone in five minutes, try Roman chamomile or true lavender.

Typical treatment: Five drops in one teaspoon of carrier oil. Apply to temples or sniff.

•**Hot flashes.** Use clary sage, fennel, geranium or rose.

Typical treatment: Ten drops in two cups of water in a spray bottle. Spray on face during hot flash.

•**Insomnia.** Use ylang ylang, neroli or rose.

Typical treatment: Five drops in a diffuser placed in the bedroom.

•**Lower-back pain.** Use lemongrass. If you feel no relief in 20 minutes, try rosemary or spike lavender.

Typical treatment: Five drops in one teaspoon of carrier oil. Apply to the painful area every three hours.

•**Menstrual cramps.** Use geranium.

Typical treatment: Five drops added to one teaspoon of carrier oil. Rub on the lower abdomen and lower back every three hours.

•**Muscle spasms.** Use clary sage, sage or try lavender.

Typical treatment: Five drops added to one teaspoon of carrier oil. Apply to the affected muscles at least every three hours.

•**Osteoarthritis.** Use frankincense, rosemary or true lavender.

125

Typical treatment: Five drops added to one teaspoon of carrier oil. Apply to the painful area every three hours.

WHAT TO BUY

Aromatherapy is most effective when the essential oils are prepared with no extraneous ingredients.

A good brand is Scents & Scentsibility (*www.scentsibility.com*). Their essential oils are also available in health-food stores.

USING AROMATHERAPY SAFELY

Some essential oils can irritate or burn skin if applied undiluted. Always dilute oils before using topically. If skin stings or becomes red, dilute with a plain carrier oil and wash with unperfumed soap.

Essential oils are flammable. Store them away from candles, fires, cigarettes and stoves. Don't pour oil on lightbulbs to scent a room.

Caution: Essential oils can be lethal if they are ingested—even in tiny doses. Keep away from children and pets. People with asthma or epilepsy and pregnant women should consult their doctors before using aromatherapy.

Vitamin C May Help Block Ulcers

Joel A. Simon, MD, MPH, FACN, associate professor of clinical medicine and epidemiology, University of California, San Francisco, School of Medicine, and staff physician, San Francisco Veterans Affairs Medical Center.

James Everhart, MD, chief, epidemiology and clinical trials branch, division of digestive diseases and nutrition, National Institute of Diabetes & Digestive & Kidney Diseases, National Institutes of Health, Bethesda, MD.

Journal of the American College of Nutrition.

People who consume large amounts of vitamin C to try to protect themselves from colds might also be defending their stomach and intestines against ulcers.

The higher a person's blood levels of ascorbic acid, another name for vitamin C, the lower their risk of gastrointestinal trouble, according to a study.

"We are not the first to show this," admits Dr. Joel A. Simon, an associate professor of clinical medicine and epidemiology at the University of California, San Francisco, School of Medicine and a staff physician at the San Francisco Veterans Affairs Medical Center. "But it could be the largest study" so far.

THE STUDY

Simon and his team of researchers examined the Third National Health and Nutrition Examination Survey (NHANES III) and discovered that almost one-third of the 6,746 adults who were evaluated had antibodies against *Helicobacter pylori*. This strain of bacteria is now believed to cause most peptic ulcers.

Chronic infection with *H. pylori* is an important risk factor, Simon notes, for both peptic ulcer problems and gastric cancer.

Researchers found that higher blood levels of ascorbic acid in the people studied were associated with lower rates of H. pylori infection, Simon says.

After the researchers accounted for factors that might affect the relationship, including age and body mass index, they still found that the subjects with the highest blood levels of ascorbic acid had a 25% lower risk of having the infection.

When the researchers looked at infection with especially virulent strains of H. pylori, there was a 69% lower risk for those with higher blood levels of ascorbic acid.

NO CAUSE-EFFECT LINK DISCOVERED YET…

Simon does not know why vitamin C may work, although animal studies have found that ascorbic acid inhibits the growth of H. pylori.

If there is a true association, he says, higher intakes of vitamin C might help prevent infection and, in turn, ulcers. Simon's study was supported by a donation from Roche Vitamins Inc. and a Public Health Service grant.

"It's an interesting finding," says Dr. James Everhart, chief of the epidemiology and clinical trials branch of the division of digestive diseases and nutrition at the National Institute of Diabetes & Digestive & Kidney Diseases.

"But I think the results were not terribly strong." And it still doesn't prove cause and effect, he adds.

Every year, there are as many as 500,000 new cases of peptic ulcer disease in the United States, according to the American Gastroenterological Association.

In addition to infection, many ulcers are the result of irritation from nonsteroidal anti-inflammatory drugs (NSAIDs), such as aspirin and ibuprofen.

Contrary to popular belief, ulcers are not caused by eating spicy food.

For information on H. pylori and ulcers, visit the National Digestive Diseases Information Clearinghouse at *http://digestive.niddk.nih.gov.*

Echinacea Questioned As a Cold Fighter

Bruce Barrett, MD, PhD, associate professor of family medicine, University of Wisconsin-Madison.

James N. Dillard, MD, DC, former assistant clinical professor at Columbia University College of Physicians and Surgeons and past medical director of Columbia's Rosenthal Center for Complementary and Alternative Medicine, both in New York City. He is now in private practice in New York City and East Hampton, NY.

Annals of Internal Medicine.

E chinacea, the well-known herb that is used as a popular cold treatment, isn't very effective in shortening the duration of the common cold or the severity of its symptoms, according to researchers from the University of Wisconsin.

But they acknowledge that more research is needed before they can recommend that people who have colds shelve their echinacea.

SOME DISAGREE WITH STUDY

Advocates of the herb suspect that it increases the activity of the immune system, helping it to fight off a cold.

Despite the study results showing no benefit to the herbal treatment, the lead author, Dr. Bruce Barrett, an associate professor of family medicine, says he's not ready to give up on echinacea—a favorite of North American Plains Indians who used it often for medicinal purposes.

THE STUDY

The researchers gave the herb or a placebo, in capsule form, to 142 otherwise healthy college students who had just come down with colds. Without knowing whether they were getting the herb or the placebo, the students took the pills for up to 10 days.

No differences were found in the severity of symptoms, such as cough, nasal congestion, fever and aches, or in the duration of the cold. In each student, the cold symptoms lasted two to 10 days.

Among the limitations of his study, Barrett says, was the type of herb used. He used a mixture of herb and root, which has not previously been tested. He says it may be ineffective because of a low bioavailability—the degree to which the mixture can be used by the body for its intended purposes.

LIQUID FORM MAY HELP

If you are going to try an herbal remedy, Dr. James Dillard, former assistant clinical professor at Columbia University College of Physicians and Surgeons in New York City, recommends that the liquid form—called a tincture—of echinacea be used.

"There have been many studies to show echinacea works, but many people don't take it the right way, which is why they don't always get results," Dillard says.

Using echinacea daily as a preventive won't help because it begins losing its effectiveness after about 10 days, experts say. Instead, "take one large dose at the first symptom of a cold and you can cut the duration significantly," Dillard suggests.

■ ■ ■ ■

Alarming Tylenol Danger

A ccidental poisonings from *acetaminophen* (Tylenol) are rising. Acetaminophen is one of the safest painkillers when taken in the correct dose, but it can cause serious—even fatal —liver damage when dosing directions aren't followed. Adults should take no more than 4,000 milligrams (mg) of acetaminophen a day (the equivalent of eight extra-strength Tylenol pills). It's easy to exceed the maximum when you're feeling under the weather and perhaps using multiple products with acetaminophen without realizing it.

Example: 1,000 mg of acetaminophen every six hours from Tylenol Cold & Flu Severe, 500 mg per dose from Excedrin and another 1,000 mg from Nyquil Cold/Flu at bedtime puts you well above the 4,000 mg/day limit.

Caution: Some prescription drugs contain acetaminophen.

Examples: Percocet contains 325 mg per pill...Vicodin ES contains 750 mg.

Anne Larson, MD, associate professor of medicine, University of Texas Southwestern Medical Center, Dallas.

■ ■ ■ ■

Daily Aspirin

Daily low-dose aspirin therapy affects men and women differently.

Men: One aspirin a day reduces heart attack risk by 32% but has no effect on stroke risk.

Women: An aspirin a day reduces stroke risk by 17% but has no significant effect on heart attack risk.

Jeffrey Berger, MD, cardiologist, department of cardiovascular medicine, Duke University, Durham, NC, and leader of an analysis of 95,456 patients, published in *Journal of the American Medical Association*.

■ ■ ■ ■

Infection Fighter

To help fight infections, take probiotics. These beneficial bacteria—which reside naturally in the body—can boost your immunity.

Example: The bacteria *Lactobacillus acidophilus* fights digestive tract infections, including *rotavirus* and *clostridium difficile*. You can get probiotics from live-culture yogurt, sauerkraut, miso and kefir, and from supplements. Choose a supplement with *Lactobacillus acidophilus* and *bifidobacterium*, with at least two billion organisms per dose. Take according to label directions.

Mark A. Stengler, ND, naturopathic physician in private practice, La Jolla, CA...adjunct associate clinical professor at the National College of Natural Medicine, Portland, OR...author of 16 books, including *The Natural Physician's Healing Therapies* (Bottom Line Books) and coauthor of *Prescription for Natural Cures* (Wiley)...and author of the *Bottom Line/Natural Healing* newsletter.

Silicon Improves Bone Density

Mark A. Stengler, ND, naturopathic physician in private practice, La Jolla, CA...adjunct associate clinical professor at the National College of Natural Medicine, Portland, OR...author of 16 books, including *The Natural Physician's Healing Therapies* (Bottom Line Books) and coauthor of *Prescription for Natural Cures* (Wiley)...and author of the *Bottom Line/Natural Healing* newsletter.

Silicon dioxide, also referred to as silica, is a nutrient that is present in vegetables, whole grains and seafood. It is used by the body to keep bones, cartilage, tendons and artery walls healthy. The average intake of silicon in adults is 14 mg to 21 mg per day. A recent study found that supplementing with silicon improved several markers that reflect bone and connective tissue breakdown. The study investigated the effect of a low dose of supplemental silicon on markers of bone breakdown and bone-mineral density in 114 women with osteopenia (mild bone loss) or osteoporosis over 12 months.

The study participants were divided into four groups. All received 1,000 mg of calcium and 800 international units (IU) of vitamin D-3 (cholecalciferol) each day. Three of the groups also took supplements of 3 mg, 6 mg or 12 mg of a usable form of silicon, sold as BioSil (distributed by Jarrow Formulas and available at local and on-line vitamin retailers). Researchers found that the silicon supplement enhanced the benefits of the calcium and vitamin D supplementation. Although bone-mineral density of the spine did not change significantly, a subgroup of 81 women who took 6 mg of BioSil per day and whose thighbone density score was lower than average at the start of the study showed significant thighbone density improvements.

For people with low bone-mineral density and those at risk for osteoporosis—that is, people with a strong family history of osteoporosis, thin bones or a history of eating disorders as well as those who have used steroids (such as *prednisone*) for long periods or who smoke—I recommend a supplement of 6 mg to 12 mg of silicon daily in addition to calcium, magnesium, vitamin D, B vitamins and essential fatty acids, all of which support bone metabolism.

Melatonin Reduces Blood Pressure

Mark A. Stengler, ND, naturopathic physician in private practice, La Jolla, CA...adjunct associate clinical professor at the National College of Natural Medicine, Portland, OR...author of 16 books, including *The Natural Physician's Healing Therapies* (Bottom Line Books) and coauthor of *Prescription for Natural Cures* (Wiley)...and author of the *Bottom Line/Natural Healing* newsletter.

A study of melatonin involved 18 women, ages 47 to 63, half with hypertension being successfully controlled with ACE inhibitor medication and half who had normal blood pressure.

For three weeks, participants took either 3 mg of time-released melatonin (a supplement typically used to promote sleep) or a placebo one hour before bed. They were then switched to the other treatment for another three weeks. After taking melatonin for three weeks, 84% of the women had at least a 10 mm/Hg decrease in nocturnal (nighttime) systolic and diastolic blood pressure, while only 39% experienced a decrease in nocturnal blood pressure after taking the placebo. The reduction was the greatest in those with controlled hypertension. In both groups, no change was found in daytime blood pressure readings. Previous studies have found similar results when men with untreated hypertension took melatonin.

My view: Melatonin, a hormone produced by the pineal gland in the brain, is secreted in response to darkness and promotes a normal sleep cycle. A deficiency of melatonin may prevent relaxation of the cardiovascular and nervous systems, increasing blood pressure. (Normally, heart rate and blood vessel constriction decrease at night.) While people with hypertension often monitor their daytime blood pressure, they usually are unaware of their readings at night. This can be a mistake. High nighttime blood pressure is just as important as high daytime pressure.

For people with high blood pressure whose levels also tend to be elevated at night, I recommend taking 3 mg of time-released melatonin one hour before bed. To determine if you have elevated blood pressure at night, use a home blood pressure monitor to test levels several times during the day and twice a night (at midnight and 4:00 am) for three days.

Caution: Consult your doctor before trying melatonin. It may require an adjustment to your blood pressure medication. Women who are pregnant or breastfeeding, as well as those taking birth control pills, should not use melatonin.

The Truth about Vitamin E

Mark A. Stengler, ND, naturopathic physician in private practice, La Jolla, CA...adjunct associate clinical professor at the National College of Natural Medicine, Portland, OR...author of 16 books, including *The Natural Physician's Healing Therapies* (Bottom Line Books) and coauthor of *Prescription for Natural Cures* (Wiley)...and author of the *Bottom Line/Natural Healing* newsletter.

F or more than 30 years, vitamin E has been one of the most widely used supplements. It's been touted as a key antioxidant, helping to prevent heart disease, certain cancers and other serious illnesses. But two years ago, vitamin E became quite controversial, because a few studies showed that it could be harmful. So it left many people wondering, *Is vitamin E safe? Is it effective? For what conditions? And what type of vitamin E should one use?*

Vitamin E is found naturally in wheat germ, nuts, seeds, whole grains, egg yolks and leafy, green vegetables. Animal products are a poor source of vitamin E. The recommended dietary allowance for vitamin E is 15 mg, or approximately 22 international units (IU), per day. Serious vitamin E deficiency is rare, although many Americans don't get enough of the vitamin. People on low-fat diets are susceptible to low vitamin E levels, because fat is needed for absorption of vitamin E. And people with the genetic condition cystic fibrosis have trouble absorbing vitamin E.

Vitamin E has been shown to be important as a supplement for people with specific diseases, such as Alzheimer's and diabetes, and those with a high susceptibility to certain conditions, such as bladder cancer and eye disease. Vitamin E prevents LDL "bad" cholesterol from becoming oxidized (damaged), thereby helping to guard against plaque formation in the arteries, known as atherosclerosis. Also, low vitamin E levels are associated with an increased risk of major depression, rheumatoid arthritis and preeclampsia (a condition during pregnancy characterized by high blood pressure and swelling of the hands and face).

CONTROVERSIAL STUDIES

Two well-publicized studies have raised questions about vitamin E. The first was a meta-analysis (a study of other studies) led by researchers from the Johns Hopkins School of Medicine. The researchers reviewed 19 vitamin E studies that followed almost 136,000 patients. Most of these studies targeted populations at high risk for a chronic disease, usually coronary heart disease. Nine of the 19 studies focused on vitamin E alone, while the other 10 studies combined vitamin E with other vitamins or minerals. These studies ranged from 1.4 to 8.2 years in length. Vitamin E dosage varied from 16.5 IU to 2,000 IU per day, with a median dosage of 400 IU per day. The meta-analysis found that those taking 400 IU or more of vitamin E daily for at least one year were 10% more likely to die from all causes than those who took a smaller dose.

There are several problems with this analysis. First, researchers combined data that used both natural supplements (which provide the same type of vitamin E as that found in food) and synthetic forms of supplemental vitamin E. Previous research has shown that natural forms of vitamin E are better utilized by the body than cheaper, synthetic forms. The Cambridge Heart Antioxidant Study used only a natural form of vitamin E and found that a dose of at least 400 IU daily substantially reduced the rate of nonfatal heart attacks after one year of use.

The biggest criticism of the meta-analysis was that most of the studies included elderly people who had existing health problems such as cancer, Alzheimer's disease, heart disease and other potentially fatal illnesses. Even the authors of the study stated, "The generalizability of the findings to healthy adults is uncertain. Precise estimation of the threshold at which risk increases is difficult."

Another study, which was published in the *Journal of the American Medical Association*, focused on patients age 55 or older with vascular disease or diabetes. The study concluded that for people with vascular disease or diabetes, long-term supplementation with natural vitamin E does not prevent cancer or cardiovascular events and may increase risk for heart failure. This study provides no evidence that vitamin E is unsafe for people who are healthy.

POSITIVE FINDINGS

Many studies exist that demonstrate both the safety and effectiveness of vitamin E (in natural and synthetic forms). *A few examples…*

•**A Harvard study of more than 80,000 healthy, female nurses** ages 34 to 59 found a 41% reduction in the risk of heart disease in those who had taken daily vitamin E supplements of 100 IU or more for at least two years.

•**A study of almost 40,000 male health professionals** ages 40 to 75 found that those who took daily vitamin E supplements of at least 100 IU for more than two years experienced a 37% lower risk of heart disease.

•**A National Institute of Aging study** focusing on 11,000 people between the ages of 67 and 105 found that those who used vitamins C and E supplements in various dosages had a 53% reduction in mortality from heart disease and a 42% reduction in death from all causes, compared with nonusers.

•**One study of moderate-severity Alzheimer's patients** conducted at Columbia University in New York City showed that a very high daily dose of vitamin E (2,000 IU) delayed the progression of Alzheimer's disease.

DIFFERENT TYPES

Vitamin E really refers to a family of compounds. There are more than 12 vitamin E compounds found in nature (currently eight forms are available in supplement form). There are two main groups of compounds—*tocopherols* (found in foods such as corn, soy and peanuts) and *tocotrienols* (found in rice, barley, rye and wheat). Many foods contain a blend of these two groups. Both have subgroups called *alpha, beta, gamma* and *delta*.

The most commonly used natural supplement form is *alpha-tocopherol*, and most studies have researched this form. But taking just alpha-tocopherol can reduce blood levels of gamma- and delta-tocopherols, which is not beneficial.

Epidemiological (population) studies indicate that higher blood gamma-tocopherol levels correspond to the reduction of prostate cancer and coronary heart disease. Also, delta- and gamma-tocotrienols reduce the liver's production of cholesterol. One of the positive aspects of the negative vitamin E studies I mentioned earlier is that they have pushed researchers to look deeper into what vitamin E supplements should really contain.

I spoke with Barrie Tan, PhD, president of American River Nutrition, Inc., and adjunct professor of food science at the University of Massachusetts, Amherst, who is a specialist in the production and supplementation of vitamin E. He explains that 70% of (dietary) vitamin E consumed by North Americans is the gamma-tocopherol form due to the abundance of soy and corn in our diets. He believes that vitamin E supplements used for disease prevention should be a blend of both tocopherols and tocotrienols. I agree with this view, because these forms are more similar to what we find in food.

One example of a full-spectrum vitamin E product that has a good ratio of tocopherols and tocotrienols is Now Foods' Tru-E BioComplex. To find a health-food store that sells this product, call 888-669-3663 or go to *www.nowfoods. com*. A good dosage for anyone, healthy or not, is 200 IU daily. Consult with your doctor before using dosages above 200 IU, especially if you are taking a blood-thinning medication, such as *warfarin* (Coumadin)—vitamin E can have a blood-thinning effect.

Alpha Lipoic Acid A True Cure-All?

Mark A. Stengler, ND, naturopathic physician in private practice, La Jolla, CA...adjunct associate clinical professor at the National College of Natural Medicine, Portland, OR...author of 16 books, including *The Natural Physician's Healing Therapies* (Bottom Line Books) and coauthor of *Prescription for Natural Cures* (Wiley)...and author of the *Bottom Line/Natural Healing* newsletter.

The nutritional supplement *alpha lipoic acid* (ALA) is touted as a treatment for cancer, chronic fatigue syndrome, diabetes, glaucoma, HIV/AIDS and liver disease.

ALA was identified as a vitamin-like substance more than 50 years ago. It is produced in the cells of the body and also is found in small amounts in certain foods, such as broccoli, spinach, tomatoes, peas, Brussels sprouts and liver.

ALA is a unique antioxidant that neutralizes free radicals (potentially harmful negatively charged molecules). ALA is absorbed into water-soluble and fat-soluble tissues, thereby providing antioxidant protection to all cells of the body.

Another important feature of ALA is that it facilitates the regeneration of antioxidants. This is helpful because antioxidants become inactivated after neutralizing free radicals. ALA reactivates these antioxidants, including vitamins E and C, coenzyme Q10 and *glutathione,* a group of nutrients considered to be the most powerful of the antioxidant network.

THE SCIENTIFIC EVIDENCE

There is reliable research supporting the use of ALA in the treatment of type 2 diabetes. Daily supplementation with ALA has been shown to improve blood sugar (glucose) uptake by cells and insulin resistance (allowing insulin to transport glucose into cells more effectively) and reduce nerve damage and pain associated with diabetic neuropathy.

A four-week, placebo-controlled multicenter study measured the effects of ALA on insulin sensitivity (the ability of the body's cells to recognize and respond to insulin). Seventy-four patients with type 2 diabetes were randomized to receive either a placebo or 600 mg of ALA once, twice or three times daily. Blood glucose and insulin levels were measured before and at the end of the study. Those receiving ALA had a 25% improvement in insulin sensitivity after the four weeks of treatment. All three doses of ALA had the same effect.

There is additional research showing that ALA at doses of 600 mg to 1,200 mg daily is helpful in alleviating diabetic neuropathy, a condition in which nerve damage causes pain, burning or numbness, especially in the lower legs and feet. Improvement with ALA can take three to five weeks.

In one Russian study, nearly half of glaucoma patients who took 150 mg of ALA daily for one month experienced improved vision. It is thought that the antioxidant properties of ALA improve the health of eye tissue and help the vision of people with glaucoma.

DOSAGE

For the treatment of type 2 diabetes and diabetic neuropathy, I recommend taking 600 mg to 1,200 mg of ALA daily. For glaucoma, cancer, chronic fatigue syndrome and liver disease, I recommend 300 mg to 1,200 mg of ALA daily. Its antioxidant and blood sugar–regulating properties support better immune function as well as energy production. ALA also can be taken at a dosage of 50 mg to 100 mg daily by anyone who wants to benefit from its immune-boosting property.

For optimal absorption, take supplemental ALA on an empty stomach. There are two main supplemental forms of ALA. The R form is found in plants and animals. The S form is a synthetic version. Recent data has found the R form to be more active in the body than the S form. I recommend taking the R form, which is commonly available in tablets at health-food stores. Side effects, including skin rash and digestive upset, are rare.

Toxic Vitamins: Are You Taking Too Much of a "Good" Thing?

Laurie Tansman, MS, RD, CDN, clinical nutritionist, Mount Sinai Medical Center, New York City.

Jyni Holland, MS, RD, clinical nutritionist, New York University Medical Center, New York City.

In our quest to fight colds, build muscle or have smoother skin, some of us believe that taking extra doses of vitamins and minerals is the best way to go. But taking large doses of any one supplement can do us more harm than good, experts say.

"Unless you are suffering from a severe deficiency, if you have a disease or disorder that is causing you to be nutrient-deficient, the most you are going to need is a high-quality multivitamin supplement, to be taken as insurance, and not used as your main source of nutrients,"

says Laurie Tansman, a clinical nutritionist at Mount Sinai Medical Center in New York.

Most people won't get into trouble taking a high-potency multivitamin. But problems can occur, experts say, when you start playing around with individual doses—even when recommended by some diet and fitness programs.

VITAMINS

Vitamins A, D and E are among those causing the most concern because they are fat-soluble, can be stored for long periods of time in the body—mostly in the liver—and a cumulative buildup can occur, turning your vitamin regimen from healthy to toxic.

•**Vitamin D is one of the most toxic supplements,** and in very large amounts can lead to liver and kidney failure, says Jyni Holland, a clinical nutritionist at New York University Medical Center.

•**Take too much *vitamin A* and you could end up with hair loss,** nausea, vomiting and significant joint pain. And there is evidence to show that too much vitamin A may cause birth defects, so it is recommended that pregnant women take no more than what comes in their prenatal vitamins.

•**Too much *vitamin E* can thin the blood so much it could lead to internal hemorrhaging,** particularly if you are taking any blood-thinning medication for a cardiac or hypertension problem.

•**Vitamin K has the reverse effect—causing blood to clot.** However it, too, can cause problems when used by people who are taking blood-thinning drugs.

•**The *B vitamins* and *vitamin C* are water-soluble and therefore don't build up in tissues and rarely reach toxic levels on their own.** They are considered relatively safe, even in high doses—unless you are also taking iron supplements.

Because vitamin C enhances iron absorption, taking large doses of both could increase your risk of a toxic reaction.

In very high levels, vitamin B-6 has been associated with neurological symptoms such as nerve tingling, while vitamin B-3—also known as niacin—could be a problem if you suffer from heart disease.

MINERALS

•*Calcium* **has been linked to the formation of kidney stones** and it can be packed with vitamin D, which helps the body absorb calcium. "If you are megadosing on calcium, you may also be megadosing on vitamin D and setting yourself up for some toxic reactions without even realizing you are doing so," Tansman says.

•*Iron* **supplements are commonly used by menstruating women,** and are also sometimes used by body builders and athletes who are seeking to fight fatigue. "What most people don't realize is iron is an oxidant. And when it's exposed to oxygen inside the body, it becomes a free radical," Holland says. Free radicals cause an oxidation process that eventually damages cells and can increase the risk of certain diseases, including cancer.

Both Tansman and Holland agree that overdosing on supplements can be easier than you think, and that the best way to get all the nutrients you need is to take one multivitamin daily and eat plenty of vitamin-rich foods.

The Case Against Vitamins

Robert M. Russell, MD, director and senior scientist at Jean Mayer USDA Human Nutrition Research Center on Aging at Tufts University, Boston, is former chairman of the Institute of Medicine's Food and Nutrition Board.

At least half of American adults take vitamins and other supplements regularly, spending more than $23 billion a year on these nutritional aids in the belief that supplements can help prevent disease and improve health. However, evidence suggests that many supplements may be ineffective—and, in large doses, some may even do more harm than good.

Here's what you need to know now...

MULTIVITAMINS

According to a recent report by a panel of advisers at the National Institutes of Health, there is not enough evidence to recommend the use of multivitamin and mineral supplements to prevent chronic disease. And most people taking multivitamins don't really need them.

Reason: These individuals tend to be health conscious anyway, getting important nutrients from the food they eat.

There are, however, some people who do need supplements...

•**Anyone who eats fewer than 1,500 calories per day** should take a daily multivitamin that contains 100% of the Recommended Dietary Allowance (RDA) of all key nutrients.

•**Women who are trying to conceive** and those who are in the first trimester of pregnancy should take a daily prenatal multivitamin—which has 400 micrograms (mcg) of folic acid. Folic acid has been shown to reduce the risk of birth defects.

•**People over age 50** should take a B-12 supplement or a multivitamin containing at least the RDA of 2.4 mcg of B-12 if they don't get that amount in fortified foods, such as cereals. That's because as people age, the stomach produces less acid to digest food, making it difficult to absorb B-12 from food.

•**Those over age 70** have trouble getting enough calcium and vitamin D from food.

Example: To get the recommended amount of calcium, they would have to drink a quart of milk a day. People in this age group should have at least 600 international units (IUs) of vitamin D (15 mcg) and 1,200 milligrams (mg) of calcium a day.

MEGADOSES

The real concern is with the millions of Americans who consume nutrient-specific supplements in dosages that far exceed the RDAs.

Examples: Many people take vitamin C pills in hopes of boosting immunity and preventing colds...vitamins B and E to protect their hearts...beta-carotene and other antioxidants to help fight cancer.

Below are common supplements and the possible health problems that may result from taking high doses...

•**Vitamin E.** Although this antioxidant has been touted to improve heart health, recent "gold-standard" studies—randomized trials in which participants who are not aware of whether or not they are taking a supplement or a placebo are carefully tracked—show the opposite may be true. One meta-analysis, led by researchers from the Johns Hopkins School of Medicine, analyzed 19 previous trials involving almost 136,000 people and found that vitamin E supplements—especially in the often-sold daily dosage of 400 IUs—caused a slight increase in death from heart attack. In another study of 9,500 people, those who took vitamin E had a 13% higher risk of heart failure.

Another danger: Vitamin E supplements could interfere with chemotherapy or radiotherapy by suppressing free-radical production, which is necessary to kill cancer cells.

•**B vitamins.** Until recently, the belief was that vitamins B-6, B-12 and folic acid reduced the risk of heart attack and stroke by lowering the level of *homocysteine* in the blood, a well-documented risk factor for coronary artery disease. However, one study published in *The New England Journal of Medicine*, which followed people who had had a heart attack, found that the risk of a second attack increased after taking B-vitamin supplements.

Another danger: In animal studies, high doses of B vitamins seemed to stimulate cancer growth. There is no proof of this effect in humans, but there is a theoretical risk.

•**Vitamin C.** Contrary to popular wisdom, there's no credible evidence that vitamin C supplements help prevent colds, although they may shorten the duration by a day or so. For people who eat healthfully, supplementing with vitamin C does not seem to boost immunity.

Dangers: Vitamin C supplements raise the risk of kidney stones. As with vitamin E, vitamin C supplements should be avoided by cancer patients who are undergoing chemotherapy or radiotherapy.

•**Vitamin A and beta-carotene.** Vitamin A comes in two forms—as preformed vitamin A or as one of several carotenoids, of which beta-carotene is the best known. Both forms of vitamin A supplements have proved risky.

Beta-carotene supplements have been found to speed the risk of death from lung cancer and heart disease in people who smoke. More recently, a study of 75,000 people found that

supplements of preformed vitamin A—as well as diets rich in vitamin A—increased the risk of hip fractures by 48%. This was observed with dosages just slightly above the RDAs of 900 mcg for men and 700 mcg for women.

Other dangers: Unless you are deficient in vitamin A—rare in the US—taking supplements containing more than 3,000 mcg (10,000 IUs) can cause liver damage. In pregnant women, high-dose vitamin A supplements may cause birth defects.

•**Glucosamine and chondroitin sulfate.** In a federally sponsored clinical trial, the often-used combination of glucosamine and chondroitin sulfate, once believed to reduce osteoarthritis knee pain by rebuilding cartilage, proved no more effective than a placebo for most of the 1,583 participants. Only a small group of patients with severe arthritis experienced slight relief.

Dangers: Mild gastrointestinal upset is a possible side effect. Theoretically, people with seafood allergies may be allergic to glucosamine, which is derived from shellfish.

•**Saw palmetto.** Although taken by millions of men with an enlarged prostate, the herb saw palmetto didn't relieve symptoms any better than a placebo in a well-respected randomized trial published in *The New England Journal of Medicine.*

Dangers: Saw palmetto should not be taken with blood thinners, such as aspirin or *warfarin* (Coumadin). Possible side effects of saw palmetto include stomach pain, nausea, diarrhea and impotence.

•**Zinc.** Another antioxidant nutrient, zinc was once believed to help boost immunity and prevent colds. However, in most studies, supplements seem to benefit only those with zinc deficiency, which is rare among Americans eating a balanced diet.

Danger: Zinc supplements lower the body's copper levels, which in turn may increase the risk of cardiac arrhythmia.

•**Copper.** In adequate amounts—the RDA of 0.9 mg—copper helps in the formation of red blood cells, nerve fibers and collagen for healthy skin and bones. It also acts as an antioxidant. However, in higher amounts, copper may work as a pro-oxidant, promoting free-radical damage that could contribute to Alzheimer's disease—especially in people who eat a high-fat diet.

In a six-year study of 3,718 people whose average age was 75, published in *Archives of Neurology*, the rate of memory loss and other cognitive decline was equivalent to 19 years of aging in those who consumed 2.75 mg of copper per day—levels found in some multivitamins—and ate a diet rich in saturated and trans fats. However, copper intake wasn't associated with mental decline in people who ate low-fat diets.

Another danger: The risk of liver damage occurs with dosages above 10 mg a day.

THE BOTTOM LINE

Although high levels of certain nutrients help prevent disease and improve health, the benefit typically comes from diets rich in those vitamins and minerals. Foods also contain health-protecting *phytochemicals*—some of which have not yet been identified—and these substances are not in supplements.

The old advice still is best—eat a healthful, well-balanced diet to meet the RDAs of necessary nutrients.

Supplements Can Save Your Life

Mark A. Stengler, ND, naturopathic physician in private practice, La Jolla, CA...adjunct associate clinical professor at the National College of Natural Medicine, Portland, OR...author of 16 books, including *The Natural Physician's Healing Therapies* (Bottom Line Books) and coauthor of *Prescription for Natural Cures* (Wiley)...and author of the *Bottom Line/Natural Healing* newsletter.

Even if you are careful about eating a well-balanced diet, you can still be deficient in important vitamins and minerals that are crucial in helping to prevent illness. In fact, in a major article published in the *Journal of the American Medical Association*, researchers from Harvard Medical School reported that most adults have mild nutritional deficiencies and recommended a daily multivitamin/mineral supplement.

Every older adult should take a daily multivitamin/mineral supplement as well as additional supplements to support normal immune function and prevent chronic disease.

As valuable as many supplements are, use your common sense—don't overdo it. More isn't necessarily better. Always discuss dosage, safety and health value with your doctor first.

CHOOSING A MULTISUPPLEMENT

Look for a product that contains a broad base of vitamins and minerals. For each vitamin, the amount in the supplement should cover 100% of the Daily Value (DV), the daily amount you need as set by the FDA. In most brands, the amounts in a single capsule or tablet won't be 100% for every vitamin—otherwise, the pill would be so big that it would be hard to swallow. To get the right daily amounts, you'll probably need a formulation that requires more than one pill a day.

The right formulation will also provide 100% of many important minerals, such as zinc and selenium.

Important: Unless your doctor has diagnosed you with iron-deficiency anemia, choose a multisupplement that does not contain iron. Extra iron, beyond what you get from your food, can cause inflammation, liver damage, joint pain, fatigue and premature heart disease.

Note: Multisupplements sold in health-food stores and vitamin shops are generally better than those sold in pharmacies and grocery stores. In many cases, the formulations are more comprehensive and ingredients are higher quality and more potent.

SUPPLEMENTS FOR BONE HEALTH

The amounts of calcium and magnesium in a daily multisupplement are small—only about 10% of the DV. In addition to a daily multi, I strongly recommend that women and men add a separate product containing 500 milligrams (mg) of calcium, 250 mg of magnesium and 400 to 600 international units (IU) of vitamin D to maintain bone health.

Vitamin D is also important for immune system support, and solid research indicates it has a role in preventing cancer. Don't exceed 2,000 IU of vitamin D a day. Excessive amounts cause liver damage and possibly kidney damage. For best absorption, take this supplement at a different time of day than your multi.

VITAMIN B-12

Numerous studies have shown that 20% of Americans age 65 and older have very low blood levels of vitamin B-12. Others may have levels on the low side but don't yet show symptoms of deficiency. Vitamin B-12 is essential for making healthy red blood cells, maintaining mental acuity and protecting your heart, among other things. It is found in animal foods, such as eggs, dairy products and meat, but only in very small amounts that become increasingly hard to absorb as we age. I suggest a daily under-the-tongue supplement containing 1,000 micrograms (mcg).

DANGEROUS INTERACTIONS

While the amounts of vitamins and minerals in a daily multisupplement are unlikely to cause any drug interactions or toxicity, be cautious about adding extra supplements, especially…

•**Vitamin E and vitamin K.** If you take a blood-thinning medication, such as *warfarin* (Coumadin), you need to avoid extra vitamin E and extra vitamin K. Vitamin E is in every multisupplement formulation and vitamin K is in some. The amounts in your daily supplement probably aren't enough to interfere with warfarin. Do not take additional doses of these vitamins unless your doctor recommends them.

•**Vitamin A.** Avoid taking additional vitamin A—too much can be toxic. Up to 5,000 IU daily is safe for most people. Nursing mothers, pregnant women and anyone with liver disease should avoid these supplements.

WHAT ELSE YOU MAY NEED

•**Fish oil.** I also strongly recommend a daily fish oil supplement for most people. Studies have shown that fish oil helps prevent stroke, heart disease and Alzheimer's and other memory problems. Fish oil also has an anti-inflammatory effect that's helpful in protecting your joints. Choose a steam-distilled product (check the label) that contains a total of 500 mg of both eicosapentaenoic acid (EPA) and docosahexaenoic acid (DHA), the active omega-3 fatty acids in fish oil.

Caution: Fish oil can thin your blood. Do not take fish oil supplements if you are on a blood-thinning medication.

•**Super greens.** "Green products"—powdered supplements that contain super-green foods, such as chlorella, wheatgrass, spirulina and alfalfa—are a great way to get the nutritional benefits of green vegetables in a concentrated way. These green plants are very high in chlorophyll, minerals, fiber and plant nutrients, such as lutein, which helps protect your eyes against the sight-robbing disease called macular degeneration.

Super greens help with bowel regularity, have valuable antioxidant properties that protect against cell damage and help your body remove toxins and waste products. Many older adults don't get the recommended five or more servings of fresh vegetables every day.

Green products are available in powdered form (you can mix the powder into juice and other drinks) or capsules. I recommend Kyo-Green (*www.kyolic.com*) or Greens+ (*www.greensplus. com*), which are available at health-food stores. Follow the directions on the label. To avoid digestive upset, start with a small dose and gradually increase it to one tablespoon a day.

•**Joint supplements.** Because osteoarthritis is common among older adults, I recommend taking 1,500 mg of glucosamine sulfate, 1,200 mg of chondroitin sulfate and 2,000 to 3,000 mg of methylsulfonylmethane (MSM) daily to support healthy cartilage in the joints and reduce pain and stiffness. These nutrients provide essential building blocks for repairing damaged cartilage. Numerous studies have shown their safety and effectiveness, and the results of the government-funded Glucosamine/Chondroitin Arthritis Intervention Trial showed that glucosamine and chondroitin were very effective for relieving moderate to severe arthritis pain.

Cautions: Because glucosamine supplements are derived from shellfish shells, avoid them if you're allergic to shellfish. Also, MSM has a mild blood-thinning effect, so check with your doctor if you're on a blood-thinning medication.

•**Liver supplements.** The average older American takes at least one prescription drug, and many take three or more, daily. Many of these drugs stress or damage the liver. I recommend milk thistle, an herb that has been shown to protect the liver and kidneys, to anyone who regularly takes prescription medicine. Look for a product that contains 80% to 85% silymarin (the active ingredient in milk thistle) extract. Take 250 mg twice daily.

Are Your Supplements Working or Worthless?

Tod Cooperman, MD, president of ConsumerLab.com, a company that conducts independent testing of health, wellness and nutrition products. General test results are available at no charge to the public. *www.ConsumerLab. com*. He is also the founder of PharmacyChecker.com (*www.pharmacychecker.com*), an evaluator of Internet pharmacies, and editor of *Health, Harm, or Rip-Off? What's Really in Your Vitamins & Supplements*. Bottom Line Books.

S upplement manufacturers are not required to test their products for safety or purity. And the US Food and Drug Administration (FDA) is not required to test supplements unless an adverse effect, such as heart attack or liver failure, has been reported.

Problem: About one out of four supplements contains either less—or more—than the amount of active ingredient listed on the label…is contaminated with pesticides or heavy metals, such as lead or arsenic…or doesn't disintegrate as it should for proper absorption. Some manufacturers correct such problems when they become aware of them, but others do not.

To learn which supplements were deemed most reliable in testing, we spoke with Tod Cooperman, MD, president of ConsumerLab.com, an independent evaluator of supplements.*

MULTIVITAMIN/MULTIMINERAL

Supplement makers can legally exceed the tolerable upper intake levels (ULs) for vitamins and minerals—without warning consumers. The UL, set by the National Academies of Science, is the maximum daily intake of a nutrient that is likely to pose no risk for adverse effects in healthy people. Of 32 multivitamin/multiminerals recently tested by ConsumerLab.com, 12 contained at least one nutrient exceeding the UL.

*The products listed here have been evaluated by ConsumerLab.com. Other evaluators of supplements include the US Pharmacopeia (USP) and NSF International. Talk to your doctor before taking any nutritional supplement.

Test results: WEIL Andrew Weil, M.D. Daily Multivitamin…NOW Adam Superior Men's Multi …and Vitamin World Time Release Mega Vita-Min were among the products that exceeded the UL (35 milligrams [mg] per day) for the B vitamin niacin, with one (Swanson Daily Multi-Vitamin & Mineral) containing 100 mg. These niacin amounts were listed on the product labels. Excess niacin can cause skin flushing and tingling…very high amounts can cause liver damage. (Although 1,000 mg of niacin daily may help lower cholesterol, such high-dose therapy should be taken only under a doctor's supervision.)

Reliable products include…

•**Kirkland Signature** Daily Multi, with Lycopene & Lutein and Calcium.

•**Centrum Silver** Specially Formulated Multivitamin/Multimineral for Adults 50+.

•**Nutrilite Daily** Multivitamin and Multimineral.

GLUCOSAMINE AND CHONDROITIN

Glucosamine combined with chondroitin sulfate slows the joint deterioration and pain associated with osteoarthritis. Glucosamine helps build and repair cartilage, while chondroitin helps preserve the elasticity of cartilage. In a well-publicized study of 1,583 people with knee osteoarthritis, a combination of the supplements helped people with moderate to severe knee pain more effectively than the prescription anti-inflammatory drug celecoxib (Celebrex) or a placebo.

Some glucosamine/chondroitin combination supplements skimp on the chondroitin content, probably because it's expensive to produce (chondroitin is predominantly derived from cow cartilage). Of the 20 combination products we recently tested, six contained less chondroitin than listed on the label. Swanson Health Products Premium Brand, while claiming to contain 250 mg per dose of chondroitin sulfate, contained only 20 mg of chondroitin.

Helpful: Products that list an exact amount of "chondroitin sulfate" per dose typically are more reliable than those labeled chondroitin "complex" or "blend." In general, 1,200 mg of chondroitin sulfate and 1,500 mg of glucosamine sulfate or glucosamine hydrochloride daily are recommended for joint pain.

Reliable products include…

•**Puritan's Pride Triple Strength** Glucosamine 750 & Chondroitin 600 Dietary Supplement.

•**Cosamin DS Chondroitin Sulfate** Glucosamine HCl 500 mg/Chondroitin Sulfate 400 mg.

•**Vitamin World Triple Strength** Glucosamine 750 mg/Chondroitin 600 mg.

GINKGO BILOBA

In clinical trials, ginkgo biloba has been shown to fight the cognitive decline associated with dementia as well as circulation problems, ringing in the ears (tinnitus), depression and asthma. These benefits have been traced to powerful antioxidants known as *flavonol glycosides* and *terpene lactones*, compounds that appear to bolster brain activity as well as dilate blood vessels.

Not all ginkgo supplements contain sufficient amounts of these antioxidants.

Of the 13 ginkgo products tested, seven failed because of inadequate amounts of active ingredients. Three of these seven also contained high levels of lead.* All of the lead-contaminated ginkgo supplements contained ginkgo leaf powder and ginkgo leaf extract.

Helpful: To avoid possible lead contamination from ginkgo leaf powder, stick with ginkgo products made only with ginkgo leaf extract. The extraction process appears to remove lead.

The typical daily dosage is 120 mg of the extract, taken in doses of 40 mg or 60 mg over the course of the day. Choose a supplement standardized to contain 24% flavonol glycosides and 6% terpene lactones—the concentrations used in most clinical trials.

Reliable products include…

•**Nature's Bounty** Ginkgo Biloba (120 mg).

•**Vitamin World** Ginkgo Biloba (120 mg).

•**Puritan's Pride** Ginkgo Biloba (60 mg).

GREEN TEA

Studies show that antioxidants found in green tea—including *epigallocatechin gallate* (EGCG) —may help prevent cancers of the stomach, lung, liver, breast and colon.

*More than 0.5 micrograms per day, as determined by the state of California, the only state to require a label warning for lead contamination in supplements.

Most green teas are caffeinated, so people who are caffeine sensitive should use the tea with caution. The seven green tea supplements we tested contained varying amounts of caffeine—from 3 mg per four-capsule dose in one product to 108 mg per four-capsule dose in another. Steeped green tea contains an average of 30 mg of caffeine per eight-ounce cup. (A cup of coffee contains about 100 mg of caffeine.)

Two of the green tea supplements we tested contained extremely high lead levels—Futurebiotics Premium Standardized Green Tea Extract with 4.5 mcg of lead per two-capsule daily dose…and Herbal Select Standardized Green Tea Extract with 6.6 mcg of lead per two-capsule daily dose. A third failed because it didn't provide the EGCG amounts listed on its label.

Caution: Recent reports have linked green tea extracts to liver damage. *Some reliable products include…*

•**Life Extension Mega** Green Tea Extract (725 mg per capsule), 2 mg of caffeine (one capsule).

•**Nature's Bounty** Green Tea Extract (315 mg per capsule), 108 mg of caffeine (four capsules).

•**Pharmanex Tegreen 97** (250 mg per capsule), 0.75 to 3 mg of caffeine (one to four capsules).

Helpful: Given the high lead content and risks for liver damage, it may be safer to *drink* green tea. The amount of lead contained in one cup is likely to be lower than that found in a concentrated supplement. The cancer-fighting potency of decaffeinated green tea has not been tested in large-scale studies.

■ ■ ■ ■

Smart Vitamin Buying

To get the most health benefit at the lowest cost from multivitamin supplements…

•**Avoid buying "mega-dose" supplements.** They provide far more than 100% of the recommended daily allowance (RDA) for vitamins, antioxidants and minerals. Such doses provide no benefit and might prove harmful.

•**Buy a basic multisupplement.** It should provide 100% of the RDA for a large number of vitamins and minerals—a "seniors' formula" containing an extra amount of vitamin B-12 and lesser amount of iron is fine.

•**Shop by price.** Generic and store brands are just as good as higher-priced name brands, and tablets are as good as capsules.

•**Look for "USP" on the label.** This indicates that the product meets United States Pharmacopeia quality standards.

•**Avoid vitamin combinations that contain herbs, enzymes and hormones.** The benefit of these is unproven and they could be harmful.

•**Don't pay more for unneeded features.**

Examples: All natural…timed release…stress formula…starch free…chelated (to promote absorption). They add no value.

Simeon Margolis, MD, PhD, medical editor, *The Johns Hopkins Medical Letter: Health After 50.* University Health Publishing.

What Supplement Makers Don't Want You to Know

James N. Dillard, MD, DC, former assistant clinical professor at Columbia University College of Physicians and Surgeons and past medical director of Columbia's Rosenthal Center for Complementary and Alternative Medicine, both in New York City. He is now in private practice in New York City and East Hampton, NY.

Samantha Heller, MS, RD, nutritionist, New York University Medical Center, New York City.

More is not better when it comes to the ingredients in your vitamin supplement. When a multivitamin pill is packed with extra nutrients or herbs along with vitamins and minerals, it's not the bargain you think it is, says Dr. James Dillard, former clinical medical adviser at the Rosenthal Center for Complementary and Alternative Medicine at Columbia University.

Why? A tablet or capsule can only hold so much, and the more ingredients in a single pill, the less of each ingredient you can have; sometimes pills have so little of each nutrient, they are hardly worth taking, he says.

That can hurt if you think you're protecting yourself, especially if you're a woman who needs extra calcium, says registered dietician Samantha Heller.

"Calcium should always be taken as a separate supplement, as they simply can't fit all a woman's needs into one multivitamin pill," says Heller, a nutritionist at New York University Medical Center.

TOO MUCH OF A GOOD THING

Vitamin supplements with nutrient levels that soar above the recommended daily amounts (RDA) can also cause problems, increasing the risk of such side effects as diarrhea and nausea, Heller says.

Too much vitamin A and D, for example, can be toxic, she notes. A vitamin supplement can even make you feel ill.

According to Dillard, nuances in the way vitamins are made, or even the source of the nutrients themselves, can affect the way you react to any specific supplement. That can result in everything from dizziness to headaches, fatigue, hives or other allergic reactions.

"If you take a vitamin supplement and don't feel well, switch brands," Dillard says.

But which brand should you take? Many experts say that the bigger, more experienced companies are more likely to give you a higher-quality product.

Also important is a product with no sugars, starches, binders or fillers.

THE DISSOLVE FACTOR

Another key concern is getting the nutrients into your bloodstream, a goal that's often defeated when supplements are made with a hard-shell coating.

"If we X-ray someone's stomach, we can often see dark shadows indicating undissolved vitamin pills," Dillard says.

Look for products that carry the US Pharmacopeia seal of approval, usually noted as "USP Approved" on the label. This means the product was tested by a government agency and will dissolve in a minimum amount of time.

Here's a home test suggested by Dillard to see how well your vitamin dissolves—mix equal parts water and vinegar in a glass and drop in your vitamin pill. Within 40 minutes, it should be well on its way to being dissolved. If it's not, he says, it's probably going to pass through your body undigested.

Finally, always check the expiration date before buying a vitamin supplement. If you don't find one, don't buy the product.

■ ■ ■ ■

Vitamin K Cuts Arthritis Risk

In a new study of 672 adults, those who had the highest vitamin K levels were less likely to have osteoarthritis of the hands and knees than people who had the lowest levels.

Theory: Insufficient vitamin K could affect proteins that build and maintain bone and cartilage.

Self-defense: Get the recommended daily intake of vitamin K—65 micrograms (mcg) for women and 80 mcg for men.

Good sources: Spinach, broccoli and olive oil.

Caution: If you take a blood thinner, vitamin K can reduce the drug's effectiveness.

Tuhina Neogi, MD, assistant professor of medicine, Boston University School of Medicine.

Avoid Dangerous Herb-Drug Interactions

Catherine Ulbricht, PharmD, senior attending pharmacist at Massachusetts General Hospital in Boston, is editor-in-chief of *Journal of Herbal Pharmacotherapy* and cofounder of Natural Standard (*www.naturalstandard.com*), a Web site dedicated to the scientific study of integrated medicine.

An increasing number of American adults now take herbs or nutritional supplements for a wide range of ailments, including arthritis, depression and nausea.

Problem: Unlike prescription drugs, herbal supplements are not regulated by the FDA, so there are no labeling requirements regarding potential interactions with prescription or over-the-counter (OTC) drugs.

Whether they are used in capsules, extracts, liquid, cream or tea, many herbal products can be harmful when combined with prescription or OTC medication.

What happens: Some herbs can interact with medications by affecting their absorption,

metabolism or by other mechanisms. As a result, drug levels may become too high or too low.

Catherine Ulbricht, PharmD, a pharmacist at Massachusetts General Hospital and one of the country's leading experts on herb-drug interactions gave this advice on commonly used herbs...*

CAYENNE

Cayenne is also known as chili or red pepper. Cayenne's active component, capsaicin, which is used as a spice in food, is commonly used as a pain reliever in prescription medicine, often for osteoarthritis, rheumatoid arthritis and diabetic neuropathy (nerve pain resulting from diabetes).

Possible interactions: When combined with aspirin, ibuprofen (Advil) or any other nonsteroidal anti-inflammatory drug (NSAID), cayenne may increase these drugs' side effects, especially gastrointestinal (GI) upset. In some people, cayenne also may enhance the pain-relieving action of NSAIDs.

Like NSAIDs, cayenne can have a blood-thinning effect, increasing the risk for bleeding. (When used topically, this risk is lessened because lower doses of cayenne are absorbed.) Do not use cayenne if you take a monoamine oxidase (MAO) inhibitor antidepressant, such as *phenelzine* (Nardil).

Caution: Avoid getting cayenne (in any form) in your eyes, nose, etc., where it can cause burning or stinging.

GINGER

Ginger is a popular antidote for nausea and/or vomiting. Research suggests that ginger also may help prevent blood clotting and reduce blood sugar levels.

Possible interactions: If you take an NSAID or antiplatelet drug, such as clopidogrel (Plavix), ginger may further increase bleeding risk.

Caution: Although there's strong evidence that it is particularly effective for nausea and/or vomiting in pregnant women, high-dose supplemental ginger (more than 1 g daily) is not recommended during pregnancy because of possible fetal damage and/or increased bleeding risk. Because of the lack of long-term studies

*Check with your doctor or pharmacist before taking any herbal product.

on ginger, consult your doctor before taking it for an extended period of time.

GREEN TEA

As scientific evidence has revealed the disease-fighting benefits of antioxidant-rich green tea, an increasing number of Americans have begun drinking it—or, in some cases, taking it in capsules or extracts. Although new research questions the health benefits of green tea, some studies have found that it may help prevent cancer, especially malignancies of the GI tract, breast and lung. More investigation is needed to confirm these findings. To read more about clinical trials on green tea, go to the National Institutes of Health's Web site, *www.clinicaltrials.gov.*

Possible interactions: Most forms of green tea contain caffeine, which may intensify the effect of any medication that increases blood pressure and/or heart rate, such as the decongestant pseudoephedrine (Sudafed). Decaffeinated green tea is available, but this form still contains some caffeine and may not have the same health benefits.

Caution: People with arrhythmia (abnormal heart rhythm) should consume no more than moderate amounts of green tea, determined by their personal sensitivity to caffeine.

LICORICE

Licorice contains a compound known as *glycyrrhizin*, which has antiviral properties. For this reason, licorice is often used to treat the common cold and herpes infections (including cold sores). However, some studies have shown that topical licorice cream does not help genital herpes.

Possible interactions: Licorice can interact with diuretics, such as *chlorothiazide* (Diuril) and *furosemide* (Lasix), and any medication that affects hormone levels, such as birth control pills.

Caution: It also may increase blood pressure and bleeding risk.

MILK THISTLE

This popular herb is used for liver problems, including cirrhosis and hepatitis. These benefits are well documented by research.

Possible interactions: Milk thistle may interfere with how the liver breaks down certain drugs, such as antibiotics and antifungals. Milk thistle also may interact with the anticonvulsant *phenytoin* (Dilantin). The herb may lower blood sugar and cause heartburn, nausea and vomiting or other GI upset.

Caution: If you take diabetes medication, do not use milk thistle unless you are supervised by a health-care professional.

ST. JOHN'S WORT

St. John's wort is commonly used for depression. Several studies show that it may work as well as a prescription antidepressant, such as *paroxetine* (Paxil), for mild to moderate depressive disorders. More research is needed before St. John's wort can be recommended for severe depression.

Possible interactions: St. John's wort may interact with drugs that are broken down by the liver, including birth control pills, the blood thinner *warfarin* (Coumadin) and migraine medications. People who take St. John's wort may experience stomach upset, fatigue, sexual dysfunction, dizziness or headaches.

Caution: St. John's wort should not be taken with prescription antidepressant medication.

Healing Herbs: What the Scientific Evidence Says About Herbal Therapies

Mark Blumenthal, founder and executive director of the American Botanical Council (ABC).

It was headline news when *The New England Journal of Medicine* published a study that cast doubt on the effectiveness of echinacea. The message to the countless consumers spending more than $300 million annually on the purported cold-fighting herb? *Save your money.*

University of Virginia School of Medicine researchers had found echinacea to be no more effective than a placebo at combating cold and flu symptoms. But don't clear out your herbal medicine chest just yet.

What went largely unreported was that study participants received only 900 mg of echinacea daily—less than one-third of the dose recommended by the World Health Organization for combating upper-respiratory infections. That's akin to expecting one-third of a dose of aspirin to relieve a headache.

What's the other side of the story? Dozens of clinical studies point to echinacea's effectiveness, including a Canadian trial in which volunteers who took echinacea at the onset of colds experienced 23% milder, shorter symptoms, such as sore throat, stuffy nose, chills and headache, than those taking a placebo—a benefit that researchers linked to a marked increase in circulating white blood cells and other cells of the immune system.

More work is needed to identify the optimal echinacea species (supplements are commonly derived from *E. purpurea*, *E. pallida* or *E. augustifolia*) and the most potent plant parts (roots, stems, leaves or flowers).

Meanwhile, best results have been achieved by taking 3,000 mg daily of an echinacea product that combines one of the above-mentioned species and parts at the first sign of cold or flu until symptoms resolve.

Caution: If you're allergic to ragweed, avoid echinacea supplements derived from stems, leaves or flowers—they may contain pollen and trigger a reaction. Use an echinacea root supplement.

Five other herbs with scientific evidence on their side…

GARLIC

What it does: Helps prevent and possibly reverse arterial plaque buildup (atherosclerosis), a major risk factor for heart attack and stroke…reduces risk for stomach and colorectal cancers…and acts as a blood thinner to reduce the risk for blood clots.

Scientific evidence: In a recent German study, 152 patients with advanced atherosclerosis who took 900 mg daily of garlic powder for four years experienced a 3% decrease in existing arterial plaques in their neck (carotid) and thigh (femoral) arteries. Those taking a placebo experienced more than a 15% *increase* in arterial plaques.

Potential side effects: Bad breath and indigestion. Because garlic has a blood-thinning effect, it should not be used if you take aspirin regularly or an anticoagulant drug, such as *warfarin* (Coumadin). To minimize bleeding

risk, ask your doctor about discontinuing garlic supplements at least one week before undergoing elective surgery.

Typical dose: One clove of fresh, minced garlic daily, or 200 mg to 300 mg of standardized garlic powder, taken in pill or tablet form, three times daily.

GINKGO*

What it does: Improves memory and concentration in people with early-stage senile dementia or Alzheimer's disease, as well as in healthy adults, by increasing blood flow to the brain. May also relieve tinnitus (ringing in the ears), vertigo and altitude sickness, as well as vascular problems such as intermittent claudication, a painful calf condition caused by decreased circulation to the legs.

Scientific evidence: An overwhelming majority of ginkgo trials have shown positive results. At least 33 randomized, controlled trials have shown this herb to enhance mental functioning or slow cognitive deterioration in older patients with dementia, while another 13 controlled studies have shown ginkgo to boost memory and cognitive performance in healthy adults.

Potential side effects: Stomach upset, headache, rash and/or dizziness. Like garlic, ginkgo should not be taken with aspirin or a prescription blood thinner such as warfarin. The herb was previously believed to increase the effects of monoamine oxidase inhibitor (MAOI) antidepressants, such as phenelzine (Nardil), but this has been refuted.

Typical dose: 120 mg daily. Nearly all positive ginkgo trials have used one of three formulations that are produced in Germany and sold in health-food stores in the US under the brand names Ginkoba by Pharmaton Natural Health Products…Ginkgold by Nature's Way… and Ginkai by Abkit Inc.

MILK THISTLE

What it does: Because of its strong antioxidant activity, milk thistle detoxifies the liver and may help regenerate liver cells. It may be appropriate for patients with alcohol-related liver damage or infectious or drug-induced hepatitis, as well as anyone who is regularly exposed to industrial pollutants.

*Check with your doctor or pharmacist before taking any herbal product.

Scientific evidence: At least 19 out of 21 clinical studies (a total of 2,200 people out of 2,400) have shown milk thistle to protect the liver against invasive toxins and possibly even stimulate the generation of new liver cells.

Potential side effect: Loose stools.

Typical dose: Take 140 mg of milk thistle three times daily.

SAW PALMETTO

What it does: Relieves the symptoms of benign prostatic hyperplasia (BPH), a noncancerous swelling of the prostate gland, which causes frequent and/or weak urination and is common in men over age 50.

Scientific evidence: In nearly two dozen clinical trials, saw palmetto has proven almost equal to prescription drugs, such as *finasteride* (Proscar) and *terazosin* (Hytrin), for relieving the symptoms of BPH. Unlike prescription prostate medications, which can cause side effects, including diminished libido, saw palmetto causes only minor adverse effects. Saw palmetto does not inhibit the production of prostate specific antigen (PSA), a protein that, when elevated, serves as an early warning for prostate cancer. (Conventional BPH drugs suppress PSA, complicating prostate cancer screening.)

Potential side effects: Stomach upset or nausea if taken on an empty stomach.

Typical dose: 320 mg daily. It requires four to six weeks to take effect.

VALERIAN

What it does: The root combats insomnia and acts as a mild sedative to relieve anxiety or restlessness.

Scientific evidence: All of the nearly 30 clinical studies to date have shown the herb to be effective against insomnia and anxiety. In a recent German trial, taking 600 mg of valerian root extract daily proved as effective as the prescription tranquilizer *oxazepam* (Serax) for improving sleep quality, but with fewer side effects. Unlike prescription sleep aids, valerian isn't habit-forming, won't leave you feeling groggy the next morning and doesn't diminish alertness, reaction time or concentration.

Potential side effects: None known. It is best to avoid combining valerian with conventional sedatives, such as *diazepam* (Valium), since the herb may exacerbate the drug's sedating effects.

Typical dose: 2 g to 3 g of the dried crushed root, infused as a tea…or 400 mg to 800 mg in supplement form, taken one-half hour before bedtime.

The Amazing Power of Fish Oil

Laurence S. Sperling, MD, associate professor of medicine and director of the section of preventive cardiology at Emory University School of Medicine in Atlanta, coauthored the paper, "Understanding Omega-3s," published in *American Heart Journal.*

Ever since scientists observed 30 years ago that Greenland's Eskimos, who subsist largely on fish, have appreciably lower rates of cardiovascular disease than nonfish eaters, the bulk of evidence has demonstrated that the omega-3 fatty acids found in fish may significantly lower the risk of developing heart problems.

Landmark study: In an Italian study involving 11,324 heart attack survivors, patients who took about 1 g of fish oil daily for three and a half years had a 30% lower risk of dying from cardiovascular disease and a 45% lower risk of having a sudden fatal heart attack. In 2000, the American Heart Association (AHA) began recommending omega-3 fatty acids to prevent heart attack and stroke.

WHAT ARE OMEGA-3s?

Omega-3 fatty acids are a kind of polyunsaturated fat found chiefly in cold-water fish, such as salmon, mackerel, lake trout, herring and sardines. The two main omega-3 types are called *eicosapentaenoic acid* (EPA) and *docosahexaenoic acid* (DHA). Another type of omega-3, called *alpha-linolenic acid* (ALA), is found in walnuts, flaxseed, soybeans and canola oil.

Studies suggest that omega-3s may protect the heart by reducing systemic inflammation, which can damage arteries and leave them susceptible to plaque buildup. Omega-3s also are believed to decrease the "stickiness" of blood platelets, lowering the risk for clots that can cause heart attack and/or stroke.

Other research indicates that omega-3s may fight mild to severe depression, as well as auto-immune disorders such as rheumatoid arthritis, psoriasis and Crohn's disease. Unfortunately, most of us just don't eat enough omega-3–rich fish to reap the benefits.

How much is enough? The AHA recommends that healthy adults consume at least two fish meals weekly to help reduce the risk for cardiovascular disease—and it urges those with existing heart disease to get 1 g of fish oil daily to prevent future attacks, preferably from fatty fish.

I suggest that patients at increased risk for cardiovascular disease—including those with diabetes or peripheral arterial disease (a condition in which blockages restrict blood circulation, mainly in arteries to the kidneys, stomach, arms, legs and feet)—also consume 1 g of fish oil daily. You can do this by eating three to six ounces of fish every day, but it's more practical for most people to take a fish oil supplement.

The advantages of taking a fish oil supplement include…

•**Consistency.** With a supplement, you generally know the amount of omega-3s you're getting. Independent testing by both *Consumer Reports* and ConsumerLab.com has shown that fish oil supplements by and large contain the levels of EPA and DHA cited on their labels. Of the dozens of products tested by these two watchdog groups, only one failed to provide the promised amount of omega-3s. (For a partial list of brands approved by ConsumerLab.com, see *www.consumerlab.com/results/omega3.asp*.) Fish, on the other hand, vary greatly in their omega-3 content. While 3.5 ounces of salmon, mackerel or bluefin tuna supply more than 1 g of EPA and DHA in total, the same amount of catfish, cod or canned light tuna provides almost none.

•**Safety.** Virtually all fish contain mercury, PCBs and dioxins. And, unfortunately, some of the best sources of omega-3s—including bluefin tuna and swordfish—also are among the fish with the most potential toxins. Fortunately, fish oil supplements appear to be generally contaminant-free. Of the 16 brands recently tested by *Consumer Reports* and the 41 tested by ConsumerLab.com, not a single product contained more than negligible levels of mercury, PCBs or harmful dioxins.

THE RIGHT SUPPLEMENT

You don't have to buy the most expensive fish oil supplement to get a quality product. Low-price store or discount brands, such as CVS and Puritan's Pride, are comparable in both quality and content to higher-priced name brands. A month's supply can cost as little as $10.

So what should you look for? *When choosing a product, consider the following guidelines (as indicated on the label and/or package insert)…*

•**It contains both EPA and DHA** (most provide both at a 1.5-to-1 ratio favoring EPA).

•**It is "molecularly distilled,"** a process used to separate the oils from any metals or other pollutants.

•**It is encapsulated under nitrogen** rather than oxygen—oxygen can turn the oils rancid, giving them a "fishy" taste and smell.

•**It is highly concentrated** to minimize the number of pills you'll need daily. Over-the-counter omega-3 supplements may contain from 30% to 90% fish oil.

•**It is approved by the US Pharmacopeia (USP),** the independent authority that sets quality standards for all US-manufactured pharmaceuticals and dietary supplements.

USING FISH OIL SAFELY

The FDA considers up to 3 g of fish oil daily to be generally safe. At or below this level, fish oil supplements are typically well-tolerated, though some people do experience gastrointestinal (GI) upset or an unpleasant "fishy" aftertaste, particularly when they first start taking them.

To minimize GI distress and the fishy aftertaste, divide the dose and take it with food twice a day. Freezing or refrigerating your fish oil supplements may minimize any stomach or intestinal symptoms, as well as any fishy aftertaste, and reduce or slow decomposition of the supplements. Fish oils, like all fats, will eventually deteriorate and turn rancid at room temperature.

Always check with your physician before beginning a supplement, particularly if you're taking any medication. If you're allergic to seafood or iodine (found in some fish and shellfish), do not take fish oil supplements. Get your omega-3s through

ALA-rich foods or supplements. *In addition, fish oil may not be advisable for people who...*

•**Take a daily aspirin** or another antiplatelet or anticoagulant drug. Because fish oil has a blood-thinning effect, it theoretically could increase your chances of bleeding, though in nearly 150 studies so far this has not emerged as a side effect.

•**Have type 2 diabetes.** Some studies suggest that high-dose omega-3s may trigger short-term increases in blood sugar in people with type 2 diabetes. However, I routinely advise my patients with diabetes to take up to 1 g of fish oil daily to stave off cardiovascular disease, and most do well on this modest dose. A person with diabetes should take omega-3 fish oil only under a doctor's supervision.

•**Have elevated LDL** ("bad") cholesterol (above 130 mg/dL). There's evidence that taking omega-3s may actually increase LDL—possibly because they decrease triglycerides. Studies have shown that lowering triglycerides may increase LDL in some patients.

If, on the other hand, you have low LDL levels (below 100 mg/dL) and very high triglycerides (above 500 mg/dL), your doctor may suggest Omacor, a new prescription drug that is a highly concentrated form of omega-3. It was just approved by the FDA to treat high triglyceride levels.

Studies show that 4 g of Omacor daily may lower triglycerides by as much as 45%. Just be sure that your doctor routinely monitors your cholesterol and triglyceride levels while you're taking this or any omega-3 fish oil at doses exceeding 3 g daily.

■ ■ ■ ■

Cough Help

Allergy medications soothe coughs better than over-the-counter (OTC) cough remedies, such as *dextromethorphan* and *guaifenesin*. OTC allergy medications, such as those that contain *diphenhydramine, chlorpheniramine* and *brompheniramine*, help to quiet a cough due to the common cold by drying the secretions in the back of the throat.

Downside: These allergy medications may cause drowsiness as well.

Also helpful for a cough: Pain relievers, such as Advil and Aleve—they may lessen the severity and frequency of the cough by inhibiting chemicals that cause inflammation.

Richard Irwin, MD, professor of medicine, University of Massachusetts Medical School, Worcester, and editor-in-chief of the American College of Chest Physicians guidelines for treatment of cough.

■ ■ ■ ■

Vitamin Warning

Vitamin C in high doses may cause kidney stones.

Recent finding: People who took 2,000 milligrams (mg) of vitamin C per day—many times higher than the recommended daily intake—for six days had a 10% or more increase in levels of *urinary oxalate*, a building block of kidney stones. If you want to take vitamin C, keep the dosage under 500 mg a day to minimize risk of calcium oxalate kidney stones.

Linda Massey, PhD, professor of human nutrition, Washington State University, Spokane, and leader of a study of 48 people who took 2,000 mg of vitamin C for six days, published in *Journal of Nutrition*.

■ ■ ■ ■

Cold Help

Zinc cold remedies should be used cautiously. There is evidence that zinc can lessen a cold's severity, but zinc products should be used only two or three times a day, primarily in the first 48 hours after symptom onset—not every three hours, as indicated on labels. Do not use zinc lozenges and nasal spray—choose one. High concentrations of zinc can cause nausea and diarrhea.

Neil Schachter, MD, professor of pulmonary medicine and medical director of respiratory care, Mount Sinai Medical Center, New York City.

■ ■ ■ ■

Drug Alert

Herbal supplements raise risks from arthritis drugs.

Examples: Echinacea can increase risk of liver toxicity in people taking the arthritis drug *metho-trexate*. Ginkgo biloba, garlic and devil's

145

claw can increase the risk of bleeding problems in people who also take nonsteroidal anti-inflammatory drugs, such as aspirin, ibuprofen and naproxen.

Self-defense: Be sure your doctor and pharmacist know everything you take—prescription and over-the-counter drugs as well as herbal supplements.

Erin Arnold, MD, rheumatologist, Illinois Bone and Joint Institute, Morton Grove, Illinois.

■■■■

Vitamin D Reduces Breast Cancer Risk

In a recent study, people who got adequate exposure to the sun, which allows the body to produce vitamin D, and also increased their intake of foods that contain vitamin D reduced their risk of breast cancer by 30%.

Foods that are high in vitamin D include: Milk, salmon, tuna and other oily fish.

Note: Unprotected sun exposure should be limited to 15 minutes a day for fair-skinned people.

Julia Knight, PhD, senior investigator, Prosserman Centre for Health Research, Samuel Lunenfeld Research Institute, Mount Sinai Hospital, Toronto, and leader of a study of 576 women with breast cancer and 1,135 women without breast cancer, presented at a meeting of the American Association for Cancer Research.

■■■■

Diabetes Guard

Calcium and vitamin D protect against diabetes.

Recent finding: Women who get more than 1,200 mg of calcium along with more than 800 IU of vitamin D daily have a 33% lower risk of type 2 diabetes than people who get less calcium and vitamin D.

Best: Have one to two servings of low-fat dairy, such as milk and yogurt, a day, and take a supplement containing 500 mg of calcium and a vitamin D pill containing 400 IU.

Anastassios G. Pittas, MD, adjunct associate professor of medicine, Friedman School of Nutrition Science and Policy, Tufts-New England Medical Center, Boston, and leader of a 20-year study of 83,779 women, published in Diabetes Care.

■■■■

Statins and Eyes

Statin drugs protect your eyes as well as your heart. Millions of Americans take *atorvastatin* (Lipitor), *simvastatin* (Zocor) or other statins to lower cholesterol and reduce the risk of heart attack and stroke.

Recent finding: Statins are associated with a 45% decreased risk of nuclear cataracts—the most common kind of cataracts—which affect the central portion of the eye.

Barbara Klein, MD, MPH, professor of ophthalmology and visual sciences, University of Wisconsin, Madison, and leader of a study of 1,299 people at risk of developing cataracts, published in The Journal of the American Medical Association.

■■■■

Vitamin D Lowers Cancer Risk

Studies show a clear link between vitamin D and the reduction of colon, breast and ovarian cancer risk. Vitamin D is found in milk, yogurt, cheese and some fortified orange juice —usually 100 international units (IU) a serving. Consider a vitamin supplement to raise your vitamin D intake to 1,000 IU per day. This is especially important for people in winter, when a lack of sunshine curtails the body's production of vitamin D, and for African-Americans, whose skin pigment limits vitamin D production.

Cedric F. Garland, DrPH, adjunct professor of family and preventive medicine, School of Medicine, University of California San Diego, La Jolla, CA.

■■■■

Immunity Help

Conjugated linoleic acid, a fat found in dairy products and meat, may boost immunity.

Recent study: People who took 3 grams of conjugated linoleic acid daily for 12 weeks had 20% to 30% higher levels of two important blood markers of immunity—IgA and IgM, both anti-infection boosters—than people who did not supplement with CLA.

Best: Take 500 mg to 1,000 mg of CLA with each meal.

Caution: Pregnant women and young children should not take CLA.

Klaus W.J. Wahle, PhD, faculty research professor, school of life sciences, The Robert Gordon University, Aberdeen, Scotland, United Kingdom, and leader of a study published in European Journal of Clinical Nutrition.

■ ■ ■ ■

B-12 Limits

Don't count on vitamin B-12 to relieve allergies. One recent clinical trial did show some improvement in symptoms—after participants got 2,500 times the recommended daily allowance of three to four micrograms of B-12 for up to six weeks. But one trial is not conclusive—more research is necessary.

Good news: Even if vitamin B-12 does not help relieve allergies, it helps to keep you healthy. But don't take huge doses of B-12 or any vitamin without consulting your doctor first.

Martha V. White, MD, director of research, Institute for Allergy and Asthma, 11002 Veirs Mill Rd., Wheaton, MD 20902.

■ ■ ■ ■

Weight-Loss Product Danger

Several "ephedra-free" diet supplements have been found to contain stimulants with potentially dangerous side effects. *Ripped Fuel* and *Lean System 7* contain mixtures of caffeine and synephrine that can potentially drive up heart rate and blood pressure. A daily dose of *Zantrex-3* has as much caffeine as about 30 cans of cola—which can cause similar effects as well as anxiety and sleep disturbances.

Tod Cooperman, MD, president of ConsumerLab.com, a company that conducts independent testing of health, wellness and nutrition products. General test results are available at no charge to the public. www.ConsumerLab.com. He is also the founder of PharmacyChecker.com (www.pharmacychecker.com), an evaluator of Internet pharmacies, and editor of Health, Harm, or Rip-Off? What's Really in Your Vitamins & Supplements. Bottom Line Books.

Arthritis Breakthroughs

John D. Clough, MD, retired rheumatologist in the department of rheumatic and immunologic disease at the Cleveland Clinic, is author of Arthritis: A Cleveland Clinic Guide. The Cleveland Clinic Press.

New developments in medications and improvements in surgery have brightened the outlook for people with arthritis. While most forms of arthritis remain incurable, many can be made bearable or better.

Arthritis is an umbrella term for nearly 100 forms of joint ("arthr") inflammation ("itis") involving warmth, redness, tenderness, swelling, stiffness and pain ranging from annoying to disabling. To complicate matters, many conditions with similar symptoms—and requiring different treatment—can masquerade as arthritis.

Examples: Fibromyalgia (muscle pain)...osteoporosis (brittle bones)...side effects of cholesterol-lowering drugs with names ending in "statin"...polymyalgia rheumatica, involving pain and stiffness in the hips or shoulders—common after age 50 (especially in women) and highly treatable with *prednisone* (Deltasone) but a cause of blindness if untreated.

Surprises: A swollen knee, hip or pain in the spine may signal tuberculous arthritis from tuberculosis contracted years before. Mild, fleeting arthritis can result from rheumatic fever following strep throat.

Ideally, arthritis is identified in its early stages and treated aggressively before irreversible damage can occur. Lab tests narrow the possibilities, but for most forms of arthritis, no single test can confirm the diagnosis.

Best bet: See a rheumatologist—a physician specializing in diseases of the joints, muscles and bones. Later, an internist or a general practitioner given the diagnosis and treatment plan can oversee your care.

To find a rheumatologist, ask your doctor, local hospital, county medical association or a friend for recommendations...or search the American College of Rheumatology Web site, *www. rheumatology.org*. Look for board certification in both internal medicine and rheumatology.

THE BIG FIVE

Equipped with a diagnosis, learn about your form of arthritis. *The vast majority (95%) of Americans with arthritis have one of five types…*

•**Osteoarthritis.** By far the most common form of arthritis in the US, osteoarthritis strikes more than half of people over age 65 and 80% of those over age 75.

What it is: Cartilage, which cushions the ends of the joint bones, disintegrates. The bones then rub together and can eventually wear out.

Most often affected: Neck, lower back… hips, knees…fingers, toes. Involvement in the ankle and elsewhere is usually triggered by an injury or surgery.

Osteo sufferers tend to take a lot of *acetaminophen* (Tylenol) and nonsteroidal anti-inflammatory drugs (NSAIDs), including *ibuprofen* (Advil, Nuprin) and *naproxen* (Naprosyn, Aleve). In large amounts, these effective and seemingly innocuous over-the-counter drugs can be toxic, even deadly. Ask your doctor how much is safe for you.

Easier on the stomach: COX-2 inhibitors, which are selective NSAIDs that block prostaglandins—hormones that cause joint inflammation. COX-2 inhibitors—*rofecoxib* (Vioxx, withdrawn from the market in 2004), *celecoxib* (Celebrex) and *valdecoxib* (Bextra, withdrawn from the market in 2005)—were welcomed with open arms in the late 1990s until a few patients had heart attacks or strokes.

You may still take a COX-2 inhibitor with your doctor's advice and monitoring. Or you may be advised to return to ibuprofen or naproxen.

Glucosamine and chondroitin, sold without a prescription, are among the building blocks of cartilage. Some osteoarthritis sufferers say that these supplements help. With your doctor's approval, you can try them if you want.

When meds no longer quell osteoarthritis pain, a trade-in may be the answer. Hip and knee replacement surgery, performed for more than 30 years, has advanced dramatically. Shoulder replacement has long been a possibility, as has elbow replacement—although the latter is not usually as successful.

On the horizon: Wrist and ankle replacement. Meanwhile, many people with osteoarthritis of the ankle are getting good results with ankle fusion, in which some ankle joints are fused together. The ankle contains so many joints that range of motion remains good.

•**Rheumatoid arthritis.** In rheumatoid arthritis, the immune system goes haywire, attacking joints throughout the body.

Results: Pain, deformity and disability.

The most exciting developments in the fight against rheumatoid arthritis and some other forms of arthritis are new drugs that fight inflammation. The remarkable tumor necrosis factor (TNF) inhibitors block a type of protein called a cytokine that triggers inflammation when present in large amounts.

TNF inhibitors are expensive but covered by Medicare Part B. They include *infliximab* (Remicade), approved for use in rheumatoid arthritis in 1999, and *adalimumab* (Humira), approved for use in advanced rheumatoid arthritis in 2002 and in psoriatic arthritis and early rheumatoid arthritis in 2005. Remicade is given intravenously in a health-care facility every six to eight weeks. Humira is self-injected every two weeks.

Another effective TNF inhibitor is *etanercept* (Enbrel), approved for use in rheumatoid arthritis in 1998 and in psoriatic arthritis in 2002. Etanercept requires an injection under the skin that can be given at home.

•**Gout.** Remember Jiggs, from the comic strip "Bringing Up Father," whose hassock-supported, bandaged foot radiated lightning bolts of pain? He had gout, a form of arthritis in which uric acid accumulates in the blood and crystallizes in a joint—often, but not always, the ball of the big toe—causing excruciating pain.

The best drug for lowering uric acid is *allopurinol* (Zyloprim). Anti-inflammatories such as *indomethacin* (Indocin) and, in chronic cases, drugs such as *probenecid* (Benemid, Probalan) that reduce the level of uric acid in the blood do wonders for gout.

Diet may help. Restrict foods containing high levels of purine, a heterocyclic aromatic organic compound that produces uric acid crystals. Limit alcohol…organ meats (liver, kidneys)… game fowl (duck, goose)…dried legumes (lentils, chickpeas)…and some seafood (scallops, sardines, shrimp, herring). For a free brochure called "Gout," with a list of food to avoid, contact the Arthritis Foundation (*www.arthritis.org*, 800-283-7800).

•**Seronegative spondyloarthropathies.** These half dozen conditions involve the spine.

Among the most common: Ankylosing spondylitis, which causes back pain and stiffness, worst in the early morning...psoriatic arthritis, which is developed by about 20% of people with psoriasis and which responds well to TNF alpha inhibitors and to the cancer drug *rituximab* (Rituxan), a monoclonal antibody.

•**Systemic lupus erythematosus (SLE).** Arthritis is the primary symptom of lupus, a dysfunction of the autoimmune system.

Relief: Prednisone, a corticosteroid...*cyclophosphamide* (Cytoxan), a cancer drug...and several other medications. These allow many lupus patients to live fairly normal lives with minimal problems.

GET MOVING

Formerly, because it hurts to move, people with arthritis sat still and got steadily worse. We now know that inactivity is a mistake. For most people with arthritis, careful exercise is recommended to keep limbs limber.

Physical and occupational therapy have an important place in treating arthritis. Applying heat and practicing strengthening and range-of-motion exercises may help. Because of the many faces of arthritis, therapy must be designed and supervised individually—and reviewed regularly—by trained professionals. What eases one person's pain may exacerbate another's.

Ask your doctor to recommend a physical therapist who can show you how to protect yourself from injury...a physiatrist, a physician specializing in physical treatments for muscular, skeletal and neurological problems...or an occupational therapist, who can explain how to protect your joints from stress during your usual activities. Swimming pools are superb exercise settings for many people with arthritis.

■ ■ ■ ■

Omega-3 Fats Fight Dry Eye

People naturally produce fewer tears as they age. This can lead to dry eye syndrome, which causes irritation and light sensitivity.

Omega-3s help maintain normal tear quality. Get them from salmon, chunk light tuna, walnuts and flaxseeds.

Neil F. Martin, MD, FACS, ophthalmologist in private practice, Chevy Chase, MD, *www.washingtoneye.com.*

■ ■ ■ ■

Herbs and Chemo

Herbs affect chemotherapy. Black cohosh, often recommended to breast cancer patients to relieve menopausal symptoms, changes the potency of some chemotherapy drugs.

Self-defense: Be sure your doctor knows all of the supplements and over-the-counter remedies you take.

To check interactions, go to the Medline Plus Web site (*www.nlm.nih.gov/medlineplus*) and click on "Drugs and Supplements."

Sara Rockwell, PhD, professor of therapeutic radiology and pharmacology, Yale University School of Medicine, New Haven, and leader of a study of black cohosh to control menopausal symptoms after breast cancer, published in *Breast Cancer Research and Treatment.*

Surgery Discovery: Potato Powder Stems Bleeding

Mark H. Ereth, MD, associate professor of anesthesiology, Mayo Clinic, Rochester, MN.
American Society of Anesthesiologists annual meeting.

The humble spud may stand poised for a major medical breakthrough. A patented starchy powder made from potatoes appears to clot blood instantly.

That could come in handy during surgeries and emergency procedures and also reduce the number of blood transfusions, say researchers at the Mayo Clinic.

"It works like a sponge for water molecules in the blood, allowing the platelets to clot almost immediately," says lead researcher Dr. Mark H. Ereth, an associate professor of anesthesiology at the Mayo Clinic.

APPROVED IN THE US

The powder, approved for most surgical uses in the United States, Canada and Europe, sidesteps problems associated with other clotting agents. It is cheaper and cleaner than clotting agents made from human and cow plasma, and it avoids the risks of disease and allergic reaction, Ereth says.

In their study, the researchers made two tiny incisions in the arms of 30 people. One incision was treated with the potato powder; the other was left to clot on its own.

The untreated cut took almost six minutes to reach hemostasis (blood clotting), while 77% of the cuts treated with the powder stopped bleeding immediately.

"In the other 23% of cases, the clotting was rapid, but there was a little bit of oozing afterward," Ereth says.

The powder, which is made of purified potato starch processed to produce tiny, absorbent particles, can help surgeons avoid blood transfusions by preventing excessive bleeding. It's particularly useful for paramedics or combat doctors who must stabilize massive wounds to prevent shock and other complications from a major loss of blood, Ereth says.

All of that from a potato.

■ ■ ■ ■

Hemorrhoid Relief

There are no dietary treatments that have been shown to consistently help or heal hemorrhoidal symptoms. In most cases, if a food causes a flare-up of symptoms, it is best to avoid that food. If you want to use topical medication, first try petroleum jelly—an inexpensive but often effective treatment. Over-the-counter (OTC) hemorrhoid medications typically contain emollients designed to facilitate easier passage of stool and protect the anal area. The best prescription hemorrhoid creams, such as Analpram-HC (2.5%) with *hydrocortisone*, contain topical steroids that decrease inflammation of the tissue overlying the hemorrhoidal veins and may reduce discomfort.

Caution: Symptoms of diseases, such as colon cancer and inflammatory bowel disease, can mimic hemorrhoidal symptoms. Rectal bleeding demands immediate attention. Consult a physician for an evaluation before beginning self-treatment.

Gary H. Hoffman, MD, senior surgeon, Los Angeles Colon and Rectal Surgical Associates, Beverly Hills, CA.

6

Your Prescriptions

Are You Taking Too Many Pills?

With our national pharmacy bill now topping $200 billion each year, and recent disclosures about harmful and ineffective drugs, more people are asking—*Are all those pills really necessary?*

To learn more, we talked with John Abramson, MD, a Harvard Medical School clinical instructor who is widely recognized for his in-depth research of the drug industry...

•**Are most Americans overmedicated?** They sure are. Americans take many drugs unnecessarily, and when drugs *are* needed, people often take the wrong ones. For example, before *rofecoxib* (Vioxx) was withdrawn from the market because it was found to cause heart attacks and strokes (and was discovered to provide no better relief of arthritis symptoms than older, much less expensive anti-inflammatory

drugs), about 80% of the Vioxx that was prescribed worldwide was used in the US.

•**Are doctors to blame?** The vast majority of physicians prescribe medication because they think it's in their patients' best interest. But there have been radical changes in the way that our medical knowledge is provided. Prior to 1980, most clinical research was publicly funded, but now most is funded directly by the drug and other medical industries, whose primary mission is to maximize the return on investments for investors.

Ninety percent of clinical trials now are commercially funded—as well as 75% of published clinical research. When a pharmaceutical company sponsors a study, the odds are five times greater that the findings will favor its product.

Drug and medical industries fund 70% of continuing education lectures and seminars,

John Abramson, MD, clinical instructor in ambulatory care and prevention at Harvard Medical School in Boston, is the author of *Overdosed America: The Broken Promise of American Medicine* (HarperCollins) and co-author of "The Effect of Conflict of Interest on Biomedical Research and Clinical Practice Guidelines: Can We Trust the Evidence in Evidence-Based Medicine?" in the *Journal of the American Board of Family Practice*.

which are among the activities that doctors are required to attend to maintain their licenses to practice. Wherever doctors turn for sources of information, drug companies dominate.

•**Who should be monitoring doctors' relationships with drug companies?** The real failure is on the part of government agencies, such as the FDA and the Agency for Healthcare Research and Quality. Medical journals and academic researchers have become dependent on drug company money and/or are vulnerable to drug company lobbying. Doctors and the public still trust these institutions to independently oversee the integrity of the medical knowledge that informs our medical care, when they simply are not able to do this anymore.

•**We all know that cholesterol-lowering statins are widely prescribed. Are they unnecessary?** Despite being on the market for 18 years and becoming the best-selling class of drugs, statins have never been shown in randomized, controlled trials to provide a significant health benefit when used by women of any age without heart disease or diabetes. The same is true for men over age 65 without heart disease or diabetes. Even so, millions of people in both groups now are taking a statin drug.

•**Is it ever advisable to take a statin?** Yes, there is good evidence that statins are beneficial for people who already have heart disease and for at least some people who have diabetes. A good case also can be made for men who are at very high risk for heart disease (LDL "bad" cholesterol approaching 200 and other risk factors).

•**What other drugs do you think are being prescribed because of drug company influence?** Antihypertensives—drugs used to treat high blood pressure—are good examples. Newer medications, such as calcium channel blockers and angiotensin converting enzyme (ACE) inhibitors, are among the most popular. One of them, *amlodipine* (Norvasc), was the second most commonly prescribed drug for older adults in 2003. But a study funded by the National Heart, Lung and Blood Institute found that diuretics, which have been around for decades, are as good or better than Norvasc in protecting against complications of hypertension, such as heart attack and stroke. A diuretic

might cost $29 per year, compared with $549 to $749 for Norvasc, depending on the dose. The patents for diuretics expired decades ago, so drug companies don't profit much from them.

•**Should everyone with high blood pressure just take a diuretic?** High blood pressure is a complex problem. Some people respond to one drug, some to another, and some need more than one. It would make sense, though, to start with a diuretic, and use expensive drugs such as Norvasc only when other alternatives haven't worked.

•**Are natural therapies a better alternative to some drugs?** If you look at the data rather than listen to the drug ads, you see that natural alternatives, such as improved diet and routine exercise, often are far more effective than drugs at achieving real health improvements, such as less heart disease and longer life.

Probably the most important test of a healthy diet's effect on heart disease is the Lyon Diet Heart Study conducted in Lyon, France. Heart attack patients were randomly counseled to eat a Mediterranean diet (high in unprocessed grains, fruits, vegetables and olive oil…very low in red meat, dairy fat and cholesterol) or a "prudent" post-heart attack diet (no more than 30% of calories from total fat and no more than 10% from saturated fat).

The people counseled to eat the Mediterranean diet developed 72% less heart disease than those in the prudent diet group over the next four years. There were 56% fewer deaths in the group counseled to eat the Mediterranean diet—that's two to three times the benefit achieved with statin drugs.

The same holds true for exercise. A study conducted at the Cooper Institute for Aerobics Research in Dallas followed 25,000 men who had undergone physical exams. Over the next 10 years, the men whose exercise endurance (as measured on a treadmill) was in the lowest 20% of the group were at a much higher risk of dying than those with high total cholesterol levels (above 240)—confirming that exercise is even more important than cholesterol control.

•**But many patients prefer pills because they're easier.** There is no question that many of us would rather take a pill than change our lifestyle. If the pills worked, it would simply be a question of how we want to spend our money. The problem is that the pills often are closer to folk medicine—empowered by our cultural beliefs but without a genuine scientific basis. About two-thirds of our health is determined by the way we live our lives, and—for better or worse—no pills can change that.

•**What's the solution?** Most doctors don't invest much time or energy helping patients to make healthy changes in diet and exercise or teaching stress reduction. If you are willing to consider these approaches before trying drug treatment, tell your doctor.

When medication is necessary, ask your doctor if a generic drug is just as effective as the expensive brand-name product. Remember, drug ads that tell you to "ask your doctor" about a particular drug have a single purpose—to sell more drugs, not to improve your health.

Prescription drug ads have become a normal part of our cultural landscape, but the US and New Zealand (with less than four million people) are the only two industrialized countries that allow them. The rest of the industrialized countries feel that assessment of the scientific information about prescription drug treatment should be left to doctors, who should work in a partnership with each patient to determine optimal medical care based on his/her individual situation.

Antibiotics: New Dangers, Latest Findings

Stuart Levy, MD, professor of medicine, molecular biology and microbiology, and director of the Center for Adaptation Genetics and Drug Resistance at Tufts University School of Medicine in Boston. He is founder and president of the nonprofit Alliance for the Prudent Use of Antibiotics (*www.apua.org*) and the author of *The Antibiotic Paradox*. HarperCollins.

By now, we've all heard about the growing threat of antibiotic-resistant bacteria. We know not to ask our doctors to prescribe an antibiotic unnecessarily, and we've been told that frequent handwashing cuts down on the transmission of bacterial infections. With such strong warnings, you might assume that antibiotic resistance is going away. It isn't.

Increasingly, bacteria that are responsible for sinusitis, ear and urinary tract infections and many types of pneumonia are resistant to one or more antibiotics. This means that many infections that were once easily cured by taking an antibiotic for a few days now can linger much longer—and even become life-threatening.

How antibiotic-resistance develops: Bacteria can become resistant to antibiotics by mutating to become insensitive to the drug. The surviving resistant organisms then multiply and create new strains of bacteria that don't respond to antibiotics that were previously effective. Emergence of resistance is enhanced when patients do not finish a full course of an antibiotic—or when antibiotics are overused or misused in general. *Latest developments…*

LAX HANDWASHING

What's new: Many people still aren't washing their hands. While 91% of American adults claim to wash their hands after using the restroom, only 83% actually do so, according to the American Society for Microbiology.

What this means for you: Since many viruses and bacteria are spread from hands to the mucous membranes of your mouth, nose or eyes, dirty hands are a prime means of transmitting infection.

Self-defense: In addition to washing your hands after using the restroom and before eating or preparing food, it's also important after handling garbage…playing with a pet…changing a diaper…blowing your nose, sneezing or coughing…and inserting or removing contact lenses.

What to do: Using soap and warm, running water, rub your hands together for at least 10 seconds. Don't forget the wrists and backs of your hands. Dry with a clean or disposable towel. Pocket-sized bottles of hand-sanitizing gels and disposable towelettes that contain alcohol are convenient ways to wash when water is not available.

MORE DRUG-RESISTANT STRAINS

What's new: The number of drug-resistant and multidrug-resistant strains of bacteria is up sharply from just a few years ago. About 70% of the bacteria that cause infections in hospitals are now resistant to at least one common antibiotic.

What this means for you: If you are hospitalized, you're now at increased risk of contracting an infection that can be difficult to treat and may even result in death. Recent studies show that 5% to 10% of hospital patients in the US get an infection during their stay, and nearly 100,000 die annually as a result. This compares with about 13,000 deaths from hospital-acquired infections in 1992.

Self-defense: Keep hospital stays as short as possible. Visitors and hospital staff should wash their hands before and after contact with you. With some infectious diseases, such as tuberculosis, visitors and staff may need to wear a mask, gown and gloves to prevent the spread of the infection.

ANTIBIOTIC BAN FOR POULTRY

What's new: The FDA has announced a ban on the use of the animal antibiotic *enrofloxacin* (Baytril) in poultry. Enrofloxacin is a *fluoroquinolone* antibiotic in the same class as *ciprofloxacin* (Cipro). The ban followed the finding that fluoroquinolone-resistant bacteria that infected poultry were becoming increasingly less responsive to Cipro in human infections caused by the same bacteria. This was the first time the FDA had banned an antibiotic used in animal health because of a potential harm posed to people by the emergence of drug-resistant bacteria.

What this means for you: Greater attention is being given to antibiotic use in agriculture, animals and people. Europe has instituted a ban on the use of all growth-promoting antibiotics. In the US, antibiotics are still given to poultry to increase growth. The FDA is currently reviewing the issue, and many experts believe the US should also ban growth-promoting antibiotics.

Self-defense: Although the FDA ban on enrofloxacin is in effect, poultry producers still can use growth-promoting antibiotics. To find poultry that is totally free of antibiotics, check with your local butcher or at a natural-food store.

NEW STAPH INFECTIONS

What's new: A drug-resistant strain of *staphylococcus* bacterium, community-acquired methicillin-resistant Staphylococcus aureus (CA-MRSA),

formerly found only in hospitals, is now increasingly being detected within communities.

What this means for you: This particular staph bacterium appears to be more virulent and spreads from person-to-person, particularly through skin-to-skin contact sports, such as football and wrestling.

Self-defense: To prevent infection, wash well with soap and water immediately after any contact sports, being especially careful to clean any cuts. Never share towels or washcloths in a gym.

CIPRO RESISTANCE

What's new: *Ciprofloxacin* (Cipro), one of the first-line antibiotics to treat anthrax (a leading bioterror weapon), is becoming increasingly ineffective against other infections.

What this means for you: For now, other antibiotics can fill the gap for ear, sinus and urinary tract infections. Experts do not believe that Cipro's effectiveness against anthrax has been compromised—but this could change in the future if the antibiotic is overused.

Self-defense: Some experts believe that doctors are too quick to prescribe Cipro when another antibiotic would do. If your doctor prescribes Cipro, ask if another antibiotic could be used.

LATEST ANTIBIOTICS

What's new: *Tigecycline* (Tygacil), the first in a new class of antibiotics called glycylcyclines is available. It was approved by the FDA as a first-line treatment for hospital-based skin and soft tissue infections caused by bacteria that are resistant to other antibiotics. A new class of antibiotics called *diarylquinolones*, which treats drug-resistant tuberculosis, is now in clinical trials.

What this means for you: Despite these new drugs, antibiotic research is getting short shrift. That's because many major pharmaceutical companies have found that it is more profitable to fund research and development for new drugs that treat chronic illnesses, such as diabetes, arthritis and high cholesterol.

Self-defense: Write to your representatives in Congress and tell them that you support efforts to boost incentives (via tax credits and other means) for pharmaceutical companies to develop new antibiotics. To write to your congressional representatives on-line, go to *www. usa.gov.* This Web site also gives mailing addresses and phone numbers for your congressional representatives.

Troublesome Side Effects Of Common Drugs

Jack E. Fincham, PhD, RPh, A.W. Jowdy professor of pharmacy care, department of clinical and administrative pharmacy at the College of Pharmacy at the University of Georgia in Athens, is also associate editor of the *Journal of Public Health Pharmacy.*

Anyone who has ever waded through the fine print on the package insert of a prescription drug knows that the list of potential side effects can be long and alarming—and difficult to understand.

Latest development: The FDA has updated the design used for prescription drug package inserts to make them easier to read. The redesigned package inserts are required for prescription drugs approved on or after June 30, 2006. For drugs approved in the five-year period prior to that date, the new format will be gradually phased in. Inserts for drugs older than that will be revised by manufacturers on a voluntary basis.

However, this good news does not change the fact that all drugs can cause side effects. Depending on the medication, there are literally hundreds of side effects that can occur, potentially affecting every organ system and bodily function.

Gastrointestinal side effects are among the most common. Dozens of drugs, including the antibiotics *ciprofloxacin* (Cipro) and *erythromycin* (E-Mycin), commonly prescribed for urinary tract, respiratory and skin infections, can cause upset stomach, diarrhea and/or abdominal pain.

Other examples: The antibiotic *amoxicillin* (Amoxil) can cause nausea…*digoxin* (Lanoxin), a heart medication, can cause vomiting…narcotic pain medications can cause constipation.

Hives and/or rashes also are common side effects. These skin conditions, which often are the first sign of an allergic reaction to a medication, can occur with aspirin, antibiotics and *atorvastatin* (Lipitor), a cholesterol-lowering drug.

Anaphylactic shock, a potentially fatal type of allergic reaction in which the breathing passages are constricted and blood pressure drops precipitously, may not occur the first time a drug is taken but rather after a third or fourth dose. Swelling (especially around the face and throat) and/or difficulty swallowing are red flags that you may be suffering from a serious allergic reaction.

Important: Each person responds differently to medication—side effects may occur in some people but not in others. It's crucial to understand the potential side effects of the medications you are taking so that you can report any adverse reactions to your doctor and/or pharmacist.

Spend the 10 to 15 minutes it typically requires to carefully read the package insert. Use reading glasses or a magnifying glass, if necessary. Checking a drug reference book (preferably one with large print) also is helpful. When picking up a prescription, ask to speak to the pharmacist about potential side effects. And of course, discuss potential side effects with your doctor when medication is prescribed.

Once you're taking a prescription drug, it's not always easy to identify side effects, because they can mimic the condition that is being treated. Usually the only way to distinguish between the two possibilities is to stop taking the drug—with your doctor's approval—to see if the side effects stop.

Side effects that are often missed by patients—and doctors…

COGNITIVE PROBLEMS

Prescription drugs that affect the central nervous system can impair thinking, memory, alertness and judgment. These include barbiturates, such as *phenobarbital* (Bellatal), prescribed for epilepsy or insomnia…anticholinergics, such as *atropine* (Sal-Tropine) and *scopolamine* (Scopace), prescribed to slow stomach motility (movement of food through the digestive system)…antispasmodics, such as *propantheline* (Pro-Banthine) and *dicyclomine* (Bentyl), for bowel spasms or cramping…muscle relaxants, such as *chlorzoxazone* (Paraflex) and carisoprodol (Soma), for muscle stiffness or back spasms…and antidepressants, such as *paroxetine* (Paxil) and *fluoxetine* (Prozac). Central nervous system stimulants, such as *methylphenidate* (Ritalin), also can affect cognition. Stimulant drugs are often used for attention deficit hyperactivity disorder (ADHD).

What you may not know: Certain blood pressure medications, such as *methyldopa* (Aldomet) and *clonidine* (Catapres), may affect heart rate and/or cardiac output (the pumping efficiency of the heart), leading to disorientation.

Cognitive symptoms to watch for: Cognitive changes, such as forgetting simple things that you normally remember, are worth noting. If family members and/or friends tell you that they see a change in your cognitive function, consult your doctor and/or pharmacist. Your doctor may be able to adjust the dosage, or it may help to take the drug at night. As an alternative, your doctor may prescribe an equally effective drug that won't trigger side effects in you.

SEXUAL DYSFUNCTION

Antidepressants, including the widely prescribed selective serotonin reuptake inhibitors (SSRIs), such as *fluoxetine* (Prozac) and *escitalopram* (Lexapro), are known to cause sexual dysfunction, including changes in libido, inability to reach orgasm and/or difficulty achieving an erection. Diuretics, such as *furosemide* (Lasix) and hydrochlorothiazide, can lead to male impotence. Some drugs that are used to treat benign prostatic hypertrophy (a condition in which the prostate gland is enlarged), such as *finasteride* (Proscar) or *dutasteride* (Avodart), also can affect sexual functioning, as can anti-anxiety agents, including *alprazolam* (Xanax), *lorazepam* (Ativan) and *diazepam* (Valium).

What you may not know: Older types of drugs used to treat acid reflux and ulcers, including H2 antagonist drugs, such as *cimetidine* (Tagamet), block androgen receptors, which are necessary for male sex hormone activity. These drugs also can decrease testosterone synthesis, leading to impotence and breast enlargement in some men. Newer H2 antagonist drugs, such as *famotidine* (Pepcid) and *nizatidine* (Axid), and some of the proton pump inhibitors, including *omeprazole* (Prilosec) and *esomeprazole* (Nexium), don't have this effect.

Symptoms to watch for: Report any changes in sexual function, including inability to have or maintain an erection, change in libido and inability to reach orgasm, to your doctor and/or pharmacist as soon as possible. Your doctor may adjust the drug dosage, prescribe an alternative medication in the same class or suggest alternative dosing schedules, such as taking the drug in the early morning.

WEIGHT GAIN

Some newer drugs, including the antipsychotic agents *olanzapine* (Zyprexa) and *quetiapine* (Seroquel), which are used to treat severe mental disorders, such as schizophrenia, may cause weight gain. The antidepressant *bupropion* (Wellbutrin), which is often used instead of an SSRI because it typically does not cause sexual side effects, also can trigger weight gain.

What you may not know: Some diabetes drugs, such as *glyburide* (DiaBeta) and *chlorpropamide* (Diabinese), can lead to weight gain.

Symptoms to watch for: If you gain more than five pounds in any four- to six-week period that you are taking a drug, speak to your pharmacist and/or doctor. Consider weighing yourself daily if you are prescribed a drug that can cause weight gain. Meanwhile, try reducing daily calories and/or exercising more to control any weight gain.

HOW TO AVOID SIDE EFFECTS

To help guard against potentially dangerous side effects, follow these steps when your doctor prescribes medication…

•**Review the dosage.** Drug dosages are usually determined by studies based on young, healthy volunteers or patients with uncomplicated diseases. People who have less body mass (under 120 pounds) don't need the same dose as someone who tops 200 pounds.

What to do: Ask your doctor if he/she is prescribing the lowest possible dose for a person your weight.

•**Mention your age.** As we age, our kidneys and liver are less efficient at metabolizing drugs.

What to do: Ask your doctor whether he is prescribing the lowest possible dose for a person your age.

Boost Your Medicine's Healing Powers

Leo Galland, MD, director, Foundation for Integrated Medicine, New York City. He is author of *The Fat Resistance Diet*. Broadway. *www.fatresistancediet.com*. Dr. Galland is a recipient of the Linus Pauling Award.

I f you're among the millions of Americans taking medication for serious conditions, you may be able to maximize the benefits… curb the side effects…and maybe even lower the dosages of your drugs by combining them with the right supplements.

Important: Consult your doctor before adding a supplement to your drug regimen. Some supplements can interact adversely with medications—for example, some research shows that fish oil can reduce the time it takes for blood to clot and should be used with caution by people taking a blood thinner, such as *warfarin* (Coumadin).

Supplements (available at health food stores) to consider using if you are taking any of the following…

ANTIDEPRESSANT

Supplement with: 1,000 milligrams (mg) to 2,000 mg daily of *eicosapentaenoic acid* (EPA), an omega-3 fatty acid found in fish oil. (Ask your doctor which dosage is right for you.)

What it does: Omega-3s are believed to enhance the ability of the brain chemical *serotonin* to act on the nervous system. In a recent British study, when depressed patients who were taking a prescription antidepressant, such as *fluoxetine* (Prozac) or *sertraline* (Zoloft), added 1,000 mg of EPA to their daily regimen for 12 weeks, they reported significantly less depression, anxiety and suicidal thoughts, as well as improved sleep, libido and energy.

Most standard fish oil supplements contain only 200 mg to 300 mg of EPA, so you'd need up to 10 capsules daily to get the recommended 1,000 mg to 2,000 mg of EPA. If you don't want to take that many capsules, take liquid fish oil—in an amount equal to 1,000 mg to 2,000 mg daily of EPA.

Also try: 500 micrograms (mcg) daily of folic acid, which promotes proper functioning of the nervous system. Low levels of folic acid have been linked to depression.

Harvard Medical School researchers report that depressed patients who had achieved remission with fluoxetine were 13 times more likely to relapse during a six-month period if they had low blood levels of folic acid.

Caution: Supplemental folic acid may mask a vitamin B-12 deficiency, which can lead to nerve damage. Take a 500-mcg to 1,000-mcg B-12 supplement daily to prevent worsening of a B-12 deficiency.

NONSTEROIDAL ANTI-INFLAMMATORY DRUG

Supplement with: 350 mg of *deglycyrrhizinated licorice* (DGL), three times daily.

What it does: Studies show that DGL may reduce or prevent the gastrointestinal (GI) inflammation, bleeding and ulcerations caused by aspirin and other nonsteroidal anti-inflammatory drugs (NSAIDs)—both prescription and over-the-counter.

Caution: Whole licorice extract also protects the stomach, but it contains *glycyrrhetinic acid*, which even in small doses may raise blood pressure. Stick with DGL.

Also try: 1,000 mg to 2,000 mg daily of vitamin C (in two divided doses) and 7 grams (g) of powdered glutamine (one heaping teaspoon dissolved in water, three times daily). Studies suggest that taking 1,000 mg of vitamin C twice daily may help prevent aspirin-induced inflammation of the small intestine.

Meanwhile, the amino acid glutamine, long used to help heal ulcers, may decrease the intestinal toxicity of other NSAIDs.

ASTHMA OR ALLERGY DRUG

Supplement with: 1,000 mg daily of *gamma-linolenic* acid (GLA) and 500 mg daily of EPA.

What it does: GLA, an omega-6 fatty acid derived from evening primrose oil or borage oil, may inhibit production of *leukotrienes*, molecules that trigger inflammation and constriction of the bronchial airways. The asthma drug montelukast (Singulair) also works by inhibiting leukotrienes.

Important: Most omega-6 fatty acids (including those found in many processed foods) increase inflammation, unless they're balanced by sufficient amounts of anti-inflammatory omega-3s. GLA, however, is an anti-inflammatory, but at high doses—and in the absence of omega-3s—it can become inflammatory. The recommended 500 mg of EPA daily creates an optimal balance of omega-6s and omega-3s.

Also try: Quercetin. In laboratory studies, quercetin has demonstrated antihistamine and anti-allergenic properties. Clinical trials are needed, but given its safety, I often recommend quercetin to my asthma and allergy patients. Try using 500 mg to 600 mg, twice daily, of quercetin—taken on an empty stomach for maximum benefit.

BLOOD PRESSURE DRUG

Supplement with: 1,000 mg of *arginine,* twice daily.

What it does: Arginine (also called L-arginine) is an amino acid used by the body to produce nitric oxide (NO), a molecule that helps keep blood vessels flexible and able to dilate—both of which stabilize blood pressure. Legumes (such as lentils, black beans and kidney beans) and whole grains (such as brown rice) contain some arginine, but you'll need a supplement to get the 2,000 mg daily that is recommended for blood vessel health.

Caution: Because some research has shown that arginine can be dangerous for people who have suffered a heart attack, it should not be used by these individuals. If you have the herpes simplex virus and want to take arginine, you may need to add 1,500 mg daily of lysine, another amino acid. The virus grows in the presence of arginine but is inhibited by lysine.

Also try: 100 mg daily of *Pycnogenol.* This plant extract appears to enhance NO synthesis in blood vessels. In a recent placebo-controlled trial, Chinese researchers found that hypertensive patients who took 100 mg of Pycnogenol daily for 12 weeks were able to significantly lower their dose of a calcium channel blocker, a popular category of blood pressure drugs.

STATIN

Supplement with: 100 mg daily of coenzyme Q10 (CoQ10).

What it does: Cholesterol-lowering statins deplete the naturally produced molecule coenzyme Q10—this depletion may lead to muscle damage.

Researchers at Stony Brook University in Stony Brook, New York, found that patients taking statins who added 100 mg of CoQ10 daily for one month reported a 40% reduction in severity of muscle pain, a common side effect of statins.

CoQ10 also may prevent oxidation of LDL "bad" cholesterol—an unfortunate side effect of statins that occurs to LDL cholesterol particles not eliminated by the drug

Also try: Fish oil that contains 1,500 mg of EPA and 1,300 mg of *docosahexaenoic acid* (DHA) daily. Studies show that these essential fatty acids raise HDL "good" cholesterol and lower dangerous blood fats (triglycerides).

The Blood Pressure Pill That's Great for Your Bones

Bruno H.Ch. Stricker, PhD, professor, Erasmus University Medical Center, Rotterdam, the Netherlands.

Felicia Cosman, MD, former clinical director, National Osteoporosis Foundation, and associate professor of clinical medicine, Columbia University, New York City.

Annals of Internal Medicine.

Thiazide diuretics that control high blood pressure can also reduce age-related bone loss and the resulting fractures, but the protection vanishes once the drugs are stopped, researchers say.

Osteoporosis, which can sometimes lead to hip fractures, is a common problem in older men and women, as bones become thinner and weaker during the normal aging process.

Studies have shown that thiazides slow calcium loss and may be a factor in preventing age-related bone erosion.

Now, Dutch investigators have clearly shown that thiazides significantly reduce the risk of hip fractures.

In a large population of elderly patients, the use of a thiazide medication "offered a substantial protection from hip fracture," says lead researcher Bruno H.Ch. Stricker, PhD, a professor at Erasmus University Medical Center located in Rotterdam.

THE STUDY

In their study, the researchers collected data on hip fractures among 7,891 men and women older than age 55.

They classified patients as those who had never used a thiazide, those who had used a thiazide for a short time and those who had used a thiazide for a year or more.

They also looked at individuals who had stopped using a thiazide for a short period and those who had stopped the medication for six months or more.

RISK REDUCED BY HALF

During up to nine years of follow-up study, Stricker and his team found that compared with patients who had never taken a thiazide diuretic, those who had taken a thiazide for more than one year had about a 50% lower risk of hip fracture.

However, this lower risk disappeared within four months after the medication was stopped, the research team says.

WHAT THE RESEARCH IMPLICATIONS ARE

Because thiazide diuretics are relatively safe, Stricker believes that they might be useful for treating older patients who have high blood pressure and who are also at risk for hip fracture.

"But I do not advise using thiazides primarily to protect against hip fracture if you do not have hypertension—not until a clinical trial has demonstrated that it is truly effective and how big that effect is," he cautions.

According to Stricker, based on the current study's findings, "it is reasonable to treat an older woman with hypertension who is also [likely] to hip fracture with a thiazide as a first medication."

FINDINGS SUPPORT OTHER STUDIES

Dr. Felicia Cosman, former clinical director of the National Osteoporosis Foundation as well as an associate professor of clinical medicine at Columbia University in New York City, comments that these findings are consistent with those of other studies.

According to Cosman, it is not surprising that the protective effect of thiazide medications wears off after use of the drug is discontinued. This is a common occurrence that can also be found with numerous other medications, she explains.

"We still need to follow the same preventive measures for osteoporosis. People need to maximize their calcium and vitamin D intake, exercise regularly and reduce any possible risk factors," she advises.

To learn more about how to prevent osteoporosis, visit the National Osteoporosis Foundation at *www.nof.org*.

ADHD Drugs May Slow Growth

James Swanson, PhD, psychologist and professor of pediatrics, University of California, Irvine.

Ernest Krug, MD, medical director, Center for Human Development, William Beaumont Hospital, Royal Oak, MI.

Pediatrics.

Children who have *attention deficit hyperactivity disorder* (ADHD) could find their height stunted by the medications used to treat this condition.

The results of a study and two years of follow-up research by scientists at the University of California, Irvine, found that stimulant medications used to treat ADHD are effective, but they may slow growth in height a bit.

THE STUDY

The randomized clinical trial, which lasted 14 months, compared the use of the stimulant medication *methylphenidate* (Ritalin) with behavioral therapy. Both Ritalin alone and behavioral therapy alone were also compared with a combination of two and with no treatment at all.

Researchers found that the children who received medication or medication in conjunction with behavioral therapy had fewer symptoms than those who received no medication. Children on medication also grew slightly less than their nonmedicated peers.

James Swanson, a psychologist and professor of pediatrics at the University of California, Irvine, and his colleagues then followed up with 540 children with ADHD who had participated in the trial.

After 24 months, the researchers interviewed the children and the parents and found that both the effects of medication and the effects of behavioral therapy were fairly consistent throughout this time period.

They also confirmed that the children who were on medication showed a slight reduction in height, but according to Swanson, the effect was less pronounced at 24 months, amounting to approximately one centimeter less per year than the children who were not taking medication.

MEDICATIONS SAFE, BUT QUESTIONS REMAIN

"Stimulant medications are really extremely safe with very few side effects," says Swanson. "I do not think this is necessarily a cause for great alarm in parents. The effect we saw was rather modest."

Swanson also notes that many questions remain unanswered.

For example, researchers don't know if children on ADHD medications will have a growth rebound later.

He adds that many children who have ADHD are larger than average for their age, so the slight growth reduction for those on medication may just put them back into the normal height range.

Dr. Ernest Krug, medical director of Beaumont Hospital's Center for Human Development in Royal Oak, Michigan, says, "Growth suppression is something we always monitor in kids on medication. This study reinforces the importance of careful follow-up of children when they're on medication. It's a good idea for these children to be seen every three to four months."

With any medication, parents should be convinced that the drug is providing beneficial effects for their children without causing unreasonable side effects, Krug says.

To learn more about ADHD, visit the Children and Adults with Attention Deficit/Hyperactivity Disorder (CHADD) Web site at *www.chadd.org*.

Counterfeit Drug Watch

Rebecca Shannonhouse, editor of *Bottom Line Health*. Boardroom Inc., 281 Tresser Blvd., Stamford, CT 06901.

Most people know there's a risk of buying counterfeit drugs on the Internet. *Problem:* Even drugs purchased from US pharmacies might be fake.

According to an FDA estimate, about one percent of the nation's drug supply—about 35 million prescriptions annually—is believed to be counterfeit.

What happens: Drugs are typically sold by manufacturers to wholesalers, who then sell them to pharmacies. However, some dishonest wholesalers tamper with drugs before selling them. Often, they buy cut-rate—sometimes phony—drugs from unlicensed or suspicious sources, explains Katherine Eban, an investigative journalist who has documented counterfeit drugs in her book *Dangerous Doses* (Harcourt).

The drugs most vulnerable to counterfeiting are commonly used and/or expensive.

Examples: The cholesterol-lowering drug *atorvastatin* (Lipitor) and the anemia drug *epoetin* (Procrit). Even common antibiotics such as penicillin have been faked. *How to protect yourself…*

•**Sign up for free E-mail alerts on fake drugs** at *www.safemedicines.org*, the Web site of the nonprofit Partnership for Safe Medicines.

•**Become familiar with the shape, color and, if applicable, taste of the drugs that you take.** Some counterfeits appear and/or taste slightly different from the real medication.

•**Note if your medicine seems to stop working or causes new side effects.**

If you suspect that a drug is a counterfeit, tell your pharmacist and physician immediately—and report it on the FDA Web site at *www.fda.gov/medwatch/how.htm*.

Low-Cost Hypertension Drugs May Work Just as Well as Expensive Ones

Jackson T. Wright, Jr., MD, PhD, professor of medicine, Case Western Reserve University, Cleveland.

Lawrence J. Appel, MD, MPH, professor of medicine, Johns Hopkins University, Baltimore.

The Journal of the American Medical Association.

You might expect newer, more advanced and costlier medications for high blood pressure to be more effective than the older and less expensive *thiazide diuretics*. But a Cleveland study found that this is not necessarily the case.

In an eight-year trial, the incidence of heart failure was lower and the risk of fatal heart disease or heart attacks was no greater for people who took a diuretic than for those who took the newer *calcium channel blockers* or *angiotensin-converting enzyme (ACE) inhibitors*.

The study may be the most comprehensive effort ever made to compare the effectiveness of different blood pressure drugs. *Here's how each drug works…*

•**Diuretics** lower blood pressure by increasing the passing of water and sodium.

•**Calcium channel blockers** widen blood vessels by relaxing the muscles around them.

•**ACE inhibitors** block the activity of an enzyme that makes arteries constrict.

Diuretics, by far the oldest drugs, are generally available as relatively inexpensive generics, while the calcium channel blockers and ACE inhibitors often are higher-priced, brand-name products.

The 50 to 60 million Americans who have been diagnosed with high blood pressure now spend an estimated $15.5 billion a year on drugs, the report says. A large proportion of patients need more than one drug, but the report says, "It is reasonable to infer that a diuretic be included in all multidrug regimens."

COST SAVINGS

A preliminary cost analysis showed that "if patients were switched from calcium channel blockers and ACE inhibitors to diuretics, the annual savings in direct costs would be between $250 and $600 per patient," says study leader Dr. Jackson T. Wright, Jr., a professor of medicine at Case Western Reserve University. There would be other savings from a reduced need for hospitalizations, Wright adds.

Diuretics have fallen out of favor with many doctors because they have potentially dangerous side effects, such as raising blood cholesterol and sugar levels, causing concern that they might actually be increasing the risk of heart disease, says Dr. Lawrence J. Appel, a professor of medicine at Johns Hopkins University.

However, the study "provides strong evidence that they should be first-line therapy," he says.

The National Heart, Lung and Blood Institute at *www.nhlbi.nih.gov/hbp* provides information on managing your blood pressure.

What Are the Odds? Some Parkinson's Drugs May Cause Gambling

Mark Stacy, MD, medical director, Movement Disorders Center, Duke University Medical Center, Durham, NC.

Jay Van Gerpen, MD, neurologist, Mayo Clinic, Jacksonville, FL.

Neurology.

A combination of some Parkinson's disease medications may produce a rare but potentially devastating side effect —addictive gambling behavior.

Researchers found nine pathological gamblers in a group of more than 1,000 people being treated for Parkinson's disease. These people said they hadn't had any gambling problems in the past.

THE STUDY

Dr. Mark Stacy, lead author of the study, says he began this study because he had two Parkinson's patients report huge gambling losses soon after Stacy had changed the doses of their medications. Stacy is the medical director of the Movement Disorders Center at Duke University Medical Center in Durham, North Carolina, but was at the Muhammad Ali Parkinson Research Center in Phoenix at the time of the study.

He and his colleague reviewed the charts of 1,184 patients with Parkinson's disease, and found seven other cases of problem gambling.

In all of the cases, the gambling was severe enough to cause financial problems.

On average, the people who had gambling problems had been diagnosed with Parkinson's disease 11 years before the start of their addictive gambling behavior.

PARKINSON'S DRUGS MAY BE IMPLICATED

All nine people were taking *levodopa* and a *dopamine agonist* when their gambling problems began.

Levodopa is a drug that changes into dopamine in the brain, and dopamine agonists help the body use the created dopamine. People who have Parkinson's disease have low levels of dopamine, which is believed to help control smooth movement. Dopamine also appears to affect mood and personality.

Of those with a gambling problem, eight were taking a dopamine agonist called *pramipexole* and one was taking *pergolide*.

None of the people who were taking levodopa alone reported problem gambling, and none of those taking a different dopamine agonist, *ropinirole*, reported any gambling problems.

Stacy says he's not sure how the medications cause addictive gambling behavior, but seven of the patients reported that their problems started within a month of when their dosage was increased. This suggests, Stacy says, that the higher doses of the dopamine agonists act as a catalyst for problem gambling behavior.

When their medications were switched, or the doses were lowered, most of the patients were able to control or stop their gambling behavior, according to the study results. Some of the patients also attended Gamblers Anonymous meetings.

DON'T BE SURPRISED BY SIDE EFFECTS

Dr. Jay Van Gerpen, a neurologist and movement disorder specialist from the Mayo Clinic in Jacksonville, FL, says he was not surprised by this study's findings.

"Medicines for Parkinson's disease may elicit unwanted side effects relating to mood and personality," says Van Gerpen. "Dopamine agonists can be associated with changes in personality, such as sexual inappropriateness, and changes in sleep cycles. Patients need to be aware of these possibilities," he adds.

Stacy says that although this side effect is rare, it's important for doctors and patients to know that higher doses of these medications may increase the risk of problem gambling.

If you think you or someone you love may have a gambling problem, find out for sure with a self-test from the National Council on Problem Gambling at *www.ncpgambling.org*.

■ ■ ■ ■

Statin Drugs Cut the Risk for Death After Heart Attack

A study of more than 170,000 heart attack patients (most of whom had never taken a cholesterol-lowering statin drug) found that those given a statin, such as *atorvastatin* (Lipitor), within 24 hours after a heart attack had a 54% lower risk of dying in the hospital than patients not given the statin therapy.

Theory: Statins increase levels of *nitric oxide*, which reduces inflammation and provides other cardiovascular benefits.

Gregg C. Fonarow, MD, professor of cardiovascular medicine, David Geffen School of Medicine, University of California, Los Angeles.

New Drug Prevents Peanut Allergies

Donald Y.M. Leung, MD, PhD, head, Pediatric Allergy-Immunology, National Jewish Medical and Research Center, and professor of pediatrics, University of Colorado Health Sciences Center, Denver.

Traci Tavares, spokeswoman, Food Allergy & Anaphylaxis Network.

American Academy of Allergy, Asthma and Immunology annual meeting, Denver.

The New England Journal of Medicine.

I t's not a cure, but a new drug may ease the worries of the 1.5 million Americans who have peanut allergies.

The experimental medication, which is called TNX-901, increases the threshold of an allergic reaction from half a peanut to approximately nine peanuts. Although that may not seem like much to peanut lovers, it has been estimated that most of the 50 to 100 deaths each year from peanut allergies occur after ingesting only one or two nuts.

Although a study on the drug was limited to those with peanut allergies, researchers say it could have a much wider impact.

"This drug may well also apply to other nut allergies and other food allergies, so it could affect six million to eight million people," says Dr. Donald Leung, colead author of the study.

People who have peanut allergies live in a culinary minefield because their condition forces them to eat defensively. They or their caregivers must examine ingredient labels with a fine-tooth comb and study the manufacturing process to determine if there are any peanuts or peanut products in the food. They also must ask detailed questions about restaurant fare. Allergic reactions are possible if even a trace amount of peanut is ingested.

PREVENTION RATHER THAN REACTION

The allergic reaction takes place when the body's immune system tries to protect itself from a substance it mistakenly identifies as harmful. The body creates antibodies against the food. The antibodies can cause something as minor as an itch or as lethal as swelling of the throat, obstructing breathing.

Avoidance has always been the best way to combat the allergy, but that's not always possible. The most common treatment for someone who has an allergic reaction is a shot of a lifesaving drug called *epinephrine*, sold under the brand name EpiPen. However, studies have found that only a small number of people with allergies carry the remedy with them.

TNX-901 is the first drug that could prevent the allergic reactions in the first place. "It's a buffer that would protect against most reactions from accidentally ingested peanuts," says Traci Tavares, a spokeswoman for the Food Allergy & Anaphylaxis Network. "Folks with a peanut allergy have never had that peace of mind."

Patients would have to get shots regularly and still watch what they eat, the investigators say.

■■■■

Steroid Warning

Corticosteroids can cause bone loss if taken for long periods and in high doses. High doses are used to treat lung disease, arthritis and other severe conditions. Patients taking corticosteroids daily for three months or longer also should take calcium and vitamin D supplements to prevent bone loss. Your doctor should arrange a bone-density test if you have been, or will be, taking high doses of these drugs or inhaled steroid drugs for asthma for longer than three months. Topical corticosteroids are usually safe.

Harris H. McIlwain, MD, adjunct professor, University of Southern Florida College of Public Health, Tampa.

■■■■

Shingles Vaccine

The first shingles vaccine, *Zostavax*, has been approved by the FDA for adults 60 and older who previously had chickenpox. If you had chickenpox, you can develop shingles, which can cause itching, burning, tingling and a red rash that develops into painful pus-filled blisters. Pain can be intense and persists in some patients for months or years. The vaccine reduces shingles incidence by half. Ask your doctor if Zostavax is right for you.

Jesse Goodman, MD, MPH, director, US Food and Drug Administration's Center for Biologics Evaluation and Research, Rockville, MD.

■■■■

Drug Warning

People who take low-dose aspirin plus *clopidogrel* (Plavix) to prevent a first heart attack or stroke are 78% more likely to die from cardiovascular causes than people who take aspirin alone. Paradoxically, the aspirin/Plavix combination can help prevent a second heart attack or stroke.

Also: Patients who have had a stent should take the aspirin/Plavix combination.

Self-defense: If you use both drugs, consult your physician about the benefits of continuing. Do not stop either drug on your own.

Eric Topol, MD, a heart researcher and former professor of genetics, Case Western Reserve University, Cleveland, and coauthor of a study of 15,603 people, published in *The New England Journal of Medicine.*

■ ■ ■ ■

New Drug Alert

New schizophrenia drugs may not be better than an older generic medicine. In a recent study, the older antipsychotic *perphenazine* worked as well as newer drugs Risperdal, Seroquel and Geodon. It was less effective than a fourth modern medicine, Zyprexa, but Zyprexa—like the other newer antipsychotics—can cause extreme weight gain and lead to heart disease and diabetes. These side effects are more pronounced in Zyprexa than in the other new drugs. Perphenazine has its own side effects, including involuntary movements, jerkiness and tremors. Ask your doctor which medication is best for you.

Jeffrey A. Lieberman, MD, chairman, department of psychiatry, Columbia University Medical Center, and director, New York State Psychiatric Institute, both in New York City, and leader of a study of more than 1,400 participants, published in *The New England Journal of Medicine.*

Sleep Apnea Helper Also Fights GERD

J. Barry O'Connor, MD, former assistant professor of medicine, division of gastroenterology, Duke University Medical Center, Durham, NC.

Ali Serdar Karakurum, MD, former chief, division of gastroenterology, Nassau University Medical Center, East Meadow, NY.

Archives of Internal Medicine.

A commonly used treatment for obstructive sleep apnea does more than help sufferers get a good night's rest. It also reduces the symptoms of *gastroesophageal reflux disease* (GERD).

Researchers at Duke University followed more than 300 patients with obstructive sleep apnea for seven years and found that 62% also had nighttime symptoms of gastroesophageal reflux. Those who used their *continuous positive airway pressure* (CPAP) machines saw major improvements in their reflux symptoms.

PRESSURE HELPS

"CPAP elevates the pressure on the esophagus and keeps acid from coming back up," says study author Dr. J. Barry O'Connor, a former assistant professor of medicine in the division of gastroenterology at Duke University Medical Center.

In obstructive sleep apnea, the soft tissue located in the back of the throat relaxes and closes the airway.

Because people can't breathe when this happens, they wake up numerous times during the night, though they might not even be aware of it.

One of the most effective treatments for sleep apnea is a CPAP machine.

Gastroesophageal reflux affects as many as one in five Americans at least once a week, according to the study. Reflux occurs when acid from the stomach backs up into the esophagus, causing heartburn. Symptoms often occur at night.

NOT PRACTICAL

"For patients who need CPAP anyway, they're killing two birds with one stone," says Dr. Ali Serdar Karakurum, former chief of the division of gastroenterology at Nassau University Medical Center in East Meadow, New York.

However, Karakurum adds, CPAP wouldn't be practical for most patients with reflux, since hoses from the machine are attached to the face during sleep. "The device is cumbersome and uncomfortable." And there are other, easier ways to manage reflux symptoms.

First is lifestyle modification. Karakurum recommends avoiding tomatoes, citrus fruits, mint, coffee and other caffeinated products, high-fat foods and tobacco.

He also says eating more frequent, smaller meals helps. Losing weight helps lessen symptoms of both reflux and sleep apnea.

If lifestyle modifications don't work for your reflux symptoms, Karakurum says, there are also effective over-the-counter and prescription medications available.

For more information on obstructive sleep apnea, go to the Web site of the American Sleep Apnea Association at *www.sleepapnea.org.*

Top Antihistamine Doesn't Work!

Karen Elizabeth Lasser, MD, MPH, assistant professor of medicine, Harvard Medical School, Boston, and Cambridge Health Alliance, Cambridge, MA. She is lead author of a study on the safety of new drugs published in *The Journal of the American Medical Association.*

A study published in *The Journal of the American Medical Association* examined all drugs approved by the US Food and Drug Administration (FDA) from 1975 to 1999. *One drug in five* was withdrawn from the market or required to have a "black-box" warning put on the package insert about serious risks.

During just one year of the study period, approximately 20 million Americans were given drugs that were later withdrawn.

The most common risks of the drugs were damage to the liver, heart and bone marrow and a variety of problems for pregnant women.

Self-defense: As long as other effective treatments are available, avoid any drug until it has been on the market for at least seven years. Approximately half of all problems with toxicity are discovered within that period.

Here is advice on common drugs to avoid—and better alternatives…

ALLERGY

Desloratadine (Clarinex). Introduced to the market in 2002, this antihistamine is essentially the same as the older drug *loratadine* (Claritin). When you take loratadine, the drug is broken down in the body into desloratadine. The manufacturer simply got a patent for the chemical by-product.

Drawbacks: Not only is there no evidence that desloratadine is clinically different from loratadine, neither drug is a particularly effective antihistamine.

In fact, when the manufacturer submitted four clinical trials to the FDA comparing doses of desloratadine with a placebo, only two of the studies found the drug to be effective.

Better choice: Over-the-counter (OTC) antihistamines, such as *chlorpheniramine* (Chlor-Trimeton) or *diphenhydramine* (Benadryl). They

are not only less expensive but they are usually more effective.

As an alternative to OTC drugs, ask your doctor about prescription nasal steroids, such as *flunisolide* (Nasalide) or *beclomethasone* (Vancenase). They quickly ease congestion without the grogginess that is sometimes caused by antihistamines.

HEARTBURN

Esomeprazole (Nexium). Introduced in 2001, esomeprazole is the fifth member of the *proton pump inhibitor* class of drugs used for gastroesophageal reflux disease (heartburn) and for duodenal ulcers that don't respond to antacids or H-2 blockers, such as *cimetidine* (Tagamet).

Drawbacks: An FDA evaluation suggests that esomeprazole is no better than *omeprazole* (Prilosec), an older OTC proton pump inhibitor that has a known safety record.

Better choice: People who have heartburn can choose among many drugs—Prilosec, Tagamet, antacids, etc.—that have been on the market for a long time and are known to be safe.

Non-drug treatments, such as not lying down after meals and avoiding chocolate or other foods known to cause heartburn, are often all that's needed.

INSOMNIA

Zaleplon (Sonata). Introduced in 1999, zaleplon was designed to help insomnia patients fall asleep without the residual grogginess that is so common with other sleeping pills. Zaleplon is quickly eliminated from the body, so you can potentially take it late at night or early in the morning and still be fully alert when you get up.

Drawbacks: It's less potent than the older *benzodiazepine* sleeping pills, such as *triazolam* (Halcion), *temazepam* (Restoril) and *flurazepam* (Dalmane).

Compared with a placebo, zaleplon decreases the time it takes to fall asleep by only eight to 20 minutes.

Zaleplon has a high risk for addiction when taken for more than several weeks.

It also has potentially serious interactions, such as excessive drowsiness, when it is taken with other drugs, including antihistamines and anti-ulcer medications.

Better choice: Behavioral and lifestyle adjustments, such as reducing caffeine intake and practicing yoga or other relaxation techniques, are much safer for treating insomnia.

For patients who need extra help for a few nights to two weeks, an older drug, such as *oxazepam* (Serax) or *zolpidem* (Ambien), can be effective.

Covered-Up Facts About Bone-Building Drugs

The New England Journal of Medicine.

Combining osteoporosis drugs may do more harm than good, according to two studies.

The studies sought to prove that combining *alendronate* and *parathyroid hormone* would work even better than using the drugs separately. Instead, it proved exactly the opposite, researchers say.

Alendronate, sold by Merck as Fosamax, helps stop any bone loss. Parathyroid hormone helps to build bone.

THE STUDIES

The first study looked at the drug combination in 238 women with untreated osteoporosis. Some got one drug, some got the other and some got both.

The study, which was conducted at several major hospitals nationwide for a year, found "no evidence of synergy" when both drugs were used. In fact, Fosamax reduced the effects of parathyroid hormone.

The second study, done at Massachusetts General Hospital, targeted 83 men with brittle bones. It, too, found that Fosamax canceled the effects of the parathyroid hormone.

Women should talk to their doctors about whether to take Fosamax alone.

BRISK WALKING BUILDS BONE MASS

According to Katarina T. Borer, professor of movement science at the Center for Exercise Research at the University of Michigan, postmenopausal women who walked three miles fast enough to become winded, five days a week for 15 weeks, increased their bone mineral density by 0.4%. This can be compared with a one percent bone-density loss in those who walked at a slower, less challenging pace.

Theory: Intense exercise triggers greater secretion of hormones that may increase bone mineralization.

Inhaled Steroids May Trigger Cataracts

Richard Bensinger, MD, spokesman, American Academy of Ophthalmology.
Robert Cykiert, MD, clinical assistant professor, New York University School of Medicine, New York City.
Robert Giusti, MD, director, Cystic Fibrosis Center, Long Island College Hospital, Brooklyn, NY.
Rajiv Luthra, MD, MPH, ophthalmologist in private practice, Rockville, MD.
British Journal of Ophthalmology.

Evidence continues to indicate that long-term use of inhaled steroids to treat asthma may contribute to the formation of cataracts. Inhaled steroids are widely prescribed for asthma and other respiratory problems, including allergies.

Cataracts are the number one cause of impaired vision and blindness in the world. But experts are divided over the amount of risk posed by the steroids.

"Steroids administered systematically are well known to cause cataracts," says Dr. Richard Bensinger, a spokesman for the American Academy of Ophthalmology.

A contrary opinion is offered by Dr. Robert Cykiert, a clinical assistant professor at New York University School of Medicine. Cykiert says, the association is "very rare. I've seen thousands of patients who have taken inhaled steroids for asthma and, of those, I've had maybe two that have mild cataracts."

THE STUDY

The authors of the study on cataracts made use of data from the United Kingdom's General Practice Research Database, which contains complete prescribing and diagnostic information for approximately 1.5 million patients in England and Wales.

Researchers looked at 15,479 people who had cataracts and 15,479 people who did not have this condition. The average age of the participants was 75 years old and approximately two-thirds were women.

In the group that had cataracts, 11.4% had been using inhaled steroids, compared with 7.6% of the group without cataracts.

The risk apparently increased with higher dosages and long-term use.

People who took up to 400 micrograms (mcg) of an inhaled steroid every day apparently had no increased risk. However, people who received doses higher than 1,600 mcg per day had a 70% increased risk.

ARE STEROIDS A NECESSARY EVIL FOR ASTHMATICS?

For many individuals who need to use inhaled steroids, this may come down to a choice between two illnesses.

"Doctors describe steroids as a wonderful awful drug," according to Bensinger. "The effects are wonderful. They're absolutely critical to the practice of medicine, but they have a lot of undesirable effects."

Cataracts are one of those effects, but it is also a very treatable condition. "Treatments are extraordinarily successful," Bensinger says. "It's not a big deal to go through. [The anesthesia for cataract surgery is] almost always local anesthetic, so it's not to be feared."

Without steroids, some asthmatics may not live long enough to develop cataracts, he adds.

A PRECAUTION

There are also ways to limit the absorption of steroids in the body.

"We have patients wash out their mouth or brush their teeth after using steroids to limit systemic absorption," says Dr. Robert Giusti, director of the Cystic Fibrosis Center at Long Island College Hospital located in Brooklyn, New York. There are also second-generation inhaled steroids that the liver metabolizes and removes from the body.

The cataract study seems to be an argument for taking the lowest dose possible for the shortest time possible.

"I have no doubt in my mind [that the inhaled steroids lead to cataracts]," says Dr. Rajiv Luthra, an ophthalmologist in Rockville, MD.

"If they're taken on a constant basis, which is every day or every other day for months to years, they will cause a problem," he adds.

The National Eye Institute at *www.nei.nih.gov* has additional information on cataracts and other eye disorders.

Alzheimer's Drug Warning

Amy F.T. Arnsten, PhD, professor and director of graduate studies in neurobiology, Yale University School of Medicine, New Haven, CTt.
Paula Bickford, PhD, professor of neurosurgery, University of South Florida Center for Aging and Brain Repair, Tampa, and past president, American Aging Association.
Neuron Online.

Experimental drugs designed to preserve memory function lost to age or brain disease may do so at the expense of other forms of recall.

Researchers believe that regional differences in the brain could undercut the effectiveness of drugs that are being developed to enhance memory in people with Alzheimer's disease and other age-related dementia.

UNDERSTANDING MEMORY

Two areas of the brain are associated with different types of memory. The hippocampus has been associated with long-term memory formation, while the prefrontal cortex has been associated with working or functional memory—such as remembering the phone number of your babysitter or remembering a phone number long enough to dial it.

In a healthy individual, the two brain systems work together. When a person gets older, however, both forms of memory can be adversely affected.

The prefrontal cortex—the working memory—naturally flags with normal aging, "so it's particularly important to see what this cortex loses, and give it back," says study author Amy F.T. Arnsten, professor and director of graduate studies in neurobiology at Yale University School of Medicine.

"There's some deterioration in the hippocampus [the long-term memory function] with normal aging, but what really erodes the hippocampus is Alzheimer's."

Experts believe that increasing the activity of an enzyme called *protein kinase A* (PKA) in the hippocampus may improve memory and other cognitive deficits. There are drugs in development that may accomplish that.

THE PROBLEM WITH DRUGS

The problem, according to Arnsten and her colleagues at Yale, is that a particular drug can have vastly different effects on different parts of the brain.

Their study found that drugs that might benefit the hippocampus might have deleterious effects on the prefrontal cortex.

"Different regions of the brain that control various kinds of learning and memory may be affected differently by drugs that are targeted at improving cognition," explains Paula Bickford, a professor of neurosurgery at the University of South Florida Center for Aging and Brain Repair in Tampa and a past president of the American Aging Association.

"They may improve one kind of cognition but impair a different type of cognition," according to Bickford.

THE STUDY

The researchers did a series of tests in rats and monkeys using drugs to increase or decrease PKA activity.

Inhibiting PKA in the hippocampus actually improved functioning in the prefrontal cortex. PKA activation in the hippocampus impaired functioning in the prefrontal cortex.

As people age, PKA activity declines in the hippocampus but increases in the prefrontal cortex, suggesting that different measures are needed to improve the situation in each area of the brain.

For more on memory and aging, visit the Memory and Aging Center of the University of California, Los Angeles, at *www.semel.ucla.edu/memory/*.

■■■■

Pneumonia Vaccine

Adults who received the pneumococcal vaccine were 40% to 70% less likely to die from pneumonia when hospitalized for the condition than patients who were unvaccinated or had unknown vaccination status. Vaccination also reduces risk for respiratory failure, kidney failure and heart attack.

Theory: Vaccination prevents invasion into the bloodstream of pneumonia-causing bacteria, lowering risk for organ failure. The CDC recommends that adults age 65 and older and younger people with risk factors, such as diabetes, asthma or kidney disease, get the pneumonia vaccine.

David Fisman, MD, MPH, epidemiologist, Ontario Public Health Laboratory, Toronto.

■■■■

Infection-Fighter After Chemotherapy

Neutropenia—a low level of infection-fighting white blood cells—is a common complication of chemotherapy.

New study: More than 1,500 patients with breast, lung, testicular or other solid tumors or lymphoma took 500 mg of the antibiotic *levofloxacin* (Levaquin) or a placebo for seven days during each of six chemotherapy cycles.

Result: The patients taking levofloxacin experienced a 27% reduction in hospitalizations for infections during all six cycles.

If you are undergoing chemotherapy: Ask your doctor about adding levofloxacin to your regimen.

Michael Cullen, MD, medical oncologist, Cancer Centre, University Hospital, Birmingham, England.

■■■■

Older Diabetes Drugs Alert

Over a five-year period, 6.8% of patients taking the older sulfonylurea drugs *tolbutamide* (Orinase) or *chlorpropamide* (Diabinese) died, compared with 6.1% of patients taking the non-sulfonylurea drug *metformin* (Glucophage) or 4% taking a second-generation sulfonylurea, *glyburide* (Diabeta).

Theory: Sulfonylurea drugs may interfere with cardiovascular health.

If you have type 2 diabetes: Ask your doctor about metformin. Cumulative research indicates that it is the best first choice for diabetes medication.

Jeffrey A. Johnson, PhD, professor of public health sciences, University of Alberta, Edmonton, Canada.

Simple Fixes for Medication Errors

Charles B. Inlander, a consumer advocate and health-care consultant based in Fogelsville, PA. He was founding president of People's Medical Society, a consumer health advocacy group active in the 1980s and 1990s. He is the author of more than 20 books, including *Take This Book to the Hospital with You*. St. Martin's.

I have been a member of a committee organized by the Institute of Medicine, a government advisory group in Washington, DC, to study and find solutions to the medication error problem in America.

Our report, based on the findings of several studies and the testimony of more than 100 experts, made front-page headlines across the country.

Among our findings: Each year, at least 1.5 million Americans are seriously harmed by medication errors (with at least 7,000 deaths). Statistically, every hospitalized patient can expect to be the victim of a medication error at least once a day for each day that he/she is hospitalized... tens of thousands of errors occur at local pharmacies each month....and more than 800,000 medication errors occur in nursing homes annually. Although the dangers of medication errors were widely reported in the media, the solutions were hardly discussed. *What you can do to help protect yourself—and your family...*

•**Keep a current list of all your medications.** One of the most dangerous medication errors involves a doctor prescribing a drug that causes a serious interaction with another drug or supplement. Most doctors do not know all the prescription and over-the-counter drugs, vitamins and other supplements their patients take, so keep a list of everything you take (and the dosage). Take the list with you to every doctor visit and hand it to the doctor before he writes a new prescription. For information on interactions, check the FDA Web site *(www.fda.gov/cder/consumerinfo/druginteractions.htm)*.

•**Double-check drugs at the pharmacy.** Pharmacy errors can occur when the pharmacist is in a rush or can't read the doctor's handwriting.

Helpful: Ask your doctor to write the name of the drug on a piece of paper along with the dosage. Compare this information with what you are handed at the pharmacy or what is delivered to you from a mail-order pharmacy. If there is a discrepancy, do not accept the drug until you have checked with the pharmacist. If the prescription is a refill, make sure the pills match those you already have.

•**When hospitalized, bring an advocate.** Studies show that error rates drop dramatically if a family member or friend is with a hospitalized patient to help oversee medications. *Your advocate should...*

1. Create a list of the drugs you were taking before being hospitalized to share with every doctor and nurse who treats you.

2. Get a list of all the drugs you are taking in the hospital and the times they should be given.

3. Monitor the drugs themselves, looking for any differences, such as size, color or dosages, and keep a log of what medication was given when.

4. Refuse any new or different drugs that have not been discussed by a doctor or nurse with you or the advocate. If you have a loved one in a nursing home or assisted-living facility, having a family member or friend visit daily to monitor the medication log will reduce errors dramatically.

Choosing the Right Drug

Marianne J. Legato, MD, founder of the Partnership for Gender-Specific Medicine at Columbia University and a professor of clinical medicine at Columbia's College of Physicians and Surgeons, both in New York City, is the author of *Eve's Rib: The New Science of Gender-Specific Medicine and How It Can Save Your Life*. Harmony.

Medical researchers have long known that men and women differ in their susceptibility to common diseases, such as diabetes, heart disease and cancer.

Now: Researchers are discovering that men and women often respond differently to the same medication.

Example: The allergy drug *terfenadine* (Seldane) was removed from the market in 1998 when it was discovered that women taking it had a higher risk for potentially deadly heartbeat irregularities (arrhythmias). Men taking the drug didn't experience the same risk.

THE GENDER FACTOR

Until recently, the pharmaceutical industry mainly tested new drugs on men. Women were not included in drug trials to protect them and any children they might conceive if pregnancy occurred during testing. Also, the hormone fluctuations experienced by women were thought to make them less desirable than men as study subjects.

In 1993, after researchers had discovered that men and women respond differently to drugs, the FDA began requiring that women be included in drug trials for medications that would be taken by them.

Among the most popular theories to explain gender-related differences in drugs...

•**Hormones.** The enzymes that metabolize drugs are affected by hormones, which differ greatly in men and women. For example, the "female" hormone progesterone, which increases just prior to menstruation, accelerates the breakdown of the steroid *prednisone* in the body. This means that a woman with asthma might require a higher dose of the drug just before her menstrual period to avoid an attack.

•**Fatty tissue.** Some drugs are stored in fatty tissue. Because women typically have a higher percentage of body fat than men, women might require a lower drug dose in some cases because the drug is stored in the fatty tissue and is available for a longer time after dosing.

Common drugs with sex-specific differences...

ANALGESICS

Women may be biologically more sensitive to pain than men—and they are known to experience more inflammation from infection and injury. Therefore, women may require higher doses of analgesics that have an anti-inflammatory component.

Women often do better with *ibuprofen* (Advil) or another nonsteroidal anti-inflammatory drug (NSAID), such as *naproxen* (Aleve), than with pain relievers, such as *acetaminophen* (Tylenol), that do not treat inflammation.

Best advice: For severe pain—following surgery, for example—women should ask their doctors for a "kappa opioid," such as *butorphanol tartrate* (Stadol), a morphine-like painkiller. This class of drugs is much more effective for women than other analgesics. In men, kappa opioids aren't as effective as other drugs.

ANESTHESIA

Women tend to wake up quicker than men following anesthesia—an average of six minutes faster—even when they're given the same dose relative to their body weight. Women experience more side effects from anesthesia than men do and are more likely than men to report some consciousness during surgical procedures.

Despite this, women tend to be given less pain-relieving medication in the recovery room following surgery.

Reason: A man's blood pressure rises when he's in pain. Doctors rely on this to indicate when to use drugs and how much to give. Women in pain frequently have a drop in blood pressure—and a more rapid heart rate as a result, which is a better indicator of how much distress they are feeling.

Best advice: Before an operation, women should request that their heart rate be monitored as a pain indicator along with blood pressure. If the heart rate increases, their doctors should consider giving more pain medication.

ANTI-ARRHYTHMICS

This class of drugs is used to treat heart arrhythmias. One popular anti-arrhythmic, sotalol (Betapace), is more dangerous for women than for men. Due to differences in the characteristics of the cardiac cell membranes in men and women, sotalol, which acts on these cell membranes, can increase a woman's risk for *ventricular tachycardia*, a potentially life-threatening arrhythmia.

Best advice: A woman who needs an anti-arrhythmic drug can sometimes be treated with another drug in the same class. If she requires sotalol, she should be advised to stay in a hospital or other facility that can provide continuous heart monitoring—and cardiac resuscitation, if necessary.

ANTIDEPRESSANTS

These days, most people with depression are treated with a selective serotonin reuptake inhibitor (SSRI) antidepressant, such as *paroxetine* (Paxil) or *fluoxetine* (Prozac). These drugs increase brain concentrations of serotonin, a neurotransmitter that regulates mood.

However, a new study shows that men don't appear to benefit from SSRIs as much as women—perhaps because men are known to have about 50% more brain serotonin than women. Therefore, increasing the levels of this neurotransmitter through drug therapy has relatively modest effects in men.

Best advice: Tricyclic antidepressants, such as *amitriptyline* (Elavil) or *nortriptyline* (Pamelor), are often better choices for men. These older drugs have a higher risk for side effects, such as weight gain and dry mouth, than the SSRIs, but are more likely to be effective in men.

ASPIRIN

Millions of healthy Americans take aspirin daily or every other day to "thin" the blood and reduce the risk for clots, which can contribute to heart attack and/or stroke. However, doctors must weigh the potential benefits of aspirin therapy against the potential risks. In both sexes, regular use of aspirin has been shown to increase the risk for gastrointestinal bleeding.

New finding: In men, daily aspirin can lower heart attack risk by 32%, according to a recent analysis of aspirin therapy conducted by researchers at Duke University Medical Center in Durham, North Carolina. Aspirin does not have this effect in all women. However, women who take a daily or every-other-day aspirin were found to have a 17% reduction in the risk for stroke.

Best advice: For men who are at risk for heart attack (due to smoking, high blood pressure or family history), aspirin therapy is often a good choice.

Women under age 65 who are concerned about heart protection alone may want to forgo aspirin therapy and focus on other protective strategies, including weight control, not smoking, regular exercise, etc.

In women over age 65, the heart benefits of aspirin therapy may outweigh the risks for stomach problems.

Because women suffer strokes about as often as men—and their risk of dying from stroke

is even higher—they should consider aspirin therapy if they have stroke risk factors, such as smoking, high blood pressure, etc.

Important: Consult your doctor before starting or discontinuing aspirin therapy.

■ ■ ■ ■

New Osteoporosis Drug

In a study of 412 postmenopausal women with low bone-mineral density, those who received injections every three to six months of *denosumab*, a fully human monoclonal antibody (a synthesized antibody identical to human antibodies), had a 3% to 6.7% increase in lumbar spine bone density after one year. This response was similar to—or slightly greater than—that in women taking once-weekly *alendronate* (Fosamax), the most commonly prescribed osteoporosis drug. The FDA will review denosumab after additional testing.

Michael McClung, MD, founding director, Oregon Osteoporosis Center, Portland.

■ ■ ■ ■

Less Expensive Drugs?

Ultra-low generic drug prices are on the way, reports consumer advocate Charles Inlander. Wal-Mart has a $4 prescription program that includes many commonly prescribed drugs. Other major chains—such as Walgreens and CVS—have lowered prices, too. Not all generics can be sold for $4, but the overall price trend is down.

Charles B. Inlander, a consumer advocate and health-care consultant based in Fogelsville, PA. He was founding president of People's Medical Society, a consumer health advocacy group active in the 1980s and 1990s. He is the author of more than 20 books, including *Take This Book to the Hospital with You.* St. Martin's.

■ ■ ■ ■

Welcome Side Effect

Celebrex may lower colon cancer risk. Celebrex is prescribed for pain, particularly arthritis pain, but it has been associated with increased risk of heart problems.

Recent finding: Celebrex lowers risk of growths that lead to colon cancer.

Best: People with a family or personal history of colon cancer should talk to their doctors to determine if the benefits of the drug outweigh the risks. Celebrex is not appropriate for people who have only average or slight risk for colon cancer.

Samuel Meyers, MD, clinical professor of medicine, Mount Sinai School of Medicine, New York City.

■ ■ ■ ■

Open-Heart Surgery Warning

Before cardiac surgery, be sure to ask your doctor not to give you *aprotinin* (Trasylol), a drug that has been proven to double a patient's risk of kidney failure and increase the risk of heart attack, heart failure and stroke.

Aprotinin has been given to an estimated one million cardiac surgery patients to limit bleeding. Using the cheaper (one-tenth the cost) and safer generic alternatives *aminocaproic acid* or *tranexamic acid* provides the same benefit without the adverse side effects.

Caution: Just because a drug has FDA approval doesn't make it safe—the FDA and the manufacturers don't necessarily do continuing studies after it's on the market.

Dennis T. Mangano, MD, PhD, Ischemia Research and Education Foundation (IREF), an independent nonprofit medical research foundation dedicated to performing quality medical scientific research that saves and extends lives, San Bruno, CA.

Dangerous Medication Risks for Seniors

Robert N. Butler, MD, professor of geriatrics, Mount Sinai School of Medicine, and president, International Longevity Center (*www.ilcusa.org*), both in New York City. He won the Pulitzer Prize for his book *Why Survive? Being Old in America* (Johns Hopkins University). He is also coauthor of *Aging and Mental Health* (Allyn & Bacon) and *The New Love and Sex After 60* (Ballantine).

Modern medications are so powerful that they both save lives and endanger them. After age 50, just when people are most

likely to take several medications prescribed by multiple health professionals who often don't communicate with each other, they become increasingly vulnerable to adverse drug reactions.

Reasons: Aging slows recovery…diminished liver and kidney functions result in altered metabolism and excretion.

Also: Reapportionment of fat and lean body tissue changes drug distribution.

Surprising: The drugs most commonly implicated in adverse drug reactions are time-honored medications prescribed for chronic conditions.

Examples: Diuretics (water pills), such as *hydrochlorothiazide* (HydroDiuril) and *furosemide* (Lasix), to reduce fluid retention and blood pressure…oral anticoagulants (blood thinners), such as *warfarin* (Coumadin), to limit clotting after a heart attack or stroke.

DANGEROUS INTERACTIONS

An often-quoted study published in the *Journal of the American Medical Association* found that in the US, more than 2.2 million people a year have serious adverse reactions to prescribed drugs and 100,000 of them die, making drug interactions one of the leading causes of hospitalization and death. *Watch out for these…*

•**Drug-food interactions.** Some labels say, "Take with food." Which food? Grapefruit juice often triggers a drug-food interaction that may be good (helps the body absorb certain AIDS drugs) or bad (deactivates some blood pressure drugs and cholesterol-lowering drugs). Oat bran also can make blood pressure medication less effective.

Solution: Ask your doctor or pharmacist which foods might affect the actions of your medications and how.

Although taking drugs with a meal may reduce stomach upset, food may delay the drug's absorption, alter its characteristics or make its actions less predictable. Speak up—ask whether this applies to any medication you take.

Reduced body mass and increased fat make older people more sensitive to alcohol, which interacts with many commonly prescribed drugs and many commonly prescribed sleep aids, such as sedatives and hypnotics.

Danger: Alcohol is a major ingredient in many liquid medications, especially cough syrup.

•**Drug-drug interactions.** Prescription drugs known for interacting with other drugs include cholesterol-lowering statins, such as *atorvastatin* (Lipitor) and *pravastatin* (Pravachol), and blood pressure-lowering antihypertensives, such as *furosemide, propranolol* (Inderal) and *clonidine* (Catapres).

Self-defense: Find out which potential interactions apply to each medication you take now…and whenever a new one is prescribed, ask your doctor and/or pharmacist which drugs or foods not to take with it. Perhaps just separating the food and the drug by two or three hours would be safer.

Over-the-counter (OTC) drugs can wreak as much havoc as prescription drugs.

Examples: Antacids, antihistamines and heavy use of nonsteroidal anti-inflammatory drugs (NSAIDs), such as aspirin and *ibuprofen* (Advil, Motrin). According to an estimate by James Fries, MD, of the Stanford University School of Medicine, NSAID-induced gastrointestinal bleeding sends about 76,000 Americans to the hospital each year…and kills about 10% of them.

Antacids (Milk of Magnesia, Tums, Amphojel) can reduce the effectiveness of antibiotics, such as *tetracycline* and *ciprofloxacin* (Cipro)…antihypertensive drugs, such as *propranolol* and *captopril* (Capoten)…and heartburn drugs, such as *ranitidine* (Zantac) and *famotidine* (Pepcid AC). But antacids can also increase the potency of *valproic acid* (Depakote/Depakene), for seizures and bipolar disorder…*sulfonylurea* (Glucotrol), for diabetes…*quinidine* (Quin-Release), for arrhythmias…and *levodopa* (Larodopa), for Parkinson's disease.

The older (first-generation) antihistamines, taken widely for allergies, colds and flu, can have dangerous interactions when taken with other drugs that cause drowsiness, such as antidepressants, alcohol, pain relievers, muscle relaxants and medications for seizures or anxiety.

Examples: *Brompheniramine* (in Robitussin Allergy & Cough) and *doxylamine* (in NyQuil).

The examples listed above are drops in the bucket. Check your own medications.

PERILOUS FALSE ALARM

Some drugs can drain certain vitamins from the body. If these vitamins aren't replaced, resulting symptoms may mimic those of dementia or other age-related conditions.

Examples: Tuberculosis drugs can deplete vitamin B-6, leading to amnesia, and vitamin-B complex, leading to apparent senility. Seizure drugs (anticonvulsants) can deplete vitamin D, leading to hearing and walking problems and general weakness. An older person displaying characteristics that are associated with dementia may just have an easily corrected vitamin deficiency.

MEDICATION ERRORS

More than 7,000 deaths in US hospitals were caused by medication errors in a single year, according to a major report published by the Institute of Medicine.

As it happens, the drugs found by the United States Pharmacopoeia* to be most frequently implicated in medication errors are commonly taken by seniors.

Examples: *Insulin* (for diabetes)…*warfarin* and *heparin* (to control clotting, such as in cardiovascular disease)…*albuterol* (Proventil, for asthma or bronchitis).

The Joint Commission asked hospitals to start providing every hospital patient with a list of all his/her prescribed medications and instructions for taking new ones. Patients, the Joint Commission said, should be encouraged to show the list to everyone providing care in the hospital, at any follow-up facility and after going home.

Have an advocate—a family member or friend—with you when you're in the hospital. Anyone hospitalized in my family is attended by a relative night and day.

Potentially fatal danger: Poor communication about meds when a patient is moved, such as from a critical-care unit to a general medical unit or from one health-care facility to another…or when nurses or other caregivers change shifts.

Self-defense: If you don't get a list from the hospital, maintain and hand out a list of your own. A free form is available on-line from The Joint Commission at *www.jointcommission.org*.

*The nonprofit public standards–setting authority for prescription and OTC medicines, dietary supplements and other health-care products made and sold in the US.

Also, question every drug you're given by anyone, anywhere, anytime.

For the most expert care, find a geriatrician—a physician specializing in seniors' medical needs. Medication needs differ as we age.

Example: A child's dose of *digoxin* (Digitek), used for congestive heart failure and other cardiac conditions, may be sufficient after age 65.

MEDICATION STRATEGIES

•**Brown-bag it.** You'll get your doctor's appreciation and attention by bringing in a bag containing every drug you currently take. Include prescription and over-the-counter drugs, vitamins, herbal supplements and nutritional supplements (such as chondroitin for joint pain). Go through the bag together.

Once you've agreed on which ones, if any, to change or drop, make a list of the ones remaining. Include the drug name, dose (amount and interval) and the name, specialty and phone number of the health professional who prescribed it. With every change, update the file.

•**Tell the world.** Post your master list on your refrigerator in case of a medical emergency at home. Keep a copy in your wallet near your driver's license. Give a copy to all your health-care providers, including surgeons, anesthesiologists and dentists. If you go to the hospital, take several copies and give them to all your health-care providers, including every nurse who hands you a pill or adds meds to your IV line. Ask to have a copy placed in your file or clipped to your chart.

•**Collaborate in your own care.** Our health system has no good mechanism for coordinating medical care. It's your job to give all your health-care providers the full picture.

Patients underestimate physicians' willingness to collaborate. Doctors are rushed, but they care. *Ways to help yourself…*

•If you suspect a possible interaction between drugs you're taking, either from symptoms or research, call the doctor immediately.

•Don't be afraid to raise concerns. You may be able to switch to a different drug that doesn't interact with your other meds.

•If you have trouble getting your doctor's attention, ask an office nurse to field medication-related questions.

•If your doctor is routinely unwilling to discuss your medications and to look up what he/she doesn't know, find one who will.

•Submit all prescriptions to the same pharmacy or chain. Typically, pharmacy computer systems automatically flag potential drug interactions. Ask your pharmacist.

EASY STEPS TO REMAIN SAFE

Prevention is far better than cure. *Keep medication crises at bay proactively…*

•**Use your eyes.** When you pick up a prescription, open and examine it on the spot.

Example: Coumadin, a brand-name product of the blood thinner warfarin, comes in nine doses. Is yours correct?

Before taking a new drug, read the side effects and interaction warnings in the patient information enclosure. Print too small? Type the drug name into Google or another search engine to find the manufacturer's Web site.

•**Don't take others' medications.** Doctors determine the best drug and dose according to age, weight, medical conditions and other drugs taken. What works well for someone else, even with the same condition, might be dangerous for you.

•**Drink lots of water.** Aspirin's tiny flakes can lodge in the esophagus, causing inflammation. *Acetaminophen* (Tylenol) in high doses can cause liver damage. Nonsteroidal anti-inflammatory drugs (NSAIDs), such as *naproxen* (Anaprox DS, Aleve), can cause ulcers. To reduce the risk, take pills with a large glass of water and drink several more glasses throughout the day.

•**Economize, but wisely.** Request a prescription for double the dose you need—a 10-milligram (mg) pill for a 5-mg dose, 20 mg for a 10-mg dose, etc. Cut each pill in half with an inexpensive pill cutter. You'll be taking the right amount at a lower cost per dose.

Warnings: Don't cut capsules or pills coated to prevent nausea or cut your prescription, taking half the prescribed dose, to save money. Ask an expert—your pharmacist will know whether your pills can safely be cut.

Popular Drugs That Steal Nutrients

Frederic Vagnini, MD, director of Heart, Diabetes and Weight Loss Centers of New York, in New York City and Westbury, NY. Dr. Vagnini is coauthor of *The Side Effects Bible: The Dietary Solution to Unwanted Side Effects of Common Medications*. Broadway.

Depletion of nutrients is among the most common—and overlooked—side effects of both over-the-counter (OTC) and prescription drugs.

Here's what happens: Medications can cause improper absorption of vitamins and minerals—or they can accelerate the elimination of nutrients from the body. The consequences may range from bothersome symptoms, such as fatigue or stomach upset, to serious heart, muscle or nerve damage.

Most doctors are aware of some minerals that are depleted through the use of diuretics (water-excreting drugs). However, few doctors are aware of the dangers of nutrient depletion caused by many other types of medication, because the problem is not widely reported.

Popular drugs that deplete the body of nutrients…

ANTIBIOTICS

The most commonly prescribed antibiotics include *azithromycin* (Zithromax), *amoxicillin* (Amoxil), *ampicillin* (Omnipen), *ciprofloxacin* (Cipro), *ofloxacin* (Floxin) and *erythromycin* (Eryc).

Nutrients depleted…

•**B vitamins.** The B vitamins are essential for normal metabolism as well as immune and nervous system functioning.

•**Vitamin K.** This vitamin is critical for blood clotting and bone strength.

•**"Friendly" intestinal bacteria** known as *Bifidobacterium bifidum* and *Lactobacillus acidophilus*. Antibiotics kill not only harmful bacteria but also "good" bacteria that promote gastrointestinal health and help balance immune response.

If you are prescribed an antibiotic: Ask your doctor about also taking a B-complex

vitamin—50 mg…vitamin K supplement—60 micrograms (mcg) to 80 mcg…and probiotic supplements providing 15 billion live B. bifidum and 15 billion live L. acidophilus organisms daily.*

In addition, eat more vitamin B–rich foods, such as beef, liver, chicken, pork, fortified breads and cereals, whole-grain pastas, legumes, nuts and dark, leafy greens.

To increase your intake of vitamin K, eat kale…collard, turnip or mustard greens…spinach…broccoli…and Swiss chard.

Caution: Do not take vitamin K supplements or eat excessive amounts of vitamin K–rich foods if you take *warfarin* (Coumadin) or another blood-thinning drug.

For additional B. bifidum, eat more asparagus, garlic and/or onions, which stimulate growth of this friendly bacteria. For L. acidophilus, yogurt containing live cultures is your best food source.

HIGH-CHOLESTEROL DRUGS

The most widely prescribed cholesterol-lowering "statins" include *atorvastatin* (Lipitor), *fluvastatin* (Lescol), *lovastatin* (Mevacor) and *pravastatin* (Pravachol).

Nutrient depleted…

•**Coenzyme Q10 (CoQ10).** All cells require CoQ10 for the proper function of mitochondria (tiny energy-producing structures within the cells). The more energy a cell must produce, the more it depends on CoQ10. That's why cells of the heart, in particular—because it is constantly beating—require an abundance of CoQ10.

Unfortunately, statin drugs, which effectively block the production of harmful cholesterol, also prevent CoQ10 production.

Some doctors worry that long-term use of statins may worsen heart failure. Studies have found that patients with chronic heart failure have lower CoQ10 levels, and that CoQ10 supplements may improve their heart condition. Signs of CoQ10 deficiency include fatigue and muscle weakness.

If you are prescribed a statin: Ask your doctor about taking 30 mg to 100 mg of a CoQ10

*If you're taking any medications, consult your doctor before changing your diet or beginning a supplement. In rare cases, increasing a nutrient may interfere with a drug's potency or worsen your condition.

supplement daily. This nutrient also is available in some foods, including beef, chicken, salmon, oranges and broccoli.

PAINKILLERS

Millions of Americans take a nonsteroidal anti-inflammatory drug (NSAID), such as *ibuprofen* (Motrin, Advil), *naproxen* (Aleve), *celecoxib* (Celebrex) and *nabumetone* (Relafen), to help relieve arthritis and other inflammatory pain.

Nutrient depleted…

•**Folic acid.** Your body needs this water-soluble B vitamin to produce new cells and DNA and to synthesize and utilize proteins.

Several large epidemiological studies have linked low folic acid levels to increased risk for colon, breast and pancreatic cancers.

Heart health is also affected by folic acid. As folic acid levels decline, levels of the amino acid homocysteine rise. Studies suggest that elevated homocysteine can raise the risks for blood clots, heart attack and stroke.

Low folic acid levels may cause loss of appetite, irritability, weakness, shortness of breath, diarrhea, anemia, headaches, heart palpitations and a sore tongue.

If you take an NSAID regularly (daily for at least one to two weeks): Talk to your physician about also taking 400 mcg to 800 mcg of folic acid daily.

You also can get more folic acid by consuming fortified breakfast cereals, orange juice, spinach and other leafy greens, peas and beans.

BETA-BLOCKERS

Beta-blockers, such as *propranolol* (Inderal), *atenolol* (Tenormin), *betaxolol* (Betoptic S), *carteolol* (Cartrol) and *labetalol* (Normodyne), are commonly prescribed for high blood pressure or glaucoma.

Nutrients depleted…

•**CoQ10.** Not only does CoQ10 appear to improve cardiac function in patients with chronic heart failure, studies suggest that it also may prevent second heart attacks and possibly protect against Parkinson's disease.

•**Melatonin.** The hormone melatonin is essential for healthy sleep-wake cycles, and there's some early evidence that it may slow aging.

If you take a beta-blocker: Ask your physician about taking 30 mg to 100 mg of CoQ10 daily…and 1 mg to 3 mg of melatonin nightly, just before bed, if you have trouble sleeping.

ACE INHIBITORS

Angiotensin-converting enzyme (ACE) inhibitors, such as *enalapril* (Vasotec), *benazepril* (Lotensin) and *ramipril* (Altace), as well as angiotensin II receptor blockers (ARBs), including *candesartan* (Atacand) and *irbesartan* (Avapro), are prescribed for high blood pressure and heart failure, and to help prevent heart attacks in high-risk patients.

Nutrient depleted…

•**Zinc.** Zinc boosts immunity, and some studies have shown that it reduces the duration of cold symptoms.

Zinc also is necessary for wound healing, strong bones and male potency, and it may help slow the progression of age-related macular degeneration (AMD).

In a recent six-year National Eye Institute study involving 3,600 people with AMD, zinc and antioxidant supplements reduced the risk of developing advanced AMD by 25%.

If you take an ACE inhibitor or ARB: Ask your doctor about taking 50 mg to 100 mg of zinc daily and eating more zinc-rich foods, such as oysters, beef, dark-meat chicken, pork tenderloin, yogurt, milk, peas, beans and nuts. If you continue to take zinc indefinitely, do not exceed 50 mg daily.

Important: Many medications combine an ACE inhibitor or ARB with a diuretic—for example, *enalapril* and *hydrochlorothiazide* (Vaseretic) is an ACE inhibitor plus a diuretic… *candesartan* and *hydrochlorothiazide* (Atacand HCT) is an ARB plus a diuretic.

If you're taking a combination drug, you'll need to compensate not only for zinc, but also for the electrolytes and nutrients excreted by the diuretic, including potassium, magnesium, thiamine (B-1) and calcium. Ask your doctor for advice.

DIABETES DRUGS

People with type 2 diabetes are often prescribed *tolazamide* (Tolinase), *acetohexamide* (Dymelor), *glimepiride* (Amaryl) or *glipizide*

(Glucotrol)—all sulfonylurea drugs. These medications stimulate the pancreas to produce more insulin, which lowers blood sugar.

Nutrient depleted…

•CoQ10. Diabetes more than doubles your chances of dying from heart disease or stroke—and low CoQ10 levels exacerbate those risks.

If you're taking a sulfonylurea drug: Ask your doctor about supplementing with 30 mg to 100 mg of CoQ10 daily.

REFLUX DRUGS

Proton pump inhibitors, such as *esomeprazole* (Nexium), *lansoprazole* (Prevacid), *omeprazole* (Prilosec) and *rabeprazole* (AcipHex), are prescribed for chronic heartburn—also known as gastroesophageal reflux disease (GERD)—and ulcers.

Nutrients depleted…

•Vitamin B-12. Vitamin B-12 is essential for producing red blood cells and maintaining a healthy nervous system. Deficits may cause fatigue, dizziness, shortness of breath, diarrhea, tingling in the hands or feet, unsteady gait, nervousness, cognitive changes and even dementia.

Vitamin B-12 is found in red meat, fish, eggs and dairy foods, but our bodies require stomach acid to release the vitamin from these foods. Proton pump inhibitors reduce the production of stomach acid, inhibiting the release and absorption of vitamin B-12.

•Iron. Low iron reduces the amount of oxygen your red blood cells can transport to body tissues, leaving you feeling weak and fatigued. A serious iron deficiency results in anemia.

If you take a proton pump inhibitor: Ask your doctor about taking 500 mcg to 1,000 mcg of vitamin B-12 daily and for advice on the best way to increase your iron intake.

Caution: Never take an iron supplement without consulting your physician—excess iron can accumulate in your major organs and cause severe damage. Most people, however, can safely eat more iron-rich foods, including liver, beef, dark-meat chicken or turkey, legumes and fortified cereals.

Surprising Link Between Acid Suppressants and Bone Health

Andrew L. Rubman, ND, director, Southbury Clinic for Traditional Medicines, Southbury, CT. *www.naturo path.org.*

Andrew L. Rubman, ND, has long been concerned about the dangers associated with long-term use of drugs that suppress stomach acid, specifically the powerful proton pump inhibitors (PPIs) including *esomeprazole* (Nexium), *omeprazole* (Prilosec) and *lansoprazole* (Prevacid). A new study adds to the alarm about the use of PPIs. This latest research shows an increased risk for hip fractures among older patients using PPIs. The risk is especially high for people taking higher doses or for those using PPIs for longer periods—and especially for people who do both.

THE STUDY

The study, from the University of Pennsylvania, reviewed 13,556 hip fractures from the United Kingdom General Practice Research Database, a collection of electronic medical records taken from 1987 to 2003. All of the data were from people older than age 50 at enrollment. The mean age at enrollment in the database was 77, and 79% were female. Researchers found that people who had used a PPI for more than a year had an associated increased fracture risk of 44%…long-term use of higher doses was even more startling, with 2.6 times elevated risk compared with non-users. Because 20% of the cases of hip fractures lead to death within a year, and older adults are increasingly being prescribed PPIs, these findings are especially scary.

WHAT'S THE CONNECTION?

Dr. Rubman notes that PPIs are effective medicine for people who have evidence of an ulcer. But use of a PPI for more than four weeks is always a risk, and a danger to those in the study who had used the medication for a year or more. Many people take a PPI not because of ulcers but to treat gastritis, an inflammation of the stomach lining that causes pain, belching, bloating and nausea. But, says Dr. Rubman, many of them are also hoping the PPI will protect them from developing the much worse gastroesophageal reflux disease, GERD (which, in fact, only rarely happens). "I would argue," says Dr. Rubman, "that most often GERD is not present as a significant health risk and is used as a fear goad to steer the patients and physicians into the prescription."

When taken to quiet the stomach and used for more than three weeks, these drugs can end up significantly disabling the body's natural ability to produce digestive acids, says Dr. Rubman. This creates havoc in the digestive process, and intrudes on the body's ability to absorb calcium and magnesium. Both minerals are essential for strong bones, but they must be transformed in the stomach first in order to be absorbed and used in the body. This process requires a strong acidic environment, not one that has been suppressed. Without adequate levels of stomach acid, calcium and magnesium won't be absorbed properly, no matter how much you ingest.

Given the enormous popularity of PPIs, it's evident that there are many people who have compromised their stomach acid, and who may be in danger of fracture. One problem, notes Dr. Rubman, is that many older adults who have been long-term users of PPIs are likely to have become hypochlorhydric—meaning that they can no longer make enough hydrochloric acid to properly digest a meal. The solution, says Dr. Rubman, is to work with a naturopathic physician or other medical professional highly trained in enzyme use to begin rebuilding the body's ability to produce enzymes on its own. This will trigger the natural production of stomach acid. He considers this a necessity for anyone who has taken PPIs for longer than three weeks. It's possible that many people will have to take enzyme supplements with meals for the rest of their lives...but Dr. Rubman says that even in people with healthy stomachs, regular digestive enzyme use can be beneficial.

A Drug for Every Reason?

Jay S. Cohen, MD, adjunct (voluntary) professor of family and preventive medicine, University of California, San Diego. Dr. Cohen is author of *What You Must Know About Statin Drugs and Their Natural Alternative* (Square One) and *Over Dose: The Case Against the Drug Companies* (Tarcher/Penguin). *www.medication sense.com.*

The maker of *atorvastatin* (Lipitor) seems to be looking for even more new uses for its best-selling, cholesterol-lowering statin drug. The company, Pfizer, has significantly raised its profits by aggressively promoting the highest doses of Lipitor. (The 80-milligram dose costs over a third more than a 10-milligram dose.)

A Pfizer-sponsored study in *The New England Journal of Medicine* suggested that Lipitor should be taken not just by people with heart disease or by those at risk of a second heart attack, but also by people at risk of a second stroke, even if they don't have heart disease.

Jay S. Cohen, MD, author of *What You Must Know About Statin Drugs and Their Natural Alternatives*, says that while the results were positive in some respects, the real problem in this study, as in a previous trial involving high-dose Lipitor, is the overall mortality data. In this study, the risk of fatal stroke was reduced. But, when total mortality was compared against a placebo, there was very little difference between the two groups. This raises safety concerns, since Lipitor—especially at high doses—is a powerful drug with potentially powerful side effects. Dr. Cohen also points out that study authors had financial ties to Pfizer, and several were Pfizer employees, which increases the potential for the authors to attach an agenda to the results of the study.

ABOUT THE STUDY

The study involved 4,731 individuals who had experienced a stroke or transient ischemic attack (a mini-stroke with symptoms such as numbness, confusion and dizziness, that may be a warning sign of a more serious stroke in the future) in the preceding one to six months, and had no known heart disease. Participants had LDL ("bad" cholesterol) levels of 100 to 190 mg/dL. Participants were randomly assigned to receive 80 mg of Lipitor a day, a high dose, or a placebo.

During the following 4.9 years, 265 people (11.2%) taking Lipitor and 311 people (13.1%) taking placebo had a stroke. The Lipitor group experienced 218 ischemic strokes (by far the most common strokes, caused by a clot in an artery in the brain) and 55 hemorrhagic strokes (strokes caused by the rupture of an artery or a blood vessel in the brain causing bleeding). The placebo group had 274 ischemic strokes and 33 hemorrhagic strokes. The researchers concluded that, in this risk group, 80 mg daily of Lipitor decreased the overall risk of stroke, although it also resulted in what they called a "small increase" in hemorrhagic strokes. When comparing the two types of stroke that occurred in each group, hemorrhagic strokes accounted for 21% of the strokes in the Lipitor group, and only 11% of the strokes in the placebo group.

QUESTIONS RAISED

While these results are promising for stroke patients, the study also raises a number of questions. Of greatest concern to Dr. Cohen is the fact that the overall mortality rate was roughly the same in both groups. Elevated liver enzymes were also more common in those who took Lipitor, and he wonders why the study included no comparisons to lower doses of Lipitor.

Dr. Cohen also questions the use of statins—which have an anticlotting effect—in people who have had hemorrhagic strokes. Again, this raises safety concerns. Logically speaking, it seems that Lipitor and other statins would be safer for people who have had ischemic strokes. Additionally, while the study authors characterized the increase in risk as small, Dr. Cohen points out that there was in fact a 66% increase in risk of hemorrhagic stroke in those taking high-dose Lipitor, in comparison with those who were given a placebo.

Dr. Cohen's bottom line? "The improvement in ischemic strokes with maximum-dose Lipitor was tiny—1.9%. This is not a 'promising' finding. Instead, it shows a minimal effect. Another study should be done, preferably by independent researchers, to confirm the results before doctors start prescribing maximum-dose Lipitor to all stroke patients," explains Dr. Cohen.

There are many risks that must be weighed against potential rewards when it comes to Lipitor. This is no "slam dunk" for the drug company. If your doctor suggests you take it based on this study, question him/her and talk it through thoroughly.

■ ■ ■ ■

Can Antibiotics Cure Bronchitis?

After 640 bronchitis patients first saw their doctors, coughing lasted for 11 days whether they received antibiotics or not. Other symptoms, such as increased phlegm and shortness of breath, cleared up less than one day sooner in those who took antibiotics.

Bottom line: Most bronchitis is caused by viruses, not bacteria—and antibiotics are ineffective against viral infections.

Self-defense: Talk to your doctor about taking acetaminophen (Tylenol), which reduces fever and relieves sore throat and muscle pain. Inhaling steam for five minutes three times a day also may be effective.

Paul Little, MD, professor of primary care research, University of Southampton, England.

■ ■ ■ ■

Antipsychotics Danger

Antipsychotic medcations can be dangerous, according to recent research.

Background: New antipsychotic drugs, such as *risperidone* (Risperdal), recently were found to increase the risk for death in dementia patients age 65 or older, prompting the FDA to require a warning label. Antipsychotics are often used to treat dementia-related delirium, psychosis and agitation.

Now: A study of nearly 23,000 patients age 65 or older who took older antipsychotics, such as *haloperidol* (Haldol), found that the older drugs are even more dangerous (18% death rate in the first six months vs. 15% with the newer drugs). Patients taking an antipsychotic may need a review of their medication.

Philip Wang, MD, DrPH, assistant professor, department of psychiatry, medicine and health-care policy, Harvard Medical School, Boston.

■■■■

Antidepressants and Dreams

Vivid dreams can be a side effect of some antidepressants, including *fluoxetine* (Prozac), *venlafaxine* (Effexor) or *bupropion* (Wellbutrin). The dreams are caused by chemical changes in the brain associated with these drugs. If the dreams are too disturbing, patients should ask their doctors about switching to a different antidepressant.

Jack M. Rosenberg, PharmD, PhD, director, International Drug Information Center, Long Island University, Brooklyn, NY.

■■■■

Medication Expiration Dates

Manufacturers guarantee product potency only until the expiration date. The medicine may be good later—but you can't be sure. Over-the-counter products in the original unopened manufacturers' packages kept under optimal conditions may last two years or more. Most prescription medicine is dispensed by pharmacists in patient-specific packaging and probably won't last as long.

Storage conditions also affect potency.

Example: If you keep medicine in a so-called medicine chest—a bathroom cabinet—it will degrade more quickly than if you store it away from bathroom heat and humidity.

Bottom line: After the expiration date, medicine should be discarded.

Susan Winckler, RPh, Esq., pharmacist, attorney and Chief of Staff for the FDA, Washington, DC.

■■■■

How Is Drug Dosage Calculated?

For certain medications with a narrow therapeutic effect (that is, the beneficial dose is just below the toxic dose), the dosage is calculated on a body-weight basis. Examples include some drugs used to treat cancer, many pediatric drugs and certain antibiotics, such as *gentamicin* (Garamycin) and *vancomycin* (Vancocin). In general, many factors other than weight are used to determine the dose of a drug, including kidney and liver function...the stage of a disease being treated...and other drugs the patient may be taking. For some medications, the dose is based on the actual level of the drug in the blood. But for many medications, the therapeutic dose is far below the toxic dose, and a fixed dose can be used for most patients.

Caution: In some cases, the lowest dose commercially available is still too high for older patients, due to reduced kidney and/or liver function and other physiological changes. In these cases, the drug is administered less often, or the dose is cut in half if the medication is suitable for splitting.

Jack M. Rosenberg, PharmD, PhD, director, International Drug Information Center, Long Island University, Brooklyn, NY.

■■■■

Rheumatoid Arthritis Medication Dangers

Many rheumatoid arthritis patients take *infliximab* (Remicade) or *adalimumab* (Humira), known as tumor necrosis factor (TNF)-blocking antibodies, usually after other treatments have failed to treat arthritis symptoms.

New finding: Scientists reviewed studies involving 3,493 patients who took one of these drugs and 1,512 patients who took a placebo.

Result: Those who took TNF-blocking antibodies had 3.3 times the risk of developing cancer, and 2.2 times the risk for serious infections, such as pneumonia, as those who took a placebo.

Theory: The drugs interfere with the body's infection-fighting mechanisms and its ability to defend itself against cancerous cells.

Self-defense: Patients who take these drugs should watch for symptoms of infection, such as fever and chills...get their vaccinations, such as those for influenza (flu) and pneumonia...and ask their doctors about appropriate cancer screenings.

Eric L. Matteson, MD, chair, division of rheumatology, Mayo Clinic, Rochester, MN.

■■■■

How Safe Are the Drugs from Canada?

Look for a pharmacy listed on the Web site of the Canadian International Pharmacy Association (CIPA), *www.canadadrugpharmacy.com.*

CIPA pharmacies must meet standards for handling drugs, licensing, business practices and more. They sell only medicines that have been tested and approved by Health Canada—the Canadian version of the US Food and Drug Administration (FDA). Health Canada and the FDA have equivalent safety standards.

Before ordering from a Canadian pharmacy site, be sure it is licensed as required by Canadian law. It should display its provincial license on-line. All pharmacies listed at the CIPA site have the necessary licenses.

Gary Passmore, spokesperson and executive assistant to the state president, Congress of California Seniors, nonprofit senior advocacy group, Sacramento. www. seniors.org.

■ ■ ■ ■

Vaccinations for Adults

Y ou should get the Tdap vaccination every 10 years. It protects against tetanus, diphtheria and pertussis (whooping cough). This is especially important now because of recent outbreaks of whooping cough among adolescents and young adults.

If you are not in a monogamous long-term relationship, get the Hepatitis B vaccine to protect against this sexually transmitted liver disease.

Also, the new shingles vaccine has been approved by the FDA. Shingles is caused by the chickenpox virus. The vaccine is recommended for everyone age 60 and older—except those with weakened immune systems.

The pneumococcal vaccine prevents pneumococcal pneumonia. Everyone age 65 and older, as well as younger people with heart or lung disease or compromised immune systems, should get this vaccination.

An annual flu shot is recommended for people over age 50 and younger adults with diabetes, asthma, kidney disease, heart or lung disease, or a weakened immune system.

William Schaffner, MD, chairman, department of preventive medicine, Vanderbilt University School of Medicine, Nashville.

■ ■ ■ ■

Antibiotics vs. Viruses

C olds, the flu and most sore throats and upper-respiratory infections are caused by viruses—and antibiotics have no effect against them. Popping antibiotics for viral ailments not only doesn't help people recover but, over time, has been the main cause of the emergence of antibiotic-resistant bacteria, a very serious health threat today. Your doctor would be more effective if he/she recommended natural antiviral agents, such as vitamin C, echinacea, lomatium and astragalus.

Mark A. Stengler, ND, naturopathic physician in private practice, La Jolla, CA...adjunct associate clinical professor at the National College of Natural Medicine, Portland, OR...author of 16 books, including The Natural Physician's Healing Therapies (Bottom Line Books) and coauthor of Prescription for Natural Cures (Wiley)...and author of the Bottom Line/Natural Healing newsletter.

Heat Can Harm Mail-Order Drugs' Potency

Gregory T. Chu, MD, senior pulmonary and critical care fellow, Carl T. Hayden Veterans Affairs Medical Center, Phoenix.

Matthew Grissinger, RPh, director, error reporting programs, Institute for Safe Medication Practices, Huntingdon Valley, PA.

Ann Smith, spokeswoman, Medco Health Solutions, Franklin Lakes, NJ.

American College of Chest Physicians.

M ail-order drugs that are exposed to too much heat—in a car, transport truck or mailbox—may become less effective, say researchers.

THE STUDY

To test the effects of heat on medications delivered by mail, lead investigator, Dr. Gregory T. Chu, senior pulmonary and critical care fellow at Carl T. Hayden Veterans Affairs Medical Center in Phoenix, and his colleagues recreated the conditions of a scorching Arizona mailbox in their lab. In the heat of an Arizona summer, a mailbox can reach a parching 158° Fahrenheit.

"The genesis of this study was our patients were actually calling us and telling us that that drug was being delivered to them in unsuitable conditions," says Chu.

In the study, capsules of the asthma drug *formoterol* (Foradil), still in their original blister packaging, were heated to 70° Celsius (or 158°F) for four hours.

When they were inspected, the heated capsules appeared grossly distorted and the formoterol formed clumps, according to Chu. His team also tested the effectiveness of the heat-exposed medication and found it delivered less than half of its intended dose.

CAUSE FOR CONCERN

With more Americans receiving prescriptions by mail, some medication-safety experts worry that exposing certain medications to extreme heat or cold could render them ineffective.

Their concern is not just limited to prescriptions that are received by mail or to formoterol, the focus of Chu's study.

"This is far more broad than what they present it to be," explains Matthew Grissinger, director of error reporting programs at the Institute for Safe Medication Practices, a Pennsylvania-based drug safety organization.

Every prescription comes with information indicating the safe temperature for storing that medication, he notes. While some medications must be refrigerated, others should be kept at room temperature.

"Any time you exceed that temperature, there's no guarantee what you're going to get," Grissinger says.

Think about the heat and humidity in the bathroom—one of the worst places to keep prescription medications.

MAIL-ORDER PRECAUTIONS

However, Ann Smith, a spokeswoman for Medco Health Solutions, which dispenses approximately 78 million mail-order prescriptions a year, says the study fails to mention safe packaging requirements.

A mail-order pharmacy such as Medco has procedures in place for temperature-sensitive medications, including formoterol, she says. Such medications are shipped overnight in insulated packaging that includes ice or cold gel packs, depending on the type of medication and seasonal weather conditions.

For more tips on safe medication use, visit the Web site of the National Council on Patient Information and Education at *www.bemedwise.org*.

■ ■ ■ ■

Antibiotic Side Effects

A common antibiotic may cause hyperglycemia or hypoglycemia in some patients. Tequin (*gatifloxacin*) is prescribed about two million times a year in the US for pneumonia, sinus infections, urinary tract infections and some sexually transmitted diseases. If rapid heartbeat, sweatiness, nervousness, tremors, frequent urination or extreme thirst develop, contact your doctor to discuss alternatives. Tequin does not cause diabetes, as some recent reports suggested.

David N. Juurlink, MD, PhD, head of the Division of Pharmacology and Toxicology at Sunnybrook and Women's College, Health Sciences Center, Toronto, and lead author of a study published in The New England Journal of Medicine.

7

Longevity Secrets

10 Easy Ways to Add Many Years To Your Life

How old are you really? We all have a "real age" that can be much lower—or higher—than our chronological years. A 50-year-old man, for example, could have the immune system of someone 20 years younger.

More than a decade ago, I introduced the RealAge concept—a scientific way of calculating a number that reflects the overall state of your health rather than your calendar age. We are constantly updating our data to reflect new research. The lower your RealAge, the longer you are likely to live.

We discovered that some changes can be hard to achieve—such as losing 25 pounds or quitting smoking—but others are relatively easy and can have a big impact on your life span.

Latest findings: Recent research pinpoints 10 simple changes that can lower your RealAge by almost 15 years…

TAKE ASPIRIN DAILY

RealAge benefit: 2.2 years

In men over age 35 and women over age 40, 162 milligrams (mg) of aspirin daily (the equivalent of two baby aspirins) reduces the risk of heart attack by 36% and the risk of colon, esophageal, throat and stomach cancers by about 40%. We don't know how aspirin reduces cancer risk—we just know that it does.

Check with your doctor about taking aspirin. Some people can't take it because of stomach discomfort and/or bleeding. Ibuprofen may be an appropriate substitute.

Caution: Taking both aspirin and ibuprofen in the same 24-hour period blocks the protective

Michael F. Roizen, MD, chief wellness officer at the Cleveland Clinic, OH, is coauthor of *YOU: The Smart Patient* (Free Press). Dr. Roizen has cowritten *YOU: The Owner's Manual* (HarperCollins), and served on the boards of five nonprofit foundations. He is former chair of a Food and Drug Administration advisory committee and has published over 160 peer-reviewed papers.

effects. Also, don't take aspirin in combination with blood-thinning drugs such as *warfarin* (Coumadin). It increases the risk of internal bleeding.

SUPPLEMENT WITH FOLATE

RealAge benefit: 1.2 years

The B vitamin folate helps prevent errors in DNA duplication, an underlying cause of cancer. Taking 600 micrograms (mcg) to 800 mcg of folate daily could decrease breast cancer risk by 25% to 50%...colon cancer risk by 20% to 50%...and risk of childhood cancers by about 60% when taken by the mother during pregnancy. Folate also lowers levels of *homocysteine*, an amino acid linked to stroke, heart disease and other cardiovascular disorders.

Take a B-complex or multisupplement that includes 100% of the recommended daily amount of the vitamins B-6 and B-12...and add a folate supplement to get a total of 600 mcg to 800 mcg daily. You need all three to lower homocysteine—and the ability of the body to absorb B-12 declines with age.

DON'T SUPPLEMENT UNNECESSARILY

RealAge benefit: 1.7 years

Millions of Americans take iron or vitamin A supplements daily. With the exception of some people who, for specific reasons, are advised by their doctors to take extra vitamin A or extra iron, the use of these nutrients (except in a multivitamin) can take years off your life.

The average vitamin A supplement contains more than 5,000 international units (IU), an amount that causes bone demineralization and increases the risk of liver and lung cancers.

Taking iron is dangerous because as many as one in 200 Americans has hemochromatosis, a condition that causes excess iron to accumulate in tissues, increasing the risk of heart or liver failure.

I advise taking a daily multivitamin that contains all the essential vitamins and minerals but no iron unless told to by your doctor. The multivitamin should contain less than 2,500 IU of vitamin A.

EAT SPAGHETTI SAUCE

RealAge benefit: 1.9 years for men, 0.8 years for women.

Tomatoes contain the carotenoid *lycopene*, which is believed to strengthen the immune system and reduce the risk of breast and prostate cancers by 30% to 50%. Try to get 10 tablespoons (a little more than one-half cup) of tomato sauce weekly. Processed tomatoes, such as those in spaghetti sauce, confer more benefits than fresh tomatoes because processing releases the lycopene. Eat canned tomatoes or tomato sauce with a little oil—for example, by cooking the sauce with olive oil—to improve absorption of lycopene.

CONSUME FAT FIRST AT MEALS

RealAge benefit: 1.8 years.

Starting meals with a little fat increases feelings of satiety and reduces overall calorie intake by about 7%. If you are overweight, you can lose about 10 pounds in a year if you do this at every meal.

Make sure that the fat is a healthy one—olive oil, nuts, etc. To get the benefits, you need about 70 calories of fat, which is about one-half tablespoon of olive oil, six walnuts or 12 almonds. One great way to start a meal is with a salad that has olive oil in the dressing and a few chopped nuts sprinkled on top.

WASH PRODUCE—AND YOUR HANDS

RealAge benefit: 0.4 years.

More than 40 million Americans suffer from food poisoning annually, and several thousand die from foodborne illness. Washing your hands frequently—and always before meals—is a key way to prevent this.

It's also crucial to wash produce thoroughly. Even organic fruits and vegetables require washing because they contain fertilizer residue that can cause illness. Wash produce twice in lukewarm water with a little dish soap, then rinse twice in regular water. You can put greens in a salad spinner and give them three cycles of rinsing/spinning.

DRINK MODERATELY

RealAge benefit: 1.9 years.

Alcohol reduces the tendency of blood platelets to clump together and form clots in the arteries, the cause of most heart attacks. It also inhibits the oxidation of fat that contributes to the development of plaque on artery walls.

The extensive Harvard Nurses' Health Study found that women who had three or more alcoholic drinks weekly had a 40% lower rate of heart attacks and arterial disease than those who did not. Studies in men show similar results.

Caution: Moderation is the key—one-half to one drink daily for women, and one to two drinks daily for men. Don't drink alcohol if you have a history of drug or alcohol abuse.

WEAR A HELMET

RealAge benefit: 1 year.

Wearing a helmet when riding a bike or a horse or when skiing can reduce your risk of head injury and related aging by as much as 80%. The RealAge benefit of one year assumes that you engage in the activity five times a month.

GET ENOUGH SUN

RealAge benefit: 1.7 years.

Vitamin D is essential for calcium absorption and bone strength. It also helps reduce the risk of breast, colon, prostate and lung cancers. Only a few foods (mainly fatty fish) contain vitamin D in a form that can be used by the body. Sunshine is required to convert fats in the body into a usable form of vitamin D.

I advise getting 10 to 20 minutes of sun exposure without sunscreen daily. Use sunscreen when you're in the sun longer than 20 minutes to prevent premature skin aging and skin cancer.

EAT FIBER EARLY IN THE DAY

RealAge benefit: 0.6 years.

Starting the day with a high-fiber cereal or fresh fruits or vegetables helps you feel full longer and reduces calorie intake. It prevents spikes in glucose that can damage arteries and increase the risk of heart disease.

Bonus: People who get at least 25 grams of fiber a day have a RealAge up to three years younger than those who get the national average of 12 grams.

Example: In a study at Northwestern University, a 10-gram-a-day increase in cereal fiber consumption decreased the risk of heart attack by 29%.

Erase Years from Your Age in 30 Minutes a Day

Michael F. Roizen, MD, chief wellness officer at the Cleveland Clinic, OH, is coauthor of *YOU: The Smart Patient* (Free Press). Dr. Roizen has cowritten *YOU: The Owner's Manual* (HarperCollins), and served on the boards of five nonprofit foundations. He is former chair of a Food and Drug Administration advisory committee and has published over 160 peer-reviewed papers.

Walking is the single best thing you can do for your health. I view it as the fountain of youth. In my first RealAge book, I showed how aging has little to do with calendar years. A 50-year-old man could have the arteries and immune system of a 75-year-old. Someone else might be 75 but have a RealAge—measured by the risk of disease, disability or death—of a 52-year-old. Exercise is a key factor in reducing your RealAge—and just 30 minutes of walking a day can make you healthier, more energetic and, in a real sense, younger.

HEALTH BENEFITS

Walking is easy to do, doesn't require any special equipment (except walking shoes) and conveys many of the same health benefits as more strenuous exercise.

Walking helps prevent fatty buildup in the arteries. When your arteries are clogged with fatty buildup, your cardiovascular system ages more quickly, and so does your entire body. Aging of the arteries brings on cardiovascular disease, the major cause of heart attacks and strokes. It also leads to loss of energy, memory loss and, in men, impotence. Walking can help keep arteries young and healthy.

Walking every day also decreases the risk of such conditions as macular degeneration (the leading cause of blindness in people over age 50) and arthritis. The long-running Framingham Heart Study found that people with arthritis who walked daily for 30 minutes and supplemented their diets with vitamins C and D and calcium were able to stop the progression of joint damage. Walking also prevented osteoarthritis in patients who didn't already have it.

Walking can even reduce the risk of some forms of cancer by as much as 50%.

GET READY

Studies show that people who walk as little as 10 minutes a day—or even just once a week—on a regular basis have less risk of dying prematurely than those who are sedentary. For optimal health gains, you should walk for at least 30 minutes daily. People who take three 10-minute walks each day have about the same health gains as those who walk for 30 minutes straight. *Helpful...*

•**Warm up before walking.** Walk more slowly than usual for the first several minutes. This warm-up heats the muscles and makes them more flexible and efficient and less prone to injury. It also increases circulation in the joints.

•**Wear a watch.** Measure time rather than distance. Time is easy to count, and you can walk for 30 minutes at a comfortable pace. You don't need to follow a track or a premeasured route—and you won't try to force yourself to go a certain distance.

•**Don't miss a day.** Make 30 minutes a day of walking a priority. Things like yard work and housecleaning help, too, but they can't take the place of your daily walks.

Malls are terrific places to walk if the weather is bad, and most YMCAs have walking tracks and treadmills. If your budget permits, buy a treadmill so you can walk any time of the day or night without leaving home.

POSTWALKING STRETCH

Once your routine becomes ingrained, set aside two to three minutes to stretch after you're done walking. Stretching improves joint range of motion. Without a normal range of motion in the joints, daily activities become more difficult and the risk of musculoskeletal injury increases. Some people find that stretching also reduces soreness, though I can't find hard evidence to support that claim.

To perform a stretch, move slowly into the stretch position until you feel a gentle pulling sensation, not pain. Hold the stretch for 10 to 30 seconds *without bouncing*. Repeat each stretch two or three times.

Here is a sample postwalking stretch for each key muscle group...

•**Hamstring.** Sit on the floor with both feet straight out in front of you. Keep your left leg extended, and bend the right so that the sole of your right foot is against the inner thigh of your left leg. Lean forward over the left leg until you feel a gentle stretch along the back of your extended thigh, keeping your back as straight as possible. Repeat with the right leg extended.

•**Quadricep.** Stand on your right leg, and bend the left so that your left knee is pointed toward the floor. Then reach your left hand behind you and take hold of your left ankle. Your hips should be pressed forward so that you feel a gentle stretch along the front of your left thigh. (You may need to stand near a wall for balance.) Repeat, standing on your left leg with the right leg bent.

•**Buttock.** Lie on your back, and bend both legs, keeping your feet flat on the floor. Cross the ankle of your right foot just above your left knee. Lift your left foot off the floor, and bring both legs toward your chest. Hold on to your left thigh to help pull your legs closer to your chest until you feel a gentle stretch near your right hip and buttock. Repeat with the other leg.

•**Adductor.** Lie on your back, and bend both knees. Open your knees out to the sides, and place the soles of your feet together. Pull your feet in toward you, allowing your knees to drop toward the floor until you feel a gentle stretch in the groin and inner-thigh area.

•**Hip flexor.** Stand with the left foot in front of the right, with your weight centered evenly between both feet. Keeping your back straight, bend your knees slightly, lowering yourself toward the floor and tucking your hips under. You should feel a gentle stretch along the front of your right hip. Repeat with the right foot in front of the left.

•**Calf.** Sit on the floor with both feet extended in front of you. Keeping your back as straight as possible, flex your toes toward you until you feel a gentle stretch in the back of both legs.

•**Lower back.** Sit on the floor cross-legged. Keeping your head in line with your spine, lean forward with your upper body and reach your arms out in front of you until you feel a gentle stretch in your lower back.

A Calorie-Restricted Diet May Slow Aging

Mark A. Stengler, ND, naturopathic physician in private practice, La Jolla, CA...adjunct associate clinical professor at the National College of Natural Medicine, Portland, OR...author of 16 books, including *The Natural Physician's Healing Therapies* (Bottom Line Books) and coauthor of *Prescription for Natural Cures* (Wiley)...and author of the *Bottom Line/Natural Healing* newsletter.

A calorie-restricted diet could slow aging, according to new research. Investigators looked at lab reports and Doppler imaging of 25 people who had been practicing calorie restriction for about six years. The people, ages 41 to 65, consumed an average of 1,400 to 2,000 calories a day. Their blood pressure, heart function and inflammatory blood markers, including *C-reactive protein*—a measure of inflammation in blood vessels and elsewhere in the body— were compared to those of 25 people of similar age and gender with an intake of 2,000 to 3,000 calories per day, the amount in a typical Western diet. Researchers found that diastolic function of the heart in the calorie-restricted group resembled diastolic function in people about 15 years younger. (Diastolic, the bottom number in a blood pressure reading, measures the pressure when the heart is at rest, in between beats.) There was little difference in systolic function (the top number in a blood pressure reading, which measures the pressure inside blood vessels when the heart beats). Blood pressure overall and inflammatory markers were significantly lower as well in the low-calorie group.

My view: This was the first human study to show a correlation between calorie restriction and an anti-aging effect on heart function. Researchers theorize that chronic inflammation from a typical calorie-loaded Western diet, which is heavy in animal products and refined sugar but low in fruits and vegetables, causes damage to—and premature hardening of—heart muscle. More studies are needed. Keep in mind that the quality of your food choices is as important as calorie restriction. For best results, opt for fruits, vegetables, cold-water fish, lean poultry, whole grains and legumes, limited red meat—and watch your portion sizes.

The Truth About Growth Hormone

Mark A. Stengler, ND, naturopathic physician in private practice, La Jolla, CA...adjunct associate clinical professor at the National College of Natural Medicine, Portland, OR...author of 16 books, including *The Natural Physician's Healing Therapies* (Bottom Line Books) and coauthor of *Prescription for Natural Cures* (Wiley)...and author of the *Bottom Line/Natural Healing* newsletter.

For over 15 years, growth hormone (GH) has been touted as a miraculous anti-aging hormone. Some physicians prescribe it for obesity, sexual dysfunction, cognitive decline and fibromyalgia.

WHAT IS GROWTH HORMONE?

GH is secreted by the brain's pituitary gland. As its name implies, it stimulates the growth of tissues in the body. Most notably, it promotes growth in height during childhood. Most people have heard of a childhood deficiency of GH, but in rare cases, adults can lack adequate amounts of the hormone. A GH deficiency that occurs during adulthood can lead to a reduction in muscle mass, strength and bone density as well as sexual dysfunction and emotional problems, such as depression. If you have these symptoms, ask your doctor for a blood test. A GH deficiency even can increase cardiovascular disease risk.

THE ANTI-AGING CRAZE

In 1990, *The New England Journal of Medicine* reported on a six-month study in which 12 healthy men, ages 61 to 81, who showed no signs of GH deficiency were given twice the dose of GH that an adult man with a deficiency would ordinarily receive. A control group of nine men did not receive GH injections. The men receiving the injections experienced systolic (top number) blood pressure and fasting blood glucose concentrations that were significantly higher than when they started the study. On the positive side, they experienced an increase in lean body mass, a decrease in fat mass and an improvement in bone density, all of which led many people to believe that GH could be used to effectively reverse some of these troubling signs of aging. However, there have been no studies of GH's effect on longevity in humans.

SAFETY CONCERNS

I have tested many patients' blood levels of insulinlike growth factor (IGF-1)—a biomarker that is used to assess GH levels. Only occasionally have I found a patient with a serious deficiency. Typically, these patients suffer from fatigue. What concerns me is that some doctors routinely recommend GH injections for virtually all of their patients who are over age 60 without testing for a deficiency. When these doctors do run blood tests, they often diagnose a deficiency by comparing their older patients' IGF-1 levels with those of a 20-year-old. I strongly disagree with this practice. GH should not be used unnecessarily because of the side effects, which include blurred vision, burning or tingling in the legs and arms, dizziness, severe headache, back pain, chills, difficulty breathing, fever, hair loss and sleep problems.

A rapid drop in GH levels or an overt deficiency (a deficiency is characterized by IGF-1 readings below 90 µg/mL) can and should be treated, but a gradual decline over a period of years appears to be one of the body's ways of preventing cancer. Research now links elevated IGF-1 levels to increased risk for colon, pancreatic, endometrial, breast and prostate cancers.

MY RECOMMENDATION

GH is a powerful hormone that should be used only by people who have been diagnosed with a deficiency. Even in these cases, GH replacement should be monitored by a physician. To gain the benefits of extra GH without the dangerous risks, there is a much more effective—and less costly—strategy. I recommend a combination of aerobic exercise (such as walking and cycling) and weight-lifting, each performed for 30 minutes three times a week. Sleep also is important for maintaining healthy GH levels. There are a variety of supplements that claim to boost GH levels, but no good data support their use. Save your money for the gym.

■ ■ ■ ■

Human Growth Hormone (HGH) Alert

Human growth hormone (HGH), sometimes touted as an anti-aging agent, has potentially dangerous side effects. Most mainstream doctors point to higher diabetes risk, carpal tunnel syndrome, muscle pain and possible tumor growth as reasons to avoid HGH. But some alternative medicine practitioners recommend using HGH under carefully controlled and supervised circumstances. They say that daily HGH injections have sometimes resulted in improvements in blood pressure, heart ailments and other conditions. HGH costs up to $20,000 a year and is not covered by insurance.

Robert N. Butler, MD, professor of geriatrics, Mount Sinai School of Medicine, and president, International Longevity Center (www.ilcusa.org), both in New York City. He won the Pulitzer Prize for his book Why Survive? Being Old in America *(Johns Hopkins University). He is also coauthor of* Aging and Mental Health *(Allyn & Bacon) and* The New Love and Sex After 60 *(Ballantine).*

A Simple Anti-Aging Formula

Bruce Ames, PhD, professor of biochemistry and molecular biology at the University of California at Berkeley, is best known for developing the Ames Test, a widely used procedure for identifying potential carcinogenic substances. He is the recipient of the National Medal of Science.

Wouldn't it be nice if you could take a pill that would help protect you against serious ailments, including cancer and heart disease?

You can. Dozens of studies have shown that taking a daily multivitamin/mineral supplement is one of the simplest and best ways to help fight age-related disease. But it has to be the *right* multi to get the job done. Unfortunately, only one in three American adults consistently takes a multivitamin.

To learn more, we spoke with Bruce Ames, PhD, a renowned biochemist who studies the effects of vitamin and mineral deficiencies on health...

ARE YOU GETTING ENOUGH?

There's no question that a balanced diet consisting of whole grains, vegetables, fruits, fish, dairy and lean meats is our best source of the nearly 40 vitamins, fatty acids, minerals and amino acids that are essential to human health.

While most Americans consume enough of these micronutrients to avoid acute deficiency diseases, such as scurvy (vitamin C deficiency) or anemia (iron deficiency), research shows that up to 10% of us consume less than half of the recommended levels of each key micronutrient—a dangerously low level. *Also...*

• **Up to 25%** of premenopausal American women consume less than half of the recommended intake of iron.

• **More than half of us** aren't getting enough magnesium or calcium.

• **Up to 80%** of American adults with darker skin (blacks, people from India and some Hispanics)—particularly those who live in northern states, where sun exposure tends to be limited—are deficient in vitamin D. Fair-skinned people who don't get much sun exposure and don't get vitamin D from a supplement also are at risk.

These nutritional deficiencies are serious threats to our health—on par with smoking or obesity. Even a marginal deficiency of only one key nutrient can significantly change our cells in a way that can lead to cancer and other serious diseases.

THE SCIENTIFIC EVIDENCE

At our laboratory at the Children's Hospital Oakland Research Institute in Oakland, California, we study nutritional deficiencies in human cells by limiting vitamins or minerals and examining how the cells respond.

Our findings: When cells are grown so that one of the vitamins (biotin or B-6) or minerals (iron, zinc, magnesium or copper) is limited, the cells' chromosomes undergo significant damage, changes that are linked to the development of cancer.

An abundance of research shows that inadequate levels of folic acid are linked to breast, pancreatic and colon cancers...low intakes of vitamin B-6 are implicated in colorectal cancer...insufficient vitamin D increases the risk for colorectal cancer and may double the risk for prostate cancer...low zinc appears to heighten the risk for esophageal cancer...and low magnesium increases colorectal cancer risk.

If this isn't reason enough to get your daily vitamins and minerals, there's even more evidence. Nutrient deficiencies appear to disrupt the normal functioning of *mitochondria*, the tiny "engines" inside our cells that convert fuel (starches and fats) into energy. This process normally produces a small number of "free radicals," oxidized molecules that contribute to cellular aging.

However, when zinc, iron, copper, biotin or other key nutrients are in short supply, we've observed that mitochondria mass-produce free radicals. In the body, this may lead to premature aging and a raft of degenerative diseases, affecting everything from our hearts and brains to our bones.

Antioxidant nutrients may help stave off the damage, but supplying the missing nutrient is the key. In a recent Johns Hopkins University study, older people taking vitamins E and C were found to be less likely to develop Alzheimer's disease. In studies at The Cooper Institute in Dallas, patients who took multivitamins for six months had significantly lower blood levels of C-reactive protein, a marker for cardiovascular disease.

YOUR BEST DEFENSE

A multivitamin/mineral is a convenient way to fill in any nutritional gaps in your diet. An expensive brand-name supplement isn't necessary. I recently bought a year's supply for about $10 at one of the big national discount stores.

Just be sure to choose a multivitamin/mineral supplement that contains close to 100% of the Daily Value (recommended daily intake) of most vitamins and minerals.

Men and women age 50 and older who eat some red meat should choose an iron-free formulation, since most adults get sufficient amounts of this mineral in their food. Premenopausal women, who lose iron through menstruation, should choose a supplement with iron.

Be cautious about supplements providing "megadoses" (five to 10 times the recommended daily intake) of specific vitamins and/or minerals. In my opinion, there is little scientific evidence showing that the use of more than the recommended daily intake of any nutrient is beneficial for the general public (though future studies may change that). What's more, certain vitamins, especially vitamin A, and many of the minerals, including iron, manganese and selenium, are toxic at high doses.

Some manufacturers are now advertising multivitamins that offer a "bonus" ingredient—for example, the herb ginkgo to bolster memory... or the sugar-cane derivative policosanol to lower cholesterol. These combination products are generally safe, but most lack sufficient research showing that they're actually any better for you—or whether the added benefits are worth the additional costs. Talk to your doctor before starting a multivitamin with added ingredients, especially if you're taking medications.

Important: A multivitamin should be taken with food to help promote the body's absorption of fat-soluble vitamins, such as vitamins D and E.

OTHER IMPORTANT NUTRIENTS

In addition to a basic multivitamin, consider a calcium/magnesium supplement. Because calcium and magnesium are bulky, most multivitamin/mineral supplements contain no more than a small percentage of the recommended daily intake (otherwise the pills would be too big to swallow). Look for a product that offers a 2:1 ratio of calcium to magnesium—your body can't effectively use one without the other. And be sure your multivitamin contains 400 international units (IU) of vitamin D to aid absorption of these minerals.

Unless you eat three meals of cold-water fish (such as salmon, halibut, mackerel) weekly, I advise taking a fish-oil supplement with omega-3 fatty acids. These essential fatty acids promote brain and heart health.

If you feel your energy or cognition slumping, try taking two lesser-known nutrients—acetyl-L-carnitine (ALC) and lipoic acid (LA). In animal studies, these biochemicals lower oxidant levels caused by aging and improve physical and mental performance. Twenty-four clinical trials have shown ALC and LA to be safe.

Good choice: The supplement Juvenon (*www. juvenon.com*) contains both ALC and LA.

The Secret to Looking And Feeling Younger: Posture

Paul D'Arezzo, MD, a board-certified emergency physician and a posture-alignment specialist practicing in Colorado Springs, *www.posturealignment.com*, is the author of *Posture Alignment: The Missing Link in Health and Fitness*. Marcellina Mountain.

You can take years off your appearance and ease pain in your muscles and joints without expensive surgery, cosmetics or even highly demanding exercise routines.

All you need to do is spend a few minutes a day focusing on one of the most important—and neglected—aspects of a youthful appearance and an optimally functioning body…posture.

Think of your body as if it were a stack of building blocks. If the blocks are lined up unevenly, the structure is weak and is more likely to collapse. If they're carefully lined up one on top of the other, the structure is strong.

When the body is misaligned, it fails to function as efficiently as possible. Bad posture contributes to arthritis, muscle pain and injuries. These aches and pains cause us to avoid activities that we once enjoyed.

What went wrong? Modern society has evolved in such a way that we're no longer required to move as much during our day-to-day activities. And when we do move, we do so in the same repetitive ways, not utilizing all of our muscles or our full range of motion. Certain muscles get strong while others get weak—and we lose correct alignment.

BETTER ALIGNMENT

By performing the following simple exercises to correct and maintain posture, you can begin to achieve maximum physical function as you age. The following four exercises strengthen and stretch unique muscles in the body that hold us upright and stabilize us—muscles that usually aren't worked by standard aerobic and strength-training exercises.

Ideally, this alignment program should be practiced at least every other day as an adjunct to your usual aerobic, stretching and strength-training regimen.

Although it can take weeks to change posture, you will feel a difference in your alignment after doing the exercises only once.

GROIN STRETCH

Purpose: Stretches and aligns the groin muscles. Over time, it will align your hips and allow your shoulders and back to return to a more anatomically correct position.

What you need: A chair, coffee table or ottoman that is the right height so that when you lie on the floor on your back, one leg can rest on top of the object and form an approximate 90-degree angle.

What to do: Lie on your back, bend your left leg and place it on top of your "platform." Your left calf muscle should be resting on the platform. Stretch your right leg straight out on the floor, toes pointed toward the ceiling. Place your arms out to the sides, palms up. Rest in this pose for five minutes, allowing gravity to do the work, relaxing the body and letting the muscles stretch. Repeat with your right leg.

TABLE STRETCH

Purpose: Counteracts the tendency to hunch and roll shoulders forward.

What you need: A table, desk, counter or back of a chair.

What to do: Stand a few feet from the table, with feet hip-width apart and pointing straight

ahead. Lean forward and rest your hands, palms down, on the table so that your legs and torso form a 90-degree angle. Relax. Let your head fall forward between your shoulders, and let gravity do the work. Hold for one to two minutes.

CATS AND DOGS

Purpose: Increases flexibility and movement in the pelvis and lower back.

What you need: A carpet, exercise mat or other comfortable floor surface.

What to do: Get on your hands and knees so

that your back forms a small table. Place your hands directly below your shoulders, fingers pointing forward. Knees should be in line with your hips. Exhale and slowly arch your back upward like a cat, pressing your chin toward your chest. Hold for five seconds.

Then arch in the opposite direction (the way dogs do when they stretch), pulling your head and neck upward and your upper and lower back downward and lifting your buttocks into the air. Hold for five seconds. Smoothly transition from "cat" to "dog" for 10 complete cycles.

FACE THE WALL

Purpose: Stretches and aligns the muscles of the chest, shoulders and pelvis.

What you need: A wall.

What to do: Stand facing the wall with feet hip-width apart, toes turned inward and touching (pigeon-toed). Your chest and nose should almost touch the wall.

Lift your arms straight above your head, shoulder-width apart. Place the backs of your hands on the wall. Hold for one minute, eventually working up to three minutes. You will feel a stretch in your pelvis and shoulders.

At first you only may be able to reach the wall with the sides of your hands. As your muscles align and stretch, you will be able to work up to reaching the wall with the backs of your hands.

Helpful: This may be uncomfortable at first, but after a minute your shoulders will begin to relax.

Illustrations by Shawn Banner.

10 Quick Energy Boosters

Jon Gordon, best-selling author of *Energy Addict: 101 Physical, Mental and Spiritual Ways to Energize Your Life* (Perigee), *The 10-Minute Energy Solution* (Putnam), and *The Energy Bus: 10 Rules to Fuel Your Life, Work and Team with Positive Energy* (Wiley). His performance-energy consulting firm is based in Jacksonville, FL. Clients include the Atlanta Falcons, Campbell Soup, Publix and JPMorgan Chase. *www.jongordon.com.*

Three-quarters of the people I meet complain of tiredness during the day. This epidemic of exhaustion is brought about by mental and physical stress, including too much caffeine and sugar as well as too little sleep and exercise.

Here are easy ways to feel more alert and energetic…

•**Stop hitting the snooze button on your alarm clock in the morning.** Your brain goes through periods of light and heavy sleep. Falling back to sleep for just five more minutes can cut short a new sleep cycle, leaving you groggier when you do arise.

Better: Set your clock for when you really have to get up. Open your shades right away, and get as much light as possible—bright light wakes you up and invigorates you. Raise your heartbeat for at least five minutes in the morning by running in place or doing sit-ups, push-ups or jumping jacks.

•**Eat a power breakfast.** It will energize you as you start the day. My favorite power breakfast: Mix low-fat plain yogurt and one-half cup of old-fashioned raw oatmeal when you first get up. The yogurt will soften the oats while you shower and dress. Add a few chopped walnuts, one-half cup of pineapple or one-quarter cup of blueberries.

•**Sit up straight.** Bad posture can decrease your oxygen intake, and slouching exhausts your neck, shoulders and upper-back muscles.

Correct posture for sitting: Your back should be aligned against the back of the chair, so that you can work without leaning forward. Your knees should be a bit higher than your hips. Keep both feet flat on the floor and your arms flexed at a 75- to 90-degree angle.

•**Replace coffee with green tea.** The rich taste of coffee and the mental alertness it imparts make coffee drinking a tough habit to break. But coffee raises stress hormones, and just a few cups a day creates an energy roller coaster that increases overall fatigue. I have found that people who have the most success giving up coffee switch to green tea. It contains one-third the amount of caffeine (20 mg to 25 mg per six-ounce cup), so you get an energy boost without feeling irritable or experiencing a slump later on.

Bonus: Green tea is loaded with disease-fighting antioxidants.

If you have no intention of giving up your daily coffee, at least try cutting back to half regular/half decaf.

•**Consume protein with meals.** It helps your body absorb sugar at a slower rate, so your energy levels don't fluctuate so much during the day.

Examples: Fish, eggs, hummus, skinless poultry breast, lean red meat.

•**Go for a 10-minute walk after lunch.** It raises your metabolism and prevents you from falling into the familiar, post-meal "coma."

If it's inconvenient to go outside, try chair squats.

How to do that: With a chair behind you, stand with your feet positioned shoulder-width apart. Keep your back straight and your chin up. Squat down, and push out your rear as if you were going to sit in the chair behind you. Just as your rear touches the chair, return to your starting position. Repeat five to 30 times—or until you feel your muscles have had enough.

•**Take a short nap,** no more than 25 minutes. Longer than that and you move into a deeper phase of sleep, which, if interrupted, can leave you groggier than before your nap. The optimal time to take a nap is eight hours after you wake up.

•**Eat an energy snack,** such as a banana or a handful of walnuts or almonds. Avoid commercial energy drinks and energy bars—they often work by introducing caffeine and/or sugar into your system.

Helpful: I do recommend a caffeine-free, multivitamin energy powder that I use myself each day—Fatigued to Fantastic! from Enzymatic Therapy, available at health-food stores.

Cost: About $30 for a month's supply.

•**Try peppermint.** It boosts mood and motivation. Have a cup of peppermint tea, or dab peppermint oil (available at health-food stores) on your wrists.

•**Breathe.** We tend to hold our breath when we work intensely or are under stress—and this contributes to fatigue.

To practice energy-boosting breathing: Stand up straight with your arms at your sides. Inhale for two seconds as you raise your arms slowly over your head with your palms open. Continue lifting your arms until they are directly over your head with fingertips touching. Exhale for three seconds as you bring your arms down. Repeat 10 times.

The Anti-Aging Workout

Karl Knopf, EdD, an exercise physiologist and instructor, Adaptive Learning Division, Foothills College, Los Altos, CA, is the author of five books, including his most recent, *Weights for 50 Plus: Building Strength, Staying Healthy and Enjoying an Active Lifestyle.* Ulysses.

Most people know that cardiovascular exercise, such as walking and swimming, helps promote good health. Unfortunately, many neglect strength training.*

*Consult your doctor before beginning this or any new exercise routine.

People who do not perform regular strength exercises will lose 50% of their muscle mass and muscular strength by age 65. In fact, sarcopenia (age-related muscle loss) is one of the main reasons that many older adults become unable to live independently and must enter an assisted-living center or nursing home.

The following simple program, designed especially for those over age 50, is easily done at home using a stretchable rubber exercise band (about $15)…ankle weights ($10 per pair)…and dumbbells ($1 to $2 a pound). These products are available at sporting-goods stores.

Most of the following exercises recommend beginning with one- to two-pound dumbbells or ankle weights. Increase the weight when you can perform 15 repetitions easily. By performing this 30-minute full body workout two to three times a week, in addition to your regular cardiovascular exercise routine four to five times a week, you can enhance your energy, strength—and even your independence.

SIT TO STAND

Purpose: Strengthens the front leg muscles that are used to get up from a seated position.

What to do: Sit toward the front of a sturdy chair, with your feet flat on the floor. Lean slightly forward. Inhale. Exhale slowly as you stand up. If possible, do not use your hands. Cross your arms in front of your chest. Inhale and lower yourself slowly into the chair. Do six to 15 repetitions. When you can easily complete 15 repetitions, try holding a one- to two-pound dumbbell in each hand.

LUNGES

Purpose: Strengthens the legs and helps with balance.

What to do: Stand with your feet shoulder-width apart, arms at your sides, holding a one- to two-pound dumbbell in each hand. Inhale. Keeping your left leg in place, exhale and lunge forward with your right leg as far as you comfortably can while keeping your right knee in line with your right ankle. Inhale as you step back to the starting

position. Do six to 15 repetitions. Repeat with your left leg.

Modification: If you find this exercise too difficult, do it without weights, and place your hands on your hips instead. If balance is an issue, hold on to a chair when lunging.

LATERAL ARM RAISES

Purpose: Strengthens the shoulders and upper back.

What to do: Stand straight, feet shoulder-width apart and knees relaxed. Place your arms at your sides and hold a one- to two-pound dumbbell in each hand. To protect your lower back, keep your torso firm by contracting your abdominal muscles and not arching your back. Inhale as you slowly lift your arms out to each side, no higher than shoulder level. Hold for one second. Exhale as you slowly return to the starting position. Do six to 15 repetitions.

Modification: If doing this exercise with straight arms is too difficult, bend your elbows and extend them out from your sides.

Caution: If this exercise causes pain and/or a clicking sound in the shoulder area, stop right away. Consult your doctor.

MODIFIED PUSH-UPS

Purpose: Strengthens the upper body.

What to do: While on your hands and knees, move your hands forward so your torso is slanted at a comfortable angle and your hands are shoulder-width apart. Keep your back straight and pull your abdominal muscles in. Inhale. Exhale as you bend your elbows to lower your chest toward the floor. Keep your elbows close to your body. Go only as far as you comfortably can. Inhale as you return to the starting position. Do six to 15 repetitions.

TRICEPS BAND EXTENSIONS

Purpose: Strengthens the backs of the arms.

What to do: Stand straight and drape an exercise band over your left shoulder, placing your right hand on the band to secure it (begin with the easiest resistance band and work up as you get stronger). Keeping your left elbow next  to your body, grasp the band with your left hand to make a 90-degree angle with your arm, keeping the band taut at all times. Inhale. Then exhale as you slowly pull the band by extending your left arm downward. Inhale and slowly return to the starting position. Do 15 repetitions. Repeat with your right arm.

POSTURE STRENGTHENER

Purpose: Strengthens upper body muscles to improve posture.

What to do: Hold your exercise band out straight in front of your body at shoulder-height,  one end in each hand. Extend your arms out to the sides, stretching the exercise band, squeezing your shoulder blades together and making a "T" with your body. Hold for two seconds. Slowly return to the arms-in-front position. Do 15 repetitions.

SEATED LEG EXTENSIONS

Purpose: Strengthens the front muscles of the legs.

Note: If you have long legs, roll up a towel and place it under your knees.

What to do: Strap a one- to two-pound ankle weight to each ankle and sit with your back against the back of a chair. Place your hands in a comfortable position. Inhale. Exhale and slowly extend your left leg until it is almost straight (but do not lock the knee). Hold for two seconds. Inhale and slowly return your leg to the starting position. Do 15 repetitions. Repeat with the right leg.

Modification: If you find this exercise too difficult, try it without weights.

Illustrations by Shawn Banner.

■ ■ ■ ■

Don't Act Your Age

Older adults who imagine themselves 20 years younger and think, act and speak as they did two decades earlier have better memory and manual dexterity than people of similar ages who act as old as they really are. The ones who act young look younger than their real ages, too, although not a full 20 years younger.

Bottom line: Positive expectations and beliefs about aging make people healthier and more vital.

Ellen J. Langer, PhD, professor, psychology department, Harvard University.

■ ■ ■ ■

Retirement Risks

Early retirement may lead to premature death. People who retire at age 55 are twice as likely to die by age 65 as those who keep working. Until recently, it was generally thought that retiring early increased longevity.

Shan P. Tsai, PhD, manager, department of epidemiology, Shell Health Services, Shell Oil Company, Houston, and leader of a study of 3,500 Shell Oil retirees, published in *British Medical Journal*.

Medical Breakthroughs For Aging Eyes

Neil F. Martin, MD, FACS, an ophthalmologist in private practice in Chevy Chase, MD, and a clinical correspondent for the American Academy of Ophthalmology.

As we age, our vision can be affected by a number of conditions, including cataracts, glaucoma, macular degeneration and diabetes-related eye damage as well as presbyopia (age-related farsightedness) and insufficient tear production (dry eyes). Catching and treating these problems early is the key to preventing long-term vision loss.

NEW EYE TREATMENTS

A number of new drugs and lens technologies are making it much easier to treat a variety of age-related eye ailments. The following treatments have become available just within the last several years…

•**Restasis eyedrops for dry eyes.** The drug *cyclosporine A* (Restasis), used to prevent rejection in heart and kidney transplants, also relieves tear-deficiency syndrome (dry eyes) when used as eyedrops by decreasing inflammation in the tear glands. The drops are applied twice a day to increase tear production. Some people may experience slight stinging at first. Anyone with an active eye infection (such as conjunctivitis) shouldn't use the drops.

•**Improved glaucoma treatments.** A new eyedrop medication, *latanoprost* (Xalatan), reduces fluid buildup better than older eyedrops. (Glaucoma eyedrop treatments work by enhancing the eye's natural filtering process.) While very safe, latanoprost can cause occasional redness, tends to make eyelashes grow longer and may turn light-colored irises brown over time.

Other new treatments include selective laser trabeculoplasty (SLT), which uses a cool laser to enhance the eye's natural drainage canal and improve flow out of the eye without invasive surgery. SLT uses less energy than its predecessor, argon laser trabeculoplasty, lowering the risk of damaging surrounding tissue. SLT is so effective and safe that it may even become a first-line treatment for glaucoma, in place of eyedrops.

•**Eyeglasses with progressive lenses.** Progressive lenses are made by a computer to "morph" from one lens setting in the upper half of the eyeglasses (for far objects) into another in the lower half (for close objects). Progressive lenses have been around awhile, but the newest ones are a vast improvement over what was available just a few years ago.

Reason: Advanced computer designs allow a smoother transition from far to near.

•**Improved Lasik.** Lasik surgery uses an "excimer" laser that can be focused very precisely to reshape the cornea to correct nearsightedness or farsightedness.

The newest version, the Allegretto Wave, uses tiny pulses of laser light adjusted by computer to match your eye's specific curvature. It can be used to treat more severe cases of nearsightedness, farsightedness and astigmatism, previously untreatable by laser, and also causes fewer side effects (such as seeing halos around car headlights at night), with less need for corrective follow-up treatments. (To find a doctor who uses the Allegretto Wave, visit *www.allegretto-wave.com.*)

•**New replacement lenses for cataract patients.** Cataract surgery, in which the cataract-clouded natural lens is removed and replaced with an artificial lens, has long been effective at restoring distance vision. Now, several new types of replacement lenses provide improved near and intermediate vision. Each has its own strengths and weaknesses. *Discuss with your doctor which is best for you…*

•The Crystalens from Eyeonics combines the distance vision of a traditional lens implant with an ability to flex slightly and turn into a lens for near vision when the eye muscles focus on closer objects. It's particularly good at providing clear intermediate vision.

•The ReZoom lens from Advanced Medical Optics employs alternating rings of near- and far-distance lenses.

•The AcrySof ReSTOR lens from Alcon Laboratories has a series of tiny ridges that diffract light (instead of refracting it, like an ordinary lens), enhancing near and intermediate vision. This lens may be the best of the three for focusing on very close objects.

Note: Cataract surgery is extremely safe, with a success rate of more than 95% and a complication rate of less than 2%. Most complications, such as minor swelling of the cornea or retina, increased pressure in the eye or a droopy eyelid, generally resolve themselves with treatment and time. Rarely, cataract surgery can lead to severe visual loss as the result of surgery-related infection, bleeding in the eye or retinal detachment.

•**New intraocular contact lenses.** For those too nearsighted for Lasik, the FDA recently approved the first intraocular contact lens—Myopic VISIAN ICL from Staar Surgical. The lens is implanted directly in front of your own lens through a tiny incision. The procedure is safe, and the lens can be surgically removed if necessary. A similar lens for farsightedness and astigmatism is in clinical trials.

Here are some essentials for keeping your eyes healthy…

•**See an ophthalmologist for a checkup** at least every two years up to age 60, and annually after that. Be sure that the exam includes a careful check for cataracts, macular degeneration (a leaking of the blood vessels in the eyes) and glaucoma (a buildup of fluid inside the eye, which can damage the optic nerve).

•**Supplement your diet** with fish oil (2 to 3 grams daily) or flaxseed oil (one to two tablespoons daily) supplements containing omega-3 and omega-6 fatty acids. These supplements help reduce the inflammation in the tear glands that can lead to tear deficiency syndrome (dry eyes).

•**Eat dark, leafy greens,** such as spinach, collard greens and kale. These are good sources of lutein—a carotenoid (naturally occurring pigment) found in the eye's macula that absorbs dangerous blue light and may help prevent macular degeneration.

•**Eat plenty of oranges,** corn, nectarines and persimmons. These are good sources of zeaxanthin, another carotenoid.

•**Take supplements of antioxidants and zinc.** The Age-Related Eye Disease Study (AREDS), sponsored by the National Eye Institute, found that taking high levels of antioxidants and zinc reduces risk of developing advanced age-related macular degeneration by about 25% in certain at-risk patients.

The study used the following daily doses—500 milligrams (mg) vitamin C, 400 international units (IU) vitamin E, 15 mg beta-carotene, 80 mg zinc in the form of zinc oxide and 2 mg of copper in the form of cupric oxide (to prevent copper deficiency anemia, a condition linked to high levels of zinc consumption).

These antioxidant supplements should be taken in addition to a daily multivitamin. Products specifically formulated to meet AREDS levels include Ocuvite (which offers two versions—the "advanced" formula also contains lutein) and Viteyes (which also contains lutein and zeaxanthin).

•**Don't smoke.** Nicotine constricts the blood vessels in the eyes, increasing the risk of cataracts and macular degeneration.

Note: Smokers should not take beta-carotene supplements.

•**If you have diabetes,** work with your doctor to keep your blood sugar under control, and see an ophthalmologist at least annually, if not more often. Diabetes leads to damage of the eye capillaries, and ultimately to vision loss if untreated. By tightly controlling your blood sugar,

you can largely prevent this damage. If capillary damage occurs, laser treatments can help mitigate the damage.

•**Wear UV-protective sunglasses outdoors.** To prevent cataracts, wear sunglasses that offer UVA and UVB protection. If you spend significant time outdoors in ordinary eyeglasses, get a transparent UV-protective coating applied at any eyeglass store.

•**Wear shatter-resistant polycarbonate goggles** whenever you use power tools, a weed whacker or a hammer, or when playing sports like handball or squash.

•**Check with your eye doctor before using** the impotence drugs *sildenafil* (Viagra) or *vardenafil* (Levitra). In some cases, these drugs can attack the optic nerves, causing damage to vision or to the nerves.

Stay in Control of Your Health Care

Adriane G. Berg, an elder law attorney in Morristown, NJ, and New York City, and a founder of the National Academy of Elder Law Attorneys, is author of 13 books on personal finance, most recently, *How Not to Go Broke at 102! Achieving Everlasting Wealth.* Wiley.

While most of us hope to age well, we all need specialized legal documents that ensure our wishes will be carried out with regard to our money and health care in the event we become mentally or physically incapacitated.

These documents include powers of attorney and several health-care directives, which appoint surrogates to carry out our financial and health-care wishes. The most comprehensive directives—living wills—set out our wishes for end-of-life planning and incapacity.

Other key directives: Health-care proxies, also called health-care powers of attorney, which delegate responsibility for carrying out these decisions to others…"Do not resuscitate orders," which cover care in emergencies.

If you become incapacitated and don't have these documents, a court will appoint a conservator to take over your money and health-care decisions, potentially at considerable cost and heartache to you and your family.

Even worse: Strangers—doctors, medical institutions, etc.—will impose their decisions at critical times.

Careful—if these crucial documents are not drafted by an experienced elder law attorney, they can present a danger to your health and/or wealth. *Here are the pitfalls to avoid...*

Problem 1: **A power of attorney is ineffective just when you need it.** A power of attorney appoints an agent to spend your money...buy, sell or make gifts of investments and other property to people you have designated...sign your name to other documents...cash checks...file your taxes...and engage in other financially related activities. Most people sign powers of attorney for use in the event that they become incapacitated, but a traditional power of attorney is void if you become incapacitated.

Solution: Create a "durable" power of attorney, which is effective unless specifically revoked by you. The document must specifically state that it is durable and goes into effect upon your incapacity. To prevent your agent from controlling your finances right away, make it a "springing" power of attorney. This means it "springs" to life when certain conditions are met.

Example: Two physicians certify that you have become incapacitated, whether temporarily or permanently.

Your surrogate can act for you only if you are incapacitated. You can take back control when you regain competency.

Entrepreneurs: Create a separate business power of attorney. A well-thought-out business power of attorney can be flexible enough to allow you to maintain control over your business for as long as possible, even if your competency waxes and wanes.

Problem 2: **The directions on your power of attorney are incomplete or incorrect.** Many powers of attorney are "one size fits all" forms that don't take into account individual needs or wishes. For example, giving your surrogate "the power to do everything I may have done under the law" may not give him/her the right to gift your property, making it difficult or impossible to plan for government assistance programs (see Problem 3).

Solution: Clearly establish your wishes. For example, a document might say, "It is understood that it is my wish to stay in my home in the event of incapacity. Therefore, I authorize my agent to make expenditures for home renovations, at-home medical equipment, mobility devices and services of a geriatric care manager and any other expenditure needed to create a state-of-the-art environment."

Problem 3: **Your power of attorney fails to plan for long-term care.**

Solution: If you don't have long-term-care insurance, give your agent the power to plan for government benefits that cover long-term health-care costs. Strategies include giving away assets or placing them in a trust so you can be eligible for government programs.

Caution: Most people name their closest heirs as surrogates, so there may be a conflict of interest in deciding who gets a gift if assets are transferred. Consider naming as surrogate a person who won't also be the recipient of the gift.

Problem 4: **The wishes expressed in the health-care directives are too vague.** Without clear health-care directives, decisions regarding your medical care, custodial care (for feeding, toileting, bathing and mobility) and even your end-of-life planning will be out of your hands. The quality of your final years may bear very little resemblance to what you wanted.

Solution: Make sure that your agent, usually a grown child or your spouse, understands and respects your desires. The American Bar Association (800-285-2221, *www.abanet.org*) and the National Academy of Elder Law Attorneys (520-881-4005, *www.naela.org*) offer information on holding a conversation with family members about your end-of-life preferences. *Specifically express your desires with regard to long-term care and pain treatment...*

•**Long-term care.** Make sure that the agent handling your money and arranging payment for your desired care is not at odds with your health-care agent. One easy fix is to make them the same person. If you have a clause in your durable power of attorney for "aging in place" (in your home), make sure that a similar clause exists in your health-care power of attorney.

•**Pain treatment.** A typical clause gives your surrogate the power to arrange for various treatments.

Example: "The administration of pain-relieving drugs of any kind or other surgical or medical procedures to relieve my pain, including unconventional therapies that may be helpful, even though such drugs or procedures may lead to permanent physical damage, addiction or even hasten the moment of (but not intentionally cause) my death."

Problem 5: **Your surrogate reinterprets or disregards your wishes.** There are civil and criminal sanctions against surrogates who ignore your wishes deliberately or use your money for personal gain. But honest surrogates, even professional trustees, may decide to cut spending on health care because of concerns about objections from heirs.

Solution: One way to handle this is to specifically relieve your trustee or other surrogate of liability to your heirs if he spends too freely on your health care, so long as the decisions are in accordance with your expressed wishes. *Such a clause might read like this…*

"My trustee and my trustee's estate, heirs, successors and assigns are hereby released and forever discharged by me, my estate, my heirs, successors and assigns from all liability and from all claims or demands of all kinds arising out of the acts, except for willful misconduct or gross negligence, needed to carry out my wishes as expressed in clause X (*specify the relevant clause in your trust*) of this trust."

■ ■ ■ ■

Older and Nicer?

Older people get along better with others than younger people do. They also are more likely to avoid conflict by waiting for things to improve…younger people are more likely to engage in yelling and name-calling.

Kira S. Birditt, PhD, research assistant professor, Life Course Development Program, University of Michigan, Ann Arbor, and leader of two studies of interpersonal relationships in different age groups, published in Journal of Gerontology: Psychological Sciences.

How to Keep an Eye on Elderly Family Members From Afar

Jim Miller, an advocate for senior citizens, writes "Savvy Senior," a weekly question-and-answer information column syndicated in more than 400 newspapers nationwide, and is a regular guest on the NBC *Today* show. *www.savvysenior.org.*

Many new technologies have been developed to help adults ensure that their older loved ones are safe…

HOME MONITORING

A basic form of this system—the personal emergency response system (PERS)—has been around for years. With a PERS, a person wears a device (panic button) that sends out a call for help if needed. The problem is that many who have such a device don't wear it or aren't alert enough to hit the button if they fall or become ill.

High-tech home-monitoring systems (which still offer the panic-button feature) require no input from the person being cared for. They work through wireless motion sensors placed throughout the senior's home and collect information on activities of daily living, such as getting out of bed, using the bathroom, eating and taking medicine. The system establishes the person's routines so it can detect when there are changes to those patterns, such as a person failing to leave the bedroom in the morning. Alerts are sent to the caregiver via phone or E-mail. Family members also can check on their loved one's patterns via the system's secure Web site. *Companies that offer this product…*

•**QuietCare.** A leader in the industry and the first to offer this service.

Cost: Less than $300, plus about $90 a month for monitoring (varies by area). 877-822-2468, *www.quietcare.com.*

•**Healthsense.** Offers a more comprehensive monitoring system that allows you to keep an eye on just about everything. With a variety of sensors, you can monitor such things as sleep patterns, shower and toilet use, whether the stove has been left on, when your loved one has left the house, etc.

Cost: $1,300, plus $60 for monthly monitoring, though prices vary depending on tier of service and size of the home. 800-576-1779, *www.healthsense.com.*

•**GrandCare.** In addition to monitoring, this system has a small computer that connects to the Internet and plugs into the TV, allowing family members to share pictures, E-mails, appointment reminders and more on a dedicated TV channel.

Cost: $2,000 to $2,500, plus a $30 to $50/month monitoring fee, depending on the service. 262-338-6147, *www.grandcare.com.*

MEDICATION MANAGEMENT

Remembering to take medications is a challenge for many seniors. The MD.2 system can help organize medications and dispense them on schedule. It also provides multiple reminders to take the medication. Caregivers are alerted if necessary. The system can be monitored via the Internet.

Cost: $750, plus a $30 monthly monitoring fee, or it can be rented for less than $100 per month, but cost will vary by distributor. 800-549-0095, *www.epill.com.*

Helpful: *www.epill.com* offers a full line of medication-reminder products and services. 800-549-0095.

VIDEO CHAT SERVICE

An on-line video chat service allows you to speak to and see each other. It is easy to set up, though both parties need a computer, webcam and high-speed or broadband Internet connection. Two services are Windows Live Messenger (*get.live.com*) and SightSpeed (*www.sightspeed.com*).

All-in-one videophones (from such companies as *www.packet8.net* and *www.ojoservices.com*) also can provide this service.

Cost: About $400 per phone, plus $15 to $20 per month.

Fight Osteoporosis the Natural Way

Mark A. Stengler, ND, naturopathic physician in private practice, La Jolla, CA…adjunct associate clinical professor at the National College of Natural Medicine, Portland, OR…author of 16 books, including *The Natural Physician's Healing Therapies* (Bottom Line Books) and coauthor of *Prescription for Natural Cures* (Wiley)…and author of the *Bottom Line/Natural Healing* newsletter.

M isconceptions abound when it comes to osteoporosis, a dreaded disease marked by porous, brittle bones and hunched backs. Most people think of osteoporosis as a women's disease, but it's more than that. While eight million American women have been diagnosed with osteoporosis, more than two million men also are affected by it.

OSTEOPOROSIS: A SILENT PROBLEM

Osteoporosis can develop because, starting at about age 35, our bone cells do not make new bone as fast as it is broken down. Our bones become more frail and fracture more easily. Fractures, especially of the hip, spine and wrist, are more likely to occur, even without trauma. Osteoporosis has no symptoms until a bone is fractured. Many people go for decades without a diagnosis of osteoporosis—until they fall and an X-ray reveals porous bones.

Bone density can be measured with a dual-energy X-ray absorptiometry (DEXA) scan, but many people don't get this test. I recommend a baseline DEXA scan by age 50, and if results are normal, follow-ups every three to five years.

The most worrisome risk for a person with osteoporosis is a hip fracture. According to the National Osteoporosis Foundation (*www.nof.org*), an average of 24% of hip-fracture patients age 50 or older die in the year following their fractures, often as a result of long-term immobilization that leads to blood clots or infection. Six months after a hip fracture, only 15% of patients can walk unaided across a room.

Virtually every person with osteoporosis who has come to my clinic is confused about the best way to promote bone health. Conventional doctors typically prescribe osteoporosis medication, such as *alendronate* (Fosamax) and *ibandronate* (Boniva). However, these drugs can cause side effects, such as digestive upset and blood clots, and they don't address the underlying nutritional deficiencies that promote bone loss.

The natural protocol I recommend includes a healthful diet (rich in vegetables, fruit and fish and low in refined-sugar products and red meat)...weight-bearing exercise (such as walking and stair-climbing)...and good hormone balance (deficiencies of some hormones, such as testosterone, accelerate bone loss). I also suggest certain bone-protecting supplements.

Caution: People with kidney disease should not take supplements without consulting a doctor. With kidney disease, the kidneys cannot process high doses of nutrients.

My recommendations: To help prevent osteoporosis, take the first three supplements listed below. If you have osteoporosis or osteopenia (mild bone loss that can be diagnosed with a DEXA scan), take the first three supplements listed and as many of the others as you're willing to try, in the dosages recommended...

SUPER TRIO PREVENTS AND TREATS OSTEOPOROSIS

•**Calcium** is the most prevalent mineral in bone tissue. Taking supplements helps prevent a deficiency. Most studies have found that calcium slows bone loss but does not increase bone density when used alone. Women with osteoporosis should take 500 mg of calcium twice daily with meals. It should be a well-absorbed form, such as citrate, citrate-malate, amino acid chelate or hydroxyapatite. To boost absorption, take no more than 500 mg per dose. Calcium carbonate, which is widely used, is *not* well-absorbed. For osteoporosis prevention, men and women, as well as boys and girls starting at age 13, should take 500 mg daily.

Calcium supplementation for men with osteoporosis is more complicated. Some recent research has identified a link between high calcium intake (from dairy products) and increased prostate cancer risk. A meta-analysis in the *Journal of the National Cancer Institute* that reviewed 12 studies on this association concluded, "High intake of dairy products and calcium may be associated with an increased risk for prostate cancer, although the increase appears to be small." A recent study found that calcium intake exceeding 1,500 mg a day (from food and

supplements) may be associated with a higher risk of advanced, and potentially fatal, prostate cancer. The saturated fat in dairy products may raise prostate cancer risk.

Until there is more definitive information, I recommend that men who have osteoporosis, regardless of whether they have eliminated calcium-rich foods from their diets, take no more than a 500-mg calcium supplement daily. Men with prostate cancer should consult their doctors before using calcium supplements.

•**Vitamin D** promotes absorption of calcium. Deficiencies of this vitamin are more common in Americans over age 50 than in younger adults. Sun exposure prompts the body to produce vitamin D, and the kidneys help convert it to its active form. As we age, our skin cannot synthesize vitamin D as effectively from sunlight, and our kidneys become less efficient. People with darker skin, those with digestive problems (due to malabsorption conditions, such as Crohn's disease) and those with limited exposure to sunlight are also at greater risk for vitamin D deficiency. Preliminary studies indicate that an inadequate intake of vitamin D is associated with an increased risk of fractures.

For the prevention of osteoporosis, I recommend 600 IU to 800 IU of vitamin D daily. People with osteoporosis should take 800 IU to 1,200 IU daily. Vitamin D is fat soluble, meaning it is better absorbed when taken with meals (containing small amounts of fat).

For many patients with low vitamin D levels, I recommend 2,000 IU of vitamin D daily. To ensure that vitamin D levels are optimal, I monitor blood levels once or twice a year. Overdosing can lead to heart arrhythmia, anorexia, nausea and other ill effects.

•**Magnesium,** an important constituent of bone crystals, is crucial for the proper metabolism of calcium. A deficiency of magnesium impairs bone-building cells known as *osteoblasts*. Like calcium, magnesium requires vitamin D for absorption.

Researchers at Tel Aviv University in Israel looked at the effect of magnesium supplementation on bone density in 31 postmenopausal women with osteoporosis. This two-year, open, controlled trial (both the researchers and patients knew who was receiving the placebo or the supplement) involved giving the participants 250 mg to 750 mg of magnesium daily for six months and 250 mg for another 18 months. Twenty-two patients (71%) experienced a one percent to eight percent increase in bone density. The mean bone density of all treated patients increased significantly after one year and remained at that level after two years. Among an additional 23 postmenopausal women not receiving magnesium, mean bone density *decreased* significantly.

For osteoporosis prevention, take 400 mg to 500 mg of magnesium daily...for osteoporosis, take 500 mg to 750 mg daily. In both cases, take in divided doses.

IF YOU HAVE BONE-LOSS DISEASE

•**Vitamin K** has received attention in recent years for its role in treating osteoporosis. It activates *osteocalcin*, a bone protein that regulates calcium metabolism in the bones and helps calcium bind to the tissues that make up the bone. It also has been shown to inhibit inflammatory chemicals that cause bone breakdown.

Studies have shown that low vitamin K intake and blood levels are associated with reduced bone density and fractures in people who have osteoporosis. A recent meta-analysis published in the American Medical Association's *Archives of Internal Medicine* found that vitamin K supplements were associated with a consistent reduction in all types of fractures. Leafy, green vegetables, such as spinach, kale, collard greens and broccoli, are the best sources of vitamin K, yet many people do not consume these vitamin K–rich foods on a regular basis. High-dose vitamin K (above 2 mg) should be used only under the supervision of a doctor, because excess vitamin K may increase blood clotting. Vitamin K supplements should not be used by people who take blood-thinning medication, such as *warfarin* (Coumadin) or *heparin*, or by pregnant women or nursing mothers. I typically recommend 2 mg to 10 mg daily of vitamin K for people who have osteoporosis to help increase their bone density.

•**Essential fatty acids** (EFAs) have been shown to improve bone density in older women and are believed also to promote bone health in men. Many researchers theorize that osteoporosis develops because of chronic inflammation of bone tissue (due to stress, toxins, poor diet and infection). EFAs, especially those found in fish oil, reduce inflammation. Some studies show that EFAs also improve calcium absorption. I recommend that people with osteoporosis take fish oil daily (containing about 480 mg of EPA and 320 mg of DHA), along with 3,000 mg of evening primrose oil, which contains inflammation-fighting gamma-linolenic acid (GLA). Because EFAs have a blood-thinning effect, check with your doctor if you are taking a blood thinner.

•**Strontium** is a mineral that doesn't get much attention, because it is not regarded as essential for the human body. However, 99% of the total amount of strontium found in the body is located in the teeth and bones. Supplemental strontium is not the radioactive type that you may have heard about in relation to nuclear facilities. Strontium is a valuable mineral for people with osteoporosis, and I often recommend it.

A clinical trial in *The New England Journal of Medicine* found that strontium prevents vertebral fractures and increases bone density. The most common supplemental forms are strontium chloride and strontium citrate. I suggest a supplement that contains 680 mg of elemental strontium daily (similar to the dose used in most studies). Because calcium inhibits strontium absorption, strontium should be taken at least four hours before or after calcium is taken. Strontium should not be taken if you are pregnant or nursing. It is not available at most health-food stores, but you can buy it from Vitacost (800-381-0759, *www.vitacost.com*). A one-month supply costs about $20.

•**Soy,** as a supplement and/or food, has been shown in several studies to improve bone density. Soy contains *isoflavones*, estrogen-like constituents that support bone mass and relieve menopausal symptoms in women. Women and men with osteoporosis or osteopenia should take 125 mg of soy isoflavones daily in soy protein powder or supplement form and consume three to five servings of soy foods weekly. (One serving equals one-half cup of tofu...one-half cup of soy beans...or one cup of soy milk.)

Caution: Soy supplements are not well studied in women who have had breast cancer, so

201

they should avoid supplements and nonfermented soy products.

•**Vitamin C** is required for the production of the protein *collagen*, a component of bone tissue. I recommend that people with osteoporosis take 1,000 mg twice daily. Reduce the dosage if loose stools develop.

•**Silicon** is a trace mineral required for bone formation. I recommend 2 mg to 5 mg daily.

■ ■ ■ ■

Best Osteoporosis Formulas

These products contain all the vitamins and minerals described in this article, in the therapeutic doses used for osteoporosis treatment…

•**Bone Up by Jarrow.** To find an on-line retailer, call 310-204-6936 or go to *www.jarrow.com.*

•**OsteoPrime by Enzymatic Therapy.** To find a retailer, call 800-783-2286 or go to *www.enzy.com.*

•**Pro Bono by Ortho Molecular Products** is available from health-care professionals, including naturopaths, holistic MDs, chiropractors, nutritionists and acupuncturists. If you cannot locate a health-care professional in your area who sells the formula, it is available from Dr. Stengler at 858-450-7120, *www.lajollawholehealth.com.*

Healthy Brain Keeps Body Young

Gary Small, MD, professor of psychiatry and biobehavioral sciences, director of the UCLA Center on Aging and one of the world's leading physician/scientists in the fields of memory and longevity. Dr. Small has authored more than 500 scientific papers and was named one of the world's top innovators in science and technology by *Scientific American.* He is author of *The Memory Bible, The Memory Prescription* and *The Longevity Bible* (all from Hyperion).

Today's American expects to live a long life. Those who make it to age 65 are likely to survive another 17 or more years. But will they be good years? To a great extent, that's up to the individual.

It's easy to say that a genetic roll of the dice determines how rapidly and gracefully we age, but studies have shown that only one-third of the factors that predict how well we age are controlled by genetics.

I've spent more than 20 years researching the lifestyle practices that lead to quality longevity. We all know that a healthful diet is the first step, followed by regular exercise. But there are other commonly overlooked, yet simple, steps that also can make a real difference in the way you age.

A HEALTHY BRAIN

Your brain is the "operating system" of your body. When you protect it, a ripple effect is created. With a sharp memory and positive outlook, you're more likely to take the actions that contribute to overall health and longer life, such as watching what you eat…exercising…and staying attentive to other people, which strengthens your relationships.

How to keep your brain healthy…

•**Brighten your outlook.** Optimists live longer. A Mayo Clinic study found that people who scored high on optimism in a personality test had fewer physical and emotional problems and were 50% more likely to survive another 30 years.

What to do: Practice mental habits that promote positive thinking—focus on your strengths and achievable goals, rather than what's wrong or missing in your life.

•**Do more than crossword puzzles.** Although research is not conclusive, mental workouts, such as those provided by crossword puzzles, have been touted as a key to maintaining brain health. However, crossword puzzles and other brain teasers, such as the number-logic game Sudoku, are of little value unless you really challenge yourself with *difficult* versions of these and other brain exercises.

What to do: Spend at least 10 minutes each day performing some form of challenging "brain activity." If you like crossword puzzles or Sudoku, choose ones that give your brain a rigorous workout, gradually progressing to even more difficult puzzles. They should be challenging but possible to complete. If you enroll in a class to learn a foreign language, put in the study hours it demands. If you join a book club, make sure you go beyond the best-seller list.

•**Be mindful.** Staying in the moment—aware of your thoughts and bodily sensations, and what's going on around you—promotes the health of both your brain and your body. If you stay in the moment, you're less likely to do things like overeating, tripping and hurting yourself, or multitasking, which studies show can be stressful.

What to do: Keep your mind in the present to avoid worrying about the future and/or dwelling on past mistakes—it's a proven stress and anxiety reducer. To achieve mindfulness, sit down and meditate for five to 10 minutes, or simply take a few slow, deep breaths and tell yourself to focus on the present.

Also helpful: If you practice mindful awareness at mealtime, portion control—the key to weight control—will come naturally to you. Notice how your body feels before, during and after each meal. Eat when you're hungry, and stop just before you feel full.

CULTIVATE STRONG RELATIONSHIPS

Spending pleasant time with other people can add years of good health. A Harvard study of about 3,000 men and women found that people who socialized most (attended sports events, played games, went to restaurants, etc.) had a 20% better chance of living long lives than loners. In addition, they had fewer disabilities and less cognitive decline.

Close, satisfying friendships and family connections are particularly helpful. The MacArthur Study of Successful Aging, conducted by researchers throughout the US, linked emotionally supportive relationships to lower levels of stress hormones. People with close relationships recover faster from surgery and need less pain medication.

Staying in the moment when talking with others—and being aware when your mind wanders—is the heart of true communication. The more attentive you are to another person's words, expressions and body language, the better you can feel what he/she is feeling. The capacity for empathy builds strong relationships.

What to do: Try this 15-minute exercise with a spouse, family member or friend: For three to five minutes, one partner talks about something that is going on in his life, such as a crisis, chronic issue or upcoming event. The listener should maintain eye contact and stay focused on what the other person is saying and should not interrupt. Switch roles for another three to five minutes, then discuss the experience.

COMBAT CLUTTER

If your environment is confusing and disorganized, you may feel constant stress. When you can't find what you need, you face a constant reminder that you're not in control of your life.

What to do: Schedule 15 minutes a day to put things where they belong. Declutter one room—or one corner of the room—at a time. Put away rarely used items, such as clothes or sports equipment not needed until the next season. Consider donating or throwing away anything you haven't used in the last 12 months. Sort mail, groceries—anything—as soon as it comes into the house. Organize and store similar items together so they will be easy to find later.

Apply the same principle to your personal life. We often maintain friendships even when they become unfulfilling. "Declutter" your social world by staying away from people who make you feel unappreciated, guilty or who simply irritate you. Or at least see them less often. This will create time for healthy relationships.

BRAIN EXERCISE

Starting with the word WARM, change one letter at a time until you have the word FILE. Each change must result in a proper word.*

WARM

——

——

——

F I L E

———

*Solution: WARM, FARM, FIRM, FILM, FILE or WARM, FARM, FIRM, FIRE, FILE.

How to Keep Your Brain Sharp

Gene D. Cohen, MD, PhD, professor of health-care sciences and psychiatry, and director of The Center on Aging, Health & Humanities at George Washington University in Washington, DC, is founding chief of the Center on Aging at the National Institute of Mental Health, past-president of the Gerontological Society of America and author of *The Mature Mind.* Basic.

Scientists used to assume that older adults don't learn as well as younger people and children...that creativity is strongest in youth...and that mental abilities in general go south after age 50. These long-standing myths prevailed even though there was virtually no science to back them up.

New findings: The brain has enormous plasticity—the ability to form new neurons (brain cells) and new connections between neurons. Brain plasticity doesn't decline with age. It can actually increase as people get older.

Example: The hippocampus is the part of the brain that processes information and integrates thinking and emotions. Nerve endings (dendrites) and connections between dendrites (synapses) increase in this area between the ages of 50 and 80.

The brain is not immune to age-related changes. Brain cells "wear out" and die with age. Older adults can't process math problems as quickly as younger people, and they experience declines in short-term memory storage.

However, other kinds of brain changes aren't caused by aging, but by underlying conditions, such as Alzheimer's, stroke and depression. *Assuming that you take care of yourself and stay healthy, you can improve mental function by doing the following...*

STIMULATE YOUR BRAIN

People who push themselves mentally can increase synaptic connections by at least 20%. They also experience increased neurogenesis, the formation of new neurons. The result is quicker thinking, better memory, etc. Mental challenges even can delay the onset of Alzheimer's disease. A study in *The New England Journal of Medicine* reported that patients at high risk for Alzheimer's who engaged in difficult mental activities, such as playing a musical instrument or word games, significantly delayed disease onset. Apparently, they built up a brain "reserve," which kept their minds robust longer.

Choose mental activities that really push your capacities.

Examples: Learning a language or instrument...doing challenging crossword puzzles... playing Scrabble or chess.

EXERCISE

People who exercise do better mentally and diminish the risk of Alzheimer's disease and other forms of dementia than those who are sedentary. Aerobic exercise in particular improves brain circulation and oxygenation. It appears to stimulate the release of chemicals in the body that increase synaptic connections as well as the formation of new neurons.

Example: A study of older women showed that those who increased their physical activity by walking had less cognitive decline and dementia over a period of six to eight years.

More is better. Just as vigorous exercise of the brain is good for cognition, vigorous physical activity is necessary for brain health.

Exercise for 30 to 45 minutes at least four days a week. Aerobic activities, such as brisk walking and swimming, are better for the brain than weight training. Aerobic workouts improve cardiovascular fitness, which is thought to increase networks of blood vessels in the frontal part of the brain and stimulate the release of chemicals that improve brain cell survival and plasticity.

ACHIEVE MASTERY

Older adults who work hard to get good at something experience feelings of empowerment and control. These feelings produce higher levels of T cells and natural killer cells—immune cells that battle disease and help keep brain tissue and blood vessels robust.

One study compared 150 older adults, average age of 80, who were involved in rigorous arts programs with a comparable group not enrolled in the programs. People in the arts group met weekly for a period of about nine months a year for two years and completed between-session assignments.

Many of those in the arts group showed no physical or mental health declines during the study—and some showed significant improvement. Those who didn't participate in the arts programs tended to have a reduction in overall mental health.

It's less important what you do—it could be embroidery, learning how to paint or understanding your computer—than learning to do it well.

STRENGTHEN BOTH SIDES OF THE BRAIN

It isn't true that some people are "right-brained" and others are "left-brained." We use both sides of our brain throughout life, but younger adults are more likely to use only one side at a time—for things such as reading, recognizing patterns, etc. After middle age, however, people are more likely to use both sides simultaneously. This is probably a protective mechanism that allows the brain to overcome some degenerative changes associated with aging. Older adults who cultivate this capacity have quicker reaction times and improved cognitive abilities.

Best: Creative activities draw on both the right and left sides of the brain and improve the ability of both sides to work together. Take drawing classes. Join a book club. Write your autobiography.

STRENGTHEN SOCIAL NETWORKS

Close relationships are important throughout life, particularly for older adults. People who maintain active social schedules—going to church, getting together with friends and spending time with family—have lower blood pressure and less risk of stroke. They have lower levels of stress hormones, the chemicals that damage brain tissue and increase the risk of anxiety and depression.

New finding: Older adults experience negative emotions less often—including fear and anger, which interfere with relationships—than younger people. Imaging studies show that the amygdalae (the parts of the brain that generate some of our most intense emotions) get less active with age. We experience less intense negative emotions as we get older, but positive ones remain robust. We have an improved capacity to ride out emotional storms that often roil relationships.

Spend time with people you really care about. Volunteer and get involved in your community. Even people who describe themselves as wallflowers during their younger years often find that social connections get easier—and more rewarding—later in life. And they help keep your brain healthy.

■ ■ ■ ■

Keep Your Memory Strong

Keep your memory strong by using all five senses to help you remember tasks and learn new things. In addition to visualizing an object or event, imagine how it would smell, taste and feel.

Example: To remember to bring dessert to an event, imagine eating it—with all the sensations—earlier in the day.

Also: Relax—memory gets overwhelmed when the body is stressed.

And: If you cannot remember someone's name, try to recall where you were, or with whom, when you last saw the person, and the name may come to you.

Douglas Mason, PsyD, clinical neuropsychologist, Clermont, FL, and author, *The Memory Doctor*. New Harbinger.

■ ■ ■ ■

Exercise Reduces Dementia Risk

A study of nearly 1,500 men and women found that those who exercised for 30 minutes or more at least twice a week in their 40s and 50s had a 60% lower risk of developing dementia. A generally active lifestyle after age 60 also is believed to be protective, according to earlier studies.

Theory: Physical activity promotes the growth of new blood vessels, increasing blood flow to the brain.

Self-defense: Exercise for 30 minutes or more at least twice weekly at an intensity that induces sweating.

Miia Kivipelto, MD, PhD, research fellow in geriatric epidemiology, Karolinska Institute's Aging Research Center, Stockholm, Sweden.

Raise Your IQ 9 Points In 10 Minutes

Arthur Winter, MD, neurosurgeon, and director, New Jersey Neurological Institute, Livingston. He is author of *Brain Workout* (American Society of Journalists and Authors) and *Build Your Brain Power* (St. Martin's). *www. brainbody.com.*

Most people assume that everyone's mental capacities diminish with age. Fortunately, that's not true.

New studies show that cognitive decline doesn't occur in *healthy* older brains. With the right kind of physical and mental stimulation, most people can keep their cognitive abilities near maximum capacity as they age. Your brain continues to repair cell damage and form new neural networks throughout life. In fact, people who are active mentally can actually *improve* their performance on intelligence tests after age 60.

Exercises that work…

EXERCISE YOUR BRAIN

One study shows that sedentary individuals ages 55 to 70 who enlisted in a four-month aerobic exercise program did significantly better on neuropsychological tests than subjects who didn't perform aerobic exercise. Improved cognitive performance was attributed to increased blood flow to the brain.

Any aerobic exercise—walking, swimming, biking, etc.—also increase oxygenation of the brain and can improve memory as well as mood and speed of decision-making. Brisk walking for 30 minutes daily is adequate.

USE ALL YOUR SENSES

We gather information with the senses—and we are more likely to remember information when we use multiple senses.

Example: It's common to forget the name of someone you just met, partly because you only use one sense (hearing) when you're introduced. The next time you meet someone, bring more of your senses into play. Shake hands. Notice his/her scent and appearance. The more sensory details you accumulate, the more likely you are to store the name in memory.

Exercise: Sniff a bar of sweet-smelling soap, and pay attention to how it looks and feels. Then read a paragraph from a book or magazine. Sniff the soap again. The next day, smell the soap again. You'll probably recall more details of the paragraph than you would if you did not sniff the soap.

MEMORIZE SOMETHING DAILY

Memory is like a muscle—the more you use it, the stronger it becomes.

The brain stimulation that occurs while you're learning new material triggers an increase in the number of *dendrites* (spider-like sensors on nerves) as well as *synapses* (gaps between the nerve cells).

Exercise: Learn one new word a day. Write it down on a notepad, and rehearse it in your mind a few times. The next day, write down a new word and review the one from the day before. Doing this daily will increase your vocabulary as well as your ability to retain new information of all kinds.

Smart idea: Use a free on-line service, such as A.Word.A.Day. To subscribe, go to their Web site at *http://wordsmith.org/awad.* Or, choose a word you don't know from your daily newspaper.

IMPROVE MEMORY WITH MUSIC

Music is a highly effective tool for improving brain function. The type of music is not important. Music of your choice reduces emotional and mental stress, both of which interfere with memory. Singing or playing a musical instrument stimulates the cerebellum and improves your ability to organize and recall new information that is presented to you.

A study of college students reported in *Nature* found that those who listened to Mozart for 10 minutes prior to a standardized intelligence test raised their scores to 119 (from 110 following silence).

Exercise: Practice a musical instrument or sing for 15 minutes several times daily. It doesn't matter if you can't carry a tune. Just the act of singing—accompanying words with rhythm—makes information easier to remember.

Helpful: If there's something specific you want to memorize—a phone number, address or shopping list—sing it out loud. This brings different parts of the brain into play and aids memorization.

MAKE ASSOCIATIONS

The brain is thought to store related information in discrete areas. When you recall a word from your long-term memory, there's a temporary increase in nerve activity in the locations of other nearby words. That's why the practice of association—linking certain words or concepts together—is an effective technique to practice to improve memory.

Exercise: Make a list of 20 simple words—dog, cat, bird, shovel, etc. Read the list of words once, then write as many of them as you can remember on a blank piece of paper. If you're good, you'll get about half of the words.

Then try the same thing while making associations for each word. The word "dog," for example, can be associated with a picture of a black Labrador or a pet you own. The more associations you make, the more words you'll remember.

PRACTICE SPEED

Using a timer or your watch, write down as many five-letter words as you can in two minutes. Repeat the exercise daily. If you want, practice with six-, seven- or eight-letter words. Your ability to recall all information—not just words—will improve.

Six Steps to Mental Fitness

Sandra Cusack, PhD, Guttmann-Gee Research Fellow in Educational Gerontology at the Gerontology Research Centre at Simon Fraser University in Vancouver, Canada, is coauthor, with Wendy Thompson, of *Mental Fitness for Life*. Bull.

Most people, including many doctors, believe that memory and cognitive abilities inevitably decline at middle age—even though there's virtually no scientific proof to support this belief.

What most people don't realize: Even though some brain cells (neurons) die with age, the brain retains the ability to form new neurons and connections between neurons. In fact, the number of nerve endings (dendrites) in the part of the brain that processes information increases between ages 50 and 80.

Imaging tests allow us to see changes in brain physiology that occur in response to brain exercises and new learning. Age-related diseases, such as dementia—and even some medications —can lead to memory loss and reduced mental function, but such problems are not an inevitable part of aging.*

CREATING A "BRAIN WORKOUT"

People who exercise their minds regularly and develop positive psychological traits, such as optimism and self-confidence, can literally "rewire" their brains (that is, new neurons can be formed, and existing neurons can form new connections). *Here's how...*

Step 1: **Set goals.** Goals create a sense of purpose and promote feelings of self-worth. Goals that are especially meaningful or that require a good deal of effort and concentration, such as raising money for charity or researching your genealogy, are believed to promote brain health.

Goals are particularly important for older adults who have a tendency to stop challenging themselves mentally in the assumption that their cognitive abilities decline with age. Any goal that improves overall health, such as losing weight or reducing stress, contributes to brain health.

Helpful steps...

•**Write down 10 things that you want to do before you die.**

Example: Short-term goal—lose 10 pounds in the next three months...long-term goal—become a part-time teacher. Choose goals that stretch your abilities but aren't impossible.

•**Write down the advantages of reaching your goals.**

Examples: "I'll be healthier and look better if I lose weight," and,"It makes me happy to help people learn."

•**Make your goals measurable.** Suppose your goal is to complete a university degree that

*Caution: If you have experienced a sudden memory decline, consult a physician. You may need to be evaluated for a memory disorder.

was abandoned years ago. Measurable goals might include applying for admission to a local college and enrolling in courses that are challenging.

•**Set deadlines.** Choose a date for each goal, and identify key steps along the way.

***Step 2:* Be a power thinker.** Because many older adults have negative perceptions of their mental abilities, they often say things like, "I can't remember your name because my memory isn't as good as it once was." Such statements indicate a willingness to accept the status quo and often lead to a self-fulfilling prophecy.

Better: Think—and phrase things—positively. Tell yourself, "I don't want to forget names, so I'm going to take the necessary steps to retain my memory."

***Step 3:* Cultivate creativity.** We used to believe that creativity declined with age. But some people reach their prime later in life.

Examples: Goethe finished writing *Faust* at age 83…Grandma Moses began painting in her 70s.

There are many ways to be creative. Humor is a form of creativity. So is keeping a journal, cooking or rearranging furniture. Every activity is creative if you put your personal stamp on it.

Creative people are natural problem-solvers. Studies show that they engage both sides of their brains and reap the rewards of cognitive effort—including better memory and more efficient processing of information.

***Step 4:* Adopt a positive mental attitude.** In the 1960s, Mayo Clinic researchers classified 839 patients as either optimists or pessimists, depending on the number of positive words that appeared in written statements they provided. Thirty years later, many more of the optimists were still alive, having lived an average of six years longer than the pessimists. Optimism, the hallmark of having a positive mental attitude, appears to have powerful effects on mental health, which may help protect cognitive abilities.

***Step 5:* Perform memory-boosting exercises.** Memory is like a muscle—the more you use it, the stronger it gets. Brain stimulation caused by learning new, challenging material triggers an increase in the number of dendrites as well as synapses (connections between dendrites).

Helpful: Create a "brain workout" schedule.

Example: *Sunday*—Read an engaging book…visit a museum. *Monday*—Listen to tapes or CDs to learn a foreign language. *Tuesday*—Do a crossword puzzle…take a meditation class. *Wednesday*—Play bridge…write in your journal. *Thursday*—Take an art class. *Friday*—Volunteer as a tour guide at an art gallery. *Saturday*—Host a dinner party…try out a new recipe.

Also helpful: Learn one new word a day. Write it down and repeat the definition a few times. The next day, write down a new word and review the one from the day before. Review all seven words at the week's end. Doing this daily will increase your vocabulary as well as your ability to retain new information of all kinds. To receive a free word-a-day E-mail, go to *www.wordsmith.org.* Or for free Sudoku puzzles, the popular number-logic game, go to *www.free-sudokus.com.* Nintendo's "Brain Age," which includes math and logic activities, and similar video games also give your mind a good workout.

***Step 6:* Speak your mind.** People who assert themselves—by being active in their communities, meeting new people or simply feeling free to say what they're thinking—develop a tremendous amount of self-confidence. Knowing that your thoughts matter will encourage you to think clearly, critically and creatively. It's also a way of engaging the world and keeping your mind active.

Important: Take every opportunity to speak your mind. Join in casual discussions with your family and friends—everyone has something to contribute. Talk to people when you're waiting in line at the post office or grocery store—and, just as important, listen to what they have to say. As we hear different points of view, we develop mental flexibility and open-mindedness. You can practice this skill one-on-one, or in groups, such as book clubs or adult-education classes.

■ ■ ■ ■

Memory Aid

To remember a word, get physical. If a word is on the tip of your tongue, but you just can't recall it, try gesturing. Physical movement can sometimes unlock a temporary memory block. If possible, move your hands in a shape related to the word.

Example: When trying to remember a type of bird, shape your hands like wings.

Elena Nicoladis, PhD, assistant professor of psychology, University of Alberta, Edmonton, Canada.

Computer Games to Keep Your Mind Sharp

Domenic Greco, PhD, a psychologist based in San Marcos, CA, studies the effect of games on the people who play them. *Information:* CyberLearning Technology.

Don't scoff at the games kids play on computers. More and more adults are discovering that on-line games help keep their minds sharp and allow them to socialize via the Internet with people all over the world.

On-line games are by no means all fast-action electronic versions of what you once might have played at penny arcades. The Internet also gives you access to dozens of traditional games, including bridge, canasta, mah jong, hearts, dominoes, chess and backgammon.

Hundreds of Web sites let you play these and other games against a computer or real competitors.

GOOD FOR THE BRAIN

If you have any doubt that computer games are good for the brain, your skepticism might be allayed by the experience of James Rosser, Jr., MD. He's the director of the Advanced Medical Technology Institute at Beth Israel Medical Center in New York City—and he asked his staff of surgeons to periodically play video games.

Dr. Rosser recently reported that surgeons who played games three hours a week performed their medical tasks faster and more accurately than those who didn't. Rosser's findings aren't unique. Experiments at my own company, CyberLearning Technology, show that people who regularly play video games have an easier time learning new tasks.

For older people, on-line games have another benefit. They can introduce you to activities that you'll enjoy with younger members of your family.

GETTING STARTED

To best play games on-line, you need a computer with at least 128 megabytes of memory (preferably 256) and at least a 17-inch screen. A high-speed Internet connection isn't necessary, although it's helpful for some games.

In on-line games, the board or playing field is displayed on screen, often with stunning graphics and dramatic sound effects. Moves are made by manipulating the mouse or other types of controllers, such as joysticks or gamepads.

Depending on the game, winning usually requires a combination of coordination, memory and occasionally teamwork. Luck plays a role, too.

For an overview of available on-line games, visit one of the major sites, called portals, that have links to hundreds of games. Some of the biggest game portals are *http://games.yahoo. com...http://games.aol.com...*and *http://zone.msn. com.* To find other game sites, enter "on-line games" into Google or another search engine.

At least one portal, *www.aboutseniors.com. au*, has links to games traditionally popular with seniors, including bingo, solitaire, cribbage and canasta.

Before you can play, you may have to register by submitting your E-mail address and choosing a password. Most sites are free, and those that charge usually have fees of less than $100 a year.

Caution: Don't register unless a site states that it won't share your E-mail address. Also, some on-line games require you to download software that enables you to play the game on your computer. Before you do, make sure your computer has a security program that screens downloads for viruses and other unwanted bits of computer code.

Game sites usually allow you to play with people you know, who must also register, or with anonymous opponents chosen by the site on the basis of the skill level that you select.

Though your identity won't be revealed when you play, many sites have chat rooms where players can exchange messages about game strategy and other topics. In chat rooms, players usually have the option of posting their real names and contact information.

CHOOSING A GAME

•**Backgammon.** "It's Your Turn" at *www.its yourturn.com* has classic backgammon as well as several variations that you and a friend can sign up for and play for free. As in all backgammon games, winning requires you to remember complex numerical combinations and to vary your strategy as your opponent moves.

•**Battleships.** "Battleships-General Quarters II" at *www.battleships.f-active.com* has been a free site for young people and it's now attracting a multigenerational crowd. Each of two players is in command of a fleet of five ships, and the object is to "destroy" the opponent's fleet before the opponent destroys yours. The game is tricky, requiring physical coordination to work the computer's mouse as well as the ability to make quick decisions about the most likely location of the enemy.

•**Bridge.** "OKbridge" at *www.okbridge.com* has been sanctioned by the American Contract Bridge League. It is the oldest and largest on-line bridge club, with members from 100 countries.

Cost: $99 a year after a free seven-day trial. Unlike most other games, bridge is played with a partner, a feature that can hone your skill at communications and patience.

•**Chess.** "Free Internet Chess Server" at *www.freechess.org* allows you to play—free of charge—against its computer or a real person.

•**Crossword puzzles.** "Best Crosswords" at *www.bestcrosswords.com* has seven new puzzles a day. Solvers have the option of submitting their results so they can track their improvement and also compete against others. When competition results are posted, players are known only by their screen names. Like most other word puzzles, crosswords build vocabulary and remind you of words you may have forgotten.

•**Dominoes.** "GameDesire" at *www.game desire.com* has a classic domino game with 28 "bones," or pieces. Play is free.

•**Mah jong.** "GameHouse" at *www.game house.com/onlinegames* lets Internet users play a variety of solitaire mah jong games for free.

•**Zuma.** "Pop Cap" at *www.popcap.com* features Zuma, which has a reputation as one of the most addictive games in the "action puzzle" genre. To win this solitaire game, you must make your way through a visually perplexing temple in the mythical city of Zuma. It's not easy. You must use the mouse to fire magical orbs without letting them reach the golden skull in the middle of the temple. The game requires coordination and the ability to resist being distracted by the accompanying music (unless you turn off the sound).

The majority of portals let you download many types of games that you can play on your computer without actually being connected to the Internet. While some downloads are free, others require payment of a fee—usually under $25.

■ ■ ■ ■

Tuning In

Daydreaming may be able to keep Alzheimer's at bay.

Recent finding: The section of the brain that is used to daydream is where Alzheimer's disease appears later. More research is needed.

Randy Buckner, PhD, professor of psychology, Harvard University, Cambridge, MA, and lead researcher of a study of 764 people, published in *The Journal of Neuroscience.*

How Nuns Ward Off Alzheimer's

Guy McKhann, MD, professor of neurology and neuroscience and founding director of the Mind-Brain Institute at Johns Hopkins University School of Medicine, Baltimore, is author of *Keep Your Brain Young.* Wiley. He is a fellow at The Royal College of Physicians.

Doctors still don't know what causes Alzheimer's disease. *Worse:* Today's treatments are far from ideal, but thanks to the ongoing Nun Study—a one-of-a-kind study of brain diseases in the elderly—scientists are beginning to identify some of the main risk factors, which could open the door to preventive strategies and more effective treatments.

Key finding: Scientists now believe that behaviors and personality traits established early in life are strongly linked to the development of Alzheimer's in later years. Some people have a genetic predisposition to getting the disease, but other factors—such as education, staying mentally active and a history of head trauma or stroke—are thought to play a bigger role.

MANY VARIABLES

Epidemiology is the field of medicine that deals with the differences between people who get sick and those who don't. The goal is to identify factors that cause or contribute to disease, such as genetics, diet, exercise and vitamin intake.

Over the years, Alzheimer's researchers have used epidemiology to identify risk factors. The difficulty in this approach is that populations are rarely static. Individuals within a group move away or come from different places... change their habits over time...or fail to accurately recollect their previous behavior. The greater the number of variables, the harder it is to determine which particular factors have positive or negative effects.

Example: It was once widely believed that people with the highest intake of vitamin E were less likely to get Alzheimer's. Yet these are also the people who tend to have healthier habits overall. This makes it difficult to determine if vitamin E itself is beneficial or if the lower disease rates are linked to different factors altogether.

What we have learned: A recent study of blood samples from the nuns showed that vitamin E did not protect against Alzheimer's.

A STABLE POPULATION

Starting in 1986, David A. Snowdon, PhD, now a professor of neurology at the University of Kentucky, Lexington, began studying nuns of the School Sisters of Notre Dame living in Mankato, Minnesota. The study was later expanded to include nuns living in the midwestern, eastern and southern US.

The researchers hoped to identify factors in early, mid- and late life that increase the risk of Alzheimer's and other brain diseases. The Nun Study, which initially included 678 participants ranging in age from 75 to 103, is providing answers.

Unlike most populations studied by epidemiologists, the School Sisters of Notre Dame live in small, relatively uniform communities. They get similar medical care and have similar lifestyles. And because convent archives contain detailed personal histories, researchers were able to collect accurate information spanning previous decades of the nuns' lives.

The Nun Study has revealed that even though symptoms of Alzheimer's typically appear in older adults, the underlying causes may be rooted much earlier in life. *Important findings...*

STROKE/HEAD TRAUMA RISK

When scientists examined the brains of nuns who had died, they found that nearly all of those with signs of Alzheimer's, such as brain deposits of a protein called *beta-amyloid*, showed evidence of a previous stroke or other forms of brain injury, such as head trauma from a car accident.

It's not yet certain that a history of stroke increases the risk of Alzheimer's, but it does seem likely that a stroke can accelerate the onset of symptoms and cause more rapid disease progression.

Reason: We all have brain reserves, "extra" neurons that give us the ability to maintain cognitive function after neurological damage. Those who lose some of their brain reserves early in life and then go on to develop Alzheimer's will experience mental impairment more rapidly than those without previous injuries and greater brain reserves.

What to do: Prevent strokes by keeping the cardiovascular system strong—don't smoke, manage blood pressure and cholesterol, and get regular exercise. Protect against head injury—wear a helmet while biking, motorcycling and horseback riding, always wear seatbelts, etc.

FOLATE HELPS

A number of studies indicate that low levels of the B vitamin folate are linked to dementia and brain atrophy (shrinkage). The Nun Study indicates that a deficiency may be linked to Alzheimer's as well.

When researchers compared autopsy results with earlier blood samples, they found that nuns with higher blood levels of folate were less likely to show signs of brain atrophy associated with Alzheimer's.

Folate (the supplemental form is called folic acid) suppresses the amino acid *homocysteine*. Excessive homocysteine levels promote the development of atherosclerotic plaques in brain and heart arteries. These plaques increase the risk of stroke and heart attack. Homocysteine is also thought to damage neurons and increase brain atrophy in Alzheimer's patients.

What to do: Eat plenty of folate-rich foods—leafy green vegetables, legumes, fortified cereals and enriched grain products. Take a daily multisupplement that contains 400 micrograms (mcg) of folic acid for even more protection.

STAY MENTALLY ACTIVE

Scientists have learned from autopsies that people with brain changes characteristic of Alzheimer's don't necessarily exhibit impairments of cognitive function. Why do some Alzheimer's patients experience severe declines in mental abilities while others continue to function more or less normally?

When researchers analyzed biographies that the nuns wrote decades before taking holy orders, they found that those with a high "idea density"—a marker of education level and vocabulary—were less likely to develop Alzheimer's symptoms later in life, even when their brains showed signs of disease.

The brain continues to form neurons and connections between neurons throughout life. People who are mentally active form the most connections and develop brain reserves that can slow the onset of Alzheimer's symptoms.

What to do: Take classes at a local college. Read challenging books. Do crossword puzzles. Learn a new language. Mental activity increases the number of synaptic pathways, connections between neurons that enhance memory and cognitive function.

EXERCISE

Obesity and hypertension are among the leading causes of stroke. One of the best ways to reduce stroke risk—and protect brain reserves—is with daily physical activity. It's never too late to start. One of the sisters in the Nun Study, who was 91 years old when she was interviewed, attributed her longevity to an exercise program that she started when she was 70.

Exercise improves blood circulation in the brain and lowers blood pressure. It also lowers stress hormones and stimulates the release of trophic factors, brain proteins that repair neurons and keep them functioning at peak capacity.

What to do: Exercise daily. Even light physical activity, such as walking or yardwork, increases the release of trophic factors and promotes better cognitive function.

STRESS AND DEPRESSION

Depression, anger and stress increase the risk of cardiovascular disease as well as declines in cognitive function. A study of the nuns' biographies showed that those who expressed negative emotions died sooner and were more likely to have declines in mental function.

Stress and anxiety increase levels of *glucocorticoids*, hormones that damage the hippocampus, the part of the brain that controls memory. Depression saps motivation and self-esteem and can cause significant memory declines. In patients who already have Alzheimer's symptoms, depression and stress can accelerate mental declines.

Know the signs: Insomnia, changes in appetite, increasing irritability or a loss of interest in daily activities can indicate clinically significant stress/depression. See a doctor or therapist right away.

What to do: Reduce stress with activities you find relaxing, such as exercise, or even simply by taking deep breaths. Talk about your problems with friends and family. Sharing concerns with others can lower levels of stress hormones even when the source of the stress is ongoing.

■ ■ ■ ■

Alzheimer's Mystery

Alzheimer's develops more quickly in people with higher educations than in less-educated people.

Study: Although highly educated people typically are diagnosed with Alzheimer's disease later in life than less-educated people—probably because they can compensate for the memory loss for a longer time—once the disease becomes apparent, they lose their memory at a faster rate.

Nikolaos Scarmeas, MD, assistant professor of neurology, Taub Institute, Columbia University, New York City, and leader of a study of 312 Alzheimer's patients, published in *Journal of Neurology, Neurosurgery and Psychiatry.*

■ ■ ■ ■

Early Warning

Alzheimer's symptoms can occur 10 years or more before the disease is diagnosed.

Recent finding: Problems with memory and difficulty solving problems and multitasking start years before severe memory loss appears. More study is needed to determine how to detect Alzheimer's early and treat it aggressively.

William Thies, PhD, vice president of Medical and Scientific research, Alzheimer's Association, Chicago.

■ ■ ■ ■

Slowing Alzheimer's

Alzheimer's is slowed by cholesterol-lowering drugs. In a three-year study of 300 Alzheimer's patients, the disease progressed more slowly (loss of 1.5 points in a 30-point mini mental status exam, or MMSE) in those who took a cholesterol-lowering drug than it did in those not taking the medication (loss of 2.5 points in MMSE).

Theory: High cholesterol levels increase the deposition of proteins that can impair brain function.

Florence Pasquier, MD, PhD, professor of neurology, University Hospital, Lille, France.

■ ■ ■ ■

Lung Capacity and Alzheimer's

Reduce Alzheimer's risk as easily as taking a single breath.

Recent finding: For 29 years, researchers monitored the lung capacities of 1,291 women with tests that measure exhalation rates.

Result: The better the lung function in middle age, the lower the risk of developing Alzheimer's later in life.

Theory: Poor lung function decreases the amount of oxygen that reaches the brain, raising the risk for Alzheimer's.

To maintain optimal lung function: Get at least 30 minutes of moderate-intensity exercise most days of the week—and don't smoke.

Xinxin Guo, MD, PhD, researcher, department of psychiatry, Institute of Neurosciences and Physiology, Sahlgrenska University Hospital, Göteborg, Sweden.

Recognizing Early-Stage Alzheimer's Disease— Subtle Signs Often Undetected

Todd Feinberg, MD, chief of the Yarmon Neurobehavior and Alzheimer's Disease Center at Beth Israel Medical Center and professor of clinical neurology and psychiatry at Albert Einstein College of Medicine, both in New York City, is coauthor of *What to Do When the Doctor Says It's Early-Stage Alzheimer's.* Fair Winds.

Alzheimer's disease was first identified 100 years ago, but only recently have significant breakthroughs been made in recognizing the sometimes subtle mental deficits caused by the condition.

Important development: With sophisticated new brain scans and neurological tests, doctors are now able to identify telltale signs of this dreaded disease in its early stages, when treatment is potentially most helpful. *What you need to know...*

HOW IT STARTS

With normal aging, our brains begin to shrink a few cells at a time, which slows brain functioning. In patients with early-stage Alzheimer's, however, a much more insidious process occurs. For reasons that are not well understood, abnormal accumulations of protein fragments and cellular material (plaques) that contain an insoluble protein called *beta-amyloid* develop, as do brain-damaging bundles of neurofibers known as neurofibrillary tangles.

When memory lapses occur as a result of normal aging, the information can almost always be retrieved at some point later. With early-stage Alzheimer's, however, memories of recent events—those that have taken place in past weeks, days or even hours—completely disappear.

Lesser-known symptoms that also characterize Alzheimer's in its early stages…

• **Loss of initiative.** The person may lose interest in what had been favorite activities, such as gardening or taking walks. He/she may become passive and spend more time sleeping or watching television.

• **Loss of smell.** One study has linked Alzheimer's to an inability to identify certain smells—specifically, strawberry, smoke, soap, menthol, clove, pineapple, natural gas, lilac, lemon and leather.

• **Language problems.** Finding the right word or phrase becomes increasingly difficult, and vocabulary is diminished.

• **Difficulty reasoning.** This affects a person's ability to do things such as read and understand an instruction manual, balance a checkbook or follow a recipe.

People who have early-stage Alzheimer's also may have trouble making even simple decisions …take longer to perform routine tasks…or experience a change in personality (such as a person who is ordinarily very sociable becoming a recluse).

Important: Many early-stage Alzheimer's symptoms are similar to those caused by depression. Imaging tests, as well as a family history of either condition, can be used to distinguish the two.

During moderate-stage Alzheimer's disease, the patient may become less concerned with personal appearance…confuse the identities of family members (for example, thinking one's wife is one's sister)…hear, see or smell things that are not there…and/or need help with basic hygiene.

Late-stage Alzheimer's is typically characterized by loss of bladder and bowel control…an inability to recognize close family members…difficulties chewing and swallowing…and a need for total assistance with activities of daily living, such as eating, using the toilet, bathing and dressing.

MAKING THE DIAGNOSIS

People who are concerned about memory loss —or experience two or more of the symptoms listed above for early-stage Alzheimer's—should be evaluated by a neurologist, psychiatrist and/or psychologist to rule out treatable conditions that can mimic Alzheimer's. These include nutritional deficiencies (especially those involving vitamin B-12 and folate)…metabolic or hormonal disorders caused by diseases of the liver, pancreas or kidneys…lung problems that reduce oxygen flow, such as emphysema or pneumonia…and alcohol abuse. Certain drugs, such as tranquilizers and antidepressants, also can cause Alzheimer's-like symptoms.

A brain autopsy is the only definitive way to diagnose Alzheimer's disease, but doctors can now make a "probable diagnosis" that is accurate about 90% of the time by using high-tech brain scans and behavior and memory tests.

A computed tomography (CT) or magnetic resonance imaging (MRI) scan is typically used to identify loss of brain tissue and/or decreased brain activity. If results are inconclusive, three-dimensional imaging techniques known as positron emission tomography (PET) or single photon emission computed tomography (SPECT) are used.

EARLY TREATMENT

If a person is diagnosed with Alzheimer's, medication is usually started right away to help slow the progression of the disease as well as curb or stabilize the symptoms. Alzheimer's drugs include *donepezil* (Aricept), *rivastigmine* (Exelon) and *galantamine* (Razadyne). Side effects, such as diarrhea, nausea, appetite loss and insomnia, usually are mild and often diminish within a few months. More recently, *memantine* (Namenda) has been approved for the treatment of moderate and severe Alzheimer's.

PREVENTION

Certain health habits are believed to help protect against Alzheimer's…

• **Control weight, blood pressure and cholesterol levels.** A recent study of nearly 1,500 people in Finland confirmed that risk factors for Alzheimer's and cardiovascular disease are strikingly similar. Researchers found that people who were obese and had high blood pressure and elevated cholesterol levels were six times more likely to develop Alzheimer's than people without those health problems.

• **Eat the right foods.** A nutritious diet that's rich in brightly colored, antioxidant-rich fruits (blueberries, plums, strawberries, oranges, cherries, raspberries and cranberries) and vegetables (kale, spinach, broccoli, brussels sprouts, red peppers, eggplant and onions) helps curb the damage that brain cells undergo in response to disease-promoting molecules known as free radicals.

•**Stay physically active.** Any kind of physical activity is valuable. But cardiovascular exercise, including walking, is particularly good for overall circulation—and blood circulation to the brain.

■ ■ ■ ■

Walk Away from Dementia

Abnormal walking may be an early sign of dementia. In a 21-year study of people over age 75, 43% of participants who had an abnormal gait, such as short-step shuffling or unsteady walking, developed non-Alzheimer's dementia over an average period of seven years. Only 26% of those with a normal gait developed dementia.

Theory: Vascular lesions, loss of nerve cells and other brain changes that alter movement patterns can also cause damage that may lead to dementia.

If you develop an abnormal gait: See your doctor for strategies to reduce your risk for dementia.

Joe Verghese, MD, associate professor of neurology, Albert Einstein College of Medicine, Bronx, NY.

New Hope for Parkinson's Disease

Stanley Fahn, MD, H. Houston Merritt professor of neurology and director, Center for Parkinson's Disease and Other Movement Disorders at Columbia University in New York City, is also scientific director of the Parkinson's Disease Foundation. Currently, Fahn serves as chair of the World Parkinson Congress Steering Committee.

Parkinson's disease, the second most common degenerative brain disease (after Alzheimer's), affects one million Americans and typically begins between ages 50 and 79. Characterized by tremor, slowness of movement, stiffness of the limbs and trunk, difficulty walking and lack of facial expression, the disease has no known cause.

There is no preventive or cure for Parkinson's disease, but research is now making advances in both areas.

Latest development: For the first time ever, renowned neuroscientists, doctors and other health-care workers joined Parkinson's patients and family members at the World Parkinson Congress in Washington, DC, to discuss innovative therapies that show promise in controlling symptoms as well as restoring motor function.

HOW PARKINSON'S DEVELOPS

Parkinson's disease occurs when nerve cells (neurons) that control movement start to die off for unknown reasons. The result is a shortage of the brain-signaling chemical *dopamine*, which triggers the muscles that allow fluid body movements, such as lifting an arm or walking.

The decline in dopamine levels leads to tremor, incoordination, slowed, reduced movement and other Parkinson's symptoms.

Research reported at the congress…

COENZYME Q10

New finding: A small, National Institutes of Health (NIH)–funded trial of coenzyme Q10 (a natural nutrient, also known as CoQ10, that is present in all human cells) found that taking 1,200 mg daily may slow disease progression in patients with early-stage Parkinson's.

More study is needed to confirm that CoQ10 does indeed slow the progression of the disease. Because the dosage of CoQ10 that was studied is only mildly effective, additional research also is needed to determine whether a higher dose (2,400 mg of CoQ10 daily) works better.

Implication: Parkinson's patients who are eager to try all possible therapies should ask their doctors about taking 1,200 mg daily of CoQ10. No side effects have been shown at this dosage.

DOPAMINE AGONISTS

Levodopa, also known as L-dopa (Larodopa), is the gold standard in treating Parkinson's. But many patients taking levodopa eventually develop uncontrolled flailing movements—a condition called dyskinesia—and motor fluctuations, in which medication levels in the brain drop and Parkinson's symptoms return.

Some doctors prefer to hold off prescribing levodopa in favor of a drug known as a *dopamine agonist*, which mimics the effects of dopamine in the brain and causes neurons to react as though sufficient amounts of dopamine were present. Dopamine agonists reduce Parkinson's-related disabilities—and work even better when combined with levodopa.

Dopamine agonists approved by the FDA are *bromocriptine* (Parlodel), *pergolide* (Permax), *pramipexole* (Mirapex), *ropinirole* (Requip) and *apomorphine* (Apokyn). Rotigotine, the only dopamine agonist offered in patch form, is available in Europe. The FDA approved the drug in 2007. The patch may be desirable for patients who have trouble swallowing or want the convenience of using a patch once a day.

New finding: In a two-year study of 186 early-stage Parkinson's patients, brain scans of those taking ropinirole or levodopa suggest that dopamine agonists may slow the decline of Parkinson's disease. Levodopa was found to worsen the disease, although patients' symptoms improved.

Implication: Because medications may interfere with brain scan results, more study is needed to confirm these findings. Ropinirole should be considered as treatment. Among the most likely candidates are younger patients who experience motor fluctuations and dyskinesia from levodopa.

Important: Ropinirole has been shown to cause side effects, such as sleepiness, nausea, hallucinations and, in rare cases, odd behavior such as compulsive shopping and gambling.

MINOCYCLINE AND CREATINE

In an NIH-sponsored clinical trial, 200 Parkinson's patients who did not yet require medication were randomly assigned to receive 200 mg daily of the antibiotic *minocycline*, 10 g daily of *creatine* (a nutritional supplement used to increase lean body mass and strength) or a placebo for 12 months.

Minocycline was studied due to its anti-inflammatory effects. Inflammation has been detected in the brains of Parkinson's patients. Creatine is an energy booster, and decreased energy utilization is a problem in Parkinson's disease. Minocycline and creatine were found to be potentially beneficial.

Implication: More study is needed before minocycline or creatine can be prescribed as a treatment for Parkinson's disease.

DEEP BRAIN STIMULATION

New finding: An advanced surgical technique known as deep brain stimulation (DBS) has been shown to provide significant benefit to moderate and advanced Parkinson's patients for up to four years after the onset of treatment.

With DBS, a surgeon implants an electrode inside the brain to stimulate specific brain sites that control movement. The electrode is connected to a palm-sized pacemaker that is implanted beneath the skin just below the clavicle. By stimulating key parts of the brain, the pacemaker helps alleviate motor symptoms, such as tremor.

Serious complications from DBS, such as stroke, occur in fewer than 2% of patients. More common side effects include speech impairment, personality and/or mood change, depression and a decline in cognitive function in older patients.

Implication: DBS is especially helpful for people who respond to levodopa but suffer from dyskinesia and wearing off of the drug. DBS is covered by Medicare and many other forms of health insurance.

Typical cost: $30,000 to $60,000.

■ ■ ■ ■

Parkinson's Treatment Warning

Mirapex (*pramipexole*)—which mimics the brain chemical *dopamine* and helps relieve the stiffness and tremors of Parkinson's disease—may trigger compulsive behaviors, such as gambling, overeating and promiscuity, in a small number of patients.

Self-defense: Notify your doctor if you exhibit any type of compulsive behavior while taking Mirapex. Ask him/her if a lower dosage would work for you…or if you can switch to another medication, perhaps another *dopamine agonist* such as Requip, Permax or Sinemet.

Maryellen Leann Dodd, MD, leader of a study of 11 patients receiving medication for Parkinson's disease, published in *Archives of Neurology*.

Extraordinary Device Uses Mind Power to Steer Wheelchairs

New Scientist.
New Scientist news release.

A system that "reads" the electrical activity of brain cells may someday allow severely disabled people to use their thoughts to steer a motorized wheelchair.

Unlike previous devices of this sort, this system does not require surgical implants. It utilizes a skullcap that is fitted with electrodes that monitor the electrical activity of a person's neurons.

THE TEST

Researchers have tested the device by having wearers try to control a steerable robot. It took two days of training for the volunteers to learn how to use their minds to control the robot.

In the robot tests, the electrodes in the skullcap collected information about the brain's electrical activity and fed that information into a computer.

Software analyzed the person's brain activity and, using a wireless link, passed on commands to the robot.

The users can select three different commands for the robot—turn left, turn right and move forward. The software can interpret the specific command by identifying telltale brain activity associated with that command.

The scientists are working to expand the ability of the system to identify more commands from the brain.

The system was created by Swiss and Spanish scientists. If they ultimately succeed in developing the technology, it would be the first mind-controlled system that is able to operate something as complicated as a motorized wheelchair.

OTHER APPLICATIONS

Mind-controlled devices—or "brain-computer interfaces"—are the stuff of science fiction and science fact. Richmond, Virginia–based East3, Ltd., for example, is developing "advanced feedback technology" to help children develop attention and concentration skills.

The company's Attention Trainer system relies on a wireless headset that sends information about its wearer's brain activity to software in video games that the child plays. If the game involves driving, the software can modulate the player's performance depending on what the sensors perceive as his/her attention level. In the process, the child can learn to improve his focus on the game and filter out extraneous information.

"The potential benefits of advanced feedback technology, whether increasing athletic performance, attention training or reducing stress, are truly amazing and are too important not to share," says John Berger, president and chief executive officer of East3.

Younger Look with No Face-Lift

David Colbert, MD, FAAD, founder of New York Dermatology Group, a private dermatological practice and research facility in New York City, is on the teaching staffs of several New York hospitals. His patients include many people in the film and television industry.

Not long ago, men and women who wanted a more youthful appearance assumed that they would have to have a face-lift. A face-lift smooths sagging skin by pulling it up and tightening it, but the surgery doesn't give the skin itself a younger look.

Cosmetic dermatologists, on the other hand, have a number of options to create younger-looking skin by getting rid of many lines and age spots. Some of these techniques make it possible to "plump" the face to reverse the sunken look that age can cause. These techniques are all nonsurgical and safe.

FILLERS

Fillers are materials that create volume to make up for the tablespoons of facial fat people lose as they age. The filler is injected directly into deep wrinkles to plump them. The materials are effective for many people over age 60, assuming that their skin is reasonably taut. Fillers can decrease facial lines and wrinkles, treat frown lines between the eyes and also plump hollow cheeks and thinning lips.

Although there are a number of fillers, Restylane is one of the most popular along with Perlane (a thicker form of Restylane), which is used for deeper wrinkles. Procedures take about an hour. The results are immediate and last for three to six months, after which the body absorbs the material. The procedure can be a bit uncomfortable, but the only side effects are a few hours of slight puffiness in the area and sometimes small, barely visible lumps that will disappear within a few days to a few weeks. Restylane is an FDA-approved, bioengineered, non-animal, stabilized hyaluronic acid, a substance almost identical to one naturally found in the body, making it safe to have repeat procedures.

I like to combine Restylane treatments with Botox. Although many people associate Botox skin injections with the "frozen" look sometimes seen on the faces of film stars, I prefer to use it more judiciously to relax muscles and give the face a de-stressed look.

Note: I do not recommend silicone injections to smooth the skin. Unlike other fillers, silicone is permanent, meaning that you are stuck with the result and your face may not age well around it.

Cost: Restylane and Perlane cost about $750 for the first syringe with some discount for additional syringes used during the same treatment.* Most people need more than one syringe. Botox costs $400 to $600 for a single area of the face treated, also with some discount for each additional area treated.

A patient's own fat is a good filler, as well, because it gives the face an especially soft, natural look. For such fat transfer, the person's own fat is taken from another area of the body, usually the thighs or buttocks. Because this requires a micro liposuction procedure, exceptionally thin people are not candidates. Once the fat is harvested, it is frozen and remains usable for the next three years.

Fat transfer requires several treatments over a few months. Although this procedure hasn't been in use long enough for us to give a definitive time frame for the results, we are finding it to be semipermanent. And unlike synthetic fillers, natural fat tends to build up and stay—eventually eliminating the need for more injections. You may experience some bruising and swelling

*All costs are approximate and are not covered by insurance.

for a week or so after the procedure. There is a slight risk of infection. While this is a more expensive treatment (total cost is around $5,000), it is cost-effective because it is so long lasting.

PEELS

Peels are available in gentle, medium and strong intensities. All peels chemically remove skin on the face and/or hands, which exposes the under layer—new skin that has been sheltered from the sun and other elements and so looks better. The difference among peels is how deeply they penetrate.

•**Gentle peels** affect only the top layer and diminish fine lines and fade age spots. Ideally, you would have gentle peels about once a month. Many spas offer these, but technicians there may not have adequate training and use weaker chemicals than dermatologists do. You can resume normal activities immediately after gentle peels.

•**Medium peels** go deeper and more effectively remove age spots and fine lines and improve skin color and texture. They require two or three sessions over three to five weeks. You can resume normal activities immediately afterward. Results last about a year.

•**Deep (or strong) peels.** The strongest peel—either a phenol or a TCA (*trichloroacetic acid*) peel—penetrates deep into the skin. It dramatically rids the face of moderately deep lines and age spots in just one treatment. Often, just specific wrinkled or discolored areas of the face are deep-peeled.

This peel is relatively painful because it destroys the upper layer of skin and results in temporary blisters and scabbing. There is some risk of infection, so meticulous post-procedure care is necessary. People with darker skin are not candidates because these peels lighten the skin and would create too much contrast with the neck. Also, anyone who has taken the drug Accutane in the last year is not a candidate because the skin would be too sensitive for a deep peel. The recovery process takes at least three weeks.

Cost: Gentle peels run from $200 to $400 each…medium peels, from $200 to $1,200, depending on how much of the face is peeled… phenol or TCA peels up to $4,000, also depending on the amount of skin treated.

LASER AND PHOTO REJUVENATION

Laser treatment tones skin and improves texture.

Photo rejuvenation uses pulsed light to rid the face and body of age spots and undesirable pigmentation.

Laser therapy also stimulates production of collagen, the natural substance in the skin that helps keep it plump and unlined. This stimulation continues several months after the treatment, giving ever-improving results. These treatments are painless and it takes from one to three treatments to achieve desirable results.

For skin that appears leathery and discolored by sun exposure, a topical photosensitizing solution called Levulan is applied an hour before the light-based therapy session begins. Levulan allows the light to go deeper into the skin, thereby enhancing the effect of the treatment. We have not found any risks or side effects for laser or photo rejuvenation treatments.

Cost: Laser and photo rejuvenation treatments run from $200 to $1,200 depending on how much skin is treated. Adding Levulan brings the cost to $500 to $1,500.

INTENSE REJUVENATION

The most intense form of skin rejuvenation comes from an infrared light machine called the Titan.

Skin rests on support collagen that keeps it firm, but this collagen collapses and loses elasticity with age. The heat from the Titan's infrared light contracts and tightens collagen deep in the dermis (the second of the three major layers of the skin) and at the same time stimulates collagen production. The result is an overall tightening of the skin on the face, jawline, arms and/or legs with an effect that lasts from one to three years.

One to three treatments are needed, depending on the patient's age, previous sun exposure and general skin condition. I prefer to combine mild photo rejuvenation for the outer layers of skin with the Titan to tighten up the underlayer of skin.

Cost: $2,000 to $3,000 per treatment. There are no currently known risks or side effects for Titan treatments.

How to Stop Memory Loss Before It's Too Late

Gary Small, MD, professor of psychiatry and biobehavioral sciences, director of the UCLA Center on Aging and one of the world's leading physician/scientists in the fields of memory and longevity. Dr. Small has authored more than 500 scientific papers and was named one of the world's top innovators in science and technology by *Scientific American*. He is author of *The Memory Bible*, *The Memory Prescription* and *The Longevity Bible* (all from Hyperion).

Nearly half of people age 50 or older complain of mild, age-related memory problems.

Good news: Studies show that 65% of aging's effects—including memory-erasing aging of the brain—are not caused by genes but by lifestyle. That means you can take action to prevent memory loss.

A brain-healthy diet, regular exercise, stress reduction and memory-boosting techniques are four effective ways to keep your memory sharp.

Recent finding: Combining these lifestyle strategies can strengthen your brain and improve your memory *immediately*. Scientists at the UCLA Center on Aging conducted a study of 17 people, average age 53, with mild memory complaints typical of middle age. Eight participants went on a 14-day program consisting of a brain-healthy diet, aerobic conditioning, relaxation exercises and memory training...nine did not.

Before and after the program, all 17 participants were tested for memory and mental ability. They also had brain positron emission tomography (PET) scans to observe blood flow in their brains. After the 14 days, those on the brain-healthy program showed an average 20% improvement on a test of mental ability, and their scans showed an average 5% greater efficiency in a brain area that regulates memory. The control group showed no significant changes.

Here's what to do to preserve and improve your memory, starting today...

DIET THAT FIGHTS MEMORY LOSS

Healthful dietary strategies can nourish the brain...

•**Limit your calorie intake.** A high body mass index (BMI) is a risk factor for Alzheimer's and other forms of dementia. Being overweight also increases risk for high blood pressure and diabetes, which can lead to stroke or death of brain tissue, as well as resulting memory loss or dementia.

•**Eat low glycemic index carbohydrates.** Fast-digesting carbohydrates, such as sugar and white flour, cause spikes in blood sugar levels, which can lead to diabetes—a disease that reduces circulation to the brain.

Recent finding: People who have "borderline diabetes"—slightly higher-than-normal blood sugar levels—have almost a 70% higher risk of developing Alzheimer's than those with normal levels, reported Swedish researchers at last summer's International Conference on Alzheimer's Disease and Related Disorders in Madrid, Spain.

The glycemic index (GI) is used to measure how quickly carbohydrates metabolize. Slow-digesting foods that are low on the GI include most whole grains, beans, legumes, fruits, vegetables, nuts, seeds and low-fat dairy products. Make these the bulk of your diet.

•**Keep blood sugar levels steady.** Eating three smallish meals and two snacks a day helps keep blood sugar levels even. For snacks, try mixtures of healthy carbohydrates and protein, such as raisins and almonds…or fresh fruit and low-fat cottage cheese.

•**Consume ample portions of omega-3 fatty acids, and reduce omega-6 fatty acids.** Omega-3 fatty acids—in fatty fish, such as salmon, mackerel, lake trout, herring and albacore tuna, and in walnuts, flaxseeds and their oils—keep brain-cell membranes soft and flexible.

Recent finding: Dutch researchers tested the mental sharpness of 210 healthy men between ages 70 and 89 over five years. The researchers reported in the *American Journal of Clinical Nutrition* that those who regularly ate fish rich in omega-3s had a slower decline in mental function than those who didn't eat fish.

Omega-6 fatty acids—found in margarine, mayonnaise, most processed foods and fried foods—may contribute to chronic brain inflammation.

•**Favor antioxidant-rich foods.** Oxidative stress—basically, internal rust from everyday cellular wear and tear—accelerates brain aging.

Antioxidants slow that process. Fruits and vegetables are high in antioxidants.

Best fruits: Berries of all kinds, cherries, kiwi, oranges, plums and red grapes, as well as prunes and raisins.

Best vegetables: Avocados, beets, broccoli, brussels sprouts, corn, eggplant, onions and red bell peppers.

Recent finding: In a study of 1,800 older people, published in the *American Journal of Medicine*, researchers at Vanderbilt University School of Medicine reported that drinking three or more four- to six-ounce servings per week of antioxidant-rich fruit or vegetable juice cuts the risk of Alzheimer's by 76%.

THE 10-MINUTE REMEDY

Exercise improves the flow of oxygen and nutrients to brain tissues and may promote growth of brain cells. Studies show that people who are active between the ages of 20 and 60 are three times less likely to develop Alzheimer's.

Recent finding: Walking for as little as 10 minutes a day reduces the risk of developing Alzheimer's by 32%, according to a study in the *Annals of Internal Medicine.*

Try out several forms of aerobic exercise—walking, swimming, biking and other activities that comfortably raise your heart rate—and choose those that you enjoy most and that you can fit into your day. Thirty minutes of aerobic exercise most days of the week is a good prescription for brain health.

SELF-HYPNOSIS

Laboratory research shows that animals subjected to continuing stress have fewer cells in the *hippocampus*, a brain structure involved in memory and learning. In human studies, even just a few days of exposure to high levels of stress decreases memory performance.

Ways to beat stress include getting enough sleep and not having too much to do. *Also, practice stress-reduction techniques, such as the following self-hypnosis exercise…*

Sit in a comfortable position…take three long, deep breaths…and try to relax your muscles. Focus your attention on a spot on the wall or on a piece of furniture. Try to clear your mind of any thoughts. Concentrate on your focus spot, and breathe slowly. Repeatedly tell yourself that the longer you pay full attention to the spot, the deeper your sense of relaxation will be. Do this for five minutes. Build up to 10-minute sessions twice a day.

Is Alzheimer's the New Diabetes?

Suzanne de la Monte, MD, MPH, professor of pathology and medicine, Warren Alpert Medical School at Brown University and neuropathologist at Rhode Island Hospital, both in Providence, RI.

N ew research into the causes of Alzheimer's disease is showing an intriguing new direction in formal treatment—one that might lead to successful treatment in the early stages of the disease. Two studies from The Warren Alpert Medical School at Brown University identified diminished insulin availability as well as insulin resistance in the brain as a possible trigger for the brain deterioration, loss of cognitive function and buildup of plaques (protein fragments between brain neurons) and tangles (twisted fibers inside brain cells) that characterize Alzheimer's.

"We've found Alzheimer's to be a form of diabetes," says Suzanne de la Monte, MD, MPH, senior researcher on the study.

CAUSE AND EFFECT

In one study, researchers depleted insulin and at the same time produced insulin resistance in the brains of rats by injecting *Streptozotocin* (or STZ), a compound known to destroy insulin-producing cells in the pancreas. The result was overall brain deterioration in the rats.

Even more exciting: In a subsequent study using the same rats—who now exhibited symptoms resembling Alzheimer's—researchers then reversed the insulin resistance in their brains by administering three classes of drugs called PPAR (peroxisome-proliferator activated receptor) agonists. (The agonists are drugs but the receptors are normally present in the brain.)

Following this treatment, the Alzheimer's-like brain abnormalities and degeneration that the rats had displayed were either reduced or nearly disappeared. Of the three classes of agonists used, one—PPAR delta—had the most benefit in preserving brain tissues and improving learning memory. PPAR alpha was less effective. Another PPAR agonist—PPAR gamma—that is already being prescribed as a treatment in type 2 diabetes to modulate insulin response was least effective. This research has yet to be applied to humans, noted Dr. de la Monte. But she is definitely thinking ahead.

"We've seen the incidence of both type 2 diabetes and Alzheimer's disease grow in epidemic proportions, and researchers now recognize both the overlap of the two conditions and the increased risk for developing Alzheimer's in patients with type 2 diabetes." But while Dr. de la Monte refers to this as a separate process, a "type 3" diabetes or "diabetes of the brain," Andrew L. Rubman, ND, observes that the underlying collapse of the regulatory systems that are behind both type 1 and type 2 diabetes is also present in "brain diabetes."

CAN WE PREVENT ALZHEIMER'S?

Obviously, a great deal of research needs to be done before these findings lead to a solid connection between Alzheimer's and diabetes, and even more until possible treatment is available. But, Dr. de la Monte shared her thoughts on how this information might be useful in the short term. "When we think about type 2 diabetes and how much it is mediated by lifestyle and environmental factors—*and* that we know the same is true for insulin resistance in the liver—you can't help but wonder to what extent this is also true for insulin resistance in the brain, which our research showed often results in Alzheimer's symptoms."

And, she concluded, when you start thinking like that, the next question is—"What are the specific lifestyle features that contribute to this? *Now*, you're talking about prevention, which almost certainly would involve lifestyle choices."

8

Brain Boosters

A Nobel Prize Winner Unravels Mysteries Of the Brain

The human brain, which weighs about three pounds and is composed of approximately 100 billion nerve cells (neurons), is the most complex organ in the body. The brain not only controls our heart rate, breathing, blood pressure and body temperature, but also allows us to walk and talk as well as see, hear, smell, think, remember and create.

Scientists have long sought to understand the inner workings of the human brain—and, more specifically, how we process learning and memory. Among the important discoveries in this field are those of Eric R. Kandel, MD, a winner of the Nobel Prize for his lifelong research into the biological basis of learning and memory.

Originally trained as a psychiatrist at New York University School of Medicine and Harvard Medical School, Dr. Kandel has written many scientific papers on brain function and is coauthor of *Principles of Neural Science*, generally considered to be the standard textbook in the field.

We interviewed Dr. Kandel to learn more about his research and its implications for a healthier brain and a happier life...

•**What is the essence of the research for which you were awarded the Nobel Prize?** I was recognized for my work on the molecular biology of learning and memory. Throughout my career, I have been extremely interested in the biology of learning.

I have been curious to know: What changes in the brain as we learn? And, once something is learned, how is that information retained in the brain?

Eric R. Kandel, MD, co-winner of the 2000 Nobel Prize for Physiology or Medicine. Dr. Kandel is professor of physiology and cell biophysics, psychiatry, biochemistry and molecular biophysics as well as senior investigator, Howard Hughes Medical Institute, and director of the Kavli Institute for Brain Sciences at the Center for Neurobiology and Behavior, all at Columbia University in New York City. He is the author of seven books, including *In Search of Memory: The Emergence of a New Science of Mind.* W.W. Norton.

Our most basic finding was that the physical structure of the brain actually changes through the process of learning—whether it's learning to use a computer or speak a foreign language.

•**What does that finding mean in terms of memory in humans?** Over the past 50 years, my colleagues and I have delineated the biological—the molecular and cellular—basis of both short- and long-term memory in a simple experimental system, the marine snail aplysia.

Short-term memory (a memory that lasts for a few minutes) is controlled by a *functional change* in the brain—a change in the strength of communication from one nerve cell to another. This often is mediated by an intracellular "signaling" molecule, such as *cyclic adenosine monophosphate* (cAMP), that helps relay information from the synapse of a nerve cell to its nucleus.

Long-term memory (a stored memory that lasts days or even a lifetime) involves an *anatomical change*, with the growth and strengthening of synapses (connections between nerve cells). In this case, cAMP enters the nucleus of the nerve cell and stimulates memory-enhancer genes, which in turn activate the growth of these new connections. Short-term memory commonly is converted to long-term memory by repetition.

•**What are some of the implications of this research?** Based on these findings, several colleagues and I started the company Memory Pharmaceuticals in 1996 to develop drugs to treat memory loss. The company has created several families of compounds. One is for *benign senescent forgetfulness*—non-Alzheimer's age-related memory loss.

Age-related memory loss can begin in a person's 40s and worsen with time, and it affects the ability to convert short-term memory into long-term memory. For example, this could be remembering the next morning the name of a person you met at a dinner party the evening before. Another family of compounds is intended to reverse the early phases of Alzheimer's disease.

Currently, the compounds are being tested in the laboratory—some of them improve a rat's memory of a new task for months. Another few years of research and testing might lead to medications for humans that were scarcely imaginable just a few years ago.

•**What do these discoveries about short- and long-term memory tell us about human capability?** Obviously, there is a genetic predisposition for many capabilities, but superimposed upon that is a huge capability to modify predispositions through learning.

This capability allows you to change the very architecture of your brain. Since learning leads to anatomical changes, every single brain is different from every other brain—by virtue of learning.

•**What's the best way to keep one's brain healthy?** There are factors that are important for long-term mental functioning, such as not being overweight and not being physically inactive, both of which reduce blood flow to the brain.

It is also important to see life as an adventure—to see oneself not in a static state, but in a process of continual growth and a state of expanding knowledge. Otherwise, one can become intellectually lazy.

But most of all, you should stay intellectually active, through learning new things and facing new mental challenges, whether it is solving a crossword puzzle, or learning a new language.

Interacting with young people also is intellectually invigorating—they challenge your established thinking and help you think in new, fresh ways.

•**Dr. Kandel, you are one of the world's most successful scientists. What lessons have you learned that could be applied to any individual's professional life?** Three lessons have been most important to me throughout my career.

First, learn to trust your own judgment. When you reach a certain intellectual maturity—when you have developed a way of thinking that has not proven at least moderately effective—trust your instincts for new ideas.

I have often gone in directions that I felt were interesting but initially seemed to be quite "fuzzy"—yet they have turned out to be quite fruitful in the long run.

For example, I started my work on memory by studying marine snails, which seemed a wild idea to some scientists. However, I thought that the technical advantages of studying a particular species of snail were extraordinary, in part, because some of this snail's brain cells are the largest in the animal kingdom. That proved to be a sound judgment.

Second, don't be afraid to change directions, even if it involves learning a new discipline. At almost every phase of your life, you're fully capable of developing new intellectual skills. Don't be frightened of something because you're inexperienced. With time and effort, there's no reason why you can't master a new discipline.

Lastly, be willing to be bold. Within reason, take chances intellectually. If you tackle important problems in original ways—even if you fail—that's preferable to doing something everyone else can do as well as you can.

• **What will science reveal about the mind in the 21st century?** In the next 50 years, we will understand, through improvement in brain imaging and improvements in the use of animal models, many details of mental function. There will be a new "science of mind" that will revolutionize how we think about ourselves and our interactions with others.

We will begin to comprehend in biological terms the brain-based biology of behavior, social cognition, decision-making in business, our appreciation of the arts and much more.

We also will develop effective approaches, such as new medications, to treat brain diseases, including age-related memory loss, Alzheimer's disease and mental illnesses such as depression and schizophrenia.

The biology of mind—the science of mind—will enlighten all aspects of mental life, for the betterment of individuals and all of humankind.

Surprising Ways to Fight Fatigue! Boost Mood! Prevent Stroke! More

Pierce J. Howard, PhD, a leading cognitive science researcher and cofounder and director of research at the Center for Applied Cognitive Studies in Charlotte, NC, is adjunct professor of organizational psychology at University of North Carolina, Chapel Hill, and author of *The Owner's Manual for the Brain*. Bard.

T hough many of the brain's inner workings remain a mystery, scientists make new discoveries about this powerful organ almost weekly. Recent brain research has revealed ways to significantly improve memory and mental ability along with practical ways to prevent stroke and other brain diseases, including Alzheimer's.

Highlights...

BOOST PERFORMANCE WITH STRESS

Scientists used to view stress as a detriment to mental performance. They advised people who were trying to improve learning and memory skills to minimize stress—with regular meditation, yoga, etc.

New finding: People learn more efficiently when they maintain an optimal level of stress. A principle called the Yerkes-Dodson Law has shown that a certain amount of stress (arousal) motivates people to try harder.

Balance is the key. People who experience very little stress—when taking a test or writing a paper, for example—tend to make errors of *omission*, such as forgetting to complete all the answers. People who experience too much stress make errors of *commission*, such as hitting the wrong computer keys.

What to do: If you find you're making more errors than usual in completing a task, you're probably experiencing too much stress. If you're bored, your stress levels are too low. For optimal mental performance, it is best to be in between these two extremes.

How to achieve stress balance: Too much stress is typically caused by one of two factors—having too few personal resources in a demanding situation or feeling that you have no options.

In the first case, increase your resources (practice, learn new skills, find helpers) or decrease the demands made on you (change to a less demanding task, simplify the task in some way).

In the second case, talk with your associates or with a counselor or doctor to identify ways to gain more control over the situation.

Too little stress is caused by having too many resources in a situation that is not very demanding—you are overqualified for the task at hand. Address this by handicapping or otherwise limiting yourself.

Example: When my daughter was younger and I played tennis with her, I would hit to her singles court, while she hit to my doubles lanes—so the tennis became more interesting for me. Or you can increase the level of difficulty or complexity of what you are doing. For example, if you are bored writing something, try doing it without using the verb "to be."

REDUCE STROKE RISK WITH CHOCOLATE

People who consume moderate amounts of chocolate have better brain circulation and can reduce their risk of stroke. Cocoa beans—the main ingredient in chocolate—contain natural antioxidants called cocoa flavonoids. The flavonoids in chocolate are more powerful than vitamin C at limiting fatty deposits (plaque) in arteries in the brain and heart. Buildups of plaque can impair mental performance and are the main cause of strokes.

Chemical compounds in chocolate also increase the levels of *nitric oxide,* a critical compound in the blood that relaxes the inner walls of blood vessels and promotes better blood flow and lower blood pressure. A study of 470 healthy men in the Netherlands found that those who ate the most cocoa beans—in the form of chocolate bars, pudding, hot cocoa, etc.—had lower blood pressure and half the risk of dying during the study period than those who ate the least.

What to do: Have one to two cups of cocoa or two small squares of a bar of chocolate daily. The darker the chocolate, the better. According to the ORAC scale—a measure of the antioxidant levels in foods—dark chocolate has double the amount of antioxidants of milk chocolate.

FIGHT AFTERNOON FATIGUE

Nearly everyone gets sleepy after lunch. You can prevent this afternoon slump by eating protein first during lunch, then carbohydrates. The protein triggers an energy-promoting amino acid in the brain.

Foods that are high in complex carbohydrates, such as whole-grain bread, fruits and vegetables, are good for you, but they contain an abundance of the amino acid *L-tryptophan*, which promotes relaxation and sleepiness. High-protein foods, such as meats and fish, contain *L-tyrosine*, which makes you more alert and less likely to feel tired.

Your energy level after lunch will depend on which of these amino acids reaches your brain first.

What to do: Start your meal with a bite or two of protein. This allows the L-tyrosine to reach the brain before the L-tryptophan. But don't just eat protein—carbohydrates are your body's main source of fuel.

GET HAPPY WITH OMEGA-3s

In countries such as Norway and Japan, where people eat the most fish—the best source of omega-3 fatty acids—the incidence of depression and suicide is much lower than in countries where people eat less. Omega-3s can help prevent and treat a variety of disorders, including bipolar disorder and attention deficit hyperactivity disorder (ADHD).

Unfortunately, Americans get excess amounts of another fatty acid group, the omega-6s, found mainly in meats, cooking oils and soybeans. In the last century, the ratio of omega-6s to omega-3s has soared, increasing the risk of mood disorders, including depression.

What to do: Eat three to four fish servings weekly to get more omega-3s. (Avoid fish high in mercury, such as shark, swordfish, tilefish and king mackerel, as well as large tuna, such as albacore, yellowfin, bigeye and bluefin.) Or you can eat nuts if you prefer. Ten to 15 walnut halves or 15 to 20 pecan halves provide the recommended daily amount of omega-3s.

REST—BUT DON'T NAP

The inventor Thomas Edison was famous for getting by on only two to four hours of sleep a night. When he was working on a particularly difficult problem, he would rest for five to 10 minutes. In the brief period between wakefulness and sleep, he often would experience an "A-ha!" moment and find the solution to his problem.

Scientists have found that when the brain goes into an "alpha state"—characterized by brain waves that are slower than the beta waves of wakefulness—people often develop insights, along with more focus and energy.

What to do: Shut your eyes and let your mind relax for five to 10 minutes. Resting in this fashion is not sleeping. People who slip into true sleep are groggy and less alert when they wake up.

PREVENT ALZHEIMER'S WITH "IDEA DENSITY"

The important Nun Study funded by the National Institute of Aging—a long-term study of 678 members of the School Sisters of Notre Dame, ages 75 to 106—revealed that cloistered nuns with brain changes characteristic of Alzheimer's disease didn't necessarily have cognitive impairments. Why do some people with these brain changes (apparent during autopsies) develop Alzheimer's, while others do not?

When researchers analyzed short biographies that the nuns had written upon taking their vows decades earlier, they found that those with a high "idea density" (many thoughts woven into a small number of words)—a marker of educational level and vocabulary—were less likely to develop Alzheimer's symptoms later in life, even when their brains showed signs of the disease.

The brain continues to form neurons and connections between neurons throughout life. People who are mentally active form the most connections and develop brain reserves that can slow the onset of Alzheimer's symptoms.

What to do: Stay mentally engaged. Take classes at a university or community college. Read challenging books and periodicals. Keep a diary or do crossword puzzles. Learn a new language.

TAKE LEARNING BREAKS

You'll learn most efficiently when you focus on one thing at a time, then take a break before moving on to new material.

Example: Someone learning a new golf swing needs about six hours for the new neural pathways to become established. If he/she tries to learn a second swing within that six-hour window, the new information will crowd out the previous learning.

What to do: If you're in school, studying for a professional exam or just trying to learn a new skill, save the beginning of each day for major new learning. Use the rest of the day for practice and repetition.

Suppose you're learning a new language, such as Spanish. You might spend the morning memorizing verbs with "–ir" endings. Practice this during the day or practice material learned on previous days, but don't introduce verbs with "–er" endings until the next day.

Stuck in the Same Old Routine? Don't Worry, It's Good for You!

Barbara Fiese, PhD, chair, department of psychology, Syracuse University, Syracuse, NY.

Irene Goldenberg, family therapist, University of California, Los Angeles.

Journal of Family Psychology.

Many Americans regularly engage in routines and rituals, and these practices improve their mental and physical health and sense of belonging, according to an analysis of 50 years of research.

Routine events, such as dinners together as a family, provide comfort simply by being events that people can count on, says study author Barbara Fiese, chair, department of psychology at Syracuse University in New York.

Children flourish when they can predict things in their life, such as family dinners or regular bedtimes, the study found. "Even a short period of time has a positive effect. It's related to physical health in infants and children, and academic performance in elementary [school] children," Fiese says.

Rituals, on the other hand, are symbolic practices people perform that help define who they are. The meaningful, symbolic parts of rituals seem to help emotional development and satisfaction with family relationships. When rituals are continued during times of stress, such as a death or divorce, they lessen the negative impact.

"It seems that at points of transition, such as [entering] school or [getting] married, rituals can increase one's sense of security," she says.

Irene Goldenberg, a family therapist at the University of California at Los Angeles, says that therapists routinely advise people to create rituals. "They represent an order and a sense of logic. They make the family more of a unit and tend to make it clear what the values are in the family."

To learn more about the importance of rituals to family life, visit ChildCareAware at *http://childcareaware.org* or read more from the Kansas State University Agricultural Experiment Station and Cooperative Extension Service at *www.oznet.ksu.edu.*

Dr. Bernie Siegel's Happiness Boosters

Bernie S. Siegel, MD, retired surgeon and well-known proponent of alternative approaches that heal the body, mind and soul, is author of several books, including *101 Exercises for the Soul: A Divine Workout Plan for Body, Mind, and Spirit* (New World Library) and the best-seller *Love, Medicine & Miracles* (HarperCollins).

In everyday life, it's easy to lose touch with your soul. I define "soul" as the authentic self that lies deep within you.

Your soul needs regular attention because it enables you to live with enthusiasm, vigor and joy. It also increases your ability to overcome difficulties that you encounter in your life. *Here's how to strengthen your soul...*

•**Access your creative side.** Take up painting, writing, sculpting or other creative endeavors. Expressing your creativity distracts you from emotional and physical pain. It also helps bring to the surface what is trapped within you so that you are able to heal emotionally and physically.

Example: More than 25 years ago, when I painted a self-portrait, I painted my face with a surgical mask. That helped me to realize that I was covering up my emotions even in the painting. Doctors aren't trained to deal with loss and pain—so we bury it. I knew I needed to uncover my feelings and express them.

•**Define your fears.** By specifically defining your fears, you can come up with solutions so you don't feel so powerless and frightened by them.

Example: If you're afraid of losing your job, dig deeper to find what that really means. Perhaps you fear that you'll end up homeless. If so, you can take steps to secure your home, such as setting aside enough savings to cover your mortgage for a year.

•**Get rid of the clutter in your life.** Release some of the negativity of the past, and make room for emotional growth by periodically cleaning your environment and letting go of belongings.

•**Get regular massages.** Being touched is therapeutic for your body and soul because it releases muscle tension, enhances the immune system and suppresses pain. Find a massage therapist, or exchange massages with your partner. Touch can be a tool to enhance your relationship.

•**Focus on the joyful.** All too often, we remember painful experiences—the annoying client, the traffic jam—rather than the happy moments. Carry a small journal to record happy moments in your life. Share funny stories at dinner. Watch funny movies and listen to comedy CDs while driving. My favorite is Mel Brooks's *2000 Year Old Man*.

Carry your baby picture in your wallet. Most likely, it will elicit feelings of joy when you look at it. Remind yourself that even though you're all grown up, there's still a happy, lovable child inside.

•**Find your chocolate—and eat it, too.** Chocolate, particularly the dark variety, stimulates the release of natural endorphins that boost mood. If you don't like chocolate, find "your chocolate"—whatever makes you feel good when you're feeling low. It could be music, gardening, reading or talking with a loved one.

Use Your Memories to Improve Your Life

Jefferson Singer, PhD, clinical psychologist in private practice in Waterford, CT, and professor of psychology at Connecticut College, New London, is author of *Memories That Matter: How to Use Self-Defining Memories to Understand & Change Your Life*. New Harbinger.

Memories are more than just images from our past. They shape how we think of ourselves in the present and affect the direction our lives will take in the future. If you carry around numerous memories of relationships that ended poorly, you might think of yourself as unlovable. If your strongest memories are of scholastic and career successes, you probably consider yourself smart. True or not, these memory-inspired self-evaluations affect your behavior and your happiness.

MEMORIES THAT MATTER

The most powerful remembrances —what I call "self-defining memories"—come back again and again and pack an emotional punch each time. They relate in some way to issues that we're still trying to resolve or goals that we still hope to accomplish.

Example: Ray, a businessman, frequently recalls a memory from his childhood of his father leaning over his shoulder criticizing his homework. This memory is particularly likely to replay when Ray's boss offers him feedback on his job performance.

If we learn to use such self-defining memories to address shortcomings and pursue goals, negative memories lose power and we feel better about ourselves.

Example: When I was a child, it was important to me that I fit in with the crowd. For years, I relived a memory of the time some boys told me I couldn't be in their club. As an adult, one of my goals was to become more confident of my own worth. I realized I had succeeded when this childhood memory became less frequent and was no longer emotional for me when it did recur. The childhood rejection had lost its power to define me.

MAKING CHANGES

Here's how to use our memories to understand and improve our lives...

•**Reevaluate the results.** Caroline lived for years with a recurring memory of the day in divorce court when her marriage ended. The memory brought feelings of shame and failure. When I encouraged Caroline to search for something positive that came from that day, she realized it was then that she gained her freedom from a bad relationship. Now the same recurring memory brings Caroline a sense of liberation.

•**Role-play new endings.** An older couple told me that they hadn't felt close to each other in years. The memory of one particular incident haunted them both—the wife had reached for her husband's hand during an argument, but he had pulled away.

I positioned the couple just as they had been seated during that argument years before and asked them to replay the fight. Only this time, I told them to argue from each other's perspective. The reversed roles changed their take on the situation, and when the wife reached out her hand, her husband didn't pull away. They both still remember that old argument, but now

the memory concludes with the more upbeat ending we created in therapy.

•**Surround yourself with objects and images that inspire positive memories.** If the sight of a painting given to you by an ex-wife reminds you of the failed marriage, replace it with a framed copy of an award you won, so you'll instead flash back to that success.

If the picture on your desk of your family at the Grand Canyon brings back negative memories of the bickering on that vacation, select another family photo.

I know one woman who hung pictures of her schnauzer around her home because she had only positive memories of the pet.

•**Don't focus on negative memories.** Despite what you might believe, there's little evidence that avoiding bad memories has any downside. Some people find it helpful to wear a rubber band around their wrist to snap when they catch themselves reliving a negative memory—the sharp sensation can yank the mind off the negative path.

Write down a list of positive memories you can turn to when you need a shot of confidence or a way to block out the negative. Specific memories are better than general ones—recall the time that you won a Little League game with a big hit, not just how much you enjoyed playing baseball as a child.

■ ■ ■ ■

Live Longer by Meditating

Transcendental meditation (TM), a technique that produces a state of "restful alertness," has been shown to reduce stress levels and lower blood pressure. People with hypertension (average age 72) who regularly practiced TM for 20 minutes twice daily were 30% less likely to die from heart disease over an 18-year period than those who did not practice TM.

Theory: TM lowers levels of adrenaline and cortisol, stress-related hormones, in the body.

Helpful: Practice TM for 20 minutes twice daily.

Robert H. Schneider, MD, director, Institute for Natural Medicine and Prevention, Maharashi University of Management, Fairfield, IA.

▪▪▪▪
Treating Depression

Depression in the elderly is best controlled by antidepressants. Over a two-year period, regular use of *paroxetine* (Paxil) was more effective at preventing a recurrence than psychotherapy. Doctors may want to keep depressed patients over age 70 on medication indefinitely—just as they would patients with diabetes or hypertension.

Also important: A depression care manager—a nurse, social worker or psychologist—to make sure the condition is kept under control.

Charles F. Reynolds III, MD, psychiatrist and professor of psychiatry, neurology and neuroscience at University of Pittsburgh School of Medicine and leader of the study, published in *The New England Journal of Medicine.*

Antidepressants Can— And Do—Save Lives

Julio Licinio, MD, professor of psychiatry and medicine, David Geffen School of Medicine, University of California at Los Angeles.

David Fassler, MD, child and adolescent psychiatrist; clinical professor of psychiatry, University of Vermont, Burlington; and spokesman, American Psychiatric Association.

ParentsMedGuide.org.

Nature Reviews: Drug Discovery.

Despite the ongoing controversy over the potential increase in suicide among children who take antidepressants, the lifesaving benefits of medications such as Paxil, Prozac and Zoloft far outweigh their risks, according to the results of a new analysis.

THE BIG PICTURE

A comprehensive review of decades of data from the US and Europe shows that there is a close correlation between dramatic declines in suicide rates and the introduction of the *selective serotonin reuptake inhibitor* (SSRI) family of antidepressants into the marketplace.

"If these drugs were really causing suicide, the reverse should be happening," according to study author Dr. Julio Licinio, a professor of

psychiatry and medicine at the David Geffen School of Medicine at the University of California at Los Angeles.

"It's sometimes hard to see the big picture, but I think the overall effect [of SSRIs] is positive," Licinio adds.

THE STUDY

In their study, Licinio and his colleagues pored over statistics on depression and suicide, stretching back to the 1960s.

The data included US suicide rates, as well as studies reporting on the percentage of suicide victims that were found with traces of antidepressants in their bloodstream.

"To my surprise, I found that the suicide rate goes up in a straight line, year by year, from the 1960s on—right up until 1988, which is exactly the year Prozac was introduced," Licinio notes. "From then on, it goes down substantially."

"Also, we find antidepressants in the blood of less than 20% of people who died of suicide," he says. Conversely, 80% of suicide victims had no blood history of antidepressant use, suggesting that either antidepressants were not prescribed or the victims were not taking what was prescribed. Therefore, the vast majority of victims might have killed themselves because of untreated depression.

THE REACTION

Dr. David Fassler, a child and adolescent psychiatrist and spokesman for the American Psychiatric Association, says these findings "support the growing consensus that, when used appropriately, the benefits of these medications far outweigh the potential risks."

Fassler believes there's now "a real concern in the medical community that the public is getting confused by contradictory media reports [on this issue]. As a result, people may be less likely to get treatment. That would be a real tragedy, because the good news is that we can help most people who suffer from psychiatric disorders, including depression."

Isolated reports of teens committing or attempting suicide while taking antidepressants sparked Congressional debate and widespread media attention.

In 2004, a special US Food and Drug Administration (FDA) panel ordered that a "black box" warning be placed on all SSRI packaging, alerting doctors, parents and young users to the potential risk.

However, has fear pushed the pendulum too far away from a balanced assessment of these medications?

RECONSIDERATION

Gail Griffiths, a member of the FDA panel who voted "yes" to the black box warning, says she would vote differently now.

"If I would have known how sharply prescription rates were falling, I would not have voted in favor of the black box warning," says Griffiths, a parent whose son attempted suicide while on antidepressants.

"I hoped the FDA could help to inform parents, but it seems many parents have simply become fearful of antidepressants, which are so often the life jacket preventing us from being sucked under by depression's powerful undertow," she adds.

CLOSE MONITORING NEEDED

Any reaffirmation of the benefits of SSRIs should not obscure the fact that a minority of users—especially young people—may experience some increase in suicide risk while on these medications. That's mainly due to the way the drugs work, boosting energy before they ease feelings of gloom, says Licinio.

"Many people who are depressed think, 'Oh, the world would be better off without me.' But they simply lack the energy to act upon that feeling," he says. "At the beginning [of SSRI use], they begin to get that energy, however."

Licinio says that initial period is when parents and doctors should monitor young users most closely, although he stresses that monitoring must continue as long as the therapy goes on.

"Of course, suicide is always tragic on an individual level, but I look upon these drugs as I would a vaccine—another intervention that saves lot of lives," Licinio says. "We should be alert here not to throw the baby out with the bathwater."

Parents can get a free guide on the use of medication in treating childhood and adolescent depression at the ParentsMedGuide Web site, *www.parentsmedguide.org*.

■ ■ ■ ■

Getting a Lift

Botox may play a role in relieving depression. Two months after receiving Botox injections in their foreheads, nine out of 10 women previously diagnosed with depression were no longer depressed.

Theory: Injections prevented the patients from frowning. Researchers believe that there may be direct feedback between the facial frown muscles and the depression center of the brain.

Eric Finzi, MD, PhD, dermatologic surgeon and president, Chevy Chase Cosmetic Center, Chevy Chase, MD (*www.chevychasecosmeticcenter.com*), and lead author of a study of depressed patients, published in *Dermatologic Surgery*.

Bored? Restless? Can't Get Organized?

Edward M. Hallowell, MD, director, Hallowell Center, Sudbury, MA and author of many books including *Driven to Distraction*. Touchstone.

Up to 10 million American adults have attention deficit disorder (ADD), but only approximately 10% know it. *Here are some of the myths about adult ADD that I want to dispel...*

Myth #1: People with ADD can't sit still or focus properly.

The Diagnostic and Statistical Manual of Mental Disorders, the "bible" of psychiatrists, refers to attention deficit hyperactivity disorder. The term isn't entirely accurate because hyperactivity (having trouble sitting through movies, for example, or frequently tapping your fingers or feet) may or may not be present.

The other important symptoms of ADD are *inattention* and *impulsivity*.

Examples of inattention include reading a book and spacing out or staring at someone's lips while they're talking to you but not taking in what they're saying.

Examples of impulsivity include taking unnecessary risks or having trouble waiting in line. Most adults suffer from only one or two of the three primary symptoms—hyperactivity, inattention and impulsivity.

Even the term *attention deficit* is misleading. Most people with ADD can focus intensely when necessary.

Myth #2: ADD is a learning disability.

Most adults who have ADD have normal IQs. They read and absorb new information as well as people who don't have the disorder—though they may have to make adjustments for their ADD symptoms.

Example: High-energy adults with ADD often avoid careers that are detail-oriented, such as accounting, bookkeeping and secretarial work. They like to work on multiple projects at the same time to stave off boredom. These individuals create systems (calendars, notes, etc.) to stay organized.

Myth #3: Poor parenting causes ADD.

This is totally false. People with ADD have a physical problem that they're born with, but it is often not diagnosed until adulthood. The exact cause still isn't known, but ADD is believed to be primarily due to genetics.

Most people with ADD have at least one relative with the disorder. Adults whose mothers smoked cigarettes, took illegal drugs or drank alcohol during pregnancy are at an increased risk for ADD, according to recent research. People who have been exposed to environmental toxins, such as dioxins and polychlorinated biphenyls (PCBs), are also at an increased risk.

Many people with ADD have more challenging careers than those without it.

Consider David Neeleman, chairman of the board and founder of JetBlue Airways. He has found ways to compensate for his ADD. For example, he takes a physical approach to his job, frequently going out onto the tarmac and checking up on his airplanes because he gets bored sitting in the office. An assistant helps keep his schedule.

People who have ADD also tend to be creative, intuitive and highly energetic. In my own case, I have three kids, have written 11 books and do 60 lectures a year. I don't think I would have the energy for all that if I didn't have ADD.

Myth #4: ADD cannot be diagnosed with any degree of accuracy.

There isn't a single test for ADD, any more than there's a single test for anxiety or depression. But it can be diagnosed objectively by a psychiatrist, psychologist or neurologist.

First, a careful medical history is essential for an accurate diagnosis. Before ruling out ADD, doctors also should discuss the patient's symptoms with a family member. People with ADD are poor self-observers. A second point of view often reveals things that patients overlook.

To see if the patient exhibits the criteria representative of ADD, psychiatrists usually use a checklist—a sense of not meeting goals, trouble getting organized, frequent procrastination, etc.

A relatively new test known as *quantitative electroencephalography* (QEEG), which provides physical data by looking for slow brain waves in the frontal lobes, also should be administered. This test is 90% accurate in diagnosing ADD.

Myth #5: Stimulant drugs are really the only course of treatment.

Many patients do get better when they take stimulant drugs, such as *methylphenidate* (Ritalin) and *dextroamphetamine* (Dexedrine).

These drugs don't cure ADD, but they reduce many of the symptoms, such as hyperactivity, inattention and impulsivity.

The medications also stimulate the inhibitor neurons, which stop a great deal of the incoming and outgoing stimuli, allowing the patient to be more focused.

A new drug, *atomoxetine* (Strattera), is the first nonstimulant medication approved by the US Food and Drug Administration (FDA) for adults with ADD. It works differently but just as effectively as stimulants, promoting higher brain levels of *norepinephrine*, a neurochemical that helps people focus and stay calm.

Nondrug treatments also are essential. *All ADD sufferers should...*

•**Exercise for at least 20 minutes every day.** Any exercise that you enjoy, that is convenient for you and can be added to your daily routine, will be beneficial. Physical activity increases brain levels of the neurotransmitter dopamine and helps people who have ADD release nervous energy.

•**Get a lifestyle coach.** Many psychiatrists refer ADD patients to professionals who are trained to help them make lifestyle adjustments. A coach will come to your home and suggest ways to improve everything from your work area and habits to your family dynamics.

•**Talk to a psychotherapist.** A directed, focused regimen of psychotherapy can be helpful in dealing with feelings that are often experienced by adults with ADD, such as low self-esteem and self-doubt.

To find a therapist, contact the Attention Deficit Disorder Association at 856-439-9099 or *www.add.org.*

New Relief for Anxiety Sufferers!

Gregory J. Quirk, PhD, professor of psychiatry, University of Puerto Rico School of Medicine San Juan, Puerto Rico.

James L. Olds, PhD, director, Krasnow Institute for Advanced Study, George Mason University, Fairfax, VA.

Nature.

If the response in rats is any indication, researchers believe they have made a discovery that could eventually help people with anxiety and *post-traumatic stress disorder* (PTSD).

Like humans, rats learn to be scared of events or things that they relate to pain. But when researchers electrically stimulated a part of the brain, the rats "forgot" they were afraid, according to study coauthor Gregory Quirk, a professor of psychiatry at the University of Puerto Rico School of Medicine. "We've fooled the brain into thinking that it's safe."

When faced with something frightening, rats will freeze and their heart rates and blood pressures go up—a classic fight-or-flight response, Quirk says. It's a hard-wired way that organisms deal with danger. That's true across many species—people, rats, birds and lizards, he adds.

In his study, Quirk taught rats to associate an audio tone with a mild shock to their feet. They froze each time they heard the tone. Then the researchers tried to make the rats forget about their fear by playing the tone without administering the shock. The rats lost their fear of the tone after it was played many times without a shock, but as

soon as the tone was followed by a shock again—even after a lot of time had gone by—the fear and freezing response came right back, Quirk says.

The rats did a better job of forgetting their fear—and not reacting to the tone—when researchers electrically stimulated a part of the brain that's associated with learning that something is no longer scary.

HOW IT COULD HELP

The findings could help people who can't learn to stop being afraid, such as those who have PTSD, he says. "In the current therapies, you find what the person is afraid of, and keep showing it to them again and again to extinguish their fear. But with time, the fear response slowly recovers, and that's a problem," he explains.

The proposed brain stimulation may be too broad to be effective in humans, says James L. Olds, a neuroscientist and director of the Krasnow Institute for Advanced Study at George Mason University. It would turn on too many nerve cells in an important part of the brain, he says. But the findings are still remarkable and provide much insight into how the brain works, he says.

Anxiety Relief—Without Prescription Drugs

Carolyn Chambers Clark, EdD, a board-certified advanced nurse practitioner, mental health specialist and faculty member in the health services doctoral program at Walden University in Minneapolis, is the author of *Living Well with Anxiety: What Your Doctor Doesn't Tell You…That You Need to Know.* Collins.

Anxiety is a normal reaction to the stresses of everyday living. For example, everyone feels insecure or worried at times. It's also common to feel anxious about job interviews, public speaking and meeting new people. But approximately 40 million American adults experience anxiety that is so persistent or excessive at some point during their lives that it interferes with their ability to function.

Anxiety disorders are among the most common mental health problems in men and women. Health effects associated with anxiety include high blood pressure, tension headache, diarrhea and fatigue.

When people suffering persistent anxiety seek help, doctors typically prescribe anti-anxiety drugs, such as *alprazolam* (Xanax).

What many people don't realize: Drugs used to treat anxiety can be addictive and create severe withdrawal symptoms when patients try to stop using them. They also may be harmful to the kidneys and liver.

ARE YOU AT RISK?

Anxiety is first learned by being around anxious parents or caregivers. If you have an excitable personality, which may be your temperament or genetic-based, you are more prone to anxiety. Abuse victims and people who witness death, such as hospital workers, soldiers and firefighters, are prone to anxiety.

As a holistic nurse practitioner who has grappled personally with anxiety at different times during my lifetime, I've spent more than 30 years devising an effective nondrug approach to help myself and the people I treat. *Best strategies…*

REVIEW YOUR DIET

•**Caffeine** triggers the release of the brain chemical *norepinephrine*, which increases alertness. However, caffeine also causes your body to release adrenaline—just as if you're undergoing stress.

It's best to forgo caffeine altogether. Slowly withdraw over a few days. Try adding more decaffeinated coffee to your cup and less caffeinated coffee. Remember that coffee isn't the only source of caffeine. Tea, cola, cocoa and many over-the-counter medications, such as Anacin and Excedrin, may contain caffeine.

•**Sugar** is bad news for people with anxiety. It's well-known that simple sugars, found in candy, cakes, cookies and ice cream, cause your body to release too much of the blood sugar–reducing hormone insulin. This imbalance leads to a severe drop in blood sugar that causes many people to feel light-headed and anxious. But all simple sugars—including corn syrup, fructose and honey—may have this effect.

What your body really needs is complex carbohydrates to burn as energy-producing fuel. Good sources include unrefined grains, found in cereal…vegetables, such as asparagus and avocados (both are rich sources of stress-reducing vitamin B)…and fresh fruit.

•**Salt** does more than raise blood pressure in some people. It causes the body to excrete potassium, which helps keep your nervous system healthy.

Read food labels to minimize your sodium intake, and avoid salting your food. Instead, use a natural salt substitute, such as tamari (available at specialty food stores), or lemon or herbs, especially basil and oregano, for seasoning.

GET THE RIGHT MINERALS

•**Calcium** acts as a natural tranquilizer. People who are calcium deficient often suffer from heart palpitations, insomnia and nervousness. To increase your dietary intake of calcium, eat more sardines, tofu, broccoli, kale, Chinese cabbage, etc.

•**Magnesium** works with calcium to relieve anxiety. People who are magnesium deficient often experience nervousness, irritability and weakness. Magnesium-rich foods include halibut, avocados and almonds.

Eating a diet rich in the minerals potassium (salmon, cod and apricots)…zinc (whole grains, kidney beans and chickpeas)…and phosphorus (oat bran, chicken and sunflower seeds) is also important for alleviating anxiety. To ensure adequate mineral intake, take a multimineral supplement.

USE GENTLE HERBS

Because herbs can be as powerful as drugs and sometimes interact with prescription medication, I recommend those with the best safety records. Tell your health-care practitioner which herbs you are taking.

•**Chamomile** is a mild relaxant. Drink a cup of chamomile tea before bed or during a "coffee break." Start with one to two cups daily. Do not use this herb if you're allergic to plants of the daisy family.

•**Peppermint leaf** calms the nerves. Drink one cup of peppermint leaf tea after meals to help with digestion and promote relaxation.

•**Nutmeg** promotes sleep, which often is disrupted in people with anxiety. For best results, grind one whole nutmeg in a coffee grinder and place the powdered herb in empty capsules, which you can buy at health-food stores. Keep the capsules in the refrigerator and use within one week. As a sleep aid, take one nutmeg capsule four to five hours before bedtime. For daytime anxiety, take one capsule in the morning.

EXERCISE EVERY DAY

Exercise provides an ideal outlet for your body when you're exposed to excessive adrenaline due to stress. By triggering the release of "feel-good" chemicals known as endorphins, physical activity acts as a natural tranquilizer.

Everyone knows the benefits of exercise—but few people do it daily. Thirty minutes daily is ideal. If you have difficulty scheduling this, break your activity into three 10-minute sessions or two 15-minute workouts. You don't have to go to a gym—climb up and down some nearby stairs, garden or take a brisk walk at lunchtime.

To successfully integrate physical activity into your daily life, don't do the same thing all the time—instead, mix it up. For example, try swimming...yoga...weight-lifting...team sports...and dancing. The more variety, the more likely you are to stick to an exercise program.

CREATE NEW HABITS

Anxiety can encourage people to adopt bad habits, such as drinking too much alcohol and/or smoking. Do whatever you must to stop these behaviors—go to Alcoholics Anonymous, use a smoking-cessation program, etc. Subtle habits —ones that you might not realize are harmful—also contribute to anxiety.

•**Living with negative "self-talk."** Indoctrination from as far back as childhood can make for an anxious adult. *Think back:* Were you taught unhealthy beliefs, such as, "Life is dangerous" or, "I must be perfect"? Do your best to change these beliefs and replace them with affirmations.

Examples: "I am becoming more relaxed" ..."I believe in myself"..."I can relax and breathe calmly." By replacing negative thoughts that cause tension with more positive ones that calm you, anxiety is reduced.

•**Not being assertive enough.** If you tend to do too much for family members and/or friends, learn to say "no." This may be easier said than done. That's why I often recommend taking a course in assertiveness training. Call your community college or look in your local newspaper to find a course near you.

Lack of assertiveness causes people to hold in feelings, which allows anxiety to mount. Assertiveness allows you to say what is on your mind in a constructive and respectful way, which reduces the tension associated with anxiety.

•**Accepting bad relationships.** Many times, family members and/or friends mean well but replicate old patterns that create anxiety. Speak to them about your anxiety. If they don't make changes that help relieve your discomfort, avoid these people whenever you can.

If they are binding relationships, it is important to seek out therapy or learn self-help skills, such as total body relaxation or imagery, to learn how to cope.

Diet and lifestyle changes should relieve some anxiety within a few days. Assertiveness skills may take longer. If you don't get adequate relief, seek counseling with a mental health professional or a counselor skilled in behavioral change.

How to Choose a Mental Health Professional

Charles B. Inlander, a consumer advocate and health-care consultant based in Fogelsville, PA. He was founding president of People's Medical Society, a consumer health advocacy group active in the 1980s and 1990s. He is the author of more than 20 books, including *Take This Book to the Hospital with You.* St. Martin's.

Choosing the right counselor, psychiatrist or other mental health professional can be confusing. But when you face a mental health issue, it is important to get appropriate care, because primary care doctors are not trained in diagnosing and treating these problems.

•**Psychiatrist.** A psychiatrist is a medical doctor (MD) or doctor of osteopathy (DO)—two degrees with virtually the same training (four years of medical school, followed by four additional years of training in psychiatry)—who specializes in the prevention, diagnosis and treatment of mental and emotional disorders. Psychiatrists use both medication and counseling. Because of their medical training, they are the only mental health professionals allowed to write drug prescriptions. Before choosing a psychiatrist, check to see if he/she is board-certified by the American Board of Psychiatry and Neurology. Go to the American Board of Medical Specialties Web site at *www.abms.org* and enter the practitioner's name, or call 866-275-2267.

Strengths: Good medical and psychological diagnosticians who can discover or rule out medical conditions that could be affecting your mental health.

●**Psychologist.** These professionals perform psychological testing and practice psychotherapy. Most psychologists hold an advanced degree, such as a doctor of philosophy (PhD) in psychology, a doctor of psychology (PsyD) or doctor of education (EdD) in psychology, all of which require the same minimum amount of schooling. Psychologists are licensed in the state where they practice. Some states also license psychologists holding master's degrees, but a certain level of work experience is required before a license can be granted. To determine if a psychologist is licensed, contact your state's health department.

Strengths: Best trained in a wide range of diagnosed mental health problems that require counseling.

●**Mental health social worker.** Social service agencies, hospitals and crisis centers employ mental health social workers, who usually hold a master's degree in social work with an emphasis in psychology. Licensing requirements for social workers vary widely from state to state. Contact your state's health department to find out if a specific practitioner is licensed.

Strengths: Skilled at helping people adjust to a new problem, such as a cancer diagnosis, and find resources and services.

●**Family, marriage or pastoral counselor.** These are general terms that are used by psychologists, social workers or even members of the clergy who specialize in particular areas of counseling. Some states require licensing for anyone calling himself/herself a "counselor," although no states require clergy to be licensed in order to offer counseling.

Strengths: Good general counselors for less serious mental health problems.

●**Psychiatric nurse.** Registered nurses with advanced training in psychiatry are called psychiatric nurses. They are found in general hospitals, psychiatric facilities and some nursing homes. They often administer and monitor medications and facilitate patient therapy sessions.

Depression: The Hidden Health Threat

Peter D. Kramer, MD, clinical professor of psychiatry and human behavior at Brown University in Providence, RI, is the author of *Listening to Prozac.* Penguin.

Depression is one of the most misunderstood health problems. Some people still stigmatize it as a "character flaw." Others romanticize it, claiming that it lends creativity, sensitivity—even wisdom.

However: Few people are aware that depression actually fuels the development of other serious medical conditions.

Unfortunately, the 19 million Americans who suffer from depression—and their families—are paying the price for the misconceptions. Only one in eight depressed Americans gets treatment.

To learn more, we spoke with Peter Kramer, MD, a renowned psychiatrist…

●**As a health problem, how serious is depression?** In a very real sense, depression is the most devastating disease known to humankind—both in the developing world and industrialized nations. It is extremely widespread, it often strikes first in young adulthood or middle age and it frequently returns or becomes chronic. It robs more people of more years of active life than AIDS, heart disease or cancer. The disability that accompanies episodes of major depression is exceeded only in conditions such as dementia and quadriplegia.

And all this doesn't even take into account the effect that depression has on other diseases. Over the last 10 years, it's been firmly established that depression significantly raises the risk for heart attack and stroke. It also can accelerate bone loss and perhaps impair immune function. Even if depression didn't cause terrible emotional suffering, it would be important to treat it for these medical reasons.

There's also evidence that certain physical conditions and medical treatments can cause depression. In older adults, for example, tiny strokes that cause changes to the prefrontal cortex—a part of the brain that seems to be involved in depression—can lead to depression symptoms, such as altered sleep and appetite and impaired self-image. Some doctors call this "vascular depression." Thyroid disorders that affect hormone levels can be a direct cause of depression, while painful ailments, such as rheumatoid arthritis, can be an indirect cause. Fortunately, these types of depression are quite treatable with medication and other therapies. Drugs, such as the cancer medication *interferon*, steroids and some antihypertensives, can induce very severe depression.

•**Isn't depression a mental illness?** Research in the last decade has found that depression is associated with *physical* changes in the brain, similar to those that might occur with any neurological disease, such as epilepsy, Parkinson's or Alzheimer's disease. Depression causes atrophy—that is, brain cells die—and a loss of connections between brain cells. The longer the depression persists—or goes untreated—the greater the damage.

One study conducted by researchers at Washington University in St. Louis found that the hippocampus—a brain region linked to memory—was smaller in women who had a history of depression, and the longer they had suffered from the disease without treatment, the greater the shrinkage. Their loss of memory was proportional to the time they had spent depressed.

•**Can treating depression reduce the risk for heart attack, stroke and other related illnesses?** The evidence isn't as strong as we'd like, but some research does suggest that this is true. A recent study of 1,834 patients who had had a heart attack and were depressed found that the risk for death or a second heart attack over the next 29 months was approximately 40% lower in the 446 who were prescribed an antidepressant. Among stroke patients, one study conducted in Denmark showed that those who did not take an antidepressant were two to three times more likely to suffer a recurrent stroke over the next year.

•**How effective are current depression treatments?** The prescription antidepressants we have today are far from perfect, but they work pretty well. About 80% of patients who are treated properly get substantially better. But all researchers agree that depression is underdiagnosed and undertreated. Most people still don't get the treatment they deserve.

•**Aren't many people wary of antidepressants because of side effects?** Yes. However, although side effects do occur, they are usually well tolerated compared with the side effects of many other medications. For someone with major depression, minor side effects are tolerable. Although rare, antidepressants have been known to induce suicidal thoughts. When taking a new antidepressant, you should follow up with your doctor consistently.

•**How depressed do you need to be for treatment to make sense—and how do you gauge this?** Many more people should be evaluated for depression than currently are. Minor, or low-level, depression is just like major depression but with less intensity. There are many advantages to being assessed by a mental health professional to determine if you need treatment.

•**Does depression ever mimic other illnesses?** Yes. Some people may have a type of depression, often called pseudodementia, that has the pattern of a dementia illness. It resembles late-stage Parkinson's disease, resulting in problems in motivation, memory, concentration and word finding. Patients don't feel sad, but respond well to antidepressants.

•**What should a person with depression do to get help?** If you think that you—or someone close to you—might be depressed, act as you would for any serious disease and get professional help from a doctor or mental health professional. If you're under treatment for depression, expect to see some sign that it's working. With antidepressants and/or psychotherapy, you should start feeling at least somewhat better after four to six weeks. Don't settle for halfway—once you begin to improve, stay with the treatment until you and your doctor agree that you have achieved optimal results.

■ ■ ■ ■

Antidepressant Risk

People who had heart disease and were taking tricyclic antidepressants showed an increased risk of death. These antidepressants, which are known to raise the level of norepinephrine in the body, can cause heartbeat irregularities.

Self-defense: If you have heart disease and your doctor has put you on a tricyclic antidepressant, ask about alternatives.

Lana Watkins, PhD, assistant research professor of medical psychology, department of psychiatry and behavioral medicine, Duke University Medical Center, Durham, NC, and leader of a study of 921 heart patients.

When Depression Won't Go Away: Bipolar Disorder Could Be to Blame

Jim Phelps, MD, a psychiatrist in private practice in Corvallis, OR, is the author of *Why Am I Still Depressed: Recognizing and Managing the Ups and Downs of Bipolar II and Soft Bipolar Disorder.* McGraw-Hill.

Until recently, bipolar disorder has been associated only with extreme mood swings—suicidal depressions alternating with manic periods of irrational and even dangerous behavior.

Now: A "soft" form of bipolar disorder has been identified and is estimated to affect one percent to two percent of the American population.

IS IT BIPOLAR DISORDER?

Depression associated with bipolar disorder has the same symptoms as common, or "unipolar," depression—sadness, lack of energy, sleep and appetite problems, loss of interest in life, etc. However, doctors can't always tell one disorder from the other. Psychiatrists are typically best suited to make the diagnosis, but they also can miss the telltale symptoms.

If you experience symptoms of depression in repeated, brief episodes, bipolar disorder should be suspected. Even though bipolar disorder is technically defined by "hypomania" (marked by

phases of increased energy and activity), in the softer forms, hypomania can be accompanied by irritability and agitation—not just euphoria and grandiosity, the typical hallmarks.

Another red flag: People with bipolar disorder tend to eat and/or sleep more than usual, not less, when they're depressed.

THE RIGHT TREATMENT

For unipolar depression, standard antidepressants—such as *sertraline* (Zoloft), *fluoxetine* (Prozac), *bupropion* (Wellbutrin) or *venlafaxine* (Effexor)—usually reduce symptoms within days to several weeks. With bipolar disorder, an antidepressant alone can change a person's mood too dramatically—like flicking a switch from depression to mania.

The prescription drugs that work best for bipolar depression are designed to not only ease the depression but also even out the mood swings. These drugs often are combined with an antidepressant to increase the effectiveness of both medications.

Most effective mood-stabilizing drugs…

•*Lithium* is the oldest and, according to many doctors, the best mood-stabilizing drug. Side effects include tremor, diarrhea and confusion.

•*Lamotrigine* (Lamictal) is one of the newest mood-stabilizing drugs. In rare cases, it can cause a potentially fatal allergic reaction, marked by a rash.

•*Olanzapine* (Zyprexa) often reduces symptoms within hours. In some cases, it can cause major weight gain and even diabetes.

•*Valproate* (Depakote) is another tried-and-true mood-stabilizing drug. Side effects include sedation and weight gain.

A HEALTHFUL LIFESTYLE

To maximize the benefits of medication, it helps to adopt a healthful lifestyle. If your symptoms aren't too serious—for example, you're still able to work and maintain close relationships—this approach may stabilize your moods *without* the use of drugs. *Recommended…*

•**Exercise regularly.** Studies have shown that regular aerobic exercise can relieve depression as effectively as some prescription antidepressant medications.

To get started, try this simple strategy: Walk just 7½ minutes in one direction, then return. Do this every day. Gradually increase the duration if you can.

• **Consume omega-3 fatty acids.** Fish oil, the best source of these essential fatty acids, has been shown to improve depression and reduce mood swings. Try 1 g daily of *eicosapentaenoic acid* (EPA) from fish oil capsules or liquid. Right now, it's not known if the amount of *docosahexaenoic acid* (DHA) found in fish oil is significant for bipolar disorder.

Caution: Fish oil can have a blood-thinning effect, so check with your doctor if you use blood-thinning medication, such as *warfarin* (Coumadin).

• **Limit alcohol.** For many people, alcohol makes their moods more unstable. If you drink alcohol, abstain for several weeks and monitor your moods. Then slowly reintroduce it—begin with one or two drinks per week and track whether it affects you negatively.

LIGHT/DARK THERAPIES

Maintaining regular sleep habits and frequent light and dark exposure can help stabilize moods and reduce depression.

• **Light therapy** acts like an antidepressant, possibly by affecting levels of the neurotransmitter serotonin.

What to do: Expose yourself to light for 30 minutes or more per day.

Best approach: Use a light box, which can be purchased for about $175 to $300 at Costco or several Web sites, including *www.lighttherapy products.com.*

Warning: If you experience hypomania symptoms such as agitation, irritability or crowded thoughts, discontinue light therapy.

• **Dark therapy** acts like a mood stabilizer and is involved in regulating the biological clock.

What to do: Go to bed at the same time each night, keep your room as dark as possible and get up at the same time each morning. In addition, control your exposure to light. Even if you don't sit in complete darkness, keep lights low after 9 pm…don't watch TV or use the computer. Use a dawn simulator, a device that wakes you naturally by slowly turning up the lights each morning. For information about where to buy dawn simulators, check my Web site, *www.psycheducation.com.*

• **Blue light** is the wavelength that is believed to regulate the sleep-wake rhythm.

What to do: If it's past 9 pm and you want to use your computer or read without disrupting the cycle, wearing yellow-lensed sunglasses that block blue light may help, though this is still being researched. Yellow-lensed sunglasses are available at *www.lowbluelights.com.*

Eating and exercising at the same time each day also helps stabilize moods.

PSYCHOTHERAPY

Cognitive behavioral therapy (CBT), which helps identify and change thinking and behavior patterns that influence moods, has been shown to be as effective as antidepressants. When adapted for bipolar disorder, it may include strategies to help you maintain a healthful lifestyle, reduce stress and identify characteristic unhealthful thoughts.

To find a CBT practitioner near you, consult the Depression and Bipolar Support Alliance, 800-826-3632, *www.dbsalliance.org.*

■ ■ ■ ■

AA Alternatives

Alcoholism may be treated without intensive behavioral counseling.

Recent study: Alcoholics taking the oral medication *naltrexone* (Depade) who met for 20 minutes on nine occasions with a medical professional had clinical outcomes as good as those who had up to 20 psychotherapy sessions of 50 minutes each. Naltrexone costs up to $5 a day.

Mark Willenbring, MD, director of treatment and recovery research, National Institute on Alcohol Abuse and Alcoholism, Bethesda, MD, and a principal investigator of a study at 11 universities of 1,383 alcoholics, published in *The Journal of the American Medical Association.*

■ ■ ■ ■

Eating Disorder

Anorexia may be caused by dopamine overactivity in the brain.

Recent finding: Anorexia nervosa sufferers may have increased chemical activity in their dopamine receptors, which control reward and reinforcement. Dopamine affects how individuals respond to stimuli and how positive and negative reinforcement are viewed. This may explain why women with anorexia don't get any pleasure from losing weight. About one percent of American women have anorexia—it is the number-one cause of death from any psychiatric illness. Some medications that block dopamine receptors, such as antipsychotics, may benefit people with this illness, but more research is needed.

Walter H. Kaye, MD, professor of psychiatry and director of the eating disorders program at the University of California, San Diego. He was leader of a study of brain imaging, published in *Biological Psychiatry*.

Is Brain Stimulation the Best Treatment for OCD?

Ali R. Rezai, MD, director center for neurological restoration, and professor, department of neurosurgery, The Cleveland Clinic Foundation.
American Association of Neurological Surgeons annual meeting, San Diego, CA.

People who have *obsessive-compulsive disorder*, or OCD, are tormented by their own repetitive, nagging thoughts, and for many, there's no treatment that offers relief.

But an experimental procedure may provide at least some improvement for patients who have severe OCD, letting them return to work and some semblance of routine.

However, the treatment, spearheaded by a Cleveland Clinic Foundation neurosurgeon, produces significant side effects, prompting some questions about the therapy's efficacy.

The study tested deep brain stimulation as a possible treatment for OCD. Because an estimated 20% of OCD patients don't respond to drug or behavioral therapies, the researchers hoped that they would be able to find a new way of treating the condition.

THE OCD LOOP

Those with OCD feel as though their brain gets snagged on a particular thought or impulse and it keeps playing the same message over and over again. For example, some people can't resist the nagging desire to wash their hands several times an hour, while others may constantly check the stove to make sure they haven't left it on. Patients who have OCD are unable to control their intrusive thoughts.

The researchers worked with 15 severely disabled OCD patients who had been on prolonged medication and behavioral therapy.

Each patient received deep brain stimulators—electronic devices that work like pacemakers—that were implanted into a fiber bundle located at the front of the brain.

A deep brain stimulator quiets activity in two regions of the brain where OCD patients appear to have abnormal activity, the researchers say.

After receiving the therapy, the patients experienced a 54% improvement in quality-of-life scores, and several were able to return to work.

PROS AND CONS

Some of the specific benefits of the treatment included mood elevation, anxiety reduction, decreased OCD symptoms and increased alertness. But some subjects also experienced depression, memory flashbacks, nausea, vomiting, visual blurring and abnormal heart rhythms, among other side effects.

But lead researcher Dr. Ali Rezai of The Cleveland Clinic Foundation says the side effects can be controlled by changing the dosage of electricity to the stimulator.

"Deep brain stimulation has the advantage of being reversible and adjustable. These [side effects] are not chronic and can be eliminated," Rezai explains.

Rezai agrees that a longer-term study is needed before his team embarks on a larger clinical trial. "The results are encouraging, but we need more follow-up before we enroll more patients."

For information on obsessive-compulsive disorder and other related disorders, visit *www.ocfoundation.org*, an educational and self-help group based in Connecticut.

■ ■ ■ ■

Contagious Yawning

The "contagious yawning effect" is due to our ability to empathize.

Recent finding: Many people yawn after someone near them yawns. Nearly every kind of animal yawns, but only primates, including gorillas and apes, mirror each other's yawns.

Steven M. Platek, PhD, associate professor of psychology, School of Biological Sciences, University of Liverpool, United Kingdom, and lead author of a study on yawning, published in *Cognitive Brain Research*.

A Good Night's Sleep Without Pills

Peter Hauri, PhD, consultant emeritus to the Sleep Disorders Center at the Mayo Clinic in Rochester, MN, is coauthor of *No More Sleepless Nights* (Wiley), and one of the founders of the American Sleep Disorders Association, now the American Academy of Sleep Medicine, *www.aasmnet.org*.

More Americans than ever are taking sleeping pills. Last year, about 42 million prescriptions for sleep medication were filled.

Insomnia is more than an annoyance. It can wreak havoc on the immune system, contributing to serious illnesses.

Newer sleep medications, such as *zolpidem* (Ambien), *zaleplon* (Sonata), *ramelteon* (Rozerem) and *eszopiclone* (Lunesta), are believed to be safe.

However: Even these medications can cause headaches, daytime drowsiness, dizziness and other adverse effects. Older adults, who are most likely to use sleeping pills, are particularly sensitive to them.

Is there a better option? Absolutely. New studies have found that natural treatments are just as effective as sleep medication for mild to moderate insomnia.

GETTING STARTED

Most people require eight hours of sleep a night to feel refreshed and stay healthy, but some of us need as many as 10 hours and others as little as four.

If you have trouble falling asleep, staying asleep or you regularly awaken earlier than you'd like, schedule an appointment with your primary care physician. Medical problems, such as thyroid disorders, pain and allergies, can compromise sleep. Treating such conditions can improve sleep.

Depression, anxiety, a panic disorder or even everyday stress also can disturb sleep. If you suspect that psychological issues may be causing sleeplessness, mention it to your doctor and consider consulting a mental health professional.

If your doctor can't find a medical problem, you can begin a natural self-help treatment plan. To determine whether natural approaches will be effective, you must try them for at least one or two weeks—one at a time.

Helpful: Keep a log of your sleep quality for at least a week, preferably two. Use a rating scale from one to 10, with 10 being optimal. Rate your sleep each night—preferably about a half hour after you get out of bed in the morning.

When you introduce one of the strategies described below, rate your nightly sleep again for about a week or two. If the ratings improve, you know that the technique you're trying works for you.

BEHAVIORAL APPROACHES

During my 40-year career, I've treated thousands of adults with sleep complaints. *Here are the simple strategies that I've found to be most successful...*

• **Create a sleep-inducing environment.** Keep your bedroom at a temperature that is comfortable for you (cooler is typically better)...turn out all the lights (darkness promotes the body's production of the sleep-promoting hormone melatonin)—some people, however, sleep better with a night-light...and, if necessary, adjust your sound level—some people like total quiet, while others prefer soft background noise, such as a radio or a "white noise" machine.

• **Go to bed at about the same time each night so that your body gets into a rhythm.** Some insomniacs are kept awake all night worrying what time it is, so putting a clock where you cannot see or reach it is often helpful. It is counterproductive to lie in bed desperately trying to fall asleep. Distract your mind by reading.

• **Get more physical activity.** Physically fit people tend to sleep more deeply. If you have been sedentary, start performing aerobic exercise, such as brisk walking or bicycling, three times a week.

Some sleep research indicates that it's best to exercise four to six hours before going to bed.

If you exercise too close to bedtime, your body may be too stimulated for you to fall asleep.

•**Meditate.** Studies show that a period of meditation during the day or the early evening helps fight insomnia by promoting physical relaxation and/or slowing the mind.

SUPPLEMENTS

If the behavioral approaches described above don't work as well as desired, consider also trying a sleep-promoting supplement (available at health-food stores).*

Effective supplements…

•**Melatonin** has been shown to help restore a more normal sleep cycle—but it rarely lengthens the amount of time you sleep. If you have problems falling asleep, take it two hours before bedtime. If you wake up too early or in the middle of the night, take it when you awaken.

Recommended dose: Start with 3 mg once a day. If this does not work, gradually increase the dosage over a period of a month to a maximum of 9 mg daily.

Possible side effects: Headache, digestive upset and depression. Long-term use of melatonin has not been studied, so consult your doctor if you need to use this hormone for more than a few months or you develop side effects.

•**Valerian** is an herb that has been rigorously tested. It helps many people fall asleep faster and stay asleep longer.

Recommended dose: Take one-half to one teaspoon of liquid extract or 300 mg to 500 mg in powdered form or capsules about 20 minutes before bedtime.

Possible side effect: Stomach upset.

•**5-hydroxytryptophan (5-HTP)** is a compound derived from the seed of the African plant griffonia. 5-HTP is best known as a treatment for mild to moderate depression. The scientific evidence on 5-HTP's efficacy as a sleep aid is inconclusive at this time, but the compound may be worth trying if you don't get relief from the other supplements listed above. 5-HTP has helped some of my patients.

Recommended dose: Ask your doctor.

*The FDA does not regulate herbal and other natural supplements. Do not take these supplements if you are pregnant or nursing.

Possible side effect: Mild nausea.

•**Vitamin B-12 and/or calcium** can improve your sleep if you have a deficiency of either one. Both vitamin B-12 and calcium calm the nervous system and have a mild sedative effect in some people.

Recommended dose: Ask your doctor.

Possible side effects: None are known.

Important: If you are taking any medications, including prescription sleeping pills, consult your doctor before taking these supplements.

■ ■ ■ ■

Help for Sleep

The FDA-approved Pillar Palatal Implant for sleep apnea—the sleep disorder that causes people to stop breathing intermittently—requires outpatient surgery, during which three pieces of polyester string are sewn into the soft palate. This procedure causes the tissue to stiffen, which reduces sleep apnea and snoring. The procedure is comparable to somnoplasty, in which microwaves directed at the back of the throat stiffen tissue. Either operation is simpler and less painful than the standard surgery to remove excess throat and soft palate tissue.

Bruce Corser, MD, medical director, Sleep Management Institute, Cincinnati.

■ ■ ■ ■

Better Insomnia Relief

In a study of 46 people with chronic insomnia, one group was trained in cognitive-behavior therapy (CBT) techniques, including relaxation practices and stimulus (noise, light) control. Two other groups took either the sleeping pill zopiclone (Imovane) or a placebo every night.

Result: After six weeks, time spent awake dropped 52% in the CBT group compared with 4% in the zopiclone group and 16% in those taking a placebo.

Theory: CBT helps patients identify and change negative thoughts, which can be an underlying cause of insomnia.

Borge Sivertsen, PhD, researcher and psychologist, University of Bergen, Norway.

Natural Remedies For Snoring

Jamison Starbuck, ND, is a naturopathic physician in family practice in Missoula, Montana. She is past president of the American Association of Naturopathic Physicians and is a contributing editor to *The Alternative Advisor: The Complete Guide to Natural Therapies and Alternative Treatments.* Time-Life.

S noring is a problem that many of my patients suffer from but few admit to. For many of them, snoring is embarrassing. For example, Bill, a 44-year-old father of three, recently told me, "I'm just a heavy breather." However, based on the description from Bill's sleep-deprived wife, snoring was a definite problem in their household.

Snoring regularly affects 37 million Americans (about 25% female). It is defined as noisy breathing during sleep caused by air passing through a constricted airway. Mild snoring can be remedied by awakening the snorer or by changing his/her position…heavy snoring lasts most of the night, regardless of the person's position or how often he/she wakes. Snoring is not the same as sleep apnea. Sleep apnea is a breathing disorder. The sleeper (who may or may not be snoring) stops breathing and must awaken in order to start breathing again.

Chief causes of the airway constriction that triggers snoring are lack of fitness, being overweight, drinking alcohol before bed, smoking and nasal congestion. Men are more likely to snore than women, and if a first-degree relative (parent, sibling or child) snores, that also may make you more likely to suffer from snoring.

Food allergies are an often-overlooked cause of snoring. They lead to nasal congestion, allergic sinusitis and swelling in the upper respiratory tract. In Bill's case, a simple blood test revealed that eggs were a problem for him. Eliminating eggs from his diet cured his nighttime "heavy breathing" and brought peace to the household. For people who snore, dairy, wheat, eggs and soy are the most common food allergens. I've seen all of them trigger snoring in my patients. If you snore, try eliminating these foods for 10 days, one at a time, to see if your snoring is reduced. For quicker answers, ask your doctor for an allergy test. Be sure to get a blood test, which checks for IgG-mediated antibodies to common foods. Skin scratch allergy testing will not adequately determine snore-inducing food allergens.

Other helpful steps for people who snore…

•**Get fit and lose weight.** Strengthening and tightening the muscles of the throat and losing weight will open airways and diminish snoring.

•**If you smoke, quit.** Smoke irritates the tissue of the upper respiratory tract, causing the congestion and swelling that can lead to snoring.

•**Don't drink alcohol within two hours of bedtime.** Drinking alcohol relaxes muscle tension. If you drink just before going to sleep, the muscles of your tongue and throat will be too lax and your airway will be narrowed—a perfect trigger for snoring.

•**Review your medications.** Drugs that relax the body—sleeping pills, antihistamines, tranquilizers and muscle relaxants—can cause snoring. Talk to your doctor about taking the smallest dose possible. Ask your pharmacist and/or doctor whether you can take the medication several hours before bedtime to help reduce the incidence of snoring.

■ ■ ■ ■

Snoring Stopper

B est treatment for snoring depends on the cause. Snoring occurs because of a blockage anywhere from the tip of the nose to the back of the throat.

Common cause: Being overweight. Losing weight should relieve the problem.

Other causes: Deviated septum, sinus infection, floppy uvula (the fleshy lobe that hangs from the back of the soft palate). These may require surgery or, when infection is present, treatment for the infection.

Best: A doctor who looks at the whole patient.

Example: An overweight smoker with allergies who complains of snoring may need to see an allergist, an acupuncturist to help stop smoking and a dietitian for weight loss. If snoring continues, the cause can be narrowed down and treated directly—surgery for a deviated septum, for example.

Jordan S. Josephson, MD, scientist and snoring, ear, nose and throat-endoscopic sinus specialist in private practice, New York City. *www.drjjny.com.*

Use Your Dreams to Improve Your Health

Gillian Holloway, PhD, a psychologist and instructor at Marylhurst University in Marylhurst, OR, is the author of *The Complete Dream Book: Discover What Your Dreams Tell About You and Your Life*. Sourcebooks.

Dream interpretation has long been used to help people resolve troubling psychological issues.

But few people realize that dreams also can foretell health problems weeks to months before symptoms develop.

Landmark study: Vasily Kasatkin, a psychiatrist at the Leningrad Neurosurgical Institute, analyzed 10,240 dreams from 1,200 patients over a 40-year period. He concluded that illnesses, ranging from tooth infections to brain tumors, often caused distressing dreams that preceded the first symptoms.

Dreams related to health issues are typically recurring—and may include an intense physical sensation in the dream and/or pain or discomfort that lingers after awakening.

Most common health-related dreams and what they may mean...

VIOLENT INJURY

Dreams: In one version, a part of your body might get stabbed. On another night, that same body part might get branded with a hot iron. In yet a third dream, that part of your body may be shot. Although the method of injury may change, the body part you dream about remains the same.

What it means: You may be developing a health problem in that part of your body.

What to do: If the dream is a recurring one about a particular part of your body, ask your doctor for an exam.

EATING ROTTEN FOOD

Dreams: You eat food that is spoiled or has bugs all over it.

What it means: You may be overindulging in "junk food" or developing a problem involving digestion.

What to do: Ask yourself if you're under excessive stress. If so, try to change the stressful situation or take better care of yourself by getting more rest, eating a healthful diet and exercising.

SICK ANIMALS

Dreams: Your pet, former pet or a stray has become ill or suffered a violent injury.

What it means: Our pets are dream symbols of ourselves. This dream often means that some part of you is suffering. People who are in abusive relationships often have this dream. It also can mean that you have been abusing your own body by neglecting your health.

What to do: If you are in an abusive relationship, seek help from the authorities and/or a mental health professional. If you are not, take stock of your lifestyle and see if there is a way for you to improve your diet and/or get more exercise.

COLLAPSING HOUSE

Dreams: The floor in your house is collapsing, most commonly due to termites. Or perhaps the walls are crumbling. Or the stairs can't hold your weight.

What it means: Something is giving way or losing ground in your life, or you have a chronic health condition that might be worsening. For example, a woman with scoliosis (curvature of the spine) dreamed of a problem with a spiral staircase in her house at a time when her back was flaring up and needed adjustment.

What to do: Ask your doctor what therapies may be available for your condition. For example, people with chronic ailments often think that they must live with them. In some cases, there are treatments to relieve your symptoms.

CANCER DIAGNOSIS

Dreams: You go to the doctor and are told that you have cancer and have only a short time to live.

What it means: This is a very common dream, and it does not necessarily mean that you have cancer. It almost always means that you simply are overextending yourself and are anxious about it.

What to do: Reflect on what is causing anxiety in your life. If you're overloaded, delegate as much as you can to others. If you suspect cancer or have a family history of the disease, see your doctor.

■ ■ ■ ■

Some Is Not Enough

Not getting enough sleep affects mental processes as much as not sleeping at all.

Recent study: The response times and memorization abilities of people who slept six hours or less a night for two weeks were no better than those of people who stayed awake for one to two days. Most people need seven to eight hours of sleep a night.

David F. Dinges, PhD, professor of psychology, department of psychiatry, and chief of the division of sleep and chronobiology, University of Pennsylvania School of Medicine, Philadelphia, and principal investigator of a study published in *Sleep*.

■ ■ ■ ■

Recipe for Great Power Nap

Find a quiet place where you can fall asleep easily…set an alarm if you are worried about oversleeping—a nap should last 30 to 40 minutes…nap at the time of the afternoon when you normally feel sleepiest…give yourself time to wake up—be fully alert before driving or doing any demanding task…if you find it hard to get going after a nap, shorten nap time…if you find that you are having trouble falling asleep or staying asleep at night, try other afternoon pick-me-ups (some people are nappers and some are not).

Examples: A well-balanced snack, exposure to bright light, 10 to 20 minutes of moderate exercise.

Scott Campbell, PhD, director of the laboratory of human chronobiology, department of psychiatry, Weill Medical College of Cornell University, White Plains, NY.

■ ■ ■ ■

"Sleeping Sickness"

Patients with sleep apnea may stop breathing after surgery. People with obstructive sleep apnea (OSA) temporarily stop breathing during sleep. Sedatives and pain medicines used during surgery can suppress the mechanism that causes arousal and may prevent these patients from waking up during the postoperative period, resulting in respiratory arrest.

Best: Tell your doctor if you snore, have daytime headaches, fall asleep during the day or have other signs of OSA.

If OSA is suspected: After surgery, fewer sedating drugs may be used…you may be positioned on your side…and you should be monitored for apnea or low blood-oxygen levels.

Kevin Finkel, MD, a Washington University anesthesiology resident at Barnes-Jewish Hospital, St. Louis, and lead author of a paper on handling apnea patients during surgery, published in *Sleep Review*.

■ ■ ■ ■

Help for Sleep Apnea

Heart failure patients with central sleep apnea (in which breathing repeatedly stops and starts during sleep due to a brain malfunction) took either *acetazolamide* (Diamox), a mild diuretic and respiratory stimulant, or a placebo for six nights in a new study.

Result: Those who took acetazolamide slept better, had improved blood oxygen levels and were less fatigued during the day compared with those in a placebo group. Over time, treatment of sleep apnea is believed to aid cardiac function through improved oxygenation.

Shahrokh Javaheri, MD, medical director, Sleepcare Diagnostics, Mason, OH. *www.snorenomore.com*.

Stress-Proof Your Personality

Redford Williams, MD, division head of the Duke University Behavioral Medicine Research Center in Durham, NC, is coauthor of *In Control: No More Snapping at Your Family, Sulking at Work, Steaming in the Grocery Line, Seething in Meetings, Stuffing Your Frustrations*. Rodale.

Nobody escapes stress, but some fortunate people seem to be able to negotiate the shallows of life with apparent ease. They take setbacks in stride and don't waste their time or inflame their arteries by flaring up unnecessarily. They enjoy loving relationships and supportive friendships.

While their talent for living may seem mysterious, it's actually a matter of skill. Like the musician who knows how to draw lovely music from a violin, they know how to bring happiness and harmony to themselves and others.

These people have skills that put them in control of their emotions and relationships. Fortunately, these skills can be learned—at any age.

THE ADVANTAGE OF BEING IN CONTROL

Research conducted over the past three decades has shown that psychological stress increases the risk for heart disease and other major illnesses, such as depression and anxiety. Higher mortality rates are particularly linked to hostility, which can manifest as a cynical mistrust of others, a low threshold for anger and/or a high level of aggression.

New finding: A study recently published in the *American Heart Journal* found that coronary-bypass patients who underwent a training program to increase control of their emotions showed significantly less depression, anger and stress, along with more social support and satisfaction, compared with healthy people who received no training.

The trained participants' pulses slowed, and their blood pressure reacted less to stress after the training—clear signs that they were taking strain off their hearts. These factors remained unchanged or worsened in the other group.

SHORT-CIRCUIT STRESS

You can't deal with stress properly unless you recognize it. *How to cope when a negative situation arises...*

***Step 1:* Ask yourself, how important is it?** The goal is to know how to separate trivial situations that are outside your control from those that are worth getting worked up over.

Helpful: Step back and decide whether you should allow yourself to react to a setback, annoyance or obstacle. Is there anything you actually can do about it? Is it important enough to go to the mat over?

***Step 2:* Change your reaction.** If your evaluation of the stressful situation tells you that it's not that important, practice turning off the negative thoughts and calming the bad feelings.

Helpful: When you're alone and feel irritated, tell yourself to STOP! in a sharp voice. Repeat the command silently when stressful situations arise in public.

During a calm time, write a list of topics that make you feel good when you think about them—a beloved relative...a pleasant vacation spot. When you're stressed or upset, close your eyes and picture items from your list.

***Step 3:* Take action.** If your analysis leads you to conclude that the stressful situation is worth acting on, take positive steps.

Helpful: Problem-solve in a systematic way. Define the problem...list possible solutions... make a decision...and implement it.

Example: Max was not comfortable driving at night. When he found out he had a book club meeting scheduled for 8 pm in a neighboring town, he at first became anxious. After considering his options (having a friend pick him up and drive him home...not going at all), he settled on calling a taxi.

IMPROVE RELATIONSHIPS

Intimate relationships, friendships and pleasant encounters with coworkers and acquaintances provide social support—a buffer against life's difficulties.

You can improve your relationships by being considerate, treating others with respect, offering help when needed, etc. One of the best strategies is to become a good listener. People appreciate you and like you when they feel heard and understood.

To improve your relationships, practice these skills...

•**Keep quiet while others are talking.** Suppress your desire to add information, ask questions, give advice or steer the conversation to yourself. Limit your input to the occasional nod or "Uh-huh." If your mind wanders, refocus on the other person's words. Your turn will come...wait for it.

•**Use appropriate body language.** To show interest, maintain a relaxed but attentive facial expression. Relax your shoulders, uncross your arms and lean slightly forward.

•**Repeat what the other person says.** Before you comment, summarize what you think you heard, focusing on facts or feelings.

Example: "It sounds like you had a great time with your grandkids last weekend."

•**Be open.** This doesn't mean you must change your mind, only that you're receptive to the possibility. When your mental attitude is open rather than rigid, it shows. You may even learn something useful.

ACCENTUATE THE POSITIVE

Several years ago, a University of Washington study found that marriages last longer when positive communications (compliments, affectionate touching, smiling, sharing enthusiasm) outnumbered negative ones (criticism, nasty looks, withdrawal) by a ratio of five to one.

Use the same principle in all your relationships—make a conscious effort to distribute five times as many compliments as criticisms.

Most important, apply the five-to-one ratio to yourself. Overwhelm negative self-talk ("I'm unprepared…my nose is too big…their house is nicer than mine") with positive messages.

Helpful: List your five best traits and count five of your blessings. Also, become aware of your five biggest self-criticisms and pledge to stop them.

■ ■ ■ ■

Take Hold

Handholding eases stress in happily married couples. When a married woman under extreme stress reaches out and touches her husband's hand, her brain shows changes in areas involved in registering emotional and physical alarm. Women get significantly more relief from a husband's touch than from the touch of a stranger. The ones who get the most relief are those in particularly close marriages.

James A. Coan, PhD, assistant professor, departments of neuroscience and psychology, University of Virginia, Charlottesville, and leader of a study of married couples, published in *Psychological Science*.

■ ■ ■ ■

Stay Alert

Stay alert with self-applied acupressure. Use your index and middle fingers to massage stimulation points in a circular motion—90 seconds in one direction, then 90 seconds the

other way. Use a very firm touch—slight discomfort is normal.

Best places to massage: Back of the head at the hairline, on left and right sides at the same time…area between thumb and forefinger, just beyond the webbing on each hand…front of the leg, between kneecap and knee bone…just below the ball of the foot, toward the arch.

Richard Harris, PhD, division of rheumatology, University of Michigan Medical School, Ann Arbor.

Music Fights High Blood Pressure, Insomnia and Pain

Suzanne B. Hanser, EdD, chair of the music therapy department at Berklee College of Music in Boston and past president of the American Music Therapy Association and the World Federation of Music Therapy, is a research associate at the Dana-Farber Cancer Institute, an affiliate of Harvard Medical School, where she investigates medical applications of music therapy.

Everyone knows the soothing effect of listening to a favorite piece of music. But until recently, there was little scientific evidence to support its effectiveness in helping to combat specific health problems.

Now: A growing body of research has found that music can affect key areas of the brain that help regulate specific physiological functions necessary for good health. The best choice of music and the time spent listening depends on an individual's needs and preferences. *Medical conditions that can be improved by listening to appropriate music…*

HIGH BLOOD PRESSURE

The *hypothalamus* helps control the autonomic nervous system, which regulates our breathing, heartbeat and other automatic responses in the body. It also is linked to emotional activity.

How music helps: When a person listens to music that stimulates positive memories and/or images, the activity of the hypothalamus helps slow a person's heart and respiration rates as well as blood pressure.

Scientific evidence: In a study published in the *British Journal of Health Psychology*, 75 adults performed a stressful three-minute math problem. Afterward, they were randomly assigned to sit in silence or listen to classical, jazz or popular music. Those who heard classical selections had significantly lower systolic (top number) blood pressure levels. Blood pressure did not significantly improve in people who listened to the other selections.

What to do: Observe how you respond to different types of music. Match your state of mind to the tempo and dynamics.

Example: If you are agitated, listen to something with a strong, fast beat, then gradually switch to slower and softer music. This can reduce stress and lower blood pressure.

INSOMNIA

Although healthy adults typically fall asleep within 30 minutes, adults age 50 and older often have more trouble falling—and staying—asleep.

How music helps: Soft, restful music can act as a sedative by reducing the amount of the stress-related neurotransmitter noradrenaline that circulates in the bloodstream.

Scientific evidence: Sixty people ages 60 to 83 who reported sleep difficulties took part in a study at Tzu-Chi General Hospital in Taiwan. After three weeks, researchers found a 35% improvement in sleep quality, length of sleep, daytime dysfunction and sleep disturbances in subjects who listened to slow, soft music at night. The most effective types of music used in the study were piano versions of popular "oldies," New Age, harp, classical and slow jazz.

What to do: Make sure your bedroom temperature is comfortable, then lie in bed at your usual bedtime, with the lights out (light interferes with the production of the sleep hormone *melatonin*) and your eyes closed while listening to music. Experiment with different types of music until you discover what's relaxing for you. (Earphones are optional.) If you wake during the night, try listening to music again.

PAIN

Listening to music does not eliminate pain, but it can help distract your brain by creating a secondary stimulus that diverts your attention from the feeling of discomfort.

Scientific evidence: In a 14-day study published in the *Journal of Advanced Nursing*, 66 older adults with osteoarthritis pain sat quietly for 20 minutes daily, while another group listened to music. Those who listened to music reported a significant decrease in pain.

What to do: For pain reduction, it's important to identify music that engages you—that is, it should elicit memories and/or make you want to tap your foot, sway or even dance. Singing, which requires deep breathing, or using a simple percussion instrument (such as chimes or a drum), which does not require playing specific notes, also helps.

Don't Let Medical Fear Threaten Your Health

Charles B. Inlander is a consumer advocate and health-care consultant based in Fogelsville, PA. He was the founding president of the nonprofit People's Medical Society, a consumer advocacy organization credited with key improvements in the quality of US health care in the 1980s and 1990s, and is the author of 20 books, including *Take This Book to the Hospital with You: A Consumer Guide to Surviving Your Hospital Stay*. St. Martin's.

If you're like most people, you'll have some level of fear if you're scheduled for a medical test, face an operation or even have to go in for a routine exam. But for some people, the fear can endanger their health.

Studies show that up to 20% of people forgo useful medical tests, such as colonoscopies and prostate or breast biopsies, because they are afraid of experiencing pain during the procedures. In similar fashion, up to 15 million Americans refuse to go to doctors at all for fear that a serious illness might be discovered.

All too often, medical fear is based on a lack of information rather than on the facts. If we take the time to learn about a specific test, surgery or treatment option, the fear typically diminishes—and we end up making better medical decisions. *Here's my advice for overcoming medical fear...*

•**Don't be misled by statistics.** Psychologists report that most fear arises in anticipation of something that is unknown. To diminish your fear, get the facts that are relevant to *your particular case.*

Disease statistics that are widely cited in the media are usually averages and, as a result, probably do not apply to your situation. For example, many women become anxious when they hear that one in eight women will get breast cancer. That's a frightening statistic, indeed. But one in eight is just 12% of all women, and only 3% die from the disease. That means most women who are diagnosed with breast cancer are successfully treated for the condition. The vast majority of conditions *are* treatable.

What you can do: Ask your doctor to review all possible treatments—based on your age and overall health—and for literature, DVDs or videotapes that explain these options. You also can get information from groups, such as the American Cancer Society and American Heart Association, that focus on specific conditions. Some Web sites, such as the American Academy of Family Physicians' (*www.aafp.org*) and the National Institutes of Health's (*www. medlineplus.gov*), also offer excellent treatment summaries.

•**Speak up if you're afraid of experiencing pain.** A friend of mine was afraid that he'd feel pain if he got a colonoscopy. After years of urging from his doctor, my friend finally agreed to the test. It was painless. But the bad news was that he had a cancerous tumor that had spread beyond the colon, requiring extensive treatment, including radiation and chemotherapy. My friend later acknowledged that his fear had prevented an early diagnosis that probably would have meant less extensive treatment. The fact is, today's doctors and dentists can prescribe medications that make most procedures and recoveries virtually painless.

What you can do: Speak directly to your doctor about your fear of pain and ask him/her what can be done to prevent or reduce discomfort.

Taking the steps described here will reduce your stress, which so often causes people to make inappropriate decisions. By staying calm, you will have the wherewithal to get the facts, consider your options and make a decision that is right for you.

Winning Strategies to Stop Smoking

Patrick Reynolds, founder and president of the non-profit Foundation for a Smokefree America, Box 492028, Los Angeles 90049. The organization provides resources and information for smokers who want to stop. *www. tobaccofree.org* and *www.anti-smoking.org.*

For Patrick Reynolds, it was natural to start smoking cigarettes. He's the grandson of R. J. Reynolds, founder of the tobacco company that bears his name. But he made the decision to stop smoking after his father, a brother and other family members died of smoking-induced emphysema and lung cancer. Today, Reynolds heads the Foundation for a Smokefree America, an organization that is dedicated to motivating youth to stay tobacco free and to empowering smokers to quit. He knows firsthand how difficult that can be. Reynolds tried to stop smoking 11 times before he succeeded in April 1985.

After just 20 minutes of not smoking, blood pressure and pulse rate decrease, says the American Lung Association.

After 24 hours, the risk of a heart attack decreases. After 48 hours, there's improvement in the ability to smell and taste.

Between two weeks and three months after quitting, circulation improves, walking becomes easier and lung function improves. A few months later, there's less coughing, sinus congestion, fatigue and shortness of breath.

After one year, quitters run less risk of coronary heart disease, and after five to 15 years, former smokers have the same risk of a stroke as people who never smoked.

After 10 years of not smoking, the risk of lung cancer drops by as much as 50%, and there's less chance of developing cancer of the mouth, throat, esophagus, bladder, kidney and pancreas.

After 15 years, the risk of coronary heart disease is about the same as it is for people who never smoked.

Just because you've tried unsuccessfully to stop smoking, don't give up. Becoming a non-smoker will increase your chance of living a longer and healthier life.

Problem: Each time you try to stop smoking and fail, you believe more and more that quitting is impossible. In fact, the majority of former smokers made several attempts before they succeeded.

Instead of looking at failures as evidence that you can't quit, think of them as normal steps on the road to becoming a nonsmoker.

TOUGH REALITIES

The nicotine in tobacco is addictive. Giving it up can be as difficult as turning away from other powerful drugs. The biggest mistake smokers make when they decide to stop is believing that they can do it on their own. Most statistics show that chances of success double or triple for people who follow a structured stop-smoking program.

Because addiction affects people differently, a stop-smoking program that's effective for one person may not be helpful for another. But the good news is that today smokers have more ways to get help than ever before. Some of the most effective programs are listed below.

Pick a program based on your personality. If you enjoy meeting with other smokers who are trying to quit, consider a program with support meetings. If you prefer to work alone, try an on-line program or one based on written materials.

If a particular stop-smoking program doesn't work, try it again or look for another one.

KEYS TO SUCCESS

Stop-smoking methods that are proven to work...

•**Nicotine replacement.** Accessing nicotine by a skin patch, lozenge or gum satisfies the craving without exposing you to dozens of harmful substances in tobacco.

Once the craving for nicotine is satisfied, smokers have an easier time giving up tobacco products. After about one month, reformed smokers can usually reduce their use of nicotine replacement devices.

Nicotine patches, lozenges and chewing gum are now available over the counter at pharmacies.

Typical prices per day: $4 for patches, $6 to $12 for lozenges and $5 for chewing gum.

Important: Consult your doctor about this and any other type of medication or therapy.

•**Zyban (*bupropion hydrochloride*).** This prescription drug contains the same active ingredient as the antidepressant Wellbutrin and has been successful in reducing the craving for tobacco products, especially in combination with nicotine replacement.

Typical price: About $3 a day for a generic form, or less with insurance coverage.

•**Hospital programs.** Many hospitals throughout the country offer smoking-cessation programs that usually include counseling plus nicotine replacement therapy.

Typical price: Less than $200 for counseling.

A few hospitals treat smokers on an inpatient basis, including the St. Helena Center for Health in Deer Park, California (800-358-9195 and 707-963-6475, *www.sthelenahospital.org*) and the Mayo Clinic in Rochester, Minnesota (800-344-5984, *www.mayoclinic.org*).

Week-long programs include psychological services, lectures, nutritional instruction, exercise, medical assessment and a lung screening.

Price: $4,455 at the St. Helena Center, $5,550 at the Mayo Clinic.

Though inpatient programs are expensive, for people who enjoy being pampered, treatment is effective because it can reduce the stress that comes in the first days after giving up tobacco.

Some insurance plans, including Medicare, cover all or part of the cost of both inpatient and outpatient treatments.

To find convenient outpatient and inpatient programs, contact your physician, local hospitals or your state health department.

•**Nicotine Anonymous.** The organization's 12-step program—modeled to some extent on the Alcoholics Anonymous regimen—is taught at free meetings in many cities. Smokers get support from former smokers who have quit as well as from fellow smokers who are trying to quit.

Information: 415-750-0328, *www.nicotine-anonymous.org.*

•**National cessation programs.** Popular programs are run by the American Cancer Society (800-227-2345, *www.cancer.org*) and the American Lung Association (800-586-4872 and 212-315-8700, *www.lungusa.org*).

The programs offer a combination of written materials, help in avoiding triggers that stimulate the urge to smoke, advice on using medication and support by telephone hotline and/or the Internet.

Whether or not the program you choose includes the following steps, we at the Foundation for a Smokefree America have found them especially helpful…

•Deep breathing. Every time you want a cigarette, take three deep breaths, each time exhaling slowly. As you exhale, visualize the tension leaving your body.

•Drink lots of water and other nonalcoholic liquids. They help flush nicotine from your body.

•Stay away from alcohol, sugar and coffee. They can stimulate the desire for a cigarette.

•Nibble on low-calorie foods, such as celery, apples and carrots. They help satisfy the need for oral stimulation.

•Get more exercise.

•Write down 10 good things about being a nonsmoker and 10 bad things about smoking. The effort can reinforce your self-image as a person who is a permanent nonsmoker.

•Ask for support from coworkers, friends and family members. Request that they don't smoke in your presence.

Very helpful: The National Cancer Institute's toll-free Smoking Quitline. By phoning 877-448-7848, smokers can talk to professional counselors trained to help smokers quit.

Most valuable secret: Even after the urge to smoke has diminished, overwhelming surprise nicotine attacks can—and will—happen. For instance, you may be at a party and someone will light up, and you'll be tempted to have "just one." This is where most would-be quitters fail.

Knowing it will happen and being prepared for it will help ensure that you succeed.

Best plan of action: Try to wait five minutes after the onset of an urge. It will pass. Deep breathing while you wait also helps.

■ ■ ■ ■

Loner Risk

Loneliness may increase the risk of high blood pressure.

Recent finding: Lonely people over age 50 have blood pressure readings 30 points higher than similar people who aren't lonely. This underscores the benefits of relationships with family members and friends.

Best: Maintain social connections with loved ones, and do volunteer work to stay active and involved with others.

Louise Hawkley, PhD, Chicago Center for Cognitive and Social Neuroscience, and department of psychology, University of Chicago, and leader of a study of 229 people, published in *Psychology and Aging.*

Stress Kills Brain Cells

Richard O'Connor, PhD, a psychotherapist, is the author of *Undoing Perpetual Stress: The Missing Connection Between Depression, Anxiety, and 21st Century Illness* (Berkley), *Undoing Depression* (Berkley) and *Active Treatment of Depression* (Norton).

Everyone knows that stress can contribute to weight gain, diabetes and many other ailments, but few people realize just how harmful stress can be for your brain.

Latest development: Although chronic stress has long been known to trigger the release of excessive amounts of stress hormones, such as *cortisol* and *adrenaline*, new studies show that both hormones actually kill brain cells and interfere with the production of new ones.

Fortunately, new research on the brain suggests that there may be ways to minimize, slow down and perhaps even reverse this damage. For advice on the most effective brain-protection strategies, we consulted Richard O'Connor, PhD, a renowned psychotherapist who has extensively studied the harmful effects of stress.

•Why has stress become such a serious health threat in recent years? It's a long-term historical trend that involves culture and economics. Before the Industrial Revolution (in the late 18th century), people tended to awaken in the morning when it became light and to go to bed when it turned dark. They also had a great deal of leisure time. That's been changing—and just in the past 25 years, it has changed dramatically. We're working 25% longer and harder to attain the same standard of living we did a quarter of a century ago. In fact, Americans now work as many hours as anyone in the world, including the Japanese, who are known for working incredibly long hours.

•Doesn't a certain amount of stress make people more productive? Yes, people are more productive when their work provides enough of a challenge to help them grow. But when the work is too difficult or the hours are too long, or our home life provides no relief, then stress becomes chronic. Research has consistently shown that chronic stress disrupts the functions of the immune, endocrine and digestive systems. This can result in a variety of health problems, such as asthma, heart disease and immune system deficiencies.

During the last 15 years, advances in technology have given scientists an opportunity to examine the human brain in great detail. For example, imaging studies have allowed researchers to visualize the significant loss of gray matter (the brain's information processing center) that can result from years of stress-related conditions, such as depression and anxiety. Unfortunately, no one knows for sure whether these effects are permanent.

•Are most people aware of the degree to which they are suffering from stress? By no means. We have an interest in denying the effects of stress. Our society admires people who show grace under pressure, and we all want to believe we can handle whatever life dishes out.

•Given the nature of our lives today, is it really possible to avoid stress? Yes, absolutely. The first step is to believe that you have some degree of control over your own life. Many people feel out of control—as if events are driving them rather than the other way around. Many people think that they must work 60 hours a week, but that's simply not so. If your job requires long, stressful hours, consider changing professions or finding a job in your profession that has shorter hours.

The stakes are high. People who can't reduce chronic stress live shorter lives, suffer more illness and disability, have less satisfying relationships and often are plagued by anxiety and/or depression.

•What if it's not practical to make such a drastic change? Changing our thought patterns helps. This can allow us to prevent and even reverse some of the adverse changes, such as loss of gray matter, that occur in our brain's neural circuitry as a result of chronic stress. Meditation is an effective stress-reducing strategy. Research has shown that people who spend just 20 minutes a day focusing on their breath or on calming thoughts achieve such benefits as lower blood pressure, less anxiety and reduced chronic pain.

•What can be done in addition to meditation? As we all know, exercise also is an excellent stress fighter. However, few people appreciate the importance of intimate communication. When we feel like we have a partner or are part of a group, we feel safer and more secure. As a result, the stress hormone cascade is reduced. Feeling that we have a purpose in life—having a child or pet to care for, a cause that's meaningful to us, people who need us—these are good stress fighters.

In one landmark study, residents of a nursing home were split into two groups. Half of the residents were told that they were responsible for taking care of a plant. The other half were told not to worry about the plant. After one year, the people who were caring for a plant were healthier and had fewer illnesses. They also lived longer.

•How can we improve the way we communicate with others? Communication always occurs on two levels. It's not only about the content of what's being said, but also the nature of the relationship between the people. Content communication is usually conveyed through words...relationship communication comes through tone, face and body language. It's perfectly possible to say the words "I love you" but contradict the words through a dismissive tone or a frown. Content communication should be consistent with relationship communication.

•**What if these strategies aren't effective?** For some people, self-help practices are not enough. Some of the newer antidepressants, such as selective serotonin reuptake inhibitors (SSRIs), appear to reverse stress-related brain damage and help people regain the ability to grow new brain cells.

We have evidence that psychotherapy can do the same thing. Cognitive behavior therapy, which trains patients to see how their psychological problems are the result of faulty thought patterns, has been around for more than 40 years—and it works to fight the effects of stress.

To find a cognitive behavior therapist in your area, consult the Academy of Cognitive Therapy, *www.academyofct.org*, 267-350-7683.

9

Heart & Stroke Help

Five Common Misconceptions About Heart Disease Risks

One out of every five Americans has some form of heart disease. Literally millions of cases could be prevented if people had better information about the best prevention and treatment strategies.

Despite the abundance of health information reported in the media, many people are endangering their health because they are still ill-informed about key aspects of heart disease. To learn about the most common misconceptions regarding heart disease, we spoke with Barry L. Zaret, MD, one of the country's leading specialists in cardiovascular health.

Misconception 1: High cholesterol is the main risk factor for heart attack.

Fact: While high cholesterol does increase risk, recent studies show that elevated levels (3 mg per liter or higher) of *C-reactive protein* (CRP), a protein that circulates in the bloodstream, may have an even stronger link than high cholesterol to heart attack and stroke.

Everyone has at least a small amount of CRP in the bloodstream. At higher levels, it indicates the presence of inflammation—possibly caused by an underlying bacterial or viral infection that may damage the linings of blood vessels and promote the development of atherosclerosis.

Every patient with a high risk for cardiovascular disease—smokers and/or those with a family history of heart disease, for example—should have a high-sensitivity CRP blood test. This test, unlike the standard CRP test, distinguishes between inflammation due to cardiovascular disease and other inflammatory conditions, such as arthritis. The high-sensitivity CRP test is particularly important for patients who have had a previous heart attack or who have unstable angina (chest pain caused by lack of blood to the

Barry L. Zaret, MD, Robert W. Berliner Professor of Medicine and professor of radiology at Yale University School of Medicine in New Haven, CT, is coauthor of *Heart Care for Life.* Yale University Press.

heart). An elevated CRP level in these patients indicates a very high risk for heart attack—even if cholesterol levels are normal.

Misconception 2: All adults should take a daily aspirin.

Fact: Daily aspirin therapy is often recommended for patients who have an elevated heart disease risk due to family history, smoking, obesity, diabetes and atherosclerosis. Studies show that it can curb heart attack risk in men by more than 40%.

For women, the evidence is less clear. New research indicates that women who take aspirin are more likely to experience gastrointestinal upset or bleeding problems than men. Although research shows that in women age 46 or older aspirin protects against stroke, it does not reduce heart attack risk in all of these women. Aspirin has been shown to lower heart attack risk only in women age 65 or older, whether or not they have risk factors for the disease. Women of any age who smoke or have a family history of heart disease or other risk factors may benefit from aspirin therapy. The standard recommendation for women is 81 mg daily.

There's no evidence to suggest that aspirin helps prevent a heart attack in healthy women who are under age 65. For these women, not smoking, controlling body weight, getting regular exercise and maintaining a healthful diet are the best ways to guard against the development of heart disease.

This also is true for men age 64 and younger who are healthy and have no risk factors for heart disease. However, men age 65 or older, even if healthy, should take 81 mg of aspirin daily to protect against heart disease.

Misconception 3: The greatest danger of smoking is lung cancer.

Fact: Lung cancer is obviously a concern for smokers, but the risk for cardiovascular disease is actually higher. Of the approximately 440,000 premature deaths caused annually by smoking, the majority are due to cardiovascular disease, according to the Centers for Disease Control and Prevention.

Smoking increases levels of carbon monoxide in the blood, which damages artery linings and promotes atherosclerosis. It appears to lower HDL "good" cholesterol and increase blood levels of fibrinogen, a substance in the blood that promotes clotting.

Good news: One year after quitting, the risk for heart disease drops to one-half that of current smokers—and within 15 years becomes about the same as for someone who never smoked.

Misconception 4: Exercise is dangerous if you've already had a heart attack.

Fact: Heart attack patients especially benefit from regular exercise. An analysis of 22 different studies that followed more than 4,000 patients for three years found that the death rate among patients who participated in a cardiac rehabilitation program that included exercise was 20% to 25% lower than among those who didn't exercise.

Heart patients who exercise have increased endurance, fewer chest or leg pains and improved heart function. Regular exercise also lowers blood pressure, raises HDL cholesterol and lowers resting heart rate.

Patients who have heart disease or have had a heart attack, or those who have been sedentary, should get a thorough checkup before starting an exercise program. This should include a treadmill stress test, which evaluates blood flow to the heart. Once your doctor determines that it's safe to exercise, aim for 30 minutes at least three to five days a week. Aerobic exercise—fast walking, swimming, etc.—provides the most benefits for heart patients. If you've had a heart attack or other cardiac event, start your exercise routine at a rehabilitation center, if possible. Ask your cardiologist to recommend one near you.

Misconception 5: Reports saying that chocolate is good for the heart are mostly hype.

Fact: The cocoa beans used to make chocolate are extremely rich in flavonoids, plant compounds that appear to relax small blood vessels and lower blood pressure. Some of the flavonoids in cocoa also appear to inhibit the ability of platelets to form clots in the arteries.

Harvard researchers recently studied residents of Kuna (an island off Panama), who drink an average of three to four cups of cocoa a day. (They consume even more cocoa in other foods.) Hypertension among these people is almost non-existent—until they leave the island and forgo their cocoa-rich diet. At that point, their rates of hypertension and heart disease rise.

Of course, there is a downside. The high levels of fat and sugar in chocolate can lead to obesity and elevated blood sugar. But one to two small squares daily of dark chocolate that's at least 70% cocoa and low in added sugar does appear to be good for the heart.

Surprising Symptoms of Heart Attack

Joseph Ornato, MD, professor and chairman of the department of emergency medicine at Virginia Commonwealth University in Richmond. He has authored numerous scientific papers on cardiopulmonary resuscitation.

Chest discomfort in the center of the chest—the most common heart attack symptom—occurs only in about two-thirds of all heart attack sufferers. Roughly one-quarter of heart attacks produce atypical symptoms, and the rest produce no noticeable symptoms. These so-called "silent" heart attacks are detected only later on, if the person happens to undergo an electrocardiogram (EKG), a test that involves placing electrodes on the patient's chest to map the heart's electrical activity.

Recent finding: In an international study involving nearly 21,000 patients from 14 countries, including the US, researchers found that people who experience symptoms other than chest pain—for example, sweating, fainting, breathlessness, nausea or vomiting—are more likely to be misdiagnosed…are significantly less likely to receive appropriate treatments…and are three times more likely to die in the hospital than people suffering telltale chest pain symptoms.

People over age 75, anyone with high blood pressure, women and diabetics are more likely to experience atypical heart attack symptoms that elude diagnosis—but they can happen to anyone. People with heart failure (a disorder in which the heart pumps blood inadequately due to narrowed arteries or heart valve disease) also are at increased risk for heart attack accompanied by atypical symptoms.

Problem: Failure to recognize atypical symptoms results in an estimated 20,000 to 50,000 heart attacks that are *not* diagnosed in US emergency rooms and doctors' offices, leading to potentially thousands of preventable deaths annually.

RECOGNIZING THE SYMPTOMS

A heart attack, also called *myocardial infarction* (MI), usually occurs when a blood clot (often the result of fatty buildup in the arteries) blocks a vessel to the heart, depriving the heart muscle of oxygen and nutrients. In a matter of minutes or over the course of hours, the starved heart cells begin to die, typically causing a feeling of deep pressure or tightness just beneath the breastbone.

Unfortunately, most people experiencing heart attack symptoms delay seeking treatment for two to three hours or even longer—often because they don't recognize the symptoms or they fear that they'll be embarrassed if it turns out to be nothing serious.

CALL 911

About half of heart attack patients are driven to the hospital by someone they know—or, even worse, they drive themselves—instead of arriving by ambulance. But studies have consistently shown that heart attack victims who arrive by ambulance are diagnosed and treated more quickly and have better outcomes than those who arrive on their own.

If your heart suddenly stops, which happens during about 5% of heart attacks, emergency medical technicians (EMTs) can use a defibrillator (a device that delivers an electric shock to the heart) to try to get it beating again. In addition, EMTs usually know which emergency facilities in the area are best equipped to handle cardiac emergencies. And, arriving at the hospital by ambulance usually means you'll be seen immediately by a nurse or physician.

In some areas of the country, EMTs are able to perform an EKG on the way to the hospital, substantially speeding diagnosis and treatment. It sometimes takes at least two EKGs, taken 20 to 30 minutes apart, to reveal a heart attack.

A PROPER DIAGNOSIS

The EKG is an invaluable, noninvasive diagnostic tool, but it's far from perfect. The EKG is very good at detecting damage to parts of the heart that lie closest to the chest wall, but it can miss heart attacks that cause damage to the back or far left or far right portions of the heart.

If your EKG is normal—and if you don't fit the profile of the typical heart attack patient and/or you are experiencing less common symptoms, such as shortness of breath without chest pain—it's wise to ask for a more thorough workup.

A blood test, known as a troponin test, screens for cardiac markers (proteins that increase after a heart attack).

Depending on your symptoms and blood test results, other diagnostic tests may include…

•**Coronary angiography.** This common procedure involves threading a catheter through an artery in the groin or an arm and into the heart. A contrast dye is injected through the catheter and traced via X-rays to detect narrowing and blockages in the cardiac arteries.

If a significant blockage is found, coronary angiography can immediately be followed by angioplasty, a procedure in which a tiny balloon is inflated at the tip of the catheter to open the artery, and a stent may be placed to keep it open. These catheter procedures do pose a small risk for stroke, heart attack, cardiac arrest or a punctured blood vessel. But angiography and angioplasty remain the gold standard for diagnosis and treatment of many patients with blocked arteries.

Caution: People with shellfish allergies may be allergic to the contrast dye. Medication is available to prevent an allergic reaction.

•**Computed tomographic angiography (CTA).** This noninvasive test involves the injection of a contrast dye, which is then traced by a high-resolution rapid computed tomography (CT) scanner to create a three-dimensional image of the heart and blood vessels. CTA provides information similar to that obtained by angiography without the risks associated with an invasive procedure, but it is not widely available.

•**Nuclear heart scan.** This noninvasive procedure involves injecting a radioactive material into your arm and tracking the material as it moves through the heart with a special camera that performs single photon emission computed tomography (SPECT). The image that is generated often allows doctors to identify a blockage

that may lead to a heart attack or a heart attack itself that is not detected with an EKG. If nuclear scanning is available, patients often undergo this test to decide whether a more invasive test, such as angiography, is necessary.

•**Cardiac magnetic resonance angiography (MRA).** This cutting-edge technology produces three-dimensional images of the heart and surrounding vessels, revealing both structural and functional damage. Unlike CTA and nuclear scanning, which use radiation, MRA relies on electromagnetic energy, which cannot be used in patients with pacemakers or defibrillators because it may pull on iron-containing objects in the body.

As nuclear scanning as well as CTA and MRA techniques become more widely available, physicians are likely to miss even fewer heart attacks.

■ **More from Joseph Ornato, MD…**

Red Flags for Heart Attack

Any chest discomfort or pain that lasts for more than a few minutes requires immediate medical attention. *Less common heart attack symptoms…*

•**Pain or discomfort in the back,** between the shoulder blades, in the neck, the jaw, the left shoulder and/or one or both arms.

•**Shortness of breath.**

•**Cold sweats.**

•**Nausea and/or vomiting.**

•**A feeling of indigestion.**

•**Sudden fatigue or weakness.**

•**Dizziness, light-headedness or fainting.**

•**Sense of impending doom (especially in women).**

If you experience any of the above symptoms for more than five minutes—and think you may be having a heart attack—immediately call 911.

Silent Heart Disease: Every Year 500,000 Americans Have a First Heart Attack—Often Without Warning

Prediman K. Shah, MD, director of the division of cardiology and the Atherosclerosis Research Center at Cedars-Sinai Heart Center in Los Angeles, is a professor of medicine at the David Geffen School of Medicine at the University of California, Los Angeles, and was the leader of the Screening for Heart Attack Prevention and Education (SHAPE) Task Force editorial committee.

Up to 50% of people who have a first heart attack—which often results in sudden death—don't experience prior chest pain, shortness of breath or other red flags for cardiovascular disease. A heart attack is their first and only symptom.

In the past, cardiologists relied solely on the presence of risk factors—a family history of heart disease, smoking, diabetes, etc.—to identify "silent" heart disease.

New approach: An international task force of leading cardiologists has issued updated guidelines that could prevent more than 90,000 deaths from cardiovascular disease each year in the US. Most of these patients have no prior symptoms.

RISK FACTORS AREN'T ENOUGH

Most heart attacks and many strokes are caused by atherosclerosis, buildup of cholesterol and other substances (plaque) within artery walls.

Over time, increasing accumulations of plaque can compromise circulation—or result in blood clots that block circulation to the heart (heart attack) or brain (stroke).

Plaque can accumulate for decades within artery walls without causing the arterial narrowing that results in angina (chest pain) or other symptoms. Even patients with massive amounts of plaque may be unaware that they have heart disease until they suffer a heart attack or sudden death.

RECOMMENDED TESTS

Guidelines created by the Screening for Heart Attack Prevention and Education (SHAPE) Task Force call for noninvasive screening of virtually all asymptomatic men ages 45 to 75 and women ages 55 to 75.* The tests can detect arterial changes that are present in the vast majority of heart attack patients. The SHAPE Task Force identified two tests—a computed tomography (CT) scan of the coronary arteries and an ultrasound of the carotid arteries in the neck—that are more accurate than traditional risk-factor assessments in identifying high-risk patients.

Most patients require only one of these tests. Which test is recommended will depend on insurance coverage and/or other underlying health conditions and risk factors. Although these tests are widely available, health insurers do not always cover the cost, which ranges from about $200 to $400 each.

• **Coronary artery screening.** Calcium within the coronary arteries always indicates that a patient has atherosclerosis (whether or not blockages are present). Calcium is a marker of actual disease, not just the risk of disease.

What's involved: The patient is given a CT scan of the heart and three coronary arteries. Undressing isn't required—the test is noninvasive and takes about five to 10 minutes.

Dozens of images are taken during the test and then analyzed with computer software. If calcium is present, it's given a score based on severity. A score of 0 is ideal...less than 100 indicates moderate atherosclerosis...100 to 400 represents a significant problem...and more than 400 is severe.

In patients with a score of 0 (no calcium is present), the risk of having a heart attack or stroke over the next 10 years is 0.1%. Patients with a score of 400 or higher are 20 to 30 times more likely to have a heart attack or stroke than those with a score of 0.

• **Carotid ultrasound.** This test measures the intima media thickness (the gap between the inside of the blood vessel wall and a layer called the media) of the carotid arteries. It also measures the amount of plaque that may be present.

A thickening of the intima media (the values are adjusted for age and sex) is a predictor of stroke as well as heart attack. The presence of any plaque is a red flag—patients who have plaque

*Screening for adults age 75 or older is not recommended because they are considered at high risk for cardiovascular disease based on their age alone.

in the carotid arteries generally will also show evidence of plaque in the coronary arteries.

What's involved: The patient lies on an examination table while a technician moves a *transducer* (a device that emits and receives ultrasound signals) over the carotid arteries on both sides of the neck. Like the CT scan, the test is noninvasive. It takes about 45 to 90 minutes to complete.

TREATING SILENT HEART DISEASE

With screening tests, doctors can target high-risk patients more precisely—and recommend appropriate treatment. The aggressiveness of treatment should be proportionate to the risk level.

It's possible that drugs to reduce levels of existing plaque will be on the market within the next five years. *Until then, patients diagnosed with asymptomatic cardiovascular disease (based on one of the above tests) should...*

•**Get a stress test.** Patients who test positive for calcium or plaque in the coronary or carotid arteries should undergo a cardiac stress test. The test, which uses an electrocardiogram, involves walking on a treadmill or riding a bicycle. The test detects impediments in circulation through the coronary arteries and identifies abnormal heart rhythms (arrhythmias) that can occur during exercise in patients with heart disease. Nuclear stress tests (which involve the use of radioactive dye) or echocardiogram (a type of ultrasound) stress tests generally are more reliable than simple electrocardiogram tests.

Patients with significant blockages in the coronary arteries may require invasive procedures, such as angioplasty or bypass surgery, to restore normal circulation to the heart.

•**Control cholesterol and blood pressure.** They're two important risk factors for heart attack and stroke—and both are modifiable with medication and/or lifestyle changes. A patient who tests positive for asymptomatic cardiovascular disease needs to treat these conditions much more aggressively than someone without it. For cardiovascular health, aim for a blood pressure of no more than 110 mmHg to 120 mmHg systolic (top number) and 70 mmHg to 80 mmHg diastolic (bottom number). An ideal LDL "bad" cholesterol level is no more than 70.

Most patients can significantly lower blood pressure and cholesterol with lifestyle changes —exercising for 30 minutes at least three to four times a week...losing weight, if necessary...eating less saturated fat and/or trans fat...and increasing consumption of fruits, vegetables, whole grains and fish.

Other risk factors to control: Smoking, obesity, diabetes, as well as emotional stress/anger, which may lead to a heart attack or angina. It's important to control all of these risk factors because they can amplify each other—for example, a sedentary lifestyle promotes obesity, which can lead to diabetes—or have a cumulative effect that's much more dangerous than an individual risk factor.

For more on silent heart disease, consult the Society for Heart Attack Prevention and Eradication, a nonprofit group that promotes heart disease education and research, 877-742-7311, *www.shapesociety.org.*

■ ■ ■ ■

Heart Risk Predictor

A blood test that measures levels of NT-proBNP, a protein produced when the heart is under stress, helps diagnose heart failure.

New finding: In people seeking emergency care for shortness of breath, a common symptom of heart failure and heart attack, those with high levels of NT-proBNP were three times more likely to die within one year than those without.

If you suffer from shortness of breath: Ask about getting this test to help determine your long-term prognosis. A clinical trial is underway to evaluate more aggressive drug therapy for patients with high levels of NT-proBNP.

James L. Januzzi, Jr., MD, associate medical director, coronary care unit, Massachusetts General Hospital, Boston.

■ ■ ■ ■

Breath Warning

Shortness of breath may indicate heart disease—especially if it is a new symptom in someone 50 or older.

New study: People with unexplained breathing problems have more than twice the risk of dying from cardiac causes as people who report chest pain.

Reason: Patients with chest pain are more likely to be treated.

Self-defense: If you experience shortness of breath, call your doctor.

Daniel S. Berman, MD, chief of cardiac imaging/nuclear cardiology, Cedars-Sinai Heart Center, Los Angeles, and leader of a study of 17,991 patients, published in New England Journal of Medicine.

■ ■ ■ ■

It's in the Timing

Heart attack prevention may be enhanced by taking low-dose aspirin in the late evening. Heart attacks occur most often in the early morning, when platelet activity (tendency for clotting) increases due to the body's natural circadian (24-hour) rhythm. If your doctor has prescribed aspirin therapy, taking it around 10 pm provides peak anticlotting action by early morning.

Jack M. Rosenberg, PharmD, PhD, director of the International Drug Information Center at the Arnold and Marie Schwartz College of Pharmacy Health Sciences at Long Island University in Brooklyn, NY.

■ ■ ■ ■

Aspirin and Surgery

Heart and stroke patients should not stop daily aspirin therapy prior to surgery unless directed by a physician.

Reasons: Patients who stop taking aspirin have triple the risk of suffering a stroke within a month. Studies also suggest that when patients stop taking aspirin, blood becomes even stickier for a few weeks than it would have been if they had never taken aspirin in the first place. These findings raise doubts about the practice of halting aspirin therapy for the weeks prior to surgery.

Self-defense: Talk to your doctor about the risks of discontinuing aspirin therapy before surgery.

Patrik Michel, MD, director, acute stroke unit, Lausanne University, Switzerland, and leader of a study of 309 stroke patients, published in Archives of Neurology.

■ ■ ■ ■

More Evidence

Heart patients are usually told to stop taking aspirin, which has a blood-thinning effect, seven to 10 days before bypass surgery to reduce risk for excess bleeding.

New finding: Patients who continued aspirin therapy up to the time of surgery had less lung damage from the heart-lung machine (which performs the functions of the heart during surgery). Patients also were able to come off the machine six hours sooner.

Theory: Aspirin decreases thromboxane (a substance that constricts blood vessels and is released abundantly during heart surgery). If you are scheduled for bypass surgery using a heart-lung machine, ask your doctor about continuing aspirin therapy.

Important: Discontinuing aspirin therapy before eye surgery and many other surgeries is still recommended.

Rabin Gerrah, MD, cardiothoracic surgeon, formerly at Massachusetts General Hospital, Boston.

■ ■ ■ ■

Aspirin, Stat!

If you think you may be having a heart attack, take an aspirin immediately and be sure to chew it. This gets the aspirin into your system quicker.

When taking an aspirin as a preventive: Do not chew it. There is no hurry in getting it into your system, and chewed aspirin can erode tooth enamel and cause other damage to teeth.

Jack M. Rosenberg, PharmD, PhD, director of the International Drug Information Center at the Arnold and Marie Schwartz College of Pharmacy Health Sciences at Long Island University in Brooklyn, NY.

Natural Remedies to Treat And Prevent Heart Disease

Gary Null, PhD, consumer health advocate and educator for more than 30 years, is a nationally syndicated talk show host and author of more than 70 books, including Complete Encyclopedia of Natural Healing. Bottom Line. He is adjunct professor at Fairleigh Dickinson University, Teaneck, NJ, and research director of Institute of Applied Biology, New York City.

Heart disease is America's number-one killer. Yet heart disease, which is primarily caused by inflammation and an accumulation of plaque in the coronary arteries, is one of the most preventable of all illnesses.

The key is to make lifestyle changes and take natural supplements. In fact, there is scientific evidence that people who already are suffering from heart problems can reverse the effects of the disease.

Here are three all-natural programs—one for general heart health, another for high cholesterol, a third for high blood pressure. Choose one, two or all three programs.

If you are doing more than one at a time, don't double or triple up on supplements. Take no more than the highest amount called for in one program. All the supplements listed are available at most health-food stores.

Regular aerobic exercise is part of each of these programs, and I offer advice on getting the most out of exercise at the end of this article.

Important: Review these programs, including supplement dosages, with your doctor. Natural remedies are not a substitute for traditional treatment but are meant to be done in conjunction with whatever your primary doctor or cardiologist recommends.

GENERAL HEART HEALTH

Your body needs certain nutrients to counteract the effects of internal inflammation on the coronary arteries…

•**Coenzyme Q10,** one of my favorites, is a superstar in protecting the heart. It increases oxygenation to the heart and helps prevent recurrences in people who have had a heart attack.

Recommendation: 100 mg to 300 mg daily.

•**Omega-3 fatty acids** decrease the growth rate of atherosclerotic plaque, which can lead to atherosclerosis, known as hardening of the arteries. Omega-3s also reduce the risk of arrhythmias, which can lead to sudden cardiac death.

Recommendation: 3,000 mg daily.

•**L-carnitine** helps transport long-chain fatty acids, which bring energy to the heart and aid in prevention of heart disease, high blood pressure and other cardiovascular diseases.

Recommendation: 500 mg to 1,000 mg daily.

•**Vitamin E,** which has *tocotrienols* and *gamma tocopherol*, is an antioxidant that helps protect cells against damage.

Recommendation: 200 international units (IU) daily.

•**Cayenne pepper** contains the active ingredient capsaicin, a natural blood thinner that helps prevent heart attacks and strokes.

Dosage: Sprinkle regularly on food.

Caution: Check with your doctor if you are on a blood-thinning medication, such as *warfarin* (Coumadin).

•**Hawthorn berry** relaxes blood vessels, enhances circulation and helps prevent arterial hardening.

Recommendation: 100 mg twice daily.

REDUCE CHOLESTEROL

Elevated levels of cholesterol are a major marker for heart attacks. Cholesterol provides the raw material for plaque, a fatty substance that builds up inside arteries and clogs them.

Optimal levels: A combined blood cholesterol count under 200 mg/dL, with LDL levels (often referred to as "bad" cholesterol) under 100 mg/dL and HDL levels ("good" cholesterol) over 40 mg/dL.

•**L-carnosine** is an amino acid found naturally in the body. This antioxidant helps rejuvenate cells and protect them from premature aging.

Recommendation: 500 mg to 1,000 mg daily.

•**Niacin/vitamin B3,** also known as nicotinic acid, lowers LDL cholesterol and raises HDL cholesterol.

Recommendation: 100 mg daily.

•**Shiitake mushrooms** speed up the processing of cholesterol in the liver and stimulate the immune system.

Recommendation: One-half to one cup of shiitake mushrooms daily. I like them lightly sautéed in olive oil.

•**Fruits and fruit juices** are rich in *phytonutrients*, which are powerful antioxidants.

Recommendation: Two to three servings daily. Look for juices that have no added sugar.

Best: Tart cherry, pomegranate, wild blueberry.

LOWER HIGH BLOOD PRESSURE

Prolonged high blood pressure (hypertension) damages the lining of the arteries that supply blood to the heart. This can lead to atherosclerosis.

Optimal blood pressure levels: A systolic rate (the top number) under 120 mm/Hg and a diastolic rate (the bottom number) under 80 mm/Hg.

•**Calcium citrate and magnesium.** This combination supplement promotes relaxation of the muscles, including the heart.

Recommendation: 1,500 mg daily.

•**Garlic** lowers blood pressure by thinning the blood, thus enhancing circulation.

Recommendation: Two to three cloves daily. It is easiest to digest when sautéed until translucent (not brown). Or take a 1,000-mg garlic supplement, but check with your doctor if you are on a blood-thinning drug.

•**Potassium** is needed for electrolyte balance, especially if you take blood pressure medication.

Recommendation: 500 mg daily.

•**Green vegetable juices,** especially those from spinach, broccoli and kale, help thin the blood, lowering blood pressure. You can buy them at health-food stores or make them yourself with a vegetable juicer (add a pear or an apple if you like a sweeter taste).

Recommendation: Two to three six-ounce servings daily. Check with your doctor if you are on blood-thinning medication.

EXERCISE

Regular aerobic exercise, such as fast walking, reduces cholesterol, increases circulation and keeps arteries healthy. *To get the most out of exercise...*

•**Work up to 45 minutes of aerobic exercise four times a week.** This can take several months. Get a clean bill of health from your doctor before starting.

•**Take your pulse.** Take it before you exercise, then immediately upon stopping, then every five minutes until your pulse has returned to its pre-exercise level. You know you are in shape if your pulse returns to its pre-exercise level in less than five minutes.

•**When you walk or jog,** keep your feet as close to the ground as possible, almost as if you're shuffling. The higher the knee comes off the ground, the greater the pressure and the risk of injury when your leg comes down.

■ ■ ■ ■

Speak Up

To protect your body from coronary heart disease, speak up for yourself. People who feel they are typically treated fairly at work, with their ideas recognized, are less likely to have heart disease later in life than ones who feel they are not fairly treated.

Mika Kivimaki, PhD, professor, Finnish Institute of Occupational Health and University of Helsinki, Finland.

Detecting Heart Attacks Before They Happen

W. Gregory Hundley, MD, professor of internal medicine and radiology, Wake Forest University School of Medicine, Winston-Salem, NC.
Circulation.

Magnetic resonance imaging (MRI) has been used for peering at the body's organs, but scientists say it can also tell whether chest pain is a harbinger of a future heart attack.

An MRI scan creates three-dimensional images and can predict the odds of a heart attack or heart-related death in people with chest symptoms, even after accounting for risk factors such as high blood pressure, smoking and diabetes. Intriguingly, the authors of a recent study say, the device can even pinpoint reduced blood flow to the apex of the heart, a particular signal of trouble.

The MRI pictures are clearer than conventional noninvasive heart imaging, says Dr. W. Gregory Hundley, a radiologist at Wake Forest University School of Medicine in Winston-Salem, North Carolina, and leader of the research team.

Doctors generally create an image of the heart using ultrasound technology. That test is cheap and portable, but it doesn't work very well on obese people or smokers. In fact, up to 20% of patients have pictures that are difficult to read.

TESTING THE MRI

Hundley's group gave MRI "stress tests" to 279 people who had cardiovascular disease and poor sound wave images. To simulate the effects of exercise, doctors gave the patients drugs that make the heart beat faster.

People whose blood flow was reduced by 40% or more had four times the risk of a heart attack or heart-related death over the next two years than those with normal results.

Hundley's group was the first to take pictures of damage to the apex—the top of the heart. People who had such damage were six times more likely than those without injury to experience more heart attacks or to die of cardiovascular illness.

Unfortunately, MRI is not for everyone. The machines don't function properly in the presence of metal plates, pacemakers or defibrillators, so some people can't undergo the test.

Grow Your Own "New" Heart

Andreas M. Zeiher, MD, chairman, department of medicine, University of Frankfurt, Germany.

William O'Neill, MD, former director of cardiology, William Beaumont Hospital, Detroit. He is now professor and executive dean for clinical affairs, division of cardiology at the Leonard M. Miller School of Medicine at the University of Miami.

Circulation.

A study by German cardiologists has found that infusing a patient's own stem cells into a heart artery several days after a heart attack improves the heart's pumping power and speeds healing.

THE STUDY

The study found that the stem cell infusions increased the amount of blood ejected by the left ventricle, the heart's main pumping center, by nearly 20% and decreased tissue damage by 20%.

The study, by researchers at the University of Frankfurt, included only 28 patients, and the report covers just the first four months of treatment. But the results have been encouraging and have prompted a larger trial, says study author Dr. Andreas M. Zeiher, chairman of the University's department of medicine.

"We now have a 12-month follow-up, and the improvement is preserved over this time," Zeiher says. "Not a single patient in the trial developed heart failure."

Heart failure, or a progressive loss of the heart's ability to pump blood, often happens after a heart attack. The American Heart Association estimates that more than 51,500 Americans will die of heart failure this year.

ETHICAL ISSUES AVOIDED

The stem cell treatment used by the Frankfurt scientists avoids the ethical issues of fetal stem therapy because it uses the patients' own adult stem cells—Zeiher prefers the term "progenitor cells."

These cells are more limited than fetal stem cells, but they are still valuable for their ability to transform into a variety of cells, including heart muscle cells.

Some of the adult stem cells used in the study were harvested from bone marrow, and others were heart-derived cells. Both were equally effective, Zeiher says.

The long-term trial in Frankfurt includes 60 patients. Half of the patients are receiving an infusion of stem cells, the other half are getting inactive cells.

This randomized, double-blind experiment—meaning neither patients nor doctors know who is getting which treatment—is essential for verifying that the therapy works, Zeiher says. Clinical trials are now underway.

An important part of the long-term human trial will be to show that infused stem cells can migrate from an artery into the heart muscle and form new, healthy tissue, according to Dr. William O'Neill, former director of cardiology at William Beaumont Hospital in Detroit. "The more likely they are to migrate, the more likely they are to hone in on damaged areas and improve heart function," he says.

Red Wine Protects the Heart

Mark A. Stengler, ND, naturopathic physician in private practice, La Jolla, CA...adjunct associate clinical professor at the National College of Natural Medicine, Portland, OR...author of 16 books, including *The Natural Physician's Healing Therapies* (Bottom Line Books) and coauthor of *Prescription for Natural Cures* (Wiley)...and author of the *Bottom Line/Natural Healing* newsletter.

You might have read the headlines in recent years—moderate consumption of alcohol, especially red wine, decreases the risk of cardiovascular disease. Before you assume that's reason enough to consume alcohol on a regular basis, let's look at this issue more closely.

It is true that alcohol consumption provides some cardiovascular protection. For example, when researchers combined data from 51 epidemiological studies, they found that the risk of heart disease decreased by about 20% when one to two alcoholic drinks were consumed per day. (One drink of alcohol is equivalent to 1.5 ounces of liquor, 5 ounces of wine or 12 ounces of beer.) The people who seemed to benefit most from light drinking (about 1.2 drinks a day) to moderate drinking (2.2 drinks daily) were middle-aged men and women.

Red wine has additional benefits over other alcoholic beverages, studies suggest. That's because several chemicals in red wine may protect the heart, including *resveratrol*, a polyphenol (plant pigment) with antioxidant effects. (White wine has smaller amounts of resveratrol.)

The natural compounds in red wine seem to prevent buildup of plaque in the arteries by reducing inflammation and promoting good tone in blood vessel walls. The compounds also play a role in preventing blood clots, which can obstruct blood flow and cause a heart attack or stroke. Alcoholic beverages of any type increase HDL "good" cholesterol, which removes LDL "bad" cholesterol from circulation, thereby minimizing plaque formation.

Despite these positive effects, I don't recommend that people rely on wine or any alcoholic beverages for heart disease prevention. If you do not drink alcohol on a regular basis, don't start. One of the obvious risks of regular alcohol consumption is alcoholism, a very serious and common disease in our country. *Other reasons not to drink alcohol…*

• **Cancer risk.** According to the American Cancer Society, men who have two alcoholic drinks a day and women who have one alcoholic drink a day increase their risk of certain cancers—of the esophagus, pharynx, mouth, liver, breast and colon. If you enjoy drinking each day, limit consumption to half a drink for women and one drink for men so as not to increase cancer risk.

• **Heart risk.** Paradoxically, the same amount of alcohol that has been shown to have a heart-protective effect—two drinks daily for men and one for women—also has been shown to raise triglyceride levels. High levels of these fats increase heart disease risk. Excessive drinking also raises the risk of high blood pressure, heart failure and stroke.

• **Obesity risk.** Alcohol contains simple carbohydrates. Consuming large amounts of simple carbs increases the risk of obesity and diabetes.

• **Fetal risk.** Mothers who drink alcohol during pregnancy predispose their babies to birth defects.

You can dramatically reduce your risk of heart disease by not smoking, avoiding secondhand smoke, exercising regularly and consuming a Mediterranean-style diet. This diet is rich in fruits and vegetables, whole grains, nuts, seeds, legumes and olive oil—and has low to moderate amounts of dairy, fish and poultry, and little red meat. You also might take fish oil with a combined EPA and DHA total of 500 mg daily to get heart-healthy essential fatty acids.

Also drink purple grape juice. It makes arteries more flexible and reduces the susceptibility of LDL cholesterol to cause damage in patients with coronary artery disease. Purple grape juice has potent antioxidant activity and, like red wine, contains resveratrol. It is high in simple sugars, so drink only six ounces daily—with a meal to slow sugar absorption. If you have diabetes, have no more than four ounces daily with a meal.

■ ■ ■ ■

Defibrillator Warnings: Keep Cell Phones Away

Don't place a cell phone within six inches of your implanted defibrillator when the phone is on. The defibrillator could misinterpret the cell phone's signal as a heartbeat and withhold pacing. You can talk safely on the cell phone as long as it is at least six inches from the defibrillator. The defibrillator may set off airport and other types of security systems, so be sure to carry the card that identifies you as a defibrillator patient to show security personnel. Handheld metal detectors contain magnets that may interfere with defibrillators—ask security personnel to scan you for less than 30 seconds or, better yet, search you by hand. Some medical equipment also may interfere with a defibrillator—be sure your doctor and the technician know about the unit if you need an MRI or other procedure involving electromagnetic energy.

Mayo Clinic Health Letter, 200 First St. SW, Rochester, MN 55905.

The "Sugar Cure" for Heart Attacks

Iwan C.C. van der Horst, MD, cardiologist, Hospital de Weezenlanden, Zwollen, the Netherlands.

Richard C. Becker, MD, professor of medicine, and director of the Duke Cardiovascular Thrombosis Center at Duke University, Durham, NC.

Journal of the American College of Cardiology.

Giving heart cells a dose of sugar in the important first few hours after a heart attack improves the chances of survival for most patients, according to a Dutch study.

THE STUDY

An infusion of a solution that combined glucose, insulin and potassium decreased the death rate by nearly 75% for heart attack patients who did not also have heart failure, the report says. (Only 10% of heart attack patients actually have heart failure, a serious condition in which the heart progressively loses its ability to pump blood.)

In the study, only 1.2% of the heart attack patients without heart failure who were given the infusion died, compared with 4.2% of patients who did not receive the infusion. The infusion did not help the patients who had heart failure.

Sick heart cells need energy. In an ailing heart, "oxygen is not available, so free fatty acids are burned without oxygen, and the results are toxic to the myocardium [heart muscle]," says Dr. Iwan C.C. van der Horst, a cardiologist who led the study. "The infusion of glucose allows cells to use glucose as the source of energy. This prevents the toxic products [from forming], and glucose produces more energy."

The insulin and potassium also have positive effects, including widening arteries to increase blood flow, van der Horst says.

LARGER STUDIES NEEDED

The Dutch work was praised as "a landmark study for the treatment of myocardial infarction [heart attack]" by the late Dr. Carl S. Apstein of Boston University School of Medicine. But, he said, larger studies are needed.

"Since the 1960s, there have been a number of small-scale trials of this kind of therapy. The results have been promising," says Dr. Richard C.

Becker, a professor of medicine at the University of Massachusetts Medical School and a spokesman for the American Heart Association,

The pharmaceutical industry, which is a possible source of money for a large-scale trial, "is not getting excited," because the components of the infusion are cheap and common, according to Becker.

An overview of heart attack treatments is available on the American Heart Association Web site at *www.americanheart.org.*

■ ■ ■ ■

Birthday Link to Heart Attack and Stroke

Researchers reviewed the medical records of 69,493 adults admitted to hospitals for vascular events—strokes, heart attacks and transient ischemic attacks (ministrokes)—over a two-year period.

Result: Vascular events were 27% more likely to occur on patients' birthdays than on other days—and 88% more likely if the patient had a history of high blood pressure.

Theory: Birthdays can trigger emotions that can lead to higher blood pressure, a spike in adrenaline or other reactions that may cause vascular events in at-risk individuals.

Gustavo Saposnik, MD, director, stroke research unit, St. Michael's Hospital, Toronto.

■ ■ ■ ■

Better Heart Drug

High levels of C-reactive protein (CRP), a protein that is produced in response to inflammation, contribute to heart tissue damage that accompanies heart attack and stroke.

Recent research: A new drug called *bis-(phosphocholine)-hexane* has been shown in laboratory studies to block CRP's tissue-damaging effects. The drug is the first to selectively inhibit CRP. Clinical trials on bis(phosphocholine)-hexane are expected to begin within the next two years.

Mark Pepys, MD, PhD, professor, head, department of medicine, University College London Centre for Amyloidosis and Acute Phase Proteins, London.

■ ■ ■ ■

Hospital Strategy

In a two-year study of 37,233 heart attack patients, those who underwent angioplasty in a hospital that used that treatment most often had a 36% lower risk of dying in the hospital than patients who were treated in hospitals that use angioplasty or drug treatment interchangeably.

Reason: Hospitals that specialize in angioplasty (inserting a balloon and expanding it at the site of a blood clot) restored blood flow to patients' hearts with this procedure an average of 19 minutes faster than hospitals that performed angioplasty less often.

If you're at risk for heart attack: Ask your doctor which hospitals in your area specialize in angioplasty.

Brahmajee K. Nallamothu, MD, MPH, assistant professor of internal medicine, University of Michigan, Ann Arbor.

"Open-Heart" Surgery Without Opening Your Chest

Michael Argenziano, MD, director of robotic cardiac surgery, NewYork-Presbyterian Hospital/Columbia University Medical Center, New York City.
American Heart Association scientific sessions, Chicago.

Your next heart surgeon may be a robot. Well, not exactly; but instead of standing over you wielding a scalpel, the surgeon will be sitting at a console, manipulating controls to manage robotic arms that repair a damaged portion of your heart.

And the surgery will be done in a less invasive way. Instead of making a foot-long incision in the chest, as is often required for heart surgery, the surgeon will work through four small holes that keep the damage to your body to a minimum.

"This is open-heart surgery without opening the chest," says Dr. Michael Argenziano, director of robotic cardiac surgery at New York-Presbyterian Hospital/Columbia Medical Center in New York City.

Argenziano has used Intuitive Surgical's da Vinci System, which is increasingly available at medical centers in the United States and around the world.

The system costs $1 million, but Argenziano says it is clearly worth it. "We were able to perform the operation with all the benefits we expected," he says. "There was minimum pain postoperatively and the patients went home a few days earlier than expected."

European surgeons are ahead of Americans in use of the system because the US Food and Drug Administration (FDA) has stricter requirements for approval, Argenziano says.

The FDA has approved the use of the da Vinci System for repair of the mitral valve, which controls the flow of blood between the two left chambers of the heart, and its use in bypass surgery could be next.

BENEFITS OF ROBOTIC SURGERY

The robotic procedures did take longer than conventional surgery; the heart had to be stopped for an average of 34 minutes, compared with 20 minutes. The reason might be the need for the surgeon to learn how to use the new system, Argenziano says. The average stay in the intensive care unit after surgery was 18 hours, the same as for traditional surgery, but patients did get to go home much sooner.

The benefits of the robotic cardiac surgery include...

• **Instruments can be manipulated with more accuracy than fingers.**

• **Magnified images of the surgery site** are finer than the view available to the surgeon's own eye.

• **Pencil-sized instruments are minimally invasive,** and they allow for a shorter recovery time for the patient.

"Instead of being in the hospital for seven to 10 days, the patient is there for three days," Argenziano says. "Instead of a recovery time of six to 12 weeks, it is two to four weeks. This is definitely part of the future."

More information about robotic surgery can be found at the Columbia University Department of Surgery Web site at *www.columbiasurgery.org/divisions/cardiac/robot.html.*

■ ■ ■ ■

Go to the ER!

If you think you are having a heart attack, don't rely solely on the new dial-up EKG service. Get to an emergency room immediately. The *EKGuard* transmits information to the service's on-call doctor by phone so that he/she can try to decide if you really are having a heart attack.

But: The transmitting device takes time to set up, and heart attack diagnosis is not always simple. Some attacks are easy to spot, but a small one may not be, and some people have atypical symptoms.

Bottom line: Call 911 for an ambulance or have someone drive you to the nearest emergency room.

Edward Berman, MD, cardiologist in private practice, Gardena, CA.

■ ■ ■ ■

Winter Danger

Rapid decreases in barometric pressure (usually associated with precipitation, especially during winter) are linked to heart attack. In a review of 1,300 hospital admissions of heart attack patients over a three-year period, when the pressure dropped one unit on the barometer, heart attack risk was 10% greater during the next 24 hours…a two-unit drop per hour resulted in a 20% increase in risk.

Theory: A rapid drop in barometric pressure causes inflamed atherosclerotic plaque to break off and trigger a heart attack.

Philip D. Houck, MD, assistant professor of internal medicine, Texas A&M University, Temple, TX.

■ ■ ■ ■

Help for Heart Failure

There is promising new treatment for heart failure. Diuretic drugs are the standard treatment to relieve fluid buildup, but they act slowly, tax the kidneys and aren't always effective. The new treatment—ultrafiltration—removes blood, filters excess fluid and returns the filtered blood to the body.

Advantages: Faster fluid removal, shorter hospital stays, fewer repeat admissions and less stress on the kidneys.

Best candidates: Patients with substantial fluid buildup and those who have become resistant to diuretics.

For more information, contact CHF Solutions, 866-709-4030, *www.chfsolutions.com.*

William T. Abraham, MD, director of cardiovascular medicine and professor of internal medicine, Ohio State University, Columbus.

How to Get Your Life Back After a Heart Attack

Paul Kligfield, MD, medical director of the Cardiac Health Center at NewYork-Presbyterian Hospital, and professor of medicine at Weill-Cornell Medical College, both in New York City, is author of *The Cardiac Recovery Handbook: The Complete Guide to Life After Heart Attack or Heart Surgery.* Hatherleigh.

Every year, about 650,000 Americans have their first heart attack—a temporary interruption in blood flow to the heart that causes permanent damage. Thanks to improvements in emergency and hospital care, more people than ever survive. But what comes next? We asked Paul Kligfield, MD, medical director of the Cardiac Health Center at New York-Presbyterian Hospital, for answers to questions cardiologists hear most often.

DRUGS

●**What medications should I take to prevent another heart attack?**

The American Heart Association and American College of Cardiology recommend that nearly everyone who has had a heart attack take all four of the following types of drugs…

●**Blood thinners.** These important drugs reduce platelet adhesion, the first step in the formation of blood clots that can block arteries. Low-dose aspirin (81 mg) often is used, but some patients may need a higher dose (325 mg) each day. If you're at higher risk of clotting (after certain kinds of heart attack, for example), your doctor also might prescribe *clopidogrel* (Plavix).

If your heart attack caused enough damage to continue to reduce heart action or disturb its rhythm, your risk of clots may require a different blood thinner, *warfarin* (Coumadin), to prevent the kind of blood clots that form within the chambers of the heart.

•**Beta-blockers,** such as *propanolol* (Inderal) and *atenolol* (Tenormin), also are routinely prescribed after heart attacks. These drugs lighten the load on the heart by slowing the pulse and lowering blood pressure.

•**Angiotensin-converting enzyme (ACE) inhibitors** and *angiotensin receptor blockers* (ARBs) lower blood pressure and seem to have a stabilizing effect on the arteries, allowing blood to flow from the heart more easily.

•**Statins,** such as *lovastatin* (Mevacor) and *atorvastatin* (Lipitor), are powerful cholesterol-lowering drugs. After a heart attack, the acceptable level of LDL cholesterol is lower than before the attack (100 mg/dl, compared to 130 mg/dl), and it appears that bringing it down still lower (to 80 mg/dl or even lower) can cut heart attack risk further. Statin drugs also help keep arteries healthy, perhaps by blocking inflammation.

EXERCISE

•**Will I be able to be as active as I was before my heart attack?**

It depends on how bad the heart attack was, but most people can safely return to their pre-attack activities. One key factor is *cardiac rehabilitation*—a program of gradually increasing exercise. By helping the heart work more efficiently, this regimen can reduce the risk of future heart attacks, too. I usually start patients on a cardiac rehabilitation program two to four weeks after they leave the hospital.

•**What does a cardiac rehabilitation program consist of?**

A post–heart attack program usually requires that you exercise three times a week for 12 weeks, following a plan tailored by a cardiologist to your needs and capacities and under the supervision of a nurse. Your heart function will be tracked by electrocardiography to ensure exercise is at a safe level and to spot abnormalities quickly.

With this program, you can increase the level of exercise while keeping it safe. An analysis of 48 clinical trials involving nearly 9,000 patients found that cardiac rehabilitation programs significantly reduce the rate of death from all causes, including heart disease.

•**Can I do the program on my own?**

After most heart attacks, you can—as long as it's not entirely on your own. Before starting to exercise, have a full examination by your cardiologist, including a stress test, to confirm that it is safe to exercise and to determine the right level. Regular check-ins should guide you in increasing the amount and intensity of exercise as your capacity improves.

Aerobic exercise is best—brisk walking, swimming, riding a stationary exercise bike.

Rule of thumb: A good level of intensity is one that you can sustain comfortably for 30 minutes while being able to talk but not sing. Work out at least three times a week.

You may want to track your pulse rate to make sure it remains at a level your doctor says is safe, possibly with the help of a watchlike heart monitor, available in drugstores and online for between $50 and $80.

•**What danger signs should I look for when exercising?**

Chest pain or shortness of breath disproportionate to the level of exertion are signals that your heart isn't getting enough oxygen and that you should stop. If these recur or you have unusual fatigue, consult your doctor.

•**When is it safe to have sex?**

There's no one timetable that is appropriate for every heart patient. Sex makes demands on the heart that are at least as strenuous as walking up stairs, so it's usually okay to have sex once you can climb a flight or two without difficulty.

DIET

•**What foods should I eat?**

Aim for 25% to 30% of calories from fat (no more than 7% of that from saturated fat, found in meat, butter, etc.), lots of fruits, vegetables and whole grains and other complex carbohydrates. Alcohol in moderation is okay.

Even if you're taking a statin to reduce cholesterol, diet still counts. It will help the medication work better and even may enable you to cut the dose.

Perhaps the most important thing is to keep calories down enough to maintain a healthy weight. Obesity is associated with worsening heart disease.

OTHER PROBLEMS

•Are there any diseases I should watch out for?

The big two are diabetes and high blood pressure—each substantially increases your risk of having another heart attack. Work with your doctor to keep blood pressure below 130/80. If you have diabetes, use diet and medication, if necessary, to control it.

•Is there anything else I should be concerned about?

Depression, which is fairly common after a heart attack, increases the risk of dying from heart disease. Although it hasn't been proven that treating depression reduces this risk, relieving it with medication and/or therapy certainly improves life and makes you better able to take care of your heart.

Signs and symptoms of depression may include irritability, loss of interest in activities that used to interest you and excessive tiredness.

Before Saying "Yes" To Bypass Surgery, Angioplasty or Stents, Read This

Michael D. Ozner, MD, medical director, Wellness and Prevention, Baptist Health South Florida, in Miami-Dade County, is past chairman of the American Heart Association of Miami and author of *The Miami Mediterranean Diet: Lose Weight and Lower Your Risk of Heart Disease.* Cambridge House.

About 1.6 million Americans undergo heart bypass surgery, angioplasty or stent procedures annually—even though there's no evidence that these procedures prolong life or prevent future heart attacks in the majority of patients.

The three-year survival rate for most patients who have had bypass surgery is almost exactly the same as it is for patients with heart disease who don't have surgery.

Good news: With medications and lifestyle changes, the vast majority of patients with heart disease can reduce the risk of a future heart attack by up to 80%—without undergoing expensive and risky procedures.

FLAWED APPROACH

More than half a million Americans die each year from heart disease. The majority suffer from coronary artery disease (CAD). This is caused by atherosclerosis, a condition in which a buildup of fatty deposits (called plaque) in the coronary arteries causes blockages that restrict blood flow to the heart. The plaque may rupture and result in a blood clot in the artery, which can shut off the blood supply and lead to a sudden heart attack.

Many doctors view CAD primarily as a plumbing problem. When imaging tests reveal blockages in the arteries, their first instinct is to clear out the "gunk," whether or not a patient is experiencing troublesome symptoms.

This approach is often flawed. Most bypass and stent procedures are the equivalent of cosmetic cardiology. They make blood vessels appear healthy but do little to reduce heart attack risk. In fact, most heart attacks are caused by tiny blockages that can be hard to detect—and these blockages often are not in the blood vessels that triggered all the concern in the first place.

Surgical procedures are risky. The mortality rate from bypass surgery ranges from 3% to 5%. More than 50% of patients may experience cognitive difficulties after surgery, and patients who have bypass surgery are nearly four times more likely to suffer a subsequent stroke. Those are poor odds for procedures that don't necessarily prolong life or make patients healthier.

MEDICAL BYPASS

Some patients—those with unstable CAD—do require intervention, such as bypass surgery or a stent procedure.

Example: A person with critical blockages in multiple coronary arteries and a weak heart muscle.

Most patients with CAD, however, are stable and unlikely to benefit from a bypass or stent. They are the best candidates for what might be called a *medical bypass*. With medications and lifestyle changes, most of these patients can eliminate symptoms (if any) and reduce heart attack risk. Only in rare cases, if symptoms get worse, would one of these patients need to consider medical intervention.

One key factor in cardiovascular health is to have an ongoing relationship with your doctor—he/she can advise you on the best steps to take to prevent and treat heart disease. *He may recommend that you…*

•**Follow a Mediterranean-style diet.** Eat lots of fruits, vegetables, whole grains and legumes…olive oil instead of butter or margarine…several servings of fish weekly…and no more than a few weekly servings of lean meats.

The landmark Lyon Diet Heart Study, which followed more than 600 participants for almost four years, showed that people who ate a Mediterranean diet instead of a typical American diet had a 50% to 70% reduction in recurrent cardiovascular disease.

•**Relax** with yoga, meditation, exercise, etc. Doctors don't always ask patients about stress—which is why it is sometimes called the "forgotten" risk factor for heart disease. People who successfully manage stress can significantly lower blood pressure and the risk of heart disease. Stress management also lowers the risk for arrhythmias (heart rate irregularities).

•**Exercise daily** for 30 to 45 minutes. It is one of the best ways to maintain a healthy weight and prevent or control diabetes and high blood pressure. Regular exercise raises levels of HDL "good" cholesterol. It also can contribute to weight control—which can reduce inflammation in the blood vessels, a risk factor for CAD.

All forms of exercise are beneficial. Aerobic exercise, such as brisk walking, is the best choice for most people because it doesn't require a high level of fitness to do it.

•**Get your cholesterol checked**—and take cholesterol-lowering medication if necessary. Everyone should have a blood test for cholesterol annually. Research indicates that aggressive lowering of LDL cholesterol helps reduce risk of heart disease and death from CAD.

Bonus: Cholesterol-lowering statin drugs also reduce inflammation in the blood vessels.

•**Take a baby aspirin daily.** It helps prevent platelets from clumping together and forming clots that can block blood flow to the heart. The anti-inflammatory effects of aspirin are also beneficial. Since aspirin may cause gastrointestinal upset and/or bleeding, talk with your doctor before initiating aspirin therapy for CAD prevention.

•**See your dentist twice a year.** Studies have shown that patients with periodontal disease—gum inflammation that can result in tooth loss—have a higher risk of heart attack and stroke than those without it.

•**Get more omega-3s.** Most Americans are deficient in omega-3 fatty acids. Omega-3s lower inflammation and triglycerides, a fat that can put you at risk for heart disease. Omega-3s reduce the risk of arrhythmias and heart attack. Sources of omega-3s include cold-water fish, such as salmon, and plant sources, such as walnuts and flaxseed. Or ask your doctor about taking a fish oil supplement.

■ ■ ■ ■

Statins and Your Heart

Heart disease may be partly reversed with very high doses of statins. The drugs cause significant drops in LDL ("bad") cholesterol—stopping the progression of heart disease and, in some cases, reversing it. Results are preliminary and more research is needed, but reducing cholesterol levels aggressively, especially focusing on LDL, provides substantial cardiovascular benefits.

Steven E. Nissen, MD, cardiologist, The Cleveland Clinic, and leader of a study of 507 heart patients who took high daily doses of the statin Crestor for two years, presented at the annual scientific meeting of the American College of Cardiology.

■ ■ ■ ■

Statins Stat

Heart attack patients treated with statins within 24 hours of the attack were 54% less likely to die than those not given the drugs.

Reason: Statins increase the release of nitric oxide, which reduces heart damage.

If you are diagnosed as having a heart attack: Ask your physician about starting a statin immediately.

Gregg C. Fonarow, MD, professor of cardiovascular medicine and science, David Geffen School of Medicine, UCLA, director of the Ahmanson-UCLA Cardiomyopathy Center and leader of a study of 170,000 patients, published in *The American Journal of Cardiology*.

■■■■

Kids' Heart Risk

School-age children who eat out four or more times a week were more likely to develop cardiovascular risks, such as higher blood pressure, lower "good" cholesterol and changes in other markers for heart disease and diabetes, than children who eat out less often.

Karen Olson, RN, BSN, nurse and executive director, Cardiovascular Research and Education Foundation, Wausau, WI, and leader of a study of the eating habits of 621 school-age children, presented at a meeting of the American Heart Association.

■■■■

Smoking Ban Benefit

Heart attack rates have declined in cities that have banned smoking in public places.

Example: After Pueblo, Colorado, banned smoking in restaurants, bars and other public places, the number of heart attacks fell by almost 30%. Thirty-five thousand Americans die of heart disease caused by exposure to second-hand smoke.

Centers for Disease Control and Prevention, Atlanta.

■■■■

A Web Site for Heart Smarts

What you need to know about different types of heart medications, risk factors, diagnostic tests, surgical procedures and more can be found on-line at *www.texasheartinsti tute.org*.

Heart Attack Survival Checklist

Marjory Abrams, publisher, newsletters, Boardroom Inc., 281 Tresser Blvd., Stamford, CT 06901.

Choosing the right hospital can be the key to surviving a heart attack, says cardiologist Richard Stein, MD, director of the Urban Community Cardiology Program at New York City's New York University Medical Center and author of the book *Outliving Heart Disease*.

To find the best hospital in your area, he advises checking the Hospital Compare heart attack statistics at *www.hospitalcompare.hhs.gov*. Do it now before an emergency. Call hospital cardiology departments to find out which perform emergency angioplasty to open blocked arteries and if it is done less than 90 minutes after arrival at the hospital. (Medication can be used instead, but angioplasty generally is more effective if done soon after arrival.) If possible, pick a hospital where your doctor has admitting privileges.

HEART ATTACK SURVIVAL CHECKLIST

1. Know the symptoms. The classic heart attack symptoms are chest pain or discomfort that may also be felt in the neck or left arm and may be accompanied by nausea. Women are more likely than men to have atypical symptoms—shortness of breath, profound fatigue, sweating, racing heart, burning stomach.

2. Call 911 for an ambulance to take you to the hospital immediately if you experience symptoms. Don't let embarrassment or concern that it is something minor prevent you from getting checked.

3. Chew two full-strength aspirin.

4. Tell ambulance and hospital staff that you think you are having a heart attack. Don't minimize your symptoms.

5. Have the appropriate tests, including an electrocardiogram (EKG) and blood tests to measure certain cardiac enzymes. Dr. Stein notes that women with the atypical symptoms cited above (or their health advocates) may need to be assertive to get these tests.

According to Dr. Stein, accurate diagnosis may require several EKGs and/or blood tests within the first few hours. When former Vice President Dick Cheney experienced chest and shoulder pain, the initial EKG and blood tests showed no evidence of a heart attack. Several hours later, the second set of tests revealed that he had indeed suffered a minor heart attack.

6. Get the proper treatment. Treatment should begin even before all test results are in…

•Aspirin right away if you didn't take it at home.

•A beta-blocker, such as *metoprolol* (Lopressor) or *propranolol* (Inderal) should be given to most patients to decrease the heart's need for oxygen-rich blood and minimize heart damage.

•Nitroglycerin, prescribed for chest pain or if the heart is short of blood, dilates blood vessels.

•ACE inhibitor to decrease blood pressure and the heart's workload.

•Clot-busting treatments, such as the drug tPA, and/or angioplasty.

Make a copy of this page so that you can take it with you to the ER. I hope that you will never need it, but if you do, it may save your life.

Deadly Blood Clots: Deep Vein Thrombosis Kills 200,000 Americans

Geno J. Merli, MD, a leading vascular expert, is director of the Jefferson Center for Vascular Diseases at Thomas Jefferson University Hospital, and senior vice president and chief medical officer, both in Philadelphia.

Blood clots that form in the coronary arteries cause heart attacks. However, many people don't realize that clots also can form in other parts of the vascular system—particularly in the deep veins of the legs, causing *deep vein thrombosis* (DVT). These clots can be even more dangerous than clots in the coronary arteries because they are more likely to go undiagnosed.

Of the 200,000 Americans who die each year from clots due to DVT, about 80% of them experience no symptoms. The worst danger of DVT is *pulmonary embolism*, in which one or more clots travel from the legs to the lungs. One in five people who experience a pulmonary embolism dies from it.

Clots that form in veins near the surface of the skin (superficial thrombosis) are rarely serious. But those that form in the deep veins in the legs—particularly in the *femoral* (thigh), *iliac* (groin) or *popliteal* (behind the knee) veins—are often life-threatening. They rarely dissolve on their own. If anything, they're likely to keep growing—and eventually break free and travel to the lungs.

Even for patients who survive a pulmonary embolism, the risk for complications is high. About 4% to 5% will go on to develop pulmonary hypertension (high blood pressure in the lungs). Others are at risk for *venous* insufficiency, in which the leg veins are damaged, resulting in chronic leg swelling, skin thickening and skin ulceration.

MAJOR RISK FACTORS

About 10% of patients with DVT have a genetic tendency to form blood clots. *Other risk factors…*

•**Prolonged periods of inactivity** can allow dangerous blood clots to form. This can occur during lengthy (more than five hours) plane flights or car trips. Long-distance air or car travelers who have other risk factors, such as congestive heart failure, previous heart attack, obesity or a history of previous blood clots, are at even greater risk than healthy people of developing DVT.

Orthopedic surgery, particularly hip or knee replacement, causes immobilization, often for days to weeks. Anticlotting drugs are given to prevent clots from forming.

•**Lung, pancreatic or ovarian cancer.** Patients with these cancers have increased levels of procoagulants, substances in the blood that promote clotting.

•**Pregnancy and childbirth.** Pulmonary embolism is a cause of death in women during childbirth. Many women who die from pulmonary embolism during or soon after childbirth may have an underlying genetic disorder that increases the risk for clots.

Women who take the breast cancer drug *tamoxifen* (Nolvadex) or supplemental estrogen in birth control pills or hormone therapy also are at increased risk for DVT and pulmonary embolism.

DIAGNOSIS AND TREATMENT

Although patients with DVT frequently do not have symptoms, when clots completely block a vein, persistent symptoms of leg swelling, redness, increased warmth and pain develop.

Red flag: A pulmonary embolism from DVT typically causes sudden shortness of breath, chest pain or a cough that produces blood-tinged mucus. If you experience these symptoms, get to an emergency room *immediately.* About 10% of patients with pulmonary embolism die within one hour.

DVT usually can be diagnosed with ultrasound, a painless, 30-minute test that uses high-frequency sound waves to view the veins.

If your doctor suspects that you have a pulmonary embolism, he/she may recommend a pulmonary computed tomography (CT) scan, in which a dye is injected into an arm vein and computerized images are taken as the dye passes through the blood vessels in the lungs.

Most patients require medication to prevent the clot from growing—and to prevent additional clots from forming.

Typical treatment approaches…

•**DVT patients with a pulmonary embolism who are hemodynamically stable**—that is, their blood pressure and level of oxygen in the blood are close to normal—are hospitalized for five to seven days and treated with intravenous heparin, an anticoagulant medication.

Recent development: A new formulation known as low-molecular-weight heparin, which is better absorbed and lasts longer than intravenous heparin, can be given as a subcutaneous shot at home for five to seven days.

After one of these initial treatments, *warfarin* (Coumadin) is given for three to six months.

•**DVT patients with a pulmonary embolism who are hemodynamically unstable** are at the greatest risk for death—they have low blood pressure and poor oxygen saturation. These patients are typically given *tissue plasminogen activator* (tPA), an intravenous, clot-dissolving drug that is often used to treat stroke patients. This therapy is followed by intravenous or subcutaneous heparin for five to seven days. Warfarin is then given for three to six months to prevent recurrent clots.

In rare cases, when a patient can not receive anticoagulant therapy because of bleeding, recent surgery or an allergy to the medication, doctors may use a vein filter, a small metal trap that's inserted into the *inferior vena cava* (the large vein that carries blood from the lower part of the body to the heart). The filter prevents pulmonary embolism by catching clots before they can be carried to the lungs.

PREVENTING DVT

Patients at risk for DVT who are hospitalized and bedridden are usually treated with subcutaneous heparin.

If they cannot take heparin, they may be fitted with graduated compression stockings or external pneumatic compression sleeves (which inflate and deflate every 30 seconds by air compression). Both exert varying amounts of pressure along the legs to keep blood from pooling in the legs and forming clots.

Other ways to prevent DVT…

•**Rotate your ankles and flex your toes** at least every 20 minutes when traveling by plane or car. On airplanes, periodically stand and rise up on your tip-toes repeatedly. These exercises flex the calf muscles, which pushes blood out of the legs and helps prevent DVT.

•**Walk daily.** Walking, like other forms of leg exercise, keeps blood moving upward out of the leg veins. The more that blood moves, the less likely it is to form unwanted clots. It's particularly important for hospitalized patients to attempt to walk with appropriate supervision or at least move their legs while they're in bed.

Recent studies indicate that about 15% of hospitalized patients get DVT. Bedridden patients also should flex their feet, ankles and calves every 20 to 30 minutes when awake for clot prevention.

•**Drink water.** Airplane and car travelers on trips of five hours or more should drink two to four eight-ounce glasses of water during the flight or car ride. This increases blood volume, which may help prevent blood clotting.

■ ■ ■ ■

Clot Buster

Dangerous blood clots can be eliminated with a new ultrasound device. The device consists of a hair-thin wire with transducers attached. After it is positioned near a clot, the transducers emit a high-frequency sound to loosen blood fibers and force an anticlotting drug through the clot. The device is in limited use for people who have deep-vein thrombosis or arterial-bypass grafts in the leg or acute blood clots in leg arteries. It is being studied for more uses, including dissolving stroke-causing clots in the brain.

James F. Benenati, MD, medical director, Peripheral Vascular Laboratory, Baptist Cardiac and Vascular Institute, Miami, FL.

■ ■ ■ ■

Heart Risk

Common bacteria may cause heart attacks in younger men. *Chlamydia pneumoniae* causes a flu-like upper-respiratory infection that can turn into pneumonia. People infected with it produce antibodies called IgA and IgG.

New finding: Men ages 30 to 50 with high levels of the IgA antibody are more likely to have serious heart attacks. The more recent the bacterial infection, the more likely a heart attack.

Christine M. Arcari, PhD, assistant professor of population health sciences, University of Wisconsin Medical School, Madison, and leader of a study of 300 male soldiers, ages 30 to 50, who had heart attacks, published in *Clinical Infectious Diseases*.

■ ■ ■ ■

New Therapy

An injection of the blood thinner *enoxaparin* (Lovenox) is typically given to heart attack patients in the emergency room to help prevent a clot from blocking the blood flow in the coronary arteries, but it can trigger internal bleeding—a fatal complication.

New finding: Fondaparinux (Arixtra), a blood thinner also given by injection, is equally effective at dissolving a blood clot or preventing

one from forming, but with about half the risk for internal bleeding.

Salim Yusuf, MD, professor of medicine, Michael G. DeGroote School of Medicine, McMaster University, Ontario, Canada.

■ ■ ■ ■

Drug Benefit

A clot-busting drug revives cardiac arrest patients. In a study of 163 people who suffered cardiac arrest (in which electrical signals that regulate the heart become erratic due to heart attack, a blood clot in the lungs or other causes), 50 patients received the clot-busting drug tenecteplase (TNKase), while the rest received cardiopulmonary resuscitation, drugs such as Adrenalin, and an electric shock to the heart.

Result: Twenty-six percent of those treated with tenecteplase were revived, compared with 12% in the standard therapy group.

William P. Bozeman, MD, associate professor, department of emergency medicine, Wake Forest University, Winston-Salem, NC.

Abdominal Aortic Aneurysms Kill 15,000 Americans Each Year

David Tilson, MD, Ailsa Mellon Bruce Professor of Surgery at Columbia University and director emeritus of the department of surgery at St. Luke's-Roosevelt Hospital Center, both in New York City, was chairman of a recent international conference on abdominal aortic aneurysm in New York City.

Until recently, hypertension, diabetes and other chronic conditions have been identified as America's biggest health threats.

Now: As the baby boomer population ages, abdominal aortic aneurysm (AAA), a potentially far more serious condition, appears to be on the rise.

An aneurysm is a bulge in a blood vessel wall. Some aneurysms affect blood vessels in the brain. Others occur in the aorta, the main artery of the body. About the diameter of a garden hose, the aorta travels from the heart through the chest and abdomen, then forms separate branches that enter the legs. Aortic aneurysms usually form in the abdominal cavity—the artery walls may be weaker in this area.

Surgeons can repair AAAs before they rupture—if they are identified. An AAA can be discovered during tests, such as X-rays or computed tomography (CT) scans, for other conditions. But what makes an AAA so deadly is that it usually is not identified and typically causes no symptoms prior to rupturing.

Caution: If you have symptoms of an AAA—abdominal or back pain, along with a pulsating mass in the abdomen—seek immediate medical attention.

A SILENT THREAT

Most AAAs grow slowly—about 3 millimeters (mm) to 4 mm (about one-eighth inch) per year. A person can have an AAA for decades before it becomes large enough to rupture—if it ever does. Even when doctors detect an AAA, they're unlikely to recommend surgery if the aneurysm is smaller than 5 centimeters (cm)—about two inches—in diameter.

Warning: AAA patients must be closely monitored with imaging tests for the rest of their lives because the risk of dying from a rupture is so high. An AAA that's 5 cm or larger—or that's growing more than 1 cm a year—has a significant risk of rupturing and needs to be surgically repaired.

CAUSES OF AAA

AAAs have some of the same risk factors as those for atherosclerosis, the accumulation of fatty deposits (plaque) that weaken artery walls. The same measures that doctors recommend to prevent heart attacks—not smoking, controlling hypertension and cholesterol, for example—also can help prevent AAAs.

Some patients, particularly those with Marfan's syndrome (a genetic condition that's characterized by extreme height), are born with a weakness in the aorta wall. In rare cases, infection or inflammation (vasculitis) in a blood vessel can predispose patients to AAA.

For small or slow-growing AAAs, "watchful waiting" is usually best. Patients are advised to have ultrasound screenings every six months to determine whether the AAA is getting large enough or expanding fast enough to rupture.

Caution: Patients with high-risk AAAs should avoid heavy lifting and intense aerobic exercises. These activities can cause surges in blood pressure that can increase the risk for a rupture.

Researchers have investigated the use of medications—for example, beta-blockers, such as *propranolol* (Inderal), and tetracycline antibiotics—to slow the growth of AAAs. The results have been disappointing. New drugs are being investigated, but surgery is currently the best option.

NEW TREATMENT STRATEGIES

Surgery to repair an AAA involves opening the abdomen, removing the damaged section of artery and replacing it with a synthetic graft.

Newer approach: A procedure known as endovascular surgery involves the insertion of a catheter into an artery in the leg. The surgeon threads the catheter upward into the damaged section of artery. Once the catheter is in place, it's used to insert and fasten a metal-covered mesh tube (stent) that reinforces the blood vessel.

The initial success rate of both procedures—open surgery and endovascular repair—has been determined to be about 96% to 98%, respectively. However, patients who undergo an endovascular procedure spend less time in the hospital and recover more quickly.

New finding: A study of 28,000 Medicare patients, published in the *Journal of Vascular Surgery*, found that the risk for death with endovascular procedures was 1.9%, compared with 5.2% for conventional surgery. It's still not known, however, whether the stent-grafts used in endovascular repair are as durable as the repairs performed in conventional surgery.

Guidelines...

•**Relatively young,** healthy AAA patients are generally advised to have conventional surgery. These patients are typically better able to withstand the operation, and the hand-sewn repair might last longer than an endovascular graft.

•**Older patients** who may not be healthy enough to withstand conventional surgery—and who have a shorter life expectancy—will probably benefit more from an endovascular procedure.

REGULAR SCREENING

Because an AAA rarely causes symptoms but is so deadly, anyone with risk factors—men who are current or former smokers or are age 65 or older...and men and women who are age 65 or older and have a first-degree relative (parent, sibling or child) with an AAA—should undergo an ultrasound test to detect changes in the artery wall. If you have a family history of AAA in one or more relatives who was diagnosed with an AAA under the age of 65, then you should be screened at a younger age.

An initial ultrasound at age 65 for people with any of the above risk factors is recommended. Cardiovascular risk factors, such as elevated blood pressure and/or cholesterol, also may be considered. Patients with no signs of disease at this age don't require additional tests.

Exception: Patients with a family history of AAAs should be retested every five years. Their risk is at least three times higher than that of someone without a family history.

Medicare and most other health insurers will pay for ultrasound screening in patients age 65 and older who have AAA risk factors.

■ ■ ■ ■

Vitamins Help

B vitamins do prevent heart attacks, despite a report to the contrary. One study failed to show reduced heart attack risk. However, the participants included stroke and heart attack survivors and diabetics, all of whom were taking drugs that may have affected the results.

Best: Continue or start taking B-6, B-12 and folate if a homocysteine test shows that your levels are above eight. Raised homocysteine levels are a warning sign of heart disease.

Kilmer S. McCully, MD, chief of pathology and laboratory medicine, VA Boston Healthcare System, West Roxbury, MA.

■ ■ ■ ■

Bad Noise

A n excessively noisy environment can cause a heart attack.

Recent findings: Men who live in noisy areas are 50% more likely to suffer a heart attack than men who live in quiet areas. Women living in noisy areas are 300% more likely to have a heart attack than women who live in quiet areas.

Probable reason: Prolonged exposure to noise in the 65- to 75-decibel range (such as that in a city street-level apartment) causes your

body to release *adrenaline*, which drives up blood pressure. Normal conversation levels are at about 60 decibels, so if you have to repeatedly raise your voice to be heard, you're in an unhealthy noise environment.

Mehmet C. Oz, MD, founder and director of the Complementary Medicine Program and director of the Cardiovascular Institute at NewYork-Presbyterian Medical Center and professor and vice chairman of surgery at Columbia University, both in New York City, is coauthor of *You: The Smart Patient: An Insider's Handbook for Getting the Best Treatment.* Free Press.

■ ■ ■ ■

Early Warnings

W omen may experience heart attack warning symptoms more than a month before the attack. The most common symptom is overwhelming fatigue, reported by 71% of women. Other reported symptoms are sleep disturbance (48%), shortness of breath (42%), indigestion (39%) and anxiety (35%). Only 30% experience chest discomfort.

Self-defense: If you are experiencing these or any suspicious symptoms, contact your doctor.

Jean McSweeney, PhD, RN, professor, University of Arkansas for Medical Sciences, Little Rock, and lead researcher of a survey of 515 female heart attack survivors, published in *Circulation.*

The Upside to Being Overweight: Heart Attack Survival

Kristin Newby, MD, associate professor of medicine, Duke University Medical Center, Durham, North Carolina.

Terrence J. Sacchi, MD, chief of cardiology, New York Methodist Hospital, Brooklyn, NY.

Eric Eisenstein, assistant research professor of medicine, Duke Clinical Research Institute, Durham, NC.

American College of Cardiology scientific sessions.

Y ou know that being obese is bad for you. And no one should misconstrue the following information as an excuse for being fat. But there may be a short-term silver lining to all the fat that Americans typically accumulate.

Much to their surprise, scientists at Duke University Medical Center found that overweight and obese individuals actually have better one-year survival rates following a heart attack than people whose weight is within a healthier range.

Not so surprisingly, the researchers also determined that the United States had the highest combined rate of obese and very obese people, while Asia had the highest percentage of healthy-weight people.

One of the ironies in these findings is that being heavy is a risk factor for coronary artery disease, and may have been what helped land these patients in the hospital in the first place.

THE STUDY

Dr. Kristin Newby, coauthor of the study, had initially hypothesized with her colleagues that overweight and obese people would have higher mortality rates in the first year following a heart attack. But the results of the study showed that the opposite was true.

To test the hypothesis, the researchers looked at data already collected for two related international trials and divided the 15,904 participants into four groups according to their body mass index (BMI)—normal (18.5–24.9), overweight (25–29.9), obese (30–34.9) and very obese (35 and higher).

One year after a heart attack, individuals in the obese group had the lowest death rate (2.2%), followed by those classified as very obese (2.6%), overweight (2.7%) and, finally, normal bringing up the rear (4.3%). Normal-weight participants also had the highest death rate after 90 days, and a similar pattern was evident even at 30 days.

AGE vs. GIRTH

The results may have more to do with the age of the people studied than their girth, says Dr. Terrence J. Sacchi, chief of cardiology at New York Methodist Hospital in Brooklyn, New York. "It seems that the patients in the overweight and obese group were younger, and also they were treated more aggressively," he says.

"When adjusted for confounders, the findings still held up in overweight and obese people, but not in the very obese group," says Eric Eisenstein, Newby's coauthor and an assistant research professor at the Duke Clinical Research Institute. "Even after adjusting for all those factors, we still found that at one year, the overweight and obese groups had a lower hazard of death than the normal people and the very obese people," he says.

RESULTS NOT AN INDICATOR OF LONG-TERM SURVIVAL

One thing to keep in mind is that this study looked only at intermediate-term survival, not long-term survival. "I don't think anyone is advocating remaining obese," Sacchi says. "It is associated with multiple risk factors."

For a handy online calculator that quickly computes your BMI, visit the National Heart, Lung, and Blood Institute at *http://nhlbisupport. com/bmi/bmicalc.htm.*

What Your Doctor Won't Tell You About High Blood Pressure

Aggie Casey, RN, associate in medicine at Harvard Medical School, and Herbert Benson, MD, associate professor of medicine at Harvard Medical School, are coauthors of *The Harvard Medical School Guide to Lowering Your Blood Pressure.* McGraw-Hill.

High blood pressure (hypertension) has long been termed "the silent killer." That's because it usually causes no symptoms, but it sets the stage for stroke, heart attack and serious kidney damage.

Hypertension is defined as a blood pressure reading of 140/90 millimeters of mercury (mm/Hg) or higher.

Now: Data compiled from several studies indicates that risk for death from heart disease and stroke starts to increase with a blood pressure above 115/75 mm/Hg.

After reviewing more than 30 clinical trials, the National Heart, Lung and Blood Institute recently created a new category of hypertension called "prehypertension"—a systolic (top number) blood pressure of 120 to 139 mm/Hg and/or a diastolic (bottom number) blood pressure of 80 to 89 mm/Hg.

Result: An estimated 90 million Americans —including 40 million who previously were considered not to be at risk—are now said to have prehypertension or hypertension. *Medication is the most common treatment, but you can avoid medication or reduce the dosage by following these important but often-overlooked strategies...*

TAKE STRESS SERIOUSLY

When treating hypertension, doctors rarely pay attention to stress—but that's a mistake. Stress hormones, such as *epinephrine* and *norepinephrine*, make the heart beat faster and blood vessels constrict, significantly raising blood pressure.

The stress response can be triggered by driving in traffic...waiting in long lines...or arguing with a family member, friend or colleague. Many studies have demonstrated that emotional stress can contribute to high blood pressure.

Solution: Allocate time each day to elicit the relaxation response. This is a quiet state that can be brought forth by meditation or breathing exercises. Start with five or 10 minutes several days a week, and gradually increase it to 20 minutes daily.

For optimal benefit, add a "minirelaxation" exercise whenever you feel stress building.

Examples: Count slowly from 10 to zero, inhaling and exhaling slowly with each number. Or sit quietly and focus on your breathing for one minute. With every inhalation, repeat "I am" to yourself. With each exhalation, repeat "at peace."

Important: Activities that people often perceive as "relaxing," such as watching TV, do not have a quieting effect on the mind and body.

LOW-PRESSURE EATING

Most people know the basics of a healthful diet—unsaturated fats, whole grains, low-fat dairy and at least five servings of fruits and vegetables daily. But there's more.

In the landmark Dietary Approaches to Stop Hypertension (DASH) study, 459 men and women with high blood pressure were divided into three groups—one group followed the typical American diet...one added more fruits and vegetables...and the third followed a diet designed specifically for the program.

The DASH diet contained four daily servings of fruits, four servings of vegetables, two to three servings of low-fat dairy foods and a moderate intake of fish, poultry and nuts, along with a decreased intake of saturated and total fats. Blood pressure dropped most significantly in the DASH group—by an average of 11.4 mm/Hg systolic and 5.5 mm/Hg diastolic.

Researchers are unsure why the DASH diet helps control blood pressure so effectively, but they speculate that it may be the potassium, calcium and magnesium that it contains...the antioxidant compounds...and/or the fiber.

Also, most people still are consuming too much salt. The usual recommendation for daily sodium intake is 2,400 mg (approximately one-half teaspoon of salt) or less, but most Americans consume 3,300 mg or more daily.

For the 50% of people who are salt sensitive (they experience an increase in their blood pressure after eating salty foods), even 2,400 mg daily is too high.

A later DASH study found that cutting sodium intake back to 1,500 mg daily reduced blood pressure by 12 mm/Hg systolic and 6 mm/Hg diastolic.

Surprisingly, only 15% of an average person's sodium intake comes from the salt shaker. Processed foods are the biggest source.

To detect sources of hidden sodium, it's crucial to read food labels. A snack should have no more than 200 mg per serving and a meal entrée no more than 500 mg. Less is even better.

Unexpected sodium sources...

• **Processed foods** labeled "healthy" or "lean." A serving may be low in calories, cholesterol and saturated fat but include up to half your daily sodium quota.

• **Packaged meats** and soy-based meat substitutes.

• **Canned foods,** including beans, tomatoes and other vegetables as well as tuna (even if it's packed in water).

• **Breakfast cereals,** including some "heart-healthy," high-fiber or whole-grain varieties.

■ ■ ■ ■

Cola, Not Coffee, Raises Blood Pressure in Women

The association between hypertension and caffeine had been attributed to coffee, but a new study shows that caffeinated colas increase women's risk of hypertension. Researchers speculate that some other compound in soda is responsible for increased risk.

Wolfgang Winkelmayer, MD, department of pharmacoepidemiology and pharmacoeconomics, Brigham and Women's Hospital, Boston, and leader of an analysis of 12 years of data from 155,594 women, published in *The Journal of the American Medical Association*.

■ ■ ■ ■

Hypertension Alert

More than 300 men who had normal or high blood pressure (above 140/90) were given tests for verbal fluency (generating words) and short-term memory (word recall).

Result: People who were hypertensive despite taking medication performed 2.4 times worse on verbal fluency and 1.3 times worse on short-term memory.

Theory: Chronic hypertension damages small blood vessels, which interferes with blood flow to the brain.

Self-defense: Maintain a blood pressure of 140/90 or below (ideally, below 120/80) through diet and exercise and/or medication.

Christopher B. Brady, PhD, instructor in medicine, Brigham and Women's Hospital, Boston.

■ ■ ■ ■

Prehypertension Alert

Prehypertension—blood pressure of 120 to 139 mmHg/80 to 89 mmHg—usually is treated with lifestyle measures, such as weight loss, salt restriction and exercise.

New finding: In a study of 800 prehypertension patients, those who took the blood pressure medication *candesartan* (Atacand) for two years while making lifestyle changes had a 15.6% lower risk of developing hypertension than those who didn't take medication.

If your blood pressure is in the upper range of prehypertension: Ask your doctor about medication in addition to lifestyle changes.

Shawna D. Nesbitt, MD, medical director, Parkland Hypertension Clinic, University of Texas Southwestern Medical Center, Dallas.

■ ■ ■ ■

Better Blood Pressure Reading

Systolic (the top number) blood pressure averaged 14 points higher when taken shortly after a patient arrived in the exam room and sat on an exam table than when he/she sat in a chair for five minutes.

Theory: Foot and back support induce a relaxed state, which helps allow for accurate blood pressure readings.

Self-defense: The next time you have your blood pressure taken, ask if you can sit in a chair with your back supported and feet flat on the floor for five minutes. Remain in this position (instead of sitting on an exam table) while the reading is taken.

Melanie F. Turner, RN, cardiology clinic practice nurse, University of Virginia Health System, Charlottesville.

■ ■ ■ ■

Skim Milk Helps

Skim milk lowers hypertension risk according to recent research.

New finding: A two-year study of 5,880 people found that those who consumed more than two to three servings of skim milk and other low-fat dairy products daily had half the risk of developing high blood pressure of those who rarely or never consumed such foods. Whole milk products were not found to reduce hypertension risk.

Theory: The calcium, which is highly absorbable in skim dairy products, may decrease blood pressure.

Alvaro Alonso, MD, PhD, assistant professor, division of epidemiology and community health, School of Public Health, University of Minnesota, Minneapolis.

Nobel Prize Winner's Secrets for a Healthy Heart

Louis J. Ignarro, PhD, the winner of the 1998 Nobel Prize in Physiology or Medicine, distinguished professor of molecular biology at the University of California, Los Angeles, David Geffen School of Medicine, and author of *NO More Heart Disease.* St. Martin's Press.

The 1998 Nobel Prize in Physiology or Medicine was awarded to Louis J. Ignarro, PhD, for ground-breaking research into nitric oxide (NO), a naturally occurring molecule in the body that may be the key to cardiovascular health. *Bottom Line/Health* has reported on the importance of Dr. Ignarro's discovery and its relevance to heart health. Dr. Ignarro's discovery has prompted every major pharmaceutical company to conduct research into the benefit of

NO on heart and circulatory systems. *The results include...*

DRUGS FOR ERECTILE DYSFUNCTION

Viagra (*sildenafil citrate*) was the first drug to utilize the NO pathway. In the late 1980s, researchers at Pfizer who were testing a new angina (chest pain due to heart disease) drug realized that about 75% of male patients who took it reported more frequent and firmer erections. Pfizer quickly decided to market the drug for erectile dysfunction instead of angina.

TREATMENT FOR INFANTS' LUNGS

NO is now used in hospitals to treat persistent pulmonary hypertension—a form of hypertension that only affects blood vessels in the lungs—in newborns. In the past, newborns with this condition were unlikely to survive. NO gas, given via inhalation for one to five days, can *completely* reverse this condition.

ON THE HORIZON: A BETTER BETA-BLOCKER

A drug (*nebivolol*) developed in Europe—now approved by the USFDA—is the *first* beta-blocker that also elevates NO. Millions of Americans take beta-blockers (also called beta-adrenergic blocking agents), drugs for treating heart disease, hypertension and many other conditions. They cause the heart to beat more slowly and with less force, reducing blood pressure and improving circulation.

The drug is mainly used for hypertension and treating elderly patients with heart failure. Because it raises NO, it also reduces blood clots and arterial buildups that can lead to heart disease/heart attack. It's the *only* beta-blocker that produces these benefits.

HOW TO INCREASE YOUR NITRIC OXIDE LEVELS

Nitric oxide (NO) causes blood vessels to dilate, prevents blood clots, regulates blood pressure and may inhibit the accumulation of arterial plaque—the underlying cause of most heart attacks. It's possible that *most* cases of heart disease could be eliminated by elevating NO.

It isn't yet known how much NO is normally present in the body, or what levels are optimal. NO is difficult to measure because it's a gas that breaks down almost instantly with air exposure. Simpler tests will be needed before doctors can measure NO as a standard part of patient care.

It's thought that NO levels remain at normal levels until early adulthood, and then gradually decline.

Reason: Damage to the endothelial cells from factors such as lifetime exposure to high blood pressure, a high-fat diet, a sedentary lifestyle, arterial inflammation and oxidation from free radicals. Damage to the cells causes a reduction in NO.

Increasing NO is a critical component of heart-disease prevention.

The difficulty: Developing ways to administer it. Because it's an unstable gas that's destroyed by hemoglobin in the blood, it can't be taken as a drug/supplement. However, patients can take other supplements that increase production of NO in the blood vessels. Lifestyle changes, including not smoking, can cause levels to rise. Important steps...

•**Take L-arginine.** It's an amino acid found in nuts, meats, grains, fish, etc. It passes through the intestine into the blood. From the blood it enters endothelial cells, where it's converted to NO. A Mayo Clinic study found that patients taking L-arginine had significant improvements in endothelial function and blood flow, compared to those taking placebos.

Recommended: 5,000 to 6,000 milligrams (mg) of arginine daily.

Eat nuts: A cup of peanuts contains about 5,000 milligrams of arginine. Fish and soy milk are also good sources. Or take arginine supplements—2,000 to 3,000 mg, twice daily.

•**Combine L-arginine with L-citrulline.** Supplemental arginine doesn't enter cells readily unless it's combined with L-citrulline, another amino acid. Melons are the richest food sources of L-citrulline, but don't provide high enough levels to significantly increase NO. Supplemental amounts are probably required.

Recommended dose: 200 to 1,000 mg, taken once daily.

•**Get more antioxidants.** We now believe that vitamin E and other antioxidant nutrients may *protect* NO by reducing its breakdown by free radicals. This might be the *main* reason that antioxidants promote cardiovascular health. *Helpful...*

•A daily multi that includes vitamin E. Don't take high-dose vitamin E supplements; recent studies suggest that patients taking daily doses of

400 IU or more may have *more* disease than those who don't supplement at these levels. The amount of vitamin E in most multi-vitamin-mineral supplements, usually about 50 IU, is well within the safety zone—and can promote NO production.

•500–1,000 mg vitamin C daily. Like vitamin E, it reduces oxidation in the blood vessels and may cause a rise in NO. A study in the journal *Circulation* that looked at 11,000 patients found that those who consumed high levels of vitamin C experienced less thickening of the carotid arteries. A reduction in arterial plaque is associated with higher NO levels.

•**Exercise at least 20 minutes three days a week.** It stimulates endothelial cells to *continuously* produce more NO, even on days you don't exercise.

•**Minimize saturated fat.** It contributes to the accumulation of arterial plaque and impairs NO production.

Better: Olive, canola or other vegetables oils, along with the omega-3 fatty acids found in fish and flaxseed. These fats help protect the endothelium by elevating levels of beneficial HDL cholesterol and lowering the harmful, LDL form.

•**Get more fiber.** The dietary fiber in grains, fruits and other plant foods lowers blood pressure and LDL cholesterol and raises HDL, thereby protecting endothelial cells.

Bonus: Many of the foods that contain fiber are also rich in antioxidants, which can protect NO.

Recommended amount: At least 25 g fiber daily. Patients who follow the government's dietary recommendations get at least this much.

•**Enjoy a glass of red wine.** It contains resveratrol, a powerful antioxidant that can delay the breakdown of NO. It's about *1,000 times* more potent than vitamin C.

If you don't drink wine: Have a daily glass of pomegranate or grape juice. They contain many of the same antioxidants as red wine.

■ ■ ■ ■

Better Treatment for Low Blood Pressure

Orthostatic hypotension occurs when blood pressure drops rapidly upon standing. It can result in dizziness, light-headedness or fainting.

New finding: Patients with orthostatic hypotension who took *pyridostigmine* (Mestinon), either alone or with *midodrine* (ProAmatine), another medication used to treat low blood pressure, had a smaller drop in standing blood pressure than when they took a placebo.

Bonus: Unlike midodrine, pyridostigmine did not increase blood pressure when patients were lying down. In rare cases, pyridostigmine can cause digestive upset and diarrhea.

Wolfgang Singer, MD, senior resident, department of neurology, Mayo Medical Center, Rochester, MN.

■ ■ ■ ■

Nighttime Blood Pressure Risk

Congestive heart failure (CHF) risk has been linked to nighttime blood pressure. High blood pressure is a risk factor for CHF, in which the heart pumps blood inadequately. In a study of 951 men, those whose blood pressure did not drop at night (as typically occurs in healthy adults)—or whose pressure rose—were 2.3 times more likely to develop CHF over a nine-year period than those whose blood pressure fell at night.

If you have high blood pressure: Ask your doctor whether your nighttime blood pressure should be checked.

Erik Ingelsson, MD, PhD, department of public health and caring sciences, division of geriatrics, Uppsala University, Sweden.

Cholesterol Mania— Millions of Americans Are Taking Drugs They Don't Need

Mark A. Stengler, ND, naturopathic physician in private practice, La Jolla, CA...adjunct associate clinical professor at the National College of Natural Medicine, Portland, OR...author of 16 books, including *The Natural Physician's Healing Therapies* (Bottom Line Books) and coauthor of *Prescription for Natural Cures* (Wiley)...and author of the *Bottom Line/Natural Healing* newsletter.

Cholesterol-lowering "statin" drugs are big business. *Atorvastatin* (Lipitor), one of the most popular drugs in this class, is among the most commonly prescribed medications in the US. With approximately 12 million Americans using it, US sales of Lipitor totaled about $8 billion in 2005.

Why are so many people taking these drugs? It's long been known that elevated cholesterol levels are associated with an increased risk of heart disease, but now consumers are being given an additional incentive to use these drugs. The National Institutes of Health's National Cholesterol Education Program (NCEP) Adult Treatment Panel III released updated guidelines for cholesterol drug therapy. According to these guidelines, 37 million Americans—or one in five adults—are eligible for cholesterol-lowering medication. Previous guidelines recommended these drugs for 13 million Americans. I find the new guidelines very suspect. Read on, and you will understand why.

The updated recommendations are based on a review of five clinical trials using statins. One of the key changes in the new guidelines involved lowering the optimal range for LDL "bad" cholesterol in the blood in all adults to less than 100 milligrams per deciliter (mg/dL). People with cardiovascular disease or other risk factors, such as diabetes, smoking or hypertension, are told to aim for the same level—with an "optional target" of less than 70 mg/dL. It is rare for any of the patients I test—whether they are healthy or not—to have LDL levels below 100 mg/dL. I encourage my patients to strive for an LDL level of 100 mg/dL to 130 mg/dL with an HDL "good" cholesterol level of 50 mg/dL or higher.

The evidence for the new NCEP guidelines was challenged in a letter from the Center for Science in the Public Interest (CSPI), a nonprofit consumer advocacy group that conducts research in health and nutrition.

The CSPI letter, which was signed by more than three dozen physicians, epidemiologists and other scientists, urged the NIH to convene an independent panel to conduct a second review of the studies. They wrote, "There is strong evidence to suggest that an objective, independent reevaluation of the scientific evidence from the five new studies of statin therapy would lead to different conclusions than those presented by the current NCEP. The studies cited do not demonstrate that statins benefit women of any

age or men over 70 who do not already have heart disease."

The letter also cited concerns that were raised after one study showed that statin therapy significantly increases the risk of some types of cancer in the elderly. (Research has, indeed, shown that statins can increase risk of nonmelanoma skin cancer and breast cancer. Other research, however, has linked statin use to a decreased risk for some types of cancer, such as colon and prostate malignancies.)

There was another alarming discovery. Eight of the nine authors of the new LDL recommendations had financial ties to statin drug manufacturers, including Pfizer, Merck, Bristol-Myers Squibb and AstraZeneca. In response to the CSPI letter, the NIH declared that the scientific basis for the new guidelines was adequate and there was no conflict of interest for panel members.

No conflict? Is it pure coincidence that most of the authors of the guidelines had financial ties to statin manufacturers? Now millions of Americans are following these misguided recommendations for statin therapy instead of using natural treatments.

STATIN DANGERS

Statins first became available in the US in the late 1980s and were marketed as a unique treatment for elevated cholesterol—they inhibit an enzyme called *3-hydroxymethylglutaryl-coenzyme A* (HMG-CoA) reductase, which is involved in the production of cholesterol in the liver. In addition to Lipitor, other statins include *rosuvastatin* (Crestor), *lovastatin* (Mevacor), and *pravastatin* (Pravachol).

The most common side effects of statins are headache, nausea, vomiting, constipation, diarrhea, rash, weakness, muscle and joint pain, and increased liver enzymes. The most serious, but rare, side effects are liver failure and rhabdomyolysis, a life-threatening condition that causes extensive damage to muscles.

In addition, statins deplete the body of coenzyme Q10 (CoQ10), a naturally occurring substance that your body needs to create energy in cells, particularly heart cells. In one study, the CoQ10 blood levels of Lipitor users were reduced by 50% after 30 days of statin use. To prevent a deficiency of CoQ10, I recommend that my patients who use statins take 100 mg to 200 mg daily of CoQ10.

CHOLESTEROL-LOWERING THE NATURAL WAY

The general medical community pays lip service to diet and lifestyle changes as a first line of therapy for abnormal cholesterol levels—but many patients are pressured to begin drug therapy right away, while diet and lifestyle changes are only an afterthought. Conventional doctors often tell patients that they have a genetic cholesterol problem and that cholesterol-lowering medication is their only option because diet and lifestyle changes would not be sufficient. Some people, such as those who have acute cardiovascular issues or extremely high total cholesterol levels (above 350 mg/dL) and/or significantly elevated LDL levels (above 200 mg/dL), are usually not able to control their cholesterol levels through diet and lifestyle changes alone. However, many people can bring their cholesterol and lipid levels into normal range by watching what they eat, exercising and reducing their stress levels. Nutritional supplements also are an option.

If your cholesterol is mildly or moderately elevated (total cholesterol 200 mg/dL to 239 mg/dL …and/or LDL above 130 mg/dL), get a baseline cholesterol test if your levels haven't been tested in the last six months. Then try the diet and lifestyle changes described in this article for eight to 12 weeks. If you don't see at least a 10% reduction (based on a repeat blood test), add targeted nutritional supplements.

People who are unable to reduce their cholesterol levels through diet and exercise and/or who have family members with high cholesterol *are* likely to be genetically predisposed to the condition. Such people should *not* rely on lifestyle changes alone.

Better: They should combine the healthful practices described here with regular supplement use.

Important: There are times when I recommend statin therapy—immediately after a heart attack to reduce inflammation and when there is extreme elevation in total cholesterol (400 mg/dL or higher) and/or LDL cholesterol (210 mg/dL or higher), usually due to genetics.

DIET AND LIFESTYLE CHANGES

My suggestions for improving cholesterol levels…

1. Reduce saturated fat in your diet to less than seven percent of daily calories. Saturated fat is found mainly in beef, veal, pork and poultry (especially in dark meat and the skin of any meat). Saturated fat is plentiful in most dairy products, except nonfat yogurt, reduced-fat cheese and skimmed milk. Small amounts are found in coconut and palm oils, so consume these sparingly. To monitor your saturated fat intake, keep a daily record based on food label information.

Avoid products that contain trans fatty acids, which often are found in deep-fried foods, bakery products, packaged snack foods, margarines (except those with cholesterol-reducing plant stanols or plant sterols), crackers and vegetable shortening. If a product contains more than 0.5 grams of trans fat per serving, the label will list the trans fat content. Avoid foods that "hide" trans fats by using the term "partially hydrogenated" on their labels and claiming 0 grams (g) of trans fat. Common offenders include baked goods, crackers and packaged mixes. Cardiovascular disease is linked to trans fat intake because this unhealthful fat raises levels of LDL cholesterol and blood fats known as triglycerides, while lowering beneficial HDL cholesterol. Cook with organic olive or canola oil. Macadamia nut oil also is healthful.

2. Consume two weekly servings of foods rich in heart-healthy omega-3 fatty acids. Sources include some types of fish—anchovies, Atlantic herring, sardines, tilapia and wild or canned salmon. For a list of fish not contaminated with mercury or polychlorinated biphenyls (PCBs), check *www.oceansalive.org*, the Web site of The Environmental Defense Fund, a Washington, DC-based, nonprofit group dedicated to solving environmental problems.

3. Eat five to seven daily servings of fruits and vegetables. Produce contains antioxidants that prevent oxidation (cell damage from negatively charged molecules known as free radicals) of cholesterol, as well as fiber that helps lower cholesterol.

4. Consume foods that contain soluble (dissolves in liquid) fiber, such as beans, barley, oats, peas, apples, oranges and pears. Soluble fiber reduces the absorption of cholesterol from the intestines into the bloodstream. For example, a daily bowl of oatmeal can reduce total cholesterol by as much as 23%. Oatmeal also has been shown to curb LDL cholesterol levels without lowering beneficial HDL cholesterol.

5. Eat nuts, such as walnuts and almonds, which are rich in healthful monounsaturated fatty acids. A study conducted in Barcelona, Spain, showed that a walnut-rich diet reduces total cholesterol by 4.4% and LDL cholesterol by 6.4%. Macadamia nuts, pistachios, almonds, hazelnuts and pecans also have been shown to reduce cholesterol levels. Eat a handful of walnuts or any of the nuts listed above daily.

6. Add ground flaxseed (up to one-quarter cup daily, taken in two doses) to protein shakes, cereal and/or salads. Flaxseed has been shown to reduce total and LDL cholesterol. Drink 10 ounces of water for every two tablespoons of flaxseed you consume, to prevent intestinal blockage.

7. Consume 20 g to 30 g of soy protein daily (in food or protein powder form). Some studies suggest that soy protein may lower cholesterol levels in some people with high cholesterol. Because soy protein has a potential estrogen-like effect, it should be avoided by women who have breast cancer or a family history of the disease.

8. Reduce daily intake of simple sugars, such as those in crackers, cookies and soda. Found in abundance in processed packaged foods and many baked goods, they have been shown to decrease HDL cholesterol. By cutting back, you also reduce risk of elevated insulin levels, which lead to increased production of cholesterol by the liver.

9. Exercise regularly. Thirty minutes of exercise, such as brisk walking, swimming, biking or tennis, three to five times a week is effective for lowering elevated cholesterol.

10. Lose weight and body fat. Weight loss by people who are overweight reduces cholesterol levels and prevents insulin resistance, a blood sugar problem that can lead to high cholesterol.

11. Don't smoke. Smokers have lower levels of HDL cholesterol and an increased risk of heart attacks.

12. Adopt stress-reduction techniques, such as deep breathing and biofeedback. Stress has been shown to elevate cholesterol in most individuals.

You Don't Need Drugs to Control Your Cholesterol

Allan Magaziner, DO, a clinical instructor in the department of family practice at the Robert Wood Johnson University of Medicine and Dentistry in New Brunswick, NJ, and the medical director of the Magaziner Center for Wellness and Anti-Aging Medicine in Cherry Hill, NJ (www.drmagaziner.com). A past president of the American College for Advancement in Medicine, he is the author of The All-Natural Cardio Cure. Avery.

I t's widely known that low cholesterol levels help prevent heart attack and stroke. But that's only part of the story. Levels of HDL "good" cholesterol must be high enough to carry harmful forms of cholesterol to the liver to be excreted.

New finding: Research has shown that decreasing LDL "bad" cholesterol by 40% and increasing HDL by 30% lowers the risk for heart attack or stroke by 70%—a much greater reduction of risk than occurs from lowering either total cholesterol or LDL levels.

The pharmaceutical industry has worked feverishly to develop a prescription medication that significantly increases HDL levels, to be used as a complement to cholesterol-lowering statins that focus primarily on lowering LDL levels.

Latest development: The new drug *torcetrapib* was pegged as a blockbuster that increases HDL levels by 60%—that is, until late-stage clinical trials showed that torcetrapib actually increased heart problems and death rates.

What you may not know: Therapeutic doses of niacin (vitamin B-3) effectively boost HDL levels—and lower LDL and total cholesterol.

THE "CHOLESTEROL VITAMIN"

Fifty years ago, Canadian scientists discovered that high doses of nicotinic acid—a form of niacin—could lower total cholesterol. In a 1975 study of men with heart disease, niacin was shown to reduce the rate of second heart attacks. Later, niacin was found to boost heart-protective HDL levels.

Although niacin alone cannot help everyone with abnormal cholesterol levels—often it is best used in combination with a statin—the vitamin is one of the most effective nondrug therapies available.

Ask your doctor about taking niacin if after trying cholesterol-lowering medication you have suffered side effects or your cholesterol levels have not improved within three months of getting a cholesterol test. Or consider trying niacin with the nondrug therapies described below.

How to use: Start with 100 mg of niacin daily and build up over one week to 500 mg a day. Every week, increase the dose by 500 mg until you reach 2,000 mg a day, taken in three divided doses, with meals. Be certain to use nicotinic acid, not niacinamide, a form of B vitamin that does not improve cholesterol levels. Consult your doctor before taking niacin.

The most common side effect of niacin is flushing—a warm, itchy, rash-like reddening of the face, neck and chest, which lasts about 10 minutes. Flushing is caused by niacin's ability to trigger vasodilation (widening of blood vessels).

To lessen this side effect, choose a form of niacin known as inositol hexanicotinate. It helps prevent the flush without reducing niacin's effectiveness.

Caution: Niacin should be avoided by people with a history of liver disease or stomach ulcers and used with caution by patients with diabetes and/or gallbladder disease. In addition, high-dose niacin (2,000 mg or more) may interact with certain medications, including alpha-blockers, such as *doxazosin* (Cardura), and the diabetes drug *metformin* (Glucophage).

OTHER NONDRUG THERAPIES

A diet that keeps sugar and processed food to an absolute minimum and emphasizes fruits and vegetables...whole grains...beans...fish... lean meats...and nuts and seeds can help lower LDL cholesterol and raise HDL levels. So can regular exercise, such as brisk walking, and losing excess weight.

Other nondrug approaches can lower total and LDL cholesterol and boost HDL. Combine the following nondrug therapies with niacin for maximum effectiveness...

•**Red yeast rice.** This Chinese medicine—a yeast that is grown on white rice, then fermented—contains monacolins, substances that act as naturally occurring statins. Research in China shows that red yeast rice can lower total cholesterol by 11% to 30%.

Typical use: Take 1,200 to 2,400 mg a day of red yeast rice, in two to four doses, with meals.

Not recommended: Policosanol—a supplement derived from cane sugar that also contains natural statins—has been widely promoted as effective for lowering cholesterol. However, several recent studies show that policosanol has no significant effect on cholesterol.

•**Fish oil and flaxseed.** Fish oil and flaxseed supply omega-3 fatty acids, which lower total cholesterol and LDL levels and raise HDL levels.

Typical dose: For fish oil, take supplements containing a total of 3 g daily of eicosapentaenoic acid (EPA) and docosahexaenoic acid (DHA). If you take a blood-thinning drug, such as aspirin or *warfarin* (Coumadin), check with your doctor before taking this dose of fish oil. Or use one to three teaspoons of ground flaxseed a day, sprinkled on food or mixed with water or juice. Flaxseed also can help relieve constipation and ease arthritis pain.

•**Soy.** Many studies show that soy can help lower total and LDL cholesterol.

Typical use: Try to get 20 g of soy protein a day—the equivalent of eight ounces of tofu...or one cup of edamame (soy) beans.

Important: Soy ice cream and other processed soy foods don't deliver enough soy to help reduce cholesterol.

Caution: If you have been diagnosed with a hormone-dependent cancer, such as some breast malignancies, or are at risk for such a condition, check with your doctor before adding soy to your diet.

•**Plant sterols.** These natural substances, which block the absorption of cholesterol in the intestines, are found in fruits, vegetables, beans, grains and other plants. Regular intake can reduce total cholesterol by 10% and LDL by 14%. Products with plant sterols (or a similar form, plant stanols) include spreads, salad dressings, snack bars and dietary supplements.

Typical use: Aim for 1 g to 2 g daily of plant sterols.

•**Walnuts.** A study published in the medical journal *Angiology* showed that people who ate a handful of walnuts daily for eight weeks had a 9 percent increase in HDL. Walnuts contain polyphenol antioxidants, which also inhibit oxidation of LDL cholesterol.

Recommended intake: One ounce of raw walnuts three times daily.

The Cholesterol Study You Never Saw

Richard C. Pasternak, MD, director of preventive cardiology, Massachusetts General Hospital, and associate professor of medicine, Harvard Medical School, Boston.

Barry Davis, MD, PhD, director of the ALLHAT Clinical Trial Center, and professor of biometry, University of Texas School of Public Health, Houston.

Joshua S. Benner, PharmD, ScD, principal, ValueMedics Research, Falls Church, VA.

The Journal of the American Medical Association.

S tatins really do lower cholesterol, but that doesn't automatically mean a lower risk of heart problems or death compared with conventional therapy to lower blood fat, say researchers.

Still, experts say the results don't undermine the broad utility of statins, which are among the most widely prescribed drugs on the planet. Rather, the study suggests doctors need to do a better job of keeping patients on the medications if they expect the same performance produced by rigorous clinical trials.

This is not a blemish on statins, according to Dr. Richard C. Pasternak, a Harvard University cardiologist. "It's more a blemish on our ability to maintain best practice," he says.

STATIN'S STATUS

In previous studies, statins have led to marked reductions in total cholesterol and low-density lipoprotein (LDL), or the "bad," form of blood fat. However, those trials have been in tightly controlled settings that don't necessarily reflect the real world. They also typically involved people with high or extremely high cholesterol.

The latest study involved more than 10,000 people with moderately high cholesterol, high blood pressure under control with medication and at least one risk factor for heart disease, such as type 2 diabetes.

Half the patients got *pravastatin* (Pravachol); the rest received the usual advice to make lifestyle changes, such as a low-fat diet and exercise. Nearly one-third of those in the latter group switched to pravastatin during the eight-year study.

After four years, people taking the statin drug saw their total cholesterol drop by approximately twice as much as those in the other group.

However, the gap between the two groups for total cholesterol was less than half the average of eight other large studies comparing statins with other therapies.

The number of deaths in each group was essentially identical, as were the rates of nonfatal heart attacks and deadly artery trouble.

"The [clinical] trials provide a compelling case for statin use, but in the real world, it doesn't appear that patients are getting the full benefit that the trials suggest," says Joshua S. Benner, principal of ValueMedics Research, a Virginia-based consulting firm.

STATINS STILL WORK

Dr. Barry Davis, who ran the latest study at the University of Texas Health Science Center in Houston, explains that the benefits of the statin were obscured by patients switching out of the usual care group and into the statin arm of the study. That migration was prompted by the evidence of the drug's ability to prevent cardiovascular deaths made public during the late 1990s. If no one had switched, they probably would have seen a difference in death rates, he says.

You can learn more about statins at the My HeartCentral.com Website at *www.healthcentral. com/heart-disease.*

■ ■ ■ ■

Red Grapefruit Lowers Cholesterol

Red grapefruit lowers LDL (bad) cholesterol even in people who don't respond to statin drugs, such as Lescol and Lipitor.

Recent study: After eating one red grapefruit a day for four weeks, people whose cholesterol levels had failed to respond to statins lowered their LDL by 20%. People who ate white grapefruit did not benefit as much.

Caution: Chemicals in grapefruit can interfere with enzymes that break down certain drugs in your digestive system, such as Celebrex and Mevacor. Ask your doctor before changing your diet.

Shela Gorinstein, PhD, chief scientist of medicinal chemistry and natural products, The Hebrew University of Jerusalem, Israel, and leader of a study of antioxidants, published in *Journal of Agricultural and Food Chemistry.*

The Protein That Cleans Out Arteries

E. Murat Tuzcu, MD, cardiologist and professor of medicine, The Cleveland Clinic Foundation.
Roger Blumenthal, MD, cardiologist, Johns Hopkins School of Medicine, Baltimore.
The Cleveland Clinic statement.
The Journal of the American Medical Association.

A new weapon in the ongoing war on heart disease has been forged by some very healthy Italians.

A manmade form of cholesterol that mimics a protein in the Italians' blood took only weeks to reverse atherosclerosis in patients whose arteries had become clogged over decades.

REMARKABLE FINDING

If the success of this therapy continues, it could mean huge strides in the battle against heart disease—the leading cause of death in the United States. In the last decade, the gold standard of preventive medicine has been the use of statin drugs, which lower low-density lipoprotein (LDL, the "bad" cholesterol). In this study, however, the patients received an intravenous infusion of synthetic high-density lipoprotein (HDL, the "good" cholesterol).

"This is the first convincing demonstration that targeting HDL can benefit patients with heart disease," says Dr. Steven Nissen, a Cleveland Clinic cardiologist and director of a study on manmade cholesterol.

HOW IT DEVELOPED

The development of the manmade cholesterol started 30 years ago, when researchers noticed that 40 people who were living in the village of Limone sul Garda in northern Italy were heart-healthy despite having very low levels of HDL, which should have left them vulnerable to disease. They lived long lives, and their arteries were remarkably clear.

"Normally, we would get very, very concerned because [we believed people with low HDLs would be] at high risk," says Dr. E. Murat Tuzcu, a cardiologist and professor of medicine at The Cleveland Clinic who took part in the study.

The researchers discovered that these people carried a variant in a blood protein called apolipoprotein A-1, which is a component of HDL. They named it ApoA-1 Milano, after the city of Milan, where the original work was conducted. Researchers at Esperion Therapeutics Inc., a biotech firm in Ann Arbor, Michigan, derived a synthetic version of this protein. Esperion then sponsored the study of the synthetic cholesterol.

THE STUDY

The study, which was led by The Cleveland Clinic team, was done at 10 centers across the United States and involved only 47 patients, aged 38 to 82 years, who had angina or had previously had a cardiovascular event such as a heart attack.

The patients underwent ultrasound at the start of the study to determine the amount of blockage in their arteries. They were then randomly assigned to one of three groups—high-dose or low-dose synthetic cholesterol or placebo. The injections were given every week for five weeks.

After six weeks, the researchers again conducted ultrasounds on the patients' arteries. Tuzcu says those who received the therapy saw their arteries clear by 4%. "That might not sound great, but actually it is," he says. "It is the first time in a human being that we can change or regress atherosclerosis in six weeks. Incredible!"

However, more and larger studies are needed, Tuzcu cautions.

Atrial Fibrillation— You Could Have It and Not Know It

Jonathan Halperin, MD, director of clinical cardiology at Mount Sinai Medical Center and a professor of medicine at Mount Sinai School of Medicine, both in New York City, is also a spokesman for the American Heart Association, *www.americanheart.org*.

Atrial fibrillation (AF) is a common type of arrhythmia (irregular heartbeat) affecting more than two million Americans. This figure includes up to 5 percent of people over age 65, many of whom may not know they have the disease. If untreated, AF significantly increases risk of stroke and other blood-clot-related ailments. Fifteen percent of all strokes occur in people with AF, and it's the leading cause of stroke in women over age 75.

Some good news: In recent years, doctors have learned a great deal about AF. If it's detected and treated promptly, AF-related strokes can usually be prevented.

WHAT IS ATRIAL FIBRILLATION?

The job of the two upper chambers of the heart (*atria*) is to pump blood into the lower chambers (*ventricles*), which in turn pump blood to the rest of the body. Normally, a regular electric pulse courses through the heart around 60 times per minute, triggering each heartbeat. But in AF, the atria beat several hundred times a minute, causing them to wiggle, or *fibrillate*, instead of contract in a regular heartbeat.

Unlike *ventricular fibrillation*—which can cause sudden death if not treated within minutes—atrial fibrillation is not immediately life threatening. But because it causes blood to stagnate in the atria, it sharply increases the risk that a blood clot could form there, then break off

and lodge in the brain, causing a stroke, or in another organ or limb, blocking circulation.

With AF, increased electrical signals also reach the ventricles, causing them to beat more rapidly and less efficiently. This can lead to increased heart rate as well as reduced blood flow—which, in turn, may cause heart palpitations, dizziness, shortness of breath, fatigue or angina (chest pain).

These symptoms aren't always present, however, and when they are, they can vary from person to person. In some older individuals, for example, overall heart rate may not increase. Some people with AF have no symptoms at all.

Trap: Many other disorders, including other types of arrhythmias, can mimic the signs of AF.

DIAGNOSIS

While signs of AF may sometimes be detected by feeling the pulse or listening to the heart through a stethoscope, the only sure way to accurately diagnose AF is with an electrocardiogram (EKG), which will clearly show if any abnormal heart rhythm exists. In an EKG, electrodes are placed on the chest and body to record the heart's electrical impulses while the patient lies on an examination table. The test is quick and painless.

If someone has persistent AF (meaning the arrhythmia is occurring constantly), it can be uncovered by having an EKG. In the case of episodic AF (meaning the AF lasts for minutes or hours, then stops for a while before recurring), it may be necessary to wear a Holter monitor, which makes an EKG recording of the heartbeat for 24 hours, or use another type of heart monitor.

If an EKG reveals AF, then an echocardiogram (which uses sound waves, like a sonogram, to take a picture of the heart chambers) may also be done, either at the chest wall or, for more revealing pictures, via a tube inserted into the esophagus, to check for abnormalities of the valves as well as for blood clots.

TREATMENT

Treatment of AF involves several priorities...

•**Controlling the heart rate**—which can race up to 200 beats per minute during a bout of AF—is a doctor's first priority. This is done by administering one of several types of blocking agents that slow the transmission of electrical signals across the *A-V node* (connecting the atria and the ventricles), thus preventing too many signals from reaching the ventricles. Blocking agents include beta blockers, such as *propranolol* (Inderal), *metoprolol* (Toprol) and *atenolol* (Tenormin)…and calcium channel blockers, such as *verapamil* (Verelan) and *diltiazem* (Cardizem), which are preferred. If these are not effective enough or cause side effects, then the blocking agents *digoxin* (Lanoxin) or *amiodarone* (Cordarone) are used.

A Holter monitor is often employed to see how well a given medication works throughout the day. A patient may need to try several medications before finding the one that works best.

•**Administering blood-thinning medication** to reduce risk of a dangerous blood clot forming and to allow clots that have formed to dissolve. The standard medication in this case is *warfarin* (Coumadin), although patients deemed to be at low risk of dangerous blood clots (younger patients without heart disease) may be given aspirin instead. This treatment is the most important aspect of stroke prevention. The anticoagulant may continue to be prescribed for months or years, if necessary.

•**Identifying and eliminating the underlying causes of AF.**

These might include: Excessive intake of alcohol and/or caffeine on a regular basis…use of a stimulant, such as a decongestant containing *pseudoephedrine*, or an illicit drug, such as cocaine…coronary artery disease…high blood pressure…a leaky mitral valve in the heart…hyperthyroidism…pericarditis…lung disease, such as emphysema or chronic obstructive pulmonary disease (COPD)…or congestive heart failure.

If the AF persists after such causes are addressed, as is the case in about 30% of patients, then an *antiarrhythmic drug*, such as *sotalol* (Betapace), *flecainide* (Tambocor) or *amiodarone* (Cordarone), may be prescribed. These drugs work by blocking ionic channels in the walls of the heart cells. (All heart cells have channels in their walls, through which ions travel back and forth, altering the electrical charge of the cell—including sodium channels, potassium channels and calcium channels.)

These drugs have a number of side effects, such as thyroid disturbances and lung damage.

Note: These drugs can interact dangerously with a number of other drugs, including warfarin (in which case the combo can cause excessive bleeding), tricyclic antidepressants and antipsychotic medications.

If the AF still isn't corrected, then more aggressive treatments may be tried…

•**Cardioversion,** in which an electrical shock is applied to the heart using paddles externally placed on the chest and back (similar to those used for ventricular fibrillation) to "reset" the heartbeat. This restores normal heart rhythms in many patients, but the success may not last. Anesthesia is administered before the procedure to minimize discomfort. The patient "jerks," but just for a moment.

•**Ablation therapy,** in which a catheter electrode is inserted into a vein and threaded into the heart, where a hole is poked in the wall connecting the right and left atria. Radio waves are then used to create a small burn in the heart lining. In many patients, this can eliminate AF altogether.

Newest ablation techniques have yielded success rates of more than 70% (keeping in mind that this procedure is done on carefully selected patients), though the long-term recurrence rate isn't yet clear.

■ ■ ■ ■

Bacteria Linked to Dangerous Heart Rhythm

Patients who have *atrial fibrillation* (AF)—rapid, irregular rhythm in the heart's upper chambers—are 20 times more likely than others to test positive for *Helicobacter pylori* bacteria.

Self-defense: If you are diagnosed with AF, you should be checked for H. pylori. Controlling the infection using antibiotics reduces—or eliminates—the heart problem.

Annibale Sandro Montenero, MD, director, arrhythmia center, and chair of cardiology, MultiMedica General Hospital, Milan, Italy.

Overactive Thyroid Tied to Irregular Heart Rhythm

Anne R. Cappola, MD, ScM, assistant professor of medicine and epidemiology, University of Pennsylvania School of Medicine, Philadelphia.

Robert Rushakoff, MD, clinical professor of medicine, University of California, San Francisco.

The Journal of the American Medical Association.

People who have an overactive thyroid gland, but no symptoms of thyroid disease, are at an increased risk of *atrial fibrillation*, an abnormal heart rhythm, according to a recent study. But contrary to standard scientific thinking, the study found that an overactive or underactive thyroid is not linked to an increased risk of other heart problems or death in older patients.

THE STUDY

In the study, researchers collected data on 3,233 people ages 65 and older who had their *thyroid stimulating hormone* (TSH) levels measured in 1989 and 1990. Through June 2002, 82% of the people maintained normal thyroid function, 15% had a subclinical underactive thyroid, 1.6% had a symptomatic underactive thyroid and 1.5% had a subclinical overactive thyroid, according to the researchers.

People who had a subclinical overactive thyroid had almost twice the risk of developing atrial fibrillation, compared with those who had a normal thyroid. However, there was no increased risk for coronary heart disease, stroke or death.

There was no difference in the risk of heart disease, stroke or death between the people who had an underactive thyroid and those who had normal thyroid.

IMPLICATIONS

"People who have subclinical underactive thyroid do not have an increased risk of cardiovascular disease, like heart attack or stroke or mortality, compared with people who have normal thyroid function," says lead author of the study, Dr. Anne R. Cappola, an assistant professor of medicine and epidemiology at the University of Pennsylvania School of Medicine.

"However, people who have subclinical overactive thyroid do have an increased risk of atrial fibrillation. They should be treated to prevent it," she says.

Dr. Robert Rushakoff, clinical professor of medicine at the University of California, San Francisco, thinks that the risk of atrial fibrillation is not as great as the study suggests, and therefore, feels that even patients who have a subclinical overactive thyroid may not need treatment. "If there is no clinical issue, you don't need treatment," he says. "The evidence is pointing to that. There are also risks to treatment."

Many older people are being treated for an asymptomatic underactive thyroid in the belief that treatment will prevent heart problems, Cappola says. She thinks that's unnecessary. "We don't see any evidence that treatment is going to help the heart," she says.

In addition, Cappola believes older people do not even need to be screened for thyroid problems, since it is neither cost-effective nor likely to make a difference to their health.

"This is going against what people have been thinking," says Rushakoff. "When you actually look at the data, suddenly the answers are different from what people have thought. It's against all the recommendations right now, but that's where it's going."

The American Academy of Otolaryngology, Head and Neck Surgery can tell you more about thyroid disease at *www.entnet.org/HealthInformation/Thyroid-Disorders.cfm*. Or you can try the American Thyroid Association Web site at *www.thyroid.org*.

■ ■ ■ ■

Stroke Prevention Surgery Improves Brain Function

Twenty-nine patients with carotid stenosis (narrowing of the artery in the neck) underwent carotid artery stenting, in which the narrowed artery is expanded with a balloon and a metal tube known as a stent. All patients were given neuropsychological tests 24 hours before and 48 hours afterward.

Result: Cognitive function (as measured by the speed with which participants connected numbers) increased by nearly 6% after stenting.

Theory: Stenting increases blood flow to the brain, which improves cognitive function. This finding contradicts previous studies suggesting that stenting may cause a slight decrease in cognitive function. More research is under way.

Iris Q. Grunwald, MD, consultant physician, department of interventional and diagnostic neuroradiology, Saarland University Clinic, Hamburg, Germany.

■ ■ ■ ■

Aneurysms and Smoking

The US Preventive Services Task Force recommends that men age 65 to 75 who have ever smoked undergo ultrasound screening for abdominal aortic aneurysm—a ballooning of the body's main artery that can lead to fatal rupture. Such aneurysms are the 10th leading cause of death among men in this age group. Symptoms are rare until rupture is imminent, but the condition is treatable if detected early. Ultrasound screening is noninvasive and typically costs from $100 to $200. Medicare pays for this test for those who have ever smoked. Consult your doctor.

Mary Barton, MD, scientific director, US Preventive Task Force, Agency for Healthcare Research and Quality, Rockville, MD.

Are You Headed For a Stroke?

James F. Toole, MD, Walter C. Teagle Professor of Neurology and director of the Stroke Research Center at Wake Forest University Baptist Medical Center in Winston-Salem, North Carolina. He is past president of the International Stroke Society (now the World Stroke Organization).

What if people received warnings about coming strokes a week or even a month before they occurred? You might assume that such an alert would cause people to seek medical attention so that the patient and his/her doctor could take measures to prevent a stroke. Usually, that's not the case.

Each year, an estimated quarter-million Americans receive a warning in the form of a transient ischemic attack (TIA), commonly known as a "ministroke." Unfortunately, the majority of patients who experience a TIA don't recognize its importance—and fail to get prompt medical care that likely could prevent a full-blown stroke. About 11% to 20% of patients who experience a TIA go on to suffer a stroke within three months.

Good news: Patients who experience a TIA and then take preventive steps can greatly reduce their risk for further problems.

Important: A TIA is an *emergency*, and everyone should know the symptoms. If you experience one of the symptoms described below for at least five minutes, see a doctor the same day—go to the emergency room, if necessary.

KNOW THE SYMPTOMS

Like the majority of strokes, a TIA is usually caused by a blood clot and/or material that breaks free from artery walls and temporarily blocks blood flow to parts of the brain. The blockage of the artery lasts long enough to stop blood flow and cause stroke-like symptoms, but not long enough to kill brain cells.

What to watch for...

•**A dizzy spell that occurs for no obvious reason,** such as standing too quickly or dizziness from a middle ear disease.

•**Weakness and/or numbness on one side of the body**—usually in the face or an arm or leg.

•**The sensation that there's something in the eye,** causing blurriness, double vision or even temporary blindness.

•**Difficulty speaking or difficulty understanding what others are saying.**

People should *not* panic if they experience one or more of these symptoms—they aren't always caused by a TIA. Dizzy spells can be caused by something as simple as a plug of earwax. The only way to know for sure whether you've suffered a TIA is to see a doctor.

DIAGNOSING TIAS

Researchers are in the process of identifying brain enzymes that are released during a TIA. Blood tests that diagnose TIAs based on the presence of these enzymes are being developed.

In the meantime, doctors diagnose most TIAs by taking a medical history of the event—what the patient felt, how long the symptoms lasted and whether the person has stroke risk factors, such as high blood pressure, family history, diabetes or smoking.

Physical findings: Atherosclerosis (hardening of the arteries) is the underlying cause of most TIAs (and the majority of strokes). Patients who have atherosclerosis elsewhere in the body, such as in the arteries leading to the legs, kidneys, heart, etc., are very likely to also have damaged carotid arteries—blood vessels in the neck that carry blood to the brain.

In some cases, a doctor can detect problems in the carotid artery by listening carefully with a stethoscope. There are characteristic sounds (bruits) that indicate atherosclerosis.

In other cases, additional tests are required...

•**Carotid ultrasonography** uses sound waves to detect blood-vessel narrowing and/or clots in the carotid arteries. This is a good screening test for people with stroke risk factors or a family history of strokes or TIAs.

•**Magnetic resonance imaging (MRI)** also measures blockages in the carotid arteries.

If atherosclerotic blockages of 50% to 70% are found from either test, further evaluation and treatment is necessary.

TREATMENT APPROACHES

Patients with carotid artery blockages of 50% or more are usually advised to take strict steps, including the use of medication, to reduce risk. *If their disease progresses to 70% blockage, surgery is typically recommended...*

Carotid endarterectomy is an in-patient procedure in which an incision is made to expose the carotid artery, and plaques are removed from the artery. When performed by a skilled surgeon, the risk for stroke or death is less than 1 percent, and the patient recovers within a week.

Stenting is an inpatient procedure in which an expandable metal net is threaded into the carotid artery. The net presses against the artery walls...dilates the opening for better circulation...and helps prevent the artery from "shedding" more clots.

Stenting, however, has not been performed long enough for its long-term effectiveness and durability to be known. One possible risk is that a dislodged blood clot could get carried in the bloodstream to the brain.

TIA patients who don't require surgery are almost always treated with drugs to prevent blood from clotting. *Main drug therapies...*

Aspirin is most often used. Taking a regular aspirin (three times weekly) or baby aspirin (daily), depending on the patient, can reduce stroke risk by up to 20%.

Aspirin plus an anticlotting drug. Adding other active ingredients to aspirin can reduce stroke risk by an additional 3% to 5%.

Example: Aspirin plus *dipyridamole* (Aggrenox).

Aspirin alternatives, such as *clopidogrel* (Plavix) and *ticlopidine* (Ticlid), can prevent excessively sticky platelets from clumping together and forming clots. These drugs are a good choice for patients who are allergic to aspirin or who have an ulcer or acid reflux disease, which can be aggravated by aspirin.

■ **More from James F. Toole, MD...**

Stroke Prevention

Most stroke risk factors can be reduced with lifestyle modifications. *Most important...*

•**Not smoking.**

•**Limiting dietary fat.**

•**Eating fruits and vegetables.**

•**Exercising regularly.**

Patients who maintain healthy blood pressure readings (less than 120/80) and total cholesterol levels (less than 200)...avoid (or reverse) obesity...and control underlying diseases, such as diabetes, are far less likely to develop hardening of the arteries, thereby reducing their risk for TIAs and stroke.

Stroke: Survival And Recovery

Cathy Sila, MD, professor of neurology at Case Western Medical Center in Cleveland.

If you suffer a stroke, one of the most common—and devastating—mistakes is failing to seek treatment fast enough. When blood supply to the brain is cut off by a clot (ischemic stroke) or there is bleeding in or around the brain (hemorrhagic stroke), damage starts within minutes. Getting help right away could save your life—or profoundly improve your recovery.

IS IT A STROKE?

The onset of stroke symptoms is sudden and consists of episodes of neurological dysfunction. Transient ischemic attacks, or TIAs, are stroke warning symptoms that usually last 15 minutes to several hours and are not associated with permanent damage. About 10% of patients who suffer a TIA go on to have a stroke within the next three months. If you think that you may be having a stroke, call 911. Studies have shown that treatment may be delayed if you first call your doctor or hospital. While waiting for emergency help, lie down in a comfortable position that allows you to breathe freely.

Caution: It is not recommended that you take aspirin for a suspected stroke. While its clot-fighting ability may help if you are having an ischemic stroke (or heart attack), it could make things worse if you are having a hemorrhagic stroke.

THE RIGHT DIAGNOSIS

At the hospital, brain imaging is one of the first tests performed to help diagnose a stroke and determine its type. Usually, this is done with a standard computed tomography (CT) scan. This painless, noninvasive test takes multiple detailed images of the brain.

A hemorrhagic stroke is easy to identify on a CT scan. That's because blood, which pools in or around the brain during a hemorrhagic stroke, appears different from brain tissue. With an ischemic stroke, the brain can appear normal on a CT scan if swelling or damage has not yet occurred. In this case, the scan rules out other causes, and ischemic stroke is diagnosed by a clinical history and exam. A follow-up CT scan is performed a few days later to confirm the diagnosis.

ISCHEMIC STROKE

During the period immediately following an ischemic stroke, medication may be needed to stabilize blood pressure and heart rate. If the stroke sufferer has a fever, it is treated with acetaminophen (Tylenol) or a cooling blanket—even a slight fever can worsen brain damage. *Other treatments...*

•**Medication.** The clot-dissolving drug alteplase (Activase) is the most effective emergency treatment for ischemic stroke. Also known as a *tissue plasminogen activator,* or tPA, the drug works with the body's own chemicals to dissolve the clot that is blocking circulation to the brain. To be effective, tPA must be given within three hours of the first stroke symptoms. TPA also has risks. As a potent "clot buster," it can cause bleeding. About 6% of patients who receive it develop bleeding into the stroke-damaged area of the brain, which can be fatal.

Latest development: Administering clot-busting drugs via an intra-arterial route through a catheter threaded up to the blocked artery itself may extend the treatment window to six hours. This approach requires special imaging, such as angiography, to pinpoint the blockage and can be performed only at centers with such equipment and personnel trained in the technique. Although studies have shown this technique to be effective for some patients, the bleeding risk is higher (10% to 12%) than standard tPA.

•**Surgery.** After a TIA or minor stroke due to blockage of the carotid (neck) artery, other options include clearing the carotid artery to prevent another stroke. This can be performed with *carotid endarterectomy* (cutting open a blocked artery and removing the clot to restore circulation) or with *angioplasty* and *stenting* (inserting a balloon via a catheter, expanding it at the site of the clot to widen the blood vessel, and inserting a wire mesh framework to keep the artery open).

Latest development: Another new approach uses a corkscrew-shaped device called the MERCI (*mechanical embolus removal in cerebral ischemia*) Retriever. It is approved by the FDA for removing clots from brain arteries, which are causing an acute stroke. The device looks promising, but it has not been definitively shown to improve the outcomes of patients and also carries a risk of bleeding into the brain.

HEMORRHAGIC STROKE

Hemorrhagic stroke treatment first focuses on stabilizing the patient—using a ventilator, if necessary, to restore breathing and treating life-threatening heart problems caused by the stroke, such as disturbances in heart rhythm (fibrillation). *Other treatments...*

•**Medication.** Blood pressure must be brought down quickly to prevent additional bleeding in other parts of the brain. Blood pressure medications often are administered intravenously for rapid effect.

Bleeding in the space between the inner layer and the middle layer of the tissue covering the brain (subarachnoid hemorrhage) is usually caused by a ruptured aneurysm—a burst bubble in a brain artery. Your doctor may prescribe *nimodipine* (Nimotop), a calcium channel blocker that prevents arteries from going into spasm and causing more damage. After the first hemorrhage, rebleeding can occur unless corrective steps are taken.

•**Surgery.** The standard treatment for brain aneurysm is *clipping*—a surgical procedure that involves opening the skull and placing a small clip at the base of the aneurysm to close it off from blood flow. It is the preferred form of treatment for aneurysms in certain areas of the brain, particularly in medically stable patients.

Latest development: For aneurysm patients who are not medically stable, a new technique known as coiling may be the best form of treatment. With coiling, a catheter is guided up through a blood vessel to place a collection of tiny platinum coils in the aneurysm, which causes a clot to form within the aneurysm. The procedure is less invasive and safer than clipping, but some aneurysms cannot be completely treated with this technique. The risks of both procedures include rebleeding from the aneurysm.

ONGOING CARE

Perhaps the most frustrating aspect of stroke recovery is waiting to determine the extent of brain damage. During this time, an antidepressant may be needed if there are signs of depression.

For most stroke survivors, physical and/or occupational therapy over a period of months—or indefinitely—is essential to optimize functions, such as speech and the physical capacities that were impaired by brain damage.

Latest development: The importance of nutrition has only recently been fully recognized for stroke sufferers. The American Stroke Association recommends assessing and correcting nutritional problems, such as malnutrition.

Turn Around Carotid Artery Disease Before It Causes a Stroke

Claudette Brooks, MD, a neurologist at the West Virginia University Medical Center, Morgantown, is a spokesperson for the American Stroke Association.

Most people know about coronary artery disease, in which plaque builds up in the arteries feeding the heart, reducing blood flow and increasing heart attack risk. But plaque can also build up in the carotid arteries—the large arteries on both sides of the neck that carry blood to the front and middle part of the brain. This carotid artery disease significantly increases stroke risk if not treated.

Carotid artery disease has the same causes as coronary artery disease—blood cholesterol adheres to the walls of the artery over time, forming plaque deposits. These deposits can cause a stroke if a piece of plaque breaks off and gets lodged in a smaller brain artery, blocking blood flow…or the plaque cracks or becomes roughened, triggering a blood clot that blocks blood flow to the brain…or the carotid artery becomes so narrowed by plaque that the blockage itself prevents sufficient blood from getting to the brain.

WHO IS AT RISK?

Risk factors for carotid artery disease include smoking, high cholesterol, high blood pressure, diabetes, obesity, physical inactivity, previously diagnosed coronary artery disease and a family history of coronary or carotid artery disease. Age is also a risk factor. Only one out of every 200 people between age 50 and 59 has significantly narrowed carotid arteries, but this rate climbs exponentially in each decade after 65. Of those age 60 to 79, one out of 100 people has blockage. Among those age 80 to 89, one out of 10 has significant carotid artery blockage of 50% or greater.

EARLY WARNING SIGN

Most people with early-stage carotid artery disease don't realize it.

Reason: Arteries with blockages of 60% or less usually produce no symptoms. For many, the first sign that they have carotid artery disease is a transient ischemic attack (TIA). TIAs may occur when a small piece of plaque breaks off or a small plaque-related blood clot forms, temporarily reducing blood flow to the brain. These attacks typically last only a few minutes and cause no permanent damage.

Symptoms include loss of sight in one or both eyes…weakness, numbness or tingling on one side of the body…loss of coordination…dizziness or confusion…slurred speech…difficulty swallowing.

If you experience any of these TIA symptoms, seek medical attention immediately. Someone who has had a TIA is 10 times more likely to have a stroke than someone who hasn't. Even if you haven't experienced symptoms, you should be examined for possible carotid artery blockage if you have any of the above risk factors—particularly if you're older than age 45.

DIAGNOSIS

•**Stethoscope exam.** The first step in this examination, which your internist can perform, is to listen with a stethoscope to the flow of blood through each carotid artery. If the doctor hears a *bruit*—a rushing sound that indicates turbulent blood flow through the artery—then it's possible that you have carotid artery blockage. The absence of bruit does not rule out carotid artery blockage, however.

•**Carotid duplex ultrasound.** If your doctor suspects carotid artery blockage because you have heart disease, high cholesterol, high blood pressure and/or diabetes, the next step is a carotid ultrasound exam. In this test, an ultrasound image of the blood flow through the carotid artery is examined to determine whether there are blockages or other structural abnormalities. The exam is noninvasive and painless.

•**Catheter angiography and CT/MRI angiography.** If an ultrasound indicates carotid artery blockage, one of several follow-up tests is typically done to get a still-better picture of the blockage. In a *catheter angiogram*, a special dye is injected into the blood vessels of the head and neck through a catheter, and the carotid arteries are then X-rayed. In a *CT angiogram* or an *MRI angiogram*, the carotid arteries are imaged using a CT or MRI scan. In all three tests, both carotid arteries are typically scanned,

along with the two vertebral arteries in the back of the head that supply the rear brain.

Reason: 20 percent of people with carotid artery disease also have blockages in the vertebral arteries. While these tests are more invasive than ultrasound and therefore carry some risk, they give a more in-depth picture of the blockage.

Note: Catheter angiogram is considered the gold standard for accuracy and gives the clearest picture—it also has the most risk.

TREATMENT

If the carotid artery disease is asymptomatic—which is usually the case when the artery blockage is 60% or less—the first line of treatment involves controlling the underlying risk factors, including…

•**Bringing LDL cholesterol down** through a low-fat diet and cholesterol-lowering medications.

•**Controlling high blood pressure** with a low-sodium diet and antihypertensive medications.

•**Keeping blood sugar under tight control,** if you have diabetes.

•**Quitting smoking.**

•**Losing weight,** if you are overweight.

•**Getting 30 minutes or more of daily physical activity** such as walking, cycling and swimming.

Also, one or more antiplatelet medications may be prescribed to reduce the risk of dangerous blood clots—including aspirin, *dipyridamole* (Persantine), *clopidogrel* (Plavix) and *ticlopidine* (Ticlid).

SURGERY

Surgery to reduce asymptomatic carotid artery blockage is usually only recommended if the blockage exceeds 70%.

Reason: Studies have shown that for lesser blockages, risks of surgical complications (reaction to anesthesia or mid-operation stroke or heart attack) outweigh stroke prevention benefits. The main causes of mid-operation stroke or heart attack are emboli (air bubbles or particles of plaque or blood clot in the blood). The risk of serious complications is 2.3%.

The most common operation is a carotid endarterectomy, in which an incision is made in the neck at the point of the blockage—the plaque and, if necessary, the diseased artery walls are surgically removed. A shunt (tube) is used to route blood around the area being worked on. If artery tissue is removed, a length of artery is taken from the leg and grafted onto the carotid artery (similar to what's done in coronary bypass surgery). It usually involves a hospital stay of two to four days. After carotid surgery for patients with asymptomatic blockage of greater than 70%, there is a 40% reduction in risk of stroke over five years. However, other risk factors must still be treated since atherosclerosis and narrowing can return.

How to Prevent a Stroke

Patrick Lyden, MD, professor of neurosciences and director of the Stroke Center at University of California, San Diego, is chief of the Stroke Clinic at the San Diego VA Medical Center.

A stroke occurs when blood supply to a part of the brain is interrupted. Without oxygen and nutrients, brain cells die within minutes, damaging areas that control movement, speech—and even involuntary activities, such as breathing.

Stroke is the most *preventable* cause of death and disability in the US. Yet more than 750,000 Americans suffer strokes each year...about 160,000 of these people die...and 200,000 live with lasting disability. What are we doing wrong?

You can't change some risk factors, such as family history. If you have a parent or sibling who has suffered a stroke, you are at greater risk yourself. Your age also plays a role. While strokes can occur even in young children, overall risk steadily increases as we grow older. That's why more than two-thirds of strokes occur in people over age 65.

Beyond these factors, whether we suffer a stroke is largely up to us.

STROKE PREVENTION

What most affects stroke risk...

•**Smoking.** Everyone knows that smoking increases heart disease risk, but did you know that smoking is actually more likely to cause a stroke than a heart attack? Not only does smoking promote the development of fatty deposits that narrow arteries (atherosclerosis), but the nicotine in tobacco causes blood vessels in the brain to constrict.

Result: Smokers have up to four times the stroke risk of nonsmokers.

What you can do: Quit smoking. If you've tried but can't kick the habit, consider using nicotine-replacement patches or gum...or the prescription drug *bupropion* (Zyban).

•**Blood pressure.** High blood pressure gradually damages blood vessels and substantially increases the risk for both ischemic and hemorrhagic strokes. The risk is greater because high blood pressure rarely causes symptoms, so the problem goes unrecognized in 30% of sufferers.

What you can do: If your blood pressure exceeds 120/80, take steps to reduce it. Weight loss and exercise may be enough, but you also may need medication, such as diuretics or beta blockers.

•**Cholesterol.** For stroke prevention, maintain the same cholesterol levels that are recommended to reduce heart disease risk—total cholesterol under 200...LDL "bad" cholesterol under 100...HDL "good" cholesterol above 40.

What you can do: Weight loss and exercise help control cholesterol levels. If these strategies are insufficient, cholesterol-lowering medication may be needed.

•**Diabetes.** Maintaining tight control of blood sugar (glucose) will minimize small blood vessel damage that can lead to stroke.

What you can do: Work with your doctor to create a treatment plan that keeps your hemoglobin A1C (blood sugar over time) level at less than seven.

•**Diet.** Stroke risk, like heart disease risk, can be related to diet.

What you can do: Maintain a diet that's low in saturated fats (no more than 30% of total fats per day) and high in fruits and vegetables (five to nine one-half cup servings per day).

Research shows that people who are deficient in potassium are 1.5 to 2.5 times more likely to suffer a stroke. Aim for the government's recommended potassium intake of 4,700 mg daily. Although bananas are a popular source of potassium (one medium banana contains 457 mg of potassium), cantaloupe can be an even richer source (one cup of cantaloupe balls contains about 547 mg).

If you determine that sodium raises your blood pressure, limit your daily sodium intake to 2.4 g (slightly more than one teaspoon of salt).

•**Exercise.** Physical activity reduces risk for heart disease, diabetes and hypertension—and may offer stroke protection as well.

What you can do: Work with your doctor to create an exercise program based on your history of heart disease, smoking, etc.

•**Daily aspirin.** Aspirin reduces the tendency of platelets to clump, which helps prevent blood clots that can lead to ischemic stroke.

What you can do: If you're over age 55 and have diabetes, high cholesterol or other stroke risk factors, ask your doctor about starting daily low-dose (81-mg) aspirin therapy.

In patients who have never had a stroke or heart attack, and who do not have hypertension, diabetes or elevated cholesterol, the risk of hemorrhage may outweigh the potential benefits of aspirin.

•**Alcohol.** Moderate drinking has been shown to benefit the heart, but it does not curb stroke risk.

What you can do: Men should limit alcohol intake to two drinks per day...one drink per day for women. A drink is defined as 1.5 ounces of hard liquor, 4 ounces of wine or 12 ounces of beer. Risk for hemorrhagic stroke jumps substantially if you exceed this amount.

OTHER RISK FACTORS

Some medical conditions significantly raise your stroke risk...

•**Atrial fibrillation.** About 2.2 million Americans are affected by atrial fibrillation (AF), a heart rhythm disturbance that increases stroke risk five- to sixfold.

AF can cause dizziness, shortness of breath and constriction or other uncomfortable sensations in the chest. Or it may cause no symptoms and be found during a routine examination or when you have an electrocardiogram.

What you can do: Taking a blood-thinning drug, such as *warfarin* (Coumadin), can virtually eliminate AF's added stroke risk by preventing the formation of blood clots. Aspirin may be nearly as effective.

•**Transient ischemic attack (TIA).** If you have had one or more of these brief stroke-like episodes, your risk for a full-blown stroke increases dramatically. A TIA can cause dizziness, numbness or paralysis on one side of the body, difficulty speaking, double vision or other stroke symptoms that disappear after minutes or hours.

What you can do: After a TIA, ask your doctor about taking antiplatelet medication, such as aspirin, *clopidogrel* (Plavix) or *dipyridamole* and aspirin (Aggrenox).

•**Carotid stenosis.** When fatty deposits accumulate in the carotid artery, which carries blood up through the neck, they can impede brain circulation enough to cause a stroke. Up to half of all ischemic strokes are associated with carotid stenosis.

What you can do: If you have had a stroke or TIA, get an ultrasound of your carotid artery. If blockage is 70% or more, ask your doctor about surgery.

▪▪▪▪

Stroke Symptoms

Strokes affecting the right side of the brain are not always accurately diagnosed by emergency room doctors soon enough—even though these strokes are as common as those that affect the left side of the brain.

Reason: Right-sided stroke symptoms—such as vision problems, memory loss, skipping food on the left side of the plate—often are overlooked by the patient and don't appear critical to family members and doctors.

Result: Patients get to the hospital later and often don't get the treatment they need.

Self-defense: If you or a loved one experiences any stroke symptoms, seek immediate care.

Vladimir Hachinski, MD, Hon. Dr. Med, University of Western Ontario, London, Ontario, and part of a study of emergency care given to more than 750 right-brain stroke victims, published in *Neurology*.

■ ■ ■ ■

Better Stroke Therapy

In a study of 41 people who had mild to moderate impairment in one arm an average of 4.5 years after suffering a stroke, about half were enrolled in a general fitness program, and the rest underwent physical therapy while wearing a padded mitt on the stronger arm, preventing its use. After two weeks, people who were not allowed to use the stronger arm showed substantial improvement in the use of their impaired arm, while the placebo group showed no significant changes.

Theory: This type of therapy reorganizes brain function and recruits new brain areas to allow for use of the weak arm.

Edward Taub, PhD, professor of psychology, department of psychology, University of Alabama, Birmingham.

Leg Pain: A Risk for Stroke and Heart Attack

Jonathan L. Halperin, MD, professor of medicine and director of clinical cardiology services at Mount Sinai School of Medicine in New York City, was a member of the writing committee that produced the American College of Cardiology/American Heart Association *Guidelines for the Management of Patients with Peripheral Arterial Disease.*

When most people hear about the condition atherosclerosis, they think of heart attack and stroke. But the same disease process (plaque buildup in the arteries) also can impair circulation in internal organs, such as the brain, heart and kidneys, as well as in the legs. The result is a potentially life-threatening condition known as peripheral arterial disease (PAD). Unfortunately, it often goes undiagnosed and untreated, largely because symptoms seldom occur until the affected artery is more than 70% narrowed.

New development: The American College of Cardiology and the American Heart Association have just released guidelines to help doctors identify PAD and treat it effectively.

Here's what you need to know about this often overlooked condition…

ARE YOU AT RISK?

An estimated eight million Americans have symptomatic PAD, and it is estimated that 16 million have PAD with no symptoms. The most common form of PAD affects the legs. Known as lower extremity PAD, the risk factors for this condition are the same as those for coronary heart disease—high cholesterol (over 200 mg/dL)…high blood pressure (over 140/90)…and advancing age (over age 50). Smoking and diabetes significantly increase risk for the disorder.

You should be screened for lower extremity PAD during your regular physical if you are…

- **Over age 70.**
- **Over age 50 and have a history of diabetes or smoking.**
- **Under age 50 and have diabetes and one other atherosclerosis risk factor,** such as high cholesterol or hypertension.

The *ankle-brachial index* (ABI) is used to identify the disorder. To determine your ABI, your doctor takes your blood pressure on your upper arm—and at your ankle. The second systolic (top) reading should be divided by the first systolic reading. A ratio of less than 0.9 or greater than 1.65 is abnormal and is associated with a higher risk for PAD.

A less accurate way to test for lower extremity PAD is to use a stethoscope to listen to the pulse at various points on the legs—for example, the thigh, the knee and the back of the foot—to see whether the pulse is weak at any of those places or there are unusual sounds, such as a *bruit* (a murmur), that suggest blood flow is disrupted. If your doctor performs this test only, ask for the ABI.

SYMPTOMS TO WATCH FOR

The classic symptom of lower extremity PAD is *intermittent claudication.* This condition causes aching pain and/or fatigue, and sometimes burning, in the calf of one or both legs when you walk. The pain subsides when you stop.

The pain also may be in the thigh or the front of the foot. Some people say, "It doesn't exactly hurt. I just need to stop walking." In all these cases, it's crucial to see a doctor.

If you are suffering from this type of leg pain and your doctor determines that your ABI is normal, you'll need additional tests that are often performed at a vascular lab. In these tests, blood pressure in the toe is measured and/or the arteries in the abdomen are examined using an ultrasound.

If either test result is abnormal, an aggressive program to reduce risk factors for heart attack and stroke, including cholesterol-lowering medication, diet and exercise, is recommended. Your doctor also may suggest a cardiovascular evaluation, perhaps with stress testing and/or an ultrasound examination of the neck (carotid) arteries that feed the brain.

TREATING YOUR ARTERIES

If blockage is beginning to occur in your leg arteries, chances are the same thing is happening elsewhere in your body. This means that your risk for heart attack and stroke is high, and you need to act promptly to curb it—by stopping smoking, treating diabetes and/or controlling blood pressure and cholesterol levels.

Important: If you have lower extremity PAD, you should follow the same guidelines for cholesterol, blood pressure, etc., as those for people with coronary heart disease.

Example: Maintain LDL "bad" cholesterol at no more than 100 mg/dL (or 70 mg/dL if your doctor feels you are at particularly high risk), using a cholesterol-lowering statin drug to do so, if necessary.

Like someone with coronary heart disease, you may need an antiplatelet drug, such as a daily low-dose (81-mg) aspirin, to prevent tiny clots from blocking circulation.

Your doctor also may recommend an ACE inhibitor, such as *enalapril* (Vasotec) or *ramipri* (Altace). These drugs are commonly prescribed for high blood pressure but have been shown to reduce heart attack risk as well.

If you also have diabetes, good foot care—including thorough cleansing and daily inspection for cuts and infections—is especially important because poor circulation impairs healing.

REDUCING THE PAIN

When leg pain due to intermittent claudication is severe enough to cause you distress or interfere with your activities, there are ways to ease the pain.

Best options include...

•**Exercise.** A supervised exercise program (usually in a rehabilitation center) is the first step. Potential benefits of this approach, such as increasing the distance you can walk without pain, are greater than those offered by any medication. Exercise improves circulation and trains muscles to use oxygen more efficiently.

The best strategy is to walk until pain becomes moderately severe, rest until symptoms go away, then walk some more. For maximum improvement, sessions should be three times a week and last longer than 30 minutes each. The supervised program should last for six months. Afterward, exercise should be continued from home.

•**Medication.** If exercise alone isn't enough, or if you'd prefer another approach, the prescription drug *cilostazol* (Pletal) has been shown to improve circulation in the legs and can increase walking distance by 40% to 60% after three to six months of treatment. Don't use cilostazol if you have congestive heart failure—a class of drugs chemically related to cilostazol was found to increase mortality in heart failure patients. The drug *pentoxifylline* (Trental) can be taken instead, though it is much less effective.

SURGICAL OPTIONS

Arterial blockage in the legs also can be treated with procedures similar to those that are used to improve coronary circulation.

Your doctor is likely to suggest one of these procedures when exercise and medication haven't relieved symptoms sufficiently, or when tests show that the blockage occurs in a location where bypass or angioplasty is likely to be particularly effective—for example, in the abdominal artery that feeds the leg.

•**Angioplasty.** During this procedure, a catheter is inserted into the affected artery, and a balloon is inflated to open the artery. A wire mesh tube called a stent may then be inserted to keep the artery open.

•**Bypass surgery.** This operation involves reconstruction of blocked arteries with grafts taken from blood vessels elsewhere in the body or made from artificial materials, such as Gortex or Dacron.

Angioplasty or bypass is almost always necessary when the blockage has advanced enough to threaten the loss of part or all of the leg—a condition known as *critical limb ischemia* (CLI).

Important: CLI requires urgent care. See your doctor immediately if you start having leg pain even when at rest—or if you develop ulcers on your leg or foot.

■ ■ ■ ■

Brain Foods

Foods that may reduce brain damage from stroke include blueberries, spinach and spirulina, a type of green algae. These foods have high levels of antioxidants that help neutralize damaging free radicals.

Recent study: Rats that were fed diets enriched with these foods for one month prior to inducing a stroke had only half as much brain damage as rats that were not fed these foods. This study suggests that including these foods—one cup of blueberries, a big spinach salad or a few teaspoons of spirulina powder—in your daily diet may make a difference in the severity of a stroke.

Paula C. Bickford, PhD, professor of neurosurgery, University of South Florida, and James A. Haley VA Hospital, both in Tampa, and leader of the study published in *Experimental Neurology*.

■ ■ ■ ■

Stroke Strategy

Call an ambulance if you think you are having a stroke—even if you live close to a hospital.

Recent finding: Stroke victims who were transported by ambulance to the emergency room were seen and evaluated by a physician within 30 minutes, compared with 34 minutes for patients who drove themselves or were brought by friends or loved ones and 55 minutes for those who arrived by other means. With stroke, even four minutes can make a huge difference in outcome.

Yousef Mohammad, MD, assistant professor, department of neurology, college of medicine and public health, Ohio State University, Columbus, and leader of a study of 630,000 stroke patients, presented at the annual American Stroke Association's International Stroke Conference.

Caffeine–Alcohol Combo Protects Against Stroke Brain Damage

James C. Grotta, MD, director, stroke program, University of Texas Medical School, Houston.
Stroke.

What started as idle conjecture has produced a promising—and unconventional—treatment to prevent brain damage caused by a stroke.

Dr. James C. Grotta, director of the stroke program at the University of Texas Medical School in Houston, says, "One of my laboratory workers was musing about the fact that the moderate or mild use of alcohol can be effective in reducing the effect of stroke. So we started fooling around with combinations of it with other things—flavonoids and vitamin C and so [on]—and we stumbled on this."

"This" is a mixture that Grotta calls caffeinol. It consists of the amount of caffeine found in one or two cups of strong coffee and the amount of alcohol in one cocktail.

Brain damage in rats was reduced by 80% when caffeinol was given within three hours after a stroke.

POSSIBLE IN HUMANS

The first human trials have shown that the blood level of caffeinol that is effective in rats can be achieved in humans, and steps toward treatment of people have been taken.

In the study, some of the patients who got caffeinol were also being treated with a clot-busting drug that is often used for stroke. The combination appears safe, Grotta says. Although one patient did have bleeding within the brain, an independent safety officer concluded the hemorrhage was not related to caffeinol.

COMBO IS BETTER

"We think that the combination is more effective than any other drugs you look at in the laboratory, particularly for strokes that affect the cortex, the gray matter of the brain that controls language and other abilities," he says.

The next step is to combine caffeinol with the cooling of the body, a process that helps reduce stroke damage. That combination of treatments has been used safely in one patient, Grotta says.

IRISH COFFEE NOT THE ANSWER

But the caffeine–alcohol combination is for treatment, not prevention, Grotta says. "Anyone who thinks that having a cup of Irish coffee every day will help prevent stroke will find that it does not work," he says.

Vampire Bat Saliva May Add Bite to Stroke Treatment

Robert L. Medcalf, PhD, associate professor, Monash University department of medicine, Box Hill Hospital, Victoria, Australia.

Keith A. Siller, MD, medical director, New York University Comprehensive Stroke Care Center, New York City.

Stroke.

An ischemic stroke happens when at least one blood clot blocks the supply of blood to the brain. Conventional treatments are only effective when administered up to three hours after the onset of stroke. But a substance taken from the saliva of vampire bats is effective when given up to nine hours after onset, says study author Dr. Robert L. Medcalf, an associate professor at Monash University Department of Medicine at Box Hill Hospital in Victoria, Australia.

The study was done in mice, and it's not known how effective the treatment will be in humans. Moreover, some experts believe the emphasis on a longer time window obscures the necessity of treating stroke victims as quickly as possible.

"Even if this drug is better than the current one, you still need to get people treated very quickly," says Dr. Keith Siller, medical director of New York University's Comprehensive Stroke Care Center. "You have a limited time window to restore blood to the brain and that window doesn't change, no matter what you give."

SALIVA HAS NATURAL CLOT-BUSTER

Conventional clot-busting agents are beneficial, but they affect the entire circulation system, whether a clot exists or not. They pose an increased risk of cerebral hemorrhage (bleeding in the brain) and may cause brain-cell death, the study's author says. Researchers have focused on refining these agents so that they target only the clot and do not injure blood vessels.

Scientists believe they may have a candidate in the new compound extracted from vampire bat saliva. The compound takes advantage of vampire feeding principles and tries to make them work in humans. When vampire bats bite their victims, they release a clot-dissolving substance that keeps the blood flowing long enough to suck a full meal. Without the clot-buster, the victim's blood would clot and dry up, leaving the bat hungry.

In this study, the compound appeared to become active only in the presence of fibrin, the "building blocks" of a clot. In fact, its clot-busting properties increase about 13,000-fold in the presence of fibrin, whereas a conventional agent increases by a factor of 72.

This is important because blood clots and, therefore fibrin, are not actually located in the brain, so the bat-saliva compound has no effect in this vulnerable region.

The next step is a test by some of the same investigators in human stroke patients.

The Only Aspirin Dose That Actually Prevents Stroke

Mark Alberts, MD, director, stroke program, Northwestern Memorial Hospital, Chicago.

Marshall Keilson, MD, director of neurology, Maimonides Medical Center, Brooklyn, NY.

American Stroke Association conference, Phoenix.

Baby aspirin and coated aspirin might not be sufficient to prevent strokes, according to research performed at several major stroke centers.

People at risk for a stroke who take baby aspirin (81 milligrams [mg]) were less likely to reap its blood-thinning benefits than those taking an adult-sized pill. The same was true of those who took coated aspirin compared with the uncoated kind, say researchers.

This research could have major implications because it could lead to aspirin as a dose-adjusted medication, says Dr. Mark Alberts, lead author of the study and director of the stroke program at Northwestern Memorial Hospital in Chicago. Instead of a one-size-fits-all approach, he says, doctors would measure the effect of the dose and see if the patient needs a different dose.

THE ACCEPTED DOSE

Right now, doctors believe that 50 to 325 mg of aspirin may help prevent ischemic stroke, says Dr. Marshall Keilson, director of neurology at Maimonides Medical Center in Brooklyn, New York. *Ischemic* strokes are the most common type of stroke and occur when blood flow in an artery to the brain is pinched off, usually because of clotting. Aspirin thins the blood and prevents clots from forming.

Keilson says doctors use low doses of aspirin because they feel it reduces such complications as gastrointestinal upset and bleeding.

Many patients taking aspirin are still having strokes and, for that matter, heart attacks (aspirin is also thought to prevent some heart attacks). "Those episodes are indicating that the low doses that are commonly being used—around 81 mg—may not be adequate for stroke prevention," Keilson says.

In his study, Alberts and his coauthors measured how effective different doses and formulations of aspirin were at thinning blood in patients who had cerebrovascular disease.

WHAT WORKS BEST

More than half of the patients taking 81 mg a day did not have an anticlotting effect. According to Alberts, this was a significant number of people. Of those taking coated aspirin, more than 60% did not have an anticlotting effect. But only 28% of the people taking 325 mg of uncoated aspirin did not have an anticlotting effect. In other words, higher doses and uncoated formulations seemed to work better. But, there's a long way to go before these early results become routinely recommended.

The study measured only thinning of the blood, and not whether a person had another stroke. "We want to see if this is predictive of clinical results, which is the holy grail of research," Alberts says.

Keilson agrees. "Sometimes things that are done in a laboratory don't carry over in people," he says, adding that a large trial with thousands of patients is needed.

For more on the different types of stroke, visit the National Stroke Association at *www.stroke.org*. The association also has information on current guidelines for the use of aspirin in preventing strokes and heart attack.

How to Tell if Someone Is Having a Stroke

Amy Hurwitz, University of North Carolina at Chapel Hill School of Medicine.
Robert Felberg, MD, director, Stroke Center, Ochsner Clinic Foundation Hospital, New Orleans.
American Stroke Association conference, Phoenix.

Can you tell if someone is having a stroke? Yes, say researchers. The odds are good that you can, even for a complete stranger, if you know how to spot the symptoms.

Even though treating stroke patients requires extensive training, people without training can easily learn to detect stroke symptoms, says study author Amy Hurwitz, then a medical student at the University of North Carolina at Chapel Hill School of Medicine.

SPEED IS ESSENTIAL

A quick diagnosis is vital because a treatment is available for strokes caused by blood clots, but it only works if it's given within three hours of the onset of symptoms.

"Even a delay of 20 minutes can make a huge difference," says Dr. Robert Felberg, director of the stroke program at Ochsner Clinic Foundation Hospital in New Orleans.

He says that, ideally, you should get to the hospital within the first hour after symptoms appear, because doctors need time to make the diagnosis and run a computed tomography (CT) scan to confirm it before they can safely give the clot-busting stroke medication.

TESTING THE THEORY

For this study, the researchers chose 100 random visitors to the hospital and put them in a room in the emergency department where a stroke survivor and one of the researchers were waiting for him/her.

The stroke survivors still had visible symptoms, such as arm weakness, facial weakness or slurred speech.

The visitor learned how to give a three-item exam used by doctors to assess stroke victims.

1. Look at the patient's smile to see if it is symmetrical.

2. Can the patient raise both arms and keep them raised?

3. Ask the patient to speak a standard phrase.

The volunteers were then asked to decide if the patient had performed normally or abnormally on the tests.

The visitors correctly gave the test nearly all of the time.

In patients with facial weakness, they correctly identified that symptom approximately 70% of the time, arm weakness was correct in nearly all of the patients and speech problems were found nearly 90% of the time.

"The biggest problem we have is that 75% of the American population doesn't know what a stroke is," Felberg says.

10

Diabetes & Other Diseases

The Diabetes Epidemic: You May Have It—And Not Know It

The US is in the midst of a diabetes epidemic. Twenty million Americans currently have type 2 (adult-onset) diabetes, putting them at risk for such serious complications as blindness, kidney failure, heart disease, nerve damage and circulatory failure leading to amputation.

Another 41 million have prediabetes, which can turn into full-blown diabetes. The problem is that people with high blood sugar levels often don't feel any different—which is why one out of three Americans with diabetes don't even know they have the disease.

Main reason for this epidemic: More Americans are overweight and physically inactive—both of which make the body less responsive to insulin, the chemical that transports sugar from the bloodstream into the body's

various cells. This condition, known as insulin resistance, forces the body to produce more and more insulin in an effort to keep blood sugar within normal limits. Among those with genetic vulnerability (including many people who aren't overweight), this eventually causes the insulin-producing cells of the pancreas to "burn out," leaving the body unable to produce enough insulin to control blood sugar.

The result: Soaring blood sugar levels.

The good news: Complications can be avoided by catching insulin resistance early and then taking basic steps to bring your blood sugar levels within normal limits.

GET A FASTING BLOOD SUGAR TEST

The best way to learn whether you have insulin resistance is a fasting blood sugar test—a simple blood draw, taken 10 to 12 hours after you've last eaten. It should be included in your annual

Anne Peters, MD, professor of medicine, Keck School of Medicine of the University of Southern California in Los Angeles, and director of the USC Westside Center for Diabetes, is author of *Conquering Diabetes—A Cutting-Edge, Comprehensive Program for Prevention and Treatment.* Hudson Street Press.

physical. If you haven't had a fasting blood sugar test within the past year, call your primary care physician and schedule one—*especially* if you have a family history of diabetes.

A fasting blood sugar level of 126 milligrams per deciliter (mg/dl) or higher indicates diabetes, while a result between 100 and 125 mg/dl indicates prediabetes.

I always recommend a second test to confirm a high reading. If your test result is below 100, your blood sugar is within normal range, but you still may have early-stage insulin resistance—particularly if you are overweight or have close relatives with diabetes. If you and your doctor suspect this may be the case, you should follow the steps outlined below.

TEST FOR RISK FACTORS

Since insulin resistance is associated with significantly increased risk of heart disease, it's important that your doctor order a cholesterol (lipid) panel and check your blood pressure and body mass index (BMI). Body mass index is a measurement indicating how your weight/height ratio stacks up against the general population.

Triglyceride (a type of blood lipid) levels above 150 mg/dl and HDL (good) cholesterol levels below 50 (for women) or 40 (men), blood pressure of more than 130/80, and a BMI over 25 are all signs that you may be at risk for both heart disease and prediabetes/diabetes.

DEVELOP A TREATMENT PLAN

Some doctors still believe that there's nothing to worry about as long as your fasting blood sugar is less than 126. However, if one of my patients has a fasting blood sugar above 100 (or less than 100, but with other risk factors for insulin resistance or a family history of diabetes), I generally treat that patient as if he/she already has diabetes.

Reason: Damage from insulin resistance starts before blood sugar reaches "diabetic" levels.

This is why I urge everybody to ask their doctors for copies of their blood test results, rather than take a doctor's word that everything is OK. If your blood sugar is above 100, you need to discuss setting up a treatment plan with your doctor, or find another doctor if yours isn't responsive. *This plan should include five elements…*

•**Lose weight and exercise.**

•**Reduce cardiac risk associated with diabetes.** This includes taking a baby aspirin daily to reduce risk of heart attack and stroke, and, if your test results warrant, a statin drug to lower high cholesterol (Lipitor, Crestor), fibric acid derivatives (Lopid, Tricor) to lower triglycerides and ACE inhibitors (Lotensin, Vasotec, Zestril, Altace) or angiotensin receptor blockers (Avapro, Cozaar, Hyzaar, Diovan) to treat high blood pressure.

•**Test blood sugar regularly.** If your fasting blood sugar test is above 100, I recommend getting another fasting blood sugar test every three months. If your blood sugar test is above 125, you'll need to test more often. My diabetic patients do home blood tests every day, including first thing in the morning and two hours after each meal, and also get an A1C blood test every three months. This test shows what your average blood sugar level was for the previous several months. The goal is to keep your A1C below 7, and preferably between 4 and 6.

•**Consider diabetes medication.** If your blood sugar levels continue to be high despite weight loss and exercise, you and your doctor might consider *glitazone* medication—either *pioglitazone* (Actos) or *rosiglitazone* (Avandia*) —to increase your body's sensitivity to insulin.

Your doctor may also prescribe *metformin* (which reduces the liver's glucose production and can be used with glitazones) and/or alpha-glucosidase inhibitors, such as *acarbose* (Precose) or *miglitol* (Glyset), which decrease the amount of carbohydrates absorbed by the intestines. (Unfortunately, they also tend to produce large amounts of intestinal gas.) Also, the new injected drug *exenatide* (Byetta) can help lower blood sugar level and weight at the same time.

If all else fails, your doctor can prescribe daily insulin doses to supplement your body's natural insulin production.

•**Test for complications of insulin resistance.** Since cell damage from diabetes begins early, I also recommend regular tests for complications, even if your blood sugar is only slightly elevated.

*Recent evidence suggests that Avandia may increase the risk of myocardial ischemia, a condition in which the heart muscle does not receive enough oxygen-rich blood, causing symptoms like angina. In 2007, the FDA required the manufacturers to add a severe warning label that Avandia may increase the risks of heart failure.

Reason: Diabetes-related complications may be treatable early on, but once damage becomes serious, treatment becomes difficult or impossible.

Tests include: An annual dilated eye exam by an ophthalmologist...a yearly urine test for microalbuminuria (an early sign of kidney damage)...yearly cholesterol and triglyceride tests...a check for normal foot sensation at every doctor's visit, and if numbness is detected, twice daily home foot exams for cuts or sores that you can't feel.

Losing weight is the single most effective way to prevent type 2 diabetes.

Reason: Putting on even as little as 10 pounds—especially around your middle—automatically increases insulin resistance. Losing just 15 pounds reduces your risk of developing diabetes by more than half.

A simple, proven way to lose weight: Eat smaller portions. Use small (10-inch) plates at home—and therefore serve smaller portions—since studies show that people tend to finish whatever is on their plates. Also, avoid fruit juices and soft drinks as well as "white" foods (white bread, baked potatoes and French fries, pasta, white rice), all of which cause sharp rises in blood sugar. Finally, make sure that every meal contains a mix of high-fiber fruits and vegetables and high-quality protein (fish or lean meat).

Another key: Do an hour of exercise at least five times a week. A good program for most people is 45 minutes of aerobic exercise—such as walking, biking or swimming—and 15 minutes of light weight lifting.

Reason: Regular exercise encourages weight loss and increases your body's sensitivity to insulin. This effect only lasts a short time, however, which is why it's important to exercise often.

For many, these steps will be enough to prevent diabetes. If your body's ability to respond to insulin is 75% of normal and you can lower your insulin resistance by 25% through diet and exercise—a typical response—then your blood-sugar regulation will be brought back in balance.

■ ■ ■ ■

Diabetes—Tests and Symptoms to Look for

You have diabetes if any one of the following test results occurs on at least two different days...

•**A fasting blood glucose level** of 126 mg/dL or higher.

•**A two-hour oral glucose tolerance test result** of 200 mg/dL or higher.

•**Symptoms of diabetes** combined with a random (nonfasting) blood glucose test of 200 mg/dL or higher.

Symptoms of diabetes are...

- •Increased thirst.
- •Frequent urination (especially at night).
- •Unexplained increase in appetite.
- •Fatigue.
- •Erection problems.
- •Blurred vision.
- •Tingling or numbness in the hands and/or feet.

American Diabetes Association, *www.diabetes.org.*

■ ■ ■ ■

Antidepressants and Diabetes Risk

Antidepressants may increase diabetes risk. In a recent study, people at high risk for type 2 diabetes who did not take diabetes medications were two to three times more likely to develop diabetes if they were taking antidepressants than similar people who were not taking antidepressants. High-risk patients who were given the diabetes drug *metformin* (Glucophage) did not have a higher risk of diabetes. If you are taking an antidepressant and are at risk for diabetes–for example, because you are overweight or have a family history of diabetes—talk to your doctor.

Richard Rubin, PhD, associate professor, medicine and pediatrics, Johns Hopkins School of Medicine, Baltimore, and leader of a study of 3,187 people with elevated blood glucose levels, presented at the annual scientific session of the American Diabetes Association.

How Not to Get Diabetes

Robert A. Rizza, MD, professor of medicine and director for research at Mayo Clinic College of Medicine in Rochester, MN, is past president of the American Diabetes Association, *www.diabetes.org*. Winner of prestigious Banting Medal for Service.

The epidemic of type 2 diabetes is alarming—and more dangerous than many people ever imagine. The disease, which affects 20 million Americans, increases the risk for heart attack and stroke. Complications include blindness, kidney failure, impotence and poor wound healing that can lead to amputation.

Until recently, doctors diagnosed diabetes only when a patient had full-blown symptoms, which typically develop gradually over a period of years.

Now: You can stop diabetes in its tracks if you recognize and take action against "prediabetes," which affects more than 40 million people ages 40 to 74. *Here's how...*

WHEN SUGAR ISN'T SWEET

Glucose, a simple sugar molecule that is metabolized from the food you eat, is basic fuel for your body. It's broken down in cells of all kinds to produce energy that powers your muscles, lets you think and keeps your heart pumping and your lungs breathing.

The hormone insulin, which is produced by your pancreas, plays a key role, escorting glucose from the bloodstream into the cells. When there isn't enough insulin to do the job or the insulin is not effective, sugar builds up in the blood. That's when the trouble begins.

To diagnose diabetes, doctors order blood tests that measure the amount of glucose in your bloodstream. One test, fasting plasma glucose (FPG), checks the level first thing in the morning, before you've eaten anything. A normal glucose level is less than 100 milligrams per deciliter (mg/dl).

The oral glucose tolerance test (OGTT) is a bit more complicated—after fasting all night, you're asked to drink a sugary liquid, and your glucose level is tested two hours later (normal is less than 140 mg/dl).

If your FPG is 126 mg/dl or higher...or the two-hour OGTT is above 200 mg/dl, you likely have diabetes. Your pancreas no longer secretes enough insulin for proper glucose metabolism. This means that your chance of developing complications, such as heart disease, kidney failure or vision loss, has more than doubled.

AN EARLIER DIAGNOSIS

There's also an intermediate condition. Fasting blood sugar of 100 mg/dl to 125 mg/dl is called impaired fasting glucose. If the two-hour OGTT is 140 mg/dl to 200 mg/dl, it is known as *impaired glucose tolerance*.

Nowadays, these conditions are called prediabetes. With prediabetes, your insulin activity has already started to fall short of the amount your body needs. And if something isn't done, there's a good chance you'll go on to develop full-blown diabetes.

What are the odds? Fasting blood sugar between 100 mg/dl and 110 mg/dl means you have a 20% chance of developing diabetes within five to 10 years. If it's above 110, it's a 40% chance. If both the fasting blood sugar and two-hour glucose tolerance tests are elevated, the odds increase even more.

At the prediabetes level, excess blood sugar already has started to take its toll, researchers have discovered. For example, the risk for heart disease is one-and-one-half times higher than that of people with normal blood sugar.

DO YOU HAVE PREDIABETES?

To determine whether you have prediabetes, ask your doctor for a fasting glucose test—especially if you are at increased risk due to...

• **Excess body weight.**

• **Family history of diabetes** (parent, brother or sister).

• **Diabetes during pregnancy** (gestational diabetes).

• **Asian, African-American or Hispanic ethnicity.**

If any of these risk factors applies to you, have your blood sugar checked at your next physical—after age 45, do it at least every three years. Given the high rates of diabetes today, *everyone* over age 45 should consider getting tested.

TREATMENT FOR PREDIABETES

Slightly elevated blood sugar doesn't mean you're destined to get diabetes. With fairly moderate lifestyle changes, you can reduce that risk by more than 50%.

Obesity increases diabetes risk. If you are overweight, bring your weight down by 5% to 10% (an achievable goal for most people). Ideally, your weight should be brought down to the normal range, which means a body mass index (a ratio of weight to height), or BMI, of 18.5 to 24.9. To find your BMI, use the free calculator at the National Heart, Lung and Blood Institute Web site at *http://nhlbisupport.com/bmi.* Or use the formula (weight in pounds × 703) ÷ height in inches squared.

Important finding: A Finnish study of 522 middle-aged, overweight people with prediabetes found that diabetes risk among those who participated in a diet and exercise program for three years was reduced by 58% compared with a control group, who experienced no reduction.

How to stop prediabetes…

•**Diet wisely.** Consuming fewer calories than you burn is the key to weight loss. Some research also suggests that reducing saturated fat (most beef and some dairy products), and the resulting weight loss that can occur, helps reverse prediabetes, allowing your body to use insulin more efficiently. A diet rich in complex carbohydrates, such as fruits, vegetables and whole grains, will meet these goals—and is best for everyone's general health.

•**Exercise regularly.** Physical activity helps control your weight and improves your body's ability to use insulin. Aim for at least 30 minutes five or more days a week. The type of exercise doesn't seem to matter, as long as it requires modest exertion—brisk walking, swimming, riding a bike, etc.

•**Forgo medication.** Blood sugar in people with prediabetes can be reduced with prescription diabetes medication such as *metformin* (Glucophage). However, research on prediabetes suggests that this drug is not as effective as diet and exercise in preventing diabetes.

Important finding: In a *New England Journal of Medicine* study, 3,234 men and women with prediabetes were randomly assigned to a lifestyle program or the drug metformin. Weight loss and exercise reduced diabetes incidence nearly twice as much as drug treatment over the next three years (a reduction of 58% versus 31%).

■ ■ ■ ■

Diabetes Pain Reduced

Twenty-four percent of 716 people with diabetes who took an alpha-lipoic acid supplement daily for three weeks felt an improvement in pain, burning and numbness in their feet due to diabetic neuropathy (nerve damage caused by high blood sugar) compared with 16% of 542 diabetics taking a placebo.

Theory: Alpha-lipoic acid neutralizes the damage caused by small molecules that accumulate when blood sugar is elevated.

If you suffer from diabetic neuropathy: Ask your doctor about taking 1,200 mg to 1,800 mg daily of controlled-release alpha-lipoic acid, available at most health-food stores. Taking alpha-lipoic acid may alter insulin or drug requirements.

Ira Goldfine, MD, professor of endocrinology, University of California, San Francisco.

Diabetes Reversed Forever

Annals of Surgery.
University of Pittsburgh Medical Center news release.

The weight-loss procedure called gastric bypass surgery, which has been gaining popularity recently, can improve or eliminate type 2 diabetes in people who are obese, according to Pennsylvania researchers.

Laparoscopic gastric bypass surgery makes the stomach smaller. Patients lose weight because their smaller stomach can't take in as many calories as before.

THE STUDY

A study by scientists at the University of Pittsburgh Medical Center found that 83% of obese patients with type 2 diabetes who underwent the operation saw improvement in, and even total reversal of, their disease.

"Most patients in the study with type 2 diabetes who underwent bypass surgery achieved excellent biochemical [blood sugar] control and were able to reap the clinical benefits of withdrawing from most, if not all, antidiabetes medications, including insulin," says principal investigator Dr. Philip Schauer, former director of bariatric surgery.

"Younger diabetes patients with less severe disease stand to gain more from the surgery by circumventing years of progressive, debilitating disease," Schauer adds.

THE PROCEDURE

Gastric bypass surgery is intended for the estimated eight million Americans who are considered morbidly obese—100 pounds or more above their ideal weight.

Morbid obesity is believed to cut between 15 and 20 years off a person's life, according to the University of Arkansas for Medical Sciences.

Most people who have gastric bypass surgery lose approximately two-thirds of their excess body weight during the first year after the procedure. Most are able to keep that weight off for years.

SYMPTOMS

Type 2 diabetes has some symptoms similar to type 1, including frequent urination, excessive thirst and hunger, dramatic weight loss (without dieting), irritability, weakness and fatigue, and nausea and vomiting.

But there are also symptoms of type 2 diabetes that are exclusively its own, such as recurring or hard-to-heal skin lesions, gum or bladder infections, blurred vision, tingling or numbness in hands or feet and itchy skin.

Symptoms for type 2 diabetes usually occur gradually over a period of months or perhaps even years, and some people who have type 2 diabetes have symptoms that are so mild, they go undiagnosed.

TREATMENTS

There are a number of different treatments for people who have type 2 diabetes, including drugs other than insulin.

Very often patients can control their sugar and glucose levels through a diet that is recommended by a physician, as well as an exercise plan and careful daily monitoring of their blood sugar levels.

The US National Diabetes Education Program lists four steps to control diabetes on their Web site at *www.ndep.nih.gov/diabetes/control/ 4Steps.htm.*

Living Donors Help Diabetics

David E.R. Sutherland, MD, PhD, head, division of transplantation, and director, Diabetes Institute for Immunology and Transplantation at the University of Minnesota Medical Center department of surgery, Minneapolis.

If at first you don't succeed, try, try again. Such is the lesson learned from a recent experimental surgery in Japan in which doctors implanted pancreatic cells from a living donor into a woman with severe diabetes. Results so far are encouraging—the woman with diabetes is no longer insulin-dependent.

According to David E.R. Sutherland, MD, PhD, head, division of transplantation, and director, Diabetes Institute for Immunology and Transplantation at the University of Minnesota Medical Center department of surgery, a similar surgery was tried in the 1970s at the University of Minnesota Medical Center, though with unsuccessful results. The recent attempt by the Japanese team, led by Dr. Shinichi Matsumoto, of Kyoto University Hospital, and who trained at the University of Minnesota, is very encouraging for the possibility of using living donor pancreas tissue donations to aid cases of severe diabetes. To date, most pancreas replacement surgery has involved taking the pancreas from a cadaver, but results have been poor. With live tissue donation, the quality of the islets isolated is better and there is less chance of rejection.

ABOUT PANCREAS TRANSPLANTS

One function of the pancreas is to make digestive enzymes to secrete into the intestine. The other is to make insulin, which is done by little groups of cells called islets of Langerhans that are scattered throughout the gland. Dr. Sutherland describes the islets as being like BBs scattered throughout the pancreas. Fortuitously, the pancreas is shaped like a dumbbell and each half has a separate blood supply. Thus, it is possible to divide the pancreas and take one half for transplantation from a living donor, much as surgeons do routinely by removing one kidney for transplantation.

Pancreas transplants from living donors have been done successfully at the University of Minnesota since the 1970s (more than 130 cases). Using islets from living donors sounds like the future, and perhaps it will be, says Dr. Sutherland—not to make the surgery easier for the donor, but to make it minimally invasive for the recipient. We know that people can survive with half a pancreas (or for that matter, no pancreas at all—though they become instantly diabetic and must take digestive enzymes as well as insulin for life). However, even with the less invasive islet surgery, the recipient requires immunosuppressive medications similar to that of other transplant recipients.

ABOUT THE JAPANESE SUCCESS

The Japanese team removed half the pancreas of a woman, harvested the islet cells and transplanted them to the woman's 27-year-old diabetic daughter, who was suffering severe attacks of hypoglycemia from reactions to insulin injections. (Most diabetics are able to anticipate and prevent such extreme blood sugar drops, but some are not and they often pass out as a consequence—a condition called hypoglycemic unawareness.) The newsworthy aspect is that now, almost a year later, the donor is doing well and her diabetic daughter remains insulin-independent. Part of this latest success may be the fact that improved islets isolation techniques combined with the extreme freshness of tissue from a live donor enhance function, and the genetic match of the donor and recipient help prevent rejection. Dr. Sutherland says he salutes this effort for its early success but longer follow-up is needed to see if rejection is less than with cadaver tissue.

Transplant surgery is not useful for pancreatic cancer because the cancer is virtually never detected until it has already metastasized. However, for people with diabetes or whose pancreas has been removed because of severe pancreatitis, Dr. Sutherland says doctors hope that someday beta cell islet transplantation from living donors will be routine. In this country, the procedure is still considered investigational and needs approval from the Institutional Review Board and the FDA before doctors can move forward with it. We'll keep watching.

■ ■ ■ ■

New Link Seen

Diabetes and pancreatic cancer may be linked, says recent research.

Recent finding: About 1% of patients ages 50 and older were diagnosed with pancreatic cancer within three years of being diagnosed with type 2 diabetes. This rate is eight times higher than in the general population.

Self-defense: Consult your physician if you are newly diagnosed with diabetes.

Suresh T. Chari, professor of medicine, Mayo Clinic College of Medicine, Rochester, MN, and leader of a study of 2,122 people ages 50 and older, reported in *Gastroenterology*.

■ ■ ■ ■

Fertility Help?

Diabetes drug may boost fertility. *Metformin* (Glucophage), which is used to make diabetics' tissues more insulin-sensitive, can help treat infertility caused by failure to ovulate. In some women who are not diabetic, excess insulin levels interfere with ovulation. For these women, metformin may restore normal ovulation. It is considered safe for use by women trying to get pregnant. See your doctor for more information.

Marguerite Shepard, MD, reproductive endocrinology specialist and professor emerita of obstetrics and gynecology, Indiana University School of Medicine, Indianapolis.

Best Exercise to Fight Diabetes

Ronald J. Sigal, MD, associate professor, medicine and cardiac sciences, University of Calgary, Alberta, Canada.
Cathy Nonas, RD, MS, director, physical activity and nutrition, New York City Department of Health and Mental Hygiene, and certified diabetes educator.
Annals of Internal Medicine.

Most people know that exercise can help beat type 2 diabetes, but one fitness regimen might work best.

Specifically, workouts that combine aerobic and resistance training exercises appear better at controlling blood sugar than either type of activity alone, researchers say.

The finding is new, because "most other studies have looked at just one kind of exercise, either aerobic or resistance," noted lead researcher Ronald J. Sigal, MD, an associate professor of medicine and cardiac sciences at the University of Calgary, in Alberta, Canada.

THE STUDY

Dr. Sigal's team evaluated 251 adults, ages 39 to 70, with type 2 diabetes who did not exercise regularly. The participants were assigned to one of four groups: those who did 45 minutes of aerobic training three times a week, those who did 45 minutes of resistance training three times a week, those who did 45 minutes each of both forms of exercise three times a week, and those who did no exercise at all.

The aerobic group worked out on a treadmill or a bike at the gym. The resistance group also worked out at the gym doing seven different exercises on weight machines.

Dr. Sigal's team evaluated changes in A1c values—a measurement reflecting blood sugar concentrations over the previous two to three months. A1c is expressed as a percentage.

RESULTS

As expected, blood sugar control improved in all the exercise groups. In those who did either aerobic or resistance exercise, the A1c value declined by about 0.5% compared to the non-exercisers. Those who did both kinds of exercise had double that level of success, with their A1c value dropping by 0.97% compared to the non-exercising group. Non-exercisers experienced no change in their A1c values over the 26-week study.

He said the decrease of nearly 1% of A1c seen in the study "translates to a 15% to 20% reduction in risk of heart attack or stroke and a 25% to 40% reduced risk of other complications, such as retinopathy," an eye problem related to diabetes.

EXPLANATION

How does physical activity fight type 2 diabetes? According to Dr. Sigal, "exercise decreases insulin resistance. It makes the transport of glucose [blood sugar] more efficient."

Cathy Nonas, RD, director of physical activity and nutrition for the New York City Department of Health and Mental Hygiene and a registered dietitian and certified diabetes educator cautions that couch potatoes often need to ease into exercise to maintain a fitness regimen over time.

The study participants built up to their 45-minute fitness sessions, Dr. Nonas noted, and the combination group ended up doing about 4.5 hours of exercise a week—an amount some might find daunting.

No More Foot Ulcers

Journal of Bone and Joint Surgery.
Washington University School of Medicine news release.

Surgery to lengthen the Achilles tendon significantly reduces the risk that people with diabetes will suffer return bouts of foot ulcers. A recent study showed that patients who had the operation cut their ulcer risk in half or more.

About 15% of people with diabetes develop ulcers on their feet. Even after treatment, these ulcers often come back.

"The return of these ulcers has been a key concern for patients and their clinicians," says principal investigator Michael J. Mueller, associate director of the program in physical therapy at Washington University School of Medicine, St. Louis.

"If these wounds don't heal, there's a greater risk that a patient will have to have a portion or all of the foot amputated," Mueller says. "This study shows that lengthening the Achilles tendon can have a dramatic effect on the problem of ulcer recurrence."

Limited ankle mobility is often a cause of foot ulcers, so lengthening the Achilles tendon, which allows greater movement, often resolves the problem of a recurrence. In addition, the cast immobilizes the foot, reducing the chances of getting an injury that may go unnoticed. Nerve damage in diabetics may cause them to lose sensation in their feet, allowing undetected injuries to occur and fester.

THE STUDY

The study included 64 people with diabetes who all had an ulcer on the ball of the foot. None had had an amputation. They were divided into two groups. The first group received a foot cast—the standard treatment—while the second group received both a cast and the surgery.

After seven months, the group that received the cast and the surgery was 75% less likely to have an ulcer recurrence than the group that received the cast only. After two years, the surgery group was 52% less likely to have an ulcer recurrence.

■ ■ ■ ■

Diabetic Foot Ulcers Helped by Acne Medication

In a study of 22 men with diabetes, more than 84% of ulcers treated with topical *tretinoin* (Retin-A), a popular acne medication, and antibacterial *cadexomer iodine gel* shrunk by at least half. In the group treated with a placebo solution and cadexomer iodine gel, 45.4% of ulcers shrunk by half.

Theory: Tretinoin stimulates blood vessel growth, which helps deliver oxygen to the wound site. Left untreated, diabetic ulcers may increase risk for amputation.

Wynnis Tom, MD, department of dermatology, University of California at San Diego.

Urgent Diabetes Drug Warning

Abhimanyu Garg, MD, professor of internal medicine, University of Texas Southwestern Medical Center, Dallas. *Mayo Clinic Proceedings.*

Type 2 diabetics with mild heart disease or kidney problems could increase their risk of developing congestive heart failure by taking certain diabetes medications, recent research has found.

The study examines six cases of congestive heart failure in people taking *pioglitazone* (Actos) or *rosiglitazone* (Avandia) to help control their diabetes.

"We could not identify any other reason for the deterioration of their status," says the lead author of the study, Dr. Abhimanyu Garg, a pro-

fessor of internal medicine at the University of Texas Southwestern Medical Center in Dallas.

Because these medications are known to cause fluid accumulation, doctors discontinued them and gave the patients diuretics to help flush excess fluid from the body. All responded to this treatment.

The current study, he says, confirms what is already known about these medications.

THE CASES

The researchers studied the records of six men between the ages of 66 and 78 years with type 2 diabetes who had gone to the emergency room at Dallas Veterans Affairs Medical Center.

All six complained of shortness of breath, swelling of their feet and weight gain, which are symptoms of congestive heart failure and pulmonary edema (fluid buildup in the lungs).

Congestive heart failure occurs when the heart can no longer pump enough blood to maintain adequate circulation. Because the heart doesn't pump properly, fluid often builds up in the lungs.

These drugs are not recommended for people who have advanced heart disease.

Four of the six people in this study had chronic renal insufficiency, which means that their kidneys weren't functioning normally. Only two of the participants had any previous signs of heart disease. Four of the six had high blood pressure.

All of the study subjects had been taking the diabetes medications for between one month and 16 months. Three of the participants developed symptoms within one to three months after the dose of their diabetes drug had been increased.

The authors conclude that anyone with a history of congestive heart failure or chronic kidney disease should avoid taking these medications, and they suggest that further study be done on them.

"If somebody is taking these medications and they develop severe swelling or severe weight gain, they are not tolerating the medication," says Garg, who recommends seeing a doctor immediately if you or someone you know is experiencing these symptoms.

Keep Down the Cost Of Diabetes

Judith H. McQuown, writer and editor in New York City who was diagnosed with diabetes in 1987. She is author of *1001 Tips for Living Well with Diabetes: Firsthand Advice That Really Works*. Marlowe & Company.

People with diabetes not only have a life-long, life-threatening ailment they have to manage on a day-to-day basis, they also bear the burden of enormous costs associated with it. Even if you have a good insurance plan, insulin and other medications can cost hundreds of dollars a year. Then there's the cost of testing strips…glucose monitors…and frequent doctor visits. It's estimated that more than 10 cents of every health-care dollar is spent on diabetes. For patients who have limited or no insurance coverage, individual costs can be staggering.

However, according to Judith McQuown, author of *1001 Tips for Living Well with Diabetes: Firsthand Advice That Really Works*, there are a number of ways that people with diabetes can save money without compromising care.

JUDITH'S SUGGESTIONS

•**Buy supplies on eBay.** There usually are hundreds of listings for test kits, glucose-monitoring devices, test strips, etc. You'll pay considerably less than retail prices.

Important: Check expiration dates on items you're buying. Also check the seller's customer feedback to make sure he/she is reputable.

•**Buy mail order.** There are a number of large, reputable mail-order pharmacies, such as Liberty Medical (*www.libertymedical.com*). Because they deal in large volumes, they typically charge less than local pharmacies.

•**Buy generics.** The Food and Drug Administration requires generic drugs to be identical to the original brand-name drugs in dosage, quality, safety and strength—and the savings can be tremendous.

Example: The average cost of a brand-name prescription drug is $77…generic, $14. That said, there have been incidents of generic drugs not being as effective as the brand-name version. Talk to your doctor to be sure the generic versions are acceptable. Then double-check that the generic version is identical to the brand-name drug.

•**Split pill doses.** Ask your doctor to prescribe pills that are double your usual dosage, and then cut them in half. Most drugs come in several doses. The cost of higher-dose pills is usually the same or only slightly higher than the lower doses. Cutting pills in half can turn one month's supply into two.

Caution: Some drugs—those with enteric coatings or timed-release ingredients, for example—must be taken whole. Ask your doctor if pill splitting is appropriate for any of the drugs you're currently taking. And, be sure to use a "pill splitter" to ensure equal distribution.

•**Participate in clinical trials.** Patients who enroll in studies to test new drugs and/or treatments usually get free checkups, tests, consultations with specialists, etc. Many clinical trials compare active drugs with a placebo. Talk to your doctor about whether a given trial would be appropriate for you—and the potential risks if you happen to be in the placebo group. The upside of being in a trial is that your overall care will be state-of-the-art and you will be very well monitored. The downside is that there is risk involved with new medications. Depending on what's being tested, it may be worth considering.

•**Know the formulary.** Most health-insurance plans have a list of brand-name and generic drugs that they'll cover. This list is known as the formulary. If your doctor prescribes a drug that's not in the formulary, you will have to pay full price.

Example: Cipro antibiotic eardrops, which weren't in McQuown's medical group's formulary, cost $134. A prescription of Cortisporin, a similar, brand-name antibiotic that was in the formulary, costs $10 for the co-pay. Since people with diabetes are prone to an array of health challenges, having the full formulary can be very helpful.

Although these strategies won't make the diabetes go away, they can help ease some of the burden of it.

Drink More Coffee, Lower Diabetes Risk

Rob M. van Dam, PhD, assistant professor of medicine, Harvard Medical School, and associate epidemiologist, department of medicine, Brigham and Women's Hospital, Boston.

More good news for latte lovers comes from researchers at the Harvard School of Public Health (HSPH). They found that people who drink coffee on a regular basis experience a substantially lower risk for type 2 diabetes.

ABOUT THE STUDY

In a retrospective review of nine studies of coffee consumption and type 2 diabetes risk, Harvard researcher Rob M. van Dam, PhD, and his colleagues looked at 193,473 regular coffee drinkers who experienced 8,394 cases of type 2 diabetes. They excluded studies of people with type 1 diabetes and studies of short-term exposure to coffee or caffeine.

Researchers calculated the relative risk of type 2 diabetes in relation to how many daily cups of coffee the participants consumed. *It turned out that the more coffee, the better...*

- **The incidence of diabetes was lowest**—0.65 (or between six and seven in 10)—for people who consumed the most coffee each day (six or more cups).
- **Those who drank four to six cups daily** faced a slightly more than seven in 10 (0.72) incidence.
- **People who drank the least coffee** (which was no consumption in US studies, and two or fewer daily cups for Europeans) had a relative risk of 0.94—or very little risk reduction.

These numbers did not differ significantly according to sex, obesity or geographic region (which in this case meant the US and Europe).

However, Dr. van Dam adds that the results were rather diverse in the lowest consumption category. He would not be surprised if future studies that are able to measure coffee consumption more precisely find a lower diabetes incidence for any amount of coffee.

MORE COFFEE, LESS DIABETES

These findings serve to underscore the results of an earlier HSPH study, in which men who drank more than six cups of coffee a day reduced their risk of type 2 diabetes by more than 50% in comparison with men who did not drink coffee...and women by 30% in comparison with women who were not coffee drinkers. This beneficial effect was observed independent of lifestyle choices such as smoking, exercise and obesity.

Scientists don't know exactly how coffee cuts diabetes risk. Paradoxically, caffeine reduces insulin sensitivity and raises blood sugar—both no-nos for diabetes. However, Dr. van Dam emphasizes that coffee is a complex beverage that contains numerous chemical compounds and minerals, which may have both helpful and harmful impacts on the body. Components other than caffeine—such as the antioxidants chlorogenic acid and magnesium—actually improve sensitivity to insulin and thus help lower diabetes risk. In animal studies, trigonelline and lignans improved glucose levels. Dr. van Dam adds that additional studies on effects of coffee components in humans are clearly needed.

WHAT ABOUT DECAF?

For those who prefer decaf, coffee still packs some protection against type 2 diabetes. Although the effect appears to be more modest, some of this discrepancy may be attributed to study limitations. Decaffeinated coffee consumption was substantially lower than caffeinated coffee consumption, and this may have affected the estimates, explains Dr. van Dam. He points out that it is easier to detect larger contrasts in consumption than smaller differences. In addition, one can expect some misclassification when you ask for the amount of coffee people consume (change over time, differences in strength and cup size, etc.).

Dr. van Dam notes that in a study on coffee consumption and C-peptide concentrations (a marker for insulin resistance), the association was actually similar for decaffeinated and caffeinated coffee consumption. He adds that it is currently unclear whether caffeine has detrimental effects on insulin sensitivity over the long term, because only short-term studies have been conducted. Nor is it clear if non-coffee sources of caffeine would have similar effects.

THE JOLT OF JAVA

Other trials have already lined up in coffee's favor, demonstrating that it can lower the risk of liver problems, gallstones, colon cancer and

Parkinson's disease. Of course, there's also a downside to coffee (which pregnant women, children and people with colitis, hepatitis and other dietary challenges should not drink), such as jitteriness, insomnia and a rapid heartbeat. (Coffee stimulates liver function, which in healthy people is fine in moderation, but those with active liver disease may have symptoms worsen when they consume coffee.)

Promising as it seems, Dr. van Dam and his colleagues do not go so far as to recommend drinking coffee to prevent type 2 diabetes. They emphasize that while coffee consumption may provide greater control over diabetes and possibly reduce the need for pharmaceuticals, it cannot replace the myriad health benefits of diet, exercise and weight management.

Many people stop drinking coffee because they think this is good for their health. Now coffee drinkers can take comfort in knowing that their daily jolt of java not only gets them up and moving, it also provides a definite health benefit.

The Amazing Healing Power of Coffee

Joe A. Vinson, PhD, professor of chemistry, University of Scranton in Pennsylvania. A specialist in food-based chemical compounds, he was the lead author of an article on antioxidants published in *Journal of Agricultural and Food Chemistry*.

When most people think of a healthful diet, fresh fruits and vegetables typically top the list.

Surprising: An eight-ounce cup of caffeinated or decaffeinated coffee contains *more* disease-fighting antioxidants than a typical serving of fresh blueberries or oranges.

Although coffee does not contain some of the other nutrients found in healthful foods, it is the main source of antioxidants in the American diet (followed by tea and chocolate, respectively). Of course, the stimulating effects of coffee's caffeine are not always desirable—some people experience nervousness, insomnia or even spikes in blood pressure.

But most people who drink moderate amounts of coffee (typically defined as one to three cups daily) seem to have a lower risk for a number of chronic conditions, including heart disease, diabetes and age-related cognitive declines.

WHAT'S IN A CUP?

The amount of caffeine that is found in coffee varies, depending on how the coffee is prepared.

Examples: One ounce of espresso contains about 50 mg…an eight-ounce cup of instant coffee has 95 mg…and eight ounces of plain, brewed coffee has 150 mg.

A serving of espresso, instant or brewed coffee each contains roughly the same amount of antioxidants. In fact, coffee contains hundreds of antioxidants, particularly *polyphenols*—plant compounds that can inhibit cell damage or inflammation, two of the main causes of many chronic diseases. The addition of milk and/or sugar does not appear to affect the antioxidant levels.

Important: Most of the research linking coffee to reduced disease rates is based on epidemiological studies, in which scientists have analyzed the past dietary habits of large groups of people.

This type of research helps to develop hypotheses that deserve further study, but definitive answers won't be possible until scientists conduct more large-scale clinical studies, in which factors such as coffee consumption are tightly controlled (rather than merely self-reported by test subjects).

What the newest research on coffee consumption tells us…

GOOD FOR THE ARTERIES

New finding: In a study published in the *American Journal of Clinical Nutrition*, Norwegian researchers found that postmenopausal women who drink one to three cups of coffee daily are 24% less likely to develop cardiovascular disease than non-coffee drinkers.

Theory: The antioxidants in coffee—like those in fruits and vegetables—are thought to inhibit the damaging effects of free radicals on cells lining the arteries.

Result: A decrease in inflammation, now thought to be the underlying cause of heart disease.

Caution: Because of the stimulating effects of caffeine, blood pressure rises temporarily (for about one hour) when regular coffee is consumed. People who drink several cups in a row may keep their blood pressure elevated, thus increasing the risk for heart disease or a heart attack.

Helpful: Space out coffee consumption. For example, have one cup in the morning and another at lunch or in the afternoon. Or switch to decaf, which doesn't cause the blood-pressure spikes of regular coffee—but offers the same health benefits, except for those that improve cognitive function.

BLOOD PRESSURE STABILIZER

New finding: An analysis published in the *American Journal of Clinical Nutrition* found that older adults (age 65 and over) who have four or more daily servings of caffeine—in the form of coffee, soft drinks, etc.—have less than half the risk of dying of heart disease than those who consume smaller amounts.

Theory: Older adults are prone to occasional *hypotension* (low blood pressure). They are especially vulnerable to drops in blood pressure after meals, which can increase the risk for heart attack. Caffeine, by quickly raising blood pressure, appears to reduce the risk for such coronary events.

Caution: The oils found in *steeped* coffee, such as that made in a French press (a glass beaker to which hot water and ground coffee are added…then a plunger is depressed, filtering out all the grounds and sediment), can significantly raise cholesterol and increase the risk for elevated blood pressure.

Better for health: Coffee that is drip brewed (water is poured over ground coffee and seeps through a filter into a pot). The filter traps most of the oils.

LESS DIABETES

New finding: Research published in the *Archives of Internal Medicine* found that among 28,812 postmenopausal women studied, those who drank four to five cups of coffee (especially decaffeinated) per day were 16% less likely to develop type 2 diabetes than women who didn't drink any coffee.

Theory: The antioxidants in coffee may protect the pancreas's insulin-producing *beta cells* from oxidative damage.

BETTER BRAIN HEALTH

New finding: Coffee appears to slow the rate of cognitive decline in elderly adults. In a study published in the *European Journal of Clinical Nutrition* researchers gave memory tests to 676 healthy men in Finland, Italy and the Netherlands, then repeated the tests 10 years later. Non-coffee drinkers had four times more cognitive decline than men who drank three cups of coffee a day.

Theory: The antioxidants in coffee reduce age-related damage to brain cells (neurons) and/or cause beneficial changes in the hormones/neurotransmitters that are involved in cognitive function.

Scientific studies also suggest that moderate consumption of coffee reduces the risk for Parkinson's disease as well as Alzheimer's disease. Researchers have yet to explain why coffee reduces risk for these two diseases, but the mechanism is thought to be similar to that associated with reduced cognitive decline.

A HEALTHIER LIVER

New finding: According to research published in the *Archives of Internal Medicine*, coffee may reduce the risk for cirrhosis (irreversible liver scarring that, in severe cases, can be life-threatening without a transplant), especially in alcoholics. This link may be due to the anti-inflammatory effects of the antioxidants in coffee.

In addition, coffee may help protect against gallstones. Specifically, data from the ongoing Harvard Nurses' Health Study found that women who drank four or more cups of coffee daily required fewer operations for gallstones than women who didn't drink coffee.

Theory: Caffeine stimulates gallbladder contractions, which cause the gallbladder to empty more often and may reduce the risk for gallstone formation.

Caution: Caffeine interacts with certain medications, causing some to become more potent or increasing the amount of time caffeine remains in the body. These drugs include certain selective serotonin reuptake inhibitors (SSRIs), such as *fluvoxamine* (Luvox)...antiarrhythmics, such as *mexiletine* (Mexitil)...and bronchodilators, such as *theophylline* (Theovert). Caffeine also may interact with the herbal dietary supplement ephedra. In addition, consumption of more than five cups of coffee daily has been linked to higher risk for bone fractures in postmenopausal women.

Avoiding Sugar Shock

Ryan Bradley, ND, clinical faculty member, Bastyr University, adjunct faculty, Bastyr Center for Natural Health, Kenmore, WA. Dr. Bradley is a former director of the Washington Association of Naturopathic Physicians (WANP).

Many people take chromium to help regulate their blood sugar levels. Given its success with people who have type 2 diabetes, researchers at the Children's Hospital in Los Angeles are looking at whether chromium picolinate will improve blood sugar (glucose) levels and weight in 12- to 18-year-olds with type 1 diabetes who are overweight and whose diabetes is poorly controlled.

AN ESSENTIAL MINERAL

Chromium is an essential trace mineral that is vital to proper insulin function and carbohydrate, fat and protein metabolism. It has been studied extensively in type 2 diabetes in adults, where evidence suggests that it improves insulin sensitivity, blood glucose control and cardiovascular risk factors. Now experts want to see if these benefits extend to youngsters with type 1 diabetes.

ABOUT THE STUDY

In the double-blind, randomized, placebo-controlled clinical trial at Children's Hospital in Los Angeles, 30 children with type 1 diabetes are taking 600 mcg daily of chromium picolinate for seven months. (An average dose for adults with type 2 diabetes is 1,000 mcg daily.) During this time, researchers will measure their glycosylated hemoglobin (HbA1c) levels (a measurement of long-term glycemic control), glucose levels, body weight, body mass index (BMI) and cardiac risk factors including lipid profiles and blood pressure.

With the results of the study, scientists hope to learn whether chromium picolinate can help children more effectively manage type 1 diabetes and improve their long-term health outlook and overall quality of life.

IMPROVING INSULIN FUNCTION AND GLUCOSE LEVELS

In type 2 diabetes, chromium picolinate has been shown to increase insulin sensitivity, helping keep blood sugar levels from rising excessively, explains Ryan Bradley, ND, a clinical faculty member at Bastyr University in Kenmore, Washington, and a former director of the Washington Association of Naturopathic Physicians. He adds that chromium picolinate is a well-tolerated supplement with few adverse effects. Other forms of chromium have not been as thoroughly investigated.

Researchers estimate that chromium picolinate also may prove to be helpful in type 1 diabetes, but for different reasons, notes Dr. Bradley. In this form of diabetes, the problem is not insulin resistance but insufficient production of insulin. He says that the theory in this case is that chromium picolinate will make insulin function more efficiently in the body, which will contribute to keeping blood sugar on an even keel.

Only time will tell whether chromium picolinate can benefit youngsters with type 1 diabetes—but it's well worth looking into a safe, simple and affordable supplement that can help control such a devastating disease. Speak to a trained professional for proper guidance.

New Weapon Against Diabetes

Bruce N. Ames, PhD, professor of biochemistry and molecular biology, University of California, Berkeley; senior scientist, Children's Hospital Oakland Research Institute, Oakland. Read more about Dr. Ames' research at *www.juvenon.com*. He was appointed member, President's Committee, National Medal of Science.

One of the more popular supplements to come along is alpha-lipoic acid (ALA). Although studies are ongoing, this is one of the better-researched supplements, with demonstrated benefits as a disease-fighting antioxidant and as a treatment for diabetes.

Bruce N. Ames, PhD, a professor of biochemistry and molecular biology at the University of California in Berkeley, has conducted a number of studies of alpha-lipoic acid. *His thoughts about its many health benefits…*

A VERSATILE ANTIOXIDANT

As you probably already know, antioxidants protect our bodies from the cellular damage caused by unstable oxygen molecules called free radicals. Left unchecked, this damage can lead to ailments including cardiovascular disease, diabetes, arthritis, cataracts and Alzheimer's disease. Because it is soluble in both fat and water, alpha-lipoic acid is an especially valuable antioxidant. It can reach both tissues composed primarily of fat (including the brain and nervous system) and those of water (such as the heart). ALA also enhances the action of other well-known antioxidants—vitamins E and C.

A BRAIN FUNCTION BOOSTER

As we grow older, there is a drop in mitochondrial function in the body's cells. According to Dr. Ames, mitochondria—the power plants of cells—provide energy for basic cell processes, and their decay with age impairs cellular metabolism and leads to performance decline. At UC Berkeley, scientists have demonstrated that ALA can help reverse this type of age-associated decline as it relates to brain function. In laboratory experiments, old rats that were given high doses of ALA along with another supplement—N-acetyl-L-carnitine, typically used as an anti-aging supplement to enhance mental functions such as memory and improve the symptoms of Alzheimer's disease—experienced improved cellular function, which in practical terms translated into better performance on memory tasks. Clinical trials in people are just getting under way.

AN AID TO THE LIVER

In hospitals, ALA is administered intravenously to treat cases of mushroom poisoning and heavy metal poisoning. With its antioxidant abilities, ALA assists the liver in flushing toxins from the body. This supplement helps to shield the liver from harmful cell changes and offers protection against disorders such as hepatitis and cirrhosis.

WEAPON AGAINST DIABETES AND ITS COMPLICATIONS

Many studies of ALA have taken place in Germany, where this compound is commonly prescribed to treat diabetic neuropathy (a frequently agonizing complication of diabetes that begins with pain and numbness in the feet). ALA has been shown to increase blood flow to nerves and fine-tune the transmission of nerve impulses. Even more important, it improves insulin function and thus blood sugar regulation by expediting the more efficient removal of glucose from the blood. Poorly regulated, chronically high levels of blood sugar contribute to complications of diabetes including diabetic neuropathy and heart disease.

A FAT FIGHTER?

A new study at the University of Ulsan College of Medicine in Korea suggests that ALA may even play a role in combating obesity. When ALA was added to the food of rats, it reduced their food intake and body weight. This research is still in its infancy, with clinical studies in humans not yet planned.

HOW TO USE ALPHA-LIPOIC ACID

Tiny amounts of ALA are present in foods such as spinach, liver and yeast…however, only supplements provide substantial benefits such as antioxidant effects. Suggested dosages of ALA vary. As an antioxidant, a typical range is 10 mg to 50 mg daily. Therapeutic doses for problems such as diabetes can be as high as 600 mg daily. But be careful. While very promising, doctors do not yet have full information on side effects or long-term effects of ALA usage at "normal" and at "high" doses. While you should work closely with your doctor to monitor usage, be aware that few conventional doctors are experienced in ALA's usage at this point in time. According to Dr. Ames, side effects are very rare—mainly a mild rash in one in 300 people. The most important interaction is with the dosage of diabetes medications. It's not contraindicated for anyone, but you should, of course, consult your doctor about taking it (especially if you have diabetes).

■ ■ ■ ■

New Diabetes Drug

New diabetes drug spurs insulin production after a meal. *Exenatide* (Byetta) is the synthetic version of a protein in the saliva of the Gila monster, a lizard. People with type 2 diabetes inject the drug twice daily to supplement the action of *metformin* (Glucophage) or other oral medications.

Most common side effect: Nausea. Dosages of older drugs may need to be reduced to avoid low blood-sugar levels (hypoglycemia).

David M. Nathan, MD, director of Massachusetts General Hospital Diabetes Center and professor of medicine, Harvard Medical School, both in Boston.

▪▪▪▪

Dementia Risk

High blood sugar levels seem to dramatically increase the risk of dementia. Researchers studied patients with type 2 diabetes to determine if elevated glycosylated hemoglobin, a marker of blood sugar control, correlated with increased dementia risk. Compared with those with normal levels (less than seven), those with levels greater than 12 were 22% more likely to develop dementia. Those with levels greater than 15 were 78% more likely to get dementia.

Rachael Whitmer, PhD, research scientist, Kaiser Permanente division of research, Oakland, CA.

▪▪▪▪

Important Little-Known Diabetes Test

The A1C test shows average blood sugar levels over the past 180 days. It is done by a lab or in your doctor's office in addition to home monitoring of blood sugar. The A1C test tells whether diabetes treatment is working effectively—but 61% of diabetics recently surveyed did not know what it was. The A1C test can help diabetics adjust diet, activity and medication to avoid possible complications of the disease. Ask your doctor how often you should have an A1C test.

Robert A. Rizza, MD, professor of medicine and director for research at the Mayo Clinic College of Medicine in Rochester, MN, is past president of the American Diabetes Association, *www.diabetes.org*. Winner of prestigious Banting Medal for Service.

▪▪▪▪

Better Insulin Therapy

In a recent five-year study, researchers followed 1,300 diabetes patients who received insulin therapy using either syringes to inject insulin extracted from a vial…or insulin pens, which contain a needle and a premeasured dose of the drug. The insulin pen group had average annual health care costs nearly $17,000 lower than those who used syringes (due to lower total hospital costs, for example, and fewer trips to emergency rooms).

Theory: When using an insulin pen, there is less risk of getting an incorrect dose.

If you use a syringe for insulin therapy: Ask your doctor if switching to an insulin pen would be appropriate for you.

Rajesh Balkrishnan, PhD, professor of pharmacy, Ohio State University, Columbus.

Is Diabetes Seeping Into Our Systems?

Duk-Hee Lee, MD, PhD, assistant professor in the Department of Preventive Medicine and Public Health, School of Medicine, Kyungpook National University in South Korea. She is a medical doctor and epidemiologist who has written extensively about the relationship of persistent organic pollutants (POPs) and diabetes.

Scientists know that elements in the environment often interact with elements of our own physiology to cause serious problems. And new research is emerging that suggests we may be seeing this phenomenon with diabetes.

We've long known that obesity is a major risk factor for diabetes. But now it appears that exposure to pollutants can seriously aggravate the risk, and—in combination with obesity—may be associated with the increased risk of becoming diabetic. A recent study in the journal *Diabetes Care* looked at the connection between six persistent organic pollutants (known as POPs) and diabetes…and what they found was dramatic.

THE STUDY

Lead researcher Duk-Hee Lee, MD, PhD, and her team divided the 2,016 subjects into groups based on five levels of pollutants. Group 1 had the lowest levels and group 5 had the highest levels. The results showed that the prevalence of diabetes increased by 14- to 38-fold as the concentrations of the sum of the six POPs increased, irrespective of participants' weight, says Dr. Lee.

Compared with group 1 (which had a .4% incidence of diabetes), group 2 had a 6.7% incidence of diabetes, while group 5 had an astonishing 25.6% incidence of the disease (groups 3 and 4 ranged in between). Dr. Lee says that while obesity remains a risk factor for type 2 diabetes, the obese and overweight people with very low concentrations of POPs had a much lower incidence of diabetes. Could obesity and pollutants interact to cause diabetes?

RESEARCHERS' THEORIES

"It's our hypothesis that obesity might be only weakly associated with diabetes among people with very low serum concentrations of POPs," says Dr. Lee. She explains that while her research concentrated on only six specific pollutants out of about 50 POPs identified in the National Health and Examination Survey, there was a striking connection between the blood concentrations of these six toxins and the prevalence of diabetes.

This is not the first time that such a connection has been demonstrated. Earlier research from Sweden also found that exposure to POPs may contribute to the development of type 2 diabetes. Prior research also demonstrated that exposure to at least one toxin—a dioxin called TCDD—increases the risk of diabetes and insulin resistance. It's believed that these toxins may interfere with glucose metabolism.

POLLUTANTS EVERYWHERE

Persistent organic pollutants (POPs) include certain chemical byproducts, PCBs and certain insecticides. They have been linked to cancer, neurobehavioral impairment, endocrine problems and reproductive disorders. Previous researchers looked at groups who are occupationally or accidentally exposed to high levels of these pollutants, for example, Vietnam veterans. (The US Department of Veterans Affairs includes type 2 diabetes in its list of presumptive diseases associated with exposure to the dioxin-containing Agent Orange.) But Dr. Lee's study is the first to examine the cumulative effect of most commonly detected POPs among a random low-level exposure in the general population. The six toxins in the study are found in the environment, and they move through the air and water to accumulate in the environment.

Dr. Lee was careful not to say that pollutants by themselves necessarily cause diabetes, and she expressed the usual researcher's caution about jumping to strong conclusions based on one or two studies. "Plenty of people have exposure to these pollutants and don't get diabetes," she explains. "But the strong connection between high levels and increased incidence is very hard to ignore, as is the fact that there are such low levels of diabetes among those with low levels of exposure, even among the overweight and obese." Could genes be a factor? "It's prudent to act as if everyone is at risk, regardless of genetic makeup," she says.

HOW TO LIMIT EXPOSURE

How do we get exposed to these chemicals in the first place? "Exposure to POPs comes mostly from animal fatty food consumption," says Dr. Lee.

Her recommendation: "A low intake of animal food and a higher intake of plant food may be beneficial. And, aside from trying to avoid POPs, preventing obesity is still very important because the toxicity of POPs appeared to synergistically increase the risk of type 2 diabetes among obese persons."

Diabetes Drug Increases Cardiovascular Risk

Steven E. Nissen, MD, chairman of the department of cardiovascular medicine, Cleveland Clinic, OH, and past president of the American College of Cardiology.

After a study involving a top-selling diabetes drug, *rosiglitazone* (Avandia), pharmaceutical giant GlaxoSmithKline started marketing the drug as a medicine to prevent type 2 diabetes in those with prediabetes (impaired glucose tolerance or impaired fasting glucose). But clinical trials can backfire. In this case, rosiglitazone did successfully lower the risk of diabetes, but at the cost of an increased risk of cardiovascular (CV) events.

This is a disturbing finding, notes Steven E. Nissen, MD, chairman of the department of cardiovascular medicine at the Cleveland Clinic and past president of the American College of Cardiology. Dr. Nissen says that drugs to prevent and treat diabetes should *decrease* cardiovascular events, not increase them, since 65% of all diabetics die from cardiovascular complications.

THE STUDY

In the trial known as DREAM (*Diabetes Reduction Assessment with Ramipril and Rosiglitazone Medication*), researchers found that rosiglitazone reduced by 62% the number of individuals with prediabetes who developed diabetes. Elevated blood sugar (higher than normal), referred to as prediabetes, has received increasing attention from medical experts in recent years, since it puts people at a higher risk of developing full-blown diabetes. Unfortunately, that benefit was offset, as rosiglitazone also slightly increased the incidence of adverse cardiovascular events—such as heart attacks, stroke and most notably heart failure.

The results were very surprising, given that rosiglitazone is not a new drug, says Dr. Nissen. It has been available for many years, and is used by hundreds of thousands of Americans. While the increase in cardiovascular problems overall did not meet the standard for statistical significance (with the exception of heart failure), in Dr. Nissen's view, it still raises serious concerns.

SAFER ALTERNATIVES

Based on his analysis of the DREAM study, use of rosiglitazone to prevent diabetes should not be recommended, says Dr. Nissen. He adds that it should now be used cautiously in diabetics, particularly in those with a CV history. Fortunately, this is not your sole alternative. Dr. Nissen points out that lifestyle alterations (a healthier diet, regular exercise, weight management, etc.) have met with excellent results in preventing or treating type 2 diabetes. And, if necessary, other medications, including *metformin* (Glucophage) have also proven effective in controlling high blood sugar.

Are You at Risk for Hidden Bone Loss?

Harris H. McIlwain, MD, adjunct professor, University of South Florida College of Public Health in Tampa, is coauthor of *Reversing Osteopenia: The Definitive Guide to Recognizing and Treating Early Bone Loss in Women of All Ages*. Owl Books.

Calcium alone won't protect you from *osteopenia*—early osteoporosis. Most women—as well as men—who are past age 50 know that they are at risk for osteoporosis, the leading cause of bone fractures in older adults. But few older adults realize that they also are at risk for a precursor to osteoporosis known as *osteopenia*.

New finding: Estimates suggest that half of all women over age 45 and about 30% of men of the same age group have the mild bone loss that characterizes osteopenia.

Painful bone fractures, which are commonly associated with osteoporosis, also can occur in people who have osteopenia. These fractures can cause spinal deformities…hand or wrist disability…and severe hip injury.

SAY GOODBYE TO BONE

In women and men, new bone is constantly being produced and old bone broken down in a process called remodeling.

Until recently, doctors believed that a woman's peak bone-building years began in her childhood and extended to her 20s or 30s.

New finding: Bone growth slows significantly about 10 years earlier than previously thought.

For women, when estrogen levels decline at menopause, bone loss accelerates greatly. In the first five years after menopause, some women lose up to 25% of bone density.

Typically, men start to lose bone 10 years later than women. Testosterone deficiency and the use of certain steroid medications, such as *prednisone* (Deltasone), are some of the most common causes.

RISK FACTORS

A sedentary lifestyle, not getting enough bone-building calcium and vitamin D, and low body weight in women (less than 127 pounds) are the main causes of osteopenia.

Other key risk factors…

•**Very low-calorie diets.** Men and women who severely restrict calories—for example, consuming fewer than 1,000 to 1,200 calories daily—may not get enough dietary protein to ensure healthy bone growth.

•**Cola consumption.** Research has shown that drinking more than one, 12-ounce cola daily significantly lowers bone density. That may be because cola contains phosphoric acid, which blocks calcium absorption.

•**Smoking.** It doubles the risk for osteopenia in women and men.

EARLY DETECTION

All menopausal and postmenopausal women as well as women and men of any age with two or more of the risk factors listed above should get a bone density test.

The most accurate test is dual-energy X-ray *absorptiometry* (DEXA). It is painless and takes only about 10 minutes and exposes patients to less radiation than that used for a chest X-ray. It usually costs $100 to $125 and is covered by most insurance plans.

DEXA measures bone mineral density and converts the measurement into a standardized value called a T-score. The result shows how a patient's bone density compares with that of a typical 25-year-old woman. A higher T-score means stronger bones. A normal T-score is above -1.0…osteopenia, -1.0 to -2.5…and full-fledged osteoporosis, less than -2.5. If your results are abnormal, the test should be repeated every one to two years.

MAINTAINING BONE STRENGTH

Patients can stop further bone loss—or, in some cases, reverse osteopenia—with lifestyle steps…

•**Get adequate calcium.** You've heard it before—but there's no way around the importance of calcium. From age 25 to menopause, women need 1,200 mg daily, and 1,500 mg daily thereafter. Men need 1,000 mg daily from age 30 to 65, and 1,500 mg daily thereafter.

Dairy foods, including milk, have long been the most popular sources of calcium. An eight-ounce glass of milk provides about 300 mg—but only 25% to 30% of the mineral is actually absorbed.

What most people don't know: Juice can be a better calcium source than milk. An eight-ounce glass of calcium-fortified orange juice contains 350 mg (36% absorption).

Absorption rates are useful to know, so you can choose your calcium sources wisely. However, total daily calcium intake is based on the food product's available calcium rather than its absorption rate.

Supplements are acceptable if you don't get enough calcium in your diet. Calcium citrate and calcium carbonate supplements are equally effective. Calcium citrate can be taken at any time…calcium carbonate should be taken with meals. You can only absorb 500 mg to 600 mg of supplemental calcium at one time. If you're taking more, divide it into several daily doses.

•**Don't skip vitamin D.** Most younger adults synthesize adequate vitamin D from the sun, but older adults are less efficient at converting vitamin D into calcitriol, the hormone that stimulates calcium absorption.

What most people don't know: If vitamin D levels are low, bone building can be compromised.

Because it can be difficult to get enough of this vitamin, I recommend taking a 400-international-unit (IU) supplement of vitamin D daily up to age 65…and 800 IU daily thereafter.

•**Eat vitamin K-rich foods.** Vitamin K aids calcium absorption.

Good sources: Red meat, eggs, cereals, fruit (prunes and blueberries) and vegetables (kale and spinach).

Caution: Sudden increases in vitamin K intake may decrease the effect of *warfarin* (Coumadin).

What most people don't know: Eating a single daily serving of vitamin K-rich green, leafy vegetables cuts the risk for hip fracture by 50%, compared with eating one serving weekly, according to the landmark Nurses' Health Study.

•**Perform strength training.** In addition to performing weight-bearing exercises, such as walking, running or using the stairs, back-strengthening exercises performed two to three times weekly can significantly increase bone strength.

What most people don't know: Bone responds better to heavier loads than frequent repetitions when weight-lifting.

Example: It's better to lift 25 pounds 10 times than to lift five pounds 50 times.

Important: If lifestyle measures are not adequate, medications, such as *alendronate* (Fosamax), *raloxifene* (Evista) or *calcitonin* (Miacalcin), may be needed.

Good News About Multiple Sclerosis

Moses Rodriguez, MD, professor of neurology and immunology at Mayo Clinic College of Medicine in Rochester, MN, is the author of over 300 scientific papers on multiple sclerosis.

Multiple sclerosis occurs when immune cells target and destroy the myelin sheath that covers nerve cells in the brain and spinal cord, causing scarring that interferes with normal nerve-signal transmission. Depending on the location of the scarring, patients may suffer muscle spasms, vision loss, slurred speech, bladder, bowel or sexual dysfunction, dizziness, depression, numbness or tingling, cognitive problems and/or extreme fatigue.

Until recently, multiple sclerosis (MS) has been viewed as a debilitating disease that can condemn sufferers to wheelchairs and nursing homes.

Now: New studies at the renowned Mayo Clinic in Rochester, Minnesota, offer reason for optimism.

Background: Each year, more than 10,000 Americans are diagnosed with MS, an inflammatory disorder of the central nervous system. About 90% of MS patients have the "relapsing-remitting" form, suffering intermittent attacks of symptoms such as difficulty walking, visual disturbances, numbness, tingling and memory loss. Flare-ups are sometimes separated by years, followed by full or partial recovery.

The remaining 10% of patients have "primary-progressive" MS, which causes more continuous symptoms and a steady deterioration over a period of 10 to 20 years.

Researchers at Mayo Clinic have studied MS in Olmsted County, Minnesota (population 100,000), for 100 years. We've literally gone door to door to identify every person in the county with MS—and for the past 25 years we have tracked the progression of the disease in more than 170 confirmed patients. This method allows us to study patients with absent or mild MS symptoms, who are often missing from clinic-based studies that use only patients whose disease is active.

Our findings for the 90% of patients with the relapsing-remitting form of MS...

• **MS is benign in up to one-third of these patients,** causing minimal or no disability even after decades. For reasons that are still under investigation, these patients seem to have an intrinsic ability to repair themselves following acute MS flare-ups.

Although there is no way to predict at the onset whether MS will prove benign or progressive, we do know that people who do not suffer disability, including deficits in fine motor skills and coordination and bowel and bladder problems during the first five years, have a less than 10% chance of seeing their condition worsen over the next 10 to 30 years.

• **Another 50% of patients develop mild to moderate disabilities,** such as arm and/or leg weakness, tingling and/or numbness and mild incoordination, but are still able to walk unassisted after 10 or more years with MS.

• **Less than one-quarter of the patients with relapsing-remitting MS** ultimately suffer significant declines in their ability to function. Even for these patients, medications can alleviate symptoms.

IS MEDICATION NECESSARY?

In 2005, a new medication that had shown significant promise in early clinical trials—reducing the incidence of MS flare-ups by as much as 67%—was linked to two deaths. As a result, the drug *natalizumab* (Tysabri) was abruptly recalled just three months after receiving FDA approval.

National Multiple Sclerosis Society (NMSS) guidelines call for all patients with relapsing-remitting MS to begin treatment with older drugs to slow the disease's progression when a diagnosis is made. Patients are diagnosed after suffering two isolated attacks at least one month apart that damage more than one area of the central nervous system myelin—the sheath that surrounds and protects nerve fibers.

Recall, however, that our studies show that for one-third of MS patients who have the relapsing-remitting form, there will be minimal or no disease progression, even without treatment. This is no small consideration. The disease-modifying drugs prescribed for MS, including *glatiramer* (Copaxone), can reduce the frequency of MS attacks by 30% but can cost more than $20,000 annually and may not be covered by insurance. They must be injected as often as every other day and can produce serious side effects, including nausea, vomiting, fatigue, muscle aches and liver damage.

DR. RODRIGUEZ'S VIEW

The NMSS and many experts in the MS field believe that MS demands early intervention with these powerful drugs because the disease is so unpredictable. Based on our new research, however, I recommend that newly diagnosed patients take a wait-and-see approach when considering medication. If the patient experiences more than two attacks a year or shows signs of neurological deterioration, such as deficits in coordination and fine motor skills, we will initiate drug therapy.

For patients who go years between flare-ups, recover fully from attacks and experience minimal or no disability, the cost and side effects of drug treatment may be more damaging than the disease itself. For patients with this type of benign or mild MS, self-care measures can help keep the disease in check. *Key strategies...*

•**Reduce stress.** Studies have shown that stress can compromise healthy immune functioning, increasing your risk for MS flare-ups. Get plenty of rest and adequate sleep, and practice daily relaxation exercises, such as deep breathing or meditation.

•**Keep cool.** Many MS patients are heat-sensitive. Increases in body temperature brought on by warm weather or physical activity exacerbate their symptoms. Studies suggest that lowering body temperature by a degree or two can help bolster nerve-signal transmission. This may help relieve fatigue and improve mental functioning and muscle strength in MS patients. Cooling can be achieved with special garments (vests, hats, scarfs, etc.) designed for people who work in high-heat conditions. For more information, contact the Multiple Sclerosis Cooling Foundation, *www.mscooling.org.*

•**Take aspirin.** In a Mayo Clinic trial, we showed that taking high-dose aspirin twice daily significantly improves MS symptoms.

Researchers are unsure of aspirin's mechanism but believe it may work by reducing body temperature.

•**Exercise.** While heat-sensitive patients may need to limit vigorous aerobic activity, research confirms that moderate exercise greatly improves mobility and mood in people with MS. Swimming is an ideal choice, because the water prevents overheating.

•**Take vitamin D.** Studies suggest that not getting enough vitamin D through sun exposure or diet—in foods such as milk or sardines—is a significant risk factor for MS. Aim to get 15 or 20 minutes of sun exposure daily, before applying sunblock. Or take a daily supplement that provides 400 international units (IU) of vitamin D.

Ample evidence supports the use of these lifestyle changes, combined with a healthy diet (and avoiding smoking and alcohol), to help slow or halt the progression of mild to moderate MS.

Others with more serious symptoms or emerging disabilities should practice these measures and take a disease-modifying drug, such as *glatiramer, interferon beta-1a* (Avonex, Rebif) or *interferon beta-1b* (Betaseron).

The immune-suppressing drug *mitoxantrone* (Novantrone) also has recently been approved for treating steadily worsening relapsing-remitting MS. But this drug should be used with caution, due to serious potential side effects, including aggressive leukemia or lymphoma. There is still no approved treatment for primary-progressive MS.

ON THE HORIZON

New research suggests that estrogen and cholesterol-lowering drugs may prove useful in treating MS. In one small but promising study, the Alzheimer's drug *donepezil* (Aricept) improved memory in MS patients.

Kidney Miracle Works Better than Dialysis Clinics

Christopher Chan, MD, medical director, Home Hemodialysis, Toronto General Hospital, and associate professor of medicine, University of Toronto, Ontario, Canada.

Nathan W. Levin, MD, medical and research director, Renal Research Institute, and professor of clinical medicine, Albert Einstein College of Medicine, New York City.

Research suggests that home-based, while-you-sleep dialysis may allow thousands of patients who have end-stage kidney disease to be freed from the daytime hours they spend at clinics strapped to machines that clean their blood of toxins.

"We train the patients to administer the therapy at home, but it's essentially the same machine we use in the clinic," explains Canadian researcher Dr. Christopher Chan, medical director of home hemodialysis at Toronto General Hospital.

THE STUDY

His team of researchers tracked 14 patients who had end-stage kidney disease for one year and found "encouraging" results from their use of nighttime home dialysis, noting improvements in cardiovascular markers that are not achieved by standard, three-times-a-week clinic-based dialysis.

As for survival, Chan says only 10 of 110 patients have died during the 10 years they have been using nocturnal hemodialysis in Toronto.

Some doctors say that the while-you-sleep protocol seems to be the most promising option for patients.

In the Canadian study and in other studies, "many claims have already been made" supporting the effectiveness of nighttime dialysis, says Dr. Nathan W. Levin, medical and research director of the Renal Research Institute, and professor of clinical medicine at Albert Einstein College of Medicine in New York City.

"First, it lowers blood albumin, a protein which is a very sensitive indicator of outcomes in dialysis patients. It may also increase hemoglobin, another important indicator of survival in cardiac disease," Levin says.

Chan's research also found that unlike standard dialysis, sleep-time dialysis prevented the buildup of calcium phosphate within arteries—a major risk factor for cardiovascular disease in these patients.

ENCOURAGING BUT CAUTIOUS

These findings, however encouraging, still took place within the context of a small trial that did not involve a control group, notes Levin.

"Without a control group you can never be sure whether there's selection bias," he says, "and with a small sample size, you can't really be sure of an effect."

To combat these potential problems and verify the results, the US National Institutes of Health (NIH) is helping sponsor the first major randomized, controlled study of both nocturnal dialysis and "short daily dialysis," where patients visit the dialysis clinic six times per week, for an average of just two hours per session. In standard, three-times-per-week dialysis, each session usually lasts three to four hours.

According to Levin, short daily dialysis has some advantages over both longer, thrice-weekly dialysis and nocturnal home dialysis. First, he says, "It's being done in the clinic—we know only a fraction of patients can learn how to go home and dialyze themselves."

Short but more frequent dialysis also keeps a patient's fluid buildup to a minimum, he adds. And chronic fluid buildup is strongly associated with cardiovascular disease, the major killer of kidney patients.

Finally, because most toxin removal occurs within the first two hours of dialysis, shorter duration treatments should not impair the quality of blood cleansing, Levin says.

To learn more about kidney disease and kidney dialysis, visit the National Kidney and Urologic Diseases Information Clearinghouse at *http://kidney.niddk.nih.gov.*

Kidney Stones: New Prevention Strategies

Glenn M. Preminger, MD, is professor of urologic surgery and director of the Comprehensive Kidney Stone Center at Duke University Medical Center in Durham, NC. He is vice chairman of the American Urological Association Nephrolithiasis Guidelines Panel.

A kidney stone is a hard mass that forms when certain minerals—calcium, oxalate and uric acid—fail to dissolve in the urine and then accumulate into solid crystals. Normally, urine contains chemicals, such as citrate, that inhibit stone formation. But some people are prone to stones due to diet, lifestyle and certain medical conditions, such as inflammatory bowel disease. Kidney stones can trigger sudden, searing pain in the back and side, often accompanied by blood in the urine, nausea and/or vomiting.

When a kidney stone creates a blockage in a ureter (one of the tubes that connect the kidney to the bladder), it can be excruciatingly painful. Each year, more than 250,000 Americans are hospitalized because of this condition. Fortunately, new research is identifying highly effective prevention and treatment options.

Recent findings…

•**Lemonade fights kidney stones.** Researchers recently tracked stone-prone patients for up to four years and found that those who drank two quarts of lemonade daily had fewer new stones…and little or no growth of existing ones.

Why it works: Lemon juice contains high amounts of *citrate*, a substance that inhibits kidney stones by reducing urine acidity and binding with urinary calcium. Potassium citrate, in pill or liquid form, is routinely prescribed for stone prevention. Lemonade isn't as potent as potassium citrate, but it does appear to be a viable alternative for patients who can't take or tolerate the drug (people with impaired kidney function, for example), or for those who wish to avoid another medication.

To reap the study-proven benefits, you need to drink two quarts of homemade lemonade daily. The lemonade should be made by mixing two quarts of water with four ounces of reconstituted lemon juice. To reduce or eliminate sugar and/or calories, consider using artificial sweeteners. Since stone formers are advised to drink three quarts of fluid daily as a preventative, you'll benefit even more if two of those quarts are lemonade.

•**Alpha blockers can speed stone passage.** For years, researchers have searched for ways to facilitate spontaneous passage of kidney stones that are stuck in a ureter so that patients would be spared stone removal via a procedure such as an endoscopic technique, using a thin, telescopic tube.

Good news: In multiple trials conducted over the last five years, alpha blockers—prescription drugs traditionally used to treat an enlarged prostate—have proven to be remarkably effective for speeding and easing the elimination of small stones (less than six millimeters in diameter) from a ureter. These drugs increase the likelihood of spontaneous passage of small stones by about 90%.

Alpha blockers work by relaxing smooth muscle cells lining the ureter, improving urine flow and preventing the painful contractions that can slow or block stone movement. It's now become the standard of care to start most ureteral stone patients on a trial of alpha blockers. In a majority of cases, the drugs allow the stones to pass spontaneously. A small percentage of patients who take alpha blockers experience orthostatic hypotension—light-headedness when quickly standing up.

•**Obesity and weight gain elevate kidney stone risk.** Several recent studies confirm that being overweight and/or gaining weight significantly increases kidney stone risk. A large-scale, long-term study shows that obese men are 44% more likely, and obese women 90% more likely, to develop stones than are their leaner counterparts. Gaining more than 35 pounds during adulthood also heightens risk (by 39% for men and up to 82% for women), compared with maintaining a stable weight.

What's the connection between kidney stones and weight gain? As recent studies show, many adults who are significantly overweight also have type 2 diabetes (often undiagnosed) or are insulin resistant—that is, their bodies have a reduced ability to respond to insulin, which causes the pancreas to secrete excessive amounts of insulin. Insulin resistance and diabetes raise the acid levels in urine—a primary risk factor for stones. Losing weight is the ideal antidote. But if that's not possible, alkali therapy, in the form of potassium citrate, may be prescribed to reduce the acid load in urine to prevent stones.

DIETARY MEASURES

For prevention, people with a personal or family history of kidney stones should…

•**Drink three quarts of fluid daily,** mostly noncaffeinated. Coffee and tea are fine in moderation.

•**Get enough calcium.** Though stone formers had long been advised to limit calcium intake, recent studies link insufficient calcium to increased risk for stones.

That's because calcium can bind with stone-producing oxalates in the digestive tract, preventing these minerals from concentrating in the urine. Aim for two to three servings daily of low-fat milk, cheese, yogurt or calcium-fortified juice or cereal.

Caution: Calcium supplements may not be the best source. Studies show that they may raise urinary calcium excretion, a risk factor for stones. If you have a personal or family history of kidney stones and wish to take calcium supplements, have your urine tested after three months to check for elevated calcium levels.

•**Limit salt.** Excess sodium steals calcium from your bones and causes it to accumulate in your urine, increasing your risk for kidney stones. Don't add salt to your food...and avoid highly processed, prepackaged foods.

•**Avoid high-oxalate foods,** such as spinach, tea, chocolate, nuts, asparagus and rhubarb. Our bodies also convert some vitamin C into oxalates, and studies suggest that too much can raise urinary oxalate levels. Stone formers should not exceed 2,000 mg (2 g) of vitamin C daily.

•**Cut back on meat.** Animal protein, particularly from red meat, raises acid levels in the urine, increasing kidney stone risk. Aim for three or fewer red meat servings weekly.

Silent Kidney Disease: Doctors Don't Always Recognize the Symptoms

L. Ebony Boulware, MD, MPH, an internist and associate professor of medicine and epidemiology at the Welch Center for Prevention, Epidemiology and Clinical Research at Johns Hopkins University School of Medicine in Baltimore, was lead author of a study on physicians' recognition of the signs and symptoms of kidney disease. Dr. Boulware won a Clinician Investigator Award from the Society of General Internal Medicine.

It's widely known that diseases such as high blood pressure (hypertension) and diabetes can go undetected for quite some time. But few patients—and a relatively small percentage of doctors—realize that chronic kidney disease (CKD) is equally threatening and often remains hidden.

Danger: CKD—and subsequent kidney damage—can be markedly slowed with medications and also by controlling the underlying causes. Yet many primary care physicians don't fully understand how to diagnose this condition or how to assess the main risk factors.

Result: Many of the estimated 20 million Americans with CKD aren't diagnosed as early as they could be. By the time symptoms appear, the kidneys could have lost more than 75% of their normal function. At that point, the damage may be so extensive that patients will eventually require dialysis or a kidney transplant—or they die waiting.

Simple blood and urine tests can detect most cases of early CKD. Patients who are diagnosed and referred to a nephrologist (kidney specialist) early are often able to delay dialysis or transplant, or even avoid them altogether.

WHAT'S GETTING MISSED?

One of the main functions of the kidneys is to eliminate wastes, such as urea, from the body. In CKD, damage to the filtering units (nephrons) in the kidneys is typically caused by hypertension or diabetes, usually over a period of decades. About 45% of CKD cases are caused by diabetes, while 27% are caused by hypertension. Because CKD causes no symptoms, laboratory tests are the only way to detect it early.

That's why patients with hypertension, diabetes or other risk factors for CKD should have tests for kidney function during annual exams. But even that might not be enough. A new study reports that many doctors miss the signs of early CKD even when those signs should be apparent to them.

The study: Researchers at Johns Hopkins University School of Medicine asked 304 randomly selected US doctors, including kidney specialists, internists and family physicians, to evaluate the medical files of a fictitious patient.

The doctors also were given the raw data needed to calculate the glomerular filtration rate, an important measure of kidney function. They were asked to calculate this number themselves using accepted equations.

Result: Of the kidney specialists surveyed, 97% accurately diagnosed CKD, and 99% of those said they would have recommended that a primary care physician refer the patient to a kidney specialist. Among the internists, only 78% made the proper diagnosis of CKD, and 81% of those recommended a referral to a kidney specialist. Even worse, only 59% of the family physicians made an accurate diagnosis of CKD, and only 76% of those recommended a specialist referral.

The implications of this study are troublesome. Delays in diagnosing CKD greatly increase the risk for complications, including heart disease.

New finding: CKD promotes atherosclerosis and is an independent risk factor (like smoking, diabetes or hypertension) for cardiovascular disease.

SELF-PROTECTION

Blood and/or urine tests, when interpreted properly, can easily detect early CKD, but doctors don't order these tests as often as they should. Patients who have been diagnosed with diabetes or hypertension should insist on getting tested for CKD. This is particularly important for African-Americans. They are six times more likely than Caucasians to develop hypertension-related kidney failure. People age 60 or older—even if they don't have diabetes or hypertension—also may want to be tested, because they are at higher risk for CKD. The testing can be done by a primary care physician. *Main tests...*

•**Serum creatinine.** CKD curbs the ability of the kidneys to remove wastes from the body. One such waste is creatinine (a substance derived from protein metabolized in muscle). Elevated levels in the blood indicate kidney disease.

Trap: Creatinine alone is not a good marker of kidney function. An older adult, or someone with a small frame, could have a normal level of creatinine and still have CKD. An additional step (below) is needed for accurate results.

•**Modification of Diet in Renal Disease equation.** Many physicians aren't aware of this equation. It's considered the gold standard for calculating glomerular filtration rate, the best measure of kidney function. The equation, which is available to physicians on the National Kidney Foundation Web site (*www.kidney.org*), takes into account the creatinine level as well as the patient's age, gender, race and other factors.

•**Albumin.** This is a protein that's often present in the urine of patients with CKD. It's detected by dipping a test strip in a urine sample. The presence of albumin usually indicates kidney damage caused by diabetes. This test is mainly recommended for patients with diabetes or other risk factors for CKD.

•**Cystatin C.** This is a relatively new test—and might be more accurate than creatinine for diagnosing CKD. Cystatin C is a protein that's normally filtered out of the blood by the kidneys. Elevated levels indicate that the kidneys aren't working at optimal levels.

TREATING CKD

Apart from a transplant operation, there isn't a cure for CKD. The most important strategy is to control (or prevent) hypertension and diabetes through medication and lifestyle changes, such as following a low-fat, low-salt diet. These conditions can double or triple the risk of CKD—and accelerate the damage in patients who already have it.

Because many patients with CKD also have hypertension, doctors often prescribe blood pressure medication. Lowering blood pressure to below 120/80 mmHg can significantly slow the progression of CKD. These drugs also are helpful for patients with CKD caused by diabetes.

Important: Studies have shown that using an angiotensin converting enzyme (ACE) inhibitor, such as *captopril* (Capoten) or *ramipril* (Altace), or angiotensin II receptor blocker, such as *irbesartan* (Avapro) or *candesartan* (Atacand), can slow the progression of CKD by as much as 30%. These drugs are effective even in CKD patients who don't have hypertension or diabetes.

What Most Doctors Don't Know About Heartburn

Lauren Gerson, MD, an associate professor of medicine at Stanford University School of Medicine, Stanford, CA. Dr. Gerson is the recipient of the Gastroenterology Research Group Young Investigator Clinical Research Award.

Most doctors tell patients who suffer from the searing, shooting pain of heartburn to avoid spicy foods, alcohol and chocolate. But new research has shown that for the majority of heartburn sufferers, switching to a bland diet doesn't eliminate pain-causing acid reflux.

SURPRISING NEW RESEARCH

Heartburn occurs when acid from the stomach backs up into the esophagus through a relaxed lower esophageal sphincter (the valve that prevents stomach acid from entering the esophagus). For decades, physicians have told heartburn patients to stop eating foods that can cause the sphincter to exert less pressure—namely, spicy, fried or fatty foods, as well as citrus, caffeinated or alcoholic beverages.

However, in my own practice, most of my patients who severely limited their diets for heartburn relief still had reflux. With this in mind, my colleagues and I set out to determine whether food avoidance actually has any benefit.

In an analysis recently published in *Archives of Internal Medicine*, we reviewed more than 2,000 studies published between 1975 and 2004 and found no evidence that removing specific foods or beverages from the diet would eliminate heartburn in most people.

A small percentage of heartburn sufferers do have triggers.

Example: Red wine causes immediate heartburn in sensitive patients, possibly because of its acid content. Such people should avoid red wine and/or take preventive medication.

Some so-called heartburn triggers, such as caffeine-rich coffee and chocolate, as well as tea and cola, have been linked to relaxation of the esophageal sphincter. However, our findings suggest that the sphincter would relax regardless of the types of food eaten. Therefore, avoiding caffeinated foods won't eliminate heartburn.

We found the same to be true for spicy foods, citrus, alcoholic beverages and even smoking—no studies have shown that eliminating these "triggers" caused an actual reduction in heartburn symptoms. More research is needed to determine systematically if food avoidance can benefit heartburn sufferers, since very few published studies have been designed to examine this question.

LIFESTYLE CHANGES

Although diet had no effect on reflux relief, our research found that there are two factors that could reduce the incidence of heartburn—weight loss and elevating the head of the bed. Try these approaches—and other proven strategies—for four to six weeks before taking heartburn medication, which can cause headache, diarrhea and other side effects.

• **Weight loss.** Excess body weight places additional pressure on the abdomen, which may cause the lower esophageal sphincter to relax.

Researchers have found that normal-weight adults in the Nurses' Health Study who gained 20 pounds developed acid reflux or worsened existing symptoms. Risk increased with greater weight gain.

Fortunately, studies have shown that weight loss brings relief. Portion control is more important than the foods you select.

• **Raise your head at night.** Elevating the head of the bed at least six inches by putting blocks or bricks under the frame guards against heartburn by helping keep acid out of the esophagus. If you don't feel comfortable raising the bed frame, buy a foam wedge pillow six to eight inches thick to place under your pillow. Wedges can be found in pharmacies or on-line at sites such as *www.medslant.com* (800-346-1850)…or *www.foamcenter.com*.

Typical cost: $20 to $90.

• **Avoid large meals.** Overeating can aggravate heartburn, since the stomach produces more acid for digestion. Additionally, fatty foods can delay emptying of the stomach, and that can lead to reflux.

• **Stop eating three hours before going to bed.** Late-night eating may cause problems for some people. A few studies have shown that heartburn didn't disappear when patients skipped late-night meals, but the pH level of acid in the esophagus improved, indicating that less acid was present.

• **Exercise.** Staying active can help you lose weight, which can offer relief. Some people find that vigorous physical activity worsens heartburn—exercise can slow stomach emptying and interfere with gastrointestinal absorption, but low-impact exercise, such as walking, typically does not have that effect.

HEARTBURN MEDICATIONS

If the above steps don't work within several weeks (or longer if you're trying to lose weight), try…

•**Antacids.** Start with fast-acting over-the-counter (OTC) antacids, such as Tums or Mylanta. Use them for intermittent reflux, not for long-term treatment (six weeks or more).

Warning: The calcium in Tums can cause constipation, and the magnesium in Mylanta can cause diarrhea. Check with your pharmacist if you're taking other medications—antacids can interfere with the absorption of some drugs.

•**H2 blockers.** When antacids aren't strong enough, consider an H2 blocker, such as *famotidine* (Pepcid) or *ranitidine* (Zantac), both of which are available OTC. Side effects, such as headache and diarrhea, are uncommon.

•**Proton pump inhibitors.** If heartburn isn't squelched by other medications, try a proton pump inhibitor, such as *omeprazole* (Prilosec) or *lansoprazole* (Prevacid). Side effects, including headache and diarrhea, are rare.

A recent study examined whether the use of proton pump inhibitors was linked to infection with *Clostridium difficile*, a bacterium that can cause diarrhea, fever and abdominal pain. These drugs reduce the amount of stomach acid, so researchers thought some C. difficile bacteria that would normally be killed in the stomach could survive, causing intestinal problems. Additional research is needed.

DRUG-FREE ALTERNATIVES

Some people who want to relieve heartburn without medication try consuming papaya juice or ginger. No studies have examined the relationship between these products and heartburn, but ingesting them shouldn't cause health problems.

SCREEN FOR CANCER

Long-term heartburn sufferers are at increased risk of developing Barrett's esophagus, a precancerous condition caused by years of acid being regurgitated into the esophagus. Barrett's can lead to esophageal cancer. People with chronic reflux lasting more than six to 12 months should get an endoscopy (in which a flexible, lighted tube is used to examine the digestive system) to screen for Barrett's and esophageal cancer.

Natural Heartburn Relief

Ara DerMarderosian, PhD, professor of pharmacognosy (the study of natural products used in medicine) and is director of the Complementary and Alternative Medicine Institute at the University of the Sciences in Philadelphia.

Many people who suffer from heartburn take over-the-counter antacids or expensive prescription medication, such as *esomeprazole* (Nexium) and *lansoprazole* (Prevacid). These treatments can help but often cause side effects, such as diarrhea and dry mouth.

Heartburn, a sharp, burning pain under the rib cage, occurs when stomach contents "back up" (reflux) into the esophagus.

Chamomile, ginger and deglycyrrhizinated licorice have long been used (in tea, extract and tincture) to relieve heartburn as well as indigestion and intestinal irritation. Their effectiveness is supported by anecdotal evidence.

For relief proven in clinical studies, try pectin, a substance found in the outer skin and rind of fruits and vegetables. Apples and bananas are among the best sources of pectin. If you suffer from heartburn, try eating an apple (do not choose green or other tart varieties) or a banana to see if it relieves your symptoms.

Pectin supplements, which are available at most health-food stores, are another option. Take at the onset of heartburn until it subsides. For dosage, follow label instructions. Pectin supplements are generally safe but may interfere with the absorption of some medications, so check with your doctor before trying this supplement.

Caution: Chronic heartburn (more than twice a week) may indicate gastroesophageal reflux disease (GERD), a condition that should be treated by a gastroenterologist.

■ ■ ■ ■

Heartburn Drug Warning

Drugs for heartburn and reflux disease increase risk of intestinal infections. Medications such as *esomeprazole* (Nexium), *lansoprazole* (Prevacid), *cimetidine* (Tagamet) and *ranitidine* (Zantac) suppress the stomach acid that fights bacteria.

Side effect: A two- to threefold increase in risk of a *Clostridium difficile* bacterial infection, which can cause diarrhea, colitis and other intestinal problems.

Self-defense: If you use a heartburn or reflux drug, be vigilant about washing your hands, which will kill C. difficile bacteria. Consult your physician if you have frequent diarrhea containing mucus or blood. C. difficile infections are treated with antibiotics.

Sandra Dial, MD, assistant professor of medicine, McGill University, Montreal, Quebec, Canada, and leader of a study, published in *Journal of the American Medical Association*.

■■■■

Fatty Foods Lead to Heartburn

High-fiber, low-fat diet may prevent heartburn, according to research.

Recent finding: People who ate four servings of fat were twice as likely to have heartburn than those who ate one serving. Heartburn, which affects about one in five Americans, is caused when stomach acids enter the esophagus. Fat may increase reflux by filling the lower end of the esophagus, thus making it easier to reflux. It also promotes obesity, which is a risk factor for reflux. Fiber may bind to some of the fat, making reflux less harmful. If left untreated, heartburn can lead to ulcers, bleeding in the esophagus and esophageal cancer.

Hashem B. El-Serag, MD, MPH, professor of medicine, Baylor College of Medicine, Houston, and leader of a study of 371 people with and without heartburn symptoms, published in *Gut*.

Nausea? Heartburn? Stomach Pain? You Might Have a Hernia

Robert Kozol, MD, FACS, is professor and chair, department of surgery, University of Connecticut Health Center, Farmington, and is part of the colon cancer prevention program team. He has been a member of the European Union Hernia Research Cooperative and participated in the Veterans Administration Cooperative Hernia study, published in *The New England Journal of Medicine*.

Most hernias cause no symptoms or only mild discomfort. Many people don't even know that they have one until it is discovered during tests for other problems. Some hernias,

however, cause nausea, heartburn or abdominal or testicular pain. Some can be life-threatening.

A hernia is the protrusion of an internal organ into an area where it's not supposed to be. For example, part of the intestine can poke through the diaphragm or protrude into the groin or through the abdominal wall.

The most common types of hernia and best treatments...

HIATAL HERNIA

A hiatal hernia occurs at the opening in the diaphragm (the hiatus), where the esophagus passes through to join the stomach. If the opening is larger than it should be or the surrounding tissue is weak, the upper portion of the stomach can bulge through the diaphragm into the chest cavity.

One-quarter to one-half of Americans have hiatal hernias. They are four times more common in women than men. Most cause no symptoms. In a minority of cases, they result in gastroesophageal reflux disease (GERD), which causes heartburn and occasionally nausea or cramping. *Two main types...*

Sliding hiatal hernias, which account for at least 90% of cases, occur when the hiatal junction—the area where the esophagus meets the stomach—slides into the chest cavity. These require treatment only when they cause severe or persistent GERD.

Paraesophageal hiatal hernias account for less than 10% of cases, but they are more dangerous. Part of the stomach protrudes into the chest, but the hiatal junction remains in the abdomen. There's a risk that the stomach and junction will twist and block circulation, causing stomach or esophageal tissues to die.

Warning: See your doctor immediately if you have severe pain in the upper abdominal or lower chest areas...suddenly have trouble swallowing...or can't eat more than a few bites at a time. These are signs that the stomach has twisted. You may need emergency surgery.

SELF-CARE

Patients without symptoms don't need treatment. If you're experiencing GERD, lifestyle approaches, such as eating smaller meals, avoiding fatty foods and not lying down within three hours of eating, can help relieve it. *If these steps don't work, try...*

•**Over-the-counter antacids,** which neutralize acidity in the esophagus and reduce heartburn in most patients. *If they don't work, your doctor may prescribe...*

•H2 blockers, such as *famotidine* (Pepcid), *cimetidine* (Tagamet) and *ranitidine* (Zantac), which reduce stomach acid and usually are taken before meals. These are available over-the-counter and in stronger prescription strengths.

•Prescription and over-the-counter proton pump inhibitors, such as *lansoprazole* (Prevacid) and *omeprazole* (Prilosec), which reduce stomach acid secretion and are taken once a day.

SURGERY

You may need surgery if medications and lifestyle changes don't control GERD...or if the stomach has twisted...or there's pressure on the esophagus that is causing bleeding or obstruction.

The surgery, *Nissen fundoplication*, usually is done laparoscopically through small incisions in the abdomen.

The top of the stomach is wrapped around the esophagus, and the opening in the diaphragm is sutured or stapled to make it smaller so the stomach can't protrude.

Most patients who have this procedure spend one or two nights in the hospital and recover fully within a month. GERD symptoms disappear in more than 90% of cases.

INGUINAL HERNIA

This type of hernia occurs when an organ pokes through a weak point in the groin. It can be painful, especially when you cough or lift a heavy object.

In men, the weak spot often occurs along the inguinal canal. This is where the spermatic cord enters the scrotum. Men are almost 10 times more likely to develop these hernias than women.

In women, the inguinal canal carries a ligament that helps hold the uterus in place. Hernias may occur where connective tissue from the uterus attaches to tissue surrounding the pubic bone.

Most inguinal hernias get larger over time. Though they can be excruciatingly painful, they aren't dangerous. However, a loop of intestine may get trapped in the weak point in the groin and obstruct the bowel or block circulation to the intestine. This condition—strangulation—can kill bowel tissue and is a life-threatening emergency. Warning signs include severe pain at the hernia site, skin redness and vomiting.

SELF-CARE

You may notice a bulge in the groin or the scrotum from the protruding intestine. You also may experience groin or scrotal pain when bending over, coughing or lifting. *You can temporarily relieve mild discomfort by...*

•**Lying on your back** and gently pushing the bulge into the abdominal cavity.

•**Sleeping with your hips higher than your abdomen** to make the intestine less likely to protrude.

SURGERY

If the hernia is painful or growing larger, your doctor may recommend surgery. *There are two main types...*

•**Herniorrhaphy.** The surgeon makes an incision in your groin and pushes the protruding intestine back into your abdomen, then repairs the weakened area by sewing it together. It may take as long as six weeks before you're able to resume normal activities.

•**Hernioplasty.** This is like patching a tire—a piece of synthetic mesh is sutured or stapled over the weak area. It closes the opening and prevents the intestine from protruding. It can be performed conventionally with a single long incision or laparoscopically with several small incisions. With laparoscopic repair, most people are back to work within a few days. Laparoscopy might not be an option if you have a very large hernia or if your intestine is pushed down into the scrotum.

PREVENTION

Some hernias are caused by congenital (inborn) weakness in the tissue walls. Other hernias are caused by "wear and tear." *To reduce your risk...*

•**Maintain a healthy weight.** Obesity puts extra pressure on weakened tissue.

•**Treat a cough.** A chronic cough increases abdominal pressure. This is another reason to quit smoking.

•**Avoid heavy lifting** to reduce pressure on the abdomen.

•**Eat a high-fiber diet** and drink water to avoid constipation. Straining can worsen hernias.

Herbal Remedies For Flatulence

Anil Minocha, MD, professor of medicine and director of the division of digestive diseases at the University of Mississippi Medical Center in Jackson, is the author of *Natural Stomach Care*. Avery.

Eating certain foods, such as beans and some fruits and vegetables, can lead to flatulence (gas or air in the stomach or intestine that is expelled through the anus). Fortunately, dozens of carminative (gas-reducing) herbs can help relieve flatulence. Use them one at a time or in combination. *Best choices...*

•**Chamomile** relaxes the bowel, which reduces intestinal spasms. Steep a tea bag in hot water for about 10 minutes. Drink one cup before bedtime.

•**Ginger** is an antispasmodic that reduces the force and frequency of intestinal contractions. It's good for most digestive complaints, including gas. Peel and slice one inch of ginger root and boil in three cups of water for 20 minutes. Drink one to three cups daily. Or take 500 mg of ginger capsules or powder three times a day.

•**Fennel seeds** calm an upset stomach and reduce gas. Munch on a handful of seeds to ease or prevent gas. They're available at health-food stores. *For additional relief...*

•**Massage your abdomen** when you have painful gas. With moderate pressure, use your palms to massage your abdomen clockwise—the direction that food moves through the gastrointestinal tract—for five to 10 minutes. Massage pushes out gas and relieves discomfort.

•**Try a simple yoga posture** to help purge gas from your intestine.

What to do: Lie on your back, pull your knees to your chest and rock in a circular motion.

•**Perform daily exercise** to help move gas out of the intestine and reduce painful pressure.

Best: Walking, tai chi and bicycling.

The Covered-Up Cause of IBS

Nancy Kraft, RD, clinical dietitian, University of Iowa, Iowa City.

Theodore M. Bayless, MD, professor of medicine, Johns Hopkins University, Baltimore.

American College of Gastroenterology annual meeting, Baltimore.

Cutting back on sugar and fat makes sense for people trying to control their weight, but there may be another health benefit. Two studies suggest that fat and fructose, the sugar in fruits and honey, also can contribute to gastrointestinal discomfort.

Irritable bowel syndrome (IBS) is a common disorder of the intestines that leads to pain, gassiness, bloating and changes in bowel habits, according to the American Gastroenterological Association. The disorder can lead to constipation in some and diarrhea in others. Some people experience both. Another common symptom may be a crampy urge to move the bowels.

In the first report, Nancy Kraft, a clinical dietitian from the University of Iowa, and her colleagues say some patients who have IBS are fructose-intolerant, and restricting that type of sugar can improve their symptoms.

Kraft says fructose intolerance often is an overlooked component of IBS.

Her colleague Dr. Young Choi says that, "a fructose-restricted diet significantly improved symptoms in patients with IBS and fructose intolerance. Fructose intolerance is yet another piece of the IBS puzzle."

THE STUDY

In the study, the 14 patients with IBS who followed a fructose-free diet for one year experienced a significant reduction in abdominal pain, bloating and diarrhea.

However, IBS symptoms remained the same for the 12 patients who did not stick with the diet, the researchers report.

Kraft believes these results are encouraging, because "people who limit their intake of fructose see their symptoms improve or disappear," but that further study is needed.

SECOND STUDY

Researchers from the Mayo Clinic in Rochester, Minnesota, led by Dr. Yuri Saito, collected data on the diets of 221 adults, aged 20 to 50 years. Of these patients, 102 had gastrointestinal disorders and 119 were healthy.

The research team found that patients with IBS or dyspepsia (indigestion) reported eating more monounsaturated fats compared with healthy patients. These patients also ate fewer carbohydrates than their healthy counterparts.

The Mayo investigators concluded that "future studies are needed to determine whether fat intake causes gastrointestinal symptoms."

Dr. Theodore M. Bayless, a professor of medicine at Johns Hopkins University, is not surprised that fat and fructose are linked with IBS and dyspepsia.

He notes that both fat and fructose are hard to digest and can aggravate both conditions. But Bayless does not believe that restricting fructose cures IBS; it may only relieve symptoms.

He advises his patients to avoid fatty foods and foods that contain high levels of fructose, such as grapes, dates, nuts, honey and apple and pear juice. He also advises patients to increase fiber intake.

Your Mind Can Ease Your IBS Symptoms

Olafur S. Palsson, PsyD, associate professor, medicine, Center for Functional GI & Motility Disorders, University of North Carolina at Chapel Hill.

Jeffrey M. Lackner, PsyD, assistant professor, medicine, University at Buffalo School of Medicine & Biomedical Sciences, Buffalo, NY.

International Foundation for Functional Gastrointestinal Disorders, Milwaukee.

When standard lifestyle adjustments such as dietary changes and drug therapy don't provide relief from the pain, bloating and other unpleasant gastrointestinal symptoms of irritable bowel syndrome, patients may want to try a different approach.

Recent studies show that using one's own thoughts, as taught in cognitive behavioral therapy, may help ease symptoms. Using hypnosis to visualize the pain and imagine it seeping away can be a powerful treatment strategy, too.

People with IBS experience chronic or recurrent constipation or diarrhea—or bouts of both. While the exact cause of the condition isn't known, symptoms seem to result from a disturbance in the interaction of the gut, brain and nervous system.

Doctors generally advise patients to avoid certain foods and may prescribe different medications. But these approaches don't always provide adequate relief.

Jeffrey M. Lackner, PsyD, assistant professor of medicine at the University at Buffalo School of Medicine & Biomedical Sciences is a behavioral medicine specialist whose research focuses on gastrointestinal disorders, particularly IBS.

For many patients, cognitive behavioral therapy, which uses the power of the mind to replace unhealthy beliefs and behaviors with healthy, positive ones, may be the answer. He and his colleagues set out to devise and test a treatment program that IBS patients could administer themselves.

THE COGNITIVE BEHAVIORAL STUDY

Seventy-five women and men were divided into three groups. One group was placed on a "wait list" for 10 weeks while they monitored their symptoms. Another group received the standard treatment of 10 cognitive behavioral therapy sessions over weekly. The third group had once-a-month therapy sessions over four months and practiced relaxation and problem-solving exercises at home.

Not surprisingly, people on the wait list did not do well at all, while those in the weekly and monthly sessions showed significant improvement. "They said at the end of treatment they had achieved adequate relief from pain and adequate relief from bowel problems, and a significant proportion of patients said they improved their symptoms," Dr. Lackner explained.

THE HYPNOSIS STUDY

Hypnosis may be another option. A pair of Swedish studies found that patients who received "gut-directed hypnotherapy" had significant improvement in symptoms compared with those who did not receive this intervention.

Hypnosis treatment has been reported to improve symptoms of the majority of treated IBS patients in all published studies, noted Dr. Olafur S. Palsson.

RECOMMENDATIONS

For patients who have tried the diet-and-drug regimen to no avail, Dr. Palsson said he would recommend either of these two psychological treatments.

"If a patient's main goal is substantial relief of bowel symptoms, hypnosis is probably the better choice," he said.

On the other hand, he added, if a patient wants to cope better with the illness or improve mental well-being, then cognitive behavioral therapy is equally good or perhaps even the better treatment option.

Keep Your Liver Healthy

Howard J. Worman, MD, associate professor of medicine, anatomy and cell biology at Columbia University and associate attending physician at New York-Presbyterian Hospital/Columbia, both in New York City, is the author of *The Liver Disorders Sourcebook*. McGraw-Hill.

The liver, which weighs about three pounds, is the body's second largest organ (after the skin). It purifies the blood by breaking down and/or filtering out toxins and pollutants. The liver also breaks down nutrients for absorption by cells…creates proteins that transport nutrients and hormones through the bloodstream…stores vitamins and minerals…and helps regulate insulin and other hormones.

The liver is capable of performing most of its functions—including regenerating damaged cells—even when it's harmed by infection or inflammation.

Caution: Popular medications are one cause of potential liver problems.

Examples: Cholesterol-lowering statins… anticonvulsants such as Dilantin…birth control pills…and anabolic steroids used to treat such conditions as anemia or weight loss associated with a severe illness. Overdoses of *acetaminophen* (Tylenol)—the recommended maximum daily dose is 4 g, or eight extra-strength tablets —also can harm the liver.

Other facts you should know…

SUBTLE SYMPTOMS

People with liver disease usually have only mild symptoms, such as fatigue or abdominal pain (often in the upper-right abdomen, where the liver is located)—or none at all.

Red flag: Jaundice (yellowing of the skin and whites of the eyes) and/or dark urine often are the first signs of acute liver disease. With chronic liver disease, jaundice may not appear until the liver is severely damaged—often decades later.

Often-overlooked symptoms: Unexplained itching or bruising…and red dots on the skin above the waist with "legs" radiating from the center (spider angioma). If you have any of the above symptoms, consult your primary care physician, who can refer you to a liver specialist, if necessary.*

FATTY LIVER DISEASE

Nonalcoholic fatty liver disease is a silent disorder that is estimated to affect up to one-third of American adults. It often occurs in people with hypertension and obesity, particularly abdominal fat.

Over a period of years, high levels of fat accumulate in the liver and cause severe inflammation that can lead to cirrhosis (irreversible scarring) or liver failure. The deposits usually can be detected with an ultrasound or computed tomography (CT) scan.

What you may not know: For many people, losing weight (about one to two pounds a week) reduces the amount of fat in their livers. For other people, it requires less weight loss.

CARDIAC CIRRHOSIS

Some people with congestive heart failure (CHF) are misdiagnosed with cirrhosis of the liver.

What you may not know: Because the heart is unable to pump blood effectively in people who have CHF, blood can back up (congest) in the liver, possibly resulting in scarring or "cardiac cirrhosis." Treating the heart disease with medication or surgery is the only way to prevent subsequent liver damage.

VIRAL HEPATITIS

Hepatitis A, B and C are the most common viruses known to infect the liver.

*The American Liver Foundation, 800-465-4837, *www. liverfoundation.org*, can give you a list of local chapters that can provide the names of liver specialists in your area.

•**Hepatitis A** is usually transmitted by food and/or water contaminated by infected fecal matter. In rare cases, it also can be passed during sexual activity with an infected partner. Hepatitis A can cause extreme fatigue and muscle and/or joint pain but usually clears up on its own in a few months.

Self-defense: Wash your hands often if you live with someone with hepatitis A...use a condom during sex...avoid undercooked shellfish (which may be contaminated by water that harbors the virus)...and in countries where sanitation is questionable, drink bottled water and avoid raw, unpeeled produce.

•**Hepatitis B** is more serious than hepatitis A—5% of adults infected with the hepatitis B virus go on to develop the chronic form of the disease, which can result in permanent liver damage or liver cancer. Hepatitis B also causes extreme fatigue and muscle and/or joint pain. It is mainly transmitted by unprotected sex with an infected partner or via blood-contaminated needles.

Self-defense: Use a condom during sex... use sterile needles...and don't share razors or toothbrushes.

•**Hepatitis C** often causes no symptoms for 20 to 30 years, at which point permanent liver damage and/or liver cancer may have developed. Many of the 4 million Americans infected with the hepatitis C virus contracted it from blood transfusions prior to 1990 (when screening became routinely available) or via contaminated needles. Body piercing and tattoos given with unsterilized instruments also may transmit the hepatitis C virus.

Most doctors choose to use drugs to fight the hepatitis C virus because there's no way to predict which people will go on to develop severe liver problems later in life. Injections of *pegylated interferon*, a cancer drug, often combined with oral doses of the antiviral drug *ribavirin* (Rebetol), can eliminate the virus in about half the cases. Side effects of interferon include muscle aches, fatigue and depression, while ribavirin can cause anemia, birth defects and nausea.

What you may not know: A relatively new vaccine, Twinrix, protects against both hepatitis A and B. Health-care workers and people who travel to areas where sanitation is not regulated are among those who should consider receiving the vaccine. There is no vaccine to prevent hepatitis C.

ALCOHOLIC LIVER DISEASE

Alcohol is more dangerous for women than men because women produce less *alcohol dehydrogenase*, an enzyme that breaks down alcohol.

Studies indicate that men who average two drinks or fewer a day and women who average one drink or less daily are unlikely to develop alcohol-related liver problems.

What you may not know: Some drinks poured in bars, such as martinis, can contain the equivalent of three servings of alcohol. Two of these drinks may contain six servings of alcohol—the level at which the risk for liver disease sharply rises.

Natural Therapies for Ulcers

James N. Dillard, MD, DC, former assistant clinical professor at Columbia University College of Physicians and Surgeons and past medical director of Columbia's Rosenthal Center for Complementary and Alternative Medicine, both in New York City. He is now in private practice in New York City and East Hampton, NY.

If you've got an ulcer, chances are you're taking an over-the-counter (OTC) antacid and/ or prescription medication to neutralize gastric acid or inhibit its production. These medications include proton pump inhibitors (PPIs), such as *esomeprazole* (Nexium) and *lansoprazole* (Prevacid), and H2-blocking drugs, such as *cimetidine* (Tagamet) and *ranitidine* (Zantac).

What most people don't realize: There are several natural, complementary remedies that help reduce ulcer symptoms and promote healing while conventional treatment is under way. Some of these treatments also can help prevent ulcers in some patients.

WHAT CAUSES ULCERS

It's been more than 20 years since doctors learned that an infectious disease—rather than emotional stress—was the primary cause of most ulcers.

A screw-shaped bacterium, *Helicobacter pylori*, or *H. pylori*, burrows through the protective mucous lining in the small intestine and/or stomach, allowing harsh digestive fluids to accumulate and ulcerate the lining. About 50% of Americans over age 60 are infected with H. pylori. The bacterium doesn't always cause ulcers—but about 60% of patients with ulcers harbor H. pylori.

The remainder of ulcers are caused by regular use of stomach-damaging nonsteroidal anti-inflammatory drugs (NSAIDs), such as aspirin, *ibuprofen* (Advil) and *naproxen* (Aleve)...alcohol...and/or smoking. Excessive alcohol wears down the lining of the stomach and intestines. Nicotine causes the stomach to produce more acid.

Best complementary treatments...*

NONDRUG THERAPIES

•**Probiotics.** The intestine contains up to four pounds of "friendly" bacteria, which aid digestion. There's some evidence that maintaining adequate levels of beneficial bacteria helps create an inhospitable environment for H. pylori and makes it harder for this ulcer-causing bacterium to thrive.

Self-defense: Take a probiotic supplement that contains *Lactobacillus acidophilus* and *Bifidobacterium bifidus*. These organisms create a healthful mix of bacteria and can inhibit the growth of harmful organisms. Probiotics are helpful if you've taken antibiotics, which can kill off some beneficial bacteria.

The optimal dose for probiotics hasn't been determined. Preliminary research cites a daily dose of up to 10 billion organisms—the amount usually included in one to two capsules. Probiotics are available at health-food stores.

•**Cabbage juice.** This folk remedy has some evidence to support it. Cabbage is high in vitamin C, which seems to inhibit growth of H. pylori. It also contains *glutamine*, an amino acid that may strengthen the protective lining in the stomach.

A small Stanford University School of Medicine study found that ulcer patients who drank about a quart of cabbage juice daily healed significantly faster than those who didn't drink it.

Self-defense: If you have an active ulcer, consider drinking a quart of cabbage juice (about the amount in half a head of cabbage) once daily for up to two weeks.

*Check with your doctor before taking supplements. They can interact with prescription medications.

•**Deglycyrrhizinated licorice (DGL).** Herbalists often recommend fresh licorice root to heal ulcers. Licorice contains *mucin*, a substance that protects the stomach lining, and antioxidants that may inhibit H. pylori growth.

However, natural licorice can increase the effects of *aldosterone*, a hormone that promotes water retention and can increase blood pressure in some people. DGL supplements (available at health-food stores) are a better option, because the substances that increase blood pressure have been removed.

Self-defense: Take one DGL tablet before meals, and another before bed. DGL may be effective for people with ulcers whose H. pylori has been successfully treated with antibiotics but who still have some stomach irritation.

•**Vitamin A.** Vitamin A helps repair damaged mucous membranes. A report in the British medical journal *The Lancet* suggests that ulcers heal more quickly in patients given supplemental vitamin A.

Caution: High-dose vitamin A therapy can be toxic, so get your vitamin A from dietary sources along with a daily multivitamin—*not* from a separate vitamin A supplement.

Self-defense: Get 10,000 international units (IU) of vitamin A daily if you're undergoing ulcer treatment. (A multivitamin typically contains 3,500 IU to 5,000 IU of vitamin A.)

Good food sources: Beef liver (1½ ozs. contains 13,593 IU)...carrots (one raw carrot contains 8,666 IU)...and spinach (one cup of raw spinach contains 2,813 IU).

•**Zinc.** Like vitamin A, zinc is involved in tissue healing. In Europe, a drug compound made with zinc plus an anti-inflammatory is often used for treating ulcers. Early studies indicate that zinc alone can speed ulcer healing and possibly even help prevent some ulcers.

Self-defense: Don't exceed the recommended daily intake (15 mg) of zinc. Take a daily multivitamin that includes zinc...and get adequate intake from dietary sources (five medium fried oysters, 13 mg...¾ cup fortified breakfast cereal, 15 mg...three ounces lean beef tenderloin, 5 mg).

ANOTHER WAY TO FIGHT ULCERS

NSAIDs alleviate pain by inhibiting the production of pain-causing chemicals called prostaglandins. However, the body produces several kinds of *prostaglandins*, including some that protect the stomach lining. That's why NSAIDs, which block the production of pain-causing *and* stomach-protecting prostaglandins, make people who regularly use the drugs more susceptible to ulcers.

Self-defense: If you require regular pain relief, start with *acetaminophen* (Tylenol). It relieves pain without depleting stomach-protecting prostaglandins.

Caution: Taking more than the recommended dosage or drinking alcohol with acetaminophen can cause liver damage.

Also helpful: Ask your doctor about taking Arthrotec, a prescription drug combination that includes the NSAID *diclofenac* along with *misoprostol*, which protects the stomach and intestinal lining. One study found that patients taking Arthrotec experienced up to 80% fewer ulcers than those taking an NSAID alone.

How to Treat Overactive Bladder

Rebecca G. Rogers, MD, director of the division of urogynecology at the University of New Mexico Health Sciences Center, and associate professor of obstetrics/gynecology at the University of New Mexico School of Medicine, both in Albuquerque, is the coauthor of *Regaining Bladder Control*. Prometheus Books.

People with bladder problems are often too embarrassed to report their symptoms to their doctors—and feel that it is just a problem they must learn to live with. Not true.

Bladder problems aren't life-threatening, but they can be *life-altering*. Patients with overactive bladder (OAB)—increased urinary urgency and/or frequency with or without incontinence—often are ashamed...and they're *always* uncomfortable.

An estimated 34 million American adults have OAB (it affects men and women equally), yet only one in 25 sufferers seeks medical treatment.

Good news: Up to 85% of patients who undergo OAB treatment experience significant improvement or are cured.

BRAIN-BLADDER DISCONNECT

The bladder normally holds approximately eight to 12 ounces of urine before it sends the "have to go" message to the brain. In patients with OAB, as little as a few ounces can trigger the urge to urinate.

Patients with OAB have one or more of the following symptoms...

• **Frequency**—the need to urinate more than eight to 10 times in a 24-hour period.

• **Urgency**—an extremely strong need to urinate immediately.

• **Nocturia**—the complaint that one has to wake more than one time at night to urinate.

About 90% of cases of OAB are idiopathic, meaning the cause is unknown. The remaining cases may be due to spinal cord injuries, neurological diseases (such as Parkinson's), interstitial cystitis (irritation of the bladder wall), a urinary tract infection or a prolapsed (dropped) uterus in women or an enlarged prostate gland in men.

DIAGNOSING OAB

Most cases of OAB can be diagnosed with a medical history. The doctor will ask questions about the frequency of urination, the urgency of sensations, etc. In addition, he/she will diagnose or rule out any identifiable underlying causes for the symptoms.

Tests may include...

• **Urinalysis** to identify a urinary tract infection.

• **Abdominal and/or vaginal or rectal exam** to identify possible obstructions, such as uterine prolapse (descent of the uterus into the vagina) or an enlarged prostate gland.

• **Postvoid residual volume measurement** to determine how completely a patient's bladder empties. Incomplete emptying can result in excessive urinary frequency/urgency. For this outpatient test, the doctor uses a catheter or ultrasound wand to measure the volume of residual urine in the bladder after the patient urinates. A large volume of residual urine could indicate an obstruction or problems with the nerves/muscles in the spine or bladder.

TREATMENTS

Most patients with OAB improve with a combination of behavioral and physical therapies, plus medication in some cases.

Important: Patients with OAB symptoms should keep a voiding diary for at least three days. The diary should include how much you drink...how much and when you urinate (your doctor can provide a plastic "hat," which attaches under the toilet seat, or a urinal, to measure urine output)...whether you've had incontinence episodes, etc. This diary can aid your doctor in making an accurate diagnosis. Also, many patients naturally improve once they become more aware of their urinary habits and may modify the volume and timing of fluid intake and other behaviors.

Best treatment choices for men and women who suffer from OAB...

•**Dietary changes.** Alcohol as well as caffeine, including that found in chocolate, tea and cola, can trigger symptoms in some people. Eliminate these offenders one by one to see if symptoms improve.

•**Pelvic-floor exercises.** Known as Kegels, these simple exercises reduce OAB by strengthening the urinary sphincter (a circular muscle that constricts to retain urine or relaxes to allow urine to pass from the urethra to outside the body) as well as the muscles of the pelvic floor. Contracting pelvic-floor muscles prompts the spinal column to send a message to the bladder to stop contracting.

What to do: Imagine that you're trying to stop the urine flow in midstream. Tightly squeeze the muscles that control urine flow...hold for a count of three...relax for a count of 10...repeat. Do the exercise for five minutes twice daily.

Helpful: Perform Kegels when you feel a sudden sense of urgency. They can help prevent urine leakage on your way to a bathroom.

•**Timed voiding.** Urinate "by the clock" instead of in response to internal signals. Your doctor might advise you to urinate every hour for several days...then every two hours...working up to every two and a half to three hours during the day. Timed voiding trains the bladder to hold more urine for longer periods of time.

•**Medications.** They're often used when behavioral techniques do not work or as an adjunct to these therapies to help patients gain better control—and may be the first choice for some patients with nocturia (since behavioral therapies cannot be used while sleeping). *OAB medications include...*

Anticholinergic and antispasmotic drugs, such as *tolterodine* (Detrol), *oxybutynin* (Ditropan), *solifenacin* (Vesicare), *trospium* (Sanctura) and *hyoscyamine* (Levsin). These medications relax the bladder and reduce sensations of urgency. Some studies have found tolterodine to be slightly more effective than the other drugs.

Main side effects: Dry mouth and constipation. Some older patients may suffer temporary cognitive impairment. Newer drugs in this class, such as solifenacin and trospium, may be less likely to cause cognitive difficulties.

•*Imipramine* **(Tofranil).** This anti-depressant reduces bladder contractions and also increases the "holding power" of the urethra. Imipramine is typically used to treat nocturia.

Main side effects: Extreme sedation. When used by older patients, it may increase the risk for low blood pressure and falls.

TREATMENTS ON THE HORIZON

Preliminary studies indicate that inserting a cystoscope into the bladder to inject Botox (normally used to treat wrinkles) in the bladder wall blocks the release of chemicals that cause the bladder to contract. The procedure involves 20 to 30 injection sites and may require anesthesia. Risks include urinary retention.

•**Electrical stimulation.** Electrodes temporarily placed in the vagina or rectum deliver electrical impulses that inhibit nerves in the bladder wall from firing inappropriately. Most patients receive the treatments in a doctor's office once weekly for six to eight weeks. I recommend electrical stimulation, but it has not been well studied and the long-term effects are not known. It's mainly used as a last resort for patients who don't respond to other methods.

Urinary Incontinence: Treatments that Work

Jonathan M. Vapnek, MD, urologist, associate clinical professor of urology and director of neurourology at Mount Sinai School of Medicine in New York City, is a member of the American Urological Association.

For the estimated 13 million Americans with urinary incontinence, poor bladder control can severely disrupt daily life. Some people don't always make it to the bathroom in time or they can't hold it in when they cough or sneeze. Some even curtail social activities because they don't have reliable bladder control.

Yet the majority of people with this condition never see a doctor—either because they're too embarrassed to discuss it or because they assume that it's a normal part of getting older.

Not true. About 80% of patients can regain nearly normal bladder control with lifestyle changes or, if necessary, medication or surgery.

TYPES OF INCONTINENCE

As the bladder fills with urine, it eventually sends signals to the brain that tell the person "it's time to go." Before that happens, the bladder walls relax to permit urine to accumulate. This gradual process is what allows most people to wait hours before going to the bathroom. Urinary control also is achieved by a ring of muscle called the urinary sphincter. It contracts to keep urine in, then relaxes to let it out.

Incontinence occurs when there's a problem with either muscular or nervous system control—or a combination of both. Women are about twice as likely as men to have incontinence, although men who have prostate enlargement or have had prostate surgery have an increased risk of incontinence.

The main types…

•**Stress incontinence** is most common, affecting at least 50% of the women who have urinary incontinence. It occurs when the urinary sphincter isn't strong enough to hold in urine, particularly during activities that cause an increase in abdominal pressure, including laughing, coughing, sneezing and exercise.

Stress incontinence frequently occurs during pregnancy and can persist in women who have had several vaginal births. Large babies and long labors can stretch and weaken the pelvic floor muscles and/or damage some of the bladder nerves. The drop in estrogen that occurs after menopause can weaken the urethra, inhibiting its ability to hold back the flow of urine.

•**Urge incontinence** often is caused by inflammation or irritation of the bladder or urethra—due to infection, urinary stones or, in men, irritation of the prostate gland. This causes frequent (and sudden) urges to urinate. This type of incontinence also may be caused by bowel problems and neurological problems, such as stroke or Parkinson's disease.

•**Overflow incontinence.** Patients with nerve damage (from diabetes, for example) or damage to the bladder may constantly dribble urine because they're unable to empty the bladder completely when they urinate.

Other potential causes of incontinence are an enlarged prostate gland, a tumor in the urinary tract or bladder cancer. The majority of patients have either stress or urge incontinence—or a combination of both, known as mixed incontinence.

DIAGNOSIS

Most cases and types of incontinence can be diagnosed with a medical history alone. Keep a bladder diary for a week or two before you see your doctor. Write down how often you urinate…when you leak…and if you have trouble emptying your bladder. The answers to these questions usually are sufficient to allow a definitive diagnosis.

Tests may be required to provide additional information. *Most common…*

•**Stress test.** The doctor examines the urethra while the patient coughs or bears down. A leakage of urine indicates that the patient has stress incontinence.

•**Urodynamic testing.** There are a variety of tests that measure pressure in the bladder and how much fluid it can hold.

Example: The doctor might insert a catheter into the bladder, inject small amounts of fluid and measure changes in bladder pressure. Sudden increases in bladder pressure and/or spasms could indicate urge incontinence.

Patients may require an ultrasound to check how well the bladder empties. Your doctor also should perform urinalysis to check for blood or signs of infection in the urine.

TREATMENT

Some forms of incontinence are transitory and will go away when the underlying problem (an infection or inflammation, for example) improves. Most incontinence requires one or more of the following treatments, which can bring about significant improvement for most patients.

•**Behavioral techniques.** These techniques are used to help patients achieve better bladder control and are considered the mainstay of treatment. *Examples...*

•*Bladder training* requires patients to avoid going to the bathroom for longer and longer periods. A person might try to wait an extra 10 minutes when he/she has the urge to urinate. The goal is to lengthen the waiting time over a period of days or weeks. With practice, most patients are able to wait several hours. This is for patients with bladder overactivity and frequent urination.

•*Timed urination* means going to the bathroom at specific intervals—say, once every hour, even if you don't feel as though you have to go. This might be used for frail, elderly people who tend to wet themselves because they can't hold it once the urge hits. The idea is to void before the bladder hits that point of no return.

•*Kegel exercises.* Patients are advised to tightly squeeze the same muscles that they would use to stop the flow of urine. Contract the muscles for three to five seconds, relax, then repeat again. Do the cycle several times daily, working up to more repetitions each time. Kegels are helpful for men and women and for both stress and urge incontinence cases.

•**Medications.** Antispasmodic drugs reduce bladder contractions that contribute to urge incontinence. These drugs often cause dry mouth as a side effect. They're usually used in combination with behavioral treatments.

•**Surgery.** If behavioral changes and medications don't adequately control incontinence, patients may require surgery. *Main approaches...*

•*Tension-free vaginal tape (TVT) procedure.* This is standard for women with stress incontinence. A mesh-like tape is slung under the urethra like a hammock. It compresses the urethra to prevent leaks.

•*Bulking injections.* Collagen or synthetic bulking agents are injected into tissue surrounding the urethra or urinary sphincter. The extra bulk causes surrounding tissue to tighten the seal of the sphincter. The procedure usually needs to be repeated every six to 18 months because collagen is absorbed by the body over time.

•*Sphincter replacement.* An artificial, doughnut-shaped device is implanted around the urethra. When patients are ready to urinate, they press a valve that causes the device to deflate and let out urine. This procedure is mainly used for men who have had prostate surgery.

■ ■ ■ ■

Side Effects

Incontinence drugs are linked to cognitive impairment.

New finding: In an eight-year study of 372 men and women age 60 and older, mild cognitive impairment was diagnosed in 80% of those who took an anticholinergic, a class of medication used to treat incontinence as well as cardiovascular and psychiatric disorders.

Theory: These drugs block the release of the neurotransmitter acetylcholine, which aids learning and memory.

If your cognitive performance has declined since beginning an anticholinergic drug, talk to your doctor.

Marie-Laure Ancelin, PhD, senior research fellow, Inserm, Montpellier, France.

Common Medications And Diarrhea

Douglas L. Seidner, MD, is director of the Center for Human Nutrition and associate professor of medicine, Vanderbilt University Medical Center, Nashville. Dr. Seidner has contributed to *The American Journal of Gastroenterology* and the *Journal of Parenteral and Enteral Nutrition*, among others.

Diarrhea—bowel movements that are looser and more frequent than usual—is the second most common medical complaint (after respiratory infections) in the US.

Most people associate a bout of diarrhea with a viral infection or food poisoning.

Now: Researchers are identifying new—and sometimes surprising—triggers, including the use of some medications.

Latest development: The *Journal of the American Medical Association* recently published a study that links the use of acid-lowering heartburn drugs, such as *omeprazole* (Prilosec), *lansoprazole* (Prevacid) and *ranitidine* (Zantac), to increased infection with the bacterium *Clostridium difficile*—a cause of severe and persistent diarrhea.

In an unexpected finding, the same researchers identified an association between diarrhea and regular use of nonsteroidal anti-inflammatory drugs (NSAIDs). More study is needed to confirm this NSAID-diarrhea link.

HOW DIARRHEA DEVELOPS

What's left of food after most of it has been digested reaches the large intestine as a sort of slurry. There, the body absorbs water from this material, creating a solid mass to be excreted. Normal stool is 60% to 90% water. Diarrhea occurs when stool is more than 90% water.

When stool does not remain in the large intestine long enough, it is excreted in a watery form. This "rapid transit" diarrhea can be caused by stress, overactive thyroid (hyperthyroidism) and certain drugs, such as antacids and laxatives that contain magnesium, and chemotherapy for cancer.

Other types of diarrhea...

•**Osmotic diarrhea** occurs when too much food remains undigested or unabsorbed. Water is drawn into the colon to dilute unabsorbed chemicals, which makes the stool looser.

Large amounts of certain fruits and beans as well as sugar substitutes (sorbitol and xylitol) that are used in some brands of fruit juice, chewing gum and candy are common causes of osmotic diarrhea. When the diarrhea sufferer stops eating the offending food, the condition stops.

Lactase deficiency—a lack of the enzyme needed to break down milk sugar (lactose)—is another cause of osmotic diarrhea. Most people know if they have this deficiency and avoid milk products.

Osmotic diarrhea also may develop in people taking antibiotics. That's because the drug eliminates beneficial bacteria that live in the intestinal tract, allowing harmful bacteria to proliferate. These microorganisms normally help the body process and absorb the small amount of food that hasn't been digested yet. Diarrhea usually develops within a few days of treatment. If it's bothersome enough, your doctor may prescribe a different antibiotic.

More rarely, diarrhea develops toward the end of antibiotic treatment—or even up to a month later. This may be caused by C. difficile or another bacterium that can flourish and cause inflammation of the large intestine when beneficial bacteria are eliminated.

Helpful: This infection is usually treated with the antibiotics *vancomycin* (Vancocin) or *metronidazole* (Flagyl).

•**Secretory diarrhea** occurs when an excessive amount of water, salt and digestive fluids are secreted into the stool. Viral infections, bacterial toxins that cause some types of food poisoning and rare tumors of the small intestine and pancreas can trigger the secretions that lead to secretory diarrhea.

With food poisoning, excess secretions are stimulated by chemicals produced by bacteria that have contaminated something you ate. This diarrhea usually lasts for 12 to 24 hours and stops without treatment. If it persists, your doctor may order tests, such as stool cultures, to determine whether a virulent bacterium, such as *Salmonella*, *Shigella* or *Campylobacter*, is involved and will require medication.

Travelers' diarrhea has a similar cause. The culprit is generally a mild strain of a toxin-producing bacterium, such as *Escherichia coli*, that is present in food and/or water. Natives of the region you're visiting have been exposed to the microorganism for years and usually are immune to it. You're not. Traveler's diarrhea typically goes away within one to two days.

•**Exudative diarrhea** occurs when the large intestine's lining becomes inflamed. This triggers the release of blood, mucus, proteins and other fluids. Infection with the bacterium Shigella can cause this type of diarrhea. Crohn's disease (chronic inflammation of the small bowel or colon) and ulcerative colitis (chronic inflammation and ulceration of the colon) can also cause exudative diarrhea.

An antibiotic is sometimes used to treat a bacterial infection. Medication, such as the corticosteroid *prednisone* (Deltasone), and sometimes surgery are used to treat the inflammatory conditions.

Seek medical attention if any of these danger signs appear...

•**The diarrhea is severe** (six or more stools a day), especially if there are signs of dehydration (parched lips, sunken eyes).

•**The diarrhea is bloody or includes mucus,** rather than just water.

•**It has lasted more than two days**—if mild, two weeks.

•**You have a fever over 101.5° F.**

•**Diarrhea is accompanied by severe abdominal pain** (anything more than moderate cramping).

BEST RELIEF STRATEGIES

In some cases, diarrhea can be a sign of a serious infection and should be treated by a doctor. *Even though most types of diarrhea run their course within a few days, the following steps can hasten the process and ease your discomfort...*

•**Eat right.** If food poisoning is the problem, you should abstain from all food until symptoms resolve, usually one to two days.

For other acute diarrhea, follow the "BRAT" diet: bananas, rice, applesauce and toast. Bananas and applesauce contain *pectin*, a water-soluble substance that helps firm up the stool...the carbohydrates in white rice and white toast are easy to digest. If you eat other foods, stick to small portions and avoid dairy products.

Yogurt is an exception. If it's made from live and active cultures, such as *Lactobacillus bulgaricus* and *Streptococcus thermophilus*, yogurt may replace beneficial bacteria in the colon, helping to relieve antibiotic-related diarrhea.

When the diarrhea subsides, return to your normal diet cautiously. For the first few days, avoid fatty foods (they're harder to digest).

Important: Drink 64 ounces of fluids daily to replace what you're losing. Choose weak tea, water and/or small amounts of clear juice or soda, such as apple juice or ginger ale.

If diarrhea is severe: Drink "replacement fluids," such as CeraLyte, Pedialyte or Enfalyte. These contain salt and simple sugars that help the body retain water. Diarrhea-related dehydration isn't a danger for most adults, but it is a danger for children and many adults over age 65. Young children do not have as large a reserve of water in the body as healthy adults. Older adults may have heart or kidney disease, which can be exacerbated by dehydration.

•**Medication.** Several over-the-counter preparations can help relieve diarrhea...

•*Loperamide* (**Imodium**) is a semi-synthetic narcotic that slows food as it passes through the bowel, allowing more time for water to be absorbed. Try loperamide if diarrhea is mild and hasn't been resolved in one to two days. It should not be taken if you have a fever or the stools are bloody.

•*Bismuth subsalicylate* (**Pepto-Bismol, Kaopectate**) absorbs toxins—it's quite effective for traveler's diarrhea. It should not be taken with aspirin. Do not take it if you have a fever or bloody stools. Children should not take this product.

Natural Remedies For Constipation

Mark A. Stengler, ND, naturopathic physician in private practice, La Jolla, CA...adjunct associate clinical professor at the National College of Natural Medicine, Portland, OR...author of 16 books, including *The Natural Physician's Healing Therapies* (Bottom Line Books) and coauthor of *Prescription for Natural Cures* (Wiley)...and author of the *Bottom Line/Natural Healing* newsletter.

Constipation is one of the most common digestive complaints, accounting for about 2.5 million doctor visits every year. But it occurs much more frequently than this number indicates because the majority of people with constipation treat it at home with over-the-counter laxatives.

Big mistake: Regular use of certain laxatives can make constipation worse by damaging the large intestine, making it "lazier" and even less efficient.

Most patients who experience constipation can prevent it permanently with dietary changes and other natural approaches. Even patients who have had constipation for years often can restore normal bowel function within two weeks.

WHAT'S NORMAL?

In a healthy body, waste travels through the digestive tract in a predictable, regular cycle, over a period of six to 24 hours. Most people have one to three bowel movements daily. Others have as few as three bowel movements a week. There's a lot of individual variability—what's normal for you might not be normal for someone else.

Red flag: Any change in your normal bowel habits. See a doctor if the frequency of bowel movements changes...you have blood in your stool…or you are experiencing intense abdominal pain. Constipation by itself is rarely dangerous, but it may be a sign of other problems, including colon cancer.

Stool in the intestine contains bacteria, fungi and metabolic by-products of digestion. If it remains in the colon for too long, these harmful substances cause a number of uncomfortable symptoms, such as bloating, painfully hard stools and a general sense of fatigue.

SUPPLEMENTS & FOODS

The right diet and supplements can relieve constipation. *Best choices…*

•**High-fiber foods,** including brown rice, whole-wheat bread, oatmeal, fruits, vegetables and legumes, such as beans and lentils. Fiber absorbs water in the intestine, which makes the stool bulkier. This triggers the intestinal contractions that cause bowel movements. Fiber also makes the stool softer, so it is easier to pass.

If you don't eat a lot of plant foods, you can supplement with an over-the-counter product containing psyllium (such as Metamucil), following the directions on the label. Or take one teaspoon of ground psyllium seed husks twice daily. Psyllium acts as a bulking agent and increases the frequency—and comfort—of bowel movements. Be sure to drink plenty of water or juice to avoid making constipation worse.

Ground flaxseed also works. It's a highly concentrated source of fiber, with the added benefit of supplying healthful omega-3 fatty acids. Have one to two tablespoons of ground flaxseed daily. You can sprinkle it on yogurt or cereal or just eat it plain. Be sure to drink at least 10 ounces of water with it. Don't eat whole flaxseed. It has a tough outer coating that is not broken down during digestion.

Some people take stool softeners. Common ones, such as *docusate* (Colace), are not laxatives and not habit forming, but you can get similar results with flaxseed oil. Take one to two tablespoons daily. The oil can go in a shake or on a salad.

•**Magnesium.** People with constipation often are deficient in this mineral. Magnesium helps in three ways—it increases the strength and regularity of the intestine's muscular contractions…it relaxes the nervous system…and at higher doses, it promotes the accumulation of water in the intestine, which boosts bowel function.

Foods high in magnesium: Green, leafy vegetables (such as spinach), brown rice, avocado, berries, cabbage, broccoli and bananas.

If you have acute constipation, take 250 mg of magnesium two to four times daily. Don't take supplemental magnesium for more than about a week. It can lead to dependence—reducing the colon's natural ability to contract—and can interfere with the normal absorption of nutrients. Don't take supplemental magnesium if you are pregnant unless authorized by your doctor.

•**Fermented foods.** People who eat sauerkraut, live-culture yogurt and/or kefir (a fermented milk) are less likely to experience constipation because fermented foods contain probiotics. These beneficial organisms crowd out harmful microbes that may impair digestion and elimination.

Eat fermented foods daily, or take a probiotic supplement. Look for a product that provides at least four billion active organisms, preferably a combination of *Lactobacillus acidophilus* and *bifidus bacteria*.

•**Milk thistle (*Silybum marianum*).** A traditional remedy for hepatitis, milk thistle improves the flow of bile, a digestive juice that breaks down fats in the intestinal tract. Bile improves the colon's motility (the ability of the colon to contract and eliminate wastes).

Dose: 200 mg to 250 mg of a product standardized to 80% *silymarin* (the active ingredient) with meals twice daily for six to eight weeks. Don't take it if you are pregnant or breastfeeding.

HOMEOPATHY

In homeopathy, individuals are given very small amounts of substances that would produce the same or similar symptoms of an illness in a healthy person if given in larger doses. These remedies stimulate the body's defenses to prevent or treat an illness.

It can be a challenge to find the right homeopathic remedy for constipation—but when it works, the results can be impressive. It's safe to self-medicate with homeopathy, but people tend to have better results when they work with a trained practitioner who can match specific remedies with symptoms. *Remedies to try…*

•**Alumina** is recommended for patients who typically go several days without having a bowel movement.

• **Calcarea Carbonica** is for patients with chronic constipation who often feel cold, have clammy hands and/or feet and experience a lot of stress.

• **Lycopodium** is helpful for patients who experience gas and bloating along with constipation.

For each remedy, take two pellets of 30C potency twice daily for two weeks (or follow directions on the label).

GIVE UP DAIRY

A *New England Journal of Medicine* study of 65 children with chronic constipation reported that cow's milk was the cause in two-thirds of cases. It contains the protein casein, which has been shown to cause constipation.

Also, reduce the amount of saturated fats in your diet. A diet high in saturated fat slows motility—and the longer the stool stays in the intestine, the more likely it is to harden and interfere with normal bowel movements.

DAILY EXERCISE

Mild-to-moderate aerobic exercise—a 30-minute brisk walk, for example—helps stimulate intestinal contractions. It also reduces stress and relaxes the nervous system, which improves muscle movements in the intestine and helps prevent or treat constipation.

STRESS CONTROL

Yoga, Pilates, meditation and other stress-reducing activities can reduce constipation. Studies show that people who experience high levels of stress often have reduced intestinal efficiency. In addition, people with high stress levels often have hectic lifestyles and don't take the time for regular bowel movements. Every day, set aside time for mental and physical relaxation.

Tired All the Time?

James L. Wilson, ND, PhD, cofounder of the Canadian College of Naturopathic Medicine in Toronto and a leading expert in adrenal fatigue, is the author of *Adrenal Fatigue: The 21st Century Stress Syndrome*. Smart Publications.

Most people know very little about their adrenal glands, but their proper functioning can have a profound effect on health.

The adrenal glands, located on top of the kidneys, are only about the size of walnuts but produce more than 40 different hormones, including the stress hormones *cortisol* and *adrenaline*. Cortisol is involved in a variety of functions, including adapting your body to—and protecting it from—stress, while adrenaline is a short-acting hormone involved in the "fight-or-flight" response.

People who experience high levels of chronic stress can develop "adrenal fatigue." With this condition, the hormone-producing cells of the adrenal glands are unable to keep up with the unremitting demand of chronic stress, which can be due to serious health problems, for example, or a high-pressure job.

People with adrenal fatigue may experience unusual tiredness, difficulty waking or getting up in the morning along with an afternoon lull, low blood sugar, lack of concentration and, in some cases, mild depression.

Some of these symptoms can be related to a variety of conditions, including general fatigue and thyroid disorders, so it is common for these patients to be misdiagnosed or go undiagnosed. But when these symptoms appear as a group—especially consistent morning fatigue—adrenal fatigue should be suspected.

A CONTROVERSIAL DIAGNOSIS

Most conventional doctors have never heard of adrenal fatigue—or deny that it's a legitimate medical problem. Unlike Addison's disease, a recognized condition in which cortisol levels drop precipitously due mainly to autoimmune problems, adrenal fatigue causes relatively modest declines in cortisol. It isn't life threatening, and conventional doctors rarely test for it.

Research has confirmed the link between low cortisol levels and fatigue. Researchers have noted that patients with low cortisol also have less resistance to disease. They are even less likely to survive a heart attack than those with normal levels.

WHAT CAUSES ADRENAL FATIGUE?

Levels of cortisol fluctuate in the body throughout the day. Levels typically are highest in the morning, drop in midafternoon, rise slightly about 6 pm, then gradually decrease until the next morning. People with adrenal fatigue may have unusually low cortisol levels at night, which prevents them from getting the deep, restorative sleep they need.

Result: Because a good night's sleep is important for the adrenal glands' recovery, the hormone-producing cells in these glands don't get a chance to recoup their ability to respond to the body's needs. Without adequate rest periods, the cells get overwhelmed and stop producing efficiently.

TESTING AND TREATMENT

The blood and urine tests that are used to diagnose Addison's disease aren't sensitive enough to detect adrenal fatigue. Saliva hormone testing is more useful because it measures the amount of cortisol that's actually available to cells.

The test requires saliva samples that are collected by the patient four times throughout the day—usually at 8 am, noon, 4 pm and 11 pm. (Cortisol levels for people who work night shifts would be measured at different times during the 24-hour period.) The samples are placed in test tubes and analyzed in a laboratory. It's a good idea to repeat the saliva hormone testing every six months after you have begun treatment.

Based on my experience with adrenal fatigue patients, approximately 80% to 90% will improve significantly in six months to two years after starting a program that includes lifestyle changes and the use of dietary supplements that promote a more normal output of adrenal hormones.

My recommendations…

•**Sleep in at least one day a week.** Adrenal cells undergo repair and recovery during sleep. Sleeping in between 7 am and 9 am—even for only one day a week—allows the adrenal glands to rest during a time when high demands are ordinarily placed on these glands.

•**Use herbs.** A number of herbs help the body normalize the production of cortisol. Follow label instructions. *Try the following herbs until symptoms subside…**

•Licorice root stimulates the adrenal glands to produce more cortisol.

Caution: Because licorice root can raise blood pressure, check with your doctor about blood pressure monitoring.

*The FDA does not regulate herbal supplements. Check with your doctor before taking any of these products. They can interact with prescription medications. Pregnant women should avoid most herbal supplements.

•Ashwagandha root, from a plant found in India, is an adaptogen, a substance that helps the body return to a normal state. It's helpful for adrenal fatigue because it can stimulate the adrenal glands to produce normal levels of cortisol.

•Siberian ginseng, a popular medicinal plant grown in Siberia, Japan, Korea and China, normalizes adrenal function and increases the body's resistance to stress.

•**Take vitamins.** Even though most health-conscious adults take multivitamins, certain vitamins are needed in higher doses to fight adrenal fatigue. Best choices…

•Vitamin C is used by the adrenal glands to help manufacture stress hormones. Vitamin C is also an antioxidant that helps prevent and repair damage to hormone-producing cells.

Recommended daily dose: 2,000 mg of time-released vitamin C.

Helpful: If your bowel movements become loose while taking high-dose vitamin C, reduce the amount of vitamin C you take daily by 500 mg until your stool is normal. Take a vitamin C supplement that includes 250 mg of bioflavonoids per 500 mg of vitamin C. The combination makes vitamin C more active.

•B vitamins affect the ability of the adrenal glands to function at peak capacity—this includes, for example, the formulation of coenzymes and other substances required for the production of cortisol.

Recommended daily dose: A B-complex supplement with 50 mg to 100 mg of vitamin B-6…and 75 mg to 125 mg of vitamin B-3.

•Combine protein, fat and carbohydrates with every meal. Each of these provides energy to cells at different rates. Combining them at each meal ensures that your blood sugar will be stabilized. Good combinations include peanut butter and whole-grain bread…cheese and rice crackers…and a chicken sandwich topped with vegetables.

Also helpful: Be sure to chew food slowly—at least 30 times per mouthful—to aid digestion and metabolize nutrients more efficiently.

■ ■ ■ ■

Bloat Buster

Natural remedy for bloating: Boil two tablespoons of fennel seeds in two cups of water for at least three minutes. Strain the seeds, add honey to taste and drink. Bloating should be relieved in one to two hours. Fennel promotes gastrointestinal motility and acts as an antispasmodic. Fennel seeds are available at health-food stores.

Birgit Rakel, MD, integrative physician, Jefferson-Myrna Brind Center for Integrative Medicine, Thomas Jefferson University Hospital, Philadelphia.

■ ■ ■ ■

Natural Help for IBS

A good diet and having stress under control can help with your digestive symptoms. Improvements—including less gas, bloating, cramps and firmer stool—can be seen within 30 days of using the supplements. The supplements I recommend include *aloe vera juice* (one or two tablespoons daily)...*L-glutamine* (3,500 mg twice daily on an empty stomach)...and *DGL*, a special type of licorice root (350 mg to 400 mg at least 20 minutes before meals).

I also suggest a *digestive enzyme complex* (one capsule with or at the end of each meal) and bitter herbs, such as *gentian root* (10 drops in two ounces of water or a 300-mg capsule taken 10 to 15 minutes before each meal). All of these are nontoxic and can be used for an indefinite amount of time, if necessary.

Mark A. Stengler, ND, naturopathic physician in private practice, La Jolla, CA...adjunct associate clinical professor at the National College of Natural Medicine, Portland, OR...author of 16 books, including *The Natural Physician's Healing Therapies* (Bottom Line Books) and coauthor of *Prescription for Natural Cures* (Wiley)...and author of the *Bottom Line/Natural Healing* newsletter.

Your Spouse's Smoking May Kill You

Melissa D. Katz, MD, assistant professor of medicine, division of endocrinology, diabetes and metabolism, Weill Medical College of Cornell University and attending physician at New York-Presbyterian Hospital, New York City.

S moking may be a risk factor for developing diabetes. But could breathing in someone else's smoke also put you at risk? Yes, according to a multicenter US study.

THE STUDY

Researchers tracked 4,572 men and women in four American cities for 15 years. They divided participants into four categories—current smokers...previous smokers...never smokers with exposure to secondhand smoke...and never smokers without such exposure. Not surprisingly, at the 15-year follow-up, smokers had the highest incidence of glucose intolerance—impaired fasting glucose or diabetes—at 21.8%. However, second place went to the never smokers who were exposed to passive smoke—17.2%...followed by the previous smokers (14.4%)...and then never smokers who were not exposed to secondhand smoke (11.5%).

ANOTHER PERSPECTIVE

That sounds pretty convincing. Endocrinologist Melissa D. Katz, MD, assistant professor of medicine in the division of endocrinology, diabetes and metabolism at Weill Cornell Medical College in New York City, says it is an interesting study—as far as it goes. Yet, in spite of its 15-year duration, the study has serious limitations, which the authors also acknowledge. It was partly based on self-reporting—participants relay the information about their habits—and this is always problematic, says Dr. Katz. People don't often keep good records and they also tend to make themselves look better by claiming they eat better and exercise more and smoke less than they do. There is really no way to know what participants actually did. And of course, as Dr. Katz points out, people exposed to secondhand smoke are likely to live with smokers, who often don't have the healthiest lifestyle.

Likely cause of secondhand smoke increasing risk: The study authors speculate that because secondhand smoke "is produced at different temperatures and different reducing conditions," toxins can be more concentrated in passive smoke than smoke that goes straight into the lungs. It's possible, the researchers say, that smoking is linked to diabetes because toxins in tobacco smoke can affect the pancreas, the organ that produces insulin. Nonetheless, she adds, the study does show once again the critical role lifestyle plays in helping prevent or control diabetes.

11

Cancer Fighters

The 7 Big Cancer Myths

Despite all the medical information in the media, many people are misinformed about the realities of cancer. These misconceptions can prevent people from getting appropriate treatment. *Here, the truth behind common myths about cancer...*

***Myth 1:* Cancer usually is fatal.** In a recent American Cancer Society (ACS) survey, 68% of respondents said that they believe the risk of dying of cancer is increasing. Not true. Though the number of Americans diagnosed with cancer has increased (because the US population is increasing and getting older), the risk of dying of cancer has decreased due to early detection and improved treatment. More than half of people diagnosed with cancer survive the disease—and for some cancers, such as lymphoma and leukemia, the cure rate is between 70% and 80%.

Cancer isn't a single disease. It includes many types of tumors, all of which behave differently.

Some tumors, such as those in the breast, are very responsive to chemotherapy and other treatments. Lung tumors are more resistant to treatment. The likelihood of a cure depends not only on the type of tumor but how far advanced it is at the time of diagnosis.

***Myth 2:* Cancer runs in families.** Only about eight percent of cancers are genetically linked. These usually are cancers that occur in younger patients, such as sarcoma or early-onset colon cancer. The vast majority of cancers occur without a known cause or are related to lifestyle.

A family history does increase risk for certain cancers. For example, if a woman has a first-degree relative (such as a mother or sister) who developed the BRCA1 form of breast cancer at an early age, her risk for getting that cancer is increased.

However, only about 10% to 20% of women diagnosed with breast cancer have a family history of the disease. That's why it's important for

---

Gregory Pennock, MD, a medical oncologist, is medical director of clinical research at M.D. Anderson Cancer Center, Orlando, FL.

every woman to undergo regular mammograms and do breast self-exams on a regular basis.

***Myth 3:* Stress causes cancer.** There's a long-standing belief that people who experience a lot of stress or lack a positive attitude are more prone to cancer. A survey of long-term breast cancer survivors in Canada found that 42% attributed cancer to stress. This causes many people with cancer to blame themselves or feel that they always have to be upbeat to prevent a recurrence.

There's no evidence that stress or a negative attitude causes cancer. In a study reported in the journal *Cancer*, 8,500 people were scored on factors such as fatigue, irritability, etc. After following the participants for almost nine years on average, researchers found no link between emotional distress and cancer risk.

However, positive thinking may play a role in recovery. Patients with a positive attitude are more likely to do things that improve outcomes, such as following medical instructions and maintaining a healthy lifestyle.

***Myth 4:* Surgery causes cancer to spread.** In the ACS survey, 41% of respondents said they believe that cancer spreads through the body during surgery. In reality, the risk of cancer spreading during surgery is close to zero. This myth probably started in the days before early detection of cancer. It was common for doctors to find advanced cancers during surgery—even in patients who may have had only mild symptoms. Patients and their families concluded that the surgery itself made the disease worse.

Some cancers in the abdomen or ovaries produce large amounts of malignant fluid. In those cases, it's theoretically possible for cancer cells to spread if the fluid leaks into the abdomen during surgery, but there is no actual evidence of that happening.

***Myth 5:* Injuries cause cancer.** More than one-third of respondents in the ACS survey thought that injuries such as a bruised breast or a hard fall could cause cancer later in life.

These types of injuries don't cause cancer. What may happen is that people hurt a part of the body, see a doctor about the injury and then learn that they have a tumor—but the tumor was already there. The injury just triggered the discovery.

That said, a few cancers are caused by certain types of injuries. A serious sunburn during childhood, for example, increases the risk of skin cancer later in life. Chronic reflux disease (heartburn) can burn the esophagus and increase the risk of esophageal cancer.

***Myth 6:* It's okay to keep smoking after a lung cancer diagnosis.** Some people believe that because the damage is done, they don't have to quit smoking—but those who continue to smoke after a lung cancer diagnosis have significantly poorer outcomes than those who quit. There's also evidence that the chemicals in cigarette smoke interfere with radiation and chemotherapy. People with lung cancer who quit smoking respond better to the treatments.

Important: Lung cancer is the leading cause of cancer deaths in men and women. Lung tissue gradually returns to normal when people quit smoking. Ten years after quitting, lung cancer risk is reduced to one-third of what it was.

***Myth 7:* Cell phones cause brain cancer.** Large population studies have shown no evidence that cell phones cause any kind of cancer, including brain cancer.

Cell-phone use today is vastly greater than it was a decade ago. If there were any truth to the cancer/cell-phone link, we would be seeing an increased incidence of brain cancers by now, but that hasn't happened.

What People with Cancer Want You to Know

Lori Hope, a three-year lung cancer survivor in Oakland, CA, and author of *Help Me Live: 20 Things People with Cancer Want You to Know* (Celestial Arts), is managing editor of *Bay Area Business Woman News.*

One in two men and one in three women will get cancer during their lifetimes, according to the American Cancer Society. The advent of new treatments has allowed many cancer patients to live relatively normal lives, and about nine million Americans are cancer survivors.

When someone has cancer, friends and family members want to help and give support, but sometimes they unknowingly say things that may be disturbing. There are many ways to express concern and love when someone is faced with cancer or any serious illness…and just as many ways to make someone cringe. *Here's what cancer survivors wish people would do…*

BE PRESENT

People may disappear or withdraw when a loved one gets sick. Some are afraid of saying or doing the wrong thing. Others are geared toward fixing problems and get frustrated when they can't help. Still others have experienced their own tragedies with cancer and don't feel strong enough to face the emotional turmoil again.

Though it's uncomfortable to confront a person's outpourings of fear and grief, make the effort. Cancer patients need to cry and release their pain. One of the greatest acts of love is to be with him/her, to listen as he shares his fears.

If you live far away, call or write. Let him know that he's loved…that he matters…and that your heart is with him.

If you simply can't be there, at least explain why the situation is too difficult for you to cope with.

GIVE HOPE

People often talk about their own experiences when they meet a person who has cancer. Their intention may be to show empathy or unload their own burdens, but the stories can hurt more than help.

Example: When people heard about my diagnosis, many said things like, "Lung cancer—that's really bad." A waiter at an Italian restaurant even told me that his wife died of the same cancer. He shared all the gruesome details—about the surgery, how the cancer returned and how she died. It brought back all of my own terror.

People who have cancer don't need to be reminded that they could die—they live with that fear every day. They would rather hear stories of hope and success.

Better: When I told my cousin about my diagnosis, she told me about one of her professors who had had the same cancer 20 years before—and who is still alive and healthy.

When I told my best friend, with whom I have always taken an annual vacation, she said that we would still be vacationing together when we're old ladies. That's the type of encouragement people with cancer need to hear.

ASK PERMISSION

Few of us ask permission before sharing our feelings or advice, but asking permission is important when you are dealing with someone who has a life-threatening illness. That's when people are at their weakest and most vulnerable.

People say things like, "You really should try this immune-boosting herb" or, "You should ask your doctor about this new treatment I read about." The word "should" suggests that the person with cancer would be remiss not to take your advice.

Instead, ask him if he is interested in your advice or information or wants to hear your stories. Back off if he says no. *Possible ways to ask…*

"I have been looking into this type of cancer. Would you like to hear some of the treatment options I've read about?"

"A friend told me about an herb that might help. Would you like to hear about it?"

LAUGH

We all tend to be overly serious when we're with people who have serious illnesses. That's appropriate some of the time, but not all the time. People with cancer may want to forget the pain and just laugh and be happy.

I interviewed a woman who received a cancer diagnosis on a Friday. She had all weekend to worry before she saw her doctor again on Monday, so to make herself feel better, she went to a video store and rented a bunch of comedies.

Going through cancer is not all about fear. There's always room for humor and joy.

DON'T HARP ON POSITIVE THINKING

It's normal to be angry, depressed or sad when you have cancer. No one feels positive all the time. Nevertheless, friends and family members often nag cancer patients about the importance of positive thinking and tune them out when they express worries, pessimism or fear.

The implication is that the cancer is somehow the patient's fault or that he can control the outcome. There's a myth that some people have a "cancer personality." There's no truth to it—and it implicitly blames the patient for causing the disease.

It is important to understand that people who have cancer need to allow themselves to feel everything. They shouldn't have to hide their true emotions. It's okay to feel rotten sometimes.

SPARE THE PLATITUDES

Platitudes are reassuring words that usually are said without much thought or understanding.

Everyone with cancer has heard things like, "You never know how much time any of us has—you could go outside tomorrow and get hit by a truck."

One woman I talked to had heard this cliché at least 10 times from people she knew—even from her doctor. Her comment? "Okay, so then in addition to the fact that I could die from cancer, I might also get hit by a truck." That isn't comforting.

No one who has had cancer sees it as "a gift." Cancer patients don't want to hear how lucky they are or what they can learn from the experience. They just want to get better.

Silence and compassion are more helpful than empty words.

The New Integrative Cancer Prevention Plan

D. Barry Boyd, MD, director of the Integrative Medicine Program at Greenwich Hospital-Yale New Haven Health System, and the Boyd Center for Integrative Health, both in Greenwich, CT, is the author of *The Cancer Recovery Plan: Maximize Your Cancer Treatment with This Proven Nutrition, Exercise and Stress-Reduction Program*. Avery.

The best surgery, chemotherapy and radiation therapy are not always enough to prevent a cancer recurrence. In an estimated four out of every 10 cancer cases, the malignancy comes back despite state-of-the-art medicine.

To maximize the effectiveness of standard cancer treatment, seek an *integrative* program that includes a healthful diet, emotional support and regular exercise. This type of approach may give the 9.8 million Americans who are cancer survivors the best possible chance of avoiding a recurrence—and help protect people who have never had cancer and want to do all they can to prevent it.

THE MYSTERY OF METABOLISM

Conventional oncologists usually advise patients to avoid weight loss, a significant side effect of chemotherapy and radiation. But for most people with cancer, avoiding weight gain is just as important. Research shows that excess weight increases the risk for the development and recurrence of many cancers as well as associated mortality.

What's the link between weight and cancer? Insulin resistance is one theory that is being extensively studied. Insulin, a hormone produced by the pancreas, is vital for glucose (blood sugar) metabolism—it brings this simple sugar into the cells to be broken down for energy. Trouble develops when the cells become less sensitive to insulin, usually as a result of a person being overweight and/or underactive. The pancreas responds by producing more insulin, and higher levels of the hormone remain in the bloodstream.

Excessive insulin levels have been linked to persistent, low-grade inflammation, which releases chemicals that stimulate the growth of cells. Many experts believe that inflammation also stimulates the growth of cancer cells. Cancer and some cancer treatments, such as hormone therapy, may increase insulin resistance as a result of decreased metabolism, reduced activity levels and changes in nutritional intake.

People diagnosed with cancer, especially if they are overweight, should be tested for insulin resistance by checking levels of fasting blood sugar, insulin and lipids, and seek treatment with medication if necessary.

A CANCER-FIGHTING DIET

Weight control is one of the most important ways to help your body fight cancer and promote recovery. Unfortunately, many cancer patients seek fattening comfort food, or their doctors tell them to eat whatever they want.

The ideal cancer-fighting diet consists of 45% complex carbohydrates, 25% protein and no more than 30% fat. Strong evidence has shown that this kind of balanced diet is associated with lower rates of cancer and cancer recurrence.

The Mediterranean diet—including ample amounts of fruits and vegetables, whole-grain cereals and olive oil—is a wise choice. Small meals eaten four to six times a day also are recommended. That's because people who consume their food over the course of the day—rather than in one to three big meals—tend to take in fewer calories and stay healthier.

The same guidelines are important if your appetite is diminished by nausea caused by chemotherapy or the cancer itself. In these cases, a balanced diet is important because it helps prevent nutritional deficiencies that can result from appetite loss.

To create a cancer-fighting diet…

•**Choose the right carbs.** The amount of carbohydrates you consume isn't as critical as the kind. Sharply limit pastries, candies, beverages containing high-fructose corn syrup, such as soft drinks and some fruit-juice drinks, and refined grain products, such as white rice and bread made from white flour. The carbohydrates in these foods are broken down immediately and deposited into the bloodstream, triggering an insulin surge. With repeated exposure to insulin peaks, cells become less sensitive to the hormone.

Complex carbohydrates, such as fruits and vegetables, beans, brown rice, whole-grain cereals and whole-grain baked goods, are digested and absorbed gradually. Insulin is produced at a steady, moderate rate, fueling the body's cells with maximum efficiency. What's more, the fiber in complex carbs fills you up, so you can satisfy your hunger with fewer calories.

•**Eat a variety of vegetables and fruits.** Specific "superfoods," such as beans and blueberries, have received a great deal of attention for their healing properties, but it's crucial to get a broad selection of healthful foods.

Fruits and vegetables should be a mainstay of your diet—the American Cancer Society recommends at least five daily servings. Nine daily servings are even better. One-half cup is the standard serving size. In addition to fiber and complex carbohydrates, fruits and vegetables contain chemicals known as phytonutrients that protect against carcinogens and enhance the body's own healing powers.

Broccoli, cauliflower and cabbage have different phytonutrients than garlic and onion. Berries, citrus fruits and leafy, green vegetables each have their own nutrients. Eating a variety of fruits and vegetables ensures that you get them all.

•**Avoid dangerous fats.** Saturated fats, found mostly in meats and high-fat dairy products, promote insulin resistance, so limit your meat intake to two servings (three ounces per serving) of lean red meat per week and consume only low-fat or nonfat dairy products (one to three servings daily). Good protein sources include poultry, fish, nuts and legumes.

Trans fat, found in many baked goods and processed foods, also causes inflammation.

Beware: Even in food products that claim "0" trans fat on the food labels, small amounts may be present and listed as "partially hydrogenated oil."

On the other hand, omega-3 fatty acids, found in cold-water fish, such as salmon, sardines and herring, have been shown to reduce inflammation and provide a range of other anticancer benefits. Other sources of omega-3s include walnuts and flaxseed.

Important: Food is the best way to get vitamins, minerals and other nutrients. High-dose supplements should be taken only under the supervision of a health-care professional who is knowledgeable about nutrition and cancer care.

EMOTIONAL SUPPORT

Serious illness, such as cancer, can trigger the release of stress hormones that increase your risk of developing excessive insulin levels.

My advice…

•**Get emotional support.** In a Yale study that followed more than 300 women with breast cancer for 10 years, those who felt free to talk about their illness with others were significantly more likely to survive. Don't be reluctant to ask friends and family for help in performing difficult chores and for company during doctor visits.

•**Choose a doctor who gives you hope.** Hopelessness and helplessness are the worst stressors for people with cancer. Make sure your care is directed by a medical professional who focuses on the most positive possible outcome, even if the disease is severe.

EXERCISE IS ESSENTIAL

Exercise reduces insulin resistance by building up lean, metabolically active tissue—which is better than fat tissue for cancer prevention.

In a study of 2,987 breast cancer patients, women who walked three to four hours a week had a 50% lower risk of dying from breast cancer than women who did little or no exercise. Researchers believe that physical activity also helps fight other types of malignancies.

For cancer prevention, strive for 30 minutes of brisk walking per day—or its equivalent in comparably strenuous activities, such as swimming or cycling.

Cancer-Free in a Week

Mark Kaminski, MD, professor of internal medicine, division of hematology and oncology, University of Michigan Cancer Center, Ann Arbor.

Marshall Lichtman, MD, retired executive vice president, research and medical programs, The Leukemia & Lymphoma Society, White Plains, NY.

The New England Journal of Medicine.

Just one week of radioactive-based therapy put 75% of people who had advanced follicular lymphoma into complete remission.

BACKGROUND

The radioactive-based therapy, known as *131 I-tositumomab*, is currently approved for people who have relapsed after having chemotherapy. Of the patients who use the therapy after chemotherapy, 20% to 38% go on to have a complete remission, and 47% to 68% have some kind of response to the treatment. Approximately 30% of these patients have remissions that last between one and 10 years.

THE STUDY

Given the success of 131 I-tositumomab as a follow-up treatment, Mark Kaminski, lead author of the study, and his team decided to test it as an initial treatment on 76 patients who had stage III or stage IV follicular lymphoma. Each participant got two infusions, one week apart.

RESULTS

Overall, 95% of the patients showed some response, and 75% went into complete remission. Of those who had a complete remission, 77% remained disease-free after five years. The percentage of people who relapsed decreased each year.

"Instead of a 30% complete response rate, we're now up to 75%, and the complete response is very much key in getting a long remission," says Kaminski, professor of internal medicine in the division of hematology and oncology at the University of Michigan Cancer Center in Ann Arbor.

The duration and ease of the treatment is almost unknown in cancer treatment. Kaminski notes that he knows of only one other instance where a quick treatment induced a remission—and that was for hairy cell leukemia, a rare form of cancer.

The 131 I-tositumomab contains an antibody tagged with a radioisotope that emits radiation. Scientists believe that when the compound is injected into the bloodstream, the antibody binds to a certain protein on the tumor cells, so the radiation from the radioisotope can kill those cells. The antibody itself can also kill tumor cells, resulting in a lethal one–two punch to the cancer.

While the results achieved with this treatment were similar to those achieved with other therapies, there has been no head-to-head comparison with other treatments.

The results of this trial may push the treatment, currently approved for use after chemotherapy, toward being a first-line treatment, says Kaminski.

"It hasn't been compared to the best current therapy, so we still don't know what role this agent would play," says Dr. Marshall Lichtman, retired executive vice president of research and medical programs at The Leukemia & Lymphoma Society. "Would it be used alone, used initially, used with chemo? It had pretty substantial activity, so one could begin thinking about using it earlier."

The patients in this trial were also younger than the average population, which could skew results. "This may be the very best therapy for a subset of patients and may be a very useful addition to other therapies for other subsets. All of these details have to be worked out," Lichtman explains.

IMPLICATIONS

Kaminski is optimistic. "I think this is going to open the door to people feeling more comfortable...and treating patients with this earlier."

"I think it's an important incremental step," Lichtman says.

STATS

Follicular lymphoma, the second most common form of non-Hodgkin's lymphoma, is diagnosed in approximately 15,000 adults in North America each year, with more than 90% of those diagnoses made when the disease is already in an advanced, often incurable stage.

The Lymphoma Information Network has more on follicular lymphoma at *www.lymphoma info.net/nhl/follicular.html.*

■ ■ ■ ■

Bladder Cancer Test

There is a new test for bladder cancer. The BladderChek test screens urine for high levels of the protein NMP22, which is associated with bladder cancer. The test costs about $50. It can be done in a doctor's office, and results are available within 50 minutes. It is good for detecting a recurrence of bladder cancer and useful as a supplement to other tests for diagnosing it initially. Bladder cancer is the fourth most common cancer in American men and the 10th most common in women—about one American in 600 has had it. BladderChek is appropriate for people over age 40 who have hematuria—blood in urine—one of the first signs of bladder cancer. Smokers with hematuria should have the test even if they are under age 40.

H. Barton Grossman, MD, professor of urology and cancer biology, University of Texas M.D. Anderson Cancer Center, Houston, and leader of a study of 668 bladder cancer patients, published in *Journal of the American Medical Association.*

■ ■ ■ ■

Uneven Care

The cancer care you receive often varies depending on where you live.

Example: More than twice as many patients with stomach cancer survive for five years in Hawaii—where doctors remove an average of 15 lymph nodes when treating the disease—as in Utah, where the average removed is six. Cancer researchers are developing standard care recommendations in hopes of getting all patients the best available care.

Ezekiel J. Emanuel, MD, PhD, chair, department of clinical bioethics, Magnuson Clinical Center, National Institutes of Health, Bethesda, Maryland, and liaison between the American Society of Clinical Oncologists and a Rand Corporation–Harvard team that studied US cancer care by geographic area.

Doctors Destroy "Inoperable" Tumors

Thomas Jefferson University Hospital news release.

A new kind of radiation technology called *shaped beam surgery* allows doctors to destroy brain and spinal tumors that cannot be treated using conventional surgery.

BETTER APPROACH

Shaped beam surgery, available at only a few US medical centers, including Thomas Jefferson University Hospital in Philadelphia, can mold radiation beams to match the exact size and shape of a tumor.

"Shaped beam surgery is a major advance in treating both benign and malignant tumors in the brain and the spinal cord regions," says Dr. David Andrews, a professor of neurosurgery at Jefferson Medical College and director of the division of Neuro-oncologic Neurosurgery and Stereotactic Radiosurgery at Thomas Jefferson University Hospital.

So far, this new technology has been used mostly to destroy benign brain tumors that couldn't be treated before.

"Shaped beam surgery gives us infinite flexibility to deal with lesions from the top of the head to the bottom of the spine," Andrews says. "We can wrap doses around structures, such as the spinal cord, and can create a very high dose of radiation and leave the cord untouched. There's no other technology out there that can do this."

■ ■ ■ ■

Proton-Beam Promise

A new cancer treatment is much more effective than radiation. *Proton-beam therapy* is best for tumors that can't be controlled with low doses of radiation and that are in or near sensitive areas, such as the prostate, chest, lungs and brain. There are proton-beam facilities in California, Florida, Indiana, Massachusetts and Texas. Treatment costs more than standard radiation but is covered by most insurers.

James D. Cox, MD, professor and head of the division of radiation oncology, M.D. Anderson Cancer Center, Houston, TX.

■ ■ ■ ■

Better Colon Cancer Screening

The fecal occult blood test (FOBT) detects blood in feces and often is used as a preliminary screening test for colon cancer.

However: False-positive results can result from eating red meat or such vegetables as radishes, turnips, beets or broccoli. Aspirin and other nonsteroidal anti-inflammatory drugs (NSAIDs), such as *ibuprofen* (Advil), also may cause a false-positive result. A diet high in vitamin C can cause false negatives.

Self-defense: Avoid these foods and medications within three days of the FOBT.

David Lieberman, MD, professor of medicine, chief, division of gastroenterology, Oregon Health & Science University, Portland.

New Technique Studied For Inoperable Liver and Lung Cancers

Riccardo Lencioni, MD, professor of diagnostic and interventional radiology, University of Pisa, Italy.

Jeff Geschwind, MD, associate professor and director of interventional radiology, Johns Hopkins University School of Medicine, Baltimore.

Society of Interventional Radiology annual scientific meeting, New Orleans.

For the many Americans diagnosed with inoperable lung or liver cancer each year, two new techniques may offer hope for longer survival, according to a pair of studies.

THE FIRST STUDY: LUNG CANCER

An Italian research team used *radiofrequency ablation*, in which a heated needle is inserted through the chest wall directly into the tumor site, to effectively "cook" the malignancy. The technique was performed on 106 patients who had a total of 186 malignant, inoperable tumors measuring 3.5 centimeters in diameter or smaller.

Researchers report the minimally invasive heated probe was successful in eradicating inoperable tumors in 93% of the cases.

Of the patients enrolled in the study, 91% were still alive two years after the intervention, the researchers report.

Further, complications linked to the procedure were minimal and easily managed.

IMPLICATIONS

That technique "is creating a new chapter in oncology," says Dr. Riccardo Lencioni, lead researcher and professor of diagnostic and interventional radiology at the University of Pisa located in Italy.

He stresses that surgery must still be the first option for people who have lung cancer whenever it is feasible.

However, because of late detection and/or poor cardiovascular health, surgery is often out of the question for many patients, he says.

According to Lencioni, the best candidates for radiofrequency ablation are "patients with early-stage, limited disease. Whether radiofrequency ablation could be used to also treat patients with more advanced tumors is not defined yet."

Lencioni says the value of radiofrequency ablation against other cancers was less known, but he did say "the treatment has been shown to be successful in treating tumors in the liver."

The treatment is beginning to catch on in the United States, Lencioni adds, especially at large teaching hospitals, but "many more doctors need to be trained to have the procedure widely available."

THE SECOND STUDY: LIVER CANCER

According to the American Cancer Society, approximately 22,000 cases of *primary* liver cancer originate within the organ itself.

However, up to 100,000 Americans each year develop secondary, metastatic tumors in their livers after battling cancer in other parts of their bodies.

More often than not, detection comes too late for surgery, says Dr. Jeff Geschwind, a researcher at Johns Hopkins University School of Medicine.

For these patients, systemic chemotherapy—with its often painful side effects—is the only treatment available.

"A lot of these patients present with far-advanced disease and they have no other options," Geschwind says.

His team of researchers hopes to change that scenario, however.

Geschwind's study looked at 149 liver cancer patients who had inoperable tumors. They were treated with a new technique called *chemoembolization*.

"This involves the delivery of highly concentrated chemotherapy suspended in an oily medium," Geschwind explains.

At the same time, doctors used tiny microspheres, which served as obstructing agents to temporarily prevent the tumor from getting its full blood supply.

"In our data, we've shown an extended mean survival of about six years, when otherwise, patients usually only survive without treatment for maybe one year, at most," according to Geschwind.

Because it is so localized, chemoembolization is also much easier on patients than systemic chemotherapy, which affects tissues throughout the body.

"We really have the ability to target the tumor while preserving healthy tissue," he says.

TECHNIQUE AVAILABLE, BUT NOT USUAL TREATMENT

The technology is currently available at most academic medical centers throughout the United States.

"Unfortunately, many patients and many primary-care physicians don't yet know about the success of this therapy," Geschwind says.

"I'm not saying it's a cure for liver cancer, but when you see the results in terms of prolongation of life, it's quite significant," he adds.

"I think we're on the cusp of something even bigger," he adds, "because now we have at our disposal new drugs that can be even more cancer-specific."

For more on these and other non-surgical breakthroughs in cancer care, visit the Society of Interventional Radiology at *www.sirweb.org*. Click on "patients."

■■■■

Fever Signals

Fever of unknown origin may signal cancer, according to research from Denmark.

New finding: Patients hospitalized with fever of 101.5° F or more for which a cause never was determined were twice as likely to be diagnosed with cancer within the next year as the general population. The increased risk was high for cancers of the liver, brain, kidney, colon and/or pancreas as well as sarcoma (cancer of soft tissue).

Reason: Cancer can cause fever through inflammation and infection.

Self-defense: If you are hospitalized due to a fever of unknown origin, ask your doctor whether cancer could be a cause.

Henrik Toft Sorensen, MD, professor, department of clinical epidemiology, Aarhus University Hospital, Denmark.

■■■■

Cancer Vaccine

A new cervical cancer vaccine has been proven effective.

New finding: In two large-scale, placebo-controlled studies, the new vaccine was 100% effective after a 17-month follow-up when three doses were given over six months (as recommended by the vaccine maker) and 97% effective after an average two-year follow-up when one dose was given. The vaccine, called Gardasil, blocks infection caused by both *human papilloma virus* (HPV) 16 and 18, the two types of HPV that together cause 70% of all cervical cancers. The vaccine is not intended to replace regular Pap smears to screen for cervical cancer. The FDA approved Gardasil in 2006.

Kevin Ault, MD, associate professor of obstetrics and gynecology, Emory University School of Medicine, Atlanta.

Deadly Skin Cancer

Perry Robins, MD, professor emeritus of dermatology at New York University Medical Center, New York City, and founder and president of the Skin Cancer Foundation, is author of *Sun Sense: A Complete Guide to the Prevention, Early Detection and Treatment of Skin Cancer.* Skin Cancer Foundation.

Melanoma is the deadliest type of skin cancer. The incidence of melanoma is increasing so fast that it has been called one of the nation's most serious epidemics.

Since 1986, the diagnosis rates of melanoma have more than doubled. This is partly due to an increased awareness of skin cancer. More people are being tested, so more cases are detected. But the real numbers also are rising. The population is aging, and half of adults diagnosed are in their 50s.

Melanoma is more likely than other cancers to spread (metastasize) to other parts of the body. About 12% of patients with melanoma die from the cancer.

Important: No one needs to die from skin cancer. With regular screenings, melanoma can be detected and removed before it has a chance to spread.

KNOW THE SIGNS

Telltale signs of melanoma and other skin cancers...

A. Asymmetrical shape. Normal moles have a uniform appearance. Moles with irregular shapes are more likely to be cancerous.

B. Border that is irregular. The edges of the mole might be notched or scalloped.

C. Color changes. Moles should have a uniform color. If a mole has different colors, it could be melanoma.

D. Diameter. A mole larger than about one-quarter-inch (six millimeters) across should be checked.

The Skin Cancer Foundation recommends annual skin exams for people age 40 and over. An exam every three years is enough for younger people. The doctor should examine every inch of skin and note or diagram suspicious moles or skin changes for future evaluation and/or treatment.

CAUSES

Melanoma occurs in cells (melanocytes) that produce melanin, the "tanning" skin pigment. When you spend time in the sun, these cells produce more melanin as a protective mechanism against sun damage. However, excessive sun exposure (along with other, still unknown factors) can damage the DNA in melanocytes and result in cancer.

The sun produces three types of UV radiation. Both UV-A and UV-B rays have been linked to melanocyte damage and melanoma. The third type of radiation, UV-C, is absorbed in the atmosphere and doesn't reach Earth.

Melanomas usually form on parts of the body that aren't regularly exposed to sun. Low levels of melanin in these areas make cells more sensitive to damage. Men tend to develop melanomas on the back. Women are more likely to get them on the legs. Less often, melanomas may occur under a finger- or toenail or in the eye or in mucous membranes that line the nose, mouth, esophagus, anus, urinary tract and vagina.

Heredity also plays a role in melanoma risk. About one out of every 10 patients diagnosed has a family member who has had the disease.

PREVENTION

Most melanomas can be prevented with simple precautions...

•**Apply sunscreen before going outdoors year-round.** Use it on all exposed skin, including the face, ears, backs of the hands, etc. Apply it a half-hour before going outdoors so that it penetrates the skin and provides maximal protection. Use a product that filters out both UV-A and UV-B rays.

Certain sunscreens may cause a reaction in some people.

Self-test: Apply a small amount to the inside of your arm at night. In the morning, check for a rash, itching or other signs of sensitivity. If there are no changes, the sunscreen should be safe for you.

•**Use a product with an SPF (sun-protection factor) of 30.** Don't pay extra for products with higher SPF numbers—they provide little or no additional protection. Apply a thin layer of sunscreen every two or three hours. Apply it more often if you're swimming or perspiring heavily.

•**Wear protective clothing.** Sunscreens don't completely block UV radiation. Wear a cap or broad-brimmed hat…tightly woven clothing…and sunglasses that block both UV-A and UV-B rays.

•**Stay away from tanning beds.** Some tanning salons advertise that they are safe, but that is not true.

•**Perform monthly self-exams.** Stand in front of a full-length mirror, and examine your skin. Use a hand mirror to check hard-to-see areas. Check the soles of your feet and the spaces between your toes, as well as the scalp, groin, etc. New growths…moles that have changed…and sores that don't heal should be checked by a doctor.

TREATMENT

Nearly everyone with melanoma survives when it's detected at an early stage, before it has spread.

The only effective treatment for melanoma that hasn't spread is surgical removal. This usually can be done in a doctor's office and with a local anesthetic.

Very small melanomas may be entirely removed during the biopsy. For larger ones, the doctor will remove the cancer, and an additional amount of healthy tissue may be removed.

If melanoma has spread: Patients may require chemotherapy, radiation therapy or other treatments, along with surgical removal of the original cancer.

There are a number of new vaccines that can extend life by several years in patients who have melanoma that has spread. However, they don't eliminate the cancer and are not a cure.

New Hope for Brain Tumor Patients

Michael Vogelbaum, MD, PhD, associate director of the Brain Tumor and Neuro-Oncology Center at The Cleveland Clinic in Ohio, is also director of the institute's Center for Translational Therapeutics, which conducts studies to evaluate the ability of new drugs to reach their targets in brain tumors.

P rimary brain tumors—those that originate in the brain rather than metastasizing from other parts of the body—are among the most virulent of cancers. The most common type, glioma, tends to strike otherwise healthy adults with seeming randomness and is often fatal.* An estimated 17,000 to 20,000 Americans will be diagnosed with a primary brain tumor this year.

Good news: Recent research is giving these patients reason for hope. *If you or a loved one has been diagnosed with a brain tumor, here's what you need to know…*

TREATMENT ADVANCES

The most aggressive of all gliomas, *Glioblastoma multiforme* (GBM), is also the most common, with about 10,000 to 12,000 diagnosed in the US annually, most after age 50. The median survival time for someone with GBM is about one year.

These tumors rapidly spread and infiltrate normal parts of the brain, so it's impossible to excise them completely. The traditional approach to treating GBMs has been to surgically remove as much of the tumor as possible and then administer radiation therapy. When the tumor regenerates, as GBMs often do, doctors have prescribed chemotherapy to slow the growth.

Breakthrough: In a recent trial by Canadian and European researchers, GBM patients who were given radiation therapy and the chemotherapy drug *temozolomide* (Temodar) following surgery did significantly better than those who received radiation alone. A full 26.5% of the patients who received combination therapy were living two years after their diagnoses, versus only 10.4% of the control group. These results were so positive that this approach is now the standard of care for all GBM patients in North America and Europe. More studies are needed to determine its long-term efficacy and safety.

On the horizon: It may soon be possible to identify which GBM tumors will respond optimally to the new protocol. In reviewing their trial data, Canadian and European researchers noticed that patients whose tumors had an inactivated gene, known as 06-methyl-guanine-DNA methyltransferase (MGMT), did markedly better on the combination therapy than those whose tumors had an active MGMT gene. The

*Meningioma, a type of brain tumor that is usually benign, is about twice as common as glioma.

median survival among patients with inactive MGMT was nearly 22 months, and an astounding 46% of them were alive at two years. Those who had an active MGMT gene survived for a median of nearly 13 months. The gene enables cancer cells to repair themselves after being damaged by certain chemotherapy drugs, rendering the chemotherapy ineffective. We're exploring ways to safely "turn off" the gene in patients for whom it remains active.

OTHER RESEARCH ADVANCES

All cancers are in part genetic, since genes play a role in the development and progression of the disease. Genetic variations also appear to affect whether and to what extent another type of tumor, called an *oligodendroglioma*, will respond to chemotherapy. This slow-growing tumor is rare and typically occurs in middle-aged adults.

We've long known that an estimated two-thirds of these tumors are sensitive to chemotherapy drugs, while the remaining one-third are largely impervious. Researchers at Massachusetts General Hospital, in collaboration with Canadian colleagues, discovered in 1998 that responsive oligodendrogliomas had one thing in common—loss of parts of chromosomes (cell structures that carry genetic information), specifically chromosomes 1p and 19q. For reasons that are not yet clear, parts of these chromosomes "disappear" in some of these tumors. About 50% of patients with oligodendrogliomas lack these chromosomes. Virtually all oligodendrogliomas lacking both of these chromosomes will have a prolonged response to treatment, while those that retain them, particularly the 1p chromosome, are unlikely to have durable responses to treatment.

While patients with oligodendrogliomas are now routinely screened for loss of 1p and 19q chromosomes, doctors have yet to reach a consensus on how best to treat tumors lacking them. Some still recommend aggressive surgery to remove the bulk of the tumor, followed by radiation and chemotherapy. Others suggest starting with chemotherapy, hoping that patients may be able to avoid surgery and radiation. Both approaches are meeting with success. The median survival rate for these patients now exceeds seven years. Clinical trials are under way to study these treatment approaches.

CLINICAL TRIALS MATTER

All new therapies—surgical, radiological, pharmacological—must prove safe and effective in clinical trials before being prescribed to the general patient population.

One big challenge we face in advancing brain cancer therapies is making patients aware of the clinical trials that may benefit them personally…or lead to lifesaving treatments for future generations. For patients whose brain tumors do not respond to traditional treatment, an investigational therapy may be their best hope.

To learn more about clinical cancer trials, or to find a trial that may be right for you or a loved one, consult the National Cancer Institute, 800-422-6237, *www.cancer.gov*, or the American Cancer Society, 800-227-2345, *www.cancer.org*.

■ ■ ■ ■

Cancer Warning

Hiccups are a surprising sign of cancer, according to a report from Europe.

Recent finding: 27% of esophageal cancer patients had experienced persistent hiccups prior to diagnosis. People who have hiccups for more than 48 hours—especially if accompanied by swallowing problems and/or weight loss—should see their physicians. The incidence of this very serious cancer is on the rise.

Thomas Noel Walsh, MD, leader of a study of 99 esophageal cancer patients.

The Fastest-Growing Cancer Threat

Herman Kattlove, MD, retired medical oncologist and retired medical editor with the American Cancer Society.

Cancer rates are generally declining in the US, but the incidence of adenocarcinoma, the most common type of esophageal cancer, has increased more rapidly since the 1970s than any other cancer.

Until recently, cancer of the esophagus—the foot-long muscular tube that carries food from the mouth to the stomach—has been considered deadly, though relatively rare. Now both of these beliefs are being challenged.

At one time, people diagnosed with esophageal cancer who underwent surgery had a low chance of surviving for five years. That survival rate is now as high as 50%, most likely due to earlier screening and diagnosis.

Fortunately, healthy lifestyle changes can reduce your risk of developing esophageal cancer.

WHO IS AT RISK?

As with many cancers, the risk for esophageal cancer increases with age—nearly 80% of new cases are diagnosed in people ages 55 to 85.

There are two main types of esophageal cancer—*squamous cell carcinoma*, which develops in the cells that line the entire esophagus, and *adenocarcinoma*, which occurs in the part of the esophagus closest to the stomach.

More than half of all squamous cell carcinomas are linked to smoking. Risk of adenocarcinoma is doubled in people who smoke a pack of cigarettes or more per day. Carcinogens in tobacco are believed to enter the bloodstream and contribute to the development of esophageal cancer. Excessive alcohol consumption—more than two drinks daily—also increases the risk for the squamous cell type of cancer, although it is not known why.

Tobacco *and* alcohol are a potentially deadly combination. A person who drinks excessively and smokes one to two packs of cigarettes a day has a 44 times higher risk of getting esophageal cancer than someone who does neither.

A diet low in fruits and vegetables accounts for approximately 15% of esophageal cancer risk. To help avoid the disease, eat at least five daily servings. Some scientific evidence suggests that berries, particularly black raspberries, which are rich in cancer-fighting antioxidants, protect against esophageal cancer.

Body weight also is a factor. Obese men are twice as likely to die from adenocarcinoma of the esophagus as men of normal weight.

THE HEARTBURN CONNECTION

Frequent heartburn, known as gastroesophageal reflux disease (GERD), is caused by stomach acid backing up into the esophagus. Up to 14% of Americans experience heartburn at least weekly, while 44% suffer from it monthly. GERD is linked to nearly one-third of esophageal cancer cases.

An additional factor for esophageal adenocarcinoma is a condition called *Barrett's esophagus*, in which cells of the esophagus begin to resemble those that line the stomach. People with Barrett's esophagus are about 50 times more likely to develop esophageal cancer than those without the condition.

People who suffer from chronic heartburn (three or more times per week for more than three months) should be screened for Barrett's esophagus. If they are found to have the condition, screenings every year may be recommended to detect esophageal cancer.

Screening involves the use of *endoscopy,* an invasive procedure that requires sedation. During the test, the doctor passes a thin, flexible tube (endoscope) through the mouth to view the entire length of the esophagus.

Prompt and effective treatment of GERD might reduce the risk for esophageal cancer, although this has never been proven. A number of effective prescription and over-the-counter GERD remedies, which block the production of stomach acid, are available. These include H2 blockers, such as *ranitidine* (Zantac) and *famotidine* (Pepcid), and proton pump inhibitors, such as *omeprazole* (Prilosec).

SYMPTOMS AND DIAGNOSIS

Difficulty swallowing is the most common symptom of esophageal cancer. If you notice that swallowing has become even slightly harder—you must swallow more firmly or food doesn't go down properly—see your doctor immediately. It could save your life.

Weight loss commonly occurs because of difficulty swallowing and loss of appetite. Frequent bouts of hiccups, another sign of esophageal cancer, may result when cancer irritates the nerves leading to the diaphragm. More advanced cancer may compress the nerves that control the vocal cords, which can lead to hoarseness.

If your doctor suspects cancer, endoscopy will be performed and a biopsy taken. Additional tests may be necessary—endoscopic ultrasound, a procedure that involves the use of high-frequency sound waves, to pinpoint the tumor thickness…and a computed tomography

(CT) scan and a positron emission tomography (PET) scan to determine whether the tumor has spread to nearby lymph nodes.

TREATMENT

Surgery is the main treatment for esophageal cancer. Most often, the surgeon will perform *esophagectomy*, in which the cancerous part of the esophagus and nearby lymph nodes are removed, or *esophagogastrectomy*, in which the lower part of the esophagus and upper part of the stomach are removed. With both procedures, the remaining part of the esophagus is reconnected to the stomach, often with a segment of the large intestine.

These procedures are extremely complex and demand a high degree of surgical expertise, as well as a skilled team of nurses and other personnel to provide after-care. Choose a major cancer center that performs more than 10 esophageal cancer surgeries a year.

Chemotherapy and radiation before surgery have been shown to improve the outcome, possibly because they destroy microscopic tumor tissue before it can spread.

In one study of 802 patients, 42% of those who had two rounds of chemotherapy before surgery were still alive two years later, compared with 34% of those who had surgery alone.

New finding: A long-term clinical trial showed that esophageal cancer patients who received so-called "triple therapy"—treatment with two cancer drugs (*5-fluorouracil* and *cisplatin*) and daily radiation for five weeks before surgery—had a 39% chance of surviving for five years, compared with 16% of patients who received only surgery.

■ ■ ■ ■

Bladder Cancer Danger

Of 214 patients who had their bladders removed within 93 days of being diagnosed with cancer that had invaded the bladder wall muscle, 39% died, and the rest had a 51% chance of living for three years. When surgery was performed after 93 days, 54% died, and the rest had a 38% chance of living for three years.

Self-defense: Bladder removal for this type of cancer should be done within three months.

Cheryl Lee, MD, director, bladder cancer program, University of Michigan Comprehensive Cancer Center, Ann Arbor.

The #2 Cause of Cancer

Julie Parsonnet, MD, professor of infectious diseases at Stanford University School of Medicine in Stanford, CA, is the editor of *Microbes and Malignancy: Infection as a Cause of Human Cancers*. Oxford University.

People tend to think that cancer is caused only by unhealthful habits, such as smoking, or environmental factors, including exposure to asbestos or excessive sunlight. They don't realize that cancer often is triggered by an infectious disease.

The shocker: At least 25% of malignancies are caused by viruses, bacteria and parasites. After smoking, infection is the leading cause of cancer.

Although millions of Americans are infected with cancer-causing organisms at some time during their lives, most of these people don't develop cancer as a result. There are additional risk factors that work in tandem with infectious microbes to trigger the biological changes that lead to cancer.

THE INFECTION LINK

Viruses are the main cancer-causing organisms, followed by bacteria and parasites.

Primary ways that these organisms cause cancer…

•**Genetic changes.** Viruses can't replicate on their own. When viruses enter your body, they inject their own genetic material into your cells and take over the cells' inner workings.

Some viral genes, known as *oncogenes*, cause cells to divide much more rapidly than usual. Rapid cell division increases the odds of genetic "mistakes" that can lead to cancer. Viruses also inhibit our body's natural ability to destroy damaged cells, which may otherwise continue to grow and divide in ways that make us more vulnerable to cancer.

•**Chronic inflammation.** Some organisms, such as those that cause stomach and liver cancer, irritate tissues and trigger persistent inflammation. Inflammation causes cells to divide at a faster rate than normal, increasing the likelihood that they will mutate and undergo changes that lead to cancer.

CANCER-CAUSING INFECTIONS

Numerous cancers are believed to be caused, in part, by infectious organisms. *The most common cancer-causing infections—and steps you can take to protect yourself...*

•**Helicobacter pylori.** Between 30% and 40% of Americans are infected with *Helicobacter pylori*, a screw-shaped bacterium that burrows into the stomach lining and causes chronic inflammation. About 20% of these people will eventually develop ulcers—another 5% will develop stomach cancer.

Infection with H. pylori is a very strong risk factor for cancer, presumably because the bacterium causes inflammation and cell proliferation. More than 80% of stomach cancer cases are caused by H. pylori. Infection with this bacterium increases your risk of developing stomach cancer by at least eightfold.

Self-defense: Ulcer patients are routinely tested for H. pylori and treated with antibiotics if infection is present. Once the bacterium is eliminated, the risk for ulcers drops significantly. It is not yet known if treating bacteria will help prevent stomach cancer. Patients with a family history of stomach cancer should talk to their doctors about getting tested for H. pylori.

Also helpful: Eat a nutritious diet that is rich in fruits and vegetables and low in salt and food preservatives known as nitrates. Such a diet may reduce cancer risk.

•**Epstein-Barr virus.** The Epstein-Barr virus (EBV) causes infectious mononucleosis, which leads to extreme fatigue and other flu-like symptoms. EBV is found in the tumors of a significant number of patients with Hodgkin's disease (a form of lymphoma that strikes most often between the ages of 15 to 35 and after age 55).

The risk that an individual patient who has had mononucleosis will go on to develop Hodgkin's disease—or non-Hodgkin's lymphoma, which also is associated with the EBV virus—is still very low.

The main risk for non-Hodgkin's lymphoma appears to be in patients who have severely compromised immune systems—for example, those who have undergone transplant surgery and/or are taking immune-suppressing drugs.

Self-defense: Transmission of EBV is impossible to prevent because many healthy people can carry and spread the virus for life. People who receive transplants and immune-suppressing drugs should ask their doctors about symptoms of EBV-related malignancies. Decreasing immunosuppression can often reverse lymphoma when caught early.

•**Hepatitis B.** The hepatitis B virus (HBV) is spread by contact with body fluids of an infected person, including blood, saliva, vaginal secretions and semen.

At greatest risk: People who have sex with infected partners...and drug users who share needles.

Most cases of HBV are acute, lasting six months or less. This form of hepatitis is not linked to cancer. However, the *chronic* form of HBV, which is almost always acquired in childhood and lasts for more than six months, greatly increases the risk for cirrhosis (destruction of normal liver tissue) as well as liver cancer.

Self-defense: All newborns are now given the HBV vaccine. It's also recommended for children ages 18 years or younger who weren't previously vaccinated. Adults don't require the vaccine for cancer prevention—but it is recommended for those in high-risk groups because it can reduce the risk for long-term liver disease.

Among those who should get the vaccine: Health-care workers...those who are sexually active with people who may have HBV and/or have household contact with them...and dialysis patients.

•**Hepatitis C.** Most people with the hepatitis C virus (HCV) were infected by tainted blood transfusions prior to 1992, when blood-screening tests first became available. HCV also can be transmitted by having sex with someone who is infected...sharing contaminated hypodermic needles...and receiving nonsterile tattoo or body-piercing procedures.

About 5% of patients with HCV will develop liver cancer. A much higher percentage will develop cirrhosis or other chronic liver diseases—usually decades after the initial exposure.

Self-defense: In addition to the high-risk practices mentioned above, do not share razors, toothbrushes or nail clippers in households with an HCV-infected person. Patients who received a blood transfusion prior to 1992, or who engage in high-risk practices, should be tested for HCV.

Treatment depends on the type and extent of the HCV infection. For example, a combination of *interferon* (such as PEG-Intron) and an antiviral drug called *ribavirin* (Rebetol) can eliminate infection in 50% to 80% of cases.

•**Human papilloma virus.** A majority of sexually active American women will be exposed to one of the many strains of human papilloma virus (HPV) at some time during their lives. HPV is a sexually transmitted infection that may cause no symptoms itself but increases the risk for cervical cancer.

Fortunately, only a small percentage of women with HPV go on to develop cervical cancer. There also are relatively harmless forms of HPV, such as those that cause genital warts—these do not increase cancer risk.

A new HPV vaccine appears to be extremely effective. It is now available.

The use of condoms and other safe-sex practices aren't very effective at preventing the spread of HPV. That's because condoms may not cover enough of the penis to prevent exposure. The virus also can be transmitted by hand-to-genital contact.

Self-defense: Women should get regular Pap tests to look for precancerous changes in the cervix. The American Cancer Society recommends an HPV test in addition to a Pap smear for women ages 30 and older. The cure rate for cervical cancer is about 90% when it's detected at an early stage.

Vitamin A vs. Cancer

John Erdman, PhD, professor of food science and human nutrition in the division of nutritional sciences at the University of Illinois in Urban, has participated in more than 100 scientific studies and authored 140 scientific publications on vitamin A and other areas of nutrition.

Vitamin A has traditionally been known for its role in helping to prevent night blindness (a condition in which you cannot see well in dim light).

In fact, that's why carrots, which are rich in beta-carotene (a vitamin A precursor), are said to be so good for your eyes.

Now, scientists are identifying new health benefits of the vitamin.

Recent finding: Researchers at the Harvard School of Public Health analyzed the diets of 450 men without prostate cancer. Among those under age 65, the men with the highest dietary intake of beta-carotene were 36% less likely to develop prostate cancer than those with the lowest intake.

How vitamin A could potentially help you…

WHAT VITAMIN A DOES

Vitamin A was discovered in 1920. As one of the first known vitamins, it was designated by the first letter of the alphabet.

Vitamin A helps prevent night blindness because it is a crucial component of *rhodopsin*, a light-sensitive molecule in the eye. It also helps maintain the health of the cornea (the front of the eye), guarding against the development of blindness, especially in children.

In addition to its beneficial effects on vision, vitamin A helps keep almost all the surfaces of the body healthy—the skin, the mucous membranes and the linings of the respiratory, urinary and intestinal tracts.

Vitamin A also improves the function of the immune system by supporting the action of various infection-fighting immune cells, such as neutrophils, macrophages and natural killer cells. In addition, it helps with reproduction, aiding the production of sperm and the development of eggs.

WHERE VITAMIN A IS FOUND

Foods of animal origin (egg yolks, liver and milk products) contain a preformed version of vitamin A known as *retinol*. Some fortified foods, such as low-fat milk and breakfast cereals, are supplemented with this highly usable form of vitamin A.

Vitamin A also can be produced in the body when you consume foods that contain *beta-carotene*, including sweet potatoes, pumpkin, mangoes, cantaloupe, apricots, tomatoes, red peppers, peas, peaches, papayas, winter squash, spinach and kale.

HOW MUCH DO YOU NEED?

The federal government sets a daily recommended dietary allowance (RDA) for vitamin A.

This amount includes vitamin A derived from retinols (found in foods of animal origin) and carotenoids, such as beta-carotene (derived from brightly colored fruits and vegetables).

For women age 19 and older, the RDA is 2,310 international units (IU). For men age 19 and older, it is 3,000 IU. The RDA for pregnant women is 2,565 IU…for lactating women, it's 4,300 IU.

Approximately 56% of Americans do not meet the RDA for vitamin A, according to the US Department of Agriculture. This segment of the population is believed to have a generally poor diet that includes significant amounts of fast foods and other low-nutrient food products.

Because vitamin A is *fat-soluble* (that is, it is stored in the liver and does not dissolve in water), it takes longer for a deficiency to develop than it would with a water-soluble vitamin, such as vitamin C.

Many Americans may suffer from a *subclinical* deficiency, a low level of vitamin A that has no observable symptoms. This type of deficiency could diminish a person's ability to recover from significant stress, such as a major illness or operation.

People who have illnesses that inhibit the absorption of nutrients, such as Crohn's disease (an inflammatory bowel disorder) and celiac disease (an intolerance to gluten, a protein found in barley, wheat and rye), should ask their doctors whether they would benefit from a vitamin A supplement. Vegans, who consume no foods derived from animals, including eggs and dairy products, also may need a vitamin A supplement. A multivitamin typically is a good choice.

CAN YOU GET TOO MUCH?

Vitamin A toxicity has been well studied by scientists.

Most important findings…

•**Vitamin A and bones.** A handful of studies over the past five years have shown that postmenopausal women who got approximately twice the RDA of vitamin A were at greater risk for osteoporosis and had an increased rate of hip fractures compared with women who received the RDA. A study from Sweden showed the same result in men.

It's important to remember, however, that while these studies show an association between increased intake of vitamin A and bone problems, they do not prove that the nutrient causes bone loss.

Best advice: Postmenopausal women who are concerned about vitamin A-related bone loss should make sure that the nutritional supplements they take do not contain a total amount of vitamin A that exceeds the RDA.

•**Vitamin A and lung cancer.** By the 1990s, 24 out of 25 epidemiological studies of various populations had shown that smokers who consumed the most beta-carotene-rich fruits and vegetables had the lowest levels of lung cancer. Researchers theorized that the nutrient functioned as an antioxidant, protecting lungs from cellular damage.

To test the theory, in two studies conducted a decade ago, men at high risk for lung cancer (those who smoked a pack a day or more for decades…and/or were exposed to lung-damaging asbestos) were given 20 mg to 30 mg daily of supplemental beta-carotene for approximately six years. More of these men got lung cancer than a similar group who did not receive beta-carotene supplements.

Researchers explain this increased lung cancer risk by noting that the high-risk men who were studied had received 80 times more of a highly absorbable form of supplemental beta-carotene than the amount usually consumed from fruits and vegetables in a typical diet found in the epidemiological studies. As the study participants' bodies attempted to break down and eliminate this high dose of beta-carotene, harmful byproducts were created that promoted the development of cancer in the lung.

Best advice: Get your beta-carotene from food.

VITAMIN A AS MEDICINE

•**Acne and psoriasis.** Retinoids (synthetic derivatives of vitamin A) are used to treat acne, psoriasis and other skin disorders.

Caution: The acne drug isotretinoin (Accutane) can cause severe side effects, including birth defects, and should be used only under close medical supervision.

•**Breast cancer.** Another synthetic derivative of vitamin A—4-hydroxyphenylretinamide (4-HPR)—is being used experimentally to prevent the recurrence of breast cancer.

■ ■ ■ ■

Surgery Alternative

Some brain tumors can be eliminated without surgery. Doctors use imaging technology to reconstruct a tumor on a computer. Based on the model, focused radiation is delivered to the site. This procedure, done while the patient is awake, is virtually painless and successfully shrinks tumors 90% of the time.

David Baskin, MD, neurosurgeon and residency program director, Methodist Neurological Institute, Houston.

■ ■ ■ ■

Another Reason Not to Smoke

Nicotine prevents the most common lung cancer drugs from working, laboratory tests show. This raises the possibility that nicotine gum and patches might have a similar effect.

Better for lung cancer patients: Use a smoking-cessation program that focuses on behavioral modification rather than nicotine replacement.

Srikumar Chellappan, PhD, professor, drug discovery program, H. Lee Moffitt Cancer Center and Research Institute, Tampa, and leader of a study, published in *Proceedings of the National Academy of Sciences.*

■ ■ ■ ■

Melanoma Recurrence

Patients treated for melanoma have an 11% risk of recurrence within the first year. People who suffer a second occurrence have a 31% chance of developing a third tumor in the first five years.

Self-defense: Have frequent skin screenings by a dermatologist, and perform routine self-examinations.

Cristina R. Ferrone, MD, division of surgery, Massachusetts General Hospital, Boston, and leader of a study of 4,484 melanoma patients, published in *Journal of the American Medical Association.*

■ ■ ■ ■

Curry vs. Skin Cancer

In a lab study of human cells, curcumin (the compound that makes curry yellow) was shown to interfere with the development of melanoma cells. Past studies have shown that people who eat curry in abundance have lower rates of lung, colon, prostate and breast cancers.

Theory: Curcumin curbs inflammation, a risk factor for cancer.

Self-defense: Eat a half tablespoon of curry daily.

Bharat B. Aggarwal, PhD, professor, department of experimental therapeutics, University of Texas M.D. Anderson Cancer Center, Houston.

■ ■ ■ ■

Statins and Cancer

Statins don't reduce cancer risk. Previous studies had suggested that the cholesterol-lowering drugs could reduce risk because of their anti-inflammatory properties, but two recent studies found no difference in cancer rates among people using statins, versus those who didn't use them.

C. Michael White, PharmD, associate professor of pharmacy, University of Connecticut at Storrs, and leader of a statin study, published in *Journal of the American Medical Association.*

■ ■ ■ ■

Heat vs. Cancer

Heat may kill some cancer cells directly and render others more responsive to radiation.

Recent finding: Treating superficial (or "contained") tumors in tissue of the breast, cervix, head, neck and skin with hyperthermia— gradually increasing the temperature of the cancerous tissue to between 105°F and 113°F— reduced the risk of recurrence by 68%.

Ellen Jones, MD, PhD, associate professor, department of radiation oncology, Duke University Medical Center, Durham, NC, and leader of a study of 109 patients with recurrent, superficial cancers, published in *Journal of Clinical Oncology.*

■ ■ ■ ■

Customized Chemo

Customized chemotherapy is just around the corner. A new study shows that genomic tests, which analyze a cancer's molecular traits, are 80% accurate in predicting which drugs will be most effective in destroying tumors from breast, lung and ovarian cancers. Trials are also under way for prostate cancer. The tests may be widely available for use within the next few years.

Advantages: In many cases, physicians won't have to try out drugs one by one to see what works. Treatment should progress faster—and patients will be exposed to fewer toxic drugs.

Anil Potti, MD, is assistant professor, Institute for Genome Sciences and Policy, Duke University Medical Center, Durham, NC, and leader of a study of more than 350 tumors, published in *Nature Medicine*.

■ ■ ■ ■

Prostate Cancer Recurrence Rate Lowered

Advanced prostate cancer patients who received radiation within 16 weeks of surgery had a 50% lower risk of recurrence over 10 years than men who did not receive radiation.

Bonus: After five years, long-term side effects, including urinary dysfunction, were the same in patients regardless of whether they received radiation.

Gregory Swanson, MD, associate professor of radiation oncology and urology, University of Texas Health Science Center, San Antonio.

■ ■ ■ ■

Oral Exams

In a recent study, when dentists and other health-care workers visually examined patients for signs of oral cancer, they uncovered numerous otherwise hidden cases, reducing risk for death by 79% compared with an unscreened control group. Researchers estimate that regular screening of the oral cavity by visual inspection once every three years could prevent at least 37,000 oral cancer deaths annually.

Self-defense: Make sure your dentist or general practitioner carefully examines the inside of your mouth at least once every three years.

Rengaswamy Sankaranarayanan, MD, head, screening group, International Agency for Research on Cancer, Lyon, France.

■ ■ ■ ■

Safer Rays

Radiation therapy for breast cancer no longer damages women's hearts. In the past, women with breast cancer on the left side who received radiation treatment risked heart attacks. Recent improvements now allow radiation to be delivered more accurately. Nearly 40% of women with breast cancer are treated with radiation therapy following surgery.

Sharon Giordano, MD, MPH, assistant professor, University of Texas MD Anderson Center, Houston, and lead researcher of a study of the records of more than 26,000 women with breast cancer, published in *Journal of the National Cancer Institute*.

■ ■ ■ ■

Cancer Test Warning

New lung cancer test may lead to unnecessary invasive procedures. The spiral, or helical, CT scan can detect tumors that are small enough to be treated successfully.

Problem: The baseline test yields false-positives as much as 60% of the time—although physicians experienced in interpreting CT scans can reduce the number of postscan invasive procedures. Cancer researchers are studying ways to make spiral CT scans more accurate.

Thomas J. Glynn, PhD, director of cancer science and trends, American Cancer Society, Washington, DC.

■ ■ ■ ■

Better Cooking Methods

Researchers who evaluated cooking methods found that steaming boosted broccoli's levels of *glucosinolates*, which are believed to reduce cancer risk, while boiling increased the release of disease-fighting *carotenoids* from carrots.

Theory: Boiling and steaming release health-promoting compounds in vegetables.

When cooking vegetables: Boil or steam them until they are crisp-tender.

Nicoletta Pellegrini, PhD, associate professor, department of public health, University of Parma, Italy.

■ ■ ■ ■

Missed Diagnosis

Sigmoidoscopies miss advanced precancerous colon growths in almost two-thirds of women—a failure rate twice as high as that in men. Sigmoidoscopies evaluate only one-quarter or one-half the colon and do not allow for removal of precancerous growths.

Self-defense: Everyone age 50 and over—and women, in particular—should have regular colonoscopies to screen for colon cancer. Many insurers will cover only sigmoidoscopies—colonoscopy is more expensive ($500 or more, depending on location) and requires use of a sedative.

Philip Schoenfeld, MD, associate professor of internal medicine, University of Michigan, Ann Arbor, and chief, division of gastroenterology, Ann Arbor Veterans Affairs Health System. He is leader of a study of 1,463 women, published in *The New England Journal of Medicine*.

■ ■ ■ ■

Chicken Lowers Colon Cancer Risk

In a study of 1,520 people, those who ate the most chicken (an average of four servings daily) had a 21% lower risk for colorectal adenomas (growths that can be precursors of colon cancer) than those who ate the least chicken (less than one serving daily).

Theory: Chicken eaters may consume smaller amounts of processed meat, which has been found to increase colon cancer risk.

Self-defense: Substitute chicken for processed meats, such as cold cuts and hot dogs.

Douglas J. Robertson, MD, MPH, assistant professor of medicine, Dartmouth Medical School, Hanover, NH.

The Shocking Truth About Deodorants and Cancer

Philippa D. Darbre, PhD, senior lecturer on oncology, University of Reading, England.
Bert Petersen, MD, breast surgeon and former director, Family Risk Program, Beth Israel Medical Center, New York City, co-founder and managing partner of Global Cancer Control, New York.
Cosmetic, Toiletry and Fragrance Association.
Journal of Applied Toxicology.

The most common group of chemical preservatives that are in cosmetics and deodorants has been found in human breast cancer tissue.

Although the discovery links breast tumors and this group of chemicals, called parabens, it is not clear what the relationship is and whether the use of these products might be hazardous.

The US Food and Drug Administration (FDA) has called parabens the most widely used preservatives in the United States. They are common in shampoos, foundations, facial masks, hair-grooming aids, nail creams and permanent-wave products.

Previous studies on animals and in the laboratory have shown that parabens can mimic the actions of the hormone estrogen. That has raised red flags because estrogen is known to fuel breast cancer.

The latest, apparently groundbreaking, research takes those findings one step further.

"We have always been assured that parabens could not get into the body. This study shows that they do. To my knowledge, no one else has done that," says Philippa D. Darbre, lead author of the study and a cancer specialist at the University of Reading, England.

RESULTS CAN'T BE IGNORED

"It's preliminary, but I think that it's a little worrisome. And I think there's definitely enough data here to suggest that more work needs to be done to look at this issue," adds Dr. Bert Petersen, a breast surgeon and former director of the Family Risk Program at Beth Israel Medical Center in New York City. "I don't think it can be dismissed."

THE STUDY

Darbre has been studying breast cancer for 20 years, but could not get funding for a study on parabens.

"I was told that I wouldn't find anything," Darbre recalls. So, she galvanized friends and colleagues in the medical community, who helped her gain access to analytic machinery and to breast tissue.

Eventually, Darbre was able to analyze samples of 20 human breast tumors with high-pressure liquid chromatography followed by tandem mass spectrometry.

In four of the 20 tumors, the total concentration of parabens was more than twice the average level.

The form the chemicals were found in suggests that they entered the body topically, not orally, the researchers add.

**DON'T TOSS YOUR
DEODORANT...YET**

Of particular concern to many people are underarm products, such as deodorants and antiperspirants, which are applied topically and absorbed through the skin.

But the Cosmetic, Toiletry and Fragrance Association defends the safety of parabens.

"There is no evidence of harm from the use of deodorants or antiperspirants. They are safe, and consumers should not be unnecessarily alarmed," according to the Association.

The study authors acknowledge that many issues need to be resolved before any definitive conclusions can be reached.

Researchers need to determine levels of parabens in normal breast tissue as well as in other parts of the body. Also, more samples should be examined.

"It would be interesting to see if women [who do not have breast cancer] have very low levels of parabens," Petersen says. "Then you might start to believe maybe this isn't just an association. It might be cause and effect here."

■ ■ ■ ■

Teflon and Cancer?

Teflon has not been found to cause cancer. *Perfluorooctanoic acid* (PFOA), a chemical used in the synthesis of Teflon, has been labeled a "likely carcinogen" by a panel advising the Environmental Protection Agency. But Teflon pans do not emit PFOA when used properly.

Teflon cookware might emit a small amount of PFOA when heated to extreme temperatures—for example, when a frying pan has been left empty on a heated burner for an extended period. Even then, it has not been established that overheated Teflon produces a dangerous amount of PFOA. Still, it wouldn't be unreasonable to dispose of a Teflon pan that has been left empty on a heated burner.

Approximately 95% of the population has some amount of PFOA in their bloodstream—but most of this PFOA likely comes from

stain- and water-repelling treatments used on carpets and fabrics. Grease-resistant food packaging, such as microwave popcorn bags and cardboard fast-food boxes, also might contain small amounts of PFOA.

The fact that PFOA is in our bodies does not mean that we're all going to die from PFOA-related cancers. Individuals who have worked in factories where PFOA is produced, and perhaps some people who live in neighboring areas, seem to have the highest levels of PFOA.

Ronald Melnick, PhD, senior toxicologist with National Institute of Environmental Health Sciences, a division of the National Institutes of Health, Research Triangle Park, NC. He is currently conducting experiments on chemicals related to PFOA.

■ ■ ■ ■

Chemotherapy and Hot Flashes

When breast cancer patients experiencing chemotherapy-induced hot flashes took 900 mg daily of the anticonvulsant *gabapentin* (Neurontin), they reported a 46% reduction in the frequency and severity of their hot flashes.

Theory: Gabapentin may work directly in the central nervous system, where body temperature is regulated. Gabapentin appears to be as effective as hormone therapy, which is used to treat hot flashes in menopausal women, but without the potentially harmful side effects.

Self-defense: Chemotherapy patients who experience hot flashes should ask their doctors if gabapentin is appropriate for them.

Kishan J. Pandya, MD, professor of medicine and oncology, James P. Wilmot Cancer Center, University of Rochester, NY.

■ ■ ■ ■

Colon Cancer and Your Diet

High magnesium consumption may help prevent colorectal cancer. In a new analysis of 61,433 women ages 40 to 75, those with the highest daily intakes of the mineral had a 40% lower risk of developing the disease than those with the lowest daily intakes.

Theory: Magnesium lowers levels of insulin (a hormone produced in the pancreas that regulates blood glucose). Elevated insulin levels are associated with colorectal cancer risk.

Self-defense: Eat food containing 300 mg to 400 mg of magnesium daily. Good sources, which contain 50 mg of magnesium per serving, include one cup of cooked or one-half cup of raw spinach…one large banana…one-half cup of cooked oatmeal…two slices of whole-grain bread…and one-half cup of beans. If you include magnesium-rich foods in your diet, there is no need to take a magnesium supplement.

Susanna C. Larsson, PhD, researcher, division of nutritional epidemiology, National Institute of Environmental Medicine, Karolinska Institute, Stockholm, Sweden. Her study was published in the *Journal of the American Medical Association*, 515 N. State St., Chicago 60610.

■ ■ ■ ■

Prostate Cancer and Surgery

Most surgeons prefer to wait for post-biopsy inflammation to subside before surgically removing a cancerous prostate gland. There's little cause for concern, however. A new study of nearly 4,000 patients undergoing radical prostatectomy (removal of the prostate) within a year of diagnosis found that the time between the biopsy and surgery did not affect the success of the surgery or the risk for cancer recurrence.

James A. Eastham, MD, associate professor, department of urology, Memorial Sloan-Kettering Cancer Center, New York City.

■ ■ ■ ■

Massage for Cancer?

In a three-year study of the effect of massage on more than 1,000 cancer patients—the largest study to date of massage used for cancer patients—patients rated their symptoms immediately before and after a single treatment of massage therapy.

Result: Anxiety declined by 52%…pain, 40% …fatigue, 41%…depression, 31%…and nausea, 21%. Massage was as effective as standard drug therapy for these symptoms.

Helpful: Insurance companies are more likely to pay for massage therapy if a doctor writes a referral to a certified therapist or if treatment is part of a hospital in-patient therapy.

To locate a massage therapist in your area, contact the American Massage Therapy Association, 877-905-2700, or visit *www.amtamassage.org.*

Barrie R. Cassileth, PhD, chief, Integrative Medicine Service, Memorial Sloan-Kettering Cancer Center, New York City.

■ ■ ■ ■

Alcohol and Colon Cancer

Some research suggests that alcohol is a factor in developing colon cancer, but the evidence has not been consistent and the mechanism of alcohol-induced colon cancer risk is not clear.

Theory: Heavy drinkers (typically more than two drinks daily) may be more susceptible to colon cancer due to a general immune deficiency and poor dietary intake of cancer-preventing foods. Also, alcohol by-products may build up to high concentrations in the colon and interfere with the absorption of cancer-preventing substances. Several dietary factors may be involved in the development of colon cancer, including diets low in fresh vegetables and fruits and high in red meat. A deficiency of the B vitamin folic acid is thought to play a role in the development of colon cancer.

Self-defense: Get 400 micrograms of folic acid daily in your diet or through the use of a supplement.

Samuel Meyers, MD, clinical professor of medicine, Mount Sinai School of Medicine, New York City.

■ ■ ■ ■

Magnesium and Colon Cancer

In a 17-year study of 42,000 women ages 55 to 69, those who ate more than 351 mg of magnesium a day were 23% less likely to develop colon cancer than those who ate less than 245 mg daily. The women got most of their magnesium from food. The current recommended daily magnesium intake is 400 mg.

Theory: Magnesium may decrease risk factors, such as insulin resistance (in which the body is less able to respond to insulin) and cell proliferation.

Self-defense: Women who are concerned about colon cancer risk should eat a diet that is high in magnesium. Magnesium-rich foods include artichokes, avocados, bran cereal, cashews, dark chocolate, lentils, spinach and wheat germ. Previous research has shown that fiber, antioxidants and other nutrients in foods rich in magnesium also contribute to lower colon cancer risk.

Ching-Ping Hong, senior analyst and programmer, division of epidemiology and community health, University of Minnesota, MN.

■ ■ ■ ■

Vitamin D and Prostate

Vitamin D, which the body manufactures as a result of exposure to ultraviolet light in sunshine, has been found to prevent the onset and growth of prostate and other types of cancer, including breast and colon cancer. For years, scientists have known that men who live in more-northern states with less sun exposure have a higher incidence of prostate cancer than those who live in southern states. Scientists are researching how giving prostate cancer patients high-dose intravenous vitamin D may help fight existing cancers.

Self-defense: It is important for men to get regular sun exposure, especially when they're young, but to keep it to a reasonable and safe level (usually 10 to 15 minutes of sunshine daily without using sunscreen) to avoid increased risk for skin cancer.

Sheldon Marks, MD, microsurgical specialist and diplomat of the American Board of Urology, in private practice in Tucson, AZ.

■ ■ ■ ■

Multiple Myeloma Treatment and Tiredness

Tiredness is common in patients with newly diagnosed multiple myeloma (a type of cancer characterized by an abnormal growth of plasma cells, usually in the bone marrow). These patients frequently have low red blood cell counts, or anemia. The red cells in your blood are responsible for delivering oxygen to the tissues. If you have anemia, your tissues may not have enough oxygen, resulting in fatigue.

What to do: A prescription drug, *epoetin* (Epogen), stimulates the production of red cells in the bone marrow and can be used in myeloma patients to improve anemia and the resulting

fatigue. It is also important to stay on a healthful diet and regular exercise program. While patients with myeloma need to be cautious not to harm the bones, which are usually weakened by the cancer, exercises that don't impact the spine, such as walking or swimming, are advisable. You should also consult your doctor about taking a multivitamin.

Melissa Alsina, MD, head, myeloma program, H. Lee Moffitt Cancer Center and Research Institute, Tampa.

■ ■ ■ ■

Breast Thermography vs. Mammogram

Thermography should not be used as a substitute for mammography. In thermography, special infrared cameras are used to detect and map heat that is produced in different parts of the body. Some cancers show up as "hot spots" because new blood vessels are forming rapidly there.

However: The technique is unreliable. The rate of false-negatives (cancers that go undetected) and false-positives (nonmalignant areas that show up as hot spots and require further testing) is unacceptably high.

Mammography remains the most useful breast-cancer screening test. The American Cancer Society recommends annual mammograms for women over age 40—and earlier or more frequently for women at increased risk.

Phil Evans, MD, FACR, professor of radiology and director of the Center for Breast Care, University of Texas Southwestern Medical Center at Dallas. He is a member of the American Cancer Society's Board of Directors.

■ ■ ■ ■

Herbs for Cancer

Essiac actually is a blend of four herbs—burdock root, slippery elm inner bark, sheep sorrel and Indian rhubarb root. The formula was named for Rene Caisse (Essiac is Caisse spelled backwards), a Canadian nurse who worked with cancer patients in the early 1900s. The formula is believed to have originated in native Canadian Ojibway Indian medicine.

Essiac, of course, is not a cure for cancer. It does, however, support the normal detoxification pathways of the liver, kidneys and lymphatic system, which helps immune function. Essiac is nontoxic, so I don't oppose using it as a dietary supplement. Take the dosage recommended on the label—and as always, before starting a new supplement, check with your doctor.

Mark A. Stengler, ND, naturopathic physician in private practice, La Jolla, CA...adjunct associate clinical professor at the National College of Natural Medicine, Portland, OR...author of 16 books, including *The Natural Physician's Healing Therapies* (Bottom Line Books) and coauthor of *Prescription for Natural Cures* (Wiley)...and author of the *Bottom Line/Natural Healing* newsletter.

■ ■ ■ ■

Mushrooms for Cancer Prevention

Mushroom extracts are used by health practitioners around the world to prevent cancer and enhance immune function in people who already have cancer. Some mushroom extracts, such as Coriolus versicolor (*Trametes versicolor*) and maitake (*Grifola frondosa*), are considered cancer drugs in China and Japan, since they have been so well studied. Various mushroom extracts are used to treat and prevent different cancers. Coriolus, for instance, is used specifically as an adjunct treatment along with chemotherapy, radiation and surgery, and as a preventive for esophageal, lung, stomach and colon cancers. Many studies support its use. Maitake is used specifically to support conventional treatment of breast, prostate, liver and lung cancers. Be sure to tell your primary care doctor and your oncologist if you are taking mushroom extracts. In some cases, they may interfere with immune-suppressing drugs, such as those taken after a transplant.

Mark A. Stengler, ND, naturopathic physician in private practice, La Jolla, CA...adjunct associate clinical professor at the National College of Natural Medicine, Portland, OR...author of 16 books, including *The Natural Physician's Healing Therapies* (Bottom Line Books) and coauthor of *Prescription for Natural Cures* (Wiley)...and author of the *Bottom Line/Natural Healing* newsletter.

12

Men's Health

The Medical Tests Every Man Should Have

I was speaking recently with emergency physician and Temple University clinical instructor Richard O'Brien, MD, about how men are reluctant to go to the doctor unless they are seriously ill or badly injured. "Many men know the maintenance schedules of their cars better than they know their own bodies' maintenance schedules," he lamented. *Among the medical tests that men need regularly...*

• **Annual prostate-specific antigen (PSA) test starting at age 50** (earlier for African-Americans and men with a family history of prostate cancer).

• **Annual digital rectal exam (DRE)** to check for enlarged prostate, starting at age 40.

• **Electrocardiogram** every three or four years, starting at age 40 (earlier if there is a family history of heart disease).

• **Colonoscopy** every 10 years—or sigmoidoscopy every five years—starting at age 50 (earlier if there is a family history of colon cancer).

• **Testosterone level screening,** including blood test and lifestyle questionnaire, starting at age 40. Discuss the appropriate frequency for you with your physician.

• **Monthly testicle and breast (yes, breast!) self-exams** to check for potentially cancerous lumps. See your physician if you find anything suspicious. Don't just hope that lumps will go away.

Staying informed is key. According to the US Department of Health and Human Services, the source of most health information for men is women—wives, girlfriends and/or mothers. Women tend to get their information from doctors, television, the Internet and printed materials. *Bottom Line/Personal* and its sister publications, *Bottom Line/Health* and *Bottom Line Natural Healing,* can be valuable resources. One of my favorite all-around health Web sites

Marjory Abrams, publisher, newsletters, Boardroom Inc., 281 Tresser Blvd., Stamford, CT 06901.

is sponsored by the National Library of Medicine (*www.nlm.nih.gov/medlineplus*). It has a special section on men's health issues. Also check out the nonprofit Men's Health Network at *www. menshealthnetwork.org*.

Rich also shared with me the most important new research findings in men's health…

•**Taking daily aspirin,** *ibuprofen* or another nonsteroidal anti-inflammatory drug (NSAID) cuts in half the incidence of an enlarged prostate.

•**Low testosterone** in older men is associated with increased mortality risk. Over a four-year period, men over age 40 with low testosterone were about 70% more likely to die than men with normal levels.

•**Men with erectile dysfunction (ED)** should be watched closely for coronary artery disease (CAD). More than 90% of men with both ED and CAD reported symptoms of ED one to three years before experiencing severe chest pain.

•**About 10% of new fathers** (compared with 14% of new mothers) suffer from postpartum depression. Male or female, anyone who experiences depression for more than two weeks should seek professional help.

Women are more accustomed to consulting with physicians, having used them more than men in their younger years because of pregnancy, birth control, urinary tract infections and other common conditions in women. Men's health issues, such as prostate problems, tend to develop later in life. (Rich, who just turned 50, recently experienced his first acute problem —serious neck and shoulder pain—in more than 20 years.)

Don't be shy, men. Silence can kill. And an ounce of prevention truly is worth a pound of cure when it comes to your health.

■ ■ ■ ■

Prostate Screening

In a study of 647 men who were tested for prostate cancer, researchers found that for those whose body mass index (BMI) was 25 or above, a lower threshold for the prostate-specific antigen (PSA) density test—a measure of PSA divided by prostate volume—was necessary to accurately predict who had cancer. Researchers don't know why BMI may be linked to prostate cancer.

If you are an overweight or obese man: Ask your doctor whether you need additional screening tests for prostate cancer.

Mark Garzotto, MD, associate professor of urology, Oregon Health & Science University Cancer Institute, Portland, and director of urologic oncology at the Portland Veterans Affairs Medical Center.

■ ■ ■ ■

Reduce Prostate Cancer Risk

In a new finding, men who engaged in at least three hours weekly of vigorous physical activity, such as jogging, swimming or bicycling, had a nearly 70% lower risk of being diagnosed with advanced prostate cancer.

Theory: Exercise reduces levels of hormones, such as *insulin* and *leptin*, that may contribute to the development of prostate cancer.

For optimal prostate cancer prevention: Men should aim for at least three hours of vigorous exercise per week. Walking or other types of milder exercise have cardiovascular and other benefits.

Edward L. Giovannucci, MD, ScD, professor of nutrition and epidemiology, Harvard School of Public Health, Boston.

Prostate Cancer: Diagnosis and Treatment

J. Stephen Jones, MD, chairman of the Department of Regional Urology of Glickman Urological and Kidney Institute at the Cleveland Clinic, OH, is the author of *The Complete Prostate Book: What Every Man Needs to Know* and *Overcoming Impotence* (both from Prometheus).

Since its introduction 20 years ago, the prostate-specific antigen (PSA) blood test has become a key tool in screening men for prostate cancer.

Until the PSA test, men received only a digital rectal exam (DRE), in which the doctor inserts a gloved, lubricated finger into the rectum to feel the prostate for lumps and thickenings that suggest a tumor.

The PSA test became popular because it can help detect some prostate cancers earlier than the DRE alone. An elevated level of the PSA enzyme doesn't necessarily mean that cancer is present, but it can indicate the need for a biopsy.

Yet now, after years of use, experts disagree about whether men should receive routine PSA testing. Some medical groups, such as the American Urological Society and the American Cancer Society, advocate annual screening for all men age 50 and over—and starting at age 40 or 45 for those at high risk (African-Americans and men with a family history of the disease). Other groups, including the American Medical Association, advise doctors to spell out the risks and benefits of PSA testing and let the patients decide. Unfortunately, few men have all the facts about PSA testing. *What men need to know...*

INTERPRETING TEST RESULTS

PSA is produced by the walnut-sized prostate gland. When cancer is present, the prostate secretes more PSA than usual. But cancer isn't the *only* reason for increased PSA levels. Infection or the enlargement of the prostate that accompanies aging, known as benign prostatic hyperplasia (BPH), can do the same thing. Even ejaculation within 48 hours of the test can affect PSA levels. That's why PSA levels can be difficult to interpret.

What's a "normal" PSA level? Until the last several years, it was defined as below 4.0 ng/ml, but newer data on prostate cancer have made it clear that a man's risk often rises at lower PSA levels. Many experts now say that 2.5 or below is normal for men in their 40s...up to 3.5 for those in their 50s...up to 4.5 for men in their 60s...and up to 6.5 for men 70 and older. (PSA levels naturally rise with age—even in the absence of cancer.)

Another way of looking at PSA is a matter of percentages—one-third of men with a PSA level between 2 and 4 have prostate cancer...44% when the level is 4.1 to 7...and one-half have the disease at a PSA level of 7.1 to 10. Above 10, the chance that a man has prostate cancer rises to two-thirds.

WHAT'S WRONG WITH THE PSA?

Since screening with the PSA test (followed by other tests, such as biopsy, when indicated) catches most cancers—and early detection is generally desirable—why do many experts question whether men should have the PSA test?

The answer isn't simple, because prostate cancer isn't simple. Most prostate tumors grow very slowly, if at all—and are best left alone because they are unlikely to lead to death. Other prostate cancers need aggressive treatment to keep them from spreading. In these cases, early detection can mean the difference between life and death.

How can you tell the difference? You can't with certainty. That's why a substantial number of prostate cancers—found with the help of PSA testing—will be treated even though they are not life threatening. Treatment generally means surgery to remove the prostate and/or radiation to kill the tumor. These treatments carry significant risks for impotence and urinary incontinence.

Proponents of the PSA test point out that prostate cancer deaths have declined in the years since the test has been widely used. However, PSA skeptics say that this trend could also be the result of better treatment, not just better diagnosis.

IMPROVING ACCURACY

In recent years, several variations on the PSA test have been used to improve its accuracy at indicating prostate cancer and limit the number of men who are advised to receive a biopsy.

•**Free vs. bound PSA.** Most PSA floats through the bloodstream bound to protein molecules, while a smaller portion is free. Evidence has shown that when PSA is produced by cancer, higher levels than usual are in the bound form, and a smaller proportion is free. Less free PSA (15% or below) means a greater chance that it's cancer. This test is recommended for men who have abnormal results from the standard PSA test.

•**PSA velocity.** The rate at which PSA changes over the course of three or more annual readings is a significant predictor. The PSA level shouldn't rise more than 0.75 per year, according to the National Cancer Care Network, a consortium of cancer specialists. The group recommends a biopsy if levels rise faster.

•**PSA density.** The larger a noncancerous prostate is, the more PSA it will normally produce. So density—the amount of PSA divided by the size of the gland—also may indicate whether prostate cancer is present. High density —that is, a big number in a man with a small prostate—means more risk. A range of 0.10 to 0.15 and above indicates increased risk.

Drawback: Measuring the prostate requires rectal ultrasound, an invasive procedure that involves placing a thumb-sized probe into the rectum.

WHAT TO EXPECT FROM A BIOPSY

If your PSA results are abnormal, the next step is a biopsy. Some men receive one as soon as possible, while others wait several months and repeat the PSA test. The results of a second PSA test are different enough to warrant a third PSA test in less than 20% of cases, but it is often worth waiting for this confirmation.

Important: If your doctor suspects a prostate infection (from a clinical exam and bacterial culture), he/she should prescribe a course of antibiotics before repeating the PSA test.

If a biopsy is indicated, your doctor will refer you to a surgeon, who will perform the procedure.

What the biopsy involves: While you lie on your side, the surgeon inserts an ultrasound probe through your rectum. A needle-like device is guided through a hole in the probe to take tiny tissue samples from the prostate for examination under a microscope. An estimated 40% of surgeons only take six tissue samples, which allows cancer to be missed 30% to 50% of the time. That's why it's crucial for the surgeon to take at least 12 tissue samples, which decreases the false-negative rate to less than 20%.

Important: Injecting local anesthesia into nerves at the base of the prostate makes the procedure less painful. Not all surgeons are familiar with this technique. Before the biopsy, make sure that local anesthesia is available.

Following the biopsy, there may be slight soreness in the area around the rectum for a few days.

The risk for infection from the biopsy is 1%. To minimize this risk, surgeons should give an antibiotic beforehand.

TREATMENT

Most of the 230,000 prostate cancers diagnosed in the US each year are found when the malignancy is still confined to the prostate. Choosing a treatment at this stage isn't simple.

Active treatment—surgery and/or radiation— is highly effective, but side effects, including impotence and urinary incontinence, are common. A majority of men who undergo treatment will develop impotence either immediately or within five years. On the other hand, treatment may not even be required. While some prostate cancers are indeed dangerous and must be treated quickly and aggressively, others cause no harm. Unfortunately, it's impossible to say with certainty whether treatment—or no treatment—is more desirable.

WATCHFUL WAITING

The most misunderstood option in treating prostate cancer is "watchful waiting." Many men believe that it means "doing nothing." It does not. Watchful waiting means following the cancer very closely. It aims to minimize unnecessary treatment of tumors that cause no trouble while taking precautions to avoid giving an aggressive cancer a dangerous head start.

The most obvious candidates for watchful waiting are men whose age (typically 70 and older) and other illnesses (heart disease, for example) make it unlikely that they will live long enough to suffer ill effects from the prostate malignancy. But refinements in diagnosis have made watchful waiting a reasonable choice for some younger men as well—if it's done properly. *Here's how...*

•**Fully evaluate the tumor.** Watchful waiting should be considered only for a tumor that appears unlikely to grow quickly. The key measure is the Gleason score, which refers to the tumor "grade" (how abnormal the cells are, and how likely they are to spread). Grades are assigned to the two areas that make up the highest and second highest concentrations of cancer cells. The Gleason score (a number from 2 to 10) is expressed as the sum of the two grades (for example, 3 + 4 = 7). The lower the score, the better.

Prostate-specific antigen, the protein produced in excess by prostate tumors, also may be taken into account. When the PSA is under 10, watchful waiting may be a possibility. Past

20, few doctors would advocate it. A PSA of 10 to 20 falls in a gray zone.

•**Repeat biopsy within a year.** If the cancer has gotten worse (a PSA or Gleason score that has risen significantly) within one year of the first biopsy, it will probably continue to worsen. How often to biopsy after that depends on age and other factors. A 55-year-old man may want to have a biopsy each year, to discover quickly if treatment is necessary. A 75-year-old with a low-grade tumor may not want a third biopsy for years. In both cases, a rectal exam and PSA testing should be done at least every year.

SURGERY AND RADIATION

The most common treatments for localized prostate cancer (surgery and radiation) are comparably effective—the cancer doesn't come back in the vast majority of cases—and they both carry similar (and substantial) risks for impotence and urinary incontinence.

•**Surgery** involves removal of the entire prostate (prostatectomy). Technical advances have improved *nerve-sparing surgery*, which aims to protect potency and reduce incontinence risk by leaving the nerve bundle next to the prostate intact. It is only possible for some tumors and not always successful in preserving function.

With *laparoscopic surgery*, the entire prostate is removed, but the operation is done through a thin tube, or laparoscope. It's less invasive than conventional surgery and involves less blood loss.

Men seem to recover more quickly with laparoscopic surgery (about three weeks versus six weeks for standard prostatectomy), and some reports suggest that there's a better chance of preserving potency—but neither has been definitively shown.

Latest development: With *robotic laparoscopic surgery*, the surgeon watches the operating field on a screen and manipulates surgical instruments with precision controls. It takes years of training and experience to become truly adept at robotic laparoscopic surgery—there are few such experts nationwide. But most surgeons skilled in conventional prostatectomy can quickly master the robotic technique. It appears to be as effective as other types of surgery, but studies are ongoing.

•**Radiation therapy** includes *external beam therapy* (the oldest type, which focuses intense energy on the tumor from a number of angles to destroy it while limiting exposure of normal tissues). With brachytherapy, "seeds," or tiny pellets of radioactive material, are implanted within the prostate itself to deliver radiation to the tumor.

Latest development: *Intensity-modulated radiation therapy* (IMRT) finely adjusts an external radiation beam to conform to the shape of the tumor. And seeds now can be targeted more precisely with ultrasound imaging. Side effects include irritation to the bladder or rectum.

AN IMPROVED ALTERNATIVE

•**Cryotherapy,** which involves freezing the prostate to destroy it, is an alternative to surgery that was developed decades ago. Only recently have advances made cryotherapy a reasonable option.

The tissue-freezing instrument (cryoprobe) is smaller than before (the diameter of a pencil lead rather than a pencil), and the temperature can be adjusted more precisely, which reduces damage to other tissues.

Cryotherapy is far less invasive than surgery, and recovery is much shorter—only a week or two. For five to seven years after the procedure, studies show, survival and cancer control with cryotherapy are comparable to that offered by surgery or radiation. Cryosurgery is less likely to cause lasting urinary incontinence than other procedures.

■ ■ ■ ■

Cholesterol Risk

Men with prostate cancer are about 50% more likely to have had high cholesterol levels than men without the disease. The association is stronger for men whose high cholesterol levels were diagnosed before age 50—and for men over age 65, for whom there was an 80% greater likelihood of high cholesterol levels.

Implication: Statins (cholesterol-lowering drugs) may help lower prostate cancer risk.

Francesca Bravi, MD, epidemiologist, Istituto di Ricerche Farmacologiche Mario Negri, Milan, Italy.

How to Beat Advanced Prostate Cancer

Celestia Higano, MD, professor of medicine and urology, University of Washington, Seattle.

Bruce Roth, MD, professor of medicine and urologic surgery and section chief, solid tumor oncology, Vanderbilt University, Nashville.

Multidisciplinary Prostate Cancer Symposium, Orlando, FL.

American Society of Clinical Oncology news release.

Prostate Cancer Foundation news release.

For the first time, a vaccine therapy that harnesses the power of the body's own immune system is proving successful in the fight against metastatic prostate cancer.

Scientists say the compound, called APC8015 (Provenge), primes patients' immune systems to recognize and kill prostate cancer cells that have spread throughout the body.

THE STUDY

The Seattle study looked at 127 men who had cancer that had spread beyond the prostate and grown resistant to hormonal therapy. Eighty-two of the men received Provenge, while the remaining 45 received a placebo. The researchers tracked patient outcomes for three years.

The patients taking Provenge survived an average of 25.9 months, compared with 22 months for those not taking the vaccine, an 18% increase in survival. By the three-year mark, 34% of the men on Provenge remained alive, compared with just 11% in the placebo group.

The side effects were minimal—"some fever and shaking for a few days at the beginning of therapy, but that was transient," says study coresearcher Dr. Celestia Higano, professor of medicine and urology at the University of Washington in Seattle.

THE VACCINE

"The vaccine is composed of a person's own immune cells that have been isolated from the blood and then sensitized to prostatic acid phosphotase, which is found on 95% of prostate cancer cells," Higano says. Once infused back into the patient, these sensitized cells prime the patient's immune system to recognize and destroy prostate cancer cells that are roaming throughout the body, she adds.

PROMISING NEWS

"For those of us doing research into metastatic prostate cancer, it looks pretty great," says Higano. "We prolonged survival—that's great news. It's the first time we've seen it with a vaccine in prostate cancer," she adds.

The therapy also gives "proof of principle" to the theory that immune-based treatments can have a real impact on prostate cancer and other malignancies, experts say.

"It's the first immunological therapy to have some efficacy against metastatic prostate cancer, after years of trying," says Dr. Bruce Roth, a prostate cancer researcher at Vanderbilt University in Nashville. "There have been many failures with this kind of approach, and many have wondered if we shouldn't set the bar lower, somehow lower our expectations, and not hope for extended survival.

"But these findings are saying, 'No, looking for a survival advantage is a valid endpoint to look at for these agents,'" he says.

The US Food and Drug Administration has not approved Provenge.

Additional research and clinical trials by Provenge's developer, the Seattle-based Dendreon, are still under way.

PROSTATE CANCER RECURRENCE

When caught early, prostate cancer remains very curable. However, despite advances in early detection, the disease remains the second-leading cancer killer of men in the US, according to the American Cancer Society.

Several recent breakthroughs highlight the medical advances in prostate cancer treatment.

EXTENDING SURVIVAL

Because prostate cells depend heavily on testosterone to grow, therapies that reduce levels of circulating testosterone are often the first course of action in men who experience a recurrence.

However, prostate cancer cells gradually grow resistant to hormonal therapy, so relapse is almost inevitable. Even among men who develop the disease while it is still confined to the prostate, between 30% and 40% will experience a recurrence in years to come, experts say.

Until very recently, doctors could only offer palliative therapies once relapse occurred. However, one new chemotherapy agent—*docetaxel* (Taxotere)—was found to improve survival in patients who had metastatic disease by an extra six months, on average.

STUDY 1:
VITAMIN D AND PROSTATE CANCER

A study by researchers at Brigham and Women's Hospital and the Harvard School of Public Health suggests that higher levels of vitamin D may help protect against prostate cancer.

Comparing vitamin D levels in blood samples from more than 2,400 men, the Boston team discovered that men who had high levels of two vitamin D metabolites were at a 45% lower risk of developing prostate cancer, compared with men who had lower levels of these two metabolites or those who had a high level of only one metabolite.

"Our finding suggests that vitamin D plays an important protective role against prostate cancer," says lead investigator Dr. Haojie Li. Vitamin D is best obtained through exposure to sunlight or certain foods.

STUDY 2:
OBESITY AND PROSTATE CANCER

In another study, also from Brigham and Women's Hospital, Dr. Jing Ma and colleagues report that obesity may increase risks for death from prostate cancer. They found that, even after adjusting for other risk factors, obese men who have a body mass index (BMI) of 30 or above were twice as likely to die of the disease than normal weight men.

According to the researchers, obesity also doubled the risk of being diagnosed with metastatic prostate cancer—19% among obese men compared with 8% among normal-weight men.

"There are two possible explanations for these findings," Ma says. "First, that being obese may delay the diagnosis of prostate cancer, or, second, that being overweight or obese is associated with a biologically more aggressive form of prostate cancer."

To learn more about detecting and treating prostate cancer, visit the American Cancer Society at *www.cancer.org*.

Natural Ways to Fight Prostate Enlargement

Mark A. Stengler, ND, naturopathic physician in private practice, La Jolla, CA...adjunct associate clinical professor at the National College of Natural Medicine, Portland, OR...author of 16 books, including *The Natural Physician's Healing Therapies* (Bottom Line Books) and coauthor of *Prescription for Natural Cures* (Wiley)...and author of the *Bottom Line/Natural Healing* newsletter.

If you're a man approaching age 45, you have a nearly 50% chance of having an enlarged prostate. By age 70, the chances are almost nine in 10 that you'll have it. Called *benign prostatic hyperplasia* (BPH), the condition involves an enlarged prostate that compresses the urethra and partially blocks urine flow. BPH is the most common prostate problem among men. While it's not life-threatening—it is not, for example, related to the development of prostate cancer—symptoms can be troublesome. Fortunately, there are natural ways to prevent and treat it.

THE PROSTATE PRESSURE POINT

The job of the prostate is to produce fluid that nourishes and transports sperm. This walnut-sized gland weighs approximately 20 grams, about as much as two Fig Newtons. Located in front of the rectum and below the bladder, the prostate surrounds the urethra, the passageway that carries urine away from the bladder and into the penis.

A swollen prostate can compress the urethra like a clamp on a garden hose, restricting urine flow. It also may press upward, irritating the outer wall of the bladder. This irritation makes the bladder wall thicker and even more easily irritated. A man with BPH might start having bladder contractions, making him feel the need to urinate frequently even when there's not much urine. Over time, the bladder may lose the ability to completely empty, increasing discomfort.

POSSIBLE CAUSES

There remains a lot to be answered when it comes to the causes of BPH. One thing researchers can agree on is that hormonal factors play the largest role.

Research has focused on the hormone *testosterone* and a related substance called *dihydrotestosterone* (DHT). Some researchers believe that testosterone, an anabolic (growth-promoting) hormone, is the main culprit. Others disagree because prostate growth tends to be a problem later in a man's life, while the amount of testosterone is at its highest when males are in their late teens or early 20s.

The conversion of testosterone to DHT increases as men get older—and DHT is very potent. It stimulates the proliferation of new prostate cells and slows the death of older ones. But if DHT is a cause, why do some men with prostate enlargement have normal DHT levels? Could another hormone be involved?

Now researchers are looking at the effect of the hormone *estrogen* (especially the kind called *estradiol*) on prostate growth. Estrogen isn't just a "female" hormone. Men have it as well, and as they age, estrogen levels increase. High estrogen-to-testosterone ratios could increase the effects of DHT on prostate cells.

LOOKING FOR TROUBLE

The most common test to diagnose BPH and other prostate-related problems is a digital rectal exam. Your physician inserts a gloved finger into the rectum and feels the part of the prostate next to the rectum for any enlargement or hardness. All men over age 40 should have this test once a year.

A variety of pharmaceuticals can help relieve BPH symptoms, but each has potential side effects. Many doctors prescribe alpha-blockers, such as *terazosin* (Hytrin) or *doxazosin* (Cardura), which relax the neck of the bladder, making urination easier—but these can cause fatigue, weakness, headaches and dizziness. Another prescription drug, *finasteride* (Proscar), relieves symptoms by shrinking the prostate gland, but it can cause impotence and reduced sexual desire.

For men who have serious BPH problems that are interfering with their lifestyle, some doctors recommend surgical procedures—but surgery can lead to impotence or incontinence.

I find that drugs and surgery usually are unnecessary. As long as a man is getting his prostate checked at least once a year and there are no signs of tumor growth or urinary blockage, BPH can be treated with natural therapies. These include improved diet and supplements. Also, 30 minutes of daily exercise has been shown to reduce BPH symptoms quite significantly.

HEALING FOODS

•**Avocados** contain *beta sitosterol*, a phytonutrient that protects against prostate enlargement by inhibiting growth factors that cause prostate swelling. Avocados also are a good source of *oleic acid*, a monounsaturated fatty acid that is thought to reduce inflammation, which can contribute to BPH. Have at least two weekly servings (one-fifth of a medium avocado per serving). If you don't like avocados, you can have three half-cup servings a week of peanuts, rice bran or wheat germ.

•**Fish** is a good source of *eicosapentaenoic acid* (EPA), a powerful omega-3 fatty acid that helps reduce swelling and inflammation. Eat at least two three-ounce servings of trout, salmon or sardines each week.

•**Ground flaxseed** has been shown to reduce estrogen levels, and it contains anti-inflammatory omega-3 fatty acids. I advise men to take one or two tablespoons daily along with 10 ounces of water (to prevent constipation). Ground flaxseed has a mild, nutty flavor and can be added to salads, cereals, yogurt, smoothies and protein shakes or just eaten plain.

•**Pumpkin seeds** are natural sources of zinc. This mineral helps keep your prostate healthy by reducing the activity of the enzyme *5-alpha-reductase*, which produces DHT. Sprinkle a tablespoon or two of pumpkin seeds—raw or roasted, with or without the hulls—on salad, yogurt, cereal, etc. four times weekly.

•**Soy** contains a number of phytoestrogens (plant chemicals that balance estrogen), including *genistein*, which can help control prostate enlargement. I prefer fermented soy foods, such as miso, tempeh and fermented soy protein powder, which provide a form of genistein that can be readily absorbed by the body. Have at least one-half cup serving daily.

•**Tomatoes** are rich in the disease-fighting antioxidants known as *carotenoids*. Preliminary scientific research has suggested that tomatoes and tomato products help prevent prostate cancer. They also may have a beneficial effect on prostate enlargement. Consume two servings of fresh tomatoes and two servings of cooked tomatoes (e.g., tomato paste/sauce) weekly (one serving equals one-half to one cup of tomatoes and/or tomato sauce). If you don't like tomatoes, eat watermelon or cantaloupe.

Foods to avoid: Men with BPH should avoid caffeinated beverages and alcohol—they irritate and inflame the prostate. Also reduce your intake of foods that contain harmful fats, such as hydrogenated or partially hydrogenated oils, that promote inflammation. Stay away from packaged foods that are high in sugar, which also can worsen inflammation.

NATURAL SUPPLEMENTS

The following supplements are listed in order of importance—start with the first and move down the list until you find what works best for you. Many formulas contain a blend of two or three of the ones listed.

•**Saw palmetto berry extract** is a mainstay in the natural treatment of BPH and alleviates most symptoms. It was first used medicinally by Native Americans for prostate and urinary tract problems. Recently, researchers have found that saw palmetto helps the prostate by reducing activity of the DHT-producing enzyme 5-alpha-reductase. A review of 18 randomized, controlled trials involving 2,939 men found saw palmetto to be as effective as the BPH drug *finasteride.*

It can take six to eight weeks before this natural prostate protector begins to fully take effect. I recommend a product that is standardized to contain 80% to 95% fatty acids (check the label) and a total daily dosage of 320 mg, which can be taken all at once. Two brands I recommend are Nature's Way Standardized Saw Palmetto Extract and Enzymatic Therapy Super Saw Palmetto, which are widely available at health-food stores. It is best to take it on an empty stomach. A small percentage of men get stomach upset from saw palmetto. If this occurs, try taking it with meals.

•**Pygeum africanum,** an extract that comes from the bark of the African plum tree, decreases the need to urinate at night and improves urine flow during the day. I prefer a formula that combines pygeum with saw palmetto, such as Ultra Saw Palmetto and Pygeum by Jarrow Formulas (800-726-0886, *www.jarrow.com*). The daily pygeum dosage is 100 mg.

•**Nettle root** can provide modest benefits. The nettle-containing product from Nutrilite, Saw Palmetto with Nettle Root, produced good

results in a UCLA study. Over six months, the 44 men in the study showed modest improvements in BPH symptoms. The Nutrilite formula includes saw palmetto, nettle root, beta-carotene, pumpkin seed oil and lemon bioflavonoid concentrate (Quixtar, 800-253-6500, *www.quixtar.com*). Take one softgel three times daily.

•**Rye grass pollen extracts** seem to relax the muscles of the urethra and improve the ability of the bladder to contract. The extract most widely tested is from Graminex (877-472-6469, *www.graminex.com*). Take three 63-mg tablets twice daily for a total of 378 mg.

•**Fish oil** can help reduce prostate swelling and inflammation. Take 3,000 mg to 5,000 mg daily in addition to two weekly servings of fish. If you prefer a vegetarian source of omega-3 fatty acids, use one to two tablespoons of flax-seed oil.

Caution: Fish oil should not be used by anyone who takes blood-thinning medications such as *warfarin* (Coumadin).

COMMON SYMPTOMS OF BPH

•**A need to urinate frequently.**

•**Urination that is hard to start or stop.**

•**Weak urination or "dribbling."**

•**Sensation of an incompletely emptied bladder.**

•**Increased need to urinate at night.**

•**Burning pain accompanying urination.**

•**Recurring bladder infections.**

■ ■ ■ ■

Pomegranate Juice May Slow Prostate Cancer

A study of 50 men who had been treated for prostate cancer, and who afterward drank eight ounces of pomegranate juice a day, tracked their PSA (prostate-specific antigen) levels, a marker of the advance of the disease.

Finding: The average amount of time in which it took their PSA levels to double increased significantly, to 54 months (after drinking the juice) from 15 (before drinking the juice).

Key: Pomegranate juice contains polyphenolic flavonoids, antioxidant chemicals that may have cancer-preventing benefits.

Allan J. Pantuck, MD, associate professor of urology at the University of California, Los Angeles.

■ ■ ■ ■

Enough Saw Palmetto?

Saw palmetto doesn't help enlarged prostate symptoms when taken at a typical dosage, a new study shows. It doesn't reduce the frequent urge to urinate or other enlarged prostate symptoms, such as a weak urinary stream. The typical dosage is 160 milligrams twice a day. A higher dose might alleviate mild symptoms—a new study on this is in the final planning stages.

Best: For now, don't stop taking saw palmetto if it seems to help.

Stephen W. Bent, MD, assistant professor of medicine, University of California, San Francisco.

■ ■ ■ ■

Prostate Cancer Warning

Men with low-risk prostate cancer that hasn't spread should not have hormone therapy.

Reason: Hormone therapy lowers levels of testosterone that feed prostate cancer—but it also can quickly raise risk of heart disease and diabetes. For younger men who have been treated for tumors confined to the prostate or nearby lymph nodes and who have no signs of the disease other than a rise in *prostate-specific antigen* (PSA), hormone therapy may be riskier than monitoring the cancer. Hormone therapy remains the treatment of choice if the cancer has spread to the bone.

Nancy Keating, MD, MPH, associate professor of health-care policy and of medicine, Harvard Medical School, Boston, and leader of a study of 73,000 prostate cancer patients, published in *Journal of Clinical Oncology*.

■ ■ ■ ■

Prostate Help

Potential prostate cancer patients benefit from osteoporosis drug.

New study: More than 100 prostate cancer patients treated with androgen deprivation therapy, which lowers testosterone levels and often causes bone loss, took either the osteoporosis drug *alendronate* (Fosamax) or a placebo for one year.

Result: Bone mass in the spine increased by 3.7% in those taking alendronate compared with a decline in the placebo group.

Susan L. Greenspan, MD, director, Osteoporosis Prevention and Treatment Center, and associate program director General Clinical Research Center, University of Pittsburgh.

■ ■ ■ ■

Safe Surgery

Prostate surgery is safe for older men. Men over age 70 who have prostate cancer are less likely to undergo radical prostatectomy to remove the prostate gland.

Recent finding: Age alone does not make prostate surgery more risky.

But: Men who have heart disease or high blood pressure or who are obese are more likely to die of complications after prostate surgery. Other alternatives for early-stage prostate cancer include radiation treatment, which some studies have indicated has similar outcomes to surgery…and watchful waiting (also known as active surveillance), in which the patient is monitored for signs that the cancer is worsening before any treatment is begun.

Durado Brooks, MD, MPH, director of prostate and colorectal cancers, American Cancer Society, Atlanta.

■ ■ ■ ■

Prostate Risks

Prostate cancer survivors—watch your weight. Prostate cancer progressed more rapidly in obese patients, according to a study of prostate cancer surgery patients.

Also: The disease was more likely to recur in men who had gained an average of three and a half pounds a year, starting at age 25 (the mean age of diagnosis was 60 years).

Sara S. Strom, PhD, associate professor of epidemiology, M.D. Anderson Cancer Center, University of Texas, Houston, and leader of a study of 526 prostate cancer patients, published in *Clinical Cancer Research*.

■■■■

New Prostate Cancer Test Is More Accurate

The current test for prostate cancer, which measures blood levels of prostate-specific antigen (PSA), detects 85% of prostate cancer cases but gives a "false positive" (a test result that wrongly indicates the presence of disease) in 80% of cases.

New study: Researchers tested 330 men for elevated levels of early prostate cancer antigen-2 (EPCA-2).

Result: EPCA-2 detected 94% of prostate cancer cases with only a 3% false-positive rate. EPCA-2 testing could be available to the public within two years.

Robert H. Getzenberg, PhD, director of urology research, Johns Hopkins University School of Medicine, Baltimore.

■■■■

Fertility Danger

Insecticides reduce male fertility, according to new research.

Recent finding: Men with higher levels of exposure to the lawn and garden insecticide *chlorpyrifos* or its metabolite (TCPY) were found to have lower levels of testosterone, which may affect reproductive health.

Best: Limit exposure to pesticides.

John D. Meeker, PhD, assistant professor, environmental health sciences, University of Michigan, Ann Arbor, and author of a study of 336 men, published in *Epidemiology*.

Testosterone: Is Yours Too Low?

Culley C. Carson III, MD, Rhodes Distinguished Professor and chief of urology, University of North Carolina School of Medicine, Chapel Hill, is editor in chief of *Contemporary Urology*.

If you're a middle-aged or older man and feel irritable, depressed or fatigued…have trouble concentrating…if you are losing muscle mass and strength and/or putting on more body fat…losing bone density, as indicated by a bone-density test…or experiencing a decreased sex drive or difficulty achieving or maintaining an erection…you might be one of the estimated five million men in the US with abnormally low testosterone levels, or hypogonadism.

It's estimated that only one out of 20 men with low testosterone is currently being treated.

Good news: All it takes is a simple blood test to determine if you have low testosterone. If you do have low testosterone, the latest form of testosterone-replacement therapy (TRT), in which the hormone is applied to the skin as a gel, is safe and effective and can begin to reverse all of the above symptoms almost immediately.

WHY IS TESTOSTERONE IMPORTANT?

The most powerful of a group of male hormones known as androgens, testosterone is largely responsible for men's growth of facial and pubic hair, deepening of the voice, increased muscle and bone mass, sex drive and, to some extent, aggressiveness. Although testosterone is present in both sexes, women typically have only one-tenth the amount of testosterone that men do.

In men, a normal blood testosterone level is generally considered to be between 300 and 1,000 nanograms per deciliter (ng/dl). Testosterone levels tend to be highest in the early morning hours, then go down somewhat as the day wears on.

As men get older, however, testosterone levels gradually decline. This occurs most acutely after age 65, but the decline can also be noticeable among men in their 50s and even 40s. Testosterone levels vary greatly from patient to patient, and drops are relative to each patient's starting level—which is usually not known. There can be many causes for decreasing levels, but the most common is testicular failure—the testicles "wear out" and fail to produce enough testosterone.

Low testosterone has long been associated with decreased sex drive, but researchers are now discovering that low testosterone levels can cause numerous other negative health effects (in addition to those already mentioned), including reduced fertility, loss of body hair, reduced muscle mass and strength, problems sleeping and increased risk of depression.

In addition, men with a number of chronic conditions are also much more likely to have low testosterone levels. These conditions include type 2 diabetes, cardiovascular disease, chronic renal failure, obesity, hypertension, insulin resistance (prediabetes) and HIV/AIDS. If you have any of these conditions, it's important to get treatment for the underlying medical problem and a blood testosterone test to see if you might benefit from TRT as well.

DIAGNOSIS AND TREATMENT

You can visit your doctor specifically to get a screening testosterone level blood test, or you can request to have it done as part of your annual checkup. The accuracy of lab tests is far better than it used to be, and testing of free circulating testosterone (not the testosterone that is bound to protein in the body) is also now available. Your doctor may also do this test if your levels in the screening test indicate a problem. Among men with low testosterone, what we typically see are levels in the 150 ng/dl range—about half of what is considered the minimum normal level. These men are prime candidates for TRT to bring blood levels into the normal range (above 300 ng/dl).

In addition to ordering a blood test, your primary care doctor can also prescribe TRT treatments. If he/she is unfamiliar or uncomfortable with TRT, however, you should consider seeing a urologist or endocrinologist for treatment.

OLDER TREATMENT METHODS

One older treatment, injection therapy, requires frequent visits to the doctor for shots and produces uneven testosterone levels, which spike drastically after injection, then decline steadily afterward. Testosterone pills carry a high risk of liver damage because of the strain put on the liver as it breaks down the testosterone. And the earliest testosterone treatment, patches (introduced in the early 1990s), were safer than pills but caused skin irritation in many patients.

The latest testosterone treatment, gels (which have been on the market for about three years), have proven to be very safe and nonirritating. They are very effective at raising testosterone levels back into the normal range. Gels are more effective than patches, which are rarely used anymore, and have fewer side effects. An added benefit of these gels is that, when applied in the morning, they come close to mimicking the normal daily fluctuations in testosterone levels —high in the morning, lower at night.

There are currently two FDA-approved gels. AndroGel is scent-free but takes up to two hours to dry completely. Testim has a slightly musky scent and dries a little more quickly on the skin.

The recommended method is to apply a five-gram packet of gel (about the size of a fast-food ketchup packet) containing 50 mg of testosterone in the morning to the shoulders, upper arms and/ or abdomen. After applying, wash your hands carefully, cover the treated area with clothing and avoid bathing or swimming for six hours.

After applying either type of gel, avoid skin-to-skin contact of that area with your partner or any other family members until the gel has dried completely. Otherwise, they may experience elevated testosterone levels as well. (If your female partner experiences any unusual acne or body hair growth, she should see her doctor immediately.)

What to expect: Initial benefits of TRT tend to be seen quickly, especially improvements in libido, mood and mental sharpness.

Example: One of my patients, a university professor, had been depressed and very forgetful, and was convinced that he had early Alzheimer's. After his blood test showed a testosterone level of 100 ng/dl, he was placed on TRT—and found that within a few weeks his mood and his mental abilities were fully restored.

Increases in muscle and bone mass occur more slowly and can be enhanced by strength training (for muscle and bone development), calcium/vitamin D supplements (for bone growth) and, if necessary, osteoporosis medication.

No long-term studies have been done on TRT —the longest was three years. But, in the three-year study, there was no indication of any risk or side effects.

Prostate alert: While TRT doesn't appear to increase the risk of prostate cancer or benign prostate enlargement, testosterone supplements may spur the growth of existing prostate tumors. For this reason, TRT should never be taken by anyone who has been diagnosed with prostate cancer.

Men on TRT should be given both a prostate-specific antigen (PSA) test for prostate cancer and a digital rectal exam twice a year. As testosterone levels move from low to normal, it's typical to experience a slight rise in PSA levels and a slight increase in prostate size, but these changes usually present no problem.

■■■■

Low-Testosterone Men Prone to Falls

In a recent finding, older men with the lowest levels of the hormone testosterone had a 40% greater risk of falling than those with the highest levels. It is too soon to say whether testosterone replacement would help prevent falls. Testosterone declines naturally with age. Older men can lower the risk of falling by increasing leg strength and coordination and by avoiding alcohol and sedatives, which may increase the risk of falls.

Eric Orwoll, MD, professor of medicine, associate vice president and associate dean for research, School of Medicine, Oregon Health & Science University, Portland. He is leader of a study of 2,587 men, published in *Archives of Internal Medicine*.

■■■■

Alcoholism Reduces Men's Fertility

Men being treated for alcoholism as in a recent study had lower levels of testosterone and more sperm abnormalities than men who did not drink at all.

Also: Seventy-one percent of alcoholics had erectile dysfunction, compared with seven percent of men who abstained from alcohol.

K.R. Muthusami, PhD, senior biochemist and laboratory manager, Institute of Laboratory Medicine, Kovai Medical Center and Hospital, Coimbatore, India, and leader of a study of 96 men, published in *Fertility & Sterility*.

■■■■

Incontinence Aid

Male urinary incontinence may be relieved by collagen injections. Incontinence is a frequent side effect of prostate surgery.

Recent finding: Transurethral collagen injections after prostate surgery improve short-term bladder control for six to seven months, at which time injections can be repeated. Injections are administered via the urethra, under local anesthesia. Collagen helps control urine leakage by bulking up the area around the urethra, compressing the sphincter.

O. Lenaine Westney, MD, associate professor, department of urologic surgery, University of Texas M.D. Anderson Cancer Center, Houston.

■■■■

Cancer Risk

Cure rates for testicular cancer are high, but the treatments may lead to an increased likelihood of tumors elsewhere in the body for at least 35 years. Most patients are diagnosed with the disease in their 20s or early 30s and treated with radiation or chemotherapy. A man diagnosed at age 35 who survives the cancer for 10 years has nearly twice the risk of the general population of developing a malignant tumor elsewhere.

Self-defense: Testicular cancer survivors should adopt a healthy lifestyle, follow screening guidelines and seek medical consultation for any changes in health status.

Lois B. Travis, MD, ScD, senior investigator, National Cancer Institute, Bethesda, MD, and leader of a study of 40,576 testicular cancer patients, published in *Journal of the National Cancer Institute* of the National Institutes of Health.

■■■■

Warning Sign

Male infertility could be a sign of testicular cancer.

Recent study: Men with low sperm counts were 20 times more likely to develop testicular cancer than men with normal counts.

Self-defense: Men whose sperm counts are low should schedule a semen analysis and cancer screening and do regular self-examinations. Speak to your doctor for information on performing testicle self-exams.

Marc Goldstein, MD, professor of urology and reproductive medicine, Weill Cornell Medical Center, New York City, and leader of a study of 4,000 infertile men, published in *Journal of Urology*.

■■■■

Cells and Sex

Excessive cell-phone use may affect a man's sperm production.

Recent finding: Radio waves such as those emitted by cell phones damaged sperm DNA in mice. DNA damage in sperm correlates to poor fertility and increased rates of miscarriage and childhood disease, including cancer. More study is needed to determine the effects in humans.

R. John Aitken, PhD, ScD, laureate professor in biological sciences, Australian Research Council Centre of Excellence in Biotechnology and Development, discipline of biological sciences, School of Life and Environmental Sciences, University of Newcastle, Callaghan, New South Wales, and leader of a study of 22 mice, published in *International Journal of Andrology*.

■ ■ ■ ■

No-Rush Hernia

Men whose hernias are not causing pain can wait to have them repaired. Their outcomes are similar to those of men who have them repaired immediately. A hernia occurs when part of the intestine bulges through a weak area of the abdomen's muscle wall.

Caution: In rare cases, when you are unable to push the hernia back and it is accompanied by cramps and vomiting, the hernia requires immediate repair.

Also: Watchful waiting is appropriate for men only. When women get hernias, the condition is more dangerous.

The late Olga Jonasson, MD, professor, department of surgery, University of Illinois at Chicago, and coauthor of a study of 720 men with hernias, published in *The Journal of the American Medical Association*.

■ ■ ■ ■

Exercise Cuts Risk of Dying

Exercise greatly cuts a man's risk of dying from heart disease.

New finding: Men at high risk for heart disease (due to hypertension, high cholesterol and/or other risk factors) who exercised for 30 minutes four to five days per week reduced their risk of dying from a heart attack or stroke by 50%.

Self-defense: Everyone—especially those who are at risk for heart disease—should perform aerobic exercise, such as walking or swimming, for at least 30 minutes four to five days a week.

Peter T. Katzmarzyk, PhD, associate professor, School of Kinesiology and Health Studies, Queens University, Kingston, Ontario, Canada.

■ ■ ■ ■

Viagra Curbs Urinary Problems

An enlarged prostate is common in men who also experience erectile dysfunction (ED).

Recent finding: In a study of 370 men age 45 or older, those who took the ED drug *sildenafil* (Viagra) for 12 weeks reported improvement in symptoms associated with an enlarged prostate, such as decreased urinary flow.

Theory: The enzyme that Viagra acts on in the penis also relaxes cells in the bladder and prostate that promote urinary flow and emptying of the bladder.

Kevin T. McVary, MD, associate professor of urology, Northwestern University Feinberg School of Medicine, Chicago.

■ ■ ■ ■

Statins May Help Men's Bones

Statins may help prevent osteoporosis in men.

New finding: In a study of more than 91,000 men, those who took a cholesterol-lowering statin had an overall 36% lower risk for fractures.

Theory: Statins improve the function of small blood vessels, which may promote bone growth and remodeling.

If you have high cholesterol: Ask your doctor about taking a statin to lower cholesterol—and to help prevent osteoporosis.

Richard E. Scranton, MD, MPH, instructor in medicine, Harvard Medical School, Boston.

■ ■ ■ ■

Sex Dysfunction

Thyroid disorders may cause sexual dysfunction in men. Hyperthyroidism (high thyroid activity) and hypothyroidism (low thyroid activity) can cause premature ejaculation, reduced desire and erectile dysfunction. Treatment for the thyroid disorder frequently reverses the sexual symptoms.

Emmanuele A. Jannini, MD, professor of endocrinology and medical sexology, University of L'Aquila, L'Aquila, Italy, and leader of a study of 48 men, published in *The Journal of Clinical Endocrinology & Metabolism*.

■ ■ ■ ■

Double Trouble

Erectile dysfunction (ED) may mean heart trouble, a new study says. There is a strong association between ED and cardiovascular disease. In a clinical trial, men older than 55 who reported a new problem with ED had a 25% increased risk of suffering a cardiovascular "event," such as a heart attack, stroke or angina, than men who had no problem with ED.

Precaution: When you seek help for ED, ask your doctor to check for heart trouble.

Ian Murchie Thompson, Jr., MD, professor and chairman, department of urology, University of Texas Health Science Center, San Antonio.

Viagra Treatment for Enlarged Heart

Richard Stein, MD, professor of medicine and director, urban community cardiology program, New York University Medical Center, New York City, and national spokesman, American Heart Association.

Hunter Champion, MD, PhD, assistant professor of medicine, Johns Hopkins University School of Medicine, Baltimore.

Nature Medicine.

Viagra, the drug best known for treating impotence, may prove effective for treating an enlarged heart.

A study showed that *sildenafil citrate* (Viagra) successfully treated enlargement and thickening of the heart in male mice—not only stopping further growth of the heart muscle, but also actually reversing the growth and damage that had already taken place.

"If, indeed, what works in mice works in humans, this will become a standard part of care," says Dr. Richard Stein, a national spokesman for the American Heart Association.

THE EXPERIMENTS

In one experiment, researchers separated male mice into two groups—one was fed Viagra and one received a regular diet. The scientists then constricted the main artery in the mice, causing the heart to pump harder. This resulted in a condition essentially the same as *hypertrophy*, the enlargement and thickening of the heart muscles.

The mice who received Viagra developed hypertrophy at half the rate of the mice who were not getting the drug. The Viagra mice also showed 67% less muscle stiffening, had smaller hearts and improved heart function.

In another experiment, the researchers gave Viagra to some mice in a group of males that already had hypertrophy. After two weeks, muscle growth almost completely disappeared in the mice given Viagra, while the hearts of the control mice continued to grow.

"By treating mice with Viagra in doses that would be similar to what a person would get, we found that we could block hypertrophy and could prevent progression to heart failure," explains study coauthor Dr. Hunter Champion, an assistant professor of medicine at Johns Hopkins University School of Medicine.

IMPLICATIONS

The findings are important because they reveal mechanisms that are involved in heart thickening and the progression to heart failure.

Prior to this study, experts did not know that PDE5A, the enzyme involved in sexual function, was also involved in heart function.

Interestingly, Viagra was originally developed to dilate coronary blood vessels in people who had angina. It didn't work for angina, but while being tested, was found to be effective for the treatment of erectile dysfunction.

Champion believes that the effect on the heart may actually be seen in the entire class of drugs, not just Viagra. "It could very well be that Levitra or Cialis would do the same thing," he says, referring to Viagra's two competitors in the erectile dysfunction marketplace.

It may be a while, though, before using these drugs as heart therapy becomes a possibility. Heart failure drug trials take time to prove measurable results.

The Secret of Half-Priced Viagra

Carmen Reitano, founder and president, Three Chestnuts Technologies Inc., Newburyport, MA.

Ira Sharlip, MD, clinical professor, urology, University of California, San Francisco School of Medicine.

US Patent and Trademark Office, Alexandria, VA.

Each diamond-shaped Viagra pill costs the same (almost $10) whether you get the 25-milligram (mg), 50-mg or 100-mg version. This flat-pricing strategy has led many in the older-than-50 crowd to buy the larger pill and try to break it up into smaller pieces.

The patient should take the dose the doctor recommends, says Dr. Ira Sharlip, clinical professor of urology at the University of California, San Francisco School of Medicine. "But I can tell you it's common practice for physicians to recommend a dose of 50 mg and write a prescription for a 100-mg tablet." Carmen Reitano, inventor and Viagra user, was involved in a conversation about the difficulties of splitting a Viagra pill.

"It explodes," complained one man.

"You cut it with a knife and it splits apart with such fury it bounces off the wall," said another.

Reitano had never tried splitting his Viagra pills, but he decided to give it a try. He went home, took out the kitchen knife and tried to cut open one of his Viagra pills. Nothing happened. He went at it with an X-Acto® knife blade. Nothing. A hammer. Still, nothing.

"It's not flat. It's awkward to hold. There's no scoring on the covering," Reitano discovered. So, to help the many frustrated Viagra users, Reitano designed the V2 Pill Splitter, for which he was awarded a patent.

Pfizer, which manufactures Viagra, did not specifically comment, but recommends against pill-splitting.

For Viagra pill splitters, please see *www.for gettingthepill.com/vsplitter.html* or *www.pillcut ter.com/pill-splitter.html.*

13

Women's Health

Natural Ways to Ease Menopause Symptoms

For decades, women relied on hormone-replacement therapy (HRT) to relieve symptoms of menopause —hot flashes, sleep disturbance, anxiety and mood swings. But several large studies have linked long-term HRT with increased risk of breast cancer, dementia, heart attack and stroke.

Fortunately, there are safer, natural alternatives to HRT.

MORE THAN JUST ESTROGEN

People typically attribute menopausal symptoms to declining production of the female hormones *estrogen* and *progesterone*. But poor eating and lifestyle habits also play a role, by overtaxing the adrenal glands. For women who are going through menopause, the adrenal glands are nature's backup system. When the ovaries decrease their production of estrogen and progesterone, the adrenals have the ability

to produce hormones to compensate. Poor diet and lifestyle choices put stress on the adrenals, creating an imbalance in body chemistry and contributing to the uncomfortable symptoms that we associate with menopause.

If you are a woman with menopausal symptoms, adopting healthier habits can help to even out these imbalances.

If you are a man and the woman you love is going through menopause, you can help by understanding that she is experiencing a profound physiological change. Your kindness and patience can ease her transition through a time that is confusing—for her as well as for you.

Common symptoms and natural solutions…

HOT FLASHES

As many as 80% of women experience hot flashes during menopause. One theory is that the hypothalamus, which controls body temperature, is triggered in some way by hormonal fluctuations.

Ann Louise Gittleman, PhD, nutritionist based in Post Falls, ID, is author of 30 books, including *Hot Times: How to Eat Well, Live Healthy, and Feel Sexy During the Change*. Avery.

•**Avoid spicy foods.** Foods containing cayenne or other peppers have a thermogenic effect, meaning that they raise body temperature.

•**Cook with garlic, onion, thyme, oregano and sage.** These seasonings contain very small amounts of phyto-estrogens (plant-based estrogens such as lignans and isoflavones that occur naturally in certain foods) and can help restore hormone balance.

•**Cut down on caffeine.** Caffeine stimulates the adrenal glands, leading to a spike in blood sugar levels followed by a plunge in blood sugar to even lower levels than before. This stresses the body and aggravates menopause woes.

If you don't want to give up coffee completely, have one cup a day with food. Don't use coffee as a stimulant between meals. Instead, eat frequent small meals for energy.

Better than coffee: Green, white and black teas have less caffeine and are high in disease-fighting antioxidants. Try substituting tea for coffee. Then transition to herbal tea or hot water with lemon.

•**Add flaxseed.** Ground flaxseed contains lignans, which seem to modulate fluctuating estrogen and progesterone levels. Aim for two tablespoons a day. Ground flaxseed has a pleasant nutty flavor—sprinkle it on cereal, yogurt and salads.

Bonus: Flaxseed reduces cholesterol, helps prevent certain cancers and relieves constipation (be sure to drink plenty of water).

•**Eat soy foods in moderation.** Some countries with diets high in soy report low rates of menopausal symptoms and breast cancer. But I'm cautious about soy. Preliminary research suggests that while isoflavones in soy appear to protect against some breast cancers, they may stimulate growth of other types of breast cancer.

I'm especially concerned about isolated soy protein, which often is added to protein powder, energy bars and supplements. This puts far more soy isoflavones into the diet than other cultures typically consume—and these high amounts may not be healthful.

If you enjoy soy foods, limit your consumption to two servings a week, and eat them in their whole-food form—as tofu, tempeh, miso and edamame.

•**Be wary of herbal remedies.** I'm cautious about black cohosh, red clover and other plant remedies with estrogen-like properties. Research has not demonstrated clearly that they help, and some can have harmful side effects if not properly monitored. However, some women do report good results from these remedies. Check with your doctor first. If you don't notice a clear change in symptoms after two to three weeks of trying a new remedy, ask your doctor about trying something else.

What men can do: Buy a dual-control electric blanket so that you both will be comfortable. Make her a cup of herbal tea. Join her in eating flaxseed—it is good for your colon and prostate.

INSOMNIA

During menopause, elevated levels of the stress hormone *cortisol* make it difficult to fall asleep and can trigger intermittent awakening throughout the night. *Natural sleep aids...*

•**Wild yam cream.** This topical cream extracted from yams grown in Mexico is a source of natural progesterone. It's available at most health-food stores and some pharmacies. Applying small amounts of wild yam cream daily may help to balance cortisol levels and enhance sleep. (The cream also helps reduce anxiety and hot flashes.)

Apply one-quarter teaspoon once in the morning and once at night. Gently rub the cream into areas where you see capillaries, such as the wrist, back of the knee and neck—these are the places where skin is thinnest and the cream is easily absorbed. Alternate where you apply the cream on a daily basis.

•**Magnesium.** Levels of magnesium, a natural sleep aid, are depleted when you consume too much coffee, cola, alcohol, sugar or salt. Foods high in magnesium include halibut...whole-wheat bread...leafy green vegetables such as spinach...nuts...and dried beans (soaked and cooked). If your diet is low in magnesium, take 200 milligrams (mg) to 400 mg in supplement form at bedtime.

•**Zinc.** This mineral can help quiet an overactive mind. Foods rich in zinc include poultry, red meat and nuts, but it is hard to get enough zinc from food. Take 25 mg to 45 mg in supplement form before bed.

•**Exercise.** One study found that women over age 50 who walked, biked or did stretching exercises every morning fell asleep more easily. Try to get a half-hour of exercise most mornings. Avoid working out in the evening—you may have trouble winding down. And don't go to extremes. Overexercising (more than two hours of strenuous, nonstop activity every day) can lead to hormonal imbalance.

What men can do: Exercise with her in the morning. Make sure there is a bottle of magnesium tablets by the bedside at home and when traveling.

MOOD SWINGS

Drinking less coffee and eating frequent small meals will go a long way toward balancing your moods by reducing spikes in blood sugar and stress on adrenals. *In addition...*

•**Eat a balanced diet.** The emotional and mental stress of menopause can lead to a vicious cycle in which stress depletes important mineral stores, further taxing the adrenals.

Among the minerals depleted by stress are copper, calcium, magnesium, potassium, sodium and zinc. To restore these minerals, eat an adrenal-supportive diet rich in bright-colored fruits and vegetables, legumes, lean meats and whole grains. Avoid sugar and other refined carbohydrates.

Recommended: Sea vegetables, such as nori, arame, wakame and hijiki. These are especially high in key minerals. Health-food stores sell them in dried form. They can be crumbled into soup and over fish, salad and vegetables.

•**Get the right kind of fat.** Though you should avoid saturated fats (found in pork, beef and high-fat dairy products) and hydrogenated fats (in margarine, shortening and many packaged baked goods), certain fats are necessary for hormonal regulation and proper functioning of the nervous system. Known as *essential fatty acids* (EFAs), these healthy fats help to stabilize blood sugar.

Strive to consume two tablespoons a day of healthy oil (use it in cooking, salad dressings, etc.). Olive, sesame, almond, macadamia and flaxseed oils are especially high in EFAs. (Flaxseed oil does not cook well.)

•**Take B-complex vitamins.** B vitamins are known as the antistress vitamins because they nourish the adrenals. Good sources of B vitamins include whole grains and dried beans (soaked and cooked). Most diets are too low in these vitamins, so supplements usually are needed to make up the deficit. Take 50 mg to 100 mg of a vitamin-B complex daily.

What men can do: Make it easy for her to avoid sugar and caffeine by cutting back on them yourself—your health will benefit, too. If she seems distant or on edge, don't take it personally. Remind yourself that it is not you—it is her biochemistry that is acting up.

WEIGHT GAIN

One reason why so many women gain weight during menopause is that the ovulation process burns calories—as many as 300 per day during the first 10 days of the menstrual cycle. When ovulation stops, fewer calories are burned and metabolism slows. *Foods to counter the slowdown...*

•**Protein.** Increasing protein intake can raise the body's metabolic rate by as much as 25%. Aim for three to four ounces of lean protein from fish, poultry, beef or lamb twice a day. Eggs and beans also are good sources.

•**Healthy carbohydrates.** Whole grains, vegetables and fruits metabolize slowly and give you energy throughout the day. Try to consume daily at least two servings of fruits, three servings of vegetables and three servings of whole grains.

What men can do: Don't nag her about her weight. Support her by not buying high-calorie foods, such as potato chips and rich desserts.

At-Home, Handheld Scanner Helps Women Spot Problems Early

Britton Chance, PhD, ScD, professor emeritus of biophysics, physical chemistry and radiologic physics, University of Pennsylvania School of Medicine, Philadelphia.

Juri Gelovani, MD, professor and chair, experimental diagnostic imaging, M.D. Anderson Cancer Center, Houston.

US Department of Defense Breast Cancer Research Program.

An experimental handheld imaging device designed for home use appears effective in detecting breast cancer in its early stages, according to a small study.

If future, larger studies prove successful, the device—tentatively called *iFind*—could be available commercially within two years.

HOW IT WORKS

The size of a deck of cards, iFind uses near-infrared light to measure how much blood is flowing in different locations in the breast, says creator Britton Chance, PhD, ScD, professor emeritus of biophysics, physical chemistry and radiologic physics, University of Pennsylvania School of Medicine, Philadelphia.

Scientists believe that tumors require new blood vessels to grow, so those areas will have more blood. iFind monitors differences in blood oxygen ratios in growing cancer tissue compared with normal tissues. In this way, it detects "hypermetabolism"—the more rapid growth rate of malignant cells. When a certain threshold is passed, the device emits a light, tone or beep, indicating a woman needs to go to her doctor for further breast screening, says Chance.

THE EVIDENCE

Chance's team tested the device on 116 women over a five-year period. The device, which takes five minutes to use, was 96% accurate when someone had breast cancer. In other words, 96% of the women who actually had cancer had an abnormal reading. All had been diagnosed by standard methods.

iFind is not meant as a substitute for mammograms or biopsies, Chance says, but might supplement those detection methods.

"The [purpose] of this device is to get the women to go to the doctor if something is wrong," says Chance. "It records what it finds on a chip when she scans it across her breasts."

He estimates iFind would cost several hundred dollars and could be especially valuable for women who have a family history of cancer or those who have the breast cancer genes, BRCA1 and BRCA2.

THE REACTION

"The results of this initial study are very encouraging," says Dr. Juri Gelovani, professor and chair of the department of experimental diagnostic imaging at M.D. Anderson Cancer Center in Houston. "Yet, large population-based studies are required to reproduce the findings to validate the technology."

To learn more about breast cancer, visit the American Cancer Society Web site at *www.cancer.org*.

■ ■ ■ ■

Birth Control Risk

Birth control pills increase heart attack risk. Women who take low-dose birth control pills are twice as likely to have heart attacks or strokes as women who don't take them. Especially at risk are women who are over 35 years old…have a high risk of heart disease or diabetes…are overweight…or have polycystic ovary syndrome—a condition characterized by menstrual disturbances, reduced ovulation rates and increased testosterone levels. Researchers believe that the risk disappears after birth control pills are discontinued.

Jean-Patrice Baillargeon, MD, professor of internal medicine, department of medicine, endocrine division, University of Sherbrooke, Quebec, Canada, and lead researcher of a meta-analysis of 14 studies of women taking oral contraceptives between 1980 and 2002, published in *Journal of Clinical Endocrinology & Metabolism*.

■ ■ ■ ■

Pill Warning

Birth control pills can cause migraines during menstruation.

Recent study: Women taking oral contraceptives containing estrogen have a 40% greater risk of suffering migraine headaches during menstruation than women who don't take oral contraceptives.

Reason: When one is on oral contraceptives, the hormone-free week causes a steep drop in estrogen levels right before menstruation, which increases the risk of migraines.

Better for migraine sufferers: Use estrogen patches during the hormone-free week, or use the oral contraceptive Mircette, which allows for a gradual decrease in estrogen. Women who get migraines with auras should avoid hormone birth control entirely.

Karen Aegidius, MD, researcher, department of clinical neuroscience, Norwegian National Headache Center, Trondheim, and leader of a study of 13,944 premenopausal women, published in *Neurology*.

Women and Low Testosterone

Culley C. Carson III, MD, Rhodes Distinguished Professor and chief of urology, University of North Carolina School of Medicine, Chapel Hill, is editor in chief of *Contemporary Urology*.

Some 30 million American women are thought to have low levels of the androgens (so-called male hormones) they need, including testosterone and DHEA.

Common causes include diminished ovarian function, estrogen supplementation (either in birth control pills or in hormone replacement therapy) and impaired adrenal function.

Symptoms include: Osteoporosis, reduced sex drive (which could be due to diminished libido or lack of interest due to pain or dryness), loss of muscle tone, low energy, lack of mental clarity and decreased enjoyment of life.

Diagnosis: To check for androgen deficiency in women, it's best to measure levels of testosterone and DHEA-sulfate (DHEA-S), another androgen. Total testosterone below 30 nanograms per deciliter and/or DHEA-S levels below 100 micrograms per deciliter may be cause to consider supplementation.

Treatment: Among women with sexual dysfunction due to low androgens, treatment with low-dose testosterone or low-dose DHEA significantly increases sex drive about 70% of the time. While the FDA has not yet approved testosterone supplements for use in women, many doctors are prescribing them anyway.

Warning: Unnecessary supplementation can lead to excessive androgen levels, resulting in heavier pubic hair growth, clitoral enlargement, acne, increased facial hair growth, lowered voice and reduced levels of HDL (good) cholesterol. Close monitoring of testosterone levels is advised.

■ ■ ■ ■

Morning-After Pill Warning

The *RU-486 pill* can cause a rare but deadly infection in women who use it incorrectly.

More than four deaths from sepsis—an infection of the bloodstream—have been reported since 2000, when the so-called "abortion pill" went on the US market. These infections occurred in women who inserted the second course of two pills vaginally, as some clinics recommend, rather than swallowing them, as the instructions state. The Food and Drug Administration says that the pill is safe when used properly and it will stay on the market.

Center for Drug Evaluation and Research, US Food and Drug Administration, Washington, DC.

■ ■ ■ ■

Drug Alert for Women

Women respond differently than men to certain drugs and should be aggressive in researching their medications. Women have been underrepresented in clinical drug studies, which long assumed that they respond to drugs as men do. But in fact, women suffer more adverse drug events than men do.

Steps: Understand the need for a drug. Ask a doctor or pharmacist about side effects and potential interactions with other drugs and be sure to understand correct dosage amounts and timing of doses.

Rosaly Correa-de-Araujo, MD, MSc, PhD, director, women's health and gender-based research, Agency for Healthcare Research and Quality (AHRQ), Rockville, MD, *www.ahrq.gov.*

■ ■ ■ ■

Depression and Menopause

As they approach menopause, women who have premenstrual syndrome (PMS) are more likely to suffer depression than women who don't suffer from PMS, a recent study found.

Self-defense: Seek medical treatment if you are approaching menopause and suffering from symptoms of depression.

Ellen Freeman, PhD, research professor, department of obstetrics and gynecology, University of Pennsylvania School of Medicine, Philadelphia, and leader of a study of 231 women, published in *Archives of General Psychiatry.*

Finally, Good News About Menopause and Memory

Peter Meyer, PhD, assistant professor of preventive medicine and director, section of biostatistics, Rush University, Chicago.
Neurology.

When women going through the "change of life" experience a memory lapse, they often blame it on a "menopausal moment." But researchers have found that the working memory and perceptual speed of women improve with age, even during menopause.

Peter Meyer, assistant professor of preventive medicine at Rush University in Chicago, and his colleagues tested the memories of 803 women each year for six years.

The women who were included in Meyer's study were aged 42 to 52 years and were tested annually on their working memory and perceptual speed. They also answered questions about their health, menopausal status, ethnicity and education.

The subjects were in different stages of pre- and postmenopause.

Premenopause is the reproductive stage of a woman's life. Perimenopause is the stage prior to menopause, when physical changes begin to accelerate due to declines in hormone production.

The working memory test asked the women to repeat increasingly long lists of numbers backward. In the perceptual speed test, the women were shown a series of symbols and a corresponding number. They were asked to match as many symbols with their corresponding number as they could in 90 seconds.

Meyer found that perceptual speed and working memory improved slightly over time for women in premenopause and early perimenopause.

Only for the perceptual speed tests was there a decrease in scores, and that was for postmenopausal women. Working memory scores for postmenopausal women did not change greatly over time.

Meyer says that, although the results are surprising, they do not indicate that women don't have problems with forgetfulness as they age.

WHAT CHANGE?

Women in the age group studied often say they have trouble remembering someone's name or coming up with the proper word, Meyer says. Why? "Verbal processing skills might be different, but not worse" with age, he says, somehow accounting for the forgetfulness.

Meyer also says that one explanation for the improvement on the tests might be that the women got better with practice.

■ ■ ■ ■

Hot Flash Relief

A drug used to control pain and epilepsy can sharply reduce the intensity and frequency of hot flashes in women with breast cancer. When breast cancer patients with chemotherapy-induced hot flashes took 900 mg daily of the anticonvulsant *gabapentin* (Neurontin), they reported a 46% reduction in the frequency and severity of hot flashes.

Self-defense: Chemotherapy patients who experience hot flashes should ask their doctors if gabapentin is right for them.

Kishan J. Pandya, MD, professor of medicine and oncology, James P. Wilmot Cancer Center, University of Rochester, Rochester, NY, and leader of a study of 420 women with breast cancer, published in *The Lancet.*

Fight the Weight Gain

Jana Klauer, MD, former research fellow, New York Obesity Research Center, St. Luke's-Roosevelt Hospital, New York City, and weight reduction physician in private practice.

For many women, as they get older, weight seems to go on more quickly and come off more slowly—no matter how much you exercise. Many women's once-lean bodies turn matronly as they reach menopause. The good news, though, is that several recent studies prove that weight gain at menopause is not inevitable.

RECENT STUDIES

The National Institutes of Health sponsored the Study of Women's Health Across the Nation (SWAN) in which researchers tracked 3,064 ethnically diverse women ages 42 to 52 over a three-year period. None had yet gone through menopause at the time the study began. At the end of the three years, the women had gained an average of 4.5 pounds, or 3% of their body weight, and increased waist circumference by about one inch. However—and this is what's really intriguing—whether or not the women had gone through menopause made no difference in their weight gain. Furthermore, the study found that women who were highly active or who became active during the course of the study did not gain weight. In fact, with activity, some lost both weight *and* inches from their waistlines.

In the second study, Harvard's famous ongoing Nurses' Health Study, researchers measured 116,686 young and middle-aged women several times during an eight-year period. They discovered that women who drank no more than one sugar-sweetened soft drink per week did not gain weight, but women who drank more put on weight. So, is it simply the age-old issue of "too much *in* results in too much *on*"?

A DIFFERENT PACE

Jana Klauer, MD, former research fellow at the New York Obesity Research Center at St. Luke's-Roosevelt Hospital in New York City and physician in private practice teaching weight control, discusses how to control weight in middle age. Dr. Klauer says that menopause does not dictate weight gain and it is crucial to avoid gaining weight at this time because postmenopausal women's cardiovascular risks go up—extra weight is an additional risk.

She acknowledges that weight can be harder to control in middle age—not because of hormones, but because metabolism slows by about 10% in these years. If unchecked, this can result in a gain of 10 or so pounds. You can indeed stop and even easily reverse that slowdown. Tests for metabolism are largely based on the body's resting rate (when the body is not in motion), she says, and the determiner of that is mostly the amount of muscle mass a person has. The more muscle you have, the higher your metabolic rate will be. The way to obtain more muscle mass is through exercise, especially strength training.

EXERCISE, A MUST

Working with weights several times a week isn't nearly enough when it comes to exercise, says Dr. Klauer. She emphasizes that exercise after age 40 is no longer an option—to stay healthy, it is a daily imperative. She recommends an hour each day of a weight-bearing exercise such as walking, jogging, cycling, dancing and the like—whatever takes you beyond the level you experience walking around your house or office. Although this may seem like a lot, if you can manage 15-minute spurts of activity throughout your day, it adds up. Be sure the activity you choose helps you build strength in your legs. Dr. Klauer points out that if the legs aren't strong, people begin to slow in their movements and balance problems set in.

SMART DIET CHOICES

After women pass age 40, their food choices also begin to play an ever-bigger role, says Dr. Klauer. Your diet should be heart-healthy and nutrient-rich. In fact, she points out that if you are eating all the nutrients you need, there won't be room in your diet for what she considers junk foods—processed foods, simple carbs, including high-sugar foods, and anything more than one drink of alcohol a day.

She reminds people that large quantities of fruits and vegetables are a wonderful way to keep weight under control because they are filling and provide much-needed fiber. She also advises eating about 60 g a day of high-quality protein.

Example: 3.5 ounces of fish has about 21 g of protein…a similar amount of chicken has 25 g…and a pint of milk has 19 g.

To get started on a healthy diet that will help you reduce or maintain a proper weight, Dr. Klauer says to record everything you eat until your new way of eating is firmly entrenched. She finds that most people are shocked to see how many little extras have crept into their daily diet, small splurges that add up to big numbers on the scale. Keeping a record will make you aware of what extra treats you are eating and help protect you from falling back into those bad habits.

No doubt, following the high level of exercise and healthy diet that Dr. Klauer describes is the surest way to control weight in and past middle age. It is also the best guarantee of a long and healthy life. And that's not a bad trade-off, not bad at all.

■ ■ ■ ■

Hot Flash Help

Hot flashes may be eased by acupuncture, says a new study.

Recent study: After seven weeks, post-menopausal women who had acupuncture twice a week for the first two weeks and once a week thereafter had a greater reduction in nocturnal hot flashes than women who had a treatment that felt like acupuncture but wasn't. Some women getting acupuncture had minor side effects, such as pain, redness and itching where needles were inserted.

Mary I. Huang, MS, clinical research coordinator of a Stanford University School of Medicine study, led by Rachel Manber, PhD, of the effectiveness of acupuncture for nocturnal hot flashes, published in *Fertility and Sterility.*

Chasteberry for Women

Mark A. Stengler, ND, naturopathic physician in private practice, La Jolla, CA...adjunct associate clinical professor at the National College of Natural Medicine, Portland, OR...author of 16 books, including *The Natural Physician's Healing Therapies* (Bottom Line Books) and coauthor of *Prescription for Natural Cures* (Wiley)...and author of the *Bottom Line/Natural Healing* newsletter.

If you were to examine some of the many "women's hormone-balancing" products in health-food stores and pharmacies, you would most likely see chasteberry (also known as *Vitex agnus castus*) listed as an ingredient. It has been recommended for female conditions, including hormone-related acne, fibrocystic breast syndrome, endometriosis, infertility, lactation difficulties, menopausal hot flashes, menstrual disorders, ovarian cysts and uterine fibroids. In other words, it is touted as helping almost all major female conditions.

The herb comes from the berries of the chasteberry tree, actually a shrub found in subtropical climates. The ancient Greeks used chasteberry as a symbol of chastity in young women, hence the name "chaste berry" or "chaste tree."

HOW IT WORKS

Chasteberry does not contain hormones. It acts on the pituitary gland in the brain to increase the production of *luteinizing hormone* (LH). LH stimulates the ovaries to release eggs, as occurs with ovulation. Ovulation triggers a surge in levels of the hormone *progesterone*. This release of progesterone is important in maintaining a balance with the other major female hormone, *estrogen*. Research has shown that some premenopausal women do not ovulate regularly. This sets the stage for what is known as "estrogen dominance"—too much estrogen relative to progesterone. By helping to normalize progesterone levels, chasteberry promotes hormone balance. This is why it is effective for so many female conditions, including premenstrual syndrome and fibrocystic breast disease as well as uterine fibroids in women of all ages, which are in large part caused by estrogen dominance.

Chasteberry also has been shown to lower levels of the hormone *prolactin*. When elevated, this hormone, which is secreted by the pituitary gland, is associated with premenstrual syndrome, irregular menstrual cycles and infertility.

DOSAGE

For all of these conditions, I commonly recommend 160 mg to 240 mg daily of a 0.6% *aucubin* or 0.5% *agnuside* extract (important active ingredients) in capsule form—available from Enzymatic Therapy (800-783-2286, *www.enzy.com*) and Natural Factors (sold by Vitacost, 800-381-0759, *www.vitacost.com*). Or I suggest 40 drops of the tincture in four ounces of water, taken once daily.

For best results, chasteberry should be used until the problem is alleviated and then for an additional three months. Women may notice improvements within two menstrual cycles.

Chasteberry often needs to be taken for four to six months or longer for long-standing cases of hormone imbalance that have resulted in infertility, amenorrhea (no menstrual cycles), irregular menstrual cycles or endometriosis.

Mild digestive upset, nausea, headaches and skin rash are infrequent side effects of chasteberry. Stop taking it if they occur.

Chasteberry should not be used by women taking birth control pills or injections. It also should be avoided by those taking drugs that block dopamine receptors, such as the antipsychotic medication *haloperidol* (Haldol).

As with most herbs, chasteberry should be avoided during pregnancy, although it is helpful for lactation in nursing mothers.

Lastly, some women experience an "adjustment phase" during the first few months of taking chasteberry. It is not uncommon for the menstrual cycle to shorten or lengthen, and flow can become lighter or heavier than what it was previously. This adjustment phase almost always normalizes after two to three months of use.

■ ■ ■ ■

Postmenopausal Incontinence

Postmenopausal women have a high prevalence of urinary incontinence.

Recent finding: Sixty percent of postmenopausal women experience one or more episodes of incontinence in a month. Postmenopausal women with diabetes are more likely to report severe incontinence—difficulty controlling urination, inability to completely empty the bladder and discomfort during urination. Treatment options for incontinence include Kegel (pelvic floor) exercises, medication and surgery.

Sara Jackson, MD, MPH, lead author of a study of 1,017 postmenopausal women, published in *Diabetes Care*.

Natural Remedies For Menopause Relief

Mark A. Stengler, ND, naturopathic physician in private practice, La Jolla, CA...adjunct associate clinical professor at the National College of Natural Medicine, Portland, OR...author of 16 books, including *The Natural Physician's Healing Therapies* (Bottom Line Books) and coauthor of *Prescription for Natural Cures* (Wiley)...and author of the *Bottom Line/Natural Healing* newsletter.

Nearly 38 million American women are between the ages of 40 and 54, according to the US Census Bureau. They all are in some stage of menopause. If you're among them, I'm sure you're wondering about the best ways to deal with the symptoms. Fortunately, several natural remedies and medicines can help. They are safe and effective—and some

work quickly, particularly if you have mild to moderate symptoms.

Menopause is a normal stage in a woman's life. Once a woman hasn't had a period for 12 consecutive months, she has reached menopause. In the US, the average age is 51. During menopause, ovaries produce less of the hormones estrogen, progesterone and testosterone. Meanwhile, there's an increase in the release of two hormones produced by the pituitary gland—*follicle stimulating hormone* (FSH) and *luteinizing hormone* (LH). Doctors believe the surge of these hormones triggers menopausal symptoms, including hot flashes (which affect three-quarters of American menopausal women) and vaginal dryness. You also may experience insomnia, depression and mood swings.

In the year or two before menopause, many women go through perimenopause, or premenopause, during which hot flashes and other symptoms usually begin. The menstrual cycle becomes irregular. A period of lingering symptoms after menopause is called postmenopause. The therapies I recommend are effective for women in any stage, from perimenopause to postmenopause—but not one of these therapies includes typical pharmaceuticals. *Here's why...*

THE HORMONE HERESY

Sixty years ago, doctors started giving women synthetic estrogen along with a synthetic form of progesterone known as progestin to control menopausal symptoms. Premarin, one of these formulas, has been one of the best-selling drugs in recent history—but I view it as one of the biggest scams of all time.

Premarin, and drugs like it, were said to offer many benefits, including prolonged youthfulness, a sound mind, improved libido, strong bones and a healthy heart. I never believed the hype, nor did many other preventive-medicine doctors.

The dangers of taking hormone formulas came to light a few years ago. Doctors and female patients were alarmed at the results of a study on the drug Prempro, a combination of Premarin and a synthetic progesterone called Provera. Prempro had been touted as a panacea for menopausal problems, but views changed in July 2002, when results of the Women's Health Initiative Study, which included more than 16,000 women, showed unexpected dangers from the drug. Investigators found significant increases in risk of heart disease, stroke, blood clots and breast cancer among women taking Prempro.

In 2003, the Women's Health Initiative Memory Study revealed that women 65 and older who had been taking Prempro had an increased risk of dementia. Premarin has been shown to increase gallbladder disease risk.

Additionally, the British Million Women Study found that the use of hormone-replacement therapy by women ages 50 to 64 over the past decade had resulted in an estimated 20,000 additional breast cancers and an increased incidence of fatal breast malignancies.

LOWER DOSAGE

The response of pharmaceutical giants makes my hair stand on end—they recommended lower dosages of the drugs, even though there were no studies showing that lower doses were safer. Companies also started promoting pharmaceutical antidepressants, such as *venlataxine* (Effexor), *fluoxetine* (Prozac), *paroxetine* (Paxil) and *sertraline* (Zoloft), for relief of menopausal symptoms, especially hot flashes. All these drugs have potential side effects—including fatigue, headache, worsening of depression and weight gain.

Fortunately, many natural therapies are readily available. Natural therapy's goal is to alleviate or reduce symptoms quickly without harmful side effects. I recommend starting with nutritional supplements—including various herbal and homeopathic therapies.

MILD TO MODERATE SYMPTOMS

Women with "mild" symptoms may be annoyed by occasional hot flashes. Those in the "moderate" category have hot flashes along with other symptoms. For example, if a woman experiences three or four hot flashes a day, doesn't sleep at night and has reduced sex drive, I consider her symptoms to be moderate. You can take these remedies one at a time or use a formula that contains some or all of the ingredients.

•**Black cohosh.** This shrub was used by Native Americans for hormonal problems. At least six studies have shown that it can help relieve hot flashes, night sweats and depression. One popular brand of black cohosh is Remifemin, which is available at pharmacies and at *www.drugstore.com*. Choose an extract standardized to 2.5% *triterpene glycosides* (an ingredient that helps control luteinizing hormone). Start by taking a dose of 80 mg daily and increase to 160 mg daily if necessary. Many women notice improvement within two to four weeks. You can take black cohosh for four to six months, then stop to see if your symptoms return. If they do, resume taking it. In rare cases, black cohosh can cause digestive upset, headache and/or dizziness.

•**Vitex (chasteberry).** This hormone-regulating herb has been recommended since the days of Hippocrates. Use vitex during perimenopause to reduce heavy bleeding and hot flashes. Take 160 mg to 240 mg of a 0.6% *aucubin* standardized extract or 40 drops of the tincture daily. Vitanica (800-572-4712, *www.vitanica.com*) offers a 0.6% aucubin extract, which is available at health-food stores. You can take it for as long as you have symptoms. Vitex should not be taken with birth control pills.

HOMEOPATHIC FORMULAS

Work with a practitioner trained in homeopathy who can match your symptoms to appropriate compounds. The following remedies are available at most health-food stores. For each, start with two pellets of a 30C potency twice daily. You should notice positive results within two weeks. After symptoms improve, stop taking the remedy unless symptoms return.

•**Sepia** helps with hot flashes, night sweats and vaginal dryness. It is recommended for women who feel short-tempered, irritable, have a low libido or when symptoms include incontinence or uterine prolapse (falling or sliding of the uterus from its normal position in the pelvic cavity into the vaginal canal).

•**Lachesis** is good for hot flashes, anxiety, headaches, insomnia, heart palpitations and irritability.

•**Pulsatilla** is for women who feel much worse in a warm room. It also is recommended if you have mood swings, weepiness or a strong craving for sweets.

•**Sulphur** helps relieve insomnia and is excellent for women who are constantly overheated, sweat easily and have a strong thirst for ice-cold drinks.

MODERATE TO SEVERE SYMPTOMS

•**Natural progesterone cream** is helpful for women with stronger symptoms. I advise perimenopausal women to apply 20 mg of the cream (about one-quarter teaspoon) on the inside of their wrists and forearms or other areas of the body one to two times daily for the last two weeks of their menstrual cycles. Do not use it during your period. If you're menopausal, apply the same amount one to two times daily. Stop using it five to seven days each month unless your symptoms return during this time. Postmenopausal women should apply 10 mg (about one-eighth teaspoon) one to two times daily, and be sure to take five to seven days off each month.

■ ■ ■ ■

Help for Yeast Infections

Menopausal women are susceptible to yeast infections because of the changes in their hormones. The use of natural estrogen (*estriol*) inserted vaginally can help prevent such infections in some women. Increasing estrogen levels locally in the vaginal area works to favorably change the pH level, so that microbes cannot grow as easily. Estriol requires a prescription from your general doctor or gynecologist. Also, some researchers think that this infection may be transmitted sexually, so cleanse the genital area before intercourse and make sure your partner uses a condom. Finally, certain homeopathic remedies work very well to reduce susceptibility to yeast infections. Consult a local practitioner of homeopathy for an individualized treatment plan. For acute infections, consider using Kreosotum, a remedy derived from beechwood. It is widely available at health-food stores and on-line. At the first sign of symptoms (itching and/or creamy discharge), take two pellets of a 30C potency up to four times daily.

Mark A. Stengler, ND, naturopathic physician in private practice, La Jolla, CA...adjunct associate clinical professor at the National College of Natural Medicine, Portland, OR...author of 16 books, including *The Natural Physician's Healing Therapies* (Bottom Line Books) and coauthor of *Prescription for Natural Cures* (Wiley)...and author of the *Bottom Line/Natural Healing* newsletter.

Less Invasive Alternatives To Hysterectomy

Esther Eisenberg, MD, MPH, project scientist, Reproductive Medicine Network, National Institute of Child Health and Human Development, National Institutes of Health, Rockville, MD, is coauthor of *Hysterectomy: Exploring Your Options*. Johns Hopkins University Press.

Over the past 25 years, advances in gynecologic surgery have caused a steady decline in the number of hysterectomies (removal of the entire uterus) performed in the US.

Now: A variety of new surgical techniques are giving women even more options for treating abnormal uterine bleeding and fibroid tumors.

ABNORMAL UTERINE BLEEDING

This condition typically occurs in women over age 45. It results from a high level of estrogen that is not balanced by progesterone. Ovulation does not occur, but the lining of the uterus (endometrium) thickens and is then shed incompletely and irregularly, causing bleeding.

In the past, abnormal uterine bleeding was treated with complete hysterectomy.

Alternatives to hysterectomy...

•**Endometrial ablation.** This approach, which requires no incision and is performed on an outpatient basis, stops uterine bleeding in up to 80% of women.

How it works: A hysteroscope (a thin, lighted telescope) is introduced through the vagina and cervix into the uterus. An electric current or laser is then used to heat and destroy the endometrium. Scar tissue may develop, which is likely to impair a woman's ability to become pregnant. Other potential risks include perforation of the uterine wall and injury to adjacent structures, such as burns to the bowel.

•**Thermal balloon ablation.** This newer technique appears to be as effective as endometrial ablation, and it typically has fewer risks. However, not all hospitals have the equipment that is required to perform thermal balloon ablation.

How it works: A balloon placed in the uterus and filled with fluid is heated until it destroys the endometrium without damaging surrounding tissue.

UTERINE FIBROIDS

Up to 40% of hysterectomies are performed to remove uterine fibroids. Although the cause of these tumors is unknown, recent research has linked them to a genetic mutation. Fibroids are almost always benign and often produce no symptoms.

However, fibroids can cause extremely heavy or frequent menstrual flow (sometimes leading to anemia)...chronic pain...bloating...pressure on the bladder and other internal organs...infertility...and/or abdominal swelling. In these cases, surgery is often the best solution. *Procedures to consider...*

•**Myomectomy.** Currently the preferred treatment for women who want to keep their reproductive options open, this procedure removes fibroids but retains the woman's uterus to allow for pregnancy.

How it works: A surgeon makes an abdominal incision, cuts the fibroid out and repairs the wall of the uterus with sutures.

•**Laparoscopic myomectomy.** This procedure is less invasive than standard myomectomy, but it may not be advisable if the fibroid is too large.

How it works: A laparoscope (a thin, lighted viewing tube) and other instruments are introduced through a small (less than one inch) abdominal incision. The fibroids are cut into fragments small enough to be removed through the abdominal incision or another small incision made through the vaginal wall. Most women can sustain a pregnancy following laparoscopic myomectomy. However, there is increased risk for uterine rupture at delivery because the laparoscopic closure of the uterine muscle may not be as effective as in a standard myomectomy.

In one out of three women who receive standard or laparoscopic myomectomy, fibroid tumors eventually recur.

•**Hysteroscopy.** An even less invasive technique than laparoscopic myomectomy, hysteroscopy is now being used for some submucous fibroids, which protrude inside the uterine cavity. (Many fibroids are embedded in the uterine muscle.)

How it works: After the cervix is dilated, a hysteroscope is passed through the cervix into the uterus, which is inflated with gas or fluid to give a better view. Because dilation is painful, local or regional anesthesia is usually administered. With hysteroscopy, fibroids are removed with an electrosurgical tool that burns the tissue so that the fibroids can be removed in pieces. The procedure, which requires no incision, is performed on an outpatient basis, and recovery occurs within two to three days.

•**High-frequency ultrasound.** This is a promising experimental procedure.

How it works: While the patient lies in a magnetic resonance imaging (MRI) scanner, a doctor uses the MRI image to aim heat-producing, high-frequency ultrasound beams at the tumor to destroy it.

The patient is awake throughout high-frequency ultrasound, and no incisions are required. Currently available at The Johns Hopkins Hospital in Baltimore, Brigham and Women's Hospital in Boston and Mayo Clinic in Rochester, Minnesota, this procedure has been found to be safe and effective in preliminary studies.

NEW HYSTERECTOMY OPTIONS

Despite the availability of newer treatments, up to 600,000 women each year still choose a hysterectomy for their gynecologic condition.

Reason: A hysterectomy provides a permanent cure for abnormal uterine bleeding and fibroid tumors and eliminates risk for uterine cancer.

Newer, less-invasive types of hysterectomy have sharply reduced hospitalization—to just two to three days for many patients—and hastened recovery to as little as a week.

•**Supracervical hysterectomy.** The uterus, but not the cervix, is removed through an abdominal incision. This surgery has fewer complications than total hysterectomy, but it still leaves a woman at risk for cervical cancer.

•**Laparoscopic hysterectomy.** The uterus is removed using a laparoscope inserted through a small abdominal incision.

•**Vaginal hysterectomy.** The uterus is removed through an incision inside the vagina.

The procedure includes removal of both the cervix and the uterus. It can only be performed on fibroids that are small enough to pass through the vagina. Vaginal hysterectomy can also be performed with laparoscopic assistance.

■■■■

Preventing Breast Cancer

Nearly 20,000 women in a recent study took either *tamoxifen* (Nolvadex), the only drug currently approved to reduce breast cancer incidence in high-risk women, or the osteoporosis drug *raloxifene* (Evista) daily for five years.

Result: Both drugs cut invasive breast cancer incidence by 50%. However, the raloxifene group developed 36% fewer uterine cancers and 29% fewer blood clots than the tamoxifen group.

Theory: Like tamoxifen, raloxifene helps moderate the hormone estrogen, but with fewer side effects. Raloxifene received FDA approval in September 2007 for breast cancer prevention.

Kathy S. Albain, MD, codirector, breast clinical research program, Cardinal Bernardin Cancer Center, Loyola University Health System, Maywood, IL.

■■■■

Screening for Older Women

Breast cancer screening and treatment for older women should be the same as that for younger women. Breast cancer is most commonly diagnosed between the ages of 75 and 79, yet many women over age 70 fail to have regular mammograms.

Also: Some physicians discourage chemotherapy because they believe older women can't tolerate it well, but this usually is not the case.

Helpful: When discussing treatment options with your physician, ask whether he/she would recommend a different treatment if you were younger and, if so, why he is not suggesting it.

J. Leonard Lichtenfeld, MD, deputy chief medical officer, American Cancer Society, Atlanta. Dr. Len's Cancer Blog can be viewed at *www.cancer.org/aspx/blog.*

Breakthrough— A Therapy That Beats Tamoxifen

Anthony Howell, the United Kingdom's first professor of cancer prevention, Christie Hospital, Manchester.

Otis W. Brawley, MD, chief medical officer of the American Cancer Society.

M.D. Anderson Cancer Center news release.

Loyola University, Chicago Stritch School of Medicine news release.

San Antonio Breast Cancer Symposium.

A newer drug called *anastrozole* could soon replace *tamoxifen* as the standard treatment for postmenopausal breast cancer patients whose cancer is fueled by estrogen, according to an international study.

Anastrozole (Arimidex) is one of a class of drugs called *aromatase inhibitors* and was significantly more effective than tamoxifen in a number of areas. More women taking anastrozole remained free of cancer than those taking tamoxifen. If cancer did recur, more time elapsed before the recurrence in patients taking anastrozole. In addition, anastrozole reduced the incidence of cancer spreading, particularly to the other breast.

THE STUDY

The study included nearly 10,000 postmenopausal women who had *localized* breast cancer—it had not spread to the lymph nodes or beyond—and had been treated with surgery.

The women were placed in three groups: Those who took tamoxifen, those who took anastrozole, and those who took both drugs. The women were followed up for five years following their initial treatment. However, after three years, the group taking both drugs was disbanded because the treatment appeared to be not as effective.

THE RESULTS

After five years, researchers found that 10% more women taking anastrozole were disease-free compared with the women taking tamoxifen. The anastrozole group also had a 20% longer period of time until the cancer recurred and 40% fewer instances of cancer spreading to the other breast than the group taking tamoxifen. In addition, the women taking anastrozole were 14% less likely to have their cancer spread to other sites in the body.

In addition, compliance rates were higher for those women taking anastrozole compared with tamoxifen, perhaps because anastrozole produced fewer side effects, although bone fractures and joint pain were more common than among women given tamoxifen, the study found.

The study did not show any significant improvement in the overall survival rates among those women who took anastrozole compared with the women who took tamoxifen. However, more time is necessary to determine if anastrozole will produce better long-term survival rates.

IMPLICATIONS

The researchers found that prescribing anastrozole immediately after surgery significantly improved results for patients, and they recommend giving anastrozole instead of tamoxifen to women for five years following their initial cancer treatment.

Currently, postmenopausal women whose breast cancer is hormone-receptor-positive—approximately 75% of all patients—take tamoxifen for five years after breast cancer surgery. The drug blunts estrogen's ability to fuel cancer growth. In contrast, anastrozole prevents estrogen from being produced. It is often prescribed for women following tamoxifen therapy.

"Results from studies suggest that it is reasonable to switch patients currently on tamoxifen to an aromatase inhibitor," say the researchers. The study was led by Anthony Howell, a professor at Christie Hospital NHS Trust, in Manchester, England.

However, some cancer experts note that aromatase inhibitors can have significant side effects, including an increased risk of osteoporosis.

Dr. Otis W. Brawley, a former oncology professor and now chief medical officer of the American Cancer Society, says, "This is the strongest of the studies I've seen so far that aromatase inhibitors are more effective than tamoxifen, and it will sway a lot of people. But

the problem is that aromatase inhibitors cause significant osteoporosis, and one worries that you might be buying a woman worse problems down the road."

Another issue, Brawley adds, is the higher cost of aromatase inhibitors compared with tamoxifen. That cost differential might lead some women to stop taking the drugs before the therapy is completed.

■■■■

Benign Breast Lesion Danger

Papillary lesions (benign growths in the milk-producing ducts) account for 1% to 3% of lesions sampled by core needle biopsies.

New finding: More than 20% of patients diagnosed with papillary lesions who underwent surgery or further imaging tests were found to harbor adjacent cells that increase breast cancer risk.

If you are diagnosed with a breast lesion: Ask your doctor what type it is and discuss whether removal is appropriate. If you have a papillary lesion that has not been surgically removed, monitor it closely with imaging tests.

Cecilia L. Mercado, MD, assistant professor of radiology, New York University Medical Center, New York City.

■■■■

Breast Asymmetry And Cancer

Researchers examined the mammograms of 252 women who later developed breast cancer and 252 women of the same age who did not develop the disease.

Result: Those who developed breast cancer had higher breast volume asymmetry (difference in volume between left and right breasts) than other women.

Theory: Estrogen, which has been linked to breast cancer, may also play a role in breast asymmetry.

Diane Scutt, PhD, director of research, School of Health Sciences, University of Liverpool, England.

Freezing Shrinks Benign Breast Tumors By 73%

Peter J. Littrup, MD, professor of radiology, urology and radiation oncology, Wayne State University, and director, image-guided therapy program, Karmanos Cancer Institute, both in Detroit.

George Hermann, MD, professor of radiology, Mount Sinai Medical Center, New York City.

Radiological Society of North America annual meeting, Chicago.

D octors are able to sharply shrink the size of benign breast tumors by using a small probe that freezes abnormal breast cells.

The procedure, called *cryotherapy*, combines ultrasound and the probe in a type of image-guided therapy that is a painless, quick and noninvasive alternative to surgery, says Dr. Peter J. Littrup, a radiologist at Wayne State University and director of the image-guided therapy program at Karmanos Cancer Institute, both in Detroit.

"We can treat major tumors on an outpatient basis with minimum discomfort. It is a great boon for patients and patient care," says Littrup, who performed the procedure in 27 women, reducing the size of their noncancerous tumors by an average of 73%.

Benign breast lumps affect approximately 10% of women, most in their late teens and early 20s, and they are twice as common in African-American women as Caucasian women, Littrup says. Although most lumps aren't removed, approximately one million are excised annually because of their size, continued growth or for cosmetic reasons, he says.

Cryotherapy is currently used to treat cancerous tumors in the prostate, Littrup says. He is also involved in trials using the procedure to remove malignant tumors in the lung and kidney.

LETHAL ICE

To perform the procedure, doctors will first numb the area around the tumor, which is visible through ultrasound.

Next, they insert a cryoprobe—similar to a large needle—into the middle of the lesion and inject liquid nitrogen into it.

An ice ball forms at the tip of the probe and continues to grow until the ultrasound confirms the entire lump has been engulfed, killing the tissue around the tumor, Littrup says.

The benefits of the procedure, according to Littrup, are that the ice is easily visible in the ultrasound so doctors can be precise in seeing the tumor, the method is painless and it doesn't affect the collagen in the breast, so it keeps its shape. Also, there is no significant scarring.

Insurers don't automatically pay for the procedure for benign lumps. "It depends on the insurers," Littrup says. But because the patients don't have to stay overnight, the procedure is cost effective, he says.

ANOTHER VIEW

Dr. George Hermann, a radiologist at Mount Sinai Medical Center in New York City, says the procedure is interesting, but he questions its use for benign breast lumps.

He says that physicians still need to do a biopsy, and then decide whether to remove any benign lumps.

Further, he says, if cryotherapy is used to remove a cancerous tumor, it's impossible to evaluate the mass afterward because it's gone. When a lump is surgically removed, you can study it, which is important to treatment, Hermann says.

But Littrup says cryotherapy has already been shown to be effective as a way to treat cancerous tumors (such as in the prostate) without surgical intervention.

■ ■ ■ ■

Breast Cancer Recovery Aid

I n a new finding, women with breast cancer who walked for at least one hour a week were 20% less likely to die from breast cancer compared with those who didn't exercise at all.

Theory: Exercise lowers hormone levels, which suppresses cancer growth recurrence.

For maximum benefit: Women with breast cancer should walk (or perform equivalent exercise, such as bicycling) a total of three to five hours per week.

Michelle D. Holmes, MD, DrPH, assistant professor of medicine, Harvard Medical School, and associate physician, Brigham and Women's Hospital, both in Boston.

Breast Cancer Patients, Walk for Your Life!

Michelle D. Holmes, MD, DrPH, assistant professor of medicine, Harvard Medical School, and associate physician, Brigham and Women's Hospital, both in Boston.

Whoever coined the phrase "walk for life" for fundraising and awareness-raising may not have realized how meaningful his/her efforts were. Many studies have established that regular exercise reduces the risk of developing breast cancer, but a recent study suggests that women battling breast cancer who exercise regularly may significantly lower their risk of dying from the disease.

THE RESEARCH

The study, led by Michelle D. Holmes, MD, DrPH, assistant professor at Harvard Medical School, analyzed data from 2,987 women with breast cancer who took part in the long-range Nurses' Health Study. This study revealed that women who walked one to three hours a week at a moderate pace had a 20% reduced risk for breast cancer death...walking three to five hours weekly reduced the risk by 50%. Interestingly, those who walked five to eight hours a week had a reduced risk of 44%...and more than eight hours a week had a reduced risk of 40%. However, according to Dr. Holmes, this may be more a factor of the data collection in the study rather than a real reduction. Most important is that, with exercise, there was significant improvement in risk for cancer death.

The immediate question, of course, is whether the women who were healthy enough to walk were more likely to survive anyway. Dr. Holmes explained that this was clearly their concern while conducting the study. Accordingly, they also conducted an analysis based on the stage of cancer, from one to three (precluding stage-four cancer, in which the disease has spread).

THE FINDINGS

Surprisingly, they discovered that the group that had the maximum benefit from walking was the stage-three group—their risk was 68% lower, apparently disproving the idea that those with more advanced disease and so poorer health wouldn't do as well. However, she cautions that there were fewer women in this group (about 260 total), and further studies are important. A contributing factor might be that women diagnosed with more advanced cancer may be more motivated to adopt a healthy lifestyle generally.

OTHER SPORTS

Although the study focused on walking, the women participated in a number of aerobic activities, including bicycling, hiking, tennis, swimming and jogging, as well as aerobics classes. The study designers evaluated these in terms of activity units and translated that to the equivalent number of hours of walking.

MODERATE AMOUNT OF EXERTION

It's encouraging for women in treatment to learn that they don't need to walk a great deal to gain benefit. Remember, a mere three to five hours a week was the optimum amount of time associated with decreased risk for death. Right now, there are many theories for why walking is so beneficial for breast cancer patients. The good news is that it does seem to be beneficial.

■ ■ ■ ■

Ginkgo and Ovarian Cancer

Taking a standard dose of ginkgo daily for at least six months decreased ovarian cancer risk by 60% or more and slowed growth of cancer cells in the lab by up to 80%. If you have a personal or family history of cancer, ask your physician about ginkgo.

Caution: Ginkgo may interact with blood thinners such as aspirin and *warfarin*.

Daniel William Cramer, MD, ScD, professor of obstetrics, gynecology and reproductive biology, Brigham and Women's Hospital/Harvard Medical School, Boston. His study of 1,389 women was presented at the American Association for Cancer Research annual meeting.

Breast Implants Linked To Higher Suicide Rates

Veronica Cornelia Maria Koot, MD, PhD, clinician, University Medical Center, Utrecht, the Netherlands.

David L. Feldman, MD, vice chair, department of surgery, Maimonides Medical Center, Brooklyn, NY.

James Wells, MD, former president, American Society of Plastic Surgeons, based in Long Beach, CA.

British Medical Journal.

Does having surgically enhanced breasts make women happier? Researchers found that Swedish women who had breast implants were 50% more likely to commit suicide than women without them.

The study showed that deaths of women with breast implants were higher than expected in the categories of suicide and lung cancer due to smoking. The authors suggested the extra deaths might be attributable to underlying psychiatric problems, something that plastic surgeons are generally on guard for. Dr. Veronica Koot, one of the study's authors and a clinician at the University Medical Center in Utrecht, the Netherlands, said that "very low self-esteem" might be to blame.

"This is not the first study to suggest that suicide rates might be higher [in women who have had breast enlargement surgery]," according to Dr. David L. Feldman, vice chair, department of surgery at Maimonides Medical Center in Brooklyn, New York. "Women are deluded into thinking that having larger breasts will change their life. It won't. It'll change their breasts."

A DIFFERENT VIEWPOINT

Not everyone agrees that the suicides can be linked to the breast implants. "That just doesn't compute with the information that we have in this country," says Dr. James Wells, former president of the American Society of Plastic Surgeons. "We don't know that we have a cause-and-effect relationship."

Part of the problem, Wells suggests, is inherent in looking at people from two different societies—in this case, the United States and Sweden.

Wells estimates that US plastic surgeons turn away clients roughly 2% to 5% of the time.

"There's an evaluation process by the physicians to try to identify those patients who seem a little unstable. Their job history isn't stable, they're bouncing from relationship to relationship," he says. "We need to spend time listening to the patient. Surgeons have a responsibility to say no as much as they have a responsibility to say yes."

EVALUATING THE PATIENTS

Koot agreed that different screening procedures could account for a difference in risk, depending on the country.

The typical woman seeking breast augmentation in the US is happily married and has several children, Wells says. "She is looking to reverse what pregnancy did in terms of her breasts and appearance," he says.

Still, identifying the "right" person can be as much art as science. "We try to avoid operating on somebody who has a propensity for suicide, but this is a tough call and some people will slip through the cracks," Feldman says. "It does point out our obligation to do a full evaluation and not just rush a person off to the operating room."

The American Society of Plastic Surgeons at *www.plasticsurgery.org* and The American Society for Aesthetic Plastic Surgery at *http://surgery.org* provide extensive overviews for women thinking about breast enlargement.

■ ■ ■ ■

Painkiller Benefit

Painkillers may reduce ovarian cancer risk. Women who regularly used nonsteroidal anti-inflammatory drugs (NSAIDs), such as aspirin, ibuprofen and naproxen, had a 28% risk reduction over a five-year period. Acetaminophen was associated with a 22% risk reduction. Not enough is known yet to recommend painkillers as a preventive. Consult your physician.

Joellen Schildkraut, PhD, associate professor of community and family medicine, Duke University Medical Center, Durham, NC, and leader of a study published in *Epidemiology.*

Nonsurgical Technique Shrinks Fibroids

Society of Interventional Radiology.

A nonsurgical treatment for uterine fibroids, known as *uterine fibroid embolization* (UFE), has a five-year success rate of 73%, according to a new study of 182 women.

UFE is an interventional radiology treatment that blocks the blood supply to fibroid tumors, causing them to shrink and die. Because it is minimally invasive, the treatment offers a faster recovery time than surgery and preserves the uterus—two factors that have made UFE increasingly popular.

THE FUTURE IS NOW?

"Some gynecologists have been waiting for long-term data before being comfortable recommending the UFE procedure, and now that we have that data, I think patients will be hearing more about UFE as a nonsurgical option," says principal investigator Dr. James B. Spies, professor of interventional radiology at Georgetown University Medical Center.

"The [study] results are comparable to *myomectomy*, a procedure in which the fibroids are surgically removed. However, UFE is less invasive, and women recover from it more quickly," Spies explains.

Myomectomy may be performed laparoscopically or through an abdominal incision.

"With any of the uterine-sparing treatments, growth of new fibroids is possible," he notes. However, the rate of recurrence after UFE is similar to that of myomectomy.

The next step is to determine which patients are best suited for each treatment, Spies says.

Uterine fibroids are common benign growths that develop in the muscular wall of the uterus. Fibroids result in approximately 200,000 hysterectomies annually.

The National Uterine Fibroids Foundation has more about uterine fibroids at *www.nuff.org*.

■ ■ ■ ■

Better Fibroid Treatment

The most common treatment for symptomatic fibroids (benign growths inside the uterus), which can result in excessive menstrual bleeding, pain and frequent urination, is hysterectomy (removal of the uterus).

Now: Magnetic resonance-guided, focused ultrasound surgery (MRgFUS) allows radiologists to precisely target fibroids without hysterectomy. The new outpatient procedure uses high-intensity ultrasound waves to heat and destroy uterine fibroid tissue. Side effects include slight cramping. The procedure is FDA-approved for premenopausal women who do not plan to become pregnant.

To locate an MRgFUS treatment center in your area, go to the Center for Uterine Fibroids Web site at *www.fibroids.net*.

Fiona M. Fennessy, MD, PhD, assistant professor of radiology, Brigham and Women's Hospital, Dana Farber Cancer Institute, Harvard Medical School, Boston.

■ ■ ■ ■

Ovarian Cancer Treatment

Researchers compared the care that gynecologic oncologists, gynecologists and general surgeons provided to 3,000 women ages 65 or older who had surgery for early-stage ovarian cancer. Patients treated by the gynecologic oncologists and gynecologists had half the mortality rate (2.1% versus 4%) of those treated by general surgeons. Women diagnosed with ovarian cancer should seek treatment by a gynecologic oncologist. To find one, contact the Society of Gynecologic Oncologists, 312-235-4060, *www.sgo.org*.

C.C. Earle, MD, associate professor of medicine, Brigham and Women's Hospital, Dana Farber Cancer Institute, Harvard Medical School, Boston.

■ ■ ■ ■

Cancer Vaccine

New cervical cancer vaccine will save many women's lives. The vaccine Gardasil protects against sexually transmitted human papilloma virus (HPV), which is responsible for 70% of cervical cancer cases. Gardasil, which is given in three doses over a six-month period, also helps prevent most types of genital warts. The vaccine is recommended for girls and young women ages 12 through 26.

Important: Vaccinated individuals should still have regular Pap tests to check for cervical cell changes caused by HPV.

William Schaffner, MD, chairman of the department of preventive medicine at Vanderbilt University School of Medicine, Nashville, is a fellow of the Infectious Diseases Society of America, and a liaison member of the Advisory Committee on Immunization Practices of the Centers for Disease Control and Prevention. He is vice president of the National Foundation for Infectious Diseases Board of Directors.

■ ■ ■ ■

Thinning Hair

Most common type of hair loss among women is *androgenetic alopecia*, in which hair thins over several months in a predictable triangle pattern. It may be caused by a hormonal imbalance and can be treated with a hair transplant or topical medication, such as Rogaine. *Telogen effluvium* occurs suddenly and strikes different parts of the scalp randomly. It often occurs after women have gone on or off hormone therapy for menopause or birth control, after pregnancy or illness, during periods of stress or when certain medications, such as blood pressure medication, are started or stopped. *Traction alopecia* is caused by tight braids or ponytails that pull on the scalp.

If your hair is falling out or thinning: See a dermatologist—simple diagnostic tests should reveal the problem.

Sandra Johnson, MD, dermatologist in private practice, Dublin, OH.

■ ■ ■ ■

Trying to Stop Hormone Therapy?

Stopping abruptly after menopause results in more hot flashes within the first three months than stopping gradually. Gradual stopping—reducing the dose by one tablet per week per month, so hormones are stopped in six months—reduces short-term hot flashes but makes them more likely after six months. Fast or slow stopping makes no difference after nine or 12 months.

Best: Work with your doctor to find the best approach.

Ronit Haimov-Kochman, MD, reproductive endocrinologist, obstetrics and gynecology department, Hadassah University Hospital, Jerusalem, and leader of a study of 91 postmenopausal women who had been on hormone therapy for more than eight years, published in *Menopause*.

■ ■ ■ ■

PMS Help

Prevent premenstrual syndrome (PMS) with vitamin D and calcium.

Recent finding: Women who had about four servings a day of skim or low-fat milk or low-fat dairy foods—which contain vitamin D and calcium—and/or calcium-fortified orange juice were 40% less likely to experience such PMS symptoms as anxiety, depression, headaches and cramps.

Elizabeth R. Bertone-Johnson, ScD, associate professor of epidemiology, School of Public Health & Health Sciences, University of Massachusetts at Amherst, and leader of a 10-year study of 3,025 women aged 27 to 44 years, published in *Archives of Internal Medicine*.

■ ■ ■ ■

Better Injections

Certain drugs and vaccines are designed to be injected into the gluteal (buttock) muscles, where they are absorbed into the bloodstream. In a new study of 50 people, only 8% of the medications injected (using a standard needle) into the women reached their gluteal muscles, while 56% of the drugs given to the men did.

Reason: Men tend to have less fat in their buttocks than women.

Self-defense: Before getting a shot, ask the doctor whether a longer needle should be used or the injection should be given in another area, such as the thigh or upper arm.

Victoria Chan, MD, registrar, clinical medicine department, Adelaide and Meath Hospital, Dublin, Ireland.

■ ■ ■ ■

Chest X-Rays Linked to Breast Cancer

In a study of 1,600 women who carry a mutation in the BRCA1 or BRCA2 gene (a known breast cancer risk factor), those who reported ever having a chest X-ray were 54% more likely to develop breast cancer than those who had never had one.

Theory: Genetic abnormalities can affect the body's ability to repair DNA damage caused by the ionizing radiation of chest X-rays.

David E. Goldgar, PhD, research professor, department of dermatology, University of Utah, Salt Lake City.

■ ■ ■ ■

Cancer Fighter

Drug fights aggressive breast cancer. Herceptin (*trastuzumab*), a treatment for advanced cases of HER2-positive breast cancer, is highly effective in preventing recurrences. Studies suggest that Herceptin can prevent about half of all recurrences.

Main side effect: Up to 4% of women treated with Herceptin in combination with chemotherapy may develop congestive heart failure. For most patients, the benefits outweigh the risks. Consult your doctor.

Eric Winer, MD, associate professor of medicine at Harvard Medical School and director of the Breast Oncology Center, Dana Farber Cancer Institute, both in Boston.

■ ■ ■ ■

Post-Cancer Fertility

Breast cancer survivors may be able to preserve their ability to have children. Chemotherapy often leaves ovaries unable to produce eggs, and doctors are cautious about prescribing fertility hormones to breast cancer patients because estrogen can fuel tumor growth.

Recent study: When doctors prescribed two common cancer-fighting drugs that also stimulate ovulation—*tamoxifen* and *letrozole*—before chemotherapy, all the breast cancer patients were able to produce healthy embryos that could be frozen for future pregnancies. Cancer recurrence was not increased in women undergoing in vitro fertilization using these drugs. Experts say it may be too soon to know whether the procedure is completely safe for women with breast cancer—patients are being monitored for

relapses. This procedure also can be used in women with endometrial cancer.

Best: Young women who have breast cancer and who want to be able to have children should contact a fertility specialist.

Kutluk Oktay, MD, professor of obstetrics and gynecology, and director of the Division of Reproductive Medicine and Infertility at New York Medical College, New York City, and leader of the study of 60 women, published in *Journal of Clinical Oncology*.

■ ■ ■ ■

Breast Cancer Disguise

Breast cancer may look like a skin irritation. This rare type of cancer is known as Paget's disease of the breast. Symptoms include a rash or flaking or a crusty area on a nipple.

Self-defense: Perform breast self-exams every month, and report to your physician any change—in the nipple or elsewhere—that persists for more than one month.

Carolyn M. Kaelin, MD, MPH, founding director of the Comprehensive Breast Health Center at Brigham and Women's Hospital, surgical oncologist at Dana Farber Cancer Institute and an assistant professor of surgery at Harvard Medical School, all in Boston. Dr. Kaelin is the author of *Living Through Breast Cancer* and coauthor of *The Breast Cancer Survivor's Fitness Plan* (both from McGraw-Hill).

■ ■ ■ ■

Phantom Risk

A dangerous heart disorder often does not show up on an angiogram.

New study: At least half of women with chest pain who showed no evidence of blocked arteries on an angiogram had cholesterol build-up that restricted blood flow to the heart. This disorder, *coronary microvascular syndrome*, which affects women 80% of the time, can more than triple heart attack risk.

Self-defense: If you have recurrent chest pain and an angiogram shows no blockage, ask your physician about further testing.

C. Noel Bairey Merz, MD, director of the women's heart center, Cedars-Sinai Medical Center, Los Angeles, and coleader of a study of more than 1,000 women, published in *Journal of the American College of Cardiology*.

Mastectomy Survival Rates No Better Than Alternative Surgeries

B. Jay Brooks, Jr., MD, chairman of hematology/oncology, Ochsner Clinic Foundation, Baton Rouge, LA.
The New England Journal of Medicine.

According to recent research, two types of breast-conserving surgeries have the same 20-year survival rates as the radical mastectomy. As a result of these trials, authors of an Italian study believe that approximately 300,000 women worldwide who have early-stage breast cancer will undergo breast-conserving surgery each year, rather than radical mastectomy, the previous gold standard.

"Whether a woman decides to preserve her breast or not, the chances of being alive and free of cancer 20 years from now is the same," says Dr. B. Jay Brooks, Jr., chairman of hematology/oncology at the Ochsner Clinic Foundation in Baton Rouge, Louisiana.

STUDIES IN ITALY AND PITTSBURGH

The first 20-year study, led by Dr. Umberto Veronesi of the European Institute of Oncology in Milan, Italy, looked at 701 women who had either received a radical mastectomy or a procedure known as a *quadrantectomy*, in which the quadrant of the breast containing the tumor is removed.

The result: There was little difference in the incidence of *metastasis*, or spread, of the cancer. As a result, the overall survival rate was virtually identical among women in the two groups.

Veronesi says the study shows that if breast cancer is diagnosed early enough, there's no need for radical surgery. "I believe that today the treatment of a woman with early breast cancer with a mastectomy must be considered unethical," he maintains.

The second study, conducted by the National Surgical Adjuvant Breast and Bowel Project in Pittsburgh, also used a 20-year follow-up. It compared a radical mastectomy with a *lumpectomy*, in which the tumor and a margin of tissue are removed.

Among 1,851 women, those receiving lumpectomy with radiation had the lowest incidence of a recurrence in the same breast.

The authors of the Pittsburgh study say it's unclear which of the two breast-conserving surgeries is better. The lumpectomy removed tumors that were no more than four centimeters in diameter, while the quadrantectomy excised tumors that were no more than two centimeters in diameter.

Brooks believes that the lumpectomy is the better of the two options because "it gives a better cosmetic result."

The Smarter Breast Cancer Drugs

Paul Goss, MD, PhD., director, breast cancer research, Massachusetts General Hospital and codirector, breast cancer research, Dana Farber/Harvard Cancer Center, both in Boston and formerly at Princess Margaret Hospital, Toronto, Ontario, Canada.
The New England Journal of Medicine.

The results of a major international trial of the cancer drug *letrozole* were so promising that investigators decided to stop the trial early.

Breast cancer patients taking letrozole, one of a new class of drugs called aromatase inhibitors, had about half the rate of cancer recurrences as women taking a placebo.

"The results are absolute, confirmed and credible," says study investigator Dr. Paul Goss. "An independent monitoring committee recommended that we stop the study by preset statistical boundaries, which we exceeded by at least tenfold."

TAMOXIFEN BENEFITS AND RISKS

An older drug called *tamoxifen* has helped women who have estrogen-receptor-positive breast cancer; that is, cancer fueled by the hormone estrogen.

Tamoxifen reduces the risk of recurrence by 47% and the risk of death by 26% for five years after surgery.

Unfortunately, when tamoxifen is used for longer than five years, it may actually promote the growth of cancer cells.

Women who are more than five years past surgery represent the largest subgroup of women with breast cancer, Goss says.

"What is unrecognized is that over 50% of recurrences unfortunately occur beyond five years after diagnosis," Goss says. "Because it continues to relapse almost indefinitely, there is no limit to the disease."

Doctors have lacked any appropriate tools for the hundreds of thousands of women who enter that critical post-five-year period every year. Until now.

THE STUDY

The letrozole trial started enrolling participants in 1998 and ended up with 5,187 women in Canada, the United States and Europe who were postmenopausal, had hormone-receptor-positive tumors and had been taking tamoxifen for approximately five years. All of the women had to be within three months of stopping tamoxifen and all were disease-free when enrolled. The trial was coordinated by the National Cancer Institute of Canada.

The participants in Goss's study received either 2.5 milligrams (mg) of letrozole or a matching placebo daily for five years. Letrozole reduced the risk of recurrence by 43%.

SIDE EFFECTS

The median follow-up was only 2.4 years when the trial was stopped. There are some drawbacks to stopping a trial early, including questions about side effects and the effectiveness of the drug over time.

At the time of the study's early closure, the number of women who were experiencing side effects in the placebo and the letrozole groups was approximately the same, except in the rate of bone thinning, which was slightly higher in the letrozole group.

Tamoxifen provides protection against bone fractures, but it contributes to endometrial cancer and blood clots. Women considering letrozole therapy need to discuss with their doctor ways to mitigate the risk of osteoporosis.

Letrozole has been approved by the US Food and Drug Administration (FDA) for the treatment of some forms of breast cancer.

The American Cancer Society has more information on cancer drugs at *www.cancer.org*.

What Most Women Still Don't Know About Breast Cancer

Carolyn M. Kaelin, MD, MPH, founding director of the Comprehensive Breast Health Center at Brigham and Women's Hospital, surgical oncologist at Dana Farber Cancer Institute and an assistant professor of surgery at Harvard Medical School, all in Boston. Dr. Kaelin is the author of *Living Through Breast Cancer* and coauthor of *The Breast Cancer Survivor's Fitness Plan* (both from McGraw-Hill).

Most women know to tell their doctors about any new breast lumps. But a lump is not the only potential warning sign of breast cancer. As a breast cancer surgeon who also has survived this disease, I know many subtle signs of breast cancer that initially may go unnoticed.

In my own case, the first clue was not a lump—but rather a tiny area of retracted skin on my breast. The mammogram I received the next day appeared normal, but I knew to follow up with an ultrasound (an imaging test using high-frequency sound waves). This test revealed a tumor, which a biopsy later confirmed was malignant.

Important facts that could save your life—or that of a loved one...

•**A swollen, red, warm and/or tender breast can indicate breast cancer.** Such symptoms can mean an infection, but they also can be caused by inflammatory breast cancer, a rare condition in which cancer cells clog the lymphatic channels in the breast skin, preventing the lymph fluid from draining.

Self-defense: If you're diagnosed with a breast infection that doesn't clear within one week of antibiotic treatment, your doctor should order a mammogram and arrange for a skin biopsy to check for inflammatory breast cancer.

•**Mammograms miss about 10% to 20% of breast cancers.** Even so, studies suggest that among women who undergo annual screenings, mammograms may reduce the breast cancer death rate by as much as 65%. And the technology continues to improve. According to a study published recently in *The New England Journal of Medicine*, newer digital mammography (which provides computer-generated images that can be enlarged and/or enhanced) is up to 28% more accurate than film mammography in detecting cancers in women who are under age 50, premenopausal or who have dense breast tissue (breasts that have a much greater proportion of dense tissue than fat). Digital mammography is not yet widely available in the US.

Self-defense: If you have a lump or another suspicious symptom and have already had a normal mammogram, request an ultrasound. This test can distinguish between fluid-filled and solid masses. It's a rare breast cancer that eludes both a mammogram and ultrasound.

•**Some breast cancer risk factors are not well-known.** More than 75% of breast cancers occur in women over age 50. You're at higher risk if you've been taking combination estrogen/progesterone hormone replacement therapy for at least five years...if you began menstruating before age 12 or stopped after age 55...if you've never had children or had your first child after age 30...and/or if you consume more than one to two alcoholic drinks daily. Dense breast tissue on a mammogram has recently been identified as an independent risk factor.

You also are at higher risk for breast cancer if one or more of the following is true: A first-degree relative (mother, sister or daughter) has had breast cancer...a family member was diagnosed with breast cancer when younger than age 40 or before menopause...a family member had cancer in both breasts...or you have a family history of ovarian cancer. This constellation of factors could suggest the presence of a mutated gene, such as the BRCA1 or BRCA2, which may be inherited.

STAY-WELL STRATEGIES

There's no way to predict or prevent every breast cancer, but you can lower your chances of developing or dying from the disease.

Here's how...

•**Maintain a healthy weight.** Gaining weight and being overweight raise the likelihood of developing a breast malignancy—and worsen your prognosis if you already have this type of cancer.

Reason: Body fat produces estrogen, which is one of the factors that increase breast cancer risk.

•**Stay active.** Exercise helps prevent breast cancer—probably by decreasing circulating estrogen. Newer research suggests that it also may improve long-term survival odds for those previously treated for the disease. In a recently published *Journal of the American Medical Association* study, breast cancer patients who walked or engaged in another moderate exercise three to five hours weekly were 50% less likely to have a recurrence or to die prematurely than women who exercised less than one hour weekly.

Best choice: Aerobic exercises, such as walking, jogging or cycling.

Weight-bearing exercises, such as walking or weight-lifting, also help to minimize bone loss—a significant advantage, since chemotherapy can lead to osteoporosis. (Chemotherapy can damage the ovaries, reducing estrogen levels and inducing early menopause in premenopausal women, which greatly accelerates bone loss.)

Self-defense: In addition to performing regular weight-bearing exercise, women with breast cancer should take a daily calcium supplement (1,000 mg for those ages 31 to 50...and 1,200 mg for those ages 51 or older) plus at least 200 international units (IU) of vitamin D. If you've had chemotherapy, experienced premature menopause or take an aromatase inhibitor (a drug used to treat postmenopausal breast cancer patients), ask your doctor what levels of calcium and vitamin D intake are right for you.

Tamoxifen (Nolvadex), the FDA-approved breast cancer preventive drug, also has been shown to conserve bone while reducing malignancies in high-risk women by as much as 50%.

Downside: Tamoxifen increases risk for blood clots, stroke and uterine cancer.

Some recent studies have shown the osteoporosis drug *raloxifene* (Evista) to be as effective as tamoxifen for preventing breast cancer and preserving bone in postmenopausal women—with lower risk for uterine cancer. Evista has been approved by the FDA as a breast cancer preventive and for preserving bone in premenopausal women.

Best: Ask your doctor if either drug may be appropriate for you.

LATEST ADVANCES

•**Aromatase inhibitors (AIs)** may offer even more powerful protection against breast cancer recurrence and death for postmenopausal women than tamoxifen. Whereas tamoxifen works by blocking estrogen from binding with cancer cells, AIs work by inhibiting estrogen production in fat tissues—our primary source of the hormone after menopause.

In a recent British study, breast cancer patients who switched from tamoxifen to an AI called *exemestane* (Aromasin) were 17% less likely to see their breast cancer spread to other organs, had a 15% lower chance of dying within about five years than women who stayed on tamoxifen, and had a 44% lower risk of developing cancer in the opposite breast. AIs do not appear to raise risk for endometrial cancer as tamoxifen does, but AIs do speed bone loss and are not effective for premenopausal women.

•**Newly developed tests** are enabling doctors to look at the genetic makeup of tumors and predict with increasing accuracy which are likely to recur or metastasize.

In the past, breast cancer patients had been routinely prescribed chemotherapy, usually following surgery, since doctors had no way of knowing which cancers would return and become fatal. New tests, which include "tumor profiling" (a more detailed analysis of the tumor than biopsy alone), take some of the guesswork out of deciding who will benefit most from chemotherapy and who is most likely to do just fine without it.

■ **More from Carolyn M. Kaelin, MD...**

Signs of Breast Cancer

A newly developed lump in the breast is the most common sign of breast cancer, but other red flags include...

•**Thickened, red skin in one breast.**

•**Any dimpling, puckering or retraction** (small depression) of breast skin.

•**Nipple scaling, flaking or ulceration.**

•**A newly inverted nipple.**

•**Spontaneous discharge from one nipple.**

•**A lump in the underarm.**

•**Persistent pain in one breast** (this usually indicates a benign cyst, but it should be assessed).

■ ■ ■ ■

Better Detection

Mammography plus ultrasound helps detect small cancers in dense breast tissue, which occurs in almost half of women. In the densest breast tissue, mammograms alone detect less than half of all invasive tumors. Adding ultrasound raises the detection rate to 97%.

Thomas M. Kolb, MD, radiologist in private practice, New York City, and leader of a study of breast cancer detection in 11,220 women, published in Radiology.

14

Healthy Relationships

Natural Ways to Much Better Sex

It's true that drugs can help with the mechanics of sex. A man with erectile dysfunction (ED) may have better erections when he takes Viagra. A woman with low libido may benefit from testosterone cream. Medications are only a temporary solution. They don't solve the underlying problems. Natural remedies often can.

CAUSES

Millions of men and women have impaired circulation, which can reduce the ability to have erections and diminish sexual sensation. Chronic stress dampens libido and sexual performance. Insomnia and low energy can make people too tired to enjoy sex.

Certain herbs and other natural products address these problems and have been used safely and successfully for hundreds of years. Natural remedies, taken alone or in combination, can improve all aspects of sexual energy and performance. They promote better blood flow, increase libido and make erections stronger.

Start with one supplement. Take it for a week or two. If you don't notice a difference, add a second or third supplement that works slightly differently.

Example: Combine ginkgo biloba (which enhances blood flow) with ginseng (which improves overall energy).

Always check with your doctor before taking any supplement.

Best choices...

GINKGO BILOBA

Function: Dilates blood vessels and improves circulation to the penis or vagina and clitoris. Impaired circulation is the most common cause of ED in men. In women, reduced blood flow can result in diminished sexual sensation and responsiveness. Ginkgo biloba is a very effective vasodilator, which means it opens (dilates)

Chris D. Meletis, ND, executive director, the Institute for Healthy Aging (*www.theiha.org*). He is author of several books, including *Better Sex Naturally* (HarperResource), *Complete Guide to Safe Herbs* (DK Publishing) and *Instant Guide to Drug-Herb Interactions* (DK Publishing).

blood vessels. In one study, more than 70% of men with ED who took ginkgo improved their ability to have erections.

Anyone who is taking a selective serotonin reuptake inhibitor (SSRI) antidepressant, such as Prozac, should consider taking ginkgo. It offsets the libido-dampening side effect that often occurs in people taking these drugs.

Suggested dose: 40 mg three times daily. It usually takes one to three weeks to work.

Caution: Ginkgo reduces the ability of blood to clot. Do not use ginkgo if you are taking *coumadin* (Warfarin) or other blood-thinning drugs. Patients taking daily aspirin, which also inhibits clotting, should be sure to talk to their doctors before using ginkgo.

ARGININE

Function: Increases pelvic circulation...improves erections...boosts libido and clitoral sensation. Arginine is an amino acid that is used by the body to produce *nitric oxide*, a chemical that relaxes blood vessels and promotes better circulation.

Suggested dose: 1,000 mg to 2,000 mg twice daily. People who take arginine typically notice the effects within a few days.

Caution: Patients with heart problems who are taking *nitroglycerin* should not take arginine. The combination could result in excessive vasodilation.

Also: Don't take arginine if you get cold sores from the herpes virus or have genital herpes. Arginine promotes viral replication and can increase flare-ups.

GINSENG

Function: Supports the adrenal glands, which produce hormones that affect genital circulation and the ability to have erections... modulates emotional stress...increases overall energy and libido. Ginseng safely increases levels of testosterone, the hormone that stimulates sexual response in men and women.

Suggested dose: 10 mg twice daily. People who take ginseng usually notice an increase in energy after about one week.

Caution: Ginseng is a mild stimulant that can increase blood pressure. Don't take it if you have been diagnosed with hypertension or heart disease.

YOHIMBE

Function: Improves libido and sexual response in women...promotes firmer erections in men.

Yohimbe is the only herb approved by the Food and Drug Administration for treating low libido and sexual dysfunction in men. It stimulates the release of *norepinephrine* from the adrenal glands, improving genital circulation and the ability to have erections. Women who take yohimbe experience greater sexual arousal.

Suggested dose: Follow directions on the label. Yohimbe works more rapidly than most natural products, so take it one to two hours before sex.

Caution: Yohimbe can cause sharp rises in blood pressure in some patients. It also can cause headaches and nausea. Use yohimbe only under medical supervision.

DHEA

Function: Increases sexual arousal in women...improves erections in men.

Dehydroepiandrosterone (DHEA) is a naturally occurring hormone that is converted to testosterone in the body. Testosterone and other androgens stimulate libido and sexual performance in men and women. The body's production of DHEA declines by about 1% annually after age 30, which can result in diminished sexual desire, performance and satisfaction.

Suggested dose: 5 mg daily for no more than three days a month.

Caution: Patients should take DHEA only if blood tests show that they have lower-than-normal levels. An excessive amount increases risk of side effects, such as acne, facial hair growth in women and sometimes heart palpitations. It also increases risk of tumors in the prostate gland. Men with a history of prostate cancer should not take DHEA.

WATER

Function: Increases blood volume...improves erections in men and sexual responsiveness in women.

How can good old water be an aphrodisiac? Because millions of Americans are chronically dehydrated—they don't drink enough water or they consume excessive amounts of caffeine, a diuretic that removes water from the body.

Dehydration can result in diminished blood flow to the pelvis and genitals. Adequate hydration improves blood flow and makes it easier for men to have erections. Women who stay hydrated experience greater sexual comfort and satisfaction.

Suggested dose: Drink at least eight full glasses of water daily. Limit coffee and other caffeinated beverages to one or two servings daily.

Sex After 50— Better than Ever

Dagmar O'Connor, PhD, a sex therapist in private practice in New York City. The first woman trained in New York City by Masters and Johnson, she has been practicing for more than 30 years and gives workshops around the world, and is the creator of a self-help sex therapy video and book packet: *How to Make Love to the Same Person for the Rest of Your Life—and Still Love It. www.dagmaroconnor.com.*

Most older Americans grew up not talking about sex. Through others' silence, they were taught to believe that sex was shameful and taboo. Any mention of sex between "old folks," in particular, made people shudder.

Sexual activity is a natural and healthy part of life. In fact, you can get better at sex and enjoy it more—at any age. I treat couples in their 80s and 90s who wouldn't dare tell their children or grandchildren that they're seeing a sex therapist. Typically, whatever the state of their sex life, therapy improves it.

With retirement's gift of time, you can learn how the aging body works differently from its younger self, what pleases you individually and how to please each other in new ways.

PRACTICAL MATTERS

Yes, bodies change with age. Many women start to feel old and asexual at menopause. Men may develop erectile problems. But most difficulties can be overcome.

Physical change: Chronic conditions, such as diabetes, thyroid disease, cancer, Parkinson's disease and depression, can affect sexual function. With heart disease, sex can cause chest pain, and with asthma, breathlessness.

Remember, intercourse is the equivalent of walking two city blocks. Check with your doctor first.

Physical change: Joint pain and stiffness from arthritis makes sex difficult.

Solution: Relax in a Jacuzzi or bath before sex…vacation together in a warm climate…find new positions that won't stress your sore spots.

Physical change: Many drugs—antidepressant, hypertension, heart disease and some cancer medications, as well as alcohol—can affect sexual function.

Solution: If your sex drive is down or you're having other sexual problems, ask your doctor whether your medications could be the cause and if switching might help.

Physical change: After menopause, vaginal tissue becomes less elastic, the vaginal opening becomes smaller and lubrication decreases.

Result: Discomfort during intercourse.

Solution: Don't avoid sex—increase it. The more tissue is exercised, the more it stretches and the more you relax your muscles. Using your finger or a dildo, gently widen the vaginal opening every day. If the problem persists for more than two months, see a gynecologist or sex therapist.

Meanwhile, smooth the way with a nonprescription water-based lubricant, such as Astroglide or K-Y Jelly.

Not as good: Oil-based lubricants or petroleum products such as Vaseline. They may linger in the vagina and irritate it.

Bonus: Applying lubricant may get you in the mood for sex. Or let your partner apply it as part of lovemaking. Good foreplay makes lubrication flow naturally.

Physical change: With age, men require more manual stimulation for erections, take longer to ejaculate and have a longer refractory period—the amount of time between an orgasm and the next erection.

Solution: Patience. These changes are an invitation to discover the slow, loving sex that many women, in particular, have always wanted but haven't received.

Erectile problems can be treated medically, too. Discuss the situation with your doctor. You may be referred to a urologist for medication or other treatment.

BEYOND INTERCOURSE

Couples in their 60s and 70s and older often ask me what to do about erectile problems and other issues that interfere with intercourse. I tell them to slow down—expand their sexual horizons, develop new sexual habits and start all over again. The goal is simply to feel more.

Our society fears low-level arousal—pleasurable excitement that doesn't lead to penetration or orgasm. But those who have always resisted "just touching" become gluttons for such physical connection once they realize how great it is.

Exercise: During the day or with a light on at night, one partner lies back and is touched by the other—but not on the breasts or genitals —for 15 minutes to an hour. The person being touched stipulates what's wanted in a nonverbal way. If you would like your partner to touch more slowly, put your hand over your partner's and slow it down. When the "touchee" is finished, switch places.

Simple interludes set a loving, sensual tone and encourage you both to overcome shyness about requesting what pleases you. Prolonged sensual touching without genital contact removes sexual anxieties…helps you become relaxed, sensitized and responsive…revives a sense of trust and well-being that you may not have experienced since you were stroked as a child.

You'll emerge from the interlude feeling wonderful about each other. Resentments and recriminations will evaporate. Making sensual, uninhibited love often follows naturally. If not, there's always next time.

LOVE YOUR BODY AS IT IS

Our society presumes that only the young and skinny are (or should be) sexually active. As a result, many older people avoid sex out of embarrassment about spotted skin, a protruding stomach, wrinkles and flab. (Do remember that while you are ashamed of your wrinkles and protruding belly, your partner's eyesight has probably also diminished!) A mastectomy or other surgery can interfere with self-esteem, too, especially with a new partner.

Your body is miraculous. Learn to love it the way it really looks. One woman attending my sexual self-esteem workshop said, "I did not learn to love my body until I lost it." But your body at any age is a gift. Value it for itself…not as it compares with anyone else's or to how you looked when younger.

Exercise: Stand together before a full-length mirror. Say what you like about your own body out loud. Do this exercise alone first, before sharing it with your partner. Then try the exercise with your partner, taking turns. Listen, but don't respond.

To learn to appreciate your body, admire it often. Come away from this event loving five things about your body.

If you look better, you'll feel better. I recommend exercise—walking, swimming, Pilates— to couples of all ages. Getting stronger makes both women and men look better and feel more powerful…more sexual.

EDUCATE YOUR PARTNER

The young body works without thought. As you grow older, you can—and may need to— benefit from learning more about your body and your lover's. The key to intimacy is to express your needs—once you have learned what they are—and to insist on knowing the needs of your partner so that you can try to fulfill them.

Special note to women: If you rarely initiated sex but would like to, take baby steps. Try asking for different ways of being touched, or take his hand and show him how you like to be touched.

Exercise: Turn up the thermostat, and hang out nude together. Sleep nude in the same bed even if you haven't done so for years.

Increasing Your Sex Drive—With Light!

Daniel Kripke, MD, professor of psychiatry emeritus, University of California, San Diego.

Ronald Swerdloff, MD, professor of medicine, and chief of the division of endocrinology, department of medicine, Harbor-UCLA Medical Center, Torrance, CA.

Neuroscience Letters.

Ultra-bright lamps may boost the body's ability to produce sex hormones, particularly for men, say researchers who studied the effects of light therapy on mood.

The importance of the finding is not fully established, but it's possible that light therapy could one day be used to control ovulation in women or treat people who take antidepressants and find themselves with low sex drives, the researchers say.

"It's a very promising lead," says study coauthor Dr. Daniel Kripke, a professor of psychiatry emeritus at the University of California at San Diego.

Researchers have known for decades that exposure to light affects the way animals live. Changes in the light from the sun, for example, set off hibernation in some mammals. Seasonal changes in light also control reproduction in rats and mice; they only mate during warmer months, Kripke says.

THE HUMAN FACTOR

Researchers are still working to understand how exposure to light affects humans. Kripke and colleagues discovered two decades ago that light therapy—shining powerful lamps at people's eyes—affects mood. Light therapy has become a common treatment for seasonal affective disorder, a type of depression that strikes when days grow shorter.

In his study, Kripke enlisted 11 healthy men, aged 19 to 30 years, to test whether light affects the body levels of luteinizing hormone, which is produced by the pituitary gland and also leads to the release of other hormones, such as testosterone in men. The men woke at 5 am for five days and spent an hour in front of a light box giving off 1,000 lux, much more brightness than typical indoor lighting. Later, they spent five days in front of a light box that only gave out 10 lux.

The result: Body levels of luteinizing hormone grew by nearly 70% while the men were exposed to the higher levels of light.

The researchers didn't look at women because the rapidly cycling hormones in their bodies would make it difficult to study the effect, Kripke says. However, luteinizing hormone does affect ovulation, he adds, and "we think light is potentially a very promising treatment for women who have ovulatory problems or long and irregular menstrual cycles."

TESTOSTERONE INCREASE?

Light therapy could also boost testosterone in men, potentially increasing sexual potency and muscle mass, he says. Researchers, however, did not monitor testosterone levels in the men.

A hormone expert cautioned that research is still needed. The study was small, and it's not clear whether the changes in the level of the hormone are significant enough to actually cause changes in the body, says Dr. Ronald Swerdloff, chief of the division of endocrinology at Harbor UCLA Medical Center, part of the University of California at Los Angeles School of Medicine.

For more information, visit the Society for Light Treatment and Biological Rhythms at *www.websciences.org/sltbr*.

■■■■

Stress Reducer?

Nervous about stressful situations, such as public speaking. Have sexual intercourse the night before.

Recent finding: Participants who engaged in intercourse before stressful events had lower blood pressure levels and felt less stressed the next day than those who abstained from intercourse.

Stuart Brody, PhD, full professor of psychology, University of Paisley, Scotland, and leader of a study of 50 people, published in *Biological Psychology*.

Heart Disease Patients Need Not Fear Intimacy

Holly S. Andersen, MD, department of cardiology, New York-Presbyterian Weill/Cornell Medical Center, New York City.

Exercise and sex are two aspects of normal living that men with heart disease often fear. However, a study from Italy shows that moderate exercise boosts sexual function in these men, including the quality of their erections...and they also reported improvements in their relationships with their partners.

The study included 59 men whose chronic heart failure had been stable for at least three months. Half of the men took part in a supervised exercise program of riding a stationary bicycle and stretching three times a week over an eight-week period...the other group did nothing. The couch potato group showed no improvement in either their heart disease or sexual functioning at the end of the two months, while the exercisers showed an increase in oxygen uptake during exercise (measured by a sophisticated test that shows how well the patient is absorbing oxygen) and the aforementioned improvement in sexual function. Researchers theorize that this might be because exercise improves blood vessel function and blood vessel lining (the endothelium).

IS THE STUDY BELIEVABLE?

Cardiologist Holly S. Andersen, MD, at the New York-Presbyterian Weill/Cornell Medical Center in New York City, spoke about the study. She points out that there is a much larger population of people who are living with coronary disease because medicine has become so good at keeping them alive…and that the quality-of-life issue has become especially important now. Dr. Andersen is enthusiastic about exercise for all of her patients, encouraging even the sickest ones to have some form of modest exercise. However, she specifies that they should do aerobic or stretch exercise only. Strength training increases pressure on the cardiovascular system and strains it—and it is definitely not recommended.

Dr. Andersen says that patients must start slowly and gradually build up their activity. Warming up and cooling down are also important. She stresses that patients plan their exercise activity with guidelines from the doctor who may well recommend supervised exercise to start. By performing aerobic activities such as walking, swimming or riding the stationary bike, she explains that patients allow their blood vessels to dilate, have better oxygen uptake and increase their heart performance.

Dr. Andersen says the rule of thumb is that when a patient can climb two flights of stairs (à la Jack Nicholson in the movie *Something's Gotta Give*), he is ready for sex with a familiar partner. Interestingly, relations with someone new is considerably more stressful, and likely needs a doctor's okay. She adds that patients who resume physical intimacy should be sure to continue to get some regular aerobic exercise out of bed.

Good Friends May Promote Good Health

Laverne Bardy-Pollak, author of the humor column "Laverne's View" for *50 Plus Monthly*, and a columnist for the nationally syndicated Senior Wire news service.

All the way through school, we live in constant proximity to our age peers and make friends almost without effort. Later on, especially after marriage, many adults grow apart from their friends and fail to renew or replace them.

Friends can cheer us up, provide a sense of community and continuity, share memories, offer tips for living better in a thousand ways, rejoice in our triumphs and commiserate in our sorrows. Having friends can even fortify our health. *Here's how…*

HAVING FRIENDS BOOSTS YOUR HEALTH

Considering the good feelings and stress relief that friendship brings, it's not surprising that having friends can improve your health.

In a 10-year Australian study of nearly 1,500 people age 70 and older, those with the strongest networks of friends and confidants (as measured by the degree of closeness and the number of friends, even if far away) lived longest. Contact with relatives, including children, barely affected survival rates.

A Harvard School of Public Health study of more than 3,200 people (average age 62) examined health-related effects of friendship by assessing levels in the blood of a marker for inflammation that's linked to cardiovascular disease. This was part of the ongoing, more-than-50-year-old Framingham (Massachusetts) Heart Study, supported in part by the National Heart, Lung and Blood Institute.

Results: Marker levels were lowest in the most socially active men…highest in the least socially active men. No such connection was found in women.

Another Harvard School of Public Health study, done in conjunction with the David Geffen School of Medicine, University of California, Los Angeles, found that socially active men ages 70 to 79 produced more fibrinogen, a desirable protein that aids blood clotting, than less social men (not in women).

Still, friendships may reduce heart disease in women. In a federally supported study, 503 women with risk factors for heart disease were assessed for the extent of their social relationships, tested for coronary artery disease and followed for several years to track who had died and why. Those with larger social circles had less severe disease than those with fewer friends—and were less than half as likely to die within a few years.

Conclusion: Having friends may help you to live better...and longer.

FRIENDS FOR REASONS AND SEASONS

It's unrealistic to believe that one friend can meet all our needs. Each friend meets some...or just one.

Examples: To commiserate with...see movies with...shop or dine out (or in) with...discuss troublesome issues with...and especially to laugh with.

It's fortunate that there's no limit on the number of friends we can have.

A few treasured friends—some, if we're lucky, are relatives, too—may be life-long, adding texture and richness to our lives, bolstered by decades of shared memories. Other friends enter our lives for a reason and then are gone. But even brief friendships can have purpose and value.

"DIVORCING" A FRIEND

As vital as good friends are, less-than-good friends can suffocate you and may need to be jettisoned. *How to tell the difference...*

●**Friendship should reduce your stress,** not add to it. A friendship that's hard work or feels bad is not a true friendship.

●**Real friends support you...**and help without being asked. They never judge you, belittle you or act superior to you.

●**Friends listen.** I dropped one so-called friend because her eyes always glazed over while I was talking as she waited for her next chance to speak.

●**Friends needn't agree** about politics or religion, but they must share the same values—what's important in life—or at least respect each other's.

Example: One friend who lived 20 minutes away phoned me countless times with minor problems, demanding my instant presence. I was forced to break with her. Later she insisted that she had reformed. I gave her another chance—and had to "break up" again.

Reevaluate your friendships periodically. You may have outgrown some. If any have become toxic, fix them or end them.

To fix a broken friendship: Identify what's wrong. Maybe your needs have changed. Then articulate your concerns (not easy!). If that doesn't work, give up and move on.

TRACKING DOWN LONG-LOST FRIENDS

There are no friends like old friends who knew you "when"...met your parents...matured into adulthood with you. If you miss chums from the old neighborhood, why not look them up? *Here's how...*

●**Ask mutual friends for contact information...**call their college, high school or summer camp alumni organization or visit its Web site...look on the Internet through Google or another search engine.

●**On-line phone books can help**—visit Whitepages.com...Switchboard.com...Anywho.com...Addresses.com...Reunion.com...Classmates.com...SchoolNews.com.

International: Visit Infobel.com.

●**Go to reunions.** Last year, I attended my 50th high school reunion, accompanied by my brand-new second husband. We had a blast—and I reconnected with a few old buddies. We've stayed in touch.

KEEPING FRIENDSHIPS AFTER WIDOWHOOD OR DIVORCE

When my first husband and I divorced after 23 years of marriage, I wondered which of our mutual friends would stick by me. After initial awkwardness, and to their credit, all remained loyal to both of us. To my credit, I worked at it. *Lessons I learned...*

●**Widows and divorcées pose a perceived threat** to married women friends. The suddenly single woman must put those wives at ease.

No longer appropriate: Hello and goodbye hugs and kisses with other women's husbands...playful banter...sexy clothing...double entendres. Over time, you may, selectively and judiciously, resume your playful behavior.

Common mistake: Asking girlfriends' husbands for help with home repairs or chores. Hire a handyman.

•**Relationships with couples change** when you're no longer half of a couple yourself. After divorce or widowhood, many men's social activities consist of golf or poker games. Women's get-togethers may be restricted to matinees, lunch and shopping.

Tip: If you miss your friends' spouses, invite couples for dinner occasionally.

•**When your life changes, your social circle alters, too.** In the latter decades, many people are single. Seek out unattached comrades to complement your stable of friends. You can't have too many good friends...but unless you work at it, you can easily have too few.

IDENTIFYING TRUE FRIENDSHIP

Potential friends are attracted much as lovers are—through chemistry and body language... the recognition of similar temperaments, intelligence, sense of humor, experiences, tastes and interests. The more two people have in common, the deeper their relationship promises to be. *How you'll know a true friend...*

•**Friends are people you genuinely look forward to sharing time with** and miss when you're apart for too long.

•**Friends reveal their weaknesses.** At our age, we (finally) know we're not perfect. Recognizing the same faults in ourselves strengthens the bond.

•**Friends accept each other's quirks and value their strengths.**

Example: My friends know that as a writer, I have an inordinate personal and professional craving for solitude. An old pal confided, "It's a good thing I understand your needs. Otherwise, this relationship wouldn't have lasted so long."

•**Friends reveal truths that you may not want to hear.** In turn, you can say what's on your mind without being hurtful or insulting. A solid friendship withstands well-intended criticism.

Bonus: Those who know us best may offer better personal advice than anyone else could.

•**Friends are generous and flexible.**

Example: Two old pals and I choose activities to share on our own birthdays. They love museums, plays and visits to the big city...I prefer craft shows, antiquing and being pampered at a spa. Obliging each other is part of the fun— and opens us to new experiences.

■■■■

Partner Up

Living with a partner is better for your health. People ages 30 to 69 who live alone are almost twice as likely to develop angina, have a heart attack or suffer sudden cardiac death as people who live with others. The risk is even greater for women over age 60 and men over 50. Living alone itself is not the reason for the increased risk. People who live by themselves eat more fat, are more likely to smoke and are less likely to exercise.

Kirsten Melgaard Nielsen, MD, internist, Aarhus Sygehus University Hospital, Aarhus, Denmark.

"All You Need Is Love" ...And Other Lies About Marriage

John W. Jacobs, MD, a psychiatrist and couples therapist in private practice in New York City, is an associate clinical professor at New York University School of Medicine and author of All You Need Is Love, And Other Lies About Marriage. *HarperCollins.*

Marriage is more fragile today than ever before, as evidenced by the shockingly high 48% divorce rate among American couples this past year. With so many marriages breaking up, it is clear that some of our basic assumptions about the modern institution are misguided—and even outright wrong. Understanding the realities of marriage today can help make your relationship more satisfying...

Myth: All you need is love.

Reality: Love is not enough to keep you together. Marital love is conditional and based on how you behave toward one another day after day.

What to do: First, be clear to your spouse about what you need from the relationship—what you can live with and what you cannot live with.

Ask your partner to think about that, too. Then share your views and negotiate how you each can fulfill each other's wishes.

Example: You may feel the need to go out with friends regularly without your partner, but your partner may feel hurt by this. You might negotiate to go out one night with friends in exchange for one night out with your partner.

Myth: **Talking things out always resolves problems.**

Reality: Communication has been oversold as the key to a good marriage, but many couples actually make things worse by talking things out. Brutal honesty often backfires, causing a spouse to dig in his/her heels instead of making changes in behavior.

What to do: Learn how to communicate skillfully by focusing on problems rather than fault. Use "I language," not "you language." With "I language," you take responsibility for your emotional experience rather than blaming it on your partner.

Example: "I feel anxious when we don't have things planned in advance, and it would be a big help to me if we could make dates with friends as far in advance as possible." That's better than making accusatory statements such as, "You always wait until the last minute to make plans, and then our friends are too busy to see us."

Myth: **People don't change.**

Reality: Change is always possible, and small changes often can produce big results. But most people go about trying to change their relationships in unproductive ways—by trying to get their spouses to change. Marital problems are rarely the fault of just one partner, and the biggest impediment to change is the belief that you aren't the one who needs to change.

What to do: Change your own behavior—this often is the best way to prompt shifts in your partner's behavior.

Example: If your spouse always seems to criticize you, try praising his actions on a regular basis. Eventually, he may reciprocate by praising you.

Myth: **Our culture's shift in gender roles has made marriage easier.**

Reality: The modern marital arrangement—in which both husband and wife work outside the home, and family responsibilities and decisions are handled by both partners—may be "fairer," but it has created its own problems. Confusion about roles, as well as mutual feelings of being taken for granted, can lead to resentment and conflict.

What to do: When discussing your expectations of your relationship, be on the alert for gender stereotypes, such as the idea that women cook and men take out the garbage. Apportion your duties and responsibilities fairly.

Example: You cook two days a week, and your spouse cooks two days a week. Order takeout on the other days.

Myth: **Children solidify a marriage.**

Reality: The stress of having children is a serious threat to a couple's harmony. Even when you feel that you are prepared for their impact on your relationship, your natural devotion to them will leave little time and energy for your marriage.

What to do: If you want to preserve your marriage, your children cannot always come first. Commit to regular alone time as a couple with weekly or biweekly date nights and occasional trips away from the kids.

Myth: **The sexual revolution has made great sex easier.**

Reality: Movies, television shows and advertisements have raised our expectations about sex, making it seem like everyone is having great sex on a regular basis and you're abnormal if you're not. But many married couples have sexual problems—they just don't talk openly about them.

What to do: Expect ebbs and flows in your sex life, and don't buy into the Hollywood image of what your sex life should be. Consider seeking help from a couples counselor or sex therapist if you can't resolve sexual problems on your own.

To locate a qualified practitioner, contact...

•American Association for Marriage and Family Therapy, 703-838-9808, *www.aamft.org.*

•American Association of Sexuality Educators, Counselors, and Therapists, 804-752-0026, *www.aasect.org.*

■■■■

Hang Up

Cell phones can often be a strain on personal relationships.

Recent finding: People who carry cell phones are available anytime to their employers, so the boundaries between work and personal time become blurred and family satisfaction declines over time.

Self-defense: Screen calls so they do not interfere with personal or family time…or let callers go to voice mail.

Noelle Chesley, PhD, assistant professor of sociology, University of Wisconsin, Milwaukee, and leader of a two-year study of 1,367 couples, published in *Journal of Marriage and Family.*

How to Deal with Defensive People

James Tamm, former judge and current adjunct law professor, Santa Clara University School of Law, is co-author of *Radical Collaboration: Five Essential Skills to Overcome Defensiveness and Build Successful Relationships.* HarperCollins.

A coworker responds with anger whenever someone disagrees with him. A husband retreats into silence whenever he gets into an argument with his wife. An employee buries her boss in piles of irrelevant information whenever she is asked a question.

These behaviors might appear different, but they're all just variations of the same problem—defensiveness. Additional forms of defensive behavior include habitually claiming, "I already knew that," when corrected…rationalizing or explaining away every misstep…or chronically making fun of others to deflect criticism from oneself.

Defensive people believe that their reactions protect them from outside attack. In fact, defensive people are unconsciously trying to shield themselves from their own doubts about their significance, competence or likeability.

We all get defensive sometimes and to some degree, but most of us learn to limit our defensive tendencies. Those who don't curb their defensiveness make life difficult for themselves and those who live and work with them. Their chronically defensive behavior promotes conflict and divisiveness…encourages rigid thinking that stifles creativity…and brings out the defensiveness in others.

Here's how to control your defensiveness—and better deal with the defensiveness of those around you…

DEALING WITH DEFENSIVE PEOPLE

The best way to blunt other people's defensiveness is to not become defensive yourself, even when provoked (more on that later). If you start to get upset, remind yourself that this person's defensiveness is rooted in his/her insecurities and has little to do with you. Arguing back will only make the person more insecure. *Instead…*

•**Be a good listener.** After the emotional moment has passed, offer the defensive person a chance to speak with you about the situation that led to the defensiveness. During the conversation, resist the urge to evaluate, criticize or suggest. Just listen intently, and take both the words and emotional content into account. Every now and then, summarize what you're hearing to make sure you understand—and to make sure the person knows that you're really listening.

Example: A coworker is upset with you because you criticized his proposal in a meeting. Rather than defend your position, listen to what your coworker has to say, then summarize —"You felt I misunderstood your recommendations" or "You were embarrassed in front of your colleagues."

By listening, you help the defensive person feel understood and accepted, easing his insecurities and making future defensive reactions less likely.

•**Change the way you argue.** Try "interest-based negotiation." With this strategy, your first goal is to state your opponent's underlying interests to his satisfaction. Your second goal is for him to do the same to you. Only then do you start proposing solutions. This creates an atmosphere of understanding that makes defensiveness less likely.

Example: I once mediated a labor strike in which the union insisted on a seven percent raise, though the union leaders knew that management couldn't go past four percent. The discussions became adversarial. Through interest-based negotiation, management learned that the underlying goal of the union negotiators was not the seven percent raise itself, but to make good on a promise they had made to their members to deliver a seven percent raise. The parties agreed to a seven percent raise for six months of the year, the equivalent of a 3.5% annual raise, which was within management's budget. Union members were happy with the 3.5% increase overall and pleased to have the negotiations resolved.

MANAGING YOUR OWN DEFENSIVENESS

The most difficult step in overcoming defensiveness in yourself is acknowledging that you are indeed defensive.

You probably consider your responses to perceived criticisms to be rational and justified when they occur. Reconsider them after the moment of confrontation has passed. Do they still seem appropriate, or were they unwarranted and unhelpful? If you're not certain, ask your spouse or a trusted friend—and try not to get defensive at the reply.

If you feel you tend to be defensive, identify the form your defensiveness takes. Are you belligerent? Uncommunicative? Overly talkative?

Other warning signs: Tightening in the gut …general sense of paranoia…adrenaline rush… feeling that you lack allies…a sense that you have been personally rejected, though the subject under discussion is only tangentially related to you.

To cut off defensive reactions…

•**Intercept the physical symptoms of defensiveness,** such as rapid, shallow breathing and a quickened pulse. It will be easier to alter your behavior if you can alter these physical reactions. Head to the rest room and splash cool water on your face…take a short walk to calm down…or if there's no time for a break, take a few long, deep breaths.

•**Monitor your thoughts.** If your mind is telling you, "This guy is out to get me," or, "She doesn't think I'm very smart," you're likely to become increasingly defensive. Respond to negative thoughts with positive self-talk.

Examples: "I know this is difficult, but I can get through it"…"They're entitled to a different opinion"…"If I listen carefully enough, maybe I can learn something."

•**Develop a reaction appropriate to your particular form of defensiveness.** If you tend to flood others with information when you feel attacked, force yourself to remain quiet for a full minute. If you tend to shut down, push yourself to say something. If you counterattack when you feel confronted, take a few deep breaths and find something that you can agree with in what's being said.

There are times when we must defend ourselves against verbal attacks, but these times are rare—and knee-jerk defensiveness isn't effective anyway. Defensive reactions make us feel temporarily better about ourselves but rarely paint us or our opinions in a favorable light. Defensiveness provides no defense—it only makes us seem less credible.

■ ■ ■ ■

To Wake Up Your Libido

Combine and drink equal parts of the tincture form of the herbs damiana and Panax ginseng to stimulate arousal and increase levels of the hormone testosterone. Works for women and men. Consult a health-care professional knowledgeable in herbal medicine to determine if the formula is right for you and what dosage you should use.

If that doesn't work: Ask your doctor to check you for a deficiency in *dehydroepiandrosterone* (DHEA). The steroid hormone is available at health-food stores and is a precursor to such hormones as *estrogen* and *androgen*. Ask your doctor if this is right for you.

Jane Guiltinan, ND, clinical professor, Bastyr Center for Natural Health, Bastyr University, Seattle.

Why Men Never Remember and Women Never Forget

Marianne Legato, MD, FACP, a physician and professor emerita of clinical medicine at Columbia University, New York City, and founder of Columbia's Partnership for Women's Health, is author of several books, including *Why Men Never Remember and Women Never Forget*. Rodale.

Neither men nor women can claim that their brains are "better." While men's brains are 10% larger on average, women's brains have more elaborate connections that make them more efficient. Male and female brains unquestionably are different, in terms of both structure and chemistry, and that can cause problems when we try to communicate with one another.

Most of us speak to our spouses just as we would speak to members of our own sex—then wonder why they don't seem to understand.

Here's how to communicate more effectively with the opposite sex...

NONVERBAL CUES

The female brain is good at decoding nonverbal signals, including facial expressions and tone of voice, perhaps because mothers must understand the needs of children too young to speak. When women send nonverbal signals to men, women are often dismayed to find that these signals are ignored.

Women don't realize that the typical male brain is not skilled at interpreting nonverbal communications. Men are particularly bad at identifying signs of sadness in women—though men are pretty good at spotting signs of anger and aggression.

Women: Tell him verbally when something is bothering you. A sad expression or the silent treatment won't get you anywhere. It's not that he is ignoring your feelings—he is just unaware of them.

If a man asks you what he can do to make you feel better, tell him. If you say "nothing," he'll assume that you mean nothing and he'll do nothing. He isn't trying to hurt you—men's brains just work in a more linear, literal manner. Because men often like to be left alone when they're upset, he might conclude that he is doing you a favor by giving you some space.

Men: Search for clues beyond her words when she seems unusually quiet or terse. She might be sending signals that you're not picking up. If you can't figure out the signals and she won't tell you what she needs, remind her that you really want to help, but it's hard for you to pick up her nonverbal cues.

LISTENING

The female brain seems to be better at listening than the male brain—women have more nerve cells in the areas that process language and put a larger percentage of their brains to work when they hear someone speak.

The more elaborate wiring of the female brain also makes women better multitaskers than men. Evolution likely made women this way so that mothers could keep an eye on the children and still get other things done. Evolution shaped the male brain to focus on one very difficult task at a time. Tiger hunts were more successful when the hunters could focus all their attention on the tiger.

Add men's inferior listening ability to their superior focus, and the result is a phenomenon most wives know well. Tell a man something important while he's watching a ball game, and he might not remember a word of it. He isn't purposely ignoring you—his brain simply isn't wired to hear what you said.

Women: Put him on alert that what you're about to say is important. If it's particularly vital information, begin with a gentle "I need you to look me in the eyes." If there are too many distractions in your present location, ask him to go with you for a walk or out to a quiet restaurant.

Men: Don't be insulted if she doesn't stop what she is doing when you want to talk. Chances are that she can pay attention to you even if she's occupied. If you want her undivided attention, ask for it.

PROBLEM SOLVING

The structure of the male brain makes men straight-ahead thinkers—when they see a problem, their instinct is to try to solve it.

Women are more likely to ruminate over decisions. They'll verbalize a problem and talk though all the implications and issues before they proceed. When women try to talk through their problems with men, they're often dismayed and insulted that the men try to tell them what to do. This confuses the men, who thought they were being asked for a solution.

Women: Tell a man the specific type of response you want before you share a problem. Are you asking the man for a solution, or do you just want to talk through the issue so it's clear in your mind? If you don't specifically tell him that it's the latter, he'll assume it's the former. If he tries to solve your problem anyway, understand that this is just how his brain responds.

As for how to respond to a man's problems, this rarely comes up. Men tend not to share their problems with anyone.

Men: Understand that women like to verbalize their thinking and don't always want you to solve their problems.

Instead, wait for a question before providing an answer. Ask what you can do to help rather than assume you know. And if your wife starts crying, holding her quietly works better than telling her she's being too emotional.

DIFFERENT INTERESTS

Women tend to expect their male partners to be interested in every subject they wish to discuss. That isn't fair. A woman wouldn't expect her female friends to chat about a subject that she knows bores them.

Women: Tailor your conversation to your partner's interests. (Men should do this, too, but because men talk less, it isn't as often an issue.) Find other conversation partners for topics that don't interest him.

Men: Encourage your partner to spend time with female friends so there's another outlet for the conversations that don't interest you. Don't get upset if she's busy with friends when you want to see her.

BETTER ARGUMENTS

During an argument, women are more likely to bring up past events. Estrogen increases the amount of cortisol, a memory-boosting hormone, released by the adrenal glands during stressful moments. Because the female brain has more estrogen, memories of old fights remain fresher in a woman's mind. The male brain finds it easier to forget emotional situations and move on. Maybe forgetting a close call on a tiger hunt made it easier for men of the past to continue to hunt.

Women: Use simple, declarative sentences, and state what you want in outline form when imparting important information to men. Leave out anecdotes and unnecessary adjectives. Take advantage of your ability to read his emotions to spot the signs of boredom. When you see them, sum up your argument with a closing statement and end the conversation. Try not to rehash old arguments.

Men: Try to keep women focused on the point under discussion. If during an argument she brings up a fight you had five years ago, tell her, "We've discussed that already and it isn't going to help to go over it again. Let's focus on the current problem."

Beat Bad Breath

Mark A. Stengler, ND, naturopathic physician in private practice, La Jolla, CA...adjunct associate clinical professor at the National College of Natural Medicine, Portland, OR...author of 16 books, including *The Natural Physician's Healing Therapies* (Bottom Line Books) and coauthor of *Prescription for Natural Cures* (Wiley)...and author of the *Bottom Line/Natural Healing* newsletter..

About half of Americans have bad breath (halitosis). Fortunately, a simple natural approach often is all it takes to eradicate the problem.

Several conditions may contribute to bad breath, including gum disease, degrading silver fillings, chronic dental and/or throat infections and ulcers and other digestive problems. It is important to work with your dentist to determine the cause because bad breath may indicate a bigger problem. *If your dentist can't find a problem, try these suggestions...*

Take one teaspoon of liquid *chlorophyll* (the green pigment in plants) straight or diluted in a glass of water after meals. Chlorophyll (available at most health-food stores) freshens breath immediately and supports detoxification of the digestive tract.

Many people who have bad breath have an overgrowth of bacteria in the mouth, which is typically caused by certain foods, sugar, lack of good bacteria and/or infection. For these cases, I recommend rinsing with *xylitol*, a natural sugar alcohol found in many fruits, berries, vegetables and mushrooms. Xylitol prevents bacteria from adhering to teeth and gums. I have seen good results with a product called Spry Coolmint Oral Rinse, which should be used twice daily. A 16-ounce bottle sells for about $5.25. It is available at many health-food stores and some dentists' offices.

When Adult Children Don't Get Along

Peter Goldenthal, PhD, a psychologist and family therapist in Wayne, Pennsylvania, is author of several books on family relations, including Why Can't We Get Along? Healing Adult Sibling Relationships. *Wiley.*

Many adults don't get along with their siblings—and sometimes it's not even clear where the bad blood began. Rivalries and hostilities among adult siblings can often be traced back deep into childhood, obscuring their origins. It's likely that your parents could be a significant contributing factor.

You're likely to have trouble getting along with your adult siblings if…

•**Your parents paid more attention** to one child than another.

Examples: A father shows more interest in the son who is active in sports than the one who prefers acting. A mother devotes more time to her son who has a serious health problem than to her healthy daughter.

•**Your parents implied that one sibling was better** than the other. There are few surer ways for parents to sabotage relations between children than to say things like, "Why can't you be more like your sister?" Even subtler, well-intentioned comments can drive a wedge between siblings.

Examples: "I'm proud of you. It's okay that you're not as successful as your brother." Or, "We should talk about money management," followed 20 minutes later by, "Your sister is saving a lot of money."

•**One sibling persistently bullied,** taunted or threatened the other, and your parents did nothing to stop it.

Sometimes these troublesome parental behaviors continue during the siblings' adult lives, sometimes they don't. Either way, the seeds of sibling rivalry have been planted.

Once siblings are grown, nothing their parents do is likely to cause a major rift between them—unless this animosity dates back to childhood.

Example: You might be unhappy that your parents visited your sister's home for the holidays this year instead of yours, but this probably won't create significant hostility unless you've always felt that your parents favored your sister.

WHAT PARENTS CAN DO

Most parents don't believe that they're to blame for problems between their grown children, but if one or more of the kids hold you responsible, citing perceived favoritism or some other reason, you might be able to help heal the situation with an apology. Say something like, "I know we made some mistakes, and we're sorry for them. It's too late to change the past, but understand that we do love you every bit as much as your sibling."

If the issue is favoritism, you might also point out that any unequal treatment that did exist was your fault, not the sibling's, so there's no reason why it should keep siblings from getting along.

It's worth noting that people who believe they were the victims of parental favoritism as children often see evidence of ongoing parental favoritism during their adult lives. Parents can keep the strained family relations from getting even worse by balancing their visits to their grown kids' homes…treating their grandchildren exactly the same (adults who feel they received less parental attention or praise growing up tend to believe that their children now get the short end of the stick from their grandparents)…and never telling a child who feels he doesn't measure up how well his siblings are doing.

WHAT ADULT CHILDREN CAN DO

If you or your sibling thinks, "My brother/sister needs to change before we can get along," your relationship is doomed. There's hope only if you can ask, "What do I need to do to make this relationship work?"

Call your sibling and say you would like your relationship to be closer. Suggest that the two of you get together and try to work through your problems. If you think your parents have poisoned the waters between you, share this idea with your sibling, but don't be shocked if the sibling doesn't agree. Siblings often remember childhood very differently.

Example: Your sibling might think that you were the golden child. While your parents were comparing you unfavorably with your sibling, they might have been doing the same to him/her.

Whatever your sibling has to say, listen without interrupting. Then, before responding, summarize what he said to make sure you understand. Discuss what you can do to improve the relationship before suggesting things your sibling can do.

Helpful: If your relationship with your sibling is so strained that you can't even call him to try to reconcile, start by seeing a family therapist. Let the therapist decide when and how to involve the sibling in the healing process.

If your parents continue to feed your competition, explain to them that they're preventing the family from being as close as it might be. Even if your parents don't agree that they're part of the problem, they might agree to be more careful about their behavior in the future for the good of the family.

Whether or not you're able to change your parents, be careful to treat your own kids as equitably as possible. People who feel that their parents treated one kid better than another often unintentionally repeat this behavior with their own children.

Is Your Parents' Marriage In Trouble? How to Help

Joseph Ilardo, PhD, and Carole Rothman, PhD, mental-health professionals specializing in elder care and family communication issues, Somers, New York, and coauthors of the recently expanded and reissued *Are Your Parents Driving You Crazy?* VanderWyk & Burnham.

Your parents have been arguing for decades—but now their marriage seems worse than ever. Or maybe they have always seemed happy together, but the marriage suddenly is on the rocks. A marriage can hit rough spots even late in the journey. When that happens, the couple's adult children typically wish to help their parents save the relationship, but what can they do to help?

STRATEGIES

When a marriage falters after decades, the best question to ask yourself is, "What's changed?" *Certain changes are particularly likely to create problems for older married couples, including...*

•**Increased togetherness.** Your mother and father probably spent many hours apart each week for most of their married lives. Retired couples often are together 24 hours a day, which can be a difficult adjustment.

What to do: Help your parents find individual hobbies. Suggest they return to activities enjoyed long ago...join clubs on their own...or spend more time with their own same-sex friends.

•**Different plans.** Perhaps one of your parents wants to travel, but the other just wants to be near the grandkids.

What to do: Help them reach a compromise by suggesting, for example, that they travel for a few months each year but spend the rest of the time at home.

•**Depression.** If one of your parents isn't happy—perhaps because of a health problem, adjusting to retirement or a child moving away—that unhappiness can taint the whole marriage.

What to do: Help this parent see that his/her marriage isn't to blame for the unhappiness. Suggest that he seek help—a therapist or support group, perhaps.

•**Financial difficulties.** Your parents' retirement savings might not have lasted as long as they had expected. Money problems can strain even the strongest relationship.

What to do: Remind your parents that they're not unhappy with each other—they're just tense about money. Help them find ways to trim expenses...offer financial support if you're able ...and point out that living separately is even pricier than living together.

•**Medication side effects.** Has either of your parents changed medications recently? Drugs sometimes cause changes in behavior or personality, potentially resulting in marital conflicts.

What to do: Consult a doctor about possible behavioral side effects of your parent's medications and alternative drug options.

•**Chronic illness or dementia.** The onset of dementia, perhaps as yet undiagnosed, can alter a person in ways that might frustrate his spouse. Illness or dementia can alter your parents' roles in ways that strain a marriage, forcing one spouse to become the caregiver and the other the dependent.

What to do: Help your parents locate appropriate support groups. If acceptable to your parents and financially feasible, consider hiring someone to ease the caregiver's burden.

•**Loss of friends.** Parents may be dealing with friends dying or retiring to different parts of the country. This can alter their social circles and outlook on life.

What to do: Encourage your parents to continue to expand their social circle by joining clubs or other groups.

•**Declining driving ability.** The loss of the ability to drive safely is a common source of arguments in older couples.

What to do: Ask a family doctor to decide if a parent can still drive safely, or let a driver's test decide so that it isn't just one parent telling the other he's not capable. Look into senior transport programs in your area, or arrange for family, friends or volunteer drivers to provide rides on a regular basis so that your parent isn't stranded.

YOUR PROPER ROLE

If your parents don't want your help with their marital problems, don't force the issue. Some parents aren't comfortable sharing their problems with their kids. When that's the case, you'll only make things worse by interfering. If you're not confident that your input will be welcomed, ask, "Is this something you would like my help with?" If the answer is no, let your parents know that you love them both…that you're there for them if they change their minds…and that you can help them find a third party to help, such as a professional marriage counselor, if they would prefer.

You won't help your parents' marriage by taking sides in their arguments. As soon as you side with one parent, the other will feel ganged up on and become wary of your continued involvement. Even if you're certain one parent is completely to blame, remember that you might not know the whole story.

Exception: If one parent is suffering from dementia or serious depression, you may need to take a more active role in helping both parents find appropriate medical and psychological help.

If your parents burden you with their problems but won't listen to your advice, tell them they must let you help or leave you out of it. Make it clear that you'll cut visits short if they can't be civil to each other. Keep in mind that you're not responsible for their marriage. If you have offered assistance and a sympathetic ear, you have done all you can do.

Do You Have a Short Fuse? Five Ways to Break the Anger Habit

Brenda Shoshanna, PhD, a psychologist and therapist for more than 25 years, is author of The Anger Diet: 30 Days to Stress-Free Living *(Andrews McMeel) and* Zen Miracles: Finding Peace in an Insane World *(Wiley).*

Expressing anger at your spouse, your boss or the driver in front of you may make you feel more powerful and less vulnerable—but only for a short time. It rarely resolves feelings and often intensifies them. Over time, anger can become addictive. You don't even recognize that you are angry or investigate why.

Even if you don't outwardly express your anger, it can be destructive. Repressed anger can be a root cause of anxiety, depression, overeating and other problems. *To reduce anger…*

1. GAIN CONTROL

The moment you begin to sense anger rising in you…

•**Regain your physical equilibrium.** Stop talking, break eye contact with the other person and/or breathe deeply.

•**Avoid personalizing the situation.** That cashier isn't just being rude to you—she is rude to everybody. If her parents, teachers and bosses couldn't teach her to be polite, how are a few words from you going to change anything? It's a waste of your emotional and intellectual energy to confront her.

•**Gain perspective** by placing your anger in a larger context. Imagine yourself looking back at the incident a year from now. Would it matter?

Example: I had a patient who had a wonderful new wife. She had a habit of talking to her friends on the phone late at night. He felt she was taking time away from him, and he would blow up at her. The next morning, he would apologize profusely, but she was left feeling wounded. He had tried asking his wife to spend less time on the phone, but she felt he was being unreasonable. I suggested that whenever he was in a rage, he write down five great things he got out of their relationship. This helped remind him of what was really important.

2. TURN A FOE INTO A FRIEND

Change your perceptions by thinking about what you can do to turn a perceived "enemy" into a friend.

Example: I had a patient who was furious because a particular employee of his kept showing up late for work. My patient saw this as a conscious refusal to be a team member and submit to the established channels of authority.

I suggested that instead of reprimanding the employee, my patient ask what he could do to help the employee arrive at work on time. It turned out that the employee was a single parent who was struggling with child-care issues but was too proud to admit it. My patient altered the man's working hours and earned an ally in his office.

3. STOP OBSESSING

Anger builds when you dwell on an incident, playing it over and over in your mind in an obsessive loop. Instead, direct your mental attention elsewhere.

Example: One patient was a hardworking manager at an insurance company. He was convinced that his boss didn't like him. The loop in his head kept saying, "You're going to be passed over for promotion." His resulting anger expressed itself in cold and distant behavior toward the boss. He turned down social invitations, kept conversations short and never smiled. In reality, his boss valued my patient's work but was turned off by his curt actions. When my patient realized how he was fueling this negative situation, he changed his self-talk. He told himself that he was doing a fine job and that his boss recognized it. He also became aware of the boss's needs and began to reach out to him and offer support. A promotion followed naturally.

4. TAKE THE HIGH ROAD

Avoid responding to an insult with an insult. It only escalates situations and can inflict long-term wounds. Realize that the other person is probably acting out of pain, fear or weakness. Respond with, "What do you need from me right now?" This cuts through the other person's anger.

Example: I worked with a couple whose arguments would escalate quickly and viciously. I suggested to the woman that the next time her husband insulted her, she not lash out but ask her husband what he needed. The next week, the woman agreed to meet her husband at a cocktail party after work. When she arrived, he snapped, "You're late." Instead of snapping back, she asked her husband what he needed. That stopped the argument cold. It turned out that he was angry because he had been uncomfortable waiting at the party alone. He didn't feel as capable as she did in social situations. He wanted her company and the warm, engaging manner in which she met people. Simply communicating this defused the anger between them.

5. LET GO OF A GRUDGE

We like to nurture old hurts because it legitimizes our ill thoughts or bad behavior.

Example: One patient had held a grudge against her husband for decades. At their engagement party more than 20 years earlier, her husband had commented in front of the entire family how beautiful her sister looked that night, but he hadn't commented on my patient's appearance. She felt deeply hurt and thought that forgiving her husband would mean she was weak and lacked self-esteem. I told her that dropping the grudge would be healing, giving her the freedom and clarity to improve their relationship. *How to let go of a grudge…*

•**Think about times when you might have behaved in a similar way.** My patient realized that she had hurt her husband's feelings in the past by talking negatively about him in front of his own family.

•**Figure out what you need to do to release your grudge.** My patient wanted her husband to acknowledge that she was beautiful to him.

•**Ask for what you want.** Express your needs clearly. My patient discussed her grudge with her husband. He responded, "I think you are the most beautiful woman in the world!" After hearing that, her anger disappeared.

15

Your Skin & Senses

Look Younger Without Surgery

Recently, the science of reducing wrinkles has been transformed by the introduction of remarkable new devices and treatments that don't involve surgery. *Here are the latest developments that could help men and women alike look and feel better if they are concerned about wrinkles...*

•**Digital imaging machine** that provides a computerized analysis of your skin. A device called Visia, made by Canfield Clinical Systems, uses a computer-aided digital camera to analyze facial skin in minute detail.

It gives doctors an unprecedented ability to diagnose skin conditions and monitor the effectiveness of various treatments.

How it works: While the patient's head is immobilized, digital photographs are taken under different types of light to identify the precise

location and depth of various skin features, including wrinkles, brown spots, enlarged pores and acne. Ultraviolet light is used to scan for latent sun damage, which will emerge as the patient gets older.

When the analysis is complete, the patient's profile is matched against a database containing thousands of profiles.

A percentile score shows how the patient's skin compares with that of people of similar age, gender and skin type. This analysis can then be used to guide doctors in prescribing and administering treatments. On subsequent visits, new digital images are taken to measure how well the skin is responding.

•**Laser treatment** that stimulates skin to renew itself. *Intense pulsed light (IPL) photorejuvenation* is becoming the treatment of choice

Barry DiBernardo, MD, a board-certified plastic surgeon; director, New Jersey Plastic Surgery, a private practice, Montclair; chief, aesthetic surgery program, Mountainside Hospital, Montclair; and associate clinical professor of plastic surgery, University of Medicine and Dentistry of New Jersey, Newark. He is a spokesperson for the American Society for Aesthetic Plastic Surgery, and past president of the New Jersey Society of Plastic Surgeons.

for eliminating fine wrinkles, brown spots, broken capillaries and birthmarks—all without any recovery time.

How it works: This treatment produces light pulses at a variety of wavelengths, which penetrate the skin to different depths, depending on the problem being treated (brown spots tend to lie near the surface, for example, while broken capillaries are slightly below).

This allows blemishes to be treated precisely without damaging surrounding tissue. Even better, IPL can penetrate below the top layer of skin (epidermis) to stimulate the cells that produce *collagen* and *elastin*—naturally occurring tissues that make skin more firm and elastic, and which we all tend to lose as we get older. IPL photorejuvenation reverses this aging effect, making skin tighter and plumper.

While IPL has been around for a number of years, a new machine called the Lumenis One (manufactured by Lumenis) represents a significant advance over previous IPL devices.

Among other things, its computer has an improved ability to deliver light at exactly the right location. This new device is so good at removing difficult-to-treat blemishes—and rejuvenating the skin—that even longtime patients praise its effectiveness.

This treatment is available in most states. To find a practitioner in your area, call Lumenis at 877-586-3647.

Sessions last approximately 20 minutes. Typically, patients undergo a series of IPL treatments over several weeks, followed by a maintenance treatment every six months.

With older IPL technology, treatments lasted 45 minutes, but the maintenance intervals were the same.

Cost: $200 to $500 per treatment.

•**Radio frequency devices** that use radio frequency to tighten the skin have been available for approximately two years, but a new device called Titan (manufactured by Cutera) represents a big improvement over previous machines—it is safer, more effective and less costly. It is available throughout the US and abroad. Radio frequency devices operate in the infrared range to heat the tissue under the skin surface, causing loose skin and its underlying collagen to contract and tighten. The treatment is effective even on large wrinkles.

Since it doesn't remove any layers of skin, there is no flaking or redness following the treatment, eliminating the need for recovery time.

Radio frequency treatment is currently approved by the US Food and Drug Administration (FDA) for use on the forehead and around the eyes. Approval is pending for use on cheek folds and the neck area.

A series of treatments may be needed for optimal results. It is not yet known how long the results will last.

Cost: $500 to $2,500 per treatment, depending on the area covered and the amount of time involved.

•**Hyaluronic filler** that replaces collagen. Deeper lines can be temporarily eliminated by injecting a filler material into the fat layer directly beneath the depressed area.

Until recently, the only filler approved for use in the US was *bovine collagen*, which is derived from cattle.

Collagen injections last approximately three months and require allergy testing before use.

The FDA has approved Restylane®, a hyaluronic acid product already available in approximately 60 countries.

Because hyaluronic acid occurs naturally in humans, it's nonallergenic, and no skin test is necessary.

In addition, Restylane injections last much longer than collagen injections—typically up to one year.

Many dermatologists and aesthetic surgeons now use Restylane exclusively, while others continue to offer both Restylane and collagen.

Cost: $500 to $1,000 per treatment.

MULTI-TREATMENT SKIN MAINTENANCE

Taking advantage of the array of new tools described above, many people are now adopting a maintenance program where they see a doctor (either a plastic surgeon, dermatologist or other medical doctor who has been trained to perform aesthetic services) every six months for IPL treatment and Botox® injections, and on every second visit—once a year—they get a Restylane touch-up. Other procedures are done as needed, including radio frequency treatment and *CO$_2$ laser resurfacing* (which produces more dramatic results than IPL, but also requires recovery time).

The final component of the program is a good home-care regimen—including regular use of sunblock to prevent ultraviolet (UV) damage, as well as products that speed up the turnover of the skin cells.

Bottom line: People who decide to follow this skin rejuvenation program not only have great-looking skin, but they also have a less invasive alternative to cosmetic surgery as they get older.

Cures for Adult Acne

Richard G. Fried, MD, PhD, clinical director of Yardley Dermatology Associates, a skin-enhancement and wellness center in Yardley, PA, is author of *Healing Adult Acne.* New Harbinger Publications.

A cne used to be rare in adults. No more. It can occur in people in their 20s and 30s—and some people continue to have acne into their 40s and 50s. In a recent study, 34% of participants who experienced adult-onset acne never had it during adolescence.

Doctors don't know why adult acne is on the rise, but one factor could be that we have busier lives and experience more stress than in the past. Stress triggers the release of hormones, such as testosterone (in women and men), and chemicals, such as neuropeptides, that increase skin oils and impair facial circulation. Contrary to popular belief, what you eat has little effect on acne.

Adult acne tends to affect deeper skin layers than adolescent acne. There's more inflammation and a greater risk of scarring.

THE ROOT OF ACNE

Acne occurs when hair follicles become plugged with oil and abnormally thick, sticky dead skin cells. Follicles are bulblike structures that encase hair roots and are attached to oil-producing glands. The oil travels up the hair shaft to the skin surface. Adults who produce excessive oil—due to high levels of testosterone, for example—may experience blockages in the follicles. The trapped oil (sebum) provides a haven for bacteria, which can cause inflammation and infection, resulting in acne.

About 54% of adults with acne are women, probably because their skin is more sensitive to testosterone's effects.

BEST TREATMENTS

To treat acne, start with step one, then move on to subsequent steps if there isn't substantial clearing in two to four weeks…

•**Step 1.** Benzoyl peroxide is the main ingredient in dozens of acne lotions, many of which are available over-the-counter. It has antibacterial/anti-inflammatory effects that usually work for mild acne. Use a 2.5% formula (such as PanOxyl AQ 2.5% Gel) for dry or sensitive skin…a 7% to 10% formula (such as Clearasil Maximum Strength medicated cream) for oily skin. Apply to affected areas once daily.

Helpful: Also apply a salicylic acid product (such as Salacid), which reduces swelling and inflammation. Use benzoyl peroxide and salicylic acid at different times of day, perhaps benzoyl peroxide at night and salicylic acid in the morning. The combination gives better results.

•**Step 2.** Retinoids, prescription topical products, such as Retin-A, Renova and Avita, help unblock hair follicles. These products may cause irritation. Apply twice weekly initially, then increase to once daily as skin adjusts.

Important: Benzoyl peroxide reduces the effects of retinoids. You can use them both, but not at the same time.

•**Step 3.** Combination ointment. Prescription products, such as Duac, contain both benzoyl peroxide and an antibiotic. Patients with mild-to-moderate acne who don't respond to other products usually do well with these.

•**Step 4.** Periostat. Available by prescription, this oral drug contains a low dose of the antibiotic *doxycycline.* It doesn't have antibiotic properties at this dose but does act as an anti-inflammatory. When used in combination with acne ointments, such as benzoyl peroxide or topical retinoids, it is very effective in most patients (though it may need to be taken for months).

•**Step 5.** *Isotretinoin* is a prescription vitamin-A derivative, taken in pill form, that can eliminate acne in most patients. It helps normalize hair follicles, so cells don't thicken and clog the pores, and can prevent acne from coming back.

Women who are pregnant or planning to become pregnant cannot take isotretinoin (Accutane, Claravis) because it increases the risk of birth defects.

•**Step 6.** Smoothbeam laser. About 40% of adults with severe acne experience substantial improvements with laser therapy. The 1,450-nanometer laser wavelength targets the sebaceous glands and can eliminate excess oil.

The procedure takes 15 to 20 minutes and is relatively painless—although there may be some irritation/redness for several days. Most patients require four to six treatments, usually given one month apart.

Cost: About $150–$500/treatment depending on the size of the area treated, not covered by insurance.

■■■■

Green Tea for Acne?

Green tea provides better acne control than traditional medication.

Recent finding: Patients with moderate to severe acne showed significant improvement after applying a specially formulated 3% green tea solution to their skin twice daily for 12 weeks. The solution cleared skin as effectively as the conventional acne medication benzoyl peroxide but with less itching, peéling and other side effects. Green tea cream is available at health-food stores.

Jennifer Gan-Wong, MD, dermatologist, Memorial Medical Center, Manila, the Philippines.

■■■■

Antibiotics Risk for Acne Sufferers

Acne sufferers who use antibiotics are more likely to get upper-respiratory tract infections than those who don't use antibiotics.

Recent finding: Patients who use oral or topical antibiotics, such as any of the tetracyclines, for more than six weeks at a time to treat acne have about twice the risk of developing an upper-respiratory tract infection, compared with those who don't take antibiotics.

David J. Margolis, MD, PhD, associate professor of dermatology and epidemiology, Center for Education and Research in Therapeutics and director, cutaneous ulcer program, University of Pennsylvania, Philadelphia.

Two New Psoriasis Treatments May Hold Key to Real Relief

University of Michigan news release.
M.D. Anderson Cancer Center news release.

Two separate approaches to treating psoriasis, a painful condition that attacks the skin, have shown promise in the lab and may be ready for human testing.

SUPPRESSING CELL GROWTH

The first treatment is an experimental drug called *benzodiazepine-423* (Bz-423)—a chemical cousin of the well-known anti-anxiety drugs Valium and Xanax.

In human skin cultures designed to model psoriasis, University of Michigan researchers found the drug suppressed the unchecked cell growth that characterizes psoriasis.

"Currently, the best treatments for skin lesions that are associated with psoriasis are topical steroids, but they affect normal cells as well," says Gary Glick, a professor of biological chemistry. "And repeated use over time can lead to tissue destruction.

"What makes our compound particularly exciting is that it has the potential to be applied topically," and it can distinguish between disease-causing cells and normal cells, adds Glick.

"So we believe the problems associated with repeated topical steroid use could possibly be alleviated with compounds like this," he says.

Glick and his colleagues hope to begin human clinical trials with Bz-423 in the near future.

EASING THE ITCH

The second treatment under study addresses the cause of psoriasis itself.

At the University of Texas' M.D. Anderson Cancer Center in Houston, scientists say they have identified a protein called STAT3 that leads to psoriasis when the body's immune system is activated to fight off a wound, burn or some other type of invasion.

That discovery led to developing a skin cream that cured the itching, redness and scaling of psoriasis—at least in study mice.

The ointment may also be able to prevent recurrence.

"We may have found an entirely new treatment option for psoriasis," says John DiGiovanni, the lead investigator of the study, who is also the director of the M.D. Anderson department of carcinogenesis.

The American Academy of Dermatology has a Web site specifically for people who have psoriasis at *www.skincarephysicians.com/psoriasisnet.*

What Your Scent Says About Your Health

Jamison Starbuck, ND, naturopathic physician in family practice in Missoula, Montana. She is past president of the American Association of Naturopathic Physicians and is a contributing editor to The Alternative Advisor: The Complete Guide to Natural Therapies and Alternative Treatments. Time-Life.

As a physician, I pay attention to many details about my patients, including body odor. If I detect anything other than a mild, almost neutral scent, my medical curiosity is piqued. Body odor tells me about a patient's health status, dietary habits and hygiene. People with liver disease may have a musty odor...infections anywhere on the body usually emit a foul smell...uncontrolled diabetes often creates a smell best labeled as sweet fermentation. People who are on high-protein diets or who eat a lot of fatty and/or fried foods, onions, garlic or curry, or drink coffee or alcohol excessively, also have particular body odors. Poor hygiene leads to its own recognizable scent.

If you're worried about your body odor, ask a trusted friend or family member to do a sniff test.

What to do: Ask the person to stand within one inch of you and inhale. If the body odor is new, quite strong or confined to a specific part of your body—for example, your mouth, ears or genitals—see your doctor for an exam and evaluation. *If body odor is a familiar, long-standing problem that's not related to an illness, try the following suggestions for 10 days (if they help, continue as needed)...*

•**Eat right.** Fresh, whole foods give your body a fresh, wholesome scent. Eat a salad daily made with dark, leafy lettuce, sprouts, raw veggies and two tablespoons of olive oil. Avoid mayonnaise and cheese-based dressings, which contain odor-producing fat. Choose brown rice or a baked potato instead of fried potatoes. Reduce protein putrification in the digestive tract by eliminating meat—or consuming no more than three ounces of red meat or poultry per day. Drink one-half ounce of water for every pound of your body weight daily.

•**Take three saunas.** Saunas make you perspire, which has a detoxifying effect that reduces body odor.

What to do: Brush your dry skin with a loofah or other skin brush. Enter the sauna and stay there until you perspire all over your body, then leave the sauna and rinse with cold water for 30 seconds. Brush your skin again and return to the sauna. End with a brisk 30-second skin brush, then wrap up in soft, warm clothing. Repeat this process two more times over the next several days.

Caution: People with high blood pressure or heart disease should avoid saunas.

•**Use chlorophyll.** This chemical compound, which is responsible for the green pigment in plants, has astringent properties and can help control the type of body odor that comes from the fermentation of food in the digestive tract. Add one tablespoon of chlorophyll (available at health-food stores) to four ounces of water and drink it at the end of each meal. If you prefer, you can eat one-eighth cup of fresh parsley daily as a substitute for liquid chlorophyll.

•**Eliminate oral bacteria.** In addition to brushing your teeth at least twice daily and flossing at least once a day, gargle each morning with a cup of warm chamomile tea mixed with one teaspoon of hydrogen peroxide. This mixture will kill bacteria living in the throat and mouth, a common cause of bad breath. After the 10-day period, gargle with the chamomile/peroxide mixture as needed for sore throats.

. . . .

Enough Sunscreen?

Most people don't use enough sunscreen. The average adult needs at least one ounce (the amount held by a shot glass) of sunscreen to adequately coat the body.

Also important: If you plan to be in the sun for more than 20 minutes (no matter what your skin type), use broad-spectrum sunscreen with a sun-protection factor (SPF) of 15 or higher that blocks both ultraviolet A (UVA) and ultraviolet B (UVB) rays...reapply it every two hours (even on cloudy days, year-round) to all exposed areas, including your ears, hands—and even your fingernails. Skin cancer also can occur on the scalp, so wear a wide-brimmed hat.

Perry Robins, MD, chief, Mohs Micrographic Surgery Unit at New York Medical Center and president and founder, Skin Cancer Foundation, *www.skincancer.org.*

. . . .

Salon Safety

Manicures at nail salons can result in infections, allergic reactions and injuries to the nail plate and cuticle.

Self-defense: Bring your own manicure tools. Cuticles should be trimmed, not removed with chemicals. Fingernails should be trimmed and filed in the same shape as toenails—flat tips with rounded corners. Periodically clean manicure tools with 70% isopropyl alcohol. Use nail polish remover only as needed—whenever possible, recoat chips with polish.

Neal B. Schultz, MD, dermatologist in private practice, clinical instructor at Mount Sinai School of Medicine and assistant adjunct physician at Lenox Hill Hospital. Dr. Schultz is coauthor, with Laura Morton, of *It's Not Just About Wrinkles.* Stewart, Tabori & Chang.

. . . .

How to Keep Hands Looking Young

You work hard to keep the skin on your face young and smooth, so don't let your hands give away your age...

•**Apply sunscreen** of SPF 30 or higher on hands every day. Use products with Z-Cote, a microfine zinc oxide. Reapply after washing, swimming or perspiring.

•**Use a bleaching product** to fade brown spots (age, sun or liver spots). Your dermatologist can give you a prescription for one, or you can try one of the milder over-the-counter products, such as Porcelana.

•**Wear gloves** whenever possible.

•**Have bulging blue veins removed** by a dermatologist with a laser, or have a dermatologist inject a sclerosing agent, which causes veins to collapse and fade.

Cost: $3,000 or more.

•**Remove fine lines** and improve the paperlike quality of aging skin with laser treatments that generate collagen—also available from a dermatologist.

Cost: $2,000 to $4,000.

Neal B. Schultz, MD, dermatologist in private practice, clinical instructor at Mount Sinai School of Medicine and assistant adjunct physician at Lenox Hill Hospital. Dr. Schultz is coauthor, with Laura Morton, of *It's Not Just About Wrinkles.* Stewart, Tabori & Chang.

. . . .

Prevent Scarring

Wash the affected area with soap and water, not peroxide—which slows healing by preventing new cells from forming. Put a protective film, such as Aquaphor or petroleum jelly, over the wound—keeping the area moist speeds healing. Instead of an adhesive bandage, use an Adaptic bandage—its plastic coating prevents gauze from sticking to the wound. Or try a liquid bandage, which seals the cut like a scab for faster healing.

Jeffrey Dover, MD, dermatologist, SkinCare Physicians of Chestnut Hill, Chestnut Hill, MAs, *www.skincare physicians.net.*

■ ■ ■ ■

Sunlight Is Good for You

Direct exposure to the sun is the health risk behind the growing incidence of skin cancer. But sunlight also is the best source of vitamin D, which is essential to good health.

In fact, research indicates that the ultraviolet radiation in sunlight, in moderate doses, may help prevent up to 16 other kinds of cancer.

Example: One 60-year study in Australia found that people who had the most exposure to sunlight had a 35% lower risk of suffering non-Hodgkin's lymphoma—a group of cancers that begin in the lymph nodes—than did those with the least sun exposure.

Safety: Avoid burning in the sun and prolonged exposure to strong sunlight (such as sunbathing) to reduce skin cancer risk. But do go out in the sun for 15 to 30 minutes each day without sunscreen while the sun is high in the sky, such as before or after lunch, to get enough sunlight to meet your body's vitamin-D needs.

Ralph W. Moss, PhD, cancer researcher based in Lemont, Pennsylvania, and author of *Cancer Therapy*. Equinox. His Moss Reports service offers alternative cancer treatment information to clients, *www.ralphmoss.com*.

Homeopathic Remedy Reduces Bruising

Mark A. Stengler, ND, naturopathic physician in private practice, La Jolla, CA…adjunct associate clinical professor at the National College of Natural Medicine, Portland, OR…author of 16 books, including *The Natural Physician's Healing Therapies* (Bottom Line Books) and coauthor of *Prescription for Natural Cures* (Wiley)…and author of the *Bottom Line/Natural Healing* newsletter.

The homeopathic remedy *arnica montana* significantly reduces bruising. In a recent double-blind clinical trial involving 29 women who were undergoing face-lifts, participants were randomly assigned to receive homeopathic arnica (12C potency) or a placebo beginning the morning of surgery. The treatment was repeated every eight hours for four days. Facial bruising and swelling were evaluated by doctors and nurses, as well as through a computerized digital-image analysis of photographs taken before and after

surgery. Subjective symptoms—those observed by the patients and professional staff—and the degree of discoloration were not significantly improved by the arnica. However, the area of bruising was significantly smaller for the group of subjects who took arnica. Although the study was on women, I would expect the same results for men and for other types of bruising.

Arnica montana, also known as leopard's bane, is a widely used homeopathic remedy for injury to soft tissues. Arnica preparations have been used in homeopathic medicine for two centuries. Sesquiterpene lactones, major active compounds in arnica, are known to reduce inflammation, decrease pain and improve circulation.

I can attest to hundreds of cases in which arnica has reduced pain and swelling. I also have seen this benefit with infants and animals—where a placebo effect is unlikely. You can use arnica for any soft-tissue injury, such as bruising after a fall or a sprained ankle. The most common dose is two pellets of 30C strength taken two to four times daily for two days. Or apply homeopathic arnica cream two to three times daily until healed. Arnica is sold at most health-food stores and some pharmacies.

Caution: Do not use topical arnica on broken skin or open wounds.

Breakthrough Treatments for Hair Loss

Mark A. Stengler, ND, naturopathic physician in private practice, La Jolla, CA…adjunct associate clinical professor at the National College of Natural Medicine, Portland, OR…author of 16 books, including *The Natural Physician's Healing Therapies* (Bottom Line Books) and coauthor of *Prescription for Natural Cures* (Wiley)…and author of the *Bottom Line/Natural Healing* newsletter.

Why do some men go bald in their 30s while others have a full head of hair until their final days? Why do some women have ever-thinning hair, while others never seem to lose a single strand?

Blame your genes, first of all. If your mom, dad or a grandparent had hair loss, chances are greater that you will, too. Even so, there are ways to slow hair loss and stimulate growth.

THE HORMONE FACTOR

You grow and shed hair all the time. Of the 100,000-plus strands of hair on your head, it is perfectly normal to lose 50 to 100 every day. Once a hair is shed, a new hair grows from the same follicle. Hair grows at a rate of nearly one-half inch per month (faster in warm weather, slower when frost is on the vine). Baldness results when the rate of shedding exceeds the rate of regrowth.

Hair loss usually accelerates when you're over age 50. One hormone, *dihydrotestosterone* (DHT), seems to be the chief culprit. DHT is a derivative of *testosterone* (the sex-determining hormone that is more abundant in men than women). In both men and women, DHT increases in the presence of the enzyme *5-alpha reductase*, which is produced in the prostate, adrenal glands and the scalp. 5-alpha reductase is more likely to proliferate after age 50. When DHT is overproduced, hair follicles are damaged. Some follicles die, but most shrink and produce thinner, weaker hairs—and the weak hairs are the ones that fall out.

An oily skin substance called *sebum*—produced by the sebaceous glands—makes matters worse. Excess sebum clogs follicles and contributes to high 5-alpha reductase activity, which stimulates production of DHT.

STRESS

Among my own patients, stress is a factor for both men and women. I have found that highly stressed women, in particular, have higher-than-normal levels of *cortisol*, a stress hormone that can contribute to hair loss.

A study published in the *Journal of Clinical Biochemistry* confirms that cortisol is indeed elevated in some women who suffer hair loss—and that when they learn to cope better with stress, hair growth improves.

For stress relief, I recommend daily exercise, such as brisk walking, as well as relaxation techniques, including deep breathing and meditation. B vitamins and ashwagandha (a stress-reducing herb from India) also can help counteract the effects of cortisol.

A regular daily dose of 100 mg of a B-vitamin complex and 250 mg to 500 mg of ashwagandha can help control cortisol levels. Look for Sensoril Ashwagandha, a patented extract formula by Jarrow Formulas, available at many health-food stores or by calling 800-726-0886 or at *www.jarrow.com.*

A PROMISING FORMULA

Taking a daily multivitamin and mineral supplement as well as the herbal remedy saw palmetto also can help slow hair loss. A daily scalp massage with essential oils is beneficial, too.

• **Saw palmetto** helps block the effects of DHT on hair follicles, strengthening hair. In a study in the *Journal of Alternative and Complementary Medicine*, researchers used a product containing saw palmetto and a plant compound called *beta-sitosterol* that is found in saw palmetto and other plants. The study included 19 men between ages 23 and 64 who had mild-to-moderate hair loss. Men in one group were given a placebo daily... and men in the other group received the saw palmetto/beta-sitosterol combination (none of the participants knew which group they were in). After five months, researchers found that 60% of the men who received the saw palmetto/beta-sitosterol combination showed improvement, while only 11% of the men receiving a placebo had more hair growth.

In my clinical experience, saw palmetto is helpful for both men and women. I recommend 320 mg to 400 mg daily of an 85% liposterolic extract. It is safe to use long term but should not be taken if you are pregnant or nursing.

For a more aggressive approach, you should also take beta-sitosterol. Source Naturals (800-815-2333, *www.sourcenaturals.com*) offers a 113-mg tablet that can be taken daily. It is available at health-food stores and at *www.iherb.com.*

• **The essential oils of rosemary and lavender** have been shown to improve hair growth when applied to the scalp. My own belief is that they improve blood flow to the scalp, ensuring that nutrients get to the sites where they're needed.

You can purchase these essential oils in separate containers. Pour some of your regular shampoo into the lid of the shampoo bottle, then add five to 10 drops of each essential oil. Massage into the scalp and leave on three to five minutes before rinsing thoroughly.

OTHER SUPPLEMENTS

If you have tried these approaches for two to three months and still aren't satisfied with the growth of your locks, here are some other supplements that can help both men and women...

• **Biotin,** a nutrient that is required for hair growth, is particularly good for brittle hair. Food

435

sources of biotin include brewer's yeast, soybeans, eggs, mushrooms and whole wheat. For supplementation, take 3,000 micrograms daily for at least two months or use a biotin-enriched shampoo daily.

•**MSM (methylsulfonylmethane)** is a great source of sulfur, an integral component of the amino acids that are the building blocks of hair protein. MSM improves the strength, sheen and health of hair. In one study, 21 adults (16 men and five women) who were assessed by a certified cosmetologist under the direction of a medical doctor were given MSM or a placebo and then were reassessed at the end of six weeks. The participants did not know who was given MSM and who was given a placebo.

Those given MSM showed significant improvement in hair health, while those taking a placebo showed few or no changes. I recommend a 3,000-mg daily dose of MSM. Look for Opti-MSM or Lignisul MSM, available from many manufacturers and at health-food stores.

Essential fatty acids keep hair from becoming dry and lifeless by decreasing inflammation. Inflammation worsens the quality of hair follicles, and essential fatty acids are needed for the proper development of hair. Food sources include walnuts, eggs, fish, olive oil, flaxseed and hempseed and flax oils. Or you can take a formula like Udo's Choice Oil Blend, produced by Flora (800-446-2110, *www.florahealth.com*). Follow directions on the label. The formula contains both omega-3 fatty acids (from flax oil or fish oil) and omega-6 fatty acids from evening primrose oil or borage oil. Don't expect immediate results, however. It can take four to six weeks to see improvement.

Not Just Wrinkles: Secrets To Younger-Looking Skin

Neal B. Schultz, MD, dermatologist in private practice, clinical instructor at Mount Sinai School of Medicine and assistant adjunct physician at Lenox Hill Hospital. Dr. Schultz is coauthor, with Laura Morton, of *It's Not Just About Wrinkles*. Stewart, Tabori & Chang.

W hen people complain about looking older, they usually talk about lines and wrinkles. However, most people who are dissatisfied with their appearance have color or texture problems as well that make them look older than they should.

Well-known treatments, such as Botox and collagen, are very effective for lines and wrinkles, but they don't affect color and texture issues. About three-quarters of patients will notice a dramatic improvement when they treat these two important factors, too.

COLOR

Color problems are among the easiest skin defects to correct. They basically fall into two categories—browns (such as age spots and freckles) and reds (usually due to engorged or broken capillaries).

•**Browns.** Brown spots go by many different names—sunspots, liver spots, age spots, etc. They're almost always caused by sun exposure, which triggers excessive activity in some of the skin's pigment-producing cells. Most brown spots appear on exposed areas of the skin, such as the face, arms and back of the hands.

On the other hand, blotchy brown areas that don't have a clear border are usually caused by an imbalance of female hormones, such as during pregnancy or in women taking birth control pills.

Virtually all brown defects can be removed with laser treatments, which cost $400 to $1,200 per treatment. A less expensive but more time-consuming approach is to lighten the brown areas with exfoliation.

Best home treatment: A product with 8% *glycolic acid* used daily. Glycolic acid is one of the alpha hydroxy acids (AHAs). It dissolves *keratin*, the uppermost layer of dead skin. Over-the-counter products, such as Aqua Glycolic Face Cream, Glytone Day Cream for Dry Skin and Kinerase Cream, lighten brown spots and stop the formation of new pigment cells.

Glycolic acid begins to work within two weeks—and will significantly reduce brownness in four to six weeks.

Important: Continue to apply a sunscreen whenever you are going outdoors. Repeated sun exposure will cause the brownness to return.

Also helpful: Twice-daily applications of over-the-counter topical vitamin C, such as Stallex C Complex Rescue Serum or SkinMedica Vitamin C Complex. Topical vitamin C lightens brown spots and blocks cell-damaging free radicals. It can be used in addition to glycolic acid.

Skin cancer warning: If there is a change in a brown spot's or a mole's size, shape or color (other than lightening from treatment) or if it bleeds, itches or becomes painful, contact your dermatologist immediately.

•**Reds.** Most people have one or more red spots or lines on their faces. They're often present on the cheeks or alongside the nose and usually are due to dilated or broken capillaries.

Common types: *Telangiectasias*, which appear as tiny straight or curved red lines…*spider hemangiomas*, which are raised red bumps with red lines emanating from the center…or *cherry hemangiomas*, flat or dome-shaped spots. Another type of redness is caused by *rosacea*—an acne-like condition that's characterized by red blotches (telangiectasias) that appear intermittently on the cheeks and nose.

Best home treatment: An over-the-counter topical sulfur preparation—such as Rezamid Acne Treatment Lotion or Sulforcin Acne Treatment Lotion. Sulfur shrinks blood vessels and helps reduce redness. This can work for rosacea, too, but test an area the size of a dime first to see how your skin reacts.

Because it's difficult to eliminate skin redness entirely, I usually advise patients to conceal it by using color-correcting makeup—a green-tinted foundation works best. Neutrogena makes a good one.

Diet: Certain foods have dilating effects on blood vessels, causing them to temporarily increase in diameter. The most common perpetrators are alcohol and spicy foods. Also, certain medications and vitamins (the most common of which is any form of *niacin*, one of the B vitamins) are known to cause dilation of facial blood vessels and thus to increase their conspicuousness.

TEXTURE

Young skin is smooth, with a noticeable "slip factor" when you run a finger across the face. Older "dull" skin feels rough, or there are "bumps" when the finger passes over enlarged pores.

Both of the main texture problems—enlarged pores and dull, flaky skin—are caused by the retention of dead skin cells. Skin cells shed every 28 days—but not all cells do this. This results in an uneven accumulation of dead cells.

Best home treatment: Exfoliation with glycolic acid. People should start with a product that has eight percent glycolic acid. The concentration can be increased to 10% or 15% if needed.

Bonus: Exfoliating can remove early precancerous cells along with the dead skin cells.

In-office exfoliation treatments: There are two types of in-office exfoliation—chemical, with a prescription glycolic acid treatment…and mechanical with microdermabrasion. The latter involves the use of a machine by a properly trained doctor, nurse or esthetician that bombards the skin with sterilized aluminum-oxide crystals. It immediately strips away dead cells and leaves the skin looking uniform and fresh.

In-office treatments cost $100 to $200 per treatment. You will need six to 10 treatments done at one- to two-week intervals.

CONTOUR

After about age 40, just about everyone notices an increase in lines, wrinkles and sagging skin. These and other contour problems usually are treated with products such as Botox and/or "filler" materials, such as collagen.

Botox can cost $400 to $1,600 per treatment, depending on the area done, and lasts about three months. Fillers are $600 to $2,000 per treatment and last three to nine months, depending on the area done and the filler used.

The main contour problems and the best treatments…

•**Frown lines** (the vertical lines between the eyes) and forehead lines (horizontal lines across the forehead) are known as dynamic lines because they're most visible when the underlying muscles move. Injections of Botox often can eliminate these types of lines, but when the injections wear off in about three months, they have to be repeated.

•**Marionette lines** run from the nose down to the corner of the mouth. They're caused mainly by the age-related loss of fat and skin elasticity. Botox can't be used for these lines because it can paralyze the entire cheek muscle and prevent smiling. A better approach is to inject collagen or another filler, such as Restylane. These products add volume to the skin and fill out the hollow contours.

•**Crow's feet,** the lines that radiate from the corners of the eyes, often can be improved or eliminated with Botox. In about 20% of cases, patients require a combination of Botox plus collagen.

•**Smoker's lines** on the lips (also called "lipstick lines" because lipstick can "bleed" into the tiny crevices) will disappear when injected with a very fine form of collagen. Most patients also are given injections of Botox to reduce muscle contractions that cause the lines.

FOUR STEPS TO BEAUTIFUL SKIN

Getting enough sleep, eating a healthy diet and finding time to relax all contribute to younger-looking skin.

In addition, everyone can have smoother, more lustrous skin with this simple, twice-a-day program, done in the morning and evening. The first three steps are the same for both times of day…the fourth is different in the morning and evening.

Step 1: Cleanse the skin to remove oils and debris. Doing this also allows the active ingredients in other products to penetrate the skin. Never scrub with a washcloth. Use your fingertips to massage a small amount of cleanser onto the face for 10 to 15 seconds, then rinse with warm water.

Step 2: Apply a toner to a soft, thin cotton makeup pad, and gently wipe. Toner removes leftover debris, along with any cleanser that wasn't removed by rinsing.

Step 3: Use the right active ingredient for your skin-care issues—glycolic acid for brown spots, sulfur for reds, etc.

Step 4 (morning): Apply sunscreen after completing the first three steps but before applying makeup. A sunscreen with an SPF of about 30 is right for most people.

Step 4 (evening): Apply a moisturizer that is right for your skin. An oil-based moisturizer is good for extremely dry skin…a water-and-oil moisturizer is good for "normal" skin…and an oil-free, water-based moisturizer is best for oily skin.

■ ■ ■ ■

Telltale Link?

Psoriasis is linked to heart attack risk. In a study of patients ages 20 to 90, a patient who is 30 years old with severe psoriasis has more than three times the risk of heart attack as a person the same age without psoriasis. Risk also is elevated—but not as much—in older patients and people with mild psoriasis.

Likely link: Both psoriasis and heart disease are associated with high levels of inflammation. If you have psoriasis, ask your doctor to evaluate your risk factors.

Joel M. Gelfand, MD, medical director of the clinical studies unit and assistant professor of dermatology, University of Pennsylvania School of Medicine, Philadelphia. His study of 130,976 people was published in *The Journal of the American Medical Association*.

■ ■ ■ ■

Psoriasis Relief

Natural remedy for psoriasis, *Reliéva*, a homeopathic product containing Oregon grape extract, reduces skin redness and scaly patches associated with mild-to-moderate psoriasis Because it has no side effects, Reliéva is worth trying even for severe psoriasis before moving on to stronger treatments. Oregon grapes contain an alkaloid chemical that fights cell proliferation, which is what occurs in psoriasis. Reliéva now is being studied for eczema, too.

Mark A. Stengler, ND, naturopathic physician in private practice, La Jolla, CA…adjunct associate clinical professor at the National College of Natural Medicine, Portland, OR…author of 16 books, including *The Natural Physician's Healing Therapies* (Bottom Line Books) and coauthor of *Prescription for Natural Cures* (Wiley)…and author of the *Bottom Line/Natural Healing* newsletter.

■ ■ ■ ■

Better Block

New sunscreen protects against UVA rays longer than traditional sunscreens. Anthelios SX, made by L'Oréal, is also effective against UVB rays.

Downside: It costs more than other sunscreens and washes off in water.

However: Sweat doesn't interfere with its effectiveness. It is available at *www.anthelios.com*.

Nelson Lee Novick, MD, clinical professor of dermatology, Mount Sinai Medical Center, New York City, and author of *Super Skin*. iUniverse.

■ ■ ■ ■

Acne Aid

Over-the-counter acne creams are just as effective for mild to moderate acne as prescription oral antibiotics.

Bonus: Use of topical creams—such as Clearasil and Oxy Acne Cream—does not lead to antibiotic resistance.

Hywel C. Williams, PhD, professor of dermatology, University of Nottingham, England, and leader of a study comparing commonly used acne treatments, published in *The Lancet*.

■■■■

Hair Restoration?

Fight hair loss by getting more iron. You normally shed about 100 hairs a day, but if hair comes out in clumps, get screened for iron deficiency. Getting more iron (through diet or supplements) may limit shedding and promote regrowth.

Caution: Do not take supplements without consulting a physician—too much iron can lead to heart disease, liver disease and diabetes.

Leonid Trost, MD, physician in private practice, Palm-Beach Dermatology, Florida, and coauthor of a research review published in *Journal of the American Academy of Dermatology*.

How I Won the War on Toenail Fungus

Dwight Thomas, PhD, a medical writer and former toenail fungus sufferer in Savannah, is author of *The War Against Toenail Fungus*, a book about his battle to cure his own toenail problems. Monterey Square Press.

I contracted toenail fungus and spent nearly four years and several thousand dollars searching for a cure. Eventually, I found a treatment that worked, and my toenails now have been healthy for more than three years.

Millions of Americans suffer from toenail fungus. It's caused by *Trichophyton rubrum* (T. rubrum), the fungus responsible for athlete's foot. Affected toenails thicken and become discolored and crumbly. The nail bed can become so scarred after a few years of infection that the nail won't grow at all. People with diabetes who suffer from toenail fungus face increased risk of ulcerations on the toes and even gangrene.

Older people are more likely to get toenail fungus. Young people's toenails tend to be strong enough to prevent the fungus from getting into the nail bed below. But as we age, our toenails and the surrounding skin are increasingly likely to develop cracks or cuts that offer a point of entry—and the heat and moisture in our shoes allow the fungus to thrive.

Also, some people seem genetically predisposed to the fungus—if you have had athlete's foot, you also may be susceptible to toenail fungus. I had athlete's foot many times before I got toenail fungus.

THE CURE

I tried several different medications. The two most effective are Lamisil tablets and a topical nail lacquer called Penlac. Both are prescription drugs, and they are expensive for those like me who don't have health insurance—a full regimen of either can cost well into the hundreds of dollars.

I tried both medications individually, but my toenail fungus wasn't cured until I used Lamisil and Penlac at the same time for a full year. Studies in Europe have reported success rates as high as 88% for people who combine a systemic treatment (that is, a pill) with a topical treatment.

The good news is that you don't have to use both of these expensive medications each day for the full course of treatment.

Penlac is effective when applied three times a week for the first month, twice a week for the second month and once a week thereafter. Lamisil is effective when taken once each day for the first month, followed by daily doses one week in four thereafter, with three weeks off between. Neither medication has significant side effects for most people, though Lamisil can be dangerous for those suffering from severe liver problems.

If you don't have health insurance and/or aren't willing to spend hundreds of dollars on expensive medications, consider asking your podiatrist to grind the damaged nails down to a normal thickness, a process known as "debridement." I did this. It won't cure the infection, but it can make the nails more presentable and allow shoes to fit more comfortably.

PREVENTION

Take these steps to prevent the fungus, especially if you have had toenail fungus before or you have had athlete's foot and you're past age 40…

•**Apply antifungal powder to your feet each day before you put on your shoes.** Zeasorb

Powder (available over-the-counter) is particularly effective, I have found.

• **Choose loose, breathable shoes** such as canvas sneakers or sandals. Avoid tight, pointed shoes as well as leather shoes, such as boots and dress shoes.

Shingles Prevention: New Strategies

Albert Lefkovits, MD, associate clinical professor of dermatology and codirector of the cosmetic dermatological surgery training program at Mount Sinai School of Medicine in New York City, lectures widely at national and international medical conferences.

Few people realize that a severe case of shingles—a viral infection characterized by a rash, blisters and sometimes excruciating pain—can lead to serious complications, such as blindness or hearing impairment.

That's why physicians are doggedly pursuing new ways to prevent shingles, and stressing the importance of early treatment to lessen its severity and duration.

Latest development: Recently, the FDA approved a new vaccine, called Zostavax, that promises to reduce the risk of developing shingles in adults age 60 or older. However, the vaccine may not be appropriate for everyone who is at risk for the condition.

Here's what you need to know...

SIGNS AND SYMPTOMS

Shingles is caused by the varicella-zoster virus, the same virus that causes chicken pox. After an attack of chicken pox (usually in childhood), the virus remains dormant in nerve tissue until it is reactivated by the onset of a serious illness, such as leukemia or lymphoma...weakened immunity, even from a bad cold...or normal aging.

Each year, approximately one million Americans develop shingles. The virus primarily attacks people over age 60, but it also can occur in children and teenagers. Half of all people age 80 or older can expect to develop shingles.

The first signs of shingles are easy to miss because they can mimic flu symptoms—chills, fever, nausea, headache, even difficulty urinating. Within a week, the virus spreads to the skin, causing the emergence of fluid-filled blisters in a band on one side of the body. The location of the blisters and pain correlates with the area of skin served by the infected nerve. While the rash and blisters usually appear on the trunk, they can appear on the face, near an eye, in the genital area or anywhere else on the body. The blisters usually dry and begin to scab about five days later. But the pain can continue for weeks, months or even years.

Shingles itself is not contagious. However, anyone who has never had chicken pox can develop chicken pox if he/she is exposed to the live virus in the skin of a shingles patient. The virus primarily is transmitted via direct contact with blisters that haven't completely dried. Airborne transmission, while rare, may occur.

Although the reason is unclear, doctors tend to see multiple patients with shingles at the same time—coinciding with a seasonal outbreak of chicken pox in grade-school children, typically in the fall or spring.

IF SHINGLES IS SUSPECTED

If you suspect that you may have shingles (based on the signs and symptoms already described), you should seek prompt medical attention (within 72 hours) either from your family doctor, a dermatologist or a neurologist.

Antiviral medication, which is generally taken for seven to 10 days, can be an extremely effective treatment for shingles. The antiviral agent *acyclovir* (Zovirax) is now available in a generic form, so it is the least expensive antiviral available. However, some people find acyclovir inconvenient to use because it must be taken five times a day. Both *famciclovir* (Famvir) and *valacyclovir* (Valtrex) can be taken three times a day. They are not available in generic forms and cost about $255 to $270 for a seven-day supply. If you start the medication right away, you'll decrease the odds of needing a painkiller later on. Side effects of antivirals may include nausea, headache and diarrhea.

When shingles pain does occur, sufferers describe it as itching, burning or cutting. At its extreme, the pain can be so severe that people contemplate suicide or are willing to undergo radical surgery (which entails cutting the infected nerve's roots) to relieve it. The standard painkillers used for shingles include topical and systemic steroids, the antidepressant *amitriptyline* (Elavil) and the antiseizure drug *gabapentin* (Neurontin).

A NEW VACCINE

As people grow older, their immunity tends to decrease. The new shingles vaccine contains a small dose of a live but weakened varicella-zoster virus. With exposure to the varicella-zoster virus, the recipient's immune system is stimulated to create antibodies against it. This helps protect people who receive the vaccine from developing shingles. The vaccine costs about $150 per dose, not including your physician's fee for the office visit.

Recent finding: In a study of almost 40,000 people age 60 or older, half of whom received a placebo, the vaccine reduced the occurrence of the virus by about 50%. The vaccine reduced postherpetic neuralgia (PHN), extreme nerve pain that can last for months or years after the rash is healed, by 66%. About 20% of shingles patients develop PHN, according to the Varicella-Zoster Virus (VZV) Research Foundation. However, in my experience, the incidence rate and the severity of PHN symptoms have decreased since the introduction of antiviral drugs to treat them.

Who should get the vaccine? That still hasn't been clearly established. The chance for a recurrence is low (about 5%), so people who have already had shingles do not need the shingles vaccine.

Because shingles responds well to treatment when it is initiated within the first 72 hours, I recommend using the new vaccine for adults over age 80 who are generally in good health but very frail. They are most likely to contract shingles and develop PHN.

The studies conducted thus far suggest that the vaccine has only mild side effects, such as redness, pain and tenderness, swelling at the site of the injection, itching and headache. However, many doctors—myself included—are prescribing cautiously because, like other live-virus vaccines used for other conditions, the live varicella-zoster virus can infect others.

Those who are at greatest risk of becoming infected after exposure to a person who has received the varicella-zoster virus vaccine include people with weakened immune systems due to cancer or AIDS and pregnant women, whose fetus could be harmed by a chicken pox infection. Anyone who gets the shingles vaccine should avoid the people mentioned above for about three months following vaccination.

Although doctors are optimistic about the potential of Zostavax, many of us are waiting to see whether widespread use results in yet-unreported adverse side effects.

BEST PAIN RELIEF

Shingles often causes severe pain. In a new survey conducted by the American Pain Foundation, 35% of 401 shingles sufferers reported "severe" pain…11% said it was "very severe"… and six percent called the pain "intolerable" during the first few weeks of the illness.

Dr. Lefkovits recommends…

•**Take an over-the-counter (OTC) pain-killer.** Some doctors recommend a nonsteroidal anti-inflammatory drug (NSAID), such as aspirin or *ibuprofen* (Advil), to help curb skin and nerve cell inflammation as well as pain. Because these medications are known to cause stomach problems, I tell most of my shingles patients to try *acetaminophen* (Tylenol). It has little effect on inflammation but is a very effective pain reliever.

To avoid possible liver damage: Do not exceed the maximum daily dose of 4 g (eight extra-strength tablets)—or 2 g daily if you're age 70 or older.

•**Use topical steroids.** Skin inflammation as well as burning and itching can be relieved with OTC creams and lotions that contain hydrocortisone (1%). These treatments can be used up to three times daily and do not cause side effects, such as weight gain, that are generally associated with oral steroids. If you must take oral steroids for an extended period, you should be closely supervised by your doctor.

•**Take warm baths.** Do this several times daily, if necessary. Warm baths are soothing and help relieve pain.

•**Go to a pain clinic.** People who cannot get adequate pain relief on their own should consider going to a pain clinic, where anesthesiologists, neurologists and other specialists will recommend different pain relief methods. Acupuncture also may be helpful.

For more information, contact the Varicella-Zoster Virus (VZV) Research Foundation, 212-222-3390, *www.vzvfoundation.org*.

∎ ∎ ∎ ∎

Shingles Self-Defense

Shingles is a painful rash caused by the re-activation of the varicella virus that causes chicken pox. Typically, shingles start as vesicles (small blisters) that may look like small pimples. Oftentimes, you will experience an itching, tingling or burning sensation. Shingles is usually unilateral, meaning that it follows a nerve and therefore will not cross the midline of the body. The rash will always be on the left or right side.

Self-defense: The best treatment is an oral antiviral, such as *acyclovir* (Zovirax), *valacyclovir* (Valtrex) or *famciclovir* (Famvir). It is important to take one of these medications within 48 to 72 hours of the onset of symptoms for it to be effective. After 72 hours, use a warm compress to relieve symptoms and a topical antibiotic ointment, such as *mupirocin* (Bactroban), to prevent infection.

Leon Kircik, MD, clinical associate professor of dermatology, Indiana University School of Medicine, Indianapolis.

Surprising Causes of Fungal Infections

John R. Perfect, MD, infectious disease specialist and professor of medicine at Duke University School of Medicine in Durham, North Carolina. Dr. Perfect is director of Duke's mycology research unit and leads the antibiotic trials unit. He has authored over 250 publications in the field of medical mycology.

Most people blame viruses or bacteria when they get an infection. Fungi is another—often-overlooked—possibility. Fungal infection is more common than most people realize.

Example: *Candida*, a fungus that causes yeast infections, is the fourth most common microorganism found in the blood of hospitalized patients. Candida can infect the mouth, causing white, painful patches on the tongue and inside the cheeks (thrush). In the hospital or during serious illnesses, these mild fungal infections can develop into potentially fatal ones, which can affect the heart or brain.

Fungi are normally present on the skin and in the intestinal tract. Local fungal infections, such as athlete's foot, are common and relatively easy to treat. Mild infections also can occur in the other places that fungi normally inhabit, such as the vagina, mouth, groin area or in fingernails or toenails.

It's rare for someone who's healthy to get a serious fungal infection. Those at greatest risk include people with compromised immune systems, such as hospitalized patients and individuals with diabetes, lung disease, kidney failure, cancer, human immunodeficiency virus (HIV) or some other chronic illness…as well as anyone who has undergone an organ or bone-marrow transplant.

•**How difficult is it to diagnose a fungal infection?** Infections of the skin usually can be diagnosed just by looking at them. *Dermatophytosis* (ringworm), for example, usually appears as scaly, red ring-shaped patches. Systemic infections (that have spread into several organs) usually require taking a sample of body fluid, such as sputum from the lungs or blood, and culturing it in a laboratory and/or examining specimens under a microscope for fungal forms.

Caution: Fungal infection in the lungs can be mistaken for cancer on an X-ray. The only way to distinguish the two is by taking a biopsy.

•**Are fungal infections contagious?** Some fungal infections of the skin, such as ringworm, can be passed from one person to another by sharing towels or clothing or having direct contact with a rash. Most other fungal infections occur when microscopic spores in the air come in contact with the skin or are inhaled. Many fungi reproduce and spread through these microscopic spores.

•**Is there any way to protect yourself from developing a fungal infection?** We live in a virtual "sea of fungi," so it is impossible to avoid them. The vast majority cannot cause disease. The best prevention is for your doctor to be aware of these infections and for you to get treatment early if one develops.

•**Does a skin/nail infection indicate that there's a more serious underlying problem?**

Usually not. It's possible that someone with a serious, underlying illness will get a nail or skin fungal infection—but it's unlikely that the infection would be the first sign. The most dangerous fungal infections, such as *aspergillosis* and *cryptococcosis*, tend to occur in patients who are already sick and perhaps undergoing extensive medical treatments. Both of these infections primarily affect the lungs but occasionally spread to other areas of the body.

Someone with cancer or diabetes might be more likely to develop a severe Candida infection because he/she may be in a hospital receiving intravenous antibiotics or chemotherapy, which may allow fungi to proliferate in the body. Although Candida most often causes yeast infections, in more serious cases, it can invade the bloodstream or certain organs.

Some fungal infections may be important warning signs. Therefore, anyone who's getting fungal infections more than twice a year or has an infection that doesn't respond to treatments needs to consider the possibility that his/her immune system isn't working well—and see his doctor right away.

•**Aren't fungal infections difficult to treat?** Fungi are very hard to kill. Like humans, fungi are eukaryotes (single-celled or multicellular organisms whose cells contain a distinct membrane-bound nucleus). This means that we share the same kinds of "cellular machinery." It's difficult to develop drugs that will kill a fungus without killing human cells at the same time. Fungi grow slowly and protect themselves inside host cells. Despite this, there has been great improvement in the drugs we have for invasive fungal infections. However, some antifungal medications can be costly—about $300 for a month's treatment.

Latest development: The newest class of antifungal drugs, known as candins, include *caspofungin* (Cancidas), *micafungin* (Mycamine) and *anidulafungin* (Eraxis), which are used to treat aspergillosis and serious Candida infections. These medications inhibit a component that fungi require to create cell walls. Since human cells don't have that component, they aren't affected by these drugs. Because of this, the candins are less likely to cause toxicity and/or side effects than older antifungal agents, such as polyene drugs, including *amphotericin B* (Fungizone).

Topical antifungal drugs are effective, but they don't necessarily work quickly. It's common for patients with athlete's foot to apply the creams for weeks or months. Treating a nail fungus may require oral antifungal drugs.

•**What happens if a fungal infection goes untreated?** That depends on the severity of the infection. Mild skin fungal infections sometimes clear up on their own—and even if they don't, they may require minimal treatment. A patient with a nail fungus, for example, might choose to ignore it, since the only symptom—usually yellow, green or brown nail discoloration—is cosmetic.

Athlete's foot, jock itch and vaginal yeast infections, on the other hand, can be itchy and uncomfortable. They respond well to over-the-counter topical agents, such as *clotrimazole* (Gyne-Lotrimin or Mycelex) or *miconazole* (Monistat).

An invasive fungal infection, which usually begins in the lungs or bloodstream, can spread rapidly to other parts of the body and always requires treatment. The drugs may be given orally or intravenously. In the highest-risk patients, such as those getting chemotherapy, an antifungal drug can be given prophylactically—that is, to prevent an infection from occurring.

■ ■ ■ ■

Razor's Edge

Multiblade razors may give a smoother shave, but they also promote razor burn by pulling hair and cutting it below the skin. When the hair grows back, it may do so at a curve, causing painful bumps.

Self-defense: Use a single- or double-blade razor, and always shave in the direction in which the hair grows.

Bruce P. Robinson, MD, dermatologist in private practice, New York City.

■ ■ ■ ■

Cellulite Creams Don't Work

Clinical experiments have found that anticellulite formulations are no more successful than placebos at reducing cellulite, the fatty dimples that make skin on the hips and thighs appear lumpy. The only treatment proven to temporarily reduce cellulite is *endermologie*—a somewhat painful process in which a suction device squeezes and kneads the affected skin between two rollers. A course of 15 to 20 treatments over several months produces a temporary visible reduction in cellulite. Monthly sessions are required to maintain results. Each treatment can cost up to $125. Some physicians are testing a new procedure called *thermage*, which attempts to eliminate cellulite by the application of heat.

Barney J. Kenet, MD, dermatologic surgeon, New York-Presbyterian Hospital/Weill Cornell Medical Center, New York City. Dr. Kenet is the president and founder of the American Melanoma Foundation and coauthored (with his wife, Patricia Lawler) *Saving Your Skin.* Thunder's Mouth Press.

Natural Ways to Protect Your Vision

Mark A. Stengler, ND, naturopathic physician in private practice, La Jolla, CA...adjunct associate clinical professor at the National College of Natural Medicine, Portland, OR...author of 16 books, including *The Natural Physician's Healing Therapies* (Bottom Line Books) and coauthor of *Prescription for Natural Cures* (Wiley)...and author of the *Bottom Line/Natural Healing* newsletter.

Millions of Americans have lost some or all of their sight to cataracts, glaucoma, macular degeneration and other eye diseases. Medications and surgical procedures can help, but the results are rarely optimal.

Fact: Up to 80% of all diseases can be prevented with natural approaches—and there is evidence that nutritional treatments can halt or even reverse underlying vision problems.

Sun exposure is one of the main causes of vision loss. Everyone should wear sunglasses that block the sun's damaging ultraviolet (UV) rays.

Other measures to combat vision loss include eating certain foods and taking supplements. The antioxidants described below (*lutein, zeaxanthin* and the recommended vitamin supplements) help prevent and treat most eye conditions. The other remedies described can help specific problems. You can take all the supplements listed here (available at health-food stores), but it is always wise to consult with your physician before taking any supplement.

LUTEIN

Spinach, kale and other leafy greens contain an antioxidant called lutein, which reduces damage caused by unstable molecules known as free radicals. Smoking and exposure to UV light are two common sources of free radicals. Decreasing damage from free radicals can reduce the risk of cataracts and macular degeneration.

Recommended: One to two servings of leafy greens daily, or supplement with 15 mg of lutein daily. I usually have my patients take a daily supplement that combines lutein (15 mg) with zeaxanthin (3 mg), another antioxidant. A study of 876 older adults found that those with the highest levels of these antioxidants were less likely to develop age-related macular degeneration.

VITAMINS C & E

Individually, these vitamins are among the most potent antioxidants. Taken together, they're very effective at preventing vision loss. Vitamin E blocks free radicals in the fatty parts of cells, such as in the macula of the eye, while vitamin C fortifies the watery portions in the cornea and retina.

For optimal protection, I recommend to my patients supplements of vitamins C and E, along with zinc and beta-carotene. Patients who take this combination daily can reduce their risk of vision loss. In patients who have age-related macular degeneration, these supplements can slow the disease's progression.

Recommended: Daily supplements with 400 IU of mixed natural vitamin E (a mixture of tocopherols and tocotrienols), 500 mg of vitamin C, 80 mg of zinc and 15 mg of beta-carotene.

GINKGO BILOBA

The herb ginkgo biloba blocks free radicals and dilates blood vessels, increasing circulation to the optic nerve. There is some evidence that it can improve peripheral vision in patients with glaucoma.

Recommended: 120 mg of ginkgo daily. Choose an extract that is standardized to 24% flavone glycosides.

Caution: Do not take a supplement with ginkgo if you are taking a prescription blood-thinning medication, such as *warfarin* (Coumadin).

N-ACETYL CARNOSINE

This naturally occurring molecule is composed of two amino acids.

A recent study found that N-acetyl carnosine (NAC) eyedrops improved visual acuity and glare sensitivity in patients with cataracts. During the two-year study, 90% of the eyes treated with NAC had significant improvements in vision.

Recommended: Patients with cataracts should ask their doctors about using topical NAC drops.

FISH OIL

About half of the retina consists of *docosahexaenoic acid* (DHA), a component in fish oil that provides the main structural support in cell membranes. DHA causes a significant drop in intraocular pressure—important for patients with glaucoma. Another component in fish oil, *eicosapentaenoic acid* (EPA), has anti-inflammatory effects and is thought to play an important role in maintaining visual acuity.

Recommended: Eat fish twice a week. Avoid fish high in mercury, including shark, swordfish, tilefish, king mackerel and large tuna, such as albacore, yellowfin, bigeye and bluefin. Or take a fish-oil formula daily that includes 600 mg of EPA and 400 mg of DHA. Check with your doctor if you are on a blood thinner, such as *warfarin*.

MAGNESIUM AND CHROMIUM

Each of these minerals dilates blood vessels in the eye and reduces pressure from glaucoma. Chromium is particularly important for patients with diabetes, a common cause of vision loss. Chromium supplements help maintain an optimal blood-sugar balance and reduce the risk of glaucoma.

Recommended: Take 250 mg of magnesium (citrate or chelate) and 200 mcg of chromium (polynicotinate or picolinate) twice daily.

DIGESTIVE ENZYMES

Cells in the retina have an extremely high rate of metabolism. They require high levels of nutrients (along with blood and oxygen) for optimal function and to repair normal damage. Older adults often get insufficient nutrients, in part because levels of stomach acid decline with age and impair normal digestion.

Supplements that contain *betaine hydrochloride* mimic the hydrochloric acid normally produced by the stomach and can improve the digestion/absorption of eye-protecting nutrients, which are particularly helpful in the prevention and treatment of macular degeneration.

Recommended: One or two capsules of betaine hydrochloride with each meal.

Also helpful: One or two capsules of a full-spectrum plant-based enzyme (such as Longevity Science Total Gest) during or at the end of meals.

Caution: Patients who have active ulcers should not take digestive enzymes.

Devices Improve Eyesight

Eleanor E. Faye, MD, an ophthalmologist in private practice and ophthalmic surgeon emeritus at the Manhattan Eye, Ear and Throat Hospital in New York City, is the author of *Clinical Low Vision*. Little, Brown & Company. Dr. Faye is medical director of Lighthouse International, has two Merit Awards from the American Academy of Ophthalmology, and the Distinguished Service Award from the American Optometric Association.

Low vision, a permanent vision impairment that cannot be improved by standard eyeglasses, surgery or medical treatment, affects approximately 14 million Americans. Ninety percent of the eye diseases that lead to low vision—macular degeneration, diabetic retinopathy, glaucoma and cataracts accompanied by additional eye problems—occur in people over age 50.

Now: Vision aids—devices that provide magnification, light and/or contrast—can help people with low vision perform tasks that otherwise would be difficult or even impossible. Few doctors prescribe these aids for their patients—so only about 20% to 25% of people with low vision are using them.

GET A PROPER EVALUATION

If you have vision loss due to macular degeneration, diabetic retinopathy, glaucoma or cataracts, it is a good idea to consult an ophthalmologist (a medical doctor who diagnoses and treats eye diseases) or optometrist (a doctor who treats eye conditions not needing surgery) who specializes in low vision.

To find a low-vision specialist in your area, consult the free referral service sponsored by the American Academy of Ophthalmology, the American Optometric Association and Lighthouse International, a not-for-profit organization that provides education, research, advocacy and rehabilitation services, 800-829-0500, *www.lighthouse.org* (click on "Vision Services," then "Find Help Near You").

The doctor will perform a detailed evaluation of your visual function, including your contrast sensitivity and visual field. Based on his/her findings—and your lifestyle needs—the doctor will prescribe vision aids that best suit you. The products most widely used for low vision—including aids that do not require a prescription—are available at Maxi-Aids, 800-522-6294, *www.maxiaids.com*…and Independent Living Aids, 800-537-2118, *www.independentliving.com*.

Best vision aids for the following eye conditions…

MACULAR DEGENERATION

The most common cause of low vision, macular degeneration occurs when the macula (the central part of the retina, which is responsible for sharpness, color and daylight vision) is damaged by gradual degeneration of retinal cells or hemorrhaging of underlying blood cells into the retina.

Best vision aids: Macular degeneration destroys central vision, so magnification is necessary for most people who have this disease. Magnifiers can be handheld ($10 to $150)…placed on a stand ($20 to $150)…or even attached to your television or computer screen ($50 to $200). Tiny telescopes ($50 to $300) that magnify objects ranging from reading distance to far away can be held up to the eye or mounted on eyeglasses (by prescription only) to help you see better at the movies or the opera or while watching television.

Computer screen magnification is available with software such as ZoomWare ($149), which enlarges on-screen text up to two times its original size. The software can be purchased at Enable Mart, 888-640-1999, *www.enablemart.com*.

DIABETIC RETINOPATHY

A complication of advanced or long-term diabetes, diabetic retinopathy results in peripheral and central vision loss. It is caused by leaking blood vessels that damage the entire retina, including the macula.

Best vision aids: Diabetic retinopathy affects each individual differently, but most require a variety of aids, such as magnifiers and large-print books and periodicals.

Vision aids that help patients administer insulin are good for those with moderate vision loss from diabetic retinopathy. The Count-a-Dose syringe-filling device ($79.95) makes a clicking sound that can be heard for each dosage increment. The Magni-Guide Magnifier and Needle Guide ($8.95) magnifies syringe markings and helps guide the syringe needle into an insulin vial.

GLAUCOMA

Increased eye pressure, resulting from a buildup of fluid in the eyes that damages the optic nerves, often leads to the progressive eye disease known as glaucoma. In late-stage glaucoma, the optic nerve damage can cause an irreversible loss of peripheral vision.

Although glaucoma patients typically retain their central vision, it is impaired because their ability to see contrast is significantly reduced. This makes it difficult to distinguish edges, such as those on a curb or steps.

Best vision aids: Good lighting and contrast enhancement are crucial for people with glaucoma. They usually need double or triple the amount of light that a person with normal vision would use. For reading, good options are lighting that simulates the full spectrum of daylight, increasing clarity and reducing glare.

Warning: Regardless of whether you have low vision, never use halogen light for reading. Halogen is fine as an incidental light, but it is too intense as a direct reading light and can potentially damage the retina.

CATARACTS

Although cataracts can be surgically removed, some people must delay or even forgo surgery because of other health problems, such as stroke or a broken hip. For these cataract patients, low-vision aids can be helpful until surgery can be performed.

Best vision aids: Magnification makes reading easier, and polarized sunglasses ($12 to $35) eliminate glare and are helpful for people who have had cataract surgery.

Also helpful: To increase contrast on steps, sinks and bathtubs, mark the edges with brightly colored tape. Reduce glare by installing adjustable blinds on windows and covering shiny surfaces with dark tablecloths or towels.

Protect Your Vision

Melvin Schrier, OD, an optometrist who practiced in New York City for 40 years. A past president of the New York Academy of Optometry, he is now a vision consultant based in Rancho Palos Verdes, CA.

Every person over age 45 should have an annual eye exam—even if you don't have any apparent eye problems. Cataracts, macular degeneration and glaucoma often cause no symptoms in the early stages but can be detected with an exam. Our eyes also can indicate hypertension, diabetes and some types of tumors. Even dizziness or clumsiness can be related to an eye disorder.

Schedule a checkup with an optometrist (a doctor of optometry, or OD, who examines, diagnoses, treats and manages eye disorders) or ophthalmologist (a medical doctor, or MD, who specializes in eye diseases and surgery).

GETTING STARTED

Many people experience episodic eye problems that they forget to mention during an exam.

What you can do: Make a list. Is your vision occasionally blurry? You may have cataracts. Do you sometimes feel dizzy? You may have *hyperphoria*, a condition in which one eye sees higher than the other.

Also, don't allow your doctor to depend solely on an intake form that you fill out in the waiting room.

What you can do: Even if your doctor doesn't ask, tell him/her how you use your eyes. Do you golf? Drive? Use a computer? Read a lot?

EYE EXAM

Your doctor should carefully assess the health of your eyes using various instruments, including an ophthalmoscope (an instrument for examining the interior of the eye). The cornea (the front of the eye), the lens (the central part of the eye) and the retina (which consists of nerve tissue and blood vessels at the back of the eye) are evaluated. A cloudy lens may indicate cataracts, and abnormal nerve tissue could suggest diabetes, macular degeneration or, in rare cases, a tumor.

What you can do: If your doctor says that the blood vessels in your eyes are unhealthy, you may have problems in the vessels throughout your body. This could indicate high blood pressure, which could lead to a heart attack or a stroke. See your primary care doctor.

You also should be tested for glaucoma (loss of vision due to abnormally high pressure in the eye). The test measures the pressure in your eyes. Eye pressure of 10 to 18 millimeters of mercury (mm/Hg) is considered normal…25 and higher can indicate glaucoma.

What you can do: If you have a borderline reading of 19 to 24, get your eye pressure rechecked approximately every three months if your doctor doesn't prescribe follow-up care (usually eye drops).

Eye-muscle tests (there are six muscles that move each eye) determine if your eyes are working in tandem. If they are not, you may have eye discomfort or a headache.

What you can do: If your doctor does not perform eye-muscle tests during your exam, ask for them.

VISION EXAM

Your eyes should be tested for near visual acuity (for activities such as reading, sewing and looking at a map)…and distance visual acuity (for driving, watching movies and playing golf). People in their 50s may begin to have trouble with their middle-distance vision (for using a computer, shopping and seeing the dashboard on their cars).

What you can do: Before going to your appointment, measure the distance from your eye to the object you view most frequently from an intermediate distance. Is it 20, 25 or 30 inches away? You may want a pair of glasses for intermediate distance alone. Or you may prefer trifocals (lenses with three vision zones—the top for distance, middle for intermediate distances and the bottom for reading).

Important: If you are not seeing clearly and comfortably within a week of receiving any new vision prescription, insist on a recheck from your doctor.

To locate an optometrist in your area, contact the American Academy of Optometry, *www.aaopt.org*. To find a local ophthalmologist, contact the American Academy of Ophthalmology, *www.aao.org*.

New Treatments to Save Your Sight

Lylas G. Mogk, MD, founding director of the Visual Rehabilitation and Research Center of the Henry Ford Health System in Detroit, and chair of the American Academy of Ophthalmology's Vision Rehabilitation Committee, is coauthor of *Macular Degeneration—The Complete Guide to Saving and Maximizing Your Sight.* Ballantine Books.

The leading cause of vision impairment in adults is age-related macular degeneration (AMD). It's terrifying to think about, much less have.

Good news: In its very early stages, damage from wet AMD can be minimized and new treatments are now available.

AMD is a gradual, progressive eye disease. It affects the macula, which sits at the center of the retina and is responsible for central vision. AMD affects the sight of more adults than glaucoma, cataracts and diabetes combined. One out of 25 Americans over 65—nearly 1.75 million people—already have significant vision loss from AMD, and another 200,000 Americans' vision is significantly affected each year.

HOW IT WORKS

Doctors don't know for sure what causes AMD. But contributing factors include exposure to (nonultraviolet) blue light, which passes through the lens into the retina, where it creates free radicals—destructive, electrically charged particles. (People with blue or light-colored eyes are at greater risk of AMD.) Other stresses that cause free radical formation in the retina include air pollution, pesticides and, particularly, cigarette smoke. Studies have shown that smoking doubles the risk of developing AMD—and living with a smoker increases the risk, even if you don't smoke.

AMD occurs when the layers of tissue beneath the retina—the retinal pigment epithelium (RPE), Bruch's membrane and the third layer, called the choroid—stop functioning properly. The macula's cells then become deprived of oxygen and clogged with waste particles, causing them to die.

Result: Central vision gradually diminishes, making it difficult to read, make out faces or read signs.

Most cases of AMD are the so-called "dry" version, characterized by deposits of small, fatty particles, called drusen, in the macula. Over time, these deposits can enlarge and coalesce, forming a scar in the center of the retina. Ten percent to 15% of people with dry AMD go on to develop "wet" AMD, in which abnormal blood vessels form in the underlying layers and leak fluid into the retina. This fluid reduces vision in and of itself, and also contributes further to cell damage in the macula. Late-stage wet AMD can also cause retinal scarring.

MONITORING AMD

If you get examined every two years after age 40 by an ophthalmologist—as recommended by medical experts—he/she should spot telltale signs of drusen in the macula (indicating early-stage AMD) before any vision loss. The first symptom is often difficulty reading, recognizing faces and seeing in low light or low contrast conditions, such as reading ATM screens or a car dashboard.

If you have AMD, the best tool for checking subtle changes in your central vision is an Amsler grid (below, with instructions).

SELF-CHECK FOR MACULAR DEGENERATION

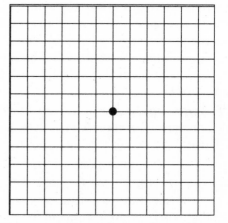

1. Put on your regular reading glasses, and use adequate lighting each time.

2. Cover your right eye, and look only at the dot in the center of the grid.

3. If any lines around the dot appear wavy, choppy or distorted, tell your ophthalmologist immediately.

4. Cover your left eye and repeat the same steps.

Important: See an ophthalmologist every two years.

TREATING WET AMD

The primary treatment for wet AMD used to be photodynamic therapy (PDT), in which a laser is used to cauterize the blood vessels leaking fluid into the retina. This method has been in use for about eight years, and was a big improvement on the older "hot laser" treatment.

How it works: A photosensitive dye is injected into the patient's arm and gravitates to the newly formed blood vessels beneath the retina. A cool laser is then focused on one blood vessel at a time, and the light of the laser activates the dye, causing it to destroy the vessel without damaging the retina—unlike with a hot laser.

While PDT can eliminate existing blood vessels, it can't stop more from forming. So, patients may need to come back for repeated treatments, ranging from every year to as often as every six weeks, depending on frequency of new blood vessel formation.

Your doctor may want a fluorescein angiogram or indocyanine green angiogram (ICG) before laser treatment. These both involve injecting dyes that make the offending blood vessels show up clearly in photographs, allowing the doctor to "map" the blood vessels before treating them.

Good news: Two newly approved drugs can help prevent new blood vessels from forming beneath the retina—Macugen (*pegaptanib sodium*), in use for over a year, and Lucentis (*ranibizumab*), approved by the FDA just recently. Both drugs block the effects of endothelial growth factor, a naturally occurring chemical that triggers the growth of new blood vessels. In the studies, Lucentis did restore some newly lost vision as long as the cells in the macula had not already died. Macugen could stop new vessels from forming but couldn't restore vision.

Avastin (*bevacizumab*), a much cheaper drug currently approved for colorectal cancer, is being used and may work just as well as Lucentis, even though it has not been studied for macular degeneration specifically.

The medication is injected through the white of the eye, with supplemental injections every six to 12 weeks. This is not painful.

Downside: Macugen and Lucentis cost around $1,000 per shot. Although Medicare typically covers 80%, this still leaves the patient with a sizable monthly expense. Avastin, on the other hand, is about $17 per shot.

Latest: Research on gene interference for macular degeneration is currently in clinical trials.

TREATING DRY AMD

For the 85% of patients with dry AMD, the progression of the disease is slower, but vision loss can eventually become significant. About 20% of people with dry AMD develop a blind spot in the shape of a ring or donut at the center of their vision. While dry AMD can't be reversed, trials are under way to see if its progress can be slowed by using low-intensity lasers to destroy the drusen particles in the retina. One preliminary study found that when 64 patients had their drusen lasered, progression of dry AMD was halted for at least two years.

THE RIGHT NUTRITION

Evidence also suggests that nutritional supplements can help. A large National Institutes of Health study found that loss of visual acuity was slowed in 30% of people who had either wet or dry AMD who took the following combination of over-the-counter nutrients each day—25,000 international units (IU) beta carotene (only recommended for non-smokers), 500 milligrams (mg) vitamin C, 400 IU vitamin E, 80 mg zinc and 2 mg copper. A number of companies now sell this full combination in pill form.

Other studies suggest that progression of wet and dry AMD may be slowed by taking six grams to 20 grams per day of lutein—a nutrient, found mainly in kale, that's active in the retina—and 1,000 mg daily of the omega-3 fatty acids DHA and EPA (contained in fish oil and flaxseed oil). I recommend taking daily capsules of both lutein and either fish oil or flaxseed oil, since it's difficult to eat enough kale or oily fish each day to get the needed amounts.

Also promising are dried wolfberries, available in some health food stores and on-line. I recommend sprinkling a handful each day into dry cereal or oatmeal. These berries, taken for centuries by the Chinese for eye health, contain high amounts of zeaxanthin, a nutrient similar to lutein that's particularly active in the macula.

PROTECTING YOUR RETINA

Finally, in addition to the precautions listed earlier, you should wear sunglasses that screen out ultraviolet (UV) rays to protect against cataracts. For protection against AMD, use amber, orange or yellow tints to screen out blue light, which contributes to damage to the retina. Those tints also provide high contrast.

KEEP LIVING FULLY!

Even with vision loss, it's important to keep up your normal activities. Vision rehabilitation—training and counseling to maximize existing sight—can help.

For services in your area, visit Lighthouse International (800-829-0500, *www.lighthouse.org*).

Mike's Miracle Vision Cure

Ione Fine, PhD, assistant professor, Keck School of Medicine, University of Southern California, Los Angeles.

Ivan Schwab, MD, professor of ophthalmology and visual sciences, University of California, Davis, and spokesman, American Academy of Ophthalmology.

Iqbal Ahmad, PhD, professor of ophthalmology and visual sciences, University of Nebraska Medical Center, Omaha.

Nature Neuroscience.

A chemical accident left Mike May completely blind at the age of three. But his real challenge began when he was finally able to see again.

In 2000, 43 years after May lost his sight, he had an experimental limbal stem cell transplant in his right eye that restored his vision. The procedure is rare, performed in perhaps 100 people each year in the United States.

Now that May, a California businessman, can see, he has found that sight is not that simple. His world consists of colors and abstract forms, not three-dimensional shapes. He can't identify his wife from her face alone, nor can he tell the difference between male and female faces most of the time. Facial expressions remain a mystery.

May's experience represents an unprecedented opportunity to glean information about how vision works.

Until now, scientists knew only that people blind for a long time whose vision returned had difficulties making sense of what they saw. But they didn't know why. Using advanced imaging techniques, researchers now have an idea of the effects of long-term blindness on various parts of the brain.

THE STUDY

Functional magnetic resonance imaging (fMRI) revealed that the parts of May's brain normally responsible for processing faces and objects were inactive. When he was shown something moving, however, that part of his brain showed high levels of activity.

"It's very much a wiring thing," says study author Ione Fine, who led the project while she was a researcher at the University of California at San Diego. "He can see. He just can't make sense of it."

Because he lost his sight at such a young age, May's brain never "learned" how to see. "Infants just out of the womb see poorly," says Dr. Ivan Schwab, professor of ophthalmology at the University of California, Davis, and a spokesman for the American Academy of Ophthalmology. "The brain has to put it all together and the early years are very important."

"You might be able to go ahead and restore vision, but if the brain has not been conditioned to make sense of the information coming from the retina, then it will be very difficult for the patient," says Iqbal Ahmad, an associate professor of ophthalmology at the University of Nebraska Medical Center in Omaha.

A DIFFERENT LIFE

May says he's better now at guessing what he is seeing than he was when he first got his sight back. He has also become better and faster at figuring out what something is, in large part because he's amassing an internal library of information.

May was a champion skier when he was blind (a guide skied ahead of him and shouted directions), but he had to close his eyes the first time he skied as a sighted person because the experience was so terrifying.

For more on blindness and how people cope with it, visit the Prevent Blindness America Web site at *www.preventblindness.org*.

■ ■ ■ ■

Beware of Glare

Open wide—squinting causes itchy, tired, dry eyes.

Reason: It reduces blinking, which allows eyes to rewet themselves with tears and reduces eyestrain. Even slight squinting can cut blinking rates by half. Many computer users squint while looking at the screen.

To reduce squinting: Reduce glare by positioning monitors so windows are to the side, not behind…use lower-wattage bulbs in lamps.

James E. Sheedy, OD, PhD, director of Pacific University's Optometry Research, Forest Grove, OR, and leader of a study of computer users, published in *Optometry and Vision*.

The Whys of Dry Eyes— And How to Get Relief

J. Daniel Nelson, MD, professor of ophthalmology at the University of Minnesota in Minneapolis.

A healthy adult produces tears every minute during waking hours. Tears protect and lubricate the surfaces of the eyes (corneas), remove dust and other particles, and flush out inflammatory chemicals that accumulate when the eyes are irritated.

But about 15% of Americans over age 65 suffer from dry eyes. The problem occurs most often after age 50, as our tear production declines with age. Symptoms of dry eyes include stinging or burning sensations…eye fatigue when reading…mucus in or around the eyes…or the sensation that there's sand or gravel in the eyes.

What most people don't know: Tears help people see. By spreading across the eye surface to create a "tear film," tears work in tandem with the cornea to provide the major optical surface. That's why long-distance vision may be impaired in people who have chronic dry eyes.

If you think you have dry eyes, see an ophthalmologist (a medical doctor who specializes in eye diseases and surgery). He/she usually can diagnose dry eyes after taking a medical history and noting your symptoms. There may not be a cure for dry eyes, but treatment can minimize discomfort and help protect your vision.

CAUSES OF DRY EYES

Tears are composed of 90% water and small amounts of salts or electrolytes and proteins that are secreted by the lacrimal glands located at the top outer edge of each eye. Tears also contain mucus and blood fats (lipids) produced by the *meibomian glands* located on the edge of the eyelids.

Main causes of dry eyes…

•**Blepharitis.** This inflammation of the eyelids is often caused by a blockage of the lipid-producing meibomian glands or by the secretion of oils that are unusually thick and don't flow properly.

•**Medications.** Many prescription and over-the-counter (OTC) drugs cause dry eyes.

Main offenders: Antihistamines, decongestants, diuretics and some antidepressants, such as *amitriptyline* (Elavil). If you experience dry eyes after starting a new medication, talk to your doctor about alternatives.

•**Inflammation.** When allergies or exposure to environmental irritants, such as dust or wind, or chemicals found in household cleaning products irritate the eyes, cells release inflammatory chemicals called cytokines. In normal eyes, the flow of tears dilutes the concentration of inflammatory cytokines and may counteract their effect, thereby reducing irritation. But in allergy sufferers and other people with chronic inflammation, there aren't enough tears to dilute the cytokines. Treating allergies or other sources of eye irritation may eliminate dry eyes—but not always.

•**Sjögren's syndrome.** This autoimmune disease occurs when a person's antibodies damage the lacrimal glands, which reduces tear production. Drug treatments for Sjögren's help relieve dry eyes, but do not cure them.

DIAGNOSIS AND TREATMENTS

If you've been diagnosed with dry eyes, here are the best ways to treat the condition…

•**Lubricate the eyes.** Patients who experience only mild dryness of the eyes usually can get relief by using "artificial tears" one to four times daily. These OTC products are available in liquid and gel forms. Both are equally effective.

Caution: The preservatives, such as benzalkonium chloride, added to many products can damage eye cells if used more than four times daily.

For more frequent use, choose a preservative-free product, such as Refresh Liquigel, Systane or Tears Naturale Free, or one with a "vanishing preservative," such as GenTeal. The preservative disappears as soon as the drops come into contact with the tear film.

•**Reduce inflammation.** People with inflammatory conditions, including Sjögren's syndrome, may require anti-inflammatory medications to diminish dryness. Steroid or immunosuppressant eye drops, such as *cyclosporine* (Restasis), control the inflammation response and significantly reduce dry eye symptoms in many patients. These drugs are typically used for a few months to several years.

Caution: Because topical steroids can cause an increase in eye pressure and cataracts, patients must have their eye pressure measured monthly while using these drops.

•**Wear "moisture chamber" eyeglasses.** They are designed to create a high-humidity environment by fitting snugly to prevent moisture in the eyes from evaporating. They also minimize exposure to wind or dust. Some patients can get by with tight-fitting, wrap-around sunglasses. If these don't help, an eye-care professional can make special moisture-chamber glasses.

Cost: As high as $250 in addition to the cost of the lenses and frames. Many insurance policies pay for them.

Also helpful: Put a humidifier or vaporizer beside your bed, desk or any area where you spend a lot of time.

•**Practice blinking.** Four times a day, blink 20 times. Many people with dry eyes experience subconscious discomfort when they blink—as a result, they get in the habit of not blinking completely. Blinking is essential because it causes the eyes to secrete protective oils…wipes away dead skin cells…and increases tear production.

•**Take an omega-3 supplement.** The omega-3 fatty acids found in cold-water fish and flaxseed have anti-inflammatory effects and often reduce eye dryness. Because it can be difficult to get adequate amounts of these essential

fatty acids in your diet, I recommend taking TheraTears Nutrition or ProOmega capsules, formulas that contain a good mix of fatty acids for eye health. Such products are usually found in the eye-care section of pharmacies. Take two capsules twice daily.

If your dry eyes don't improve enough with these therapies, you may be advised to undergo *punctal occlusion*, a simple outpatient procedure in which the tear drainage ducts are either sealed with silicone plugs or permanently closed. This causes tears to remain in the eyes longer and can reduce dry eye symptoms by up to 50%. Possible side effects include watery eyes and increased inflammation.

Caution: This procedure should only be done if your doctor determines there is no eye inflammation. Otherwise, inflammatory chemicals stay in contact with the eyes longer and *increase* irritation.

■ ■ ■ ■

Cataract Breakthrough

New lens implants allow people with cataracts to see near, far and in between. Previous lenses corrected for either distance or reading. Multifocal intraocular implants could cost from $2,000 to $3,000 more per eye than traditional ones. Health insurers pay only up to the cost of traditional implants.

Gina Gladstein, MD, section head of ophthalmology, Greenwich Hospital, Greenwich, CT.

■ ■ ■ ■

Children's Vision

Distance glasses can worsen nearsightedness in children. They are prescribed routinely by some doctors when children start to become nearsighted. Some children can become nearsighted because they spend excessive time on computers or playing video games. That can cause eyestrain and focusing problems. Most nearsightedness (myopia), however, is genetic in nature. Doctors often prescribe distance lenses to clear the blur, but the lenses may aggravate the problem by bringing everything closer, forcing the child's vision to refocus and strain. This may lead to a need for stronger lenses every year or two. If other visual tests show that the eyes are under stress, children should be given nearpoint, or "plus," lenses for reading, using the computer and playing video games. Reading lenses tend to push things farther away, allowing the focusing muscles to relax.

Also: Don't be afraid of bifocals for children if your optometrist recommends them—they can play a big part in limiting myopic changes.

Melvin Schrier, OD, an optometrist who practiced in New York City for 40 years. A past president of the New York Academy of Optometry, he is now a vision consultant based in Rancho Palos Verdes, CA.

■ ■ ■ ■

Contact Lens Risk

Contact lenses can increase the risk of eye infections.

Recent finding: One of every 2,500 contact lens wearers will develop an infection.

Especially risky: Wearing contacts while sleeping—they impede the flow of oxygen to corneas.

If you don't often remove your lenses before bed: Switch to the new silicone hydrogel lenses, which allow more oxygen to reach the eyes and reduce risk of infection fivefold over traditional lenses.

Thomas Steinemann, MD, associate professor of ophthalmology, Case Western Reserve University, and cornea and external eye disease specialist, MetroHealth Medical Center, both in Cleveland.

■ ■ ■ ■

Vision Savers

A new drug fights vision loss, reports George A. Williams, MD. The wet form of age-related macular degeneration (AMD)—a major cause of blindness—is characterized by growth of abnormal leaky blood vessels in the retina. The drug *ranibizumab* (Lucentis) blocks blood vessel growth, preventing further deterioration in AMD patients. The medication is injected inside the eye monthly for three months. Anesthetizing eyedrops prevent pain.

George A. Williams, MD, director of Beaumont Eye Institute, Royal Oak, MI, and a spokesperson for the American Academy of Ophthalmology, *www.aao.org.*

■ ■ ■ ■

Carb Danger

Carbohydrates can increase the chances of developing cataracts.

Recent study: People who consumed 200 grams or more per day of any kind of carbohydrate for more than 14 years had more than twice the risk of developing cataracts as those who consumed the USDA-recommended 130 grams per day. Carbohydrates are found in such foods as bread, cookies, white potatoes and rice.

Theory: The excess glucose liberated within the body from the digestion of dietary carbohydrates may damage proteins in the lens of the eye and lead to cataracts.

Allen Taylor, PhD, professor of nutrition, biochemistry and ophthalmology, USDA Human Nutrition Research Center on Aging, Tufts University, Boston, and leader of a study of 417 women, published in *The American Journal of Clinical Nutrition.*

■ ■ ■ ■

Glaucoma Link

High blood pressure and glaucoma may be related.

Recent study: Among people with glaucoma, 29% also had high blood pressure—a significantly higher percentage than in the population as a whole. If you have hypertension, watch your weight, eat healthful foods, exercise regularly and ask your doctor about medication.

Michael J. S. Langman, MD, professor of medicine, University of Birmingham, Queen Elizabeth Hospital, Birmingham, England.

■ ■ ■ ■

Eye Strain

New animated 3-D films can cause eye pain, headaches and visual discomfort in children and adults. Watching a 3-D movie can be stressful to the eyes if a person's prescription is significantly different in one eye than the other. Images do not fuse easily or at all, causing the brain to use extra effort to focus.

Melvin Schrier, OD, an optometrist who practiced in New York City for 40 years. A past president of the New York Academy of Optometry, he is now a vision consultant based in Rancho Palos Verdes, CA.

■ ■ ■ ■

Vision-Friendly Diet

Diet can reduce the risk of age-related macular degeneration (AMD)—a leading cause of blindness among people over age 55. There's no cure for AMD, but the right foods may help prevent it. A new study of more than 5,000 people over age 55 found that those who had above-average intake of each of four nutrients—vitamin C, vitamin E, zinc and beta carotene—reduced their AMD risk by 35%.

Best sources: For vitamin C, oranges and fruit …for vitamin E, almonds and peanut butter…for zinc, turkey, chicken and fortified cereal…for beta carotene, sweet potatoes, apricots and peaches.

Jacqueline C. M. Witteman, PhD, associate professor of epidemiology, Erasmus Medical Center, Rotterdam, the Netherlands.

Natural Cures for Nasal Congestion

Jamison Starbuck, ND, naturopathic physician in family practice in Missoula, Montana. She is past president of the American Association of Naturopathic Physicians and is a contributing editor to *The Alternative Advisor: The Complete Guide to Natural Therapies and Alternative Treatments.* Time-Life.

When cold weather arrives, decongestants and boxes of tissue are familiar standbys for people with stuffy, runny noses. The common cold is often the culprit. With a cold, the nose can become congested as the body tries to eliminate the virus that is causing the illness. But there are other irritants that also cause nasal congestion. *Fortunately, you can get at the root cause of your nasal congestion and avoid taking decongestants, which only temporarily mask symptoms, by following these steps…*

•**Identify respiratory irritants.** One of my patients recently complained of congestion when she vacuumed her house. Although she has a cat, she claimed to not be allergic since she does not sneeze or get congested when she spends time with her pet. As an experiment, I asked her to visit a friend who doesn't have pets

and spend a little time vacuuming. When she did not become congested, my patient agreed that the cat dander released in the air from the vacuum could be the problem. A simple dust mask worn while vacuuming prevented any other bouts of congestion. Dust masks made of paper (less than $1 each) work nicely for reducing sneezing and/or runny noses triggered by dust, pollen, pet dander, smoke, grass, hay or fallen leaves. If potentially harmful vapors, such as fumes from paint, varnish or cleaning compounds, bother your nose, use a carbon-filtration mask, available in paint stores from $40–$42. They trap vapors, removing them from the air breathed.

•**Test for food allergies.** If you're chronically congested, or regularly get a stuffy nose after eating, ask your doctor for a food allergy blood test to check for IgG-mediated—or delayed sensitivity—food allergens. These allergies cause generalized inflammation, leading to congestion.

Most common food allergens: Dairy, wheat, peanuts and soy.

•**Eat the right foods.** To soothe and strengthen the mucous membranes of your nose and upper-respiratory tract, eat lots of *proanthocyanidins*, a type of plant pigment with anti-inflammatory, antiviral and antiallergenic properties. Blueberries, blackberries, Marion berries or raspberries (fresh or frozen) are great sources of proanthocyanidins. If you suffer from chronic nasal congestion, eat one-half cup daily.

•**Drink hot tea.** For a gentle decongestant, try a tea made from equal parts dried linden, elder and chamomile flowers. Combine the herbs and use three teaspoons of the mix per 10 ounces of boiling water. Steep, covered, for 10 minutes. Strain and flavor the tea with honey and lemon, if desired. Drink one cup twice daily until congestion is eliminated.

•**Use a neti pot.** In Ayurvedic (Indian) medicine, neti pots, which cost about $20 and resemble small watering cans, are used to pour a saline solution through each nostril, to reduce congestion. You can buy saline solution at drugstores or make your own (follow the instructions that accompany the pot). Use once or twice daily—upon waking and/or at bedtime, when congested or exposed to allergens.

■■■■

Sinus Treatment Warning

New treatment for sinusitis has not yet been proved effective. *Balloon sinuplasty* involves inflating a small balloon in the sinus cavity to open inflamed and infected sinuses, similar to the technique used to open coronary arteries. Sinuplasty has been promoted as less invasive and requiring a shorter recovery time than traditional sinusitis surgery.

But: Sinuplasty costs more, and no clinical trials have yet proved its lasting effect. Two studies have been done, but one involved only cadavers and the other was based on 10 patients, eight of whom also had conventional surgery at the time of the sinuplasty.

David W. Kennedy, MD, vice dean for professional services and senior vice president, director of rhinology, department of otorhinolaryngology, Hospital of the University of Pennsylvania, Philadelphia, and president of the American Academy of Otolaryngology—Head and Neck Surgery.

■■■■

Hearing Loss

Hearing loss may be caused by the brain, not the ears. In some older people, when sound reaches the brain, it is not processed correctly due to various factors, including aging itself. Specialized hearing tests can determine where the problem occurs.

Robert D. Frisina, PhD, associate chair for research and professor, otolaryngology department, University of Rochester Medical Center, Rochester, NY.

Sudden Hearing Loss: The Symptom You Should Never Ignore

Gordon B. Hughes, MD, program officer, clinical trials, National Institute on Deafness and Other Communication Disorders, National Institutes of Health, Bethesda, MD. Dr. Hughes former is secretary of the Polizer Society (an international society of ear surgeons) and is coeditor of a landmark book, *Clinical Otology*. Thieme Medical Publishers.

Don't confuse a temporary, normal loss of hearing—the kind you get from a head cold or an airplane's descent—with sudden hearing loss (SHL), in which your hearing gets worse over a few hours or days without an obvious cause. SHL is an emergency that can result in permanent ear damage. SHL usually affects just one ear. Approximately half of patients with SHL also experience dizziness, light-headedness, a sensation of spinning and/or ringing in the ear (tinnitus).

•**See a doctor immediately.** The optimal window for treatment is within two weeks. About one-third of SHL patients experience significant improvement if they are treated within this period. Even with rapid treatment, however, less than 20% of patients return completely to normal.

It's estimated that more than 80 conditions can cause SHL. *Main causes...*

VIRAL INFECTIONS

Viruses, particularly the herpes viruses, can cause SHL. Mumps, measles and chicken pox/shingles viruses have been linked to SHL. A viral infection affecting the inner ear can cause inflammation that damages the *organ of Corti*, the structure that generates hearing impulses and sends them to the brain.

Red flag: SHL accompanied by a cold sore may be due to the *herpes simplex* virus. SHL patients who also have herpes symptoms may be treated with antiviral drugs, such as *acyclovir* (Zovirax), *valacyclovir* (Valtrex) or *famciclovir* (Famvir)—but it's not known for sure if antivirals affect the outcome of SHL.

Primary treatment: Oral *prednisone* for 10 to 14 days. About one-third of patients given this powerful anti-inflammatory steroid experience significant improvement, even if the underlying causes are not known. It's a first-line treatment for most cases of SHL. Side effects can include excitability, increased appetite, increased urination and facial flushing.

New treatment: A national study is under way to determine whether inner-ear injections of *methylprednisolone*, a prednisone-like drug, work as well as, or better than, oral treatments for SHL.

CIRCULATORY PROBLEMS

The cochlea, a snail-shaped structure in the inner ear that translates sound vibrations into signals to the brain, requires a steady flow of blood. Reductions in blood flow can disrupt cochlear function in as little as one hour.

Treatment: People who have circulatory disorders may be given drugs to improve circulation—as well as prednisone.

ACOUSTIC NEUROMA

About 3% of SHL cases are caused by a slow-growing, noncancerous tumor (neuroma) that puts pressure on the acoustic nerve. It is not known why hearing loss is sudden when the tumor is slow-growing.

SHL accompanied by dizziness, tinnitus and/or unsteadiness may be due to a neuroma. An MRI of the brain stem and hearing nerve will show if an acoustic neuroma is present. Hearing loss caused by a neuroma usually can't be reversed. Treatment is recommended if the tumor continues to grow…hearing loss gets progressively worse…or other symptoms are present. Otherwise, your doctor may recommend watchful waiting—having an MRI once or twice a year to check the neuroma's progress.

Treatment: Surgery or radiation therapy.

EXCESSIVE FLUID

Fluid buildup in the inner ear is usually due to Meniere's disease, in which excessive fluid causes fluctuating SHL along with vertigo and balance difficulties. Meniere's disease can be diagnosed from a health history (two or more episodes of vertigo lasting at least 20 minutes… ringing in the ears…and hearing loss), along with a hearing test and electronystagmography (ENG), a diagnostic test that evaluates balance by detecting abnormal eye movements.

Treatment: Most patients are put on a low-salt diet and given diuretics for 10 to 14 days. Those with Meniere's disease continue treatments indefinitely.

EARWAX

Some SHL cases are caused by compacted wax in the ear canal.

Common cause: Cleaning inside the canal with a cotton swab. Wax naturally migrates from the inner to the outer canal. Cleaning inside the canal pushes wax downward and compresses it into a plug that prevents sound waves from reaching the eardrum.

Treatment: Over-the-counter solutions containing *hydrogen peroxide* or *carbamyl peroxide*

soften wax and make it easier to flush out with a bulb irrigator. If home treatments don't help, the wax has to be removed by a doctor with a curette (a small metal loop at the end of a metal handle) or a suction device.

MEDICATION SIDE EFFECTS

Approximately 200 drugs can cause SHL, including aspirin, quinine and the aminoglycoside antibiotics *gentamicin* and *neomycin* (usually prescribed for serious infections and given intravenously). SHL caused by these "ototoxic" drugs can range from mild to severe—and may be permanent in some cases.

Red flag: Hearing loss that occurs in both ears simultaneously following the use of these or other medications.

Hearing can improve when patients discontinue or take lower doses of certain drugs. The risk of permanent hearing loss is higher with aminoglycoside antibiotics.

■ ■ ■ ■

Ear Infections

Kids with recurrent ear infections may benefit from seeing an osteopathic physician (DO) trained to perform osteopathic manipulation to relieve pressure in the eustachian tube. Osteopaths are licensed to practice medicine just as MDs are.

Recent study: Children who received osteopathic manipulations in addition to routine care—antibiotics, ibuprofen, ear tubes, etc.—had fewer ear infections and were less likely to need antibiotics or surgery than ones given routine pediatric care only.

Miriam V. Mills, MD, clinical professor of osteopoathic manipulative medicine, College of Osteopathic Medicine, Oklahoma State University, Tulsa.

■ ■ ■ ■

Hearing Aid News

Invisible hearing aids are here. *Completely in the Canal* models fit deeply into the ear. The microphone picks up less wind noise than other hearing aids do. Controls can be hard to adjust, but some models come with remote controls. Open ear fit models are placed behind the ear and are barely noticeable. In *Behind the Ear* (BTE) models, the casing is concealed by hair. Sound ID (866-768-6343, *www.soundid.com*) makes a unit that doubles as a wireless cell-phone headset.

Paul Pessis, AuD, past president of the American Academy of Audiology, Reston, Virginia, and founder of North Shore Vestibular Lab, Highland Park, IL.

■ ■ ■ ■

Easier Dentistry

Afraid of the dentist? Some dentists with special training now use sedation pills, such as *triazolam*, to treat patients who are afraid of having dental work done. The pills lead to conscious sedation—relaxation so deep that even patients with strong fear of the dentist can relax while work is being done. Such sedation does not reduce pain, so there is still a need for a local anesthetic, such as novocaine.

For information, contact Dental Organization for Conscious Sedation, 866-592-9618, *www.sedationdocs.com.*

Matt Smith, DDS, The Center for Esthetic Dentistry, Commack, NY.

■ ■ ■ ■

Quick Fixes for Tooth Trouble

Consider these temporary fixes for dental problems.

If a tooth is sensitive to cold or sweets: Rinse with warm water.

If you have swelling from an injury: Apply ice—a half-hour on, a half-hour off.

If swelling is from infection: Apply a heating pad or hot washcloth, or hold hot salty water in your mouth—the heat stimulates blood flow to the area, which helps remove toxins.

If you lose a filling: Rinse your mouth with warm water and place cotton dipped in oil of cloves in the cavity—the clove oil eases pain.

If a crown pops off: Use denture adhesive or tooth cement—available at most drugstores—to reattach it temporarily. See a dentist as soon as possible for any of these problems.

Irwin Smigel, DDS, president and founder, American Society for Dental Aesthetics, and a dentist in private practice, New York City.

■ ■ ■ ■

Filling Alert

Mercury fillings are not safe, despite recent reports that they are. Studies at the University of Calgary have found that mercury vapor from fillings enters the body and may cause brain-cell degeneration and immune suppression, among other problems.

Self-defense: Have your dentist use mercury-free white composite fillings, and try to have existing amalgam ones replaced over time by a "biological dentist."

Mark A. Stengler, ND, naturopathic physician in private practice, La Jolla, CA...adjunct associate clinical professor at the National College of Natural Medicine, Portland, OR...author of 16 books, including *The Natural Physician's Healing Therapies* (Bottom Line Books) and coauthor of *Prescription for Natural Cures* (Wiley)...and author of the *Bottom Line/Natural Healing* newsletter.

Natural Ways to Care for Your Gums

Jamison Starbuck, ND, naturopathic physician in family practice and a lecturer at the University of Montana, both in Missoula. She is past president of the American Association of Naturopathic Physicians and is a contributing editor to *The Alternative Advisor: The Complete Guide to Natural Therapies and Alternative Treatments.* Time-Life.

For years, I've observed that far too many otherwise health-conscious people neglect their oral health. That's a mistake. Gum (periodontal) disease occurs in 50% of people over age 55. Even though we all know the importance of regular brushing and flossing, it often takes more than conventional tooth and gum care to keep our mouth tissues healthy. The mildest form of periodontal disease is gingivitis. This inflammatory condition, which is primarily caused by poor oral hygiene, typically leads to red, swollen gum tissue that often bleeds.

If you have these symptoms, see your dentist for a checkup. If you've got periodontal disease, and it is left untreated, surgery may be needed. The first step I recommend is to reduce your sugar intake. Sugar increases plaque formation and feeds the harmful bacteria that dwell in your gums.

Taking the right nutritional supplements also can help reverse gingivitis, often within three months. This could eliminate the need for costly periodontal surgery. *My favorite supplements for gum health…*

•**Vitamin C.** It strengthens gum tissue and enhances your white blood cells' ability to fight inflammation-promoting microorganisms in your mouth. To restore gum health, take 3,000 mg daily in divided doses for three months. If this amount of vitamin C causes diarrhea, cut back on the dose. If you have high iron levels, do not take a vitamin C supplement—it increases iron absorption. For healthy gum maintenance, take 1,500 mg of vitamin C daily.

•**Zinc.** Like vitamin C, zinc improves gum health by enhancing white blood cell activity. This mineral also inhibits plaque buildup (which increases inflammation) and speeds the healing of bleeding gums. To treat gingivitis, take 40 mg of zinc daily for three months. For healthy gum maintenance, take a daily dose of 20 mg of zinc.

•**Folate.** A deficiency of this B vitamin is common and increases risk for gingivitis. To treat gingivitis, add a daily dose of 1 mg of folic acid along with 500 micrograms (mcg) of vitamin B-12 to your supplement regimen for three months. Taking folic acid alone can mask a possible B-12 deficiency. Bleeding gums also improve with a 0.1% solution of liquid folic acid, which is available at health-food stores. Brush your teeth, then swish one-half ounce of the solution in your mouth twice daily for 60 seconds and then spit it out. For optimal gum absorption, do not eat or drink anything for at least 15 minutes after swishing. To maintain gum health, take 800 mcg of folic acid along with 400 mcg of vitamin B-12 daily.

•**Coenzyme Q10.** This powerful antioxidant helps our cells function efficiently. Studies show that CoQ10 not only protects the heart and brain, but also the gums. For periodontal disease, take 100 mg of CoQ10 daily for three months. Take 60 mg for gum maintenance. It is available wherever vitamins are sold.

■ ■ ■ ■

Raisins Good for Your Teeth

Oleanolic acid, a plant chemical found in raisins, was shown to inhibit the growth of two species of oral bacteria, Streptococcus mutans, which causes cavities, and Porphyromonas gingivalis, which is associated with gum disease. This finding refutes the long-standing belief that raisins promote tooth decay.

Christine D. Wu, PhD, professor and associate dean for research, periodontics department, University of Illinois at Chicago College of Dentistry.

■ ■ ■ ■

Best for Your Teeth

Avoid all-natural toothbrushes, made with boars' hairs. The hairs are hollow and retain bacteria. Beyond that, it doesn't matter if you use a manual or electric nylon, rounded-bristle brush.

Also: Any toothpaste will clean teeth and remove bacteria—just be sure it has fluoride to help prevent decay—but some have minor enhancements.

Examples: Tartar-control toothpaste may be slightly better at preventing the formation of tartar…sensitivity toothpastes contain ingredients that may be helpful if your teeth are extremely sensitive to heat and cold…whitening toothpastes may make teeth slightly whiter if used according to the manufacturers' directions.

Sheldon Nadler, DMD, dentist in private practice in New York City.

■ ■ ■ ■

Tongue Problem

Black hairy tongue is an overgrowth of the tongue's normal bumps (papillae), making them look similar to hair. It is a harmless but embarrassing problem. The papillae can grow five to six millimeters high.

Causes: A diet of primarily soft foods, poor oral hygiene and taking antibiotics, which can disrupt the mouth's healthful bacteria. Drinking coffee and tea as well as smoking can aggravate the condition.

To get your tongue back to normal: Scrub your tongue with a toothbrush or tongue scraper twice a day, and continue to brush your tongue even when the problem goes away. Eat healthful foods, such as raw vegetables and whole-grain cereal.

Also helpful: The acid from fresh pineapples.

Selene Yeager, health journalist, Emmaus, PA, and co-author of more than two dozen health books, including *The Doctor's Book of Food Remedies*. Rodale Books.

■ ■ ■ ■

Hiccup Cures That Work

Stick a finger into each ear—this stimulates the vagus nerve, which runs from the brain to the abdomen and controls hiccups. Use a cotton swab to draw a line gently down the roof of your mouth—the tickling stops the throat spasm that causes hiccups. Breathe into a paper bag to produce carbon dioxide, which helps calm the diaphragm—but do this only if someone is with you, in case you get light-headed. Get distracted—have someone ask you a nonsensical question or try to make you hiccup at an exact moment.

Health, 2100 Lakeshore Drive, Birmingham, AL 35209.

■ ■ ■ ■

Wait for Nasal Surgery

Cosmetic nasal surgery for teenagers should be done only after the nose is structurally stable and the teenager is psychologically mature. For most girls, this means at least age 15...for boys, who tend to develop later than girls, at least age 17. Be sure the teen is comfortable altering his/her appearance and is not being pushed into surgery by peers or family members.

Robert Kotler, MD, FACS, clinical instructor, University of California, Los Angeles, and author of *Secrets of a Beverly Hills Cosmetic Surgeon*. Ernest Mitchell.

16

Food Smarts

The Healing Power Of Spices

Traditional medicine has recognized the medicinal benefits of spices for thousands of years.

Now: A growing body of scientific evidence supports the use of spices to prevent—and even help treat—various diseases, such as arthritis, diabetes, cancer and Alzheimer's.* *New findings...*

CAYENNE PEPPER

What it does: Lowers cholesterol...helps prevent atherosclerosis...and reduces allergic responses. An extract from the pepper, called capsaicin, can be used in a topical cream to treat pain from arthritis, shingles, bursitis, low-back ache and neuropathy (nerve pain). Cayenne's benefits can be attributed to the antioxidants, flavonoids and carotenoids it contains, all of

*Check with your doctor before using spices for medicinal purposes. They can interact with prescription medication.

which have anti-inflammatory effects and enhance circulation. Capsaicin depletes nerve endings of *substance P*, a neurotransmitter that facilitates nerve transmission of pain.

Scientific evidence: A four-week study published in the *Journal of Rheumatology* found that patients with osteoarthritis of the hands who applied capsaicin cream four times a day experienced reduced pain and tenderness.

Typical dose: Cayenne is available as a supplement in capsules and tincture. Take one capsule of cayenne pepper up to three times a day...or add three to eight drops of cayenne tincture to four ounces of water and drink two to four times a day. Apply topical cream containing capsaicin to painful areas, as directed on the label. You also can season your food with powdered cayenne pepper or hot sauce.

Possible side effects: Cayenne pepper can cause gastric upset. To avoid pain and burning,

David Winston, a Washington, New Jersey–based registered herbalist (RH) and professional member of the American Herbalist Guild, is coauthor of *Herbal Therapy and Supplements: A Scientific and Traditional Approach*. Lippincott.

460

do not let topical capsaicin come in contact with your eyes or other mucous membranes. If you take *warfarin* (Coumadin), do not use cayenne pepper supplements.

CINNAMON

What it does: Helps prevent heart disease and type 2 diabetes.

Due to its antioxidant properties, cinnamon helps people with metabolic syndrome (a cluster of factors, including excessive abdominal fat, high blood sugar and elevated blood pressure, which increase the risk for cardiovascular disease and type 2 diabetes) use the hormone insulin in their bodies more efficiently.

Scientific evidence: A US Department of Agriculture clinical study found that consuming capsules containing 1 g, 3 g or 6 g of cinnamon daily (about ¼ teaspoon, ¾ teaspoon or 1¼ teaspoons, respectively) for 40 days lowered blood levels of glucose and triglycerides (fats in the blood) by about 25% in adults with type 2 diabetes. It also reduced LDL "bad" cholesterol by up to 27%.

Typical dose: Use ½ to one teaspoon of powdered cinnamon daily on cereal or toast or mix into yogurt…take one capsule twice a day…or add 20 to 40 drops of tincture to one ounce of water and drink three times daily.

For tea, mix ¼ to ½ teaspoon of powdered cinnamon with eight ounces of boiling water. Steep for 10 to 15 minutes, covered. Drink a four-ounce cup up to three times a day.

Possible side effects: Because cinnamon can affect blood glucose levels, people with diabetes should carefully monitor their blood sugar and ask their doctors if their medication needs to be adjusted.

GINGER

What it does: Reduces the pain and swelling caused by rheumatoid arthritis and osteoarthritis…helps prevent the nausea and vomiting associated with motion sickness or pregnancy…enhances digestion and circulation…and eases intestinal gas.

Scientific evidence: Two clinical studies found that ginger relieved pain and/or swelling in 75% of arthritis patients.

Typical dose: Take one to two capsules with meals two to three times daily…or add 10 to 30 drops of the tincture to one ounce of water and drink three to four times daily.

For tea, mix ¼ to ½ teaspoon of powdered ginger (or use a ginger tea bag) with eight ounces of boiling water. Steep for 10 to 15 minutes, covered. Drink four ounces up to three times daily.

Possible side effects: Ginger can have a blood-thinning effect, so check with your doctor before using it if you take an anticoagulant, such as *warfarin* (Coumadin). Ginger may cause an upset stomach in people who take larger doses than those described above.

TURMERIC

What it does: Helps prevent atherosclerosis, some types of cancer and Alzheimer's disease… reduces the pain and stiffness of rheumatoid arthritis and osteoarthritis…eliminates indigestion…and eases the symptoms of inflammatory bowel disease and irritable bowel syndrome. The beneficial effects of turmeric (also found in curry) are due to its anti-inflammatory compounds known as *curcuminoids*, as well as the essential oils and carotenoids it contains.

Scientific evidence: In a double-blind, placebo-controlled study, 116 people with indigestion took either a 500-mg capsule of curcumin (the substance that gives turmeric its yellow color) or a placebo four times a day. Nearly 90% of those taking curcumin experienced full or partial relief after seven days.

Typical dose: Take 250 mg to 500 mg of curcumin (standardized to 80% to 90% curcumin) three times daily…or add 40 to 60 drops of the tincture to one ounce of water and drink three to four times daily.

For tea, mix ½ teaspoon of powdered turmeric with eight ounces of boiling water. Steep for 10 to 15 minutes, covered. Drink four ounces up to four times a day.

Possible side effects: Turmeric stimulates liver function, so it should be avoided by anyone with gallstones or any other bile-duct obstruction. Preliminary studies show that curcumin may lessen the effectiveness of chemotherapy drugs, such as *doxorubicin* (Rubex) and *cyclophosphamide* (Cytoxan). If you are undergoing chemotherapy, talk to your doctor before taking curcumin.

■ ■ ■ ■

Spices Fight Cancer

Adding fresh rosemary leaves to ground beef has been found to lower production of cancer-causing compounds during cooking by up to 60%.

Theory: Antioxidants in rosemary reduce levels of heterocyclic amines, known carcinogens found in protein-rich meat that has been grilled, broiled or fried. Basil, oregano and thyme also are believed to confer this benefit.

J. Scott Smith, PhD, professor, Animal Sciences & Industry, Food Science Institute, Kansas State University, Manhattan, KS.

Is Your Diet Deficient?

C. Leigh Broadhurst, PhD, research scientist at the University of Maryland in College Park, and a research geochemist at the US Department of Agriculture, has published scientific research on diabetes, polyunsaturated fats and medicinal plants.

With all the processed food now consumed in the US, getting the necessary nutrients from our diet has become increasingly difficult. Of course, we can turn to nutritional supplements, but research has consistently shown that fresh food—with an abundance of healthful compounds that are believed to work synergistically—is usually our best source of valuable nutrients.

What most people don't realize: Choosing the right foods and food combinations allows you to consume these vital nutrients in a form that is most bioavailable, meaning the food components are efficiently digested, absorbed and assimilated.

What you must know to maximize the bioavailability of nutrients in your food...

•**Iron.** This mineral is critical for brain function and helps your immune system function normally by increasing your resistance to stress and disease. Iron can help you avoid symptoms of fatigue, weakness and irritability.

Plant foods are rarely a good source of iron. For example, the iron from spinach is a net loss. Even though spinach is a good source of magnesium, bone-building vitamin K and other important nutrients, the fiber and plant chemicals in the spinach leaf bind to iron, inhibiting the mineral's bioavailability.

Helpful: When shopping for meat, look for dark meat products, such as liver, beef or dark meat turkey. They are the best sources of iron. Tofu and seafood (especially clams and shrimp) also are rich in iron.

•**Zinc.** This mineral is essential for a healthy immune system. It is highly bioavailable in red meat, though some zinc also is found in nuts (almonds and walnuts). Poultry is another good source of zinc.

Helpful: Consider adding oysters to your diet. They are one of the richest sources of zinc.

Caution: Raw oysters are often contaminated with bacteria.

•**Magnesium.** Up to 75% of Americans are deficient in this vital mineral, which is needed for heart health, strong bones and blood sugar control.

Helpful: Vegetables are among the richest sources of magnesium. Eat raw or lightly steamed vegetables—highly processed or overcooked veggies lose their magnesium content. Whole grains are also much richer sources of magnesium than refined grains.

•**Calcium.** Many people advocate green, leafy vegetables for calcium, but these foods do not provide ample amounts of the mineral in a bioavailable form.

Sardines are an often-overlooked source of calcium, but they are not standard fare for many Americans.

Dairy foods remain the best regular source of calcium. Milk with one percent or two percent fat is a good choice. Skim milk is not recommended. That's because the bioavailability of fat-soluble vitamins, such as vitamin D, is diminished when you remove all the fat from milk.

Helpful: Avoid "fat-free half and half." This product provides no nutritional value—it is usually filled with corn syrup and other sugars to give it the creamy feel of real half and half.

•**Selenium.** The number-one source of this cancer-fighting mineral is the soil in which plants are grown. Soil in the Great Plains states contains adequate levels of selenium, so products made from whole-grain wheat, which is typically harvested in this area, are generally good sources of selenium.

Helpful: If you are at increased risk for cancer (due to family history, exposure to second-hand smoke or other carcinogens), consider taking a 50-microgram (mcg) to 200-mcg selenium supplement.

Important: If you are currently undergoing treatment for cancer, talk to your doctor before taking selenium.

•**Chromium.** This mineral, shown in dozens of studies to help control blood sugar levels, is poorly absorbed. Unless you eat organ meats, such as liver, it's best consumed in a supplement.

Helpful: Everyone should consider taking a 200-mcg chromium supplement daily for general health. If you have diabetes, ask your doctor about taking 1,000 mcg of chromium daily.

•**Carotenoids.** More than 600 nutritious plant compounds known as carotenoids can be found in vegetables and fruits.

Examples: Lycopene, found in tomatoes, watermelon and pink grapefruit, may help prevent prostate cancer...and lutein and zeaxanthin, found in dark green, leafy vegetables and corn, may help prevent and treat macular degeneration. This disease is the leading cause of vision loss in people over age 65.

Helpful: Because carotenoids are fat-soluble nutrients (that is, they require some amount of dietary fat for optimal absorption), consume carotenoid-rich foods with olive oil or other healthful fat sources. Low-fat salad dressings can be used, but try to stay away from no-fat versions.

Also helpful: Steam or lightly simmer vegetables. Raw fruits and vegetables contain valuable enzymes, but cooking breaks the cell walls, increasing the bioavailability of many valuable nutrients.

Examples: To maximize the amount of cancer-fighting lycopene from tomatoes, cook them in a sauce.

•**Protein.** On the bioavailability scale, meat, poultry, fish and eggs are among the best sources of protein. Although the protein found in lunch meats, such as ham and bologna, is bioavailable, these foods typically contain high levels of sodium and harmful fillers and preservatives known as nitrates.

Aim for 50 g to 120 g of protein daily (one-half of a salmon fillet contains 42 g...one-half of a chicken breast contains 27 g...three ounces of top sirloin contains 25 g).

Helpful: To maximize the bioavailability of nutrients found in beef, prepare it medium rare.

For a convenient protein source that lasts for several days, roast a turkey breast or chicken in an oven cooking bag, slice it up and use it during the week.

As an alternative to meat, consider using whey protein powder—an excellent source of protein derived from milk. Look for "cold filtered" and "ion exchanged" on the label, which indicates that the processing has removed lactose (milk sugar) and casein (a highly allergenic protein found in milk). This breaks down the whey, making it more absorbable. Next Nutrition as well as Jarrow each make excellent whey products. Only two percent of people with dairy allergies are allergic to whey protein.

Whey protein powder can be easily added to a smoothie.

What to do: Mix one scoop of protein powder (typically 20 g of protein) with eight ounces of water, milk or juice and ice in a blender. Add frozen blueberries or other fruit, if desired.

If you are allergic to whey protein, consider soy powder—the protein in soy powder is more easily utilized than that in other soy foods. Soy powder also can be used in smoothies.

Important: If you eat a vegan diet (no animal products of any kind), take a multivitamin as nutritional insurance. Plant-based diets do not contain adequate amounts of all nutrients.

SuperFoods That Prevent Heart Disease, Cancer, Diabetes, More

Steven G. Pratt, MD, senior staff ophthalmologist at Scripps Memorial Hospital in La Jolla, CA, is coauthor of two best-selling books, including *Bottom Line's Super-Foods Rx*. Bottom Line Books.

You know that spinach and broccoli are good for you. But did you know that dark chocolate can lower blood pressure? Or that avocados can prevent migraine headaches?

Steven G. Pratt, MD, has added dark chocolate, avocados and seven other foods to the original list of 14 that he presented in his best-selling *Bottom Line's SuperFoods Rx*.

Together with exercise, weight control, healthy sleep habits and stress reduction, these foods can help you live a long and healthy life...

APPLES

Apples can reduce your risk of heart disease, certain cancers, high blood pressure and type 2 diabetes. They are particularly good for the respiratory system, helping to prevent lung cancer and asthma.

Why are apples so beneficial? They are a great source of fiber, potassium and disease-fighting antioxidants, such as vitamin C and polyphenols. But evidence suggests that it is the complex synergistic interactions among these various elements that make the fruit so healthful.

Eat as wide a variety of apples as possible—and don't remove the peels. A study in *Journal of Agricultural and Food Chemistry* confirmed that the concentration of antioxidants in an apple's skin is several times greater than in its flesh.

Best: An apple a day, just as the saying goes.

AVOCADOS

Avocados have a remarkable ability to help the body absorb nutrients from food. You'll get substantially more health benefits from the carrots and tomatoes in your salad if you toss in half an avocado as well. This is probably because the monounsaturated fat of the avocado increases the body's absorption of fat-soluble carotenoid phytonutrients, such as beta-carotene.

Avocados also contain lots of magnesium, which helps prevent type 2 diabetes and migraine headaches, as well as plenty of potassium, which promotes low blood pressure and good circulation.

Though relatively high in calories (48 calories per ounce), avocados help fight obesity because they boost satiety—the feeling of fullness that signals us to stop eating and thus helps control calorie intake.

Best: One-third to one-half an avocado two to three times a week.

DARK CHOCOLATE

Dark chocolate contains plenty of polyphenols, such as flavonols, which lower blood pressure. (Milk chocolate does not appear to lower blood pressure.) Chocolate also is a natural anti-inflammatory.

A study published in *American Journal of Clinical Nutrition* showed that the effects on blood flow from drinking one cup of cocoa rich in flavonol were comparable to those from taking a low-dose aspirin (though the benefits didn't last quite as long). This suggests that a bar of dark chocolate can be used to treat a mild headache or other minor pains.

Newman's Own Sweet Dark Chocolate has significantly more polyphenols than many other dark chocolates. Next on the list are Dove Silky Dark Chocolate...Endangered Species Chocolate Company Wolf Bar...Cadbury Royal Dark Indulgent Dark Chocolate...and Hershey's Special Dark Mildly Sweet Chocolate. The higher the percentage of cocoa solids in your dark chocolate, the more polyphenols it contains.

Despite its high fat content, dark chocolate does not seem to increase blood cholesterol levels.

Best: Chocolate is a high-calorie food, so consume no more than 100 calories of chocolate per day—that's about half of a 2.8-ounce Newman's Own Sweet Dark Chocolate bar.

OLIVE OIL

The single most healthful change people can make to their cooking habits is to use extra-virgin olive oil in place of other oils and fats. While most fats and oils are bad for us, olive oil has been shown to reduce the risk of breast and colon cancer, lower blood pressure and improve cardiovascular health. Select an extra-virgin olive oil that is cold pressed and greenish in color—this suggests that it has a high level of polyphenols.

Best: One tablespoon most days.

GARLIC

Eating garlic on a regular basis helps reduce blood pressure, triglyceride levels and your LDL (bad) cholesterol—and it may increase HDL (good) cholesterol. Garlic is an anti-inflammatory that can help control arthritis. It has been shown to have significant antibiotic properties, decreasing the incidence and severity of bacterial infections.

There's even some evidence that garlic consumption might reduce the risk of certain cancers, including colorectal, gastric and prostate cancer, though more research is needed on this subject.

Best: About one clove of garlic several times a week. Fresh garlic is better than dried garlic or garlic supplements. Raw garlic offers the most health benefits, but cooked is fine, too.

HONEY

Daily honey consumption increases the amount of antioxidants in the blood, which appears to reduce the risk of heart disease and cancer. It also helps prevent constipation and reduces cholesterol and blood pressure.

Honey even does a better job of maintaining energy levels than other sweeteners. While consuming sugar typically provides only a very brief spike in blood sugar, a study found that athletes given honey after a workout maintained optimal blood sugar levels for a full two hours—and their muscles recovered faster from the workout than those who consumed other sweeteners.

Darker honeys tend to have more antioxidants—and more flavor.

Best: One to two teaspoons, taken several times a week.

KIWIS

Kiwis contain massive amounts of vitamins C and E. Vitamin C can reduce our risk of asthma, osteoarthritis and colon cancer. It also can boost our immune systems. Dietary vitamin E appears to lower the risk of Alzheimer's disease—and unlike most vitamin E–rich foods (nuts, oils), kiwis aren't high in fat or calories.

Kiwis are an excellent source of the antioxidant *lutein*, which is associated with lower risk of cataracts and macular degeneration. And they have been shown to reduce the risk of blood clots.

Best: One kiwi two to three times a week.

ONIONS

Onions deliver many of the same benefits as garlic. They can help reduce blood pressure, cholesterol levels and the risk of heart disease. They're useful as anti-inflammatories and have antibiotic properties. There's some research to suggest that onions might reduce the risk of colon cancer.

After you cut open an onion, let it sit for five to 10 minutes before cooking. Applying heat sooner will deactivate the *thiopropanal sulfoxide* in the onion. That's the compound that contributes to the onion's ability to help our hearts, among other health benefits. In general, you will get the greatest benefits by eating the most pungent onions.

Best: Dishes containing onions at least three times a week.

POMEGRANATES

Pomegranates are phytochemical powerhouses, and they are packed with potassium, which can help lower your blood pressure. Studies even suggest that pomegranates can slow the progression of prostate cancer and reduce the risk of atherosclerosis, the narrowing and hardening of the arteries.

Best: Four to eight ounces of 100% pomegranate juice several times each week. Avoid brands that contain added sugar.

■ ■ ■ ■

Dr. Pratt's SuperFoods

Here are 14 additional superfoods that can keep us healthy…

Beans	Soy
Blueberries	Spinach
Broccoli	Tea
Oats	Tomatoes
Oranges	Turkey
Pumpkin	Walnuts
Wild salmon	Yogurt

Some Cancer-Fighting Foods Are Much Better Than Others

Karen Collins, RD, a registered dietitian and nutrition adviser to the American Institute for Cancer Research (AICR) in Washington, DC, is the author of *Planning Meals That Lower Cancer Risk*. AICR.

Only about 10% of all cancers are due to genetics. The remaining 90% of malignancies are related to diet, weight and exercise…smoking…and/or environmental factors.

Even though most people realize that diet can affect cancer risk, few regularly consume a variety of the foods that contain large amounts of *phytochemicals*, substances that actually can inhibit the cellular damage that leads to cancer.

Eating a combination of cancer-fighting foods is the best approach because no single food supplies all the available protective substances—vitamins, minerals, phytochemicals and fiber.

BLACK BEANS

Beans (legumes) have high levels of a cancer-fighting compound called phytic acid. They're also rich in fiber and saponins, chemical compounds that reduce the ability of cancer cells to proliferate.

The landmark Nurses' Health study found that women who ate four or more servings of legumes weekly were 33% less likely to develop colon polyps than those who consumed one or fewer weekly servings. In people already diagnosed with colon polyps, those who ate more beans reduced their risk for a recurrence by 45%, compared with those who ate fewer beans.

Bonus: Beans are very high in protein. They're a good substitute for people who want to reduce their consumption of red meat—a major source of saturated fat, which can increase cancer risk.

Other cancer-fighting legumes: Small red beans, red kidney beans, pinto beans and garbanzo beans.

Helpful: If you don't want to spend time cooking dried beans, you can get many of the same benefits by eating canned. To reduce the sodium in canned beans, empty them into a colander and rinse thoroughly with cold water.

Recommended: Eat one-half cup of beans at least four times weekly.

BLUEBERRIES

Berries are rich sources of vitamin C and other antioxidants. People who regularly eat berries have a lower risk for malignancies of the colon, bladder, esophagus and prostate. Berries also may lower the risk for lymphoma and premenopausal breast cancer.

Blueberries are an excellent choice for cancer prevention because they are among the richest sources of antioxidants, chemical compounds that protect cells from free radicals that can damage cell DNA—the first step in cancer development.

Much of this nutritional power comes from their high levels of *anthocyanidins*, a type of antioxidant that reduces the ability of carcinogens to damage DNA.

Bonus: Because berries are both filling and low in calories, they can be substituted for other sweet snacks to promote weight loss—which further reduces the risk for many cancers.

Other cancer-fighting berries: Blackberries, strawberries, raspberries and cranberries.

Helpful: Keep frozen berries in the freezer. They can be kept almost indefinitely without spoiling and provide virtually the same nutritional benefits as fresh berries.

Recommended: Aim for at least one half-cup serving of berries per week.

BROCCOLI

Broccoli is a cruciferous vegetable that is rich in *isothiocyanates*, a family of phytochemicals linked to a reduced risk for colon, prostate, lung and premenopausal breast cancer. One of these phytochemicals, *sulforaphane*, reduces the ability of carcinogens to cause cell damage—and may increase the tendency of cancer cells to self-destruct, a process called apoptosis.

A study published in the *Journal of the National Cancer Institute* reports that men who consumed three or more weekly servings of broccoli (raw or cooked) were 41% less likely to get prostate cancer than those who consumed less than one weekly serving.

Other cancer-fighting cruciferous vegetables: Cauliflower, brussels sprouts, cabbage and kale.

Helpful: If you don't like the strong taste (and smell) of cooked broccoli and other cruciferous vegetables, eat them raw or lightly sauté them in olive oil or canola oil for three to four minutes.

You also can microwave or steam them. (Long cooking, such as boiling for 15 minutes or more, causes the release of strong-smelling/tasting sulfur compounds.)

Recommended: Aim for three to five half-cup servings per week of cruciferous vegetables.

GARLIC

Garlic is an allium, which is a family of plants that contain *allyl sulfides*, phytochemicals not found in any other foods.

The Iowa Women's Health Study found that people with the highest intake of garlic (at least one serving weekly) had a 32% lower risk of developing colon cancer than those who never ate garlic. Garlic has also been linked to a lower risk for prostate, lung, breast and skin cancers.

Bonus: Garlic can be used as a flavor enhancer to make healthful foods—vegetables, beans, whole grains, etc.—more enjoyable… and it reduces the need for unhealthful flavorings, such as salt and butter.

Other cancer-fighting alliums: Onions (all types), leeks and chives.

Helpful: To reduce the strong taste, use cooked garlic (by sautéing or roasting it, for example) rather than raw. The flavors mellow with long cooking. Wait 10 to 15 minutes after chopping garlic before cooking, to allow the active form of the protective phytochemicals to form. The cancer-fighting properties of jarred garlic are unknown.

Recommended: Aim to eat one to three cloves of garlic per week.

WALNUTS

Walnuts provide fiber and are rich in omega-3 fatty acids, the same healthful, anti-inflammatory fats that are found in fish. Reducing inflammation in the body helps prevent cell damage that can lead to cancer.

Other cancer-fighting nuts: Almonds and hazelnuts.

Helpful: Buy packaged or bulk shelled, unsalted nuts (raw or roasted). Substituting nuts for other snacks improves the body's ratio of omega-3 to omega-6 fatty acids—important for lowering inflammation and cancer risk.

Recommended: Eat three to five one-third-cup servings weekly.

WHOLE-GRAIN BREAD

Whole-grain bread is high in fiber. As fiber and certain starches resistant to digestion are fermented in the colon, substances are produced that block the cancer-promoting effects of bile acids. In addition, whole grains are higher in antioxidant vitamins (including vitamin E) and phytochemicals called *phenols* than are refined grains.

When scientists analyzed and combined the results from 40 different studies, they found that people who ate the most whole-grain bread and/or other whole grains had a 34% lower risk for cancer overall than those who consumed less.

Other cancer-fighting whole grains: Whole-wheat pasta, whole-grain breakfast cereal, brown rice, bulgur, kasha and quinoa.

Helpful: When shopping for whole-grain bread or cereal, don't be misled by terms like multigrain, which merely means that more than one type of grain is included…and don't judge by brown color, which can result from added caramel coloring. Check the ingredients list to make sure a whole grain is listed first, such as whole wheat or whole rye. "Flour" or "wheat flour" means that the product contains refined flour made from wheat—not whole-grain flour.

Recommended: Aim for three daily servings—one-half cup of whole grains or a slice of whole-grain bread counts as one serving.

■ ■ ■ ■

The Truth About "Healthier" Snacks

Food companies are marketing candies and snacks that they say are better for your health, but only a few are truly worthwhile…

Best: Snacks that have less salt, trans fats and high-fructose corn syrup. *Examples…*

•**LesserEvil popcorn snacks,** 99¢ for a 1.75-ounce single-serving pouch and $3.49 for a 3.65-ounce carton.

•**Bearitos Tortilla Chips,** $3.50 for a 16-ounce bag.

•**Barbara's Bakery Fig Bars,** $3.50 for a 12-ounce package.

Worst: Fortified candies, including jellybeans, that have vitamins C and E and electrolytes. Electrolyte-replacement products, including sports drinks, are of little use to all but elite athletes. Added C and E are of questionable value for anyone who eats well or takes a multivitamin/mineral supplement.

Suzanne Havala Hobbs, DrPH, RD, clinical assistant professor, School of Public Health, University of North Carolina at Chapel Hill. She is the author of *Get the Trans Fat Out: 601 Simple Ways to Cut the Trans Fat Out of Any Diet.* Three Rivers.

Best Breads for Your Health

Evelyn Tribole, RD, a nutritionist in private practice in Newport Beach, CA, is the author of *Stealth Health* (Penguin) and coauthor of *Intuitive Eating: A Revolutionary Program That Works* (St. Martin's).

The new USDA dietary guidelines recommend that most Americans get six ounces of grains daily, and that half of that—at least three one-ounce servings (one slice of bread equals about one ounce)—should be from whole-grain sources. Of course, eating only whole grains to meet the quota is even better.

Breads can be a source of whole grains, but knowing which ones are most healthful is difficult.

WHOLE VERSUS REFINED

Grain products, including pasta, oatmeal, hot and cold breakfast cereals and bread, are divided into two subgroups—whole and refined. Whole grains, by definition, contain the entire grain—the bran (outer coating), germ (seed embryo) and endosperm (also called the kernel, it makes up most of the seed). Examples include whole-wheat flour, cracked wheat (bulgur) and brown rice.

Whole grains are rich in fiber, which has been shown to reduce risk for heart disease, diabetes and some cancers. They provide large amounts of vitamins and minerals that are sometimes lacking in our diet, including magnesium, selenium, potassium, zinc, vitamin E and chromium.

Refined grains are milled to remove the bran and germ, which gives them a finer texture and lengthens their shelf life. This process is also nutritionally devastating—it removes the healthful fiber, iron and many B vitamins and other vitamins and minerals found in whole grains.

Since refined grains are digested more quickly than whole grains, they can cause spikes in blood sugar and insulin secretion, which can increase hunger—and diabetes risk. Refined grains include white flour, white rice and white bread.

IS IT WHOLE GRAIN?

When buying any type of bread, look for whole-grain flours in the list of ingredients. These include bulgur, whole wheat, whole rye, whole oats, barley, brown rice and buckwheat. Less common whole grains include amaranth, millet, quinoa, sorghum and triticale (a hybrid of wheat and rye). One of these flours should appear first in the list of ingredients—this means it is the primary ingredient by weight.

Caution: Just because a bread package says "multigrain," "stone-ground," "100% wheat," "seven-grain" or "bran," it does not mean it is made from whole grains.

Important: Serving sizes can be deceiving. Some breads list one serving as one slice, others as two slices.

White bread, which is made from refined grains, will list enriched wheat flour as the first ingredient.

Typical nutritional data per slice: 66 calories, 0.6 g fat, 0.6 g fiber, 170 mg sodium.

Important: Sourdough bread does not cause the spikes in blood sugar that result from eating other refined breads. That's because it has a lower glycemic index, an indicator of how quickly carbohydrates are digested.

The following breads can be among the most healthful available. Just check the ingredients to ensure that they're made from whole grain.

Nutrient-dense breads…

WHOLE WHEAT

What to look for: Whole wheat is typically the first ingredient, but it could be whole oats, whole rye or millet.

Typical nutritional data per slice: 90 calories, 1 g fat, 3 g fiber, 180 mg sodium.

Good brands: Arnold Natural 100% Whole Wheat…Oroweat 100% Whole Wheat…Stroehmann Dutch Country 100% Whole Wheat.

Important: Some "wheat" breads are made with enriched wheat flour. Enriched means that after the grain was refined, only five nutrients that were removed in the refining process were added back in—thiamin, riboflavin, niacin, iron and folic acid. However, fiber, magnesium and other vitamins and minerals are not restored to the flour.

RYE

What to look for: Whole rye should be the first ingredient.

Typical nutritional data per slice: 100 calories, 0.5 g fat, 3 g fiber, 200 mg sodium.

Good brands: Rubschlager 100% Rye, Rye-Ola Black Rye…Genuine Bavarian Organic Whole Rye.

PUMPERNICKEL

What to look for: Whole rye should be the first ingredient. Long, slow cooking causes the natural sugar in rye flour to darken and sweeten the bread.

Typical nutritional data per slice: 100 calories, 0.5 g fat, 3 g fiber, 200 mg sodium.

Good brands: Mestemacher Genuine Westphalian Pumpernickel…Rubschlager 100% Rye, Rye-Ola Pumpernickel.

■ ■ ■ ■

What "Whole Grain" Really Means on Food Labels

Don't be misled by labels on cereals, bread and other foods made from grain…

• **"Made with whole grain"** means that the food contains some whole grain, either a little or a lot.

• **"Good source of whole grain"** on a cereal box means as little as eight grams of whole grain per serving, and "excellent source" means as little as 16 grams. Since the typical cereal serving is as large as 55 grams, a "good source" may be as little as 15% whole grain, and an "excellent source" as little as 30%.

• **"Whole grain"** means that at least 51% of the flour is whole grain—up to 49% may not be.

• **"100% whole grain"** means that no refined flour is used.

Note: These terms are being used this way voluntarily by cereal makers until the government makes an official rule.

Michael F. Jacobson, PhD, executive director, Center for Science in the Public Interest, and executive editor, *Nutrition Action Healthletter*, 1875 Connecticut Ave. NW, Washington, DC 20009.

■ ■ ■ ■

Get More from Food

Ounce for ounce, the drying process used for fruit nearly doubles the antioxidant content and increases levels of fiber.

Smart idea: Mix chopped prunes into your morning oatmeal…sprinkle dried cranberries into salads.

Important: Dried fruit contains twice the calories of regular fruit.

Caution: Dried fruit may contain sulfites, preservatives that may trigger allergic reactions, especially in asthmatics.

Joe A. Vinson, PhD, professor of chemistry, University of Scranton, PA.

Don't Be Fooled by Food Labels

Suzanne Havala Hobbs, DrPH, RD, clinical assistant professor, School of Public Health, University of North Carolina at Chapel Hill. She is the author of *Get the Trans Fat Out: 601 Simple Ways to Cut the Trans Fat Out of Any Diet*. Three Rivers.

If you are confused about the claims that manufacturers are now making on food labels, you are not alone.

"ORGANIC"

The term organic is hotly debated. The US Department of Agriculture's (USDA) current definition states that organic foods are those plants produced without the use of pesticides, sewage sludge (for fertilization) or synthetic fertilizer...or those animals raised without hormones or antibiotics.

To read the complete definition, go to the USDA's Web site at *www.ams.usda.gov/nop/NOP/standards.html.*

Organic foods, including produce, meat, milk and other dairy products, typically cost more than nonorganic varieties.

The FDA has linked pesticides to some types of cancer, and numerous other studies have linked them to Parkinson's disease. There's also strong evidence from the American Medical Association that bacteria are becoming resistant to some antibiotics because they are used in meat production.

What you may not know: In October 2005, the Agricultural Appropriations Conference Committee voted to allow synthetic ingredients into foods labeled "organic." Therefore, yogurt, pudding and other items may be considered organic even if they contain synthetic additives.

What you can do: Whenever possible, buy organic meats and dairy products.

For produce, choose organic varieties if you're buying one of the items found by the Environmental Working Group (a nonprofit group of researchers who investigate environmental health threats) to be among the most contaminated.

If you must buy nonorganic, choose produce that is least likely to be contaminated. Wash the nonorganic produce vigorously under running water to remove as much potentially harmful residue as possible. (Organic produce also should be washed.)

If you must buy nonorganic meat, choose the leanest cuts available and, whenever possible, remove the skin from poultry (toxins from hormones and antibiotics tend to accumulate in fatty tissue).

"NATURAL"

"Natural" is a word used for marketing purposes—it is not a term that is defined by the government.

What you may not know: Natural does not mean that a food product is necessarily "healthful."

Example: Breyers labels its ice cream "all natural," but it is high in fat and saturated fat.

What you can do: Read food labels carefully to determine the levels of fat and saturated fat as well as other ingredients in products that are labeled natural.

"LOW"

Many dairy products and some processed foods, such as soup, frozen entrees and snacks, use the term "low" or some variation thereof. *What these terms mean...*

Low fat: 3 grams (g) or less of total fat per serving.

Low saturated fat: 1 g or less of saturated fat per serving.

Low calorie: 40 calories or less per serving.

Low cholesterol: 20 milligrams (mg) or less of cholesterol and 2 g or less of saturated fat per serving.

Low sodium: 140 mg or less of sodium per serving.

Very low sodium: 35 mg or less of sodium per serving.

Nonfat: Less than 0.5 g of fat per serving.

"LEAN" AND "EXTRA-LEAN"

"Lean" and "extra-lean" refer to the fat content of meat, poultry and seafood. *What these two terms mean...*

Lean: Less than 10 g of fat, including no more than 4 g of saturated fat and less than 95 mg of cholesterol per 3.5-ounce serving.

Extra-lean: Less than 5 g of fat, including no more than 2 g of saturated fat and less than 95 mg of cholesterol per 3.5-ounce serving.

OTHER TERMS

Reduced: The food contains at least 25% less of an ingredient (such as fat, cholesterol, sodium or added sugar) or calories than the regular product.

Example: Reduced Fat Fig Newtons have at least 25% less fat than the original recipe.

High: The food contains at least 20% of the Daily Value (recommended daily intake) for a particular nutrient.

Example: The Daily Value for fiber is 25 g. If a food product contains 5 g of fiber per serving, it might say "high fiber" on its label.

■ ■ ■ ■

When to Buy Organic

When does it make sense to spend the extra money for organic produce? Take a look at the lists of the most—and least—contaminated fruits and vegetables, and spend your money wisely.

MOST CONTAMINATED PRODUCE

Apples	Peaches
Bell peppers	Pears
Celery	Potatoes
Cherries	Red raspberries
Imported grapes	Spinach
Nectarines	Strawberries

LEAST CONTAMINATED PRODUCE

Asparagus	Kiwi
Avocados	Mangoes
Bananas	Onions
Broccoli	Papaya
Cauliflower	Peas (sweet)
Corn (sweet)	Pineapples

Environmental Working Group. *www.ewg.org.*

What Those Food Labels Really Mean

Suzanne Havala Hobbs, DrPH, RD, clinical assistant professor, School of Public Health, University of North Carolina at Chapel Hill. She is the author of *Get the Trans Fat Out: 601 Simple Ways to Get the Trans Fat Out of Any Diet.* Three Rivers.

The claims made on food labels can't always be taken at face value. There are rules that govern how certain words can be used on food packaging, but these rules often leave room for deception. Food companies eager to sell their products take full advantage of these loopholes.

Among the most potentially confusing food label terms...

•**Free range.** Some people feel better about eating eggs or poultry that come from "free range" birds. They imagine these birds living relatively normal lives, not confined to pens. Unfortunately, this might not be the case.

According to the US Department of Agriculture (USDA), poultry can be labeled "free range" as long as outdoor access was made available to the bird "for an undetermined period each day." A single door to a large coop might have been opened for a few minutes, with only a small percentage of the birds making the dash outside.

There's no USDA definition at all for the term "free range" when it comes to eggs. It's possible that the bird that laid your "free range" eggs never saw the light of day.

•**Fresh.** The word "fresh" often means exactly what it seems to—that a food has not been frozen, heated or chemically preserved. But when the word is used as part of the phrase "fresh-baked," the only guarantee is that it is fresh until the sell-by date.

When "fresh" is used as part of the phrase "fresh frozen," not only has the food been frozen, it might have been blanched—quickly scalded—as well. Blanching deactivates enzymes in vegetables that might otherwise cause loss of color, flavor and texture.

•**Light.** Very specific rules govern the terms "light" and "lite." In general, the food must be reduced in calories by one-third or have half the fat or sodium. "Light" potato chips have 50% less fat than regular chips. Food makers also are allowed to use this word to describe foods that are light in other ways—a fruitcake labeled "light" simply might have been made with white sugar rather than brown sugar. The product's label must then state which attribute "light" is referring to—for example, "light in color" or "light in texture."

•**Natural.** This word implies healthy or even, to some people, organic. But because government regulators have not officially defined "natural," food makers for the most part are free to use it however and whenever they like, rendering the term meaningless.

The only exceptions are meat and poultry products. When these foods are labeled "natural," they must not contain any artificial flavorings or colorings and must be only minimally processed.

471

•**Organic.** Organic food is growing in popularity, but what does "organic" really mean? It does not necessarily mean that all of the ingredients were grown or raised in organic fashion, with limited or no use of pesticides, synthetic fertilizers, antibiotics and hormones. It just means that at least 95% of the ingredients were produced that way. A component of these foods might contain pesticides. For example, 95% of the ingredients in a breakfast cereal may be organic, but the remaining 5% may have been conventionally grown.

Rules for using the phrase "made with organic ingredients" are even less stringent, guaranteeing only 70% of the ingredients to be organic. If a product is labeled "100% organic," you can be more confident that you're getting something fully organic.

•**Reduced.** For a food to be labeled "reduced" or "less," as in "reduced fat," "reduced sugar" or "less sodium," it must contain at least 25% less of that item than you would find in the manufacturer's original version of the product. But that's no guarantee of healthfulness—if the manufacturer's original product was exceptionally high in fat, sugar or sodium, this reduced version still might be less healthy than competing products that are not labeled "reduced." Compare labels.

•**Serving size.** Many consumers overlook the fact that nutritional data on food labels is in per-serving terms. A large cookie might be labeled "200 calories" or "10 grams of fat" per serving—but if the label shows the cookie is equal to two servings, the calorie and fat contents in the whole cookie are actually double that amount.

•**No trans fat.** Government regulations now require most food manufacturers to list on the nutrition facts label the number of grams of trans fat in packaged foods. Trans fats, often listed as "partially hydrogenated vegetable oil," can increase your risk of heart disease by increasing your total and LDL ("bad") cholesterol.

Label loophole: If the trans fat totals less than one-half gram per serving and no label claims are made about fat, fatty acids or cholesterol, trans fat information doesn't have to be listed. Even if trans fat is included in the product, if the amount totals less than one-half gram per serving, manufacturers can list the amount as zero and advertise the food as having no trans fat. Eating several servings could result in an intake of a few grams of trans fat.

How to Save Money on Organic Food

Ronnie Cummins, national director of the Organic Consumers Association, a nonprofit organization that promotes food safety, children's health and environmental sustainability, Finland, MN, is the author of *Genetically Engineered Food: A Self-Defense Guide for Consumers.* Marlowe & Company.

Many people who would like to eat organic fruits, vegetables, dairy, meat and poultry are put off by the high prices. Organic foods can cost 25% to 100% more than regular foods—but if you're willing to do a bit of sleuthing and look beyond traditional grocery stores, you can find organic products for much less.

My group's Web site, *www.organicconsumers. org,* has links to most of the resources suggested below…

•**Compare prices of conventional and organic foods** when shopping at regular grocery stores. Occasionally, the price gap narrows dramatically, or organic foods may even be cheaper.

•**Shop at a farmers' market.** You can find bargains if you prowl around the stalls of your local farmers' market. You'll save even more if you haggle. Farmers may be especially willing to negotiate prices if produce is misshapen or closing time is approaching.

Sample savings: Organic apples at a farmers' market often are 25% to 50% cheaper than organic apples at grocery or natural-food stores.

•**Consider purchasing a share in a community-supported agriculture program (CSA).** There are more than 1,000 of these programs around the US. Through a CSA, you purchase produce from an organic farmer in a region near you. You'll receive a weekly basket that contains produce, flowers and perhaps even eggs and milk. A share in a CSA typically costs several hundred dollars for one growing season, which could last half a year (prices vary dramatically depending on location). In mild regions, such as California, you can receive just-picked produce year-round. Each week, it's fun to discover what goodies are in the basket.

Sample savings: In rural Minnesota, where I live, I pay $450 for the season and split my weekly harvest with another family. This is at least 50% cheaper than store prices.

Helpful: Most CSAs deliver produce orders to a central location. You may be able to reduce the price of your weekly delivery if you allow your front porch to serve as a delivery spot for your neighborhood.

CSAs can be found at the Web site of Local Harvest (*www.localharvest.org*), as well as on my Web site.

•**Join a food co-op.** Co-ops typically offer high-quality organic food and produce at a discount for members. You may be required to volunteer your time for a certain number of hours each month. For a list of co-ops, see my organization's Web site.

•**Buy in bulk.** This is a great way to save money on long-lasting and nonperishable organic food, such as dried beans, lentils, pasta, rice, cereals, trail mix, nuts and even peanut butter. Health-food stores, Whole Foods, and even some supermarkets sell bulk items.

Cheaper still: Join a wholesale buying club (regular yearly membership fee is between $35 and $50). The minimum order for the club I belong to is $1,000 every three months, so I share a membership with several families in my area.

Typical savings: 30% to 50% off retail.

There is no national directory of buying clubs. Ask your local natural-food store for the names of its organic-food suppliers and contact them.

•**Eat seasonally.** You're sure to overpay if you buy organic fruits and vegetables off-season. That's when you want to buy frozen or canned. When produce is bountiful and cheap, you may want to can, freeze or dry it for the coming months.

■ ■ ■ ■

Almonds Aid Memory

Eating more almonds may help improve your memory.

Recent study: Mice with a disease similar to Alzheimer's that were fed an almond-rich diet fared better on memory tests than mice fed a diet without almonds. Almonds contain substances similar to those found in drugs used to treat Alzheimer's.

Neelima Chauhan, PhD, research assistant professor, department of anatomy and cell biology, University of Illinois, Chicago, and leader of a study presented at the annual meeting of the Society for Neuroscience.

Apple Cider Vinegar: A Cure-all?

Mark A. Stengler, ND, naturopathic physician in private practice, La Jolla, CA...adjunct associate clinical professor at the National College of Natural Medicine, Portland, OR...author of 16 books, including *The Natural Physician's Healing Therapies* (Bottom Line Books) and coauthor of *Prescription for Natural Cures* (Wiley)...and author of the *Bottom Line/Natural Healing* newsletter.

Patients often tell me that apple cider vinegar has helped them with a variety of ailments. This intrigued me because, until recently, there was little research to back up these claims.

CURE-ALL?

Apple cider vinegar has been singled out as beneficial for a variety of conditions, including leg cramps, stomach upset, sore throat, sinus problems, high blood pressure, obesity, osteoporosis and arthritis. It also has been used to help rid the body of toxins, improve concentration, slow aging, reduce cholesterol and fight infection.

It is used topically to treat acne, sunburn, shingles and insect bites...as a skin toner...and to prevent dandruff. Many women add it to bathwater to treat vaginitis. Two of its most common uses are for weight loss and arthritis.

THE SCIENTIFIC EVIDENCE

Recent studies have found that consuming apple cider vinegar can improve insulin resistance, a condition in which muscle, fat and liver cells have become resistant to the uptake of the hormone *insulin* and the blood sugar *glucose* needed to provide fuel for energy.

This is common among people who have diabetes as well as in some people considered prediabetic—that is, their blood glucose and insulin levels are approaching the numbers that define diabetes. People with insulin resistance are more likely to be overweight and have increased cholesterol and triglyceride levels as well as high blood pressure.

A study at the University of Arizona examined the effects of apple cider vinegar on 29 participants (10 had type 2 diabetes, 11 had signs that they could become diabetic and eight were healthy but "insulin sensitive"). All participants fasted and were randomly asked to drink either a vinegar solution (two tablespoons or 20 g of apple cider vinegar, some water and a bit of saccharin for flavor) or a placebo drink. The drinks were followed by a high-carbohydrate meal of one white bagel, butter and orange juice.

Researchers found that postmeal spikes of insulin and glucose in the vinegar group were significantly lower in those who had insulin resistance and slightly lower in those who had diabetes, compared with those in the placebo group. Other research has shown that apple cider vinegar helps control insulin and glucose spikes in healthy people.

HOW IT WORKS

Researchers theorize that the *acetic acid* in any vinegar, including apple cider vinegar, interferes with the enzymes that digest carbohydrates, so carbs pass through the digestive tract without being absorbed. Acetic acid also has been shown to affect enzymes that alter glucose metabolism in liver and muscle cells, reducing insulin spikes.

Because high levels of insulin promote inflammation, taking vinegar to maintain better insulin levels will control any inflammatory response in the body. This may explain why vinegar eases arthritis pain.

DOSAGE

People can try apple cider vinegar for weight loss, blood sugar balance and other traditional uses, including arthritis relief. Dilute one to two tablespoons (some people use as little as two teaspoons to start with) in an equal amount of water, and drink it at the beginning of a meal.

Sometimes it is more convenient to take it in supplement form. A good product is Apple Cider Vinegar Plus, which is made by Indiana Botanic Gardens (800-644-8327, *www.botanic choice.com*). Take one capsule with each meal for a total of three capsules a day. Ninety capsules cost $14.49.

Apple cider vinegar can cause digestive upset in some people. If you have active ulcers, use caution when taking apple cider vinegar.

Those Amazing Bananas

Ara DerMarderosian, PhD, professor of pharmacognosy (the study of natural products used in medicine) at the University of the Sciences in Philadelphia. He also is the scientific director of the university's Complementary and Alternative Medicines Institute. Dr. DerMarderosian has published more than 100 scientific papers and chapters in books as well as two books.

Most people know that bananas are an excellent source of potassium (one ripe banana supplies more than 10% of an adult's daily requirement of the mineral). That's important because people with a low dietary intake of potassium are 28% more likely to suffer a stroke than those who consume higher levels, according to a study conducted at Tulane University.

Lesser-known medicinal uses of bananas…

•**Depression.** Bananas are a good source of tryptophan (a precursor to serotonin, a brain chemical that helps regulate mood).

•**Diarrhea.** Unripe bananas and plantains (high-starch, green bananas that are typically cooked) are a rich source of tannins, astringent plant compounds that help stop water accumulation in the intestines, thus diminishing diarrhea.

•**Heartburn and ulcers.** Bananas neutralize acidity and soothe and coat esophageal tissue with pectin (a substance used as a thickener and stabilizer in jellies).

Important: In rare cases, bananas may cause an allergic reaction. Bananas with blackened skin can increase blood sugar levels. Because bananas have high levels of potassium, people with kidney problems should check with their doctors before eating this fruit.

■ ■ ■ ■

Berry Good

Blueberries protect the heart. Of all fruits, blueberries have the highest level of anti-oxidants. Antioxidants relax blood vessels, improving blood flow and keeping blood pressure down. Eat between one-half and one cup every day for maximum benefit.

Dorothy Klimis-Zacas, PhD, professor of clinical nutrition, department of food science and human nutrition, University of Maine, Orono, reported in *The Federation of American Societies for Experimental Biology (FASEB) Journal.*

■ ■ ■ ■

Broccoli May Prevent Blindness

Sulforaphane, the naturally occurring antioxidant in broccoli and broccoli sprouts, protects the eye from damage caused by the sun's ultraviolet rays. This damage is believed to be a primary cause of age-related macular degeneration.

Paul Talalay, MD, professor of pharmacology and molecular sciences at Johns Hopkins University School of Medicine, Baltimore, and coauthor of a study of antioxidant protection in cells, published in *Proceedings of the National Academy of Sciences of the USA.*

Coffee: Now the Miracle Health Drink?

Tomas de Paulis, PhD, coffee chemist and former research assistant professor of psychiatry, Institute for Coffee Studies, Vanderbilt University Medical Center, Nashville.

The health benefits from drinking coffee continue to be reported—to the point where many of the results seem almost too good to be true.

Coffee reduces diabetes risk. Drinking six cups a day slashed risk of diabetes by 54% for men and 30% for women in an 18-year Harvard study. Even drinking only one cup a day was found to reduce risk by several percent.

At least six other studies indicate coffee drinkers reduce their risk of Parkinson's disease by up to 80%. In addition, other studies have reported that drinking at least two cups of coffee a day can reduce risk of developing colon cancer by 25%, risk of gallstones by 50% and risk of liver cirrhosis by 80%.

There's even evidence that coffee drinking offsets some of the health damage caused by smoking and excessive drinking—those who engage in such health vices but also drink coffee have been reported to suffer less heart and liver damage than those who don't.

And other studies have indicated coffee may help control asthma, relieve headaches, lift spirits and even prevent cavities.

Coffee also increases athletic performance and endurance—until recently, it was a controlled substance at the Olympic Games.

Moreover, coffee is even good for children. One study in Brazil indicated that children (age 12 average) who drank coffee with milk were less prone to depression and were more alert in school. No study indicates that coffee consumed in reasonable amounts is in any way harmful for children.

■ ■ ■ ■

Coffee Plus

Coffee has more antioxidants than any other food or beverage in the American diet. The average adult receives more than four times the amount of antioxidants from coffee—regular or decaf—daily than from black tea (the second-most consumed source), followed by chocolate, bananas, beans and corn.

Joe A. Vinson, PhD, professor of chemistry, University of Scranton, Pennsylvania, and leader of a study of 100 different foods, presented at the 230th national meeting of the American Chemical Society.

■ ■ ■ ■

A Cup or Two

Coffee may help prevent cirrhosis. Cirrhosis is the irreversible scarring that prevents the liver from filtering toxins properly. It is common in heavy drinkers. On average, coffee reduces the risk of cirrhosis by 20% for people who drink one cup per day...and reduces risk by 80% for those who have four cups daily. Coffee drinkers—whether or not they drink alcohol—

also have better results on blood tests used to measure liver function.

Reason: Unknown.

Arthur Klatsky, MD, adjunct investigator, Kaiser Permanente Division of Research, Oakland, CA, and leader of a study of more than 125,000 people, published in *Archives of Internal Medicine*.

■ ■ ■ ■

Java Jumps

Drinking too much coffee may cause heart trouble.

Recent finding: People who drink three or more cups of coffee a day have twice as many signs of abnormal arterial pressure and stiffening of the arteries as those who drink less coffee.

Possible reason: Caffeine may interfere with the metabolism of adenosine, a substance that relaxes arteries.

Self-defense: Drink no more than two cups of regular coffee a day, especially if you have high blood pressure.

Charalambos Vlachopoulos, MD, staff cardiologist, first department of cardiology, Athens Medical School, Hippokration Hospital, University of Athens, Greece, and leader of a study of 228 people, published in *The American Journal of Clinical Nutrition*.

■ ■ ■ ■

Dairy and Diabetes

A recent study revealed that men's diabetes risk dropped by nine percent for each additional serving per day of low-fat dairy, such as milk and yogurt.

Frank B. Hu, MD, PhD, professor of nutrition and epidemiology, Harvard School of Public Health, Boston, and coauthor of a 12-year study of dairy intake by more than 41,000 male health professionals, published in *Archives of Internal Medicine*.

■ ■ ■ ■

Figs Protect Your Heart

Dried figs protect your heart. They can help you meet daily fruit and fiber recommendations and, like all dried fruits, provide a big dose of polyphenols, potent antioxidants that help prevent the formation of artery-clogging plaque.

Best: Eat five or six dried figs a day. Add them to sweet potato and squash dishes, oatmeal and salad, or enjoy them just as they are.

Joe A. Vinson, PhD, professor of chemistry, University of Scranton, Pennsylvania, and leader of a study of antioxidants in dried fruit, published in *Journal of the American College of Nutrition*.

■ ■ ■ ■

Fish Curbs Appetite

In a study of 23 men ages 20 to 32, those who ate fish (salmon) for lunch consumed 11% fewer calories at dinner than those who ate beef for lunch. The lunches contained the same number of calories and the same ratio of proteins, carbohydrates and fats.

Theory: Fish protein takes longer to digest than beef (or chicken) protein, so eating fish may help you feel full longer.

Stephan Rossner, PhD, professor obesity unit, Huddinge University Hospital, Stockholm, Sweden.

■ ■ ■ ■

When Ginger Works As Well as Aspirin

In a recent study, participants who took two 500-milligram (mg) tablets of gingerol, the component that gives ginger its bite, twice a day for three months experienced the same reduction in inflammation as when they took aspirin for three months.

Caution: Ginger can thin blood, so consult your doctor.

American Chemical Society news release.

■ ■ ■ ■

Ginger Helps Arthritis Pain

Ginger relieves arthritis pain Ginger supplements soothe osteoarthritic joints by inhibiting production of pain-causing prostaglandins.

Best: Take a 100-mg supplement, such as Gingerforce, one to three times a day.

Sung Woo Kim, PhD, associate professor of animal nutrition and digestive physiology, department of animal science, North Carolina State University, Raleigh, and leader of a study published in *Journal of Medicinal Food*.

■■■■

Ginger Eases Nausea

In a review of studies involving a total of 363 people, those who were given at least 1 g of powdered gingerroot capsules one hour prior to surgery were one-third less likely to suffer nausea and vomiting during the first 24 hours after the operation than those who got a placebo capsule.

Theory: Ginger may suppress the neurotransmitter serotonin, which plays a role in triggering nausea and vomiting.

Nathorn Chaiyakunapruk, PhD, associate professor, department of pharmacy practice, Naresuan University, Phitsanulok, Thailand.

■■■■

Ginseng for Breast Cancer

A new study suggests that ginseng (a popular herb that supports energy production within cells) improves survival rates and quality of life for breast cancer patients. Researchers studied 1,455 women in Shanghai who had received at least one type of conventional cancer treatment, such as chemotherapy or radiation. Compared with women who had not used ginseng before their diagnoses, those who had taken ginseng had a higher overall survival rate (88.6% vs. 80%) and a higher disease-free survival rate (83.8% vs. 77.4%).

My view: This study and others suggest that red or white Asian ginseng (*Panax ginseng C.A. Meyer*) and American ginseng (*Panax quinquefolius*) help boost immune function and aid recovery from conventional breast cancer treatments. Women with breast cancer should consider supplementation under a doctor's guidance, since appropriate dosages will vary. I also recommend ginseng for women who have a strong family history (two or more relatives on the same side of the family) of breast cancer.

Mark A. Stengler, ND, naturopathic physician in private practice, La Jolla, CA...adjunct associate clinical professor at the National College of Natural Medicine, Portland, OR...author of 16 books, including *The Natural Physician's Healing Therapies* (Bottom Line Books) and coauthor of *Prescription for Natural Cures* (Wiley)...and author of the *Bottom Line/Natural Healing* newsletter.

■■■■

Grapefruit Lowers Cholesterol

Heart disease patients who were nonresponsive to cholesterol-lowering drugs ate balanced meals that included one grapefruit daily. Those who ate red grapefruit lowered their total cholesterol by 15.5%, and white-grapefruit eaters reduced cholesterol by 7.6%. Those not eating grapefruit showed no cholesterol decrease.

Caution: Grapefruit can adversely interact with certain medications. See your doctor.

Shela Gorinstein, PhD, chief scientist, The Hebrew University of Jerusalem.

■■■■

Grape Seed Extract Lowers Blood Pressure

Twenty-four patients with metabolic syndrome (a cluster of heart disease risk factors, including high blood pressure, excess abdominal weight and elevated blood sugar) took a 150-mg or 300-mg capsule of grape seed extract or a placebo daily for one month.

Result: Those who took either dose of the extract experienced an average drop in systolic pressure (top number) of 12 mmHg and 8 mmHg in diastolic pressure (bottom number).

Theory: Grape seed extract boosts the production of nitric oxide, a heart-protective enzyme. If you have prehypertension (120–139 systolic and 80–89 diastolic), ask your doctor about trying grape seed extract.

C. Tissa Kappagoda, MD, PhD, professor of cardiovascular medicine, University of California, Davis.

■■■■

Honey-Biotic?

Honey acts as a natural antibiotic, according to Peter Molan, PhD.

How it works: Honey's natural acidity creates an inhospitable environment for germs... and it contains a small amount of germ-killing hydrogen peroxide.

Important: Heat can destroy honey's beneficial properties, so buy the raw and unpasteurized kind. Honey can be used on most wounds. If you have a puncture wound, consult your doctor.

What to do: Work one tablespoon of warmed honey into a four-inch by four-inch gauze pad, then place it on the wound. Change the dressing at least twice daily until the wound heals.

Caution: Infants younger than age one should not eat honey.

Peter Molan, PhD, professor of biological sciences, University of Waikato, Hamilton, New Zealand.

■ ■ ■ ■

Put the Squeeze on Alzheimer's

Juice may ward off Alzheimer's, says a researcher.

Recent finding: People who drank three or more servings a week of fruit and/or vegetable juice had 76% lower risk than those who drank less (the risk reduction was greatest in people with a family history of Alzheimer's).

Likely reason: Polyphenols—antioxidants that protect brain tissue—are in fruits and vegetables. Apples, grapes and oranges have high concentrations.

Qi Dai, MD, PhD, assistant professor of medicine, Vanderbilt University Medical Center, Nashville, and leader of a study of 1,836 people, published in *The American Journal of Medicine*.

■ ■ ■ ■

Meat a Factor in Gout?

Meat eating is linked to gout. In a study of more than 41,000 men, those who consumed the most meat (beef, poultry, pork and seafood) increased their risk for gout, a common form of inflammatory arthritis that often occurs in joints of the feet and ankles, by 41%.

Theory: Uric acid, which causes gout, is created in the body as meat is metabolized.

Self-defense: Limit your meat intake to four to five ounces daily.

Gary Curhan, MD, ScD, associate professor of medicine, Harvard Medical School, Boston.

Is It Time to Become A Vegetarian?

Neal D. Barnard, MD, president and founder of the Physicians Committee for Responsible Medicine, Washington, DC.

The average American consumes 220 pounds of meat each year, but the mad cow disease scare made many people think twice about this practice.

Even before the latest questions were raised regarding the safety of the US meat supply, 10 million Americans identified themselves as vegetarians.

Here are answers to some commonly asked questions about vegetarianism from Dr. Neal D. Barnard, president and founder of the Physicians Committee for Responsible Medicine, an independent, nonprofit health research and advocacy group...

•**Why do you favor a meat-free diet?** It's been scientifically proven—in epidemiological studies of people who selected their own diets, and in clinical trials where people were assigned vegetarian diets—that a vegetarian regimen is the most healthful diet.

Studies of Seventh-day Adventists—people who don't smoke, use alcohol or eat meat and who exercise regularly—have shown that a vegetarian diet (excluding their other healthful lifestyle practices) allows them to live about 10 years longer than nonvegetarians.

Other studies show that vegetarians have a lower incidence of cardiovascular disease, diabetes and hypertension. Vegetarians also are 40% less likely to develop cancer, especially of the colon and prostate.

•**In your opinion, what are the greatest health risks associated with eating meat?** Many factors should discourage you from eating meat. Cooking meat at higher temperatures, such as those used during grilling or broiling, generates *heterocyclic amines*, carcinogens that can be formed when animal tissue is heated. Because of these carcinogens as well as the harmful effects of fat and cholesterol, a meat eater has three times the risk for colon cancer as a person who rarely eats meat.

Meat also is devoid of key nutrients, like fiber and vitamin C. Because it consists of little more than fat and protein, meat is one of the most calorie-dense foods. Fat contains nine calories per gram of weight, whereas protein, such as beans, and carbohydrates, such as breads and pasta, have only four calories per gram.

•What do you consider to be the most healthful type of vegetarian diet? A vegan diet—one that includes no animal or dairy products whatsoever—is the most healthful. From a health standpoint, there is no reason to add these foods to your diet. They typically are high in cholesterol and fat, and can be easily replaced with healthier alternatives, such as soy products or rice milk.

There's plenty of protein in most types of beans…and grains, such as rice and oats. If your concern is calcium, green vegetables and beans are a better source than milk because they also provide antioxidants and fiber.

As for meat being "low-fat," that's simply not true. The leanest beef is 28% fat. The leanest chicken—breast, with the skin removed—is 23% fat. The fat content of fish varies widely, from 10% to more than 50%. Compare that with beans, at 4%.

In a study of 59 people who ate either a vegan diet or less than six ounces of meat per day, the vegans got more iron from eating green vegetables and beans.

•What foods are allowed on a vegan diet? If you adopt this form of vegetarianism, you'll be eating from four food groups—whole grains, vegetables, fruits and legumes, such as beans and peas. Eat these in whatever proportions you like, and you'll lose weight as well.

Eat spaghetti marinara, bean burritos, vegetarian chili, many kinds of Asian dishes—the list of possibilities is almost endless. If you're time-pressured, have a Veggie Delite (on Italian bread) at Subway or a veggie burger (without mayonnaise) at Burger King.

To ensure that you're consuming all your essential nutrients, take a multivitamin specifically formulated for vegetarians (marked on the label). Also take a vitamin B-12 supplement (six micrograms daily) or eat B-12–fortified foods, including some cereals and some meat substitutes.

•What's the best way to start a vegetarian diet? First, speak to your doctor. If you get his/her OK, then jump in all at once, rather than simply cutting back on meat. This is safe to do, but be aware that you may experience intestinal gas if you eat a lot of beans.

Within three weeks, your taste buds will have adjusted, you'll have lost a few pounds and you'll be glad you made the change.

•What basic food items should be included in a vegetarian's pantry? Pasta, rice and couscous are good staples to have on hand. For legumes, I recommend dried lentils, split peas and pinto beans, as well as canned chick peas and black beans.

My favorite produce items include potatoes, carrots, celery, yellow onions and raisins.

Baked tofu, vegetarian hot dogs and veggie burgers are delicious meat substitutes. Tortillas and pita bread also are convenient. If you want snack foods, try rice cakes, popcorn or pretzels.

■ ■ ■ ■

Eat Healthier

The Mediterranean diet reduces Alzheimer's risk. Elderly patients who strictly followed the diet were 40% less likely to develop the disease than similar patients who did not.

Theory: The diet—which is high in monounsaturated fats (such as olive oil), produce, fish and legumes and low in meat and dairy—is associated with lower rates of cardiovascular disease and inflammation, both of which increase risk of Alzheimer's.

Nikolaos Scarmeas, MD, assistant professor of neurology, Columbia University Medical Center, New York City, and lead author of a study of 2,258 elderly patients.

■ ■ ■ ■

Mushrooms Rich in Antioxidants

In a new study, researchers measured the amount of two antioxidants—polyphenols and ergothioneine—in a variety of mushrooms.

Result: Portobello, cremini and white button mushrooms have more antioxidant activity per gram than carrots and several other vegetables.

Self-defense: To ensure that you get a wide variety of disease-fighting antioxidants, include washed, store-bought mushrooms among nine daily servings of fruits and vegetables.

Joy Dubost, PhD, RD, a member of the international team of the Tropicana Nutrition Institute Nutritionist Network.

■ ■ ■ ■

Crunch vs. Cholesterol

Nuts and seeds contain cholesterol-lowering compounds.

New finding: In a study of 27 popular nuts and seeds, the levels of phytosterols (plant chemicals shown to lower cholesterol) were highest in wheat germ, sesame seeds, pistachios and sunflower seeds.

Helpful: Add wheat germ to cereal or yogurt…eat tahini (ground sesame seeds), an ingredient in hummus…or snack on a handful of unsalted sunflower seeds or pistachios.

Katherine M. Phillips, PhD, research scientist, department of biochemistry, Virginia Polytechnic Institute and State University, Blacksburg.

■ ■ ■ ■

Eating Oranges Reduces Disease Risk

A review of the literature finds that eating citrus fruits can reduce risk of mouth, larynx and stomach cancers by up to 50%. Moreover, one extra serving of citrus fruit a day (on top of the recommended minimum five daily servings of fruits and vegetables) can reduce risk of stroke by almost 20% while reducing risk of cardiovascular disease and diabetes.

Key: Citrus fruits are high in antioxidants, which strengthen the immune system and inhibit tumor growth.

Best: Oranges have the most antioxidants.

Katrine Baghurst, PhD, Food Standards Australia New Zealand Board, Adelaide, Australia.

■ ■ ■ ■

Frozen Edge

Frozen orange juice has about 25% more vitamin C than ready-to-drink juice.

Reason: At refrigerator temperatures, oxygen slowly destroys vitamin C in ready-to-drink juice. This reaction is prevented by the colder temperatures needed to store frozen juice. Once a container of any type of citrus juice is opened and exposed to air, it may lose all of the vitamin C within a month.

Carol Johnston, PhD, RD, professor of nutrition, Arizona State University, Mesa.

■ ■ ■ ■

Pomegranate Juice and Your Heart

A study of 10 people with type 2 diabetes (and 10 healthy people) found that drinking 50 milliliters (ml)—1.7 ounces—of pomegranate juice daily for three months significantly reduced markers of oxidative stress (cell damage caused by negatively charged molecules) among the diabetic patients.

My view: People with diabetes are prone to forming more free radicals, which cause LDL cholesterol molecules to oxidize—and this contributes to the formation of plaque in the arteries. Anyone who is concerned about heart health—even in the absence of diabetes—should drink 1.7 to two ounces of pomegranate juice a day.

Mark A. Stengler, ND, naturopathic physician in private practice, La Jolla, CA…adjunct associate clinical professor at the National College of Natural Medicine, Portland, OR…author of 16 books, including *The Natural Physician's Healing Therapies* (Bottom Line Books) and coauthor of *Prescription for Natural Cures* (Wiley)…and author of the *Bottom Line/Natural Healing* newsletter.

The "Cooking Oil Cure" For High Blood Pressure

Mark A. Stengler, ND, naturopathic physician in private practice, La Jolla, CA…adjunct associate clinical professor at the National College of Natural Medicine, Portland, OR…author of 16 books, including *The Natural Physician's Healing Therapies* (Bottom Line Books) and coauthor of *Prescription for Natural Cures* (Wiley)…and author of the *Bottom Line/Natural Healing* newsletter.

Using sesame oil instead of other cooking oils helps reduce high blood pressure and lower the amount of medication required to control high blood pressure, according to a study by researchers in India.

The study looked at the effect of sesame oil on 328 people with hypertension who were taking 10 to 30 milligrams (mg) a day of the calcium channel blocker *nifedipine*, which lowers blood pressure by relaxing arterial membranes.

The average age of the people in the study was 58 years, and they had moderate to severe long-term hypertension but no history of stroke or heart disease.

They consumed an average of 35 grams of sesame oil a day for 60 days. Their blood pressure was measured at the start of the study, every 15 days during the study and on day 60.

The study found that by using sesame oil as their sole cooking oil, participants lowered their blood pressure readings from an average 166/101 to 134/84.6.

The average dose of nifedipine taken by the study participants was reduced from 22.7 mg per day to 7.45 mg per day by the end of the study.

WHAT DO THE BLOOD PRESSURE NUMBERS MEAN?

The American Heart Association says that in blood pressure readings, the top (systolic) number represents the pressure while the heart is beating and the bottom (diastolic) number represents the pressure when the heart is resting between beats. The association says normal blood pressure should be below 120/80.

■ ■ ■ ■

Oil Reserves

After 12 months under supermarket lighting, levels of tocopherols and carotenoids, two disease-fighting antioxidants found in extra-virgin olive oil, were found to be reduced by 30%.

Reason: Exposure to light allows oxygen molecules to attack nutritive properties.

Self-defense: Buy olive oil sold in tinted glass or in metal containers…and store in a cool, dark place. Do not use past the expiration date on the label.

Francesco Caponio, associate professor of food technology, University of Bari, Italy.

■ ■ ■ ■

Pepper Upper

Red chili pepper fights cancer. It contains *capsaicin*, an anti-inflammatory that is effective against cancer cells. In tests, capsaicin caused cancer cells to die without damaging normal ones. Though clinical trials are needed before a recommendation to eat chili pepper can be made, it can be enjoyed as part of your regular diet.

Sanjay K. Srivastava, PhD, assistant professor of pharmacology, University of Pittsburgh School of Medicine, and leader of a study of capsaicin and pancreatic cancer cells.

Pekoe Boo! How a Cup Of Tea Scares Away Bacterial Infections

Jack F. Bukowski, MD, PhD, assistant professor of medicine, Harvard Medical School, and staff rheumatologist, Brigham and Women's Hospital, both in Boston.
Jeffrey B. Blumberg, PhD, professor of nutrition and director, Antioxidants Research Laboratory, and scientist, Jean Mayer USDA Human Nutrition Research Center on Aging, Tufts University, Boston.
Proceedings of the National Academy of Sciences.

Drinking tea may help prime your immune system and enable you to more easily fight off bacterial infections, say researchers.

Their study adds to the growing list of health benefits researchers have attributed to tea.

Previous research had found that the drink can help ward off heart disease and cancer, probably because of its abundant supply of antioxidants.

THE SCIENCE OF TEA

Some teas may fight infection, however, because they contain a substance called *L-theanine*, which is broken down into a group of chemicals called *alkylamine antigens*. Antigens produce antibodies that fight infections.

The researchers studied the effects of these antigens on *gamma-delta T-cells*, one of the immune system's infection fighters.

The study was small, cautions the lead author, Dr. Jack F. Bukowski, an assistant professor of medicine at Harvard Medical School and staff rheumatologist at Brigham and Women's Hospital in Boston at the time of the study.

And although his team proved that tea drinkers produced more disease-fighting chemicals than coffee drinkers, the researchers did not track whether the tea drinkers actually had fewer infections.

EXPOSING THE CELLS

His team first did work in the laboratory, exposing some human gamma-delta T-cells to an alkylamine antigen but not exposing others. Then they exposed the cells to bacteria, simulating an infection.

The cells exposed to the antigen produced a lot of interferon, an infection fighter, in the first 24 hours, Bukowski says, while those not exposed did not produce it.

The study also proved that these cells have a memory, he says, and can recognize bacteria the next time and fight them.

Next, Bukowski and his team asked 11 people to drink five to six cups of black tea every day, and another 10 people to drink the same quantity of instant coffee. The subjects did this for either two or four weeks.

The researchers tested the blood of the coffee and tea drinkers by exposing it to bacteria in the lab. The tea drinkers made five times more interferon after they started drinking tea, Bukowski says. The coffee drinkers showed no enhanced production of interferon.

But not all teas contain L-theanine, Bukowski cautions. Green, black, oolong and pekoe teas do, he says.

If the research bears out, tea drinking may protect against skin infections caused by bacteria, bacterial pneumonias and food poisoning, among other ailments, Bukowski says.

PRIMING THE RESPONSE

Another expert who has researched tea and its antioxidant benefits says the study results make sense.

"These compounds may prime our immune cells so that when they see [bacteria], they are better able to respond," says Jeffrey B. Blumberg, professor and director of the Antioxidants Research Laboratory and scientist at the Jean Mayer USDA Human Nutrition Research Center on Aging at Tufts University.

For more on the health benefits of tea, visit *www.teausa.org*.

Drinking Soda Linked to Hypertension

Mark A. Stengler, ND, naturopathic physician in private practice, La Jolla, CA...adjunct associate clinical professor at the National College of Natural Medicine, Portland, OR...author of 16 books, including *The Natural Physician's Healing Therapies* (Bottom Line Books) and coauthor of *Prescription for Natural Cures* (Wiley)...and author of the *Bottom Line/Natural Healing* newsletter.

A 12-year study reported in the *Journal of the American Medical Association (JAMA)* has found a link between regular consumption of carbonated, caffeinated soda, including diet soda, and hypertension (high blood pressure). Interestingly, the researchers—who surveyed and later examined about 155,000 women, ages 25 to 67, who had no recorded history of hypertension—originally intended to study the link between caffeine in beverages (not soda specifically) and high blood pressure. Coffee was exonerated, but soda was implicated.

More than 30,000 of the women in the study were diagnosed with hypertension at the end of the 12 years. Age seemed to be an independent factor—the oldest women, ages 43 and older at the start of the study, were most likely to develop hypertension, but soda consumption was an additional factor. Among this older group, those who consumed four or more cans or glasses of caffeinated, sugared soda daily had a 44% greater risk of hypertension than those who drank less than one can a day. Drinking four or more cans of caffeinated diet soda per day increased risk of hypertension as well, but by less—16% in the older group.

There was no increased risk of hypertension with any kind of coffee—regular or decaffeinated—so the researchers speculated that "it is not caffeine but perhaps some other compound contained in soda-type soft drinks that may be responsible for the increased risk of high blood pressure."

My conclusion: The high sugar content of regular soda pop could increase insulin levels and thus elevate blood pressure, but that does not explain why diet soda also seemed to increase the risk of high blood pressure. The mystery is not yet solved—but since neither regular nor diet soda has any nutritional value, I recommend avoiding both.

■ ■ ■ ■

Diet Soda Danger

We all know that sugary soft drinks are bad for our teeth, but did you know that even diet soda causes cavities? One of the best ways to prevent cavities is to curb your intake of acidic drinks, such as soda. The average American drinks more than 56 gallons of soft drinks a year. And a shocking 20% of one- and two-year-olds drink an average of seven ounces of soda per day.

Soft drinks, even diet sodas with artificial sweeteners, have high acidity—meaning a low pH level, or a measure of the balance between acids and bases. The low pH erodes tooth enamel, causing calcium to be leached out of teeth. This makes cavities more likely. If you are prone to cavities, dilute orange and grapefruit juice with an equal amount of water—their acidity is similar to that of soda.

Regular soda, in addition to containing acids, has sugars that feed bacteria in the mouth, creating an acidic environment. Diet soda is not as acidic as regular soda, but it still has quite a low pH—Classic Coke has a pH of 2.53 and Diet Coke has a pH of 3.39. A neutral pH—the pH of water—is 7.0.

Colas in general—both regular and diet—are worse for your teeth than other sodas, since they often have a pH of 3.5 or less. To neutralize a glass of regular cola, you would need to consume 32 glasses of water!

■ ■ ■ ■

Tomato Extract Lowers Blood Pressure

In a study of 54 adults with moderately high blood pressure (above 135 mmHg/80 mmHg), a dietary supplement derived from tomatoes reduced average systolic (top number) readings by 12 mmHg and diastolic (bottom number) readings by 6 mmHg after two to four weeks.

The 250-mg capsule given daily was equivalent to eating four medium tomatoes.

Theory: High levels of lycopene and vitamins C and E improve function of the arterial wall, which can lower blood pressure.

Esther Paran, MD, head, hypertension unit, Soroka University Hospital, Ben-Gurion University of the Negev, Israel.

■ ■ ■ ■

Veggies and Cancer

Certain vegetables may lower lymphoma risk, says researcher.

Recent study: People who ate more than three servings a day of vegetables had a 42% lower risk of developing non-Hodgkins lymphoma, a type of cancer, than those who ate less than one serving a day. Eating lots of antioxidant-rich vegetables, such as leafy green vegetables, broccoli, cauliflower and cabbage, was especially beneficial. Dietary zinc from poultry, beans, whole grains and nuts also has been associated with lower lymphoma risk.

Linda E. Kelemen, RD, ScD, division of population health and information, Alberta Cancer Board, Calgary, Alberta, and leader of a study of people with non-Hodgkin's lymphoma, published in *The American Journal of Clinical Nutrition*.

■ ■ ■ ■

Foods for Lungs

An unhealthy diet has been linked to lung disease.

New finding: In a study of more than 50,000 men and women, those who ate a diet high in sodium, saturated fats, meats and refined carbohydrates, such as noodles and white rice, were 43% more likely to develop bronchitis symptoms (cough with phlegm) than those who ate a more healthful diet. Chronic bronchitis often precedes or accompanies chronic obstructive pulmonary disease (COPD), persistent airway obstruction.

To improve lung health: Eat more foods with lung-protecting antioxidants, such as fruits, vegetables, soy foods and whole grains.

Stephanie London, MD, principal investigator, National Institute of Environmental Sciences, Durham, NC.

Whole Truth About Coffee, Eggs, Sweeteners ...And More

Marion Nestle, PhD, MPH, professor of nutrition, food studies and public health at New York University, New York City, is author of *What to Eat*. North Point.

We're bombarded with conflicting information about foods and health. The result is confusion. Is milk good for our bones or bad for our hearts? Is fish a source of healthful fats or dangerous toxins? Are artificial sweeteners smart low-calorie alternatives to sugar or dangerous chemicals?

Here, a closer look at the controversies about common foods...

FISH

Fish is a wonderful source of protein, vitamins, minerals and omega-3 fatty acids, but the nutritional benefits of omega-3 fatty acids fall short of their hype. Some scientists claim that they are great for the heart as well as for children's ability to learn, but all we can say for sure is that omega-3s may be beneficial.

Also, because of water pollution and some fish-farming techniques, fish can contain *methylmercury* and PCBs. High amounts of these chemicals can cause children to have muscle weakness, fatigue, headaches and severe developmental problems.

Bottom line: Eat fish if you enjoy it, with certain caveats...

•**Limit consumption of large predatory fish** likely to contain the most methylmercury (shark, swordfish, king mackerel, albacore tuna and tilefish) to no more than twice a week. Do not eat the fish at all if you are or might become pregnant—and don't feed these fish to children.

•**Select wild fish over farm-raised.** Farm-raised fish, salmon in particular, can have higher concentrations of PCBs than the same fish raised in the wild.

•**Don't regularly eat fish caught in freshwater** without checking first with state health or wildlife officials. Unless you know that the water the fish came from is safe, assume it's not. Consuming a few fish a year from a local lake or stream should be fine, but the health risks climb the more you eat.

COFFEE

It's full of caffeine, a mild "upper," and millions of people down it by the quart every day—surely coffee must be bad for us. In fact, there's little evidence that there's anything in coffee that's harmful to our health, and it may even be good for us. Coffee contains antioxidants believed to promote good health.

Bottom line: You can enjoy coffee without guilt, but don't load it with sugar, milk or cream. A 12-ounce caffe latte breve at Starbucks has 420 calories and 23 grams of saturated fat—more fat than you should consume in a day. If you become nervous or shaky when you drink coffee, you may be sensitive to caffeine. Reduce your intake or switch to decaf.

EGGS

Eggs are widely considered unhealthy because they're high in cholesterol—higher than any other food. But when eaten in limited quantities, eggs are good for you. They're relatively low in calories and are a good source of protein.

Some producers feed the hens flaxseed and fish oil to boost the eggs' omega-3 content—but these "omega-3 eggs" cost more, and it's not clear that they actually are any better for you. *Note:* There's no difference between a brown egg and a white egg aside from the color of the shell.

Bottom line: The American Heart Association recommends no more than one egg per day from all sources. If your doctor has warned you to watch your cholesterol, cut down on eggs or eat egg whites, which have no cholesterol.

MARGARINE

Margarines do have significantly less saturated fat and cholesterol than butter, so a nonhydrogenated (no trans fats) margarine is a healthy alternative. It certainly is cheaper than butter. But if you are not eating much of either, this decision isn't going to have a major effect on your health. Personally, I prefer butter. I just don't eat much of it. If you like margarine, you can choose from vegan or organic margarines, omega-3 margarines and "light" low-calorie/

low-fat margarines—but these cost significantly more than standard margarines, and the difference they make to your health will be small, at best.

Bottom line: If you like margarine, choose one with no trans fats.

ARTIFICIAL SWEETENERS

The FDA has approved artificial sweeteners because there is no compelling evidence that they cause harm at current levels of intake. But I am not a fan of them. I can't believe any food with that kind of chemical taste can be good for you. Their single virtue is the absence of calories, but there is not much evidence that their use has helped people lose weight. Perhaps people who use them compensate by eating more calories from other sources, or artificial sweeteners reinforce our preference for sweets. Personally, I prefer sugar—just not much of it.

Bottom line: If you are trying to lose weight, it is best to eat less, move around more and avoid junk foods.

MILK

For decades, dairy trade associations and lobbying groups have told Americans that drinking milk strengthens bones. Now they claim that dairy helps us lose weight. As with many aspects of nutrition, the evidence linking dairy foods to health conditions is complicated and contradictory. Dairy foods may have lots of calcium and other nutrients, but they are high in saturated fat (the bad kind) and calories.

Bottom line: If you want to avoid the fat and saturated fat, choose nonfat options. If you don't like or can't tolerate milk, you can get the nutrients it contains from other foods. Consuming dairy foods is not the key to bone health. The best advice for bone health—and for just about any other health condition—is to eat a diet with plenty of fruits, vegetables and whole grains, don't smoke cigarettes, be active and don't drink alcohol to excess.

These good habits mean more to your health than the effects of any one food that you might choose.

■■■■

Know Your Foods

Check what's in your food using software from the US Department of Agriculture's free database at *www.ars.usda.gov* (click on "Food Nutrion," then "What's in the Foods You Eat," then "Download Software"). The information, which can be kept on a PC or handheld device, provides a detailed listing of nutrients—such as calories, protein, fat, carbs, sugars, vitamins and minerals—in almost 7,000 foods, including processed and fast foods.

Examples: Oscar Mayer fat-free hot dogs (per serving of one hot dog), 36 calories, 6.3 g protein, 0.3 g fat, 2.15 g carbs...General Mills Cheerios cereal (per cup), 111 calories, 3.6 g protein, 1.8 g fat, 22.2 g carbs.

■■■■

Raspberries May Prevent Oral Cancer

The pulp of black raspberries contains antioxidants and anti-inflammatory acids that may slow the growth of—or even eliminate—cancerous lesions in the mouth. Researchers now are testing a raspberry-based gel for treatment of lesions. Oral cancer, generally associated with alcohol and tobacco use, causes 8,000 deaths in the US each year.

Russell J. Mumper, PhD, the John A. McNeill Distinguished Professor, molecular pharmaceutics division, University of North Carolina, Chapel Hill.

■■■■

Well Done

Raw and undercooked sprouts can be as risky as undercooked beef and eggs. They may carry *E. coli* and *salmonella*, which can be especially dangerous for children, elderly people and those with weakened immune systems. The FDA is developing stricter safety standards for sprouts.

Michael Doyle, PhD, professor of food microbiology and director, Center for Food Safety, University of Georgia, Griffin.

Millions of Americans Are Getting Too Much Salt...Are You?

Mark Houston, MD, clinical professor of medicine at Vanderbilt University Medical School and medical director at the Hypertension and Vascular Biology Institute and the Life Extension Institute at Saint Thomas Hospital and Medical Center, all in Nashville, TN, is the author of *What Your Doctor May Not Tell You About Hypertension: The Revolutionary Nutrition and Lifestyle Program to Help Fight High Blood Pressure.* Warner.

For years, Americans have been warned that excessive use of salt (sodium chloride) can elevate blood pressure in some people.

Now: Doctors are becoming increasingly concerned about the amount of salt consumed by Americans and fear that it is contributing to even more health problems than previously believed.

Latest development: The American Medical Association has recommended that the FDA require food manufacturers to place warning labels on high-sodium foods.

SOURCES OF SODIUM

Sodium is a mineral that is found naturally in most foods. Everyone is aware of high-sodium foods, such as soy sauce, pickles, potato chips, most canned foods, frozen dinners and lunch meats.

However, few people realize that sodium is found in most carbonated drinks, including many diet sodas. Many brands of tomato juice contain significant amounts of sodium.

Example: Campbell's V8 contains 590 mg of sodium (more than one-quarter of the recommended daily total) per eight-ounce serving. Small amounts of sodium are even found in the tap water of many US municipalities.

Healthful foods, including poultry, dairy products and vegetables, also contain sodium.

Caution: Sodium is found in many over-the-counter medications.

Examples: Alka Seltzer (567 mg per tablet)...and Bromo Seltzer (959 mg per packet).

Our bodies require sodium to help regulate fluid balance. The mineral also is essential for nerve and muscle function. Sodium works with the mineral potassium, which counters the adverse effects of sodium, to keep the proper amount of liquid and electrolytes (minerals needed for proper functioning of the body) inside the body's cells. These minerals are excreted via sweat and urine. Imbalances can occur when too much sodium remains in the body in relation to potassium.

DANGERS OF TOO MUCH SODIUM

Even though high blood pressure (hypertension) is the most commonly recognized health risk associated with excessive sodium intake, there are other potentially serious conditions that can result.

Even in someone who does not have hypertension, excessive sodium intake increases risk for congestive heart failure (inadequate pumping action of the heart)...kidney disease...hardening of the arteries (arteriosclerosis)...swelling of the lower legs, ankles and feet (edema)...and ischemic stroke (impaired blood flow to the brain) as well as hemorrhagic stroke (bleeding into or around the brain).

Consuming too much sodium also may increase your risk for osteoporosis. That's because sodium and bone-strengthening calcium metabolism are linked. High sodium intake may increase the excretion of calcium, which is removed from the body—along with excess sodium—via urine. Over time, calcium stores in the bones will be reduced. This can lead to a calcium deficiency that often results in osteoporosis.

SAFE SODIUM LEVELS

The average American consumes at least 4,000 mg of sodium daily, but research shows that this is far too much. Our bodies require only about 500 mg of sodium daily to maintain normal functioning.

To avoid potential dangers, healthy adults should limit their sodium intake to 2,300 mg (approximately one teaspoon) daily, according to the American Heart Association (AHA).

In my opinion, everyone should limit sodium intake to 1,500 mg daily—especially older adults (age 65 or older), people with hypertension (blood pressure of 140/90 or above) or prehypertension (blood pressure of 120/80 to 139/89), diabetics, obese patients and people with kidney disease or a history of heart failure.

SALT SENSITIVITY

Salt sensitivity is a measure of how blood pressure responds to changes in salt intake. An estimated 60% of Americans with high blood pressure—and 25% of Americans with normal blood pressure—are salt sensitive.

In a recent study, salt sensitivity was found to increase a person's risk for death as much as high blood pressure, regardless of whether blood pressure actually was elevated.

In the study, salt sensitivity was measured by giving study participants a saline solution followed by a diuretic (a water- and salt-excreting drug) and testing blood pressure volume (the fluid content within blood vessels) over a two-day period as salt in the body was increased and then decreased. Unfortunately, there is no test available to the public for salt sensitivity.

Simply putting away the salt shaker is not the full solution. Salt added to food by the eaters themselves accounts for only about 15% of the average American's total daily sodium intake. About 75% comes from sodium in processed and restaurant food, while the remaining 10% of a person's total sodium intake comes from the natural sodium content of food.

Cutting back on canned and processed foods, including fast food, while increasing your intake of fresh fruits and vegetables can substantially lower your sodium intake—most produce contains small amounts of sodium and increases levels of sodium-balancing potassium. To reduce sodium intake when dining in a restaurant, ask that no salt be added to your food.

SALT SUBSTITUTES

Our bodies function most efficiently when we maintain a five-to-one ratio of potassium to sodium. In addition to fruits and vegetables, most unprocessed natural foods, including whole grains and legumes, contain more potassium than sodium. Maintaining this dietary ratio promotes healthy blood pressure.

Some salt substitutes, such as Nu-Salt and NoSalt, contain potassium chloride rather than sodium chloride. These substitutes, available at most grocery stores, taste much like table salt and can be used without potential health risks by most people.

Caution: Potassium chloride-based salt substitutes can be harmful to people who have kidney disease, which can inhibit the proper excretion of potassium and lead to heart and nerve problems. In addition, if you're taking drugs that cause potassium retention, including those for high blood pressure or congestive heart failure, consult your doctor before using a salt substitute. *Good alternative:* A seasoning blend such as Mrs. Dash, which does not contain potassium chloride.

Herbs and spices also add flavor to food. Instead of mimicking the taste of sodium with salt substitutes, try using garlic, lemon juice, flavored vinegar, cumin, pepper, tarragon and/or oregano in food. After a few weeks of reducing salt intake, most people no longer miss it.

■ ■ ■ ■

Shorter Flu Recovery

In a new study, flu patients who were given elderberry extract four times daily for five days recovered in four days compared with eight days for those given a placebo.

Theory: Elderberry prevents the flu virus from attaching to cells, which stops it from replicating.

Self-defense: Take four tablespoons of elderberry extract or four elderberry lozenges daily at the onset of flu symptoms and for the duration of the illness.

Vivian Barak, PhD, head of the immunology lab for tumor diagnosis, Hebrew University-Hadassah Medical School, Jerusalem.

■ ■ ■ ■

Honeycomb Helper

Honeycomb prevents hay fever. Honeycomb works as a desensitizer and antiallergen. About two months before hay fever season begins for you—and that depends on which plants you are allergic to—chew a one-inch square of local honeycomb for 10 to 15 minutes (then discard) twice a day. Purchase honeycomb from a local beekeeper or at your neighborhood health-food store.

Caution: People who are allergic to bee stings or honey should consult a physician first.

Joan Wilen and Lydia Wilen, authorities on folk remedies, New York City, and authors of *Bottom Line's Healing Remedies*. Bottom Line Books.

■ ■ ■ ■

Cholesterol-Lowering Foods

Thirty percent of 66 people who adhered to a diet rich in soy protein, oats, barley, margarine with plant sterols, and almonds for one year lowered their LDL "bad" cholesterol by more than 20%—the same drop seen in those who took a cholesterol-lowering statin for one month.

Reason: Soy protein reduces cholesterol production by the liver...fiber in oats and barley washes out metabolized cholesterol...plant sterols block its absorption...and almonds do all of the above. This food combination is especially well suited for people with slightly elevated cholesterol levels.

David Jenkins, MD, PhD, Canada research chair in nutrition and metabolism, University of Toronto.

■ ■ ■ ■

Rice Padding

Believe it or not, rice cakes can cause weight gain.

Reason: Even though they are low in calories, they boost blood-sugar and insulin levels, causing the body to store extra sugar as fat.

Other products to avoid for the same reason: Mashed potatoes, instant rice, dried dates, fruit roll-ups and jelly beans.

Men's Health, 33 E. Minor St., Emmaus, PA 18098.

■ ■ ■ ■

Anti-Inflammatory Cherries

Cherries fight inflammation. In a recent study, 18 healthy men and women ate 280 g of bing sweet cherries (about 50 fresh cherries) daily for 28 days. Researchers measured levels of *C-reactive protein* (CRP), a marker of inflammation associated with diabetes and cardiovascular disease, in participants' blood during the study and for one month afterward.

Result: After one month, CRP levels dropped by 25% on average.

Theory: Cherries are rich in polyphenols that have strong antioxidant and anti-inflammatory properties.

Darshan S. Kelley, PhD, research chemist, Western Human Nutrition Research Center, US Department of Agriculture, Davis, CA.

A Mineral Imbalance Can Harm Your Heart, Brain, Kidneys...And More

W. Rex Hawkins, MD, a staff surgeon at Methodist and Park Plaza Hospitals in Houston, is the author of *Eat Right—Electrolyte: A Nutritional Guide to Minerals in Our Daily Diet*. Prometheus.

Our bodies require a properly balanced intake of key mineral elements known as electrolytes to maintain normal functioning of the heart, brain, kidneys, nerves and muscles. Unfortunately, the typical Western diet, steeped in salty, processed foods, provides an overabundance of sodium and marginal amounts of calcium, potassium and magnesium. This electrolyte imbalance contributes to a variety of ailments, including high blood pressure (hypertension), osteoporosis and kidney stones.

Because our diets are high in sodium and low in calcium, potassium and magnesium, one in three American adults has hypertension—a condition that increases the risk for heart attack, stroke and dementia. As a retinal disease ophthalmologist, I've seen how hypertension also can lead to blood vessel problems within the eye and can hasten the onset of macular degeneration, a leading cause of blindness in people over age 65. Hypertension also contributes to diabetic retinopathy (a disorder of the retina resulting from diabetes—and the leading cause of visual loss in people ages 20 to 65). *My advice...*

THE RIGHT DIET

The Dietary Approaches to Stop Hypertension (DASH) study, published in *The New England Journal of Medicine*, showed that a healthful diet—eight to 10 daily servings of fruits and vegetables and two to three daily servings of low-fat dairy foods—lowers systolic (the top number) blood pressure by an average of 5.5 points.

When compared with the typical US diet, the DASH diet provides 250% more calcium and 70% to 100% more potassium and magnesium. Sodium consumption was kept at a daily intake of 3,000 mg to exclude the effect that sodium has on blood pressure. Even without sodium restriction, increasing other dietary electrolytes helps lower blood pressure.

Researchers tested the effect that dietary sodium exerts on blood pressure. Volunteers who followed the DASH diet and restricted sodium to 1,150 mg daily experienced an even greater drop in systolic blood pressure of 8.9 points—a result on par with that of blood pressure medications. This may not sound like a significant reduction, but my calculations show that if every American adult with hypertension lowered his/her blood pressure by just this amount, we'd see 46% fewer strokes and prevent nearly one-third of all heart attacks.

The DASH studies confirm that electrolytes play a critical role in the maintenance of normal blood pressure.

DANGERS OF TOO MUCH SODIUM

More is at stake than cardiovascular health. Excessive dietary sodium also causes you to waste calcium. Research studies show that for every 1,000 mg of sodium we consume, the kidneys excrete 10 mg to 25 mg of calcium in our urine.

In an Australian study published in *American Journal of Clinical Nutrition*, bone loss from osteoporosis in postmenopausal women was prevented by restricting sodium consumption to 2,110 mg daily and increasing calcium intake. (The average adult in the US consumes 3,500 mg of sodium daily.)

Not surprisingly, osteoporosis has climbed to epidemic proportions. Studies show that nearly 90% of women at age 80 have lost approximately 50% of the calcium in their bones. Furthermore, an Italian study published in *The New England Journal of Medicine* showed that limiting sodium to 1,150 mg daily prevented recurring kidney stones nearly twice as effectively as the traditional approach of limiting calcium.

Additional evidence suggests that lowering your sodium intake may reduce your risk for stomach cancer and help ease bronchial symptoms in asthmatics.

According to the US Department of Agriculture, healthy adults should consume no more than 2,300 mg of sodium daily. People with hypertension or those at increased risk (African-Americans, older adults, etc.) should consume no more than 1,500 mg of sodium.

STRIKING THE RIGHT BALANCE

The problem is that most Americans consume far too much sodium—most of it hidden in processed and prepackaged foods. Half a can of soup can contain 800 mg of sodium, while a fast-food burger provides 1,200 mg to 2,000 mg—and that is not counting the fries!

For most of us, putting away the salt shaker will eliminate only about 20% of dietary sodium. To make an even bigger dent, you must cut back on processed foods, such as deli meats and cheeses, canned vegetables and soups, sauces and marinades. Choose fresh foods whenever possible… or packaged foods without added salt.

CALCIUM

Calcium is required for normal muscle contraction, heart rhythm, blood clotting and bone formation. Adults over age 50 should aim for 1,200 mg daily, though most consume only about half this much.

Dairy products contain abundant calcium. An eight-ounce glass of skim milk contains about 300 mg. Much of your daily calcium requirement also can be met with plant sources, such as cabbage, kale, spinach and broccoli. Other good calcium sources include tofu and calcium-fortified juices.

POTASSIUM

In addition to helping to control blood pressure, potassium transmits nerve impulses throughout the body, keeping your muscles contracting, your heart beating and other systems functioning normally.

The recommended daily intake of potassium is 4,700 mg, but most Americans consume only about half this amount. You can reach recommended potassium levels by consuming eight daily servings of fruits and vegetables. Excellent potassium sources include bananas, apricots, honeydew melons, spinach, tomatoes and fish (salmon, cod and flounder).

Caution: The liquid in canned vegetables leaches up to 30% of the potassium from the food. Choose fresh vegetables whenever possible…or frozen without added salt.

Because potassium is readily available in common foods, supplements are generally not recommended for healthy adults.

MAGNESIUM

Magnesium helps maintain normal muscle and nerve function, regulates heart rhythm, bolsters energy and immune functioning, and aids calcium absorption. It also helps regulate blood sugar levels, possibly protecting against diabetes. Magnesium may play a vital role in controlling blood pressure by relaxing blood vessels.

Women require 320 mg of magnesium daily, while men need about 420 mg. You can easily meet these levels by consuming magnesium-rich foods, such as spinach and whole-grain breads and cereals…legumes, such as kidney beans, and unsalted nuts.

■ ■ ■ ■

Diet and Vision

In a study of 4,170 people, those who ate the most foods rich in beta-carotene, vitamins C and E and zinc were 35% less likely to develop age-related macular degeneration (the leading cause of blindness in people over age 65) than those who ate less of these nutrients.

Theory: The antioxidants in these foods help protect against free radical damage to the retina.

Self-defense: Eat generous amounts of foods that contain the above nutrients, such as whole-grain cereal, eggs, poultry and olive oil.

Redmer van Leeuwen, MD, PhD, resident in ophthalmology, Erasmus Medical Centre, Rotterdam.

■ ■ ■ ■

Surgery Recovery with Gum

In a new study, 62 patients who underwent intestinal surgery chewed gum for 15 minutes four times daily, while 40 other patients who received the same type of surgery did not chew gum.

Result: The gum chewers had their first bowel movements 12 hours earlier and left the hospital almost a day earlier than those who did not chew gum.

Theory: Gum chewing triggers the production of digestive juices that may result in earlier recovery of gut motility (movement of muscles in the gastrointestinal tract).

If you are scheduled for abdominal surgery: Ask your doctor whether you should chew gum three to four times a day as soon as possible after surgery.

Harry Papaconstantinou, MD, section chief, colon and rectal surgery, division of surgical oncology, Scott & White Clinic, Texas A&M University System Health Center, Temple.

■ ■ ■ ■

Clean Your Veggies

Fruits and vegetables contaminated with bacteria such as salmonella and E. coli now cause more illness than raw chicken or eggs. The contamination comes from the use of manure as a fertilizer or from cross-contamination in home and restaurant kitchens.

Precaution: Wash fruits and vegetables under running water, use separate cutting boards for raw meat, poultry, fish and produce, and thoroughly wash countertops on which unwashed produce had been placed.

Caroline Smith DeWaal, food safety director, Center for Science in the Public Interest, Washington, DC.

Eating Breakfast Lowers Your Disease Risk by 50%

Linda Van Horn, PhD, professor of preventive medicine, Northwestern University, Chicago.

Alice H. Lichtenstein, DSc, professor of public health and family medicine, Tufts University, Boston.

American Heart Association's annual conference, Miami.

Sugar-laden cereals and high-fat muffins in the morning may not be ideal fare, but eating anything for breakfast seems healthier than skipping the first meal of the day, researchers report.

THE STUDY

For eight years, researchers tested study participants for insulin resistance and assessed them for obesity and abnormal glucose levels, elevated blood pressure and elevated lipid values. Researchers also took into account physical activity, smoking, age and sex.

Although the best results were achieved by those who ate whole-grain cereals and other nutritious breakfast items, "eating breakfast at all was preferential to not eating," says study author Linda Van Horn, a professor of preventive medicine at Northwestern University.

Breakfast eaters are up to 55% less likely than their non-breakfasting counterparts to develop problems such as diabetes or obesity, the study suggests.

RESULTS

Alice H. Lichtenstein, a professor of public health and family medicine at Tufts University in Boston, says the study supplies interesting information, but "we need to know a lot more about dietary patterns."

She would like to see more detailed monitoring of what the people in the study ate and their actual glucose levels.

Still, there is an assumption, which this study seems to confirm, that eating in the morning prevents binge eating later in the day.

"People have been told for years that you're better starting off your day with breakfast," Lichtenstein says.

The wise will heed this advice, which is easy and makes a difference, Van Horn concludes. "One simple thing you can do to cut heart disease risk in half is eat breakfast," she says.

■■■■

Best Yogurt

To find yogurts that have live active cultures, look for the *Live & Active Cultures* (LAC) seal from the National Yogurt Association. The seal is an easy way for consumers to identify yogurts that have significant levels of live and active cultures, which can help to boost the immune system.

Note: Some yogurt products may have live cultures but don't display the seal, so always check labels. Look for the words *contains active yogurt cultures* or *living yogurt cultures*. Among brands with live cultures are Stonyfield Farm, Yoplait, Dannon and Nancy's.

The National Yogurt Association, *www.aboutyogurt.com.*

■■■■

Healthy Wine Trend

Natural wines—made with as little technological intervention as possible—are becoming popular. Grapes for these wines are generally —but not always—organically grown without chemical pesticides and herbicides and usually are picked by hand. Enzymes usually are not added, although some sulfites may be included late in the process as a preservative. If properly stored—at cool temperatures, like any other wine—they will last as long. Many natural wines are available nationally.

Two of the better ones: Pierre Breton Bourgueil (red) and Huet Vouvray (white).

David Lillie, owner, Chambers Street Wines, New York City. *www.chambersstwines.com.*

■■■■

Beer Builds Better Bones!

Dietary silicon, found in whole grains and their products (such as beer), reduces bone loss and promotes bone formation. Beer is an especially good source because it is readily absorbed. Other sources of silicon include oat bran, barley and rice.

Warning: More than two drinks per day for men or one for women is considered harmful.

Ravin Jugdaohsingh, PhD, research fellow, biomedical and health sciences, Kings College, London.

Don't Fall for the Hype of "Functional Foods"

Rebecca Shannonhouse, editor of *Bottom Line Health.* Boardroom Inc., 281 Tresser Blvd., Stamford, CT 06901.

Supermarket shelves are now filled with "functional foods"—products designed to provide health benefits beyond the food's basic nutritional value.

Examples: A new version of Tropicana orange juice contains 3 g of fiber per serving… a spread called Benecol contains cholesterol-lowering plant stanols…and a yogurt called

Activia contains a strain of beneficial bacteria that helps promote regular bowel movements.

Some cereals, breads and other staples have been fortified with vitamins and minerals for decades. But the new functional foods have some nutrition experts worried.

"People who start adding foods to their diets because they're 'good for them' could end up consuming more calories if they do not eliminate other foods," says Alice H. Lichtenstein, DSc, professor of public health and family medicine at Tufts University in Boston. The health risks from obesity could far outweigh any of the likely benefits, she explains.

Other potential drawbacks...

•**Foods that are clearly bad for people,** such as soft drinks, could be marketed as "healthy," once they're spiked with vitamin C, calcium or other nutrients.

•**Foods can be less reliable and/or less convenient** than supplements for getting some substances, such as plant stanols.

Even though functional foods may be tempting to try, you're better off following the tried-and-true nutritional advice we all grew up with: Eat a diet rich in vegetables, fruits and whole grains...include cold-water fish, such as salmon or mackerel, two times per week...and balance the calories you eat with those you burn.

■ ■ ■ ■

Soybean Protein Lowers Blood Pressure

In a study of 302 adults with a median blood pressure of 135/85 mmHg (normal is below 120/80 mmHg), those who ate one cookie containing 40 g of soybean protein a day for 12 weeks had a 4.31-point drop in systolic (top number) pressure and a 2.76-point drop in diastolic (bottom number) pressure compared with those who ate a placebo cookie.

Theory: Soybean protein may influence the sympathetic nervous system, sodium excretion and insulin resistance, all of which affect blood pressure.

Implication: Soybean consumption may be an effective alternative to medication for lowering blood pressure in otherwise healthy people with mild hypertension.

Jiang He, MD, PhD, associate professor and chair, department of epidemiology, Tulane University School of Public Health and Tropical Medicine, New Orleans.

The Healing Power Of Herbal Teas

Brigitte Mars, an herbalist and nutritional consultant in Boulder, CO, is the author of 12 books, including *Healing Herbal Teas* (Basic Health) and a professional member of the American Herbalist Guild (AHG).

Herbal teas, which are generally rich in vitamins, minerals and other healthful compounds, have been used as healing agents for thousands of years.

However, because of the prevalence of over-the-counter and prescription medications, most Americans don't think of drinking tea to treat common ailments. That's a mistake.

Dozens of scientific studies have supported the use of herbals for a wide variety of health problems.* Herbal teas have the same active ingredients as herbs sold in capsules, powders and extracts. Herbal teas also have fewer side effects than medication and can be much less expensive.

Loose tea herbs, which are available at health-food stores, tend to be more potent than tea bags. To prepare tea with loose herbs, use one heaping tablespoon of dried herb or three tablespoons of fresh herb in eight ounces of boiling water. Steep for 10 minutes.

For best results, drink four eight-ounce cups of herbal tea per day until the problem subsides. If you are age 65 or older, do not exceed three cups daily...or two cups daily if you are age 70 or older.

Best teas for treating common health conditions...

COLDS AND FLU

Echinacea, which has an aromatic, earthy flavor, promotes white blood cell production... acts as an anti-infection agent...and stimulates the immune system.

*Check with your health-care practitioner before drinking herbal tea, especially if you are a pregnant woman, nursing mother or have a chronic medical condition. Some herbal teas should not be combined with certain drugs.

How to use: Echinacea should be used for no more than 10 consecutive days, because it loses its effectiveness when taken continually. Drink echinacea tea at the onset of cold or flu symptoms, such as sore throat, sneezing and/or nasal congestion.

Caution: Echinacea stimulates the immune system, so people with autoimmune diseases, such as lupus, should consult a doctor before using this herb. People who are allergic to plants in the daisy family, such as ragweed, are more likely to have an allergic reaction to echinacea.

Other teas that fight colds and flu: Elder-flower and elderberry.

DIGESTIVE DISORDERS

Peppermint, which has a zesty, fresh taste, calms muscle spasms…eases intestinal cramping …contains antibacterial compounds…soothes ulcers…and freshens breath after a meal.

Caution: Do not drink peppermint tea if you are suffering from an acute episode of a digestive disorder, such as a gallstone attack. Seek immediate medical attention.

Other teas that fight digestive disorders: Cardamom, ginger and cinnamon.

HEADACHE

Lemon balm, which has a gentle lemon flavor and aroma, acts as an anti-inflammatory and antispasmodic…and contains magnesium, which acts as a muscle relaxant.

Caution: This herb may inhibit thyroid function. If you have low thyroid function (hypothyroidism), avoid lemon balm tea.

Other teas that fight headache: Feverfew and rosemary.

INSOMNIA

Linden flower, which has a sweet flavor and jasminelike aroma, is rich in vitamin C…calms nerves…and promotes rest. In Europe, linden flower tea often is given to patients before surgery to help them relax.

Other teas that fight insomnia: Chamomile and passionflower.

LOW LIBIDO

Oat seed, which has a slightly sweet, milky flavor, relaxes the nerves…and is often used as an aphrodisiac.

Caution: Oat seed contains gluten, so this herb should be avoided by people with gluten intolerance.

Other teas that fight low libido: Cinnamon and raspberry leaf.

■ ■ ■ ■

More Than Milk

Drinking milk isn't enough to build strong bones.

Recent finding: Women who drank one or more glasses of milk per day were just as likely to fracture a hip or wrist as those who drank less than one glass of milk per week.

Reason: Most women don't get enough vitamin D, which is necessary for calcium absorption.

Best way to get adequate vitamin D: Sit in the sun for 15 minutes a day, without sunscreen—sunlight is necessary for the skin to manufacture the body's own supply of vitamin D. Vitamin D also can be found in fortified orange juice, certain fortified cereals and fatty fish, such as salmon and sardines. The recommended daily intake for vitamin D is 400 international units (IU), but many researchers now believe that much higher daily intakes are necessary.

Diane Feskanich, ScD, assistant professor, Channing Laboratory, department of medicine, Brigham and Women's Hospital and Harvard Medical School, both in Boston, and leader of an 18-year study of 72,000 women, published in *The American Journal of Clinical Nutrition*.

Five Rules for Healthful Snacking

Jamison Starbuck, ND, naturopathic physician in family practice and a lecturer at the University of Montana, both in Missoula. She is past president of the American Association of Naturopathic Physicians.

I'm a three-meals-a-day type of person. But many of my patients love to eat a little something between meals and often ask for my advice in selecting healthful snacks. That's why I've developed a set of rules for healthful snacking—and a list of tasty, fun foods that make good snacks.

Rule 1: Drink water first. Often, we head for a snack when we're actually thirsty. Drink a

12-ounce glass of water and wait 10 minutes. If you are still hungry, select a healthful snack.

***Rule 2:* Choose a snack food that still bears a resemblance to its original form.** Natural food—the most healthful food—comes from the earth or an animal. Lettuce grows in the dirt. Oranges and nuts hang from trees. Corn, wheat and oats grow in fields. The fillet or steak you're having for dinner was part of an animal before it landed on your table. When you apply this concept to snacks, it's fairly easy to make healthful choices. Cheetos, for example, are a long, long way from the corn from which they are made—many synthetic ingredients are added. An unsweetened rice cake, on the other hand, still looks quite a bit like rice.

***Rule 3:* Avoid fat- and sugar-laden snacks.** If a sweetener or oil is the first or second ingredient on the label list, skip this snack.

***Rule 4:* Keep portions small.** The more fat or sugar in the snack (cheese, nuts and dried fruit), the smaller the portion should be. Recommended snack size is one ounce of cheese... eight nuts...or two tablespoons of dried fruit. Watery, fiber-rich snacks, such as fresh fruit or vegetables, can be eaten in larger portions—½ cup to one cup is reasonable.

***Rule 5:* Drink a cup of hot mint tea with your snack.** It aids your digestion, promoting absorption of nutrients, which improves the satisfaction you derive from the food. *My snack suggestions...*

•**Raw almonds, hazelnuts or pecans... whole fruit...celery sticks, carrots or a rice cake** covered with a tablespoon of nut butter (almond, sesame, cashew) or hummus (mashed chickpeas flavored with lemon juice, garlic and oil).

•**Whole-grain muffin** (no bigger than a tennis ball) containing fruit, nuts and/or ground seeds and made with honey or cane sugar—not corn syrup.

•**Vegetable salads,** such as cooked and chilled beets drizzled with olive oil and a sprinkle of goat cheese or cole slaw made with oil and vinegar rather than mayonnaise.

•**Air-popped popcorn**—plain or seasoned with garlic or a pinch of sea salt.

•**Small baked potato,** seasoned with herbs and a sprinkle of oil (put extra potatoes in the oven when you make dinner and refrigerate them for snacks that can be eaten later).

•**Rice**—½ cup, with nuts and a dash of oil.

Experiment with different healthful and delicious oils—⅛ teaspoon of 100% virgin pistachio oil goes a long way to make a baked potato taste pretty special. Sesame, hazelnut and pumpkin seed oils are also tasty and add a special flavor to vegetable salads or whole-grain snacks.

■■■■

Prepare Meals in Advance

Prepare a month's worth of dinners in one two-hour session at Dream Dinners (*www. dreamdinners.com*). There are about 600 of these meal-assembly operations nationwide, where participants measure and scoop precut, precooked ingredients into resealable bags or aluminum trays. Popular meals include lasagna and cassoulet (made with sausage, chicken and white beans). Cooking instructions are included.

Cost: Between $80 and $300, with the average cost being about $200 for 72 servings.

For a list of other meal-preparation companies, go to *www.easymealprep.com*.

Sweetener Alert

Rebecca Shannonhouse, editor of *Bottom Line Health.* Boardroom, Inc., 281 Tresser Blvd., Stamford, CT 06901.

Splenda, which has been in use in the US for nearly 10 years, is the nation's best-selling artificial sweetener—and one of the most controversial. Some consumer groups argue that Splenda was given FDA approval without adequate toxicity studies and that it may increase the risk for cancer.

Sucralose (the main ingredient in Splenda) is an amalgam of sugar molecules spliced together with chlorine—and chlorine can potentially damage cellular DNA. Yet there's no evidence—either from case reports or scientific studies—that sucralose poses any real increased risk for cancer.

"When you consider the number of people who consume Splenda, the fact that cancer hasn't appeared suggests that the risk, if any, would likely be very modest," explains David L. Katz, MD, founder of the Yale Preventive Research Center in New Haven, Connecticut.

But there are other reasons to be concerned about—and to avoid—any artificial sweetener, Dr. Katz says. For example, some studies indicate that people who use artificial sweeteners (or products that contain them) consume more—rather than fewer—calories.

Possible reason: Artificial sweeteners are 300 to 600 times sweeter than sugar. People who consume them can develop a higher "threshold for satisfaction"—and wind up consuming excess amounts of regular sugar-rich foods.

Splenda and other artificial sweeteners don't appear to pose significant health risks—but they don't ensure calorie control either.

If you're trying to lose weight: Avoid artificial sweeteners and curtail your intake of regular sugar.

■ ■ ■ ■

Olive Oil Benefit

Olive oil may help stop some types of breast cancer cells from growing and dividing. It is already known to be good for heart health—it boosts HDL (good) cholesterol and lowers LDL (bad) cholesterol. To get more olive oil in your diet, sauté vegetables in olive oil instead of butter, and use salad dressing containing olive oil.

Ruth Lupu, PhD, associate professor of medicine, Robert H. Lurie Comprehensive Cancer Center of Northwestern University, Evanston, IL.

■ ■ ■ ■

Beef and Pork Linked to Pancreatic Cancer

In a seven-year study, people who reported eating the most beef or pork were 50% more likely to develop pancreatic cancer than those who reported eating the least.

Possible reasons: Carcinogens caused by cooking red meat at high temperatures…or nitrites used as preservatives in processed meats. Further research is needed to confirm a link.

Bonnie Liebman, MS, director of nutrition, *Nutrition Action Healthletter*, 1875 Connecticut Ave, NW, Washington, DC 20009.

Best Wines for Your Health

Roger Corder, PhD, professor of experimental therapeutics at the William Harvey Research Institute, Queen Mary's School of Medicine and Dentistry in London. The author or coauthor of more than 100 scientific studies, his primary research interests are the relationship between diabetes and heart disease, and the health benefits of wine.

For years, scientists theorized that the "French Paradox"—the phenomenon of relatively low rates of heart disease among the French, who are known for their rich, fatty foods—may be due, in part, to the daily consumption of red wine.

Now: The cumulative body of scientific evidence shows that moderate consumption of red wine not only reduces the risk for heart disease, but also for stroke and metabolic syndrome (a constellation of health problems that can lead to heart disease and diabetes). Wine also helps people live longer and avoid dementia. Only recently, however, have scientists begun to identify the specific compounds in red wine that confer health benefits.

Trap: Mass-produced, sweet red wines with high alcohol content (above 14%) do *not* offer high levels of health-promoting chemicals.

What you must know to choose the most healthful wines—and the best options for non-drinkers…

WINE'S PROTECTIVE EFFECTS

Recent research shows that white wine may offer some of the same health benefits of red wine, such as protection from heart disease, but the bulk of scientific evidence focuses on red wine.

Latest developments: Animal experiments show that *polyphenols*—chemicals found abundantly in dark and/or colorful foods, such as red and purple grapes, cocoa and pomegranates—can stop atherosclerosis (fatty buildup in the arteries). That's because polyphenols affect the *endothelium* (cells lining the arteries), causing blood vessels to widen (vasodilate), increasing blood flow.

Breakthrough: English scientists published a paper in *Nature*—a renowned scientific journal—showing that…

•**The most potent polyphenols in red wines** are *procyanidins*, healthful plant substances that over time become condensed *tannins*, compounds that give an astringent taste to wine. The more procyanidins consumed, the greater degree of vasodilation that occurs.

•**Regions in Europe with the highest rates of proven longevity** produce wines with two to four times more procyanidins than do other regions.

Examples: Many varieties of Bordeaux wines from France and Chianti wines from Italy.

What you may not know: *Resveratrol* is often mentioned as the key heart-protecting component of red wine. But to get enough resveratrol to benefit the heart, you would need to drink 1,000 quarts of wine a day. Resveratrol supplements haven't been proven safe or effective.

HEART-FRIENDLY WINES

Many factors influence the level of procyanidins in red wine.

Certain varieties of grapes, including cabernet sauvignon and malbec, are higher in procyanidins than other red and white grapes. Other positive factors include the altitude of the vineyard (the higher, the better)…a slower ripening process…a lower yield (the amount of grapes produced per vine)…and older vines.

Useful: Wines described as having "firm" tannins are more likely to have high levels of procyanidins than wines with "soft" or "ripe" tannins. Look for this description in wine reviews and at the Web sites of wine retailers, such as K&L Wine Merchants (*www.klwines. com*) and Wine.com, Inc. (*www.wine.com*).

DRINK WITH MEALS

The most healthful way to drink red wine is in the classic French style—one or two small glasses at lunch and/or with dinner, as food slows alcohol absorption. Most research shows that women should not exceed five ounces of wine per day, and men should limit their daily consumption to 10 ounces.

When red wine is consumed in excess, its health benefits are outweighed by the risks associated with alcohol abuse, including increased risks for many types of cancer, as well as heart disease, obesity and diabetes.

Caution: Drinking wine quickly or on an empty stomach speeds alcohol absorption, increasing the risk for high blood pressure.

NONALCOHOLIC PROCYANIDINS

If you prefer not to drink red wine, consider these procyanidin-rich foods…

•**Dark chocolate.** Look for a bittersweet or extra-dark chocolate, with 70% to 85% cacao. One ounce of dark chocolate delivers the amount of procyanidins in four ounces of red wine.

Caution: To limit calories, don't eat more than one ounce to one-and-a-half ounces of dark chocolate daily.

•**Apples.** Red Delicious and Granny Smith have high levels of procyanidins. One medium-sized apple is equivalent to four ounces of red wine.

•**Cranberry juice.** An eight-ounce serving of juice containing 25% cranberry is roughly equivalent to a four-ounce glass of red wine. Choose low-sugar versions with at least 25% cranberry content.

Other sources of heart-healthy procyanidins: Raspberries, blackberries and strawberries, Concord grape juice, pomegranates, walnuts, pinto beans and cinnamon.

HEALTHFUL WINES

Laboratory analyses of more than 400 red wines at William Harvey Research Institute show that the following have high levels of healthful procyanidins…

•**Argentina.** Cabernet sauvignon, from Bodegas Catena Zapata.

•**Australia.** Cabernet sauvignon, from Wynns.

•**California.** Cabernet sauvignon, from Robert Mondavi Napa Valley Reserve…and many other Napa Valley cabernets.

•**Chile.** Cabernet sauvignons from Veramonte.

•**France.** Large numbers of Bordeaux wines —both at the top end of the market and modestly priced—have high or better-than-average procyanidin levels.

•**Italy.** In Tuscany, wines made from the Sangiovese grape that tested well include Il Colombaio di Cencio's Chianti Classico Riserva.

In Sardinia, where wine drinkers are particularly long-lived, a good choice is Rosso Superiore del Mandrolisai.

17

Fitness Savvy

The Fat-Resistance Diet

Weight loss isn't only —or even mainly— about calories. Surprisingly, we gain weight when natural weight-control mechanisms are disrupted by inflammation, a low-grade inflammatory response caused by poor diet and environmental toxins.

When people gain weight, the extra fatty tissue produces *leptin*, a hormone that suppresses appetite and speeds metabolism. In theory, this should cause people to lose the extra weight.

Instead, inflammation in fat tissue and blood vessels stimulates the production of anti-inflammatory chemicals. These chemicals disable leptin's ability to suppress appetite and speed metabolism. This is called *leptin resistance*.

To combat leptin resistance, I have developed a fat-resistance diet based on cutting-edge research at premier institutions such as Harvard, Johns Hopkins and Rockefeller universities. Eating the proper foods can eliminate chronic inflammation and reprogram the body's weight-loss mechanisms.

ANTI-INFLAMMATORY FOODS

The focus of the diet isn't calorie control. The idea is to eat foods that supply anti-inflammatory nutrients. A major problem with most weight-loss diets is the use of artificial sweeteners and fat substitutes to reduce calories. Substituting these products for real foods deprives your body of key anti-inflammatory nutrients. *Main principles...*

•**Eat fish at least three times weekly.** The omega-3 fatty acids in fish have powerful anti-inflammatory properties. Fish that are rich in omega-3s and relatively low in mercury include anchovies, conch, herring (fresh or pickled, not creamed), mackerel (Atlantic only), sablefish, salmon (fresh, canned or smoked, wild or farmed), sardines (Atlantic), sturgeon and tuna (fresh or canned bluefin—not albacore).

Leo Galland, MD, director, Foundation for Integrated Medicine, New York City. He is author of *The Fat Resistance Diet*. Broadway. *www.fatresistancediet.com*. Dr. Galland is a recipient of the Linus Pauling Award.

497

•**Balance essential fatty acids.** The optimal ratio of omega-6 fatty acids to omega-3s is about 4:1. The ratio in the average American diet is closer to 20:1. A relative excess of omega-6 fats in tissues leads cells to produce excessive levels of pro-inflammatory chemicals called *prostanoids*. The best approach is to decrease intake of omega-6s and increase intake of omega-3s.

Foods high in omega-3s: Fish, flaxseed, walnuts and beans—navy, kidney and soybeans.

Foods high in omega-6s: Red meat, chicken, milk, eggs and most vegetable oils, including corn, sunflower and safflower.

•**Cut back on unhealthy fats.** Saturated fat—primarily found in beef, pork, lamb, dairy products and poultry skin—should be limited to no more than 10% of total calories. Don't eat any trans fat—this means avoiding any foods made with hydrogenated or partially hydrogenated vegetable oil. These include most commercial baked goods and some fast foods. Both saturated fat and trans fat greatly increase levels of inflammatory chemicals.

•**Get 25 grams of fiber daily.** A high-fiber diet helps control appetite and reduce inflammation. A study by the Centers for Disease Control and Prevention found that people who consume the most fiber have lower levels of *C-reactive protein* (CRP), which indicates the presence of inflammatory chemicals in the body. All plant foods contain some fiber. Among the best sources are beans, whole grains and vegetables.

•**Eat colorful fruits and vegetables.** Get at least nine servings daily. Produce with deep colors and intense flavors is high in flavonoids and carotenoids, chemical compounds that have anti-inflammatory effects.

Important: Have at least one serving of blueberries, cherries or pomegranates a day. These contain *anthocyanins*, which are among the most potent anti-inflammatory agents.

•**Choose alliums and crucifers.** Crucifers are strong-flavored vegetables, including broccoli, cauliflower, cabbage and kale. Alliums include onions and garlic. Both classes of vegetables reduce chronic inflammation and lower the risk of cancer, particularly breast cancer. Eat at least one serving of each daily.

•**Use only egg whites or unbroken egg yolks.** The cholesterol in yolks has relatively little effect on cholesterol in the blood—but if the yolk is broken, the cholesterol is oxidized and produces inflammatory by-products. Poached or boiled whole eggs are fine. Avoid scrambled eggs and whole-egg omelettes.

•**Favor herbs and spices that are potent anti-inflammatories.** These include basil, cardamom, cilantro, cinnamon, clove, ginger, parsley and turmeric. Use them every day. Avoid chiles, cayenne pepper and jalapeños, which can trigger inflammation.

THREE STAGES

The diet progresses in phases…

•**Stage 1.** Eat as much as you want of such foods as arugula, bell peppers, broccoli, cabbage, carrots, leeks, onions, romaine lettuce, scallions, shiitake mushrooms, spinach and tomatoes—as well as blueberries, cherries, grapefruit and pomegranates.

Eating three four-ounce servings of high-protein foods each day helps suppress appetite and maintain muscle mass. Choose fish, egg whites, poultry and plain, fat-free yogurt. Meat lovers can eat red meat twice a week but should marinate beef with cherry or pomegranate concentrate (this reduces inflammatory chemical compounds produced during cooking). You can have a tablespoon or two each day of nuts or seeds (especially flaxseed, walnuts and almonds). During this stage, get 25 grams of fiber, primarily from vegetables.

Avoid grains, even whole grains, because they tend to raise insulin levels, increasing leptin resistance. Most people stay in this stage for two weeks and lose six to 10 pounds.

•**Stage 2.** The long-term weight-loss part of the diet. Stay on this until you reach your goal weight. Expect to lose one to two pounds per week.

In addition to the Stage 1 foods, add some whole grains, such as oats and brown rice, and beans, lentils and other legumes (about two to three cups a week of each).

•**Stage 3.** The lifelong maintenance phase. Increase variety by adding potatoes, pasta and whole-grain breads.

How to Break the Weight-Gain Cycle

Ray D. Strand, MD, author of *Healthy for Life* (Real Life) and *What Your Doctor Doesn't Know About Nutritional Medicine May Be Killing You* (Thomas Nelson). Dr. Strand has devised a 15-month wellness program that is available on-line at *www.releasingfat.com*. More about his work at *www.drraystrand.com*.

In a country obsessed with dieting and weight loss, we have a disproportionately large number of overweight people. In fact, two-thirds of American adults and nearly one-third of children are overweight or obese, putting them at increased risk for an array of health risks.

Ironically, according to Ray D. Strand, MD, we continue to ignore the root cause of obesity—insulin resistance and the inability to properly process glucose and fat stores. He believes that if people were able to tame insulin resistance, they would lose weight and at the same time prevent obesity-related health problems.

The earlier you get on top of insulin resistance, the greater the chance you have of reversing it and avoiding diabetes or high blood pressure. How to go about this?

It's simple: Develop a healthy lifestyle.

INSULIN RESISTANCE— A PRIMER

In order to get to the bottom of insulin resistance, let's first take a closer look at insulin's proper role in the body. Insulin is normally released into the bloodstream in response to elevated glucose (blood sugar) levels after you eat. Its role is to push glucose out of the bloodstream and into the cells of the body, where it is converted into energy. When you develop insulin resistance, however, this system goes awry and the body no longer can make efficient use of insulin. The result is uncontrollable food cravings, increased emotional eating and an inability to lose weight no matter how hard you try.

When you suffer from insulin resistance, it is as if your body holds on to fat like a sponge holds on to water, says Dr. Strand. He adds that insulin resistance and its devastating consequences are no sudden, random occurrence. They sneak up over the course of many years, gradually eroding your health. Their roots lie in the way most Americans eat.

A VICIOUS CYCLE—CARBOHYDRATE ADDICTION AND INSULIN ABUSE

The typical American diet includes far too many fast foods, chips, cookies, doughnuts, bread and soft drinks. Atkins high-protein craze aside, we've become carbohydrate addicts in this country, warns Dr. Strand. Simple sugars quickly flood the bloodstream, and in response, the body furiously pumps out insulin. This, in turn, leads to an abrupt crash in blood sugar and a drop in energy that leaves you craving more carbs, and the vicious cycle continues—more carbs, more blood sugar, more insulin, etc.

As time goes on and insulin converts excess glucose into fat, you put on weight, which makes the body's cells more resistant to insulin. The pancreas responds by pumping out still more insulin in an increasingly vain attempt to try to force glucose into cells. The bloodstream is left awash in excess glucose.

In people with insulin resistance, blood sugar is not high enough (yet) to constitute diabetes, but it is higher than normal. If you do nothing to change your ways and break the cycle, eventually you will tip over into the abnormal metabolic state known as metabolic syndrome (also called Syndrome X). Characteristics of this devastating syndrome—shared by 25% of the adult population of the US—include obesity, diabetes, high blood pressure, abnormal cholesterol, elevated triglycerides, cardiovascular disease and, in women, polycystic ovarian syndrome (PCOS).

HOW TO TAME INSULIN RESISTANCE

Full-blown metabolic syndrome doesn't develop overnight, emphasizes Dr. Strand. It is a result of years and years of poor daily food and activity choices. The good news is that you can break the vicious cycle of carbohydrate addiction and insulin abuse, slowing down and even reversing the development of obesity and type 2 diabetes. However, there's no quick fix, no easy pill to pop—the only way you can overcome these obstacles is by developing and following a healthy lifestyle.

WATCH THE WARNING SIGNS

According to Dr. Strand, there are a number of measurable warning signs for insulin resistance, in which case you need to take action. *Warning signs of insulin resistance are...*

•**Expanding waist size.** Beware of a waist circumference of 29 or more inches in women and 34 or more inches in men.

•**Any slight elevation in blood pressure.** Even a measurement of 130/85 can be an early sign of insulin resistance.

•**Elevated blood sugar.** Ask your doctor to give you a fasting blood sugar test. A result above 100 (or even approaching 100) is a red flag.

•**A decrease in HDL or good cholesterol** (below 50 for women, or below 40 for men), which is often accompanied by increasing triglyceride levels. Dr. Strand calculates a simple ratio by dividing a person's triglyceride level by his/her HDL level. If the resulting triglyceride/HDL ratio is greater than two, this is another warning sign.

THREE STEPS TO REVERSING INSULIN SENSITIVITY

Once you and your physician have identified the problem, the answer is to promote a healthy lifestyle that enhances insulin sensitivity and works to reverse the problem and reduce long-term health risks. *Dr. Strand advises...*

1. Follow a healthy diet that does not spike blood sugar. Generally, 40% to 50% of calories should come from low-glycemic carbohydrates ...30% from fat...and 20% to 30% from protein.

While you don't need to weigh your food or starve yourself, you do need to make healthy food choices. *This means...*

•Eat good complex carbs such as antioxidant-rich fruits, veggies and whole grains, and avoid high-glycemic carbs that send your blood sugar soaring, including white bread, white rice, highly processed cereal and white potatoes.

•Replace the bad saturated and trans-fats in hamburgers and french fries with good alternatives such as monounsaturated fats (for example, olive oil, avocado and macadamia nuts) and essential fatty acids (EFAs), including cold-water fish (salmon, sardines, etc.), flaxseed oil and walnuts.

•Choose good sources of protein such as nuts, hard-boiled eggs, avocados, beans, soy, legumes, fowl with the skin removed and cold-water fish. Dr. Strand notes that the poorest sources of protein are red meats and dairy products.

•Drink eight to 10 glasses of purified water every day.

•Never go hungry. Small, frequent meals will help control spikes in blood sugar. As you feel better, you should decrease meal frequency and increase content. If you're still hungry between meals, snack on an apple, a hard-boiled egg or a handful of raw almonds.

2. Develop a moderate, consistent exercise program. Physical activity is the second step to insulin sensitivity. It doesn't matter what you choose to do, says Dr. Strand. At first, consistency is the most important thing.

Your ultimate goal: Gradually work your way up to 30 to 40 minutes of aerobic exercise such as brisk walking five days a week. Every step you take will bring you one step closer to improved insulin sensitivity. To be on the safe side, Dr. Strand recommends consulting your physician before beginning an exercise program.

3. Take high-quality nutritional supplements. To boost cellular nutrition, Dr. Strand recommends taking a high-quality antioxidant with each meal. He explains that we require antioxidants to protect our bodies from oxidative stress and free radical cell damage that lie at the bottom of chronic degenerative diseases such as diabetes and cardiovascular disease. Dr. Strand in particular recommends vitamins C and E to ward off oxidative stress created by elevated levels of insulin and glucose following a rich meal high in bad fats and carbs (for example, steak and mashed potatoes). Other beneficial supplements are chromium, magnesium and selenium. Consult your physician about exact dosages.

MORE EFFECTIVE THAN A PILL— A HEALTHIER LIFESTYLE

As Dr. Strand sees it, modern medicine relies too much on drugs to control the consequences of elevated insulin levels without addressing the underlying problem—insulin resistance. He speculates that this may be because there is no FDA-approved pill to cure insulin resistance. In the parlance of conventional medicine, where there's no pill, there's no disease.

However, if you follow these three simple steps to a healthier lifestyle, says Dr. Strand, your body will gradually begin to release fat, and you will see triglyceride and blood pressure numbers start to drop. It won't happen overnight, any more than insulin resistance develops overnight…but over the months, you'll find that you feel better overall and have more energy. Without a pill, without drugs or their side effects, you will have taken charge of your health and brought your body back into balance.

Surprising Reasons We Overeat

Brian Wansink, PhD, director of the Food and Brand Lab at Cornell University, Ithaca, NY, is author of *Mindless Eating: Why We Eat More Than We Think*. Bantam. *www.mindlesseating.org.*

Our minds, not our stomachs, control our eating habits—but our minds don't always do a good job of making food decisions. Most people put on weight because their minds don't accurately keep track of how much they have eaten, not because they lack the willpower to put down their forks.

Surprisingly, when our minds tell us which foods we enjoy, it's often for reasons that have little to do with how they taste.

Example: Approximately one-third of World War II veterans who served in the South Pacific love Chinese food 50 years later. A similar percentage hate it. It turns out that almost all the veterans who love Chinese food did not experience frequent heavy combat when in Asia, but those who hate it did.

Brian Wansink, PhD, a noted food psychologist, has done extensive research on how our minds trick us into unhealthy eating habits. *Here are some of the ways…*

•**If it looks like a small meal, it feels like a small meal.** Our eyes, not our stomachs, tell us when we're full. In a study conducted by our research team, when we replaced eight-inch dinner plates with 12-inch plates, diners consumed 20% to 35% more because their portions looked smaller on the larger plates. After the meal, they were certain that they hadn't eaten any more than usual.

What to do: Use smaller plates, bowls and spoons if you want to eat less. Drink from tall, thin glasses—not short, fat ones—so you will think you are drinking more. When possible, serve food over a bed of lettuce so that the plate looks full.

•**We feel full when there's visual evidence that we have had a lot to eat.** In one study, we gave chicken wings to graduate students while they watched the Super Bowl. When we left the bones in front of the students, they ate an average of four wings apiece. When we cleared the bones away frequently—removing the visual evidence of earlier consumption—each student ate an average of six wings. After the game, students in both groups estimated that they had only four wings each.

What to do: When you're eating—particularly when you're snacking—leave out candy wrappers, peanut shells and other evidence of snacking so that your eyes can warn you about how much you have eaten.

•**When there's no distance to the food, there's no thinking before eating.** Office workers consumed an average of nine Hershey's Kisses per day when we put bowls of the chocolate candies on their desks. Their consumption dropped by more than 50% when these bowls were positioned just six feet away. Six feet is only two steps, but even a short distance forces us to think twice before we eat.

What to do: At home, fill individual plates at the stove, and leave the leftovers on the stove or a sideboard. The more hassle it is to eat, the less we eat. You will have fewer additional helpings if you must stand up to get them. A bowl of salad or vegetables can be brought to the dinner table because second helpings of these foods won't add many calories.

With snack foods, pour a serving into a bowl rather than eating straight from the bag. Then if you want more, you have to go to the kitchen to get it.

•**"Comfort foods" cause overconsumption.** Comfort foods improve our moods. These foods pick us up when we're feeling stressed or unhappy and serve as rewards when we're feeling good.

Women's comfort foods tend to be unhealthy dessert or snack items, while men's comfort foods are more likely to be hot meals. Why the difference? Men tend to associate home-cooked meals with someone taking care of them, because men's meals often are prepared by their wives. Women associate home-cooked meals with the chore of cooking, so they prefer prepared snack foods and desserts.

What to do: We get nearly as much emotional benefit from a small serving of a comfort food as from a large one—for example, a single scoop of ice cream instead of a pint.

Also, we get nearly as much emotional benefit from our second- or third-favorite comfort food as from our absolute favorite. If your top comfort food is chocolate ice cream but tomato soup is a close second, keep plenty of microwavable tomato soup in the house so that low-calorie comfort is just seconds away.

•**We underestimate beverage calories.** When people are asked to gauge the calories in a drink, they typically undershoot by 30% or more. Beverages don't seem to be filling, so we don't assume that they have as many calories as they actually do.

What to do: As a rule of thumb, estimate that you're consuming 10 calories per ounce for "thin" beverages, such as juice, soda and milk…and 20 calories per ounce for "thick" beverages, such as smoothies and meal-replacement shakes. That adds up quickly when you're drinking a 32-ounce soda—to an estimated 320 calories.

Interestingly, if you load that drink with ice, you'll actually burn off a few of those calories. Since your body has to use energy to heat up an iced beverage, you actually burn about one calorie for every ice-cold ounce you drink. If you drink the recommended eight eight-ounce glasses of water a day and if you fill those 64 ounces with ice, you'll burn about 70 extra calories a day, the equivalent of about seven pounds a year.

•**Exercise might make you fatter.** You have forced yourself to jog three miles every day for months—yet you weigh just as much as when you started. What are you doing wrong?

Most exercisers overestimate the calories their exercise burns and reward themselves with high-calorie foods after their workouts because they think they've earned it. They don't realize that the six Oreo cookies they treat themselves to as a reward have more calories (around 320) than the number of calories they burned while running three miles (around 300).

What to do: If you need a reward, opt for nonfood treats, perhaps a half-hour doing something you enjoy, such as reading a good book or watching a favorite TV show.

•**Birth order might affect your eating habits.** Oldest children and only children tend to save their favorite foods for last. Give them a chocolate chip cookie, and it might become a special treat for after dinner.

Youngest children and middle children of large families are more likely to polish off favorite foods as soon as they receive them—probably to ensure that older siblings won't snatch the food away. These birth-order eating patterns tend to continue into adulthood.

For adults who are the youngest or middle children, the result can be unnecessary pounds. Favorite foods tend to be unhealthy foods, and people who eat unhealthy foods as soon as they get them may be inclined to eat larger quantities in the long run.

What to do: Don't bring favorite snacks into the house in large quantities, especially if you are a youngest or middle child. You might polish off a box in a single sitting.

Secrets of Thin People

Stephen Gullo, PhD, health psychologist and president of the Center for Healthful Living, New York City, is former chairman of the National Obesity and Weight Control Education Program of the American Institute for Life-Threatening Illness at Columbia-Presbyterian Medical Center and author of *The Thin Commandments Diet.* Rodale.

Do you know people who never gain an ounce and yet don't seem to have to watch what they eat? Good genes play a role—if your parents were thin, more than likely you will be, too. But in helping thousands of patients slim down, Stephen Gullo, PhD, author of *The Thin Commandments Diet*, has found that though most of us assume thin people never give their weight a second thought, they actually rely on a number of strategies to keep the pounds from accumulating. *Here, the secrets of thin people, which can help anyone who is trying to lose weight or maintain a healthy weight…*

•**Thin people don't skip meals.** They don't allow themselves to get so hungry that they become compulsive eaters rather than selective eaters. Thin people have structured eating habits. They eat three meals and one to two healthful snacks a day to keep blood sugar stable and prevent the body from secreting large amounts of *insulin*, the hunger hormone. Stable blood sugar levels also help the body metabolize calories efficiently and prevent cravings for sweets.

•**Thin people eat the right breakfast.** The National Weight Control Registry, which monitors people who have lost weight and successfully kept it off, found that 78% of those who have maintained their weight loss eat breakfast every day. But the wrong breakfast isn't helpful. A breakfast high in simple carbohydrates, such as a sugary cereal, stimulates appetite. That's because blood sugar is low in the morning. If you eat a sugary breakfast, blood sugar levels rise and then crash rapidly, making you hungry. A breakfast that contains protein and fiber—such as oatmeal and skim milk or low-fat yogurt with fresh fruit—is better. It satisfies your appetite, keeps blood sugar levels on an even keel and helps you feel full longer.

•**Thin people act quickly.** If they gain a few pounds, they immediately cut back on portion sizes and exercise more. I tell my patients that a mark of a winner at weight control is to own only one size of clothing. When thin people think their clothing is getting too tight, they don't buy larger clothes. They change the habits that are creating the problem. It's far easier to lose three or four pounds than it is to lose 20.

•**Thin people weigh themselves regularly.** Most people who have lost weight and kept it off weigh themselves at least once a week. A gain of even two to three pounds motivates them to shift into a more restricted eating plan for a few days. I weigh myself on Monday, right after the weekend, when my eating habits tend to be more liberal, and again on Friday. If I don't

like what I see on Monday, I make changes in my diet. I eat lighter meals, such as broiled fish and chicken, egg white omelets and steamed vegetables without oil or butter, and I don't eat sweets. I weigh myself again on Wednesday to see if my weight is coming down.

•**Thin people don't deprive themselves.** They devise creative strategies to limit consumption of high-calorie foods. They don't stock the house with them. When they do buy them, they select individual portions or serve them only when they have company or on weekends. A patient of mine only buys her children cookies containing peanuts because she doesn't like peanuts. Other people eat desserts only in restaurants.

•**Thin people get enough sleep.** Being sleep-deprived stimulates the appetite, especially carbohydrate cravings. Researchers at the University of Chicago studied young men who got only four hours of sleep per night for two nights. The researchers measured levels of the hormone *leptin*. An increase in leptin signals the brain that no more food is needed…a decrease triggers hunger. The sleep-deprived men had an 18% *decrease* in leptin. The researchers also found that levels of *ghrelin*, a hormone that causes hunger, increased by 28%.

The sleep-deprived men were not only hungrier, they also craved carbohydrates, such as sweets, and salty foods, such as chips. They may have wanted sweets because of lower blood sugar levels. The salt cravings may have been because sleep-deprivation lowers blood pressure. Salty foods raise blood pressure and may have temporarily made the young men feel more energetic.

•**Thin people move a lot.** Studies show that people who lose weight and keep it off exercise regularly. They may not work out in a gym or have a structured program, but they walk a lot, garden or take the stairs instead of the elevator. The National Weight Control Registry found that people who keep off weight burn about 11,830 calories per week through physical activity—the equivalent of walking more than 20 miles.

Researchers at the Mayo Clinic have reported that lean people expend about 350 more calories per day, on average, than sedentary obese people—and not just through exercise, such as walking. They fidget, tap their toes and so on.

•**Thin people exercise portion control.**
They know which foods they can eat in generous amounts, such as lean protein, fruits and
vegetables. If they overeat, they do it at a special restaurant or on a holiday. There's nothing
wrong with overeating on Thanksgiving, but
there is something destructive about consuming
a pint of ice cream every night. Thin people also
consider how food is prepared. They know that
a healthy, low-calorie filet of sole, for example,
is neither healthy nor low-calorie if it's fried in
oil or sautéed in butter.

•**Thin people don't use food to deal with
emotion.** Many of my patients don't really enjoy the foods that are making them heavy. They
use food to cope with anger, depression and
stress. People who stay trim over a lifetime don't
use food as therapy. They also don't eat because
of boredom or out of habit, such as when they
go to the movies or they're watching TV.

Instead, they have other ways to deal with
their emotions. They may go for a walk, take
a bath, play a computer game or browse in a
store. Mental diversion turns off the food switch.
If they associate watching television with food,
they chew on a stick of gum or eat cut-up vegetables. Or they allow themselves a sensible
portion of a low-cal snack, such as a small bag
of low-fat popcorn.

Dieting Myths

Mark Hyman, MD, editor-in-chief of *Alternative Therapies in Health and Medicine*, is author of *Ultrametabo-
lism: The Simple Plan for Automatic Weight Loss* (Scribner)
and coauthor of the best-seller *Ultraprevention: The Six-
Week Plan That Will Make You Healthy for Life* (Atria).

Losing weight can be hard work. People
feel they have to count calories, endure
hunger pangs and work up a sweat. It's no
wonder so many give up and regain their hard-
lost pounds. It doesn't have to be that way. The
reason we are losing the battle of the bulge is
that we have bought into some common myths
about weight loss. *Here, six of those myths and
what to do instead...*

Myth 1: **The less you eat, the more weight
you'll lose.**

Our bodies are made up of hundreds of genes
that protect us from starvation. That's why we end
up gaining weight if we start out eating too few
calories. You can starve yourself for only so long
before your body engages a primitive response
that compensates for starvation by making you
overeat. In my experience, the average person
who goes on a diet actually gains five pounds.

What to do: Never go on a diet. Instead,
eat foods that turn on your metabolism. These
are whole foods that come from nature, such
as vegetables, fruits, whole grains, nuts, seeds,
beans and lean animal protein. If you eat only
these foods, you won't have trouble with your
appetite—it will self-regulate, and the triggers
that drive overeating will be under control.

Myth 2: **It doesn't matter what kind of
exercise you do, as long as you exercise.**

It's true that any kind of exercise is better than
no exercise, but interval training is the most effective for weight loss. Interval training consists
of short bursts of intense activity followed by
longer periods of lighter activity. This kind of
training tunes up your metabolism so you burn
more calories all day and while you sleep, not
just when you are exercising.

What to do: Aim for 20 to 30 minutes of interval training two to three days a week. Exercise
as vigorously as you can for 30 to 60 seconds,
and then slow your pace for three minutes, repeating this pattern for about a half hour.

If you are over 30, have a physical before you
start interval training. If you are out of shape, ease
into a regular exercise routine first—you might start
by walking for 30 minutes five times a week.

Myth 3: **You can control your weight by
counting calories.**

Many people believe that all calories are the
same when it comes to weight control—that if
you substitute 100 calories' worth of, say, cookies
for 100 calories of carrots, you'll come out even.
But food isn't just about calories. Everything that
you eat contains "instructions" for your DNA,
your hormones and your metabolism. Different
foods contain different information.

For instance, the sugar in soda enters your
blood rapidly, increasing insulin levels. Insulin is
a hormone that promotes more fat storage around
the middle and raises inflammation levels in the
body, which in turn promotes more weight gain.

On the other hand, the same amount of sugar from kidney beans enters your blood slowly. Because the sugar is absorbed over time, your insulin levels remain stable and more of the calories are burned and fewer are stored.

What to do: Don't focus on the number of calories you are consuming. Losing weight is not about counting calories—it's about eating the right calories.

Myth 4: Eating fat makes you fat.

Dietary fat does not correlate with excess body fat. Any weight loss resulting from a low-fat diet is usually modest and temporary. The amount of fat Americans eat has dropped from 42% to 34% of total calories on average, but we still are getting fatter. That's because all fats are not created equal. There are good fats, bad fats and ugly fats. Good fats actually can help you lose weight, but many of us have nearly eliminated them from our diet.

Two examples of good fats are omega-3s and monounsaturated fats. Omega-3s are found in fish, flaxseed and flax oil, and nuts and seeds, such as walnuts and pumpkin seeds. Monounsaturated fats are found in olive oil, avocados and nuts.

Bad fats include refined polyunsaturated vegetable oil—such as corn and safflower—and most saturated fat, found in meat and animal products, such as butter.

The ugly fats are trans fats, often found in snack foods and packaged baked goods. Trans fat comes from adding hydrogen to vegetable oil through a process called hydrogenation.

What to do: Eat good fats. These improve your metabolism by activating genes that help you burn fats. Saturated and trans fats turn off fat-burning genes. The Inuit people of Greenland used to eat a diet that was very high in fat—primarily omega-3 and monounsaturated fats—and they were thin and healthy. Now they have shifted to a diet that is lower in fat and high in carbohydrates from junk food, and many are obese, with higher rates of heart disease and other illnesses.

Myth 5: Going low-carb makes you thin.

Carbohydrates are the single most important food you can eat for long-term health and weight loss. They are the source of most of the vitamins, minerals and fiber in our diet—and all the *phytonutrients*, plant compounds that are key regulators of our health. Phytonutrients turn on the genes that help us burn fat and age slowly. They contain disease-fighting nutrients. Some examples are the *isoflavones* in soy foods, *polyphenols* in cocoa and *glucosinolates* in broccoli.

However, just as there are different fats, there are different types of carbohydrates.

What to do: Eat complex carbohydrates—vegetables, fruits, nuts, seeds, beans and whole grains. These tend to have low glycemic loads, which means they are absorbed slowly and don't raise blood sugar quickly, so you feel full longer. Refined carbs, such as white flour, rice and pasta, along with sugary foods, make your blood sugar spike so that you feel hungry sooner.

Myth 6: It doesn't matter when you eat.

Sumo wrestlers look the way they do because they fast during the day, then overeat at night and go to bed. Like Sumo wrestlers, we eat most of our calories late in the day. When you eat late, calories are stored instead of burned.

What to do: Don't eat within two to three hours of going to bed, because you need to give your body time to digest and burn off your food. Also, eat throughout the day to keep blood sugar levels stable. Breakfast is important. I can't tell you how many people I have helped to lose weight by having them eat breakfast. The National Weight Control Registry, which is tracking long-term weight-loss maintenance in more than 5,000 people, has found that 96% of those who have maintained weight loss for six years eat breakfast regularly.

■ ■ ■ ■

Diet Soda Backfire?

Diet soda drinkers in a long-term study were more likely to become overweight than people who drank full-calorie beverages.

Recent finding: 57% of normal-weight people who drank two or more cans of diet soda a day became overweight after eight years, versus 47% of those who drank regular soda.

Possible reasons: Diet soda drinkers may feel that they're saving enough calories, so they can splurge elsewhere in their diet...or diet sodas may—in some as yet undetermined way—increase hunger in some people.

Sharon Parten Fowler, MPH, coauthor of the review of data from the San Antonio Heart Study of 1,177 people, presented at a recent meeting of the American Diabetes Association.

The Easiest Way to Lose Weight Without Changing Your Life!

Jeffrey Friedman, MD, PhD, head, Laboratory of Molecular Genetics, Rockefeller University, New York City.

James Hill, PhD, director, Center for Human Nutrition, University of Colorado Health Sciences Center, Denver.

Adam Drewnowski, PhD, spokesman, American Dietetic Association, and director, Center for Public Health Nutrition, University of Washington, Seattle.

Science.

Researchers are still trying to determine whether it is genetics or a growing affinity for fast food and a sedentary lifestyle that is behind the growing number of obese Americans.

Dr. Jeffrey Friedman, head of the laboratory of molecular genetics at Rockefeller University in New York City, argues that the tendency toward obesity is rooted in evolution. According to Dr. Friedman, early survival meant being able to withstand periods of famine. Therefore, individuals who were able to store fat well had a better chance of surviving. And now, many Americans can thank (or curse) their ancestors for their battles with weight. Friedman adds that eating is a powerful, primal drive, one that wins out over the desire to be thin in people predisposed to obesity.

"The feeling of hunger is intense and, if not as potent as the drive to breathe, is probably no less powerful than the drive to drink when one is thirsty," Friedman says. "This is the feeling the obese must resist after they have lost a significant amount of weight."

ANOTHER OPINION

Although Friedman's published remarks argue that genetics is the primary determinant for obesity, James Hill, director of the Center for Human Nutrition at the University of Colorado Health Sciences Center in Denver, points to a different culprit—the environment.

For contemporary Americans, adults and children, that means super-sized portions, calorie-dense fast food, hours in front of a video screen, too little exercise and too much to eat.

EVEN A SLIGHT ADJUSTMENT CAN HELP

Hill has proposed a simple solution to halt the creeping weight gain—eat 100 fewer calories a day. That's equal to the calories in a cookie or three bites of a fast-food burger.

It takes just a slight energy imbalance to cause a gradual increase in weight, Hill says. Say you ate just 50 more calories every day than you burned during physical activity. That means five extra pounds in a year.

"We believe that what we've been doing isn't working," Hill says. "We have to stimulate people to think differently about this."

Adam Drewnowski, a spokesman for the American Dietetic Association and director of the Center for Public Health Nutrition at the University of Washington in Seattle, says he believes the environmental argument more than Friedman's genetic argument, because genetics doesn't explain why minorities, the poor and people with little education have the highest rates of obesity.

"In the last 20 years, as obesity has doubled and tripled, the genetic pool has remained the same," he says.

Lifestyle changes, not medical interventions, will ultimately stem the tide of obesity in this country, Drewnowski says. "It all comes back to this issue of eating less and exercising more."

The Ultimate Natural Weight-Loss Aid

Stephen Bloom, MD, professor of medicine, Hammersmith Hospital, Imperial College, London.

David Cummings, MD, associate professor of medicine, University of Washington, Seattle.

The New England Journal of Medicine.

Injections of a natural protein significantly trimmed a person's urge to eat, a study found. The discovery could lead to effective obesity treatments.

The protein, normally secreted in the intestine, is called *peptide YY* (PYY), and it cuts food intake by sending satiety signals to the brain. Previous research had shown that normal-weight people don't eat as much when injected with PYY prior to a meal. The latest study has found that the effect is equally potent for the obese, cutting short-term food intake by about 30% in both groups.

"We didn't know whether PYY would work in the obese," says Dr. Stephen Bloom, a diabetes expert at London's Imperial College and leader of the study.

"But when we administered PYY, it was fully effective. That is the first step for trying to establish it as a therapy for obesity," he adds.

THE STUDY

Bloom and his colleagues studied the effects of PYY in 12 fit and 12 obese men and women. The obese subjects had roughly 40% lower levels of the peptide than their slim peers.

Bloom says the difference explains why obese people have a greater tendency to eat. "They don't have the same level of satiety hormone that thin people have," he says.

Why PYY was so low in the obese study subjects, however, isn't clear. It could reflect prolonged overeating or it could be the cause of the overeating.

Dr. David Cummings, an appetite expert at the University of Washington in Seattle, is concerned about touting the results of Bloom's study. "Does PYY help you avoid one meal, or is it a regulator of body weight over the long haul?" asks Cummings, who studies another appetite hormone called *ghrelin*. Ultimately, he says, drug treatment for obesity will likely be a cocktail of medicines that target several pathways to appetite regulation.

Myths of Low-Carb Dieting

Sandra Woodruff, RD, author of *Secrets of Fat-Free Cooking, The Good Carb Cookbook* and *Secrets of Good-Carb/Low-Carb Living.* Avery.

These days, supermarket shelves and restaurants are filled with low-carbohydrate food choices, which many people believe virtually guarantee weight loss. Not true.

Just as many consumers assumed a few years back that they could load up on low-fat cookies, cakes and crackers and still lose weight, the low-carb craze has perpetuated many potentially dangerous myths...

Myth: **All carbohydrates are "bad."**

Reality: Carbohydrates—the sugars and starches in foods—have an undeservedly bad reputation.

One reason is that consuming too much of the *wrong* kinds of carbohydrates causes the body to produce too much insulin, the hormone that helps regulate sugar (glucose) in the body.

High insulin levels encourage the body to store fat rather than burn it. Excess insulin production has been linked to heart disease, type 2 diabetes and breast, colon, prostate and other cancers.

However, not all carbohydrates are bad. It's true that some, including those found in processed foods, such as white bread, white rice, low-fiber breakfast cereals, many snack foods, sodas and sweets, enter the bloodstream quickly, causing a rapid increase in blood sugar and insulin levels.

But the carbohydrates found in vegetables, whole grains and many fruits enter the bloodstream more slowly, and, unlike processed foods, these "good" carbs are loaded with fiber and disease-fighting nutrients.

Myth: **Eating "low-carb" versions of high-carbohydrate foods, such as bread and pasta, will help you lose weight.**

Reality: Manufacturers have succeeded in taking out carbs by replacing flour with wheat gluten and other proteins, plant fibers, poorly digested starches and other bulking agents. However, these foods still contain calories. Ounce for ounce, these modified foods may contain fewer carbs but may—or may not—have fewer calories.

The same can be said for "sugar-free" desserts, which often contain generous amounts of added fat to make up for qualities lost when sugar is removed. Ultimately, calories still count, and it pays to compare labels.

Myth: **A low-carb diet is "heart-healthy" because it helps lower cholesterol.**

Reality: The truth is that cholesterol levels typically drop on any reduced-calorie diet (including a low-carb/high-saturated-fat diet). That's the body's response to being in a state of semistarvation.

This does not mean that a regular diet of bunless bacon cheeseburgers is healthy. Diets high in saturated fat have been linked to serious health problems, including colon cancer, type 2 diabetes and Alzheimer's disease. Moreover, when weight loss stops or the pounds creep back on, cholesterol levels often will rise again.

Myth: **When cutting carbs, there's no such thing as too low.**

Reality: Some diets—most notably Atkins—initially suggest a carbohydrate intake of as little as 20 grams (g) per day. This type of diet can cause health problems, especially for people who have kidney disease or gout or those who take medications for diabetes or high blood pressure.

Anyone interested in following a very-low-carb diet should do so only under a physician's supervision.

A reduced-carb diet is a much healthier option that provides more flexibility and is easier to stick with over the long term. Reduced-carb diets provide about 40% of their calories from carbs—about 120 to 160 g per day—during the weight-loss phase. The carbohydrates should come from nutrient-dense vegetables, fruits and whole grains. Reduced-carb diets leave ample room to eat at least eight servings of vegetables and fruits a day.

Myth: **You don't have to worry about the fat content of high-protein foods.**

Reality: If you eat a low-carb, high-protein diet that allows greasy meats, high-fat cheese, butter, cream and similar foods, you're still consuming artery-clogging saturated fats that will increase your risk for heart disease and many other health problems.

On the other hand, eating a low-carb diet that includes skinless poultry, fish, lean meats, unsaturated fats, low-fat dairy products, nuts, seeds and fiber-rich fruits and vegetables will lower your risk for many diseases.

Myth: **If you are on a diet that limits carbohydrates, it always is a good idea to eliminate dairy products.**

Reality: Unfortunately, many low-carb diets do not recommend dairy foods, such as milk and yogurt.

Not only does this create a calcium deficit, it also may thwart weight-loss efforts.

Researchers have found compelling evidence that the calcium that is contained in dairy products helps stimulate the fat-burning machinery in the body through a complex series of hormone reactions.

One study published in the *Journal of the American College of Nutrition* found that each 300-milligram (mg) increase in daily calcium intake—the equivalent of one cup of low-fat milk—was associated with approximately six fewer pounds of body fat in adults.

The best way to meet your calcium intake requirements is to eat low-fat versions of milk, yogurt and cheese.

It is best to aim for three one-cup servings of milk or yogurt or 1.5 ounces of low-fat cheese per day. Some good nondairy sources of calcium include kale and calcium-fortified soy foods.

Is There a "Magic Bullet" For Weight Loss?

Sandra Woodruff, RD, author of *Secrets of Fat-Free Cooking, The Good Carb Cookbook* and *Secrets of Good-Carb/Low-Carb Living.* Avery.

Some dieters put their hopes in pills that promise to "burn," "block," "flush" or otherwise eliminate fat from the system.

But science has yet to come up with a low-risk "magic bullet" for weight loss. Some pills may help control the appetite, but they can have serious side effects. Amphetamines, for example, are highly addictive and can have an adverse impact on the heart and central nervous system. Other pills are utterly worthless.

The Federal Trade Commission (FTC) and a number of state attorneys general have successfully brought cases against marketers of pills claiming to absorb or burn fat.

The US Food and Drug Administration (FDA) has banned 111 ingredients once found in over-the-counter diet products. None of these substances, which include alcohol, caffeine, dextrose and guar gum, have proved effective in weight-loss or appetite suppression.

Beware of the following products that are touted as weight-loss wonders...

•**Diet patches.** Worn on the skin, these have not been proven safe or effective. The FDA has seized millions of these products from manufacturers and promoters.

•**"Fat blockers"** purport to absorb the fat and mechanically interfere with the fat that a person might eat.

•**"Starch blockers"** promise to block or impede starch digestion. Not only is the claim unproven, but users have complained of nausea, vomiting, diarrhea and stomach pains.

•**"Magnet" diet pills** allegedly "flush fat out of the body." The FTC has brought legal action against several marketers of these pills.

•**Glucomannan** is advertised as the "weight loss secret that's been in the Orient for more than 500 years." There is little evidence supporting the effectiveness of this plant root in helping people lose weight.

•**Some bulk producers or fillers,** such as fiber-based products, may absorb liquid and swell in the stomach, thereby reducing hunger. But some fillers, such as guar gum, can prove harmful, causing obstructions in the intestines, stomach or esophagus.

•**Spirulina,** a species of blue-green algae, has not been proven effective for losing weight.

PHONY DEVICES AND GADGETS

Phony weight-loss devices range from those that are simply ineffective to those that are truly dangerous to your health.

Some of the fraudulent gadgets that have been marketed to hopeful dieters over the years include...

•**Electrical muscle stimulators,** which have a legitimate use in physical therapy treatment, do not help weight loss or body toning. In fact, when used incorrectly, they can cause electrical shocks and burns. The FDA has even taken a number of them off the market.

•**Appetite-suppressing eyeglasses** are common eyeglasses that have colored lenses that claim to project an image to the retina that decreases the desire to eat. There is no evidence that these work.

•**Magic weight-loss earrings** and devices that are custom-fitted to the purchaser's ear purport to stimulate acupuncture points that control hunger. These claims, of course, have never been proven.

---

10 Surprising Ways to Stay Healthy and Control Your Weight

Mehmet C. Oz, MD, founder and director of the Complementary Medical Program and director of the Cardiovascular Institute at New York–Presbyterian Medical Center and professor and vice chairman of surgery at Columbia University, both in New York City, is coauthor, with Michael F. Roizen, MD, of You on a Diet: The Owner's Manual for Waist Management. *Free Press.*

Whether you're trying to lose weight or simply find a healthful eating plan you can stick with, you're bound to fail if you try to stay on a diet. Invariably, people on diets end up depriving themselves of certain foods and/or scrupulously counting calories.

Problem: Virtually no one can maintain long-term deprivation because our bodies are programmed to avoid this type of ongoing discomfort. And calorie restriction causes your metabolism to slow down in order to preserve energy, often resulting in more stored fat.

The secret is to work with your body's chemistry rather than against it, so healthful eating becomes automatic, not forced.

Recent development: Body weight used to be considered one of the best indicators of overall health.

Now: Research has shown that your waist measurement (at or just below your navel) may be more reliable. That's because abdominal fat is especially harmful due to its proximity to your vital organs, where it can lead to harmful increases in cholesterol and triglyceride levels. Fat in this area has been linked to heart disease, cancer and diabetes. Studies have found that men should strive for a waist measurement of 35 inches or less, while women should aim for 32½ inches or less. When these measurements are exceeded, health risks increase. For example, risk for metabolic syndrome (a group of conditions, including hypertension and abdominal obesity, that raises diabetes and cardiovascular disease risk) increases by 40% at 40 inches for men and 37 inches for women.

Important: Even if your weight is ideal, you still can benefit from some of the strategies described below because they promote healthy cholesterol and blood pressure levels. *My recommendations...*

1. Spice up your morning eggs. Cayenne and other forms of red pepper contain capsaicin, a substance that suppresses appetite signals, increases metabolism and decreases the desire for food later in the day. In addition, eggs are high in protein, which tends to induce feelings of fullness.

2. Consume fiber early in the day. Fiber increases levels of appetite-suppressing signals in the small intestine. Eating fiber early in the day makes people less hungry in the afternoon—the time when most of us tend to eat snacks and other calorie-dense foods. Consume about 30 g of fiber daily in the form of high-fiber cereals, fruits and vegetables, and 100% whole grains.

3. Eat nuts. The monounsaturated fat in nuts stimulates the production of cholecystokinin (CCK), a chemical messenger that slows the rate at which the stomach empties and reduces appetite without putting your body into starvation mode—that is, the point at which it starts conserving calories, rather than burning them. Before lunch and/or dinner, have about six walnuts, 12 almonds or 12 hazelnuts.

4. Drink coffee instead of soft drinks. Coffee (caffeinated and decaffeinated) is a rich source of antioxidants, and Americans consume more of it than any other antioxidant-rich food. Coffee is much lower in calories (if you don't add a lot of sugar and/or creamer) than sugary soft drinks.

Bonus: Caffeine stimulates the release of norepinephrine, a hormone that suppresses appetite and promotes calorie burning by increasing heart rate and metabolism. Green tea also is a rich source of antioxidants and caffeine.

5. Supplement with 5-hydroxytryptophan (5-HTP). Related to the amino acid tryptophan and sold as a weight-loss supplement, 5-HTP increases brain levels of serotonin, a neurotransmitter

that controls appetite. In one study, people taking 5-HTP for six weeks lost an average of 12 pounds, compared with only four pounds in a control group.

Recommended dose: 300 mg daily.

Bonus: 5-HTP has mood-enhancing benefits.

6. Turn up the thermostat. One reason that people tend to eat more during the cold months is that cold temperatures stimulate appetite. Also, people with naturally low body temperatures tend to have a slower metabolism and are more prone to weight gain. Staying warm may be a natural form of appetite control, particularly if you increase body temperature with exercise. Every one degree increase in body temperature increases metabolism by 14%.

7. Ask your doctor about Tagamet. The active ingredient (cimetidine) in this heartburn drug is thought to activate appetite-suppressing CCK. One 12-week study found that people taking a prescription form of Tagamet (400 mg, three times daily) had about a 5% decrease in waist size.

Important: Tagamet is unlikely to cause significant side effects, but should be taken to aid weight loss only if you have heartburn symptoms.

8. Consider using nicotine. It's common for people who quit smoking to gain weight, probably because the nicotine in tobacco suppresses appetite, increases metabolism and damages taste buds, which makes food less appealing. Studies have shown that nicotine—in the form of patches and gum, not from cigarettes—when combined with small amounts of caffeine, can help some people lose weight.

If you've hit a weight plateau: Talk to your doctor about combining a nicotine patch with two cups of coffee daily. Even for nonsmokers, this approach can be used temporarily (to avoid possible addiction risk) to jump-start weight-loss efforts.

9. Smell grapefruit. Grapefruit oil, available from aromatherapy shops, emits an aroma that is thought to affect liver enzymes and help promote weight loss. In preliminary research, animals exposed to grapefruit scent for 15 minutes, three times weekly, had a reduction in appetite and body weight.

10. Control emotional stress. People who live with chronic stress (due to family pressures, a fast-paced job, etc.) produce high levels of cortisol, a stress hormone that increases the propensity for the omentum—a structure located near the stomach—to store fat. Excessive fat in the omentum can significantly increase waist size.

Important: Exercise is among the best ways to lower stress—and curb accumulations of omentum fat.

Recommended: A 30-minute walk and five minutes' worth of stretching daily...and three weekly sessions that include basic exercises, such as push-ups, shoulder shrugs, abdominal crunches, etc.

■■■■

Fat Burner

Vitamin C helps you burn more fat when you exercise.

Recent study: People who took 500 milligrams (mg) of vitamin C daily burned 39% more fat while exercising than people who took less. Since it is difficult to get enough vitamin C just from fruits and vegetables, take a vitamin C supplement to be sure you get at least 500 mg per day.

Carol Johnston, PhD, professor and chair, department of nutrition, Arizona State University, Mesa, and leader of a study published in *Journal of the American College of Nutrition*.

■■■■

A Connection Between Drinking and Weight

A recent study found that people who drink one alcoholic drink a day, including wine, beer and mixed drinks, are 54% less likely to be obese than those who don't drink at all. Those who have two drinks are 41% less likely to be obese.

But: Don't overdo it—people who drink four or more drinks a day are 46% *more* likely to be obese than nondrinkers. Binge drinkers, who sometimes have five or more drinks per day, are 80% more likely to be obese.

Ahmed Arif, MD, PhD, assistant professor of family and community medicine, Texas Tech University Health Sciences Center, Lubbock, and leader of a study of the link between obesity and alcohol consumption in 8,236 nonsmokers, published in *BMC Public Health*.

Don't Gain Weight on Your Vacation

Peter Greenberg, travel editor of NBC's *Today* show and host of the nationally syndicated *Travel Today* radio show, is author of *The Traveler's Diet: Eating Right and Staying Fit on the Road*. Villard.

Many people return from vacation dismayed to find that they gained several pounds. Peter Greenberg, travel editor of NBC's *Today* show, can sympathize. The travel guru, who logs 400,000 miles a year, found it difficult to eat sensibly on the road, and he weighed more than 280 pounds.

Then, during a TV shoot, the prime minister of Jamaica, who was watching Greenberg swim with dolphins, joked that the dolphins were swimming with "a whale." That was the motivation Greenberg needed to lose weight.

After consulting with personal trainers and nutritionists, Greenberg has lost 42 pounds since last August. He is determined to drop another 38 pounds or so. *Here are some of his favorite strategies...*

DIET

•**Don't starve yourself before your trip.** Dramatically cutting calories will send your body into starvation mode, which means it will burn fewer calories to conserve energy.

•**Choose airport food carefully.** The best airports for healthful food, according to a survey by the Physicians Committee for Responsible Medicine, are Chicago's O'Hare, followed by Detroit Metropolitan, San Francisco, New York's JFK, Dallas–Fort Worth and Denver.

If you have time only for fast food, try Burger King's vegetarian burger. If you skip the mayo, it has only 310 calories and seven grams of fat.

•**Drink water.** Bring several bottles on every flight. Water will keep you hydrated and also curb your appetite. Drinking bottled water also can reduce your chance of getting sick. One in six airplanes has unsafe drinking water.

•**Be leery of "healthy" menus.** Just because a restaurant labels an entrée "healthy" doesn't mean it is. Order grilled chicken or fish with sauce on the side. Order salad with dressing on the side—then use it sparingly.

•**Pay attention to portion size.** Pick two appetizers but no entrée, or choose an entrée but skip the starters. And eat dinner before 8 pm.

•**Don't open the hotel mini bar.** Either have it removed or don't accept the key. The snacks are fattening and expensive.

•**Watch what you drink.** Cream, soda pop or a drink mixer can add several hundred calories to that of the alcohol alone. Stick with wine or light beer. Or have a mixed drink with club soda or water.

I used to drink several cans of Diet Pepsi a day, but I have stopped. According to recent research, drinking two cans of diet soda a day increases your chance of becoming overweight by 55%.

Likely reason: You think it is OK to eat more.

EXERCISE

•**Burn calories at the airport.** You won't break a sweat by sitting and reading a magazine, but you can by walking through the airport to, say, meet a connecting flight. Recently, at Miami's airport, I had to go through customs. I then walked to my flight in the next terminal, which was a mile away.

•**Buy a pedometer.** With this gadget, you can monitor how many steps you're taking daily. Aim for 10,000 steps a day for weight loss.

•**Use hotel gyms.** If you expect a long layover between flights, why not work out? You may be able to buy a day pass for the gym at an airport hotel. Passes start at $10 a day.

■ ■ ■ ■

Yoga May Slow Midlife Weight Gain

People in their 50s who regularly practiced yoga lost about five pounds over 10 years, while those who did not practice yoga gained about 13 pounds. Most yoga exercises do not burn enough calories to account for the weight loss, but some practitioners believe that yoga keeps people aware of their bodies and eating habits.

Alan Kristal, DrPH, researcher, Fred Hutchinson Cancer Research Center, Seattle, and leader of a study of 15,550 people, published in Alternative Therapies in Health and Medicine.

■ ■ ■ ■

Smart Snacks

One hard-boiled egg with half a slice of toasted wheat bread—total 109 calories… one-half cup of ice milk or sherbet—100 calories…a large rectangular graham cracker with one-and-a-half teaspoons of peanut butter— 105 calories…one-ounce slice of angel-food cake with half a cup of fresh strawberries—95 calories…one cup of chicken noodle soup with two saltine crackers—100 calories…these are all healthier than 100-calorie packaged snacks.

Woman's Day, 1633 Broadway, New York City 10019.

■ ■ ■ ■

Amazing Eggs

Eggs can help you stick to your diet. People who have eggs for breakfast consume fewer calories throughout the day than people who don't eat eggs but get the same number of calories. An egg-based breakfast may help maintain a feeling of satiety longer.

Nikhil V. Dhurandhar, PhD, associate professor, department of infections and obesity, Pennington Biomedical Research Center, Baton Rouge, LA, and leader of a study, published in Journal of the American College of Nutrition.

■ ■ ■ ■

Fresh Is Best

Canned and dried fruit have twice as many calories from sugar as their fresh counterparts.

Best: Eat fresh fruit or canned fruit that is packed in its own juice or extra-light syrup to limit added sugars. Eat at least one-and-a-half to two cups of fruit each day.

Environmental Nutrition, 52 Riverside Dr., New York City 10024.

■ ■ ■ ■

Fat Risks

Being overweight in your early 40s increases risk of Alzheimer's disease decades later. Also, the location of fat matters—people with high levels of fat in the arms and back were nearly three times as likely to develop Alzheimer's as people with less fat in those areas.

Self-defense: Maintain proper weight at all ages to protect the brain and the cardiovascular system.

Rachel A. Whitmer, PhD, research scientist, Kaiser Permanente Division of Research, Oakland, CA, and leader of a study of data on more than 10,000 people, published in *British Medical Journal.*

■■■■

Weight and Kidney Disease

In a review of the health data of 320,252 adults, those with a body mass index (BMI) of 25 to 29.9 (moderately overweight) were nearly 90% more likely than those of normal weight to develop end-stage renal disease (ESRD), which typically requires a kidney transplant or dialysis.

Theory: Excess body weight puts more demand on the kidneys, and people who are overweight are more likely to develop diabetes and high blood pressure, two risk factors for ESRD.

Chi-yuan Hsu, MD, associate professor in residence, division of nephrology, University of California, San Francisco.

Add 20 Wonderful Years to Your Life

Steven G. Aldana, PhD, former professor, Brigham Young University and CEO and founder of WellSteps (*www.wellsteps.com*).

Everyone knows that a healthful lifestyle—eating right, exercising, not smoking, etc.—is the key to disease prevention. What people may not realize is that each healthful change can add years to your life. By making several changes, you may be able to add 20 years or more.

People don't have to completely turn their lives around to get significant benefits.

Example: Someone who exercises for 30 minutes six times a week can gain 2.4 years of life, even if he/she remains overweight or doesn't adequately control his blood pressure.

Making multiple changes can give exponential (rather than just additive) gains. Studies have shown that if you eat nuts regularly, you add 2.5 years to your life, and if you reduce high blood pressure, you gain 3.7 years. Add that to the 2.4 years you gain from exercising, and the total is 8.6 years—but the increase in life span can be even greater.

Not smoking is probably the most important change. Men who smoke a pack a day lose an average of 13 years of life, while women lose 14 years.

The earlier in your life that you start to make changes, the better—but it is never too late. *Important steps…*

NUTS

Studies show that eating one-quarter cup of nuts five times a week can add years to your life. Tree nuts and peanuts (though technically a legume) are high in beneficial fats, antioxidants and other protective phytochemicals. One study found that women who ate peanut butter five or more times a week had a 21% reduction in diabetes risk.

A nut-rich diet can lower LDL cholesterol by about one-third—the same amount achieved with some statin drugs.

Eat a variety—walnuts, pecans, almonds, etc.—to get a greater number of protective chemical compounds.

Lengthens life by: 2.5 years.

FRUITS AND VEGETABLES

People who increase their consumption of fruits and vegetables from two to five servings a day can reduce by half their risk of many cancers—including pancreatic, colorectal and endometrial cancers. Produce also greatly reduces the risk of heart disease, diabetes, hypertension and Alzheimer's disease.

The fiber in produce binds to potential carcinogens in the intestine and prevents them from entering the bloodstream. Fruits and vegetables are the best sources of antioxidants and other phytochemicals that inhibit oxidation and inflammation—triggers that cause normal cells to become cancerous.

Have a serving of fruit with breakfast every day…snack on a handful of dried fruit…eat carrot sticks at lunch…and have a vegetable salad with dinner.

Lengthens life by: Two to four years.

FIBER

For every 10 grams (g) of fiber you consume per day, your risk of heart attack goes down by 14% and risk of death from heart disease drops by 27%. People who eat as little as two servings of fiber-rich whole grains daily can reduce their risk of stroke by 36%.

Fiber-rich foods also reduce colon cancer risk. Fiber speeds digested food through the intestine and reduces the time that the colon is exposed to carcinogens. It also binds to excess estrogen and promotes its excretion in stool—this is important for preventing estrogen-dependent breast cancers. Fiber causes a drop in LDL cholesterol and reduces the risk of atherosclerosis, blockages in the arteries that promote heart disease.

Get at least 25 g to 30 g fiber daily. Whole grains are good sources. *Example:* Two slices of whole-grain bread plus one cup of whole-grain cereal, such as Cheerios, can provide up to 10 g of fiber.

Lengthens life by: Two to four years.

"GOOD" FATS

People who increase their intake of mono- and polyunsaturated fats and cut back on saturated fat can achieve drops in cholesterol that are comparable to those achieved by taking statin drugs. Improvements in cholesterol translate into a 12% to 44% reduction in the risk of heart disease and stroke.

Mono- and polyunsaturated fats, along with the omega-3 fatty acids in cold-water fish such as salmon, appear to reduce blood vessel inflammation that causes clots, the cause of most heart attacks.

Get 20% of total daily calories from healthful fats (in olive oil, nuts, fish, etc.). Limit saturated fat (in butter, red meat, whole milk, etc.) to 10% or less.

Important: Eliminate trans fats (often called "partially hydrogenated" and found in many margarines and commercially baked goods). Americans get an average of 3% of total calories from trans fats. If we cut that percentage to 1%, the risk of heart disease would be reduced by half—and there would be 347,000 fewer deaths each year.

Lengthens life by: Three to five years.

WEIGHT LOSS

Excess weight greatly increases the risk of cancer, diabetes and hypertension. A person who is 20 pounds over his/her ideal weight is 50% more likely to develop heart disease—and the risk increases as weight increases.

In addition to regular exercise…

• **Eat most meals at home.** Restaurant food tends to be higher in calories.

• **Drink water instead of soda.** The sugar in soft drinks is a main contributor to weight gain—and artificial sweeteners have not been proven safe.

• **Don't eat in front of the TV.** Studies show that people who engage in "mindless" eating take in far more calories.

• **Weigh yourself weekly** to track your progress—or identify backsliding.

Lengthens life by: 11 years. (This is the difference in life span between obese and normal-weight adults.)

EXERCISE

Vigorous exercise is ideal, but it's not realistic for many of the 78% of Americans who describe themselves as sedentary. People who engage in moderate exercise at least three to five times a week can reduce their blood pressure by an average of 10 points and dramatically lower their risk of diabetes.

Studies show that even mild exercise, such as walking for 30 minutes a day, can increase life span by two to five years. Any kind of exercise, even working in the yard, is beneficial.

Lengthens life by: Two to five years.

The 5 Most Common Exercise Mistakes— How to Avoid Injury

Wayne L. Westcott, PhD, fitness research director at the South Shore YMCA in Quincy, MA, and strength-training consultant for the American Council on Exercise, the US Navy and the American Association of Health and Fitness, is the author of *Building Strength and Stamina* and *Strength Training Past 50* (both published by Human Kinetics).

More people start an exercise program in January than at any other time of the year. Within weeks or months, most of them have called it quits—often because of injury. Unfortunately, many people exercise in such a way that almost guarantees injuries or even chronic pain. But this common problem can be avoided.

How much exercise do you need? Opinions differ, but the American College of Sports Medicine recommends 20 minutes of aerobic exercise three days a week...and two 20-minute weight-lifting sessions a week. This level of exercise—along with ordinary activities such as going for occasional walks and working in the yard—is sufficient for fitness as well as disease prevention.

Avoid these exercise mistakes...

Mistake 1: **Stretching before workouts.** At one time, trainers advised everyone to stretch before exercise. It doesn't help—and actually increases the risk for injury.

Tendons have a limited blood supply. It takes them longer to warm up than muscles. Performing stretches before a workout—when tendons are cold—increases the risk for microtears in the connective tissue in or around the tendon. These tears are painful and slow to heal.

Recommended: Stretch after—not before—vigorous activities. Warm up by performing the exercise at a slower pace and reduced resistance for three to six minutes. For example, if you plan to bike for 35 minutes, begin by riding at a slow, comfortable pace for three to six minutes.

Mistake 2: **Using a barbell** (a bar with an adjustable weighted disk attached to each end and held with two hands). Experienced weight lifters can safely use barbells, but a dumbbell (a short bar with weight at each end and held in each hand) is better for injury prevention. That's because the wrists are less likely to move into a fully supinated (palms facing up) or pronated (palms facing down) position, which may strain your elbows. Just about every exercise that you perform with a barbell can be done with dumbbells.

Recommended: If you're using a barbell, keep your hands in your peripheral vision. If they're so far apart that you can't see them, the wrist will be cocked at an angle and more vulnerable to strain.

Mistake 3: **Performing repetitions too quickly.** People who use weight machines or lift free weights tend to go too fast—either to minimize time spent in the gym, or because accelerating the pace generates momentum and

makes it easier to lift heavy loads. Fast lifting greatly increases stress on the joints, especially when people neglect proper form.

Recommended: A six-second repetition speed. When lifting weights, take about two seconds to raise the weight, then lower it to a count of four. This pace is slow enough to maintain good form throughout the movement, and fast enough to complete about 10 repetitions in one minute—the recommended number of repetitions for most workouts.

Mistake 4: **Lifting too much weight.** This is among the most common causes of joint, muscle and tendon injuries.

Recommended: Warm up by lifting lighter-than-usual weights. For example, if you are going to do curls with 15-pound dumbbells, begin with eight to 12 repetitions with five-pound dumbbells. After warming up, lift no more than 70% to 80% of your *one-repetition maximum*. That's the heaviest weight you can lift one time.

Example: If the most you can lift one time with dumbbell bench presses is 20 pounds in each hand, use 75% of that—about 15-pound weights. You'll know you're in the right range if you can complete eight to 12 repetitions. If you can't complete eight repetitions, the weight is too heavy...if you can easily complete 12 or more, the weight is too light.

Mistake 5: **Neglecting to cool down.** The cool-down period is even more important than the warmup period—not just for injury prevention, but also to protect the heart.

The elevation in heart rate that occurs during exercise continues for several minutes after you stop.

A larger-than-usual volume of blood is being pumped from the heart throughout the body. Without continued muscle activity to help pump it back into circulation, the blood tends to pool in the legs and feet. The heart has to work harder to restore normal circulation, which can trigger high blood pressure.

Recommended: After finishing any exercise or vigorous activity, keep moving for a few minutes at a slower rate—by walking in place or biking at a reduced resistance or slower pace, for example.

Bonus: Activity during cool-down helps flush lactic acid from the muscles. This metabolic byproduct increases during exercise and can result in muscle discomfort.

Since muscles and tendons have the best blood flow and elasticity during cool-down, it is a good time to stretch. A basic gentle stretch that targets many of the body's muscles is the "Figure 4." It stretches the muscles of the calves, hamstrings, hips, lower back, upper back and shoulders.

What to do: Sit on the floor with your legs extended. Bend your right knee and place your right foot just below your left knee. Bending at the waist, reach forward with your arms as far as you comfortably can toward your left ankle or foot. Hold for 20 seconds. Repeat with the opposite leg. The full cool-down should last about four to eight minutes.

Illustration by Shawn Banner.

Fat-Burning Math— Exercise for Maximum Efficiency

Jonny Bowden, MA, CNS, author of *Living the Low Carb Life: Choosing the Diet That's Right for You from Atkins to Zone* (Sterling) and *The 150 Healthiest Foods on the Planet* (Fairwinds). Bowden is a board-certified nutritionist and weight-loss coach. His CD set, *Change Your Body Change Your Life*, can be found at *www.jonny bowden.com*.

The next time you sweat your way through your workout on the elliptical machine at the gym, try playing with the computerized programs and choose "fat burning." The computer will ask you to grasp the handlebars so it can measure your heart rate. To your utter amazement, it may tell you you're working too hard. Even more amazing is how low the machine wants your heart rate to be in order to be in the target zone. You'll feel like you're not even working hard. It will seem too good to be true.

The "weight-loss coach," nutritionist and fitness expert Jonny Bowden, explains why.

TRUTH VS. MYTH

"The conventional advice about working at a lower heart rate to burn more fat is based on a complete misunderstanding of how the body works," Bowden said. "Yet that information continues to get passed around in gyms and aerobics classes. It's even made its way into the computer programs on exercise machines." Bowden explained that at every level of activity—from sleep to running a marathon—you're always "burning" some mixture of fat and carbohydrates, with just the tiniest bit of protein thrown in for good measure. "There's always a mix of these two fuels," Bowden explained. "The confusion about *fat burning* arose because many aerobics teachers don't understand the differences between percentages and absolute numbers."

FUELING YOUR SYSTEM

Here's how it works. You're always burning calories, even when you're sleeping. It "costs" calories to grow toenails, digest food, breathe and perform even the most basic metabolic activities. Those calories have to come from somewhere—and at rest, the highest percentage of them come from fat (or, more accurately, fatty acids, which circulate in the bloodstream and get stored in the hips, thighs and tummy). "But the total number of calories burned at rest—and at low levels of activity—is very small," Bowden explained.

"The average person burns about a calorie a minute—or 60 calories an hour—sitting around watching television. Now the *percentage* of that 60 calories that comes from fat is pretty high—around 70%. But the total number of calories burned is very small. As you work harder, the *percentage* of fuel that comes from fat goes down somewhat, but the total number of calories burned goes way up." The result? You actually burn more total calories—and fat—when you're working harder even though the relative percentage of fat burning drops.

THE ARITHMETIC

"In seminars, I always ask the following question," said Bowden. "Would you rather have 90% of all the money I have in my pocket, or 10% of all the money Donald Trump has in the bank? Obviously, everyone chooses the Trump option, even though I'm offering a higher percentage of the money in my pocket. Why? Because clearly, the payoff in dollars for the person choosing a lower percent of a huge number is going to be way higher than the payoff for the person choosing a high percent of a low number! And it's the exact same thing with calories.

"At a high level of exertion, you might be burning as many as 12 calories per minute, or 720 calories per hour. At that level of exertion, 30% of your calories are probably coming from fat. That sounds like a pretty low percentage, doesn't it? But the number of fat calories burned is actually 216 calories (30% of 720). Now at a very moderate rate of exertion, like they tell you to do on the 'fat burning programs,' you might burn only five calories per minute, or 300 calories per hour, and sure, a greater percentage—say 50% of those 300 calories—is coming from fat. But 50% of 300 calories is only 150 fat calories. That's not bad, but you did better working harder!"

BOWDEN'S BOTTOM LINE

The picture isn't as simple as how many calories you burn from fat during the exercise session. "People get very caught up in the concept of where their calories are coming from during the exercise session, but in the long run it doesn't much matter," he said. "Ultimately, to lose weight, you want to burn—or spend—more calories during the day than you take in. At some point in the day you may be using more fat calories, and at others you may be using more calories from carbs, but if you're in the red, calorically speaking, you're going to pay that debt from your savings account, which in this case is the fat around your waist, hips and thighs!

"If you want to lose weight," Bowden told me, "you want to work out as hard and as long and as frequently as you can." Of course, always check with your doctor before starting any exercise program.

So is there ever a reason to work out at lower levels of effort? "Absolutely," said Bowden. "It's always good to mix and match levels of intensity. Sometimes you go for a long, slow run, other times you go for a series of sprints. Long and slow, or short and fast, doesn't really matter. Just burn the calories."

■ ■ ■ ■

More Reason to Exercise

Exercise controls triglyceride levels. Eating high-fat foods, such as whipped cream and chocolate, causes triglyceride levels to spike, increasing heart disease risk.

Recent study: Triglyceride levels of all participants who ate high-fat foods rose, but the levels of those who exercised for 90 minutes before eating were 25% lower than the levels of nonexercisers.

Jason M.R. Gill, PhD, researcher, department of vascular biochemistry, University of Glasgow, Glasgow Royal Infirmary, Scotland, and leader of a study of triglycerides, published in *Journal of the American College of Cardiology.*

Proven Depression Buster—Regular Exercise

Madhukar Trivedi, MD, director, UT Southwestern Medical Center mood disorders research program, professor of psychiatry, Dallas.

For many people, exercise is a surefire way to get energized and even beat vague feelings of depression. Given that fact, the question for some researchers has been, "How far can exercise go in improving symptoms of depression for those who have been diagnosed as clinically depressed and who are undergoing treatment with either a form of psychotherapy, medication or both?"

The answer: Quite far.

RECENT STUDY RESULTS

Psychiatrist Madhukar Trivedi, MD, director of UT Southwestern Medical Center's mood disorders research program, conducted the study with 80 people, all of whom had been diagnosed as clinically depressed with mild to moderate levels of the disorder and were not physically active. The researchers separated the participants into five groups: Two groups did moderately intense aerobics on the treadmill or stationary bicycle for either three or five days a week...two groups did lower-intensity aerobics, either three or five days a week...and the last group did 15 to 20 minutes of stretching and flexibility exercises three days per week.

After 12 weeks, the group doing the higher intensity level of aerobics, whether three or five days a week, had an average 47% decline in depressive symptoms. The low-intensity aerobics group had a 30% reduction in depressive symptoms…and the stretching/flexibility group had a 29% reduction.

INSIDE THE RESULTS

Dr. Trivedi explained that public health guidelines were used to determine the intensity for the higher level aerobics group. These guidelines recommend 30 minutes a day three times a week…but this is based on the amount of physical activity needed to burn an additional 1,200 calories a week if you weigh about 155 pounds. Because the formula is derived from a calorie-to-weight ratio, heavier people must burn more calories per week. Dr. Trivedi clarified that only members in the group who worked at this higher level experienced more meaningful relief of depression. Furthermore, whether they accomplished that in three days or five depended on how intensely they worked out at each session.

This is very encouraging news for those suffering from depression. However, Dr. Trivedi is emphatic about the need for depressed people to work with a health-care professional on building exercise into their treatment regimen. In particular, those taking prescription medications to assist their depression should have their medication and performance monitored closely when starting an exercise program. Exercise—yes. But do it with guidance.

The 15-Minute Workout To Prevent Back Pain

Renée Daniels, a medical exercise specialist and trainer in New York City, is a former member of the Alvin Ailey dance troupe and coauthor of *Straighter, Stronger, Leaner, Longer.* Avery.

About 80% of Americans suffer from back pain at some point in their lives. Some have obvious medical problems (such as a herniated disc), but most get a clean bill of health from their doctors—yet their backs still hurt.

Back pain isn't always caused by a specific injury or activity. It can be due to the ways we use our bodies over time. People who sit for long periods, for example, often have pain because sitting puts more pressure on the back than standing.

Regular exercise helps prevent pain—but generalized workouts aren't sufficient. Back patients do better with *functional* exercise—workouts that mimic the ways we move in real life. To prevent back pain, perform the following exercises and stretches three times a week. They take about 15 minutes to do.

TRUNK FLEXION STRETCH

Most people who have back pain need to elongate and strengthen muscles in the lower back and hips. This stretch hits all of the lower back muscles. It also relieves pressure on the sacroiliac joint, which connects the triangular bone at the base of the spine (the sacrum) with the pelvis (iliac crest).

How to do it: Sit on the floor with your knees bent and your heels on the floor. Grip the tops of your shoes with both hands. Keeping your knees pointing toward the ceiling, pull your upper body forward toward your feet. Bend your elbows as you pull forward, keeping your knees outside your shoulders.

Tuck your head down so that the top of your head is aimed at the floor.

Flex your spine as far forward as you comfortably can. Hold for a count of three. Repeat five times.

HOOK LYING

People who have weak backs and pelvic floor muscles tend to walk with the pelvis thrust slightly forward. This produces a slight sway in the lower back that increases muscular stress and the risk of injury. This exercise targets muscles in the abdomen, back and pelvic floor and improves posture.

How to do it: Lie on your back with your knees bent and your feet flat on the floor. Reach your arms straight out behind you, flat on the floor, palms up. Tighten your stomach muscles so that there's as little space as possible between your spine and the floor. This move is called a pelvic tilt.

Keeping your arms straight, lift your head, neck and shoulders off the floor, reaching forward with your hands until they touch your knees.

While in this position, aim to complete 10 "pulses" (tightening and releasing the stomach muscles), maintaining the pelvic tilt with the small of the back remaining on the floor. Then return to the resting position. Increase the number of repetitions as you get stronger.

UPRIGHT ROTATION

Strengthening the core muscles in the abdomen and lower back is the best way to reduce or prevent back pain. Trainers often recommend lying crunches for strengthening the core.

Better: A standing rotational exercise that involves more than one plane of movement and mimics the ways we move in real life.

How to do it: Stand with your legs hip-width apart and your arms extended about shoulder-width apart. Hold a rope, towel or resistance band tautly between your hands. Tighten your stomach muscles and rotate your body to the right as far around as you comfortably can. As you move, lift the heel of your left foot and pivot on the toes. Keep your right foot stable.

Repeat the movement in the same direction 10 times. Then repeat the movement going in the opposite direction.

QUADRUPED

This therapeutic movement is especially good for people with chronic back pain. It stretches while strengthening muscles that stabilize the spine.

How to do it: Get on your hands and knees, with your arms directly under your shoulders and your feet hip-width apart. Lift and straighten your right arm and left leg simultaneously, keeping shoulders down. Stretch the arm and leg as far as you comfortably can. Hold for five seconds. Repeat 10 times.

Reverse the movement by lifting and straightening your left arm and your right leg.

Also important: Get at least 20 minutes of aerobic exercise most days of the week to improve circulation to weak and/or sore muscles and to trigger the release of pain-relieving endorphins. At health clubs, the elliptical machine—which is a cross between a stair climber and a cross-country ski machine—is ideal for aerobic exercise because it doesn't stress the lower back. Also good are bicycling, walking and tai chi.

Illustrations by Shawn Banner.

Healthy-Back Exercise

Karl Knopf, PhD, instructor, Adaptive Learning Division, Foothills College, Los Altos Hills, CA, and author of five books. His latest is *Weights for 50 Plus: Building Strength, Staying Healthy and Enjoying an Active Lifestyle.* Ulysses.

Eighty percent of Americans have some form of a back problem—leading to $24 billion spent in medical costs each year directly related to low-back pain. Karl Knopf, PhD, a leading authority on exercise for baby boomers and author of *Weights for 50 Plus: Building Strength, Staying Healthy and Enjoying an Active Lifestyle* (Ulysses), explains exercises that are easy on the back.

POSTURE FIRST

Poor posture is a major contributor to back pain. Dr. Knopf believes that the first order of business for strengthening and rehabilitating the back are posture exercises, which can be practiced absolutely anywhere. "Stand upright with your weight evenly distributed over the balls of your feet and heels, with legs slightly bent. Then tilt your pelvis slightly forward so your tailbone is slightly tucked under your hips. Make the distance from your belly button to your sternum as far as possible by letting the chest rise and open, countering the "hunched over" effect. Your chin, sternum and belly button should be lined up from the front. From the side it should look like your earlobes are over your shoulders, which are over your hips." Practice that alignment whenever you are standing. When you sit, the alignment should be the same. Make sure you sit on the "sit bones" of the buttocks, not on the tailbone.

GUIDE WIRES FOR YOUR BACK

The back alone can't hold your body upright. "Think of standing a pencil upright on your desk balanced on the eraser," Dr. Knopf instructs. "You could make it stand—but it would take a lot of work and balance. How much more efficient to have guide wires? Well, the guide wires are the muscles that help keep the back aligned. These need strengthening to build a strong support system for the back."

The three basic "guide wire" muscle groups for the back are the abdominals, the gluteals (buttocks) and the perispinals (the muscles that run up and down the spine). "While many baby boomers are aware of the importance of training their abs, they often neglect the buttocks muscles, which are the other side of the guide wires." *To strengthen the abs, back and glutes, Dr. Knopf recommends the following exercises...*

Buttocks strengthener: Lie on your back with knees bent and feet flat on the floor. Tighten butt muscles and lift the butt off the floor slowly. Hold for a few seconds, return. Do 10 repetitions.

Hamstring stretch: Lie on your back, feet straight out. Pull your right knee into the chest and hold it there for a few seconds. Then gently extend the leg toward the ceiling until you feel a stretch in the hamstrings. Hold, return to start and repeat with the other leg.

This stretches the hamstrings.

Mad cat: Get on your hands and knees. Arch your back like a cat. Keep your neck in a relaxed neutral position. Hold for 10 seconds, then release.

Note: Don't do this if you have a ruptured disc.

OTHER GENTLE EXERCISES

When choosing other exercises that are gentle on the back, Dr. Knopf recommends exercises that are done with the back supported and no "load" (or weight) on the spine.

Dr. Knopf has high praise for two specific forms of exercise. "The recumbent bike is my all-time favorite," he maintains. The recumbent bike, found in almost all gyms, is a bicycle (in either stationary or outdoor road versions) that allows you to sit on the bicycle as you would in a chair with your back supported, instead of upright or hunched over the way traditional bicycles do. Dr. Knopf also loves water exercise.

"Vertical water exercise allows you to work all muscle groups without putting any stress or strain on the back whatsoever," he stresses.

As for strength-training exercises, again, Dr. Knopf recommends those in which the back is supported and that avoid putting any "load" on it. *His favorites...*

1. Seated chest press.
2. Lat pulldowns to the front.
3. Sit-to-stands.
Avoid: Military or shoulder press...squats.

CAUTIONS

"You have to be careful with leg exercises," Dr. Knopf insists. "If there's injury or pain, I'd prefer you do *sit-to-stands*." In this exercise, you sit on the edge of a chair, then stand up and sit down again. It's a "no load" version of the squat that works the front of the legs without putting any strain on the spine. You could work up to holding dumbbells in your hands to increase the resistance and build more strength.

For anyone with chronic back pain who wants to exercise and eliminate pain, Dr. Knopf strongly suggests finding a physiatrist. "They are the most underused medical specialty I know of," he says. A physiatrist is a medical doctor who treats chronic pain and chronic conditions using a nonsurgical approach that often includes exercise. "They have no vested interest in doing surgery, and are usually very open minded to medical interventions such as chiropractic and acupuncture," says Dr. Knopf. "I've had back pain for years, and I always make the physiatrist the captain of my ship when it comes to back-pain treatment."

Don't Feel Like Exercising? Secrets to Staying on Track

Gabe Mirkin, MD, a physician with a specialty in sports medicine and a former associate professor of pediatrics at the Georgetown University School of Medicine in Washington, DC, is the author of eight books, including *The Healthy Heart Miracle: Your Roadmap to Lifelong Health*. HarperCollins.

We all know that regular physical activity is crucial for good health—it reduces our risk for heart disease, diabetes, stroke, certain types of cancer, mental disorders, including depression and anxiety, and even premature death.

Problem: Nearly nine out of every 10 people who start an exercise program drop out within six weeks, typically due to injuries and/or lack of social reinforcement. But these aren't the only reasons that people give for skipping workouts.

In my 46 years as a practicing sports medicine physician, I've heard all kinds of excuses for not exercising. *Here are the most common excuses and the rebuttals I give my patients to get them back on track...*

***Excuse:* I'm so out of shape that I wouldn't know where to begin.**

My rebuttal: No matter how out of shape you might be, you'll immediately begin getting fitter once you engage in any regular physical activity. If you haven't exercised in a long time, start by simply getting a bit more physical activity each day and gradually increasing it.

The most popular recommendations are to park a block from where you're heading and walk the rest of the way and/or to take the stairs instead of the elevator.

Other possibilities: Do gardening or yard work...vacuum and wash your car...walk around the inside and/or outside of your house...tackle a cleaning project you've been putting off...ride a bike to nearby destinations instead of driving...and/or stroll around a park or mall.

When you're ready to start a more formal exercise program, don't choose an activity that requires a great deal of skill or strength you don't yet have, such as in-line skating, jumping rope or rock climbing. Instead, try a low-risk activity that you already know how to do. Walking is great for most people.

Other good choices: Swimming, cycling, jogging and/or dancing (aerobic or ballroom).

Start with just a few minutes a day. Begin very slowly and continue until your muscles start to hurt or you feel uncomfortable, then quit for the day. Do this every day until you can exercise continuously for 30 minutes daily without feeling sore. You can always add more challenging activities to your program later.

***Excuse:* I'm afraid that I'll strain my heart.**

My rebuttal: It's true that heart rate and blood pressure rise during exercise, but this doesn't pose a danger for most people. A recently published Johns Hopkins study of healthy older people with mild hypertension (130–159 mmHg/85–99 mmHg) found that the short-term spike in blood pressure they experienced during moderate exercise (the equivalent of brisk walking plus weight training) didn't harm their hearts in any way. Since regular physical activity helps lower your heart rate and blood pressure when you're not exercising, being physically fit actually results in less overall strain on your heart.

Important: Always check with your doctor before starting any exercise program. If you ever develop chest pain, shortness of breath or dizziness during exercise, stop at once. If your symptoms go away as soon as you stop, check with your doctor as soon as possible. If symptoms continue, consult a doctor immediately.

***Excuse:* I can't find time in my schedule to exercise.**

My rebuttal: There's no "best" time to exercise. The ideal time is any time that you will do it. It really doesn't matter whether you exercise first thing in the morning, during your lunch break or sometime in the early evening. And you don't have to exercise for long stretches at a time to get tremendous benefits. Multiple short bouts of exercise can be as effective as long sessions in strengthening your heart. Perform longer workouts (one hour or more) on the weekends, when you are more likely to have the time.

For some people, keeping an exercise diary is helpful. Use a calendar to schedule your workouts. After every workout, jot down what you did, how long you did it and how much distance you covered, if applicable. Tracking your progress will give you a sense of accomplishment and keeps you focused on your goals.

***Excuse:* I started to exercise once but got injured.**

My rebuttal: It's true that almost two-thirds of people who start an exercise program end up dropping out because of an injury. Jogging is especially hard on your knees, hips and other joints because your feet hit the ground with a force greater than twice your body weight. However, the more slowly you run, the lower the shock. If you approach your exercise prudently, you probably won't get injured.

Examples...

•**Take up swimming or tai chi.** These activities put little or no stress on your joints—while delivering significant fitness benefits. Swimming improves cardiovascular health, while tai chi strengthens muscles.

•**If you enjoy cycling,** consider buying—or getting your gym to buy—a recumbent stationary bike, which provides back support while you pedal.

Typical cost: $500. You can use it year-round indoors, and it's considered one of the safest types of exercise equipment available. This type of exercise is ideal for most people with back problems.

Excuse: **I get bored.**

My rebuttal: Exercise can be a great social activity itself—and can lead to a more interesting social life in general. Studies have shown that the people who stick to their exercise programs are more likely to meet regularly with other exercisers in some formalized way.

You don't have to exercise with others every day—but try to meet one or more people at least once a week. Join a walking, running or cycling club that has regular weekend events…agree to meet with one or more friends at a regular time each week for a group walk, swim, bike ride or gym workout…or set up a weekly session with a personal trainer. You won't be bored.

Ballroom dancing and cycling are both great activities for couples. My wife and I like to ride bikes together, but we cycle at different speeds. So we bought a tandem bike that lets us ride together—each of us pedaling at our own level of effort—and joined a club that holds group tandem rides on the weekend.

Exercise Secrets from Jack LaLanne

Jack LaLanne, author of *Revitalize Your Life: Improve Your Health, Your Sex Life & Your Looks After Fifty* (Hastings House) and creator of eight exercise videos and DVDs. His new book of healthy recipes is *Cooking with Jack–Eat Right and You Can't Go Wrong.* His Web site is *www.jacklalanne.com.*

When Jack LaLanne began his fitness career more than 70 years ago, most Americans were not even aware of the health benefits of exercise. LaLanne, now a legend in the fitness world, opened the first modern health club in 1936, invented many of the kinds of equipment used in gyms today, such as the first leg extension machine and pulley machine using cables, starred in his own fitness show on television for 34 years and became known as the "Godfather of Fitness." Today, his goal remains the same as it always was—to help people stay fit and healthy.

Jack LaLanne's latest secrets to staying fit…

YOU DON'T HAVE TO GO TO THE GYM

It's great to belong to a gym and have a personal trainer, but many people don't have the time or money for this. Fortunately, there are many activities you can do at home that take only minutes to complete.*

What you can do: Walk up and down the stairs until your muscles tire. This is one of my favorite exercises. It works your leg muscles and your heart and lungs. If you feel unsteady, use a handrail.

•**Standing around?** Run or walk in place by bringing your knees as high as you can toward your chest. This gets your heart beating and targets your abdominal muscles.

•**Do you sit in a chair behind a desk?** Stand up and sit back down 10 times quickly. Now, slow it down and do it five more times.

Also: Stand up with your feet shoulder-width apart. Make a fist with your fingers and raise your fists to shoulder height. Punch your arms toward the ceiling, bring your fists back to your shoulders and repeat. Start with 10 repetitions and work up gradually until you can do three sets of 10.

•**Watching television?** Scoot down in your chair and hold on to the sides. Bring one knee to your chest, then the other, alternating and pumping like you're riding a bicycle. This works your abs, back, thighs, heart and lungs. Remember to start slowly and rest when your muscles tire.

Also: Do sit-ups. Lie on the floor or your bed so that your back is flat. Bend your knees, keeping your heels as close to your buttocks as possible. With your hands either behind your head or across your chest, try to sit up. Exhale as you

*Check with your doctor before starting this—or any—exercise program.

raise up. Inhale as you lie down. Start slowly with five repetitions and work up to 10.

Important: Increase your workout intensity gradually.

MIX UP YOUR WORKOUTS

Sticking to the same old routine can become boring, making it harder to stick to regular exercise. Also, by doing the same routine your muscles eventually stop getting stronger.

What you can do: Change your workouts every three to four weeks, so that you are challenging your muscles to work harder. Without resistance, your muscles become complacent.

Example: If you walk regularly, walk up hills after you become used to walking on a level surface.

Also helpful: Try walking a short distance with your feet turned inward. Then repeat with your feet turned outward. All of these strategies provide resistance, which strengthens your muscles.

ADOPT HEALTHFUL EATING HABITS

You are never too old to learn to eat more nutritiously. You must replace bad habits with good ones.

What you can do: Avoid foods with added sugar and salt.

Also: Instead of cooking with oil, sauté in chicken or vegetable broth to cut calories. If you use oils, canola, olive and peanut oils are the best—they have low cholesterol. Eat plenty of whole grains, fresh fruits and raw vegetables. If raw vegetables are difficult for you to digest, lightly steam them.

How I do it: My wife, Lala, and I eat out regularly. For lunch, I usually have four hard-boiled eggs and eat only the egg whites. I also have soup with no cream and four pieces of fresh fruit. For dinner, a usual meal consists of a salad with eight to 10 raw vegetables, fresh fish and brown rice. Whenever I can, I bring my own salad dressing—a mixture of vinegar, canola oil, honey, soy sauce and a little sesame oil. On the road, we stick to oil and vinegar.

SET NEW GOALS

Keep challenging yourself by making gradual increases in your fitness routine. For example, if you don't get much exercise, aim to walk a block the first day, a block and a half or two the second day, etc. Each day, walk a little farther, and before you know it, you'll be walking a mile. If you miss a day, reset your goals.

Exercising for 20 to 30 minutes three to four days a week is adequate to keep most people healthy and fit. Remember, our body is the only machine where the more you work it, the stronger it gets.

How I do it: My personal workout consists of one hour of weight lifting in my gym and one-half hour of exercises and/or lap swimming in the pool each day. I do not expect everyone to follow my regimen—but I have been doing this for more than 70 years, so I want to see how long I can continue.

JACK'S CARROT AND GINGER SOUP

I love soup and have it at least once a day, sometimes twice. My mother made delicious soup, and her specialty was carrot soup. *Her recipe, which follows, is my favorite...*

1 medium onion, diced
4 garlic cloves, minced
2 Tbsp. olive oil
2 lbs. carrots, cut into 1-inch chunks
2 Tbsp. gingerroot, peeled and chopped
1 quart chicken stock, defatted
Plain yogurt and sesame seeds for garnish

Sauté the onion and garlic in oil for five minutes. Add carrots, cover and cook for 15 minutes. Add half of the ginger and all of the stock. Simmer 15 minutes. Add the rest of the ginger. Purée soup in a food processor or blender. Pour into bowls and garnish with yogurt and sesame seeds. Serves six.

A "No-More-Excuses" Exercise Plan

Jamison Starbuck, ND, naturopathic physician in family practice and a lecturer at the University of Montana, both in Missoula. She is past president of the American Association of Naturopathic Physicians.

Whenever I encourage a patient to start exercising, I brace myself for the inevitable comeback: "I've tried, but I just can't stick with it." It's no secret that regular exercise reduces the risk for heart disease, diabetes and cancer—and that it speeds weight loss, lessens menopausal symptoms and alleviates depression. But there are some secrets to creating an exercise program that can be maintained. *Here's what I recommend…*

•**Set a goal.** Keep it simple. Perhaps you'll walk two miles per day three times per week with the hope of hiking a nearby mountain this summer. If you like, hire a personal trainer to give you specific strength and cardiovascular goals…learn a new sport…or join a recreational team. Devise a program that's within your physical limits, affordable and enjoyable.

•**Avoid injury.** To keep your muscles limber, alternate aerobic workouts, such as biking or using a treadmill, three times weekly, with stretching exercise, such as yoga or qi gong (a combination of postures, breathing techniques and meditation), twice weekly.

•**Get enough protein.** Low blood sugar impairs athletic performance and can make you feel fatigued, light-headed or dizzy during a workout. Blood sugar levels tend to be low in the early morning before breakfast and in the late afternoon. If you exercise at these times, consuming a small amount of protein powder 30 minutes before your workout will help stabilize your blood sugar. Whey, soy and rice protein powders are available at health-food stores. Mix a portion that contains about 20 g of protein into water, milk or soy milk.

•**Take minerals.** If you exercise regularly, consuming minerals each day is important for aiding muscle contraction and heart function. In my opinion, mineral-fortified sports drinks, such as Gatorade and POWERade, contain too much sweetener and too many synthetic ingredients to be healthful. The average adult who exercises regularly should take one or more daily mineral supplements that contain approximately 300 mg of magnesium, 600 mg of calcium, 99 mg of potassium, 25 mg of zinc, 200 micrograms (mcg) of chromium, 200 mcg of selenium and 2 mg of copper.

•**Use topical arnica.** Keep homeopathic arnica (available at health-food stores) on hand for occasional sprains, strains or tendinitis. This remedy speeds the healing of musculoskeletal injuries by supporting circulation and immune function. If you sustain a minor injury, rub arnica onto the affected area twice daily for up to one week.

•**Soak in Epsom salts.** This is one of my favorite post-exercise treats. Epsom salts help relax muscles and soothe mild muscle injuries. Add one cup to your tub and soak for 15 minutes daily, if desired. A quick cold rinse at the end of the bath will improve circulation. Taking an Epsom salt soak before bed also will help you sleep well.

Small Moves Mean a Lot

David Zemach-Bersin, training program director, Feldenkrais Method Professional Training Program and author of *Relaxercise*. HarperCollins. He studied with Feldenkrais in the 1970s.

Frederick Schjang, a guild-certified Feldenkrais practitioner in New York City.

I t may be hard to imagine that an exercise method of small, almost imperceptible movements may create important results. However, the Feldenkrais Method is just that. Developed more than 50 years ago by Russian-born Israeli physicist Moshe Feldenkrais, the method isn't really exercise—it's a process that uses movement. With Feldenkrais, students develop new body awareness that changes their overall posture and the way they move. It also improves their physical and psychological performance.

Today, the popularity of Feldenkrais is on the rise—athletes and musicians are using it to correct problems in how they hold themselves…people with arthritis are turning to it to facilitate freer, more flexible movement…and many others are converts for the way it teaches them relaxation, focus and overall enhanced movement.

David Zemach-Bersin, former president of the Feldenkrais Guild of North America and author of *Relaxercise*, studied with Feldenkrais for 12 years. Feldenkrais developed his method after a series of accidents left him barely able to walk. He thought if he could understand how his nervous system learned to walk in the first place, he might be able to find information that would help him relearn to walk. Armed with a broad understanding of movement based on his background as a physicist and his long-time study of Judo, he devoted himself to studying how body movement develops in humans, including analyzing infants in motion. Ultimately, he designed a method made up of thousands of exercise lessons.

FELDENKRAIS BASICS

Feldenkrais has two basic components, which may be used alone or in combination. Awareness Through Movement (ATM) is generally conducted through 30- to 60-minute classes as well as through audio- and videotapes, while Functional Integration (FI) is always conducted during hands-on private sessions.

In ATM, practitioners provide verbal instructions for highly specific sequential patterns of movement that students follow, paying careful attention to how their musculoskeletal system is responding. The lessons start with one small movement, perhaps with students moving one shoulder up and down from a prone position. The lesson adds a gradually expanding sequence of movements through which students begin to learn to involve their whole body, even for small functions such as turning the shoulders or the head. The result is that students instinctively create all motions using their body as a whole rather than as independently functioning parts.

PRIVATE LESSONS

In FI, the instructor works one on one with the student, using gentle, light movements to manipulate his/her body parts. People typically seek this out because of some kind of injury or other acute problem. It can help many people recover function, including after stroke or neurological injury, as well as after accidents and other less serious problems.

WHO CAN DO IT?

Zemach-Bersin has found that people of all ages can do Feldenkrais. He has worked successfully with people who suffer from multiple sclerosis or cerebral palsy, and he calls it extraordinarily useful for older adults who may be developing mobility problems. Students see the results of the method—easier and more fluid movement—often in the first lesson, he says, because it directly affects the nervous system. Frederick Schjang, a Feldenkrais instructor in New York who came to the method as a fitness professional, says that within the first seven minutes of his first experience with it, he realized that this was something entirely different

and that it brought into question everything he thought he knew about body movement. He compares practicing Feldenkrais with eating a healthy diet—over time, it applies to and improves everything you do.

EXPERT RESOURCES

There are about 3,000 practitioners in North America, says Zemach-Bersin. The skill of the Feldenkrais practitioner is critical. To become one takes extensive study over a four-year period, and about 20% of practitioners are physical therapists, notes Zemach-Bersin.

How often do you need "treatment?" Feldenkrais' goal was to empower people to be their own movement guides. According to Zemach-Bersin, the number of FI sessions needed to address problems depends on the severity of the problem and how long ago it started. As to ATM, there is no reason not to partake in sessions for a lifetime if you wish. Each session costs from $10 to $20.

Don't throw out your aerobics shoes just yet. However, integrating Feldenkrais into the exercise regimen will be a great addition.

You can get information about Feldenkrais in your area by calling 800-775-2118…or going to *http://www.feldenkrais.com.*

Where You Work Out Does Matter

Liz Neporent, MA, CSCS, an exercise physiologist and cofounder of Wellness 360, a wellness consulting company in New York City, and is a contributing editor at iVillage.com and a regular health columnist for the New York Daily News. The author of Fitness for Dummies (Wiley), her latest book is The Fat-Free Truth (Houghton Mifflin).

It's easy to forget how great you feel every time you exercise outside until the next time you do it. Whether it's a planned workout like a run, or simply a vacation activity such as kayaking or riding bicycles—activities that you might not mentally categorize as a "workout"—you feel invigorated and energized in a very different way than from your usual indoor routines.

"There are some significant differences when you exercise outside," explains exercise authority

Liz Neporent, MA, CSCS, "though they have very little to do with calorie burning. Exercising outside is just more exciting and interesting. A rowing machine is just not going to be the same as rowing on the river. The movement on a machine is relatively predictable, but outdoors you're actually dealing with the elements—with the sun on your face, with pretty landscape going by and with getting rocked by the water. Navigating the outdoor elements actually causes extra movement, which also makes it more of a challenge." Plus you get your fill of vitamin D from the sun, which improves your energy, calcium management and mood.

TREADMILL MYTH

Neporent says that people believe that they burn more calories running on a treadmill than outdoors, but that this really isn't true. "There's a slight difference between running up a hill and running on a treadmill," she explains. "You will burn slightly more calories on the real hill due to wind resistance and terrain changes. For the average person, it is hardly enough of a difference to matter, but physiologically speaking the difference is there," Neporent says. Other than that, she says, running/walking outdoors versus the treadmill test out virtually the same in terms of calorie burn.

But Neporent points out that exercising indoors has many advantages—safety being one of them. "Running on a treadmill in a gym is a lot safer than running outside in some neighborhoods, particularly at night," Neporent points out. "And the great thing about cardio machines is that they give you feedback about your speed, distance, pace and calorie burn, which helps ensure you exercise at an adequate level. It is also motivating, especially if you're one of those people who likes facts about your workout." And of course indoors often takes less time.

Some people who regularly work out outdoors skip strength-training exercises. "You don't have to limit your outdoor workout to cardio," Neporent insists. *Some suggested exercises to mix in with cardio for a terrific outdoor circuit workout...*

- **Find a bench and do step-ups.**
- **Stop and do some push-ups.**
- **Do tricep dips off a bench.**
- **Do a set of squats or lunges.**

So what's best? Variety. A little bit of both. When time is tight, or the weather is bad, stay inside. But, on a beautiful sunny day, get out and enjoy the rich experience of an outdoor workout.

Most critical: Just keep moving every day.

■ ■ ■ ■

Coffee and Your Workout

Drinking coffee before exercise may be dangerous.

New finding: The equivalent of two cups of coffee 50 minutes before exercise reduces by 22% the body's ability to boost blood flow to heart muscles.

Theory: Caffeine blocks the release of adenosine, a compound produced during exercise that opens the arteries. This finding is especially important if you have coronary artery disease or other conditions that reduce blood flow to the heart.

Philipp Kaufmann, MD, professor of nuclear medicine and cardiology, University Hospital, Zurich, Switzerland.

■ ■ ■ ■

Optimum Workout

Exercise in the late afternoon for the best results.

New finding: Lung performance, which is governed by circadian (24-hour) rhythms, drops in the early morning and again at about noon. In the late afternoon (4 pm to 5 pm), lung function is 15% to 20% more effective than at noon.

Important: Although your lungs may function most effectively in the late afternoon, it's still advisable to exercise whenever you can.

Rubin Cohen, MD, codirector of the Asthma Center, Long Island Jewish Medical Center, New Hyde Park, New York.

■ ■ ■ ■

10,000 Steps the Easy Way

By walking 10,000 steps or more each day, you'll be able to build and maintain fitness. *Here's how...*

- **Measure** how much you walk with a pedometer.

Cost: $15 to $30. Less-expensive ones are often not accurate, and more-costly ones are unnecessary.

•**Take a walk** at lunchtime every day.

•**Park** in an inconvenient spot.

•**Get together** with friends to walk, not to drink coffee.

•**Use stairs** instead of an escalator or elevator.

•**If you bike, row or swim,** count every 10 minutes of exercise as 1,000 steps.

Katrien De Cocker, staff academic assistant, department of movement and sports sciences, Ghent University, Belgium.

■ ■ ■ ■

Burn More Calories by Walking Slower

A new study has found that obese individuals who walked one mile at a leisurely pace burned more calories than if they walked a mile at their normal pace. In addition, those who walked at two miles per hour rather than three miles per hour reduced the load on their knee joints by up to 25%. The message is that by walking more slowly, obese individuals can burn more calories per mile and may reduce the risk of arthritis or joint injury.

Ray Browning, PhD, department of integrative physiology, University of Colorado at Boulder.

Home Exercise Equipment Basics

Colin Milner, health and fitness expert for more than 23 years, and chief executive officer of the International Council on Active Aging, in Vancouver, British Columbia, which promotes healthier lifestyles for adults. *www.icaa.cc.*

Not long ago, home-exercise equipment was for young guys preparing for a summer at the beach. Today, men and women of every age are benefiting from treadmills, dumbbells and other home-exercise equipment.

Bulging biceps are no longer the main objective, though building up arm strength can indeed be helpful to people over age 50. Exercise equipment can also help improve your cardiovascular system, strengthen respiratory functions and help you lose weight.

Exercising on home equipment can have big advantages for people who don't enjoy the atmosphere of health clubs or for those without a club nearby. It's also a plus for people who live in areas with cold winters, where outdoor sports—or even walking—are difficult.

Even if you're a member of a health club and live in a warm climate, home equipment has the benefit of convenience. It allows you to exercise in the middle of the night, before breakfast or any other time you want.

Important: Be sure to consult your physician before you start an exercise program.

BUILDING A HOME GYM

Don't make the mistake of buying lots of equipment right away. Start with basic devices to gain strength, and then—if you still enjoy exercising at home—work up to more demanding and sophisticated equipment. *Road map…*

•**Step 1.** If you haven't exercised regularly in a few years, start again by increasing your strength. That type of exercise is relatively easy, the equipment is inexpensive and building strength will give you the ability to go to the next step—cardiovascular exercise.

•Resistance bands are the simplest type of upper-body equipment. These are bands of expandable materials with hand clasps at both ends. Stretching the band builds up strength in your arms and upper body.

•Dumbbells are also effective in building up muscles in this area, and they're usually preferable to barbells.

Reason: Dumbbells are weights lifted individually by each arm. Since you're probably stronger in one arm than the other, a dumbbell lets you concentrate on the weaker arm.

That's nearly impossible with a barbell, which is one long bar with weights at each end. Moreover, if you lose control of a barbell, it could fall on your chest and even roll back on your throat. If you have problems lifting a dumbbell, you can simply drop it on the floor.

Weight-lifting guideline: Start with about 70% of the greatest amount of weight you can lift. Then increase the amount slowly—one pound a week, for example.

As you improve your fitness, also consider a "multigym," a device with one or two weight stacks, plus attachments that let you exercise arms as well as legs in many different ways.

•**Step 2.** Once you've increased your upper-body strength, work also on improving your cardiovascular system.

•Pedometers aren't usually thought of as a piece of gym equipment, but they can serve in that role by encouraging you to take more steps, even around the house.

Some pedometers, including Digi-Walker, record the number of steps you take and estimate how many calories you burn. Most people over 50 take about 2,000 to 4,000 steps a day, and only 1,000 steps more are known to improve heart and lung functions.

•Treadmills can be an even better way to burn calories and improve the cardiovascular system. You can adjust a treadmill to move at varying speeds, so you can start at, say, one mile per hour (mph) and slowly increase the pace and/or the length of your exercise.

•Stationary bicycles and recumbent steppers (which exercise your muscular and cardiovascular systems from a sitting position) also help improve the cardiovascular system. They are safer than treadmills, which entail the risk—however slight—of falling.

General rule: If you have a problem with balance or if you haven't exercised in several years, opt for a stationary bike or recumbent stepper.

•Elliptical machines (motion is similar to a bike but you pedal while in a standing position) are a good addition to your home gym once you've worked out for several months—or if you're already physically fit. By requiring you to move in elliptical patterns, this relatively new device gives you the opportunity to improve your cardiovascular system while also getting a particularly safe workout as you stand.

If you doubt that you're exercising at the right level, use the "talk test." If you can't talk comfortably while exercising, you're probably pushing yourself too hard.

TEST, THEN BUY

With so many different types of exercise equipment on the market, it's easy to spend big bucks for a device that winds up as a coatrack. The solution is to visit retailers that sell exercise apparatus, and try out different types of equipment.

Major retailers are usually listed in the Yellow Pages under "Exercise Equipment" and include Gym Source and OMNI Fitness Equipment, Inc. Exercise devices are also sold by Sports Authority and other large sporting-goods outlets, as well as by Sears and Wal-Mart.

Most stores have several types of exercise equipment set up on the floor and allow customers to try them out there.

Look for equipment that challenges you but doesn't cause pain or require exertion that you can't perform. Be cautious of machines with expensive gadgets that you're unlikely to use, such as a treadmill device that tells you "how far you've gone," just as though you were on a track. All you really need is a timer and speed indicator so that you can pace yourself at, say, four mph for 20 minutes.

But, if you enjoy using gadgets, they could be valuable motivators that inspire you to work out.

Don't fall into the trap of buying equipment that's difficult to use on the theory that you won't benefit much without a major challenge. In fact, equipment that's overly demanding often falls into disuse.

Instead, consider devices that let you start with easy exercises and then work up incrementally to more demanding ones.

Example: A weight-training machine that starts at 10 or 15 pounds and allows you to work up in five-pound increments.

What about exercise equipment advertised on TV? The problem is that you can't test it like you can at a store where you can compare three or four types of equipment.

My advice: Never buy anything advertised on TV unless you have the right to return it and get a complete refund, including shipping charges.

Regardless of where you shop, the cheapest equipment will rarely be as long-lasting as more expensive models, but the most costly devices will probably have unneeded bells and whistles. Even though you don't need to buy the most expensive equipment you can find, it's still worth investing in good quality. So expect to pay up to $2,000 or $3,000 to get something durable that has what you need.

Be sure that you have room for the equipment in your home. It's easy to underestimate the space you'll need, especially when you try out equipment on a large showroom floor. For a treadmill, make sure that you have at least five feet between the device and the wall behind it. That will prevent the treadmill from pinning you against the wall in case you should fall down on it.

Information for assessing fitness equipment can be found at my organization's Web site at *www. icaa.cc/welcomeback/equipment.pdf.*

■ ■ ■ ■

Running in Reverse

Running backward works the lungs more efficiently than running forward, burns more calories and lets bones absorb shock more effectively. Backward running also helps recovery from sprained ankles, pulled hamstrings and other leg and knee injuries, because it puts less impact on joints.

Best: Start slowly, until you build confidence.

Dean Karnazes, San Francisco–based ultra-marathoner and author of *Ultra-Marathon Man: Confessions of an All-Night Runner.* Tarcher.

■ ■ ■ ■

Calorie Tracker

Know how many calories you're burning with a glance. The *BioTrainer* clips onto your waistband and with a small motion detector keeps track of how active you are. It instantly calculates the amount of calories you're burning and displays it on a small digital screen in real time. Stores up to nine days of data. Great for keeping track of your exercise goals.

Cost: $39.99

For information 561-208-6906, *www.biotrainerusa.com.*

Creating Balance

Fuzhong Li, PhD, researcher, Oregon Research Institute, Eugene, OR.

Falls are one of the biggest dangers to elderly people. In older people, even a simple broken bone can have disastrous consequences, resulting in a permanently diminished quality of life, or short- or long-term stays in a nursing home. A good way to reduce the risk is by practicing the ancient Chinese martial art of tai chi.

THE STUDY

In a study at the Oregon Research Institute in Eugene involving 256 elderly people (average age 77), it was found that those who practiced tai chi experienced 28 falls, whereas control group participants who instead practiced standard stretching exercises had 74 falls.

The incidence of falls was counted during six months of formal exercise training and for six months following the end of the trial. All study participants had been physically inactive for three months prior to the study, and most patients reported their overall health as good or better at the start of the study.

Lead researcher Fuzhong Li, PhD, correlates the significantly lower number of falls for the tai chi group with their overall improvement in balance and coordination. These were measured by functional balance tests at the beginning of the trial, at three months, at six months and again at a six-month post-intervention follow-up. The tai chi practicers who improved on the functional balance tests after six months of practice were the ones who had significantly less risk of falling during the six-month post-intervention period, said Dr. Li.

GOOD NEWS

An encouraging postscript to the study is that 66% of the tai chi group continued to perform some exercise after the study ended, while only 20% of the control group continued exercising. This suggests that, in addition to aiding balance, tai chi positively affected these formerly sedentary people to change to a more physically active lifestyle.

GENTLE, YET EFFECTIVE

A tai chi exercise program consists of a series of flowing, gentle movements, which involve constant weight shifting from one leg to the other. Tai chi requires a person to continually coordinate lower body and upper body movements. In effect, a tai chi session is training in maintaining balance.

Today, it is fairly easy to find a tai chi instructor. Tai chi classes have become common offerings at local Ys and continuing-education programs at high schools and colleges. Although tai chi is certainly low-impact exercise, it's always a good idea to check with your physician before beginning a new exercise regimen.

Tai Chi—In a Chair!

Cynthia Quarta is a tai chi instructor based in Montana, and the author of Tai Chi in a Chair. *Fair Winds Press.*

Western doctors have long dismissed the ancient Chinese concept of chi (life energy) as mere superstition.

But a growing body of scientific evidence supports the salutary effects of Eastern healing techniques—especially the traditional exercise known as tai chi. By stimulating the body's nervous system, tai chi triggers a biochemical cascade of beneficial endorphins.

Tai chi combines slow, rhythmic movements with deep breathing and visualization techniques to enhance the flow of chi. Disruption of chi flow is thought to be the source of illness and pain.

People often think of tai chi as a group activity that is best performed in a park. In reality, you can practice it anywhere, anytime. Here is a 15-minute tai chi program that can be performed while seated.

The exercises can be done on their own or as a warm-up or cool-down to your normal exercise routine.

Tai chi in a chair will tone and stretch your muscles without putting stress on your knees, feet, hips or back. The movements are less complex and easier to maintain than traditional tai chi postures. That's why it's a good form of exercise for everyone, regardless of age or fitness level.

Like traditional tai chi, the chair exercises often produce surprising gains in muscular tone, endurance and coordination.

In fact, a recent University of Connecticut study showed that older adults who practiced tai chi had greater balance and strength gains than a similar group who performed strength training.

Begin each movement sitting in a chair. Press your back against the back of the chair and place your feet flat on the floor, shoulder-width apart.

Perform each movement slowly and smoothly while breathing in through your nose and out through your mouth.

You can do the exercises in the morning while you wait for coffee to brew, at your desk during the day or while watching TV at night.

BALLOON BREATHING

This exercise strengthens the diaphragm.

Close your eyes, and place both palms on your lower abdomen. Feel your diaphragm expand and contract as you breathe.

As you inhale deeply, visualize a disk in your lower abdomen (just below your belly button) spinning faster and faster as it releases energy into your body. Mentally guide these sparks of energy up into your chest. Picture them circling around your lungs. While exhaling, envision the toxins that have collected in your lungs exiting through your mouth. Repeat nine times.

BRUSHING TREE TRUNK

This pose stretches your neck muscles.

Extend your arms and reach for the ceiling as you breathe in deeply. Swing your right arm down and across your chest to your left side while turning your head in the opposite direction, looking as far toward the ceiling as you can.

As you twist, visualize your internal organs being squeezed and massaged. Exhale as you bend forward and tighten your abdomen. Return to the starting position. Repeat nine times on each side.

CENTERING CHI

This movement focuses energy.

As you do this exercise, imagine that you're collecting bits of energy from all over your body and returning them to your lower abdomen.

Hold your hands above your lap, palms upward. Breathe in deeply as you pull your abdomen inward, contracting your diaphragm. (This is the only exercise in which your diaphragm is not expanding as you inhale.) As you tighten your abdomen, raise your arms out to the side, and then extend them up over the center of your head so that your palms are facing the ceiling.

Allow your arms to drop gently to the side in an arc. As they drop downward, exhale until there is no breath left in your lungs and relax your abdomen.

Return to the starting position. Repeat three times.

FLOWER BUD OPENS

This is a great way to achieve deeper inhalation.

Hold your hands in front of your chest with palms facing each other. Raise your arms upward, inhaling deeply and visualizing energy circulating through your shoulders, arms, neck and head. As you lift your arms above your head, arch your back away from the chair and extend your arms outward. Then press your arms down to the side, palms facing the floor. Finish the inhalation by relaxing your arms and pulling them behind you.

Exhale and return to the starting position. Repeat nine times.

GREEN DRAGON

This exercise strengthens the shoulders and arms. It is especially good for firming up the backs of your upper arms.

Bring both arms over your left shoulder so that your right palm is almost touching your left shoulder, and your left hand is next to your left ear.

Move your right hand across your chest and down, until it rests just outside your right thigh, palm facing down. At the same time, move your left hand in front of your upper chest so that it is perpendicular to the floor, with the palm facing to the right. By the time your left hand reaches this position, the muscles in your left arm should be taut.

Repeat on the opposite side. Move your arms so that your left palm almost touches your right shoulder and your right hand is next to your right ear. Sweep your left arm downward so that it is alongside your left thigh, and position your right hand in front of your chest.

Repeat nine times on each side.

NEEDLE AT THE BOTTOM OF THE SEA

This movement stretches back muscles and helps tone your legs. During this exercise, visualize energy circulating from the top of your head to the bottoms of your feet.

Inhale deeply while extending your left leg so that your knee is straight. Keeping your leg straight, relax and exhale, bending forward from your hips while extending your right hand between your legs and reaching for the floor. Allow your left arm to hang totally relaxed. Repeat nine times on each side.

■ ■ ■ ■

Muscle Up

Muscles don't turn to fat when you stop working out. When people stop exercising, their muscles begin to shrink. This makes some people believe that muscle turns to fat. In reality, the ratio of fat to muscle simply changes.

Gerard P. Varlotta, DO, clinical associate professor, department of rehabilitation medicine, New York University Medical Center, New York City.

Oprah's Trainer Tells How Very Busy People Can Find Time to Exercise

Bob Greene, an exercise physiologist and personal trainer. He is the author of Bob Greene's Total Body Makeover. *Simon & Schuster.*

Over the past two decades, I have worked with many incredibly busy people to help them lose weight and get in shape.

All of them have overcome their weight and fitness "demons." They became aware of what they truly wanted—and what they were willing to do to achieve it.

No single fitness plan works for everybody, but there are steps all busy people can take to begin an exercise program and stick with it.

DESIGNING YOUR FITNESS PLAN

If your goal is to lose weight and keep it off, you don't have to give up everything else in your life to reach your fitness goals. The key to getting into better shape is to regularly challenge the body to improve strength.

You simply need to engage in a physical activity that exercises the heart muscles for 15 to 20 minutes, five times a week. In fact, many of my clients get in better shape when they cut their workout time in half because they exercise at a much higher intensity.

Any time you start or modify an exercise program, consult your doctor to be sure that the program is safe for you.

Next, select a "primary" aerobic exercise that is relatively convenient and enjoyable to perform. The most effective ones are those in which you support most of your own weight.

Best: Power walking, jogging, aerobic dance and stair-stepping.

Also choose one or two alternative exercises that can help tone different muscles and prevent boredom on intermittent days. If power walking is your primary exercise on three days, do stair-stepping on the other two.

Good alternatives: Outdoor or stationary cycling, rowing, cross-country skiing or swimming—although they are a bit less intensive aerobically.

To lower risk of injury, warm up for three to five minutes...followed by about five minutes of stretching. Do each stretch twice, and hold it for four seconds. Have a two-second interval in between. After your workout, it is important to stretch for another five to 10 minutes.

Hamstrings: Lie on your back with one leg bent and the corresponding foot on the floor. Raise the other leg until you feel a gentle tension. Repeat with the other side.

Buttocks and lower back: While on your back, grab the backs of both legs just above the knee and pull them toward your chest. Hold and repeat.

Shoulders and chest: Stand with your head, shoulders and hips aligned, hands clasped behind you and knees slightly bent. Bring your hands up toward the ceiling until you feel a gentle tension.

OTHER CONSIDERATIONS

•**Exercise in the morning.** Your place of exercise should be within a few minutes of your home or work. This eliminates excuses not to exercise that inevitably arise during a busy schedule.

•**Do some physical activity on your days off.** Consistency is an important key to maintaining interest in exercise. Although the body needs a rest from vigorous training, I ask my clients to add an enjoyable activity, such as a stroll or bike ride, on their days off.

•**Work toward your results zone.** To lose weight and strengthen your body, perform aerobic exercise at a level of intensity that pushes your physical limits without causing injury. This level is what I call the results zone.

Strategy: Picture a scale from 0 to 10, with 0 equal to the feeling you have at rest and 10 equal to the feeling of all-out exercise—fatigue, labored breathing, etc.

Aim for a 7—a feeling of fatigue, deep breathing with the ability to carry on a conversation, although you don't necessarily want to. If you are physically able, you can shoot for an 8—exercising very vigorously with very deep breathing.

•**Weight training can be added in two or three months.** The greatest benefit of resistance training is to combat the effects of aging. It prevents muscle and bone loss, strengthens the body and helps control excess weight.

Surprisingly, lifting weights can significantly increase your appetite, while aerobic exercise suppresses appetite. Add weights only after your eating is under control and aerobic exercise is fully incorporated into your schedule.

STICKING WITH IT

Busy people often find it difficult to stick with an exercise program. The secret to maintaining a high motivational level is to become more self-aware.

•**Take responsibility.** All my busy clients who have changed their lives have stopped blaming external causes, such as demanding careers, their kids, etc. Instead, they have taken responsibility for their actions and made time for exercise. Positive change is possible only through conscious decisions.

To change your mind-set: Think about the three best decisions you've ever made. For each decision, write down if it was difficult, if you considered other options and why you valued your decision.

Think about how the decision affected your life and how your life would be different if you hadn't made it. Do the same for the three worst decisions you've made.

•**Anticipate setbacks.** As you embark on a new fitness program, expect the following to occur...

•Aches and pains are part of training and demonstrate that you are working hard. If they are extreme, back off a bit and do a similar activity at a lighter level.

Example: Walking can help alleviate sore muscles that come from stair-stepping.

- Physical fatigue can occur from time to time and usually indicates your body needs rest. After a rest day, you can come back stronger and resume your training.

- Mental fatigue is often a sign of stress or boredom. Varying your fitness routine, refocusing your goals or taking a day off can help eliminate it.

- **Remember why exercise is important.** This will help you define your level of commitment and keep you motivated to strive continuously for positive change.

To prioritize your life, draw a large circle and divide it into eight equal sections.

Within each section, write the eight most important areas of your life. These will likely include family, health, fitness, community, etc.

Next to each section, write down three things you can do daily to improve that area. Even if you are able to do only one of these daily steps, you will significantly improve your life.

Exercises Designed for People with Arthritis

Ian Fraser is a Victoria, Australia–based writer and coauthor of *Exercise Beats Arthritis*. Bell Publishing Company.

If you have arthritis—discomfort and stiffness may make you want to sit down and stop moving. But that only leads to disability.

Better idea: Do gentle exercises designed specifically for people with arthritis.

When I developed osteoarthritis years ago, one of the most helpful things I did was to follow a program of simple exercises done at home or in a pool. They worked so well that I wanted to spread the word.

My coauthor—skilled physical therapist Valerie Sayce—and I wrote a book describing and depicting exercises that have helped many people with arthritis.

These exercises are also useful as light exercise for anyone who wants to remain supple, active and mobile in later years.

The exercises shown here were developed for long-term mild-to-moderate arthritic problems.

They may not be suitable for people with severe joint deformities or for those whose arthritis greatly hinders normal daily activities. To adapt these exercises for more severe arthritis, consult your doctor or a physical therapist.

GROUND RULES

- **Exercise for an uninterrupted 15 to 30 minutes a day.**

- **Choose a time when you're feeling near your best,** not tired or in pain.

- **Wear comfortable clothes that allow full movement.**

- **Don't exercise right after you have eaten.**

- **If you take pain medication,** exercise half an hour after a regular dose, when the medication is working best.

- **If you feel pain, stop.** Consult your doctor or a physical therapist. Don't take extra medication to mask pain during exercise. If your exercise-induced pain lasts for more than two hours, do fewer repetitions next time.

- **Clear a wide space.**

- **Begin with two to four repetitions of each exercise,** gradually adding one repetition a week until you reach five or six—as long as your joint doesn't become too tender.

- **For floor exercises, use a mat.** For exercise involving a chair or stool, use one whose seat is at the right height to support your thighs with your feet flat on the floor.

LEAP OVER THESE ROADBLOCKS

Occasional discouragement is normal, but don't stop just because you...

- **Lose enthusiasm.** Progress may be slow, but it will be sure. Keep plugging away.

- **Fear physical effort.** Deep down, you may believe that exertion is harmful. If you feel pain when exercising, stop. See your health professional or call the local chapter of the Arthritis Foundation.

- **Get bored.** Try exercising to medium-speed music that you like. Tired of exercising by yourself? Join a water exercise class or similar group.

MOVE IT OR LOSE IT

Once you start to exercise, keep going. You are making a lifestyle commitment—and a commitment to improving your own life. What better incentive could you have?

HANDS

1. Tuck in your elbows. Place your palms facing each other. *Then...*

•Bend your wrists forward, bringing the fingers of one hand toward the matching fingers of the other hand.

•Bend your wrists back so that your palms face front.

2. Place your hands in front of you. Look at your palms. *Then, one hand at a time...*

•Stretch your thumb across your palm. Gently close your fingers over it.

•Stretch open your fingers and thumb.

•Gently fold your fingers into your palm and close your thumb over them. Do not make a tight fist.

•Stretch open your fingers and thumb again.

3. Do each hand individually.

Touch the tip of your thumb to the tip of each other finger in turn. Make the circle as round as you can. Straighten your fingers after touching each finger.

HIPS

1. Stand, holding onto the back of a chair with both hands. Keep your body upright as you lift one leg out to the side, with your foot flexed and toes pointing out. Lower slowly and repeat with the other leg.

2. Stand, holding onto the back of a chair with one hand.

Caution: If you have had a hip replacement, do not lift your leg above hip level.

Keep your back straight and lift your outside knee.

Straighten your knee as you stretch your leg behind you, with your toes just off the floor. Turn around to work the other leg.

3. Lie on your back with your knees bent and your feet and knees comfortably apart. Push through your feet and slowly lift your buttocks off the floor. Lower slowly, rolling your spine onto the floor from the top down.

KNEES

1. Sit up straight on a chair with your thighs fully supported.

Flex your foot back and straighten your knee. Keep your back straight and your thigh on the chair. Hold for three to five seconds, then lower slowly.

2. Lie on your back with one leg bent. Flex back the other foot and tighten your knee. Lift your straight leg about two feet off the floor. Lower it slowly, touching the floor with your calf first.

Contact the Arthritis Foundation, 1330 W. Peachtree St., Atlanta 30309, 800-283-7800. To find an Arthritis Foundation chapter by zip code, visit *www.arthritis.org.* Click on "Questions & Answers" for additional information and materials.

■ ■ ■ ■

Exercise Your Knees

Osteoarthritis of the knee is a leading cause of disability among seniors—but a new study suggests exercise may be the best "medicine."

Facts: Persons with a history of knee surgery who faced high risk of osteoarthritis were divided into two groups, one that exercised their knees three times a week for four months and another that did not.

Result: The exercisers reported fewer joint symptoms and better knee functioning, while MRI scans of their knees showed improved quality and strengthening of their cartilage not found in the nonexercisers.

Key: Like muscle and bone, cartilage also responds to the stress of exercise by increasing its content of supportive building blocks (or matrix molecules).

Leif Dahlberg, MD, PhD, department of clinical sciences, Malmö University Hospital, Malmö, Sweden, and Ewa M. Roos, PT, PhD, Lund University, Lund, Sweden.

Lose Weight with Your Palm® and Other PDA Tricks

David Boyer, research editor, *Bottom Line/Personal*, Stamford, CT.

Most people use personal digital assistants (PDAs) to keep track of phone numbers and appointments, but there are many more ways that your PDA can help you.*

*These programs are available for Palm PDAs, Windows Mobile devices and some mobile phones.

In addition to the Web sites listed below, there are others where you can find, try out and buy software for your PDA. Great places to start are *www.palm.com...www.handmark.com...*and *www.handandgo.com.*

- **Create a universal remote.** If your PDA has an infrared port for sending data, you can probably use it as a remote control for your TV, VCR, DVD player and more. *Salling Clicker* (*salling.com*, $24) and *NoviiRemote* (*www.novii. tv*, $15 to $36, depending on the operating system and device) are good choices. Salling Clicker also lets you control a PowerPoint presentation with your PDA.
- **Watch TV.** If your Palm has WiFi capability (and you have a wireless Internet service account), you can watch live TV with *MobiTv* (*www. mobitv.com*, $10/month). More than 35 channels are available, including MSNBC, ESPN, TLC, The Discovery Channel and The Weather Channel.
- **Eat and be entertained.** *Zagat to Go* is available for $29.95 a year at *mobile.zagat.com*. With the subscription, you get ratings for more than 30,000 domestic and international restaurants and entertainment venues, as well as contact information and maps.
- **Know your way around.** *Express Maps* offers maps, news, weather, movie showtimes and more for handheld devices at *express.hand mark.com*. The cost is $7/month or $70/year.
- **Stick to your diet.** Enter your height, weight and age...select a diet plan and weight-loss goal...and the *Diet & Exercise Assistant* will create a personalized plan for you. It also lets you track calories, carbohydrates, protein, fiber, etc. (*www.keyoe.com*, $24.95).

■■■■

On a Treadmill?

For a better treadmill workout, gradually increase the treadmill incline as you run or walk at a brisk pace. To warm up, set the incline at an angle you can sustain comfortably—about a 2% incline for most people. After 10 to 15 minutes, increase the incline up to 3% to 5% over the course of one minute. Run or walk at that incline level for five to 10 minutes. Increase the incline as many as two to three times more, and run or walk for five to 10 minutes at each level. You can take a break before increasing the incline by walking for two to three minutes at a 2% incline. Then go to the next interval. As you progress, increase the total lengths of your intervals.

Caution: Stay on the front of the belt. Running or walking at the back of the belt can result in injuries.

Also: Always check with your doctor before beginning an exercise program.

Derick Williamson, co-founder and partner, Source Endurance located in Austin, TX. He is pursuing a graduate degree at the University of Texas in sports science and nutrition. His Web site is www.source-e.net.

How I Lost 172 Pounds

Tricia Cunningham, a former hospice nurse who is now a weight-loss coach and motivational speaker. She is coauthor of The Reverse Diet *(Wiley), with Heidi Skolnik, MS, CDN, FACSM.* www.reversedietsolution.com.

In August 1999, 27-year-old Tricia Cunningham weighed 292 pounds. The mother of two had tried numerous diets without success and was becoming increasingly despondent about her size. One day that August, Cunningham decided that since everything about her relationship with food was wrong, she would completely reverse the way she ate. For starters, she would eat breakfast for dinner and dinner for breakfast.

Within one week of reversing her meals, she began losing weight. By March of the next year, she had lost more than half her body weight—and has kept the weight off ever since.

Cunningham explains how her "reverse diet" works...

REVERSING MEALS

Like most people, I used to eat my biggest meal of the day at dinner. Trouble was, I didn't burn many calories between dinner and bedtime, so my body stored most of the meal in the form of fat. Eating a large dinner also meant my body was still digesting as I tried to get to sleep at night. I didn't know this at the time, but it turns out that it's difficult to sleep soundly while digesting...and it's even harder to lose weight when we don't get enough sleep. We are less likely to remain active when we're drowsy during the day, and sleep deprivation reduces our bodies' production of the hormones that assist in weight regulation.

To compensate for a big meal at night, I ate only a small meal for breakfast, sometimes skipping breakfast entirely. But this, too, was a mistake. Skimping on breakfast left me feeling energy-deprived all day, which meant that I was less likely to exercise. Plus, I was so hungry, I ate more at lunch and dinner. Nutritionists refer to this as "residual hunger"—when we undereat early in the day, our bodies send out hunger signals with such insistence that we're prone to overeat later.

With the Reverse Diet, the first meal of my day is the largest meal, and the final meal of my day is the smallest. I feel less hungry and more energetic all day. Some people who try this diet tell me that they have so much more energy, they no longer need to drink coffee in the morning to get started.

WHAT TO EAT

The best choices are whole grains, fruits and vegetables, lean cuts of pork or beef, poultry and fish. Avoid processed foods and canned or boxed foods, which often have lots of salt and/or sugar.

Breakfast: I love to start my day with a piece of salmon and a baked potato…whole-wheat pasta with lightly sautéed shrimp…a salad… even a steak. Traditional breakfast foods, such as omelets or whole-wheat French toast, also are perfectly acceptable. Just make sure your breakfasts are high in protein and big enough so that you feel full but not stuffed.

Lunch: Eat enough at lunch so that you're not hungry in the afternoon, but eat less than you ate for breakfast. I might have a turkey breast sandwich for lunch or grilled tuna over mixed greens.

Dinner: Demote dinner from your major meal to little more than a healthy snack. Appropriate dinners include traditional breakfast foods, such as a bowl of oatmeal…two hard-boiled eggs…or a fruit smoothie made with low-fat yogurt. Or consume foods that typically are treated as a small part of a larger dinner, such as a bowl of soup or a salad.

Rule of thumb: If your caloric intake is 1,400 calories per day, then breakfast should be about 500 calories…lunch about 400…and dinner 300…with two 100-calorie snacks in between, such as one-half cup of fat-free cottage cheese with one-half cup of peaches or a handful of almonds or walnuts. Though the Reverse Diet doesn't really promote calorie counting, most people need to limit themselves to 1,400 to 1,800 calories a day to lose weight. I also walk at least 30 minutes a day.

OVERCOMING CHALLENGES

•**Late-night snacking.** If you feel the need to snack later in the evening, try increasing the size of your evening meal slightly, say, from two hard-boiled eggs to three. If that doesn't do the trick, at least favor fruits and vegetables.

Better yet, prepare yourself a cup of hot lemon water. For more flavor, add mint sprigs…vanilla and cinnamon…a touch of honey…or artificial sweetener.

•**No time in the morning.** I do most of my cooking at night, making regular dinners for my family. Then I microwave my big breakfasts in the morning. Sometimes, I cook seven meals at once and freeze them so that I'm set for the week.

•**Eating out.** Most restaurants serve large portions for dinner. I just eat a little and get the rest packed to go for my breakfast the next morning.

Caralluma for Weight Loss

Mark A. Stengler, ND, naturopathic physician in private practice, La Jolla, CA…adjunct associate clinical professor at the National College of Natural Medicine, Portland, OR…author of 16 books, including *The Natural Physician's Healing Therapies* (Bottom Line Books) and coauthor of *Prescription for Natural Cures* (Wiley)…and author of the *Bottom Line/Natural Healing* newsletter.

Legend has it that hunting tribes of Western India chewed the edible *Caralluma* cactus to suppress hunger and thirst when on long hunts. Today, Caralluma extract is being marketed as a weight-loss product that suppresses appetite and enhances metabolism.

For centuries, *Caralluma fimbriata*, the most common form, which grows in Africa, the Canary Islands, Arabia, southern Europe, Sri Lanka, Afghanistan and India, has been a normal part of the daily diet in India. It is commonly found growing wild in urban centers, as roadside shrubs and as boundary markers in gardens. It can be eaten in several forms—raw, cooked as a regular vegetable or used in preserves, such as chutney. There have been no reports of adverse side effects over centuries of use.

Two recent studies investigated a concentrated extract of Caralluma known as *Slimaluma*. In the first—a randomized, double-blind, placebo-controlled study—25 overweight or obese participants received 500 mg of Caralluma twice a day (a dosage that is equivalent to the traditional Indian intake of 100 grams of raw cactus) and another 25 participants received a placebo for eight weeks. No other changes were made in the study participants' diets, and all were advised to walk 30 minutes every morning and 30 minutes every evening.

There was slightly greater average weight loss in the Caralluma group (1.94 pounds) than in the placebo group (1.12 pounds). More impressive was the decrease in waist circumference—an average loss of 2.75 inches in the participants taking Caralluma, versus 1.29 inches in those taking the placebo.

Also, researchers found that there was a statistically significant decrease in body fat, blood pressure and hunger in members of the Caralluma group but not in the placebo group.

The second study consisted of 19 overweight patients who were given 500-mg capsules of Slimaluma twice daily—once before breakfast and once before dinner—and seven patients taking a placebo for one month. More than 60% of those taking the cactus extract lost six pounds or more in the month. Three of the seven participants in the placebo group lost an average of one pound...the other four gained weight or stayed the same.

I spoke with Ronald Lawrence, MD, PhD, a former assistant clinical professor at UCLA School of Medicine, who reviewed the research on Slimaluma and has recommended the extract to many patients. He told me that most patients lose two pounds per week for the first one to two months of use, with no side effects, and most report an increase in energy.

We don't know exactly how Caralluma suppresses appetite and stimulates weight loss. Researchers theorize that substances in Caralluma known as *pregnane glycosides* prevent fat accumulation by blocking *citrate lyase*, an enzyme involved in fat formation. Pregnane glycosides also may inhibit the hunger mechanisms in the brain.

I believe that Caralluma fimbriata will become popular in the US because it is one of the few weight-loss supplements that has sound clinical data demonstrating its effectiveness.

Several companies offer the Slimaluma extract, including Country Life (800-645-5768, *www.country-life.com*), which sells a product known as Genaslim.

Cost: $40 to $50 for one month's supply. The recommended dosage of Slimaluma is 500 mg twice a day—30 to 45 minutes before breakfast and 30 to 60 minutes before dinner.

As with all supplements, pregnant or nursing mothers and children should use this only under a doctor's supervision.

Subject Index

Medications Index

Subject Index

M

Macular degeneration. *See* Age-related macular degeneration (AMD)

Magnesium
  anxiety and, 233
  bioavailability of, 462
  for bone health, 135, 200–201
  for cancer prevention, 367–368, 368–369
  for constipation relief, 343
  for heart health, 260
  for menopausal symptoms, 388
  role of, 490
  for vision protection, 445

Magnetic resonance angiography (MRA), 256

Magnetic resonance-guided, focused ultrasound surgery (MRgFUS), 404

Magnetic resonance imaging (MRI), 214, 261–262

Mammograms, 369, 408–410

Manicures, 433

Margarine, 484–485

Marijuana, and mental health, 78

Marriage. *See also* Personal relationships; Sex
  communication in, 419, 422–423
  death and divorce in, 417–418
  helping your parents', 425–426
  myths about, 418–420

Massage therapy, 369

Mastectomies, 407

Meat, 462, 463, 470, 478–479, 495. *See also specific meats*

Mechanical embolus removal in cerebral ischemia (MERCI) retriever, 292

Medical care
  active participation in, 5
  complaints about poor, 13–14
  cost of, 19–23
  medical history for better, 68

Medical exams, wasting time during, 1

Medical offices, 69. *See also* Hospitals

Medical tests
  for adrenal fatigue, 345
  for allergies, 78
  for Alzheimer's disease, 214
  for aneurysms, 274–275, 290
  for atrial fibrillation, 287, 288
  for attention deficit disorder, 231
  benefit versus harm from, 7
  for bladder cancer, 353
  for blood count changes, 95
  for bone density, 321
  for breast cancer, 369, 389–390, 399, 408–409
  for carotid artery disease, 294
  for colon cancer, 354
  cost of, 20
  for deep vein thrombosis, 272
  for diabetes, 303–305, 306, 318
  for esophageal cancer, 359–360
  eye-related, 445–446, 447, 448, 450
  during heart attack, 270–272
  for heart disease, 253, 256, 257–258, 265
  for kidney disease, 327
  for lung cancer, 365
  for men, 371–372
  for overactive bladder, 337
  for prostate cancer, 10–11, 371, 372, 381
  for stroke, 291, 292
  before surgery, 27
  for testosterone levels, 371, 382
  for tuberculosis, 75, 96, 97

Medicare, 14, 24

Medications. *See also* Medications Index; Over-the-counter remedies; Vaccinations; *specific conditions*
  for acid suppression, 177–178 (*see also* Heartburn)
  affecting marriages, 425
  for birth control, 82–83, 390, 391
  caffeine in, 3, 147, 233
  from Canada, 180–181
  causing skin disease, 82
  choosing, 169–171
  cost of generic, 171
  counterfeit, 160
  errors in taking, 169, 173–174
  foods interacting with, 172
  gender difference in response to, 391
  herbs interacting with, 140–141, 145–146, 149
  during hospitalization, 14, 15, 19, 21
  keeping list of, 17, 169, 173, 174
  mail-order, 181–182
  measuring and storing, 3
  multiple uses for, 178–179
  nutrients depleted by, 175–177
  reaction to, 82
  remembering to take, 199
  snoring caused by, 242
  supplements interacting with, 140–141
  before surgery, 27
  taking too many, 151–153
  for travel, 68
  understanding how to take, 2

Meditation, 228, 241. *See also* Breathing exercises

Melanoma, 53–54. *See also* Skin cancer

Melatonin, 66, 176, 241

Memory. *See also* Brain health
  almonds improving, 473
  gender differences in, 423
  menopause affecting, 392
  painkillers and loss of, 121–122
  positive and negative, 227–228
  science of, 222–223
  stopping loss of, 219–221
  strengthening, 205, 208–209

Men
  aspirin benefits for, 128, 254
  bone health in, 384
  communication tips for, 422–423
  dangerous symptoms for, 51–52
  drugs for women versus, 169–171
  fertility of, 383–384
  heart health of, 384, 385
  helping menopausal partners, 388, 389
  hernias in, 384 (*see also* Hernias)
  medical tests recommended for, 371–372
  nipples of, 5
  prostate health in, 372, 377–380, 384 (*see also* Prostate cancer)
  sexual dysfunction in, 372, 384–385, 386
  sleeping after sex, 25
  snoring by, 25
  testosterone levels in, 381–383
  yeast infections in, 75–76

Menopause. *See also* Women
  depression and, 391
  incontinence after, 395
  memory and, 392

Medications Index